C000186198

ISBN 978-1-5278-7306-3
PIBN 10922602

1 MONTH OF
FREE
READING

at

www.ForgottenBooks.com

By purchasing this book you are eligible for one month membership to ForgottenBooks.com, giving you unlimited access to our entire collection of over 1,000,000 titles via our web site and mobile apps.

To claim your free month visit:

www.forgottenbooks.com/free922602

English
Français
Deutsche
Italiano
Español
Português

www.forgottenbooks.com

Mythology Photography **Fiction**
Fishing Christianity **Art** Cooking
Essays Buddhism Freemasonry
Medicine **Biology** Music **Ancient**
Egypt Evolution Carpentry Physics
Dance Geology **Mathematics** Fitness
Shakespeare **Folklore** Yoga Marketing
Confidence Immortality Biographies
Poetry **Psychology** Witchcraft
Electronics Chemistry History **Law**
Accounting **Philosophy** Anthropology
Alchemy Drama Quantum Mechanics
Atheism Sexual Health **Ancient History**
Entrepreneurship Languages Sport
Paleontology Needlework Islam
Metaphysics Investment Archaeology
Parenting Statistics Criminology
Motivational

SESSIONAL PAPERS

VOLUME 20

FIFTH SESSION OF THE TWELFTH PARLIAMENT

OF THE

DOMINION OF CANADA

SESSION 1915

VOLUME L.

ALPHABETICAL INDEX

TO THE

SESSIONAL PAPERS

OF THE

PARLIAMENT OF CANADA

FIFTH SESSION, TWELFTH PARLIAMENT, 1915.

See also Alphabetical List, Page 1.

LIST OF SESSIONAL PAPERS

Arranged in Numerical Order, with their titles at full length; the dates when Ordered and when presented to the Houses of Parliament; the name of the Senator or Member who moved for each Sessional Paper, and whether it is ordered to be Printed or Not Printed.

CONTENTS OF VOLUME D.

Fifth Census of Canada, 1911,—Agriculture, Volume IV.   Presented by Hon. Mr. Foster, February 8, 1915.. .. ..*Printed for distribution and sessional papers.*

CONTENTS OF VOLUME 1.

(This volume is bound in three parts).

1. Report of the Auditor General for the year ended 31st March, 1914, Volume I, Parts A, B and A to L ; Volume II, Parts M to U ; Volume III, Parts V to Z.   Presented by Hon. Mr. White, February 9, 1915.. .. .. ..*Printed for distribution and sessional papers.*

CONTENTS OF VOLUME 2.

2. The Public Accounts of Canada, for the fiscal year ended 31st March, 1914. Presented by Hon. Mr. White, February 9, 1915 .. .. ..*Printed for distribution and sessional papers.*

3. Estimates of sums required for the service of the Dominion for the year ending on 31st March, 1916.   Presented by Hon. Mr. White, February 8, 1915.
Printed for distribution and sessional papers.

4. Supplementary Estimates of sums required for the service of the Dominion for the year ending on the 31st March, 1915.   Presented by Hon. Mr. White, March 9, 1915.
Printed for distribution and sessional papers.

5. Further Supplementary Estimates of sums required for the service of the Dominion for the year ending on the 31st March, 1915.   Presented by Hon. Mr. White, March 27, 1915.
Printed for distribution and sessional papers.

5a. Further Supplementary Estimates for year ending 31st March, 1916.   Presented by Hon. Mr. White, March 31, 1915.. .. ..*Printed for distribution and sessional papers.*

CONTENTS OF VOLUME 3.

6. List of Shareholders in the Chartered Banks of the Dominion of Canada as on 31st December, 1914.   Presented by Hon. Mr. White, February 9, 1915.
Printed for distribution and sessional papers.

CONTENTS OF VOLUME 4.

7. Report on certified cheques, dividends, unclaimed balances and drafts or bills of exchange remaining unpaid in Chartered Banks of the Dominion of Canada, for five years and upwards prior to 31st December, 1913.   Presented by Hon. Mr. White, April 10, 1915.
Printed for distribution and sessional papers.

CONTENTS OF VOLUME 5.

(This volume is bound in two parts).

8. Report of Superintendent of Insurance for year 1914. Presented by Hon. Mr. White, 1915.
Printed for distribution and sessional papers.

9. Abstract of Statement of Insurance Companies in Canada for year ended 31st December, 1914.   Presented by Hon. Mr. White, 1914.
Printed for distribution and sessional papers.

CONTENTS OF VOLUME 6.

10. Report of the Department of Trade and Commerce for the fiscal year ended 31st March, 1914: Part I.—Canadian Trade. Presented by Sir George Foster, 8th February, 1915.
Printed for distribution and sessional papers.

CONTENTS OF VOLUME 7.

10a. Report of the Department of Trade and Commerce for the fiscal year ended 31st March, 1914: Part II.—Canadian Trade with (1) France, (2) Germany, (3) United Kingdom, and (4) United States. Presented by Sir George Foster, 8th February, 1915.
Printed for distribution and sessional papers.

10b. Report of the Department of Trade and Commerce for the fiscal year ended 31st March, 1914: Part III.—Canadian Trade with foreign countries (except France, Germany, the United Kingdom, and United States.) Presented by Sir George Foster, 8th February, 1915.. .. .. .: .. ..*Printed for distribution and sessional papers.*

10c. Report of the Department of Trade and Commerce, for the fiscal year ended 31st March, 1914, (Part IV, Miscellaneous Information.) Presented by Sir George Foster, March 27, 1915.. .. ..*Printed for distribution and sessional papers.*

10d. Report of the Board of Grain Commissioners for Canada. Presented by Sir George Foster, 1914... .. ..*Printed for distribution and sessional papers.*

CONTENTS OF VOLUME 8.

10e. Report of the Department of Trade and Commerce for the fiscal year ending 31st March, 1914. Part VI.—Subsidized Steamship Services, with statistics showing steamship traffic to 31st December, 1914, and Estimates for the fiscal year 1915-16. Presented by Sir George Foster, 1915.. .. ..*Printed for distribution and sessional papers.*

10f. Report of Trade and Commerce for fiscal year ended 31st March, 1914. (Part VII.—Trade of Foreign Countries, Treaties and Conventions.) Presented by Sir George Foster, 1915... .. ..*Printed for distribution and sessional papers.*

CONTENTS OF VOLUME 9.

11. Report of the Department of Customs for the year ended 31st March, 1914. Presented by Hon. Mr. Reid, February 11, 1915.. .. Printed for distribution and sessional papers.

CONTENTS OF VOLUME 10.

12, 13, 14. Reports, Returns and Statistics of the Inland Revenues of the Dominion of Canada, for the year ended 31st March, 1914 (Part I.—Excise). (Part II.—Inspection of. Weights and Measures, Gas and Electricity). (Part III.—Adulteration of Food). Presented by Hon. Mr. Blondin, March 1, 1915.
Printed for distribution and sessional papers.

15. Report of the Minister of Agriculture for the Dominion of Canada, for the year ended 31st March, 1914. Presented by Hon. Mr. Burrell, February 8, 1915.
Printed for distribution and sessional papers.

CONTENTS OF VOLUME 11.

(This volume is bound in two parts).

15a Report of the Dairy and Cold Storage Commissioner for the fiscal year ended 31st March, 1914. (Dairying, Fruit, Extension of Markets and Cold Storage). Presented by Hon. Mr. Burrell, 1915.. .. ..:*Printed for distribution and sessional papers.*

15b. Report of the Veterinary Director General for the year ending 31st March, 1915. Presented by Hon. Mr. Burrell, 1915.. .. ..*Printed for distribution and sessional papers.*

16. Report of the Director and Officers of the Experimental Farms for the years ending 31st March, 1914. Presented by Hon. Mr. Burrell, March 1, 1915.
Printed for distribution and sessional papers.

CONTENTS OF VOLUME 12.

17. Criminal Statistics for the year ended 30th September, 1913. (Appendix to the Report of the Minister of Trade and Commerce for the year 1913.) Presented by Sir George Foster, 1915.. .. ..*Printed for distribution and sessional papers.*

18. Return of By-elections for the House of Commons of Canada, held during the year 1914. Presented by Hon. Mr. Speaker, March 12, 1915.
Printed for distribution and sessional papers.

CONTENTS OF VOLUME 13.

CONTENTS OF VOLUME 14.

CONTENTS OF VOLUME 15.

CONTENTS OF VOLUME 16.

CONTENTS OF VOLUME 17.

CONTENTS OF VOLUME 18.

CONTENTS OF VOLUME 19.

(This volume is bound in two parts)

CONTENTS OF VOLUME 1

CONTENTS OF VOLUME 1.

CONTENTS OF VOLUME 1.

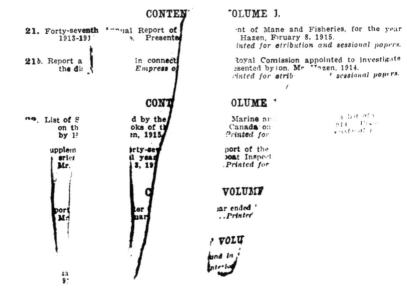

CONTENTS OF VOLUME 20.

CONTENTS OF VOLUME 21.

CONTENTS OF VOLUME 22.

CONTENTS OF VOLUME 23.

CONTENTS OF VOLUME 24.

CONTENTS OF VOLUME 25.

CONTENTS OF VOLUME 26.

CONTENTS OF VOLUME 27.

CONTENTS OF VOLUME 28.

CONTENTS OF VOLUME 28—*Continued.*

CONTENTS OF VOLUME 23—*Continued.*

of convicts; dates of conviction; crime of which convicted; sentences passed; by whom sentenced; sentences commuted, and if so, to what.   3. For a return showing all persons in Canada, and each province, convicted during the above mentioned period of murder whose sentences have been mitigated, or who have received a free pardon, together with a statement of the offences of which they were severally convicted, with the name of convicts; dates of conviction; nature of offence; sentences; and extent of mitigation of sentences and dates.   4. For a return of instances, during the above mentioned period, in which appeal has been made on behalf of the persons convicted of capital offences to His Excellency, the Governor in Council, for the exercise of the Royal Prerogative of pardon, or mitigation of sentences, with the name of convicts; dates of conviction and place; crime of which convicted; sentences; dates of appeal; and the result.   Presented 9th February, 1915.—*Mr. Wilson (Laval).. ..Not printed.*

54. General Rules and Orders of the Exchequer Court of Canada made, respectively, on the 23rd September, 1914, and the 18th June, 1914.   Presented by Hon. Mr. Coderre, 9th February, 1915.. .. ..*Not printed.*

54a. General Rules and Orders of the Exchequer Court of Canada made on the 15th February, 1915.   Presented by Hon. Mr. Coderre, 16th March, 1915... .. ..*Not printed.*

55. Ordinances of the Yukon Territory passed by the Yukon Council in the year 1914.   Presented by Hon. Mr. Coderre, 9th February, 1915... .. ..*Not printed.*

56. Return to an Order of the House of the 18th May, 1914, for a return showing the details of moneys paid to J. F. Farrington, $248.25; B. H. Smith, $469.50, and H. C. Dash, $182.40, as set forth in *Hansard* of this session, page 3071.   Presented 9th February, 1915.—*Mr. McLean (Halifax)... .. ..Not printed.*

57. Return to an Order of the House of the 16th March, 1914, for a copy of instruction sent to Mr. Wm. Flynn, advocate, to hold investigations into charges made against employees of the Department of Marine and Fisheries in Bonaventure County, and reports made by him in such investigations.   Presented 9th February, 1915.—*Mr. Marcil (Bonaventure).. .. ..Not printed.*

58. Return to an Order of the House of the 27th April, 1914, for a copy of all documents bearing upon the application made to the Department of Marine and Fisheries for the dismissal of Ulric Dion, lightkeeper at St. Charles de Caplan, Quebec, and the appointment of Omer Arsenault in his place, and on the action taken by the Department in that connection.   Presented 9th February, 1915.—*Mr. Marcil (Bonaventure).*
Not printed.

59.—Return to an Order of the House of the 9th February, 1914, for a copy of all agreements made and entered into between the Department of Marine and Fisheries or the Government and Railway and Express Companies, including the Intercolonial Railway, relating to the transportation of fresh fish by fast freight or express, since the year 1906; also a copy of all guarantees given to railway and express companies by the Government or any Department thereof, relating to such transportation, together with a statement of all disbursements made by the Department of Marine and Fisheries each year under the terms of such agreements or guarantees, distinguishing between disbursements made on account of fast freight and disbursements made on account of express shipments; also the number of refrigerator cars, subject to guarantee, by Department of Marine and Fisheries, forwarded by fast freight from Mulgrave or Halifax to Montreal, each calendar year since 1906, and the number of tons of freight carried by such cars each year.   Also the number of refrigerator express cars forwarded from said points, Mulgrave and Halifax to Montreal, up to December 31, 1913, under the terms of an agreement made since 1911, between the Department of Marine and Fisheries and the railway or express companies or both.   Also the number of tons of fresh fish carried by express companies, prior to December 31, 1913, under the last mentioned agreement; and the amount paid up to December 31, 1913, by the Department of Marine and Fisheries, under the last mentioned agreement.   Also the number of tons of fresh fish carried by express companies from Mulgrave and Halifax to points west since 1906, on which the Government paid one-third, but not under the terms of the said agreement made as aforesaid, since 1911.   Presented 9th February, 1915.—*Mr. Sinclair.. .. ..Not printed.*

60. Return to an Order of the House of the 20th April, 1914, for a return showing all the post offices in the several counties in the province of Nova Scotia for which a rent allowance, or a fuel fund, and light allowance is made, specifying the amount of such allowance in each case.   Presented 9th February, 1914.—*Mr. Chisholm (Antigonish).*
Not printed.

61. Return to an Order of the House of the 16th March, 1914, for a copy of all correspondence, letters, telegrams, etc., in the year 1913, relating to the carrying of the mails between Grand River Falls and Grand River, county of Richmond, and the awarding of the contract to Malcolm McCuspic.   Presented 9th February, 1915.—*Mr. Kyte.*
....Not printed.

CONTENTS OF VOLUME 28—*Continued.*

CONTENTS OF VOLUME 28—*Continued.*

CONTENTS OF VOLUME 28—*Continued.*

CONTENTS OF VOLUME 28—*Continued.*

91. Report of Board of Officers on boots supplied to the Canadian Expeditionary Force. Presented by Hon. Mr. Hughes, 15th February, 1915............*Not printed*

92. Regulations under "The Destructive Insect and Pest Act" Presented by Hon. Mr. Burrell, 16th February, 1915............*Not printed*

93. Report on "The Agricultural Instruction Act," 1913-14, pursuant to Section 8 of the above named Act. Presented by Hon. Mr. Burrell, 16th February, 1915.
Printed for sessional papers only.

93a. Supplementary Return to an Address to His Royal Highness the Governor General of the 9th February, 1914, for a copy of all arrangements made between the Government and the various provinces under the Agricultural Instruction Act. Presented 19th February, 1915.—*Sir Wilfrid Laurier*............*Not printed.*

93b. Return to an Order of the House of the 20th April, 1914, for a copy of all documents, correspondence, letters, petitions, reports, etc, exchanged between Dr. C. C. James, Mr. J. C. Chapais and each of the Provincial Ministers of Agriculture, in connection with the distribution and the administration of the federal subsidy granted to the provinces for agricultural purposes since the granting of same Presented 23rd February, 1915 —*Mr. Lapointe (Kamouraska)*............*Not printed.*

94. Return to an Order of the House of the 11th February, 1914, for a copy of all telegrams, correspondence, instructions, recommendations, and other documents that passed between the Shellfish Fishery Commission of 1913, and the Department of Marine and Fisheries, from the date of the appointment of said Commission to 31st December, 1913, excluding such documents as have been printed in the published report of said Commission. Presented 16th February, 1915.—*Mr Sinclair*............*Not printed*

95. Return to an Order of the House of the 16th March, 1914, for a copy of all correspondence, tenders, telegrams, complaints and of all other documents in any way referring to the collecting of spawn for the Margaree Lobster Hatchery during the years 1911-12, 1912-13 and 1913-14 Presented 16th February, 1915.—*Mr. Chisholm (Inverness)*
Not printed

96. Return to an Order of the House of the 10th February, 1915, for a return showing the amount of coal imported into Alberta, Saskatchewan and Manitoba, respectively, from the United States during the year 1914; also the amount of duty collected in each of the said provinces during the same year. Presented 16th February, 1915.—*Mr. Buchanan*............*Not printed.*

97. Copy of the Eighth Joint Report of the Commissioners for the Demarcation of the Meridian of the 141st Degree of West Longitude Presented by Hon. Mr. Roche, 18th February, 1915............*Not printed.*

98. Return to an Order of the House of the 20th April, 1914, for a copy of the agreement between the Government of Canada and the Canadian Pacific Railway Company at the time the special land grant was made whereby the Canadian Pacific Railway Company were enabled to get their land grant in one block for the purpose of establishing their present irrigation system east of Calgary, province of Alberta. Presented 18th February, 1915 —*Mr. Burnham*............*Not printed.*

99. Return to an Order of the House of the 23rd March, 1914, for a copy of all letters, telegrams and other documents in connection with the sale of any timber on Parry Island, Parry Sound District, and of advertisements, agreements for purchase and any other documents connected with such sale or grant of timber to any person or persons. Presented 18th February, 1915.—*Mr. Arthurs*............*Not rpinted.*

100. Return to an Order of the House of the 11th February, 1914, for a return showing reasons for the dismissal of Mr. Larivière, Dominion Lands Agent at Girouard; the date of his appointment and of dismissal and salary at time of dismissal; also the name of agent appointed in his place, with date of appointment and salary Presented 18th February, 1915.—*Mr. Oliver.*............*Not printed.*

101. Annual Return respecting Trade Unions under Chapter 125, R.S.C, 1906 Presented by Hon. Mr. Coderre, 18th February, 1915............*Not printed.*

102. A detailed statement of all bonds or securities registered in the Department of the Secretary of State of Canada, since last return (21st January, 1914) submitted to the Parliament of Canada under Section 32 of Chapter 19, of the Revised Statutes of Canada, 1906. Presented by Hon. Mr. Coderre, 18th February, 1915............*Not printed.*

CONTENTS OF VOLUME 28—*Continued.*

CONTENTS OF VOLUME 28—*Continued.*

CONTENTS OF VOLUME 28—*Continued.*

CONTENTS OF VOLUME 28—*Continued.*

CONTENTS OF VOLUME 28—*Continued.*

CONTENTS OF VOLUME 28—*Continued.*

150. Return to an Order of the House, of the 11th February, 1915, for a return showing the names and addresses of all persons in Antigonish County to whom the bounty under the Fenian Raid Volunteer Bounty Act has been paid; the names and addresses of all persons from said county whose applications have been rejected, and a list giving names and addresses of all applications from said county whose applications have not yet been disposed of. Presented 8th March, 1915 —*Mr. Chisholm (Antigonish).*
Not printed.

151. Return to an Order of the House, of the 3rd March, 1915, for a return showing :—1. Who were the different officers commissioned to the 17th Nova Scotia Regiment at Valcartier before they sailed for England? 2. Who are now the commissioned officers of said reg.-ment. Presented 8th March, 1915.—*Mr Macdonald.............Not printed.*

152. Return to an Order of the House, of the 9th February, 1915, for a copy of all accounts of the transfer of the storm signal at Shippigan, N.B, from its former position on land to the public wharf, showing the total cost of said transfer during the months of October and November in 1911. Presented 8th March, 1915.—*Mr. Turgeon.*
Not printed.

153. Return to an Order of the House, of the 4th May, 1914, for a copy of all correspondence, telegrams, petitions, including the signatures of such petitions, and all other documents and papers in the possession of the Department of Trade and Commerce, or the minister of said department, or in the possession of the Prime Minister, relating to any application made between 1st November, 1913, and date hereof by parties in Nova Scotia asking for Government assistance towards the transportation of fresh fish between ports in Nova Scotia and the United States. Presented 9th March, 1915.—*Mr. Sinclair.*
Not printed.

154. Statement of Mr. H. C. Crowell, staff correspondent of the Halifax *Chronicle,* and correspondence in connection with statements appearing in the press referring to alleged ill-treatment of the 17th Regiment of Nova Scotia, at Salisbury Plains. Presented by Sir Robert Borden, 9th March, 1915..................*Not printed.*

155. Return to an Order of the House, of the 3rd March, 1915, for a return showing :—1. The estimated cost of fitting up the works of the Canadian Car and Foundry Company, Limited, at Amherst, N S., for military purposes. 2. The rent or other remuneration being paid, or will be paid, this company for the use of its buildings. 3. Who are to supply the military provisions, including food for men, coal for heating and cooking, and food and other supplies for horses quartered on these premises, and at what prices. 4. Whether it is true that forms for tendering for such military supplies could only be obtained from the office of the sitting member for Cumberland County, and in several cases forms of tender were refused to applicants. 5. Whether the Government is aware that in the case of the supplying of hay, as alleged, not only Liberals were not allowed to tender for same, but supporters of the Government were informed they would not secure any part of the contract, if any of the hay to be supplied was to be purchased from a Liberal.- Presented 11th March, 1915.—*Mr. Copp......Not printed.*

156. Return to an Address to His Royal Highness the Governor General, of the 1st March, 1915, for a copy of all correspondence of the Imperial authorities on the subject of loans from the Imperial Treasury to the Canadian Government. Presented 11th March, 1915.—*Mr. Maclean (Halifax)..................Not printed.*

157. Return to an Order of the House of the 3rd March. 1915, for a copy of all correspondence, recommendations, letters and telegrams relating to the appointment of H. W. Ingraham as Assistant Registrar of Alien Enemies at Sidney, N.S., and to his dismissal from the said office. Presented 12th March, 1915.—*Mr. Kyte..........Not printed.*

158. Return to an Address to His Royal Highness the Governor General of the 11th February, 1915, for a copy of all correspondence relating to the purchase of, and payment by the Government for two submarines authorized by Order in Council dated the 7th August, 1914, and of any other Order or Orders in Council relating thereto, and also of all reports received by the Government or any department thereof referring to said submarines. Presented 12th March, 1915.—*Mr. Pugsley ....Printed for distribution only.*

158a. Supplementary Return to an Address to His Royal Highness the Governor General, of the 11th February, 1915, for a copy of all correspondence relating to the purchase of, and payment by the Government for two submarines authorized by Order in Council dated the 7th August, 1914, and of any other Order or Orders in Council relating thereto; and also of all reports received by the Government or any department thereof referring to said submarines. Presented 15th March, 1915 —*Mr. Pugsley.*
Printed for distribution only.

CONTENTS OF VOLUME 28—*Continued.*

CONTENTS OF VOLUME 28—*Continued.*

CONTENTS OF VOLUME 28—*Continued.*

CONTENTS OF VOLUME 28—*Continued.*

CONTENTS OF VOLUME 28—*Continued.*

CONTENTS OF VOLUME 28—*Continued.*

CONTENTS OF VOLUME 28—*Continued.*

CONTENTS OF VOLUME 28—*Continued.*

CONTENTS OF VOLUME 28—*Continued.*

CONTENTS OF VOLUME 28—*Continued.*

CONTENTS OF VOLUME 28—*Continued.*

267. Return to an Order of the House of the 17th March, 1915, for a copy of all petitions, letters, documents, etc., between persons in the province of Nova Scotia and the Department of Trade and Commerce since 1st August last, with regard to Atlantic ocean freight rates on subsidized, steamers or otherwise. Presented 10th April, 1915.—*Mr. Maclean (Halifax)*... ... . *Not printed.*

268. Return to an Order of the House of the 22nd February, 1915, for a copy of the report of investigation held about 1st June, 1914, by T. R. Ferguson, as special commissioner, into the allotment of homesteads on the area cut out of the Riding Mountain Forest Reserve in the year 1908 or about that time. Presented 10th April, 1915.—*Mr. Cruise.* *Not printed.*

269. Copy of Order.in Council dated 6th April, 1915.—Regulations in respect to steam trawlers clearing from ports on the Atlantic seaboard of Canada. Presented by Hon. Mr. Hazen, 10th April, 1915.. ... . *Not printed.*

270. Return to an Order of the House of the 15th February, 1915, for a copy of all tenders in connection with the supply of lumber to the Department of Militia for the training camps at Medicine Hat and Calgary, and of the invoices for the material supplied. Presented 12th April, 1915.—*Mr. Buchanan*.. ... ... *Not printed.*

271. Return to an Order of the House of the 17th March, 1915, for a copy of all correspondence and reports relating to the purchase of 25,000 shovels of special pattern, mentioned in Order in Council P.C. 2302, dated 4th September, 1914, on page 38 of memoranda respecting work of the Department of Militia and Defence, and also relating to any further purchases of such shovels. Presented 12th April, 1915.—*Mr. Hughes (Kings, P E.I.)*.. ... . *Not printed.*

272. Return to an Order of the House of the 15th March, 1915, for a return showing the names of the persons who bought the horses which were sold by auction at Valcartier camp, giving the price paid for each horse. Presented 12th April, 1915.—*Mr. Kay.* *Not printed.*

273. Return to an Order of the House of the 24th February, 1915, for a return showing:—1. If the Government ever leased any land at or near Shelburne, Nova Scotia, known as the Barracks property, to the town of Shelburne? 2. If, so, at what rental, and for how long? 3. If said lease is now in force? 4. If the Government has sold any of the standing timber on this property? 5. If so, when, to whom, and at what price? 6. How long the purchaser has to remove it? 7. What is the minimum size at the stump sold? 8. If the Government has ever had the property cruised by competent timber cruiser? 9. If so, by whom, and when? 10. If the timber on said property was advertised for sale, and if tenders were asked for, or any opportunity afforded to other prospective buyers to bid for this timber? 11. If any other offers were received? 12. If the town of Shelburne was notified before the sale took place. If so, on what date? 13. How much timber the Government estimates to be on this property? 14. What steps the Government intends to take to compute the quantity of timber cut from this property? 15. If the Government is aware that timber is now being cut from this property by a person or firm who are cutting timber from private property adjoining said Barracks property? 16. What steps are being taken by the Government to be sure that in this case the logs are kept separate from those coming from the adjoining lot, for the purpose of having accurate count and scale? 17. If the Government will bring down a copy of all correspondence, cruisers reports and contracts in relation to the sale of this timber? Presented 12th April, 1915.—*Mr. Law*.. ... ... *Not printed.*

274. Return to an Address to His Royal Highness the Governor General, of the 11th February, 1915, for a copy of all correspondence, telegrams, Orders in Council, petitions and any other documents in connection with the removal of Edward N. Higinbotham from the position of postmaster at Lethbridge, Alberta. Presented 13th April, 1915.—*Mr. Buchanan*.. ... . *Not printed.*

275. Return to an Order of the House of the 10th March, 1915, for a copy of all petitions, correspondence and other documents in connection with the dismissal of Emile Cyr, postmaster at St. Hermas, county of Two Mountains. Presented 13th April, 1915.— *Mr. Ethier*.. ... . *Not printed.*

276. Return to an Order of the House of the 7th April, 1915, for a return showing:—1. Who the mail carriers are for the rural mail in the counties of Chicoutimi and Saguenay? 2. The salary of each such mail carrier, and the trip that each has to make? 3. Who the mail carriers are for the rural mails in the parishes of St. Prime and St. Louis de Metabetchouan, and their respective salaries? Presented 13th April, 1915.—*Mr. Lapointe (Kamouraska)*.. ... . *Not printed.*

277. Return to an Order of the House of the 29th March, 1915, for a copy of all documents, letters, telegrams, testimonials, reports. etc., relating to the claim of Télesphore Paradis, of the city of Lévis. arising from the burning of his wharf and mills which were set on fire by a locomotive of the Intercolonial Railway. Presented 13th April, 1915.— *Mr. Bourassa*.. ... . *Not printed.*

CONTENTS OF VOLUME 28—*Continued.*

CONTENTS OF VOLUME 28—*Continued.*

DEPARTMENT OF THE INTERIOR

ANNUAL REPORT

OF THE

TOPOGRAPHICAL SURVEYS BRANCH

1913-14

PRINTED BY ORDER OF PARLIAMENT.

OTTAWA
PRINTED BY J. DE L. TACHÉ, PRINTER TO THE KING'S MOST
EXCELLENT MAJESTY
1915.

[No. 25b—1915.]

TABLE OF CONTENTS

5 GEORGE V., A. 1915

PAGE.

ILLUSTRATIONS.

MAPS AND PROFILES.

5 GEORGE V, A. 1915

12. Sketch map of the fifteenth base line, ranges 22 to 27, and of sixteenth base line, ranges 1 to 27, west of second meridian, surveyed by E. S. Martindale, D.L.S., 1913.

13. Sketch map and profile of ninteenth base line, ranges 1 to 17, west of third meridian, and of third meridian, townships 69 to 72, surveyed by A. Saint Cyr, D.L.S., 1913.

14. Sketch map and profile of twenty-first base line from the fourth to the fifth meridian, surveyed by F. V. Seibert, D.L.S., 1913.

15. Sketch map and profile of twenty-second base line from the fourth to the fifth meridian, surveyed by G. H. Blanchet, D.L.S., 1913.

16. Sketch map and profile of twenty-fourth base line, ranges 1 to 11, west of fourth meridian, surveyed by J. B. McFarlane, D.L.S., 1911, 1912 and 1913.

17. Sketch map and profile of twenty-fifth base line, ranges 1 to 12, west of fourth meridian, surveyed by J. B. McFarlane, D.L.S., 1913.

18. Sketch map and profile of the twenty-fourth and twenty-fifth base lines, ranges 18 to 21, and of the twenty-sixth base line, ranges 18 to 20, west of fifth meridian, surveyed by J. R. Akins, D.L.S., 1913.

19. Profile of each boundary of range 22, townships 89 to 92, west of fifth meridian, surveyed by J. R. Akins, D.L.S., 1913.

20. Sketch map and profile of twenty-seventh base line, ranges 9 to 22, west of fifth meridian, surveyed by J. R. Akins, D.L.S., and J. A. Fletcher, D.L.S., 1913.

21. Sketch map and profile of twenty-eighth base line range 18, and of east boundary of range 18, townships 89 to 108, west of fifth meridian, surveyed by J. A. Fletcher, D.L.S., 1913.

REPORT

OF THE

SURVEYOR GENERAL OF DOMINION LANDS

1913-14

DEPARTMENT OF THE INTERIOR,
TOPOGRAPHICAL SURVEYS BRANCH,
OTTAWA, August 7, 1914.

The Deputy Minister of the Interior,
    Ottawa.

SIR,—I have the honour to submit the following report of the Topographical Surveys Branch for the year ended March 31, 1914.

The survey operations in the field were continued on about the same scale as during the previous year. The surveys carried out under the direction of this branch may be dealt with under the following heads: block outlines, township subdivision, inspection of contracts, delimitation of interprovincial boundary, levels, topographical work, stadia traverses, corrections and resurveys, settlement and townsite surveys, timber berth and mineral claim surveys, Yukon surveys.

BLOCK OUTLINES.

The unsurveyed portions of the provinces of Manitoba, Saskatchewan, and Alberta are wooded lands interspersed with extensive marshes, with here and there tracts of good land. Except along the main waterways and the surveyed lines of the Dominion lands system, this country is practically unknown. It is certain that much of the land is unsuitable for occupation, but with a view to the subdivision of the scattered tracts of good land as they are required for settlement, the efforts of the department have been directed towards the extension of the system of base lines and meridian outlines upon which the system of Dominion lands surveys is built up.

The tide of settlement in recent years has set strongly towards the Peace River district. Extending northerly from this district, the Peace and Athabaska rivers afford two natural highways along which the pioneers of future settlement will naturally proceed. There is already a persistent demand for surveys at Fort Vermilion and McMurray.

The meridian outline between ranges 17 and 18, west of the fifth meridian was surveyed northerly from the twenty-third base to the twenty-eighth base. From this meridian outline the intervening base lines were run across the valley of Peace river, thus enabling the department to proceed with the subdivision of lands along the valley as they are required.

Between the fourth and fifth meridians the twenty-fourth and twenty-fifth base lines were run westerly across the valley of the Athabaska. The survey of the twenty-first and twenty-second bases between these two meridians was also completed.

West of the Athabaska and south of McMurray the country is very wet, large muskegs extending back from the river as far as range 23. These muskegs as a rule can be easily drained, and when dry will make excellent agricultural lands. Extensive

5 GEORGE V., A. 1915

areas of good farming land lie along the valley of Wabiskaw river, which flows
northerly in the vicinity of the fifth meridian, and empties into the Peace near Fort
Vermilion. Fire has swept a great part of this north country, leaving only small
patches of good timber here and there in the muskegs.

The district north of McMurray is not suited for farming on account of the
muskegs and summer frosts, but ranching can be carried on successfully.

The sixteenth base line was run from the second to the third meridian, and the
nineteenth base west of the third meridian across nineteen ranges. The production
of these base lines was necessary to enable the department to subdivide lands to meet
the needs of the scattered settlements in these districts. Exceptional difficulties were
met with by the survey parties in both cases due to the extensive swamps encountered,
and to the lack of horse feed along the base lines. The soil all through the country
is good, but extensive drainage operations will have to be completed before much of
the land can be used for agricultural purposes. Jackpine is the prevailing timber, but
some areas of spruce up to thirty inches in diameter were seen.

The construction of the Hudson Bay railway, which is now under way, has created
a demand for the survey of lands along the route. To meet this demand a network
of base and meridian outlines had to be established north of lake Winnipeg.

The principal meridian was run north from the nineteenth to the twenty-first base
line, and the twentieth and twenty-first base lines were run east a few ranges from
the meridian, and the twentieth base line three ranges west of the meridian. The
seventeenth, eighteenth, and nineteenth base lines were projected westerly from the
principal meridian across the Hudson Bay railway, and the sixteenth base line was
run from range 26, west of the principal meridian, to the second meridian.

The land along the principal meridian is mostly dry and rolling, and much of it
is fit for agriculture. Along some of the lines surveyed, swamps prevail, the soil
being mostly clay covered with moss. Timber as a rule is stunted, but occasional
belts of jackpine and spruce up to twenty-six inches are found. Water-powers exist on
all the streams, and fish abound in the lakes. Fishing will be a very profitable industry
when the markets are made available by the completion of the railway.

The second meridian was extended northerly from township 78 to township 85.
Little of the land along this part of the meridian is fit for agriculture, the soil being
mostly sandy, with frequent outcroppings of rock. A few good areas, however, lie
along Churchill river.

The proposal to extend a railway northerly between lakes Winnipeg and Winnipegosis towards Grand Rapids, and the demand for lands in the vicinity of this settlement, make it necessary to establish the base lines between the lakes. The thirteenth
and fourteenth base lines were, last season, produced as far easterly as the shore of
lake Winnipeg, and it is proposed to complete the survey of the remaining base lines
the coming season.

TOWNSHIP SUBDIVISION.

Subdivision surveys were made under contract mostly in the Peace River district
and between Athabaska (formerly Athabaska Landing) and Lesser Slave lake. The
projection of railways throughout these districts has stimulated settlement, and extensive subdivision surveys were necessary to keep ahead of the demand for land.

The reports received from the surveyors indicate as a rule that these lands are
good for agricultural purposes. They are mostly heavily timbered, but this will not
greatly retard settlement, as all the prairie lands of Western Canada are already
subdivided, and to a great extent alienated.

A number of townships were subdivided along Athabaska river north of Athabaska
to meet the requirements of settlement extending northerly along the valley. A few
townships north of Battleford, and a small number near lake Winnipegosis and east

of lake Winnipeg were also surveyed. In all, twenty-seven parties were employed on contract subdivision. Subdivision surveys, of such a nature that they could not conveniently be executed under contract at the regular rates fixed by Order in Council, were made in the foot-hills of the Rocky mountains in southern Alberta. All the land lying east of the Rocky Mountains Forest reserve was also subdivided. These surveys were undertaken to meet the demand of farmers and ranchers for land in the foot-hills and in the valleys penetrating the mountains.

Several townships or portions of townships in the vicinity of Fort Vermilion were subdivided. Some excellent prairie land lies in that locality, and settlement there is rapidly increasing. Squatters had been on the land for years, and were urgently asking that the lands be subdivided so that their claims might receive consideration before the influx of settlers caused complications.

The country bordering the southern section of the Hudson Bay railway consists of narrow ridges separated by wide areas of swamp and muskeg, and is not suitable for subdivision in block. It is essential, however, that a few sections on each side of the right of way shall be laid out, and during the past season, the work was carried on as far north as the sixteenth base line. A number of unsurveyed fractional townships around the Porcupine Forest reserve were also completed.

In the railway belt, British Columbia, seven parties were employed on township subdivision. The work was mostly in compliance with the demands of the Dominion lands agents and the settlers. Lands along the right of way of the Canadian Northern and Canadian Pacific railways were subdivided. Township subdivision in British Columbia includes in many cases, the survey of timber berths, village and town lots, and the retracement of Indian reserves and provincial lot boundaries. Owing to the mountainous character of the country the surveys are not suitable for execution under contract. In the Revelstoke and New Westminster districts, land is so valuable that it is usually allotted to settlers in 40-acre parcels. To mark the boundaries of such parcels sufficiently involves several miles of additional survey in each township. Land along the Fraser is excellent for fruit farming, and this industry is making rapid strides, though the lack of transportation is a great drawback.

By an Act of the Legislature of British Columbia, passed in 1883, the province granted the Dominion three and one-half million acres of land lying east of the Rocky mountains and adjoining the Northwest Territories. The boundaries of the block were surveyed a few years ago. On account of the excellent land in the block and the prospect of railway construction across it in the near future, settlers are flocking to the district. To meet the requirements of the newcomers, subdivision surveys are required of the prairie openings here and there. Several hundred quarter-sections were surveyed last season, and the fact that lands are available in that fertile district will no doubt stimulate settlement.

INSPECTION OF CONTRACT SURVEYS.

Subdivision surveys performed under contract during the year were examined by five inspectors. Their reports indicate that contractors have generally performed their surveys in fair conformity with the provisions of the Manual of Survey, and of their contracts with the department.

INTERPROVINCIAL BOUNDARY SURVEYS.

The boundary between the provinces of British Columbia and Alberta follows the Rocky mountains from the international boundary to the 120th meridian; thence it runs due north along this meridian to the 60th parallel of latitude.

At the request of the province of British Columbia arrangements were made for the delimitation of this boundary as a joint survey under Mr. A. O. Wheeler, B.C.L.S., Mr. R. W. Cautley, A.L.S., and Mr. J. N. Wallace, D.L.S., representing the provinces of

5 GEORGE V., A. 1915

British Columbia and Alberta, and the Dominion, respectively. The survey was begun last year in the vicinity of the main passes. The line was established and marked across Kicking Horse pass, Vermilion pass, Simpson pass, and Crowsnest pass. Pyramids of concrete, two feet high and covered by galvanized iron, were erected to mark the boundary where surveyed. Above timber-line, stone cairns five to seven feet high were substituted for the cement pyramids.

LEVELS.

Five thousand three hundred miles of line have now been levelled by surveyors of meridian outlines and base lines in the western provinces. As a result, much information previously lacking is now available for dealing with future extensions of railways, utilization of water-powers, improvement of navigable rivers, drainage, and development of natural resources. The results show that many areas of wet land, reputed to be of little value, can be drained readily into neighbouring streams, and become fit for agriculture. These lines of levels, having been commenced in unsettled lands where no altitudes were previously known, are dependent on the running of other lines for their connection to sea-level, and to one another. Twelve hundred miles of these connecting lines have already been run. These have joined the greater part of the levels to sea-level, thus improving their accuracy, and have furnished new information for the partly settled lands. The results are now being tabulated and will be published shortly.

TOPOGRAPHICAL SURVEYS.

At the request of the Director of Forestry, a topographical survey of the Crowsnest Forest reserve on the eastern slope of the Rocky mountains was begun last season. It is expected that the map of the reserve, when published, and the data collected by the survey, will be of great benefit, not only to the Forestry Branch, but also to the numerous holders of oil, coal, timber, and mineral claims.

In 1886 and 1888 a topographical survey was made of the country in the vicinity of Banff, Alberta. A scheme of lots was prepared in conformity with the topography, but only a few of the corners were marked. Mr. Mawson, an expert on town planning, has been engaged on the amended scheme for the subdivision. The villa-lot section and the townsite at Banff have been retraced. Roads have also been located, and scattered surveys made throughout the Rocky Mountains park.

In 1913 part of the townsite of Jasper in Jasper park was surveyed. A topographical survey of the surrounding country was commenced in order to obtain information for the preparation of a suitable scheme for the development of the park. The work is being continued this year.

STADIA SURVEYS.

Eight parties were employed in the prairie regions on stadia surveys of lakes and ponds that have been gradually drying up, and of rivers that have changed their courses. These surveys were undertaken for the purpose of amending the official plans of the townships so that they may represent all lakes, ponds, and rivers as they are at the present date, and give the correct area of land available.

A party on stadia surveys consists of a Dominion Land surveyor in charge, a surveyor's pupil, two rodmen, and a cook. A district is assigned to each party, and they are expected to investigate and report upon all bodies of water over five acres in extent in each township in which they carry on operations. If a body of water is over five feet deep, or if it does not dry up in the fall, the banks are traversed and a plot thereof forwarded to the head office. Rivers over a chain wide, and all islands, are accurately surveyed.

To avoid delay in issuing amended official plans, the surveyor is required to plot his traverse in camp and send it to the head office at the earliest opportunity. The sur-

SESSIONAL PAPER No. 25b

veyor is provided with special field books suitable for field notes of stadia surveys, and with convenient portfolios containing paper and drawing board for making traverse plots. Complete detailed instructions for making stadia surveys, for keeping field notes, and for preparing plots have been printed and furnished to each surveyor.

The eight parties employed last season made traverses or investigations in 442 townships; 3,360 miles of traverse were run.

CORRECTION AND RESURVEYS.

Some of the early surveys in the western provinces were badly executed; lines which are shown on the official plans as running north and south or east and west are found to be very much out in direction, and quarter-sections returned as 160 acres each are sometimes more than 40 acres over or under the area returned by the surveyor. When authorized by the provisions of the Dominion Lands Surveys Act, corrections are made by our surveyors. Last year two surveyors were employed to travel from place to place to make corrections or such small original surveys as could be done by a surveyor and assistant without a party. They made surveys in about seventy townships.

In many .townships surveyed twenty-five or thirty years ago not a trace can be found of the original survey. Where the marks have disappeared it is difficult for newcomers to locate the lands. It is the policy of the department to renew the lines in townships now being colonized after an investigation has shown that it is impossible to locate the lands without a new survey. Three parties were employed on resurvey work during the past season.

Base lines and initial meridians run many years ago are also found to have been badly surveyed. These lines being the governing lines of the Dominion lands system it is very necessary that their survey be accurate and reliable. To determine the nature and extent of some of the discrepancies, the retracement of the old base lines and meridians was commenced in 1912. In 1913 the second base line was retraced from the principal to the second meridian, as well as other lines in Manitoba and Saskatchewan. In 450 miles of line retraced the five largest errors found were of twenty-seven chains, seventeen chains, eight chains and eleven chains. The error of twenty-seven chains was made in measuring distance, but the remaining four were errors in direction.

SETTLEMENT AND TOWNSITE SURVEYS.

In the summers of 1911 and 1912 a survey party was engaged in surveying settlements along the Athabaska and Slave rivers. The work was continued during 1913, and the surveyor in charge will remain in the field till the autumn of 1914. It is expected that the survey of all the settlements along these rivers will be finished by that time.

A settlement was also surveyed at Wabiskaw, Alberta, and a summer resort at Wymark, Saskatchewan.

TIMBER BERTHS.

Under the present regulations the surveys of timber berths are made by the department before the berths are offered for sale. The cost of the surveys is included in the upset prices of the berths. The berths are surveyed by surveyors working under contract, or by the surveyors employed regularly during the season under daily pay, as may seem most economical. Fifty-two miles of timber berth boundaries were surveyed in 1913.

MINERAL CLAIMS.

Every mineral claim is designated by a lot number in the group to which such lot belongs. The claimant, after staking his claim, is required to apply to the Surveyor General to have instructions issued to a Dominion land surveyor to have the boundaries of the claim run out, measured, and marked on the ground. Lot and group numbers

5 GEORGE V., A. 1915

for the claim are furnished the surveyor with the instructions for survey. After completing the work on the ground, the surveyor must forward to the Surveyor General a plan of the claim on tracing linen, accompanied by complete field notes. He must furnish as well the necessary duplicates, the plan for filing with the mining recorder and for posting on the claim.

Twenty-two mineral claims outside of the Yukon Territory were surveyed last season. Thirty-one additional were surveyed in the Yukon Territory. In the latter district the group and lot numbers are furnished to the surveyor by the Commissioner of the Yukon, and the returns of the survey must be filed with the commissioner.

YUKON SURVEYS.

Dominion land surveys in the Yukon Territory are under the direction of a Director of Surveys who has his office at Dawson; he has a staff of two draughtsmen. The work is mostly in connection with mining claims.

During the year 167 miles of base lines and connecting traverses were made along The work is mostly in connection with mining claims.

STATEMENT OF MILEAGE SURVEYED.

The following is a comparison of the mileage surveyed each year since 1911:—

Nature of Survey.	April 1, 1911, to March 31, 1912	April 1, 1912, to March 31, 1913.	April 1, 1913, to March 31, 1914.
	Miles.	Miles.	Miles.
Township outlines	2,011	2,718	3,760
Section lines	10,098	10,365	7,918
Traverse	2,577	3,509	5,748
Resurvey	2,317	2,586	1,632
Total for season	17,033	19,178	19,058
Number of parties	61	72	66
Average miles per party	280	266	289

The following tables show the mileage surveyed by the parties under daily pay, and by the parties under contract:—

WORK OF PARTIES UNDER DAILY PAY.

Nature of Survey.	April 1, 1911, to March 31, 1912.	April 1, 1912, to March 31, 1913.	April 1, 1913, to March 31, 1914.
	Miles.	Miles.	Miles.
Township outlines	992	1,619	2,074
Section lines	823	1,358	1,695
Traverse	498	992	4,179
Resurvey	2,237	2,538	1,613
Total for season	4,550	6,507	9,561
Number of parties	29	35	39
Average miles per party	157	186	245

SESSIONAL PAPER No. 25b

WORK OF PARTIES UNDER CONTRACT.

Nature of Survey.	April 1, 1911, to March 31, 1912.	April 1, 1912, to March 31, 1913.	April 1, 1913, to March 31, 1914.
	Miles.	Miles.	Miles.
Township outlines..........	1,049	1,099	1,695
Section lines............................	9,275	9,077	6,214
Traverse	2.079	2,517	1,569
Resurvey.............	80	48	19
Total for season	12,483	12,671	9,497
Number of parties..............:................... . .	32	37	27
Average miles per party... .... :...	390	342	352

Owing to the nature of their work, twelve parties are not included in the statement of mileage for the year ended March 31, 1914.

COST OF SURVEYS.

The following statement shows the average cost per mile of surveys executed by surveyors under daily pay, and by surveyors under contract :—

	Surveyed under daily pay.	Surveyed under contract.
Total mileage surveyed.....	9,561	9,497
Total cost.................... ,,................	$542,297	$278,707
Average cost per mile....	$56·72	$29·35

CONTRACT SURVEYS.

Section 53 of the Dominion Lands Surveys Act provides that the township sub-division survey of Dominion lands shall be performed under contract, either at a rate per township, per mile, or per acre, to be fixed, from time to time, by the Governor in Council, or by competitive tender, as the Governor may, from time to time, direct; provided that in special cases, where circumstances render it advisable, the Governor in Council may order the survey of a township or townships to be otherwise performed.

In my opinion the time has come to abandon the system of contract surveys and to have the subdivision surveys of the Dominion executed by surveyors and parties paid by the day.

The system of Dominion land surveys is an adaptation of the United States system. The method of surveying under contract was one of the features borrowed from the United States; it had several advantages and as land had little value, it was believed that the imperfection of the surveys was of small consequence. The system was cheap and, as little or no inspection was made, it gave no trouble for the time being. Surveyors were ready to undertake surveys for almost any remuneration. At one time, tenders were called; the rates asked by the surveyors were so absurdly

5 GEORGE V., A. 1915

low that they have since been fixed by Order in Council at a figure sufficient for doing the work irrespective of what the surveyors would be ready to accept. A consideration which had great weight when a rush of immigration set in was that the amount of surveying which could be performed under the contract system was unlimited. With work paid by the day, the amount was limited by the number of qualified surveyors available; there was no such limitation with contractors.

The objections to surveys made under contract are many. The cost of a subdivision survey cannot be estimated in advance; it depends upon the nature of the ground and upon other circumstances unknown both to the Government and to the contractor, and which cannot be foreseen. No schedule of rates can be devised which will afford fair remuneration to the contractor in all cases without being excessive in any case. A contractor may make large profits if he happens to strike good country and is favoured by circumstances, while another may lose money through no fault of his own, if circumstances are against him. If he is unable to pay the wages of his men or his bills for supplies, the creditors ask payment from the Government and are aggrieved when it is refused.

Before a contractor is paid for a survey, some one should go over the lines in order to make sure that the survey for which payment is asked has actually been made. This inspection is never made for the obvious reason that it costs as much to inspect a survey line as to survey it in the first instance, the inspection involving the same measurements as the survey itself. If all the lines were inspected, the inspector might as well survey them himself and dispense with the survey of the contractor, thus saving the cost of the contract.

In the early days, very little inspection was made; the word of the contractor that the survey had been correctly executed was accepted and he was paid. We are now going over these old surveys; many of them are incorrect. Sometimes we can find no trace of a survey, and it is a question whether the original survey, which was paid for, was ever made.

At present, an inspection is made of a few miles in each contract. If nothing wrong is found, it is assumed that the remainder of the contract has been executed and that the survey is correct, but there is no direct evidence that such is the case.

There are five inspectors and a chief inspector of surveys; the cost of inspection is over $68,000 a year. The expenditure on contract surveys during the year was about $240,000, so that the inspection costs more than one-quarter of the work inspected. It is true that the inspectors do some little work besides inspection, but it does not amount to much.

Some surveyors do good work under contract; others do not. When a contractor's work is found defective, he is invited to correct it. He corrects the defects pointed out by the inspector, after which a new inspection is made and new defects are discovered. This may happen again and again, until so many inspections are made that it would have been cheaper for the inspector to make a new survey.

When the survey is very bad, the situation is most embarrassing. The bond given by private sureties for securing the advances does not appear to have much value; we have lost the cases that were brought before the courts. Surety companies are the only ones from whom we have recovered because they prefer paying to being sued by the Government. Practically we have the alternative of accepting bad work or losing our advances.

A large proportion of the appropriation for Dominion land surveys is now being expended in resurveying townships imperfectly subdivided under contract. The lands being settled and occupied, the resurveys are very intricate, unsatisfactory to the settlers, and most expensive. Money would have been saved if the surveys had been properly made in the first instance. For this reason alone, if for no other, the contract system should be abolished.

SESSIONAL PAPER No. 25b

Land has become too valuable for the imperfections of the contract system. The value of one or two acres in a quarter-section represents many times the difference in cost between a good and a bad survey.

After he has finished the survey in the field and received 75 per cent of the amount of the contract, the contractor attends to the preparation and correction of his field notes when he is not otherwise engaged. This is the cause of serious delays; it is seldom less than two years before the township plans are issued and the lands thrown open to settlers.

With competent surveyors and properly organized parties, there is no reason why subdivision surveys paid for by the day should cost much more than if executed under contract. The contract system was discarded in 1910 by the United States. The report of the Commissioner of the General Land Office for 1911 contains the following remarks:—

"June 30, 1911, was the close of the first fiscal year under the direct system, and it is gratifying to be able to report that it has been an unqualified success. When the change in method from the contract to the direct system was first considered, it was expected that the cost of production would not be greater than that in the procedure which it was proposed to abandon. It was conceded that greater expedition would ensue and better work be accomplished, and this alone would have justified the change. The work of last season and this season, however, has shown that the average cost of survey of a township under the direct system is $750, or a saving of about $5 per mile, the average cost of surveys under the contract system being $15 per mile.

"There is, in addition, a saving from one to two years in time, counting from the time of the appropriation to the completion and adoption of the survey."

Again in his report for 1913, he states:—

"The third season of field operations under the direct system has fully demonstrated the wisdom of abandoning the contract system."

BOUNDARY MONUMENTS.

The corner of a section or quarter-section is marked by an iron post and four pits, with or without a mound. The mound and pits become obliterated in time, or are wilfully destroyed; the post, which is a 3-foot length of half-inch iron pipe, is easily pulled out. A person who has an interest, for some purpose of his own, in removing land marks, can easily do it, and evidence is not lacking of the destruction of a large number of survey monuments. When the monuments are gone, a new survey must be made and, if the land is alienated, it is a most unsatisfactory and expensive undertaking.

A more substantial boundary post, and one that cannot be so easily removed is very desirable, but the improvement will involve some expense. Not only will the initial cost of the post be greater, but the post will be heavier, and transportation will be expensive. Land has become so valuable and the troubles due to lost corners are so far reaching that the outlay for improving corner marks will prove a wise investment.

CORRESPONDENCE.

The correspondence consisted of: letters received, 13,588; letters sent, 17,000.

ACCOUNTS.

Number of accounts dealt with, 1,616; amount of accounts, $1,073,655; number of cheques forwarded, 3,651.

5 GEORGE V., A. 1915

OFFICE WORK.

T. Shanks, Assistant Surveyor General.

In previous reports, attention was called to the deplorable condition of the office staff. The situation has not improved; on the contrary, it is becoming worse. Last year twelve permanent technical employees left our service; their names are: J. P. Cordukes, A. S. Thomas, L. O. R. Dozois, G. O. Vogan, T. S. Mills, S. D. Robinson, Jas. Hill, G. N. Clarke, O. E. Fournier, J J. Freeland, J. A. S. King, L. G. Smith.

Twenty temporary employees were secured through the Civil Service Commission for filling the vacancies. Of these ten left before their period of probation had expired, and before we had a chance of appointing them permanent; their names are: W. B. George, G. B. Stewart, A. H. Bick, L. C. Prittie, G. A. George, J. Mooney, A. J. Boucher, L. Leclerc, H. S. Van Patter, R. J. Gauley.

Comments are superfluous. Employees do not abandon their positions in such large numbers unless there is something radically wrong in the conditions of their employment. This has been going on for years. The disastrous consequences of this policy are set forth in last year's report; I can only repeat that efficient administration with a staff continually changing is not to be thought of.

As an office, our first duty is towards the settler on Dominion lands. It is important that his homestead shall be correctly laid out and marked by proper monuments. While the subdivision of Dominion lands appears to be an operation of extreme simplicity, actual experience has proved that it can be done only by properly qualified men equipped with instruments specially designed for accurate work. Facilities have now been provided in one of the divisions of the office for instruction in special astronomical work, and for the testing and inspection of surveyors' instruments. The results have amply justified the additional attention given to this department of our work.

The preparation of detailed instructions, many of technical nature, covering the work of a field staff of seventy or eighty surveyors, requires the services of men who are thoroughly conversant with survey methods, and with the history and records of the old surveys. Unfortunately, few of our staff have been in the service long enough to acquire these qualifications.

Experience has shown that better results have been obtained by a separation of the draughting offices from the other technical work of the branch. The number of properly qualified draughtsmen looking for positions is very small, and there is great difficulty in getting competent men for the salaries offered. Many of the best technical men are poor draughtsmen and, on the other hand, very few of the expert draughtsmen are qualified for the examination of survey returns, the checking of astronomical data, and the compilation of topographical and geographical information. It has proved a decided advantage to have the compilation of maps and plans prepared by men possessing technical qualifications for the purpose, and to have the draughting done by others specially trained for that work.

It is desirable that the surveys shall be confirmed, and the plans thereof issued as soon as possible after the field work is completed. Delays lead to misunderstandings between the settler and the department, and it is frequently a matter of surprise to the former that it is not possible for him to secure patent as soon as the lines are marked on the ground. Where the matter is particularly urgent the surveyor is instructed to forward returns from the field as soon as the survey is completed, but this can be done in comparatively few cases without seriously interfering with the field work. The cost of a party in the field is so great that it is not advisable to keep the surveyor employed on clerical work which, under ordinary circumstances, can be much better done in an office where there are proper conveniences for the purpose, and without keeping the party idle.

Inquiries from the general public for information as to the localities covered by subdivision or exploration surveys are being received in increased numbers. An attempt is made to print the surveyors' descriptive reports as soon as possible after they are received. The results are not entirely satisfactory as the subdivision reports are not forwarded by the surveyor until the season's work is completed, and the delays in compilation and printing are sufficient to considerably impair the freshness and value of the reports when issued. Little has been done to prepare for publication the reports covering the districts into which subdivision has not been extended, although in many cases these localities have been fairly well covered by the explorers who are now attached to block outline parties. The sketch maps showing the exploration and the general report of the surveyor in charge of the party are published in the annual report of the branch. This information, however, is not in convenient form for reference, as it can be obtained for any particular district only by searching the reports for several years. With additional office help it should be possible to compile much valuable information in such a form as to be of the greatest value to the public. A start has been made in this respect by issuing a pamphlet covering the Peace River district. The demand for this publication indicates the need for further work along the same lines.

DIVISION OF SURVEY INSTRUCTIONS AND GENERAL INFORMATION.

(H. G. Barber, Chief of Division.)

The work of this division consists, in general, of the preparation of instructions for the surveyors who are engaged in the field operations, the entering of all survey returns in the various registers, the issuing of all preliminary plans except for the townships in the railway belt of British Columbia, the compilation of the annual report of the branch, and the answering of requests for information received from the general public and from other branches and departments.

During the year the total number of draft letters and memoranda was 8,293, an increase of more than 30 per cent over the preceding year.

Two hundred and ninety-five drafts of instructions to surveyors for the execution of surveys were issued, involving the preparation of 2,628 sketches and 234 maps and tracings.

Two thousand and seventy-eight communications from settlers and others, and inquiries from other branches and departments were dealt with, an increase of more than 40 per cent over the number during the preceding year. This necessitated the preparation of 588 sketches, 92 maps and plans, and 386 pages of field notes. Three thousand one hundred and sixty-one sketches were also made for the information of other branches.

Twelve descriptions of parcels of land were drafted, and a number were checked and revised for other branches.

Preliminary plans were issued for 316 townships. These plans allow of the land being opened for entry at once without waiting for the final examination of the surveyors' returns and the issue of the official plans.

Plans of 672 townships and of thirteen townsites or settlements were received from the lithographic office, entered in the various registers and distributed. One hundred and eight sectional maps and 151 miscellaneous plans were also received and distributed.

During the year there were received from the surveyors in the field, and entered in the office registers, 1,304 progress sketches, 368 books of field notes for township surveys, 414 books and 762 plans for miscellaneous surveys, 219 timber reports, 107 statutory declarations, and returns for 125 magnetic observations, 90 azimuth observations, and for 11 timber berths. General reports on their survey operations were received from all the surveyors under daily pay.

5 GEORGE V., A. 1915

Their examination having been completed, 456 field books of township surveys and 93 books and 105 plans of miscellaneous surveys were placed on record.

For reference in the work of the office, there were received from the Survey Records Branch, 5,480 field books and 630 plans, and from the Registration Branch, 1,734 files.

Two new publications were issued, namely, the new edition of the Manual of Instructions for the survey of Dominion Lands, and the second edition of the pamphlet entitled " Description of the surveyed townships in the Peace River district in the provinces of Alberta and British Columbia." Already nearly two thousand of the latter publication have been distributed.

A new kind of work was commenced in 1911-12 in the preparation of topographical maps of Banff, Woodhaven, and Jasper (Fitzhugh) townsites, and of Bankhead cemetery, on which schemes of subdivision were laid down, and from which working plans for the surveyors were prepared. This work was continued during the year just passed and, in addition, similar maps and plans were prepared for summer resorts in Madge, Clear, and Elk lakes. A new and comprehensive scheme of subdivision for Banff and its vicinity is now under consideration.

DIVISION OF EXAMINATION OF SURVEYS.

(T. S. Nash, Chief of Division.)

The work of this division comprises the returns of survey of all Dominion lands other than those in the railway belt in British Columbia.

The first returns received from the surveyor are sketches showing the progress of his work. These sketches are examined to see that correct methods are being employed and that satisfactory results are being obtained, 304 progress sketches from contractors, 533 from men employed by the day, and 149 from inspectors of contract surveys were examined, making a total of 986 sketches.

Following the change in the method of dealing with water areas in the prairie provinces, outlined in the last annual report, eight surveyors were employed during this year in the investigation and retraverse of lakes and former lake-beds. This retraverse of lakes by stadia added materially to the work of this division. As this branch of work was new, and the instructions to surveyors were of a tentative nature, it was necessary to examine the returns of survey as soon as received with a view to the revision of the instructions in order to get the most desirable results. As the examination progressed, a comparative analysis of the results was made in order to arrive at a working basis for showing the new land areas and water areas on township plans. One hundred and thirteen field books and 789 plots comprised the final returns of survey of the lakes in 458 townships. The examination of these, together with the preparation of the new township plans, involved so much additional work that it was necessary to employ six of the stadia surveyors after quitting the field.

Including these stadia surveys, examination has been made of 704 subdivision surveys, 95 miscellaneous, and 243 township outlines. Four hundred and three memoranda on examination of survey returns were sent to surveyors and 407 replies were received and the necessary corrections made. Compiled plans of 549 townships were completed, of which 241 were first editions. Compiled plans of thirty-six miscellaneous surveys, twelve settlements and six timber berths were also completed. The number of draft letters prepared was 1,850. Forty-three accounts for contract surveys were prepared and closed, as the work was shown by the inspectors' reports to be satisfactorily performed.

The new plan of the town of Banff was completed, and considerable time was spent on the compilation of surveys in the adjoining villa-lot district.

With regard to the maps of the Yukon Territory, one sheet has been completed, and ten are practically finished, having been held up awaiting a further tie between existing surveys. These latter sheets are south of Dawson in the vicinity of the Yukon and Stewart rivers. Twenty group lot surveys, twenty-four base lines and reference traverses in various parts of the territory, and a triangulation survey of part of the lower watershed of Klondike river were reveived and examined.

Requests for information from other branches of the department involved the writing of 145 memoranda, the preparation of sixty-one sketches and the calculation of 394 areas. The field notes were examined and plans prepared for six timber berths comprising fifteen blocks whose boundaries totalled 140 miles of survey and whose area was approximately 54 square miles. The returns of eighteen other timber berths were examined. The plans of road diversions submitted by the Provincial Governments have been examined to the number of 405. Regarding railways, 110 plans of right of way were examined, the mileage of which was 1,917. As many of these plans were in duplicate or triplicate, the gross mileage of plans examined was equivalent to 4,584. The final returns of twenty-six mineral claims outside of the Yukon Territory were received and examined.

DRAFTING AND PRINTING DIVISION.

(C. Engler, Chief of Division.)

Township Plans.

The preparation of township plans for printing is the most important work of this division. The issue of the preliminary plan of a township allows settlers to initiate proceedings towards obtaining title to their lands, but the title cannot be obtained until the issue of the official plan. It follows that the full value of surveys has not been obtained until such plans have been issued and,. consequently, any delay in the issue of the official plan is equivalent to holding back the results and benefits of the survey. It is therefore essential that plans be issued as promptly as possible, and although the work on such plans has become more or less of a routine character, it is to be remembered that they constitute the most important part of our work even though other work may be more inviting and attractive.

The number of township plans prepared for printing was 724. The work on plans of second or subsequent editions is becoming in some respects simpler, in others more complex. As all areas of patented lands are now omitted, the plans have fewer areas, but the notes affecting the plan are more complex.

Plans of Settlements, Townsites, Subdivision and Miscellaneous Surveys.

The number of such plans was seventy. These plans vary in size and scale and, as a rule, require more time to prepare than township plans. In designing them the size, scale, and the arrangement of the notes, north point, border, and margin are subject to the following considerations:—

1. The scale must conform to the requirements of the Manual of Surveys.

2. No sheet can be fed into our lithographic presses larger than 25½ inches by 36½ inches.

3. The top of the plan should be to the north if possible.

4. To prevent waste of paper, plans must, as far as possible, be adapted to the sizes of lithographic paper kept in stock.

5. The arrangement of the borders, notes, etc., of a plan must be such as to reduce to a minimum the number of negatives necessary to reproduce it.

5 GEORGE V., A. 1915

The first and second of the above considerations are absolute, i.e., the scale of a plan cannot vary beyond certain fixed limits, and the size of the sheet of paper is limited. It follows that when a plan covers a very large area it must be printed in sections and, if necessary, joined afterwards. When plans are to be reduced by photography, the amount of such reduction must also be kept in mind by the draughtsman. On a plan too much reduced, letters and figures become so small as to be illegible, and fine lines become so thin as to be almost indiscernible. To offset this the draughtsman must make his letters and figures large enough and his lines heavy enough so that the reduction will make them just right.

It will be seen from the above that when a plan is to be copied for photographing and printing the proposition confronting the draughtsman is not simply that of making a neat copy. He must do this, of course, but at the same time he must keep in mind the processes and operations through which the plan must subsequently pass, in order to save extra labour and expense in these operations, and to give the best result when printed. This is especially true of plans in several colours.

Plans to accompany Orders in Council.

These plans are usually small and in several colors. As the Orders in Council are bound in a volume eight inches by thirteen inches the plans are printed on paper of this size, if possible. In copying them, care is taken to follow the original as closely as possible, as in many cases the plans deal with matters of which we have no official knowledge, and we have no other guide but the plan itself. To copy the original is not always easy, for originals are often very dim and obscure in some details, and letters and figures are not always clear and unmistakeable. Twenty-five such plans were printed.

Exploration Sketches.

During recent years, surveyors of base lines have furnished sketch maps of explorations of the country twelve miles on each side of the line. These are printed in black, blue, and brown on a scale of six miles to an inch, with an accompanying profile on a scale of 1,000 feet to an inch, and are appended to the annual report of the branch. These maps and profiles give a very good idea of the country.

Mounting Plans.

Plans printed in the early days of our lithographic experience were on a soft paper, well suited for making fine prints but not calculated to stand the wear to which copies for office use are subjected. We now use a much more durable paper (though one harder for the lithographers to print on), and for copies likely to have hard usage we use buckram. The office copies of the early plans, however, are in many cases badly torn, and to remedy this we have them mounted on cotton. We have already mounted 140 plans.

Miscellaneous Work.

This work is very varied in character. One of our draughtsmen was formerly an engraver, and during the year his services were frequently requisitioned for numbering the instruments, tapes, etc., of the Special Surveys Division. The number of tapes and instruments engraved was 500. Seven designs in colour for covers of publications for the Immigration Branch were made from time to time by our artist.

SESSIONAL PAPER No. 25b

The paper used by the lithographers is ordered by this division. Most of it comes from England, but some is made in Canada. It has to be ordered some time in advance as it is not so liable to change its shape or dimensions while being printed if it has been for some time in the same atmospheric conditions which prevail in the press room. Well seasoned paper is especially desirable where maps are in several colours, and the fitting or register of the colours requires to be very accurate.

The indexing and filing of plans of value takes up considerable time. When a plan is returned from the photographer it is filed away so that if more copies are required it has only to be photographed again and printed. It usually happens that changes can be effected without making the whole plan over again. We have now over 5,000 plans of townships and over 300 miscellaneous plans filed for future use. We also have a small library of over a hundred volumes, consisting of catalogues, departmental reports, and text books bearing on our work. The supply of printed sectional maps is also in charge of this division.

Supervision and Proof Reading.

As stated above, the draughtsman must plan his work out to suit the subsequent operations of the photographer and lithographer. This being the case, the draughting room may be looked upon as having an interest in the evolution of a printed plan throughout its whole course. This has become more and more apparent as the work has grown in proportion. It has come to be an established custom to look to this division for information on all matters relating to the progress of a plan towards its final printed form. Proofs of all plans are read here and, if necessary, sent for a second reading to those most concerned in their issue, and instructions are given as to the photographic reduction and details of lithographing.

BRITISH COLUMBIA SURVEYS DIVISION.

(E. L. Rowan-Legg, Chief of Division.)

The work of this division has been the preparing of preliminary plans from sketches sent in by surveyors, showing the progress of their work in the field, the examination of surveyors' field notes and plots, the compiling of township and other plans, the comparing of fair copies of township and other plans, and replying to requests for various information.

The work done has been as follows:—

Preliminary plans compiled, 55, and copies made, 275; surveyors' field notes of subdivision surveys examined, 25; plots, 36; of mineral claims, 7; of miscellaneous surveys, 14; township plans compiled, 97; townsite plans compiled, 3; miscellaneous plans compiled, 7; fair copies of compiled plans compared, 85; various plots and sketches made, 267; odd jobs and requests for various information dealt with, 368; draft letters and memoranda written, 667.

For the publication of reports of the surveyors engaged during the last few years in the inspection and classification of the lands in the railway belt, the detailed and general reports were collected and handed over to the Superintendent of British Columbia Lands by whom they are being edited.

For this publication, which is to be issued in pamphlet form in three volumes, maps are being prepared upon which will be shown the classification of the lands inspected, as well as all lands disposed of, timber berths, reserves, and other lands reserved from entry.

Two of these maps, for the first volume, have been compiled. This volume covers the railway belt as far westerly as the fifteenth range, inclusive, west of the sixth meridian.

For each of the two remaining volumes a similar map will be required. These have not yet been undertaken.

MAPPING DIVISION.

(J. Smith, Chief of Division.)

Part of the staff of this division is engaged solely on mapping, the remainder on compiling pamphlets of information about newly surveyed districts in the western provinces.

The usual work has been continued on sectional maps.

Nine new sheets were compiled and printed, taking in the country adjacent to Dunvegan and Fort St. John, and also along Athabaska river as far north as McMurray.

Twenty-five other sheets were revised and reprinted, most of them being in the more settled parts of the provinces. They show new railways, post-offices, roads, etc. Two of these sheets are in the British Columbia railway belt, covering the country adjacent to Vancouver and to Lytton.

The map to accompany the report on the Peace River country was also revised for a new issue, and a map of part of the railway belt was prepared, to accompany Mr. Bridgland's report on the triangulation of the Rocky mountains.

Among numerous smaller jobs may be mentioned a tracing of the contour map of Banff and vicinity, on a scale of 400 feet to an inch; a map of Eastern Ontario; a map of the Atlantic ocean between Canada and Northern Europe; preparing a new edition of the " Index map "; collecting and compiling information for a new map of Banff and vicinity on a scale of one mile to an inch.

The compilation in pamphlet form of all the useful and available information regarding the newly surveyed sectional districts in the West as well as the reports of all the surveyors who have worked in these districts, has been carried out.

The material for the publication of four such pamphlets has all been made ready. These pamphlets were not printed owing to the lack of suitable maps to accompany them. A map of the St. Ann sectional district, which is to be used as a sample in the preparation of all sectional maps for these pamphlets, was compiled in this office.

A pamphlet containing the surveyors' reports of the townships surveyed between July, 1911, and July, 1912, was prepared, edited, and published.

The pamphlet containing the surveyors' reports of all townships surveyed between July, 1912, and July, 1913, was prepared and edited, and is now in the hands of the printers.

A great many of the reports on townships which are to be included in the 1914 pamphlet have been typewritten, put in proper form, and made ready for publication.

One member of this division, Mr. John Brigly, died. Mr. Brigly's death, which occurred on March 12 after a short illness, is much regretted. He was in the prime of life, was of steady, vigorous habits, fond of athletic sports, popular amongst his associates, and a good man in the office.

SPECIAL SURVEYS DIVISION.

(G. Blanchard Dodge, Chief of Division.)

Base Line Surveys.

An examination is being made of the returns of survey of all base lines and meridians. This has been found necessary for the purpose of checking as nearly as possible the latitudes and longitudes of points and lines in the Dominion lands system and comparing their positions, as found on the ground, with the corresponding theoretical positions. As stated in last year's report, a number of errors of considerable magnitude were discovered in the older surveys in and around Manitoba, these errors being largely due to imperfect facilities in the earlier days of survey for testing surveyors' chains and other instruments. An investigation of all the surveys is therefore being made with the object of locating all such errors and, as far as possible, correcting them.

SESSIONAL PAPER No. 25b

Triangulation Survey.

A reduction has been made of the triangulation of the British Columbia railway belt between the Kootenay and Salmon Arm bases. In order to carry the triangulation over the summit of the Selkirks, it was found necessary, in general, that the stations should be situated on the highest peaks. In some cases the long and hazardous climbs were fraught with considerable danger, and the exposed top of a high mountain peak presents many difficulties to rapid and accurate observing. The weather conditions, also, were all against accurate work, and often a hard climb would be undertaken only to find that the stations on neighbouring peaks were invisible or indistinct, and that good work at that station would necessitate another long climb. Under such conditions it has been extremely gratifying to find that the untiring energy and perseverance of the surveyor has enabled him to maintain a high degree of accuracy throughout the survey.

The survey necessitated the observing of angles from sixty-five stations, the accurate measurement of two bases, each about five miles in length, astronomical observations for latitude and azimuth, and considerable subsidiary triangulation and traverse work. The triangulation network extends over a length of about 160 miles of the Canadian Pacific railway, and embraces an area of approximately 5,000 square miles.

When the last results of the angle and base measurements were received at this office during the early part of the year, an adjustment of the whole survey was commenced. This has now been completed in accordance with the degree of accuracy of the angular measurements, by dividing the triangulation network into sections and adjusting by the method of least squares. It was then found that the length of the Salmon Arm base, as computed through the triangulation from the Kootenay base, differed from its measured length by about six inches. A secondary adjustment was made to correct for this slight discrepancy.

Much minor triangulation and traverse work had also to be reduced to provide ties between triangulation posts and other surveys.

As the object of the triangulation was to replace the meridians and base lines as a basis for Dominion land surveys, it was required to compute the position each station would occupy in the Dominion lands system. To do this, it was necessary to form an estimate of the unknown deflections of the vertical at the points of astronomical observations, and to make corrections for the altitude above sea-level at which the Dominion lands surveys are made. The position of each station in the Dominion lands system was then computed from its latitude and longitude by means of tables IV and X of the Supplement to the Manual.

The elevations of the stations, as determined by the observing of vertical angles, have also been computed and adjusted.

A complete report of the triangulation work and adjustment has been prepared, and is ready now for printing.

Magnetic Survey.

Forty-six surveyors were instructed to observe for magnetic declination, and during the miscellaneous surveys made by R. C. Purser, D.L.S., and G. A. Bennett, D.L.S., observations for magnetic dip and total force were taken at fifty-two stations. The results are given in Appendix 58. The instrumental constants of the dip circles, as determined both at the beginning and at the close of the season's work, show a probable error of less than 0.0001 c.g.s. in each case, from the mean of six observations. At nearly every station a complete set of observations was duplicated and the average range was found to be comparatively small.

The index error of every transit used was determined both at the beginning and at the end of field operations. Every observation for declination has been checked,

5 GEORGE V., A. 1915

reduced to the mean of the month by means of the daily records of the declinometer at Agincourt, and plotted on a large scale map.

Besides the ordinary trough compass, as described in Appendix No. 50 of the annual report of this branch for 1911-12, a telescopic pattern was used this season. The compass was first submitted to the officer in charge of the Magnetic Observatory for examination and report, and was highly approved by him. The outer shell of the compass is a brass tube, on one end of which an ordinary Ramsden eye-piece is attached. There is a glass diaphragm on which are etched two close parallel vertical lines. The needle is of the regular edge bar type, with one end bent up at right angles and ground to a very fine edge. This end swings sufficiently close to the glass diaphragm to give a good definition of the bent up edge of the needle when the eye-piece is focussed on the lines on the diaphragm. A pointing is made by bisecting the space between the two vertical lines with the needle. Only one end of the needle can, of course, be read. It is found, however, that this is more than compensated for by the increased accuracy of the readings. The needle lifter is operated by means of a milled-headed screw at the end of the compass remote from the eye-piece. The method of fastening this compass to the standard is an improvement on that used with the trough compass, and assures better permanency of the index correction.

The director of the Meteorological Service expects to establish a self-recording declinometer this season, somewhere in the province of Alberta. This will be of great value in the reduction of our observations.

```
Returns for magnetic declination received to date for 1913..........   1,295
Previous returns, since 1908 ......................................   4,119
Total returns, to date ............................................   5,414
Dip observations received for 1913    ............................     145
Previous returns, since 1908 ......................................     144
Total force observations for 1913       ...  .................  .....      94
Previous returns, since 1908 ......................................     120
```

Astronomical Work.

Azimuth Observations.—All the azimuth observations taken on base lines and meridians during the summer season of 1912 and the winter season of 1912-13 have been received at this office and examined during the year. The effect of the careful examinations made and the strict supervision which has been exercised by this office in regard to the accuracy of the meridians and base lines run, is now becoming evident in the great increase in the accuracy of the work being done. The following table shows a brief résumé of the azimuth work of the four seasons 1909-12:—

	1909.	1910.	1911.	1912.
	$''$	$''$	$''$	$''$
Average correction per mile of line	5·5	6·5	2·7	2·1
Miles of line per azimuth station....	4·3	3·8	3·9	4·5
Average number of observations per azimuth station.... .	1·6	2·0	2·4	2·6
Average range of observations at an azimuth station.	17″	14″	11″	9″

The greatly reduced average corrections to the lines run in the different seasons illustrate very clearly that much greater skill and care are being exercised to run an accurate line on the theoretic bearing. No less important is the fact that the determinations of azimuths are much more accurate than formerly, as is evidenced both by the smaller range of the observations and by the greater number of observations taken at

SESSIONAL PAPER No. 25b

a station. Thus where, a few seasons ago, the azimuth of the line was often determined and a correction applied on the result of one comparatively poor observation with an uncertainty of fifteen or twenty seconds, it is now customary to take two or more observations at a station determining the azimuth usually to within five seconds. The objectionable practice of making corrections to the line on the result of a single observation is now but seldom resorted to.

The instruments used for observing during the seasons 1909-12 were, with but one or two exceptions reiterating instruments, having a six-inch circle with three verniers reading to 0·004 degrees (14″·4). The new pattern of transit now being used by all base line surveyors, furnished with a micrometer eye-piece and micrometer microscopes, should result in a still further improvement in the accuracy of the azimuth determinations and of the azimuths of the lines run. From the examination of the 1913 observations already received, this expectation would seem to be fully realized.

The larger parties now being employed, and the faster progress usually attained, often make it difficult for a surveyor to observe at such frequent intervals along the line as formerly; under these conditions it is necessary that a close supervision be kept, to ensure that no surveyor shall allow other considerations to stand in the way of his attaining a requisite degree of accuracy in his surveys.

The more northern latitudes in which the meridians and base lines are now being established, and the greater precision required in the azimuth observations, have necessitated a revision of the azimuth observing books and an extension of the tables of addition logarithms as given in table XVII of the Supplement to the Manual.

Star List.—In observing for latitude by Talcott's method, the latitude of the point of observation governs the stars eligible for making the determination; and since an observation may be required at any point north of the international boundary, it follows that a large number of suitable stars must be available. The various ephemerides and star catalogues published, as a whole, contain this information; but the number, size, and weight of the books prohibit their use in the field, where transportation is always so difficult. Also the fact of having to refer to so many separate books was decidedly inconvenient.

To obviate these difficulties, a Catalogue of Stars has been prepared embodying in one book the information of the different ephemerides and star catalogues, and this information has been reduced to the common epoch 1910·0 and put in the form most convenient for latitude work.

The Star Catalogue comprises over 5,000 suitable latitude stars, and the work involved in compiling the list was considerable, being in excess of 66,000 separate computations. Much data useful in latitude computations are given in the catalogue, and the various methods of star reductions are explained.

In conjunction with the revised and extended 1914 edition of the Star charts, this Star catalogue gives all the information necessary for latitude work in the field.

Astronomical Field Tables.

On account of the large amount of subdivision work now being made in the Peace River district, it has been found necessary to extend the Astronomical Field Tables from township 80 to township 140. In addition to giving the altitude and azimuth of Polaris, the field tables gave the sun's apparent right ascension for each day, and the right ascensions of forty-five bright stars for time observations.

As the apparent path of Polaris, due principally to precession and aberration, is such that the star has almost the same position in January, February, and March of one year, and April, May, and June of the next, taking a mean position of the star for these periods introduces no great error. Similarly a mean position may be taken for November and December, September and October, and July and August of three

5 GEORGE V., A. 1915

consecutive years. In order that the tables may be issued in time, they must be computed almost a year before required. The Nautical Almanac is supposed to be published two years ahead, but every year the computation of the tables has been delayed by the difficulty experienced in getting it, and each year this difficulty has increased. The right ascension and declination of Polaris can be extrapolated from the positions of former years, giving no appreciable error in the mean position of the star. In the same way the positions of the time stars can also be found sufficiently accurately from former values. But this method was not applicable for finding the right ascension of the sun. It was therefore decided to make a change in the form of the tables, the sun's right ascension being omitted from the Polaris tables and given separately for a whole year. The change was first made for the 1914 tables.

In the past two years a number of surveyors have been employed making traverses of lakes, etc. Often they spend only a short time at one place. On account of cloudy weather, frequently they have been unable to observe the pole star and have been compelled to resort to sun observations. Tables were therefore prepared giving the sun's apparent declination.

The maximum error in the table for the azimuth of Polaris is now much greater than when the tables were first prepared. Extending the tables from township 80 to township 140 has increased it by over 16 per cent. The change in the path of Polaris has produced a still greater effect, and as the error due to this cause is increasing, an investigation will be made with the purpose of finding a more suitable arrangement of months.

Levelling.

The levelling operations of the branch are now under the direction of Mr. J. N. Wallace at Calgary, but as he was not in a position during the past year to plot profiles from the levels, this work has been done here.

Profiles have been made showing levels run along 1,324 miles of base lines and meridians. These profiles are made on a large scale for office use, and on a smaller scale for publication in the annual report.

Surveying Instruments.

The work of this division includes the outfitting of surveyors with surveying instruments, such as transit theodolites, precise levels and levelling rods, stadia rods, steel measuring tapes, clinometers, aneroid barometers, sidereal watches, surveying cameras, etc. These are all of special design, adapted to the conditions and requirements of Dominion lands surveys. A complete stock of instruments is maintained, and they are packed and shipped, as required, to the surveyors in the field. Repairs to surveyors' instruments are also made under the supervision of this office. As upwards of seventy survey parties have to be cared for each season, a considerable amount of work is involved. To give some idea of this, it may be stated that 393 packages, weighing about 16,500 pounds, or 8¼ tons, were shipped out by express last year, and 142 packages, weighing about 8,200 pounds, or over 4 tons, were received.

Surveys Laboratory.

During the past year ten block survey transits, fifty-four D.L.S. subdivision transits, and eighteen levels have been tested, adjusted, and the constants determined. Forty-nine sidereal watches have been tested for isochronism and temperature compensation. In addition to the regular work, a large amount of time was devoted to the installation of the new apparatus at the Comparator building. A special cut-out arrangement for the new Cooke astronomical transit has been designed and constructed, and also a low temperature box for watch testing.

FIG. 2.
Transit Micrometer—Drum on Right.

FIG. 3.
Transit Micrometer—Drum on Left.

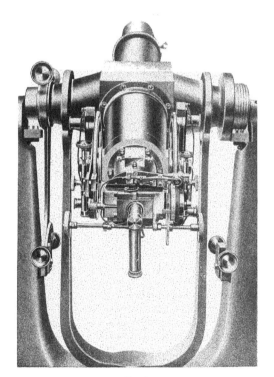

FIG. 4.
Astronomical transit with Transit Micrometer.

SESSIONAL PAPER No. 25b

All the watches purchased by the department and afterwards sold to surveyors for use on Dominion lands surveys are submitted to test before being accepted. The test is of forty-four days' duration, divided into eight periods of five days each, with four intermediate and extra days.

1. Watch in the vertical position, pendant up, temperature 65°.
2. Watch in the vertical position, pendant right, temperature 65°.
3. Watch in the vertical position, pendant left, temperature 65°.
4. Watch in the horizontal position, dial up, temperature 40°.
5. Watch in the horizontal position, dial up, temperature 65°.
6. Watch in the horizontal position, dial up, temperature 90°.
7. Watch in the horizontal position, dial down, temperature 65°.
8. Watch in the vertical position, pendant up, temperature 65°.

The four intermediate days when the rate of the watch is not recorded are at the commencements of the fourth, fifth, sixth and seventh periods, which are extended one day each for that purpose.

The watches are set going and allowed to run for a week in the dial-up position before the tests begin.

The conditions of the tests are as follows:—

1. The mean daily variation of the mean daily rate in any period must not exceed 2 seconds.

2. The mean error α of the mean daily rates for all the periods must not exceed 0.75 seconds.

3. The mean daily rate in any one of the five position tests must not differ from the mean of the mean daily rates in the five positions by 7.5 seconds.

4. The mean error β of change of rate for change of position must not exceed 3.5 seconds.

5. The mean daily rate at 40° F. must not differ from the mean daily rate at 90° F. by more than 0·3 seconds per degree F.

All watches which fail to meet these conditions are not accepted. The conditions are pretty severe for ordinary commercial watches; only the most skilled workmen in the factories are able to adjust the watches with the required delicacy. Of the forty-nine tests made during the year, five were special tests, and forty-four regular. Twenty-three watches passed the test, and as two of these were examined twice, 25 or 57 per cent of the tests were successful as against 15 or 25 per cent for the preceding year. The much larger percentage of watches which passed during the last year is undoubtedly due to the fact that the makers now realize that greater care must be given to the adjustments, if the watches are to be accepted.

In reference to the conditions of the test, conditions 1 and 2 are the tests for isochronism, 3 and 4 for position, 5 for temperature compensation. Of the nineteen watches which failed, four were withdrawn before their tests were completed. Of the remaining fifteen, five failed to fulfil condition No. 1, five condition No. 2, seven condition No. 3, and seven condition No. 4, or seven watches failed in isochronism, nine in position, and one in temperature compensation.

Comparing the average errors of the watches which passed with those for 1913 we have the following:—

	1913.	1914.
Average error for isochronism	0.59	0.45
Average error for position	2.58	2·03
Average error for compensation	0.14	0·10

5 GEORGE V., A. 1915

The average errors for isochronism of the twenty-three watches which passed were as follows:—

P.U	P.R.	P.L	D.U. 40°	D.U. 65°	D.U. 90°	D.D.	P.U.
0s 59	0s.50	0s.42	0s.44	0s.47	0s.38	0s.32	0s.48

The smallest error for α was 0s.26. Ten were less than 0s.4 and two less than 0s.3. It is interesting to note that both in the watches which passed and in those which failed the average error is lowest in the dial-down position and highest in the pendant-up position. In the temperature tests the lowest errors for isochronism were in both cases in the 90° temperature box.

The average errors for position of the watches which passed are as follows:—

P.U	P.R.	P.L.	D.U.	D.D.
1s.84	2s.46	2s.65	1s.59	1s.81

The smallest error for β was 0s.72. Eleven were less than 2s.0 and two less than 1s.5. Both in the watches which passed and in those which failed the largest average error is in the pendant-left position.

The compensation for temperature is remarkable. The average temperature coefficient is 0s.09. One watch had a coefficient of 0s.02, and one a coefficient of 0s.03. Of the forty-nine tested, only one exceeded the limit.

The results of the trials of the twenty-three watches which passed is given in Appendix 59.

Past experience has shown the hot-water temperature box to be preferable to the straight electric type. Being unable to purchase a temperature box from any standard line to run at 40° F., it was decided to have one constructed locally to our own specifications. It was considered advisable to provide a much larger ice chamber than usually supplied, also as perfect insulation as possible. Figure 1 shows a section through the temperature box as finally constructed.

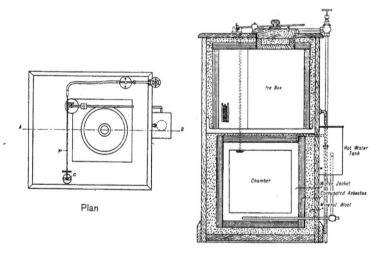

Plan

Section through AB

Fig. 1.—Temperature box, 40° Fahrenheit, for watch testing.

Surrounding the ice-box and temperature chamber is a special insulating material, 1¼-inch thick, of corrugated asbestos sheathing, affording five alternate air spaces and sheathings of asbestos. Between this special insulation and the wall of the temperature box is a space varying from 1-inch to 1¾-inch, filled with mineral wool. The chamber of the temperature box is fitted with two tight-fitting doors, with an air space between them.

The water jacket surrounding the chamber has been increased 50 per cent above that used in ordinary temperature boxes of this type. The increase in water space decreases the liability to any sudden change of temperature in the chamber. One other special feature is the addition of a small separate chamber in the ice-box compartment from which the cold water flows to the jacket surrounding the chamber. Before the water from the ice chamber can enter this compartment it passes through a fine sieve to remove any dirt and prevent clogging of the piping inside.

The regulator parts, proper, are very similar to those used on the Hearson temperature boxes. A capsule inside the chamber expands or contracts with slight changes in temperature, and causes the feed pipe " P " to swing to the right or to the left, as necessary to correct the temperature and the water flows into the hot-water tank or ice chamber and from there to the water jacket. When the temperature is correct in the chamber, the feed pipe remains in a central position and the water flows away through the waste pipe " O ".

Some difficulty was experienced in obtaining a liquid sufficiently volatile to be used in the capsules at 40° F. Rhegolene was first used, as it boils below this temperature, but it was found the vapour pressure was not great enough to be used in the ordinary capsule. Ether is now used in place of rhegolene. The capsules can only be filled during the cold weather.

The temperature box has been in operation for some time and has given excellent results, the variation in temperature in the chamber being less than ¼° F.

Time observations for checking the rate of our clock have been taken in the past with a small portable transit made by Messrs. Troughton and Simms. The instrument is very old, and at some time has evidently received very rough usage and is in bad repair. This year a new instrument was purchased from Messrs. Cooke and Sons. The telescope has a 3-inch objective of 36 inches focal length, and is fitted with a transit or registering micrometer. The instrument has a beautiful telescope and the workmanship on the whole transit is very fine, but the transit micrometer as furnished was not complete in that no cut-out was provided and no means of identifying the various contacts. After using the instrument for some time in this way, it was finally decided to design a cut-out apparatus ourselves and have the necessary alterations to the micrometer made locally. The principle of the cut-out design is somewhat similar to that used by the United States Coast and Geodetic Survey at Washington. The mechanical construction, however, is entirely different owing to the fact that no arrangement was provided by the makers for such a device on the instrument. It was found difficult to place the mechanism in a neat and compact manner.

While installing the cut-out, the opportunity was taken of improving the recording device, which was of the break-circuit type. The standard voltage of the chronograph is four volts and, with a small voltage of this nature in conjunction with the break circuit, misleading records are liable to occur due to any dirt or irregularity on the contact surfaces, unless an unduly high pressure is maintained between them. The recording device was changed to the make-circuit type, the micrometer transmitting its records through a relay to the chronograph. This permits the use of a strong current through the contact points of the micrometer head, ensuring the record of each contact and a minimum pressure upon the micrometer head by contact spring.

The cut-out provides that the micrometer transmits no records except those made within an accepted space on either side of the line of collimation and forming the observations of transit of the star.

5 GEORGE V., A. 1915

Figures 2 and 3 show the construction as finally adopted. In Figure 4 is shown the complete instrument, with attachment.

The micrometer screw which carries the slide with the movable wire is geared to the hand wheel shaft (s) by a two-to-one gearing. Mounted on the micrometer screw is the micrometer drum (c), worm gear (d), and ebonite drum (e) with contact strips (f). On the end of the telescope is mounted a fibre bracket (g) which carries the break-contact device, and gear (h), the gear engaging with the worm gear (d). This turning of gear (h)—of which the upper part is slotted—by the worm gear, causes lever (l) to break the contact at proper intervals. One special feature of gear (h) is that the upper half may be removed and replaced by another part giving different periods of contact. A second feature is the double pitch of the worm gear (d) which ensures a rapid make and break contact.

The instrument with this mechanism is now in use and is giving entire satisfac-. tion.

The Comparator building has been completed and the comparator installed. While the equipment is not yet altogether complete, it is possible to make very precise measurements and to verify the tests of our D.L.S. subsidiary standards with confidence. That a building of this nature is needed for the engineering profession in Canada is evident from the number of requests which have been received from surveying instrument dealers and others to have measures verified. Although the comparator has been in operation but a short time, 153 tapes have been tested for outside parties at their request. For Dominion lands survey purposes, 112 D.L.S. subsidiary standards have been standardized, and also eighteen surveying tapes for base line surveyors. Four precise levelling rods have also been tested. A description of the apparatus and method of testing will be published later in separate monograph form.

Correspondence.

The number of draft letters prepared was 1,808. Seventy letters of instructions to surveyors were prepared, and 490 memoranda written.

PHOTOLITHOGRAPHIC OFFICE.

(H. K. Carruthers, Process Photographer.)

About 1887 saw the beginning of the photographic office. All maps and plans were reproduced by the wet-plate process, and from these negatives the photo-litho transfer was made.

A specially prepared India paper was coated and sensitized, and when dry was exposed to the light through the negative. Afterwards this print was inked over with a thin coating of lithographic transfer ink and washed under the tap, when a complete fac-simile of the original was obtained. Immediately this was transferred to the prepared stone previous to its being printed in the power press.

This system had many drawbacks, as after sensitizing the paper it had to remain over night to dry, and should the following day be dark or rainy, exposures could not be made. This was before arc lamps were installed. If this print was incorrectly exposed, it meant a spoiled paper. Another big disadvantage was the copying of a map in sections. After passing through many stages of wettings no two sections were alike in size and had to be faked in the joining.

In 1903 the first and present up-to-date photolithographic plant was installed. Negatives ranging from 18 inches by 20 inches down to 8 inches by 10 inches were made. All plans and townships were drawn on larger sizes and reduced to proper scales, making the final results clear and sharp. Thin sheets of fine-grained zinc were used in printing from the negatives, and these could be stored away indefinitely for future use. Larger printing frames were installed with 5,000 c.p. arc lamp, and a large tournette for the coating of the zinc plates. The largest zinc plate used at this time was 18 inches by 20 inches, larger plates being unnecessary, as the camera did not accommodate larger sizes.

To facilitate handling the township plans, which were increasing in numbers, a special iron bed was obtained for the printing press. This bed was the thickness of standard litho stone, and with the clamps attached to each end, the zinc plates, with the image thereon, were securely fastened on, ready for the run. This method obviated the necessity of pulling transfers and materially increased the output in the printing department. The average number of impressions taken from each township was 225.

In 1910 the department installed a large offset printing press, taking plates 49 inches by 32 inches and steps were taken to enlarge the size of our camera to take negatives 28 inches by 32 inches. A large vacuum printing frame, 62 inches by 38 inches and four 50-inch mercury vapour tubes were installed, the dark-rooms and sinks being increased in size.

The townships were photographed on glass 15 inches by 18 inches. Three of these negatives were placed side by side and exposed on the 49 by 32-inch sheet of zinc. Three-mile sectional maps that had previously been copied in two sections were now done on one negative with headings and footnotes complete. These were placed on the press and printed without any further preliminaries.

Ten years ago the average number of negatives made monthly was fifty-four. During the month of March, 1914, a total of 275, ranging in size from 24 inches by 32 inches to 8 inches by 10 inches, was the output.

The staff at present consists of the photographer, four assistants, and two apprentices.

A schedule of the work for the year is given in Appendix No. 7.

PHOTOGRAPHIC OFFICE.

(*J. Woodruff, Chief Photographer.*)

General photographic work has increased about 50 per cent over that of last year. It has grown to such an extent that more help and larger quarters must be secured or the work will have to be curtailed. Even now it has been found necessary to curtail some of the work which we have been doing for other branches of the department. For the Forestry Branch alone nearly 10,000 prints were made, and about 1,000 negatives developed.

The space in the top floor of the Metcalfe Street building being required by the process photographer, most of the apparatus belonging to the chief photographer was moved to the basement, the blue-print and Vandyke work only being now done on the top floor.

A new camera (**Fig. 5**), specially designed for enlargements has been installed in the basement. Accuracy and a wide range of usefulness are its two outstanding features.

5 GEORGE V., A. 1915

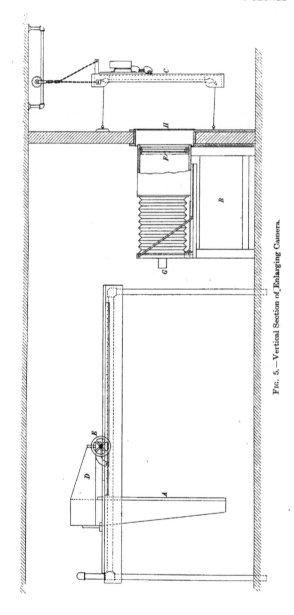

Fig. 5.—Vertical Section of Enlarging Camera.

The whole arrangement consists of three parts, the easel A, on which the sensitive paper is placed, the camera B, which carries the negative F and lens G, and the light C, which illuminates the negative, H being ground glass betwen the negative and the light. The easel is supported on a frame of steel tubing with four $2\frac{1}{2}$-inch posts, the lower ends of which are embedded in the concrete floor, making the frame perfectly rigid. The dimensions of the frame are 5 feet wide and 11 feet long. A steel track I (Fig. 6) runs the length of the frame on each side. A rack J runs on

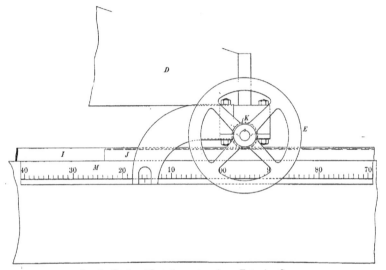

Fig. 6.—Rack and Scale for easel carriage—Enlarging Camera.

the frame supporting the carriage D which carries the easel, and enabled it to be moved forward or backward by means of a hand wheel E and pinions K which engage the rack.

The easel is 4 feet by 5 feet, and will take an enlargement of that size.

5 GEORGE V.. A. 1915

The camera is 4 feet long and 2 feet square, and will take a negative up to 20 inches square. It is supported on a heavy frame bolted to the floor. Adjustment is provided for by the crank *N* (Fig. 7), operating pinion *O* on rack *P*.

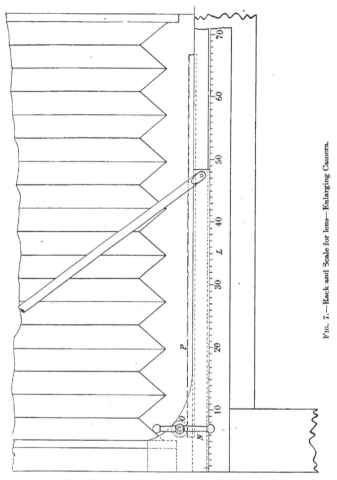

Fig. 7.—Rack and Scale for lens—Enlarging Camera.

The camera and easel are fitted with scales *L* and *M*, graduated to millimeters. This does away with all focussing, as the apparatus is simply set to scale for any size of enlargement.

The camera is also used for making lantern slides and transparencies of all sizes.

The light *C* (Fig. 5), consists of five Cooper Hewitt mercury vapour tubes which give a fine even illumination, and is much more satisfactory than daylight. A ground glass H is placed in front of the light, behind the negative, to diffuse the light still further.

A great deal of time is saved by this camera in reducing or enlarging maps, plans, etc., to the required scale; work which formerly required weeks to perform is now done in a few hours, and in a much more satisfactory manner.

The numerical strength of the staff is the same as last year, one clerk resigning and one being appointed.

LITHOGRAPHIC OFFICE.

(A. Moody, Foreman.)

The work of the lithographic office continues to increase steadily, as shown by the statement of work done, in Appendix 8. Two power presses are used, one a flat-bed machine capable of printing either from stone or from zinc plates, the other a rotary offset press printing from zinc plates only. One essential difference between the presses is that for the flat-bed press the work on the plate or stone is reversed, so that when the sheet of paper to be printed comes in contact with the work and receives a print, the print reads correctly. With the offset press the work on the plate reads correctly; a reverse print is made to a rubber blanket which in turn prints a correct copy on the paper. It is therefore necessary in preparing work for these presses to keep in mind this difference, as any plate prepared for one press must be reversed before the other press can print it. This reversing may be done by transferring but this usually thickens up the work and causes a loss of sharpness. A preferable way is to reverse by photography, and as most of the work is photographed, it is merely necessary to determine upon which press a job is to be printed, and the photographer arranges the matter by copying either direct or through a mirror as desired. The offset press is a later development in lithography and is capable of a higher rate of speed than the flat-bed. It is therefore used in long runs. The printing of annual report maps and of township plans forms the bulk of the work turned out. Of the latter, 203 copies only are printed; 3 on linen, 170 on thin paper for mailing purposes, and 30 on thick paper for ordinary office use.

More time is required for preparation and adjustment of press to meet the conditions relative to the printing on each kind of paper than would be required for a straight run on only one kind of paper. The same would apply regarding the necessity for frequent changes when more than one colour is used in printing a plan or map.

The flat-bed press is easier to change from one colour to another, and is consequently used much for colour work or for short runs. The printing of the 3-mile sectional maps in three colours, black, blue, and brown, has been undertaken, and provides considerable additional work for the flat-bed press. Reprints of township plans originally issued in colours have also given much colour work.

The largest size of paper used is 24 inches by 34 inches, so that the maximum size of map which can be printed is about 22 inches by 32 inches, varying a little with the allowance for margin.

GEOGRAPHIC BOARD OF CANADA.

(A. H. Whitcher, Secretary.)

The twelfth annual report of the board, containing a consolidation of the decisions published in previous reports up to June 30, 1913, has been published and distributed. This report is now printed as a supplement to the report of this department, as the chairman of the board is the Surveyor General. The secretary is also a member of the staff of the Topographical Surveys Branch.

Regular meetings of the board have been held throughout the year, and the bulletins containing the decisions published from time to time in the *Canada Gazette*. A number of these bulletins have also been published separately and distributed by the secretary.

25b—3½

       DEPARTMENT OF THE INTERIOR

5 GEORGE V., A. 1915

BOARD OF EXAMINERS FOR DOMINION LAND SURVEYORS.

(*F. D. Henderson, Secretary.*)

Two meetings of the Board of Examiners were held during the year. The first was a special meeting for the examination of candidates, and lasted from April 28 to May 29, 1913, inclusive. Examinations were held at Ottawa, Toronto, Calgary, and Edmonton. The second was the regular annual meeting of the board provided for in section 9 of the D. L. S. Act. It lasted from February 9 to April 1, 1914, inclusive Examinations were held at Ottawa, Halifax, Montreal, Kingston, Toronto, Winnipeg, Regina, Calgary, Edmonton, and Dawson, Y.T. The total number of candidates examined was 287. The following table shows the number who tried at each centre, and the number who were successful:—

Places.	Full Preliminary.		Limited. Preliminary.		Final.		D. T. S.		Total.	
	Tried.	Passed.	Tried.	Passed.	Tried.	Passed.	Tried.	Passed.	Tried.	Passed.
April-May, 1913.—										
Ottawa................	19	6	.....	....	21	12	.....	....	40	18
Toronto..............	5	2	....	....	8	6	.....	....	13	8
Calgary..............	8	6	3	2	4	2	. . .	....	15	10
Edmonton....	11	4	1	0	4	1	...	....	16	5
February, 1914.—										
Ottawa.......	29	6	4	2	19	9	4	1	56	18
Halifax....	2	1	.....	.... ..	2	2	....	....	4	3
Montreal	21	8	1	0	.....	.....	.....	......	22	8
Kingston	28	6	... ..	....	.. ..	.. ..	....	.....	28	6
Toronto....	24	4	2	0	9	3	.	....	35	7
Winnipeg..	5	2	... ..	.... ..	1	0	....	.....	6	2
Regina....	5	3	.....	....	1	1	....	.....	6	4
Calgary	11	3	1	1	10	1	....	.....	22	5
Edmonton....	19	4	.....	....	3	0	....	....	22	4
Dawson.......	2	0	.....	....	.....	....	...	....	2	0
Total	189	55	12	5	82	37	4	1	287	98

Following are the names of the successful candidates:—

Full Preliminary and Limited Preliminary Examinations (60).

Alexander, John Bentley, Calgary, Alta.

Bannister, George William, Ottawa, Ont.
Beach, Floyd Kellogg, Calgary, Alta.
Biddell, Cecil Henry, Regina, Sask.
Bonham, John C., Kingston, Ont.
Bostock, Achilles, Banff, Alta.
Buck, Cameron Alexis, Edmonton, Alta.
Burfield, Francis Robert, Calgary, Alta.

Calder, Leslie Raymond, Nanaimo, B.C.
Carroll, John, Toronto, Ont.
Carter, John Lark, Calgary, Alta.
Cohoon, Carl William, Ottawa, Ont.
Cole, William Stanley, Brockville, Ont.
Crowell, Clement William, Yarmouth, N.S.

DesBrisay, Eric Merrill, Vancouver, B C.
Donaldson, Garnet Hilliard, Ottawa, Ont.

Lindsay, Charles Crawford, Quebec, P.Q.
Lyon, John Edward, Ottawa, Ont.

Martin, Frederick John, Winnipeg, Man.
Meitz, Walter H., Pembroke, Ont.
Mills, Arthur McIntosh, Ottawa, Ont.
Mills, Thomas Stanley, Kingston, Ont.
MacKenzie, Hugh Ross, Regina, Sask.
McDonald, William Sutherland, Embro, Ont.
McFarlane, Maynard Deedes, Montreal, P.Q
McIntosh, John Stuart, Morrisburg, Ont.

Nelson, Edward, Streamstown, Alta.

Parker, Henry Albert, Havelock, Ont.
Patterson, George B., London, Ont.
Paul, John McNeill, Calgary, Alta.
Pelletier, Henri Burrough, Montreal, P.Q.
Perry, Alfred Melville, Banff, Alta.
Prittie, Lloyd Conn, Pembroke, Ont.

SESSIONAL PAPER No. 25b

Fawcett, Thomas Gordon, Ottawa, Ont.
Frame, William Tay'or, Vancouver, B.C.
Fullerton, James Thornton, Victoria, B C.

Gammon, Albert Osborne. Calgary, Alta.
Gass, Lawrence Henderson, Iroquois, Ont.
Gray, Edwin Roy, Toronto, Ont.
Guignard, Ernest Auguste, Ottawa, Ont.

Jones, Cyril, Calgary, Alta.
Joslyn, Cecil Earl, Sintaluta, Sask.

Keep'ng, Kimball F Murray Harbour P. E I.
Kezar, George Lennox, Britannia Heights, Ont.
Knight, Albert Matthew, Edmonton, Alta.

Lawrence, Charles Albert Rutter, Toronto. Ont.

Prinsep, Garnet T. T., Ottawa, Ont.

Ramsay, James Harold, Ottawa, Ont.
Riddell, John Morrison, Toronto, Ont.
Richer, Cuno Edward, Ottawa, Ont.
Robertson, James, Lach.ne P.Q.
Russell, John, Edmonton, Alta.

Scandrett, Frederick Raymond, Calgary, Alta.
Sharpe, David Neville, Winnipeg, Man.
Smith, Gordon J., Kingston, Ont.
Tory, Charles Howard, Edmonton, Alta.
Trelle, Hermann William, Edmonton, Alta.

Wall. George, Albert, Crescent, Alta.
Wilkins, Arthur G., Ottawa, Ont.
Wright, Harold Colin, Sandhurst, Ont.

Final Examination (37).

Alport, Frederic, Orillia, Ont.
Bartley, Thomas Holmes, Toronto, Ont.
Barton, Harold Miall, Ottawa, Ont.
Bingham, Harold Carr, Moosejaw, Sask.
Bolton, Lambert Ernest Stanley, Wiarton. Ont.

Clarke, Roger Fyfe, Hamilton, Ont.
Coté, Joseph Martial, Ottawa, Ont.

Dozois, Leo Oswald Ross, Calgary, Alta.
Dynes, Richard Fforde, Pembroke. Ont.

Edwards, William Muir, Edmonton, Alta.
Ewan, Hedley Jenkins, Yarmouth, N.S.

Grant, Alexander Macdonald, Ottawa, Ont.
Griffin, Albert Dyke, Elk Lake, Ont.

Fredette, Joseph Fredelin, Ottawa, Ont.

Huffman, Karl, Toronto, Ont

Johnston, Robert Henry, Toronto, Ont.

King, James Albert Shirley, Ottawa. Ont.

LeBlanc, Pierre Maxime Henri, Ottawa, Ont.

Logan, Robert Archibald, Middle Mosquodo-
boit, N.S.
Macdonald, Colin Stone, Ottawa, Ont.
Macdonald, James Atwood, Ridgetown, Ont.
Morency, Georges, Lévis, P.Q.
Moulton, Hazen Parker, Ottawa, Ont.
MacIlquham, Walter Lloyd, Ottawa, Ont.
MacRostie, Norman Barrie, Metcalfe, Ont.
McGarry, Patrick Joseph, Merritton, Ont.
McKnight, James Henry, Simcoe, Ont.

Norrish, Wilbert Henry, Guelph, Ont.

Pierce, Benjamin Clifford, Kingston, Ont.
Pounder, Irvine Rudsdale, Ottawa, Ont.

Roberts, Otto Beer, Murray Harbour, P.E.I.

Sharpe, George Pearce, Agassiz, B.C.
Steers, Francis Paul, Ottawa, Ont.
Squire, Richard Lane, Ottawa, Ont.

Van Skiver, Leighton Adelbert, Fish. Lake, Ont.

Wrong, Frederick Hay, Chatham, Ont.

Young, Stewart, Owen Sound, Ont.

Examination for Certificate as Dominion Topographical Surveyor.

Rannie, J. L., Ottawa, Ont.

The examinations at all the centres are held simultaneously and according to a time-table approved by the board; and the presiding examiners have instructions to transmit each night to the secretary at Ottawa, the answer papers received during the day. As the papers are received at Ottawa they are distributed to the members of the board. The members being busy during the day with departmental business, the papers have to be read at night, and where the number of candidates is large, as it has been for some years, the work becomes very arduous.

At the meeting in April and May, complete sets of papers were prepared for use at the examination in February, 1914, and at the meeting in February other sets were prepared for the examination in April and May, 1914.

For some time it has been felt by the members of the board that the writing of candidates who came before them is very bad and that the answer papers also left much to be-desired in the way of neatness and orderly arrangement. After consider-able discussion it was decided to amend the rules and regulations so as to provide for a subject "Penmanship and Neatness," for which a certain number of marks would

DEPARTMENT OF THE INTERIOR

be allowed on each paper. "Penmanship" is taken to be "the quality of ordinary writing;" and "neatness," "the clean, orderly, and tidy condition of the written answers to the questions." It is hoped by this means to secure not only more creditable papers from candidates, but to impress upon these young men seeking to enter the surveying profession the need of legible writing and of neatness and care in the preparation of the returns of survey.

Several college graduates applied to be admitted to the shorter term of service as provided in section 22 of the D.L.S. Act. Favourable decisions were given in the case of a graduate in civil engineering of the University of Colorado and in the case of a graduate of the Nova Scotia Technical College at Halifax.

Mulford's "Boundaries and Landmarks" and Cautley's "Descriptions of Land, a Textbook for Surveying Students" were added to the list of books of reference for final candidates.

Thirty-nine commissions as Dominion Land Surveyors were issued to those who had passed the final examination and had furnished the oath of office and oath of allegiance and bond as required by section 25 of the Act.

Thirty-two standard measures were issued during the year. Twenty-eight of these went to Dominion Land surveyors and two to provincial surveyors.

A list of Dominion Land surveyors who are in possession of standard measures, corrected to March 31, 1914, will be found in Appendix No. 10.

The correspondence of the board was as follows: letters received, 1,727; letters sent, 920; circular letters, pamphlets, notices, etc., sent, 1,654.

The following table shows the number who have tried the various examinations each year since 1900, and the number and percentage of successful candidates.

Fiscal Year.	PRELIMINARY.			FINAL.			D.T S.			TOTAL.		
	Tried.	Passed.	Per cent Passed.	Tried.	Passed	Per cent Passed.	Tried.	Passed.	Per cent Passed.	Tried.	Passed.	Per cent Passed.
1899-00......	7	6	86	5	4	80	....	.....	....	12	10	83
1900-01... ..	5	5	100	5	5	100	.....	.....	....	10	10	100
1901-02......	30	26	87	10	9	90	.....	.....	....	40	35	88
1902-03......	31	22	71	8	8	100	....	.....	.. ..	39	30	77
1903-04......	43	37	86	18	13	72	.....	.....	....	61	50	82
1904-05......	57	42	74	23	20	87	1	0	....	81	62	77
1905-06......	36	25	70	27	19	70	4	0	....	67	44	66
1906-07......	20	15	75	20	15	75	1	0	....	41	30	73
1907-08......	132	67	51	28	21	75	1	0	....	161	88	55
1908-09......	224	88	39	52	27	52	3	1	33	279	116	42
1909-10......	289	97	34	72	37	51	1	0	....	362	134	37
1910-11......	186	64	34	69	38	55	2	1	50	257	103	40
1911-12......	195	57	29	71	48	68	2	0	....	268	105	39
1912-13......	187	56	30	83	44	53	1	0	.. ..	271	100	37
1913-14......	201	60	30	82	37	45	4	1	25	287	98	34

APPENDICES.

The following schedules and statements are appended:—

No. 1. Schedule of surveyors employed and work executed by them from April 1, 1913, to March 31, 1914.

No. 2. Schedule showing for each surveyor employed from April 1, 1913, to March 31, 1914, the number of miles surveyed of township section lines, township outlines, traverses of lakes and rivers and resurvey; also the cost of the same.

SESSIONAL PAPER No. 25b

No. 3. List of lots in the Yukon Territory, surveys of which have been received from April 1, 1913 to March 31, 1914.

No. 4. List of miscellaneous surveys in the Yukon Territory, returns of which have been received from April 1, 1913, to March 31, 1914.

No. 5. Statement of work executed in the Topographical Surveys Branch.

No. 6. List of new editions of sectional maps issued from April 1, 1913, to March 31, 1914.

No. 7. Statement of work executed in the photographic office from April 1, 1913, to March 31, 1914.

No. 8. Statement of work executed in the lithographic office from April 1, 1913, to March 31, 1914.

No. 9. List of Employees of the Topographical Surveys Branch at Ottawa, on April 1, 1914, with the name, classification, duties of office and salary of each.

No. 10. List of Dominion Land Surveyors who are in possession of standard measures.

Nos. 11 to 57. Reports of surveyors employed.

No. 58. Results of observations for magnetic declination.

No. 59. Results of watch trials.

MAPS AND PROFILES.

The following maps and profiles accompany this report:—

Map showing surveys to March 31, 1914.
Maps to accompany reports of surveyors.
Profiles of meridians and base lines.

I have the honour to be, sir,

Your obedient servant,

E. DEVILLE,
Surveyor General.

TOPOGRAPHICAL SURVEYS BRANCH

SCHEDULES AND STATEMENTS

APPENDIX No. 1.

Schedule of Surveyors employed and work executed by them from April 1, 1913, to
March 31, 1914.

Surveyor.	Address.	Description of Work.
Akins, J. R.	Ottawa, Ont..	Survey of the east outlines of townships 89 to 92, range 22, the twenty-fourth and twenty-fifth base lines. across ranges 18 to 21, the twenty-sixth base line across ranges 18 to 20, and the twenty-seventh base line across ranges 10 to 18 and part of range 9, all west of the fifth meridian.
Allison, C. B..	South Woodslee, Ont.	Contract No. 25 of 1913. Subdivision of townships 33, ranges 11 and 12, and the south two-thirds of townships 34, ranges 11, 12 and 13, west of the principal meridian.
Aylsworth, C. F..	Madoc, Ont.	Resurvey in township 16, range 6, east of the principal meridian; townships 20 and 21, range 3, townships 21 and 22, range 4, and township 23, range 5, west of the principal meridian.
Baker, J. C.	Kingston, Ont..	Contract No. 20 of 1913. Subdivision of townships 57, 58, 59 and 60, range 15, and the north two-thirds of township 60, range 14, west of the third meridian.
Bélanger, P. R. A.	Ottawa, Ont..	Inspection of contracts Nos. 19, 22, 23, 28, 31 and 32 of 1912 and No. 20 of 1913. Subdivision in townships 54 and 55, range 12, west of the third meridian.
Bennett, G. A.	Tillsonburg, Ont.	Correction surveys in townships 10 and 11, range 13, townships 10, ranges 14 and 16, east of the principal meridian; townships 17 and 18, range 20, and townships 20, ranges 21 and 22, west of the principal meridian; township 19a, range 1, township 11, range 6, township 19, range 8, township 7, range 10, townships 19 and 20, range 12, townships 3 and 4, range 18, and township 16, range 30, west of the second meridian; townships 15 and 16, range 2, township 13, range 5, and township 18, range 18, west of the third meridian; township 2, range 19, west of the fourth meridian. Subdivision surveys in townships 18 and 19, range 1, townships 23, ranges 15 and 16, west of the third meridian; township 17, range 5, township 9, range 16, townships 1, ranges 28 and 29, west of the fourth meridian; township 19, range 4, west of the fifth meridian. Retracement

DEPARTMENT OF THE INTERIOR

5 GEORGE V., A. 1915

APPENDIX No. 1—*Continued.*

SCHEDULE of Surveyors employed and work executed by them from April 1, 1913, to March 31, 1914—*Continued.*

Surveyor.	Address.	Description of Work.
		surveys in township 10, range 8, township 20, range 12, west of the second meridian; township 23, range 9, west of the third meridian; townships 18 and 19, ranges 9, 10 and 11, and townships 1 and 2, ranges 12 and 25, west of the fourth meridian. Resurvey in township 21, range 11, west of the principal meridian; township 24, range 5, townships 25, ranges 5 and 6, and township 22, range 9, west of the third meridian. Traverse in township 10, range 15, east of the principal meridian; township 25, range 9, west of the principal meridian; township 10, range 8, west of the second meridian; townships 25, ranges 5, 6 and 9, township 23, range 15, west of the third meridian; township 17, range 5, and township 2, range 25, west of the fourth meridian; township 24, range 1, west of the fifth meridian. Investigation in township 25, range 9, west of the third meridian.
Blanchet, G. H.. .. .. ..Ottawa, Ont...		Survey of the twenty-second base line from the fourth to the fifth meridian.
Boivin, E.. .. ..Chicoutimi, Que.. ..		Resurvey in township 42, range 28, west of the fourth meridian. Retracement survey in township 53, range 27, west of the fourth meridian. Correction survey in township 49, range 14, west of the fifth meridian.
Boulton, W. J. .. ..Mattawa, Ont.. ..		Subdivision in township 3, range 30, west of the fourth meridian; townships 4 and 12, range 1, townships 8, 11, 14 and 15, range 2, townships 8, 10, 13, 14, 15 and 16, range 3, townships 8 and 16, range 4, and township 8, range 5, west of the fifth meridian.
Bowman, E. P... .. ..West Montrose, Ont. ..		Investigation and traverse of lakes in township 34, range 11, townships 31, 32 and 34, range 12, townships 29, 30, 31, 33, 34, 35 and 36, range 13, townships 31, 33, 34, 35, 36 and 37, range 14, townships 30, 31, 32, 33, 34, 35, 36, and 37, range 15, townships 31, 32 and 33, range 16, townships 27, 28, 30, 32, 33, 34, 35, 36, 37, 38 and 39, range 18, townships 28, 29, 30, 32, 33, 35, 36, 37, 39, 40 and 41, range 19, townships 29, 30, 31, 34, 35, 36, 37, 38, 39, 40 and 41, range 20, townships 30, 31, 33, 35, 39 and 47, range 21, and townships 47 and 48, range 22, west of the third meridian.
Brenot, L.. .. ..Ottawa, Ont...		Survey of the east outlines of townships 81, 82, 83 and 84, range 17, townships 81, 82 and 83, range 18, and townships 81, 82 and part of 83, range 19, west of the sixth meridian. Subdivision in townships 83 and 84, range 20, township 84, range 21, township 83, range 22, and township 82, range 25, west of the sixth meridian. Survey of timber berth No. 2052 in townships 80 and 81, ranges 15 and 16, west of the sixth meridian. Mounding in township 79, range 14, west of the sixth meridian.
Bridgland, M. P. .. ..Calgary, Alta..		Photo-topographical survey of the northern part of the Crowsnest Forest Reserve.

APPENDIX No. 1—*Continued.*

SCHEDULE of Surveyors employed and work executed by them from April 1, 1913, to March 31, 1914—*Continued.*

Surveyor.	Address.	Description of Work.
Brown, C. D..	Winnipeg, Man.. ..	Contract No. 19 of 1913. Subdivision of townships 79, 80 and westerly half of township 78, range 22, townships 78, 79 and 80, range 23, west of the fifth meridian.
Buchanan, J. A..	Edmonton, Alta. ..	Contract No. 1 of 1913. Subdivision of townships 85 and 86, ranges 5 and 6, townships 86 and 87, ranges 7 and 8, west of the sixth meridian.
Calder, J. A..	Lytton, B.C..	Subdivision in townships 15, 16 and 17, ranges 24 and 25, township 15, range 26, townships 15, 16, 17 and 18, range 27, and townships 17 and 18, range 28, west of the sixth meridian. Resurvey in townships 15 and 16, range 25, and township 18, range 27, west of the sixth meridian. Traverse in townships 15, 16 and 17,. ranges 24 and 25, township 15, range 26, townships 16, 17 and 18 range 27, and township 18, range 28, west of the sixth meridian.
Chase, A. V...	Orillia, Ont..	Subdivision in townships 12, 13 and 14, range 26, townships 12, 13, 14 and 15, range 27, and township 12, range 28, west of the sixth meridian. Resurvey in townships 12 and 13, range 26, and townships 13 and 14, range 27, west of the sixth meridian. Traverse in townships 12 and 13, range 26, townships 12, 13 and 14, range 27, and township 12, range 28, west of the sixth meridian.
Christie, Wm..	Prince Albert, Sask.	Contract No. 22 of 1913. Subdivision of townships 57, ranges 1, 2, 3, 4 and 5, west of the third meridian.
Coltham, G. W..	Aurora, Ont..	Investigation and traverse of lakes in townships 50 and 52, range 9, townships 49, 50, 51 and 52, range 10, townships 47, 49, 50, 51 and 52, range 11, townships 47, 48, 49, 50, 51 and 52, range 12, townships 47, 48, 51 and 52, range 13, west of the fourth meridian.
Cowper, G. C..	Welland, Ont.	Investigation and traverse of lakes in townships 14 and 15, range 19, townships 12, 14 and 15, range 20, townships 12, 13, 14, 15 and 16, range 21, townships 12, 13, 14, 15, 16 and 17, range 22, townships 12, 13, 14, 16 and 17, range 23, townships 12, 13, 14, 15 and 16, range 24, townships 13, 14, 15, 16 and 17, range 25, townships 12, 13, 14 and 16, range 26, township 14, range 27, all west of the third meridian; townships 12, 13, 15, 16 and 17, range 1, townships 1, 8, 13, 14, 16 and 17, range 2, townships 1, 8, 9, 13, 14, 15 and 19, range 3, townships 1, 9, 18, 19 and 20, range 4, townships 8, 14, 15, 17, 18 and 19, range 5, townships 9, 10, 15 and 18, range 6, townships 3, 4, 5, 18, 20 and 21, range 7, townships 3, 4, 5, 9, 15, 18, 20, 21 and 22, range 8, townships 3, 5, 16, 20 and 21, range 9, townships 18, 19 and 21, range 10, townships 9, 10, 15, 16 and 18, range 11, townships 9 10 and 19, range 12, townships 5, 9, and 10, range 13, townships 5 and 9, range 14, west of the fourth meridian.

5 GEORGE V., A. 1915

APPENDIX No. 1—*Continued.*

SCHEDULE of Surveyors employed and work executed by them from April 1, 1913, to March 31, 1914—*Continued.*

Surveyor.	Address.	Description of Work.
Cumming, A. L..	Cornwall, Ont..	Survey of the boundaries of the townsite of Nordegg in township 40, range 15, west of the fifth meridian. Resurveys in township 45, range 23, west of the third meridian, and townships 26 and 27, range 15, townships 50 and 51, range 27, west of the fourth meridian. Correction surveys in township 48, range 22, west of the third meridian; township 65, range 5, townships 58 and 59, range 6, township 55, range 8, and township 50, range 12, west of the fourth meridian. Investigation and traverse of lakes in township 48, range 22, townships 44, 45 and 46, range 23, west of the third meridian; township 55; range 8, township 69, range 10, township 68, range 16, township 38, range 28, west of the fourth meridian; township 38, range 1, townships 51, 52, 53 and 55, range 2, and township 52, range 3, west of the fifth meridian. Survey of timber berth No. 2066 in township 64, range 27, west of the fourth meridian.
Davies, T. A..	Edmonton, Alta.	Contract No. 15 of 1913. Subdivision of townships 70, 71 and 72, ranges 18 and 19, west of the fourth meridian.
Day, H. S..	Edmonton, Alta.	Contract No. 16 of 1913. Subdivision of townships 73, 74, 75 and 76, range 18, west of the fourth meridian.
Deans, W. J..	Brandon, Man..	Inspection of contract No. 7 of 1911 and No. 23 of 1913. Survey of the 212 foot contour line at Point du Bois falls on Winnipeg river in township 15, range 14, and townships 14 and 16, range 15, east of the principal meridian. Subdivision in townships 45 and 46, range 9, townships 47 and 48, range 10, and townships 14 and 15, range 27, west of the second meridian. Correction survey in township 14, range 29, west of the second meridian. Traverse in township 16, range 14, east of the principal meridian, and township 1, range 20, west of the principal meridian.
Evans, S. L..	Corinth, Ont..	Subdivision in township 17, range 3, townships 16, 17, 18, 19 and 20, range 4, township 23, range 5, and township 19, range 7, west of the fifth meridian. Survey of summer resort lots in township 19, range 19, and township 30, range 30, west of the principal meridian. Traverse in township 19, range 19, townships 26 and 27, range 30, west of the principal meridian; township 17, range 4, west of the fifth meridian.
Fawcett, A.	Gravenhurst, Ont.	Contract No. 17 of 1913. Subdivision of township 77, range 18, and townships 75, 76 and 77, range 19, west of the fourth meridian. Survey of east outline of township 74, range 20, west of the fourth meridian.
Fawcett, S. D..	Ottawa, Ont..	Settlement surveys at Fort Resolution on Slave river and at Fort Simpson, Fort Wrigley, Fort Norman and Fort Good Hope on McKenzie river.

APPENDIX No. 1—*Continued.*

SCHEDULE of Surveyors employed and work executed by them from April 1, 1913, to March 31, 1914—*Continued.*

Surveyor.	Address.	Description of Work.
Fletcher, J. A..	Ottawa, Ont..	Survey of the east oulines of townships 89 to 108, range 18, the twenty-seventh base line across ranges 19 to 21 and the east half of range 22 and the twenty-eighth base line across range 18, west of the fifth meridian.
Fontaine, L. E..	Lévis, Que..	Inspection of contracts Nos. 1, 2 and 3 of 1913. Subdivision in township 84, range 21, and township 83, range 22, west of the fifth meridian; township 71, range 5, townships 71, 72, 78 and 79, range 6, townships 79 and 80, range 7, west of the sixth meridian. Traverse in township 85, range 21, west of the fifth meridian.
Francis, John..	Portage la Prairie, Man.	Contract No. 28 of 1913. Subdivision of part of township 17 and southerly two-thirds of township 18, range 12, southerly two-thirds of township 18, range 13, township 17 and southerly two-thirds of township 18, range 14, and west half of township 17, range 15, east of the principal meridian.
Galletly, J. S..	Oshawa, Ont..	Subdivision in townships 109 and 110, ranges 3 and 4, township 108, range 6, townships 108 and 109, range 11, township 108, range 12, and township 109, range 13, west of the fifth meridian. Survey of the east outline of township 109, range 17, part of the east outline of township 107, range 16, the north outlines of townships 107, ranges 11, 12, 13 and 14, west of the fifth meridian. Traverse in townships 109 and 110, range 3, townships 108, 109 and 110, range 4, township 108, range 6, townships 108, ranges 11 and 12, township 109, range 13, townships 108 and 109, range 14, and township 109, range 15, west of the fifth meridian.
Gibbon, Jas..	Vancouver, B.C..	Contract No. 18 of 1913. Subdivision of townships 60, ranges 10, 11 and 13, and townships 58 and 59, range 14, west of the fifth meridian. Survey of the east boundary of township 60, range 15, west of the fifth meridian.
Green, T. D..	Ottawa, Ont..	Contract No. 14 of 1913. Subdivision of townships 70 and 71, range 23, and townships 69 and 70, range 24, west of the fourth merdian.
Herriot, G. H.	Ottawa, Ont..	Survey of the eighteenth base line across ranges 1 to 16 and the nineteenth base line across ranges 1 to 6 and part of 7, west of the principal meridian.
Hunter, A. E.	Wiarton, Ont.	Subdivision in township 8, range 25, and townships 8, 9 and 10, range 26, west of the sixth meridian. Resurvey in townships 7, 8, 9 and 10, range 26, west of the sixth meridian. Traverse in township 8, range 25, and townships 8, 9 and 10, range 26, west of the sixth meridian.

5 GEORGE V., A. 1915

APPENDIX No. 1—*Continued.*

SCHEDULE of Surveyors employed and work executed by them from April 1, 1913, to March 31, 1914—*Continued.*

Surveyor.	Address.	Description of Work.
Jackson, J. E..	Hamilton, Ont..	Contracts No. 23 and 24 of 1913. Subdivision of townships 38, 39, 40 and 41, range 24, and part of township 41, range 25, west of the principal meridian. Partial subdivision of townships 40, 41 and 42, range 18, townships 38, 39, 40 and 41, range 19, townships 39, 40 and the northerly third of township 38, range 20, west of the principal meridian.
Johnston, C. E..	Toronto, Ont.	Investigation and traverse of lakes in townships 15,. 16, 17, 18, 19, 20, 21 and 22, range 2, townships 15, 16, 17, 18, 19, 20, 21 and 22, range 3, townships 15, 16, 17, 18 and 19, ranges 4 and 5 townships 15, 16, 17, 18, 19 and 20, range 6, townships 15, 16, 17, 18, 19, 24, 25 and 26, range 7, townships 24, 25, 26, 27 and 28, ranges 8 and 9, townships 25, 26, 27 and 28, ranges 10 and 11, all west of the third meridian.
Johnston, J. H..	Edmonton, Alta. ..	Contract No. 7 of 1913. Subdivision of parts of townships 72, ranges 4 and 5, townships 72 and 73, range 6, part of township 73, range 7, township 74 and part of townships 72 and 73, range 8, townships 72, 73, 74 and parts of townships 71 and 72, range 9, and township 72 and part of township 71, range 10, west of the fifth meridian.
Johnston, W. J..	St. Catharines, Ont.	Subdivision in townships 5, 6, 7 and 8, range 26, townships 4 and 5, range 27, townships 3, 4 and 5, range 28, west of the sixth meridian; townships 4 and 5, range 5, west of the seventh meridian. Resurvey in townships 5, 6, 7 and 8, range 26, townships 4 and 5, range 27, and township 4, range 28, west of the sixth meridian. Traverse in townships 5, 6 and 7, range 26, township 4, range 27, and townships 3 and 4, range 28, west of the sixth meridian; township 4, range 5, west of the seventh meridian.
Lighthall, A..	Vancouver, B C..	Contract No. 26 of 1913. Subdivision of townships 24 and 25, ranges 8 and 9, and the southerly two-thirds of township 26, range 9, east of the principal meridian.
Lonergan, G. J..	Buckingham, Que.	Inspection of contracts Nos. 14, 15 and 37 of 1912, and 5, 6, 7, 8, 9, 10 and 18 of 1913. Traverse in township 75, range 14, west of the fifth meridian. Survey of Lesser Slave Lake and Wabiskaw settlements.
MacLeod, G. W..	Edmonton, Alta.	Contract No. 3 of 1913. Subdivision of township 72 and northerly two-thirds of township 71, range 1, east half of northerly two-thirds of township 71 and east half of township 72, range 2, township 73, northerly two-thirds of township 70 and southerly third of township 71, range 4, northerly two-thirds of township 70 and southerly third of township 71, ranges 5 and 6, township 69, range 9, township 69 and southerly two-thirds of township 70, range 10, west of the sixth meridian.

SESSIONAL PAPER No. 25b

APPENDIX No. 1—*Continued.*

SCHEDULE of Surveyors employed and work executed by them from April 1, 1913, to March 31, 1914—*Continued.*

Surveyor.	Address.	Description of Work.	.
Martindale, E. S..	Kingsmill, Ont... .. .	Survey of the fifteenth base line across ranges 22 to 27 and the sixteenth base line across ranges 14 to 27, west of the second meridian.	
Matheson, H..	Ottawa, Ont..	Surveys along the Canadian Northern railway in townships 47 and 48, ranges 17 and 18, west of the fifth meridian. Survey of Fitzhugh townsite, villa lots at Pyramid and Patricia lakes and corrals at Jasper in township 45, range 1, west of the sixth meridian. Correction survey in Lake St. Anne settlement in township 54, range 3, west of the fifth meridian. Topographical survey in Jasper Forest Park in townships 44 and 45, range 1, and township 45, range 2, west of the sixth meridian. Traverse of road from Jasper to Pyramid and Patricia lakes, and traverse of Pyramid and Patricia lakes in township 45, range 1, west of the sixth meridian.	
McFarlane, J. B..	Toronto, Ont.	Survey of the twenty-fourth base line across ranges 7 to 11 and part of range 6, and the twenty-fifth base line across ranges 1 to 12, west of the fourth meridian.	
McGrandle, H.	Wetaskiwin, Alta. .. .	Contract No. 11 of 1913. Subdivision of townships 69 and 70, ranges 25, 26 and 27, west of the fourth meridian.	
McKay, R. B..	Vancouver, B.C.. .. .	Subdivision in townships 1, ranges 28 and 29, west of the sixth meridian; townships 17, 19, 21, 22 and 25 east of the coast meridian; township 39 west of the coast meridian. Resurvey in townships 1, ranges 28 and 29, west of the sixth meridian; townships 14, 17, 19, 21, 22, 23, 25 and 40 east of the coast meridian: and township 39 west of the coast meridian. Traverse in townships 1, ranges 28 and 29, and township 3, range 30, west of the sixth meridian; townships 22, 23 and 24 east of the coast meridian; and township 39 west of the coast meridian.	
Miles, C. F..	Toronto, Ont.	Inspection of contracts Nos. 13 and 33 of 1912, and 11; 12, 13, 14, 15, 16 and 17 of 1913. Traverse in township 73, range 19, west of the fourth meridian. Subdivision in townships 45, ranges 9 and 10, west of the second meridian; township 70, range 18, and township 73, range 19, west of the fourth meridian.	
Narraway, A. M.	Ottawa, Ont..	Retracement surveys in townships 6 and 7, range 30, west of the third meridian; townships 5 and 6, ranges 3, 4 and 5, township 6, range 6, townships 1 and 2, ranges 9 and 10, and township 21, range 10, west of the fourth meridian. Resurveys in townships 18 and 19, range 9, townships 18, 19, 20 and 21, range 10, township 21, range 11, townships 21 and 22, range 12, and townships 2 and 3, ranges 14 and 15, west of the fourth meridian. Subdivision surveys in townships 18 and 19, range 10, township 21, range 11, and townships 21 and 22, range 12, west of the fourth meridian. Traverse in townships 8, ranges 22 and 23, township 10, range 24, townships 9 and 10, range 25, and township 9, range 26, west of the fourth meridian.	

DEPARTMENT OF THE INTERIOR

5 GEORGE V., A. 1915

APPENDIX No. 1—*Continued.*

SCHEDULE of Surveyors employed and work executed by them from April 1, 1913, to March 31, 1914—*Continued.*

Surveyor.	Address.	Description of Work.
Neelands, R..	Hamiota, Man..	Investigation and traverse of lakes in townships 39 and 40, range 17, townships 39, 40 and 41, range 18, townships 38, 39, 41, 42, 44, 45 and 45a, range 22, townships 38, 39, 40, 41, 42 and 44, range 23, townships 38, 39, 40, 41, 42, 43 and 44, range 24, townships 38, 39, 40, 41, 42 and 43, range 25, townships 39, 40, 41 and 49, range 26, townships 46 and 49 range 27, township 46, range 28, west of the second meridian; township 46, range 1, west of the third meridian.
Neville, E. A..	Vancouver, B.C..	Contract No. 6 of 1913. Subdivision of townships 72, 73 and part of township 71, range 11, townships 72, 73 and 74, range 12, townships 73, ranges 13, 14 and 15, west of the fifth meridian.
Palmer, P. E..	Dorchester, N.B.. ..	Subdivision in township 52, range 29, townships 50 and 51, range 30, township 50, range 31, and townships 49 and 50, range 32, west of the principal meridian; townships 48, 49 and 50, range 1, townships 47 and 48, range 2, and townships 46 and 47, range 3, west of the second meridian. Survey of the east outlines of township 49, range 30, and townships 49, 51 and 52, range 31, west of the principal meridian; townships 46, 49 and part of township 45, range 2, township 48, range 3, and townships 47 and 48, range 4, west of the second meridian. Retracement of the east outlines of townships 45 and 46, range 3, west of the second meridian. Survey of the north outlines of township 49, range 31, west of the principal meridian, and of township 47, range 1, west of the second meridian.
Pearson, H. E..	Edmonton, Alta. ..	Contract No. 12 of 1913. Subdivision of townships 71 and 72 and part of township 73, range 26, west of the fourth meridian; township 72 and parts of townships 70, 71 and 73, range 1, and part of township 70, range 2, west of the fifth meridian. Survey of part of east outline of township 70, range 27, west of the fourth meridian.
Pierce, J. W..	Ottawa, Ont..	Contract No. 21 of 1913. Subdivision of townships 57 and 58, range 13, townships 57 and 58 and the southerly two-thirds of township 59, range 14, west of the third meridian. Survey of the east outlines of townships 59 and 60, range 13, and of township 60, range 14, west of the third meridian.
Pinder, Geo. Z..	Edmonton, Alta. ..	Contract No. 10 of 1913. Subdivision of townships 67, 68 and 69, range 1, the northerly two-thirds of township 67 and parts of townships 68 and 69, range 2, west of the fifth meridian.
Plunkett, T. H..	Ottawa, Ont..	Survey of the thirteenth base line from the northeast corner of township 48, range 28, west of the principal meridian easterly to the western shore of lake Winnipeg, and the fourteenth base line from the northeast corner of township 52, range 28, easterly to the western shore of lake Winnipeg.

APPENDIX No. 1—*Continued.*

SCHEDULE of Surveyors employed and work executed by them from April 1, 1913, to March 31, 1914—*Continued.*

Surveyor.	Address	Description of Work.
Ponton, A. W..	Edmonton, Alta.	Contract No. 5 of 1913. Subdivision of townships 76, ranges 7, 8, 9 and 10 and parts of townships 75, ranges 7, 8 and 9, west of the fifth meridian.
Purser, R. C..	Windsor. Ont.	Subdivision in township 33, range 6, township 39, range 19, and township 34, range 25, west of the third meridian. Resurveys in township 29, range 15, west of the principal meridian; township 27, range 24, west of the second meridian; township 42, range 6, and township 26, range 12, west of the third meridian. Correction surveys in township 47, range 14, township 42, range 16, and township 33, range 28, west of the second meridian, and township 51, range 27, west of the third meridian. Retracement in township 33, range 31, west of the principal meridian; township 26, range 11, township 42, range 16, and township 25, range 27, west of the second meridian; township 30, range 3, township 47, range 4, townships 47, 48 and 55, range 5. township 29, range 17, townships 40, ranges 23 and 24, and township 51, range 27, west of the third meridian, and township 34, range 21, west of the fourth meridian. Traverse in township 29, range 15, and township 33, range 31, west of the principal meridian; townships 25, ranges 4 and 5, township 33, range 10, townships 26 and 33, range 11, and township 33, range 12, west of the second meridian; township 37, range 1, township 33, range 6, township 53, range 7, township 50, range 23, and township 34, range 25, west of the third meridian. Investigation in township 29, range 17, west of the second meridian; township 45, range 23, and township 51, range 27, west of the third meridian; and township 33, range 10, west of the fourth meridian.
Rinfret, C..	Montreal, Que.	Investigation and traverse of lakes in townships 4, 5 and 7, range 19, townships 2, 3, 4, 5, 7 and 8, range 20, townships 2, 3, 4, 5, 6, 7, 8 and 9, range 21, townships 2, 3, 4, 5, 6, 7 and 8, range 22, townships 2, 3, 4, 5, 6 and 7, range 23, townships 4, 5, 6 and 7, range 24, townships 3, 4, 5, 6 and 7, ranges 25 and 26, townships 3, 4, 5 and 6, range 27, townships 4, 5 and 6, range 28, townships 3, 4, 6 and 9, range 29, and townships 3, 4, 5 and 6, range 30, west of the second meridian. Retracement surveys in township 2, range 21, and township 6, range 25, west of the second meridian.
Robinson, E. W..	Ottawa, Ont..	Production of the second meridian from the northeast corner of township 78 to the quarter section post on the east boundary of section 13, township 85.
Rolfson, O.	Walkerville, Ont..	Survey of the sixteenth base line across ranges 26 to 31, and the seventeenth base line across ranges 6 to 20, west of the principal meridian.

DEPARTMENT OF THE INTERIOR

APPENDIX No. 1—*Continued.*

SCHEDULE of Surveyors employed and work executed by them from April 1, 1913, to March 31, 1914—*Continued.*

Surveyor.	Address.	Description of Work.
Roy, G. P. J.. .. .. ..Quebec, Que..	Quebec, Que.	Subdivision surveys of the parts of township 41, range 13, township 37, range 3, township 37, range 4, and township 39, range 9, west of the second meridian; and townships 36, ranges 30 and 31, west of the principal meridian not included in the Porcupine Forest Reserve. Survey of timber berth No. 2055, blocks 1 and 2 in townships 42 and 43, range 11, west of the second meridian. Retracement of part of the north outline of township 35, range 31, west of the principal meridian, north outlines of townships 36, ranges 3 and 4, and part of the east outline of township 37, range 5, west of the second meridian. Traverse in township 37, range 4, west of the second meridian.
Saint Cyr, A.. .. .. ..Ottawa, Ont..	Ottawa, Ont.	Survey of the third meridian from the eighteenth to the nineteenth base line, and the nineteenth base line across ranges 1 to 17, west of the third meridian.
Saint Cyr, J. B.. .. ..Montreal, Que. ᐧ.. ..	Montreal, Que.	Investigation and traverse of lakes in townships 32 and 33, range 14, township 32, range 15, townships 34 and 35, ᐧrange 16, townships 34, 35, 36, 37 and 38, range 17, townships 34, 35, 36, 37 and 38, range 18, townships 35, 36, 37, 38 and 39, range 19, townships 31, 34, 37 and 38, range 20, townships 29, 38 and 39, range 21, townships 35, 36, 37, 38, 39 and 40, range 22, townships 34, 35, 36, 37, 38, 39 and 40, range 23, townships 35, 36 and 37, range 24, townships 35, 37 and 41, range 25, townships 36, 37, 40 and 41, range 26, townships 34, 36, 39 and 40, range 27, townships 36, 37, 39, 40, 41 and 42, range 28, west of the fourth meridian; townships 40, 41, 42 and 43, range 1, west of the fifth meridian.
Segré, B. H.. .. .. ..Toronto, Ont..	Toronto, Ont.	Investigation and traverse of lakes in township 25, range 18, townships 23, 24, 25 and 26, range 19, townships 20 and 25, range 20 townships 20, 21, 25 and 26, range 21, townships 17, 18, 20, 21, 24, 25 and 26, range 22, townships 17, 18, 20, 21, 22, 23, 24, 25, 26 and 28, range 23, townships 18, 22, 23, 24, 25, 26, 27 and 28, range 24, townships 17, 18, 19, 25, 26, 27 and 28, range 25, townships 19, 20, 21 and 22, range 26, townships 22, 23, 25 and 26, range 27, and township 18, range 30, west of the second meridian; township 18, range 1, west of the third meridian.
Seibert, F. V.. .. .. ..Edmonton, Alta. ..	Edmonton, Alta.	Survey of the twenty-first base line from the fourth to the fifth meridian. Retracement of the east outline of section 36, township 80, range 1, west of the fourth meridian.
Steele, I. J.. .. .. ..Ottawa, Ont..	Ottawa, Ont.	Contract No. 4 of 1913. Subdivision of townships 76, ranges 11, 12 and 13 and parts of townships 75, ranges 10, 11, 12 and 13, west of the fifth meridian.

APPENDIX No. 1—*Continued.*

SCHEDULE of Surveyors employed and work executed by them from April 1, 1913, to
March 31, 1914—*Continued.*

Surveyor.	Address.	Description of Work.
Stewart, N. C..	Ottawa, Ont..	Subdivision of townships 23 and 24, range 17, and township 23, range 18, west of the fifth meridian; townships 23, ranges 2, 3, 4, 5 and 6, township 18, range 8, township 20, range 9, townships 18 and 21, ranges 10 and 11, townships 21 and 25, range 12, townships 24 and 25, range 13, and township 25, range 14, west of the sixth meridian. Resurvey in township 23, range 18, west of the fifth meridian; township 23, range 1, townships 22 and 23, range 2, townships 23, ranges 4 and 5, townships 19 and 20, range 9, townships 18 and 21, range 10, township 21, range 11, townships 21 and 25, range 12, and townships 25, ranges 13 and 14, west of the sixth meridian. Traverse in townships 22 and 23, range 2, townships 23, ranges 3, 4 and 5, township 21, range 11, township 25, range 12, township 24, range 13, and township 25, range 14, west of the sixth meridian.
Stock, J. J..	Ottawa, Ont..	Contract No. 8 of 1913. Subdivision of township 66 and parts of townships 67 and 68, range 3, townships 65, 66 and part of township 67, range 4, and township 65 and southerly half of township 66, range 5, west of the fifth meridian. Survey of timber berth No. 1935 in township 62, range 4, and townships 60 and 61, range 5, and timber berth No. 1918 in township 59, range 12, west of the fifth meridian.
Street, P. B..	Toronto, Ont..	Subdivision in township 61, range 20, township 60 and 61, range 21, townships 59 and 60, range 22, townships 58 and 59, range 23, townships 57 and 58, range 24, township 54, range 26, and townships 53 and 54, range 27, west of the principal meridian. Traverse in township 61, range 20, township 60, range 21, townships 59 and 60, range 22, townships 59, range 23, township 58, range 24, township 54, range 26, township 53, range 27, and township 54, range 27, west of the principal meridian.
Stuart, A. G..	Buckingham, Que.	Retracement of the second base line from the principal to the second meridian, the east boundary of range 31 from the international boundary to the northeast corner of township 24, and the fifth, sixth and seventh base lines across ranges 31 to 33, west of the principal meridian; the third base line across ranges 1 to 7 and the east boundary of range 7 from the northeast corner of township 8 to the northeast corner of township 16, east of the principal meridian.
Taggart, C. H..	Kamloops, B.C..	Subdivision in townships 16 and 17, range 13, townships 18 and 19, ranges 14 and 15, township 21, range 18, township 20 and 21, range 19, townships 21, ranges 20 and 21, township 22, range 22, townships 21 and 22, range 23, townships 18, 19 and 21, range 24, townships 18, 19, 20, 21 and 22, range 25, townships 19, 20 and 21, range 26, and township 20, range

5 GEORGE V., A. 1915

APPENDIX No. 1—*Continued.*

SCHEDULE of Surveyors employed and work executed by them from April 1, 1913, to March 31, 1914—*Continued.*

Surveyor.	Address.	Description of Work.
		27, west of the sixth meridian. Resurvey in townships 18 and 19, range 15, townships 21, ranges 18, 19, 20 and 21, township 22, range 22, townships 17, 18, 19, 20 and 21, range 24, townships 18, 19 and 21, range 25, and townships 20, ranges 26 and 27, west of the sixth meridian. Traverse in township 19, range 15, townships 21, ranges 18 and 21, townships 22, ranges 22 and 23, townships 17, 18, 19, 20 and 21, range 24, townships 18, 19, 20 and 21, range 25, and township 21, range 26, west of the sixth meridian.
Taylor, W. E..	Toronto, Ont..	Contract No. 27 of 1913. Subdivision of townships 21, 22 and 23, range 9, and parts of townships 21, 22 and 23, range 8, east of the principal meridian.
Tipper, Geo. A..	Brantford, Ont..	Contract No. 2 of 1913. Subdivision of townships 85, 86 and 87, range 23, townships 86 and 87, ranges 24, 25 and 26, west of the fifth meridian. Survey of the east outlines of townships 88, ranges 23 and 24, and of townships 85 and 88, ranges 25 and 26, west of the fifth meridian.
Tremblay, A. J..	Edmonton, Alta	Contract No 13 of 1913. Subdivision of township 72, range 23, and townships 71 and 72 ranges 24 and 25, west of the fourth meridian. Survey of the east outlines of townships 70, ranges 24 and 26, west of the fourth meridian.
Waddell, W H..	Edmonton, Alta.	Contract No. 9 of 1913. Subdivision of township 72 and part of townships 73 and 74, range 2, townships 73 and part of townships 74, ranges 3, 4 and 5, township 74 and part of townships 75 and 76, range 6, all west of the fifth meridian.
Walker, C. M.	Guelph, Ont..	Surveys of cemeteries at Banff and Bankhead Alberta and Field, B.C. Traverse, levels and supervision of the construction of roads in the neighbourhood of Banff. Survey of small parcels of land for leaseholds in township 25, range 12, township 28, range 18, and township 26, range 26, west of the fifth meridian. Survey of golf links and recreation grounds at Banff. Contour survey and a survey for the location of improvements in the villa lot section of Banff.
Wallace, J. N.	Calgary, Alta..	Levelling along Athabaska river from Athabaska to Lesser Slave lake; along Athabaska river down stream from Athabaska to the twentieth base line west of the fourth meridian; along the Canadian Pacific railway from Edmonton to Calgary; along the Canadian Northern railway from Edmonton to Lloydminster; along the Hudson Bay railway northeast from Hudson Bay Junction to the fifteenth base line west of the principal meridian; along the Canadian Northern railway east and south from Hudson Bay Junction to Swan River.

SESSIONAL PAPER No. 25b

APPENDIX No. 1—*Concluded.*

SCHEDULE of Surveyors employed and work executed by them from April 1, 1913, to March 31, 1914—*Concluded.*

Surveyor.	Address.	Description of Work.
Waugh. B W.	..Ottawa, Ont..	..Production of the principal meridian from the northeast corner of section 24, township 72, to the northeast corner of township 80 ; the twenty-first base line across ranges 1 to 9 east of the principal meridian, and the twentieth base line across ranges 1 to 3, west of the principal meridian, and ranges 1 to 7, east of the principal meridian.

APPENDIX No. 2.

SCHEDULE showing for each surveyor employed from April 1, 1913, to March 31, 1914, the number of miles surveyed of township section lines, township outlines, traverses of lakes and- rivers and resurvey, also the cost of the same.

Surveyor.	Miles of section.	Miles of outline.	Miles of traverse.	Miles of resurvey.	Total mileage.	Total cost.	Cost per mile.	Day work or contract.
						$	$ cts.	
Akins, J. R	....	147	....	....	147	23,377	159 03	Day.
Allison, C. B	180	30	7	....	217	6,146	28 32	Contract.
Aylsworth, C. F....	....	....	....	195	195	10,533	54 02	Day.
Baker, J. C....	200	52	25	....	277	8,717	31 47	Contract.
Bennett, G. A	16	4	54	158	232	5,267	22 70	Day.
Blanchet, G. H	....	152	....	7	159	25,589	157 27	"
Boulton, W. J	132	12	9	44	197	12,890	65 43	"
Bowman, E. P. . .	....	....	214	....	214	7,027	32 84	"
Brenot, L	100	74	43	....	217	26,767	123 32	"
Brown, C. D........	227	58	....	....	285	9,060	31 68	Contract.
Buchanan, J. A......	339	185	....	....	524	17,601	33 59	"
Calder, J. A	121	....	52	3	176	8,314	47 24	Day.
Chase, A. V	42	....	56	8	106	8,346	78 74	"
Christie, Wm........	202	54	93	. . ...	349	9,167	26 27	Contract.
Coltham, G. W	....	... ...	373	....	373	7,281	19 52	Day.
Cowper, G. C.......	....	... ...	425	....	425	5,489	12 92	"
Cumming, A. L	1	....	77	122	200	8,754	43 77	"
Davies, T. A........	241	86	88	....	415	13,094	31 55	Contract.
Day, H. S..........	168	60	74	....	302	8,887	29 43	"
Evans, S. L..........	129	6	20	3	158	9,559	60 50	Day.
Fawcett, A.........	168	72	28	....	268	8,182	30 53	Contract.
Fletcher, J. A.......	....	152	....	....	152	24,542	161 46	Day.
Francis, J	166	42	36	....	244	7,236	29 66	Contract.
Galletly, J. S	181	87	119	... ...	387	15,755	40 71	Day.
Gibbon, Jas	208	36	56	....	300	9,047	30 16	Contract.
Green, T. D........	168	36	....	....	204	6,789	33 28	"
Herriot, G. H.	....	133	....	....	133	19,549	146 98	Day.
Hunter, A. E.......	44	. ...	57	3	104	8,240	79 23	"
Jackson, J. E........	385	127	215	....	727	18,018	24 78	Contract.
Johnston, C. E	....	....	259	....	259	5,872	22 67	Day.
Johnston, J. H	263	55	63	....	381	11,159	29 29	Contract.
Johnston, W. J......	52	....	55	2	109	9,779	89 72	Day.
Lighthall, A........	138	30	62	....	230	6,591	28 66	Contract

5 GEORGE V., A. 1915

APPENDIX No. 2—*Concluded.*

SCHEDULE showing for each surveyor employed from April 1, 1913, to March 31, 1914, the number of miles surveyed, &c.—*Concluded.*

Surveyors.	Miles of sections.	Miles of outline.	Miles of traverse.	Miles of resurvey	Total mileage.	Total cost.	Cost per mile.	Day work or contract.
MacLeod, G. W......	427	52	123	16	618	17,574	33 93	Contract.
Martindale, E. S.....	....	196	....	....	196	26,820	136 84	Day.
McFarlane, J. B.....	....	105	....	1	106	23,132	218 23	"
McGrandle, Hugh...	196	52	48	....	296	8,325	28 13	Contract.
McKay, R. B	42	....	23	24	89	10,091	113 38	Day.
Narraway, A. M. ...	46	....	64	450	554	9,632	17 39	"
Neelands, R..	....	....	572	....	572	7,313	12 78	"
Neville, E. A........	261	12	33	....	306	9,366	30 61	Contract.
Palmer, P. E........	211	156	8	12	387	12,680	32 76	Day.
Pearson, H. E.......	218	47	99	....	364	10,710	29 42	Contract.
Pierce, J. W.	190	72	74	....	336	9,127	27 16	"
Pinder, G. Z...	244	28	39	....	311	9,139	29 39	"
Plunkett, T. H ...	....	211	....	....	211	20,592	97 59	Day.
Ponton, A. W.	206	54	14	....	274	8,783	32 05	Contract.
Purser, R. C........	2	....	46	43	92	7,053	76 66	Day.
Rinfret, C....	....	....	506	....	506	6,017	11 89	"
Rolfson, O...	....	117	....	....	117	25,093	214 47	"
Roy, G. P. J	121	....	9	25	155	12,495	80 61	"
Saint Cyr, A	....	126	....	....	126	26,394	209 48	"
Saint Cyr, J. B.....	....	....	603	....	603	6,862	11 38	"
Segré, B. H	....	....	407	....	407	6,745	16 57	"
Seibert, F. V	....	153	....	1	154	26,022	168 97	"
Steele, I, J	221	39	36	....	296	7,732	26 12	Contract.
Stewart, N. C.... ..	84	....	32	9	125	10,220	81 76	Day.
Stock, J. J	272	51	12	....	335	11,866	35 42	Contract.
Street, P. B........	196	70	61	....	327	13,094	39 95	Day.
Stuart, A. G........	....	....	....	490	490	8,704	17 76	"
Taggart, C. H	189	....	35	13	237	10,772	45 45	"
Taylor, W. E.......	139	28	53	3	223	6,041	27 09	Contract.
Tipper, G. A........	305	174	139	....	618	16,800	27 18	"
Tremblay, A. J . .	206	80	69	....	355	11,113	31 30	"
Waddell, W. H. .	276	83	83	....	442	12,437	28 14	"
Waugh, B. W.......	....	164	....	....	164	29,636	180 70	Day.
Total......... .	7,918	3,760	5,748	1,632	19,058	821,004		

APPENDIX No. 3.

LIST of lots in the Yukon Territory, survey returns of which have been received from April 1, 1913, to March 31, 1914.

GROUP 2.

Lot No.	Acres.	Surveyor.	Year of Survey.	Date of Approval.	Claimant.	Remarks.
348	100·00	F. H. Kitto..... .	1913	Sept. 25, 1913...	Patrick Roach......... .	Surface.
351	160·00	"	1913	Mar. 20, 1914...	Joseph Rousseau...	"
357	40·00	"	1913	" 20, 1914 ..	"	"
363	51·65	"	1912	July 28, 1913 ..	Amanda Savory....	Virgin mineral claim
364	30·23	"	1912	" 28, 1913...	"	Virgin No. 2, M.C.
366	10·89	"	1913	Jan. 22, 1914 ..	Lone Star Limited... . .	Surface.

SESSIONAL PAPER No. 25b

APPENDIX No. 3—*Concluded.*

GROUP 3.

21	160·00	F. H. Kitto......	1914	Feb. 23, 1914...	V. E. Ferry..............	Surface.
24	51·68	"	.....	1913	Mar. 26, 1914 ..	Donald McKinnon, *et al.*..	Lion, M. C.
25	51·31	"	......	1913	" 26, 1914...	" "	....Thistle, M.C.
26	51·31	"	.....	1913	" 26, 1914 ..	" "	. ..Hidden Treasure, M.C.
29	40 27	"	.....	1913	" 26, 1914...	" "	. . Talisman, M.C.
30	160·00	"	.....	1913	Feb. 17, 1914 ..	Donald McKinnon.	Surface.
31	51·63	"	...	1913	Mar. 26, 1914 ..	Donald McKinnon, *et al.*..	Argyle, M.C.
32	51·65	"	....	1913	" 26, 1914	" "	....Drumkinnon, M.C.
33	51·52	"	.....	1913	" 26, 1914	" "	....Roseneath, M.C.

GROUP 4.

9	160·00	F. H. Kitto......	1913	Dec. 19, 1913....	Geo. Grenier.............	Surface.

GROUP 10.

34	141·70	F. H. Kitto.	1913	Mar. 26, 1914....	M. H. Boulais & Jos. Vinu.	War Eagle, M.C.
35	98·00	"	....	1913	" 26, 1914....	" " Paul Guité	Bunker Hill, M.C.
36	36·00	"	....	1913	" 26, 1914....	L. A. Herdt.............	Susie, M.C.
37	41·11	"	......	1913	" 26, 1914....	Victor and Joseph Dupont.	Glenlivet, M.C.

APPENDIX No. 4.

List of miscellaneous surveys in the Yukon Territory, returns of which have been received from April 1, 1913, to March 31, 1914.

Year.	Surveyor.	Description of Survey.
1912	F. H. Kitto. ...	Base line on part of Tenmile creek, a tributary of Sixtymile river.
1913	" ..	Base line on part of Barlow and Clear creeks.
1912	"	" " Minto creek.
1912	" ..	Reference traverse from mouth of Clear creek, on Stewart river to mouth of Fla creek on Klondike river.
1913	"	Reference traverse on McKinnon creek, a tributary of Indian river.
1911	"	Triangulation topographical survey on Klondike watershed.
1913	H. G. Dickson..	Ibex river reference traverse Whitehorse district.
1912	" ..	Base line on Nansen creek a tributary of Nisling river.
1912	" ..	" Summit " Nansen creek.
1912	" ..	" Courtland " "
1912	" ..	" Dolly
1912	" ..	" Webber "
1912	" ..	" Cabin
1912	" ..	" Center "
1912	" ..	" Newbauer "
1912	" ..	" Discovery pup "
1912	" ..	" Shaw creek " "
1912	" ..	" Eliza " "
1912	" ..	" Rush " "
1912	" ..	" Slate " ..
1912	" ..	" East Fork " "
1912	" ..	" South " "
1912	" ..	" Victoria creek a tributary of Nisling river.
1912	" ..	" Dome " "
1912	" ..	" Back .. "

5 GEORGE V., A. 1915

APPENDIX No. 5.

STATEMENT of work executed in the Topographical Surveys Branch.

Letters of instruction to surveyors	365
Progress sketches received and filed	1,304
Declarations of settlers received and filed	107
Returns of timber berths received	11
Plans received from surveyors	762
Field books received from surveyors	782
Timber reports received	219
Observations for magnetic declination received	1,295
Preliminary township plans prepared	371
Sketches made	7,971
Maps and tracings made	236
Plans of Yukon lots received	20
Plans of miscellaneous Yukon surveys received	25
Returns of surveys examined—	
Township subdivision	729
Township outline	243
Road plans	405
Railway plans	36
Yukon lots	20
Miscellaneous Yukon surveys	25
Mineral claims	26
Timber berths	24
Correction and other miscellaneous surveys	95
Township plans compiled	97
Townsite settlement and other plans compiled	10
Proofs of plans examined	42
Township plans printed	910
Townsite and settlement plans printed	13
Miscellaneous plans printed	151
Descriptions written	12
Areas calculated	394
Pages of field notes copied	386
Applications for various information dealt with	2,446
Files received and returned	1,734
Letters and memoranda drafted	11,964
Books received from Record Office and used in connection with office work	5,712
Books returned to Record Office	5,068
Plans other than printed township plans received from Record Office and used in connection with office work	944
Plans returned to Record Office	537
Volumes of plans received from Record Office and used in connection with office work	53
Volumes of plans returned to Record Office	52
Books sent to Record Office to be placed on record	549
Plans other than township plans sent to Record Office to be placed on record	105
Sectional maps (3 miles to 1 inch)—	
Revised and reprinted	25
Reprinted but not revised	7
New maps compiled and printed	9
Sectional maps (6 miles to 1 inch)—	
Reprinted	59
New maps printed	9

APPENDIX No. 6

LIST of New Editions of Sectional Maps compiled from April 1, 1913, to March 31, 1914.

Scale, 3 miles to 1-inch.

No.	Name.	No.	Name.
10	Port Moody.	216	Sullivan Lake.
11	Yale.	220	Nut Mountain.
15	Lethbridge.	264	Brazeau.
18	Wood Mountain.	266	Ribstone Creek.
21	Turtle Mountain.	269	Prince Albert South.
22	Dufferin.	270	Pasquia.
23	Emerson.	313	Brulé.
61	Lytton.	315	Edmonton.
65	Macleod.	320	Carrot River.
68	Swift Current.	363	Baptiste.
71	Brandon.	413	Iosegun.
72	Portage la Prairie.	414	Saulteux.
73	Winnipeg.	415	Tawatinaw.
119	Regina.	461	Moberly.
120	Qu'Appelle.	463	Smoky River.
121	Riding Mountain.	465	Pelican.
122	Manitoba House.	466	Landels.
163	Donald.	511	St. John.
165	Rosebud.	512	Montagneuse.
170	Yorkton.	516	McMurray.
214	Rocky Mountain House.		

Scale, 6 miles to 1-inch.

No.	Name.	No.	Name.	No.	Name.
10	Port Moody.	120	Qu'Appelle.	270	Pasquia.
11	Yale.	121	Riding Mountain.	313	Brulé.
14	Pincer Creek.	122	Manitoba House.	314	St. Ann.
15	Lethbridge.	163	Donald.	315	Edmonton.
18	Wood Mountain.	164	Morley.	320	Carrot River.
21	Turtle Mountain.	165	Rosebud.	363	Baptiste.
22	Dufferin.	166	Sounding Creek.	364	Ft. Assiniboine.
23	Emerson,	168	The Elbow.	365	Victoria.
24	Lake of the Woods.	170	Yorkton.	366	Saddle Lake.
61	Lytton.	171	Duck Mountain.	367	Meadow Lake.
65	Macleod.	214	Rocky Mountain House.	368	Green Lake.
66	Medicine Hat.			413	Iosegun.
68	Swift Current.	215	Red Deer.	414	Saulteux.
69	Moosejaw.	216	Sullivan Lake.	415	Tawatinaw.
70	Moose Mountain.	219	Humboldt.	416	La Biche.
71	Brandon.	220	Nut Mountain.	461	Moberly.
72	Portage la Prairie.	262	Yellowhead.	463	Smoky River.
73	Winnipeg.	263	Jasper.	464	Giroux.
74	Cross Lake.	264	Brazeau.	465	Pelican.
114	Calgary.	265	Peace Hills.	466	Landels.
115	Blackfoot,	266	Ribstone Creek.	511	St. John.
118	Rush Lake.	267	Battleford.	512	Montagneuse.
119	Regina.	269	Prince Albert South.	516	McMurray.

APPENDIX No. 7.

STATEMENT of work executed in the Photographic Office from April 1, 1913 to March 31, 1914.

	3¼ x 3½	3¼ x 5½	5 x 7	8 x 10	10 x 12	11 x 14	15 x 14	16 x 18	18 x 20	20 x 24	24 x 32	25 x 35	30 x 36	36 x 42	42 x 48	Total
Dry plates and films	22		1,042	2		4										2,022
Bromide prints		952	44	148	615	1,492		251	220	101	22		75	63	85	3,118
Solio "			1,019	222		7										1,948
Velox "	212	8,583	5,300	380		52										14,536
Artura "				13												13
Vandyke "			4	19	8	127		66	140	77	98		140	109	141	959
Blue "			8	54	25	313		326	117	197	228		260	200	85	1,813
Lantern slides	148		157					16	8	2						148
Photographs mounted				265		292	1,271		200	57	51					448
Wet plate negatives				156					125	20		5				2,027
Photo-litho plates													653			803
	382	9,535	7,574	1,268	648	2,287	1,271	659	810	454	399	5	1,128	374	311	27,105

APPENDIX No. 8.

STATEMENT of work executed in the Lithographic Office from April 1, 1913, to March 31, 1914.

Month.	MAPS.			TOWNSHIP PLANS.			FORMS.		
	No.	Copies.	Im-pressions.	No.	Copies.	Im-pressions.	No.	Copies.	Im-pressions.
1913.									
April............	8	1,325	2,150	58	11,600	12,400	7	5,275	5,275
May............	15	4,800	5,475	65	13,000	13,000	8	5,541	5,541
June..	8	3,500	3,500	59	11,800	12,000	....	....	....
July............	3	225	600	28	5,600	5,800	5	35,000	35,000
August..........	7	16,875	75,775	36	7,200	7,200	3	1,650	1,650
September........	11	15,925	63,950	72	14,400	14,600	4	3,500	3,500
October	54	23,425	24,025	43	8,600	8,600	5	1,600	1,600
November.... ...	45	18,925	19,650	84	16,800	17,600	5	9,100	10,300
December.... ...	9	3,375	3,525	64	12,800	12,800	3	3,500	3,500
1914.									
January..........	17	27,540	71,550	174	34,800	35,.00	4	8,750	8,750
February.	14	28,380	97,725	142	24,300	24,300	2	600	600
March...	15	2,810	4,935	85	17,000	24,600	10	26,200	26,200
Total.......	206	147,105	372,860	910	177,900	188,000	56	100,716	101,916

RECAPITULATION.

—	No.	Copies.	Impressions.	Cost.
Maps	206	147,105	372,860	3,425 74
Townships	910	177,900	188,000	3,776 00
Forms....	56	100,716	101,916	927 76
Grand total	1,172	425.721	662,776	8,129 50

NOTE.—In the above schedule, the figures given for "cost" cover only the wages of the lithographers and printers : they do not include the cost of paper, machinery, supplies, rent, etc.

APPENDIX No. 9.

LIST OF EMPLOYEES of the Topographical Surveys Branch at Ottawa, on April 1, 1914, with the name, classification, duties of office and salary of each. (Metcalfe street, corner of Slater.)

NAME.	CLASSIFICATION.		Duties of Office.	Salary.
	Division.	Sub-division.		
				$
Deville, E., D.T.S., LL.D	1	A	Surveyor General	3,950
Shanks, T., B.A.Sc., D.L.S	1	A	Asst. Surveyor General	2,800
	Correspondence.			
Brady, M.	1	B	Secretary	2,600
Cullen, M. J	3	A	Clerk	1,200
Moran, J. F	3	A	"	1,050
Williams, E. R.	3	A	"	1,050
Addison, W. G.	3	A	Stenographer	950
Renault, J. F	3	B	"	750
Pegg, A.			Messenger	800
O'Meara, M. T.			"	650
	Accounts.			
Hunter, R. H	2	A	Accountant	2,100
Lemay, A.	2	A	Asst. Accountant	1,650
McPhail, N R.	2	B	" "	1,000
	Field work.			
Brown, T. E., B.A	1	B	Supervisor of field work	2,750

DIVISION I.

Survey Instructions and General Information.

Barber, H. G., Grad. S.P.S	1	B	Chief of division	2,200
Rice, F. W., Grad. School of Mining	2	A	Technical clerk	2,000
MacIlquham, W. L., B.Sc	2	A	"	2,000
Weld, W. E.	2	A	"	2,000
Peaker, W. J., Grad. S.P.S	2	A	"	1,700
Carroll, M. J., Grad. S.P.S	2	A	"	1,700
Rochon, E. C	2	A	"	1,650
McRae, A. D., B.A., B.Sc.	2	A	Supply clerk	1,650
Grant, A. W., B.A.	2	A	Editor	1,650
Hayward, H. E., B.Sc.	2	A	Registration clerk	1,600
MacMillan, J. P., B.E	2	B	Technical clerk	1,400
Wadlin, L. N., B.Sc., D.L.S	2	B	"	1,150
Gagnon, J. N. H., B.A.S	2	B	"	1,150
Armstrong, W. B, B.Sc	2	B	"	1,300
Nevins, L. A., B.A.	2	B	"	1,300
McDonald, J. F., B.A	2	B	Registration clerk	1,300
Sammon, J. J., B.A.	2	B	"	1,250
Fleming, A. C., B.A	2	B	"	1,250
Quinlan, L. J., B A.Sc	2	B	Technical clerk	1,250
Lawrence, J., B.Sc.	2	B	"	1,200
Gallaher, O. G., B.Sc	2	B	"	1,200
Miller, A. H., B.A.	2	B	"	1,200
Burkholder, E. L	3	A	Clerk	1,050

SESSIONAL PAPER No. 25b

APPENDIX No. 9—*Continued.*

DIVISION II.

Examination of Survey Returns and Compilation of Plans.

Name.	Classification.		Duties of Office.	Salary.
	Division.	Sub-division.		
				$
Nash, T. S., Grad. S.P.S., D.L.S . .	1	B	Chief of division	2,750
Dennis, E. M., B.Sc.	1	B	Surveys examiner.	2,100
Hill, S. N., Grad S.P.S	1	B	"	2,100
Elder, A. J., Grad. S.P.S., D.L.S	2	A	"	2,000
Genest, P F. X., Q.L.S	2	A	"	2,000
Kitto, F. H , D.L.S	2	A	Director of surveys (Yukon)	1,700
McClennan, W. D	2	A	Surveys examiner	1,700
Roger, A., O.L.S	2	A	"	1,700
Sutherland, H. E., B Sc	2	A	"	1,650
Ault, H. W	2	A	"	1,650
Bray, R. P	2	A	"	1,650
Spreckley, R. O	2	A	"	1,600
Goodday, Leonard	2	A	"	1,500
Harrison, E. W	2	B	"	1,400
Lytle, W. J	2	B	Recorder	1,150
LaBeree, E. F	2	· B	Surveys examiner	1,150
Jones, G. S., Grad. S.P S., O.L.S	2	B	"	1,150
Bradley, J. D	2	B	"	1,150
Kirwan, G. L., B.A.Sc	2	B	"	1,250
Callender, R., B.Sc	2	B	"	1,200
Cram, R. M., B.Sc	2	B	"	1,200
Timbrell, E. G., B.Sc	2	B	"	1,200
Macdonald, J. A	3	B	Clerk	800

DIVISION III.

Drafting and Printing, Imperial Building, Queen Street.

Name	Division	Sub-division	Duties	Salary
Engler, Carl., B.A., D.L.S	1	B	Chief of division	2,300
May, J. E . . . . :	2	A	Draughtsman	2,000
O'Connell, J. R	2	A	Draughtsman and engraver . .	1,800
Moule, W. J	2	B	Litho-designer	1,600
Helmer, J. D	2	B	Draughtsman	1,200
Dawson, R. J	2	B	Stamper	1,200
Archambault, E	2	B	Draughtsman and stamper . . .	1,200
Watters, James	3	A	Printer	1,200
McLennan, A. G	3	A	Recorder . . . . —	1,200
Brown, A	3	A	Stamper	1,050
Ebbs, E. J	3	A	"	1,050
Baril, C	3	A	Clerk	900

DIVISION IV.

British Columbia Surveys, Imperial Building, Queen Street.

Name	Division	Sub-division	Duties	Salary
Rowan-Legg, E. L	2	A	Chief of division	2,100
Gillmore, E. T B., Grad. R.M.C	2	A	Surveys examiner	2,100
Morley, R. W . . . . :	2	A	"	2,000
Wilson, E. F. D., B.Sc	2	A	"	1,750
Harris, K. D	2	A	"	1,600

5 GEORGE V., A. 1915

APPENDIX No. 9—Continued.

DIVISION V.

Mapping, Imperial Building, Queen Street.

Name.	Classification. Division.	Classification. Sub-division.	Duties of Office.	Salary.
				$
Smith, J..	1	B	Chief of division	2,750
Begin, P. A..	2	A	Draughtsman	2,050
Blanchet, A. E.	2	A	"	1,650
Côté, J. A., Grad. R.M.C	2	A	Editor of reports	1,750
D'Orsonnens, A	2	A	Draughtsman	1,700
Flindt, A. H	2	A	"	1,800
Davies, T. E. S	2	A	Recorder	1 600
Purdy, W. A.	2	A	Draugh sman	1,600
Bergin, W.	2	B	"	1,200
Blanchard, J. F.	2	B	Technical Clerk	1,200
Colquhoun, G. A., B. ~c	2	B	"	1,300
Davy, E.	2	B	Draughtsman	1,500
Howie, Jas	2	B	"	1,150
Perrin, V.	2	B	"	1,600
Squire, R. L.	2	B	Technical Clerk	1,200
Villeneuve, E.	2	B	Draughtsman	1,200

DIVISION VI.

Special Surveys, Imperial Building, Queen Street.

Dodge, G. B., D.L.S	1	B	Chief of division and Supt. Surveys Laboratory	2,750
Watt, G. H., Grad. S.P.S., D.L.S.	2	A	Computer	2,000
Way. W. C., M.Sc	2	A	Asst. Supt. Sur. Laboratory.	1,650
Milliken, J. B., B.A., B.Sc., D.L.S	2	A	Examiner of baseline surveys.	1,600
Parry, H., B.Eng., D.L.S	2	A	Mathematician	1,600
Wardle, J. M., B.Sc	2	B	Laboratory assistant	1,250
Fredette, J. F., D.L.S	2	B	" "	1,200
Hughson, W. G., B.Sc..	2	B	" "	1,250
Cannell, H. W., D.L.S.	2	B	Computer	1,250
Cousineau, A., B.Sc	2	B	"	1,200
Herbert, W. H., B.Sc.	2	B	"	1,300
Roe, B. J.	2	B	Computer	1,250
Ross, R. C., B.Sc	2	B	"	1,300
Lynch, F. J.	3	B	Stenographer	800
Watson, J. W.	3	B	Clerk	800
Pick, A. C.			Messenger	650

Chief Inspector of Surveys Office, 98 Wellington Street.

Hubbell, E. W., D.L.S	1	B	Chief inspector	2,800
Sylvain, John	2	A	Assistant	1,800
Stalker, Miss M. W.	3	A	Stenographer	1,050

Board of Examiners for D.L.S.

Henderson, F. D., Grad. S.P.S., D.L S.	1	B	Secretary	2,100
Nolan, Miss A. A.	3	B	Stenographer	500

APPENDIX No. 9—*Concluded.*

Geographic Board, Woods Building, Slater Street.

Name.	Classification.		Duties of Office	Salaries.
	Division.	Sub-division.		
				$
Whitcher, A. *H.*, F.R.G.S , D.L.S....	2	A	Secretary.	2,100

Photographic Office, Metcalfe Street, corner Slater Street.

Carruthers, H. K...	2	A	Process photographer . ..	2,000
Woodruff, John....	2	A	Chief "	2,000
Collins, G. H. A.............	2	B	Photographer......	1,000
Whitcomb, H. E	3	A	"	1,200
Morgan, W. E................	3	A	"	1,200
Kilmartin, A.....	3	A	Asst. photographer..........	1,050
Ouimet. E. G.....	3	B	"	950

Lithographic Office, Imperial Building, Queen Street.

Name.	Occupation.	Salaries.	
Moody, A..........	Foreman ....∴.................	$27 00	per week,
Burnett, E...	Lithographer..................	25 00	"
Thicke, C. R......	"	23 00	"
Deslauriers, J. H......	Transferrer.....	20 00	"
Bergin, J.........	Printer..........	21 00	"
Thicke, H. S....................................	"	20 00	"
Boyle, S......... . ...•	Stone polisher	15 00	"
Gagnon, J.......	Press feeder	12 00	"
Kane, P.....	"	9 50	"
Easton, R. M............................	Printer..	19 50	"
Hare, F. H.......	Asst. photographer...........	15 00	"

5 GEORGE V.. A. 1915

APPENDIX No. 10.

LIST of Dominion Land Surveyors who are in possession of Standard Measures.

Name.	Address	Date of Birth.	Date of Appointment or of Commission.	Remarks.
Akins, James Robert...	Ottawa, Ont..... .	Sept. 2, '76	Mar. 14, '10	
Allison, Calvin Bruce	South Woodslee, Ont.	June 16, '84	Mar. 28, '10	O.L.S.
Ashton, Arthur Ward.........	Ottawa, Ont........	Nov. 5, '80	May 29, '08	B.C.L.S.
Austin, George Frederick	Not known...... ...	....	April 14, '72	
Aylen, John.	North Bay, Ont....	....	May 29, '85	
Aylsworth, Charles Fraser....	Madoc, Ont...	April 21, '62	May 13, '86	O.L.S.
Baker, James Clarence	Vermilion, Alta....	May 12, '78	May 18, '06	A.L.S.
Baker, Mason Heimon.. . .	St. Thomas, Ont....	July 9, '84	Aug. 6, '08	O.L.S.
Bartlett, Ernest....	Medicine Hat, Alta.	——— '83	Jan. 16, '11	A.L.S.
Bayne, George A......	Winnipeg, Man.....	Oct. 25, '50	April 14, '72	M.L.S.
Beatty, David...	Parry Sound, Ont...	Dec. 22, '42	April 14, '72	O.L.S.
Begg, William Arthur. ·. ...	Hamilton, Ont......	July 15, '82	June 8, '09	S.L.S.
Belanger, Phidime Roch Arthur	Ottawa, Ont	Mar. 5, '53	May 17, '80	Inspector of Surveys, Topographical Surveys Branch, Dept. of the Interior.
Belleau, Joseph Alphonse . .	Ottawa, Ont.......	Sept. 30, '56	May 15, '83	Land Patents Branch, Department of Interior.
Belyea, Albert Palmer Corey..	Edmonton, Alta....	....	July 14, '09	A.L.S.
Bemister, George Bartlett.....	Winnipeg, Man	....	June 11, '78	M.L.S. Engineering Dept. C.N.R.
Bennett, George Arthur... ..	Ottawa, Ont.......	May 18, '86	Aug. 25, '10	A.L.S.
Berry, Edward Wilson..	Seaforth, Ont	Aug. 26, '81	May 18, '11	
Bigger, Charles Albert	Ottawa, Ont	Aug. 15, '53	Mar. 30, '82	B.C.L.S., O.L.S., Assistant Superintendent Geodetic Survey
Bingham, Edwin Ralph.. ...	Fort William, Ont..	——— '78	Oct. 25, '06	O.L.S.
Blanchet, Guy Houghton......	Ottawa, Ont.......	Feb. 12, '84	Mar. 10, '10	.
Boivin, Elzear....	Edmonton, Alta....	June 13, '57	Nov. 13, '83	
Boswell, Elias John	Montreal, Que...	Sept. 26, '70	Mar. 18, '03	O.L.S., M.L.S.
Boulton, William James. . .	Wallaceburg, Ont..	Oct. 2, '84	Mar. 7, '12	
Bourgeault, Armand	St. Jean Port Joli, Que.............	Feb. 23, '58	Mar. 29, '83	Q.L.S.
Bourgault, Charles Eugene....	Lauzon, Levis, Que..	Sept. 6, '61	Feb. 21, '88	
Bourget, Charles Arthur......	Lauzon, Que.......	Aug. 26, '51	May 14, '84	Q.L.S.
Bowman, Edgar Peterson....	West Montrose, Ont.	Sept. 29, '83	Sept. 26, '07	O.L.S.
Bowman, Herbert Joseph	Berlin, Ont........	June 18, '65	Feb. 16, '88	O.L.S.
Brabazon, Alfred James ...	Ottawa, Ont.......	....	May 13, '82	Boundary Surveys, Dept, of the Interior.
Bray, Samuel................	Ottawa, Ont.......	Nov. 5, '46	Nov. 14, '83	O.L.S., Chief Surveyor, Dept. of Indian Affairs.
Bray, Lennox Thomas	Edmonton, Alta....	Mar. 14, '77	Feb. 18, '03	O.L.S., A.L.S.
Brenot, Lucien	Ottawa, Ont	Aug. 31, '87	Mar. 18, '10	
Bridgland, Morrison Parsons..	Calgary, Alta.	Dec. 20, '78	Mar. 10, '05	A.L.S.
Broughton, George Henry.....	Penticton, B.C.....	Aug. 12, '86	June 3, '09	B.C.L.S.
Brown, Charles Dudley.. ..	Winnipeg, Man.....	Feb. 25, '83	April 4, '10	A.L.S., S.L.S.
Brown, Edgar Carl...........	Winnipeg, Man....	Nov. 28, '86	May 23, '11	A.L.S., S.L.S.
Brown, Thomas Wood........	Saskatoon, Sask....	Nov. 10, '79	June 21, '09	A.L.S., S.L.S.
Brownlee, James Harrison....	Vancouver, B.C....	Mar. 22, '56	April 15, '87	M.L.S., B.C.L.S.
Buchanan, John Alexander....	Edmonton, Alta....	Mar. 4, '87	May 17, '12	A.L.S.
Burd, James Henry..........	Weyburn, Sask....	Sept. 7, '71	May 18, '11	O.L.S., S.L.S.
Burgess, Edward LeRoy	Kamloops, B.C....	May 5, '78	Feb. 23, '05	O.L.S.
Burnet, Hugh..	Victoria, B.C......	....	June 22, '85	O.L.S., B.C.L.S.
Burwash, Nathaniel Alfred....	Toronto, Ont. .	Sept. 28, '79	Mar. 6, '07	O.L.S.
Burwell, Herbert Mahlon.....	Vancouver, B.C....	Oct. 23, '63	Feb. 17, '87	B.C.L.S.
Calder, John Alexander.	Lytton, B.C..... .	June 2, '86	May 21, '12	
Cameron, Charles Scott......	Beaverton, Ont.....	Dec. 6, '84	Mar. 15, '13	
Campbell, Alan John.........	Sidney, B.C.......	Oct. 1, '82	April 13, '09	B.C.L.S., A.L.S.
Campbell, Alexander Stewart..	Kingston, Ont......	Mar. 7, '80	Mar. 6, '09	O.L.S.
Carbert, Joseph Alfred	Medicine Hat, Alta.	Feb. 4, '56	May 12, '80	O.L.S., A.L.S., District Engineer and Surveyor, Dept. of Public Works, Alberta.
Carpenter Henry Stanley......	Regina, Sask. . .	Feb. 8, '74	Feb. 20, '01	O.L.S., S.L.S., Department of Public Works.
Carroll, Cyrus	Regina, Sask.. .	Dec.. 6, '34	April 11, '72	O.L.S , S.L.S.

SESSIONAL PAPER No. 25b

APPENDIX No. 10—*Continued.*

LIST of Dominion Land Surveyors who are in possession of Standard Measures.—*Continued.*

Name.	Address.	Date of Birth.	Date of Appointment or of Commission.	Remarks.
Carson, Percy Alexander	Calgary, Alta	Dec. 25, '77	Feb. 22, '06	Hydrographic Survey.
Carthew, William Morden	Edmonton, Alta	Oct. 19, '86	Mar. 29, '10	A.L.S.
Carthew, John Trewalla	Edmonton, Alta	Feb. 15, '91	Mar. 15, '13	
Cautley, Reginald Hutton	Edmonton, Alta	Dec. 6, '79	May 1, '05	A.L.S.
Cautley, Richard William	Edmonton, Alta	Aug. 3, '73	Sept. 2, '96	A.L.S.
Cavana, Allan George	Orillia, Ont	Jan. 22, '58	Nov. 16, '76	O.L.S.
Charlesworth, Lionel Clare	Edmonton, Alta	Nov. 17, '73	Mar. 24, '03	O.L.S., A.L.S., Dept. of Public Works, Alberta.
Chase, Albert Victor	Orillia, Ont	Mar. 4, '83	Oct. 11, '10	O.L.S.
Chilver, Charles Alonzo	Walkerville, Ont	Feb. 8, '83	Feb. 22, '07	
Christie, William	Prince Albert, Sask	Feb. 13, '76	Mar. 22, '06	S.L.S.
Clarke, Frederick Fieldhouse	Toronto, Ont	Aug. 22, '78	Feb. 18, '08	O.L.S.
Clarke, Charles Wentworth	Regina, Sask	Nov. 19, '75	Mar. 21, '10	S.L.S.
Cleveland, Ernest Albert	Vancouver, B.C.	May 12, '74	June 27, '99	B.C.L.S.
Coates, Preston Charles	Victoria, B.C	May 16, '81	April 19, '07	B.C.L.S.
Cokely, Leroy S	Duncan, B.C	Nov. 23, '84	Mar. 22, '10	B.C.L.S.
Coltham, George William	Aurora, Ont	Feb. 19, '89	Mar. 15, '13	O.L.S.
Cond, Fritz Thomas Piercy	Vancouver, B.C.	May 16, '86	May 18, '11	B.C.L.S.
Côté, Joseph Adélard	Prince Albert, Sask	June 5, '64	May 14, '81	S.L.S.
Côté, Jean Léon	Edmonton, Alta	May 6, '67	Mar. 21, '90	A.L.S.
Côte, Joseph Martial	Ottawa, Ont	Aug. 25, '89	May 13, '13	
Cotton, Arthur Frederick	Massett, B.C	Aug. 8, '52	May 11, '80	O.L.S., B.C.L.S.
Cowper, George Constable	Welland, Ont	Oct. 20, '86	Mar. 11, '11	
Craig, John Davidson	Ottawa, Ont	Jan. 30, '76	Feb. 24, '02	Boundary Surveys, Dept. of the Interior.
Cumming, Austin Lewis	Edmonton, Alta	Aug. 25, '82	Mar. 3, '10	A.L.S.
Cummings, Alfred	Fernie, B.C	July 3, '80	Mar. 3, '09	B.C.L.S.
Cummings, John George	Cranbrook, B.C.	Nov. 19, '73	Feb. 17, '04	B.C.L.S.
Dalton, John Joseph	Weston, Ont	June 12, '54	Apr. 17, '79	O.L.S., D.T.S.
Davies, Thomas Attwood	Edmonton, Alta		Feb 22, '06	A.L.S.
Dawson, Frederick James	Kamloops, B.C	Sept. 22, '86	Sept. 12, '10	B C.L.S.
Day, Harry Samuel	Edmonton, Alta	Nov. 14, '85	Mar. 9, '10	A.L.S.
Deans, William James	Brandon, Man	May 4, '60	May 13, '86	O.L.S.
de la Condamine, C	Calgary, Alta	Feb. 13, '75	May 4, '10	A.L S.
Dennis, John Stoughton	Calgary, Alta	Oct. 22, '56	Nov. 19, '77	D.T.S.
Denny, Herbert C	Not known.		Apr. 1, '82	
Dickson, Henry Godkin	Whitehorse, Y.T.	Mar. 29, '64	Mar. 19, '89	M.L S.
Dickson, James	Fenelon Falls, Ont.	Oct. 30, '34	Apr. 14, '72	O.L.S.
Dobie, James Samuel	Thessalon, Ont.	Oct. 15, '73	Mar. 22, '06	O.L.S.
Donnelly, Cecil	Winnipeg, Man.	Oct. 18, '89	Mar. 15, '13	M.L.S.
Doupe, Jacob Lonsdale	Winnipeg, Man.	Sept. 14, '67	Oct. 6, '88	M.L.S., A.L.S., S.L.S., Asst. Land Commissioner for C.P.R.
Drewry, William Stewart	Victoria, B.C	Jan. 20, '59	Nov. 14, '83	O.L.S., B.C.L.S.
Driscoll, Alfred	Edmonton, Alta	July 2, '65	Feb. 23, '87	B.C.L.S., A.L.S
Drummond, Thomas	Montreal, P.Q	1856	June 24, '78	D.T.S.
D uc William A	Winnipeg, Man	April 4, '52	Mar. 30, '83	O.L.S., M.L.S.
Dumais, Paul T. Concorde	Hull, P.Q.	Jan. 2, '47	Mar. 29, '82	Q.L.S.
Earle, Wallace Sinclair	Vancouver, B.C	Feb. 8, '89	May 18, '11	B.C.L.S., O.L.S.
Edwards, George	Ponoka, Alta.	June 13, '42	Apr. 14, '72	O.L.S., A.L.S.
Edwards, William Milton	Lethbridge, Alta.	June 21, '79	Apr. 5, '10	A.L.S.
Ellacott, Charles Herbert	Victoria, B.C	Dec. 24, '66	Feb. 22, '99	B.C.L.S.
Ellis, Douglas Stewart	Kingston, Ont.	Mar. 16, '85	May 17, '12	
Empey, John Morgan	Calgary, Alta.	Apr. 16, '74	Feb. 23, '05	O.L.S., A.L S.
Engler, Carl	Ottawa, Ont.	Sept. 30, '72	Feb. 23, '05	T. S. Branch, Dept. of Interior.
Evans, Stanley Livingstone	Corinth, Ont.	Jan. 14, '84	Feb. 13, '11	
Fairchild, Charles Courtland	Edmonton, Alta.	Feb. 21, '67	Feb. 20, '01	O.L.S., A.L.S.
Farncomb, Alfred Ernest	Edmonton (South) Alta	May 22, '73	Mar. 12, '02	O.L.S., A.L.S.
Fawcett, Adam	Gravenhurst, Ont.		Feb. 22, '93	
Fawcett, Sydney Dawson	Ottawa, Ont.	Oct. 29, '82	May 18, '11	
Fawcett, Thomas	Ottawa, Ont.	Oct. 28, '48	Nov. 18, '76	O.L..S., D.T.S., Boundary Surveys, Dept. of Interior.

5 GEORGE V., A. 1915

APPENDIX No. 10—*Continued.*

LIST of Dominion Land Surveyors who are in possession of Standard Measures—
Continued.

Name.	Address.	Date of Birth.	Date of Appointment or of Commission.	Remarks.
Ferguson, George *H*endry	Toronto, Ont......	Jan. 20, '83	June 2, '09	
Findlay, Allan..	Winnipeg, Man....	Oct. 15, '80	Mar, 21, '08	M.L.S.
Fletcher, James Allan	Fletcher, Ont.....	Mar. 26, '89	May 18, '11	
Fontaine, Louis Elie..........	Levis, P.Q.........	Oct. 3, '68	Nov. 30, '92	A.L.S., Inspector of Surveys, Dept. of Interior.
Francis, John................	Portage la Prairie, Man.............	Dec. 22, '52	June 17, '75	M.L.S.
Galletly, James Simpson ...	Brooklin, Ont.. ..	Apr. 15, '88	May 18, '11	
Garden, James Ford.........	Vancouver, B.C. ...	Feb. 19, '47	May 13, '80	B.C.L.S.
Garden, George *H*..........	Lethbridge, Alta....	....	Apr. 14, '72	Deputy Surveyor for N.B.
Garden, Charles ,.........	Not known.......	....	Apr. 14, '72	Deputy Surveyor for N.B.
Garner, Albert Coleman......	Regina, Sask.	Sept. 6, '78	May 27, '07	S.L.S., A.L.S., Chief Surveyor Surveys Branch Land Titles Offices.
Gauvreau, Louis Pierre	Not known	....	Apr. 14, '72	
Gibbon, James...............	Vancouver, B.C. ...	June 25, '60	Feb. 12, '91	O.L.S.
Glover, Arthur Edward.......	Edmonton, Alta ..	Mar. 4, 87	Mar. 11, '11	A.L.S., S.L.S.
Gordon, Maitland Lockhart...	Vancouver, B.C....	Sept. 27, '82	Feb. 18, '04	B.C.L.S.
Gordon, Robert John	Lethbridge, Alta....	June 18, '69	Mar. 12, '02	A.L.S.
Gore, Thomas Sinclair	Victoria, B.C. ...	1852	Apr. 19, '79	B.C.L.S.
Graham, John Robertson	Vancouver, B.C.....	Apr. 18, '87	May 26, '10	B.C.L.S.
Grassie, Charles Andrew......	Medicine Hat, Alta.	Dec. 24, '83	Dec. 27, '10	A.L.S.
Gray, James Edward	Edmonton, Alta....	Oct. 12, '81	Mar. 11, '11	A.L.S., S.L.S.
Green, Alfred *H*arold.	Nelson, B.C........	Jan. 20, '79	Feb. 23, '05	B.C.L.S , A.L.S.
Green, Thomas Daniel........	Rocky Mountain House, Alta ..	Dec. 21, '57	May 19, '84	O.L.S.
Green, Frank Compton... ..	Victoria, B.C......	May 4, '73	May 8, '03	B.C.L.S.
Griffin, Albert Dyke	Elk Lake, Ont....	Dec. 14, '60	May 13, '13	O.L.S.
Grover, George Alexander.....	Toronto, Ont	....	Feb. 18, '04	
*H*aggen, Rupert Williams....	Quesnel, B.C	July 29, '87	May 18, '11	B.C.L.S.
*H*amilton, Charles Thomas....	Vancouver, B.C....	July 29, '84	May 18, '11	B.C.L.S.
*H*amilton, James Frederick....	Lethbridge, Alta....	April 4, '69	June 2, '09	A.L.S.
*H*arris, John Walter	Winnipeg, Man.....	Feb. 26, '45	April 14, '72	O.L.S., M.L.S., Assessment Commissioner and City Surveyor.
*H*arrison, Edward	Calgary, Alta......	....	May 14, '10	A.L.S.
*H*arvey, Charles	Kelowna, B.C	May 5, '76	Feb. 17, '04	B.C.L.S.
*H*awkins, Albert *H*oward.. ...	Listowel, Ont......	July 27, '62	Mar. 6, '06	
*H*eaman, John Andrew	Winnipeg, Man.....	June 3, '75	July 15, '09	O.L.S.
*H*eathcott, Robert Vernon ..	Edmonton, Alta....	July 7, '81	May 13, '07	A.L.S.
*H*enderson, Walter..........	Not known.........	....	Nov. 17, '83	
*H*erriot, George *H*enry.... .	Souris, Man........	Feb. 23, '83	Sept. 18, '09	M.L.S.
*H*euperman, Frederick Justinus	Calgary, Alta.......	July 23, '87	Mar.. 13, '11	A.L.S.
*H*euperman, Lambertus Fred.	Calgary, Alta.	Sept. 20, '81	Mar. 29, '10	A.L.S.
*H*oar, Charles Millard......	Calgary, Alta.....	Sept. 26, '85	Mar. 9, '11	A.L.S.
*H*obbs, Wilfrid Ernest........	Winnipeg, Man.....	Mar, 12, '87	Mar. 5, '12	M.L.S.
*H*olcroft, Herbert Spencer.....	Toronto, Ont	Sept. 4, '77	Feb. 18, '03	O.L.S.
*H*opkins, Marshall Willard....	Edmonton, Alta....	May 24, '61	Feb. 20, '01	O.L.S., A.L.S.
*H*ubbell, Ernest Wilson......	Ottawa, Ont........	Nov. 5, '62	May 19, '84	Chief Inspector of Surveys, Dept. of Interior.
*H*unter, Albert Ernest........	Wiarton, Ont..... ..	Nov. 8, '87	Mar. 7, '12	
Inkster, Oluff.	Edmonton, Alta	Mar. 23, '85	May 18, '11	A.L.S.
Jackson, John Edwin.	*H*amilton, Ont	Dec. 27, '81	May 18, '11	O.L.S.
James, Silas	Toronto, Ont	June 19, '34	April 14, '72	O.L.S.
Jephson, Richard Jermy	Brandon, Man......	Feb. 5, '54	May 12, '80	O.L.S., B.C.L.S., M.L.S.
Johnson, Alfred William.....	Kamloops, B.C	Feb. 23, '74	Mar. 12, '02	B.C.L.S.
Johnson, Percy Nowell........	Edmonton, Alta	Oct. 4, '75	May 10, '09	
Johnston, James *H*omer......	Edmonton, Alta	Aug. 23, '87	May 17, '12	A.L.S.
Johnson, William James	St. Catharines, Ont..	Jan. 31, '81	Mar. 11, '11	
Keith, *H*omer Pasha	Edmonton, Alta	Aug. 30, '85	Feb. 1, '11	A.L.S.
Kimpe, Maurice	Edmonton, Alta	Jan. 17, '76	May 13, '07	A.L.S.
King, William Frederick	Dominion Observatory, Ottawa, Ont.	Feb. 19, '54	Nov. 21, '76	D.T.S. Chief Astronomer, Dept. of Interior.

APPENDIX No. 10—*Continued.*

LIST of Dominion Land Surveyors who are in possession of Standard Measures—
Continued.

Name.	Address.	Date of Birth.	Date of Appointment or of Commission.	Remarks.
Kirk, John Albert............	Summerland, B.C...	Jan. 9, '54	May 11, '80	O.L.S., B.C.L.S.
Kitto, Franklin *H*ugo.........	Dawson, Y.T... ...	Mar. 28, '80	Mar. 6, '08	
Klotz, Otto Julius	Dominion Observatory, Ottawa, Ont.	Mar. 31, '52	Nov. 19, '77	O.L.S., D.T.S., Astronomer, Dept. of Interior.
Knight, Richard *H*	Edmonton, Alta	June 7, '77	Feb. 18, '04	A.L.S.
Lamb, Frederick Carlyle . . .	Saskatoon, Sask.....	Dec. 11, '85	May 17, '12	
Lang, John Leiper.........	Sault Ste. Marie, Ont	Aug. 18, '84	Oct. 14, '08	O.L.S.
Latimer, Frank *H*erbert.	Penticton, B.C......	May 23, '60	Nov. 13, '85	B.C.L.S.
Laurie, Richard C	Battleford, Sask	Jan. 31, '58	April 27, '83	S.L.S.
Leblanc, Pierre Maxime *H*enri	Ottawa, Ont........	Oct. 1, '84	May 13, '13	
Lemoine, Charles Errol......	Ville Montcalm, P.Q.	....	Mar. 31, '82	Q.L.S.
Lighthall, Abram............	Vancouver, B.C...	Mar. 30, '78	Dec. 25, '09	
Lindsay, James Herbert	Prince Albert, Sask.	Nov. 27, '82	May 18, '11	S.L.S.
Lonergan, Gerald Joseph.	Buckingham, P.Q...	Oct. 8, '71	Feb. 28, '01	Q.L.S., A.L.S., Inspector of Surveys, Dept. of Interior.
Loucks, Roy Wm. Egbert.	Saskatoon, Sask.....	Oct. 31, '84	Mar. 1, '12	A.L.S., S.L.S.
Lumsden, *H*ugh David.	St. Andrews, N.B...	Sept. 7, '44	April 14, '72	O.L.S.
Macdonald, Colin Stone..	Ottawa, Ont.......	May 26, '87	Mar. 10, '14	
Macdonald, Gordon Alexander.	Muirkirk, Ont.....	May 24, '85	May 17, '12	B.C.L.S.
MacLennan, Alexander L....	Toronto, Ont	May 10, '78	Feb. 23, '05	S.L.S.
MacLeod, George Waters......	Edmonton, Alta	'38	Mar. 1, '12	A.L.S.
MacPherson, Charles Wilfrid..	Dawson, Y.T.......	Sept. 6, '71	Mar. 7, '00	O.L.S.
Magrath, Charles Alexander ..	Ottawa, Ont.......	April 22, '60	Nov. 16, '81	O.L.S., B.C.L.S., D.T.S., Member International Waterways Commission.
Martindale, Ernest Smith.....	Kingsmill, Ont.	May 20, '86	Mar. 11, '11	
Martyn, Oscar William.	Regina, Sask.......	Dec. 2, '88	Mar. 11, '11	S.L.S.
Matheson, *H*ugh............	Ottawa, Ont.......	May 2, '79	May 9, '11	
McArthur, James Joseph.	Ottawa, Ont........	May 9, '56	April 17, '79	Boundary Surveys, Dept. of Interior.
McCaw, Robert Daniel.. . ..	Sidney, B.C . ..	May 24, '83	Mar. 23, '09	O.L.S., B.C.L.S., A.L.S.
McColl, Gilbert Beebe	Winnipeg, Man.....	Oct. 8, '82	Mar. 20, '07	M.L.S. D.T.S.
McColl, Samuel Ebenezer....	Winnipeg, Man.....	July 17, '86	May 18, '11	M.L.S.
McDiarmid, Stuart Stanley....	Vancouver, B.C	Aug. 4, '81	Feb. 23, '05	B.C.L.S.
McDonald, *H*arold French....	Winnipeg, Man.....	Nov. 22, '85	Mar. 3, '13	M.L.S., S.L.S., A.L.S.
McElhanney, Thomas Andrew.	Vancouver, B.C	April 21, '86	Mar. 17, '12	
McEwen, Duncan Findlay	Edmonton. Alta ...	Aug. 7, '76	May 18, '11	A.L.S.
McFadden, Moses	Vancouver, B.C	Aug. 26, '26	April 14, '72	O.L.S., M.L.S.
McFarlane, Walter Graham. .	Peace River Landing Alta	Sept. 28, '75	May 19, '05	A.L.S.
McFarlane, John Baird.... ...	Toronto, Ont... ..	Feb. 25, '79	June 3, '08	A.L.S.
McFee, Angus	Red Deer, Alta......	July 14, '46	April 19, '79	A.L.S.
McGeorge, William Graham...	Chatham, Ont......	Mar. 22, '87	Mar. 31, '10	O.L.S.
McGrandle, *H*ugh	Wetaskiwin, Alta....	Mar. 12, '57	Mar. 30, '83	O.L.S., A.L.S.
McKay, Robert B............	Vancouver, B.C	April 21, '83	May 21, '12	
McKnight, James Henry......	Simcoe, Ont...... .	July 13, '85	May 13, '13	
McLellan, Roy Alexander.....	Toronto, Ont. ...	July 31, '89	Mar. 15, '13	
McMaster, William Angus Alexander	Prince Albert, Sask.	Feb. 1, '85	July 6, '10	A.L.S., S.L.S.
McMillan, George............	Finch, Ont.........	Dec. 9, '69	Feb. 22, '06	
McNaughton, Alexander L....	Kelowna, B.C	Sept. 30, '81	Feb. 23, '05	O.L.S., B.C.L.S.
McPherson, Archibald John...	Regina, Sask:	—, '70	Feb. 21, '01	S.L.S.
McPhillips, Robert Charles...	Winnipeg, Man.....	April 24, '56	May 17, '80	M.L.S.
McVittie, Archibald W.	Victoria, B.C......	May 5, '58	Mar. 30, '82	B.C.L.S.
Meadows, William Walter.....	Maple Creek. Sask..	May 27, '73	Feb. 23, '05	O.L.S., S.L.S.
Melhuish, Paul.........	Vancouver, B.C	April 14, '87	May 18, '11	B.C.L.S.
Miles, Charles Falconer..	Toronto, Ont.	Jan. 30, '38	April 14, '72	O.L.S. Inspector of Surveys, Dept. of Interior.
Mitchell, Benjamin Foster	Edmonton, Alta....	June 16, '80	April 16, '08	A.L.S.
Moberly, Harford Kenneth....	Yorkton, Sask	—, '69	April 21, '03	S.L.S.
Montgomery, Royal *H*arp	Prince Albert, Sask.	May 20, '82	Feb. 23, '05	O.L.S., S.L.S.
Moore, *H*erbert *H*arrison......	Calgary, Alta.......	Dec. 1, '69	Feb. 17, '04	A.L.S.
Morrier, Joseph Eldedge	Prince Albert, Sask..	Aug. 29, '74	May 16, '07	S.L.S.

25b—5½

DEPARTMENT OF THE INTERIOR

5 GEORGE V., A. 1915

APPENDIX No. 10—*Continued.*

LIST of Dominion Land Surveyors who are in possession of Standard Measures—
Continued.

Name.	Address.	Date of Birth.	Date of Appointment or of Commission.	Remarks.
Murray, Ernest William	Regina, Sask......	Mar. 20, '84	May 31, '10	S.L.S.
Narraway, Athos Maxwell	Ottawa, Ont	July 19, '88	May 18, '11	
Neelands, Rupert A.	Hamiota, Man.....	Aug. 26, '84	Mar. 5, '12	
Nelles, Douglas Henry......	Ottawa, Ont	Mar. 26, '81	Mar. 9, '07	
Nesham, Edward Williams...	Ottawa, Ont ...	June 10, '88	Mar. 15, '13	
Neville, Everett A	Vancouver, B.C. ..	Jan. 8, '87	May 18, '11	B.C.L.S
O'Hara, Walter Francis......	Ottawa, Ont	....	Feb. 19, '95	O.L.S.
Ord, Lewis Redman..........	Hamilton, Ont.....	Oct. 17, '56	April 1, '82	O.L.S.
Palmer, Philip Ebenezer	Dorchester, N.B. ..	May 6, '88	Mar. 7, '12	
Parsons, Johnstone Lindsay R.	Regina, Sask......	Jan. 18, '76	Feb. 23, '05	O.L.S., S.L.S.
Patrick, Allan Poyntz...	Calgary, Alta	July 18, '49	Nov. 19, '77	B.C.L.S., D.T.S., A.L.S.
Patten, Thaddeus James	Little Current, Ont..	Feb. 4, '59	Mar. 29, '83	O.L.S.
Pearce, William...	Calgary, Alta..	Feb. 1, '48	May 10, '80	O.L.S., B.C.L.S., A.L.S.
Pearce, Seabury Kains.......	Calgary, Alta	Dec 6, '87	Mar. 9, '11	A.L.S.
Pearson, Hugh Edward.	Edmonton, Alta...	Oct. 17, '87	May 17, '12	A.L.S.
Pequegnat, Marcel	Berlin, Ont	April 27, '86	June 6, '10	O.L.S.
Peters, Frederic Hatheway....	Calgary, Alta.. ...	Nov. 4, '83	Mar. 4, '10	A.L.S., Com. of Irrigation
Phillips, Edward Horace. ...	Saskatoon, Sask....	Dec. 19, '78	Feb. 24, '02	S.L.S.
Phillips, Harold Geoffrey,.....	Regina, Sask.	Sept. 3, '87	April 23, '10	S.L.S.
Pierce, Benjamin Clifford......	Kingston, Ont......	Nov. 5, '90	Mar. 13, '14	
Pierce, John Wesley.	Ottawa, Ont.......	July 14, '85	Dec. 24, '09	O.L.S.
Pinder, George Zouch.	Edmonton, Alta....	Mar. 5, '81	Mar. 15, '13	
Plunkett, Thomas Hartley	Meaford, Ont	June 1, '78	Mar. 12, '08	
Ponton, Archibald William....	Edmonton, Alta ...	Jan. 25, '59	May 18, '81	O.L.S , A.L.S.
Powell, William Henry......	Vancouver, B.C.....	Dec. 22, '84	Feb. 22, '11	B.C.L.S.
Proudfoot Hume Blake......	Prince Albert, Sask	June 23, '58	Mar. 28, '82	O.L.S., S.L.S.
Purser, Ralph Clinton	Windsor, Ont.......	April 7, '86	Feb. 2, '11	
Rainboth, Edward Joseph.....	Ottawa, Ont	.	May 19, '81	Q.L.S., O.L.S.
Ransom, John Thomas	Toronto, Ont.......	Aug. 24, '88	Jan. 14, '11	O.L.S.
Reilly, William Robinson. ...	Regina, Sask.......	Aug. 10, '57	Nov. 17, '81	O.L.S., M.L.S., S.L.S.
Richard, Joseph Francois.. ...	Ste. Anne de la Pocatière, P.Q...	....	May 13, '82	Q.L.S.
Rinfret, Claude...............	Montreal, P.Q	Jan. 5, '86	Mar 20, '08	Q.L.S.
Rinfret, Raoul	Montreal, P.Q......	July 16, '56	Feb. 20, '00	Q.L.S.
Ritchie, Joseph Frederick	Prince Rupert, B.C	May 23, '63	Jan. 7, '89	B.C.L.S.
Roberts, Sydney Archibald....	Victoria, B.C.	April 10, '48	May 16, '85	B.C.L.S.
Roberts, Vaughan Maurice....	Goderich, Ont	Mar. 22, '64	May 17, '86	
Robertson, Donald Fraser. ...	Ottawa, Ont........		'80 May 25, '09	Dept. of Indian Affairs.
Robertson, Henry H.	N.Timiskaming, P.Q	Sept. 13, '47	April 14, '72	Q.L.S.
Robertson, Edgar Doctor.	Edmonton Alta.....	Sept. 12, '85	Mar. 15, '13	
Robinson, Ernest Walter P..	Ottawa, Ont	May 8, '80	May 1, '08	
Robinson, Franklin Joseph....	Regina, Sask. ...	Oct. 20, '70	Feb. 20, '00	S.L.S.. Deputy Minister of Public Works.
Robinson, William Andrew....	Winnipeg, Man.....	Feb. 21, '81	Oct. 2, '11	S.L.S. M.L.S.
Rolfson, Orville	Walkerville, Ont....	Feb. 26, '85	July 11, '08	
Rombough, Marshall Bedwell	Morden, Man.. .	Oct. 14, '35	April 14, '72	M.L.S.
Rorke, Louis Valentine..	Toronto, Ont......	Feb. — '65	Aug. 13, '91	O.L.S., Inspector of Surveys for Ontario.
Ross, George	Welland, Ont.	June 12, '53	Nov. 21, '82	O.L.S.
Ross, Joseph Edmund.	Kamloops, B.C.....	Jan. 9, '61	Feb. 12, '91	O.L.S., B.C.L.S
Routly, Herbert Thomas	Toronto Ont	Jan. 20, '78	Feb. 15, '11	O.L.S.
Roy, George Peter..	Quebec, P.Q.......	Oct. 1, '52	Nov. 17, '81	Q.L.S.
Roy, Joseph George Emile,....	Quebec, P.Q.......	Mar. 14, '86	May 25, '10	Q.L.S.
Russell, Alexander Lord.... ...	Port Arthur, Ont....	....	April 14, '72	O.L.S
Saint Cyr, Jean Baptiste ..	Montreal, P.Q......	Dec. 17, '66	Feb. 17, '87	Q.L.S.
Saint Cyr, Arthur............	Ottawa, Ont.	Nov. — '60	Feb. 17, '87	
Saunders, Bryce Johnston.. ...	Edmonton, Alta ...	Oct. 17, '60	Nov. 16, '84	O.L.S.
Scott, Walter Alexander......	Calgary, Alta... .	Aug. 8, '85	Mar. 9, '09	A.L.S., S.L S
Seager, Edmund...'........	Kenora, Ont ...	Nov. 22, '38	April 14, '72	O.L.S.
Segré, Beresford Henry......	Davidson, Sask	Feb. 19, '86	May 8, '12	
Seibert, Frederick V	Edmonton Alta	Nov. 5, '85	Mar. 11, '11	O.L.S. S.L.S.
Sewell, Henry DeQuincy.......	Toronto, Ont.	April 18, '48	May 16, '85	O.L.S.
Seymour, Horace Llewellyn. ...	Red Deer, Alta.....	June 11 '82	Feb. 22, '06	O.L.S. A.L.S. S.L.S

SESSIONAL PAPER No. 25b

APPENDIX No. 10—*Concluded.*

LIST of Dominion Land Surveyors who are in possession of Standard Measures.—
Concluded.

Name.	Address.	Date of Birth.	Date of Appointment or of Commission.	Remarks.
Shaw, Charles Æneas... ...	Greenwood, B.C.. . .	Nov. 16, '53	May 10, '80	O.L.S., B.C.L.S.
Shepley, Joseph Drummond..	N. Battleford, Sask...	Sept. 13, '79	Mar. 12, '06	S.L.S.
Smith, Charles Campbell.....	Vancouver, B.C.....	Jan. 1, '73	Feb. 22, '06	O.L.S.
Smith Donald Alpine.........	Regina, Sask	Sept. 22, '80	April 21, '10	S.L.S.
Smith, James Herbert... ...	Edmonton, Alta.	Nov. 9, '76	Feb. 23, '05	A.L.S., O.L.S.
Soars, Henry Martin Robinson	Edmonton, Alta.....	April 22, '77	Nov. 2, '08	A.L.S.
Speight, Thomas Bailey......	Toronto, Ont.......	Feb. 8, '59	Nov. 16, '82	O.L.S.
Starkey. Samuel M..........	Codys, N.B....	Sept. 4, '37	April 14, '72	P.L.S. for N.B.
Steele, Ira John.	Ottawa, Ont.	April 6, '81	April 16, '08	O.L.S. S.L S.
Stewart, Elihu..	Collingwood, Ont.....	Nov. 17, '44	April 14, '72	O.L.S.
Stewart, Lionel Douglas N ..	Fort Frances, Ont....	Sept. 15, '83	Jan. 27, '10	O.L.S.
Stewart, Will Malcolm......	Saskatoon, Sask....	Nov. 26, '84	June 6, '07	S.L.S.
Stewart, Louis Beaufort......	Toronto, Ont..........	Jan. 27, '61	Nov. 22, '82	O.L.S., D.T.S. Professor of Surveying and Geodesy, University of Toronto.
Stewart, Alexander George...	Edmonton, Alta..	Aug. 16, '87	Mar. 14, '10	A.L.S.
Stewart, George Alexander...	....		April 14. '72	O.L.S.
Stewart, Norman C........	Vancouver, B. C.....	Jan. 9, '85	March 7, '12	B.C.L.S.
Stock, James Joseph........	Ottawa, Ont........	Aug. 16, '87	March 2, '10	
Street, Paul Bishop.........	Toronto, Ont........	Dec. 3, '81	Mar. 29, '10	
Stuart, Alexander Graham...	Buckingham, P.Q ...	July 16, '88	May 9, '11	
Summers, Gordon Foster.....	Haileybury, Ont. ...	....	Oct. 20, '10	O.L.S.
Swannell, Frank Cyril......	Victoria, B.C........		May 10, '04	B.C.L.S.
Taggart, Charles Henry	Kamloops, B.C.....	.... .'83	May 9, '11	
Talbot, Albert Charles. ...	Calgary, Alta.........	April 5, '56	May 13, '80	A.L.S.
Taylor, Alexander......., .	Portage la Prairie, Man	Aug. 6, '75	June 9, '04	M.L.S., S.L.S.
Taylor, William Emerson....	Toronto, Ont	Aug. 3, '81	Dec. 16, '10	O.L.S.
Teasdale, Charles Montgomery	Moosejaw, Sask.....	Oct. 18, '79	March 9, '06	S.L.S.
Thompson, William Thomas..	Grenfell, Sask........	Nov. 1, '53	Nov. 19, '77	D.T.S., S.L.S.
Tipper George Adrian........	Brantford. Ont.......	July 25, '86	May 18, '11	A.L.S.
Tracy, Thomas Henry.......	Vancouver, B.C. ...	June 25, '48	April 14, '72	O.L.S., B.C.L.S.
Tremblay, Alfred Joseph.....	Montmagny, P.Q.....	....	Feb. 18, '90	
Tremblay, Albert Jacques....	Edmonton, Alta.....	July 25, '87	March 1, '12	A.L.S.
Turnbull, Thomas......	Winnipeg, Man......	May 26, '57	Mar. 29, '82	O L.S.
Tyrrell, James William....	Hamilton, Ont.......	May 10, '63	Feb. 16, '87	O.L.S.
Underwood, Joseph Edwin...	Saskatoon, Sask.....	Nov. 3, '82	May 18, '11	S.L.S.
Van Skiver, Leighton A.....	Fish Lake, Ont.......	.......'74	May 13, '13	
Vaughan, Josephus Wyatt...	Vancouver, B.C.....	Oct. 17, '45	June 11, '78	B.C.L.S.
Vicars, John Richard Odlum.	Kamloops, B.C......	April 16, '58	May 17, '86	O.L.S., B.C.L.S.
Vickers, Thomas Newell......	N. Battleford, Sask...	April 19, '90	May 17, '12	S.L.S.
Von Edeskuty, Joseph Otto..	Vancouver, B.C.	Oct. 27, '84	March 3, '13	
Waddell, William Henry.....	Edmonton, Alta.....	March 23, '83	Mar. 25, '07	O.L.S., A.L.S.
Waldron, John	Moosejaw, Sask......	Aug. 1, '72	April 2, '07	S.L.S.
Walker, Claude Melville.....	Guelph, Ont.........	Oct. 16, '84	Mar. 11, '11	
Wallace, James Nevin.......	Calgary, Alta.	Aug. 21, '70	Feb. 20, '00	O.L.S., A.L.S.
Warren, James.............	Walkerton, Ont.	Nov. 7, '37	April 14, '72	O.L.S.
Warrington, George Albert...	Winnipeg, Man..	.......'83	Mar. 15, '13	M.L S.
Watt, George Herbert.... ...	Ottawa, Ont	Feb. 5, '76	Feb. 24, '02	
Waugh, Bruce Wallace	Ottawa, Ont........	March 24, '88	May 28, '12	
Weekes, Abel Seneca.......	Edmonton, Alta.....	Feb. 17, '66	Feb. 11, '92	A.L.S., S.L.S., O.L.S.
Weekes, Melville Bell	Regina, Sask.........	Nov. 28, '74	F-b. 18, '03	O.L.S., S.L.S.
Wheeler, Arthur Oliver......	Sidney, B.C..........	May 1, '60	Nov. 21, '82	O.L.S., B.C.L.S., M.L.S., A.L.S.
White-Fraser, George W. R.M.	Victoria, B.C........	.......'61	Feb. 21, '88	D.T.S., B.C.L.S.
Wiggins. Thomas Henry.....	Saskatoon, Sask....	Aug. 24, '63	Feb. 18, '96	O.L.S., S.L.S.
Wilkins, Frederick, W. B....	Norwood, Ont.......	June 27, '54	May 18, '81	O.L.S., D.T.S.
Wilkinson, William Downing	Hamilton, Bermuda...	Mar. 22, '64	Feb. 22, '93	
Williams, Guy Lorne	Enderby, B.C........	March 3, '79	June 24, '08	B.C.L.S.
Wilson, Reginald Palliser....	Winnipeg, Man......	July 9, '72	Jan. 26, '11	M.L.S.
Woods, Joseph Edward	Pincher Creek, Alta...	Oct. 13, '61	Nov. 14, '85	A.L.S.
Wrong, Frederick Hay......	Windsor, Ont.......	Aug. 22, '86	May 18, '11	
Young, Stewart	Regina, Sask.........	Sept. 2, '84	May 17, '13	S.L.S.
Young Walter Beatty..	Winnipeg, Man.......	July 6, '80	Mar. 25, '05	M.L.S.
Young William Howard......	Calgary, Alta.........	June 8, '78	May 17, '07	A.L.S. District Engineer

REPORTS OF SURVEYORS.

GENERAL REPORTS OF SURVEYORS

1913-1914

APPENDIX No. 11.

REPORT OF J. R. AKINS, D.L.S.

BASE LINE SURVEYS IN THE VALLEY OF PEACE RIVER.

OTTAWA, March 2, 1914.

E. DEVILLE, Esq., LL.D.,
  Surveyor General,
    Ottawa, Canada.

SIR,—I have the honour to submit the following report on the survey of the meridian outline between ranges 21 and 22, from the 23rd to the 24th bases and parts of the 24th, 25th, 26th, and 27th bases, all west of the fifth meridian.

I left Edmonton with my party on February 28, 1913, and reached Peace River Crossing on March 13. The route followed was by the Canadian Northern railway to Athabaska, up Athabaska river to Mirror landing, up Little Slave river and over the portage to Lesser Slave lake, across the lake to Grouard, and from there to Peace River Crossing by trail.

Hay was known to be very scarce along Peace river on account of the dry weather and fires during the previous season. It was therefore decided to haul the hay from Grouard, a distance of eighty-five miles. Most of the packhorses would work in harness, so when we were at Grouard, extra sleighs were purchased and used for freighting, each team hauling about a ton.

At Peace River Crossing arrangements were made with the Peace River Trading and Land company to have a scow ready to take supplies down stream to the work as soon as navigation should open. This scow was later used for moving the party and supplies between bases. In the fall it was brought up to the Crossing, loaded with supplies, horses, sleighs and oats and sent down to Vermilion. This scow was built very strongly with a flat bottom and square ends and carried about twelve tons.

In the meantime as the starting point of the work was about thirty-five miles down stream from Peace River Crossing, the outfit was hauled down the river and afterwards the teams were used hauling freight from the Crossing while the main party commenced work on the meridian outline which ran nearly parallel to the river and about five miles west of it. As the snow was still deep in the woods the cache was left on the river, and was moved down as the work proceeded.

As the line advanced trails were cut from the river to intersect it, and on these trails supplies were brought from the river to the camp. When the ice began to melt the cache was moved down to where the 24th base was expected to cross the river and placed on the east side of the river. All but ten of the horses were also put on the east side. This necessitated making two trips each day camp was moved while working west of the river, but it eliminated the risk of transportation being stopped by running ice when the survey of the 24th base line should reach the river. This proved to have been a wise precaution, for when the river was reached on April 19 the ice, although strong enough in the morning to chain over, broke up in the afternoon. The river was open along the west shore, and as the horses could not cross, a canoe was used to get the camp from the shore to the ice. Several men were engaged in getting it across when the ice began to move. They had considerable difficulty in getting the outfit off the moving ice, but nothing was lost. It is a fine sight to see the ice on those northern rivers go out. It is of great thickness and when a jam occurs great blocks roll up on the shore.

The northeast corner of township 92, range 18, was reached on May 5 with forty-nine miles of line run. Here we met Mr. J. A. Fletcher, D.L.S., with his party, and the two parties working together produced the meridian outline to the 25th base, where the parties separated. After twelve miles of this base had been run Peace river was reached again. The water was now very high and driftwood was running so thick that the Hudson's Bay company would not take the horses across in their boats. As the horses could not swim, the twelve miles on the west side of the river was done by man packing, after which the party was moved to the 26th base. When eighteen miles of this was run the outfit was again moved north and work commenced on the 27th base. I was instructed to run this line far enough west to establish a township corner on the west side of the river. One range was found sufficient for this, after which the line was produced eastward.

On receiving your telegram of August 6, stating that some of the horses should be wintered at Fort Vermilion, I endeavoured to get one of the settlers to take charge of them for the winter, but they claimed that it was too late in the season to get sufficient hay cured. I therefore hired a wagon, mowing machine and rake, and left a small party at Buffalo Head prairie to put up hay while the remainder continued on the line. On account of the wet fall weather and the short days considerable difficulty was found in curing the hay, but in about a month one hundred and thirty loads were gathered. The horses are wintering there, two men being in charge. They have built stables and a shack and by their latest reports the horses are doing well.

On September 26 we reached Wabïskaw river. Up to that time we had independently completed 147 miles of line. On the following day the party started for Fort Vermilion. Previous arrangements had been made with the Hudson's Bay company by which they promised to have their last boat leave Vermilion on October 1, that being the latest date on which they said they would risk starting up stream as they were afraid of meeting running ice. When the arrangement was made much stress was laid on the fact that they were not to keep us waiting. The later the appointed time of starting the better, if they were sure to start on the day appointed. I offered to contract with them that I would pay any expense which they would incur if I kept them waiting providing they would pay ours if we had to wait on them. They would not make this contract but assured us that they would leave at the time appointed. This trip was arranged especially for the surveyors in the country, we having guaranteed to give them a certain number of passengers and freight. But when we got to the Fort no boat had yet arrived. We waited four days and then decided that we would wait no longer, as an accident might have happened to the boat, and if we stayed longer we might be unable to get out, which would place us in a serious position as there was only a limited amount of supplies.

A scow was fitted up, and on October 3 we started tracking up the Peace. On the 6th we met the boat coming down. Six days later it picked us up and we arrived at the Crossing on the 16th.

Owing to the wet season the trail to Grouard was in a very bad condition. As high as seven cents per pound was being paid to get freight across, and it was difficult to get freighters to make the trip. We were therefore fortunate in getting two teams to go the day after we arrived. The progress was very slow because of the mud and water. On the 21st information was received that the lake boat had just come to Grouard and would leave the following morning. If this boat was missed it would be about a week before another would leave, and if the weather turned cold we might not get one at all. It was therefore decided to travel at night and Grouard was reached

SESSIONAL PAPER No. 25b

.at three o'clock in the morning. The boat transported the party to Soto landing. From there the party walked to Mirror landing, while the baggage was brought over in wagons. From Mirror landing to Athabaska the transportation was by scow. Edmonton was reached on October 28.

Route.

Settlers can get to Peace river any time of the year, but the month of March is the best. At that time of the year the trail is generally good and the weather not very cold. There are stopping-places all along the way which have bunk-houses for the travellers and stables and feed for the horses, but each person must carry his own blankets. At other times of the year the trails are often in a very bad condition, but it will only be a couple of years before the railroad will have reached Peace river.

In summer it is easy to get from Peace River Crossing to Fort Vermilion. A settler can build a raft, pile on his effects and quietly float for a distance of 330 miles, at a rate of from two and a half to four miles an hour. There are three ways of getting out from Fort Vermilion: (1) by boat, (2) by tracking up the river when the water is low, (3) by a pack trail which connects Fort Vermilion with the Crossing. This trail is on the northwest side of the river and is in places about forty miles from it.

There are two boats on the river: one owned by the Hudson's Bay company and one by the Peace River Trading and Land company. The latter company's boat was compelled to tie up the greater part of last summer on account of the boiler bursting. These boats run a freight and passenger service from Vermilion chutes to Hudson Hope. The following is the tariff :—

Distance in Miles.	From Vermilion chutes to	Freight Tariff per 100 lbs.		Passenger Tariff each person.	
		Up.	Down.	Up.	Down.
		$ cts.	$ cts.	$ cts.	$ cts.
50	Fort Vermilion	1 00	0 75	5 00	2 00
330	Peace River Crossing.	4 00	1 75	30 00	17 00
400	Dunvegan............................	5 00	2 50	40 00	22 00
530	Fort St. John.	7 00	4 00	55 00	32 00
570	Hudson Hope..............	9 00	6 00	65 00	37 00
240	Chipewyan..	3 00	1 50	30 00	20 00

A good road would greatly assist in settling the country. A road from Athabaska via Wabiskaw to Fort Vermilion is now under consideration by the Provincial Government. If a road were built on the northwest side of the river from Peace River Crossing to Fort Vermilion it would make most of the good country accessible.

Description of Country.

Almost the entire valley of Peace river, consisting of a strip from thirty to sixty miles wide, is suitable for settlement. The west side of the river has the larger proportion of good soil. The land could be easily cleared as it is generally lightly wooded with spruce, poplar and scrub, and there are also many open patches which grow fine hay.

The 27th base enters a prairie in range 15. This prairie is not large but it grows an abundance of peavine and blue-joint which makes the best of horse feed, and there is no difficulty in cutting it with a machine. About one and a half miles south of the

5 GEORGE V., A. 1915

base in range 10, there is a much larger prairie, about four miles wide and twenty long. Between these two prairies the line passes through a peculiar country. When heavy rains fall much of it becomes flooded and large streams which have their source in the Buffalo Head hills suddenly spread all over the country. In the first part of their course they have well-marked channels but when they spread out there is no channel whatever. It was very disagreable work running this part of the line as there had been heavy rains on the Buffalo Head hills and we had to work knee-deep in the cold water for several miles. A few miles north of the base line this water is all collected by Bear river. On the east side of Loon river there is little feed, the country being mostly covered with moss. A full description of the different parts of the country is shown on the sketch map which accompanies this report.

Resources.

Agriculture will probably be the chief industry of the country. Farming has been tried many places around Fort Vermilion with considerable success. Mr. S. Lawrence, who has been in the country for many years, finds farming a paying proposition. He has three hundred head of cattle, seventy-five horses and one hundred pigs. Last year he raised over three thousand bushels of wheat, besides oats and barley. He sells the wheat at one dollar and a half a bushel, and it is ground at the Fort. The Hudson's Bay company have a modern electrically lighted flour mill; the flour is either used in the vicinity or shipped to the northern ports.

The experimental farm in charge of Mr. Jones suggests wonderful possibilities for the country, and leads to the conclusion that it will be only a short time before the whole valley will be settled with prosperous farmers.

There were no minerals seen during the season except traces of gypsum.

There will be enough timber to supply the needs of the settlers but not enough to be of any commercial value.

Game.

Game is quite plentiful, moose abounding in the vicinity of the Buffalo Head hills. Bears are also plentiful, and in the fall many were seen along Peace river, where they come to look for berries. Prairie-chickens and several species of grouse were noticed, but they were not very plentiful.

Fur.

There are many fur-bearing anmials in the country, consisting of foxes (black, silver, cross and red), mink, marten, weasels and some beavers. The last mentioned are not very numerous at present, but the work which they have left shows that they have been very plentiful in the past. On the Buffalo Head hills there are quite a few timber wolves, and in very severe winters these come down to the plains to look for food.

Photo by J. A. Fletcher, D.L.S.

Twenty-seventh Base Line in Range 22, West of Sixth Meridian.

Photo by J. A. Fletcher, D.L.S.

Survey Cache on Peace River in Township 105.

These caches are built at convenient points, as near as possible to the place where the

SESSIONAL PAPER No. 25b

The following is a record, obtained from the Hudson's Bay company at Fort Vermilion, of the conditions of the river at that place for the last twenty-four years:—

Year.	Ice starts moving.	First crossing in open water.	Ice starts drifting.	First crossing.	Year.
1890	May 4	May 8	Nov. 16	Nov. 30	1890
1891	Apr. 23	" 1	Oct. 29	" 12	1891
1892	May 11	" 15	Nov. 4	" 8	1892
1893	" 3	" 10	Oct. 31	" 4	1893
1894	Apr. 29	" 6	Nov. 1	" 10	1894
1895	" 25	Apr. 29	" 7	" 15	1895
1896	May 2	May 5	" 7	" 10	1896
1897	Apr. 20	Apr. 26	Oct. 10	" 1	1897
1898	" 23	" 27	" 27	" 1	1898
1899	May 5	May 10	" 20	" 12	1899
1900	Apr. 14	Apr. 20	Nov. 4	" 15	1900
1901	" 26	May 3	" 2	" 6	1901
1902	May 1	" 6	" 4	" 8	1902
1903	" 3	" 13	" 11	" 19	1903
1904	Apr. 17	Apr. 24	" 16	" 30	1904
1905	" 27	" 30	Oct. 23	" 1	1905
1906	" 20	" 22	Nov. 10	" 16	1906
1907	May 6	May 13	" 8	" 13	1907
1908	Apr. 30	" 6	Oct. 28	" 2	1908
1909	" 20	Apr. 22	Nov. 5	" 13	1909
1910	" 25	" 28	" 1	" 9	1910
1911	" 29	May 3	Oct. 31	" 9	1911
1912	" 29	" 1	Nov. 1	" 9	1912
1913	" 25	" 2			1913

I have the honour to be, sir,

Your obedient servant,

J. R. AKINS, D.L.S.

5 GEORGE V., A. 1915.

APPENDIX No. 12.

ABSTRACT OF THE REPORT OF C. F. AYLSWORTH, D.L.S.

RESURVEYS IN MANITOBA.

I organized my party and procured my outfit at Winnipeg, and on May 5 I left by the Canadian Northern railway for Eriksdale. My first work in this district was to determine the necessity for a resurvey of township 21, range 3, west of the principal meridian.

I next began the resurvey of township 22, range 4. This township is rather stony, but wood for fuel and building material is plentiful. When the stones are removed the soil will be excellent for any desired purpose. There are a number of settlers in the township but as yet the majority of them have not made much progress toward the cultivation of their land. We completed this resurvey on August 1. We then began the resurvey of township 23, range 5.

We experienced some difficulty in this survey owing to the many large and small floating muskegs in this township. The high land is rather stony, but there is an abundance of fuel and building material to be had. The hay in the numerous sloughs is of a poor quality and affords a barely sufficient supply for the present requirements. There are a number of new settlers of a good class, but they have not made much progress yet. When the stones are removed the soil will be good for mixed farming. A number of people were looking for homesteads in this township while we were there.

The northeast quarter of this township abounds with game such as moose, deer and elk, but it is doubtful if many of them will remain there after this winter's hunting.

The past season was dry, and as there are not many wells in the district it was difficult to obtain water for domestic purposes, but this disadvantage can be remedied as the water to be obtained from this soil is excellent.

On September 20 we proceeded to township 16, range 6, east of the principal meridian, to complete the resurvey of the township. We then returned to township 21, range 3, west of the principal meridian, and proceeded with the resurvey of this township.

The progress of our work was expedited by the early freeze-up, and we were able to travel on the ice as early as October 20.

The land in this township is stony, and I would estimate that about 50 per cent of it is muskeg and water. There is some good land in the northeast quarter of the township. An abundance of wood for fuel and building purposes and considerable first-class hay is to be found. The township lies about midway between the Oak Point and the Grosse Isle branches of the Canadian Northern railway, and the locomotive whistle from each branch can be heard in this township.

Old timers inform me that much of the comparatively high land is liable to be flooded by excessive rains, and that years ago a number of settlers who lived there were compelled to leave and abandon their homes. The many abandoned shacks and clearings we saw bear mute testimony to the correctness of this information. There are, however, many desirable homesteads in the northwest quarter of this township.

We completed our work in this township on December 2, after which I disbanded the party, made the necessary arrangements for wintering the outfit, and left for home, where I arrived on December 10.

SESSIONAL PAPER No. 25b

APPENDIX No. 13.

ABSTRACT OF THE REPORT OF P. R. A. BELANGER, D.L.S.

INSPECTION OF SURVEY CONTRACTS IN SASKATCHEWAN.

I began the organization of my party at Prince Albert on Monday, May 12, 1913, and after spending a week in hiring men, buying supplies and securing my transport outfit from Henribourg, I shipped the whole outfit by rail to Dumble, a siding on the Big River branch of the Canadian Northern railway.

From Dumble we drove easterly for nearly three days over a trapper's road, meandering around numerous lakes and sloughs before we reached township 55, range 5, west of the third meridian, where we pitched camp on the north bank of Sturgeon river.

Our work there consisted of the inspection of contract No. 19 of 1912. This contract comprises township 54, range 5, and townships 55 and 56, ranges 4 and 5, and covers a hilly country which is situated at the height of land between watercourses running southerly to the Saskatchewan and northerly to Montreal lake.

The land is still generally heavily timbered, but small openings are found along Lofthouse creek in township 55, range 5, while larger ones are found in township 54 of the same range along Sturgeon river, where good homesteads can be located. Scattered mixed farms could be established at intervals along the streams above mentioned or in the vicinity of a few lakes where hay is found in fairly large quantities. This country can be reached from the west by the road we followed, or from the east by the surveyors' road, branching in township 56, range 1, from the Prince Albert-Montreal lake trail.

From this contract I proceeded on June 10 westerly to contracts Nos. 31 and 32 of 1912. I followed the Green lake trail to Witchekan lake and from there to Edam, a small town on the Canadian Northern railway northwest of Battleford, where I secured supplies before continuing my journey northerly via Brightsand and Makwa lakes.

The road which I followed from Witchekan lake to Brightsand lake passes through thriving settlements where farmers were busy breaking land or seeding; but from Brightsand lake northwesterly the road enters a bush country which extends to Makwa lake and which is unoccupied, except in the northern part of township 57 and the southern part of township 58, range 21. There a few settlers are found and a few more could settle to advantage. This applies also to the lands at Makwa lake, where good mixed farming could be carried on. Hay grows in large quantities and the land is of first quality.

From Makwa lake I followed a surveyor's trail northerly to the south bank of Beaver river, and by cutting a small piece of road down the bank I reached the river flat and crossed the river in section 6 of township 61, range 22, on a strong raft which I built for that purpose. From that crossing, by cutting about three miles of road northerly I found the surveyor's road which leads through both contracts.

The inspection of these two contracts kept the party busy from July 1 to the 30th, both days inclusive. The country covered by these contracts comprises townships 62 and 63, range 21, townships 61, 62 and 63, ranges 22 and 23, and townships 63 and 64, range 24, west of the third meridian. · With the exception of a practically clear opening extending east and west in the centre of township 62, range 22, where a small colony of settlers could locate at once to advantage, the townships inspected are more or less timbered and need clearing.

5 GEORGE V., A. 1915

This part of the country can be reached by the road which I followed but better roads are found running due north from Fort Pitt. Upon one of these a ferry was established last summer, crossing Beaver river. It is also easily reached from Cold lake by an Indian trail running easterly to Lac des Isles and Waterhen lake. Good milling spruce is found along the road in township 62, range 23, near Lac des Isles. This lake abounds with fish.

On July 31, not knowing of any short road which would take us directly to our next work, the inspection of contract No. 28 of 1912, in townships 63 and 64, range 16, and townships 62, 63 and 64, range 17, west of the third meridian, we returned to Makwa lake, whence we followed an Indian trail branching easterly to Meadow lake. Before reaching the latter place we passed through a belt of exceedingly rich land which is occupied by only a few ranchers.

From Meadow lake we followed the Green lake trail northerly and northeasterly for about twelve miles and thence branched off to Morin's ranch in the valley of Beaver river where we crossed the river in a row-boat, and entered contract No. 28.

The country we passed over in this contract may be described as heavily timbered and unfit for immediate settlement, though the land is fair; but at "the narrows," on the north shore of Waterhen lake, as well as along Waterhen river near where it empties into the lake, are found stretches of meadow land where large quantities of hay can be obtained. A few families of Indians were the only inhabitants we met in this country; they live on game and fish which is abundant in the vicinity. They are great believers in offering guns, rifles and material of all kinds to the great Manito for the success of their hunting excursions. They appeared very anxious to know whether they would be disturbed in their wilderness by settlers who might take their land. This district is reached by the road we followed or by an Indian trail from Cold lake to the west side of Waterhen lake.

On August 19, having completed the inspection of contract No. 28 I proceeded to my next work, the inspection of contract No. 23 of 1912, comprising townships 53 to 56, range 13, and township 56, range 12, west of the third meridian. This country was reached by following a long circuitous route via the Battleford-Green lake trail from Meadow lake to Birch lake, and thence by the Chitek lake trail to township 53, range 13, where we commenced work.

Fifteen days were occupied in the full inspection of four townships out of the six comprised in this contract. The Battleford-Chitek lake trail runs across a large meadow in townships 53 and 54, range 13, where thousands of tons of first class hay can be cut, principally near the southern end of Chitek lake where a large dairy industry could be established with great advantage. This place is used by a rancher from Rabbit lake, as winter quarters for his cattle. The eastern half of township 53, as seen along the road, is very suitable for mixed farming though in need of clearing. Good soft water is found in creeks and in Chitek lake which is full of whitefish, jackfish and pickerel.

Having completed the inspection of contract No. 23 we entered contract No. 22 in range 12, on September 15, to make the inspection of the part of the contract surveyed. In passing Boutin post office, however, I received instructions to limit my operations in this contract to the inspection of the monuments marking corners in townships 55 and 56, range 11. I therefore temporarily abandoned this inspection, and proceeded to contract No. 20 of 1913, comprising townships 57 to 60 inclusive, range 15, and two-thirds of township 60, range 14.

To reach this work we followed an old branch of the Battleford-Green lake trail along the east shore of Chitek lake as far north as the north end of the lake where we branched off westerly by cutting a road which took us to section 4 of township 57, range 15, where we set up camp on the north bank of Alcott creek. This new road crosses several creeks along which are found good hay meadows which would warrant

SESSIONAL PAPER No. 25b

the establishment of a few mixed farms. The remainder of the country along this road, as well as in contract No. 20 is, with the exception of a few small openings in the valley of Alcott creek, more or less heavily timbered and broken by extensive muskegs, and consequently not fit for immediate settlement.

The only way to enter this part of the country with wagons at present is by following the road which we used, but it could also be reached from Meadow lake by an Indian pack trail along which a wagon road could easily be cut.

On October 8, having completed the inspection of contract No. 20, we returned from range 15 to range 12 to complete the subdivision of townships 54 and 55, range 12, and also to continue the inspection of contract No 22, in townships 55 and 56, range 11. This inspection and the subdivision work in the two townships above referred to kept the party busy until November 29. The whole of township 55 was completely subdivided, while in township 54 our work was limited to the survey of the north boundary of the township, together with the tier of sections adjoining it on the south side. This fractional part of township 54 as well as the two southern tiers of sections in township 55, is all rolling country, timbered with a second growth of poplar, birch and willow, partly dry and easy to clear for immediate settlement. The land is fair and well watered by marshes and several lakes, the largest being Chitek lake which encroaches on sections 5, 6, 7, 8, 17, 18 and 19 of township 55, and section 31 of township 54; this lake abounds with fish of all kinds.

The remainder of township 55, range 12, is more or less heavily timbered. The soil is light and generally unfit for immediate settlement, but the timber can be used for building purposes, railway ties, and cordwood.

With the exception of the northern tier of sections, township 54 forms part of contract No. 22 which I inspected, and may be described as open and generally suited for farming purposes in the eastern half, but the western half is more timbered and broken by muskegs, which render it unsuitable for immediate settlement. The south-east quarter of this township, as well as the northeast quarter of township 53, is occupied in summer by a rancher of the south settlements, who brings his cattle in to fatten them for the market.

On November 10, owing to the serious illness of my wife, it became necessary for me to return home. My party was left in charge of Mr. E. W. Hubbell, D.L.S., for the remainder of the season.

Before closing my report I would like to make special mention of the valley of Beaver river, which has in the past been the breeding home of the industrious animals from which it derives its name, and which by their yearly damming of the river have converted its valley into immense hay meadows where dairy farmers and ranchers can secure thousands of tons of the very best hay, principally on the west side of the mouth of Meadow creek, where a few small ranchers are already located. I cannot emphasize too strongly the great advantage offered in this river valley to settlers who do not care for grain cultivation. For those in search of mixed farming land, I would recommend the country in the vicinity of Meadow lake.

No minerals of any kind were found during the survey, but large game, such as moose and deer, is still plentiful, and partridges, ducks and rabbits are abundant. Good water is also found everywhere.

APPENDIX No. 14.

REPORT OF G. A. BENNETT, D.L.S.

MISCELLANEOUS SURVEYS IN MANITOBA, SASKATCHEWAN, AND ALBERTA.

TILLSONBURG, ONT., January 14, 1914.

E. DEVILLE, Esq., LL.D.,
> Surveyor General,
>> Ottawa, Canada.

SIR,—I have the honour to submit the following report upon the miscellaneous surveys performed by me in the provinces of Manitoba, Saskatchewan, and Alberta, during the past season.

These surveys were very varied in character. They consisted in restoring and re-establishing obliterated and lost monuments, traversing lakes and rivers whose beds and channels have considerably altered since the original survey, surveying the beds of lakes which have dried up and yielded many acres of valuable hay and farm land, making original surveys of coal-mining leases and park boundaries, destroying duplicate and river-lot monuments, investigating various matters in connection with the survey of Dominion lands and locating and correcting where possible, errors in original surveys, under the provisions of section 57 of the Dominion Lands Surveys Act. When it was found impossible to alter the original surveys, retracement surveys were made to obtain a true record of the metes and bounds of the lands as defined by the misplaced monuments of the original survey, so that the areas could be shown correctly upon the official plans.

The field operations were begun by a resurvey of part of township 18, range 18, west of the third meridian, to correct a small error in the original survey. Township 15, range 2, west of the third meridian, was next visited to investigate reported errors in the original survey. Large errors were found affecting much of the township, so upon petition of the settlers and with the consent of all the owners affected, a correction survey was made. Valuable improvements were thereby affected, as the boundaries of several improved quarter sections were moved over forty rods. To make a peaceful adjustment of the various claims, the settlers held a meeting one evening and upon their request, I attended. There I explained the provisions of the law, as contained in the Dominion Lands Surveys Act, and gave authoritative statements of the various improvements changing ownership from the correction of the survey, thus preventing exorbitant demands. After considerable discussion, a friendly settlement of their claims was effected. Agreements, in writing, were then drawn up stating definitely the payment to be made in each case, and these were signed by the parties interested.

Small retracement surveys were next made, in township 19 A, range 1, west of the second meridian, to destroy a false duplicate monument; in township 18, range 20, west of the principal meridian, to investigate the position of a section corner as defined by a witness monument of a recent survey, and to correct the error found; and in township 20, range 22, west of the principal meridian, to investigate and verify the position of a section corner as defined by a witness monument of a recent survey. These townships are wooded and are settled by Ruthenians and Galicians. Rapid progress has been made by these industrious settlers in clearing their farms and to-day they are building modern dwelling houses with large barns, and they possess fine horses and many cattle.

On June 25, a resurvey was begun in township 16, range 2, west of the third meridian, upon a petition of the settlers there. A complete correction of the known errors in the survey of this township was made, and payment for transferred improvements was agreed upon by the owners interested.

An investigation of reported errors in township 7, range 10, west of the second meridian was then made. In this township very large discrepancies were found in the original survey. Most of the township was retraced and the largest errors corrected, consequently some improvements of small value changed ownership. The original survey was so erroneous (some of the monuments being one-quarter of a mile from where they should have been) that the settlers had disregarded the old survey monuments and divided the land as equally as they could among themselves.

As much of the land in this township is held by absentee speculators, the settlers are few and scattered. Little progress has been made in road building or the drainage of numerous sloughs, so that it was difficult to drive across the township last year after the June rains. The municipal authorities informed me that they had hesitated to build roads on account of the crookedness of the section lines arising from errors in the original survey, but that the accumulated appropriations for this work would be spent immediately upon the resurveyed road allowances. This district is noted for its rich clay loam soil, and the fact that fine crops have been obtained over a term of years is attested to by the fine buildings and stock of the prosperous farmers.

According to the Dominion Lands Surveys Act the consent of all owners of lands affected must be obtained before a resurvey may be made to correct the original survey. Generally all resident owners are anxious to have an erroneous survey corrected, but the indifference and suspicion of absentee owners render it difficult to carry out the wishes of the settlers. When the errors in the survey are discovered before improvements have been made or lands patented, the corrections are usually readily accomplished.

On July 23, I retraced the north boundary of Katepwe park in township 20, range 12, west of the second meridian and restored the boundary monuments. Mr. Norman Ross, chief of the Tree Planting Division, Indian Head, who has charge of the park, requested me to also survey the east boundary. However, as this necessitated the measurement of several lines across Katepwe lake, which was impracticable at this season, the survey was not completed until December, when the lake had frozen. On the surveyed boundaries of the park, fences have now been erected to preserve to the people of eastern Saskatchewan, the beautiful shady groves along the lake, which render this place so attractive. Several hundred people were enjoing themselves there during July and the park is certain to become more popular when people learn of its existence.

I proceeded to Alberta on July 29 and began the retracement of both sides of the fifth correction line through ranges 9, 10 and part of 11, west of the fourth meridian, to ascertain the extent of the errors in the outline surveys. This district has been recently homesteaded and the dry weather in June rendered the settlers' crops on new breaking poor. However, the farmers, who had started into mixed farming were not complaining and their stock looked well.

The survey of the boundary of the Rocky Mountain Forest reserve through townships 1, ranges 28 and 29, west of the fourth meridian, was next completed. It appears that most of this rough country had once been covered with forest, but bush fires have denuded many of the mountain slopes. Much fine grazing land has resulted and cattle by the hundred and sheep by the thousand were noticed feeding upon the rich pasturage near and in the forest reservation. The cattle were doing little injury to the forest growth, but the sheep were destroying most of the vegetation and so largely preventing reforestation.

The traverse of the banks, by-channels and islands of Bow river through sections 13 and 14, township 24, range 1, west of the fifth meridian, was completed by

5 GEORGE V., A. 1915

September 6. The topography was found to have very materially changed during the interval of thirty years, since the original survey.

From here, I proceeded to township 1, range 12, west of the fourth meridian, and completed the retracement of part of the township. Then a survey was made of that part of township 17, range 5, omitted by the original survey. South Saskatchewan river was also traversed throughout the township and twenty-three river-lot monuments destroyed. These old river lot mounds have proved confusing to the settlers and in consequence one homesteader had built his house off his homestead.

A considerable portion of this district appears to be more adapted for ranching than grain growing. Wheat farming has not proved, as yet, very successful, but the settlers engaged in mixed farming are prosperous. Many ranchers are irrigating land to grow alfalfa. A beautiful meadow of 100 acres was noticed in township 1, range 12, on the Milk river flat, the water used being obtained by damming Red Deer creek. This small scheme has proved a success. Along the South Saskatchewan several other schemes were noticed. Here the water is obtained by pumping it from the river to the top of the river flats. Gasoline engines are used to run the pumps, and the high cost of the power so obtained renders the practical success of these schemes somewhat doubtful. However, a rancher, Mr. Lokier, showed me where gas was bubbling up through the water of the South Saskatchewan in township 17, range 4. This proved on test to be largely methane gas, therefore it is probable that the settlers may obtain natural gas here at a moderate depth and then have a cheap fuel for power. Many seams of coal were noticed in the river banks in township 17, range 5. This coal is used for fuel by the neighbouring settlers. The veins are numerous, and some lignite veins are five feet thick, but the coal of best quality occurs in veins about two feet thick. On account of the distance from railways and the lack of local demand, no commercial mining has been done.

On September 25, I began the survey of coal leases in township 19, range 4, west of the fifth meridian. An investigation into the location of some old coal claims surveyed twenty years ago showed that these claims were placed approximately one mile in error upon the map of the old survey. Because of this mistake in the former survey, these claims occupy part of the land that was supposed to be open for leasing.

The work in Alberta was completed by three more small surveys, the traverse of St. Mary river through township 2, range 25, a resurvey to correct one section line in township 2, range 19, and an investigation and necessary surveys of a dry lake shown by the original survey as Horsefly lake in township 9, range 16, all west of the fourth meridian.

On October 18, I began the investigation of Whitebear lake in townships 23, ranges 15 and 16, west of the third meridian. The lake was found to have completely dried up, and the dry bed was surveyed so that the land might be disposed of. Similar surveys were made to deal with Pelican lake, in townships 18 and 19, range 1, which has become dry. These dry lake bottoms are of little value until improved. The old beaches are very stony and the bottoms are grown up with foxtail or wild barley, which is practically useless for hay or pasture.

The following surveys completed the operations in Saskatchewan: A small resurvey upon petition to correct errors in the original survey of township 18, range 8, the survey of Swan lake and retracement of a large part of township 10, range 8, on account of large errors found in the original survey, the investigation of a reported error in the returns of the survey of townships 3 and 4, range 18, the completion of surveys in connection with Katepwe park townships, 19 and 20, range 12, and a small resurvey in township 11, range 6, all west of the second meridian; the traverse of one bank of the South Saskatchewan through townships 25, ranges 5 and 6, a restoration survey upon petition of owners of lands affected in township 25, range 5, and the retracement survey of a small portion of township 23, range 9, all west of the third meridian.

SESSIONAL PAPER No. 25b

On December 16, operations were begun in Manitoba by an investigation of the survey of township 25, range 9, west of the principal meridian. It was found that considerable worthless swamp land had not been correctly surveyed by the original survey. This district is so wet that it is very difficult to make surveys until late fall or winter. The settlers here are generally from Iceland and appear to be fairly prosperous. They cut hay around the marshes for their stock and grow but little grain. The winter fishing on lake Manitoba is another important source of income to the people of this district.

The following surveys were made to correct errors found by the inspectors in surveys recently made under contract; the resurvey of one section line in township 21, range 11, west of the principal meridian, the survey of a small lake omitted in the original survey of township 10, range 15, and the re-marking of posts and placing of mounds in townships 10, ranges 13 and 16, east of the principal meridian. Investigation showed that the posts reported wrong were correctly marked in townships 11, ranges 13 and 14.

In addition to the miscellaneous surveys, observations were taken whenever opportunity permitted, for magnetic declination, inclination and total force, these observations not materially retarding the regular work. Sixty-three observations for declination were obtained in forty-one different townships with a Bausch and Lomb trough compass attached to the standards of a Watts transit.

The observations for magnetic inclination or dip and total force were made with a Dover dip circle according to Dr. Lloyd's method. Twenty-six stations were occupied, a total of seventy-nine observations for inclination and forty-nine observations for total force being obtained.

Before and after the field operations, the correction to be applied to the readings of magnetic declination of my compass and the "A factor" of the total force readings were obtained personally at the Magnetic Observatory, Agincourt, Ont. As my assistant took many of the observations for dip and total force, he also determined the constants of the dip circle at Agincourt in order to correct for personal equation.

I have the honour to be, Sir,

Your obedient servant,

G. A. BENNETT, D.L.S.

5 GEORGE V., A. 1915

APPENDIX No. 15.

ABSTRACT OF THE REPORT OF G. H. BLANCHET, D.L.S.

SURVEY OF THE 22ND BASE LINE WEST OF THE FOURTH MERIDIAN.

The organization of the party having been completed we left Edmonton on February 12, 1913, for Prince Albert and from there we proceeded via the Canadian Nórthern railway to Big River settlement.

From Big River to Isle à la Crosse, a distance of 165 miles, the Isle à la Crosse Fish Co. have opened up a good winter trail by which fish are brought out from the northern lakes and merchandise is taken in, to be distributed in summer by water.

Beyond Isle à la Crosse there was no trail and it was reported that hay was scarce and the ice bad. The winter had been very severe in this country, the snow being over two feet deep and a cold north wind blowing almost continually. Under these conditions it was difficult to hire freighters, but finally seven teams were obtained which with my own three were able to handle the outfit. Owing to the difficulty we had breaking trail with the heavy freighting teams, I decided it would be impossible to use bob-sleighs on the line with my light horses, so I disposed of my sleighs and replaced them by flat sleighs.

On March 11, the post at Methye lake was reached and the freighters were sent back. A day was spent outfitting toboggans and pressing hay, and then we proceeded by the dog trail to our starting point at Garson lake, reaching there on the 14th. After establishing the meridian across the lake, the base line was begun on the 15th.

The height of land between the Churchill (Hudson Bay drainage) and the Athabaska occurs about the centre of range 2, being marked by extensive muskegs rather than an elevation. The region included in this watershed has little economic value, the timber being small and the land too wet for agriculture, but it is useful in conserving the water supply.

The muskeg country extends westward to Christina river which crosses the line near the centre of range 4. This river flows in a northeasterly direction, discharging about 1,500 cubic feet per second, and it is broken by many rapids from here to its juncture with Clearwater river. It drains the country lying between the height of land and the "Little Rocky mountains," its basin extending south to township 74. Its immediate valley first becomes appreciable about three miles south of the line and from there it increases rapidly to about six hundred feet in depth at its juncture with the Clearwater. Along the river flats there are some small groves of excellent spruce and upstream there are some good hay sloughs. There are also many areas of good agricultural land along this river and its tributaries.

Farther west the country rises towards the "Little Rocky mountains" from which many fairly large streams flow northeasterly into the Christina. In general the soil on the ridges is rather light, and in the valleys where not too wet it is good. Much of this district hes been fire-swept but some areas of good timber remain, notably along Grégoire river.

The "Little Rocky mountains" are roughly triangular in shape, the vertex being about nine miles north of the base line at the west side of range 8, whence lines extending southeast and southwest mark the limits of the elevated area. Proceeding southward they become broader and flatter, the south boundary being a curve with Christina river occupying the valley to the south. The northerly border of the "mountains" is marked by escarpments with rock exposures where they are cut by creek valleys. Extensive lake-like muskegs which give rise to many streams occupy most of the top of the plateau. These streams cut deep valleys through the borders of the plateau which is, consequently, very rough. The drainage is northeasterly into the Christina and thence via the Clearwater into the Athabaska, and north and northwesterly through Hangingstone and Horse rivers into the Athabaska.

Photo by G. H. Blanchet, D.L.S.

Beaver Meadow on Twenty-second Base Line West of Fourth Meridian.

These beaver meadows are formed by deposits of silt carried down by the river and stopped by the beaver dams. Extensive flats of very rich land were thus formed and, as there are no trees, the snow melts very early in spring. Horse feed can thus be obtained on these flats long before the snow disappears in the woods, where the evergreens prevent the heat of the sun from reaching the snow.

In range 10 the line left the high lands of the mountains, dropping to a country which continues almost level to the Athabaska. The drainage here is poor and, consequently, the land is principally muskeg. The only horse feed obtainable was in the beaver meadows along the small streams. The country south of the base line continues the same till the slope of the mountains is reached. Two principal branches of Horse river rise in the mountains to the south and cross the line, one in range 12 and the other in range 14, and after flowing north for a few miles they both turn easterly, flowing in parallel courses and finally uniting in range 10. From there the stream swings off to the north, emptying into the Athabaska. There is considerable good land lying along its course.

After crossing the westerly branch of Horse river the line enters what is known locally as "Twasinaw" muskeg, which is a peculiar lake-like area about ten miles across and almost surrounded by poplar and jackpine ridges. Algar lake is situated near the centre of this muskeg, and lies just south of the line. Two branches of Algar river rise here and, after crossing the line in range 15, unite about two miles north and flow in a northerly direction into the Athabaska, which at this place is about fifteen miles north of the line and flows in an easterly direction. The sleigh road from Horse river to McMurray passes through this muskeg and crossing the line at the westerly side of range 14 practically follows Horse river down to McMurray.

Athabaska river crosses the line about the centre of range 17, and is approached through an extremely wet stretch of muskeg broken by islands and ridges of jackpine. The line passes just north of "Grand" rapids and across "Little Grand" rapids which extend down stream for about two miles. These rapids form the chief obstacle to navigation on this section of the river which here, becoming wide and shallow, flows through a bed of sandstone. An island about a quarter of a mile long divides the river where the greatest fall occurs into two unequal channels. The westerly, though the wider and fairly straight, is unnavigable, being shallow and strewn with large boulders, while the east channel through which the scows are taken is narrow and crooked. "Little Grand" rapids, though rough, are not very dangerous. As far as power development is concerned the situation is somewhat similar to the Lachine rapids on the St. Lawrence and might, perhaps, be similarly treated. "Grand Rapids" settlement, situated on the east bank of the river here, was crossed by the line. The river valley is about 400 feet deep.

Westward from the river the country has been badly burnt, though some areas of timber, protected by muskeg, remain. The country bordering the river is much cut up by deep creek valleys but contains some good agricultural land.

After the abrupt rise out of the Athabaska valley the country ascends gradually to the west for about fifteen miles, and is drained by many small streams rising in the muskegs several miles back from the river. These have deep abrupt valleys where they enter the Athabaska valley, and in consequence the country bordering the river is very rough in places. There are also several fairly large rivers with more extensive drainages, the chief of which are the Loon, Three rivers and the Little Buffalo. Loon river rises about ten miles west of the Athabaska and flows northeasterly into it at the head of the Grand rapids. Most of its valley has been fire-swept but a few bodies of good timber remain. The stream is about twenty-five feet wide at its mouth. About six miles north of the line three fair-sized streams flow northeasterly into the Athabaska, all entering it near the same point. They all rise in lake-like areas of muskeg in the interior. Little Buffalo river rises in a lake of the same name in the northerly part of township 86, range 20, and flows easterly into the Athabaska near where it makes its big bend from a northerly course to an easterly one. In several places at the mouth of this river natural gas escapes through cracks in the earth in sufficient quantities to keep up a brisk flame. With the exception of the strips of dry land bordering the river and its tributary streams as far back as they hold their valleys, the country is principally muskeg.

5 GEORGE V., A. 1915

The rainfall in July was excessive and this, combined with the swampy surface, practically flooded the country, especially the hay meadows, and these conditions finally made it advisable to postpone the completion of the line till after freeze-up. The party was therefore taken out to Edmonton and discharged.

The autumn of 1913 was remarkably fine and mild. The ice on the lakes and rivers did not become safe till December, and the snow was very scanty till the end of that month. After organizing a new party I left Edmonton on December 2 and proceeded to the work by way of Athabaska and Wabiskaw, reaching the latter place on December 8. There was practically no snow there, and Wabiskaw river was reported to be open. It was therefore necessary to open up a sleigh road from the north end of Wabiskaw lake to the line, a distance of about sixty miles by the route we travelled. The line was reached on December 18 and the next day we started working on the line and bringing up the caches. During the interval while we were out, one of the caches was broken into and the contents stolen; this left us very short of supplies for a time.

The height of land between the Athabaska and Wabiskaw rivers was crossed in range 20. This is covered by an extensive tamarack muskeg which drains easterly through the Three rivers and Loon river into the Athabaska and westerly via the Wood Buffalo into Wabiskaw river. The country in the neighbourhood of the "height of land" is practically level and consequently all muskeg. Some interesting features may be observed there. The dry land, lakes and rivers, found ordinarily, are here represented, respectively, by spruce muskeg, lake-like areas of tamarack muskeg and tamarack runs. With an outlet that would give efficient drainage the country would soon rid itself of its excessive moisture, but the problem of draining an extensive level district is a difficult one. In considering the problem of reclaiming the muskegs of the north country the question of muskeg subsoils is an important one, and investigation reveals some interesting conditions. From the amount of sand forming the surface in many parts of the north and from the fact that precipitation is not ordinarily excessive one would expect natural absorption to go on to a much greater degree. This is prevented to a greater extent by an impervious stratum of clay with a thickness varying from a few inches to several feet lying on top of the sand. It is probable that the clay is of recent origin as it lies generally in the depressions, the underlying sand coming to the surface in the ridges. This sand may not have a great depth as is suggested by the fact that it sometimes is of a quicksand nature. The ice which remains most of the year under the moss in muskegs lies on top of the clay. The most important considerations in facilitating drainage are, first the removal of the surface moss to cause the ice to melt more quickly and allow freer flow, and secondly to increase absorption, if possible, by ditches cut through the impervious clay. The usual profile of the northern swamp lands is more that of a shallow plate than of a bowl such as is usually found in Northern Ontario. Wabiskaw river crosses the line in range 23. It has no immediate valley but occupies the bottom of a wide shallow valley which is about fifteen to twenty miles wide. Much of this valley is muskeg but areas of good land occur along Wood Buffalo river floing northwesterly into the Wabiskaw north of the line and Trout and Bear rivers flowing easterly, south of the line. These three rivers, which are each from a chain to a chain and a half wide, form, with the addition of the Wabiskaw lake drainage, the principal sources of the upper Wabiskaw. There are some stretches of merchantable timber along each. There is also an area in townships 82, ranges 23 and 24, known locally as "the mountain" consisting of ridges and islands on which there is a good growth of poplar and spruce and which contain considerable land of agricultural value.

There are many small rapids along the Wabiskaw but probably none producing water-powers of economic value.

The fifth meridian was reached on January 26, 1914, and on the 28th, the work of closing having been completed, the party left for Edmonton, arriving there on February 7.

APPENDIX No. 16.

REPORT OF W. J. BOULTON, D.L.S.

SUBDIVISION SURVEYS IN SOUTHERN ALBERTA.

CALGARY, ALBERTA, March 2, 1914.

E. DEVILLE, Esq., LL.D.,
    Surveyor General,
        Ottawa, Canada.

SIR,—I have the honour to submit the following report on my operations in the field during the past season.

Having completed the organization of my party I left High River, Alberta, on May 17, 1913, and two days later arrived at my first work, in township 16, range 3, west of the fifth meridian.

The work in this township lay in the westerly and southerly parts, which are mostly covered with willow brush and poplar. The township is well supplied with splendid water, being traversed in its northerly sections by Pekisko creek, a stream about fifty links in width, and by many other smaller creeks which are well distributed throughout the township.

After completing this work, I did some subdivision in townships 15, ranges 2 and 3, and township 14, range 3, in the order named. Two small lakes were traversed in township 15, range 2.

Townships 16, 15 and 14, range 3, are quite similar in their general characteristics, varying from rolling and hilly to rough and mountainous, the ravines and coulées being mostly covered with willow, poplar, jackpine and a few spruce.

From a rough estimate I should say that only twenty-five per cent of the territory included in these townships can be classified as open, but that part affords an abundance of rich grass. This feature together with the provisions made by nature for water and shelter, makes the country one that is especially adapted for the grazing industry. This industry has been taken up by a few ranchers in this vicinity, and their efforts have been very successful. The soil is generally very good, ranging from sandy to black loam, but on account of the short growing season and the ever present frosts, it is not suitable for agricultural pursuits. Plenty of fish, partridges and prairie-chickens are found in these parts. Access to these townships is rendered very easy by excellent trails leading from both High River and Nanton.

On September 4, I started south to do some subdivision work in townships 8, ranges 2, 3, 4 and 5, as I wished to finish the mountainous work before October 15, which date, generally marks the advent of the stormy season in the foot-hills of southern Alberta. In going to this work, we followed a well-beaten wagon trail practically straight south, in range 2, until we arrived in township 10, where we crossed the north fork of Oldman river, turned west for about four miles and thence south on a splendid trail to township 8, range 2, where we stopped and completed the subdivision in this township. This being done, we continued on this trail which joined the Crowsnest trail, about one and one-half miles east of Burmis, a small town on the Crowsnest division of the Canadian Pacific railway. This latter trail is macadamized right through the Crowsnest pass, and is used by automobiles.

The work in township 8, range 5, was first completed, after which that in township 8, range 4, was begun. This latter work practically followed the top of Bluff

5 GEORGE V., A. 1915

mountain, and although it was very rough, and at times very treacherous, some excellent closings were effected, having of course to resort to triangulation in many instances. Bluff mountain is practically covered with spruce varying from six inches to two feet in diameter, but on account of the precipitous nature of the country lumbering there would be quite difficult.

Having completed this work, we moved to a small abandoned village called "Lille" from which point we did the work in township 8, range 3. The main part of this work consisted in running north on the meridian, which forms the eastern boundary of sections 5, 8, 17, 20, etc. To run the actual meridian itself was impracticable. So after running one mile north I started triangulating and traversing. I succeeded in again getting back on the line about one and one-half miles south of the northeast corner of section 32 and from there I ran due north to the northeast corner of section 29, where I deviated my bearing to hit the post at the northeast corner of section 32, finally effecting a closing of two inches in departure at this point. This township is practically all limestone ridges, with deep valleys and ravines. The valleys contain burnt timber only, which is at present used for mine props. Coal mining was an important industry at one time in this township, but has of late years been abandoned.

There are many good indications of coal in townships 8, ranges 4 and 5, and many small seams were noticed, but it has all been taken up and will eventually be worked by the companies operating in these parts.

On October 25, we left Lille for township 4, range 1, west of the fifth meridian. We left the Crowsnest road at Burmis and travelled in a southeasterly direction along a splendid wagon road, to Mountain Mill, thence south to section 7, township 5, range 1. From this point several trails provide a means of access to township 4, range 1. The country through which we passed on our way is well settled and is practically all under cultivation, and judging from improvements and the general prosperous appearance of the farms, the yield is very good.

I encountered four settlers in township 4, range 1, and ascertained from them that hay is the only thing that can be grown successfully there, the short season and intense early frost preventing any extensive agricultural operations. Ranching is engaged in to a slight extent. The westerly and southerly parts are practically all limestone ridges, with intervening valleys of green and dry spruce timber, varying from four to twelve inches in diameter, while the remaining part is rolling to hilly, mostly covered with willow brush and poplar, thus rendering the grazing possibilities only fair.

After completing the subdivision in this township, which consisted of that part lying immediately outside the forest reserve, we went to township 3, range 30, west of the fourth meridian, and completed similar surveys there. The general characteristics of this township are similar to those of the one previously mentioned. Streams of considerable size, varying from thirty to forty links in width, would provide an adequate supply of water for ranching purposes. Township 3, range 30, is very well occupied by settlers, but there are practically no improvements.

Game such as partridges, prairie-chickens, bears, mountain goats, and mountain sheep is more plentiful in this district than in any other through which I passed during the season.

The work in township 3, range 30, west of the fourth meridian, having been completed, I started north again to township 10, range 3, west of the fifth meridian. This township, which is located near the "gap" in the Livingstone range of mountains, was reached by following an excellent wagon trail to Pincher creek, thence to Cowley, and from there to our destination where we arrived on November 22.

My work in this township consisted in running south from the correction line for five miles along the boundary of the Dominion Forest reserve, and connecting up the corners on the chords to the east, all of which I completed by December 1. The meridian followed a very deep valley, which was covered by spruce, jackpine, willow

SESSIONAL PAPER No. 25b

brush and poplar. There are a few settlers in this township, but they have made no noticeable advancement or improvements. It is an exceedingly rough country, and there are several good indications of steam coal in the northerly part,

Deer are quite numerous in this locality, many hunters being attracted there during the open season.

The months of October and November were very stormy, and we were frequently compelled to cease work on account of the high winds, which I understand are quite prevalent in the foot-hills at this time of year.

I next completed the survey of the boundary of the Dominion Forest reserve, in township 11, range 2, and also that part in the southwest corner of township 12, range 1.

Having completed this work, I again returned to the locality in which I had been working during the summer months and finished the survey of the boundary of the forest reserve in townships 13 and 14, range 3, after which I moved to township 14, range 2, and completed the subdivision of that township.

During the season we succeeded in running 211 miles of line, including traverse and trial lines.

On January 12, 1914, I again arrived at High River, where I stored my outfit and made suitable arrangements for the wintering of my horses. This having been done, I, with one assistant, went to Coleman, Alberta, and completed a small survey there, returning to High River on January 17.

I have the honour to be, Sir,

Your obedient servant,

W. J. BOULTON, D.L.S.

APPENDIX No. 17.

ABSTRACT OF THE REPORT OF E. P. BOWMAN, D.L.S.

STADIA SURVEYS IN WESTERN SASKATCHEWAN.

The work on which I was engaged during the season of 1913 was an examination of the lakes and other bodies of water in the district lying south of Battleford.

I arrived in Battleford on May 17, and spent several days there in organizing my party and purchasing horses, wagons and the outfit required for the work. The party left Battleford on May 23, reaching our first work in township 40, range 19, west of the third meridian, on the 24th.

The lakes and other bodies of water in sixty-two townships were examined during the season; those which were considered permanent were traversed, and others were investigated as to their depth, locality, nature of the water, and any other points worthy of note. Camps were located at suitable points for reaching the work, usually one camp being located in each township, unless time could be saved by doing two or more townships from one camp.

Magnetic observations were taken whenever possible without hindering the regular work to any extent. Astronomical observations were also taken as often as possible when the weather was favourable. In all sixty-one magnetic and forty-two astronomical observations were obtained during the season.

In accordance with instructions the condition of the monuments in each of the townships was noted, and as much territory covered in each as was possible without loss of time on the regular work, thus serving the double purpose of seeing as many monuments as we could, and of locating bodies of water not shown on the township plans.

I closed my operations in the field on December 10 and returned to Battleford, where I discharged my men and made arrangements for wintering the horses and storing the outfit.

Most of the bodies of water examined in the prairie country have no springs or other permanent sources of supply. The quantity of water in them is variable, depending on the annual rainfall and snowfall. Many are shallow, and contain water in the spring but dry up during the summer, excepting in wet seasons. In some districts particularly in fairly level, open country, the lakes seem to have permanently dried up. In one district four such townships were observed in each of which at least one lake and several marshes existed at the time of the original survey about ten years ago, but at the time of our survey not a drop of water was found in any of them, the land being suitable for agriculture. One of these lakes which covered an area of two thousand acres or more at the time of the original survey, was found entirely dry, and part of it was producing grain crops. In other districts, where the land is more rolling, the change is not so marked, but many of the lakes now produce slough and marsh grass and large portions of the old beds have become suitable for hay or pasture land. An occasional deep lake was found, however, which will be permanent for a number of years, and in some districts springs exist which feed the lakes and tend to keep them at a more constant level. A number of alkaline lakes were also found. Very little change occurred in the limits of vegetation around such lakes even where practically dry owing to the alkaline soil. These alkaline flats require to be dry for several years before vegetation begins and then the first growth is usually foxtail and other weeds.

The settlers claim there is more water in the lakes this year and last year than there has been for the preceding three or four years. This is probably due to the wet season of 1912, which filled the lakes and sloughs to a greater depth than usual, and saturated the soil to a higher level so that percolation does not proceed as rapidly as it did during the preceding dry years.

The condition of settlement varies in different parts of the country. In general, however, practically all of the Government lands are taken up by settlers, except in those sections where the land is unsuitable for farming, owing to its stony or hilly nature. In some districts, the country is very well settled, almost all of the land being under cultivation, while in other parts farther removed from the railways the settlement is in its initial stages. In the better settled townships good roads are being constructed along the road allowances, and the settlers have good buildings and prosperous looking farms.

The difficulty of obtaining water in some districts is a serious drawback to the settlers. Many of them have to haul water for their stock and general use for several miles. In one instance a settler was hauling it from a spring seven miles from his home. The cost of drilling wells is usually too great for the early settler as in many cases it is necessary to drill from two hundred to three hundred feet to obtain water.

The farmers in this district are engaged chiefly in grain growing although many of them have recently been devoting more attention to stock raising and mixed farming. This seems to be advisable owing to the uncertainty of the crops on account of frosts or hail and also because of the gradual exhaustion of the soil caused by continuous grain production. Mixed farming is carried on in those districts more remote from the railways where the cost of hauling grain to the elevators becomes a serious item of expense and in hilly and wet districts where the land is hard to till.

5 GEORGE V., A. 1915

APPENDIX No. 18.

REPORT OF M. P. BRIDGLAND, D.L.S.

TOPOGRAPHICAL SURVEY OF THE CROWSNEST FOREST RESERVE.

CALGARY, ALBERTA, February 23, 1914.

E. DEVILLE, Esq., LL.D.,
      Surveyor General,
            Ottawa, Canada.

SIR,—I have the honour to submit the following general report on the operations of my party during the season of 1913, while engaged on the topographical survey of the northern part of the Crowsnest Forest reserve.

On June 2, the party started for Claresholm, from which point it had been decided to enter the northern part of the reserve. From there camp equipment and supplies were freighted in to a point near " The Gap", which is a narrow pass about forty miles southwesterly from Claresholm, where Oldman river flows through the Livingstone range. While this was being done, the horses were driven down from Okotoks to " The Gap."

Later it was learned that a better way of reaching " The Gap " was by way of a wagon road from Lundbreck or Cowley, on the Crowsnest branch of the Canadian Pacific railway. This route is shorter and is not nearly so hilly as the other.

Owing to the necessity of testing camera levels, and of determining the focal length of cameras and the speed of the photographic plates, some delay followed our arrival at the Gap. Consequently it was not until June 13 that actual survey work was started. During this time, however, the bulk of the camp equipment and supplies was moved by pack train farther into the mountains, so that no more delay would be caused by difficulties of transportation. A temporary cache was made at the ranch of Mr. R. Macdonald, about a mile west of the Gap.

From June 15 to August 6 work was carried on from this point. Trips were made up Oldman river, Dutch creek, and Livingstone river and its tributaries. It was then decided to move south towards the railway, surveying the other valleys on the way. The valleys of Racehorse, Vicary, and Daisy creeks were covered, thus completing the drainage basin of Oldman river. While the railway and the adjacent land is not included in the reserve, the boundaries are so irregular that it was decided to partially cover all the country rather than to adhere strictly to the reserve. Another reason for this decision was that as the elevations of all stations were to be based on a traverse of the railway, it was necessary to occupy stations adjacent to it in order to carry the elevations to the more distant peaks. Seven stations south of the railway were occupied in order that they might be connected with the traverse and used as a basis for elevations of future stations in the southern part of the reserve.

While no organized system of triangulation was carried out, angles were read to connect different stations as well as possible. Advantage was taken of any old signals that could be located. Stations adjacent to the railway were fixed by a traverse of the railway, and a sufficient number of the more remote stations were connected with the posts of the Dominion lands system to control the survey.

The season of 1913 was, on the whole, favourable for the work. The party left Calgary on June 2 and returned on September 25. During this time 114 triangulation stations (exclusive of section corners or secondary camera stations) were occupied and twenty-two miles of railway traversed. Only eighteen days were completely lost owing to bad weather, though work was frequently interrupted on other occasions. No delay was caused by smoke and no prolonged delay by bad weather. On account of the low elevation, the hills were seldom covered with clouds, although the higher peaks to the west were often clouded. Work on the summits was frequently interrupted by local

SESSIONAL PAPER No. 25b

thunderstorms, but these rarely lasted more than a couple of hours. The worst difficulty was due to incessant high winds, which rendered good work extremely difficult. In the absence of sharply defined topographical features, on sunny days the distance was often rendered indistinct by haze, particularly in the direction of the sun.

The northern part of the Crowsnest forest reserve covers an area of about 650 to 700 square miles and lies chiefly in townships 9 to 14 inclusive, ranges 3, 4, and 5, west of the fifth meridian. Nearly all of this area is drained by Oldman river. The chief tributaries of this river, which are Livingstone river, Racehorse and Dutch creeks, join the main stream before it flows through the Gap. This part of the reserve consists principally of rolling hills, the higher summits rising slightly above timber line. On the west side, running in a northerly and southerly direction, there is a limestone range forming the summit of the Rocky mountains and the boundary between British Columbia and Alberta. The peaks of this range vary from 8,500 to 10,000 feet in elevation. Adjacent to this range there is a series of lower hills where the highest summits run from 7,000 to 8,000 feet above sea-level. About fifteen miles east of the main range and running almost parallel to it, lies the Livingstone range, also a limestone formation. This range is slightly higher than the intervening hills, especially south of the Gap. Farther east the hills rapidly become lower.

The country as a whole is comparatively open. There are good trails which are practically free from steep grades, bad swamps, or muskegs, in all the main valleys. In many cases horses can easily be taken through country where no trail exists. In most sections feed is very plentiful, the valleys as a rule being " U " shaped, with large meadows in the bottoms. In addition many of the hillsides are open and are covered with a luxuriant growth of grass and pea-vine. During the past summer the upper part of Livingstone valley was used as a range for several hundred cattle. Wild flowers of many varieties are abundant, particularly on some of the upper slopes near the timberline. Edible fruits are scarce, soapberries (if these can be called edible) and wild black currants being the only varieties seen in any quantity.

Timber of commercial value is not plentiful. A bad fire a few years ago burned over much of the country and did a great deal of damage to the standing timber. There is some spruce near the heads of Oldman and Livingstone rivers, but the greater portion of these basins has been burned over and is either bare or is covered with a growth of small jackpine. In the southwest part of the reserve near the heads of Dutch, Racehorse and Vicary creeks, and along the valley of Allison creek, there is a considerable quantity of spruce about eighteen inches in diameter. East of Livingstone range the country is more open and there is no timber of commercial value. The varieties of trees usually seen are spruce, small poplar and jackpine in the valleys, scattered fir, spruce and jackpine on the hillsides, and spruce, balsam and pine on the upper slopes.

So far as could be learned no minerals other than coal have been discovered. Much of the country is held under lease for coal rights, and stakes were frequently seen. In only one place, however, were surface outcrops seen by any member of the party.

Trout abound in Oldman river and its tributaries, but are not as plentiful as in former years. During the fishing season of 1913 the Gap and its vicinity was visited by many fishing parties, and there is no doubt that as the attractions of this locality become better known the number of parties will increase and the number of trout will correspondingly decrease. At the present time there are very few fish in Crowsnest river or its tributaries at the southern end of the reserve. Large game does not seem to be very plentiful. Deer were seen on several occasions, and some mountain goats were encountered on the main range. There are a few bears, but berries and wild fruit are too scarce to offer them much inducement to remain in the country permanently.

I have the honour to be, Sir,

Your obedient servant,

M. P. BRIDGLAND, D.L.S.

5 GEORGE V. A. 1915

APPENDIX No. 19.

REPORT OF J. A. CALDER, D.L.S.

SUBDIVISION SURVEYS AROUND KAMLOOPS.

ASHCROFT, B.C., January 15, 1914.

E. DEVILLE, Esq., LL.D.,
      Surveyor General,
            Ottawa.

SIR,—I have the honour to submit the following general report on my surveys in the railway belt, British Columbia during the season of 1913.

I left Kamloops, where my party was organized, on May 9, 1913, and commenced the season's work in township 17, range 25, west of the sixth meridian. There I surveyed suitable grazing lands along Twaal creek, and retraced a part of Cooks Ferry Indian reserve No. 6. This portion of the township is very hilly and broken, and nearly all the land surveyed is suitable only for grazing. There is fair bunch-grass on all the lower slopes. Some benches along the east boundary of the township are cultivated, and the quality of the soil is generally excellent, but the scarcity of water for irrigation discourages more extensive farming.

I next subdivided certain sections along Pimainus creek in township 17, range 24, consisting for the greater part of a narrow valley, which save for some stony bench land in sections 21, 22 and 15, contains no land which could be tilled profitably. There is good grazing along the creek but the sides of the valley might be too steep in places for stock.

Most of this township consists of an elevated plateau, well timbered with fir and jackpine, and is nearly all covered with a good growth of timber grass, or pine grass as it is sometimes called. Unfortunately cattle and horses do not thrive on it, and it is generally considered worthless for grazing. I have been credibly informed, however, that sheep do well on this grass and if this be so, large tracts of the central plateau of British Columbia, which hitherto have been considered worthless, may in future provide a very valuable addition to the food supply of the province.

Deposits of gypsum have been discovered in various places along Pimainus creek. Since this mineral is of small value in proportion to its weight, the expense of transportation is likely to prohibit the development of these claims for a long time.

There are several fair-sized lakes at the head of Pimainus creek in township 17, range 23, which are well stocked with good trout.

On June 10, I moved to Drynoch and began work in township 16, range 25. The right bank of Thompson river was traversed from the north boundary of Cooks Ferry Indian reserve No. 2 to the south boundary of the township; such lines as were necessary to complete the survey of the sections adjoining the river were run and several Indian reserves retraced and tied in. The portion of this township which lies west of the Thompson is very rough and broken, so that it was difficult to run some of the lines.

I also subdivided nearly the whole of the east half of this township, which lies mostly on a rolling and hilly plateau between the Thompson and Nicola valleys. This plateau is generally well timbered with fir and bull pine, interspersed with some open patches; it is nearly all fair to good grazing land, and considerable areas in places, are arable. The elevation averages from 3,400 to 4,000 feet above sea-level, and nothing more delicate than hardy cereals and vegetables can be grown. The Indians on Nicoamen Indian reserve No. 10 raise most of the ordinary vegetables successfully, as well as

SESSIONAL PAPER No. 25b

grain, but the latter sometimes does not ripen before the fall frosts set in. There are a number of good springs throughout the township, and while the amount of water is not sufficient to be useful for irrigation, they constitute a most valuable asset for a stock range. Strawberries grow in great profusion, ripening about the first of July. Bands of wild horses range over this plateau, furnishing considerable diversion for the Indians, who often endeavour to capture some of them with but indifferent success. Even when captured young, it is almost impossible to break them. Blue and willow grouse also abound in this district.

Subdivision was extended southerly to include grazing lands in the northeast quarter of township 15, range 25, and such portions of Indian reserves as fell within the lands surveyed were retraced and tied in. Both banks of the Thompson were traversed through this township, and the survey of the sections along the river was completed where necessary.

Miscellaneous surveys along the Fraser, from Lytton to the north limit of the railway belt, occupied practically the remainder of the season. The country there is very mountainous and broken, especially on the west side of the river.

In townships 17, ranges 27 and 28, a number of small benches occur in the sections surveyed on the lower slopes of the mountains. Many of these have been cleared and are cultivated by Indians. These Indians seem to be, as a rule, good farmers. Practically all the suitable land within their reserves is utilized, and they have gone to considerable pains constructing ditches and flumes for irrigation purposes. There is no wagon road along the west side of the river, and any farm produce they may raise has to be brought to market, or at least part of the way, on packhorses. For this reason beans are the principal crop grown, as their value is great in proportion to their bulk, and they stand rough handling well. Until a road is built along this side of the river extensive development cannot take place.

I subdivided such lands along McGillivray creek, in township 18, range 27, as I considered valuable. The best land is a sloping bench in the east half of section 8 and the grazing is generally good throughout this section.

In township 18, range 28, I completed the survey of section 15 including the establishment of half a mile of the north limit of the railway belt, and the traverse of the right bank of Fraser river through this section. Some subdivision was also made on the east side of the river, including some patches of good land, suitable for settlement, in sections 26, 23 and 14.

This portion of the Fraser valley is very suitable for general farming. There are many thriving orchards, and dairying is carried on very successfully by a few ranchers. Bees do well, and give good returns with apparently little attention. The climate is excellent, and there are no summer frosts. This district being in the "dry belt", irrigation is essential, and generally the amount of water available is not sufficient to supply all the cultivable land. In many places this condition of affairs could be improved by constructing reservoirs at suitable places along the streams, wherever dams could be built economically, and thus conserve much of the water which now is lost in the spring.

Considerable prospecting is being done along McGillivray creek, and some fair samples of platinum and gold have been found, but not in paying quantities. Many of the bars along the Fraser are occasionally worked on a small scale for gold by Indians, who generally make fair wages. Several benches of what must have been fine agricultural land, close to the river, have been washed for gold in years gone by, and there is now left only a waste of rounded small boulders and stones. It is doubtful if the amount of gold thus obtained compensates in the long run for such wanton destruction of one of the province's most valuable assets.

After completing a few small surveys near the town of Lytton, I decided to discontinue field operations for the season: the remaining lands to be surveyed were at a considerable elevation and the snow was deep.

25b—7

5 GEORGE V., A. 1915

I arrived at Kamloops on December 15, where I discharged the party on the following day.

Although an unusual quantity of rain fell during the summer months, the season generally was very favourable for surveying and the fall was ideal from a surveyor's point of view.

I have the honour to be, Sir,

Your obedient servant,

JOHN A. CALDER, D.L.S.

SESSIONAL PAPER No. 25b

APPENDIX No. 20.

ABSTRACT OF THE REPORT OF A. V. CHASE, D.L.S.

SURVEYS IN THE RAILWAY BELT, B.C., SOUTH OF LYTTON.

I organized my party at Kamloops, and on May 22, 1913, we left for township 14, range 27, west of the sixth meridian where our first surveys were to be made.

The valley of Fraser river in this township is narrow and flanked by steep mountains to the east and west, and averages scarcely more than one mile in width. In this valley may be found land suitable for settlement. Small areas of bench land at varying elevations are found throughout the valley and are composed almost without exception of a good quality of light sandy loam soil. Some areas include also a considerable quantity of sandy gravel. The timber in this township is not of merchantable value. It is composed throughout of bull pine and fir up to twenty-four inches in diameter, the quality being generally better to the west of the river. Much of it in accessible places has been cut by settlers but it still covers most of the main valley except in the vicinity of lands which have been cleared and improved. The average size would scarcely be considered of any value for lumbering.

Our next work was in township 13, range 27, and in townships 12 and 13, range 26. The valley of the Fraser through these townships conforms to the general character of the valley in this locality except in the southern part of township 12 where the mountains to the east recede to a greater distance from the river, leaving areas of bench and bottom land as far as two or two and one-half miles from the river. Bench land fit for cultivation was found adjoining the river in the southern part of township 13 and throughout township 12. Considerable settlement has taken place in this neighbourhood and other settlers are waiting for the vacant lands to be sufficiently surveyed for disposal to make homestead entries thereon.

I then decided to move into the valley of Nahatlatch river in townships 12, ranges 26, 27, and 28, and do as much work there as could be accomplished before the uncertain fall weather set in. To this end I moved by wagon to the cable ferry of Messrs. Wordenhoff & Co. at Keefers, B.C., where my outfit was transported across the Fraser. From the ferry I moved to the end of the wagon road by team and wagon, but was disappointed by the non-arrival of packhorses for which I had arranged but which had strayed into the hills. I was able, however, to move sufficient of the outfit into the valley by man pack to supply us with food and shelter for the night, and the next day, August 23, the remainder of the outfit was moved down to the valley by pack horses, and camp was set up in the southeast quarter of section 13, township 12, range 27.

The valley of Nahatlatch river and lakes is essentially, as far as these surveys were carried, a narrow defile between steep mountain ranges to the south and north, but small areas of workable bench land are found along the valley. These when close to the river bottom are inclined to be very sandy and somewhat stony, but such benches as are at a slightly higher elevation are composed of a very good quality of sandy loam and light sandy loam soil. Most of this class of land is found in range 27, the mountains in ranges 26 and 28 rising as a rule from points close to the water's edge. In township 12, range 26, in this valley, are to be found several areas of excellent bench land at from 500 to 600 feet above the river, but this land is nearly all disposed of. Only one bona fide settler was found in this valley west of range 26.

25b—7½

5 GEORGE V., A. 1915

The timber in the Nahatlatch valley is scarcely of sufficient value to warrant lumbering operations. In the river bottom bull pine, white pine, fir and cedar are found in fair size and quantity, but as the elevation increases white pine and cedar disappear and the timber is composed mainly of scrub, bull pine and fir, with jackpine in the higher altitudes.

This valley can be reached by wagon road from Keefers to the divide between Fraser and Nahatlatch rivers and thence by a good pack trail to Hannah lake, in section 19, township 12, range 27. From this point the pack trail is not fit for loaded horses and supplies must be carried westward on the lakes by means of rafts or dug-outs. At the western end of the lakes the pack trail is again fit for use by loaded horses, and access may be had by it to the western limit of the railway belt.

The physical features of the land surrounding the western part of Nahatlatch lake suggest the advisability of a micrometer traverse, and as I did not have the necessary instruments with me, I left this work to be carried out at a later date.

On October 30, I returned to the Fraser valley to complete before the end of the season certain surveys for which there was an immediate necessity in township 12, range 26, and in township 13, range 27, and on November 28 I moved camp to Lytton to complete some work omitted earlier in the season in township 14, range 27.

This ended my work for the season. I disbanded my party on December 6 and left at once for Orillia, Ont., where I arrived on the 11th.

APPENDIX No. 21.

ABSTRACT OF THE REPORT OF G. W. COLTHAM, D.L.S.

STADIA SURVEYS IN CENTRAL ALBERTA.

On May 26, 1913, we left Edmonton, where I had organized my party, and proceeded easterly over the Canadian Northern railway to Sickman lake, in township 52, range 13, west of the fourth meridian.

Surveys of lakes in the following townships were completed during the season:—

Townships 50 and 52, range 9, townships 49, 50, 51, and 52, ranges 10 and·11, townships 47, 48, 49, 50, 51, and 52, range 12, and townships 47, 48, 51 and 52, range 13, all west of the fourth meridian. An inspection was made of township 50, range 13, but no bodies of water of sufficient importance to warrant a survey were found, No lakes exist in township 51, range 9, or township 49, range 13.

Sickman lake is surrounded by hills which rise gradually from the shore. About a mile from the southerly end of the lake they attain a height exceeding 100 feet. Small fresh-water springs are found along the shore, and these serve to partially offset the effects of evaporation of the lake water. The lake level, however, has fallen in recent years as the old shore is visible in many places more than a chain from the water's edge. The shore is composed of sand and gravel and rises very slightly for some distance. The water is slightly alkaline, and the greatest depth found was about fifteen feet but soundings indicate that the bed is uneven. The bays are very shallow.

The soil in this township is a sandy loam, and while not very suitable for the cultivation of cereals is well adapted to the production of potatoes and garden vegetables. The greater part furnishes splendid grazing land for cattle and horses. Small scattered areas of poplar, a few acres in extent, furnish fuel to the surrounding settlers.

Township 52, range 12, contains a great many lakes; those in the northerly part are all surrounded with poplar of small dimensions while the shores are obstructed with dry fallen timber. In several small lakes ranging from nine to twelve feet in depth portions of dry trees were standing, indicating that they are of comparatively recent origin.

The surrounding country is rolling, broken by small hills, and not well adapted to cultivation, but furnishes good summer pasture for cattle.

A small lake formerly existing in the southwest quarter of section 7 has entirely dried up, and the old lake bed is covered with grass. The only apparent cause of its disappearance is evaporation, as no surface outlet or inlet is visible. A lake lying in sections 2 and 11 contains upwards of thirty islands, and has only narrow channels of open water. These islands lying a few feet above the water are thickly timbered with small poplar. The lake water though almost free from alkali is stagnant, and is filled with small green particles of vegetable matter which in the presence of the sun's heat impart a putrid odour to the water, and give it a most unpleasant taste. The depth is fairly uniform averaging about ten feet. The shore line is timbered, and low hills rise from the water's edge. The surrounding country is settled largely by Russians and Galicians, who have as yet tilled only a few acres of their farms, the land in fact being too rough and broken for profitable cultivation but well suited for cattle ranching. The soil in general is a light sandy loam.

The lakes in townships 52, ranges 11, 10 and 9 contain water which is almost free from alkali and which, after boiling is quite potable. A lake in sections 19 and 20, range 11, has a hard level bed of sand and gravel and open shores and contains fine clear

5 GEORGE V., A. 1915

drinking water of temporary hardness. The other lakes are surrounded by small scrubby poplar and have nearly level shores. Many of these lakes are fed by springs which seem to maintain a fairly constant level. .

The surrounding country is rolling, and near Vermilion river the hills are rather precipitous. The soil consists of sand and clay loam on which grain thrives but cultivation is difficult. The land is perhaps quite as valuable for grazing purposes. Poplar timber which occurs in scattered areas ranges from two to seven inches in diameter.

Vermilion river drains a large area but in the month of July it was only twenty to thirty feet wide and three feet deep, with a sluggish current. The river valley ranges from ten to twenty chains in width, with abrupt banks rising from fifty to one hundred feet in height. Small scattered spruce and poplar fringe the summit of the bank.

The lakes in townships 51, range 10, and the easterly part of range 11, were found to have dried up considerably, the open prairie country and shallowness of the water promoting active evaporation. The shores are sandy and quite level while the water contains in solution a high percentage of alkaline salts. The depths range from one to four feet and under present conditions these lakes will disappear in a few years.

The country is quite level and well adapted for grain growing although only a very small fraction of the available land is under cultivation. The settlers in this district follow mixed farming and raise a large number of cattle and horses.

In the westerly part of townships 51, range 11, and the northerly part of range 12, the lakes are different in character, having greater depths and being surrounded by rough hilly country, covered to a large extent with small poplar and scrub. A depth of forty feet was found in a lake lying in sections 26 and 35, range 12. This was the greatest depth noted in any lake during the season's work. Dry timber standing in several feet of water near the shore of this lake indicated that the water had risen quite recently. The shore is rough, and covered with dead timber. The water is rather stagnant and slightly alkaline. The small lakes in sections 10, 11, 14 and 15, range 12, contain less than two feet of water and must under present conditions eventually disappear. Incrustations of alkaline salts are found along the shores. The lakes in sections 21, 28, 29 and 33 of this township are quite picturesquely situated and contain clear sparkling water which however is alkaline to the taste.

A lake lying in sections 31 and 32, township 51, range 12, and partly in township 52 was completely dry in the month of June, but contained several inches of water two months later, after the summer rains had fallen. No survey was made as it was thought that it will soon be permanently dry.

The township is similar in its general topography to the one adjoining it to the north. The small town of Ranfurly on the line of the Canadian Northern railway from Edmonton to Vermilion is situated in the southeast quarter of section 15. It has one grain elevator, two stores, and a hotel and a population of about one hundred.

Township 51, range 13, is rolling in character, the land being light and arid, and consequently grain farming is not pursued. It would appear however to be suitable for sheep ranching.

Birch lake extending into townships 50 and 51, ranges 11 and 12, was the largest than two feet of water and must under present conditions, eventually disappear. Incrusbody of water surveyed during the season. This lake with a maximum width of nine miles in an easterly and westerly direction, presents so many long inlets connected with the main body by narrow channels, that the amount of shore line is very great compared with the water area. The west shore in range 12 is sandy and the land rises gradually from it. A fringe of poplar extends to within a few chains of the water's edge. The shore line here indicates that the water has fallen three to four feet within the past few years. Several small bays originally connected with the large westerly bay of the lake are now isolated from the main body forming separate shallow lakes with level sandy shores. The land adjoining the shore is rolling, but not too rough for cultivation,

SESSIONAL PAPER No. 25b

though it might prove more profitable if used for grazing as the soil is sandy. The farmers in this section have experienced some difficulty in obtaining a sufficient supply of good water. The southerly shore of the lake is similar in its general characteristics to the westerly shore. The land adjoining the inlets of the lake is low and wet during the greater part of the year. In range 11 the land is rolling and in parts too rough for profitable tillage, but furnishes good pasture.

Masses of limestone were found strewn along the north shore in several places, but it is evidently too easily disintegrated by weathering agencies to prove valuable as a building material. A steep precipitous clay bank ranging from fifty to one hundred feet in height extends several miles along the north shore. The small adjoining lakes have evidently been connected originally with the main body. The greatest depth noted was thirty-five feet; this was found at a point a few chains south of the larger island in the large easterly bay extending northward.

A large ranch containing about 6,000 acres comprises the area along the north shore between the two great bays. The greater part of this land is rough and hilly with long narrow coulees affording fine natural shelter for stock in winter. At present about 1,000 acres are under cultivation. Springs of clear hard water are found along the lake shore in section 34, range 11. The lake water is soft containing a high percentage of solids in solution and although alkaline is not unsuitable for stock. Owing to the presence of free ammonia in the water it has been found that fish will not thrive. According to the testimony of the surrounding farmers several of the islands in the lake have appeared only within the last ten years, showing that the lake level has fallen three or four feet at least in that time. The town of Innisfree situated on the Canadian Northern railway in section 2, township 51, range 11, has a population of about four hundred and owing to the proximity of the lake attracts quite a number of summer campers from Edmonton and neighbouring centres.

Townships 50, ranges 10 and 11, consist of open rolling and undulating prairie. The soil is chiefly clay loam and is exceptionally well suited to the production of wheat and oats. All the land open for entry is being farmed, with large areas already under crop.

Townships 49, ranges 10 and 11, contain very rolling land, with good clay soil in several sections; but it is too rough for extensive cultivation. Good farm land is found in the south part of range 11, where the surface is undulating with several quite level sections. Alice lake in this township is evidently slowly drying up; evaporation is very active, leaving the water in the lake extremely alkaline, so that it is even unsuitable for stock. The adjoining small lakes are very shallow and will probably soon disappear. In range 9 the surface is very rolling in character.

Townships 47 and 48, ranges 12 and 13, contain some of the best wheat producing land in Alberta. The surface is level or in places sufficiently undulating to afford good natural drainage. The soil is clay and clay loam which seems especially suitable for the production of wheat and oats, the common crops in this locality. The settlers here are principally Norwegians who have adopted modern, and even scientific farming methods with surprising rapidity and remarkable success.

The town of Viking, situated on the main line of the Grand Trunk Pacific railway, in the northeast quarter of section 36, township 47, range 13, has a population of about four hundred, and is a thriving agricultural centre with three grain elevators, which during the month of November were receiving grain at the rate of 5,000 bushels per day.

Thomas lake, the largest in this district, presents some peculiar features. The depth is variable, while springs of water of a higher temperature than that in the lake rise in various places from the lake bed, which is very soft and composed of alkaline clay and mud. The lake level however appears to be gradually lowering.

The lake in section 10, township 47, range 13, was found to have entirely dried up. Evaporation and cultivation of the surrounding soil appear to be active agencies in

5 GEORGE V., A. 1915

drying up most of the shallow lakes that came under our observation, while the element of rainfall seems to exert comparatively little effect on the level of many of these lakes. Various large sloughs which according to the testimony of settlers existed four or five years ago have entirely disappeared. In most instances this has proved of great benefit to the farmers as the land now produces heavy crops of good hay.

The lakes on the northerly part of township 52 and the northeasterly part of township 51, range 12, seem to have maintained their present level for a long period, and in a few cases appearances seem to indicate that new lake bodies have been formed comparatively recently.

Game was plentiful throughout the whole area where surveys were performed. Ducks of various species were plentiful on nearly all the lakes and sloughs while flocks of geese frequented the larger bodies of open water. Several flocks of pelican were seen, as well as various kinds of snipe and small aquatic birds which frequented the shallow lakes with open shores. Prairie-chickens were everywhere abundant while a few ruffed grouse were noticed in the timbered areas. Rabbits were very numerous particularly in township 52, range 12. Jumping deer, though not plentiful, are to be found in township 52, range 12, and the vicinity of Birch lake, but no moose are to be found in this region. For feathered game this district is considered to be one of the best hunting grounds in the province.

The weather, during the months of June and July was rather damp, although the actual rainfall was not heavy; but the warmer weather in August and September together with the absence of early frosts which often occur in the district, combined to make the season one of the most favourable that the farmers have experienced for over ten years. It was noticed that in the low flat sections frosts occurred earlier and were much more severe that in the higher and more hilly parts.

The weather conditions however are such as to permit of the raising of practically all the common kinds of vegetables and small fruits, where proper methods of preparation and culture of the soil are pursued.

On November 24, owing to unfavourable weather conditions, operations were suspended.

APPENDIX No. 22.

REPORT OF G. C. COWPER, D.L.S.

STADIA SURVEYS IN SOUTHERN SASKATCHEWAN AND ALBERTA.

OTTAWA, February 27, 1914.

E. DEVILLE, Esq., LL.D.,
  Surveyor General,
    Ottawa, Canada.

 SIR,—I have the honour to submit the following report on the stadia survey of lakes carried on by my party in southern Alberta and Saskatchewan during the past season.

 I left Welland on May 5, 1913 and proceeded to Medicine Hat, where I organized my party. On the 20th of the month I left for township 9, range 8, west of the fourth meridian, the scene of my first operations. My work consisted of the traverse by stadia of all lakes of a permanent character over five acres in area and the investigation of all lakes and marshes which had dried up since the original surveys or which were likely to dry up. These surveys were carried on in sixty-three townships in Alberta, extending from townships 1 to 22 and ranges 1 to 14, west of the fourth meridian.

 From township 9, range 8, I worked east to township 8, range 2. The country passed through is well settled and few homesteads remain to be taken up. Townships 8, ranges 2, 3, and 5, are rougher than the others and are largely under lease for cattle and horse grazing. The remaining townships are homesteaded, the settlers going in for mixed farming.

 The only body of water of any importance in these townships is Elkwater lake, in township 8, range 3. This lake is two miles long by a mile and a half wide and is composed of three arms. The deepest sounding taken was twenty-one feet. The water is cool, clear and well stocked with pike. It is prettily situated at the foot of a high wooded hill and part of the south shore is laid out as a summer resort. The lake is only thirty-five miles from Medicine Hat, and as there is a good trail to that city, a large number of people from there use it as a summer resort.

 From Elkwater lake I moved south by way of Medicine Lodge coulee to township 1, range 2. This coulee runs north and south and varies from one to two miles in width, with banks from 100 to 400 feet high. The coulee and the land immediately east is well settled as far south as township 5, but from there to township 1 the country is rougher and is practically all under grazing lease, and the ranch houses are widely separated.

 Township 1, range 2, is well settled by Americans, who on account of the great distance to the nearest railway in Canada do most of their trading in Montana. This will largely be overcome on the completion of the Weyburn-Lethbridge branch of the Canadian Pacific railway.

 Milk River lake in this township is about three miles long and varies in width from ten chains to half a mile. It is very shallow, and at the time of my survey, June 23, contained only a little over a foot of muddy water. In a dry season it will completely dry up, but it will not produce hay.

 From this township westerly to Comrey, in township 2, range 6, the country is rough and is sparsely settled with ranchers. From there northerly to Pakowki lake, in townships 3, ranges 7, 8, and 9, townships 4, ranges 7 and 8, and townships 5, ranges 7, 8, and 9, the country is well settled with homesteaders. This lake was originally

5 GEORGE V., A. 1915

a large body of water. The main body of the lake was ten miles long and from two to six miles wide; it had two long arms, the one at the southwest end being seven miles long and three-quarters of a mile wide, and the other at the northwest end being four miles long and about half a mile wide. It has dried up considerably in the last few years and is very shallow, three feet being the greatest depth found. The land formerly in the lake and now dry is gumbo soil and is covered with foxtail. The water is milky and unfit for use. There are a number of creeks flowing into the lake but there is no outlet.

The country around the lake, with the exception of the north end, where there is a large sheep ranch, is well settled. A large number of Americans, who came into this district in 1910, are following mixed farming, and although at present fifty miles from the railway they are meeting with success. The new branch of the Canadian Pacific railway from Weyburn to Lethbridge runs just north of the lake.

From Pakowki lake I moved to Crow Indian lake, in townships 5, ranges 13 and 14, passing through a well settled country. This lake is about four and a half miles long and 20 chains wide. It is situated in a long coulee about a mile wide with banks about 200 feet high. The greatest depth found in this lake was six feet, and the water is fresh and good. The area covered by water is fairly constant except at the west end where the lake runs out into a long marshy flat. The overflow from this lake reaches Pakowki lake.

From Crow Indian lake I moved north to the town of Grassy lake, in township 10, range 13. For the first ten miles after leaving Crow Indian lake there are practically no settlers, but from there north to South Saskatchewan river the country is well settled. In townships 9, ranges 11, 12, 13, and 14, and townships 10, ranges 11, 12, and 13, only one lake was found to contain water, all the other lakes having dried up. These now form valuable hay meadows.

The next townships investigated were those situated between the main line of the Canadian Pacific railway and Red Deer river and from South Saskatchewan river west to range 12. The largest lake shown on the map for this district is Tide lake which originally covered half of township 18, range 10. This lake was found to be completely dry and its bottom which is gumbo soil was covered with more or less vegetation. I investigated seventeen townships in this district in which all the lakes were dry, and in ten others some of the lakes were dry and some were found to still contain water the year round. The only lake in this district of which special mention may be made is Old Channel lake in townships 14 and 15, range 5. This lake is in the form of a horseshoe and is about two miles from end to end and ten to twenty chains wide. It was evidently at one time the channel of the South Saskatchewan, but the river has cut a new channel. The lake is very shallow, varying from one to two feet deep, but it has never been known to be completely dry.

In townships 20, ranges 4, 7 and 8, township 19, range 3, and townships 17 and 18, range 5, a number of alkaline lakes were traversed. These lakes contained very little water, but their bottoms are composed of very soft white alkaline mud which, even when the water disappears, do not become dry, nor do they produce any vegetation. In some cases the settlers have these lakes fenced off to prevent their stock from becoming mired in them.

This district is becoming very well settled. New houses were noticed going up in all the townships, and new land is being broken. The branch of the Canadian Pacific railway from Swift Current to Bassano runs through this district. Some of the townships are rough and broken and are under lease for horse and cattle ranching. There are no sheep ranches in the district.

The next area investigated was in townships 12 to 17, ranges 1 to 3 inclusive. In these townships about half of the lakes were found to be dry while the remainder still contain some water. These townships, with the exception of townships 14, ranges 2 and

Photo by J S Galletly, D L S

Hudson Bay Store and Factor's Residence at Fort Vermilion.

The building in the foreground is the Factor's residence, while away in the background can be seen the flour mill. The store is about half-way between the residence and the mill.

Photo by G. C. Cowper, D L.S.

Alkaline Mound in Southern Saskatchewan.

This mound, on the shore of a lake in township 16, range 25, west of the Third meridian, is about eight feet high and fifteen feet in diameter It is snowy white and is composed of clear crystalline salts which on exposure to the air break up into a fine white powder which covers the mound to a depth of about one inch The mound appears to be formed from salt springs When the lake fills up the mound dissolves, the salt spreading over the bottom of the lake, and when the lake dries up the mound forms again.

SESSIONAL PAPER No. 25b

3, which are rough and hilly, are well settled, mostly by Germans. There are no large or important lakes. A number of summer camps for sheep were seen.

On September 19 I finished the survey of the lakes in township 12, range 1, thus completing my surveys in Alberta.

My surveys in Saskatchewan were confined to the block of townships composed of townships 12 to 16, ranges 20 to 26, west of the third meridian, in which I surveyed and investigated all the lakes. These townships are situated immediately north and east of Maple Creek settlement and the townships are with a few exceptions well settled.

The settlers in this district go in for mixed farming and very few of them depend altogether on the growing of grain. There are still a number of ranches in this block. Township 12, range 23, and township 13, range 20, are both entirely under grazing lease. Township 14, range 24, and townships 16, ranges 23 and 24, are largely composed of sand hills. At one time there was some fairly large timber in these townships, but the settlers have cut practically all of this and now very little except scrub remains. The ranchers in this district raise horses, cattle and sheep

Crane lake, in townships 13, ranges 22, 23 and 24, is the largest body of water in this district. It is about eight miles long and five miles wide at the widest part. On account of a thin coating of ice I was unable to sound it, but it is said to be twenty feet deep. The water in the lake is slightly alkaline but it is used for stock. The lake is fed by Bear creek and has no outlet. Crane lake has dried up somewhat in the last few years. This is most noticeable on the south side where the land is low and flat.

Bigstick lake, in townships 15, ranges 24 and 25, is also a large body of water, but it is drying up rapidly although it has no outlet. This is accounted for by the fact that the water in Maple creek, which is the lake's only source of supply, is being used for irrigation purposes. The water is also slightly alkaline and the greatest depth found was nine feet. The east end of this lake is very shallow and the land rises very gradually. As the water recedes it leaves good hay lands. In both Crane and Bigstick lakes moderate quantities of pike and sucker are to be found, and both of these lakes are frequented in the fall by a large number of ducks, geese and cranes.

In township 16, range 25, a very unique lake was found. This lake is about two miles long by half a mile wide, and at the time of my survey, October 8, was dry except for a few inches of water at the north end. The bottom of the lake is covered with a coating of hard crystalline and alkaline salt varying from a few inches to a foot in depth. At the south end of the lake there is a large mound of alkaline salt of snowy whiteness, about fifteen feet in diameter and eight feet high, and close to it there is a smaller mound about three feet high. The mounds are composed of clear crystalline salts which on exposure to the air break down to a white powder, and this powder covers the mounds to a depth of an inch. I cut about a foot into the larger mound without finding any change in its composition, but on cutting six inches into the smaller one, water spouted out and continued flowing. On returning next day this mound was found to be again sealed up. These mounds are apparently formed by salt springs, which on coming to the surface deposit the salt. The mounds are said to disappear and to be built up again, and one settler informed me that he had seen five of these mounds at one time. It appears that when the lake fills up in the spring with the fresh snow water and the heavy rains, these mounds are dissolved and the salt is then deposited over the lake bottom.

Vincent lake in townships 14 and 15 range 22, which is approximately the same size as the last mentioned lake has practically the same bed formation, but there are no mounds in it. A number of smaller lakes were examined which had the same hard crystalline salt bottom, but in none of these were any springs noticed.

In sections 30 and 31, township 15, range 20, there is a fairly large lake with a hard crystalline bottom. About twenty chains south there is a much smaller lake without any water but with a very soft white alkaline mud bottom, and about fifteen

5 GEORGE V., A. 1915

chains east of this there is a fresh-water lake. The lake with the hard crystalline bottom is in a small valley, while the other two are in another valley but they are not connected.

In these townships a large number of lakes were surveyed which were practically free of water but the bottoms were soft white alkaline mud. These lakes carry water so long each season that their beds never become really dry, and vegetation has no chance to grow. In a few cases where the lakes have remained dry, vegetation appeared to be starting.

The deepest lake encountered during the season was Freefight lake, in townships 16 and 17, range 23. It is about two miles long by half a mile wide, and is surrounded by high rolling prairie. It is fed by a fresh-water creek but the lake itself is strongly alkaline. It was found to be over sixty feet deep.

Practically all the lakes surveyed during the season were found to cover a smaller area than they did at the time of the original surveys, from ten to thirty years ago. This may be partly accounted for by the fact that the land is becoming more broken each year, thus allowing the surface water to sink in. Virgin prairie is almost impervious to water.

A large number of the prairie lakes have no well-defined inlets or outlets. They are simply pot-holes, varying from a few acres to a few square miles in area. The surface water from the melting snows and the spring rains fill them and evaporation is their only outlet. As the land becomes more valuable and proper drainage is instituted many of these lakes will be reclaimed for hay meadows and in some cases for the growing of grain.

The one great drawback of this southern country to the homesteader is the uncertainly of the rainfall for the ripening of his crops, and to the rancher the uncertainty of having an abundant supply of fresh water for his stock.

The game consists of ducks, geese and cranes in large numbers, and an occasional antelope in the less settled districts.

As to the accuracy of the stadia for traverse surveys, I would mention that I closed a large number of my traverses by latitudes and departures and found the closing errors in many cases to be little in excess of that which would be expected with a transit and chain. In one case I retraced three miles of a base line with the stadia and differed by only seven links from the theoretic at the end of that distance.

During the season I completed the survey and investigation of the lakes in ninety-two townships and partly investigated eleven other townships.

I completed operations in the field on December 20 and reached my home in Welland on the 24th.

> I have the honour to be, Sir,
>
> Your obedient servant,
>
> G. C. COWPER, D.L.S.

APPENDIX No. 23.

ABSTRACT OF THE REPORT OF A. L. CUMMING, D.L.S.

RESURVEYS IN SASKATCHEWAN AND ALBERTA.

My work during the season of 1913 consisted of resurveys, retracment and restoration surveys of townships, the original surveys of which were performed twenty or thirty years ago.

I organized at Edmonton and shipped my outfit to Strome, Alta., on July 7, 1913. My first work was to renew the monuments adjoining Wavy lake in townships 44 and 45, range 15, west of the fourth meridian. Upon completion of this work I drove by way of Content and Red Deer to Cygnet lake which lies in township 38, range 28. This lake was reported to have been greatly lowered by a ditch which had been constructed by the railway company whose grade crosses this lake. The ditch has lowered the water in the lake by about two feet but has not caused any great change in the shore line, except that in a dry season some valuable hay sloughs would be available. I inspected the monuments surrounding the lakes and replaced a number of iron posts that were missing.

My next work was on the correction line between townships 26 and 27, range 15, where I corrected the positions of the monuments. I shipped most of my outfit to Munson by Canadian Pacific and Canadian Northern railways and drove across country lightly loaded. I passed through a flourishing well-settled farming country. Mixed farming is increasing in every district; this method of farming practically guarantees the farmer a fair year, even if his grain suffers some from an early frost. Due to the poor service over the new road from Stettler to Munson I was able to complete my work before my freight arrived.

I reloaded my outfit at Munson and shipped it to Maidstone, Saskatchewan, where I made a retracement and restoration survey of township 45, range 23, west of the third meridian. The surface of this township is hilly, the northeastern portion being rough. Approximately two-thirds of it is settled, and mixed farming is being carried on extensively. The soil is a good loam from four to eight inches deep with a clay subsoil. There are numerous lakes in this township, one of which is salty, but the majority have potable water. Every settler has a good well. I found the majority of the old markings, but due to the hilly nature of the country they were hard to locate without re-running the lines. I found the original work very good, but practically all the posts had to be renewed.

From this work I moved north into township 48, range 22, where I retraced the southerly two-thirds of the township and traversed the lakes. The surface is gently rolling and covered with willow and poplar bush. There are a number of lakes in the township partly surrounded with good hay sloughs. The water in the larger lakes is fresh. The soil is a light brown loam from two to six inches deep with a sandy subsoil and mixed farming is largely carried on. Every settler has a good well, water being available at a depth of twenty to forty feet. A large amount of breaking and fencing has been done and considerable land is under crop.

On the completion of this work I shipped the outfit to Sprucegrove, west of Edmonton, and drove to my next work which was a small correction survey in townships 50 and 51, range 27, west of the fourth meridian. I then returned to Edmonton and dismissed my party on October 5, 1913.

5 GEORGE V., A. 1915

From this date until I closed operations on Februray 9, 1914, I was employed on miscellaneous surveys and the traversing of lakes. The first lakes to be traversed were in townships 51, 52 and 53, range 2, west of the fifth meridian. The work progressed somewhat slowly at first due to the scarcity of help and the lack of ice on the lakes, but as soon as the ice would carry us we made good progress. We also had a few days' work in township 55, range 2.

My next work was to survey the townsite of Nordegg at the Brazeau coal mines in township 40, range 15. I lost considerable time in reaching the work due to the unreliable transportation facilities but the railway has reached the mines and regular mixed trains are running now. This country is being rapidly opened up. A number of settlers are locating south and southeast of the Rocky Mountain House district, and a few have homesteaded west of this point along the right of way. The Brazeau Mines company are counting on spending large sums of money in developing their properties and building a model town to be known as Nordegg. The company employs at present approximately one hundred and fifty men and will greatly increase this number as soon as they start to ship their coal. In December, there were thirty-four thousand tons of coal on the dumps ready for shipping. The company has selected an ideal townsite surrounded by magnificent mountain scenery.

Upon my return from the Brazeau coal fields I left by way of Athabaska for Heart lake, situated northeast of lac LaBiche, in township 69, range 10, west of the fourth meridian. There is a great rush for homesteads in lac LaBiche district due to the construction of the Alberta Great Waterways railway to McMurray. A great deal of this country is very suitable for cattle raising and mixed farming. A great number of settlers have already got their title for their farms, but development has been retarded due to the long distance from a railway or a market. A fine class of mixed farming country extends from lac LaBiche, in townships 67 and 68, ranges 13 and 14, south to within twenty miles of the Canadian Northern railway. My next work was in the Cold lake district. There one sees a large number of up-to-date houses and farms. The only drawback is the great haul to a railway or a market. Every settler I met expressed the greatest confidence in the country. The farmers are for the most part going in for mixed farming. This winter has been exceptionally fine and warm, so that farmers were able to keep their stock out for most of the winter. In some locali- . ties they did not commence to feed hay until the end of January.

APPENDIX No. 24.

ABSTRACT OF THE REPORT OF W. J. DEANS, D.L.S.

MISCELLANEOUS SURVEYS AND INSPECTION OF SURVEY CONTRACTS IN MANITOBA AND EASTERN SASKATCHEWAN.

On June 2, 1913, I left Winnipeg with my party for Point du Bois via Lac du Bonnet, arriving at the latter place the same evening. I was delayed there two days on account of a breakdown on the tram line running to Point du Bois, so that I did not arrive at my work until the 5th.

The city of Winnipeg has a hydro-electric power plant located at Point du Bois falls on Winnipeg river, and has applied for certain lands above the falls for flooding purposes.

It has been agreed between the engineers of the city of Winnipeg and the department that an elevation of 212 feet above Winnipeg city datum would be required.

In order to deal with the application of the city it was necessary to measure the area in each quarter-section which would be flooded by the dam. To determine these areas the 212-foot contour had to be located on the side of the river and on the islands in the river.

This work was started by the late William Ogilvie, D.L.S., but owing to his death it was not completed.

My first camp was located about four miles above the power station on the south side of the river, and from this point I was enabled to traverse some ten miles of the contour. There are a number of bench marks along the river from which I obtained the height of the water. I then set a water gauge and noted any change in the level; from the water level I obtained the position of the contour.

The land surrounding that portion of the flooded area which I surveyed is mostly rocky, with patches of soil in places, and is covered with a thick growth of jackpine, balsam, hemlock and poplar, varying in diameter from two to ten inches. In many places the windfall was high and the underbrush thick, and as we had to cut lines through this, our progress on some days was very discouraging. The land is of no use for farming purposes, and as the timber is too small and too scattered for lumbering, it could be utilized only for fuel. The waters of Winnipeg river teem with fish and the forests abound with large and small game. There is a saw-mill located at Point du Bois which affords employment to a considerable number of men. The logs are obtained from a point down the river and are brought to the mill in booms. The lumber is shipped to outside points, first over the tram lines owned by the city of Winnipeg to Lac du Bonnet and thence by the Canadian Pacific railway.

The Hydro-electric power plant at Point du Bois is quite extensive, and has been instrumental in reducing the cost of electric lighting to the citizens of Winnipeg and furnishing them with cheap power for manufacturing purposes. Notwithstanding this, it pays at the present time, and, when fully developed will be a money-making proposition for the city of Winnipeg, and will make the city a great industrial centre.

On July 26 I finished the traverse of the 212-foot contour, and on the 28th moved my outfit down to the tram lines, loaded it on and, with my party, went to Lac du Bonnet. The next day I started for Tisdale by way of Winnipeg, stopping on the way at Portage la Prairie to pick up my horses and wagons which had been left near this place. After loading the horses and outfit I proceeded to Tisdale, arriving there on July 31. I was delayed there until August 5 awaiting the arrival of my outfit by freight.

5 GEORGE V., A. 1915

On the following day I started for township 48, range 10, west of the second meridian, and got as far as Arborfield, where I was delayed by heavy rains. On the 9th I received a telegram instructing me to re-inspect contract No. 7, of 1911. As the telegram stated that it was imperative that this work should be done at once, I immediately returned to Tisdale and loaded my outfit on the train for Bannock, arriving at that place on the 19th. From Bannock I recut an old pack trail to section 33, township 45, range 9, west of the second meridian, and moved part of my outfit there. The land in that vicinity is well adapted for mixed farming. The soil is a black loam, with clay subsoil, and is covered with small poplar, willow and some scattered tamarack. There are numerous open patches of high land, an abundance of hay in the meadows, and good water in the numerous small lakes. The Prince Albert branch of the Canadian Northern railway runs through township 45, affording good transportation facilities. At Bannock and Mistatim stations saw-mills are located which would provide a market for any produce raised in the locality and which furnish employment for the settlers when not engaged on the land.

On September 16, I moved the outfit by train from Bannock water tank to Tisdale, on my way to township 48, range 10, and on the 18th reached Burntout creek, where I was compelled to stay for nearly a week on account of heavy rains which rendered travelling over the trail almost impossible. On September 27 I started for township 48, and after a hard day's travel through mud up to the axle, we arrived late at night within a few miles of where I intended to start work. The next day I moved to section 7, township 48, range 10, and on the following day started to subdivide the northerly two-thirds of this township, which I completed on October 23. There are quite a number of settlers in this township, attracted there by the numerous inducements offered in the way of good soil, plenty of hay for cattle raising, and sufficient timber for building purposes and fuel. Small game is very plentiful and also large game such as moose, elk and bears. Small fruits, such as raspberries, currants and cranberries grow in profusion. The greatest drawback to the settler is the lack of good trails or road. At the present time travelling out for provisions and supplies is attended with a good deal of hardship and inconvenience.

On October 25 I arrived at Tisdale, and on the 27th shipped my outfit to Regina on my way to Buttress. It was necessary for me to wait in Regina until the car arrived, so that I could get it transferred to the Canadian Pacific railway and billed to destination.

I arrived at Buttress with party and outfit on November 1.

My work in that locality was to make a restoration and retracement survey, which I finished on November 8, and on the 11th moved to Johnston lake, in township 14, range 29, where I was to make a correction survey. The land in this township is nearly all settled, but as yet the amount cultivated is very small. I did not see any graded roads in the township, but the trails are good. The nearest and most available railway station is Caron, on the Canadian Pacific railway.

On November 17 I loaded my horses and outfit on a car at Buttress and shipped them to Boissevain by way of Brandon. The outfit and party arrived at Boissevain on November 19, and I at once started for Max lake, situated in township 1, range 20, west of the principal meridian.

My work in this township was to lay out a number of lots along the northerly shore of Max lake in the Turtle Mountain Forest reserve. This lake is situated in the heart of the mountains at an elevation of about 2,400 feet above sea-level, and is two miles long and about the same in width. The shores are mostly sandy or gravelly. In some places the water is shallow, while in other places it is quite deep, so that bathers can choose the water which is deep and cold or that which is warm and shallow. The waters of the lake abound with jackfish, muskallonge, trout and black bass, which are of a very superior quality and flavour. This lake is fast becoming a well-patronized summer resort, and, when better known, will undoubtedly 'become one of the most popular resorts in Manitoba. The lake may be easily reached from Boissevain by automobile or carriage, being sixteen miles distant from that place. I laid out twenty-nine lots, a small parcel for a picnic ground, and a road. These lots are leased at a yearly rental, subject to a building regulation. I completed the work there on November 29, and on December 1 I loaded my outfit and horses on the train and shipped the same to Fishtown siding, arriving there on the 3rd.

My work was to inspect contract No. 23 of 1913. I recut ten miles of trail, moved to the contract on December 6, and finished the inspection of the same on the 12th. We were in that locality during the big game hunting season, but the hunters did not get as far east as we were, preferring to remain within easy distance of the railway track. The moose were very plentiful, and a good many were shot.

There is some good agricultural land in spots throughout this contract. Township 41, range 25, west of the principal meridian, is mostly level, with ridges of poplar and occasional clumps of tamarack and spruce large enough for lumber. The soil is a black loam, with clay subsoil, and there are many meadows which would produce hay for a large number of cattle. The water is good throughout the township.

Township 41, range 24, is much the same as the last described township, with the exception that the hay marshes are more extensive.

Townships 39 and 40, range 24, contain some good agricultural lands, but are better adapted for cattle raising, as there are many extensive hay marshes throughout these townships. Swan lake occupies a portion of the northeast part of township 40, Birch river, Wood river, and Swan river all flow north and east through this township and empty into Swan lake. These streams all have good banks at a sufficient height above the water to afford a means of drainage for the low lands and swamps.

On December 16, I took the train at Fishtown siding for Swan river, where I paid the party off, and after storing the outfit and making a contract for wintering the horses, I started for Brandon, arriving there on December 22.

The season throughout was favourable for field operations. We had a long spell of warm weather which lasted on into December.

On January 5, 1914, I received your telegram asking me to go to Moosejaw, and settle up the survey affairs of the late Mr. C. E. Johnston, D.L.S. I started that evening, and on the 6th was at work on the accounts. I paid off the men, and made a contract for wintering the horses and storing the outfit. Mr. A. D. Stewart, assistant, took all papers and books to Ottawa.

I arrived back in Brandon on January 14.

5 GEORGE V., A. 1915

APPENDIX No. 25.

ABSTRACT OF THE REPORT OF S. L. EVANS D.L.S.

SURVEYS IN SOUTHERN ALBERTA.

After outfitting at High River I left on May 23, 1913, for township 17, range 3, west of the fifth meridian where my first survey was located.

Work in this township was started on May 26 and was completed by June 7, The surface of the township is open hilly prairie and is rather too rough for agricultural purposes, although in the northern part there are a few quarter-sections that might be worked. The soil consists of a black loam with clay subsoil. Ranching is already carried on in a profitable manner and seems to be the most suitable occupation for the district, not only owing to the roughness of the township, but also to the high altitude. Summer frosts are usual in this district.

My next work was the completion of the subdivision of the parts of townships 16, 17, 18, 19 and 20, range 4, west of the fifth meridian which lie outside the Rocky Mountains Forest reserve. Townships 16 and 17 which were completed by July 24 are very rough and hilly and are covered for the most part with burnt poplar and spruce. A fire in 1910 completely burned over this district leaving very little green timber. These townships lie very close to the Highwood range of the Rocky mountains and farming, especially grain growing, is not feasible. The hills and valleys are covered with a good growth of grass and afford splendid opportunities for ranching which, at the present time, is carried on very successfully; horses and cattle can range the year round. Highwood river crosses township 17. This stream has a very swift current and no doubt in the future, when the district is settled, will offer opportunities for the development of water-power.

Townships 18, 19 and 20, range 4, were next subdivided. This work was completed by the end of September. Ranching is carried on successfully in these townships, but the country is too rough and hilly and at too high an altitude for grain growing. This district has been the centre of an oil rush during the past season. Oil has been found in the "Black Diamond" well at "Black Diamond" in township 20, range 2. From the opinion of geologists it would appear that the strata in which the oil at "Black Diamond" has been found dips upwards and runs in a northwesterly direction. That would put these townships close to the oil deposits. Prospectors have been busily engaged all summer looking for likely locations in this district.

While engaged in the subdivision of township 19, range 4, I moved camp to township 19, range 7, and ran the north half of the east boundary of section 14. A good pack trail runs up the south fork of Sheep river to Burns' coal claims in this township. A railroad is now being located into this district and it is expected that the coal mines will be opened in the near future.

After the completion of townships 19 and 20, range 4, I moved camp to township 23, range 5, and completed the subdivision of the township. Much of the land in this township is swamp, but the settlers along Bragg creek are ranching successfully. No grain has yet been ripened in the district, as summer frosts are frequent, due no doubt to the closeness of the mountains and the high altitude. This work was finished on October 21, after which I took the party to High River where the men were paid off on the 27th.

From October 27 I was engaged on miscellaneous surveys. A proposed summer resort on Madge lake in township 30, range 30, west of the principal meridian, was surveyed and a topographical survey of the area made. This was finished on November 26.

My next work was a topographical survey of a proposed summer resort in township 19, range 19, west of the principal meridian. This was completed on December 12.

I next proceeded to township 26, range 30, west of the principal meridian where a traverse of Assiniboine river was made across this township. This was finished on December 31 and after storing the outfit I left for home arriving there on January 8, 1914.

APPENDIX No. 26.

ABSTRACT OF THE REPORT OF J. A. FLETCHER, D.L.S.

BLOCK OUTLINE SURVEYS IN THE PEACE RIVER VALLEY.

My work during the past season consisted of the survey of the west boundary of range 17, west of the fifth meridian from the twenty-third to the twenty-eighth base lines.

I left Edmonton where my party was organized, on March 3, 1913, and proceeded by way of the winter trail across Lesser Slave lake and through Grouard to Peace River Crossing. From Peace River Crossing we followed Peace river down to Cadotte river. This stream was passable for sleighs as far as the junction of the north and south branches, a distance of about four miles from its mouth. The packhorses were used as much as possible to freight in the outfit, but they were too light for teaming and I considered it advisable not to overtax their strength in view of the expected shortage of feed in April and May. The services of three freighters were therefore secured to supplement the work of the packhorses. One team weighing about 2,700 lbs. was taken from Edmonton through to Cadotte river and their weight was very effective in breaking trail on Peace river. Another team was hired from Athabaska to Grouard. The third took a load of supplies from Peace River Crossing to Cadotte river. From there on, considerable difficulty was experienced in securing sufficient feed for the horses, so they were spared as much as possible. Deep snow rendered foraging difficult and frozen grass-at best has little nourishment. The outfit was packed up the north bank of Cadotte river and freighted across country on sleighs to the vicinity of our work. Owing to the deep snow and the extensive windfall and timber in this district trail cutting entailed considerable labour, and freighting was tedious and laborious.

Work was commenced on the line on April 8 and, shortly afterwards the snow disappeared, several warm days from the 10th-13th, leaving only a few patches of snow in the shaded localities. The remainder of the month was fine, and the horses were able to get the dry feed with very little difficulty. Sufficient oats were taken along to last, with careful distribution, till the first grass began to appear, toward the end of May, but before it became plentiful in June, the horses failed considerably and not until well on in July, after a month's feed on the splendid meadows northeast of Carcajou, did they regain what they lost during the spring work. However, the convenience with which we got in as far as Cadotte river and the early commencement of the survey in April well repaid the trouble experienced with the horses in April and May. The work proceeded without interruption till September 26, when the survey was completed.

The fall of 1912 had been quite dry and forest fires had started in several localities. West of Peace River Crossing these fires did considerable damage, burning up large quantities of hay. This caused a scarcity of hay in the succeeding winter and spring around Peace River Crossing, prices rising as high as $50 and $60 a ton. What was used was brought largely from Grouard where the price was $25 a ton. When the snow disappeared in the spring the water went off very quickly, surface water bothering very little. The dry weather which followed caused the fires, which had smouldered in some patches of moss in several localities throughout the winter, to break out afresh in the latter half of May and the first half of June. They were burning in several directions. One of our coaches was barely saved, but in saving it two horses were cut off by the fire and subsequent search did not locate them. Trouble was experienced with

SESSIONAL PAPER No. 25b

smoke and also with fires about June 5, but shortly after this, between the 10th and 20th, and at intervals thereafter rain fell very opportunely anad checked them. At Fort Vermilion the crops and the gardens received the rain to mature before the frosts in the fall.

The extensive rains which fell between Peace River Crossing, Grouard and Wabiskaw in 1913 were not experienced farther north, where the rainfall was sufficient but not excessive. The growth of all vegetation was very rapid in June and July. The month of August was very pleasant. Light frosts were experienced for three nights, the 15th, 16th and 17th, but they were not heavy enough to damage the wheat at Fort Vermilion; after that date the temperature was steadily above freezing point for most of September, which was a rather wet month. The rains though not heavy, fell often enough to interfere materially with the curing and stacking of hay.

The Hudson's Bay Co. arranged to take the party out, promising to leave Vermilion on October 1 for Peace River Crossing, but owing to indifference on the part of some of the officials, their steamer, the *Peace River,* was unable to pick up the party until the 12th, causing an unnecessary and tedious delay of ten days. The trip was made from the twenty-seventh base, up to Peace River Crossing in six days. The two boats plying on Peace river, are both stern wheelers and burn cordwood. The steamer *Grenfell,* operated by the Peace River Trading and Land Co., was running from Fort Vermilion to Fort St. John on a twenty-one day schedule but was incapacitated in the fall owing to an accident to the boilers.

The party crossed the portage to Grouard, two teams being hired, each taking about 1,000 pounds. This trail was in a very bad condition. Owing to the wet summer experienced here, the trail in places was flooded a great part of the summer. In some places it is clay and is graded to a rather flat crown no special attention has been paid to drainage. The road bed thus becomes soaked with rain and once started, soft holes quickly work bigger. The road has been partially corduroyed, but after the heavy traffic of the last few years this corduroy is largely worn out and worn out corduroy is worse than none. In the fall of 1913, this trail for some considerable distances, was well nigh impassable, being a succession of broken patches of corduroy and bog holes. Numerous settlers came to grief, attempting to go in with their effects and supplies. The trail in the winter is very good, sufficient snow falling and enough traffic passing over it, to keep it well broken for the entire distance. March is an excellent month for travel on this trail.

The Northern Transportation company's boat was used across Lesser Slave lake, the boat going down Lesser Slave river as far as Soto landing. Teams were taken across the portage to Mirror landing, a distance of sixteen miles. Several hard frosts occurred in the latter part of October and on reaching Mirror landing, the Athabaska was found to be running full of drift ice. A gasoline boat operated by Mr. Patterson was used in Athabaska. The water was quite shallow and the presence of so much running ice in the river rendered navigation difficult. However, the boat was solidly made and bumped over the rocks without serious injury. It was driven by side paddle wheels and these wheels lost most of the paddles on the trip down, one wheel being entirely destroyed and only half the paddles being left on the other. The party reached Edmonton on November 3 and was paid off.

Townships 89, 90 and 91 in the vicinity of our line are drained to the southwest and west, largely by Cadotte river which flows into Peace river. Nearing the Peace, its current is swift, and as the bed is full of stones, it forms almost a continuous rapid. The valley itself is from a mile to two miles wide and the banks are quite steep. Little Cadotte river which empties into the Cadotte is about a chain wide and in the upper stretches the current is somewhat sluggish, meandering considerably in a more or less direct valley. Numerous beaver workings, some hay meadows, and some good spruce characterize this valley. Fire has passed through this country in recent years and large areas are covered with windfall. Throughout this region, spruce and poplar up to eighteen inches in diameter, alternate with smaller spruce and tamarack in the

5 GEORGE V., A. 1915

swamps and muskegs. Probably forty per cent of this district is muskeg, but as Peace river is approached the muskegs become less numerous and extensive. Some hay is to be found along the creeks, especially around the old beaver dams. The height of land between the drainage basin of Cadotte river and Cache creek to the north is passed in townships 91 and 92. Several lakes and some sloughs were passed there and creeks thread the most of the country. After draining and clearing, this district would be suitable for agriculture.

Townships 92, 93 and 94 are somewhat freer from muskeg, although stretches of swamp are to be found. The drainage in these townships is largely to the north and parallel to Peace river. The basin of Cache creek is good loam. In townships 95, 96, 97 and 98 between Cache creek and Peace river a large area of light soil with ridges of jackpine and brulé, interspersed with sloughs is to be found, but it is generally too light for good agricultural land. East of Cache creek in the same townships some very good land was seen, and also some rich land bordering Wolverine river. In townships 100 and 101, there is some good merchantable spruce up to thirty inches in diameter near Wolverine and Buffalo rivers. In range 16, there is some open land with rich vegetation and a few meadows. Townships 102,103 and 104 are quite lightly wooded, and could be easily settled. Hay meadows are numerous and extensive.

The survey line passed about six miles from the Buffalo Head hills, where the country is rough and broken. After crossing Peace river in township 105, an area of light soil, jackpine ridges and interlying swampy meadows with numerous sloughs and lakes extends northward for seventeen or eighteen miles. This area extends in a north-easterly and southwesterly direction being bordered roughly by the trail from Keg river to Fort Vermilion. This trail is a wagon road as far as range 18 and west of there it is a good pack trail. The branches of Boyer river have numerous beaver dams. In August there was practically no current in either of the branches northwest of the Keg river trail. The country drained by these branches is good agricultural and grazing land. Hay meadows are numerous and the country is practically free of muskeg.

During the season, several moose and bears, both brown and black, were seen. Foxes and wolves were observed several times in the vicinity of the twenty-seventh base and beaver and muskrat workings were seen in many places. Fur-bearing animals are sufficiently numerous in this country to make fur trapping so attractive that several members of my survey party returned to the lower Peace river to trap during the winter.

In township 105, just north of the twenty-seventh base line some fossilized remnants of trees were found. Shale outcroppings were also noticed at the edge of Peace river in this district.

APPENDIX No. 27.

ABSTRACT OF THE REPORT OF L. E. FONTAINE, D.L.S.

MISCELLANEOUS SURVEYS AND INSPECTION OF CONTRACTS IN THE PEACE RIVER DISTRICT,
ALBERTA.

I left home on May 20 for Edmonton, Alberta, where I outfitted and organized my party. On June 11, I left for Spirit River settlement, travelling by the Canadian Northern railway to Athabaska, thence by the Northern Transportation Co.'s steamer to Grouard, at the west end of Lesser Slave lake, and from there on by means of my own transport to our destination, which we reached on July 8.

As a number of squatters had located on the unsurveyed part of township 78, range 6 west of the sixth meridian, subdivision in this township was urgently required. While running the necessary outlines, I noticed that the south third of township 79 range 6 was also well suited for settlement, I therefore, decided to subdivide it. I completed the surveys in these townships on September 15.

The next surveys undertaken consisted of the examination of partially dry lake beds in townships 71 and 72, ranges 5 and 6, together with the surveys of four islands along the course of Wapiti river in township 70, range 7.

On the completion of these surveys I was advised that survey contracts in the district were ready for inspection. I therefore inspected contracts Nos. 3, 1 and 2 of 1913, in the order mentioned, and then returned to Peace River Crossing where I arrived on December 9.

While in that vicinity I ran that part of the east outline of township 83, range 22, west of the fifth meridian, not already run and completed the subdivision of township 84, range 21. I suspended operations on January 7, 1914 and left for Edmonton where I arrived on the 17th.

The district through which I worked appears to have a great future in store for it. Great changes have taken place during the past twelve months and if railway construction progresses as rapidly as expected this part of the country will soon have the benefit of railway facilities which should greatly assist in its future development, and afford innumerable openings for private enterprise.

5 GEORGE V., A. 1915

APPENDIX No. 28.

ABSTRACT OF THE REPORT OF J. S. GALLETLY, D.L.S.

SURVEYS IN THE FORT VERMILION DISTRICT.

The greater part of my work, during the summers of 1912 and 1913 and the intervening winter, consisted of the subdivision of townships in the Peace river valley in the vicinity of Fort Vermilion.

On February 12, 1912 I arrived in Edmonton where I organized my party.

Supplies sufficient for eighteen months were ordered, the major part being shipped direct to North Vermilion. Some difficulty was experienced in getting men to hire for the length of time desired. This may have been partly due to the fact that there were several other parties organizing at the same time, and that I could offer only the same rate of wages as those who were going out for one season. Finally, however enough men were found willing to engage for two years' work and we were able to make a start on the afternoon of February 28.

My assistant, Mr. J. H. Patterson was in charge of the party till they reached Athabaska. In the meantime I settled my affairs in Edmonton and then proceeded to Athabaska arriving there before the outfit and in sufficient time to arrange accommodation for it. I engaged freighters there to take us to Peace River Crossing. Mirror Landing was reached on the 7th. and Sawridge two days later. At the latter place we pitched camp and made a survey of Dog Island in Lesser Slave lake opposite the entrance to Lesser Slave river.

This survey with its connection to the township in which it lies occupied about two days, and we were able to proceed on our way on the morning of the 13th. The trails were good and we had but little difficulty in reaching Peace River Crossing, where we arrived on the night of March 19.

Next day we commenced work, retracing part of the survey of the Peace River Landing settlement. The following afternoon I went to examine the north boundary of section 19, township 83, range 21, to see if conditions on the ground were such that a road could be opened up, by producing this line through lot 41, of the addition to Shaftesbury settlement. Such a road would run over the high bank of Peace river. As it was with difficulty that my assistant and I walked up this hill at the point where the line would cross, I concluded that I would not be justified in putting this line through.

Navigation on Peace river usually opens about the beginning of May, so that I had at least five weks in which to work in this vicinity before I could proceed to Fort Vermilion. With this in view I laid out the work in what seemed to be the most advantageous manner.

While the packers went to Spirit River settlement for the remainder of our transport outfit, I employed the rest of the party in running the north boundary of township 83, range 21. On the return of the packers we moved north to run the east boundary of township 84, range 21.

In the meantime I was trying to arrange for some means of transport to take us to Fort Vermilion. I was strongly advised against rafting and there was only one scow in the vicinity. The price asked for this was $400.00 which I considered unreasonable; moreover it was not large enough to take all the outfit. After some delay I obtained the use of two scows which were brought from Fort Vermilion by the steamer, but they

SESSIONAL PAPER No. 25b

did not arrive until late in May and it was June 1 before we could start on our journey north. Before leaving Peace River Crossing we completed the south third and all the portion west of Peace river in township 84, and the north third of township 83, range 21, together with a school site and a site for the Church of England mission. I would have preferred to have made the last two rectangular in shape but conditions on the ground were such that to have done so would have been to defeat, to a great extent, the purpose for which they were intended.

We were fortunate in our passage to Fort Vermilion, as we took only three days and a half to make the journey of 300 miles. We travelled continuously day and night, with the exception of two stops of about six hours each, one when we tied up the first night and the other when a strong head wind drove us into the bank and compelled us to stay there till it subsided.

We arrived at North Vermilion on the morning of June 5, and after we had unloaded and stored our supplies in a warehouse lent us by Messrs. Revillon Freres. I returned the scows to the Hudson's Bay Co. across the river. Next day we moved into township 109, range 13, to commence subdivision.

My next step was to endeavour to locate the different settlers who were occupying unsurveyed lands in this district. The settlers themselves lent no aid in this matter: they were at first not only indifferent, but in some cases actually tried to avoid the survey altogether. It was not until late in the summer that I acquired a fair knowledge of their approximate positions. As I found that they were stretched over a range of territory from township 107, range 15, to township 109, range 11, and nearly all close to Peace river, I thought it best to leave this part of the work till the river was low.

We continued the subdivision in townships 109, ranges 14, 15 and 16, as we found a good stretch of country just north of the south branch of Boyer river, and as part of the first and last of these townships was desired for Indian reserves. By the beginning of October our surveys had reached Prairie point, in township 107, range 15, and from there we gradually worked our way along Peace river as far as township 109, range 11, surveying all the lands actually occupied. It was not till July of the following year that this work was completed.

In March, 1913, I sent a small party, in charge of my assistant, to traverse Boyer river, and in June I took another small outfit and went back to do the mounding we had left during the winter months.

Our horses were wintered at North Vermilion, as this was the most central point, and it was also the base of our supplies. Stable accommodation was scarce and therefore expensive, so that when Revillon Freres offered to provide the land and the logs for a stable and give us the use of the building on condition that we would provide the floor and roof and perform the labour, I accepted the offer. The season of 1912 was poor, and I had considerable trouble getting the amount of hay necessary to put the horses through the winter.

In July, 1913, we left Fort Vermilion to go to the post at the junction of Mikkwa (formerly Red) and Peace rivers, in order to survey some land in that vicinity which were desired for an Indian reserve. While passing the Vermilion chutes, I was met by a settler there who asked to be included in the survey. In order to do this I had to omit part of the work on the reserve at Fox lake.

We arrived back at the Vermilion chutes at the beginning of September and surveyed here a sufficient area to include one settler, though we were unable to include his partner, due to the latter's absence at the time of the survey.

During that month I received information that a guide whom I had engaged to take me overland to Trout lakes, was sick and would be unable to accompany me: I therefore had to arrange to have my party taken out by steamer over the usual route.

With the expectation that a steamer would be leaving Fort Vermilion for Peace River Crossing on September 27, we left the chutes on the 20th for Fort Vermilion,

5 GEORGE V., A. 1915

and arrived there on the 26th. Our information was incorrect, and after waiting in vain for a steamer we left Fort Vermilion in company with J. R. Akins, D.L.S., and his party on October 4. The steamer passed us on the 6th on its way to Fort Vermilion, and picked us up on its way back on the 12th, permitting us to reach Peace River Crossing on the 17th. We had difficulty in obtaining teams to take us to Grouard, but we managed to leave on the 19th. The trail was in bad shape, and it took up seven days to make the trip of ninety miles. We left Grouard on the 28th, and after considerable trouble reached Edmonton on November 3.

Most of the country surveyed at Peace River Crossing was very rough, and would be suitable only for grazing or mixed farming. The surface is covered usually with poplar varying in size from scrub to about twelve inches in diameter, with willow underbrush and occasional spruce. The soil, which is second-class, usually consists of about four inches of black loam overlying a stiff blue clay. On the west bank of Peace river, just north of Peace River Crossing, there is an extensive outcrop of sandstone of reddish colour which is suitable for building material.

At Fort Vermilion, most of the country is covered with a growth of poplar varying in size from scrub to about fifteen inches in diameter, with willow and spruce, the latter reaching a maximum of about twenty-four inches. Some open patches occur in every township surveyed, but with the exception of townships 109, ranges 11, 14, 15 and 16 they are almost entirely taken up by the present settlers. The greater part of the settlement is in townships 108, ranges 13 and 14 and many farms can be seen there which would do credit to a community much nearer railway communication.

The country is generally level, the only hills being on the banks of Peace and Boyer rivers, where they are seldom more than fifty feet high. With the exception of township 109, range 11, there is a good wagon road leading into each township from one of the settlements.

The soil which is a light sandy loam except on a few river flats where the black loam is found to a considerable depth, is usually about four inches deep overlying a sandy clay mixutre. It is especially a wheat-growing soil, and it has in some instances yielded large returns. There is a slight amount of alkali all over the district, but in the majority of cases, it does not seem to produce evil effects.

It has usually been assumed that wheat can be grown successfully there every season, but this is open to doubt. The crop for 1912 amounted to about 500 bushels, an average of less than one bushel for each acre sown. This was due mainly to lack of rain, but a severe frost in July did not improve matters any. Mr. R. Jones, who is in charge of the experimental farm at Fort Vermilion, states that wheat can be successfully raised every season and that lack of methods suitable to the needs of the district is the cause of most failures. Those in charge of the Roman Catholic mission, however, state that a crop is sure only once in five years, and the evidence would indicate that this is more nearly correct.

On account of the recent failures of the wheat crop, the flour mill of the Hudson's Bay company has been temporarily shut down.

Oats seem more difficult to raise than wheat, but barley is probably the surest of the grain crops. Rye has never been tried in this district. Potatoes, turnips, mangolds, carrots, sugar beets, cabbage, cauliflower, and celery do exceedingly well. Tomatoes ripen occasionally. Small fruits such as currants, raspberries, etc., thrive, but strawberries have not been successful. Flowers are among the successes of the district, and many varieties are to be seen blooming in the garden of the experimental station at Fort Vermilion. Timothy and broom grass grow well, but alfalfa is always a failure.

Slough hay or upland hay is difficult to obtain anywhere near the settlements and most of the settlers are drawing their hay from a considerable distance.

Horses, cattle and hogs are plentiful in the district and do exceedingly well. Considerable numbers of the horses rustle all winter, but it is usual to feed the cattle during the extremely cold weather.

Photo by J S Galletly, D L S

Flour Mill at Fort Vermilion.

This flour mill, built and operated by the Hudson's Bay company, is said to be the farthest north flour mill in America if not in the world.

Photo by J. S. Galletly, D L S.

Bringing a Scow up Vermilion Chutes.

These chutes or falls are situated on Peace river about fifty miles east of Fort Vermilion. The total fall is about twenty-four feet, extending over a mile and a half; the falls consist of two rapids and one perpendicular drop, each of about eight or nine feet. Unloaded scows run down the chutes easily, but are seldom brought back, as the expense of taking one up is about as great as making or purchasing a new one.

At the present time these animals may be purchased at a reasonable price, but any sudden demand would cause the price to rise considerably. Chickens are successfully raised in this district, but wolves, coyotes, foxes and dogs are too plentiful at present to permit sheep-raising.

One has to go a considerable distance from the settlement to obtain much game, but we saw signs of mink, marten, weasels, foxes, coyotes and wolves. Black bears and moose were seen on several occasions. Ducks, prairie-chickens, ruffed grouse and ptarmigan were the only feathered game seen.

No coal of any kind was seen but wood is everywhere plentiful for fuel though in some of the most settled parts of the community is has to be hauled a considerable distance.

No minerals of economic value were found, but there is a deposit of clay suitable for making brick, which has been used for that purpose within the limits of the settlement survey at Fort Vermilion.

The summers are comparatively cool and of late years have been remarkably dry, too dry in fact to permit successful crop raising. The temperature does not often exceed 75 degrees F. in the shade. The shortness of the season is compensated for by the long daylight which in the middle of the summer lasts about twenty-two hours.

Seeding commences about the first of May, and haying commences about the middle of July. By the end of September the weather turns decidely cold and winter may be said to start with the beginning of October. Until Christmas the weather is not often excessively cold, though one may expect to see the thermometer register 40 degrees below zero occasionally. January and February are excessively cold, and temperatures from 30° to 70° below are prevalent during these months. In March the temperature rises, but owing to the high winds which prevail we found this the most trying period of the winter. By the end of April the snow is usually all gone even in the bush.

The average depth of snow during last winter in sheltered spots and in the bush was about eighteen inches, but on Peace river and on some of the open places the snow drifted to a considerable depth.

Mosquitos, black flies, and bull-dog flies are numerous in summer especially in swampy parts of the country.

The country surveyed near Mikkwa (formerly Red) river is poor. In the vicinity of Fox lake immense quantities of hay could be cut and this township would be best suited for ranching. The remaining country surveyed in the vicinity of Mikkwa river is largely flooded, the creeks having been dammed by beaver.

There are immense deposits of limestone at the Vermilion Chutes in township 108, range 6.

Peace river which flows through a large part of the country in which we worked varies in width from half a mile to about two miles, and its depth in places will reach fifty feet. It is open for navigation from about May 15 to October 15. Above Vermilion chutes the current is about three miles an hour, between the rapids and the chutes it is about six miles an hour and below the chutes about two miles an hour. Immense quantities of power can be developed at the chutes. Boyer river which empties into the Peace in township 109, range 12, will average about a chain wide and its depth will vary from a few inches to ten feet. Fish are scarce in these rivers, but can be obtained in large quantities from the lakes in the Caribou mountains about sixty miles from Fort Vermilion.

The Roman Catholic mission at Fort Vermilion in addition to the regular church work, conducts a boarding school for the children in the neighbourhood and there is a small hospital ward in their school building. The Church of England mission conducts two schools, one at Fort Vermilion and one at Stony point, seven miles from Fort Vermilion.

The Hudson's Bay company have a modern grist mill, and also a small saw-mill at Fort Vermilion.

5 GEORGE V., A. 1915

Mr. Sheridan Lawrence also has a small sawmill and grist mill, and rough lumber may be purchased at $20 per thousand feet b.m. The Roman Catholic mission has small mills but these have not been in operation-for some time.

The best route for a settler to take to Fort Vermilion is via Peace River Crossing. From Athabaska the usual route is followed along Athabaska river to Mirror Landing, then up Lesser Slave river to Sawridge, across Lesser Slave lake to Grouard, then overland to Peace River Crossing. From this point Peace river is followed to Fort Vermilion. A settler with an outfit will find it to his advantage to make the trip to Peace River Crossing in winter. He should arrive there not later than March 20, in order to take advantage of the roads when at their best, and also to get a raft assembled and ready to be put in the water when the ice goes out. It is the custom of the trading companies to send loaded scows from Peace River Crossing to Fort Vermilion on the first open water, and a settler with his raft and outfit ready could follow in their wake thus saving the expense of a guide. Rafting on this river is not to be recommended for a very large outfit. In such a case it would be advisable to ship by the steamers which ply on the river, or to obtain the use of scows if possible. The distance from Peace River Crossing to Fort Vermilion by river is 300 miles, and it usually takes six days on a scow or two days on the steamer to make the trip.

The Provincial Government has voted a sum of money to be spent on cutting a winter trail from Fort Vermilion to Trout lakes where it will connect with the winter trail from there to Athabaska, but this route is not yet open.

APPENDIX No. 29.

ABSTRACT OF THE REPORT OF G. H. HERRIOT, D.L.S

BASE LINE SURVEYS IN NORTHERN MANITOBA.

My work during the past season consisted of the survey of parts of the eighteenth and nineteenth base lines west of the principal meridian.

I left Edmonton on February 20, 1913, for the purpose of taking in supplies to a point near the eighteenth base line. These supplies were purchased in Winnipeg and shipped over the Canadian Northern railway to Pas. I left Winnipeg for Pas on the 28th, arriving there the following day. I at once arranged with McMillan Bros., contractors on the Hudson Bay railway, to have my supplies freighted out along the right of way to a suitable point, where I proposed to cache them. It was, however, not until March 10 that three teams finally left Pas with my freight. The intervening time was spent in securing, from Hudson Bay railway engineers, prospectors, trappers and guides familiar with the country near Setting lake, all the available information covering this district, and preparing therefrom such sketch maps as were deemed useful. The Northwest Mounted Police also furnished me with a record showing the earliest dates at which dog travel was possible in this region, for a period of several years prior to 1913.

Just here it may be pointed out that wherever a surveyor is dependent on the waterways of a country for his transportation any time spent in securing maps and information covering the area is well spent. It may save many long, round-about trips and much advance exploration on the part of the canoe men. The maps covering Northern Manitoba are in places very incomplete and very inaccurate and any additions, that can be made to them through the knowledge of those who have travelled new routes and waterways are to be strongly advised. It might also be suggested that a surveyor going into this district should familiarize himself with all the available reports covering this district.

On March 18 the freight reached McMillans' cache No. 13 at mileage 141 from Pas. I decided to leave my supplies in their care at this cache for two very important reasons. First, because it was located near where the eigtheenth base line was expected to cross, and on the bank of Goose creek, a small stream navigable for large canoes from this point to the nineteenth base line, and second, because the supplies would be ensured against the danger of loss from thieves and fire, both of which were grave dangers in the vicinity of the right of way.

I went along with my freight in order to make sure that it would get through as far as I desired, and to be certain that such perishable supplies as the dried fruit and meats were properly cared for. In addition I hoped to add to my knowledge of the character of the country by personal observation.

After caching my supplies I returned to Pas, arriving there on March 24 and two days later left for Winnipeg which place I reached on the 27th.

On May 16 I again left my home for Winnipeg in order to organize my party so as to be ready for the departure of the first boat to cross lake Winnipeg.

On May 24, with a party of nineteen men, I left West Selkirk and after a rather exciting trip through large ice floes, we reached Warren's landing on the 26th. The Hudson's Bay company's boat did not arrive until the 28th, when we were permitted to load a small portion of our freight and my party in a York boat, and to tow my canoes behind. In this way we were towed down the Nelson, across Great Playgreen lake, and down the east branch of the Nelson to Norway House. The next two days

5 GEORGE V., A. 1915

were spent in getting the remainder of the freight down to Norway House and storing it, and in trying to hire Indian guides to assist us down the river.

No Indian guides could be secured so we were compelled to find our way down the river to Cross lake the best way we could. My transport consisted of six large canoes and one small one. These carried about a month's supplies together with the surveying outfit and the camp equipment. At Cross lake I was able to engage two Indians as guides and on June 6 we proceeded down the Nelson, reaching the point at which the principal meridian crosses Sipiwesk lake, the following day. On the 9th my Indian guides piloted us up small winding creeks and across a small lake to our first camp, within a quarter of a mile of the northeast corner of township 68, range 1, west of the principal meridian.

This corner falls in a deep creek and is marked by a witness monument eight chains south. On June 10, after first retracing a mile of the meridian, the eighteenth base was turned off as an offset line, nine chains south of its theoretical location. After producing this offset line about half a mile west it was possible to turn north to the true base line. This was first opened back to the meridian and then its production westward was commenced.

The first thirteen miles of the base line entailed man packing, but the canoes were able to loop around from the end of the base line to a small lake, about the middle of range 1, which they entered by way of a small creek from Sipiwesk lake. Again supplies were brought by the canoes to within a mile of the muskeg lake in range 2. From the crossing of the first bay on Sipiwesk lake in range 3, until Bear island was reached in range 4, the canoes were used to shift camp, the next camp being made on Duck lake, which was reached by a mile portage from below Red Rock rapids on the Nelson over the height of land to Duck lake. A 300 yard portage from Duck lake to the Nelson below Duck falls, made it possible to use canoes as transport from this point until our last camp was reached on an island, near the eighteenth base line leaves the upper bay of Sipiwesk lake in range 6. There it was found that further production westward would entail a great deal of man packing and as the nineteenth base line offered excellent canoe routes, I decided to proceed to it immediately.

The following day we started across Sipiwesk lake, and down the Nelson on our way to the nineteenth base. We packed across Cross portage, which is one and a half miles long, put our canoes into a small lake connecting with Landing lake and following westward along the south shore of Landing lake, we reached the point where the principal meridian crosses that lake about noon on August 11.

The northeast corner of township 72, on the principal meridian, falls in Landing lake and is marked by a witness monument four chains south of its true position. On the afternoon of August 11, the nineteenth base was turned off as an offset line three chains south and parallel to its theoretical location, and produced across a bay of Landing lake. For the first ten miles of this base line canoes were used to transport the camp and supplies, the camp being moved frequently to bays of Landing lake in order to keep close to the end of the line. From Landing lake everything had to be carried one and a quarter miles across Thicket portage into Wintering lake, and the next fifteen miles of line were produced from camps located on small creeks flowing northward into Wintering lake. During the survey of the next six miles back-packing being necessary, only enough supplies were carried to last until the line should reach Halfway creek, in range 5. While the line was being opened across this stretch, the four canoemen were engaged taking the canoes and some of the freight around by Wintering lake across two very wet portages, one and a quarter miles in length, into Paint lake and thence up Grass river and Halfway creek to our anticipated crossing. The canoemen had each to handle a large canoe and tow a small canoe. In crossing Wintering lake they encountered a very heavy wind, and the small Peterborough canoe broke its tow line and was swamped, attempts to recover it proving futile. Halfway creek and Grass river were used for moving camp until the last crossing of

SESSIONAL PAPER No. 25b

a bay of Grass river in section 34, range 6, was reached. From this point man packing was again resorted to, although an attempt was made to bring in supplies by Soab creek and Frozen lake.

On October 11, the nineteenth base line had reached a point about thirty-five chains west of the northeast corner of section 35, township 72, range 7. The muskegs in ranges 6 and 7 were very wet, and the snowfall on October 10 so protected these from frost that a delay seemed inevitable. This combined with the rapid approach of winter, made it advisable to close operations on the nineteenth base line and to return to the eighteenth where it had been discontinued on the west side of Sipiwesk lake. It was therefore decided to start back on October 13. The party returned over the first stretch, back-packing the necessary supplies, consisting of the camp equipment and surveying outfit, to a point where the canoes had been left. Four of the party made the trip to Frozen lake about three miles south of the northeast corner of township 72, range 7, where they picked up one of the canoes which had been left at that point, and started to make their way to the mouth of Soab creek. Ice was soon encountered, however, and they were compelled to leave the canoe and pack across to Grass river, where they met the remainder of the party with two large chestnut canoes. From this point on the progress was very difficult, it being necessary in places to drag the canoes over the newly-frozen ice. Finally, however, the canoes had to be left behind and along with them the iron posts, instruments, and part of the camp equipment. The remainder of the outfit, including the men's beds, sleeping tents and enough supplies with which to reach the right of way, had to be back-packed. Several days of very trying travel ensued, caused by the heavy loads and the many wide detours around open lakes or bays. Not infrequently men broke through the ice on the lakes, each of which was a source of danger and delay. However, on October 20, the Hudson Bay railway was reached at a point not far distant from McMillans' cache No. 14. The following day the party arrived at cache No. 13, where an abundant supply of food was stored.

In September while still at work on the nineteenth base line the cook and two Indians left the party thus reducing it to seventeen men. Moreover, the Hudson's Bay company wrote advising me that it was impossible for them to purchase the dogs I had asked for. It was therefore necessary for me to go to Winnipeg in order to purchase my transport outfit for winter work and to hire more men. Accordingly on September 14, I left the party in charge of my assistant and proceeded to Winnipeg, where I engaged five more men and purchased a number of dogs.

On October 3 I left Selkirk with my men and dogs and after many vexing delays arrived at McMillan's camp near Sipiwesk lake, on the 15th. Great difficulty was experienced in getting across Sipiwesk lake owing to the formation of ice in the bays and the calmer water of the lake. By October 20, we were able to get twenty-one dogs and the freight across the lake to a point a short distance west of where the Nelson flows from Duck lake. There we found that the whole western arm of Sipiwesk lake had already frozen, so that we could proceed no farther with the canoes. We therefore endeavoured to return for the remaining ten dogs, but we found that the ice had formed so rapidly in our wake that immediate return was impossible. We accordingly cached the canoes, loaded most of our freight on the toboggans and started westward across the long bay of Sipiwesk lake to where the eighteenth base line leaves it. After a rather perilous passage during which the toboggans broke through occasionally, and frequent portages had to be cut out over different points in order to avoid the weak ice, we managed to reach the west shore by evening. The following day we proceeded due west, with two men cutting trail ahead of the dogs and on the evening of October 22 we reached cache No. 13, where the remainder of the party was awaiting us.

The following day the dog teams went north to pick up the outfit which the main party had been compelled to leave behind. New trails had to be opened so that it was not until four days later that the teams returned. The next day the outfit was moved east to within a mile and a half of what was then the end of the eighteenth base line. Each man had to pack his own dunnage as the transport was unable to handle everything in a single trip. On the 28th the production of the line was begun and the work went steadily forward without delay until January 5, 1914, when the northeast corner of township 68, range 17 was reached.

During this period of the survey, dog transport was used throughout. The supplies were hauled from McMillans' cache No. 13 and the dog feed consisting of fish was hauled from a cache on Setting lake. Six dog trains handled by four dog drivers were used during the first six weeks, and from then till the end of the survey five teams were used. The trips after supplies and feed were so arranged as not to interfere with the regular work of moving camp.

As soon as Setting lake was sufficiently frozen for fishing I started two of my regular men at work fishing for dog feed. The fish were very plentiful and by December 12, working with about a dozen nets, they were able to catch enough fish to supply the dogs till the survey was completed. About 4,200 fish, mostly whitefish, were taken during this period. Although the work of fishing reduced my party by two men, it was by far the cheapest method of securing dog feed. Moreover, it assured good wholesome feed and this kept the dogs in condition to handle the transport. As stated before, the northeast corner of township 68, range 17, was reached on January 5. As the supplies were then practically exhausted, and the limit of economical haul for our transport had been reached, it was decided to close operations. Accordingly on the following day we started for Pas which we reached on the 10th. There the men were paid off, each being allowed his time and fare to Winnipeg.

Taken as a whole the season of 1913 was only an average one for survey work. The months of July, August and September were decidedly wet, daily showers being quite the usual order. The month of October was exceptional as during the early part several snow storms were experienced, the heaviest of the year occurring on the 10th. On the 12th, the smaller lakes and creeks began to freeze up and by the 20th many of the larger lakes and swifter streams were frozen hard enough to be crossed by the dog trains. The heavy snowfall before the freeze-up so protected the swamps and muskegs that these did not freeze solid until near the end of November. The period following this heavy snowfall and until the muskegs became frozen was far from pleasant for work, as the men were constantly breaking through, but from the end of October until the completion of the survey in January the weather conditions were the very best. It is worthy of note that the freeze-up in 1913 was about six days earlier than any previous record for twenty-five years. The country traversed by the nineteenth base line in its production across the first six ranges is fairly uniform in character, except that it is much broken by large lakes, such as Landing, Wintering and Paint lakes. Ranges 1 and 2 are very similar in character. The surface is generally rolling and mostly dry, except along the shore of Landing lake, where it is more broken. The soil is a clay loam suitable for agriculture. The greater part of this area has recently been burned over, the surface soil being badly burned. To the north of the base line the country is broken by Landing lake, a beautiful rock-bordered lake about thirty miles long and from a half to one and a half miles wide, with a few deep bays breaking its otherwise regular contour. This lake is reached from Nelson river by way of Cross portage which is one and a half miles long, and from Wintering lake to the west, by way of Thicket portage, which is one and a quarter miles long. The surplus water of the lake finds its way into the Nelson to the east through Landing river. In section 32, range 2, the west shore of Landing lake is reached and from this point westward the timber is dense and consists of spruce, jackpine, poplar, willow and birch, with tamarack in the low places. Townships 73 and 74 in ranges 2 and 3, are much cut up by Wintering lake, with its many deep bays. This lake has a most irregular shore line with two deep bays, about eight miles long extending southwest. It is approximately sixteen miles long and averages about two miles wide. Many islands add to its picturesqueness.

The surface of ranges 3 and 4, in townships 73 and 74, is more broken by rock ridges which frequently rise to fifty or sixty feet above the surrounding level. Adjacent to Wintering lake the Huronian rocks outcrop in many places. The soil in the less broken areas is clay overlaid with moss. In range 4, there is a large moss swamp interspersed with stretches of tamarack swamp. This range is therefore not suitable for agriculture. In range 3 the soil is much better, and areas suitable for agriculture are found close to the right of way of the Hudson Bay railway, which is crossed by the base line in section 35. McLaren creek which is about one chain wide and ten feet deep traverses this range and empties into Wintering lake. It drains McLaren lake which is three miles long and one-half mile wide.

Range 5 is broken by Halfway creek, a stream about sixty links wide, with a marked current which flows northerly through section 35 and connects with Grass river about four miles farther north. In section 31 a deep bay of Grass river is crossed. The river there appears to be a series of long narrow lakes, connected at the sides instead of the ends by a stream from fifty to one hundred feet wide. Where the stream is thus contracted the current is very swift and falls of from ten to forty-five feet, are not infrequent. The banks are in many places almost perpendicular cliffs, from ten to thirty feet in height. The surface throughout the range is rolling, rising at intervals into rock ridges. The soil on the ridges is rich clay wherever the rock does not outcrop, while in the hollows small muskegs occur. The general slope of the country is to the north, while the ridges run nearly due north and south. In section 33 a marked ridge occurs which is covered with very good spruce from ten to twenty-four inches in diameter. Elsewhere the country is densely timbered with smaller spruce, jackpine, poplar and tamarack.

Range 6 is very similar in its eastern half to the preceding one, while the western portion is more rocky, with more muskeg between the rock ridges. The line crosses another bay of Grass river in section 34. The last two miles of the range is practically all muskeg covered, in places, with water from one to two feet deep. The soil is clay loam on the ridges, but in the swamps this is covered by one or two feet of moss.

In range 7 the rocky ridges seem to continue to the west. Several small lakes could be seen to the south of the base line. The muskeg between the ridges was deeper and wetter than at any time earlier in the season, owing no doubt to the heavy rains and snowstorms in the latter part of September and the early part of October.

The first three ranges of the eighteenth base line west of the principal meridian are gently rolling, with the surface generally dry, and the soil is clay loam suitable for agriculture. A large portion of the country is covered with standing fire-killed timber, consisting of spruce and jackpine. When Sipiwesk lake is approached, however, this gives place to dense spruce, birch, poplar and willow. Throughout the next three ranges the base line crosses channels and bays of Sipiwesk lake. The soil is mostly clay on the islands and the timber is largely very dense small spruce, birch, poplar and jackpine. Across ranges 7 to 12, inclusive, the country is undulating, except where it is broken by the configuration of lakes such as Setting and Goose lakes, and by an occasional rocky ridge. In ranges 13 to 16, inclusive, the country is very broken by the frequent occurrence of rocky ridges which in general follow a northerly and southerly trend.

When the lakes in the district traversed by these two base lines are made accessible by the construction of the Hudson Bay railway, commercial fishing may become an important industry. These lakes, comprising Setting, Sipiwesk, Landing, Wintering, Cross, Paint, Wekusko and Halfway, together with Nelson and Grass rivers, teem with fine whitefish, jackfish and some lake trout, while Sipiwesk lake and Nelson

5 GEORGE V., A. 1915

river have long been famous for sturgeon. As the lakes are comparatively small it will, however, be necessary to guard these fisheries by the proper restrictions in order to avoid depletion of these waters.

Throughout the greater part of the country traversed practically the only merchantable timber to be found is in patches and fringes on the islands and along the lakes and rivers. The larger timber is mostly spruce but smaller spruce, jackpine, poplar and birch suitable for pulp wood is to be found almost everywhere

It is only in recent years that the great clay belt, of which this district forms a part, has been known to exist, and the average citizen to-day still regards this clay area as more or less of a myth. However, the existence of it has been proven beyond all doubt. Although the season of growth may be shorter than farther south, the longer hours of daylight more than compensate for this short season. Experience has shown that most garden vegetables can be grown, as evidenced by the gardens at the two Hudson's Bay company's posts at Nelson House and Cross Lake. The Nelson House post is situated north of the district traversed by the eighteenth and nineteenth base lines while Cross Lake post is south of it. Wheat, oats and barley have been successfully grown, on a small scale, at Cross Lake. The surface of the country is generally rolling and even where only gently undulating, there seems to be sufficient slope to make drainage possible.

It is the hope of those who are interested in the development of this district that minerals of economic value will be found. There is considerable to encourage that hope, as the area traversed by our survey, is crossed by several belts of Huronian rocks. The most important of these are belts at the north end of Wekusko lake and around Wintering lake. Prospectors have been busily engaged around Wintering lake so that now nearly all the land fronting on the lake has been staked as mineral claims. The chief indication is of copper with its allied minerals. Development alone can determine whether or not these claims will prove of any commercial value.

Water-powers in the immediate vicinity of the lines surveyed are to be found on practically all the streams and rivers. The more important ones, however, are those on Nelson and Grass rivers. Those on the Nelson are by far the most important on account of the great volume of water. A table covering the falls on Nelson river compiled from the 1911 report of the Conservation Commission, is given below:—

Name of Rapid.	Approximate Head in feet.	Estimated Horse-power.
Limestone rapid...	85	1,140,000
Long Spruce rapid..	85	1,140,000
Kettle rapid...	96	1,290,000
Gull rapid......................	67	900,000
Birthday rapid...	24	320,000
Grand rapid...	20	270,000
Rapids above Sipiwesk lake	31	416,000
Bladder rapid..	10·6	147,000
Whitemud rapid..	30	403,000
Ebb and Flow rapid..	11	148,000
Rapids above Cross lake	45	605,000

These figures are based on a volume of 118,369 cubic feet per second at low water, determined by measurements taken across Nelson river just below Sipiwesk lake. Below the point where these measurements were taken the Nelson is swollen by such rivers as Clearwater, Armstrong, Grass, Burntwood, Kettle and Limestone. These rivers would materially increase the volume and therefore the horsepower of all rapids below Split lake, including Birthday, Gull, Kettle, Long Spruce and Limestone.

No definite data can be found covering the falls on Grass river, but the following is a table showing the aproximate height of the falls between Reed and Paint lakes.

Location or Name of Rapid.	Approximate Head in feet.
1st Rapid below Reed lake......	10
2nd " " " "	6
3rd " " " "	48
1st " " Wekusko lake....	12
2nd " " " " (known as Kanisoto or 2 Rapids)	15
3rd " " " "	8
4th " . " " " (known as White Forest)	
5th " " " " (" " Skunk)...............................	
6th " " " " (" " Whitewood)..............................	40
1st " " Setting " (" " Sasagin)	12
2nd " " " " (" " Pisew or Lynx Falls)	50
3rd " " " " (" " Kwasitchewan Falls)	45

Halfway creek although carrying only a comparatively small amount of water has five distinct falls ranging from three to fifteen feet.

To anyone familiar with river navigation the number of rapids as indicated above suggests very definitely a great many portages. Portages are without a doubt the curse of river transportation. Throughout the season my canoe men crossed over the portages given below, and in several cases some of these portages were travelled a number of times.

Name or Location.	Approximate Length of Portage.
Sea falls on Nelson river.	150 feet.
Sugar falls on Nelson river......................	300 "
Three small rapids on Nelson river........	30 to 50 feet.
Ebb and Flow " " "	¼ mile.
Whitemud falls " " " ....·....	Nearly ½ mile.
Bladder rapid " " "	¼ mile.
Over the Hill " " "	300 feet.
Red Rock rapid " " "	Either 2 portages 50 and 300 feet or ⅔ mile.
Chain of Rocks " " "	100 feet.
Cross Portage from Nelson river to Landing lake....	1½ mile.
Thicket Portage from Landing lake to Wintering lake	1½ mile.
Portage from Wintering lake to small lake between Wintering and Paint lakes....	1¼ mile.
Portage from same small lake to Paint lake.	1¼ mile.
Six small portages on Halfway river, each......................	About 100 feet.
Portage to avoid Kwasitchewan falls, Grass river..................	½ mile.
Portage from Grass river to Halfway lake.....................	1¼ mile.
Strawberry portage from Thicket river to Jim creek............ ...	2 miles.
Portage from Leach lake to Halfway lake......................	3 miles.
Portage from Nelson river to Duck lake.........	1 mile.
Portage from Duck lake to Nelson river below Duck falls............	300 yards.
Portage past the first rapid above Duck lake	¾ mile.

Of the fur-bearing animals, mink, foxes (red and black, silver and cross), lynx, wolves, weasels, muskrats and beavers are to be found in great numbers. The winter of 1913-14 has been an especially good one for foxes of all shades and colours. Red foxes were taken in great numbers and nearly every trapper had taken at least one or more silver foxes and not a few cross foxes. Black bears, otter and martin although not plentiful are to be found in the district. Moose and the woodland caribou are quite common although not nearly so numerous as in some parts of the country. Some jumping deer were seen in the valley of Grass river. Wild fowl such as geese and ducks are to be found on the lakes and rivers, but not in great numbers. Several varieties of grouse are fairly numerous.

5 GEORGE V., A. 1915

APPENDIX No. 30.

ABSTRACT OF THE REPORT OF A. E. HUNTER, D.L.S.

SURVEYS IN THE RAILWAY BELT, BRITISH COLUMBIA, IN THE VICINITY OF YALE.

I organized my party at Kamloops and proceeding from there located my first camp at Saddle Rock, five miles south of Spuzzum, on May 18, 1913. On the following day the survey of the east boundary of township 8, range 26, west of the sixth meridian, was commenced from the northeast corner of section 1.

The hills along this boundary are very precipitous, and some difficulty was experienced in obtaining men suitable for carrying on the work.

Having completed the survey of the lands adjoining the Canadian Northern railway right of way in this locality, camp was moved five miles north on June 26.

On August 6 camp was again moved across to the right bank of the Fraser, and as the cables and ferry in this vicinity had been carried away by the high water in June, canoes had to be used for crossing.

On September 2 camp was moved to Camp Sixteen, and here the crossing of the Fraser was greatly facilitated by making use of a cable car formerly operated by the Northern Construction company. At Camp Sixteen the Canadian Pacific Railway company has in operation a stone-quarry, and grey granite of excellent quality for building purposes is shipped from that point.

On November 21 I moved to Spuzzum, and on the 24th completed the survey of Spuzzum townsite.

While engaged in this latter work I received instructions to retrace the Canadian Pacific railway through townships 10 and 9, range 26. I completed this retracement on December 3.

I then completed the survey necessary for the disposition of lands adjoining the Canadian Pacific and Canadian Northern railways in township 10, range 26.

The season was then too far advanced to do further work advantageously, so operations were brought to a close on December 15.

The general characteristics of the country along Fraser river in townships 8, 9 and in township 10 as far north as the north boundary of section 14, range 26, are very similar. The hills rise abruptly from the river or from narrow benches along the river, and are cut through by small streams in deep canyons. Level or slightly sloping benches of a few acres in extent are found in places along the river, but the greater part of these arable areas has been set aside as Indian reserves or surveyed into Group Lots.

The soil on these benches is generally a sandy loam with a sand or gravelly subsoil overlying the solid rock, and although the rainfall in May and June is abundant, the drainage is so rapid that a few hot days in July are sufficient to destroy the vegetation. When properly irrigated, however, the land is very productive and the common vegetables and fruits may be grown to advantage.

Many of the Indian reserves appear to be deserted, the results obtained from cultivation apparently being incommensurate with the outlay for irrigation.

Fir from two to five feet in diameter is found on the benches and creek valleys and in strips on the rocky hillsides, but the timber on the benches has been fairly well culled in the construction of the railways. On the hills, the timber is too difficult of access to be taken out conveniently. Some cedar and hemlock are also found, but not in great quantities.

Some prospecting has been done for gold in the southeasterly part of township 8, range 25, but although surface indications appeared favourable, no strikes of any importance have been made.

Salmon of many varieties come up the Fraser as far as section 27 in township 9, but the river above this has been so filled up in places by the construction of the railroads as to exclude all but a very small percentage of the fish which have run that far.

Marten, bears, deer, mountain goats, rabbits and partridges are found in the hills adjoining the river.

In the construction of the railroads the wagon roads in these townships have been so cut off as to render wagons practically useless except for short hauls.

APPENDIX No. 31.

ABSTRACT OF A REPORT ON THE SURVEYS PERFORMED BY THE LATE C. E. JOHNSTON, D.L.S., PREPARED BY HIS ASSISTANT A. D. STEWART.

STADIA SURVEYS AND INVESTIGATION OF LAKES NORTH AND EAST OF SWIFT CURRENT.

The party left Swift Current the place of organization, on May 30, 1913, to commence work near Ernfold in township 17, range 7, west of the third meridian. From that town, the party worked eastward, and investigated the lakes in a block of about thirty townships in the vicinity of Chaplin.

While traversing Chaplin lake, wooden witness posts were placed at points in fractional sections 3, 4, 8, 9, 16 and 17, of township 17, range 5. It was found that the south half of this lake becomes dry during part of the year so it was not traversed.

While investigating townships 22, ranges 2 and 3, instructions were received to traverse the group of lakes formerly known as Red Deer lakes. Accordingly on October 20 camp was moved to Macrorie, in township 27, range 8, and work was started at Coteau lake, the most southerly of the group on the 23rd. The adjoining townships were investigated, and on November 20, the party moved to township 26, range 11 and examined this township and township 26, range 10.

Camp was then moved back to Macrorie, and later on to Manna and Luck lake, while townships 24 to 26 ranges 7, 8 and 9 were investigated and their lakes traversed. Luck lake was not traversed as it was found to dry up each year.

On December 29, the party returned to Macrorie where the outfit was left and where arrangements were made for wintering the horses; we then moved to Moosejaw where the party was disbanded.

The townships surrounding Chaplin have for the most part good agricultural soil of sandy or clay loam. The surface however in townships 18, ranges 4 and 7 and townships 17 ranges 2 and 3 is to a large extent heavily rolling. In the immediate vicinity of Chaplin lake while the soil is very light, south of the lake the country is very dry and fresh water difficult to obtain. Although the area of this lake has decreased considerably owing to its gradual subsidence, the greater part will apparently always remain useless, and the remainder will for the most part be suitable only for grazing purposes for some years.

In several townships there seems to be arable land which is still open to settlers. Except just north of Parkbeg and at a few other odd points, the farm buildings are not as large and prosperous looking as those in other parts of the country the one-room shack seems to predominate.

Thunder creek valley which lies about twelve or fifteen miles northeast of Chaplin lake seemed prosperous, with large farms, and good soil. The valley seems to be thickly settled, and there is apparently no open land except school lands or Hudson's Bay Co. property. The buildings are nearly all large and provide generously for livestock and crops.

Around Coteau, Stockwell and Anerley lakes the open land has been nearly all taken up. There is a good deal of what appears to be fine farming land still vacant, but it is held by speculators and the railway companies. The soil is generally sandy to clay loam. The buildings are not all that could be desired but as the land is proved up and the owners' financial positions improve the homesteader's shack is gradually giving way to comfortable homes and larger farm buildings.

SESSIONAL PAPER No. 25b

In the neighborhood of Luck lake the soil is sandy or clay loan. The district is well settled, the lake being surrounded by prosperous-looking farms with ample and attractive buildings.

During the past year there seems to have been a general financial depression apparently due to poor crops and the low price of wheat. Oats were grown by some farmers and this crop did not seem to suffer to the same extent as the others. The price given for wheat in the fall months by the local elevators was generally 65 cents a bushel. Twenty-five bushels to the acre was considered a heavy crop for the districts passed through and fifteen to twenty bushels was the average.

Vegetable growing does not seem to be in favour in these parts of the province and the towns have to send away for such as they need. Potatoes were very scarce. One farmer had obtained only three bags where previously he had over one hundred. The price varied from 75 cents a bushel in summer to $1.50 in winter.

Chicken raising seems to be successfully carried on and turkeys and ducks are also commonly seen. Fresh eggs are generally hard to obtain and sell at from 30 to 40 cents a dozen as a rule.

A prairie fire which originated some distance west, burned out a few settlers in townships 25 and 26, ranges 9 to 11 and caused losses to others of haystacks and pasturage.

Hail destroyed the crops southwest of Dinsmore, but only touched a few sections of township 26, range 11.

The farmers in the district surveyed seem favorably inclined toward mixed farming, and all spoken to were unanimous in saying that it will prove the most paying proposition in the long run.

Despite the poor crops of the past year, the settlers are of the opinion that a good crop this year will prove a panacea for all financial ills.

The lakes and ponds in the districts examined are generally dried up. Ponds and marshes that formerly had some depth of water all the year round are dry now for a good part of the year. In fact in late summer and fall the settlers in some districts have to go quite a distance to obtain water.

Most of the bodies of water investigated had at least traces of alkali, generally too much for domestic use though not enough to prevent its use for stock. Fresh water was found fairly often though non-alkaline stagnant water was seen only a few times.

No signs of minerals, quarryable stone, oil or natural gas were noticed.

In the townships investigated, bituminous coal is the common fuel. The Canadian Northern Railway company is introducing lignite but as yet it is not extensively used.

Lumber is imported into all these townships as there is no bush. Along South Saskatchewan river, there are a few small trees up to two inches in diameter, and the settlers for long distances around haul this brush for kindling purposes. The growth is being rapidly cut down and will probably be gone in a few years if no attempt is made at conservation. There also a few small clumps of bush scattered along the group of lakes which comprises Coteau lake and those lying to the west of it, but the trees are not over two inches in diameter; in fact there are very few approaching that size.

A branch of the Canadian Northern railway between Elrose Junction and Elrose, about forty miles west of Macrorie has been completed and put in operation, and several new towns are springing up along it. The line has also been continued from Macrorie through Elrose Junction to Dunblane, a new settlement in township 26, range 7.

The branch of the Grand Trunk Pacific railway from Moosejaw to Mawer in the Thunder creek valley is also constructed and in operation.

The Canadian Pacific railway line running north from Chaplin through the upper Thunder creek valley in township 20, range 6 has been surveyed, and location stakes of

5 GEORGE V., A. 1915

various other projected lines were also seen. In the vicinity of Luck lake several lines were run and some were noticed also near Dinsmore.

In Thunder creek valley lines have been surveyed for the Moosejaw water-supply canal.

If this proposition be carried through as projected, it should afford opportunities for the generating of cheap electric power.

Well-graded roads lead north and south from Ernfold on the Canadian Pacific railway, and some good roads run north of Chaplin. A road with the necessary bridges has been built south across Chaplin lake, but it is poor on account of the sandy soil. Another trail leading southeast is poor for the same reason. Three good trails lead out from Ernfold, one to Parkbeg, one to Tugaske and one in a northerly direction. Roads were surveyed during the season west of Chaplin lake and south from Parkbeg through township 17, range 2 into township 16, range 2, where there are now several good roads. North of Thunder creek valley there are generally good roads or trails in all directions. From Tugaske good roads run to South Saskatchewan river, and on the north bank of the latter at Elbow trails lead off in several directions through the sand hills which make hauling very heavy. Around Luck and the group of lakes consisting of Coteau, Stockwell and Anerley, the roads and trails are very fair except in townships 25 and 26 ranges 9 and 10 where there are only poor trails through rolling country.

Exceptionally fine weather prevailed all summer and fall. In the latter part of December it became threatening, and it was decided to close operations on completion of the work then in hand.

APPENDIX No. 32.

REPORT OF W. J. JOHNSTON, D.L.S.

SUBDIVISION IN THE YALE DISTRICT OF THE RAILWAY BELT, BRITISH COLUMBIA.

CHASE, B.C., July 24, 1914.

E. DEVILLE, Esq., LL.D.,
    Surveyor General,
        Ottawa, Canada.

SIR,—I have the honour to submit the following report on my work for the season of 1913.

I left Vancouver for Hope, in township 5, range 26, west of the sixth meridian, on May 12, 1913, via the Canadian Pacific railway, and established my first camp on the north side of Fraser river, near Hope station. There I completed what subdivision was possible, traversed a few miles of the right bank of the Fraser and retraced the boundaries of a few Indian reserves. On May 30 I moved my camp across the river and began subdivision there. The boundaries of a few Indian reserves were retraced and provincial lot No. 873 was surveyed. The left bank of the Fraser in section 34 and an inland at the mouth of Silver creek were traversed, and the points of intersection of all surveyed section lines with the Canadian Pacific and Canadian Northern railway lines were determined. These railways run almost parallel on opposite sides of the Fraser.

From this camp I also subdivided part of township 6, range 26, on the east side of the Fraser, and traversed the left bank of the river. For transport we used a hand car on the Canadian Northern railway track, which was laid and ballasted at that time.

On July 26 I moved my camp by wagon to Choate siding over the old Yale-Cariboo road, which is gradually getting into bad shape through neglect. There I commenced subdivision on the west side of the Fraser in township 6, range 26. The boundaries of the Indian reserves and provincial lots were retraced, and Strawberry island and a portion of the right bank of the Fraser were traversed. The points of intersection of all surveyed section lines with the Canadian Pacific railway were determined.

On August 21 we moved to Yale over the Yale-Cariboo road. From this camp I subdivided lands on both sides of the Fraser, in township 7, range 26, and traversed both banks of the river through the Yale canyon. I used a hand car over the Canadian Pacific and Canadian Northern railways for transport. The work in this township was rather difficult and slow, owing to the rugged nature of the country.

The valley through townships 5, 6 and 7, range 26, averages about a mile in width, though in many places the mountains run down to the water's edge. The land is covered with scattered fir, cedar, and spruce up to three feet in diameter, with a heavy undergrowth. The soil is a sandy loam with a gravel subsoil. The best land is taken up by Indian reserves and provincial lots, and in most cases no development has been made on them. Irrigation farming is being undertaken on lot 65, group 1, and it is proving a success. Fishing is good in the mountain streams, mountain trout being very plentiful, though small. There was a large run of salmon in the Fraser during the months of July, August, and September. Game was rather scarce, though deer are more plentiful in the fall, when they are driven down by the snow.

No water-powers were seen. Mosquitoes are very scarce, owing to the streams being so cold and swift. There was a heavy rainfall during the summer months, chiefly at night.

On October 6 I moved my camp via the Canadian Pacific railway to Hope, from where I retraced two miles of Indian reserve boundaries on Yale Indian reserves Nos. 13 and 14. While there we experienced almost two weeks of steady rain.

On October 16 we moved by wagon to St. Elmo over the Yale-Westminster road, which is in good condition. From this camp I ran a few miles of subdivision in townships 4, ranges 27 and 28 and traversed some islands in the Fraser. The soil is a sandy loam, and is very rich. The valley on the left of the Fraser extends back about a mile and is covered with timber, chiefly of second growth. Mixed farming is followed and there is an abundance of fruit.

On November 3 we moved to Pitt river over the Canadian Pacific railway and by launch up Pitt river to Pitt lake in township 4, range 5, west of the seventh meridian. There I surveyed timber berth No. 559. This berth is at an elevation of 3,000 or 4,000 feet and is very rough in places. Some fine cedar, fir and hemlock, up to four feet in diameter, were seen. Owing to a two-foot fall of snow I had to abandon the work before completion and return to Ruby creek where I arrived on November 28.

There we began subdivision in township 4, range 28 and township 5, range 27, west of the sixth meridian on the right bank of the Fraser. In township 4, range 28, the land was rough and mountainous to the river's edge. The right bank of the Fraser was traversed.

Only a few miles of subdivision were run in township 5, range 27. There is very little farming being done there yet, but some good land was subdivided. The soil is a sandy loam with a gravel subsoil.

On December 20 I disbanded my party and returned to Vancouver.

I have the honour to be, Sir,
Your obedient servant,

W. J. JOHNSTON, D.L.S.

APPENDIX No. 33.

REPORT OF G. J. LONERGAN, D.L.S.

INSPECTION OF CONTRACTS IN ALBERTA AND NORTHERN MANITOBA.

BUCKINGHAM, QUE., February 21, 1914.

E. DEVILLE, Esq., LL.D.,
    Surveyor General,
        Ottawa, Can.

SIR,—I have the honour to submit the following general report on my last season's operations.

My first work was the inspection of contracts Nos. 14 and 15 of 1912, comprising the townships through which Carrot river flows in ranges 7, 8, 9 and 10 west of the second meridian. From Tisdale we followed a well-graded road almost due north to Arborfield passing through a well-settled district where mixed farming is successfully followed. From Arborfield the only trail running to the northeast is the one made by the surveyors. It passes through a country that was at one time heavily timbered but fires destroyed the timber about fifteen years ago, and there is now a second growth of poplar and willow, scarcely exceeding four inches in diameter, with considerable windfall in places. The soil is chiefly a loam from three to five inches in depth with a clay subsoil and the surface is almost level. There is ample drainage provided by small creeks, the valleys of which seldom exceed six feet in depth. They flow northerly emptying into Carrot river which is not navigable at this point. In low water it can be forded at almost any place. After completing the inspection I returned to Edmonton.

My next work was the inspection of the mounds in contracts No. 35 and 36 of 1912. These contracts are situated northeast of Holmes' Crossing along Athabaska river. Knowing that the trail from Belvedere west would be in a very bad condition and that there was no horse feed in the country I decided that the cheapest and quickest way to get there was to go west on the Grand Trunk Pacific railway to Hinton and then paddle down the Athabaska in canoes. The upper part of the Athabaska is not navigable for steamboats and in low water there is just sufficient for canoes drawing twelve inches of water. The current is very swift and there are many small rapids. The first one hundred and twenty-five miles can be covered in two days, after that thirty to forty miles per day is fair travelling, much depending on the wind and the height of the water. At Holmes' Crossing I engaged teams to take the camp outfit to contract No. 36 and on the following day we started the inspection of the mounds. When this was completed we returned to the Crossing, and going down stream we inspected contract No. 35 from the river. · Northwest of Holmes' Crossing along the Assiniboine flats there is a large settlement of people from Dakota. They have but recently gone in there and their progress is somewhat slow as there is but little open country. However, they report that they are not troubled with frost and everything they have tried so far has been successful, particularly garden vegetables; the small patches of grain that they put in have ripened thoroughly. A railway location was surveyed in the winter of 1911 crossing the Athabaska at Holmes' Crossing and heading for Sawridge. From what I could find out it runs parallel to the Calgary and Edmonton railway and about fifty miles west of it. Although I could get no information concerning the road the fact that a survey has been made is a start, and such a good country cannot remain much longer without railway facilities. Having com-

5 GEORGE V., A. 1915

pleted the inspection I continued down the Athabaska in canoes to Athabaska settlement then by train to Edmonton.

In connection with this trip I would like to mention that there is one place west of where the Athabaska crosses the trail to Grande Prairie that is a remarkably good site for power development. The river turns at right angles and enters a narrow gorge about two hundred feet deep and from three hundred to four hundred feet wide; the banks and bottom are sandstone. A dam could be built across and the water held back forming an immense reservoir insuring a uniform supply during the whole year. Gravel for the dam could be had a short distance back from the proposed site. There is no doubt this is a national asset that is worth while looking into and preserving.

My next work was to extend the lots of Lesser Slave Lake settlement to the shore of the lake. Owing to the extremely low water, navigation was late in starting and the large accumulation of freight made it impossible to secure accommodation on the steamboats, so I started overland with my horses and wagons. The road is so bad that it does not pay to travel it after the frost is out, particularly with any kind of a load.

There is a lot of good country yet to be taken up along the south side of Lesser Slave lake in the vicinity of Swan river and west of it. It is equal to the Peace river valley and has the advantage of being close to navigation and to a railway that is almost constructed at this date. An abundant supply of hay can be cut and there is ample rainfall in this district.

My next work was a settlement survey at Wabiskaw lake. There are three routes to reach this place. The first is a winter trail from Athabaska direct to Wabiskaw which follows the frozen lakes and marshes and is impassable in summer. The second goes down the Athabaska to Pelican river, and up that river. By this route I am told there are fourteen portages varying in length from a few hundred yards to three miles, and some of the portages are over muskegs and swamps which are not practical for heavy loads. However all the spring catch of fur that is taken after the roads break up is taken out this way. The fur-dealers of Wabiskaw have their goods brought down to the mouth of Pelican river during summer and stored, then freighted to Wabiskaw by teams during the winter. The third route, which was the one I chose, is a pack trail from the mouth of Martin river on Lesser Slave lake. While waiting for my pack saddles to arrive from Edmonton I started my men opening up this pack-trail into a wagon road. In this way we were able to use wagons for about thirty miles and pack-horses for the remainder of the distance. As I had but eight horses to pack for twelve men I cut the outfit down to one blanket to each man with what clothes he was wearing, using only one tent for the party and taking provisions for ten days. This with the iron posts, instruments and other necessary articles made a maximum load for the horses.

Wabiskaw is situated on the north side of a channel joining two lakes. This channel flows through a marsh which varies in width from one to two miles. When I arrived at the south side of this marsh, which at that time was covered with water from four to six feet deep, I had considerable difficulty in attracting attention but I finally got an Indian who was hunting ducks to take me across in his canoe. I then rented boats to take the men and outfit over and swam the horses, nearly drowning one of them. On the following day, we started work.

The settlers at Wabiskaw are mostly half-breeds and Indians with white people in charge of the three stores and the missions. The total amount of land under cultivation is about seventy-five acres while the total length of wagon road is less than a mile. Upon inquiring into the cause of this backward condition, the fur dealers told me that successful hunters made as much as two thousand five hundred dollars during the season with furs, and that it did not pay them to cultivate land. Labour is worth two and a half dollars and board per day; but two to four days was as long as any person would work at one time; they would then take a holiday. Goods are sold at from five to six hundred per cent higher than in Edmonton. There are three trading posts,

SESSIONAL PAPER No. 25b

Church of England and Roman Catholic missions and a monthly service mail from Sawridge by packhorses.

Wabiskaw is located in the centre of an immense saucer-shaped tract of land, and during a wet season all the water drains down into the lake, and as there is but one small outlet the water rises and floods the hay marshes, and does not go down again until November, when it is too late to cut hay. This could be easily remedied as the outlet of the lake is Wabiskaw river, and half a mile from the lake the river is a succession of rapids; all that is necessary is to widen the channel, not to deepen it. By this means the overflow of water would run out, and the depth of the lake would be maintained, thus protecting the fishing industry. This industry is not followed at present, not for lack of fish, but because the freight rates are prohibitive. Such a conditions of affairs will not last for more than a couple of years as a direct communication will then be opened up with the Edmonton and Dunvegan railway at Sawridge.

The land in this vicinity is covered with scrub and scattered poplar from four to eight inches in diameter with a few spruce in places. I saw no timber fit for milling purposes, but was told that there is a sufficient supply for future settlers, though not enough to warrant the erection of a large saw-mill. The only means of cutting it at present is the slow process of whip-sawing. When the land is cleared it will be as productive as any other part of the province. The Roman Catholic mission people are at present raising oats, barley, wheat and all kinds of garden vegetables, all of which ripen. The soil is a clay loam. The first twenty miles along the trail from Wabiskaw to the mouth of Martin river has been burned over, and a farmer could start easily, more particularly if he had a few head of stock. Good water may be had in abundance everywhere.

The survey being completed, I started on my return journey. I swam my horses across the marsh a little west of the mission, then struck south about three miles, again swimming Willow river and heading in a westerly direction through the bush until I reached the trail by which I came in, and finally arrived at the mouth of Martin river on Lesser Slave lake. At this place I started the inspection of contracts Nos. 5 and 9 of 1913. We soon ran out of provisions, however, and had to move to Sawridge. On my arrival there I found that the supplies I had left in the Northern Transportation company's warehouse had been destroyed by the unusual and extreme high water. As it was impossible to purchase supplies there, and as there were three contracts to be inspected along Athabasca river, I left my transport at Sawridge and went to Edmonton by boat and train. I purchased supplies and went by train to Hinton, where I started on a second trip down the Athabaska in canoes. I inspected the three contracts along that river, and followed the river down as far as Mirror Landing, then moved up Lesser Slave river and thence to the west end of Lesser Slave lake, and commenced working eastward. I made use of the canoes on this trip as I knew the high water had flooded the trail around the lake, and that the railway grade which crosses the trail so often would make it almost impossible to use wagons. This trip was successfully made in canoes and the work was completed.

I arrived at Mirror Landing on November 1 to find the Athabaska full of running ice. I found out by telegraph that it was impossible to cross on the ferry at Athabaska, and as the railway company had a scow working at Mirror Landing I made arrangements with them to cross my outfit. This we did by putting one team in the scow at a time and tracking it up half a mile along the shore and then working it across with poles while drifting down. I drove to Edmonton along the new Edmonton and Dunvegan railway line, and on my arrival stored the outfit, placed my horses in winter quarters, and paid off my party.

I have the honour to be, Sir,

Your obedient servant,

G. J. LONERGAN, D.L.S.

5 GEORGE V., A. 1915

APPENDIX No. 34.

REPORT OF E. S. MARTINDALE, D.L.S.,

BASE LINE SURVEYS IN EASTERN SASKATCHEWAN.

AYLMER, Ont., July 31, 1914.

E. DEVILLE, ESQ., LL.D.,
   Surveyor General,
      Ottawa, Canada.

SIR,—I have the honour to submit the following general report on my survey operations during the season of 1913-14.

Instructions for the survey of the sixteenth base line from the third meridian to the second were received early in February, 1913. I left for Prince Albert immediately, in order to have the season's supplies cached at suitable places before the winter broke up, and also that I might be able to run the base line across Montreal lake on the ice, thereby avoiding the long and difficult triangulation which would be necessary in the summer. It was found upon making inquiry, that a proposed railway, known as the Hudson's Bay Pacific railway, now abandoned, had been surveyed northeasterly from Prince Albert for a distance of over one hundred and thirty miles. This line crossed the fifteenth base line in range 18, and from there was reported to run almost due north. I arranged to have a cache established in the vicinity of the sixteenth base line on this railway line by making use of the road, cut out at the time of the survey, for freighting in the supplies. My assistant took charge of this work but, because of the excessive depth of snow and the lateness of the season, he succeeded in reaching a point only about two miles north of the fifteenth base line, where the supplies were cached. In the meantime I had organized a small party, and, with a hired transport outfit, left for Montreal lake to carry out the other part of the work which it was advisable to complete before the break up. After arriving at Montreal lake, a trail was cut westward nearly to the meridian, and the survey of the base line was commenced. The snow at this season was very deep and retarded progress to some extent. The line was run to the east side of Montreal lake, a distance of about fourteen miles, by April 5. A cache was built there, and the supplies which had been forwarded by the Hudson's Bay company from Prince Albert to their post at the south end of the lake, were then freighted up the lake and stored; this work was completed by April 9. By that time the snow had practically all disappeared, and travelling with our sleighs was very heavy. Prince Albert was reached on the 13th, and the party paid off the following day. I then proceeded to Ottawa for observing practice, and while there completed my final returns for surveys of 1912.

In the meantime I had been instructed to complete the fifteenth base line by running east from the third meridian to the east boundary of range 22, before again taking up work on the sixteenth base line.

On June 7, 1913, I again left for the West. Horses and transport outfit were collected from Edmonton and Lac la Biche, Alberta, and from Bowsman, Manitoba, and shipped to Prince Albert where the party was organized. On the 26th, the outfit was sent out with teams in charge of the assistant to the "Red Deer Forks" on the Montreal lake road, near our point of commencement, and a pack trail was cut to the third meridian. By June 24 our horses had all arrived at Prince Albert and on the following day I left there with the packers, reaching camp July 3. We moved to the meridian and commenced survey work the next day. Four days of almost continuous rain beginning on the 10th flooded the country and made the swamps and muskegs almost impassable for horses.

Our work on the fifteenth base line was completed on September 25. A trail was then opened out from the west side of Candle lake northerly to a lake on the northerly boundary of township 58, range 23, then westerly to the east shore of Montreal lake and thence north along the lake shore to the sixteenth base line where work had been discontinued in the spring. The survey of this base line was then carried on to its completion at the second meridian, the final closing being made on June 20, 1914.

Horse feed along the base line was very scarce and of poor quality, and, after freeze up, hay and oats had to be freighted in from Prince Albert by way of Hudson Bay Pacific trail. Our inability to get in touch with this trail until December, and the failure of freighters to get through with horse feed, caused us to lose considerable valuable time in December and the beginning of January. Practically no snow fell to the south of the fifteenth base line until late in January, and it was difficult to get freighters to venture on long trips with wagons at that time of the year.

Horse toboggans or flat sleighs were used for transportation during the winter months and also in the spring until the frost was practically all out of the muskegs, and they proved most satisfactory for the purpose. Our sleighs were two feet wide, twelve feet long, made of one and a half inch oak and were fitted with shafts. Loads of from five to ten hundred pounds were hauled, depending on the state of the trail and three men had no difficulty in handling the outfit of eight sleighs. In the spring after the snow was gone, the ponies hauled from three to four hundred pounds. Extra heavy canvas should be used for covers in this work and special attention should be given to the lashing of the loads in order to prevent damage to camp outfit and loss of supplies.

The intersection of the sixteenth base line and the second meridian falls in Namew lake and it was necessary to make the closing on the meridian at the northeast corner of section 25, township 60.

The survey being completed, the outfit was loaded on a barge and taken by steamer down through Namew and Cumberland lakes and Saskatchewan river to Pas, where it was shipped via Canadian Northern railway to Prince Albert, reaching there on June 23. The men were paid off, the outfit stored and arrangements were made to pasture the horses for the summer.

Routes.

There are two main transportation routes into that portion of the north country lying between the second and third meridians, one following more or less closely each meridian. At the west the Montreal lake road runs northerly from Prince Albert past Shoal Creek headquarters camp of the Prince Albert Lumber company, situated a little north of the fourteenth base line and west of the meridian, and then crosses the fifteenth base in range 1 and the meridian in township 57, thence northeasterly to the small settlement at the south end of Montreal lake. The winter trail then runs north, crossing Montreal lake, to lac La Ronge. From Prince Albert to the Shoal Creek camp the road is in fair condition nearly all year, but north of this it passes through many swamps and muskegs and in consequence used but little in summer. In the winter, however, a large number of teams are employed in freighting the yearly supply of provisions and merchandise for the various trading companies located at Montreal lake, lac La Ronge and Fort Stanley.

Along the second meridian a sleigh road, following rivers and lakes for the most part, runs from Pas to Cumberland House, thence northerly across Cumberland, Amisk and other lakes to Pelican narrows on Pelican lake, from which place the northern freight is distributed by water route in the summer. This road which crosses the

5 GEORGE V.. A. 1915

sixteenth base line in range 2 was opened out from Cumberland lake north in the winter of 1912. In the summer this country can best be reached by water from Pas up Saskatchewan river to Cumberland lake and through Whitey and English narrows to Namew lake. Numerous steamers and gasoline launches are now operating on this route catering to the needs of the prospectors going into the recently-discovered gold fields of Amisk lake, which are reached from Namew lake by means of a newly-cut portage (wagon road) fourteen or sixteen miles in length.

The Hudson Bay Pacific railway trail runs northeasterly from Prince Albert crossing the fourteenth base line in range 21, the fifteenth in range 18 and the sixteenth in range 16. The end of this trail is reported to be about fifteen miles northeasterly from its crossing on the sixteenth base line. This road has practically never been used, except by a few trappers, since it was first cut. Summer travel is difficult on account of swamps and muskegs, while between the fifteenth and sixteenth base lines it follows rough broken and hilly country making winter travelling also heavy. It is joined a few miles north of Torch river by a road from Fort à la Corne.

Another wagon road runs northerly and easterly from Prince Albert to the south end of Torch lake. By this route the country in the vicinity of the fifteenth base line in range 23 may be reached but in summer it is necessary to complete the trip from Torch lake to the base line by water.

Description of the country adjacent to the fifteenth base-line from range 27 to range 22 west of the second meridian.

From the third meridian to Bittern lake in range 26 the country varies from rolling hills, covered with small birch, poplar and spruce in the western part of range 27, to low level swamp and muskeg with low jackpine ridges. To the north of the base line, tamarack, swamps and muskegs extend nearly to Montreal lake, while to the south it is more rolling with a few small areas of good spruce. To the south of the base line in range 27 drainage is to the southwest through Spruce river and emptying into the Saskatchewan at Prince Albert, while the water to the north flows through Bittern river and finally into the Churchill. Bittern lake is a long, deep, narrow body of water about twelve square miles in extent, which overflows through Bittern river. It is reported to be well stocked with whitefish and pike. Several small streams flow into the lake, namely, Bittern creek from the west, Wolftrap creek from the south and McLean creek from the east and south. A small tract of good milling spruce is found at the south end of the lake. Bittern river, from one to two chains in width, follows a tortuous route from Bittern lake to the south end of Montreal lake and is not navigable by canoe throughout its whole length because of numerous small shallow rapids. A wagon road has been cut between the two lakes and is used by the Indians from Montreal lake who fish at Bittern lake in the winter. An Indian reserve has been set apart at the south end of Montreal lake; this includes several hundred acres of very good spruce and poplar running from ten to twenty inches in diameter. Located there are the trading posts of the Hudson Bay company, Révillon Frères, and one or two other independent traders, also a small mission day school for the Indian children.

Range 25 is low and wet with the exception of a low poplar ridge crossing the base line and extending for a distance of about three miles on either side of the line. McLean creek, about eight feet in width and from three to six feet in depth, was crossed in section 31 in an open swamp. To the south of the line the country appears to be higher and more rolling and is mostly covered with small jackpine, while to the north it is fairly level consisting of spruce muskegs separated by low jackpine ridges; there are also some large areas of very thick small spruce. Clearsand lake, or as it is sometimes called " West Candle lake ", covers an area of about eight square miles and drains to the east into Candle lake. Range 24 is higher and more rolling; it is mostly covered with birch and poplar from three to eight inches in diameter and also some jackpine up to nine inches in diameter. There is also an area of about one hundred acres, thickly covered with spruce and poplar up to twenty-four inches in diameter, a short distance south of the base line in this range. To the south are jackpine ridges with spruce muskegs and tamarack swamps.

Candle lake was crossed near the north end in range 23. This is a fine body of water covering an area of sixty or seventy square miles. Whitefish and pike are caught but not to the same extent as was the case a few years ago. Torch lake, to the south and west of, and in close proximity to Candle lake, covers eight or ten square miles and drains into the latter through Fisher creek, a deep narrow stream about three miles in length. This lake is surrounded to the northwest and northeast by large hay meadows which, however, are subject to flooding in wet seasons. A considerable area of good milling spruce lies to the south of the northwest portion of Candle lake which, I understand, has already been disposed of as a timber berth. Torch river flows from Torch lake through the southeast arm of Candle lake into Saskatchewan river near Cumberland lake. To the north and east of Candle lake the country rises about 190 feet in crossing range 22. There spruce muskegs alternate with low jackpine ridges. Along the east shore of the lake is a narrow strip of poplar and spruce up to eight inches in diameter.

The soil on the ridges and on the higher ground is a sandy loam throughout, while on the lower lands it is a vegetable muck. There is some good agricultural land in the vicinity of Candle lake and at a few points along the base line, but at present, this country generally, is too wet to be of much value for agricultural purposes.

A farm has been taken up at the mouth of Fisher creek on Candle lake where vegetables such as potatoes and turnips are successfully grown.

Description of the country adjacent to the sixteenth base line, from the third to the second meridian.

At the point of commencement of the base line at the third meridian is a tract of good milling spruce from eight to twenty inches in diameter, extending to the east a distance of thirty chains to a branch of Burntwood river. The greater portion of this area appears to lie to the west of the meridian. East to Montreal lake the country is rolling with a descent of approximately one hundred feet in the seven miles from the meridian to the water in the lake. For the most part it is wet and swampy with occasional poplar and jackpine ridges. The western shore of the lake is low, mostly spruce and tamarack muskegs. To the north and west of the base line the land appears to be higher and more rolling. The soil is a vegetable mould varying from two to six inches in depth, underlaid by a sandy subsoil. Burntwood river, which is about a chain in width, is crossed in section 33, range 27, and flows south between steep banks to its junction with Crean creek, thence easterly to Montreal lake. A few small lakes were noticed in this district.

Montreal lake, nearly seven miles in width where it is crossed by the base line, has a length of over thirty-two miles and an area of nearly one hundred and seventy square miles, and is comparatively shallow. Fish are not plentiful and are of poor quality. To the east of Montreal lake the country rises six hundred feet or more to the height of land between the Churchill and the Saskatchewan near the west boundary of range 18.

The east shore of the lake is also swampy to a large extent. There are a few patches of good spruce to the south of the base line not far from the lake. Farther south are also a few small hay meadows. A lake about two miles in extent, is situated in township 59, range 23, and is well stocked with whitefish; to the west of the lake are several hay meadows where hay is put up by the Montreal Lake Indians. There is also some good agricultural land in this vicinity, the surface being rolling and wooded with small poplar and spruce.

25b—10

5 GEORGE V., A. 1915

In range 24 a strip of good timber two miles wide, and with an area of about ten square miles, was crossed by the base line. The trees which are mostly spruce, jack-pine and poplar, are from eight to twenty inches in diameter and are clean and straight. In ranges 23 and 22 the land is gently rolling, mostly spruce and tamarack muskegs with occasional clumps of small spruce and poplar and low jackpine ridges. An open swamp one and a half miles wide from ten to twelve miles long was crossed in range 23.

In range 21 the country both to the north and south of the line becomes more broken. To the north the surface is broken by deep ravines, and is wooded mostly with small poplar, spruce, birch and jackpine, while to the south are spruce muskegs and jackpine ridges, the latter becoming more prominent and numerous. A series of three large lakes known as the " White Swan " lakes lie to the south of the line in this range. Drainage from these lakes is to the southwest into the lake in township 59, range 23, and thence to Candle lake. The height of land there is but a short distance south of the line and runs approximately east and west. Ranges 20, 19, 18, 17 and part of 16 are from rolling to hilly, being broken by deep ravines running nearly at right angles to the base line, and are covered, generally speaking, with a thick growth of small spruce and jackpine with occasional small areas of birch and poplar four or eight inches in diameter. A few small patches of good spruce were also noticed in these ranges. To the south near the correction line is a well-defined range of sand hills running nearly east and west. It is reported that this broken country extends northwesterly to Pipe-stone lake, a large body of water lying a short distance southeast of lac la Ronge. To the south of the line in ranges 18 and 17 the country has been burned over within recent years. There are numerous small lakes along this part of the line.

From the height of land an elevation of 2,242 feet above sea-level, the country drops rapidly to the east to the large muskegs at the east of range 16 with an elevation of 1,434 feet. The Hudson Bay Pacific railway survey, crossed in section 36, range 16, marks the easterly limit of the higher hilly country. In range 16 there is some poplar and birch averaging eight or ten inches in diameter; the surface both to the southwest and northeast is wooded with jackpine from four to eight inches in diameter.

From Montreal lake to range 16 the soil consists of a layer of vegetable mould underlaid by a loose sandy subsoil except in the hilly country and on the ridges, where it is inclined to be heavier and stony.

From range 16 to range 2 the nature of the country is practically uniform, the greater part being low, apparently level, and wet, with tamarack swamps, spruce mus-kegs, quaking bogs, occasional low jackpine knolls and ridges and patches of small spruce. The south branch of Mossy river was crossed in range 15. It has an average width of forty feet and joins the main stream some distance farther east. Along the banks of this river are a few large spruce trees. This river which is the main drainage outlet of the district, was crossed at three points on the line, first in range 13 and twice in range 11; it has a width of from two to three chains and on account of numerous small rapids is difficult for navigation even with canoe. Brougham creek, from thirty to fifty feet wide and flowing south to Mossy river was crossed in range 7. To the east of this creek in the same range is another small area of spruce and jackpine of eight to twelve inches in diameter. Lakes in this stretch of country are few in number and are small and marshy. From a point about half a mile south of the second crossing of Mossy river in range 11, an old flat-sleigh trail runs easterly to "Pine bluff" which lies about nine miles up Muskeg river from Cumberland lake. A winter dog trail from " Pine bluff " running north, crosses the line in range 6.

A small Indian reserve has been laid off at "Pine bluff," and outposts of the Hudson's Bay company and Revillon Freres are located there.

A lake in township 62, range 6, is reported to be large and deep and well stocked with fish. Grassberry river was crossed in range 5. This stream varies from one to

SESSIONAL PAPER No. 25b

two hundred feet in width and is six feet deep, except at the numerous small rapids where the shallow water makes canoe travel difficult and tedious. It flows south-westerly from a lake about ten miles north of the base line joining Mossy river at "Pine bluff." These waters flow into one of the several channels of the Saskatchewan leading to Cumberland lake.

An old sleigh trail, cut from Cumberland lake to the lake in township 62, range 6, as a means of freighting fish from the latter to Cumberland House many years ago, was crossed in a large quaking bog in range 4. Mackenzie lake, in ranges 4 and 3 south of the line, has an area of about twelve square miles and is almost entirely surrounded by muskegs. It drains into Cumberland lake through a small creek at the southwest corner. According to all reports, it is well stocked with jackfish.

In range 3, along the base line and to the north of it the proportion of dry land to muskeg begins to increase. The surface is gently rolling, and the limestone ridges first noticed in range 6 become more prominent. From the base line south to Cumberland lake there is practically no dry land except near the lake shore. The winter portage from Cumberland lake to Amisk lake is crossed in section 32 range 2. From the base line to Cumberland warehouse on the north shore of the lake, the road runs almost continuously through quaking bogs. Near the lake are some well-defined ridges made up of limestone and granite boulders, evidently carried there and deposited by the ice.

Across ranges 2 and 1 east of O'Leary lake the country is fairly level and dry, being partly covered with jackpine from six to ten inches in diameter. There is also some dry spruce muskeg with tamarack swamps both to the north and south of the line. Several lakes with areas of about five square miles lie in these two ranges and are well stocked with jackfish. The base line closes on the second meridian in Namew lake, a large body of deep water with rocky (limestone) shores. Excellent whitefish and jackfish are caught, and sturgeon fishing was an important industry on this lake a few years ago.

The soil in ranges 1 and 2 is a clay loam which to all appearances is well suited for farming. From range 16 to range 2, however, the soil is mostly a vegetable muck which, if drained and exposed to the sun, would no doubt in time become valuable for agricultural purposes. No hay meadows whatever were seen in the immediate vicinity of the base line throughout its whole length.

No traces of economic minerals were seen. Large game, such as moose, deer and caribou, are plentiful, while elk are frequently seen in the neighbourhood of Torch lake. Bears and the other important fur-bearing animals such as lynx, mink and foxes are frequently seen. Timber wolves were also heard during the winter. Rabbits were unusually plentiful during the winter of 1913-14, but they are commencing to die off. Spruce and birch partridges are common in some localities, and occasional prairie-chickens and ptarmigan were also seen. Wild fowl such as ducks and geese were very scarce at the western end of the line, but were plentiful in the swamps nearer the second meridian.

The summer of 1913 was unusually wet. The winter following was mild, except for a few cold snaps of short duration; snow was not as deep as usual, being about two feet on the level, and it did not come until late in the season. Summer frosts are frequent, as is the case in all the newer parts of the Canadian West, but otherwise the climate is very much the same as it is farther south on the prairies.

I have the honour to be, Sir,

Your obedient servant,

E. S. MARTINDALE, D.L.S.

5 GEORGE V., A. 1915

APPENDIX No. 35.

ABSTRACT OF THE REPORT OF H. MATHESON, D.L.S.

SURVEYS IN THE VICINITY OF JASPER, ALBERTA.

On May 21' 1913, I left Edmonton, Alberta, for Jasper, where I arrived on the morning of the following day. After examining the country and consulting Col. Rogers, Superintendent of Jasper park. I commenced a survey of the townsite on May 23.

At that time the town consisted of only a few scattered shacks situated in the vicinity of the railway station. It was a typical railway construction town. The only permanent buildings were those belonging to the Grand Trunk Pacific Railway company consisting of a station, roundhouse, and some smaller buildings.

These buildings were situated on a flat about half a mile wide and about two miles long, lying along the left or west bank of Athabaska river just below its junction with the Miette.. This flat is fairly level and is about sixty feet above the level of the Athabaska river bed. It is bounded on the north and west by a hill which is from two hundred to three hundred feet high and which rises to a rolling plateau broken by small creeks and numerous small lakes. The largest of these lakes are Cabin, Pyramid and Patricia lakes. Cabin creek drains Cabin lake, and runs across Jasper flats; it is used as a source of water supply for the town.

Practically, the whole of Jasper flats consists of boulders and gravel. Consequently it has good natural drainage. It is a very suitable location for a townsite, even though excavation for sewerage and waterworks systems is difficult on account of the great number of boulders. Excavation for building foundations is also difficult, but the boulders obtained in the excavation can be used for building purposes, and when properly used greatly enhance the architectural beauty of the buildings. My surveys were considerably retarded by the boulders, as a hole had to be made for every iron post planted to mark the townsite. I do not think that any post could have been driven to its proper striking depth without striking a boulder.

Jasper flats, except the parts cleared for townsite purposes, are covered with timber consisting mostly of small jackpine and a few large Douglas fir. The fir, on account of their thick bark, have been able to withstand the forest fires which have occasionally swept the country, destroying all the other timber. On the rolling plateau west and north of Jasper there is much brulé and dead standing timber, mostly spruce and pine up to two feet in diameter. Some of this is also found on Jasper flats. The Douglas fir is not found much farther east than Jasper, but live specimens as large as four feet in diameter are found in that vicinity. On account of forest fires, very little large green timber of any other variety is found except where it is protected in deep gullies.

The townsite is situated west of the Grand Trunk Pacific railway, adjacent and parallel to the right of way. The railway depot is opposite the centre of the townsite. The avenues are parallel to the railway track and the streets approximately perpendicular to it. It consists of twelve blocks and ten reserves.

I completed my survey of Jasper townsite on June 27, and then moved my outfit into the Brazeau district to complete some work which I had started in 1912. The work to be done lay in townships 47 and 48, ranges 17 and 18, west of the fifth meridian. A Canadian Northern railway location line runs through the district. I surveyed sufficient section lines to tie in the right of way in these townships.

To reach this work I proceeded by train from Jasper to Bickerdike, and thence by the Alberta Coal branch to the Pacific Pass Coal mines (now called "Lovett"). From the mines I travelled northeast for three days by pack train to my first work in township 48, range 17.

SESSIONAL PAPER No. 25b

The townships surveyed consist mostly of wide low ridges separated by shallow muskeg. They are thickly timbered with spruce, jackpine and some poplar and willow. Tamarack is found in the muskegs. Most of the large timber has been ruined by fire, and now lies as brulé. The difficulty of travelling over this fallen timber was the greatest handicap to the work. The soil is generally a sandy loam with few boulders, and would be very productive if it were cleared, and the muskegs drained. However the general elevation of the district is high, so that it is subject to summer frosts, and it will not likely be used for agricultural purposes for some time. I completed my work in this district on September 9 and then moved my whole outfit back to Jasper.

I found conditions at Jasper considerably changed. Many of the houses were moved on lots in the townsite. Considerably progress had been made in grading the streets and a new administration building was about half completed. This is a handsome building constructed of boulders. A road was also built to Pyramid and Patricia lakes.

My first duty was to traverse the road to the lakes and then to lay out villa lots one hundred feet by one hundred and fifty feet, around the lakes. Pyramid lake is somewhat crescent shaped, and has an area of about three hundred acres. It is drained from the north end by a creek. A number of small creeks run into it through a muskeg on the south side. The southern and eastern shores of the lake consist of muskeg flats and benches up to ten feet in height. On the north and west sides fairly high steep hills rise from the water's edge. There is a small well wooded island in the lake, which is very beautiful. Patricia lake is long, narrow and fairly straight, and has an area of about one hundred and twenty acres; the average width is about nine hundred feet. It has no visible outlet or inlet, and its water has a bitter taste. In some parts steep hills rise from the water's edge, while in other parts of the shore there are benches not more than twenty or thirty feet above the level of the lake.

These lakes will make very fine summer resorts as they are suitable for boating. There is a good choice of lots; they can be had on low benches, high benches or on hillsides of various slopes. The front and back lines of the lots are curves and tangents parallel to the lake shores. Patricia lake is approximately three and a half miles and Pyramid lake four miles from Jasper. The new road from Jasper has an easy grade and is suitable for automobiles.

I completed my survey of villa lots on October 21. I then surveyed four corrals of about one acre each, and one of about two acres, situated behind Jasper townsite near the foot of the hill. The small corrals are to be leased to packers who furnish transportation and act as guides to tourists. The large corral is for the governmnet transportation outfit. The corrals form block "A" of Jasper townsite.

After completing the survey of the corrals, I commenced topographical work, which I did by the transit-stadia method. Closed traverses were run, and from the stations of the traverses numerous side shots were taken to locate the contours. Rough sketches of the country were made. From the traverse notes and sketches regular topographical maps were afterwards constructed. I first traversed Cabin lake and a considerable area around it. I afterwards traversed Miette river for a distance of about four miles, commencing at its mouth; I also traversed both sides of Athabaska river for a distance of about four miles above and below the town, and the chain of lakes on the east side of the river. I ran other traverses to locate contours in the country adjacent to the lakes and rivers. I used the Grand Trunk Pacific Railway bench marks as data for elevations. I checked my elevations obtained by stadia by ties on these bench marks wherever convenient. I also ran a line of levels from one of them to Cabin lake.

On January 6, I had completed all of the work on the flats of Athabaska and Miette rivers, which could be conveniently done from my camp at Jasper. I therefore closed operations and on January 8 arrived in Edmonton, where I disbanded my party.

5 GEORGE V., A. 1915

APPENDIX No. 36.

ABSTRACT OF THE REPORT OF C. F. MILES, D.L.S.

INSPECTION OF CONTRACT SURVEYS AND MISCELLANEOUS SUBDIVISION.

The surveys performed by my party during the past season were distributed over the provinces of Manitoba, Saskatchewan and Alberta.

I arrived at Prince Albert on May 19, 1913 and after organizing my party and purchasing supplies left on the 22nd for Mistatim by the Canadian Northern railway.

My first work consisted of making corrections in townships 45 and 46, ranges 9 and 10, west of the second meridian. Much of this land is burned-over swamp and is not suitable for immediate settlement without drainage. We were engaged on this work until June 21 and on the 23rd left for Dauphin. From there we went to Winnipegosis where we secured a sailing vessel, and left for contract No. 13 of 1912 in townships 34, 35 and 36, ranges 16 and 17, west of the principal meridian. It is a pleasant sail up lake Winnipegosis; the water is not very deep along the route we followed, the main channel for vessels lying more to the west. I was informed that great quantities of whitefish are caught and shipped by rail from Winnipegosis every fall and winter, giving employment to many fishermen and teamsters. Settlements are extending along the west shore of the lake, but as yet only a few settlers are located on the east side. However, now that the country east of the lake has been subdivided, there is a fair promise of it becoming settled. During the inspection of this contract we had a good deal of rain and cloudy weather, so that it was impossible to observe for azimuth, except on the morning of June 6 before our departure for Winnipegosis.

We then returned to Dauphin, arriving there on the evening of the 7th. The country between Winnipegosis and Dauphin appears to be very flat, and owing to frequent rains there was much water on the surface, and the creeks and river were full. We left Dauphin on the morning of July 8, arriving at Edmonton on the following morning.

I had been in communication with the Hudson's Bay company's transport department in order to ascertain the quickest method of reaching McMurray where my next work was located. I was informed that their scow brigade would probably leave Athabaska about July 15, but at Edmonton I learned that it would probably not start until some days later. This delay gave me ample time to secure pasture for my horses. Transport and other articles of our outfit were deposited in the Government storehouse. Necessary supplies having been purchased I started with my party for Athabaska on the 15th. When we arrived I repaired to the Hudson's Bay company's transportation office to make necessary inquiries. There I was informed that twenty-seven scows had to be loaded with about two hundred and fifty tons of freight before they would be ready for departure.

The scows used on the Athabaska are each capable of carrying about nine tons. Each scow is fitted out with four big clumsy-looking cars and one sweep, about thirty feet long and nine inches in diameter at the thickest part, which is manipulated in the stern by the steersman. The scows are fifty feet long and have a beam at the widest part of about thirteen feet. The oars in the scows are not used for propulsion except when it is intended to land, or when some obstruction has to be avoided. The sole motive power is the stream, down which they float day after day, the crews landing only for the preparation and consumption of mid-day meals and for the night.

SESSIONAL PAPER No. 25b

We left Athabaska on the afternoon of July 22 and during the first afternoon drifted about six miles camping below Six-Mile island; after that the average was approximately forty miles a day. On the 23rd we passed Calling river where there is a small settlement of half-breeds, comprising four or five families, who live in houses, although retaining the Indian habits and customs of hunting, trapping and fishing. In summer, during the season of navigation, they are employed as boatmen on the different scow brigades, which are owned mostly by fur traders who take their goods down almost to the farthest limit of fresh-water navigation. These scows are rarely ever brought back, the steamboats that run below McMurray being utilized for the return trip as far as McMurray. Above this point the free traders, as distinguished from the Hudson's Bay company, have to bring their furs up to Athabaska in their own scows by tracking, the company declining to carry a free trader's furs in their scows.

In summer the mail is carried by canoe once a month from Athabaska to McMurray, but there are no offices on the river between these two points. In winter it is carried by dog-train via Lac LaBiche settlement to McMurray.

At Calling River settlement there is a general store, fairly well stocked with provisions, dry goods, etc. Mr. Peter Prudens the owner of this store does some farming on a limited scale; he grows sufficient oats for his own use, as well as potatoes, cabbages, turnips, carrots, etc., both for his own use and for sale. He has grown wheat very successfully but there is no market for it. The Dominion Government telegraph line crosses the river here and the right of way is cut out all the way from Athabaska. Most of it is passable for wagons, but the banks of Deep creek cannot be crossed with teams. The telegraph line is said to be opened as far as the nineteenth correction line.

We passed two oil-boring outfits, the first one on the right bank, and the next one on the left bank near Pelican portage. Neither of these outfits have struck oil yet but the one at Pelican rapids has struck a considerable flow of natural gas. The first oil-boring outfit is about eleven miles and the other about three miles above the rapids. There is another outflow of natural gas about twenty miles below Grand rapids, near Buffalo river, on the left bank of the Athabaska; there at the edge of the river the gas exudes, and can be lighted with a match. At Pelican portage just below the rapids there is a settlement of seven or eight families, nearly all half-breeds. From there a winter road leads to Wabiskaw Lake settlement. Goods are brought down from the Athabaska by steamer in summer and when winter sets in are freighted across the portage with sleighs to Wabiskaw, a distance of about seventy miles.

Forty-one miles below Pelican rapids is the mouth of House river, which is as far as the Hudson's Bay company's steamer *Athabaska* runs. A quantity of freight is usually taken there by the steamer when the water is fairly high and is then freighted by team over the trail to McMurray. This trail was at one time an Indian pack-trail, but recently it was opened out as a sleigh road. The Hudson's Bay company have at House river a large shed covered with tar paper and there are in the vicinity three or four half-breed families engaged in hunting and trapping. The soil there has not been cultivated to any extent, although potatoes have been grown successfully.

Nine miles below House river the Grand rapids commence. These are very formidable rapids, having a fall of about fifty feet in half a mile. An island lies in the rapids, and by far the greater body of water passes down on the west side of the island. The channel on the east side is not more than three chains wide. The loaded scows are all tied up about a mile above the island whence they are run down singly between big boulders and rocks, to the head of the island, where there is a tramway laid up to near the water's edge. The freight is then loaded on a car and pushed down to the foot of the island, while the empty scows are run down the east channel to some comparatively still water which lies behind a point of land jutting out from the east immediately below the island. At the foot of the island floats in the shape of logs, are attached to the end of a long rope and thrown into the water. They float down through part of the turbulent water into the eddy behind the point jutting out from the east, where

5 GEORGE V., A. 1915

they are taken aboard a scow, which is allowed to float out into the current. Fifty or more hands then take hold of the rope, now attached to the scow, and pull her up to some bare rocks jutting out from the lower end of the island where she is again loaded with freight. This work does not occupy as much time as one might imagine, but every parcel of goods has to be carried on a man's back from the tramcar to the scow, a distance of two or three chains. Merchandise and provisions are as a rule done up in fair-sized packages, but there are other articles, such as stoves which are of considerably greater weight; they have also to be carried on the backs of the men, some of whom may be seen running down the incline with three, four or even up to five hundred pounds of flour on their backs. It is not a smooth path either, as the men have to step from stone to stone and rock to rock.

All of the twenty-eight scows were reloaded by the afternoon of August 2, when we continued our journey down stream. The banks of the river appeared to increase in height as we proceeded down the river, and at a point not far from McMurray the aneroid reading showed the depth of the valley to be over 500 feet. After passing all the remaining rapids, of which the Cascade is the most formidable, we arrived at McMurray, on the morning of August 5.

From this place I proceeded to the inspection of Mr. Tremblay's contract No. 33 of 1912. I hired two canoes and left McMurray in the afternoon and after tracking, poling and paddling up a very rapid current arrived at our destination seven miles up Clearwater river. We camped on the twenty-third base line where it intersects the Clearwater in section 36, township 88, range 9, west of the fourth meridian.

The immediate banks of the Athabaska at McMurray and for some distance up are not very high. The settlement lies on a plateau about forty feet above the level of the river and extends easterly for several miles. There are four stores at McMurray proper, besides a Roman Catholic mission; about two miles farther east there is another store or two. At this place which is called "The Prairie," there are a number of settlers, carrying on farming on a small scale. Up the Clearwater there are also a number of squatters, most of whom appear to be there for speculative purposes rather than with the intention of becoming permanent settlers. The proposed construction of a railway from Edmonton to McMurray in the immediate future, appears to have created a considerable demand for land in that district.

We concluded our inspection of this contract on August 10, and returned to McMurray that evening. On the following morning the scow brigade, now reduced to eight boats, started up stream. Six of these were laden with fur, brought up from the Hudson Bay company's most northerly stations. The other two were cook scows, one for supplying meals to the passengers, and one for the crew. Each scow was pulled up stream by a crew of ten or twelve men who tramped along the edge of the water. At the "Cascade" all the scows were unloaded as the water was considerably lower, and all the goods, principally bales of fur, and the passengers' baggage were portaged a short distance up the shore while the scows were hauled up by the combined crews. This occupied nearly a whole day.

After passing Cascade, Crooked, Middle and Brulé rapids we finally reached the foot of Grand rapids, the last and also the most formidable of all, on August 20. Here we were delayed until the 23rd, on account of all the cargoes having to be portaged about a quarter of a mile and the scows tracked up stream with a crew of fifty men each. Above the rapids we met the Hudson's Bay company's steamer *Athabaska* in which both crews and passengers, amounting to a total of between 200 and 250 persons, were taken to Athabaska where we arrived about noon on August 25.

After re-organizing my party we again left Athabaska on September 13 via Athabaska river for LaBiche river where we arrived the following day. There is a good pack trail from the mouth of LaBiche river to Lac LaBiche settlement; in fact it has the appearance of having at one time been utilized as a wagon or sleigh road. We packed along this trail about five miles, where we camped, and from there completed

Photo by H. Matheson, D.L.S.

Road to Pyramid Lake in Jasper Park, Alberta.

Pyramid lake is situated in township 45, range 1, west of the Sixth meridian four miles from Jasper. The road from Jasper, which, like all other roads in the Park, has been built for tourist traffic, is a splendid road for automobiles, and has very easy grades. In the foreground of the picture is the reddish aspen (*Populus tremuloides*).

the subdivision of that part of township 70, range 18, west of the fourth meridian, lying south of La Biche river. On September 29 I received instructions to subdivide township 73, range 19, west of the fourth meridian, I therefore sent my packers with the horses to a point near the nineteenth base line. We broke up camp the following morning, and started down the river with our scow, arriving at the nineteenth base line pack trail on the morning of October 1, the horses having arrived on the opposite shore the night before. We swam the horses across, built a stage for a cache, unloaded the scow, and got everything ready to move into the work. The next morning we moved to the southwest quarter of section 2, township 73, range 19 and commenced subdivision. On the night of the 3rd and the two following days there were flurries of snow which lodged in the trees, and made it somewhat disagreeable for the line men. On the 8th as the work was progressing favourably I started for Athabaska to lay in a further supply of provisions and to purchase some sleighs, which I knew would be required later on. We tracked up the river with a borrowed canoe, arriving at Athabaska on the 11th. I had to purchase another scow and a canoe to carry the provisions, sleighs, harness, etc., back to camp. We left Athabaska on the 18th arriving at my cache, near the nineteenth base line on the 23rd.

The party returning to camp from their day's work crossed a lake on the ice on the evening of the 25th. On the 26th snow fell all night and continued all the following day, so I sent all the party down to the river cache, to haul up the scows and secure them for the winter.

We continued the subdivision of township 73, range 19 and completed it on December 5. This township is fairly level and there is some good soil, but the larger part of it consists of swamps. Very little of the land, west of Athabaska river and below Calling river, will be available for settlement, until either a road or a railway has been constructed on that side of the river. The banks are so high, that it is almost impossible to construct a wagon or even a sleigh road from the river to the plateau above. For this reason the small areas of excellent timber which grow all along the plateau, can not be utilized at present. Judging by the signs and tracks in the snow there is game in abundance, but while we were engaged in the subdivision, four large timber wolves appeared and this had the effect of driving all the deer away. Up to November 21 the lowest temperature was 2°above zero, but on the following morning it dropped to 5° below.

On December 11 we left for the inspection of contract No. 15 of 1913 in townships 70 and 72, ranges 18 and 19, and reached there on the 15th. We completed this inspection on the 23rd and left for Athabaska on the following morning. On our way to Calling River settlement, we passed Mr. Kraemer's fox farm, on the east side of the Athabaska. He had in captivity twenty-seven wild foxes, varying from common red, to cross and silver grey, some of them quite valuable. Owing to my horses not being shod, we could not take the outfit up the Athabaska on the ice, so we had to make a detour by way of Calling lake and thence south, striking the river about twelve miles below Athabaska which we reached on December 27.

While there I purchased supplies and horse feed, engaged a freighter to carry my goods to Moose portage and had my horses rough shod for travelling on the ice.

We left Athabaska on January 2, 1914, for contract No. 14 of 1913, which we inspected and then proceeded to contracts Nos. 13, 12 and 11 of 1913, completing this work on February 18. These four contracts lay in townships 69 to 73, ranges 23 to 27, west of the fourth meridian and range 1, west of the fifth meridian. While engaged on this inspection we experienced the coldest weather of the winter, the thermometer registering 51° below zero for three days. Port Cornwall which was formerly known as Mirror Landing is a new town consisting of several hundred inhabitants situated at the junction of Lesser Slave and Athabaska rivers, in township 71, range 1, west of the fifth meridian. It has a number of stores and a telegraph office, and is on the direct road from Athabaska to Grouard. It lies opposite Smith, a still newer town consisting

5 GEORGE V., A. 1915

mostly of log buildings, on the south side of the river. This is the present terminus of the Edmonton, Dunvegan and British Columbia railway and is the point where the new railway bridge crosses the Athabaska, said to be 131 miles from Edmonton. This town appears to be the headquarters of the railway company and will be a divisional point. Trains are running on this road to Edmonton every alternate day, but only freight is hauled. Much of the freight so far comes up the river from Athabaska to Port Cornwall, thence to Grouard by way of Lesser Slave lake and on to Peace River Crossing. Sleighs and automobiles are met frequently on this trail. Nearly all the settlers along the river keep stopping-places for man and beast, and they are frequently overcrowded. Much of the country fronting on the river is burned over, the banks on both sides being considerably lower than those below Calling river. There is a fairly large settlement back of Moose portage. The soil is productive and some good crops have been grown, as well as vegetables of excellent quality. Most of the settlers combine with their farming operations, freighting, fishing, hunting, trapping and taking out railway ties, and fuel for steamboats.

We arrived back at Athabaska on February 20. After procuring further supplies and horse feed we again started down the river on the 25th for contracts Nos. 16 and 17 of 1913, both lying along the river below the nineteenth base. We reached there on March 2, and camped on section 4, township 74· range 18, west of the fourth meridian.

The valley of the river in this vicinity varies from 400 to 500 feet in depth, and the banks are generally steep. The plateau above is nearly level, and consists mostly of swamp lands, wooded with spruce and tamarack. The higher areas are covered with poplar and spruce. Small areas of very good timber are found, more particularly in the northern plateau. This will not be available for manufacturing purposes until railways are constructed to carry off the manufactured product.

Athabaska river was in excellent condition for travel at this season, freighting teams carrying loads of three tons and over. A great deal of traffic was carried on from Athabaska to Pelican portage, a distance of about 120 miles, thence to Wabiskaw, about 70 miles, and also from Athabaska to Old House, and thence overland to McMurray. This traffic affords the settlers around Athabaska a good opportunity for employment for their horses during a few months of the winter. Much of this traffic will cease as soon as the Edmonton-McMurray railway is constructed.

Access to any of the lands subdivided down the river from Athabaska can only be had by the river, which is the main highway at the present time for entering these new townships. Those subdivided up the river may be conveniently reached by the newly constructed Edmonton, Dunvegan and British Columbia railway.

APPENDIX No. 37.

ABSTRACT OF THE REPORT OF J. B. McFARLANE, D.L.S.

BASE LINE SURVEYS IN NORTHERN ALBERTA.

My work during the past season consisted of the survey of parts of the twenty-fourth and twenty-fifth base lines west of the fourth meridian.

I left Toronto on April 3, 1913, but as the ice on the Athabaska was a little later than usual in breaking up, I did not leave Edmonton until the 23rd. This early start was of little avail, as the water was very low and the trip to McMurray in scows a very laborious one. It took twice as long as the same trip the previous year. Few outfits went through without all of their boats suffering more or less damage, and some had the misfortune to have scows sunk. At Grand rapids only a small portion of a scow load could be taken through the last mile and landed at the portage. Consequently we had to make many trips. Below the rapids the water was so shallow that the scows were continually grating on rocks or gravel, and we had to leave one load behind to be brought down at high water, as we had not enough men to handle the scows quickly enough in the continuous rapids. At the Boiler rapids our steersmen successfully used a new channel. At the Little Cascades each scow stuck at the drop and had to be partially unloaded At the Cascades two-thirds of each load had to be portaged about twenty chains and lowered thirty feet over an ice cliff into the scows and even then the scows stuck at the drop, which was about six feet.

We reached McMurray on May 14, and my horses, which had left Edmonton on April 14, arrived the following day. On the 16th we camped at the mouth of Steepbank river. As practically all the country between there and the end of the twenty-fourth base line in the middle of range 6 was muskeg, we followed Steepbank river. This led us a long distance south of the base line, but as we were sure of running into no impassable muskegs, I decided that this was the quickest way to take the outfit. At the forks of the river we followed the north branch, which took us within a few miles of the end of the line. On June 5 work was commenced on the line by retracing the north boundary of section 34, township 92, range 6.

The country through which the twenty-fourth base line was run this year was about 90 per cent muskeg. A few sand ridges run north and south across the line in the west half of range 6. These mostly face the west and have most of their fall in that direction. This half range and range 7 are drained to the south by the north branch of Steepbank river and its tributary creeks.

This country is, as a rule, flat with a few low sandy or gravelly ridges. Those running north and south have their fall to the west and others scarcely rise out of the muskeg. In the summer of 1912 a fire completely overran the northeastern part of this district crossing the line from the centre of range 7 easterly. As that was a dry summer the moss in the muskegs burned well and all trees except those in the very wet tamarack swamps, were killed. The timber throughout this stretch of country was small and stunted except on the scattered ridges, where patches of good spruce, jackpine and poplar timber were destroyed.

Immediately following fires in this country the grass springs up in the burnt muskegs, and I have no doubt that if the fires were frequent enough to keep the moss and trees from growing, a good ranching country would be formed. Old patches of brulé testify that grass will grow luxuriantly on the burnt muskegs until smothered out again by the growing scrub.

5 GEORGE V., A. 1915

Township 93, range 8 and almost all of township 92, up to the high banks of Steepbank river, are drained to the north away from the river, and many creeks rising in this district flow north or northwest to join Muskeg river. Throughout this district the timber, mostly spruce, is thick and small, probably large enough for pulp-wood, but not suitable for timber except in narrow bands along some short slopes, or along creeks where the banks have sufficient drainage to allow the timber to grow.

Range 9 is crossed in a west by northwesterly direction by the deep valley of Steepbank river with the river itself coming near the line at the west of the range, but not touching it. The river valley is generally one-half to three-quarters of a mile in width with high banks and steep slopes, and the more level portions are generally well timbered with spruce. The valley is much the same from the mouth of the river bank to the forks of the north and east branches, only its depth and width gradually decrease and the timber becomes more broken with patches of small poplar and jackpine. The north branch soon loses its valley and its banks become gradu-ally lower until they form part of the muskeg. There is very little timber along this branch.

In range 10 the Athabaska crosses the line in section 35. This great river aver-ages about half a mile in width in this vicinity, and is always navigable for steam-boats past this point. Its flow at high and at low water differs immensely and an estimate of the one without the other would be very misleading. The channel is always well defined and scarcely ever is any land flooded. Patches of spruce timber up to three feet in diameter are scattered along its banks, and a small but valuable limit, easily accessible, could be had on the flats just north of the mouth of Steepbank river. The river flats are generally about a mile wide with the river sometimes on one side of the valley and sometimes on the other. Many of these flats have large lagoons or lakes with marshes or swamps around them and only a narrow neck of dry ground separating them from the river. At La Saline, about three miles north of the line, a very large hay meadow adjoins a small lake and at several other places there are smaller ones. Last summer however, was so wet that very little hay could be put up as most of the meadows in the north country were flooded.

The banks of the Athabaska valley are about two hundred feet high in this district and in some places are quite steep. There are a number of projections of limestone along the valley and in the river banks, in the vicinity of the twenty-fourth base.

Above the hill, west of the river, there is a stretch of wet tamarack muskeg reach-ing a long distance to the south and three or four miles to the north. Its width at the line was ninety chains, with only one jackpine ridge in the middle. A trail was not made across this muskeg but the line was finished, as far as instructions called for, from a flying camp in the next range. A small river known locally as Beaver river, flows almost due north along the east side of range 11, having its source north-west of McMurray and emptying into the Athabaska about a mile below Muskeg river. The valley is about thirty feet deep and less than a quarter of a mile wide with a few chains of flats. Across the remainder of this range the line followed close to a creek with popular and spruce timber averaging ten inches in diameter along its banks. Back from the creeks, which only drain the land for a short distance on either side, much of the land is muskeg with stunted spruce or tamarack. An old Indian trail for pack-horses crosses the line just west of Beaver river. It runs from McKay to McMurray, following the Beaver almost to its source, thence southeast to McMurray.

Levels were run along the line starting at the last bench-mark established in 1912. Bench-marks were established, as nearly as possible, at every half mile and check levels were run in the opposite direction between these. The elevation which starts at 2,010 feet drops gradually but almost continuously for twenty-one miles till it is 1,100 feet just above the banks of the valley of Athabaska river. The valley is a little less than two hundred feet deep the left bank being the higher. Then the elevation remains about the same until Beaver river is crossed whence there is a gradual rise to 1,292 feet at the end of the line.

On August 5 the twenty-fourth base line was completed through range 11 which was as far as instructions called for. The move to the twenty-fifth base line was then commenced. On the way down the Athabaska we stopped at La Saline for five days and put up hay, as it was impossible to get any one at McMurray to do this for us, although promises were easily obtained. A party of five men with fourteen horses and a scow load of supplies had left the twenty-fourth base line on July 10 to cut trail and pack supplies along the twenty-fifth base. After building a cache on the Athabaska in the vicinity of the latter base we followed their trail and overtook them on August 25 about the middle of range 6. This far the trail had followed close to the line but, there we had to swing to the south around a large muskeg basin and follow along some ridges which form a watershed but which are completely covered by muskeg, thence east to Firebag river and thence northeast through a range of jackpine hills. We reached our most easterly camp on the twenty-fifth base on September 8 and on the following day the east boundary of section 36, township 96, range 1, was retraced and the corners moved 4·34 chains north.

The pack trail from the Athabaska was built with great difficulty and travelled with more difficulty and almost all of the party got wet at one time or another by a horse going through or off the corduroy. Fortunately this country was frozen up fairly solid before the line was run through it.

In range 1 the base line runs mostly through sand hills and the two townships to the north are much the same. These townships were completely overrun by fire in 1912. Firebag river, which at this point is about seventy feet wide, three feet deep, and has a current of about one mile per hour, crosses the line in section 34 running northwesterly and then back again in section 33. From there it takes a sweep to the south and winds- through a large muskeg which is too wet to have timber of any size on it. In range 2, townships 96 and 97, are both crossed east and west by ranges of sand hills with a wide stretch of muskeg and long stretches of tamarack swamp between them and directly along the line. Firebag river leaves the large muskeg about the middle of the range and swings around south of the hills in township 96. It runs in a small valley through low sand ridges. Range' 3 is much the same as range 2 with muskeg along the line and sand hills to the north and also along Firebag river to the south. This river runs in a west by northwesterly direction until it is about a mile and a half south of the line at the west boundary of the range. Near the middle of township 96, range 3, it is joined by a large tributary from the south. It crosses range 4 in a west by northwesterly direction in section 33. Its width is about one hundred and forty feet, its depth two feet and it has a current of about one and a half miles per hour. The muskeg to the east follows the line to the river. The country to the south of the river is rolling and sandy with small muskegs sloping off to a large muskeg basin to the southwest. This muskeg includes the central and western part of township 96, range 4, all of township 96, range 5, and the northeast half of township 96, range 6. It is drained to the north by creeks running into Firebag river. In township 95, across these ranges, is a wide shallow depression draining to the east and to the west. North of the line Firebag river winds in a west by northwesterly direction through a narrow valley with many cut banks. A range of jackpine hills follows the north bank of the river and back of these the country is rolling with creeks or muskegs in the valleys. The greater part of range 7 is dry country. A range of rolling hills covers the eastern part of township 96, range 7. These hills become higher and rougher north of the line and widening out in range 6 and to the west side of range 7, extend north to Firebag river which turns more to the north in this range being joined by the north branch near the north boundary of township 98, range 7.

Much of this hilly country was overrun about three years ago by a fire which killed a large quantity of good spruce timber. The soil on the rougher hills to the north is mostly sand but in the vicinity of the line there was a fair coating of loam and in many places grass stood three feet high among the fire killed timber. Grass springs up quickly in the burnt muskegs and I think a large proportion of this district could easily be turned into a good ranching country.

The main branch of Muskeg river flows out of Muskeg lake which is about three miles long and a mile wide, and is located about the northeast corner of township 95, range 8. This lake is fed by a large creek from the east. The river is very crooked and from the lake flows northeasterly between dry banks in a rolling country until it nears the base line. There it turns northwesterly amidst the beginning of the large stretch of muskeg from which it derives its name. Where it crosses the base line in section 35, range 8, it is twenty-one feet wide, eight feet deep and flows one-eighth of a mile per hour. At its most northerly part it is joined by the north branch, and from there flows southwesterly across the line and keeps about the same direction to its mouth. It has very little current and is almost dead water except when flooded by rains; it then fills its low banks which are all muskeg and show nothing but vegetable formation below. The water in Muskeg river is always dark coloured and is rather stagnant in winter. Water in the small lakes also becomes stagnant in the winter but all the running creeks had good water. A continuous wide stretch of muskeg follows Muskeg river from the jackpine hills along the Athabaska northeasterly to the source of the north branch. Between the two crossings of the river the line traverses a tamarack and willow swamp.

A range of rolling hills stretches along the line from section 35, range 9, to section 32, range 10. These are covered with thick jackpine, poplar, spruce and birch averaging about ten inches in diameter. In range 9, most of these hills were overrun by a fire in the summer of 1912, which was very dry. This fire burned across the muskeg at Muskeg river and ran off towards the southeast to the twenty-fourth base line. The hills drop down to a lower level about three miles north of the base line and a low stretch of land drains towards the north branch of Muskeg river.

The Athabaska crosses this base line in section 36, range 11, running almost due north. Through townships 95 and 96 jackpine and poplar hills follow the east bank of the river. These gradually drop into muskeg about one mile south of the line. This is the point where our trail leaves the river and where we placed our cache. The river banks are about one hundred feet high and are steep. They are usually close to the channel and have but little valuable timber on them.

In ranges 11 and 12 the line ran through an undulating country covered with thick jackpine, poplar, spruce and tamarack averaging about eight inches in diameter. The country, back from the rivers and creeks is cut up by muskegs, and the creeks in some places spread out in large willow flats.

Calumet river drains the townships north of the line and Tar river those immediately to the south. Both are short streams rising in Birch mountains. This range of mountains will apparently cross the base line about half way between the west boundary of range 12 and Moose lake. They run in a northeasterly direction.

A strip of good spruce timber about twenty chains wide, with the trees averaging from fourteen to twenty inches in diameter, extends along the narrow valley of Tar river across these ranges.

A sleigh trail was cut from the Athabaska to section 35, range 12; this crosses several muskegs but probably a good pack trail could be made following Tar river which crosses the line in section 31, range 12.

Scarcely any of this country would be suitable for agriculture on account of summer frosts and the difficulty of draining and clearing it, but I think a good deal would be suitable for ranching if cleared enough to give the grass a chance to grow.

Rainfall was plentiful throughout the whole season and the snow was about fourteen inches deep on January 15, 1914. No land is flooded by creeks but the muskegs are well filled by heavy rains.

Mineral claims are numerous along the river but the only minerals much in evidence yet are salt and tar sand or asphalt. These appear to be well distributed. Wood fuel is everywhere plentiful. Game and fur-bearing animals are plentiful, and hunting and trapping is largely carried on among the Indians in this district. An industrious and capable trapper can make from one thousand to twenty-five hundred dollars in a season.

No valuable water-powers were found this season. Dams could be built but it would be difficult to get much head. No stone-quarries are opened up and no other industries are started yet although there has been considerable drilling for oil along the Athabaska.

Levels were run along the line and bench-marks established wherever possible near each half mile post and check levels were run in the opposite direction between them. From the elevation of 1,871 feet at the fourth meridian the fall is rapid, to 1,713 feet at the west crossing of Firebag river in section 33, range 1. A hill just west of the river rises to 1,773 feet. From there to the west side of range 3 there is little change in elevation. In range 4 the elevation drops steadily to 1,539 feet at Firebag river. This elevation is again reached three miles west of the river and the elevation then drops steadily to 1,344 feet at the middle of range 6. The hills at the east of range 7 reach an elevation of 1,405, but they slope rapidly to the west. At the crossing of the east branch of Muskeg river the elevation is 1,142 feet and at the crossing of the main river 1,090. Across range 9 the line follows through rolling country draining to the southeast. An elevation of 1,304 feet is reached on section 35, range 10 and from there the slope is towards the Athabaska the elevation of which was 897 feet. West of the Athabaska the land rises gradually to the Birch mountains, with only small local depressions; at the west of range 12 the elevation is 1,818 feet.

On January 15 the twenty-fifth base line was completed through range 12 and as no hay or feed was procurable at McMurray or farther north to continue the survey of the twenty-sixth base line, I decided to close operations for the season. It took four days travel to reach McMurray. We left there on January 21 and in six days and a half we reached the portage to House river. This is a new trail and is still rough. Hay was scarce at McMurray and on the trail as the Hudson's Bay company were holding all they could get in order to do their own freighting. Our horses were on short rations of hay and a moderate amount of oats until we reached Colin river where hay was plentiful. We reached Athabaska on February 5 and Edmonton the following evening.

APPENDIX No. 38.

REPORT OF R. B. McKAY, D.L.S.

SURVEYS IN THE RAILWAY BELT, BRITISH COLUMBIA.

VANCOUVER, B.C. February 11, 1914.

E. DEVILLE, Esq., L.L.D.,
　　Surveyor General,
　　　　Ottawa, Canada.

SIR,—I have the honour to submit the following general report on my survey operations for the season of 1913.

My first work which was commenced on May 17 consisted of the survey of two small parcels of land withdrawn from timber berth No. 553 in sections 30 and 32 of township 17 east of the coast meridian, which had been squatted upon and partly cleared. The land in this vicinity is rather hilly, and is timbered with fir, cedar, hemlock, alder and maple. The soil is well suited for growing fruit and vegetables. A saw-mill was being constructed preparatory to logging the timber of the locality during the following winter. These parcels are situated about three miles from Mission Junction, a town on the Canadian Pacific railway, with a population of about 1,200. It serves as a local market for the produce of the settlers who are engaged in fruit growing, dairying and mixed farming. Fruit growing is the main industry, and the district is noted for the success it has attained in this line.

On May 23 I proceeded to township 21, east of the coast meridian, to establish the east boundary of the western tier of sections in this township, and complete the survey of these sections. The eastern halves of these sections occupy the westerly slope of a steep mountain ridge covered with fir, hemlock, cedar and alder, mostly second growth, interspersed with some large burnt fir. The land for the most part is rocky and unfit for agricultural purposes. There is some good land suitable for fruit or vegetables in the westerly half of sections 19, 30 and 31, but the remainder of the township is mountainous and of no agricultural value.

On June 27 I moved camp to Coquitlam to make a preliminary survey of a proposed subdivision of land withdrawn from timber berths Nos. 77 and 86 in sections 11, 12 and 14 of township 39, west of the coast meridian. This land has been " logged." The soil is a sandy loam, gravelly in places, with gravel subsoil. It is suitable for poultry ranching and fruit land, and where not gravelly for vegetables. It should also make good home sites, as it is situated about two miles from Westminster Junction on the Coquitlam pipe line road and adjoins the limits of the growing town of Port Coquitlam which has recently experienced a boom due to the Canadian Pacific Railway company establishing railway shops and yards there. This town extends to Pitt river where dredging operations are in progress. The ship-building industry has been started and the erection of grain elevators is contemplated.

On July 22 I moved to Port Moody and thence across Burrard inlet to " Sunnyside," where I examined a parcel of land which has been withdrawn from timber berth No. 52, in sections 20, 21 and 16 of township 39, west of the coast meridian and which it is proposed to subdivide into twenty acre blocks. This land is situated about 600 feet above Burrard inlet and is reached by the old Buntzen lake trail, or skid road, which connects with the Port Moody road on the north shore of the inlet where a gravel plant is in operation. The soil is light, sandy loam, rather rocky or gravelly in places and is suitable for poultry ranching, fruit growing and gardening and should make good home sites for the people of Port Moody where lumbering and oil refining are at present the main industries.

I finished my preliminary survey at Port Moody on August 8, and after increasing my party, proceeded to Columbia valley, establishing camp in section 7 of township 22, east of the coast meridian. From this camp I made surveys of eighteen parcels of land withdrawn from timber berth No. 55 and situated in section 1 of township 19, and sections 4, 5, 6, 7, 8, 9, 15 and 16 of township 22. These parcels were from twenty to eighty acres in area, and were laid out as legal subdivisions or aliquot parts thereof, in such a way as to include the improvements of the squatters on the land. Some of these squatters were attracted to this locality over twenty years ago and although the land has not been open for entry, as it was included in a timber berth, they have remained on their holdings and have annually grown good crops of vegetables and fruit. The climate is mild and rather wet, and the soil is very fertile in many places. When the timber is removed and the land thrown open for settlement, the remaining land in the valley will be quickly taken up. There is a dense growth of large fir and cedar in parts of sections 6, 5, 4 and 9, estimated as high as 150,000 feet per acre, but elsewhere the larger trees are more scattered. The amount of merchantable timber is annually growing less as much of it is decaying and should have been logged years ago. The nearest market for the produce of the district is the town of Chilliwack, fifteen miles distant, which is reached by a road which skirts the eastern shore of Cultus lake.

On September 14 I moved up to the north end of Cultus lake, where I surveyed three parcels in sections 35 and 36 of township 22, east of the coast meridian, and two parcels in section 30 of township 25, all of which were being withdrawn from timber berth No. 55. Here also a good portion of the land will make first class fruit land when cleared. The soil is rich and suitable for garden products of all kinds.

On September 23 I moved camp up Chilliwack river to the end of the Mt. Baker wagon road, in section 34 of township 1, range 29, west of the sixth meridian. There I surveyed three parcels in sections 33, 34 and 27 of this township, and one parcel in sections 32 and 33 of township 1, range 28, all of which were being withdrawn from timber berth No. 50. There are few patches of land in the valley of Chilliwack river in this vicinity which are level enough to be of use for agricultural purposes. The soil is rich and consists usually of clay loam with clay subsoil, and is suitable for all kinds of garden products. The timber is the main resource of the district, large fir and cedar up to four feet in diameter being found on both sides of the river and particularly on the higher benches.

On October 4 I moved to Majuba hill and camped in section 29 of township 22, east of the coast meridian. From this base I surveyed one parcel in section 12 of township 19, and seven parcels in sections 20, 29, 28 and 34 of township 22. This district is easy of access, as it is served by a good road and also by the British Columbia Electric railway. Fruit raising, dairying and mixed farming are engaged in by the settlers. I completed the survey of these parcels on October 25.

I then retraced the east and north boundaries of section 27, township 23, east of the coast meridian, and the northerly boundary of Commonage Indian reserve in that section, and traversed the islands of Fraser river in sections 9, 10, and 15 of township 3, range 30, west of the sixth meridian. Some years ago the channel of Fraser river in these sections was along the left bank, but it has now shifted to its right bank, with the result that the large islands which originally existed have been practically reduced to sand bars and the former channel of the Fraser is occupied by recent deposits of gravel, sand and silt. I also made some traverses in section 4 of this township. Fraser river is navigable through these sections only in high water.

I left this district on November 7 for Deroche, where I traversed three small islands in Nicomen slough in section 8 of township 24, east of the coast meridian.

25b—11

5 GEORGE V., A. 1915

There a saw-mill is in operation, and the settlers in the vicinity are engaged in raising garden produce and dairying.

On November 10, I moved by the Canadian Pacific railway to Port Moody, where, after experiencing considerable unfavourable weather, I completed, on November 30, the subdivision of the forty-one twenty-acre lots withdrawn from timber berth No. 52, which I had investigated earlier in the season.

I then moved to Coquitlam, where I laid out thirty-four lots on the land withdrawn from timber berths Nos. 77 and 86, which I had also previously examined, and, having finished this, I returned to Vancouver and disbanded my party on December 13.

I have the honour to be, Sir,

Your obedient servant,

ROBT. B. McKAY, D.L.S.

APPENDIX No. 39.

ABSTRACT OF THE REPORT OF A. M. NARRAWAY, D.L.S.

MISCELLANEOUS SURVEYS AND RESURVEYS IN SOUTHERN ALBERTA.

On May 7, 1913, I left Medicine Hat for township 21, range 10, west of the fourth meridian.

My work there consisted of a resurvey of this township and a survey of a few section lines not run when the old river-lot lines were destroyed; this was completed on June 10.

Red Deer river runs across this township, and with the coulees on the south side which extend several miles from the river, breaks up the township very badly. It is fairly well settled and good progress is being made by the settlers especially those engaged in mixed farming. On the north side of the river there is considerable difficulty in obtaining water, and most of-it is hauled from the river. The branch line of the Canadian Pacific Railway from Bassano to Empress is now nearly completed. This will afford a ready outlet for this vicinity as it passes about five miles south of the river, and the new ferry installed this season by the Government in section 2, township 21, range 11, will accommodate those living north of the river. .

My next work, which was started on June 23 and completed on July 10, was a retracement of townships 6 and 7, range 30, west of the third meridian. To reach this location it was necessary to return to Medicine Hat, and thence go southwest past Elkwater lake, and across the Cypress hills. The country along this route is nearly all taken up and good fields of grain were seen. Elkwater lake and the small lakes in its vicinity, backed up by the thickly wooded Cypress hills to the south will make a very pretty and desirable summering place, and no doubt will be used as such by the people of Medicine Hat in the near future.

The Cypress Hills forest reserve cuts off the northerly one-third of township 7, but most of the remainder of the township is level prairie with very rich soil. There is a strip of this level land along the south boundary of the reserve from the east boundary of township 7, range 30, to the west end of the hills; this is known locally as "the bench." At present there is usually a summer frost which prevents the ripening of the grain and this land is being used for hay and green feed. It is the belief of the ranchers and settlers in this vicinity that summer frosts will disappear as the country becomes settled. It is hard to see that this will be the case on account of the large stretch of country immediately to the south which is so rough and rocky that it will probably be used for ranching and not for cultivation. There seems to be an unusual amount of rainfall along these hills which almost completely misses the country more than a few miles away. Numerous springs of excellent water are scattered throughout this district. .

My next work, which was completed on July 23, was a retracement of township 6, range 5, west of the fourth meridian. This township is nearly all taken up, and the settlers are making very good progress. They appear to be meeting with great success with their crops. Abundance of good water can be obtained and both coal and wood are convenient. Within a couple of years the Weyburn branch of the Canadian Pacific railway will pass through Manyberries a townsite within three miles of this township.

From this township I went to township 2, range 15, west of the fourth meridian where two township corners were missing and there was a road allowance of abnormal width.

25b—11½

5 GEORGE V., A. 1915

After dealing with this we moved to township 2, range 9, and retraced townships 2, ranges 9 and 10 finishing on September 3. Milk river passes through both of these townships and with its coulees, which in many cases stretch four and five miles from the river, breaks up the townships so badly that they are unfit for farming purposes. They are admirably adapted to ranching however as is shown by the good condition of the cattle and horses at present grazing there. A great many rattlesnakes are found in these townships; I have sometimes killed ten or more in one day.

From here we went back past Manyberries and retraced townships 6, ranges 3 and 4. These townships are well adapted for ranching and are being used almost wholly for this purpose at present. Feed is a little scarce, but the ranchers claim that there is a great amount of nourishment in what grows. This appears to be the case as the cattle we saw were in good condition.

These townships were completed on October 7 and we returned to Carlstadt and then went north to township 18, range 10, west of the fourth meridian. As had been reported we found that Tide lake had dried up and we produced the section lines across the land formerly covered by water. It is doubtful if this land will be of much use for some time as the settlers state that each spring it is covered with water which stays fairly late in the season.

While in this vicinity we resurveyed the south boundary of township 19, range 9, as the road allowance had been found to be abnormal in several places.

Having finished the work in this vicinity on October 30, we moved to Red Deer river to survey some section lines not run during the original subdivision in townships 21, ranges 11 and 12, and township 22, range 12, west of the fourth meridian. These townships are badly cut up by the river and its coulees. To the north of the river the country is well settled and good progress is being made in spite of the lack of rain, but south of the river the country is all used for ranching.

It is in these townships that the fossilized remains of dinosaurs and other of the prehistoric animals are to be found, and while running our lines we found some very good specimens.

We completed these townships on November 28 and then moved to Lethbridge by way of Brooks. Here we traversed the left bank of Belly river across sections 25 and 36, township 8, range 23, as the river had changed its course in several places.

From here we went to Macleod, reaching there on December 6. We commenced the traverse of Oldman river on the 10th and continued it across townships 9, ranges 26 and 25, and township 10, range 25, west of the fourth meridian, completing it on December 27. We found that the river had changed its course in many places and that some of the islands had been joined to the main land.

I closed operations for the season at Medicine Hat, and reached Ottawa on January 2, 1914.

APPENDIX No. 40.

ABSTRACT OF THE REPORT OF R. NEELANDS, D.L.S.

STADIA SURVEYS IN CENTRAL SASKATCHEWAN.

My work during the past season consisted of the stadia survey of lakes in the Humboldt and Prince Albert districts of Saskatchewan and was carried on in the following townships, all west of the second meridian: township 40, range 18; township 44, range 22; townships 38, 39, 40, 41 and 42, range 23, townships 39, 40, 41, 42, 43 and 44, range 24; townships 39, 40, 41 and 42, range 25; townships 40 and 41, range 26; township 46, range 28, and township 49, range 26. In the last named township a stadia traverse was made of the north bank of Saskatchewan river.

In this district there are many small lakes that had not been surveyed; these, as well as the larger ones that had been traversed when the townships were subdivided, were surveyed by means of stadia traverses.

The large number of these lakes is due to the frequency of enclosed basin-like hollows and depressions in a rolling country with few creeks and rivers and an almost level watershed. Few of these lakes have running inlets except in the spring or after heavy rains and fewer still have any outlets. They are subject to great variations in depth and area depending partly on the amount of precipitation, partly on the drainage effected by the cultivation of the soil and the clearing of the land, and sometimes on changes in underground drainage systems, on springs drying in some places and appearing in others, and on natural drains becoming obstructed or diverted.

The water is generally alkaline and often salty. The salt water is caused presumably by the absorption of salts from the soil, followed by excessive evaporation, but the reason why some lakes should be salt and others fresh is not easily explained. Lakes are often salty where there is no indication of alkaline salts in the surrounding lakes with running inlets and outlets are salty and others with no inlets or outlets are fresh while fresh and salt water lakes often lie close together.

Some of these lakes that are connected with Carrot river contain sucker, a species of the catostomidae but otherwise they have no fish. It is probable that some of the deeper fresh-water lakes could be successfully stocked.

In all of these townships the surface is rolling and covered with poplar bush with stretches of open or scrubby prairie. The poplar has been burnt and cut over till what is left is small, and though the growth is dense in places, the land is easily cleared as the poplar stumps soon rot, especially if cut in summer. When cleared, it is fine farming land and does not seem to be so susceptible to frost as the open prairie land. Homesteads in solid bush are now being eagerly taken up but there are still good homesteads left all through this district and good land for sale on easy terms.

The roads are fairly good considering that few of the settlers have been on the land more than ten years and that the district is still only partially settled. The greatest natural difficulty in road building is that the levelness of the country makes it hard to get good drains. The settlers realize the importance of good main roads and wisely confine their work to two or three of the road allowances in the township. The old trails, where still open, make fine roads.

More railways are needed in this district, many farmers have to haul wheat from twenty to thirty miles to market. This takes away their profits and discourages them from making improvements or increasing the area under cultivation.

5 GEORGE V., A. 1915

The settlers as a whole are making splendid progress. The majority of them have had previous experience in farming in the older provinces or in the States. Agriculture is the sole industry and grain growing is the only branch of it to which much attention is paid. The soil is good and all grain crops do well. The yield and quality are excellent.

The land is still fairly clean but the settlers hardly appreciate the necessity of making a determined and concentrated effort to keep out noxious weeds. All of the settlers keep some cattle, pigs and poultry. Around Reynaud and Bonne Madone sheep are kept for their wool, which the settlers there card and spin into yarn. There too the settlers keep bands of horses and droves of pigs. The Galicians prefer cattle raising to wheat growing and keep the greater part of their homesteads for pasture. The high price of horses has made it impossible for many of the settlers to buy them and oxen are largely used, especially by the Hungarians and Galicians. The decline in the price of horses this fall, however, has extended their use. Many settlers are ignorant of the proper care of horses and of their treatment when sick, and their losses in horses have been costly. The settlers need education too with regard to the comparative values of well-bred and scrub stock and to the wastefulness of pasturing cattle on uncultivated land.

Muskrats are the only fur-bearing animals left which are at all plentiful. Many settlers increase their winter income by trapping them. Bears are occasionally seen but coyotes are not so common as on the open prairie. Deer, elk and moose are still found and moose ranged this fall as far south as township 40 in ranges 23 and 24. Grouse, ducks, geese and cranes are plentiful.

Many Europeans or their descendants have settled in these townships. South of township 42 most of the settlers are Germans or Hungarians. Around Bonne Madone and Reynaud and in township 44, range 22, there are a number of French settlers. There is a Norwegian settlement in township 40, range 18, and township 43, range 24, is settled by Galicians. While they have different standards of comfort and prosperity the settlers get along well together; they all seem to be contented with their homesteads and prospects, while they, at the same time, appear ambitious to improve them. They are well supplied with churches and schools, are comfortably situated, live well and are making as good progress as could be expected. The prospects for the future of this district are the best.

APPENDIX No. 41.

REPORT OF P. E. PALMER, D.L.S.

SUBDIVISION ALONG THE HUDSON BAY BRANCH OF THE CANADIAN NORTHERN RAILWAY IN
EASTERN SASKATCHEWAN.

St. John, N.B., May 12, 1914.

E. Deville, Esq., LL. D.,
  Surveyor General,
    Ottawa, Canada.

Sir,—I have the honour to submit the following report on my survey operations
for the season of 1913-1914.

We left Prince Albert, the place of organization on June 2, 1913, for Hudson Bay
Junction, which was my post office and base of supplies during the whole season.

Hudson Bay Junction is a busy little town situated in township 45, range 3, west
of the second meridian at the junction of the Hudson and Prince Albert branches
of the Canadian Northern railway. It has two stores and two hotels, and is the centre
of the logging operations of the Red Deer and Ruby Lake Lumber companies, who
together employ from 1,000 to 1,500 men in the woods during the winter. It is also a
railway divisional point, and upon the completion of the line to Hudson bay it will
probably have a large increase of business and population. There is very little agricultural land in the vicinity, though within the last few years a number of homesteads
have been taken up, and potatoes and other vegetables as well as oats, hay and dairy
products, are produced to some extent.

About three miles south of Hudson Bay Junction surveys have been made on
Red Deer river with a view to developing power to be used in the manufacture of pulp.
If this industry is established it will employ a large number of men and make a
profitable use of large quantities of poplar and other wood, which is not suitable for
the best grade of lumber.

There is also the village of Ruby Lake in section 10, township 46, range 3, west of
the second meridian, on the Canadian Northern railway, six miles north from the
" Junction ". It has a normal population of about two hundred people, employees of
the Ruby Lake Lumber company and their families and has a general store, a post
office and mills.

Although the railway from Hudson Bay Junction to Pas has been completed for
about seven years, a regular service has only recently been inaugurated, and it still
leaves much to be desired. During the summer of 1913, however, many improvements
were made to the road, to enable it to stand the heavy traffic occasioned by the building
of the Hudson Bay railway.

My surveys extended along this railway from the north boundary of township 45,
range 3, west of the second meridian at mileage 5 from Hudson Bay Junction, to the
east outline of township 52, range 29 west of the principal meridian at mileage 58.

I commenced my operations by running the east outline of townships 45 and 46,
range 2, which I reached by canoe on Red Deer river from Erwood, a station on the
Canadian Northern railway, eight miles east of Hudson Bay Junction. I transported
my outfit along this line by back-packing. I then moved to Chemong in township 49,
range 1, on the Hudson Bay branch of the Canadian Northern railway. From there
I moved my camp by push car along the railway as the work required, cutting toboggan
trails from the right of way to reach the more inaccessible parts as soon as the ground

5 GEORGE V., A. 1915

had frozen sufficiently to carry horses. I established the east outline of townships 47, 48 and 49, range 2, by back-packing a small outfit along the part north of the railway, while I reached the part south of the track by toboggan trail cut from where it crosses the north boundary of township 47, range 2, to Leaf lake. I also cut a trail to run the north boundary of township 47, range 1. The east outline of townships 48 and 47, range 3, I reached by packing in from Chemong along the thirteenth base line. To run the east outline of townships 48 and 47, range 4, I cut a trail from the track near the twelfth correction line approximately to the first named line, thence north to the thirteenth base line thus avoiding many bad ravines and much rough country. From this trail I also ran part of the twelfth correction line. I lost considerable time on the east outlines of townships 48 and 47, ranges 3 and 4, owing to the heavy cutting and the difficulty of reaching them. I did the necessary subdivision in townships 46 and 47, range 3, townships 47 and 48, range 2, townships 48, 49 and 50, range 1, retraced the east outline of township 45, range 3, and resurveyed the east outline of township 46, range 3, all west of the second meridian.

This work kept me busy until December 27, when I moved my outfit to Chemong and from there to Otosquen in township 50, range 32, west of the principal meridian, running the east outline of townships 49 and 50, range 32, from those places. At Otosquen I did some subdivision in township 50, range 31, and from there moved to Cantyre, near the northeast corner of township 50, range 31. From there I cut a trail south to the thirteenth base and north to the fourteenth base line to run the east outlines of townships 49, 50. 51 and 52, range 31. I then moved to the east outline of range 30 and cut a trail to the thirteenth base line to enable me to run the east outline of townships 49 and 50, range 30. I also did subdivision in township 51, range 30, from this camp, and established the thirteenth correction line in this range. I then moved to township 52, range 29, and did some subdivision. Finally I moved back to Cantyre, from which camp I established the thirteenth correction line in range 31 and did subdivision in townships 50, ranges 30 and 31, and in township 51, range 30.

The country traversed by the railway between the limits of my work is for the most part muskeg. The soil of these muskegs is usually a fibrous peat, formed by the decomposition of peat litter moss (Sphagnum Fuscum Von Gallesceu), cup-moss (Polytricum Juniperium), Labrador Tea (Ledrum Latifolium), and spruce and tamarack trees; it is from three to twelve feet in depth over clay or gumbo subsoil. These muskegs are usually covered with a light growth of black spruce and tamarack from three to eight inches in diameter, the growth of which is very slow. Along the banks of creeks and where natural drainage exists to carry off the surplus water, the soil is usually clay or clay loam and is covered with a heavy growth of spruce and poplar, much of which is suitable for lumber and pulp. The growth of timber in this locality where suitable drainage exists, is very rapid, and when the land is cleared it will be suitable for growing vegetables, hay and the hardier grains. Along the railway, where there is some drainage, I have noticed grass growing in places where the covering of moss has been removed.

Most of the muskegs in this section could be drained, as the surface is usually slightly undulating. These muskegs freeze to a depth of about two or three feet in winter, and the frost remains in them until the first of August. There is an opportunity for the development of a peat fuel industry in this locality. and at the present prices of coal in the West, this would appear to be a subject worthy of investigation.

In connection with these muskegs, which at present seem almost worthless, I would like to call attention to the fact that the Government of the United States has imported into Alaska a number of Lapland and Siberian reindeer animals closely related to our caribou, whose food is moss, and whose natural habitat is muskeg and tundra. These animals thrive to such an extent in Alaska that there are now 42.000 of them. They have also been introduced into Labrador by Dr. Grenfell. There are enormous tracts of land in our Canadian West and more particularly in the locality of my work this year, that would make suitable ranges for these animals. The flesh of the reindeer is said to be excellent food, while its hide and horns are also valuable.

The Fasquia hills run parallel to and at a distance of three to six miles from the railway from mile 12 to mile 35. These hills are about four hundred feet above the general level of the country. The outer slopes are covered with a thick growth of poplar and birch, with some spruce and jackpine, much of which is suitable for lumber or pulp, while the higher benches have mostly been burned over thirty or forty years ago, and are covered with a second growth of jackpine, spruce and poplar. There is also a great deal of muskeg in places, covered with spruce up to ten inches in diameter. The soil in these hills is usually clay or loam, and is frequently stony. Many creeks rise there, flowing through deep ravines. On the eastern slopes, where my work was situated, these creeks all spread out to form a swamp at a distance of five or six miles from the hills and again emerge as tributaries of Pasquia and Overflowing rivers. For the most part the land in these hills is not suitable for agriculture, and with the exception of the timber on the slopes, there is, through the locality where my work was situated, very little milling timber. The lower slopes and southern extremity might be suitable for mixed farming, but are not likely to be settled for many years. These hills were explored during the summer of 1913 by the Forestry Branch for the purpose of learning if the district were suitable for a forest reserve. It would appear that this country would be more suitable for that than for any other purpose.

Pasquia river rises in the Pasquia hills and runs through township 49, range 1, west of the second meridian, and through townships 49, ranges 32 and 31, townships 49, 50 and 51, range 30, and township 50, range 29, and thence on toward Saskatchewan river. It varies in width from forty-five feet in township 49, range 1, to ninety or one hundred feet in township 51, range 30, with a current of from one to three miles per hour. It is navigable for canoes in most places east of the second meridian. There is good timber along its course in township 49, range 1. The water is good.

Overflowing river rises in the Fasquia hills and runs through townships 47 and 46, range 3, and township 46, range 2, west of the second meridian, into Leaf lake, thence towards the northeast, crossing the thirteenth base line near the east boundary of range 30, west of the principal meridian, at which point it is about one hundred feet in width and from two to four feet deep, and is navigable for canoes and small boats. There is much good poplar up to twenty-four inches in diameter along the banks, and in many places there are hay marshes and meadows which would afford plentiful pasturage for cattle. The water is good.

Leaf lake is crossed by the twelfth correction line on the east outline of range 2, west of the second meridian. It is about four and a half miles long by three miles wide and from three to ten feet in depth. The shores are marshy and clumps of reeds rise from the water in many places. It is the resort of large numbers of ducks and geese. The water is sweet and good in this lake.

Ruby lake lies in township 46, range 3, west of the second meridian and is about two and a half miles long and from one-quarter to one-half mile wide. It has no tributaries nor outlets and the water is strongly alkaline and unfit for use. The mill and plant of the Ruby Lake Lumber company are at the south end of the lake, around which their limits lie. The shores are marshy on the west, south and north sides, but mostly dry with a good beach on the east. It varies in depth from three to twelve feet.

Red Deer river runs through the southerly part of township 45, range 2, in an easterly direction. It is from four to eight feet deep, with a swift current, has many rapids and is navigable for boats and canoes. There is much good land along its banks and large quantities of poplar and spruce suitable for lumber. It is used by the Red Deer Lumber company for driving their logs.

5 GEORGE V., A. 1915

Besides the Ruby Lake mills the MacKenzie & Mann Lumber Co. have a mill at Chemong in township 48, range 1, and limits in townships 48 and 49, ranges 1 and 2. The Great West Lumber company have limits in townships 49 and 50, ranges 1 and 2. Ties were cut on permit in several places along the line during the past winter and there is still much good timber in this locality.

. There are no minerals of economic value in this district. Game is very abundant. Moose and caribou are plentiful everywhere and black and cinnamon bears, deer and elk are found in many places, while partridges, ruffed grouse, prairie-chickens, pinnated grouse and ptarmigan are constantly seen. Geese and the many varieties of ducks are found in the lakes, and the fur-bearing animals, such as muskrats, mink, ermine, otter, lynx, foxes and marten are plentiful enough to amply repay the labour of the trapper. Timber wolves are occasionally met with in the winter. There are jackfish, pickerel and gold-eye in Red Deer river and Leaf lake.

The climate appears similar to that of other parts of Saskatchewan in the same latitude. There is considerable rain in the summer and fall. The first frost occurred about August 20 and the lakes froze over about November 1, but there was very little frost in the ground before the end of December. The snowfall was light only about six inches before February 1, and not more than fifteen inches altogether. The weather during the winter was remarkably fine, only one day being lost from work on account of storm between the 1st November and the 16th of March. The lowest point registered by the thermometer during the winter was 51 degrees below zero. Survey operations can be carried on more quickly and economically in this district during the winter than at any other time.

I completed the work for which I had been given instructions on March 13, 1914 and on the 16th I paid off my party stored my outfit at Hudson Bay Junction and left for the east.

I have the honour to be, Sir,

Your obedient sevant,

P. E. PALMER, D.L.S.

APPENDIX No. 42.

ABSTRACT OF THE REPORT OF T. H. PLUNKETT, D.L.S.

BASE LINE SURVEYS IN NORTHERN MANITOBA.

My work during the latter part of the summer of 1913 and the following winter consisted of the survey of the thirteenth and fourteenth base lines from range 28 west of the principal meridian easterly to lake Winnipeg.

I organized my party in Winnipeg and obtained supplies at Winnipegosis; we left this latter place by boat on August 24. Our progress north on Lake Winnipegosis was very slow. North and west gales which had delayed us two days at Winnipegosis continued to hamper us. On August 29 we arrived at the mouth of Overflowing river with our boat leaking badly from having run on a submerged reef in the lake, thereby damaging most of our supplies.

From information I had previously gathered regarding Overflowing river I believed it easily navigable for canoes and small boats. This I found only partly correct. For a distance of about five miles up the river from its mouth, this stream is very shallow and consists of a series of rapids. Loaded canoes had to be pulled up the centre. After the rapids are passed the river is easily navigable for many miles for small boats and launches.

From my ranger, I learned that we could reach the commencement of our work by following the south branch of Overflowing river, a stream not hitherto shown on maps of the country. Accordingly we left the greater part of our outfit at the point where it was expected the base line would cross the main river and canoed up the south branch reaching a point only two miles east of the point of commencement of our work.

On September 3 work was commenced on the thirteenth base line. Many difficulties had to be contended with in range 27. Throughout the range the line crossed an almost continuous floating bog, so soft and wet that it was with great difficulty crossed by the members of my party. This bog is almost level and I doubt very much if it can be drained. The south branch of Overflowing river meanders through this country from its source, a short distance north of Red Deer lake. I believe this river has an underground connection with Red Deer lake, as it rises most abruptly, in the midst of a huge floating bog. The river appears to be well named as at high water it floods the country for miles north and west of range 27. This branch crosses the base line in section 32. It has low banks, a sluggish current, a mud bottom and a depth of eight feet.

In section 31 of range 26 the line crosses the main branch of Overflowing river, just above the series of rapids leading to its mouth. From there south along the river there are some fine locations for settlers particularly on the northerly side of the river. High land, wooded chiefly with small poplar and willow extends back on an average of from one half to one mile from the river bank. North of this strip of high land the level muskeg extending northward to the base line could be easily drained and I believe those portions of ranges 26 and 25, township 48 lying between the base line and lake Winnipegosis would afford good locations for a few settlers.

North of the base line in the southerly halves of townships 49 ranges 25 and 26 a few good patches of high land were seen, wooded with small poplar and willow, but the extent of these patches was very limited. The northerly halves of these townships as well as township 50 in the same ranges consist of floating bog, undoubtedly flooded

5 GEORGE V., A. 1915

at high water by Overflowing river. Toward the easterly limit of range 25 we began to cross a series of ridges running about due north and south. These are wooded with jackpine with a sand or gravel soil on stratified limestone. Frequent outcroppings of the rock occur. The land seems too barren to be of agricultural value. Between the ridges are floating bogs sloping toward lake Winnipegosis. These could be drained and made productive. This succession of ridges and bogs continues to the middle of range 24 where the ridges disappear and moss muskeg with a scattering of large bogs characterize the remainder of the range.

On October 2 the line had reached the northeast corner of range 24. As navigation on the north end of lake Winnipegosis closes on October 8 it was decided to discontinue work on the thirteenth base, go south to Winnipegosis and on the way down to mound portions of the twelfth base. Previous to our leaving, a cache was built on the thirteenth base to be stocked with provisions for the winter work. We reached Winnipegosis on the night of October 15. The lake froze over on the 24th.

On October 20 the party arrived at Whithorn siding on the Hudson Bay branch of the Canadian Northern railway. Preparations were at once made to complete the mounding and levelling on the fourteenth base line in ranges 28, 29, 30 and 31 which had been left unfinished the previous season. Some difficulty was experienced on this work owing to the very soft and wet nature of the country to be crossed. Man-packing was our only mode of transportation until November 3 when ice on the rivers could be used, but the almost total lack of snow greatly hampered our work. By November 6 this work was finished, and the party was now occupied in moving supplies east in order to continue the survey of the fourteenth base line to lake Winnipeg. Supplies had to be dragged over almost bare ground and consequently progress was slow.

On November 17 the line was commenced at the northeast corner of range 28 and carried on continuously thereafter as far as range 16. Until Christmas the lack of snow greatly hampered our progress and the ill effects of the rough trails on our dogs were felt throughout the winter. On December 16 Saskatchewan river was crossed in section 35, township 52, range 23.

The country between range 27 on this base line and lake Winnipeg in range 11 can best be described in three sections. The first division takes in ranges 26, 25 and 24, the second includes ranges 23, 22, 21, 20 and 19 as far east as Cedar lake and the third extends from Cedar lake to lake Winnipeg.

In the first section the line traversed a country fairly thickly wooded with spruce, tamarack and jackpine, not sufficiently large for milling, and for much the greater part, too small and stunted to be of any commercial value. Ranges 27 and 26 produce mainly spruce and tamarack from six to ten inches in diameter. In ranges 25 and 24 jackpine predominates. As a rule the jackpine was very small and dense. The whole surface of the country in this division is covered with moss from one to two feet in depth. Patches of bog are found on all sides, but these are generally small. When drained this section of the country might be of value for farming.

The second section might be called the Saskatchewan river section. Excepting a very narrow strip of land along the banks of the maze of rivers and lakes found there the country is a continuous bog. Rushes, reeds and rat houses are the common characteristics. It appears to be a flooded country, absolutely useless in its present condition from an agricultural viewpoint. It would require a much more extended study of this section than it was possible for us to give it to predict what possibility there is of its being drained

Crossing Cedar lake we found in the third division an altogether different type of country. Ranges 18, 17, 16, 15, 14 and 13 are mainly rolling and of a rock formation. In ranges 16, 15, 14 and 13 the flat limestone lies either on the immediate surface or a few inches beneath.

This is a continuous bush country producing jackpine almost entirely. Ranges 13 and 14 have been fire swept leaving for miles on either side of the base line a vast

SESSIONAL PAPER No. 25b

extent of bare limestone rock piled up with small brulé. The jackpine seldom attain a diameter of more than six inches. They appear to die for lack of soil.

Throughout this section for many miles both north and south of the line there are innumerable lakes of varying size. Almost all of these lakes have high rocky banks and gravel bottoms. The water is very clear and apparently pure. Clearwater lake in range 17 is one of the largest of these lakes. Whitefish and jackfish abound in it. Jackfish is found in almost all of the lakes. So numerous are these lakes that Indians from Moose Lake and Grand Rapids reserves are able to travel by canoe in almost any direction by making short portages.

In range 12 the elevation drops rapidly in a series of steep hills and narrow gravel benches probably old shore lines of lake Winnipeg. Throughout the greater part of this range however and through section 31 of range 11 where the base line reaches lake Winnipeg we traversed a bog and muskeg country wooded with stunted spruce and tamarack with occasional patches of jackpine. This strip of muskeg extends all along the lake shore, retaining a width of about six miles almost as far south as Grand Rapids settlement. About four miles north of the base line it becomes wider and extends northwesterly. This land undoubtedly could be easily drained and from an agricultural standpoint constitutes the only hope of this third section.

Work was carried on continuously on this base line from November 17, 1913, until February 3, 1914 when the line had been carried as far as range 16. A return was then made to the thirteenth base line in range 24 where the line had been left the previous fall.

From February until April we were occupied extending this line across ranges 23 to 14 inclusive.

From range 23 to the northeast corner of section 31, range 20, where the line intersects the shore of Cedar lake the country is wholly muskeg. The ground is covered with moss from one to two feet deep. Small floating bogs occur. The timber consists of stunted spruce and tamarack. Occasional bluffs were found with spruce up to ten inches in diameter but the quantity of timber is very limited. In the event of settlement this spruce would probably supply settlers with building timber.

In section 23, range 22, Mossy creek was crossed. This creek is about sixty feet wide, three feet deep and flows southeast with a sluggish current to lake Winnipegosis. Along the banks of this creek on a narrow strip of land spruce trees up to twelve inches in diameter are found. Larger timber consisting of spruce, poplar, birch and tamarack is found along the base line throughout range 22 and the western half of range 21. This larger timber however is not characteristic of the country and is found here only because of the proximity to lake Winnipegosis which lies about one mile south. North from the base line to Saskatchewan river the country is of the usual muskeg variety dotted with floating bogs. In this country the scrub spruce and tamarack is supplemented by a scattering of scrub cedar. Between the base line and lake Winnipegosis a very limited number of settlers could be accommodated without extensive drainage being necessary.

The easterly half of ranges 21 and 20 as far as Cedar lake is low wet muskeg of the usual type.

Cedar lake extends across ranges 20, 19, 18, 17 and range 16 as far as section 35.

From there to Saskatchewan river in section 33 of range 15 the line crosses a rocky country. The timber consists of spruce, tamarack and jackpine generally small but attaining in places a diameter of twelve inches. South of the line as one gets farther from Cedar lake the land again assumes the usual moss and muskeg characteristics.

From Saskatchewan river in section 33, range 15, to Cross lake in section 35, range 15, the line crosses a stretch of very fair land wooded with poplar, spruce, tamarack, jackpine and willow brush. This strip extends south of the base line to the river and north of the base line about four miles and would afford a few good locations for settlers.

5 GEORGE V., A. 1915

The easterly shore of Cross lake is crossed in section 31 of range 14 and from there on to lake Winnipeg the base line runs parallel to Saskatchewan river. This country is underlaid with limestone and frequent outcroppings of the rock occur. The soil is very poor. South of the base line to the river and extending north of the line an average distance of about one mile, there lies a belt of fairly good spruce, jackpine, poplar, birch and tamarack. This timber is easily available at Grand Rapids settlement and may become of value in the future development of this place which I believe has lately been incorporated as a town. In section 34, township 48, range 13, the country drops rapidly and the strip of muskeg along the shore of lake Winnipeg is crossed. This muskeg where the line crosses is only half a mile wide but becomes rapidly wider north of the base line.

The Provincial Government of Manitoba commenced a drainage scheme just west of Grand Rapids this summer with a view to reclaiming this muskeg. It is estimated that about 500 acres will be drained as an experiment. As this muskeg is typical of a vast area of the north country it may be of advantage to intending settlers to describe the methods and implements used in draining it.

The pick and shovel are of secondary importance in this work. The main ditch is first laid out the proper width, usually from six to eight feet, and marked by pickets every hundred feet. One man on either side of the drain then cuts the moss from station to station along the drain with an ordinary hay knife designed originally for cutting hay in the stack. These knives when they are to be used for muskeg ditching should be cut off about six inches below the handles and a piece of iron one foot or so in length depending on the depth of the moss welded in. A third man then cuts the moss across the ditch in strips from one to two feet in width and these strips into squares of eighteen inches or two feet. Following these three men are four others with iron hooks, lifting these squares of moss and muck permeated as they are with small roots which hold the squares together onto the bank of the ditch leaving a berm of two or three feet.

These hooks are manufactured for the purpose from five-eighths inch iron rods. Two rods are fastened togethed at the handle and also firmly banded together at the bend for the hooks. The hooks are placed at an angle of about thirty degrees with one another. Ordinary manure forks with the prongs turned at right angles to the handle were first used but were found too light to withstand the strain.

Immediately behind these men follow three others with shovels, who level the bottom roughly to grade. It has been found in very wet bogs and muskegs that when the ditch is carried up to a small slough the rush of water will scour the bottom muck out to grade. In some country where old beaver dams are found holding bodies of water it has been found very advantageous to remove only every alternate block of moss before breaking the dam, the resulting rush of water doing the rest of the work.

In the muskeg west of Grand Rapids settlement ten men were able to complete one thousand feet of main ditch in one day. At intervals depending on the level of the ground, but at least eveery fifteen hundred feet in ordinary muskeg, lateral ditches two or three feet wide are run to the main ditch. As a rule the removal of the moss is all that is required.

This system of drains enables the settlers to use horses or oxen with which to turn under the moss which is undoubtedly the cause of this boggy area. On a very large percentage of this muskeg country the drains need not be made with a view to making them permanent watercourses. There is at present ample slope for natural drainage. All that is needed is sufficiently firm footing for horses or oxen to enable the settler to get rid of the moss. Once this is removed drainage will be no more a problem here than elsewhere.

On April 6, 1914, the thirteenth base line had been surveyed across all lakes. A return was at once made to the fourteenth base line in range 16. Advantage was taken

Drainage Operations West of Grand Rapids, Manitoba.

Photo by T. H. Blanket 191-

One man goes along each side of the ditch, which is usually about eight feet wide, and cuts the moss with an ordinary hay knife. A third man cuts the moss across into strips and then into squares, each about eighteen inches or two feet. Four men follow with iron hooks and lift the squares of moss out on the bank, and three men with shovels level the bottom of the ditch roughly to grade. The rush of water carries away all loose muck left in the ditch.

of the ice and snow to reach range 16 and distribute provisions easterly in three caches to lake Winnipeg. We were just able to accomplish this before the spring break-up came. The work from range 16 to lake Winnipeg was carried on with man-packing as our means of transport.

The base line having been completed block outlines were run south along the east boundaries of townships 52 and 51, range 13, and the party then returned to Grand Rapids by canoe, our boats having arrived from Pas by the first open water. The thirteenth base line was then extended to lake Winnipeg and block outlines run north to the northeast corner of township 50 range 13. After the completion of the base lines and the adjoining block outlines tie lines were run to Grand Rapids settlement and Indian reserve.

By July 1 our work was completed. On the 4th we left by tug for Black river where we connected with the steamship *Wolverine* for Selkirk, Manitoba. The party was paid off at Winnipeg on July 6. The country traversed by these two base lines abounds in game. Moose and caribou are very plentiful throughout the whole country between the second meridian and lake Winnipeg. Scarcely a day passed without these animals being seen by members of the party. East of Cedar lake bears, marten and foxes are plentiful. Muskrats are trapped in large numbers by the Indians in the sloughs and bogs that are found on all sides, mink, lynx, weasel and otter are also taken in large numbers but beaver are rare. Small game such as ducks, geese and grouse of all kinds including ptarmigan is very plentiful.

No valuable minerals were found by the party but claims of red ochre were staked at Cross lake this spring by prospectors from Grand Rapids. The quality seems to be good but as yet it has not been found in sufficiently large deposits to be of commercial value. Samples of what appeared to be potters clay were also brought from Cross lake. East of Cross lake splendid limestone in thick strata is found throughout the country.

Fishing and fur-trading are the only industries flourishing in this country. Extensive operations are carried on on lake Winnipeg, lake Winnipegosis, Moose and Cedar lakes and on Saskatchewan river. The most valuable fish taken are whitefish. Owing to the heavy freight rates from the north end of lake Winnipeg whitefish only are taken. On lake Winnipegosis however, jackfish or pike, gold eye, pickerel and even sucker are freighted to the railway at Mafeking. The winter fishing offers wide opportunities to settlers and during some seasons summer fishing is permitted.

Excepting a few small gardens at Grand Rapids settlement no attempts have as yet been made to cultivate the soil. Potatoes and all other garden vegetables are grown successfully at the settlement.

The early fall of 1913 was very cold. The thermometer dropped to 10° below zero on October 19. After that the weather became milder and no cold weather occurred until nearly Christmas. The winter until February was mild. During that month however, the temperature dropped as low as 58° below zero. Three weeks of very severe weather extended from February 1 to 21.

The spring of 1914 was late, snow remained in the bush until the last of April and the ice on the lakes could be travelled on well into May.

It was June 1 before there were any signs of growth in the bush. Frost at night was noticed as late as June 25. Residents of the country considered this a very late spring.

As a rule the flow in rivers crossed by our lines was slow. No water-powers were noted excepting Grand rapids on Saskatchewan river at Grand Rapids settlement, and the rapids on Overflowing river near its mouth on lake Winnipegosis.

APPENDIX No. 43.

ABSTRACT OF THE REPORT OF R. C. PURSER, D.L.S.

MISCELLANEOUS SURVEYS IN MANITOBA, SASKATCHEWAN AND ALBERTA.

The surveys on which I was engaged during the season of 1913 were quite similar in their character to those I had been on during the previous year. They consisted of scattered miscellaneous surveys of every nature extending throughout the more northerly parts of Manitoba, Saskatchewan and Alberta. The greater part of my work lay in the province of Saskatchewan, and so I found it convenient to use Saskatoon as a sort of headquarters during the season. My party consisted of one assistant and myself supplemented when and where necessary by local labour. In all, thirty-one different surveys and investigations were made, my time spent in field work extending from April 23, 1913, to January 24, 1914, making an average of about one survey per week. A considerable part of the time was spent in travelling from one place of work to another, both by train and by wagon or democrat, our total mileage for the former being over seven thousand one hundred miles, exclusive of our initial and final trips to and from the West, and for the latter over eight hundred miles. We had no transport outfit of our own, hiring the same whenever necessary the advantage of this arrangement being the ease with which we could move from one part of the country to another by train, shipping our small outfit with us as baggage. Most of the surveys on which we were engaged were small, some requiring not more than one actual working day for their completion. A rough classification of the surveys made during the season would be as follows: Eleven retracements for the purpose of correcting monuments out of place or duplicate monuments; five investigations of the condition of monuments; eleven lake traverses; two investigations of lakes supposed to be dried up; one river traverse, and one investigation of timber berth lines.

The retracements first mentioned were mostly for the purpose of correcting small errors in localities where they had been petitioned for by the settlers affected.

Some of the lake traverses above mentioned were held over until cold weather had set in and the lakes had frozen up. Working over the ice did away with a great deal of line cutting which we otherwise would have had to do. In the eastern part of the province of Saskatchewan, particularly in the vicinity of Yorkton, the lakes and sloughs were all found to be filled with water to a much greater extent than they had been for years.

I traversed the left bank of Saskatchewan river through township 33, range 6, west of the third meridian. This work was done in September and owing to the almost impenetrable brush through which our traverse lines had to be cut, it lasted well over three weeks.

In township 55, range 5, west of the third meridian, a fruitless search was made for a timber berth block supposed to exist there. In reality the block did exist some twenty-four miles farther south, the discrepancy being due to a confusion of the neighbouring timber berth numbers on the original surveyor's blue prints.

In addition to the surveys above mentioned we were required to take observations for the determination of the magnetic dip and total force, whenever we could do so without interfering with our regular work. In all forty-eight sets of these observations were taken, the instrument stations here extending through a wide range of territory. At the beginning and the end of the season the instrumental constants were determined at the Magnetic Observatory at Agincourt, Ontario.

APPENDIX No. 44.

ABSTRACT OF THE REPORT OF C. RINFRET, D.L.S.

STADIA SURVEYS IN SOUTHERN SASKATCHEWAN.

I left Montreal on May 2, 1913, for Maple Creek, Sask., where I organized my party.

I then moved by trail via Swift Current to township 6, range 27, west of the second meridian, and began the traverse of Willowbunch lake on May 30.

During the month of June we traversed Willowbunch lake and the lakes in township 5, range 24, townships 6, ranges 24 and 25, and townships 7, ranges 24, 25 and 26, west of the second meridian. The part of the country northeast of Willowbunch lake is well settled and partly cultivated, yielding good crops of wheat, flax and oats. The part southwest is cut up by coulees, but has some fairly level spots so that mixed farming and ranching is carried on successfully.

The lakes in township 6, range 29, were next traversed. The country south of Montague lake is hilly and partly covered with poplar and brush.

We then proceeded to survey Fife lake and the surrounding lakes in townships 3 and 4, ranges 29 and 30. The country north and east of Fife lake is excellent for farming and is fairly well settled, although there are still a few vacant homesteads. The country south and west is hilly, but has many level spots where farming and ranching is carried on. The district around this lake is in my opinion the most suitable one for settlers seen during the season.

Our next work was in townships 4 and 5, ranges 27 and 28, and in townships 3 and 4, range 26. All of this country is rolling to hilly and farmers and ranchers are equally successful.

We then traversed the lakes in townships 3, 4 and 5, range 23, townships 5 and 6, range 24, and townships 5 and 6, range 22. Farming is the principal industry in these townships, all of the suitable land being taken up.

The traverse of Big Muddy lake was our next work. The country south of this lake is very hilly and does not seem to be settled, although ranching would be advantageous if communications with the railroads were more convenient. In township 2, range 22, north of the lake, and townships 3, ranges 22 and 23, there are some ranchers and farmers, but many good homesteads are still vacant.

We then moved to township 7, range 19. This township is all taken up and well farmed.

All the bodies of water in townships 3, ranges 20 and 21, townships 4, ranges 20, 21 and 22 and townships 5, ranges 20 and 21, were then traversed. In each of these townships from ten to thirty-five lakes or sloughs were found. These swarm with ducks and muskrats and some settlers make considerable money trapping muskrats. Most of the lakes contain potable water. That country is well adapted for mixed farming and ranching, and could be more thickly populated.

The remainder of the season was spent in investigating two or three townships which had no lakes and in traversing the lakes in townships 6, ranges 21 and 23, townships 7, ranges 20, 21 and 22 and townships 8, ranges 20 and 21. These townships are convenient to railroads and consequently well settled.

As a rule the lakes and sloughs have been drying up for the last few years, but there are a few exceptions, the most noteworthy being Fife lake which is now three feet deeper than it was some years ago. This was the only lake surveyed which has

5 GEORGE V., A. 1915

an outlet and the only one containing edible fish in sufficient quantities to be caught with nets. Glen lake situated four miles south has completely dried up.

The depth of the lakes and sloughs surveyed was generally about three feet or less, while a few were five to ten feet deep. The deepest one was fourteen feet. Most of the smaller lakes and sloughs contain drinkable water, while the big ones, with the exception of Fife lake, contain alkaline water.

In all the district travelled over, lignite coal is common and in many places it is mined and sold to the surrounding farmers at from one-fourth to one-fifth of the price of the better grades of coal sold in the neighbouring towns.

I closed operations on November 25.

APPENDIX No. 45.

ABSTRACT OF THE REPORT OF E. W. ROBINSON, D.L.S.

MERIDIAN AND BASE LINE SURVEY IN NORTHEASTERN SASKATCHEWAN.

I left Ottawa on August 8, 1912, and proceeded to Prince Albert to complete the survey of the fifteenth base line west of the second meridian. Upon my arrival at Prince Albert I discovered that the season was wet, and after ascertaining definitely that the Candle Lake trail was in an almost impassable condition I decided to leave this line until a later date, as I was anxious to make an early start on the second meridian. I therefore went to Pas and made arrangements for my winter transportation. In the meantime I had a small party mounding on the fifteenth base line east and west of the second meridian.

I decided to use horses and toboggans for the heavy freighting, keeping in the meantime a small number of dog teams for light work and where speed was necessary. Up to this time horses had never proceeded north of Pelican narrows and my venture was looked upon with considerable misgiving by those familiar with northern travel, but I am pleased to state that I found them a perfect success. When north of Churchill river my horses were inspected by a number of the Indians with curiosity, for they had never previously seen any, and one was surprised to find that they had no horns. I used the horses up to March 28 which was the latest date I could keep them so as to enable them to reach Pas before the break-up. From this date I used the dog trains until the snow went which unfortunately occurred a few days later. I was then obliged to resort to man-packing for the rest of the trip, except on large lakes where the dogs assisted. This early disappearance of the snow is exceptional in this latitude. We had considerable cold weather after that but never enough snow to enable us to use the dogs for overland transportation.

Previous to my experiment the dog train had been relied upon for all northern winter transportation, but when a survey is undertaken at this distance from railways the number required even when one has a cache of provisions reasonably close to the work, is so large that the transportation becomes unwieldy. The great disadvantage of using dogs lies in the fact that every dog team requires a driver and one team on a good trail will not carry more than 400 pounds and usually less. On the other hand a horse toboggan can be relied upon for 1,600 pounds on a good trail, and the saving of blankets. food and tent accommodation for the extra drivers is very considerable. It is undoubtedly desirable that horses should be tented, but this is not absolutely necessary. Horses of the right stamp, namely of about 1,200 pounds weight and preferably of the broncho strain, will do well if properly blanketed and tied in a sheltered situation. Heavy feeding is absolutely necessary to enable them to stand winter work of this description, which is hard on them, and all their ailments should be at once attended to. The heavy mortality amongst horses engaged in winter survey work is largely due to lack of food. It is impossible to expect a horse to work hard on dead grass and a few oats grudgingly handed out. The cost of taking in proper feed may be high but this is preferable to having the party tied up through the collapse of transportation. It seems to be more difficult to ensure against dogs dying. For one reason no general systematic attempt has been made to breed up dogs suitable for work, as is the case with horses. The husky dogs are justly famous for their stamina, but they die sometimes with very little apparent cause. There is no doubt that generally

5 GEORGE V., A. 1915

speaking dogs are over-driven, and as it does not seriously hurt a well-fed dog to go entirely without food for two days, and thus while working there is a tendency to underfeed especially if the procuring of dog feed entails some trouble. Many dogs will work when completely exhausted and show no sign of their condition particularly to an inexperienced driver while a horse shows signs of fatigue long before exhaustion comes, and he is usually unhitched and taken to camp.

We left Pas to continue the second meridian northerly from township 67, on December 24, 1912, this being the earliest date at which it was safe to leave. The country around Pas is swampy and if heavy frosts do not come before the first snowfall, it is always late before it is safe to travel with horses. We proceeded by the Cumberland House trail and thence to the northeast corner of Beaver lake where some delay was caused by the difficulty in finding a cache. We then travelled up the trail already cut by the men I had sent ahead, and arrived at our starting point on January 10, 1913. The country through which this trail passes is rolling and very rocky in places. It is fairly well timbered with small spruce, tamarack, jackpine and poplar, except where a few small fires have swept through. There are many lakes and the soil is sandy with usually a rocky subsoil.

I commenced running the second meridian on January 13. Through township 68 the meridian crosses low rocky ridges with muskegs between. The soil is sandy with considerable surface rock and is unfit for agriculture. Small spruce, jackpine and tamarack is found and a few small areas of spruce up to ten inches in diameter. Close to the north boundary of section 25 the line enters a lake which forms one of the main routes of travel to the north both in summer and winter. This lake is very irregular in shape consisting of long bays running roughly in a northerly and southerly direction. At the south end a water route leads northwesterly to Wildnest lake and another leads to the east.

Proceeding northerly through township 69 the country becomes rougher. The ridges are broken and rock bluffs are common. The soil is sandy and very rocky and consequently is of no use for agriculture, except in some low-lying sections of small extent where a fair sandy loam is found. Scrub spruce, jackpine and tamarack cover all this area. The lakes are deep with rocky shores and clear water, and are fairly well stocked with whitefish, jackfish, trout and pickerel. Fur-bearing animals seem plentiful particularly foxes and lynx. In section 29, approximately, there is a fall of about twenty-two feet between two lakes which could easily be developed into a power site and smaller falls exist at several other points.

Through township 70 the surface continues broken and rocky. The soil is sandy with considerable surface rock and is useless for agriculture. The timber is a little larger than to the south and the same varieties were seen up to ten inches in diameter. Difficulty of access and smallness of area take away their value for milling purposes. In sections 24 and 25 we crossed a bay of the lake previously mentioned and from the east side of this bay I made a horse trail running to the north end of Wildnest lake. From this point there is a well-known water route leading to Birch portage on the Sturgeon-weir river between Beaver lake and Pelican narrows.

Through township 71 the line crosses only one small lake in section 25. The surface is broken but not so rocky as to the south. The soil is very sandy on the ridges, but in the lower places where it is not muskeg we found a very fair sandy loam. On the top of the ridges there is jackpine up to ten inches in diameter and spruce, tamarack and poplar of the same size on the slopes. West of the line there is a long bay of the lake to the south, and farther west can be seen a high rocky ridge. Fish are not very plentiful there, but fur-bearing animals abound, principally foxes, lynx, mink and otter.

Entering township 72 the line drops to the valley of a lake lying mainly to the east of the line. This lake is shallow and has swampy shores in places. The long bay seen west of the line in township 71 ends here and is connected by creeks and a small lake with another lake lying for the most part in township 73. There are rapids on both the connecting creeks suitable for power development. The country through this township is broken but not so rocky as farther south. Jackpine up to six inches covers the tops of the ridges and spruce and occasional patches of poplar and birch are found on the slopes. The land drops generally in a northeasterly direction towards Kipahigan lake lying to the east and northeast.

In township 73 the line crosses two bays of Kipahigan lake. This is one of the prominent lakes of this district, and there is a small Indian settlement on the southeastern corner, at the mouth of a river about two chains wide running southeasterly. There is a water route from this settlement to Kississing lake which lies on the direct route from Cumberland House to Pukkatawagan. There is also another route leading northerly to the Indian settlement on Sisipuk lake which is a bay of Churchill river. Kipahigan lake is well stocked with whitefish, jackfish, pickerel and sucker. The district seems a good one for fur and the residents make large catches of foxes, lynx, mink and otter. On the east side of the lake the country is rough and rocky and a considerable area has been burnt over. West of the lake the surface is not so rough but there are gravel and rocky ridges timbered with small spruce, jackpine and tamarack. There are muskegs between the ridges and small lakes. The soil is sandy with considerable rock.

In township 74 the north bay of Kipahigan lake is crossed. Along the shore there is a narrow fringe of spruce from eight to ten inches in diameter. To the west of the line the country is broken and covered with small jackpine and spruce, and occasional small birch and poplar. The soil is of no use for agriculture, being sand and rock.

In township 75 a bay of Kipahigan lake stretches to the west and there are many islands carrying spruce and tamarack up to ten inches in diameter. A water route to Pelican narrows leaves the west shore. The line crosses a very rough broken rocky country and precipitous rock bluffs are common. Many of the ridges have been burnt over and are now covered with a growth of small poplar, birch, spruce and jackpine but in other places jackpine up to six inches is found. Many small muskegs occur all through the district. The soil in the depressions between the ridges, where there is no muskeg, is a light sandy loam. Fur is still plentiful, and good catches of foxes, mink, lynx and otter are made every year.

In township 76 the northern extremity of Kipahigan lake is reached and the meridian crosses a number of bays on the east shore. The country is very rocky with precipitous bluffs, and small jackpine, spruce, poplar and birch cover the ridges. The soil is sandy and very rocky except in depressions where there is a fair sandy loam. Fire has burnt over some sections. To the east the country is even more rocky and broken.

In township 77 the meridian crosses several arms of Sisipuk lake, one arm of which runs to the north along the meridian and almost reaches Churchill river, thus forming practically an island. The shores of Sisipuk lake are not so rocky as the shores of the lakes to the south, and they are generally well timbered with spruce, poplar and birch up to eight inches in diameter. The arm stretching in a northeasterly direction forms part of one of the water routes from Pelican narrows to Pukkatawagan, along which there is a considerable amount of travel. The islands are generally well timbered with spruce, tamarack and jackpine up to ten inches in diameter. It was noticed that the islands in all these lakes are usually better timbered than the mainland. The soil also is better, usually a very fair sandy loam, and the Indians living on this lake cultivate small patches on the islands. In section 24 there is an Indian settlement of six houses and both the Hudson's Bay company and Revillon Frères have traders there. A considerable quantity of fur is handled every year, foxes, lynx, beaver, mink, otter, bears and weasels being the principal varieties. All the district is apparently well stocked with fur-bearing animals and every Indian with any energy can make a good catch. The lake is well stocked with whitefish, pickerel, jackfish and sucker. The country

5 GEORGE V., A. 1915

lying to the west of Sisipuk lake is very rough and rocky and is sparsely covered with scrub spruce and jackpine.

In township 78 the meridian crosses the north end of the west bay of Sisipuk lake. Along the northeastern shore there is a strip of sandy loam covered with spruce, poplar, and birch. The surface is somewhat rolling, but there are several small areas of good agricultural land. Inland in an easterly and northeasterly direction we found a broken and rocky country with small spruce, tamarack, birch and poplar. The soil was sandy and very rocky, and of practically no use for agriculture. To the west of the bay the surface was rolling and timbered with spruce, poplar and birch up to eight inches in diameter with a few swamps and muskegs. The soil is mostly a light sandy loam with patches of a heavy clay loam. Rocky ridges are also in evidence.

In section 1, township 79, we crossed the southern shore of Churchill river. The river during this part of its course is more truly a string of irregularly shaped lakes connected by narrow channels, usually with rapids in them. The shores have a fairly gentle slope back from the water's edge, although it is very rocky in some sections. The banks are well timbered with spruce, poplar and birch up to ten inches in diameter, although most of it is under this size. The islands, of which there are a large number carry better timber of the foregoing varieties. All along both banks of the river, and more particularly on the islands, there are areas of good agricultural land. The soil varies from a sandy loam to a clay loam and is comparatively free from rock. Hay can be cut in swamps at the head of some of the bays, one good place being the bay lying to the east of the line in townships 79 and 80. The river is well stocked with sturgeon, whitefish, jackfish, pickerel, trout and sucker. As a fur country it appears good. All the Indians had good catches of beaver, foxes, mink and otter. There is a small Indian settlement of about five houses east of the meridian at the mouth of Loon river, which enters the Churchill from the north.

In township 80 after leaving Churchill river the land rises to the north and the line crosses an area of rolling land, becoming broken toward the northern part of the township. To the west of the line in the southern part of the township, the country slopes down to a bay of Churchill river but to the east it is high. A creek about sixty links wide was crossed in section 25 running southwesterly to the river. It is very unsuitable for canoe travel owing to numerous obstructions and rapids, but at high water it is passable for small canoes. It receives several small tributaries during its passage from a lake crossed in township 81 to Churchill river, and there are several falls on these which could be utilized for small water-powers. West of this creek the land is broken and cut up by ravines. Spruce up to six inches in diameter, poplar, birch and tamarack cover the slopes with jackpine on the summits of the ridges. The soil is a sandy loam and very rocky. To the east of the creek the land is high carrying spruce, poplar, birch and tamarack up to eight inches in diameter with many swamps and muskegs. The soil varies from a sandy loam to a clay loam and surface rock is usually present.

In township 81 the line crosses a lake. To the east the country is high and rolling covered with small jackpine, spruce, poplar and birch and the soil is sandy and very rocky. To the west we found a broken country with jackpine and spruce up to six inches with some poplar, birch and tamarack. There are some small patches of sandy loam land.

A small lake was crossed in section 1 township 82, and from the northwest corner a portage of about half a mile leads to the south end of a long lake lying to the west of the meridian. To the west of this lake the surface is high, rolling and rocky, covered with small spruce, tamarack, jackpine, poplar and birch and there are many small lakes. The soil is sandy with considerable rock. To the east of the meridian the country is similar with many bare ridges.

In township 83 several small lakes were crossed before reaching the south shore of Kamuchawi lake in section 24. The land on both sides of the meridian is high, rolling and rocky with many small lakes and is covered with small spruce, tamarack, jack-pine, poplar and birch. The soil is sandy with considerable rock, with the exception of fringes around some of the lakes where a fair agricultural soil is found varying from a sandy loam to a light clay loam. Kamuchawi lake is a large body of water lying partly in townships 84 and 85 and on both sides of the meridian. It is deep with clear water and is well stocked with trout, whitefish, pickerel and jackfish. Its shores are well timbered with spruce, jackpine, poplar and birch up to six inches. It is drained from the northeast corner by Loon river. This river constitutes a well known water route. It expands into a number of lakes and in its narrow parts is usually full of rapids; the portages however are good. It reaches the Churchill in township 79 east of the meridian. When it is decided to continue the second meridian farther north, this will be the best way to reach the end of the line in summer from the Churchill. At the northwest of Kamuchawi lake a bay stretches to the west and from this point there is a water route to Reindeer lake. I have been told that there is a lake of considerable size called Rabbit lake situated to the north of Kamuchawi lake. Between Kamuchawi lake and the Loon river the country is very rough and rocky with scrub spruce and jackpine growing thereon.

We finished running the line on May 12. I sent the party back over the line to do the mounding and the levelling to Churchill river while I returned to the main camp in township 81, and started from there with canoe and supplies to go by the Loon river route, to the end of line to get a latitude observation. We had a hard and strenuous trip. The lakes on this route were only partly open. I was able to pick up a jumper and when it was impossible to travel with canoe, we would cut our way through slush ice to where it was fairly solid, and then take the canoe out, place it on the jumper and travel on the ice until it became too rotten to proceed any farther. Then cutting a trench in the ice the canoe would be placed therein and forced into open water. I arrived at the north end of Kamuchawi lake on June 4 and commenced taking latitude observations. This I continued up to the 13th with excellent success. On this day, however, we unfortunately had a bush fire that burnt our camp out. We lost practically all the camp outfit, food, personal belongings, etc., but worst of all some of the records of this survey. The latitude observation records were destroyed and one azimuth observation book and some accounts and field books were partly burnt. I returned at once to the party who by this time had reached the Churchill, and as I had neither the supplies nor the outfit to stay and obtain the missing information I decided to return to Pas. I went to Pukkatawagan to obtain canoemen and an extra canoe. Pukkatawagan is a fairly large Indian reserve situated on a bay of Churchill river. It is a picturesque spot and the land, although light, seems to be productive. I was informed that all the common vegetables can be raised to perfection. The season is short but the rapid growth caused by the long days of summer compensates for this. I obtained the necessary canoemen there and returned to my main camp.

The quantity of land suitable for agriculture in the country traversed by the second meridian between townships 67 and 85 is very limited. The lakes are well stocked with whitefish, jackfish, pickerel and sucker. Fur-bearing animals abound, the principal varieties being foxes, lynx, mink, otter, beaver, bears and weasels. The barren land caribou, in their migration, reach the Churchill in winter and leave about the third week in March. These provide an excellent supply of fresh meat during the winter. The caribou seem to be coming farther south every winter. In summer time moose may be obtained as far north as Churchill river and a few stragglers even farther north. In winter time the moose all migrate to the south. It was reported to me that there are some bush caribou here, but I did not see signs or tracks of any.

On June 21, we started down to Pas travelling by Barrier, Kississing and Cumberland lakes. This is a well travelled route and the portages are fairly well cut. We arrived in Pas on June 30, and I paid off my party on July 1.

5 GEORGE V., A. 1915

I then had instructions to complete the mounding of the fifteenth base line between the second and the third meridians. The water in Saskatchewan river was very high and I knew that the swamps through which the line passed would be wet, but on July 28 I left Pas for my starting point. I found that the line was impassable and went farther up stream to two other points on the line, but the same conditions prevailed. I accordingly returned to Pas. I again left Pas on August 25 as the water had fallen considerably, and found that it was possible to get through some of the swamps. The work was slow and laborious, but I was able to bring supplies by canoe to several points by the Saskatchewan and Torch rivers, and man-packing was resorted to between these points. From range 10 the canoe work ceased and man-packing was the only method of transportation. A delay was caused by a large floating muskeg which could not be crossed until the surface was frozen. Three dog trains were used when it was possible for them to travel. The work was completed and the party returned to Pas on February 25, 1914. Two men who unfortunately had their feet frozen arrived on March 7.

APPENDIX No. 46.

ABSTRACT OF THE REPORT OF O. ROLFSON, D.L.S.

BASE LINE SURVEYS IN NORTHERN MANITOBA.

My work during the summers of 1912 and 1913 and the intervening winter consisted of the survey of portions of the fifteenth, sixteenth and seventeenth base lines west of the principal meridian.

I organized my party at Selkirk and left for Norway House on June 10, 1912, travelling by the steamer Wolverine to Warren's landing, and by the Hudson's Bay company's boat *Highlander,* the remainder of the distance.

Owing to very stormy weather on lake Winnipeg, the barge with my supplies was so delayed that it did not arrive at Norway House until June 18. As soon as it was unloaded I left with canoes travelling up Jack and McLaughlin rivers to the principal meridian and then packed north to the fifteenth base. The following day, June 27, I commenced cutting the line and continued until July 30, it being then completed to Playgreen lake.

As Kiskittogisu and Kiskitto lakes which are crossed by the sixteenth base are too large for triangulation, I moved down to Cross lake and commenced running the seventeenth base. My plan was to run enough of this line in 1912 so that it might be completed as far as necessary the following summer. After running five ranges I left a small party at Cross lake to do some miscellaneous work and moved the main party back to Norway House, from which place we commenced moving supplies to Sea falls to be ready for the winter's work along the sixteenth base.

On October 21 I commenced work on this line and continued it until April 8, 1913, by which time I had run 150 miles. The warm spring weather was then melting the snow so fast that I was compelled to cease work and move into Pas, travelling via Cormorant and Clearwater lakes, and the Hudson Bay railway grade. We moved none too soon as two of the teams broke through the ice on Cormorant lake. At Pas I disbanded the party and made preparations for completing the seventeenth base to Reed lake.

On June 6, I again left Selkirk for Cross lake by the same route as before. On the 18th, I commenced running the seventeenth base and continued until October 2, by which time it was completed to Reed lake in section 36 of range 20. I then moved to Cormorant lake via the regular canoe route and on December 9 completed the sixteenth base to the second meridian. After this I returnd to Pas and disbanded the party.

In the summer of 1912 I had all my supplies for the eastern part of the line shipped directly to Norway House and then moved to Playgreen lake and Cross lake as required for the different parts of the work. I also had supplies shipped by boat from Pas to the narrows on Cormorant lake, and placed in cache there for use on the western part of the sixteenth base. In March of 1913 I had supplies for the westerly end of the seventeenth base shipped by the railway contractors by means of horse teams from Pas to camp 7 near Limestone river, and held for me until required in the fall. I shipped supplies for the easterly end of the seventeenth base to Norway House, then took them with my own party to the beginning of the work.

During the latter part of October and until the freeze-up occurs, it is practically impossible to work in the bad swamps because standing all day in ice-cold water is beyond the limit of endurance. When winter sets in there is no more difficulty. Work in this district is both easier and more pleasant in winter than in summer. In the

5 GEORGE V., A. 1915

spring the party must disband for about two months because during the latter part of April and all of May dog teams cannot be used, and as the lakes are not yet free of ice canoes are useless.

For survey work during the winter only, horses and flat sleighs may be used to advantage for transportation, but a surveyor working all summer must use dog teams the following winter, or disband his party until about Christmas. As a general rule horses cannot be used until late in December, when the swamps are frozen, whereas dogs may be used in bush as soon as snow falls, and on the lakes as soon as they are frozen, generally about November 15. In making trail it is best to have several men walk ahead and return on snow-shoes, cutting what is necessary as they go. This will freeze at night and the next day the dog teams should be sent ahead loaded with heavy and compact supplies, the drivers wearing snow-shoes. This still further packs the snow which freezes at night leaving a good trail for moving the awkward high loads of camp equipage and dunnage. Before it is frozen, no one should be allowed on the trail without snow-shoes because the holes make hard work for the dogs.

Transportation by dog team is, under certain circumstances, the best method to use but it is always expensive. It requires one man to drive each team which haul about 400 pounds, often much less. On this basis freight moved along the line costs $1.00 per 100 pounds per seven miles.

Fish is without doubt a splendid dog food as the northern dogs are accustomed to eating it, but it is very inconvenient for use by the base line surveyors. Five working dogs should be fed two fish each day or about thirty pounds, that is eight per cent of the load they can haul. The same dogs will eat ten pounds of dog biscuit per day, that is $2\frac{1}{2}$ per cent of the load they can haul. No matter how carefully he may plan, the surveyor is never certain of getting all the fish he requires, whereas dog biscuit may be purchased from the wholesale firms and shipped to the line along with the rest of the cache. Dogs entirely unused to eating biscuits will soon relish them and keep in good condition. I have never seen biscuits fed to dogs that are making long hard trips every day, but believe they could be successfully used.

I have tried different methods of running line during the summer, but find the most successful is to move camp to the end of the work each morning, then cut line during the day and return to camp at night. In summer the men must be supplied with silk tents in order to lighten their loads. The comforts of life are few; the cook bakes without a stove, using frying pans, the men eat without dishes rather than pack the extra weight and everyone is continually wet, generally to the waist, because of wading through swamps. Man-packing is very laborious, but it the only method possible in the summer. The caches are placed on canoe routes near where the base will cross and the supplies packed along the line until the next route is reached. Those accustomed to packing with horses have no idea how much of their camp equipage and personal effects may be dispensed with.

There is no comparison between the swamps in the western country where horses are used and those where surveyors attempt to use anything else than men for packing. Last season on the seventeenth base our party ran from Muningwari lake to the grade of the Hudson Bay railway, a distance of nineteen miles, and carried their camp equipment, dunnage and supplies over very bad swamps with no possible way of getting supplies in at any intermediate point. This will, perhaps show how great is the difficulty of summer work in this district.

The country along the fifteenth base from the principal meridian to Playgreen lake is a series of spruce and tamarack swamps with granite outcrops occuring about once or twice in each mile of line. The underlying rock is all granite and the swamps lie in the depressions. There is a small amount of spruce along the banks of McLaughlin river. The soil in most places is a black muck which is unsuited for farming. There are occasional clay ridges covered with poplar and birch, but these are too scattered and small to be of great value.

Shallow Shore of Waskik Lake.

This lake is situated in township 64, range 9, west of the Principal meridian. The shore is very shallow, and the soft muddy bottom prevents even the use of canoes near the shore, unless pushed along through the mud. Though the men appear to be knee-deep in water, there is really not enough to float the canoe, as they are walking in nearly a foot of soft mud.

Photo by O. Rolfson, D.L.S.

SESSIONAL PAPER No. 25b

The first four miles of the sixteenth base crosses bad tamarack and spruce swamps but near Nelson river the land is drier and covered with spruce, jackpine, birch and poplar. Along the west side of the river the line runs for about two miles through a brulé ridge. From range 2 to Playgreen lake the country is spruce and tamarack swamp. Between Playgreen and Kiskittogisu lakes the line runs through a small belt of spruce six to twelve inches in diameter. Between the latter and Kiskitto lakes the country is swampy and covered with small spruce and tamarack.

For the first five miles west of Kiskitto lake the line runs through a mixture of spruce ridges and tamarack swamps; west of this the swamps are more extensive and the spruce occurs as knolls or islands in the swamp. For a short distance on each side of Minago river the country is burned and covered with deep windfall. From there to the beginning of range 14 it is almost all swamp. About the middle of range 14 the line runs through spruce and jackpine; a rock outcrop occurs there, the first after leaving Kiskitto lake. West of this the country is drier, the rock is limestone and the timber spruce, birch, poplar and jackpine.

Around the shore of Little Cormorant lake there is considerable limestone, which appears to be of good quality. The soil away from the rock ridges is clay and clay loam.

In the first two miles west of Cormorant lake the line runs over a limestone hill, covered with small jackpine and spruce. Ranges 24 and 25 are covered with spruce and tamarack with frequent jackpine ridges. Small lakes are numerous. In ranges 26 and 27, the line runs through a large amount of clay loam soil covered with spruce, poplar and birch. This is the best land seen along the three bases. It is distant from Pas about fifty miles.

East of Cross lake the seventeenth base runs through spruce swamp. The timber is of little value being the ordinary stunted growth generally seen in wet country. Near Cross lake on both sides and on the island crossed by the line, the underlying rock is granite, the soil clay loam and the timber spruce, birch and poplar from six to fourteen inches in diameter. West of the lake the country becomes softer and wetter and the timber gradually changes to the small spruce and tamarack of the swamps.

In range 9 near Lily lake and from there to Muningwari lake, in range 10, the soil is mostly clay loam and the timber spruce and poplar. On the west side of Muningwari lake extending for one mile east and west and nearly five miles north and south there is a belt of good spruce and jackpine from six to twenty inches in diameter. The soil is sandy, some of it being attracted by the magnet. The remainder of range 10 and ranges 11, 12 and 13 are very wet and covered with small spruce and tamarack. This is the same great swamp that is crossed by the sixteenth base in ranges 12 and 13. Through ranges 14 and 15 the line runs near Limestone river. There the soil is clay loam and the timber growing along both sides of the river is good spruce. In ranges 16, 17 and 18 the line runs through a vast spruce and tamarack swamp. Range 19 is drier being nearer Reed lake. As usual the timber also improves and near the shore good spruce grows from six to eighteen inches in diameter. The underlying rock is again granite and the soil clay loam. The rock at Norway House, Cross lake, Lily lake along Nelson and Muhigan rivers and also at Setting and Reed lakes is granite. The limestone area projects into this from the south.

At Norway House the settlers have small gardens and grow potatoes and some of the ordinary vegetables. One settler at the narrows of Cormorant lake has grown good potatoes and some of the resident engineers along the line of the Hudson Bay railway have small gardens with the ordinary vegetables. When circumstances warrant an extensive system of drainage I believe that some of this district can be used for farming.

Many of the swamps are soft and very difficult to cross in the summer, but nearly all have a hard bottom of clay, sand or rock. In mounding where the moss is thick, ice is frequently found at a depth of twelve inches throughout the summer.

5 GEORGE V., A. 1915

Partridges, prairie-chickens, ptarmigan, rabbits, rats, mink, caribou, moose and bears are plentiful. In the district near Reed lake the work of beavers is seen along many of the rivers. Large numbers of whitefish, jackfish and some pickerel and gold-eye are found in all the lakes, and large trout in Namew lake. The Indians have no difficulty whatever in obtaining all the fresh meat and fish they require, and making a good living with their traps in winter. Trappers' cabins are numerous on all the lakes and rivers.

When the railway is completed the facilities for transportation will make the fishing industry profitable where now it is carried on only for dog feed in winter and for the local supply in the summer.

On almost all the rivers there are water-powers which will some day be valuable.

The original site of Norway House was on a point north of Warren's landing but many years ago it was moved to its present situation on Norway House island. This is the district office of the Hudson's Bay company for Keewatin district, and is the scene of great activity at times in the summer when freight is arriving or leaving. The Methodist mission is on the mainland northeast of the post; the Roman Catholic mission is on the east side of the island and the English mission is on an island immediately south. There is an Indian village near and many houses are scattered up and down the river.

The Northern Fish company run two boats from Selkirk to Warren's landing at the north end of lake Winnipeg in connection with their fishing operations and the Hudson's Bay company run a boat from there to Norway House. All freight for the district north of lake Winnipeg passes through Warren's landing. From Norway House the regular route to York Factory and intermediate points is via Nelson river, to Echimamish river, then through the lakes and rivers past Oxford House and down Hayes river. The Hudson's Bay company operates a small car on a wooden track over the portage on the Echimamish. The route down the Hayes instead of the Nelson is used because of the number of rapids on the latter. The route to Split lake and Nelson House is down the Nelson from Cross lake. Freight for Oxford House, Split lake and Nelson House is taken in York boats, that for Gods lake and Island lake is sent up Jack and McLaughlin rivers in canoes.

During the summers of 1912 and 1913, most of the freight for Cross Lake post and points north was shipped to Whisky Jack by boat, then teamed across the portage and sent to Cross Lake post and points north in York boats.

Last summer the contractors for the Hudson Bay railway sent their freight from Warren's landing direct to Whiskey Jack, teamed it across the portage, and then shipped it over Cross lake in a barge towed by a gasoline launch. From there to Sipiwesk lake, a distance of thirteen miles, they hauled it on a pole track, and then towed it in another barge across the lake. During the coming summer they will be able to take freight by this means as far north as Manitou rapids. From there to Split lake and points north it will be necessary to use canoes or York boats.

A small steamer runs from Pas up and down Saskatchewan river and across Moose lake to the narrows of Cormorant lake. The most used canoe route to the north from Pas is to Limestone bay on Moose lake, across the portage. ten miles to Limestone lake, then down Limestone river to Grass river and thence into Setting lake.

The Hudson Bay railway now under construction from Pas to Port Nelson crosses the sixteenth base in range 21 and the seventeenth base in range 13. When completed this road will alter and reverse many of the present freight routes into the north.

From Namew (Sturgeon) lake, there is a winter road out to Pas via Rock and Root lakes and the easterly side of Reader lake. This is used by teamsters in hauling fish from Namew and Rock lakes to Pas.

APPENDIX No. 47.

ABSTRACT OF THE REPORT OF G. P. J. ROY, D.L.S.

SUBDIVISION IN EAST CENTRAL SASKATCHEWAN.

Our work for the season of 1913 lay mostly in the country bordering on the south limit of the Porcupine forest reserve in the eastern part of the province of Saskatchewan.

We left Tisdale on May 28 and on June 6 reached township 41, range 13 west of the second meridian where our first work was situated. On July 24 this survey was completed with the exception of the traverses which were left over for the winter.

The soil in this township is a heavy coat of yellow loam over a clay subsoil. The surface is a succession of light slopes and levels covered with areas of poplar two to five inches in diameter, interspersed with patches of brush and scrub. The principal topographical feature is Barrier lake, a long narrow body of water situated at the bottom of a valley from one hundred to one hundred and fifty feet deep. When cleared this district will be a good farming locality.

From July 25 to August 4 we were absent from our main camp running the boundaries of blocks 1 and 2 of timber berth No. 2055 situated in townships 42 and 43, range 11. We estimated these bluffs to be capable of producing nearly ten milion feet of spruce. The spruce bluffs of the berth were surrounded by poplar woods interspersed with scrubby and open spaces. Red Deer river, a swift-flowing stream one hundred feet wide and four to ten feet deep, winds southeasterly through township 42, one bend of it being only half a mile from the south edge of the berth.

On August 5 we proceeded to township 39, range 9 west of the second meridian to survey the portion lying outside of the forest reserve. We found the soil good with large areas of open country interspersed with areas of timber, light poplar and willow brush and a number of small sloughs.

From there we moved to Kelvington where we camped, while the wagons drove to Wadena to haul in supplies coming from Winnipeg. Wadena is a prosperous new town on the branch of the Canadian Northern railway running from Winnipeg to Edmonton.

On September 2 we moved to the northeast corner of section 6, township 37, range 4 west of the second meridian and commenced the survey of the western part of the township. This township contains large sloughs mainly on sections 5, 7 and 8 and the low ground in the vicinity is covered with small poplar, willow and poplar brush, section 6, as well as the northern sections, is good level land, and is covered with a growth of poplar averaging two to three inches in diameter and scattered bluffs of spruce of little value except for homestead purposes. The southern sections are lightly wooded, and have some open spaces. Intending settlers were exploring them when we left.

The part of township 37, range 3 which we surveyed is similar to township 37, range 4, that is to say lightly rolling with the same kind of soil, but the bush is denser. We completed the work there on October 20.

There is a post-office two miles south of the centre of township 37, range 4, and Preeceville, the present terminus of the branch of the Canadian Northern railway running from Swan River, was within one day's travel from any of our camps. The location line of the proposed railway from Corona to Hudson Bay Junction crosses the same township.

5 GEORGE V., A. 1915

Leaving our camp there on October 21, we camped seven days later on the bush road opened along the east boundary of township 36, range 31, west of the principal meridian where our work consisted of the survey of part of this township, and the north and east boundaries of sections 19 to 24 in township 36, range 30. This work being completed we left for Bowsman on December 9.

Township 36, range 31 is thickly wooded, the only openings being a number of small hay sloughs. Part of the two northern tiers of sections and all of the southern part is a forest of poplar, some measuring up to seven inches, but most of it being from three to five inches in diameter with extensive windfall. Evidences remain of a bush fire which had passed many years ago. The soil is good and the surface slopes slightly to the south.

An old mill site is situated on section 34 in the middle of a well-timbered area which, although partly cut during recent years, is still capable of yielding at least ten million feet of good spruce.

The sections surveyed in township 36, range 30 are all wooded with poplar and scattered bluffs of spruce. The soil is good, the surface level, and there is an abundance of building material, fuel and water.

Benito, a progressive town in township 34, range 29, is the business centre of the vicinity. Arran is the nearest railway station but the village is small and there is no station agent.

The soil in the whole of this district is good and is suitable for all kinds of grain and root crops. With timber, fuel and good water in abundance, and roads good for travel even in their primitive state, it is one of the best sections for intending settlers.

All the small towns are growing fast and constitute a good market for all farm produce as well as for horses from the remaining but fast disappearing ranches.

On December 9, we closed operations for the season and left our camp on section 12, township 36, range 21, west of the principal meridian for Bowsman, where I stored the outfit, paid off the party and left for home.

APPENDIX No. 48.

ABSTRACT OF THE REPORT OF A. SAINT CYR, D.L.S.

MERIDIAN AND BASE LINE SURVEYS IN NORTHERN SASKATCHEWAN.

My work for the season of 1913-14 consisted of the survey of the third meridian through townships 69 to 72 and the nineteenth base line west of the third meridian to the end of range 17.

I left Prince Albert, where my party was organized, on June 3, 1913, and arrived at " the forks " on the Montreal lake trail five days later. There I divided the party and instructed by first assistant to proceed to the eighteenth base line by the pack trail along the third meridian. Knowing that at many of the camping grounds along this trail the grass would be scanty, I advised him to take as many bags of oats as the horses could possibly carry, in addition to the men's outfit which had been reduced to the bare necessaries. They took sufficient provisions to last them three weeks. With four men I proceeded to the Hudson's Bay company's trading post at the south end of Montreal lake, where I had already arranged to build a boat for the transport to the line, of our supplies stored at both ends of this lake. This mode of transportation was the only one possible at that season. The boat was substantially built, special care being given to the bottom. Its dimensions were thirty feet in length, but only eight and one-half feet in width. It had to be built narrow in order, to run safely through the worst rapids where the channel is less than ten feet wide, and very tortuous in places. After the boat was built, I experienced some difficulty in securing an Indian crew, the best boatmen being at the time away from the village. Finally this matter was arranged by the agent of the Hudson's Bay company and on June 22 I made a start from the company's trading post at the south end of Montreal lake. The boat had been loaded with six and a half tons of material for the survey, and the crew consisted of four members of my survey party and several Indian canoemen picked up at Montreal lake. Sailing up the lake, I reached the north end on June 25. Loading up two and a half tons more of camp supplies I then proceeded down Montreal river.

On July 1, we reached Montreal rapids where I received news of the main party who had just reached the eighteenth base line and were commencing the survey of the third meridian. They had met with many difficulties on the road owing to the flooded state of the country; the rebuilding of bridges, rebrushing of muskegs and the opening of new trails had considerably delayed their progress. I also learned that one man had quit the party shortly after the start had been made from " the forks " and that two of their ponies had taken sick and had been left behind near a small hay meadow, the packers intending to return for the ponies later on in the season.

At the " rapids " the packers loaded enough supplies to last the party until the big boat should have been brought to a point ahead of the line, whence a pack trail might be constructed along the nineteenth base line.

While going down the " Montreal rapids " a member of the Indian crew had the misfortune to meet with a serious accident and the rest becoming frightened at the difficulties met in navigating this river, decided to return with him to Montreal Lake Indian reserve. Accordingly I sent word to the Hudson's Bay compnay's agent at Montreal lake to despatch another crew of boatmen and to instruct them to pick up a small lot of supplies which had been left behind along the river banks, at Askik rapids.

5 GEORGE V., A. 1915

Leaving Montreal rapids, we proceeded north to Sikachu lake which we reached on July 10. Here I spent some time exploring the country in the hope of locating a route passable for loaded pack ponies, but was unsuccessful, the soft and quaky nature of the ground and the extensive tracts of open bogs and treeless swamps upsetting all my plans in this respect.

My party was also experiencing great difficulties in their work and frequently had recourse to man-packing to move their camp outfit and supplies forward and the survey work that was daily carried on was due to the indomitable energy of the first assistant.

While waiting at Sikachu lake for the return of the Indian boatmen who had been sent back to Montreal rapids and Mountain rapids for some supplies that had been left at these places, I began a thorough exploration of the country northwest of the lake. Entering one of its west bays, I followed it two miles. At this distance it turns northwesterly. Noticing a gap through the hills along the west shore, I concluded that it must be the valley of a stream discharging into a bay. This proved to be Morin river which is from two to four chains wide and eight miles long. As the current was slack, we made good progress and soon came to Morin lake nearly five miles long and bearing west. This brought me within five miles of the third meridian but almost eighteen miles north of my party. However, another large stream was discovered flowing from the south into Morin lake and by ascending it five miles I came to Moose lake from which starts a portage leading to Smoothstone river. I returned to the big boat on Sikachu lake for more camp supplies and before leaving again for Moose lake I instructed the two men left in charge to overhaul all our provisions, some of which were in a fair way to spoil, and then to bring the boat to the west shore of Morin lake and there build a cache for our supplies. As the land west of this lake appeared to be fairly high I saw the possibility of opening later on, a pack trail between this cache and the line.

I returned to Moose lake in the old canvas canoe loaded with as many supplies as it could safely carry, and stored these on the west shore of this lake. Moose portage, which crosses the third meridian, begins here. Near this point I had previously left a note and sketch of the surrounding country (as we knew it then) for the explorer; it showed the location of this " cache " of supplies and advised my first assistant of my future whereabouts. On August 6, travelling westerly on Moose portage, I met seven of my men heading for the " cache " so we carried all the supplies to the first lake on the portage. These supplies were, the same night, brought to the main camp in the canvas canoe which one of my men had carried across the portage.

The northern Moose portage had been explored by me with the view of utilizing it for the transport of the supplies to Smoothstone river and thence to Snake lake, close to which we thought the nineteenth base line would run. If this could have been accomplished, it would have been of great assistance to us as my transport outfit was in a very reduced condition, no fewer than nine ponies having contracted swamp fever and an equal number being unfit for work through foot-rot. I was however unable to follow out this plan. Along Moose portage there are too many lakes surrounded by muskegs unfit for travel by horses, and no rafts could have been floated down Smoothstone river which, as we discovered later in the season, is a succession of rapids. Therefore, we frequently resorted to man-packing as our only means of transport.

The southern portage to Smoothstone river was, if possible, in a worse condition than the northern one, as it runs across a succession of quaky bogs and muskegs which do not become fit to travel over with dogs till frost has set in. The main party had up to this point been experiencing much difficulty from the wet country through which they were travelling and their horses were in very poor condition from lack of feed, the only grass obtainable being that growing in deep sloughs in which the horses had to stand in a considerable depth of water with the result that swamp fever and foot-

rot were prevalent and several animals had already succumbed. Up to that time all
medicine given to them to counteract these ailments did not appear to produce the
desired effect and no relief could reasonably be expected till the animals had been
brought to a higher country.

From Moose portage the country along the line was drier and fairly good progress
was made. When the line had reached as far north as Morin lake, seeing no prospect
of getting farther west with the big boat, I transferred supplies contained in it to
another " cache " which had been built about three miles from a lake close to which
the meridian passes.

After some exploring on August 25, I left for Montreal lake to get my mail, hire
more men and to arrange about the winter supplies. The members of my party who had
helped in taking the boat down and in exploring this country, were sent back to join
the main party. On September 6, the third meridian was completed.

Proceeding along the base line the nature of the country along the first ranges
rendered a pack-road impossible and accordingly the horses were left near some fair
feed at the south end of Lynx lake and the work was continued by means of canoe
transportation and man-packing.

Several large lakes lying west of one another with quaky bogs between, were
crossed by the first three ranges of the nineteenth base line and progress was very
slow especially as the road even when located needed a great amount of corduroying
and the building of several bridges before any freighting was practicable. Long detours
had to be made to get past some bays of these lakes.

Returning from Prince Albert I rejoined the party on October 4 at section 35,
township 72, range 2 and here found the head-packer to be very ill with what proved
to be typhoid fever. I accordingly conveyed him to the Indian village on Egg river
where there were some facilities for nursing him. To have tried to carry him to Lac
la Ronge settlement at this season when snow storms were prevalent and the only
accommodation for the night was a tent might have had very serious results.

The horses were now becoming fewer in number mostly from swamp fever
contracted earlier in the summer, and which attacked them again while in an ema-
ciated condition from lack of feed.

Returning from Lac la Ronge without obtaining my mail and with much difficulty
as the freeze-up came very early, I rejoined my party on October 28, with a dog team
and two Indians whose services had been secured by the manager of the Hudson's Bay
company's trading post at Lac la Ronge.

Meanwhile the animals used by the main party were almost unable to work and
several of them in their searches for feed became bogged in the partially frozen sloughs
in spite of the vigilance of the packers, and died from exposure. Owing to this, the
men had to carry everything on their backs and this delayed the progress of the survey
considerably. I next started on the exploration of Besnard lake and Snake lake, with
the timber cruiser and two men, since the two Indians wished to return to Lac la Ronge
with their dogs. This exploration was necessary to find the lay of the country in the
vicinity of the line and to locate and open a road for the freighters which were expected
at an early date to bring some camp supplies, especially horse feed.

These men however failed us; they were very late in starting from Prince Albert
where summer conditions were prevalent. They did not realize that in the northern part
of the province winter had long before set in. Another reason for the delay was that
they thought it absurd to use wagons and sleds on the same trip, this having never been
attempted there. They spent so much time on the trip that on January 11, when they
reached my camp in range 8, they had fed all my hay and part of the oats to their
teams, so that not a particle of hay was left for our ponies at the most critical period
of the year.

25b—13

5 GEORGE V., A. 1915

As soon as the ice became thick enough on the lakes near the line, we started to build sleds which were hauled by members of the party and in this manner the survey work was continued.

On November 16 we set to work building larger sleighs on which the men could pull a considerable load on the ice of the lakes while the horses were regaining strength; the small sleds were found too low to be of service except on absolutely bare ice. These large sleighs were afterwards used for a considerable time along the line, until we could obtain steel-shod factory-made ones.

West of range 3, the survey was carried on much more quickly, the frozen surface on the lakes assisting the transportation of supplies, etc., and such of the horses as remained got better feeding, now that the ice was solid enough everywhere to carry their weight. Still up to the close of operations in April 1914, although they were later on well looked after, they never fully recovered from the hardships they had endured in travelling across this country, and many more of them died.

I finished the exploration of Besnard and Snake lakes on December 9, and went to camp along our sled road near section 35 township 72 range 6.

There the party joined me on the following day using the horses to draw the sleighs over the ground for the first time.

On November 14, the explorer met with an accident that prevented him from doing his work, and the exploration of the country besides my other duties, devolved on me as no other member of the party cared to undertake it, one of their principal objections being the fear of meeting timber-wolves which had attacked the explorer on one of his trips across country and which are quite numerous in this locality.

Range 7 was completed and range 8 just begun by the end of the year. With the few bags of oats the teamsters from Prince Albert had brought to camp and others that I had obtained later from the mission at lac la Plonge, the remaining six ponies were kept alive for a time but two more died on February 10. To replace these I procured two oxen from lac la Plonge and with these six animals for transport the line was surveyed to range 18.

At the beginning of April the yoke of oxen had met with accidents; both of them had been snagged and our two smallest ponies were so weak that I saw the impossibility of continuing the survey of this line to the fourth meridian, I therefore decided to close operations and return to Prince Albert.

General description of the country adjacent to the third meridian from township 68 to township 72 inclusive.

The country traversed by the twenty-four miles of this meridian is somewhat varied in character.

In township 69 there is very little dry land; the country is flat, covered with stunted small trees, and short scrub, and was half flooded at the time of the survey. These wet lands extend several miles east of the meridian, but their drainage into Montreal river is largely prevented by a sandy ridge from fifty to one hundred feet high running northerly from Montreal portage to Partridge Coop lake. Where this ridge approaches the river it is at once noticed by the precipitous cut banks of stratified sand which form the left bank in several places.

In township 70 the country consists largely of spruce and tamarack swamps intersected by ridges of sand and gravel, timbered with jack pine of a diameter seldom over six inches. West of the meridian the low lands extend almost to Smoothstone river in townships 69 and 70, range 2, leaving along this stream only a narrow strip of dry land, varying from one-quarter of a mile to two miles in width and which is fairly well wooded with birch, poplar and jackpine from four to eight inches in diameter.

A stream which starts from a large lake in townships 68 and 69, range 26, west of the second meridian meanders for twelve miles in a northwesterly direction through this flat country. It is a tributary of Smoothstone river and connects several lakes. One of these is quite large and is found at one mile from the confluence of the two streams, near the centre of township 70, range 2.

In the country west of Smoothstone river the same conditions exist. Judging from the numerous brooks which discharge into the river from both sides, it seems that this wet country could be easily drained as the river is almost a continuous rapid, and the fall in a short distance of its course must therefore be very great. North of the eighteenth correction line the country becomes more rolling and township 71 contains some fair land which, although of a somewhat light soil, supports a good growth of large poplar.

In township 72, range 1, the ridges consist of granitic rocks and between these lie deep bogs, many of which are partly open. There is no hay in that section of country and except in township 71, very little grass for horse feed is to be found.

In township 70, there are several lakes; two of these, in sections 25 and 34, are on Moose portage which connects Moose lake four miles east of the meridian, with Smoothstone river in township 71, range 2. This portage is travelled every summer by the natives of Snake lake; it is fourteen miles long and follows a general north-westerly course. There are on it seven lakes from half a mile to two miles long. The two longest portages are two miles and two and one-half miles; the first one begins at the west shore of Moose lake, and the other one is adjacent to Smoothstone river. which at this point flows north across section 14, township 71, range 2. On this portage the height of land rises three miles east of the river and the drainage of many of the lakes found along the portage is carried by a swift-running but deep stream, which after a long circuitous course several miles north of the portage, returns southwards towards Moose lake where it discharges at a quarter of a mile only from the beginning of the portage. I ascended this stream several miles to the first rapids. but experienced great difficulty in paddling the canvas boat through the dense willow overhanging its low banks. I found this country covered with willow swamps inter-sected by low ridges of sand and gravel.

Lynx creek which flows out of Lynx lake in township 72, range 1, is another very crooked stream which presented the same difficulties, increased by occasional large boulders obstructing the narrow channel. It intersects the meridian in section 12 whence it winds through township 72, range 26, west of the second meridian and there enters Morin lake at the southeast corner of the same township.

In townships 70 and 71, ranges 25 and 26, west of the second meridian are many lakes, the largest one, named Morin lake, being five miles long from east to west. It lies in township 71, partly in ranges 25 and 26. Near its eastern extremity it has two large bays extending for several miles north and south.

Moose lake and Sanderson lake are both crossed by the eighteenth correction line. The first one is connected to Morin lake by a fairly large stream five miles long. The banks are very low and grassy and the current hardly noticeable. In Sanderson lake, which is east of Moose lake, there are several wooded islands; this lake drains eastward into Morin river, and a portage one hundred yards long connects the two lakes.

Morin river carries the water from the lake of the same name into the west bay of Sikachu lake. It is eight miles long, has a slack current and in two places expands into small lakes. The banks of this river are almost on a level with the water and the marshy country which adjoins it runs back a quarter mile or more to the foot of high hills timbered with jackpine, poplar and a few spruce.

Partridge Coop lake lies in the southeastern part of township 70, range 25, and drains east into Montreal river. By a portage two miles long, one can reach Sikachu lake and avoid the longer route by Montreal river. This portage passes through fairly level lands with woods of poplar six to ten inches in diameter. From the west end of Partridge Coop lake another portage leads to the valley of Smoothstone river. It bears almost west, is eighteen miles long and crosses a very wet country covered

5 GEORGE V., A. 1915

with stunted trees and short scrub, except in the vicinity of the lake, where higher
and fairly well timbered land exists.   The Indians seldom travel over this portage
before the frost has set in when it then becomes an ideal route to their hunting
grounds.   High dry land is found as a rule around all the above-mentioned lakes and
the timber, consisting mostly of poplar and pine averages eight inches.

In the south half of townships 72, ranges 25 and 26, west of the second meridian
no granite ledges were noticed.   The country in general is level with occasional low
ridges covered with small pine.   It is drained by Lynx creek where several short rapids
occur wherever it approaches the foot of the ridges.   The elevation of its banks varies
from three to six feet above the normal level of the water and at different places along
it I saw some good hay land which could be improved by clearing it of the clumps of
willow growing here and there on the grassy patches of land.   By draining the wet
sections of these hay meadows, they could be turned into fair pasturage.

The level country continues east into range 25 and extends south to the shores of
a deep bay of Morin lake where another brook discharges.   Farther north the land rises,
but among the hills there appears to be a   pass northwards towards the depression
where Besnard lake, formerly known as Trout lake, is situated.   The south shore of
the latter lake is rock bound, and granite ledges, which rise up to forty feet, are found
everywhere inland; between these are soft swamps and bogs.   All the timber is stunted
and of no commercial value.

The outlet of Besnard lake is at the northeastern corner of the lake and flows north
to Churchill river.   There are three rapids, two of which are avoided by portages.
From the Indian village situated on the north side of the narrows of Besnard lake it
takes a day and a half by canoe to go to Churchill river.   The narrows are situated
approximately in section 10, township 74, range 1.   Here four or five families of Indians live, but although the soil in that vicinity is good, they do not raise any vegetables, being very different in that respect from their relatives living at Egg lake who,
on the same kind of soil grow all the potatoes they require for their yearly consumption.   The narrows are only one and one-half chains wide.

Exploration of part of Smoothstone river and the adjacent country.

Smoothstone river is with the exception of Beaver river, the largest stream intersected by my surveys.   It empties into the south end of Snake lake as it is far
from the ordinary routes leading north, this river and the adjoining country have very
seldom been visited, except by Indian hunters.   Therefore, with the intention of exploring this country I travelled a distance of forty-miles above the mouth of the
river and reached the north boundary of township 69, range 2.

Such a journey if undertaken in the summer would have been very arduous owing
to many long rapids which begin where the river crosses the north boundary of township 71, range 4.   This work was made easy by the ice, over which I travelled quickly
and with comparative safety.   This allowed me to camp at points convenient for a
fair examination of the country east and west of the river, to determine its possibilities
as agricultural land and the value of its timber growth.   The first camp was near the
foot of the first rapids, fourteen miles above the estuary of the river.   From this camp
the exploratory line followed closely the north boundaries of townships 71, ranges 3
and 2, south of which the river flows in a general westerly direction and at distances
varying from one mile and a half in the northeast part of township 71, range 2 to
three miles in the northeastern part of township 71, range 3; thence its course is N.
60° W. to the foot of the rapids.   This exploration shows that along this part of the
river there is a strip nearly two miles and a half wide of good land wooded with
poplar.   This land has been burnt over and the trees of the second growth seldom
reach six inches in diameter.   Beyond this strip of good land are ridges with jackpine
from two to ten inches in diameter.   Back of the ridges tamarack and spruce swamps
were crossed in which the timber is of no commercial value.   At two places along the

SESSIONAL PAPER No. 25b

river banks I noticed some small clumps of spruce where a few of the trees ran up to thirty inches in diameter.

The benches along the right bank of the river often rise to fifty feet but where flats occur the banks of the river are from four to six feet high. The soil of the flats is always good as shown by the larger trees growing in such places. The width of Smoothstone river varies much. Across some of the rapids it is less than one chain and a half, while at other places it is from four to six chains wide. Its bottom is stony and the depth of the water is eight feet in many places.

The second camp was approximately in section 23, township 71, range 3, which Smoothstone river crosses from east to west. In this vicinity there are along the river some narrow flats with poplar, spruce and birch, amongst which grow thick underbrush. The benches which rise at a short distance from the river are fifty to seventy feet high and covered with second-growth poplar and jackpine. At three miles west of the river there is a lake two miles long. A dense growth of small spruce is found around this lake and it continues west another mile where a strip of good land, two miles wide lies. Ridges of jackpine and poplar divide this land from the valley of a small creek which joins the river at one mile above the first rapids. The exploration line crosses this creek at six miles from its junction with the river; at the crossing the valley is ten chains wide and covered with thick willow but beyond the creek the surface of the country is rolling. A short distance above the confluence I crossed a narrow belt of fair timber consisting of spruce from eight to fifteen inches and jackpine and balsam from six to ten inches in diameter. There is some bad windfall in this vicinity. The river benches rise to one hundred feet.

The next exploration line ran in a southwesterly direction from section 13, township 71, range 2, where Moose portage ends. Two miles and a half below it is one of the worst rapids seen on Smoothstone river. It can, however, be avoided by packing over a portage half a mile long which passes across a flat covered with scrubby birch and spruce. The country through which Moose portage passes may be described as rolling. Near one of the lakes in the middle of the portage there is a patch of spruce from ten to eighteen inches in diameter, but the timber consists mostly of jackpine from six to twelve inches; poplar running up to ten inches cover large areas. North of the portage a forest fire was still burning through the second growth of trees found there. The more level and best wooded lands are generally near the lakes, around which the soil is fair, but I did not see any hay meadows as the valleys of all the streams connecting these lakes were everywhere covered with dense willow and alder. At half a mile above the point where Moose portage reaches Smoothstone river, the high benches, which from the first rapids were a prominent feature along its banks, gradually recede from the river, leaving long stretches that are covered with willow and swamps. There are many small islands in that part of the river.

The timber cruiser who explored townships 71 and part of 70, range 2, reports crossing, after leaving the river, a strip of land two miles wide and timbered with poplar and spruce; the country farther west he describes as rolling and covered with jackpine and small spruce. The same day I travelled nine miles by the river as far as the confluence of a large brook which flows from a southeasterly direction. Here I noticed a dog trail and as the ice on the river was unsafe, I decided to follow this trail over which I could make good progress. From Smoothstone river it runs S. 20° W. for four miles and crosses a flat country sometimes covered with short scrub. At many places it is open and grassy. It extends east beyond the third meridian; a few knolls only rise from this flat swampy expanse, one lies west of the trail and another one is close to the north shore of a lake, two miles long and one mile wide. The valley of the river is not more than two miles west of the trail and is defined by low ridges wooded with pine and poplar. After crossing the lake the general direction of the dog trail is south and west and the distance to Smoothstone river is four miles, most of it through spruce swamp and a few open bogs with narrow ridges across. When within one-third of a mile from where it again strikes the river it enters a belt of jackpine and poplar from four to six inches in diameter. I was quite surprised to find that at this point Smoothstone river was entirely free from ice. It is about three chains wide; its right bank is fifty feet high, but the other bank is low, grassy and covered with willow and the country back of it appears to be swampy. A branch of the trail which I had followed in going to Smoothstone river leaves the main trail at two miles and a half north of the small lake mentioned above. It runs almost east and intersects the third meridian at the corner of section 1, township 69. This dog-trail evidently ends at Partridge Coop lake. We then went to section 30, township 70, range 1 where we found a newly-built Indian hut, and as there was no one living in it we took possession for the night. This shack is on the right-hand side of the river, and stands in a flat where spruce and jackpine from four to eight inches grow. Smoothstone river here is six chains wide and for three miles north is free from rapids. There are grassy marshes along the left bank.

The country west of the river in township 70, is fairly high for a quarter of a mile or so, but this narrow strip of dry land comes to an end a few miles farther on where the swamp back of it comes to the river. The water in the numerous brooks which rise in these swamps tastes strongly of iron.

On Smoothstone river large water-powers could be developed.

General remarks.

During my surveys I saw very little land at present suitable for settlement along the third meridian and for a considerable distance west of it. The sections of country at present fit for agriculture are very sparsely distributed in this region. The arable land consists of clay loam and is generally found in proximity to some of the largest lakes and in the valleys of the principal streams. Hay lands are also very scarce through all this district. Whenever seen they were always submerged and in most cases would be hard to reclaim, being so little above the level of the lakes and streams. Moreover these grassy stretches are more in the form of bogs than regular hay meadows. The country improves to a certain extent west of Beaver river both in the quality of the soil and also the growth of timber, which is much better in size and quantity.

At places where the land has been tilled, the crops have proved satisfactory and have never been seriously damaged by summer frosts. The principal revenue of the country is still derived from the fur trade to which has been added in recent years the produce from the yearly increasing fishing industries. The I. C. Fish Co., which is the pioneer in this province, intends to establish new fisheries and in connection with this industry have this spring erected a saw-mill at Ile-a-la-Crosse settlement. They will now be able to manufacture their own boxes of which several thousands are required, and which up to the present date have had to be brought in by teams.

All the lakes in the district are well stocked with the best species of fish including trout and whitefish. There are also quantities of pike, pickerel, carp, etc.

Water-power could be developed on Montreal river as the drop in the whole course of this stream is 350 feet, whilst at Montreal rapids which are about eight miles long the fall is 105 feet. Farther down stream at Mountain rapids the drop in two miles and a half is 40 feet.

Large game such as moose, caribou and deer, is plentiful. In one herd which I saw east of lac la Plonge I counted twenty-three head. As might naturally be surmised the predatory animals, such as timber-wolves infest this country. Of the fur-bearing animals, bears, lynx, marten, mink, coyotes, foxes and otter are often seen. The ubiqitous muskrat is still there in great numbers. Of beaver, traces only of their work were noticed on Tippo river.

No minerals were found but quarries of building stones could be opened in the granite ledges seen south of Besnard lake.

APPENDIX No. 49.

ABSTRACT OF THE REPORT OF J. B. SAINT CYR, D.L.S.

STADIA SURVEYS IN THE VICINITY OF RED DEER, ALBERTA.

My party was organized at Edmonton, and on May 14, 1913, I left for Gull lake the scene of my first work which consisted of the survey of this lake and of those in the surrounding townships.

At the south end of Gull lake which is situated in township 40, range 28 west of the fourth meridian a great number of cottages have lately been built. It is a fine summer resort, and hundreds of people from Edmonton, Red Deer, Lacombe, Ponoka and other laces spend a part of the summer there. The lake is deep, contains clear soft water, and is well stocked with pike and pickerel. Wiseville which is south of the lake is the principal village in that township. The greater part of the village is situated on section 22. All that country situated between the Blindman valley to the west of Gull lake and Lacombe and Ponoka to the east is good farming country. The surface is half prairie and half bush and is hilly and rolling. Oats are grown in that district in larger quantities than wheat. In the gardens all kinds of vegetables are grown successfully. The farmers also raise hogs and horses on a large scale .

After leaving the vicinity of Gull lake we travelled from township to township throughout the district lying east and southeast of Red Deer, traversing all the lakes which were large enough and deep enough to warrant it. During the season fifty-four townships were visited and investigated and hundreds of lakes were traversed.

In all the townships in which we worked the country is more or less open. Wheat is grown in larger quantities through the eastern part of this district than in the western part. In nearly every locality where I travelled during the summer of 1913, mixed farming was carried on by all the farmers. Every settler praises the country highly for its great agricultural possibilities. The fall was remarkably dry and mild, the sun shining almost every day for several weeks. The coldest period experienced in December was ten degrees below zero, for four or five days.

On January 6, 1914, I returned to Edmonton after eight months in the field having moved camp about fifty times and travelled over a thousand miles.

DEPARTMENT OF THE INTERIOR

5 GEORGE V., A. 1915

APPENDIX No. 50.

ABSTRACT OF THE REPORT OF B. H. SEGRE, D.L.S.

STADIA SURVEYS IN THE REGINA DISTRICT.

My work for the season of 1913 consisted of the investigation and traverse of lakes in townships north and west of Regina.

My first work was in township 17, range 22, west of the second meridian. This township is all gently undulating prairie and the lakes and marshes have either entirely dried up, or dry up in the fall of each year. The large lake formerly in section 17 of this township has completely dried up and now provides excellent grazing land for stock. To the west the country becomes more rolling towards Moosejaw creek, the valley of which is nearly 250 feet below the level of the surrounding area; west of this creek the prairie becomes less broken and no marshes were noticed.

Northerly towards township 20, range 22, the country becomes more 'and 'more rolling and there are many marshes and sloughs which contain only the surplus water of the spring and which dry up in autumn. Many alkaline lakes were found in this township, lying in valleys about fifty feet deep; these lakes are shallow and contain strongly saline water, but they are fed by springs and will be permanent.

From this township I proceeded to township 18, range 24. I found that the majority of the lakes in the township had changed very little since the original survey. Rocky lake was about six feet deep in places and its water was slightly alkaline, the surrounding country is rolling prairie becoming more and more broken to the west in range 25.

My next work was the survey of Buffalo Pound lake in townships 18, 19 and 20, ranges 25 and 26. This lake lies in a valley, the banks of which rise 300 feet above water level. The shores are marshy for the most part, and long reeds fringe them for a distance of from five to ten chains from the high-water mark; this feature is no doubt due to the shallowness of the lake, the greatest depth being eight feet. The maximum depth is reached about ten chains from shore on both sides, thus revealing a very uniform bed in the centre of the lake. A small creek enters the lake at the north end, and this together with numerous springs constitute its source of supply. It is drained through Qu'Appelle river at the south end. The slopes of the valley are covered with a dense growth of poplar and willow scrub. An abundance of grass furnishes ample pasture for stock.

This lake seems to be the dividing line between two different types of country.

The land above the valley on the west side is gently undulating prairie with good sandy loam, free from stones, while that part lying on the east side of the lake is very hilly and rolling and the soil is freely intermixed with granite boulders, requiring more expense in carrying on farming operations.

This seeming disadvantage however, is more than offset by the fact that farmers living above the valley on the west side, find great difficulty in securing water. It can be obtained only at great depths and even then it is of very inferior quality. Those on the east side on the other hand get an abundance of good water near the surface.

The water of this lake is very alkaline which no doubt accounts for the fact that there are no fish in it, although many fish are caught in Moosejaw creek which joins Qu'Appelle river just east of the lake.

Having completed the traverse of Buffalo Pound lake, my next work consisted of the investigation of small lakes and marshes in township 21, range 26. The country

Bear in Jasper Park, Alberta.

Photo by H. Matheson, D.L.S.

This small black bear up a large Douglas fir tree, near lake Annette in Jasper Park, is waiting for his lunch. Labourers constructing roads near by used to eat their mid-day lunches near this tree and feed scraps to the bear, so that he became quite tame.

25b—1915—p. 200

around these lakes is very hilly prairie, and no doubt the lakes are formed from the surplus run-off of the surrounding area. No large creeks or springs were found which could be called a source of supply, yet the lakes seemed permanent and no change in the high water mark could be noticed.

From there we moved camp to township 22, range 27, and surveyed a lake near Aylesbury. The water of this lake is slightly alkaline and lies in a valley, the banks of which rise from 50 to 100 feet above water level. There are numerous small springs along the sides which constitute the source of supply, and a small creek at the south end apparently drains the lake. The greatest depth is about ten feet. There are no fish in this lake.

From this township I crossed the valley of Arm river and after making an investigation in township 26, range 27, I moved camp to township 26, range 25. Here my work consisted in traversing a large lake near the town of Stalwart. This lake is nothing more than a large marsh filled with alkaline water, three feet being its greatest depth; the greater portion of the lake is covered by reeds. A small creek enters from the northwest forming the only visible source of supply and another small creek drains it to the southwest; this creek eventually enters an arm of Last Mountain lake. On account of the amount of weeds growing in this lake, it is the resort of a great number of ducks and other water-fowl, which nest along its banks. A number of marshes were also investigated and traversed in this township; they were all shallow and distinctly alkaline in taste. A few alkaline flats lie in the western part of this township, rendering many hundreds of acres useless for grain growing purposes. The country between this township and Last Mountain lake is gently rolling prairie; but west of this, the ground becomes more and more broken and covered by boulders. Very little road-building has been done in this township on account of the number of sloughs to be crossed. This hampers the farmer very much in the speedy transport of his grain to the railway.

We next moved camp to township 27, range 24, and investigated many small marshes in this township and also in township 28. There the country is not as hilly as is usual in this district and the majority of the marshes, having dried up, produce excellent hay. In many instances the former beds of marshes have been ploughed up and are producing grain.

Bullrush lake in township 28, range 25, was traversed from this camp. This lake resembles a large marsh, the greatest depth of water being three feet, and a thick growth of grass covering the entire bed. The water has receded in many cases and parts of the former bed are now being utilized for hay growing. There are unmistakable signs that this lake has dried up before, as old haystacks were seen in the centre of the area now covered by water, and the marks of the plough were noticed, the old furrows being now under water; the bed of the lake, however, being the natural receptacle for the run-off of a large area, is liable to flooding in wet years.

From this camp I commenced the survey of Last Mountain lake, the largest body of really fresh water in central Saskatchewan. The north end of this lake consists of three long arms, into which flow as many creeks, while along the shore numerous springs and creeks enter. These drain a very large area, and maintain the lake at an almost constant level. Soundings were taken in the north end amongst the many islands, and the greatest depth recorded was ten feet. Farther south, however, the depth increased, and from information obtained from the captain of the steamer which plies up and down the lake, I was led to believe that the greatest depth is near the southern end and is about one hundred and thirty feet.

There are numerous summer resorts along this lake, the most important being Regina beach and Saskatchewan beach, the former on the west shore, and the latter on the east shore, both served by the Canadian Pacific railway from Regina and Saskatoon. The lake provides excellent fishing during the summer; pike, pickerel and whitefish being caught in abundance. A few fisherman make a living by summer fishing,

5 GEORGE V., A. 1915

but in winter operations are carried on more extensively, about one hundred men being engaged in this occupation. The fish finds a ready market in Regina.

At the north end the shores of the lake are more or less marshy with low banks, but as we worked south along the west shore, the banks commenced to rise abruptly from the water's edge, in township 22. These banks became gradually steeper until township 21 was reached where the valley is about 250 feet deep and stretches back for a distance of from twenty to forty chains from the water's edge. Commencing in township 22 vegetation is to be found along the shores, which are for the most part sandy. Groves of ash and willow which extend to the water's edge, delayed traversing considerably in the summer; it was therefore found advisable to cease operations for the time being, when the north boundary of township 21, range 22, was reached. A return was made to the lake when the ice formed and the traverse of the west shore was completed, as well as the east shore south of township 25, range 24.

The largest body of water entering the lake is Arm river which forms a long estuary running nearly two miles from the main body of the lake. This lake is drained by a river which flows through a large marsh at the southeast end, finally joining Qu'Appelle river. During the traverse of this lake numerous investigations were carried on in the townships passed through, the majority being of shallow marshes and lakes, the water of which was alkaline, and the shores of which were covered with reeds and marsh grass. A few of these marshes have dried up and are producing hay, but the most of them contained water all through the past season. The country on the west side of Last Mountain lake is gently rolling prairie at the north end, and becomes more hilly and broken toward the south, township 21 being very rough and containing many small lakes. The water in these lakes was for the most part slightly alkaline, but wherever it was found to be not too salty, it was of great use to the farmers, providing drinking water for the stock in many districts where the obtaining of a large quantity of water is a serious problem.

After leaving the traverse of the west shore of Last Mountain lake, investigations were carried on in townships 20 and 21, range 21. A few small lakes were found which were shallow but evidently permanent. The marshes in these townships have dried up considerably, but being low spots in scrubby country are likely to hold the snow and contain water in early spring. The valley of Qu'Appelle river divides the topography of the country, the south side of the valley being gently undulating prairie, and the north side being rolling country covered by poplar and willow bluffs. In the river valley there is excellent pasture land, and it is an ideal spot for stock-raising.

Camp was next moved to township 23, range 19 where further investigations were carried on. This district is mostly rolling prairie with many shallow sloughs, quite a number of which have dried up and are now producing hay.

From there camp was moved to township 25, range 19 and once more rough rolling country was encountered.

A branch of Loon creek flows through the eastern part of this township and provides drainage for a large area. The valley of this creek is from fifty to seventy-five feet deep, and is covered with thick bluffs of poplar and willow in the southeastern end of the township. There are also several marshes in the creek valley. Three lakes traversed in sections 22 and 27 were found to be permanent, they lie in a valley from twenty to thirty feet deep and apparently receive the drainage of a large area in the northeastern part of the township. Most of the small marshes investigated are now dry and are used for growing hay. A large lake in township 26, range 19, was traversed and found to be permanent but the marshes in this township have all dried up and produce hay.

Our next camp was in township 25, range 22. All the lakes examined in this township were strongly alkaline, and are drying up: in section 29, the greater part of the former bed of the lake is now dry and producing hay. The country is very rolling in this township becoming more and more broken until Last mountain is reached in range 21, where the hills rise abruptly from 300 to 500 feet and are cut by deep valleys, which at present greatly impede traffic from the East. One large marsh at the northeast corner of this township lies at the base of Last mountain. This marsh does not exceed one and a half feet in depth, and is almost completely covered by a thick growth of reeds and marsh grass; however, it receives the drainage of a very large area, and will be permanent, although its shores may be subject to wide variations according to the season. To the south of this township many alkaline lakes were traversed, they were all shallow, but they will likely all be permanent. The country is rough rolling prairie, and there are no creeks to drain these lakes. A number of marshes were investigated in this township and also to the west; the majority appear to be drying up and are being used to produce hay.

From there, camp was again moved to Last Mountain lake in township 25, range 24, and the traverse of the east shore commenced by running south from the north boundary of the township. The shore line in the northern part of township 25 is marshy, but farther south it is for the most part sandy with banks rising from three to ten feet high from the water's edge. In township 23 the banks become steeper and more abrupt, until township 21 is reached where the valley is 250 feet deep and similar to the valley on the western shore; being covered by poplar and willow scrub and a good growth of grass affording good pasture for stock. This lake becomes gradually more shallow as the south end is reached, and at the point where the Canadian Pacific railway grade crosses it the maximum depth is three and a half feet. South of this grade there is a great change in the lake as the open water gives place to a large marsh covered by reeds and marsh grass with water one to three feet deep. The creek which drains the lake meanders through this marsh finally joining Qu'Appelle river at Craven. The land covered by the waters of the marsh is more or less useless except for water-fowl, but a strip of low land about five chains wide and one foot above water level extend along both banks of the creek and may provide pasture. On completion of this work, I made a traverse of that part of the lake in section 30, township 28, range 23. I then returned to Regina and disbanded my party.

5 GEORGE V., A. 1915.

APPENDIX No. 51.

ABSTRACT OF THE REPORT OF F. V. SEIBERT, D.L.S.

SURVEY OF THE TWENTY-FIRST BASE LINE FROM THE FOURTH TO THE FIFTH MERIDAN.

To survey the twenty-first base line it was necessary to have supplies placed near the latitude of the line and west of the fourth meridian, yet close enough to the latter to be within easy reach of the starting point of the line. With this in view my assistant left Edmonton on February 12, 1913 to build a cache on Christina river near where the line would cross and to clear the old trails and cut new ones where necessary. His route led by way of Athabaska and Lac LaBiche settlements, thence over the wagon road to Heart lake, and from there northerly to Wappau lake over the sleigh trail used by Mr. G. McMillan, D.L.S. in placing supplies for the twentieth base. From Wappau lake he expected to go down May river to Christina river and then along this river to the latitude of the line. When he reached May river, however he found that the deep snow had kept the river from freezing over in many places, necessitating more cutting than he had expected. He therefore decided to build a cache at the northerly end of Wappau lake, return to Lac LaBiche to report and have the freight sent on to the cache, and then report to me at Edmonton. He arrived at Edmonton March 11.

The following day my party left for the work, going by the Canadian Northern railway to Athabaska and thence by teams and sleighs to Lac LaBiche. When we arrived there on March 20 we found that the deep snow with the heavy crust had retarded the forwarding of freight; the larger part of the supplies were still at Lac La-Biche and the remainder had been taken about twenty miles north of Heart lake where they had been left by the freighters when their teams became exhausted.

We left Lac LaBiche on March 21 with eight teams and ten of our best pack horses, leaving the remainder there. We took nearly all the camp supplies with us and before leaving we made arrangements for more teams to follow with the remainder and sufficient hay and oats to take us to our destination.

At noon March 24 we reached the cache made by the freighters on their first trip. Up to this point it was easy travelling as the trail was broken but from there on travelling was very slow and extremely hard on the horses, as their legs soon became seriously cut by the crust, and they showed signs of playing out. We procured four sets of double harness and one set of sleighs left by Mr. Blanchet, D.L.S. on the nineteenth base line and made use of the flat sleigh we had with us. I also decided to relieve the horses to some extent by having my men break down the crust ahead of the teams. On March 28, we reached the cache built by Mr. Logan and after resting there one day, we proceeded down May river, cutting out portages where necessary. We reached Christina river on March 30.

Our supply of hay and oats was low, so I decided to return with one of my teams and all the hired teams to meet the teams coming in with more. We returned to Christina river on April 4, and my hired teams stayed with me one day more taking us about twelve miles down the river. From there I allowed them to return to Lac La-Biche. We then moved camp and supplies about twelve miles farther down the river to the crossing of the McMurray summer pack trail, getting everything there by April 15. We used the sleighs on the river for the last time on the 11th and then packed what was left over land.

In April 19 the packponies we had left at Lac LaBiche arrived and we at once started to pack to the latitude of our line cutting our trail as we went and following the east bank of the Christina. We took only the necessary supplies and outfit, and made a cache of the remainder. When we were about four miles south of the latitude of the twenty-first base line we struck an old trail running easterly which was part of the trail running from Winefred lake to McMurray. We opened up this trail as far as Cowpar lake and from there cut trail easterly to the fourth meridian pack trail on Landels river. We reached the starting point of our line on May 3 and commenced our survey on the 5th.

The supplies we took with us to the meridian lasted until we ran the line as far as the summer pack trail between Lac LaBiche and McMurray, which we reached on June 1. We were then in touch with the cache we had made in April on Christina river, which was two days' travel by pack train south of the line. During our absence this cache had been broken into and about nine hundred pounds of supplies taken, as well as a quantity of clothing belonging to myself and men. Fortunately we had still enough supplies but my men were short of the necessary clothing.

Large areas of muskeg exist in the country traversed by the twenty-first base line between the fourth meridian and Athabaska river, but nearly all of this can be easily drained. The river valleys have in most cases good land. Beginning at the fourth meridian and going west good land is to be found along Landels and Winefred rivers as well as around Cowpar lake. At the latter place a few Indian families make their permanent home. Where the line crosses it Christina river has a low valley which extends either way for about twelve miles. In some places this valley is low and wet but it could be easily drained. The land close to the river is excellent, becoming lighter, however, the farther it is from the river. The strip of land between the Little Rocky mountains and the Christina is mostly of excellent quality.

The Little Rocky mountains in ranges 6 and 7 make a distinct break in the country. They rise rather abruptly from the rolling country bordering on the Christina to a plateau composed chiefly of muskeg and sandy rocky ridges. They are more pronounced to the north running off into low hills to the south. The same formation appears in ranges 12 and 13 with the drop towards the west instead of the east as in ranges 6 and 7. They are also more pronounced to the north and barely noticeable to the south. Ranges 13, 14 and 15 contain large areas of muskeg with ridges, running northerly which to a large extent prevent the drainage from taking its natural course westward. These ridges are very little higher than the muskegs which border them on the east, but they have a decided slope to the west and give the country the appearance of being composed of a series of plateaus with a general fall to the west.

House river in range 16 has a valley which is from three hundred to three hundred and fifty feet deep. The river can be navigated with canoes a greater part of its length. Patches of large spruce are still preserved in the valley but a much larger area has been destroyed by fire.

The strip of land between House and Athabaska rivers is mostly muskeg which could be very easily drained to the deep valleys on either side.

The Athabaska which is crossed by the line in range 17 has a valley from two to three miles wide and averaging about four hundred feet deep. Here also a great deal of large spruce has been destroyed by fire, but much still remains. A fire ranger with headquarters at Pelican portage patrols the river, working in conjunction with the fire patrol boat which has its headquarters at Athabaska, and much of the waste by fire will no doubt be prevented.

Drilling has been done at Pelican portage and gas has been found in each of the four wells drilled.

On the west side of the Athabaska muskeg extends for many miles westward. This muskeg extends north as far as the correction line and south to Pelican river which flows into the Athabaska from the west. On account of the very wet summer this muskeg was impassable; and it was therefore necessary to leave this part of the line till winter.

5 GEORGE V., A. 1915

Accordingly we left the line on September 29 and tracked up the river with a scow and canoe, arriving at Athabaska on October 7 and at Edmonton on the 9th.

We left Edmonton again by the Canadian Northern railway for Athabaska on January 2, 1914 and reached there the same day. There we met four of my teams which I had sent overland by trail from Edmonton. We left Athabaska on the 5th, and following down Athabaska river, reached Pelican portage on the 10th. We rested the horses there a day, and then continued down the river reaching the crossing of the line in two days. In making the trip to this place we broke trail most of the way from Athabaska, but experienced no serious difficulty until we were within about ten miles of Pelican portage. From there we encountered rough ice most of the way to the line. At Pelican rapids the ice was in some places piled ten feet high, and it required considerable cutting to get a trail through it. With the party ahead of the teams cutting down the ice the delay was slight. Two days cutting trail from the river took us up over the edge of the valley to the centre of range 18 where we had left the line in September.

We started the line on January 16, and made good progress with its production, reaching the fifth meridian on February 23.

We cached our main stock of supplies at the river and forwarded them along the line on bob-sleighs at the river using four teams from my pack outfit for the purpose.

The country from the banks of Athabaska river about the east boundary of range 18 to the east boundary of section 32, range 23, a distance of thirty-four miles, is mostly muskeg. To the south this muskeg extends to Pelican river which follows roughly the twentieth correction line, and to the north it extends beyond the twenty-first correction line. Muskeg creek in range 20 is too small to be used by canoes, and the only way to cross this country is over the frozen muskeg. The tamarack in some parts of the muskeg and the jackpine on some small islands of sandy land is large enough for railway ties, but ninety per cent of this area is covered with timber too small for use.

West of the east boundary of section 32, range 23, the character of the country changes entirely, the surface becoming rolling. Very little muskeg exists, and some good spruce and poplar is still preserved. There is not enough timber in any one place for a timber berth, but there is sufficient for the needs of settlers. The land is good.

The line crosses north Wabiskaw lake in ranges 25 and 26. South Wabiskaw lake is about four miles south of the line in ranges 24 and 25, and Sandy lake is situated in township 79, range 23. All of these lakes contain whitefish.

The settlement of Wabiskaw lies at the southeast corner of north Wabiskaw lake. To reach it there is a choice of two trails in winter and three in summer. One of the winter trails crosses from south Wabiskaw lake over Pelican mountains to Rock Island lake, then to Calling lake, and from there to a point on Athabaska river, twelve miles from Athabaska. Another branch of the same trail leads from Calling lake to a point on Athabaska river, called the "fish camp," about seventy miles up the river from Athabaska. This branch of the trail is not used much now. There are some bad hills going over the Pelican mountains, and another leaving Athabaska river. The trip from Athabaska to Wabiskaw by this trail can be made, with moderate loads and good weather, in five days. The other winter trail is by way of Sandy lake, Pelican lake, Pelican river, and Athabaska river to Athabaska. This is a very much longer route, but has the advantage of having only one hill, which is at Athabaska river. The regular winter freight rate from Athabaska to Wabiskaw is two and a half cents per pound. In summer there is a canoe route by way of Sandy lake, Pelican lake and river, and Athabaska river. Two pack trails can be used in summer to reach this post, one by way of Calling lake, and Rock Island lake, and the other by way of Sawridge on Lesser Slave river. The latter I am told is much the better trail and is cut out for wagons part of the way.

No indications of minerals were noticed during the season.

SESSIONAL PAPER No. 25b

APPENDIX No. 52.

REPORT OF N. C. STEWART, D.L.S.

SURVEYS IN THE RAILWAY BELT OF BRITISH COLUMBIA.

VANCOUVER, B. C., January 28, 1914.

E. DEVILLE, ESQ., LL.D.,
Surveyor General,
Ottawa, Canada.

SIR,—I have the honour to submit the following report of my season's operations in the railway belt in the province of British Columbia.

After organizing my party at Revelstoke I left for township 20, range 9, west of the sixth meridian where my first work was located. I arrived there on May 8 and pitched my first camp beside the new automobile road which was being constructed between Salmon Arm and Enderby. I surveyed the east boundaries of sections 4 and 9 and moved camp by wagon along the road to Enderby about six miles, then taking a branch road which leads around Sugarloaf mountain I was able to get my outfit to the southeast quarter of section 35, township 19, range 9. The road around the mountain was very rough and steep and I required two teams to haul my outfit over it. Several fine farms surround the mountain and others were being taken up on the bench land which extends northward from this mountain for nearly three miles. I surveyed the east boundaries of sections 2 and 11 and the north boundaries of sections 1 and 12, in township 20, range 9, thus opening all that bench land for settlement. The soil is generally a light sandy loam and very stony. A muskeg about eighty acres in extent, known locally as " Mara Meadows," was found in section 12: this will need considerable drainage before it will produce hay. Marketable timber was found in parts of sections 1, 12 and 13.

On May 28 we moved to Grindrod, the nearest railway station, and took train to Chase. The following day we crossed Little Shuswap lake on the Adams River Lumber company's launch and teams were hired to take the outfit to Adams lake which was reached rather late that night. The road between the two lakes is very steep in places ascending a mountain and then descending again although I believe the difference of level between the lakes is only 150 feet. On May 30 with the aid of a small steamer and a scow we arrived at section 28, township 25, range 12. All the land in this township north of Adams lake including four miles of the north limit of the railway belt was surveyed. I triangulated across the lake on the east boundaries of sections 28 and 21, traversed a few miles of the southeast shore of the lake and ran sufficient lines to survey all the land likely to be required for agricultural purposes in the township. While there we experienced very wet weather and several severe storms.

The next work was in township 24, range 13, west of the sixth meridian. Here I again triangulated Adams lake from a post found on the north boundary of section 27 to a point on the north boundary of section 26. The land in sections 35 and 26 and the northeast quarter of section 23 was surveyed. This part of the lake which is opposite to Agate bay (known locally as " Squam bay ") is said to be the only part of the lake free from ice in the winter.

My next move was across Adams lake to Pass creek and then by wagon road to section 1, township 25, range 14, west of the sixth meridian. There I ran the north boundary of the section which is also the north limit of the railway belt. This

5 GEORGE V., A. 1915

line ran along the side of an almost perpendicular mountain which rises about 2,500 feet above the valley. I also attempted to retrace the boundaries of the Home-stake group of mineral claims which are located in this section, but most of the monuments of the original survey had disappeared.

Adams lake is more interesting from a scenic and geological than from a settler's standpoint,. as there is very little agricultural land near it, its shores being generally perpendicular cliffs. The lake is subject to sudden and violent wind storms making it dangerous for small boats and canoes.

The surveys in the vicinity of Adams lake were completed on July 17, and on July 19 camp was pitched beside Columbia river near the south boundary of section 14, township 23, range 18, west of the fifth meridian, a move of nearly 250 miles, requiring eight changes of conveyances.

My work in this locality consisted of running the south limit of the railway belt from the Columbia valley over the Beaverfoot range, and across the Kootenay valley. The Beaverfoot mountains are very picturesque from a tourist point of view but they are not so inviting to a surveyor. I opened up an old hunting trail that ran along the mountains to the north of Cedar creek and extended this trail to the headwaters of that creek, but could go no farther on account of rock bluffs around which a trail could not be built. I had two camps on the western slope. From the second camp to the summit there was a very steep ascent of about 2,000 feet. I sent the pack train with provisions around into Kootenay valley by way of Vermilion pass, the trip taking five days on account of the distance and the number of trees fallen across the trail. Meanwhile we packed the remainder of the outfit over the summit and about 2,000 feet down the other side to the first creek. We also cut a trail out to the main one along Kootenay river, thus making connections with the pack train. During the work on the summit we had very wet weather with some snow, hail and fog.

Kootenay valley is nearly four miles wide where the south limit of the railway belt crosses it. The soil is gravelly in most places, but near the river clay was found. The western side of the valley is heavily timbered with spruce, but the lower benches are chiefly covered with a jackpine brulé. The eastern side is covered with fir, spruce and jackpine.

Wild goats are very plentiful on the Beaverfoot mountains, while deer and moose were often seen along Kootenay river. Trout fishing was good in the river and in the lakes along its valley.

On August 30 we started for Leanchoil along a good trail which connects with a wagon road eleven miles from the Canadian Pacific railway. The scenery along this trail was magnificent.

From Leanchoil we moved to township 23, range 2, west of the sixth meridian, where camp was pitched about five miles southeast of Revelstoke on September 1. The surveys here included the outlines of some timber berths and were very difficult to make owing to the long climb to work, the large size of the timber and the very wet weather. The remainder of the surveys in this township were traverses of four small islands in Columbia river and a lake on the north boundary of section 14.

From September 26 to November 20 surveys were made along the main line of the Canadian Pacific railway from Boulder to Craigellachie, the work consisting of surveying all land likely to be required for settlement and making ties to the new double track survey of the railway.

From Craigellachie I. went to Enderby and thence by wagon to township 18, range 8, west of the sixth meridian, where I completed the survey of timber berth No. 558. Eight inches of snow fell while we were in this township.

On November 27 we left for Enderby and the following day moved by wagon to Salmon river and camped in section 7, township 18, range 10. There was no snow on the ground in this township which was a welcome change from the country farther east. The work consisted of running the west boundaries of sections 6 and 7. All the country from Enderby to Salmon river and down the river to Shuswap lake is thickly settled, and all the farmers seem to be prosperous.

SESSIONAL PAPER No. 25b

Section 17, township 21, range 10, west of the sixth meridian was next reached. The west and east boundaries of the section were surveyed and on December 10 we moved by wagons about ten miles into Skimikin valley and camped in the southeast quarter of section 18, township 21, range 11. The road from Tappen through this valley is in good condition; it is an old road and is therefore well known. A large bench containing some good land in section 7 on the south side of the valley was surveyed. The farmers in Skimikin valley are fairly prosperous, one of them having about 150 head of stock.

Owing to the snow and the short days I decided to disband the party, and on December 23 I left for Revelstoke arriving there the following day with my outfit.

I have the honour to be, Sir,

Your obedient servant,

N. C. STEWART, D.L.S.

25b—14

5 GEORGE V., A. 1915

APPENDIX No. 53.

REPORT OF P. B. STREET, D.L.S.

SUBDIVISION IN NORTHERN MANITOBA.

WINNIPEG, MAN., May 20, 1914.

E. DEVILLE, Esq., LL.D.,
    Surveyor General,
      Ottawa, Canada.

SIR,—I have the honour to submit the following general report of my survey in northern Manitoba during the season of 1913-14.

I reached Pas on June 20, 1913, and tried for several days to hire sufficient labourers for my party. Owing to the demand for labour on the Hudson Bay railway, I was able to secure only one man at this place. I had brought in several men from the outside points and commenced work with them in township 53, range 27, west of the principal meridian, on June 27. As soon as the work was well under way, I went to Prince Albert to secure the remainder of my party.

Our first work was the partial subdivision of townships 53 and 54, ranges 26 and 27. Pasquia river flows through these townships, emptying into Pasquia lake, a large shallow body of water, about twelve miles long and five miles wide with a maximum depth of about six feet at high water. The river leaves the lake again in township 56, range 26, and empties into Saskatchewan river. The Saskatchewan rises so high during June and July that the water is forced back up the Pasquia into Pasquia lake, which in turn overflows the surounding country, rendering it useless for agriculture. When the Saskatchewan is lowered, and this overflow is prevented, some very good farmlands can be easily reclaimed. We saw hundreds of acres of fine hay growing five and six feet high in this vicinity. Summer frosts seem to be unknown, September 8 being the first day on which frost was recorded. No timber of any value was seen in these townships. East of the Pasquia the ground is covered with deep moss, which holds back the water like a sponge and prevents drainage, but there is plenty of slope to insure natural drainage if this moss were removed. This vicinity will be most valuable as a mixed farming district when the land is thus reclaimed. During our operations in this vicinity, we moved our camps either by boat on the Pasquia, or by means of a push car on the Canadian Northern ralway which follows the same direction as the river.

On October 6, we moved north of Pas to make a partial subdivision of the townships along the Hudson Bay railway. This country is mostly swamp and muskeg, the ground being covered with a rank growth of moss, which frequently reaches a depth of six feet. Naturally drainage is impossible until the moss is removed. Ice can be found in July by removing a couple of feet of this moss, so that it is only natural to find that the spruce and tamarack which grow in these muskegs are very stunted. Occasionally patches of large spruce and tamarack are found. Gravel and rock ridges are common and are covered with spruce and jackpine. Two large lakes, Clearwater and Cormorant, lie northeast of Pas, and are nearly surrounded with rocky limestone ridges. The lands bordering on these lakes are mostly of a gravelly clay formation, covered with a very dense growth of spruce, jackpine, poplar and birch, ranging from three to ten inches in diameter. Very little of this wood is of any value for lumber but it makes a very attractive cordwood proposition. Unfortunately in clearing the right of way for the Hudson Bay railway, fires were allowed to spread, which destroyed several square miles of good jackpine timber. A large area lying between the Hudson Bay railway and Moose lake appears to be a totally useless swamp. It is regularly overflowed by the Saskatchewan at high water, and in many places it is impossible to find the bottom with a long pole. It is very doubtful if this area can be reclaimed.

We subdivided lands adjoining the Hudson Bay railway from mile 15 to mile 56. The muskegs froze about October 20, and during the next two months, we made very good progress with our work, as the weather was not very cold and there was little snow to impede our movements. After December we had frequent snowfalls until the snow attained a depth of thirty inches by April. During February, we had the usual cold spell, the thermometer for three weeks hovering between 30 and 50 degrees below zero. The lowest temperature recorded was 53 degrees below zero. During this cold period our axes suffered considerably. The blades chipped off every time a dry tree was encountered and the handles snapped in two nearly as fast as they could be replaced. Mounding on the gravel ridges was so tedious that many of the mounds were left until May. Fifty-four inches of ice formed on Clearwater lake prior to March 1.

Fishing in Clearwater, Cormorant and Moose lakes is carried on extensively every winter. Whitefish, trout, pickerel and jackfish are taken in large quantities and shipped from Pas. We saw several moose in this vicinity and a few caribou. Ptarmigan are very plentiful while the snow is on the ground, and, as might be expected, the numerous lakes around Pas are well stocked with geese and ducks of all varieties, affording excellent sport both in the spring and autumn.

The Hudson Bay railway is being built as rapidly as circumstances will allow. Crossing a muskeg country, as it does, it is very hard to get a good roadbed and the construction company have been very unfortunate in not finding suitable gravel pits for ballast. Gravel has had to be hauled for very long distances and the nature of the country requires an unusual amount of ballast to make a good road bed. The line has been well laid out with long tangents and easy curves, and when the road is finished, will be able to take care of heavy traffic.

High winds are very prevalent in this district, both in summer and in winter. We found it useless to break snow-shoe trails through the deep snow, as they are almost invariably drifted full and obliterated in a few hours. Except on the big lakes, the snow never seems to get sufficient crust to make good snow-shoeing.

By May 1, the country was becoming so wet that I decided to discontinue work as soon as I completed the necessary surveys in township 58, range 23, where I was then working. I kept a sub-party busy most of the time erecting monuments which had been left during the winter, and on May 14, we had completed our work and moved back to Pas, where I paid off the party. After storing my outfit in Pas, I left for home on May 18.

I have the honour to be, Sir,

Your obedient servant,

P. B. STREET, D.L.S.

5 GEORGE V., A 1915

APPENDIX No. 54.

ABSTRACT OF THE REPORT OF A. G. STUART, D.L.S.

RETRACEMENT OF MERIDIAN AND BASE LINES IN MANITOBA AND SASKATCHEWAN.

My work during the past season consisted of the retracement of the second base line from the principal meridian to the second; the east boundary of range 31 west of the principal meridian from the international boundary to the seventh base line; the fifth, sixth and seventh base lines from the east boundary of range 31 west of the principal meridian to the second meridian; the third base line from the principal meridian east to the east boundary of range 7, and the east boundary of range 7 east of the principal meridian from the third base line to the fifth.

These retracements were made to serve as a working base from which to investigate and locate certain errors of previous surveys which were believed to exist.

Levels were taken in connection with the surveys and elevations were established in all the towns along the railways in the vicinity of the work. These levels can easily be reduced to mean sea-level datum and added to the great network of levels already taken over the country, which will some day be used for drainage, reclamations, railway location, highways and other engineering schemes.

Good roads were found almost everywhere in the vicinity of our work. The exceptions were the very rough wooded country in the Pembina mountains, near Swan lake, near Pelican lake and some swamp areas such as that in township 8, range 6, east of the principal meridian. One long stretch of well-graded road, runs from Beausejour to the settlements southeast of lake Winnipeg, passing through a low portion of the country where much drainage has been necessary. This road has probably the heaviest traffic of any rural highway in the West and is of great benefit to the farmers.

The country passed over has a close network of railways making the city market easily available to all farmers.

Pembina mountains in the southern part of Manitoba are a series of hills and deep ravines, heavily wooded with poplar and oak of large and small diameter. There is very little rock, but there is an abundance of blue clay suitable for brick manufacture, and on account of the convenient transportation connections with the large cities, this will some day be of economic value.

At Swan, Pelican and Whitewater lakes, which are in deep ravines and are surrounded by woods, the people from the nereby cities and towns have found pleasant summer resorts.

In that part of southeastern Saskatchewan through which we worked the land is not quite as heavy and rich as in southern Manitoba, but the conditions under which the crops were raised this season seemed very favourable and the harvest was an abundant one, and was marketed early. In this district there are some very prosperous German settlements, such as Langenburg.

The country northeast of Winnipeg is settled by homesteaders from Galicia, who have cleared the land they cultivate of heavy spruce and poplar. Considerable drainage has been done and more will be necessary in order to develop this district to its full extent.

During the winter months large quantities of wood and ties are shipped from railway points south, affording a means of making ready money. The present winter, however, has been so mild with practically no snow, that this industry is almost at a standstill and this has been keenly felt in the local business centres.

The Canadian Northern Railway company has at present the right of way cut for a line extending along the southeast side of lake Winnipeg. This will help to a very marked degree in opening up this portion of the country.

APPENDIX No. 55.

ABSTRACT OF THE REPORT OF C. H. TAGGART, D.L.S.

SURVEYS IN THE KAMLOOPS DISTRICT OF THE RAILWAY BELT, BRITISH COLUMBIA.

On April 11, 1913, I left Ottawa for Kamloops, where I arrived on the 16th. I immediately commenced the organization of my party, which was completed on the 21st. On the morning of the 22nd we started for our first work in townships 19, ranges 14 and 15, and camp was pitched at the west end of Desdero lake.

The Kamloops to Okanagan wagon road runs through this township. At Holmwood post office in section 12, range 15, a branch road leads to the lands surveyed. Many fair pieces of agricultural land are to be found in this township. The settlers already located seem to be meeting with success; their chief crops being grain and hay, with some vegetables. Some good stock ranches are located along the Okanagan wagon road. It would seem that the farmers in this district would meet with greater success by introducing mixed farming on a larger scale, and making a specialty of hogs and poultry.

Our next work took us into township 17, range 13. It is expected by the residents there that the new Canadian Northern Pacific railway from Kamloops to Kelowna, on which it has been announced that construction is to commence this summer, will pass through this district. In anticipation of this fact a large portion of the land suitable for agriculture, has been purchased by a syndicate. The owners are doing little development work and seem to be holding the land simply for higher prices. On this account the district does not show much improvement. Much may be expected from it; however, with the advent of the railway and the breaking up of the large holdings into smaller farms.

Our next work was north of Kamloops lake, in townships 21, ranges 18, 19 and 20. Tranquille river flows through township 21, range 19, but its valley is very narrow and as a result no settlers have as yet located there. Two or three ranches are located higher up the valley, and there is some land under cultivation at the mouth of the river, on Kamloops lake. A new wagon road up Tranquille river is under construction; it follows the western slope of the valley, crossing to the east side in section 27. This road will give access to the country to the north in townships 22, ranges 20 and 21, and will aid very much in opening up this region. The soil on the bench lands on either side of the river, is rocky and dry and produces only a small quantity of grass.

The country in the vicinity of lac du Bois is suitable for dry farming. The soil is rich and areas of sufficient size for homesteading are to be found. A number of persons have already taken up land there and appear to be pleased with their prospects. The road from Kamloops is rather difficult to travel at present but it is said to be the intention of the settlers to try to induce the Provincial Government to improve the old road where the present grades are suitable and make diversions where they are unsuitable.

In July Tranquille river had a flow of 2·5 cubic feet per second. This water is all used in irrigating two ranches on Kamloops lake at the mouth of the stream.

Our next work was at Savona Ferry, at the west end of Kamloops lake. The main line of the Canadian Northern railway is under construction there and follows the north shore of Kamloops lake very closely. The construction of the railway along the lake shore was very expensive on account of the great amount of rock work, which had to be done. It was necessary to construct two tunnels.

5 GEORGE V., A. 1915

A considerable area adjoining Savona Ferry has been subdivided into building lots, but so far as could be ascertained, there has not been a great demand for these lots. The district west of the mouth of Deadman river is being developed as a fruit growing area, and already many thriving apple orchards may be seen. This land is watered by an irrigation flume which takes water from Deadman river at a point about the middle of township 22, range 22.

We proceeded next to the Semlin valley in township 21, range 24. The valley is very fertile and capable, under irrigation, of producing hay, all kinds of grain and vegetables, and the hardier fruits. The land in this valley, part of which has been taken up since the early days, is at present held by large ranchers. The Hon. Charles Semlin ex-premier of British Columbia, is one of the largest holders. These ranchers have extensive grazing areas, in the Cariboo district, away to the north. Cattle are kept on these ranges during the growing season, and brought to the Semlin valley, to be wintered on the hay which has been put up for them during the summer. When they are in condition to be slaughtered, they are taken to Ashcroft.

We next completed the subdivision of township 21, range 25, which is high rolling range land, and practically uninhabited. It is mostly held under lease by stock owners. The Indian reserve in the middle of the township does not appear to be used by any one.

Our work continued westward into the valley of Hat creek. The best of the bottom lands of this valley have been taken up and used for cattle ranching for many years. On account of the advent of the Pacific and Great Eastern railway which passes within about ten or twelve miles of Hat Creek settlement, this valley is receiving a new impetus. Already a considerable number of additional homesteads have been taken up.

The closing weeks of the season were spent in making surveys near Thompson river in townships 18 and 19. The Canadian Northern Pacific railway follows closely the right bank of the river there. The grade is completed and ready to receive the steel. The railway parallels the old " Cariboo road," about which something of interest may be mentioned here.

This road is one of the original trunk roads of the province. It was built in the early sixties, for the purpose of furnishing a means of transport for the gold seekers who rushed from every corner of the earth, but chiefly from the gold fields of California, into the Cariboo country in the late fifties. The Cariboo road early became a regular route for passenger and mail stages. Later on an express company was formed, known as the British Columbia Express company, but which has always been known as the " B. X." This company operated until a few months ago, carrying His Majesty's mails from Ashcroft to Fort George. These stages are still operated in much the same style as in days gone by. The vehicles are very picturesque. They are drawn by four or six spirited young horses, and make the distance in very quick time. Fresh relays of horses are put in every fifteen miles. Besides the main route to Fort George, express lines run to Lilloet, Barkerville and other points in the interior. During the summer the stage runs north only as far as Soda creek. From there to Fort George passengers and mail are carried by boat up Fraser river.

Within the last few months, however, this historic express company has practically ceased to exist. Last year the Government mail contract was captured by a newly organized company known as the Inland Express company. The original company is understood to have sold the new company all their outfit with the exception of the river boats.

The portion of the " Cariboo road" south from Ashcroft has been used but very little since the completion of the Canadian Pacific railway. As a result the road has been allowed to fall into disrepair and in many places it is now almost impassable. It will always be required as a local road however and it is not probable that it will be allowed to fall into disuse entirely.

SESSIONAL PAPER No. 25b

The district in which our work was situated lies within what is known as the " Dry Belt" of British Columbia. This belt is very irregular in shape and extends from the west end of Shuswap lake westerly including the valley of Thompson river to its confluence with Fraser river. It extends a hundred miles or so north of Ashcroft, and includes the Nicola and Okanagan districts to the south. In many places through the Kamloops district, farming can be carried on successfully without irrigation at altitudes varying from two thousand feet to twenty-five hundred feet and over. Of course, even at these altitudes crops are grown successfully only when the principles of dry farming are practised. A remarkable feature about the character of the soil in many localities is that the richer and more productive soils are found at the higher altitudes. In the district about Kamloops the soil at altitudes exceeding twenty-five hundred feet is mostly black loam similar to that found in the prairie provinces. In fact where sufficiently large areas are to be found wheat and other crops are grown as on the prairie and during the last two years when the rainfall has been more copious than usual, with equal success.

At altitudes between three thousand and thirty-five hundred feet summer frosts are of frequent occurrence so that the more tender fruits and garden crops cannot be grown with success. As an altitude of four thousand feet is reached frosts occur throughout the summer and the only dependable crops which can be grown are hay and oats, the latter having to be cut and made into hay before reaching maturity. The soil at these altitudes is usually fertile and the rainfall sufficient.

The country generally is ideal for stock raising and the climate is said to be particularly suitable for horses.

This year weather conditions in the dry belt of British Columbia were excellent for survey operations. Although probably more than the average amount of rain fell during the season it did not hinder our work materially. A considerable portion of the area covered was range land and partly open so that an unusually large area was surveyed.

DEPARTMENT OF THE INTERIOR

5 GEORGE V., A. 1915

APPENDIX No. 56.

REPORT OF C. M. WALKER, D.L.S.

MISCELLANEOUS SURVEYS AT BANFF.

BANFF, ALTA., January 28, 1914.

E. DEVILLE, Esq., LL.D.,
Surveyor General,
Ottawa, Canada.

SIR,—I have the honour to submit the following report, with reference to work done by may party during the season of 1913.

On May 12, I began my first work, the resurvey of the cemetery at Banff, Alberta, in the Rocky Mountains park. Only one section of the cemetery had been previously surveyed, though graves were to be found in the other sections, this necessitating considerable re-adjustment .

After the completion of the survey, I proceeded to lay out a cemetery in the vicinity of Bankhead on the eastern slope of Cascade mountain.

In the meantime, I had received instructions from the Department to work in conjunction with the Dominion Parks branch in the laying out and construction of roads, throughout the Rocky Mountains park.

The point at which both location and construction were begun this year, was about three and a half miles west of Banff, on the Banff Castle road. Several years ago, the road was constructed from Banff to this point, but was left in a very unfinished state. A repair gang was engaged on this portion of the road for a great part of the summer, and much work is still needed on it.

We began the final location of the road, from the point mentioned above, and continued westerly in the direction of Castle mountain. As, is to be expected, in a mountainous country, the ground surface is very much broken by ravines, ridges or rocky bluffs, thus making almost constant change in the direction of the road necessary in order that low grades might be maintained. Tangents are necessarily limited to very short distances. The measurements were all taken on the proposed centre line, and stations were placed every on hundred feet and sometimes oftener, as in case of curves where the centre line was staked, every twenty or twenty-five feet; the beginnings and ends of the curves were also marked on the ground. The profile of the centre line was then run and plotted, and the grades having been determined upon, stakes were driven marking the cut and fill. Cross-section stakes were also placed where necessary. Sheets or working sketches of the grade were made and supplied to each foreman of the several gangs employed on the construction.

Having completed the final location of the road from Banff to Castle mountain, a distance of about twenty miles, I next ran a traverse and levels over a right of way which was partially cleared several years ago, from Castle mountain to the boundary between Alberta and British Columbia, in the Vermilion pass. From this point the British Columbia Government have been constructing the road down through the Vermilion pass, to join the road running from Golden to Steele, near Windermere, in the upper Columbia valley. When this road is completed, probably two years hence, there will be thrown open to the tourist, one of the finest scenic routes on the continent.

We next moved to Field, British Columbia, in order to make some small miscellaneous surveys including the laying out of a cemetery. I also traversed the road leading from Field to Emerald lake, while in the neighbourhood.

Bridge across Miette River near Jasper, Alberta.

This bridge crosses Miette river about a mile southwest of Jasper and was constructed by the Dominion Parks Branch. The road was made during the construction of the Grand Trunk Pacific railway and afterwards improved by the Dominion Government. Goat mountain is seen in the distance.

Photo by H. Matheson, D.L.S.

This road about seven miles in length, was found to be in very good condition, and it leads to one of the beauty spots in Yoho park, that is, Emerald lake. One view alone of this beautiful lake hidden away at the back of Mount Burgess, surely repays the tourist for the time spent in reaching it.

Our next move was made to Glacier, British Columbia, to do some miscellaneous work in connection with roads. The only wagon road leading out of Glacier, is the one in the direction of Nakimu caves, which are about seven miles distant. The road is somewhat steep for carriages, and has, therefore, been constructed on the southern and western slopes of Mt. Cheops. At present the road does not go right to the caves but has stopped about one-half mile therefrom.

Only two of the caves are open to the public as yet, but surveys were being carried on this summer with a view to opening up the largest of them by means of a tunnel, from the outside, thus making it accessible to visitors at all times of the year. Up to the present time the largest cave just referred to has been accessible only when the stream which runs through it is very low and even then, there has been considerable risk attached. These caves constitute the most interesting spot for the sightseer.

Having traversed the road to the caves and completed the survey of a small parcel of land for private leasehold close to Glacier station, we returned to Castle mountain, Alberta, and began the final location survey of the auto road on the north side of Bow river, from Castle to Laggan, a distance of about eighteen miles. The country is timbered throughout the length of the proposed road, with small jackpine, spruce and scattered fir. As a general rule, however, the timber is so small that it is difficult to obtain proper timbering for the necessary culverts and wooden bridges along the road. Splendid views of the mountains are to be obtained throughout the entire route.

Just at the time when I was completing the location survey of this road I was requested by the Commissioner of Parks, to also make a road survey on the south side of the Bow, from Laggan to Castle in order that a comparison of the two routes could be made as to desirability and respective cost. Accordingly, as soon as I had reached Laggan on the north side, I began the survey of the route on the south side of the Bow, from Laggan back to Castle.

I received instructions from the Department at this time, that Mr. T. H. Mawson, the noted landscape and civic design artist, was proceeding to Banff, in order to make plans for the beautifying of Banff and vicinity, and that the Department wished me to make any surveys which Mr. Mawson might desire for the obtaining of necessary information.

On interviewing him I was informed that ten-foot contours were necessary and that they were needed at once, over an area of about six hundred acres in the villa lot section, on the south side of Bow river at Banff. Consequently about November 1, I was compelled to organize a second party to carry on the work in this connection. This party was kept busy for one month. On the completion of the survey of the road from Laggan to Castle on the south of the Bow, I moved the party to Banff, where we were engaged in making various surveys in the villa lot section. I then made a survey of the new golf course enlarging the old one sufficiently to make the grounds suitable for an eighteen link course.

A small parcel of land was also surveyed in section 29, township 25, range 12, west of the fifth meridian for purposes of picnic grounds, to be reached by a motor launch, from Banff.

Throughout the whole season, it was necessary to keep in constant touch with the construction work, on the various roads for the purpose of setting bridge levels, grades, etc.

Having completed the work for which I had received instructions I disbanded my party for the season on December 16, storing the outfit at Banff.

I have the honour to be, Sir,

Your obedient servant,

O. M. WALKER, D.L.S.

5 GEORGE V., A. 1915

APPENDIX No. 57.

ABSTRACT FROM THE REPORT OF B. W. WAUGH, D.L.S.

MERIDIAN AND BASE LINE SURVEY IN NORTHERN MANITOBA.

My work during the season of 1913-14 consisted of the survey of part of the principal meridian from townships 73 to 80 inclusive and parts of the twentieth and twenty-first base lines.

The party having been organized, and the necessary outfit obtained, we left Selkirk for Warren's landing on May 24, 1913, one-half of the party on the *S.S. Mikado* and the remainder on the *S.S. Wolverine*. The southern end of lake Winnipeg was then completely free of ice, but towards the northern end we encountered large cakes of rotten ise miles in extent. From Warren's landing we travelled to Norway House on the tug *Highlander,* and from there by canoe down Nelson river to Cross portage, and thence to Landing lake where our work commenced.

On June 11 work was started on the principal meridian at the northeast corner of section 24, township 72 and continued steadily until August 22 when the northeast corner of section 13, township 80 was reached. During this time we had succeeded in getting only a small portion of our supplies down Nelson river from Norway House, the Hudson's Bay company, on whom we were depending for our transportation, having difficulty in obtaining the necessary help from the Indians. It was deemed advisable, therefore, on account of the short season then left for navigation, that we freight our own winter supplies by canoe, and consequently we left camp for Norway House on August 26, arriving there on September 6. The canoes were loaded and started for Split lake on the following Monday. I took advantage of this opportunity to go to Selkirk to purchase dogs for the winter work.

By this time McMillan Bros. had completed a transportation route from Whiskey Jack portage, between Playgreen lake and Cross lake, to Shoal falls on the Nelson, about eight miles below Cross lake, and then were engaged in laying a pole track from there to the southwest end of Sipiwesk lake. This afforded us great assistance in our transportation, as we were able to get the remainder of our supplies to Whiskey Jack by the tug *Highlander,* across this portage by McMillan Bros'. teams and thence to Shoal falls by means of their barge. From Shoal falls our canoes took their next load of supplies to Partridge Crop lake on the twentieth base-line, where I left one man to mind cache and fish for dog-feed. The remainder of our supplies, with the exception of the dog-biscuit, we succeeded in getting across McMillan's pole track to Sipiwesk lake and from there to Split lake by our own canoes, where we were frozen in on October 19, small sluggish creeks having frozen over as early as October 12. It then became necessary for us to build hand sleighs to move our supplies and camp equipment to the end of the meridian in township 80, and work was commenced on the line again on November 10. On the 11th the twenty-first base line east of the principal meridian was turned off and produced to the end of range 9 by January 21, 1914. We then moved to the twentieth base line completing the seven ranges east of the meridian on March 9 and the three ranges west of the meridian on March 27.

During the summer canoes and man-packing were our means of transportation while in the winter dogs were used.

This summer it is the intention of McMillan Bros. to put a launch and a barge on Sipiwesk lake to run from the north end of their pole track on this lake to Manitou rapids. This will afford the best means of transport to Manitou rapids until the Hudson Bay railway is completed to that place.

General description of the country.

In crossing Landing lake, in which the northeast corner of township 72, range 1, falls, the meridian passes from a country in which rock outcroppings is the prominent feature into a clay belt; this continues as far north as township 80, the rock becoming gradually less frequent. The clay belt is rolling, with swampy valleys, and the soil is clay and clay loam. In most cases the swampy valleys would be quite easily drained into the different rivers and lakes. The hills and ridges become higher to the northward, until in township 80 they reach a height of about two hundred feet. The ridges and valleys lie in a northeasterly and southwesterly direction.

Along the twenty-first base line the clay belt continues but the country is more level east of Burntwood river and is, although fairly dry, much more swampy than that previously passed. In ranges 8 and 9 the country becomes more of the muskeg variety and to the east, south and southwest of these ranges it appears to be almost continuous muskeg with occasional jackpine ridges.

The twentieth base line to the east in range 1 passes through Partridge Crop lake and the remainder of the line passes through country with a good clay loam soil. The country is rolling with some muskeg of considerable extent. In range 7 on the east side of the Nelson the country becomes more swampy, and farther east appears to drop into the regular muskeg country.

Westward from the principal meridian on the twentieth base line the rock more nearly approaches the surface and in some cases bald rocks appear. The country consists of long ridges running in a northeasterly and southwesterly direction with broad deep valleys intervening.

Description of the principal lakes and rivers.

In section 1, township 73, range 1, the meridian crosses Landing lake, a long narrow body of water about three-quarters of a mile wide and thirty miles long. The lake is very deep and whitefish are plentiful.

Wintering lake, crossing townships 73, 74 and 75, range 2, west, Partridge Crop lake along the twentieth base line, Natawahunan lake in township 78, range 3, east and Armstrong lake in township 78, range 4, east are all well stocked with fish, the principal variety of value being whitefish. The species caught in these lakes, although inferior to the lake Winnipeg whitefish, are of good quality and no doubt, in the near future when the transportation in this country is benefited by the Hudson Bay railway, fishing stations will be established there. Small patches of timber consisting of spruce from six to ten inches in diameter, are found on some of the points on the shores of these lakes. Landing lake, Wintering lake, Partridge Crop lake and Armstrong lake and river appear to lie on rock contact depressions; the only indications of mineral however are seen in pegmatite veins which cut the granite containing pyrite, muscovite, some amber mica, chalcopyrite and molybdenum in small quantities. Some quartz veins were observed on Natawahuan lake, but in nearly all cases were found barren. A number of discovery claims have been "staked" in these places.

In section 12, township 80 the meridian crosses Burntwood river, and this river is again crossed three times by the twenty-first base line in ranges 2 and 3. Its banks are clay about fifty feet high, with occasional rock outcroppings. On the lower portion there are only three falls, the river being mostly wide and the current slow but the upper part has many rapids.

Odei river, crossing the twenty-first base line in ranges 1 and 2, east is a tributary of Bruntwood river, and is most remarkable for the straightness of the fifteen miles nearest its mouth. Its banks are from one hundred to two hundred feet high on the lower part and very low and swampy in the upper part. Over a stretch of three miles in section 2, township 81, range 1 and sections 35, 36 and 25, township 80, range 1,

5 GEORGE V., A. 1915

there is a drop of nearly one hundred feet affording good water-power but the lower part of this river is free from rapids. Whitefish and sturgeon are to be found in this river.

In range 5 the twenty-first base line crosses Witchai lake, a large shallow L-shaped body of water in which whitefish are plentiful. This lake as well as Natawahunan and Partridge Crop lakes are merely enlarged oprtions of Grass river which empties into Split lake. That portion of Grass river between Natawahunan lake and Split lake is very shallow and contains many rapids, making it a very poor canoe route.

Split lake which is an enlargement of Nelson river is a large body of water about twenty miles long and from ten to fifteen miles wide. It has a very uneven rocky -shore line making many long narrow bays, and contains many islands, hence in some places the current is strong causing heavy seas in certain winds. The whitefish in this lake are small and not plentiful.

The winter trail from Split lake to Norway House runs along this river to Natawahunan lake where it turns to the south, going overland to Landing lake and thence over Cross portage to Sipiwesk lake. Another route is to go up Grass river through Partridge Crop lake to Wintering lake, and thence by way of Thicket portage, Landing lake and Fiddle river to Sipiwesk lake.

The proposed line of the Hudson Bay railway crosses the meridian in township 74, and the twentieth base line in range 3, east of the principal meridian. Along this. railway line McMillan Bros. have a winter road cut as far north as mile 290.

No timber or minerals of value were found except those already mentioned. The timber throughout the country is invariably small spruce, jackpine and poplar on the ridges, and small spruce, tamarack and birch in the valleys.

Whitefish are plentiful in most of the larger lakes and rivers, and in Grass, Odei and Nelson rivers sturgeon are to be found.

In the fall during freeze-up caribou pass through the country around Split lake in herds, and it is a common occurrence to hear of one man shooting as many as thirty in one day. The Indians depend largely on these caribou for their winter supply of meat for themselves and their dogs. Moose are plentiful in Natawahunan lake district and a few bears are to be found there. Foxes are the chief fur-bearing animals of the district but mink, bob-cat, wolves and others are also plentiful.

The summer in this country appears to be very short, the snow leaving about the latter part of April and coming again in October. Last summer was very wet and cold and during August we had several frosts. Towards the end of the winter the snow became very deep, being from three to three and a half feet. The winters are extremely cold, the average minimum temperature often being about forty degrees below zero for a period of four to six weeks.

SESSIONAL PAPER No. 25b

APPENDIX No. 58.

RESULTS OF MAGNETIC OBSERVATIONS.

TABLE I.   DECLINATION OBSERVATIONS.

Place.	Township.	Range.	Meridian.	Date.	Declination.	Observer.
44 00 N.-NE. cor. sec.22	16	6	E. pr.	Oct. 4, '13	12 27·8	C. F. Aylsworth.
5·00 N.- " 18	10	15	"	Dec. 27, '13	9 29·7	G. A. Bennett.
5·00 N.- " 18	10	15	"	" 27, '13	30·9	"
30·00 S.- " 36	15	15	"	July 6, '13	11 05.2	W. J. Deans.
30·00 S.- " 36.	15	15	"	" 6, '13	06·8	"
30·00 S.- " 36	15	15	"	" 7, '13	02·8	"
30·00 S.- " 36	15	15	"	" 6, '13	09·7	"
20·00 S.- " 33	15	15	"	" 20, '13	9 28·1	"
20·00 S.- " 33	15	15	"	" 20, '13	10·1	"
20·00 S.- " 33.	15	15	"	" 20, '13	22·1	"
20.00 S.- " 33	15	15	"	" 20, '13	32·6	"
0·65 S.- " 32	15	15	"	" 26, '13	6 05·7	"
0·65 S.- " 32.	15	15	"	" 26, '13	5 51.6	"
1·00 N.- " 32	15	15	"	" 27, '13	6 09.1	"
1·00 N.- " 32.	15	15	"	" 27, '13	08·4	"
78·68 W.- " 35.	68	1	Pr.	June 11, '13	17 31·6	G. H. *H*erriot.
59·97 W.- " 35	68	1	"	" 12, '13	15 15·0	"
60·94 W.- " 32	68	1	"	" 17, '13	14 23·4	"
44·60 W.- " 36.	68	2	"	" 19, '13	15 30·1	"
59·80 W.- " 35	68	2	"	" 21, '13	16 12·2	"
At " 36.	72	2	"	Aug. 16, '13	16 19·2	"
55·91 W.-NE " 32	72	2	"	" 23, '13	20 17·6	"
60·00 N.- " 35	20	3	"	Nov. 5, '13	13 52·1	C. F. Aylsworth.
35·00 N.- " 4.	21	3	"	Oct. 29, '13	30·9	"
At " 18.	21	3	"	Nov. 7, '13	35·8	"
At " 22.	21	3	"	" 11, '13	50·1	"
At " 34.	21	3	"	" 13, '13	38·4	"
At " 21.	21	3	"	" 17, '13	45·9	"
20·00 N.-NE cor. sec. 19	21	3	Pr.	Nov. 25, '13	13 38·8	C. F. Aylsworth.
60·00 N.- " 3).	21	3	"	" 25, '13	38·7	"
At " 29.	21	3	"	" 27, '13	42·5	"
At " 20	21	3	"	" 26, '13	32·4	"
At " 32.	21	3	"	" 29, '13	42·8	"
10·00 E.- " 36	28	3	"	Mar. 8, '13	12 59·9	W. J. Deans.
10·00 E.- " 36.	28	3	"	" 9, '13	56·8	"
11·95 W.- " 31	68	3	"	July 4, '13	18 22·9	G. H. *H*erriot.
27·77 W.- " 35.	72	3	"	Aug. 28, '13	15 37·6	"
8·13·W.- " 34.	72	3	"	" 29, '13	14 08·0	"
48·00 N.- " 35.	21	4	"	June 27, '13	13 32·8	C. F. Aylsworth.
30·00 N.- " 12.	22	4	"	" 23, '13	40·7	"
At " 26.	22	4	"	" 24, '13	53·6	"
At " 4.	22	4	"	" 26, '13	26·0	"
At " 3. . . . : . . .	22	4	"	" 27, '13	37·2	"
At " 9.	22	4	"	" 27, '13	30·1	"
At " 4.	22	4	"	" 27, '13	21·7	"
At " 3.	22	4	"	" 27, '13	26·1	"
At " 18.	22	4	"	July 2, '13	16·1	"
20·00 W.- " 30	22	4	"	" 4, '13	14·4	"
40·00 N.- " 8	22	4	"	" 5, '13	31·5	"
At " 20.	22	4	"	" 9, '13	33·7	"
At " 29.	22	4	"	" 11, '13	30·1	"
At " 21.	22	4	"	" 17, '13	37·4	"
55·00 N.- " 22	22	4	"	" 22, '13	43·7	"
At " 3.	22	4	"	June 18, '13	34·7	"
15·00 N.- " 26	28	4	"	Mar. 5, '13	12 55·7	W. J. Deans.
15·00 N,- " 26.	28	4	"	" 6, '13	59·1	"

5 GEORGE V., A. 1915

RESULTS OF MAGNETIC OBSERVATIONS—*Continued.*

TABLE I.—DECLINATION OBSERVATIONS—*Continued.*

Place.			Township.	Range.	Meridian.	Date.	Declination	Observer.
							° ′	
56·53 W.-	,,	35	68	4	,,	July 10, '13	16 37·5	G. H. *Herriot.*
27·40 W.-	,,	36	72	4	,,	Sept. 5, '13	14 32·8	,,
25·55 W.-	,,	35	72	4	,,	,, 6, '13	14·2	,,
20·00 W.-	,,	31	72	4	,,	,, 10, '13	02·5	,,
At	,,	4	23	5	,,	Aug. 20, '13	15 32·7	C. F. Aylsworth.
At	,,	16	23	5	,,	,, 21, '13	31·3	,,
55·00 N.-NE cor. sec.	8		23	5	Pr.	Aug. 25, '13	13 27·8	C. F. Aylsworth.
At	,,	30	23	55	,,	,, 29, '13	36·8	,,
At	,,	21	23	5	,,	Sept. 1, '13	28·2	,,
At	,,	26	23	5	,,	,, 12, '13	49·5	,,
10·00 N.-	,,	23	23	5	,,	,, 8, '13	50·1	,,
At	,,	36	28	5	,,	Feb. 28, '13	07·6	W. J. Deans.
At	,,	36	28	5	,,	Mar. 2, '13	08·6	,,
At	,,	36	28	5	,,	,, 3, '13	04·9	,,
39·05 W.-	,,	32	68	5	,,	July 28, '13	18 20·8	G. H. *Herriot.*
6·97 W.-	,,	35	72	5	,,	Sept. 14, '13	13 20·3	,,
72·00 W.-	,,	36	29	6	,,	Feb. 22, '13	13 09·9	W. J. Deans.
7·00 ,,	,,	36	29	6	,,	,, 23, '13	10·4	,,
10·00 S.-	,,	36	29	6	,,	,, 20, '13	13 11·6	,,
30·00 W.-	,,	36	29	6	,,	,, 21, '13	00·0	,,
60·55 W.-	,,	34	68	6	,,	Aug. 6, '13	19 24·1	G. H. *Herriot.*
53·73 W.-	,,	33	72	6	,,	Oct. 1, '13	18 10·5	,,
20·00 W.-	,,	32	72	6	,,	,, 2, '13	16 52·7	,,
50·00 N.-SE	,,	1	31	7	,,	Feb. 16, '13	13 49·3	W. J. Deans.
,,	,,	1	31	7	,,	,, 17, '13	53·8	,,
,,	,,	1	31	7	,,	,, 18, '13	55·7	,,
67·71 W.-NE	,,	33	64	7	,,	July 1, '13	16 29·7	O. Rolfson.
49·90 W.-	,,	35	68	7	,,	Oct. 29, '13	15 15·4	G. H. *Herriot.*
21·10 W.-	,,	32	68	7	,,	Nov. 1, '13	14 52·6	,,
2·99 W.-	,,	31	68	7	,,	,, 3, '13	15 23·7	,,
16·77 W.-	,,	32	64	8	,,	July 10, '13	15 13·0	O. Rolfson.
19·89 W.-	,,	33	68	8	,,	Nov. 6, '13	17 00·2	G. H. Herriot.
40·00 W.-	,,	15	25	9	,,	Dec. 16, '13	13 21·6	G. A. Bennett.
12·00 W.-¼ cor. E by sec. 22			25	9	,,	,, 18, '13	24·4	,,
60·48 W.-NE cor. sec. 34			60	9	,,	Jan. 1, '13	16 49·0	O. Rolfson.
29·40 W.-	,,	32	64	9	,,	July 15, '13	14 49·5	,,
72·57 W.-	,,	34	68	9	,,	Nov. 12, '13	13 11·3	G. *H.* *Herriot.*
52·65 W.-	,,	35	64	10	,,	July 18, '13	13 42·9	O. Rolfson.
27·96 W.-	,,	35	64	10	,,	,, 21, '13	46·8	,,
27·96 W.-NE cor. sec. 35			64	10	Pr.	July 21, '13	13 49·7	O. Rolfson.
61·95 W.-	,,	31	64	10	,,	,, 24, '13	16 53·5	,,
0·18 W.-	,,	36	68	10	,,	Nov. 15, '13	15 11·9	G. H. Herriot.
4·20 W.-	,,	34	68	10	,,	,, 18, '13	12 07·0	,,
4·14 W.-	,,	33	64	11	,,	July 30, '13	21 02·4	O. Rolfson.
56·27 W.-	,,	31	68	11	,,	Nov. 28, '13	17 13·6	G. H. Herriot.
70·00 W.-SE	,,	6	23	12	,,	Jan. 1, '13	14 36·1	W. J. Deans.
24·03 W.-NE	,,	31	60	12	,,	Feb. 1, '13	15 49·4	O. Rolfson.
16·63 W.-	,,	32	64	12	,,	Aug. 5, '13	19 01·9	,,
36·00 W.-	,,	35	63	12	,,	Dec. 1, '13	16 29·4	G. H. *Herriot.*
74·95 W.-	,,	34	68	12	,,	,, 2, '13	17 51·5	,,
30·00 S.-	,,	2	23	13	,,	Jan. 2, '13	15 09·7	W. J. Deans.
52·90 W.-	,,	32	60	13	,,	Feb. 3, '13	18 05·7	O. Rolfson.
52·90 W.-	,,	32	60	13	,,	,, 3, '13	24·7	,,
12·34 W.-	,,	33	64	13	,,	Aug. 9, '13	16 44·5	,,
12·34 W.-	,,	33	64	13	,,	,, 9, '13	44·7	,,
4·00 W.-	,,	33	68	13	,,	Dec. 9, '13	16 03·6	G. H. *Herriot*
76·75 W.-	,,	33	68	13	,,	,, 1, '13	17 06·5	,,
70·00 W.-	,,	7	33	14	,,	Jan. 15, '13	15 14·1	W. J. Deans.
19·16 W.-	,,	36	60	14	,,	Feb. 6, '13	22 14·5	O. Rolfson.
67·00 W.-	,,	34	60	14	,,	,, 8, '13	17 17·1	,,
67·00 W.-	,,	34	60	14	,,	,, 8, '13	13·4	,,
67·00 W.-	,,	34	60	14	,,	,, 8, '13	12·5	,,
59·70 W.-	,,	35	64	14	,,	Aug. 21, '13	16 48·0	,,
17·00 N.-	,,	8	29	15	,,	Nov. 19, '13	13 59·6	R. C Purs
At ¼ cor. N. by sec. 9..			29	15	,,	,, 22, '13	59·6	,,

RESULTS OF MAGNETIC OBSERVATIONS—*Continued.*

TABLE I.—DECLINATION OBSERVATIONS—*Continued.*

Place.	Township.	Range.	Meridian.	Date.	Declination.	Observer.
					° ′	
At NE cor. sec. 36	33	15	"	June 25, '12	15 56·1	T. H. Plunkett.
75·00 S.- " 15............	33	15	"	Jan. 13, '13	14 59·6	W. J. Deans.
76 00 S.- " 3............ ...	34	15	"	" 14, '13	15 35·0	"
35·59 S.- " 13	34	15	"	June 27, '12	51·8	T. H. Plunkett.
5·44 N.- " 25............	34	15	"	" 30, '12	17 03·9	"
56·57 W.- " 35............	60	15	"	Feb. 14, '13	16 44·4	O. Rolfson.
4 49 W.- " 35............	60	15	"	" 17, '13	10·4	"
4·40 W.-NE cor. sec. 35........	60	15	Pr.	Feb. 17, '13	16 09·1	O. Rolfson.
1·53 W.- " 31............	60	15	"	" 17, '13	41·8	"
1·53 W.- " 31............	60	15	"	" 17, '13	43·8	"
50·47 W.- " 32............	64	15	"	Aug. 27, '13	17 42·2	"
48·00 W.- " 33............	68	15	"	Dec. 25, '13	16 55 0	G. H Herriot.
38·00 W.- " 32............	68	15	"	" 26, '13	48·1	"
0·73 W.- " 34............	60	16	"	Feb. 25, '13	27 28·6	O. Rolfson.
0·73 W.- " 34	60	16	"	" 25, '13	28·1	"
15·00 W.- " 34............	68	16	"	Dec. 31, '13	20 15·0	G H. Herriot
77·70 W.- " 32............	60	17	"	Mar. 5, '13	18 16·8	O. Rolfson.
8·85 W.- " 35............	64	17	"	Sept. 12, '13	16 44·6	"
56·00 E.- " 34............	40	18	"	Feb. 13, '13	17 45·4	T. H. Plunkett.
30·00 E.- " 36............	40	18	"	" 14, 13	46·0	"
23·50 W.- " 33............	60	18	"	Mar. 10, 13	18 11·2	O. Rolfson.
23·50 W.- " 33............	60	18	"	" 10, 13	11·8	"
61·05 W.- " 34............	64	18	"	Sept. 24, 13	19 09·6	"
19·95 W.- " 32............	64	18	"	" 25, '13	27·3	"
At " 33............	40	19	"	Feb. 5, '13	18 16·4	T. H. Plunkett.
63·00 E.- " 35............	40	19	"	" 8, '13	27·3	"
63·00 E.- " 35.	40	19	"	" 8, '13	27·0	"
18·05 W.- " 34............	60	19	"	Mar. 14, '13	33·0	O. Rolfson
18·05 W.- " 34	60	19	"	" 14, '13	31·9	"
56·54 W.- " 31.-..	64	19	"	Oct. 1, '13	17 36·9	"
30·00 E.-NW " 30............	1	20	"	Nov. 22, '13	14 44 1	W. J. Deans.
8·00 E. Wit. M-marked 7·78 N.-NE. cor. sec. 33..	17	20	"	June 12, '13	14 51·6	G. A. Pennett.
" " 33............	17	20	"	" 12, '13	52·2	"
" " 33............	17	20	"	" 12, '13	55·9	"
" " 33............	17	20	"	" 12, '13	53.1	"
79·00 E.-NE cor. sec. 33............	40	20	"	Jan. 31, '13	19 31·5	T. H. Plunkett.
16·67 W.- " 32............	60	20	"	Mar. 21, '13	15·2	O. Rolfson.
60·03 W.- " 31............	60	20	"	" 23, '13	18 44·8	"
60 03 W.- " 31............	60	20	"	" 23, '13	46·1	"
60·00 W.- " 18............	20	21	"	June 20, '13	15 48·2	G. A. Bennett.
18·65 E.- " 32............	40	21	"	Jan. 24, '13	17 23·1	T. H. Plunkett.
14·00 E.- " 33............	40	21	"	" 27, '13	02·1	"
43·00 E.- " 31............	44	21	"	Mar. 21, '13	11·9	"
11·41 E.- " 33............	44	21	"	" 22, '13	07 3	"
60·20 W.- " 32............	60	21	"	" 26, '13	18 17·1	O. Rolfson
60·20 W.- " 32............	60	21	"	" 26, '13	17·7	"
16·00 N.- " 24............	20	22	"	June 20, '13	16 01·2	G. A. Bennett.
53·00 E.- " 34............	40	22	"	Jan. 14, '13	20 06·3	T. H. Plunkett.
51·00 E.- " 31............	44	22	"	Mar. 17, '13	17 29·3	"
36·00 E.- " 32............	44	22	"	" 18, '13	17·2	"
18·30 W.- " 31............	60	22	"	" 30, '13	18 00·0	O. Rolfson.
18·30 W.- " 31............	60	22	"	" 30, '13	17 58·6	"
70·71 E.- " 36............	40	23	"	Jan. 8, '13	17 52·6	T. H. Plunkett.
62 00 E.- " 34............	44	23	"	Mar. 13, '13	16 56·6	"
14·30 W.- " 36............	60	23	"	" 31, '13	18 06·7	O. Rolfson.
30 00 W.- " 35............	39	24	"	Dec. 11, '13	16 40·3	W. J. Deans.
10·00 S.- " 35............	39	24	"	" 12, '13	43·6	"
28 00 E.-¼ cor. N. by sec. 31......	40	24	"	" 30, '12	17 07 9	T. H. Plunkett.
60 00 W.-NE cor. sec. 36	40	24	"	Jan. 6, '13	10·3	"
55·00 W.- " 31............	40	24	"	Dec. 9, '13	18·4	W. J. Deans.
40·60 W.- " 32	60	24	"	April 3, '13	59·5	O. Rolfson.
40 60 W.- " 32	60	24	"	" 3, '13	58·3	"
At " 36	40	25	"	Dec. 8, '13	01 5	W. J. Deans.........

5 GEORGE V., A. 1915

RESULTS OF MAGNETIC OBSERVATIONS—*Continued.*

TABLE I.—DECLINATION OBSERVATIONS—*Continued.*

Place			Township.	Range.	Meridian.	Date.	Declination.	Observer.
							° ′	
At	"	35	40	25	"	" 10, '13	16 48·6	"
15·00 S.-	"	13	41	25	"	" 8, '13	16 51·0	"
At	"	35	44	25	"	Mar. 9, '13	17 48·6	T. H. Plunkett.
60·00 E.-	"	34	57	25	"	Jan. 27, '13	19 24·2	E. W. Berry.
60 00 E.-	"	35	57	25	"	" 28, '13	17 35·6	"
5 00 N.-	"	25 ..	57	25	"	Feb. 3, '13	19 10·8	"
42·00 E.-	"	33	57	25	"	" 10, '13	19 19·5	"
40·00 N.-	"	35	57	25	"	" 12, '13	17 52·2	"
50 00 N.-	"	34	57	25	"	" 13, '13	38·4	"
20 00 W.-NE cor. sec. 34			57	25	Pr.	Feb. 17, '13	19 09·8	E. W. Berry.
8·00 N.-	"	27	57	25	"	" 17, '13	17 55·4	"
43 00 W.		22.	57	25	"	" 18, '13	19 50·6	"
20 00 S.-	"	28............	57	25	"	" 19, '13	20 58·4	"
10·00 N.-	"	29............	57	25	"	" 21, '13	29·5	"
45 00 N.-	"	33	57	25	"	" 24, '13	18 07·7	"
65 00 E.-	"	10............	57	25	"	" 27, '13	15 43·5	"
60·00 N.-	"	11	57	25	"	" 28, '13	16 58·9	"
65·00 E.-	"	11	57	25	"	Mar. 1, '13	19 05·1	"
60 00 N.-	"	2............	57	25	"	" 3, '13	15 46·9	"
50 00 N.-	"	17...	57	25	"	" 5, '13	21 32·5	"
35 00 N.-	"	18	57	25	"	" 12, '13	18 59·2	"
50·00 N.-	"	6....	57	25	"	" 13, '13	19 56·5	"
14 03 W.-	"	32............	60	25	"	April 4, '13	17 59·1	O. Rolfson.
14·03 W.-	"	32....	60	25	"	" 4, '13	18 04·7	"
35·00 N.-	"	15....	58	26	"	Jan. 16, '13	18 50·2	E. W. Berry.
75 00 E.-	"	22	58	26	"	" 17, '13	19 03·7	"
42 00 N.-	"	16............	58	26	"	" 18, '13	18 38·8	"
7·36 W.-	"	34............	60	26	"	Nov. 13, '13	17 25·7	O. Rolfson.
61·83 W.-	"	34............	60	27	"	" 20, '13	19 01·1	"
16 90 W.	"	35	60	28	"	" 22, '13	21 27·5	"
60 14 W.-	"	33	60	29	"	Dec. 1, '13	20 16·2	"
At ¼ cor. E. by sec. 5			33	31	"	June 19, '13	16 01·4	R. C. Purser.
32·41 E.-NE cor. sec. 31............			52	31	"	April 3, '12	19 19·7	T. H. Plunkett.
50·52 E.-	"	32............	52	31	"	" 4, '12	20 33·1	"
50·52 E.-	"	32.	52	31	"	" 4, '12	19·7	"
1·02 W.-	"	31............	48	1	2	Mar. 23, '12	19 57·0	"
1·02 W.-	"	31............	48	1	2	" 23, '12	56·7	"
19·30 W.-	"	35	48	2	2	May 2, '13	20 36·9	"
43·24 W.-	"	31............	48	2	2	" 16, '13	19 42·2	"
69·59 W.-	"	34	48	3	2	" 22, '12	20 19·3	"
At ¼ cor. E.- by sec. 29			25	4	2	Dec. 23, '12	18 07·7	R. C. Purser.
10·00 W. 13·00 N.-NE cor. sec. 18, Sta.								
16, Lake traverse....			25	4	2	" 24, '13	18 04·1	"
20 00 N.-NE cor. sec. 4			11	6	2	" 13, '13	39·5	G. A. Bennett.
28 00 S.-	"	7.............	10	8	2	Nov. 5, '13	03·5	"
28·00 S.-	"	7.............	10	8	2	" 5, '13	04·6	"
At	"	27.............	19	8	2	Oct. 31, '13	19 23·7	"
40 02 W.-	"	33	45	9	2	June 21, '13	20 46·7	C. F. Miles.
40·02 W.-	"	33	45	9	2	" 14, '13	36·9	"
40·02 W.-	"	33	45	9	2	" 21, '13	37·8	"
5·00 E.-	"	33.............	45	9	2	" 13, '13	36·9	"
5·00 E.-	"	33.............	45	9	2	" 13, '13	28·8	"
At	"	31....	6	10	2	July 17, '13	18 04·9	G. A. Bennet.
40·00 W.	"	11....	7	10	2	" 9, '13	17 45·3	"
40·00 E.-	"	9.............	7	10	2	" 10, '13	45·6	"
20 00 E.-	"	31....	7	10	2	" 16 '13	18 11·7	"
20·00 E.-	"	31....	7	10	2	" 16, '13	11·6	"
6·50 E.-	"	5.............	20	10	2	" 23, '13	19 02·6	"
40·00 E.-	"	10.............	48	10	2	Oct. 9, '13	37·3	W. J. Deans.
25·00 N.-	"	14..	48	10	2	" 10, '13	52·2	"
At NE	"	20.............	48	10	2	" 12, '13	20 08·0	"
50·00 W.-	"	27	48	10	2	" 13, '13	19 27·2	"
25·00 N.-SE	"	27	48	10	2	" 14, '13	46·6	"
At NE	"	23.............	48	10	2	" 16, '13	52·9	"

SESSIONAL PAPER No. 25b

RESULTS OF MAGNETIC OBSERVATIONS—*Continued.*

TABLE I.—DECLINATION OBSERVATIONS—*Continued.*

Place.	Township.	Range.	Meridian.	Date.	Declination.	Observer.
					° ′	
70·00 N.-SE cor. sec. 26..............	48	10	2	Oct. 17, '13	57·8	W. J. Deans.
20·00 N.-NE " 26	48	10	2	" 20, '13	20 33·0	"
At " 21..............	48	10	3	" 21, '13	19 58·0	"
5·00 S.- " 20	48	10	2	" 22, '13	56·9	"
At " 21..............	26	11	2	June 13, '13	18 08·9	R. C. Purser.
At " 21..............	26	11	2	" 15, '13	05·7	"
At ¼ cor. E. by sec. 28...... ...	33	11	2	Dec. 1, '13	44·0	"
17·32 W.-¼ cor. N. by sec. 22........	33	11	2	" 2, '13	47·1	"
14·99 S.-NE cor. sec. 27	33	11	2	" 3, '13	48·4	"
15·00 S.-¼ cor. E. by sec. 28.........	33	11	2	" 4, '13	49 1	"
At ¼cor. E. by sec. 2............	33	11	2	Dec. 8, '13	18 47·6	R. C. Purser.
28·50 E. 31·00 N.-NE cor. sec. 2, Sta. 11, Lake traverse...	33	11	2	" 10, '13	48·9	"
11·50 N. 4·00 W.-SE cor. sec. 1, Sta. 4, Lake traverse....	33	11	2	" 12, '13	19 21·6	"
29·30 E.-NE cor. sec. 8	20	12	2	" 10, '13	18 48·7	G. A. Bennett.
' M At " 31...............	47	14	2	July 26, '13	22 33·2	R. C. Purser.
30·00 N.- " 18	42	16	2	June 6, '13	19 31·0	"
10·00 E.- " 31..............	13	18	2	Nov. 10, '13	17 55·8	G. A. Bennett.
. . At " 22..............	40	18	2	" 19, '13	20 10·0	R. Neelands.
⌐.⌐' At Sta. 4, sec. 16	7	19	2	Sept. 15, '13	18 24·9	C. Rinfret.
39·00 N.-NE cor. sec. 8.............	23	19	2	Oct. 13, '13	19 23·9	B. H. Segre.
40·00 W.- " 22.............	25	19	2	" 23, '13	35·5	"
At Sta. 2, sec. 33....	4	20	2	" 11, '13	17 07·0	C. Rinfret.
" 33....	4	20	2	" 12, '13	10·3	"
At Sta. 3, sec. 22·	5	20	2	Sept. 25, '13	18 02·3	"
" 22..........	5	20	2	" 26, '13	17 56·0	"
At Sta. 4, sec. 31.............	7	20	2	Nov. 13, '13	18 36·3	"
At Sta. 78A sec. 6.............	3	21	2	Sept. 11, '13	03·6	"
At Sta. 2, sec. 24.............	3	21	2	Oct. 12, '13	17 45·1	"
At Sta. 3, sec. 22	4	21	2	" 15, '13	54·4	"
" 22..............	4	21	2	" 21, '13	57·0	"
At Sta. 3, sec. 15.............	5	21	2	" 1, '13	46·5	"
At Sta. 2, sec. 10.............	6	21	2	" 31, '13	18 07·9	"
At Sta. 3, sec. 18.............	7	21	2	" 31, '13	19·1	"
" 18	7	21	2	Nov. 6, '13	16·0	"
At Sta. 2, sec. 28.............	2	22	2	Sept. 6, '13	32·6	"
At Sta. 12, sec. 28.............	5	22	2	Aug. 16, '13	45·7	"
At Sta. 6, sec. 28.............	5	22	2	" 22, '13	52·4	"
At Sta. 2, sec. 17	6	22	2	" 28, '13	40·3	"
"	6	22	2	" 30, '13	38·3	"
15·00 N.-NE cor. sec. 9........... ...	20	22	2	May 22, '13	19 59·0	B. H. Segre.
19·00 S. 14·00 W.-NE cor. sec. 19......	21	22	2	Dec. 18, '13	54·0	"
At NE cor. sec. 32..	25	22	2	Nov. 8, '13	19 47·2	"
2·00 E.- ' " 17...............	44	22	2	Dec. 1, '13	21 17·9	R. Neelands.
0·60 E.- " 20	44	22	2	" 3, '13	16·8	"
40·00 N.- " 14...............	3	23	2	Aug. 11, '13	19 03·1	C. Rinfret.
At Sta. 3, sec. 29	6	23	2	Nov. 8, '13	18·4	"
40·00 W.-NE cor. sec. 35..............	21	23	2	Sept. 27, '13	20 09 2	B. H. Segre.
22·00 W.- " 32..............	22	23	2	" 7, '13	10·6	"
" 32..............	22	23	2	" 11, '13	07·4	"
40·00 S. } NE " 22.............. 21·00 E. }	22	23	2	Dec. 5, '13	03·0	"
16·00 S.- " 31..............	23	23	2	Nov. 26, '13	20 05·5	"
At " 21..............	38	23	2	July 6, '13	19 40·1	R. Neelands.
1·60 S.- " 22..............	39	23	2	" 15, '13	25·8	"
40·00 S.- " 30..............	39	23	2	" 16, '13	48·8	"
Sta. 3, Traverse Lake No. 9..........	39	23	2	" 28, '13	20 20·3	"
40·00 S.-NE cor. sec. 2	40	23	2	" 22, '13	21·3	"
39·54 W.- " 9	40	23	2	" 26, '13	24·5	"
51·00 W.- " 34	40	23	2	" 30, '13	45·4	"
8·00 SE- " 15	41	23	2	Aug. 18, '13	11·6	"
At Sta. 7, sec. 5	7	24	2	June 10, '13	18 00·1	C. Rinfret.
" 5......	7	24	2	" 13, '13	48·3	"

25b—15

5 GEORGE V,. A. 1915

RESULTS OF MAGNETIC OBSERVATIONS—*Continued.*

TABLE I.—DECLINATION OBSERVATIONS—*Continued.*

Place.	Township.	Range.	Meridian.	Date.	Declination.	Observer.
					° '	
37·00 S.-NE cor. sec. 11..............	18	24	2	May 24, '13	19 33·2	B. *H.* Segrè.
At " 24......	23	24	2	Sept. 5, '13	20 16·5	"
9·00 W.- " 33......	24	24	2	Aug. 25, '13	17·3	"
40·00 W.- " 32..............	25	24	2	" 15, '13	19·5	"
36·00 W.- " 11..............	25	24	2	Nov. 17, '13	17·8	"
At ¼ cor. E. by sec. 19....	27	24	2	July 31, '13	49 54·3	R. C. Purser.
6·50 N.-NE cor. sec. 10......	27	24	2	Aug. 6, '13	20 30·9	B. H. Segre.
30·00 S.- " 11..............	28	24	2	July 21, '13	07·2	"
At " 4..............	39	24	2	Oct. 27, '13	19 57·0	R. Neelands.
40 00 S.- " 2..............	40	24	2	July 5, '13	20 02·5	"
At Sta. 3, Traverse lake No. 1...	41	24	2	June 27, '13	20 21·1	R. Neelands.
29 00 N.- NE. cor. sec. 24	42	24	2	Oct. 8, '13	28·4	"
At " , 11..............	44	24	2	Dec. 13, '13	12 4	"
At Sta. 62, sec. 15	5	25	2	June 18, '13	18 35·8	C. Rinfret.
27·00 N.-						
22·00 W.-NE. cor. sec. 8.........	19	25	2	" 2, '13	20 16·8	B. *H.* Segre.
40·00 S.- " 28..............	26	25	2	J·ly 16, '13	41·6·	"
16·00 E.- " 12..............	39	25	2	Nov. 2, '13	53 9	R. Neelands.
At Sta. 7, Traverse lake No. 1...	40	25	2	May 27, '13	56 3	"
At NE.- cor. sec. 20	41	25	2	June 7, '13	12·2	"
At Sta. 2, Sec. 18....	4	26	2	Aug. 1, '13	18 08·1	C. Rinfret.
" 18	4	26	2	" 4, '13	10·4	"
At Sta. 5, sec. 35	5	26	2	June 2, '13	17 57·3	"
" 35..............	5	26	2	June 3, '13	53·1	"
At Sta 8, sec. 13....	5	26	2	" 21, '13	18 26·9	"
10·00 N.-						
14·00 W.-NE. cor. sec. 4	20	26	2	" 15, '13	20 11·7	B. H. Segre.
At " 10..............	40	26	2	" 7, '13	21·6	R. Neelands.
At " 32	22	27	2	July, 5, '13	26·1	B. H. Segre.
At " 10..............	25	27	2	Aug. 4, '13	19 33·4	R. C. Purser.
6·50 E.- " 33	25	27	2	July 12, '13	20 26·8	B. H. Segre.
At Sta. 141, sec. 26 ...	6	28	2	" 1, '13	19 35·2	C. Rinfret.
At Sta. 5, Traverse lake Johnston.	12	28	2	" 3, '12	31·5	"
At Sta. 14, Traverse lake No. 3 .	46	28	2	Dec. 27, '13	24 01·7	R. Neelands.
40 00 S.-NE cor. sec. 10..........	46	28	2	" 29, '13	25 13·9	"
At Sta. 75, sec. 15	3	29	2	July 24, '13	19 28·3	C. Rinfret.
At Sta. 2A, sec. 10	4	29	2	" 16, '13	21·3	"
At Sta. 2, sec. 23..........	6	29	2	" 7, '13	46·5	"
At Sta. 2A, sec. 23	6	29	2	" 8, '13	45·4	"
35·00 W.-NE. cor. sec. 33	14	29	2	Nov. 10, '13	44·8	W. J. Deans.
At Sta. 60, sec. 24...,......	3	30	2	July 17, '13	05·1	C. Rinfret.
" 24..........	3	30	2	" 19, '13	03 5	"
35·00 S.-NE. cor. sec. 36..........	16	30	2	" 7, '13	59·6	G. A. Bennett.
" 36..........	16	30	2	" 7, '13	58·6	"
At NE. cor. sec. 14..........	18	1	3	Oct. 23, '13	20 47·4	"
At " 23..........	18	1	3	" 25, '13	43 5	"
2·00 N.-NE. cor. sec. 23	15	2	3	May 25, '13	32·9	"
" 23	15	2	3	" 31, '13	27·2	"
40·00 E.- " 34..........	15	2	3	June 26, '13	41·4	"
" 34..........	15	2	3	" 26, '13	39·5	"
" 34	15	2	3	July 5, '13	37·0	"
45.00 S.- " 2..........	16	2	3	May 29, '13	35·5	"
36·00 S.- " 20...	16	2	3	Sept. 9, '13	21 24·4	C. E. Johnston.
At " 17...	16	2	3	" 19, '13	24·3	"
40·00 S.- " 19	16	2	3	" 24, '13	18·2	"
50·00 N.- " 10..........	57	2	3	Dec. 15, '13	23 33·7	E. W. *H*ubbell.
40·00 S.- " 23..........	16	3	3	Sept. 11, '13	21 14·1	C. E. Johnston
" 23..........	16	3	3	" 12, '13	12·5	"
At " 34..........	17	3	3	" 1, '13	17·5	"
40·00 S.- " 15..........	18	3	3	" 4, '13	21·1	"
40·00 S.- " 22..........	18	3	3	" 5, '13	25·1	"
" 22...	18	3	3	" 5, '13	12·5	"
40·00 W.- " 34..........	18	3	3	" 28, '13	20 55·5	"
At " 3...	19	3	3	" 27, '13	55·1	"

SESSIONAL PAPER No. 25b

RESULTS OF MAGNETIC OBSERVATIONS—*Continued.*

TABLE I.—DECLINATION OBSERVATIONS—*Continued.*

Place.	Township.	Range.	Meridian.	Date.	Declination.	Observer.
					° ′	
40·00 N.-NE. cor. sec. 3............	19	3	3	Oct., 6, '13	57·6	C. E. Johnston.
40·00 S.- " 12............	21	3	3	" 7, '13	20 39·8	"
" 12............	21	3	3	" 11, '13	34·6	"
" 12............	21	3	3	" 12, '13	37·9	"
" 12............	21	3	3	" 13, '13	36·9	"
" 12............	21	3	3	" 14, '13	36·7	"
" 12............	21	3	3	" 15, '13	36·8	"
" 12............,	21	3	3	" 19, '13	34·9	"
0 50 N.- " 28...........	30	3	3	May 30, '13	51·4	R. C. Purser.
At " 9............	30	3	3	June 2, '13	36·2	"
At " 19...........	17	4	3	July 3, '13	21 13·3	C. E. Johnston.
At " 19............	17	4	3	" 5, '13	15·7	"
At " 19............	17	4	3	" 6, '13	18·3	"
40·00 S.- " 20........	17	4	3	" 6, '13	18·9	"
40·00 W.-NE. cor. sec 9....	18	4	3	Aug. 20, '13	21 16·1	C. E. Johnston.
40 00 W.- " 2....	19	4	3	Sept. 30, '13	06·0	"
40·00 W.- " 2....	19	4	3	Oct. 1, '13	09·9	"
14·75 N.- " 7............	57	4	3	Dec. 10, '13	32·5	E. W. Hubbell.
15·00 S.- " 36............	13	5	3	May 28, '13	20 40·0	G. A. Bennett.
At Sta. 53 Chaplin lake trav. sec. 27...	16	5	3	July 17, '13	21 12·3	C. E. Johnston.
At NE. cor. sec. 12......	16	5	3	" 18, '13	10·6	"
At " 12	16	5	3	" 19, '13	14·6	"
At " 12	16	5	3	" 20, '13	13·0	"
At " 12	16	5	3	" 21, '13	14·4	"
At " 12............	16	5	3	" 21, '13	13·8	"
40·00 E.-NE. cor. sec. 32	17	5	3	June 28, '13	06·8	"
40·00 E.- " 32	17	5	3	" 30, '13	09·2	"
40·00 E.- " 32............	17	5	3	July 1, '13	07·3	"
At Sta. 34 Chaplin lake trav. sec. 1....	17	5	3	" 8, '13	16·4	"
" " "	17	5	3	" 8, '13	17·0	"
40·00 S.-NE. cor. sec. 1	17	5	3	" 10, '13	14·4	"
40·00 S.- " 1..........	17	5	3	" 12, '13	30·8	"
40·00 S.- " 1·.........	17	5	3	" 15, '13	13·0	"
40·00 S.- " 1...........	17	5	3	" 16, '13	16·2	"
42·00 S.- " 17............	17	5	3	" 22, '13	13·7	"
42·00 S.- " 17............	17	5	3	" 23, '13	16·3	"
At Sta. 60 Chaplin lake trav. sec. 3	17	5	3	" 24, '13	17·6	"
10·00 S.-NE. cor. sec. 8....	25	5	3	Nov. 27, '13	15·8	G. A. Bennett.
At N.E. " 36..........	47	5	3	Oct. 30, '13	22 39·9	R. C. Purser.
75 84 W.- " 19..	54	5	3	May 29, '13	20 27·9	P. R. A. Belanger.
22·45 W.- " 21......	54	5	3	June 9, '13	19 45·4	"
31·90N.- " 21	55	5	3	" 3, '13	47·6	"
0·15 S.- " 9	56	5	3	" 4, '13	20 22·4	"
At NE. cor. sec. 7......	57	5	3	Dec. 8, '13	20 42·0	F. W. Hubbell.
41·00 N.-NE cor. sec. 10.....	20	6	3	June 16, '13	21 33·4	C. E. Johnston.
41·00 N.- " 10............	20	6	3	" 17, '13	21 35·2	"
41·00 N.- " 10	20	6	3	" 18, '13	34·6	"
1·00 N.- " 29............	25	6	3	Nov. 20, '13	38·5	G. A. Bennett.
4·00 N.- " 14........	25	6	3	" 22, '13	45·9	"
4·00 N.- " 14.......... ..	25	6	3	Dec. 6, '13	31·0	"
At NE. cor. sec. 10	33	6	3	" 31, '13	40·9	R. C. Purser.
15·00 E. ¼ cor. N. by sec. 9..	42	6	3	June 26, '13	20 27·5	"
25·17 S.-N.E. cor. sec. 13............	15	7	3	" 5, '13	22 13·1	C. E. Johnston.
25·17 S.- " 13............	15	7	3	" 6, '13	21 57·7	"
At NE. cor. sec. 31............	17	7	3	" 1, '13	56·8	"
At " 31............	17	7	3	" 2, '13	22 19·0	"
At " 19............	27	8	3	Oct. 24, '13	00·4	"
At " 18..	27	8	3	" 26, '13	21 58·0	"
At SE. " 2	23	9	3	Dec. 3, '13	57·8	G. A. Bennett.
27·50 S.-NE. cor. sec. 35..............	24	9	3	" 25, '13	52·1	C. E. Johnston.
27·50 S.- " 35...........	24	9	3	" 29, '13	55·3	"
At Sta. 6, Red Deer lake B. trav. sec. 7	28	9	3	Oct. 31, '13	22 14·0	"
At NE. cor. sec. 8....	28	9	3	Nov. 1, '13	18·3	"
At " 8..............	28	9	3	" 2, '13	19·2	'

DEPARTMENT OF THE INTERIOR

5 GEORGE V., A. 1915

RESULTS OF MAGNETIC OBSERVATIONS—*Continued.*

TABLE I.—DECLINATION OBSERVATIONS—*Continued.*

Place.	Township.	Range.	Meredian.	Date.	Declination.	Observer.
					° ′	
At N E. cor. sec. 8...............	28	9	3	" 4, '13	16·5	C..E. Johnston
40·00 W.-NE. cor. sec. 33...........	27	10	3	" 3, '13	21 59·5	"
At N E. " 31.........	27	10	3	" 8, '13	22·5	"
At " 31.........	27	10	3	" 10, '13	56·6	"
8·00 W.-NE. cor. sec. 31	27	10	3	" 12, '13	54·7	"
8·00 W.- " 31.............	27	10	3	" 16, '13	58·3	"
40·00 N.- " 2	28	10	3	" 2, '13	22 12·0	"
24·35 S.-1°50′ E.-NE. cor. sec. 23, Sta. 17, Red Deer lake F trav.	28	11	3	" 14, '13	21 26·3	"
At N E. cor. sec. 30....	26	12	3	May 26, '13	20 11·6	R. C. Purser.
At Sta. 3 trav. of Lake A, 13·00 E. 11 00 N.-NE. cor. sec. 34.......	31	12	3	Sept. 30, '13	21 46·5	E. P. Bowman.
11·50 S.-N.E. cor. sec. 33.............	54	12	3	Nov. 12, '13	24 45·0	P. R. A. Belanger.
24·00 S.- " 10.............	55	12	3	" 3, '13	28·3	"
At NE cor. sec. 7.............	56	12	3	Nov. 22, '13	25 30·8	P. R. A. Belanger.
40·00 S.- " 3	29	13	3	Sept. 29, '13	22 07·5	E. P. Bowman.
4·00 N.- " 5	30	13	3	" 27, '13	21 34·8	"
35·00 N.- " 9.............	31	13	3	Oct. 3, '13	22 41·5	"
At N E cor. sec. 16.............	34	13	3	" 31, '13	11·2	"
40·00 S.- " 21.............	35	13	3	Nov. 14, '13	27·6	"
22·50 N.- " 17	53	13	3	Aug. 28, '13	23 46·9	P. R. A. Belanger.
At ¼ sec. cor. N by sec. 24	54	13	3	Nov. 17, '13	25 08·1	"
At NE cor. sec. 10............ ...	56	13	3	" 23, '13	49·3	"
40·00 S.- " 18.............	31	14	3	Oct. 4, '13	23 40·9	E. P. Bowman.
At " 9.............	33	14	3	" 9, '13	17·5	"
At " 32.............	34	14	3	" 18, '13	22 46·0	"
At " 32.............	34	14	3	" 23, '13	26·8	"
10 00 S.- " 21............. ..	36	14	3	Nov. 19, '13	23 34·2	"
10·00 S.- " 21.............	36	14	3	" 21, '13	25·8	"
50·00 W.- " 32.............	23	15	3	Oct. 20, '13	21 48·0	G. A. Bennett.
20·00 S.- " 15...	30	15	3	Sept. 26, '13	22 49·6	E. P. Bowman.
3·00 S.- " 10.............	32	15	3	" 25, '13	23 43·3	"
3·00 S.- " 10.............	32	15	3	" 25, '13	44·5	"
3 00 S.- " 10.............	32	15	3	" 25, '13	45·6	"
40·00 S.- " 7.............	34	15	3	Oct. 16, '13	03·8	"
22·00 W.- " 34...	68	15	3	Apr. 8, '13	25 47·6	A. Saint Cyr.
22 00 W.- " 34.............	68	15	3	" 8, '13	47·7	"
19·00 N.- " 24.............	23	16	3	Oct. 18, '13	21 59·6	G. A. Bennett.
40·00 W.- " 10	31	16	3	Sept. 20, '13	23 34·7	E. P. Bowman.
25·00 W.- " 33.............	32	16	3	" 24, '13	22 40·8	"
11·00 N.- ¼ sec. cor. E by sec. 18	63	16	3	Aug. 17, '13	26 17·3	P. R. A. Belanger.
3·00 W.- NE cor. sec. 31.	68	16	3	Apr. 7, '13	24 56·7	A. Saint Cyr.
3·00 W.- " 31.............	68	16	3	" 7, '13	24 57·2	"
36·00 W.- " 33.............	68	17	3	Jan. 25, '13	24 51·8	"
4·00 W.- " 33.............	68	17	3	" 26, '13	25 01·4	"
4·00 W.- " 33.............	68	17	3	" 26, '13	24 55·3	"
69 00 W.- " 32	68	17	3	" 27, '13	25 13·4	"
35 40 W.- NE cor. sec. 20	18	18	3	May 21, '13	21 46·2	G. A. Bennett.
20·00 S.- " 4.............	28	18	3	Sept. 14, '13	23 13·2	E. P. Bowman.
40 00 S.- " 4.............	28	18	3	" 15, '13	02·8	"
25·00 W.- " 22.............	30	18	3	" 17, '13	12·5	"
20·00 S.- " 27.............	32	18	3	" 2, '13	22 18·6	"
At " 3.............	33	18	3	" 2, '13	32·2	"
18·00 S.- " 15.............	34	18	3	Aug. 31, '13.	55·9	"
At Sta. 4 traverse of Lake Eins, 7·61 W.-E. by sec. 33	35	18	3	June 18, '13	22 15·4	"
25·00 S.- NE cor. sec. 14...............	35	18	3	" 26, '13	23 49·4	"
At " 20.............	37	18	3	" 12, '13	24 25·9	"
At Sta. 38, traverse of Aroma Lake, 30·00 S.-N. by sec. 31........	38	18	3	June 6, '13	23 38·7	"
46·00 W.- NE cor. sec. 35............	68	18	3	Jan. 31, '13	25 04·9	A. Saint Cyr.
30·u0 W.- " 31.............	68	18	3	Feb. 5, '13	26 14·1	"
35·00 N.- " 29.............	28	19	3	Sept. 11, '13	22 29·6	E. P. Bowman.
At " 34......	29	19	3	" 12, '13	31·2	"

SESSIONAL PAPER No. 25b

RESULTS OF MAGNETIC OBSERVATIONS—*Continued.*

TABLE I.—DECLINATION OBSERVATIONS—*Continued.*

Place.	Township.	Range.	Meridan.	Date.	Declination.	Observer.
15·00 S.-NE. cor. sec. 5	29	19	3	Sept. 12, '13	30·1	E. P. Bowman.
20·00 N.- 16.......	32	19	3	" 3, '13	21 41·1	"
2·00 S.- 9.............	33	19	3	Aug. 27, '13	22 59·3	"
21·00 S.- 17.............	35	19	3	July 7, '13	53·8	"
At 23.......... .	36	19	3	June 17, '13	23 45·6	"
22·00 N.- 20....	39	19	3	July 16, '13	21 19·3	R. C. Purser.
17·81 W.- 22	39	19	3	" 18, '13	34·2	"
32·00 S.- 13............ ...	39	19	3	May 28, '13	23 19·5	E. P. Bowman.
40 00 S.- 22............ ..	40	19	3	Aug. 11, '13	21 59·1	"
15·00 S.- 18.............	41	19	3	Aug. 10, '13	23 51·4	"
57·00 W.- 36	68	19	3	Feb. 6, '13	27 26·0	A. Saint Cyr.
31·00 N.- 57° E.-NE cor. sec. 34.....	68	19	3	" 8, '13	15·8	"
31·00 N.- 34.............	68	19	3	" 9, '13	08·0	"
31·00 N.- 34..	68	19	3	" 9, '13	18·6	"
31.00 N.- 34.............	68	19	3	" 9, '13	13·6	"
9·00 N.-NE cor sec. 17..	30	20	3	Sept. 8, '13	21 05·1	E. P. Bowman.
At SE cor. sec. 6.............	31	20	3	Sept. 6, '13	21 10·6	"
At NE cor. sec. 17	34	20	3	Aug. 22, '13	22 57·0	"
At Sta. 37 traverse of Tramping lake, 18·00 S., 40·00W.-NE cor. sec. 21...	35	20	3	July 12, '13	53·8	"
At Sta. 54, traverse of Tramping lake, 26,00 S., 24·00W.-NE cor. sec. 17....	36	20	3	July 15, '13	33·6	"
40·00 N.-NE cor. sec. 30.............	36	20	3	Aug. 15, '13	38.8	"
At Sta. 157, traverse of Tramping lake, 27·00 E., 17·00S.-NE cor. sec. 30.....	36	20	3	Aug. 16, '13	47·1	"
5·00 E.- " ". 19....	37	20	3	July 20, '13	46·9	"
At Sta. 127, traverse of Tramping lake, 27·00S.-11·00W.-NE cor. sec. 30....	37	20	3	July 23, '13	50·1	"
At Sta. 99, traverse of Tramping lake, 24.00N.-17·00 W.-NE cor. sec. 8.....	38	20	3	July 19, '13	33·3	"
40·00 S.NE cor. sec 3.....	39	20	3	July 28, '13	23 36·5	"
33·00 S. " " " 16	40	20	3	July 31, '13	49·3	"
7·00 N. " " " 16.............	41	20	3	Aug. 1, '13	24 29·4	A. Saint Cyr.
45·00 W. " " " 32.............	68	20	3	April 5, '13	25 32·0	G. C. Cowper.
At " " " 12	15	21	3	Nov. 14, '13	22 29·0	E. P. Bowman.
1·00 W. " " " 24	31	21	3	Sept. 6, '13	03·3	"
10·00 S. " " " 27	33	21	3	Aug. 25, '13	50·7	"
3·00 S. " " " 27...........	35	21	3	Aug. 20, '13	35·1	"
9·00 N. " " " 16....	39	21	3	Aug. 13, '13	24 18·1	"
40·00 W. " " " 9.............	47	21	3	Nov. 27, '13	25 53·1	"
16·00 S. " " " 21............	62	21	3	July 19, '13	26 00 6	P. R. A. Belanger.
25·00 W. " " " 33	68	21	3	Feb. 25, '13	25 40 0	A. Saint Cyr.
16·00 W. " " " 35.............	68	21	3	Feb. 22, '13	05·7	"
32·00 S. " " " 21.............	12	22	3	Dec. 8, '13	21 55·1	G. C. Cowper.
At Sta. 73, traverse Crane lake, sec. 30	13	22	3	Nov. 7, '13	22 18·6	"
At NE cor. sec. 11....................	13	22	3	Dec. 1, '13	11·3	"
40·00 W. " " 33	16	22	3	Dec. 15, '13	05·5	"
At Sta. 7, traverse Lake No. 2, sec. 34	16	22	3	Dec. 17, '13	22 15·0	"
20·00 E.-NE. cor. sec. 36....	47	22	3	Nov. 29, '13	25 36·2	E. P. Bowman.
At Sta 3, traverse of lake in sec. 7, R. 21 28·33 S., 1·71E.-NE cor. sec. 12.......	47	22	3	Dec. 5, '13	43·4	"
40·00 S.-NE cor. sec. 21.............	47	22	3	Dec. 9, '13	24 47·6	"
20·00 S.-NE cor. sec. 19	61	22	3	July 3, '13	25 20·7	P. R. A. Belanger.
42·00 S.-¼ sec. cor. E. by sec. 15.	62	22	3	July 15, '13	35·1	"
40·00 W.-NE cor. sec. 34.............	68	22	3	Mar. 1, '13	26 56·3	A. Saint Cyr.
40·00 W.-NE cor. sec. 34.............	68	22	3	Mar. 2, '13·	26 57·9	"
33·50 W.-NE cor. sec. 31.............	68	22	3	Mar. 3, '13	41·7	"
33·50 W.-NE cor. sec. 31	68	22	3	Mar. 4, '13	45·0	"
33·50 W.-NE cor. sec. 31	68	22	3	Mar. '13	28·6	"
At Sta. 36, traverse Crane lake, sec. 5.	13	23	3	Nov. 1, '13	22 34.4	G. C. Cowper.
At. Sta. 31, traverse Crane lake, sec. 6.	13	23	3	Nov. 2, '13	39·9	"
At Sta. 4, traverse Lake 1, sec. 36.....	14	23	3	Nov. 26. '13	16·3	"
At NE cor. sec. 17	50	23	3	Aug. 10, '13	23 59·9	R. C. Purser.
At NE cor. sec. 11	61	23	3	July 9, '13	25 39·1	P. R. A. Belanger.

5 GEORGE V., A. 1915

RESULTS OF MAGNETIC OBSERVATIONS—*Continued.*

TABLE I.—DECLINATION OBSERVATIONS—*Continued.*

Place.	Township.	Range.	Meridian.	Date.	Declination.	Observer.
					° ′	
At NE cor. sec. 24...................	62	23	3	July 21, '13	44·5	P. R. A. Bélanger.
2·37W.-¼ sec. cor. S. by sec. 4.......	63	23	3	July 30, '13	46·1	"
2·00 W.-NE cor. sec. 36.............	68	23	3	Mar. 4, '13	26 35·5	A. Saint Cyr.
17·00 W.-NE cor. sec. 36............	68	23	3	Mar. 5, '13	37·9	"
40·00 W.-NE cor. sec. 35	68	23	3	Mar. 5, '13	58·2	"
At Sta. 5, traverse of Crane lake, sec. 22	13	24	3	Oct. 30. '13	22 20 0	G. C. Cowper.
At Sta. 27A traverse of Big Stick lake, sec. 20....................	15	24	3	Oct. 18, '13	47·1	"
At NE cor. sec. 12	40	24	3	Oct. 20, '13	23·39·3	R. C. Purser.
73·00 W.-NE cor. sec. 36..............	68	24	3	April 3, '13	25 50·4	A. Saint Cyr.
At NE. cor. sec. 8..	15	25	3	Oct. 17, '13	22 38·5	G. C. Cowper.
At NE cor. sec. 22..	34	25	3	Oct. 15, '13	23 11·1	R. C. Purser.
10 00 E.- " 22...............	34	25	3	" 16, '13	09·0	"
40·00 W.-. " 21.............	13	26	3	Sept. 26, '13	22 23·9	G. C. Cowper.
40·00 W.- " 21.............	13	26	3	" 28, '13	21 25·6	"
53·50 W.- " 34........	68	26	3	Mar. 16, '13	26 10·0	A. Saint Cyr.
53·50 W.- " 34.............	68	26	3	" 16, '13	16·8	"
53·50 W.- " 34.............	68	26	3	" 16, '13	09·3	"
26·00 W.- " 32.............	68	26	3	Mar. 25, '13	27·0	"
53 00 W.- " 34	68	26	3	" 26, '13	31·8	"
53·00 W.- " 34.............	68	26	3	" 26, '13	19·7	"
53·00 W.- " 34.............	68	26	3	" 26, '13	24·8	"
53 00 W.- " 34.............	68	26	3	" 27, '13	24·7	"
53 00 W.- " 34	68	26	3	" 27, '13	21·4	"
53·00 W.- " 34.............	68	26	3	" 27, '13	20 9	"
21·00 W.: " 31.............	68	26	3	April 5, '13	56·5	"
At ¼ cor. E. by sec 22..........	51	27	3	Oct. 10, '13	23 54·0	R. C. Purser.
At ¼ cor. S. by sec. 2	51	27	3	July 3, '13	41·2	"
50·27 E.-NE. cor. sec. 35	6	30	3	June 23, '13	22 34·1	A. M. Narraway.
50·46 S.- " 29...	6	30	3	" 24, '13	25·5	"
48·00 S.- " 33...	6	30	3	July 4, '13	04·2	"
At " 11.............	6	30	3	" 9, '13	18·8	"
At " 22.............	7	30	3	June 26, '13	21 17·3	"
57·69N. " 11.............	7	30	3	July, 2, '13	53·2	"
79·80 N.- " 15.............	7	30	3	" 7, '13	54·0	"
At " 22.............	29	30	3	Sept. 9, '13	22 31·9	E. P. Bowman.
At Sta. 7, Traverse lake, No. 2, sec. 34	16	1	4	" 11, '13	23 09·5	G. C. Cowper.
2·90 S. NE cor. sec. 36.............	68	1	4	Mar. 25, '13	27 20·6	A. Saint Cyr.
56 92 W.- " 33.............	84	1	4	" 18, '13	29 54·0	G. H. Blanchet.
27·07 W.- " · 31	96	1	4	Sept. 15, '13	30 07·3	J. B. McFarlane.
At " 5.............	1	2	4	June 24, '13	22 18·0	G. C. Cowper.
76·24 W.- " 32...	84	2	4	Mar. 25, '13	29 20·7	G. H. Blanchet.
40·00 W.- " 35.	96	2	4	Sept. 16, '13	36·1	J. B. McFarlane.
24·00 E.- " 35.............	5	3	4	" 24, '13	21 30·5	A. M. Narraway.
19·00 N.- " 32	5	3	4	Oct. 1, '13	29·3	"
34·00 E.- " 32	5	3	4	" 2, '13	36·1	"
8·00 N.- " 20.............	6	3	4	Sept. 27, '13	33·9	"
40·00 N.- " 22.............	6	3	4	Oct. 3, '13	20·9	"
At ¼ cor. E. by sec. 26... ...	8	3	4	June 15, '13	22 35·0	G. C. Cowper.
At NE cor. sec. 1.............	14	3	4	Sept. 14, '13	23 08·4	"
25·46 W.- " 33............. ..	84	3	4	Mar. 30, '13	27 25 9	G. H. Blanchet.
22·12 N.- " 34.............	5	4	4	Sept. 15, '13	21 43·0	A. M. Narraway.
15·00 E.- " 21....	6	4	4	" 8, '13	58·0	"
40·50 E.- " 20.............	6	4	4	Sept. 10, '13	22 10·5	"
15·00 E.- " 7..............	6	4	4	" 12, '13	09·0	"
At ¼ cor.·N. by sec. 7.........	9	4	4	June 3, '13	45·0	G. C. Cowper.
1·00 E.- NE cor. sec 33....	19	4	4	Aug. 26, '13	23 01·3	"
76·24 W.- " 36.............	84	4	4	April 3, '13	29 54·5	G. H. Blanchet.
72·00 W.- " 33...	84	4	4	" 9, '13	27·6	"
30·00 W.- " 32.............	5	5	4	July 18, '13	22 26·1	A. M. Narraway.
50·00 S.- " 26............. ...	6	5	4	" 14, '13	22·8	"
40·00 S.- " 2.............	6	5	4	" 15, '13	26·6	"
20·00 W.- " 22.............	6	5	4	" 16, '13	21·2	"

SESSIONAL PAPER No. 25b

RESULTS OF MAGNETIC OBSERVATIONS—*Continued.*

TABLE I.—DECLINATION OBSERVATIONS—*Continued.*

Place.	Township.	Range.	Meridian.	Date.	Declination.	Observer.
					° '	
10·00 N.-NE. cor. sec. 22	6	5	4	July 21, '13	33·0	A. M. Narraway.
76·60 N.- " 27	6	5	4	" 21, '13	28·3	"
At " 30.............	8	5	4	May 29, '13	39·0	G. C. Cowper.
10·00 S.- " 30.............	8	5	4	" 30, '13	47·0	"
At " 14.............	8	5	4	June 1, '13	42·0	"
8·00 W.-NE cor. sec. 23	17	5	4	Sept. 11, '13	23 04·9	G. A. Bennett.
40·00 S.- " 14	17	5	4	" 13, '13	22 56·4	"
40·67 W.- " 35.............	96	5	4	Oct. 18, '13	29 18·1	J. B. McFarlane.
21·17 W.- " 36.............	84	6	4	Apr. 19, '13	30 23·4	G. H. Blanchet.
64·39 W.- " 33..	92	6	4	June 7, '13	28 59·9	J. B. McFarlane.
2·82 W·- " 31.............	92	6	4	" 10, '13	17·7	"
70·00 W.- " 31.........	92	6	4	" 11, '13	10·0	"
40·00 N.-· " 5.............	5	7	4	July 7, '13	22 37·2	G. C. Cowper.
28·73 W.- " 32.............	84	7	4	May 1, '13	29 55·2	G. H. Blanchet.
6·79 W.- " 34.............	92	7	4	June 13, '13	27·5	J. B. McFarlane.
67·41 W.- " 31.............	92	7	4	" 19, '13	30 24·8	"
At " 36.............	96	7	4	Nov. 6, '13	29 04·9	"
20·00 W.- " 31.............	96	7	4	" 13, '13	30 43·7	"
5·00 N.-¼ cor. E. by sec. 36....	3	8	4	July 3, '13	22 19·7	G. C. Cowper.
5·00 N.- " 36........	3	8	4	" 5, '13	18·7	"
40·00 N.-NE. cor. sec. 7.............	5	8	4	" 17, '13	44·1	"
At ¼ cor. E. by sec. 31...	9	8	4	May 22, '13	54·2	"
" 31.............	9	8	4	" 24, '13	52·4	"
At NE. cor. sec. 13.............	21	8	4	Aug. 18, '13	23 43·3	"
" 13.............	21	8	4	" 19, '13	46·0	"
72·80 W.- " 34.............	84	8	4	May 8, '13	29 47·5	G. H. Blanchet.
10·00 W.- " 35.............	92	8	4	June 21, '13	31 10·2	J. B. McFarlane.
21·64 W.- " 32.............	92	8	4	" 30, '13	30 00·3	"
At " 31......... ..	92	8	4	July 2, '13	04·8	"
" 19.	2	9	4	Aug. 21, '13	22 27·2	A. M. Narraway.
20·00 N.- " 21...	2	9	4	" 25, '13	09·0	"
15·00 N.- " 15.............	2	9	4	" 26, '13	22 00·0	"
47·00 N.- " 27.............	2	9	4	" 27, '13	01·2	"
15·00 N.- " 11.............	2	9	4	Sept. 1, '13	21 59·3	"
9·61 E.- .। 31.............	18	9	4	Aug. 1, '13	22 55·4	G. A. Bennett.
50·00 W.-SE " 6.............	19	9	4	" 1, '13	52·3	"
21·00 N.- " 4.............	19	9	4	Oct. 23, '13	23 11·8	A. M. Narraway.
At Sta. 8, Sturgis lake, sec. 18..	50	9	4	" 25, '13	25 51·1	G. W. Coltham.
At Sta. 13, Lake No. 1, sec. 26..	52	9	4	Aug. 18, '13	26 32·1	"
55·08 W.-NE. cor. sec. 31.............	84	9	4	May 16, '13	29 43·5	G. H. Blanchet.
34·00 W.- " 35.............	84	9	4	" 13, '13	31 09·2	"
22·41 W.- " 32.............	92	9	4	July 9, '13	29 35·7	J. B. McFarlane.
60·00 W.- ।· 35.............	96	9	4	Nov. 26, '13	30 32·2	"
40·88 W.- " 31.............	96	9	4	Dec. 2, '13	09·4	"
At " 33.............	1	10	4	Aug. 16, '13	22 36·0	A. M. Narraway.
49·00 S.- " 8.............	2	10	4	" 11, '13	34·8	"
10·00 E.- " 23.............	2	10	4	" 13, '13	36·7	"
At " 7.............	2	10	4	" 15, '13	26·2	"
40·00 N.- " 5	18	10	4	Oct. 14, '13	23 34·9	"
40·00 E.- " 35.........	18	10	4	July 29, '13	22·8	G. A. Bennett.
At " 33.........	18	10	4	" 31, '13	19·8	"
7·00 W.-SE. " 2.............	19	10	4	Aug. 4, '13	22 59·3	"
47·00 W.- " 2.............	19	10	4	" 4, '13	23 11·3	"
49·00 W.- " 2.............	19	10	4	" 4, '13	05·9	"
49·00 W.- " · 2.............	19	10	4	" 4, '13	06·7	"
49·00 W.- " 2........_...	19	10	4	" 4, '13	08·5	"
60·40 W.-NE. 31	20	10	4	May 16, '13	05·9	A. M. Narraway.
41·50 N.- " 25.............	21	10	4	" 14, '13	10·4	"
28·00 E.- " 32.............	21	10	4	" 21, '13	19·8	"
1·00 N.- " 7.............	21	10	4	" 26, '13	24·2	"
40·15 N.-SE. " 20.............	21	10	4	" 28, '13	14·0	"
40·00 S.-NE. " 9..	49	10	4	Oct. 31, '13	25 39·1	G. W. Coltham.
12·00 E.- " 30.............	50	10	4	" 23, '13	26 07·5	"
At Sta. 5, Lake No. 2..·.......	51	10	4	Aug. 25, '13	13·1	"

5 GEORGE V., A. 1915

RESULTS OF MAGNETIC OBSERVATIONS—*Continued.*

TABLE I.—DECLINATION OBSERVATIONS—*Continued.*

Place.	Township.	Range.	Meridian.	Date.	Declination.	Observer.
65·42 W.-NE. cor. sec. 35.............	92	10	4	July 18, '13	29 25·4	J. B. McFarlane.
20·00 W.- " 31...........	96	10	4	Dec. 15, '13	28 30·4	"
At " 36.......... .	18	11	4	July 31, '13	23 44·3	G. A. Bennett.
At SE. " 1.............	19	11	4	" 13, '13	45·7	"
23·00 W.-NE cor. sec. 34.............	20	11	4	Nov. 8, '13	23 23.4	A. M. Narraway
62·36 N.- ' " 13	21	11	4	May 20, '13	22 15.5	"
38·00 N.- " 4	21	11	4	Nov. 3, '13	23 27.1	"
7·00 N.- " 4.............	21	11	4	" 3, '13	29.8	"
At " 11.............	21	11	4	" 7, '13	09.4	"
At Sta. 6, Lake Alice, sec. 9.........	49	11	4	" 1, '13	26 18.6	G. W. Coltham
50·00 S.-N.E. cor. sec. 5.............	50	11	4	Sept. 30, '13	14.8	"
At Sta. 225, Birch lake, sec. 34.......	50	11	4	Oct. 13, '13	25 59.2	"
At Sta. 8, Lake 3, sec. 19............	51	11	4	Aug. 27, '13	26 15.8	"
At Sta. 4, Lake 6, sec. 19...........	52	11	4	July 22, '13	22.5	"
10·00 N.-NE cor. sec. 11.............	52	11	4	Aug. 1, '13	20.8	"
15·00 W.- " 34............	84	11	4	May 26, '13	30 00.8	G. H. Blanchet
15·00 " 34....	84	11	4	" 26, '13	29 41.5	"
38·60 W.- " 34	92	11	4	Aug. 1, '13	39.7	J. B. McFarlane
60·00 W.- " 32............	96	11	4	Dec. 29, '13	46.0	"
4·00 S.- " 10.............	21	12	4	Nov. 14, '13	23 18.4	A. M. Narraway
20·00 E.- " 33.............	21	12	4	" 21, '13	18.2	"
At Sta. 18, Lake Thomas.....	47	12	4	" 12, '13	26 02.7	G. W. Coltham
17·00 N.-NE cor. sec. 8.............	48	12	4	" 17, '13	10.5	"
At Sta. A, Lake No. 2.............	48	12	4	" 17, '13	14.7	"
50·00 N.-NE cor. sec. 36.............	49	12	4	Sept. 29, '13	11.8	"
At Sta. 2, Lake No. 1	49	12	4	Nov. 7, '13	15.9	"
64·00 S.-NE cor. sec. 17.............	50	12	4	Sept. 23, '13	07.3	"
10·00 S.- " 17.............	50	12	4	" 24, '13	10.8	"
At Sta. 77, Birch lake....	50	12	4	" 27, '13	07.5	"
At Station 3, Lake V..	51	12	4	" 15, '13	16.8	"
5·00 N.-NE cor. sec. 18	52	12	4	June 11, '13	21.3	"
At Sta. 2, Lake A, sec. 11.........	52	12	4	July 5, '13	24.4	"
At Sta. 9, Lake S, Sec. 11............	52	12	4	" 17, '13	20.5	"
18·20 W.-NE cor. sec. 31...	84	12	4	June 5, '13	29 43.1	G. H. Blanchet
At Sta. 4, Traverse. Indian lake, sec. 9	55	13	4	July 22, '13	22 38.2	G. C. Cowper
At Sta. 3, Lake A, Sec. 13............	51	13	4	Sept. 18, '13	26 13.3	G. W. Coltham
14·00 S.-NE cor. sec. 16.............	52	13	4	May 31, '13	06.1	"
45·20 W.-, 60·00 N.-NE cor. sec. 9.....	52	13	4	June 5, '13	03.0	"
At SE cor. sec. 2.............	3	14	4	July 30, '13	22 48.0	A. M. Narraway
9·00 W.-SE cor. sec. 5	3	15	4	Aug. 1, '13	23 09.2	"
5·00 F.- " 4	3	15	4	" 5, '13	22 03.5	"
3·84 N.- " 3.............	3	15	4	" 5, '13	03.5	J. B. Saint Cyr
At NE " 9.............	32	15	4	Oct. 15, '13	24 40.7	"
0·50 N.- " 10.............	9	16	4	" 15, '13	23 15.0	G. A. Bennett
" " 10.............	9	16	4	" 15, '13	12.8	"
At ¼ cor. E. by sec. 9............	34	16	4	" 22, '13	24 44.6	J. B. Saint Cyr
" " 16............	34	17	4	" 14, '13	27.3	"
At NE cor. sec. 34.............'..	35	17	4	" 11, '13	28.6	"
At ¼ cor. E. by sec. 23	37	17	4	" 3, '13	52.8	"
At NE cor. sec. 22.............	38	17	4	Nov. 8, '13	57.2	"
60·00 S.- " 25.............	38	17	4	" 10, '13	25 01.9	"
At ¼ cor. E. by sec. 1............	34	18	4	Sept. 24, '13	24 40.4	"
At NE cor. sec. 9.............	35	18	4	" 19, '13	30.4	"
At ¼ cor. N. by sec. 35.............	35	18	4	" 23, '13	47.6	"
At NE cor. sec. 14.............	36	18	4	" 29, '13	55.0	"
At " 8..........	37	18	4	Nov. 5, '13	55.6	"
At ¼ cor. E. by sec. 32.............	37	18	4	" 6, '13	25 18.3	"
20·00 S.-NE cor. sec. 19.............	37	18	4	" 7, '13	07.0	"
At ¼ cor. E. by sec. 17.....	36	19	4	Oct. 25, '13	24 52.5	"
At " " 30.............	36	19	4	" 30, '13	25 19.1	"
At NE cor. sec. 27	36	19	4	" 31, '13	15.6	"
At " 4.............	37	19	4	Nov. 1, '13	03.9	"
At " 5.............	37	19	4	" 3, '13	24 42.5	"
" 5.............	37	19	4	" 4, '13	25 09.1	"

SESSIONAL PAPER No. 25b

RESULTS OF MAGNETIC OBSERVATIONS—*Continued.*

TABLE I.—DECLINATION OBSERVATIONS—*Continued.*

Place.	Township.	Range.	Meridian.	Date.	Declination.	Observer.
					° ′	
At NE. cor. sec. 11.	38	19	4	Nov. 13, '13	08.5	J. B. Saint Cyr.
41·00 S.- " 10	38	19	4	" 13, '13	10.5	"
60·00 N.- " 22.............	73	19	4	" 2, '13	29 06.2	C. F. Miles
60·00 " 22	73	19	4	" 2, '13	28 57.5	"
10·00 N.-NE cor. sec. 15...	73	19	4	Oct. 19, '13	28 54·8	C. F. Miles.
20·00 S.- " " 28.............	31	20	4	Sept. 13, '13	25 04·6	J. B. Saint Cyr.
At ¼ sec. cor. W. by sec. 7.........	37	20	4	Nov. 18, '13	24 40·4	"
At NE cor. sec. 8....... ...•....	37	20	4	" 18, '13	25 05·3	"
At ¼ sec. cor. E. by sec. 22.........	38	20	4	" 15, '13	24 55·0	"
At NE cor. sec. 21...	38	20	4	" 22, '13	53·5	"
10·00 W.-NE cor. sec. 34.....	38	20	4	" 26, '13	44·7	"
78·10 " " 33.............	84	20	4	Dec. 23, '13	30 08·3	G. H. Blanchet.
6·00 E.-¼ sec. cor. N. by sec. 22... .	34	21	4	Oct. 25, '13	24 21·6	R. C. Purser.
20·00 S.-17·00 W. ¼ sec. cor. N. by sec.22	34	21	4	" 25, '13	38·5	"
At ¼ sec. cor. W. by sec. 26..........	38	21	4	Nov. 25, '13	25 03·7	J. B. Saint Cyr.
At NE cor. sec. 34	38	21	4	" 28, '13	06·5	"
At " " 27	35	22	4	Aug. 28, '13	24 58·5	"
At ¼ sec. cor. E. by sec. 8	35	22	4	" 30, '13	48·2	"
At NE cor. sec. 33..................	36	22	4	Sept. 6, '13	25 24·4	"
At ¼ sec. cor. E. by sec. 28.......	36	22	4	" 12, '13	33·1	"
At " " 19	56	22	4	" 8, '13	51·7	"
At NE cor. sec. 13.....	39	22	4	Dec. 19, '13	31·8	"
At " " 31...................	39	22	4	." 20, '13	23·5	"
At " " 19...................	35	23	4	Aug. 23, '13	18·1	"
At " " 10...................	36	23	4	Sept. 5, '13	13·1	"
At " " 21...................	37	23	4	Dec. 2, '13	23·7	"
5·00 N.-NE. cor. sec. 2............	37	23	4	" 5, '13	10·9	"
At NE cor. sec. 16....	39	23	4	" 2, '13	31·4	"
40·00 E.-NE cor. sec. 20.............	35	24	4	Aug. 11, '13	10·6	"
At NE cor. sec. 15..................	35	24	4	" 13, '13	14·6	"
At " " 17	35	24	4	" 16, '13	18·9	"
At ¼ sec. cor. E. by sec. 23............	37	24	4	Dec. 8, '13	19·0	"
At NE cor. sec. 9...	37	24	4	" 9, '13	23·7	"
12 09 E.-NE cor. sec. 35............	1	25	4	Oct. 8, '13	23 36·4	G. A. Bennett.
At Sta. 6, traverse of St. Mary's river, 27 00 E., 42·00 N. SE cor. sec. 2	2	25	4	" 11, '13	23 35·4	J. B. Saint Cyr.
At ¼ sec. cor. E. by sec. 9............	35	25	4	Aug. 7, '13	25 09·2	"
At SE cor. sec. 9	37	25	4	Dec. 13, '13	32·3	"
At NE " 21...............	37	25	4	" 11, '13	24·0	"
At " " 32....................	41	25	4	June 24, '13	26 05·6	"
At SW " 3	35	26	4	Aug. 3, '13	25 12·9	"
At NE " 11....................	36	26	4	July 31, '13	50·4	" .
39·00 S.-NE cor. sec. 31..............	40	26	4	June 29, '13	59·6	"
40·00 " " 28.	34	27	4	Aug. 4, '13	30·8	"
20·00 " " 15...............	36	27	4	July 29, '13	08·6	"
At NE cor. sec. 29...................	39	27	4	" 5, '13	58·2	"
At " " 32...................	59	27	4	" 6, '13	57·9	"
40·00 S.-NE cor. sec. 34	39	27	4	" 9, '13	26 14·3	"
39·00 E. " " 23....	39	27	4	" 11, '13	25 48·9	"
8·00 N.-¼ sec. cor. N. by sec. 23.....	39	27	4	" 14, '13	52·4	"
24·00 " E. " 6.....	39	27	4	" 18, '13	39·8	"
43·00 W.-NE cor. sec. 29............	1	28	4	Aug. 15, '13	23 58·0	G. A. Bennett.
19·00 N.- " " 33....	36	28	4	July 23, '13	25 27·5	J. B. Saint Cyr.
At NE cor, sec. 22..	36	28	4	" 21, '13	27·4	"
At NE cor. sec. 8.	36	28	4	" 28, '13	26 35·3	"
40·00 W.-E. by sec. 22 on lake shore...	40	28	4	May 23, '13	27 20·4	"
55·20 S.-NE cor. sec. 28..............	41	28	4	" 21, '13	24 55·8	"
17·00 N - " " 22..........	42	28	4	June 22, '13	25 26·5	"
13 00 W.- " " 26	1	29	4	Aug. 13, '13	24 06·3	G. A. Bennett.
40·00 N.- " " 1........... ..	2	29	4	" 10, '13	23 51·4	"

5 GEORGE V., A. 1915

RESULTS OF MAGNETIC OBSERVATIONS—*Continued.*

TABLE I.—DECLINATION OBSERVATIONS—*Continued.*

Place.	Township.	Range.	Meridian.	Date.	Declination.	Observer.
					° ′	
Base Line between lots 39 and 40......	a	a	4	Nov. 2, '11	26 11·1	H. S. Day.
" " "	a	a	4	" 20, '11	25 40·1	"
" " "	a	a	4	" 20, '11	40·5	"
38·00 E. Base Line where it crosses N. by lot 8..............................	b	b	4	June 19, '11	28 59·6	"
At intersection of Base Line with N. by lot 8.......	b	b	4	" 24, '11	01·5	"
At intersection of Base Line with N. by lot 14 ....:	b	b	4	July 5, '11	29 03·6	"
At Station 1, Trav. N. of N. by lot 7, 60·00 W. of Base Line..............	c	c	4	" 25, '11	31 18·2	"
" . " " ..	c	c	4	Aug. 8, '11	19 8	"
Base Line between lots 18 and 19......	c	c	4	. " 12, '11	25·3	"
" " 35 and 36	d	d	4	" 28, '11	29 52·5	"
20·00 W. Base Line on N. by. of settlement......................	d	d	4	Sept. 13, '11	45·9	"
At NE cor. lot 5..	e	e	4	" 29, '11	30 53·0	"
At NW cor, lot 5.	e	e	4	Oct. 4, '11	49·7	"
At T.H. 17, NW trav. Slave river.....	f	f	4	Aug. 22, '12	33 17·4	E. A. Neville.
At Alberta—NWT by Monument, W. side Slave river..................	f	f	4	" 27, '12	21·7	"
4·00 NW.-SW cor. lot 1	f	f	4	" 31, '12	13·1	"
At I.P. 24, 25, 26.	f	f	4	Sept. 5, '12	09·0	"
At SW cor. lot 49	f	f	4	" 6, '12	02·7	"
25·00 N.-NW cor. lot 66.............	f	f	4	" 9, '12	32 26·7	"
40·00 N.-SW " 60.............	f	f	4	" 10, '12	50·6	"
At T.H. Slave river...	f	f	4	" 11, '12	33 20·9	"
At I.P. 62·63 on Base Line............	f	f	4	" 7, '12	32 39·1	"
At NE cor. lot 25....................	g	g	4	July 9, '12	33 36·3	"
At NW " 22	g	g	4	" 10, '12	12·1	"
At SW " 62.....	g	g	4	" 24, '12	19·3	"
At NW " 39....	g	g	4	Aug. 4, '12	09·7	"
12·00 E.-NE cor. sec. 35	40	1	5	May 24, '13	26 14·6	J. B. Saint Cyr.
10·00 N.- " 21.............	41	1	5	" 31, '13	58·1	"
33·28 N.- " 21	42	1	5	June 6, '13	25 31·5	"
25·00 S.- " 27..............	42	1	5	" 11, '13	26 41·0	"
At ¼ cor. E. by. sec. 32.....	10	3	5	Aug. 7, '13	22 53·3	M. P. Bridgland.
At NE. cor. sec. 13................ ..	10	3	5	" 22, '13	24 07·6	"
At " 13......	10	3	5	" 22, '13	06·2	"
At " 12..............	10	3	5	" 22, '13	01·2	"
At " 6................	11	3	5	July 4, '13	26 06·5	"
At ¼ cor. E. by. sec. 7.	11	3	5	" 4, '13	24 14·1	"
At SE cor. sec. 6	11	3	5	" 5, '13	22 57·4	"
At ¼ cor. E. by. sec. 6	11	3	5	" 5, '13	23 46·3	"
At NE cor. sec. 7................	11	3	5	" 5, '13	07·2	"
At " 19	11	3	5	" 5, '13	45·9	"
At ¼ cor. E. by. sec. 19................	11	3	5	" 5, '13	11·3	"
At " " 18......	11	3	5	" 5, '13	21 48·1	"
10·00 S.-NE cor. sec. 7................	17	3	5	June 7, '13	25 14·8	S. L. Evans.
60·00 N.- " 8................	17	3	5	" 8, '13	13·5	"
0·50 N.- " 9................	17	3	5	" 8, '13	08·2	"
At NE cor. sec. 24..................	8	4	5	Aug. 27, '13	24 02·4	M. P. Bridgland.
At ¼ cor. N. by. sec. 34...............	9	4	5	" 10, '13	03·8	"
At " 34	9	4	5	" 14, '13	06·5	"
At " " 34	9	4	5	" . 14, '13	09·2	"
At NE cor. sec. 33.	9	4	5	" 10, '13	23 58·6	"
At " 33..........	9	4	5	" 10, '13	59·5	"
At " 34...........	9	4	5	" 14, '13	24 03·1	"
At " . 23..	9	4	5	" 23, '13	07·4	"
At " 23.................	9	4	5	" 24, '13	02·2	"

a Chipewyan Settlement.   *b* Pelican Settlement.   *c* Grand Rapids Settlement.   *d* McMurray Settlement.   *e* McKay Settlement.   *f* Fort Smith Settlement.   *g* Smith Landing Settlement.

SESSIONAL PAPER No. 25b

RESULTS OF MAGNETIC OBSERVATIONS—*Continued.*

TABLE I.—DECLINATION OBSERVATIONS—*Continued.*

Place.	Township.	Range.	Meridan.	Date.	Declination.	Observer.
					° ′	
At NE. cor. sec. 23	9	4	5	Aug. 24, '13	04·2	M. P. Bridgland.
At ˅ 35	9	4	5	" 24, '13	03 56·2	"
At ¼ cor. N. by. sec. 36	9	4	5	" 23, '13	47·4	"
41 00 S.-NE cor. sec. 25	10	4	5	Aug. 7, '13	23 03·4	"
At " 24	10	4	5	" 7, '13	03·9	"
0·50 S.- " 32	16	4	5	July 17, '13	25 00·7	S. L. Evans.
8·00 S.- " 33	16	4	5	" 17, '13	01·5	"
20·00 N.- " 10	17	4	5	" 5, '13	09·7	"
0·50 N.- " 9	17	4	5	" 8, '13	64·2	"
42·00 N.- " 27	17	4	5	" 16, '13	08·5	"
0.50 N.- " 28	17	4	5	" 16, '13	06·5	"
0·50 S.- " 31	17	4	5	" 17, '13	04·3	"
0·50 N.- " 9	18	4	5	" 27, '13	02·4	"
60·00 N.- " 8	18	4	5	Aug. 3, '13	02·1	"
8·00 W.- " 35	18	4	5	" 22, '13	23 33·8	"
38 00 W.- " 35	18	4	5	" 23, '13	24 59·8	"
0·50 W.- " 22	18	4	5	" 26, '13	25 06·5	"
0·50 S.- " 35	19	4	5	Sept. 1, '13	18·5	"
4·50 S.- " 27	19	4	5	" 16, '13	01·3	"
32·00 W.- " 30	19	4	5	" 26, '13	09·6	G. A. Bennett.
At NE cor. L.S. III, sec. 31	19	4	5	" 27, '13	08·5	"
17 00 S.-NE cor. sec. 30	20	4	5	" 26, '13	04·9	S. L. Evans.
At " 2	12	5	5	July 14, '13	23 46·5	M. P. Bridgland.
At ¼ cor. sec. E. by sec 13	12	5	5	" 15, '13	45·0	"
71·00 S. NE cor. sec. 18	23	5	5	Oct. 12, '13	24 56·2	S. L. Evans.
1.00 N.- " 5	23	5	5	" 20, '13	25 00·0	"
31·50 E.- " 31	104	10	5	Sept. 22, '13	30 50·1	J. R. Akins.
41·13 E.- " 31	104	11	5	" 16, '13	13·3	"
45.50 E.- " 32	104	11	5	" 17, '13	16·8	"
5·00 W.- " 34	104	11	5	" 18, '13	00·6	"
76.38 E.- " 36	104	12	5	" 15, '13	29 56·1	"
18·70 E.- " 34	104	12	5	" 12, '13	31 21·7	"
3·00 E.- " 31	104	13	5	Aug. 30, '13	33 32·0	"
48·87 E.- " 36	104	13	5	Sept. 8, '13	35·5	"
72·79 E.- " 36	104	14	5	Aug. 23, '13	34 27·1	"
22·00 E.- " 32	104	14	5	" 26, '13	33 34·0	"
6·00 E.- " 35	104	14	5	" 28, '13	16·2	"
27·36 E.- " 32	104	16	5	" 12, '13	25 10·9	"
39·00 E.- " 33	104	16	5	" 13, '13	34 53·0	"
2·00 E.· " 35	104	16	5	" 15, '13	53·4	"
67·00 E.- " 35	104	16	5	" 16, '13	35·1	"
23·25 E.- " 36	104	16	5	" 18, '13	40·6	"
20·00 S.- " 20	23	17	5	" 13, '13	25 56·0	N. C. Stewart.
27·00 N.-SE cor. sec. 28	23	17	5	" 16, '13	55·5	"
37·00 N.- " 34	23	17	5	" 20, '13	26 07·2	"
43·70 E.-SW " 2	24	17	5	" 22, '13	04·4	"
At SE " 2	24	17	5	" 23, '13	25 56·7	"
65·00 N.- " 2	24	17	5	" 25, '13	26 07·9	"
5·00 N.·· " 12	24	17	5	" 27, '13	25 58·3	"
70·00 N.- " 12	24	17	5	" 28, '13	57·1	"
16·50 E.-NE " 31	104	17	5	" 4, '13	33 48·8	J. R. Akins.
50·00 E.- " 11	23	18	5	July 21, '13	26 15·8	N. C. Stewart.
20·00 N.-SE " 13	23	18	5	" 23, '13	25 57·3	"
46·00 N.- " 13	23	18	5	" 24, '13	56·9	"
15·00 E.-NE " 13	23	18	5	" 31, '13	56 7	"
60·00 E.- " 13	23	18	5	Aug. 1, '13	50·1	"
38·10 N.- " 25	90	18	5	Apr. 23, '13	31 41·7	J. A. Fletcher.
7·25 E.- " 31	92	18	5	May 1, '13	13·6	J. R. Akins.
10·00 W.- " 35	92	18	5	" 2, '13	12·6	"
42·10 E.-·· " 35	92	18	5	" 5, '13	30·2	"
68·33 E.- " 33	92	18	5	" 13, '13	30 40·0	"
80·25 W.- " 36	96	18	5	June 5, '13	31 15·2	"
75·50 W.- " 35	96	18	5	" 6, '13	32 27·0	"
32·00 N.- " 12	96	18	5	May 31, '13	31 24·7	J. A. Fletcher.

5 GEORGE V., A. 1915

RESULTS OF MAGNETIC OBSERVATIONS—*Continued.*

TABLE I.—DECLINATION OBSERVATIONS—*Continued.*

Place.	Township.	Range.	Meridian.	Date.	Declination.	Observer.
					° ′	
26·00 N.-NE. cor. sec. 36	96	18	5	June 4, '13	30 58·1	J. A. Fletcher.
54·47 N.- " 1	97	18	5	" 5, '13	31 38·2	"
2·00 N.- " 13	99	18	5	" 19, '13	32 37·6	"
31·36 N.- " 36	99	18	5	" 24, '13	25·0	"
4·50 S.-NE cor. sec. 25	100	18	5	June 30, '13	32 40·6	"
80·00 W.- " 36	100	18	5	July 4, '13	54·5	J. R. Akins.
10·83 W.- " 34	100	18	5	" 5, '13	57·0	"
43·00 N.- " 24	101	18	5	" 12, '13	33 02·3	J. A. Fletcher.
8·80 N.- " 25	103	18	5	" 18, '13	34 41·6	"
8·00 S.- " 1	104	18	5	" 18, '13	52·6	"
46·20 W.- " 36	104	18	5	" 25, '13	33 40·5	J. R. Akins.
21·75 W.- " 34	104	18	5	" 27, '13	22·9	"
61·00 S.- " 25	107	18	5	Aug. 28. '13	34 50·1	J. A. Fletcher.
50·00 S.- " 36	108	18	5	" 13, '13	33 44·9	"
41·00 S.- " 25	108	18	5	" 15, '13	55·7	"
42·14 W.- " 34	108	18	5	" 25, '13	32 59·8	"
15·00 E.- W " 31	46	19	5	Dec. 18, '12	28 12·6	A. L. McNaughton.
2·12 E.-NE " 31	92	19	5	Apr. 28, '13	32 11·2	J. R. Akins.
4·00 W.- " 36	96	19	5	June 10, '13	33·9	"
14·32 W.- " 32	96	19	5	" 13, '13	24·3	"
1·25 W.- " 33	100	19	5	July 8, '13	33 13·6	"
19·20 W.- " 32	100	19	5	" 9, '13	32 49·9	"
20·82 W.- " 36	100	19	5	" 10, '13	48·3	"
63·42 W.- " 35	100	19	5	" 11, '13	30·6	"
12·99 W.- " 35	104	19	5	Sept. 8, '13	33 54·7	J. A. Fletcher.
73·90 E.- " 32	92	20	5	Apr. 24, '13	12·8	J. R. Akins.
62·83 W.- " 35	96	20	5	June 17, '13	32 57·7	"
38·88 W.- " 36	96	20	5	" 18, '13	39·1	"
50·13 W.- " 33	96	20	5	" 19, '13	51·2	"
3·91 W.- " 34	100	20	5	July 17, '13	18·3	"
59·50 W.- " 32	100	20	5	" 19, '13	49·5	"
46·82 W.- " 32	104	20	5	Sept. 17, '13	33 55·8	J. A. Fletcher.
53·83 N.- " 10	84	21	5	Dec. 18, '13	31 28·6	L. E. Fontaine.
60·00 E.- " 31	92	21	5	Apr. 17, '13	32 30·6	J. R. Akins.
45·65 E.- " 36	92	21	5	" 21, '13	33 27·1	"
50·00 W.- " 33	96	21	5	June 22, '13	32 18·5	"
57·35 W.- " 31	104	21	5	Sept. 22, '13	34 04·5	J. A. Fletcher.
10·00 E.-NE " 19	47	22	5	" 5, '12	27 58·3	A. L. McNaughton.
60·00 N.- " 20	47	22	5	" 7, '12	53·6	"
15·00 N.- " 19	47	22	5	" 9, '12	53·7	"
15·00 N.- " 29	47	22	5	" 7, '12	56·1	"
50·00 S.- " 19	47	22	5	" 20, '12	58·0	"
60·00 S.- " 18	47	22	5	" 27, '12	28 00·5	"
5·00 W.- " 33	47	22	5	Nov. 8, '12	27 55·6	"
32·00 S.- " 15	48	22	5	July 11, '12	28 01·4	"
10·00 S.- " 11	48	22	5	" 17, '12	01·0	"
0·93 S.- " 13	83	22	5	Dec. 11, '13	31 32·3	L. E. Fontaine.
3·00 S.- " 13	89	22	5	Mar. 27, '13	57·8	J. R. Akins.
35·77 N.- " 36	89	22	5	" 31, '13	57·5	"
30·00 S.- " 12	90	22	5	Apr. 2, '13	45·6	"
24·40 N.- " 25	90	22	5	" 5, '13	27·6	"
73·72 W.- " 36	90	22	5	" 7, '13	40·1	"
70·80 N.-SE " 1	91	22	5	" 8, '13	55·3	"
" " 1	91	22	5	" 9, '13	41·6	"
56·80 N.-NE " 25	91	22	5	" 14, '13	44·9	"
23·51 N.- " 1	92	22	5	" 15, '13	50·6	"
5·00 E.- " 24	47	23	5	Sept. 5, '12	28 04·1	A. L. McNaughton.
60·00 E.- " 24	47	23	5	" 5, '12	27 55·1	"
10·00 N.-SE " 19	47	23	5	Oct. 2, '12	28 07·8	"
13·00 S.-NE " 8	47	23	5	" 23, '12	08·1	"
6·00 N.-SE " 6	47	23	5	" 28, '12	27 57·1	"
35·00 N.- " 4	47	23	5	" 29, '12	28 02·0	"
10·00 S.-NE " 24	48	23	5	Aug. 20, '12	27 58·3	"
28·58 S.- " 20	85	23	5	Nov. 21, '13	31 28·8	L. E. Fontaine.

SESSIONAL PAPER No. 25b

RESULTS OF MAGNETIC OBSERVATIONS—*Continued.*

TABLE I.—DECLINATION OBSERVATIONS—*Continued.*

Place.	Township.	Range.	Meridian.	Date.	Declination.	Observer.
12·32 S.-NE. cor. sec. 31.............	86	23	5	Nov. 23, '13	27·8	L. E. Fontaine.
37·00 S.- " 25	46	24	5	" 2, '13	27 57·2	A. L. McNaughton.
15·09 N.- " 24............	86	24	5	" 26, '13	31 21·2	L. E. Fontaine.
21·75 S.- " 20..	87	24	5	Dec. 3, '13	42·6	"
26·43 N.- " 23..........·,....	86	25	5	Nov. 29, '13	22·8	"
7·00 E.- " 22	50	27	5	July 17, '12	27 47·2	C. A. Grassie.
21·40 N.- " 23............	50	27	5	" 18, '12	50·8	"
7·37 N.-NE cor. sec. 26............	50	27	5	July 19, '12	27°53·6	"
52·00 N.- " . 22............	50	27	5	" 28, '12	53·0	"
15·30 N.- " 27............	50	27	5	" 31, '12	47·9	"
31·50 N.- " 34...........	48	28	5	Aug. 2, '12	29·0	"
39·80 N.- " 3............	49	28	5	" 3, '12	27·9	"
30·00 E.- " 33	47	1	6	Sept. 6, '12	30·3	"
39·50 N.- " 6............	47	1	6	" 20, '12	23·6	"
10·00 N.-SE " 6	47	1	6	" 21, '12	26·2	"
31·62 E.-NE " 23............	48	1	6	Aug. 30, '12	24·4	"
45·00 N.- " 3........	48	1	6	Sept. 5, ,12	30·7	"
2·00 W.- " 24............	49	1	6	Aug. 22, '12	37·0	"
70·00 W.- " 17............	23	22	6	Sept. 5, '13	25 49·3	N. C. Stewart.
19·00 S.- " 18............	23	2	6	" 6, '13	43·1	"
62·00 S.- " 18............	23	2	6	" 8, '13	27·3	"
5·00 S.- " 7............	23	2	6	" 10, '13	30·5	"
35·00 S.- " 7............	23	2	6	" 10, '13	39.7	"
26·00 E.- " 6............	23	2	6	" 15, '13	53·5	"
44·00 E.- " 6............	23	2	6	" 16, '13	29·6	"
79·00 E.- " 7.·..........	23	2	6	" 19, '13	00·2	"
26·00 W.- " 15............	23	3	6	" 30, '13	26 08·2	"
16·00 W. centre sec. 23............	23	3	6	Oct. 4, '13	12·0	"
At NE cor. sec. 7............	23	3	6	" 9, '13	01·0	"
47·00 S.- " 7............	23	3	6	" 14, '13	25 31·3	"
23·00 W.- " 6............	23	3	6	" 15, '13	44·2	"
At " 6............	45	3	6	" 9, '12	27 30·9	C. A. Grassie.
64·07 N.- " 9............	45	3	6	" 12, '12	26·3	"
3·85 E.- " 9............	45	3	6	" 14, '12	29·7	"
42·10 E.- " 7..·..·....	45	3	6	" 22, '12	31·8	"
At " 7............	45	3	6	" 23, '12	39·1	"
47·00 W.- " 1............	23	4	6	" 18, '13	26 00·4	N. C. Stewart.
16·00 W.- " 2............	23	4	6	" 20, '13	25 28·0	"
4·00 W.- " 3............	23	4	6	" 23, '13	53·8	"
53·00 S.- " 17............	23	4	6	" 25, '13	41·4	"
43·00 N.- " 17............	23	4	6	" 29, '13	25 43·3	"
9·00 W.- " 17............	23	4	6	" 28, '13	46·3	"
73·00 W.- " 17............	23	4	6	" 29, '13	43·2	"
40·00 W.- " 20............	23	4	6	" 30, '13	37·0	"
43·00 W.- " 18............	23	4	6	" 30, '13	39·9	"
32·00 W.- " 19..	23	4	6	" 31·'13	34·6	"
18·27 N.- " 19............	70	4	6	" 7, '13	28 24·8	L. E. Fontaine.
30·00 S.- " 24............	23	5	6	" 31, '13	25 31·6	N. C. Stewart.
63·00 W.- " 24............	23	5	6	Nov. 3, '13	40·5	"
53·00 S.- " 23............	23	5	6	" 8, '13	39·3	"
3·00 W.- " 29............	23	5	6	" 11, '13	55·1	"
50·00 W.- " 29............	23	5	6	" 12, '13	26 04·0	"
11·00 W.- " 30............	23	5	6	" 13, '13	00·0	"
34·60 S.- " 15	70	5	6	Oct. 2, '13	28 54·4	L. E. Fontaine.
24·63 N.- " 11	85	5	8	Nov. 1. '13	29 45·5	"
20·00 W.- " 23............	23	6	6	" 17, '13	25 47·9	N. C. Stewart.
5·00 N.- " 24............	70	6	6	Sept. 29, '13	29 12·1	L. E. Fontaine.
67·35 E.-SE " 4............	79	6	6	Aug. 28, '13	30 25·4	"
25·70 S.-NE " 36............	85	6	6	Nov. 5, '13	12·7	"
0·83 N.- " 36............	79	7	6	July 29, '13	32 15·8	"
16·90 S.- " 36............	80	7	6	" 18, '13	31 13·8	"
15·68 N.- " 36............	85	7	6	Nov. 6, '13	30 47·9	"
57·49 S.- " 10............	87	7	6	" 12, '13	38·0	"
77·00 N.-SE " 12... ....|	18	8	6	" 26, '13	25 36·8	N. C. Stewart.

5 GEORGE V., A. 1915

RESULTS OF MAGNETIC OBSERVATIONS—*Continued.*

TABLE I.—DECLINATION OBSERVATIONS—*Continued.*

Place.	Township.	Range.	Meridian.	Date.	Declination.	Observer.
					° '	
36.56 N.-NE. cor. sec. 21..	86	8	6	Nov. 9, '13	31 18·0	L. E. Fontaine.
23·00 W.- " 25	19	9	6	May 16, '13	26 29·2	N. C. Stewart.
60·00 N.- " 35........	19	9	6	" 19, '13	20·3	"
75 00 N.- " 4.............	20	9	6	" 14, '13	25 53·6	"
At " 11.............	20	9	6	" 21, '13	39 2	"
2·00 N.- " 2.............	20	9	6	" 25, '13	57·9	"
40 00 E.- " 2.............	20	9	6	" 26, '13	26 36·1	"
16·00 E.- " 7....	21	10	6	Dec. 8, '13	25 44·0	"
26·50 E.- " 7....	21	10	6	" 9, '13	48·0	"
0·59 S.-NE. cor. sec. 32	69	10	6	Oct. 17, '13	28 02·1	L. E. Fontaine.
68·00 S.- " 12.............	18	11	6	Dec. 1, '13	25 48·6	N. C. Stewart.
20·00 S.- " 7....	21	11	6	" 13, '13.	25 27·5	"
13 00 W.- " 6.............	21	11	6	" 16, '13.	44·5	"
42·00 W.- " 6.............	21	12	6	" 17, '13.	34·4	"
7·00 E.- " 12	21	12	6	" 11, '13.	47·9	"
26 00 E.- " 12	21	12	6	" 12, '13.	37·8	"
29·00 W.- " 23	24	12	6	July 3, '13.	26 42·0	"
29 00 S.- " 29	25	12	6	June 4, '13.	39·1	"
45·00 S., 23·00 W.-NE. cor. sec. 28....	25	12	6	" 13, '13.	50·6	"
At Sta. 67, Trav. Adams lake in sec. 16.	25	12	6	" 17, '13.	27 02·9	"
71·00 N.-NE. cor. sec. 9.	25	12	6	" 24, '13.	02·6	"
36·00 W.- " 9..	25	12	6	" 25, '13.	26 47·7	"
45·00 E.-SE. " 34.....:........	16	13	6	" 3, '13.	25 39·8	C. H. Taggart.
20 00 S.-NE. " 30.............	16	13	6	" 10, '13	26 01·6	"
30·00 W.- " 31.	16	13	6	" 7, '13.	27 48·0	"
30·00 S.- " 26.............	24	13	6	July 3, '13.	26 54·7	N. C. Stewart.
29·00 N.- " 26........	24	13	6	" 5, '13.	27 19·3	"
At " 1............ ..	25	14	6	" 11, '13.	26 33·8	"
60·00 E. " 9.............	19	15	6	Apr. 30, '13.	24 57·8	C. H. Taggart.
At " 4.............	19	15	6	May 3, '13.	27 00·1	"
5·00 S.- " 4......... ...	19	15	6	" 5, '13.	28 22·1	"
30 00 N.- " 1..	19	15	6	" 24, '13.	24 10·6	"
20 00 S.- " 18.............	21	18	6	June 27, '13.	48·6	"
10 00 S.-NW. " 6.............	21	19	6	July 21, '13.	26 17 7	"
40·00 W.-NE. " 1.............	21	20	6	" 16, '13.	27 35·7	"
43 00 E.-NW. " 21.............	17	24	6	May 22, '13.	46·4	J. A. Calder.
6 00 N.-¼ sec. cor. N. by sec. 1........	17	24	6	June 5, '13.	28 47·4	"
At Sta. 9, Course 8-9, 15·00 W., 18·00 S., NE. cor. sec. 18, Thompson River	18	24	6	Dec. 7, '13.	27 30 1	C. H. Taggart.
" " " ..	18	24	6	" 7, '13.	32·1	"
" " " ..	18	24	6	" 7, '13.	30·7	"
" " " ..	18	24	6	" 7, '13.	27 31·6	"
" " " ..	18	24	6	" 7, '13.	34·7	"
" " " ..	18	24	6	" 7, '13.	29·3	"
" " " ..	18	24	6	" 7, '13.	30·3	"
" " " ..	18	24	6	" 7, '13.	29 3	"
35·00 W.-NE. cor. sec. 19.............	18	24	6	" 7, '13.	26 40·6	"
At " 7......	3	25	6	July 22, '12.	24 54 6	A. Lighthall.
T.B. 495-2.						
39 00 W. cor. sec. 6	8	25	6	June 20, '13.	25 52 1	A. E. Hunter. .
6·00 W.- " 6.	8	25	6	" 24, '13.	46·9	"
16·30 S.-¼ sec. cor. E. by sec. 26:......	15	25	6	Aug. 23, '13.	29 27·5	J. A. Calder.
16·30 S.- " 26.............	15	25	6	" 23, '13.	30·3	"
61·00 S.-NE. cor. sec. 21............	15	25	6	" 15, '13.	32 12·4	"
16·30 S.-¼ sec. cor. E. by sec. 26.......	15	25	6	" 24, '13.	29 27·1	"
" 26..... .	15	25	6	" 25, '13.	28·0	"
" 26..... .	15	25	6	" 26, '13.	30·7	"
" 26.	15	25	6	" 27, '13.	29·6	"
15·00 W.-NE. cor. sec. 17.............	15	25	6	" 13, '13.	42·3	"
6·30 E.- " 8.............	16	25	6	June 16, '13.	27 43·7	"
8·30 E.-NW. cor. Nicomen I.R. No. 10	16	25	6	" 14, '13.	17·3	"
7·00 S.- " 10	16	25	6	" 17, '13.	34·9	"
40 00 S.-NE. cor. sec. 27	17	25	6	May 15, '13.	25 40·9	"
At " 16	19	25	6	Nov. 18, '13	24 17·0	"

SESSIONAL PAPER No. 25b

RESULTS OF MAGNETIC OBSERVATIONS—*Continued.*

TABLE I.—DECLINATION OBSERVATIONS—*Continued.*

Place.	Township.	Range.	Meridian.	Date.	Declination.	Observer.
					° ′	
20·00 E.-NE. cor. sec. 33	20	25	6	Sept. 9, '13.	25 57·6	C. H. Taggart.
At '' 7....	20	25	6	Oct. 31, '13.	54·8	''
40·00 W.-¼ sec. cor. E. by sec 35.....	21	25	6	Aug. 15, '13.	27 13·7	''
40·00 S.-NE. cor. sec. 22	21	25	6	'' 19, '13.	26 56·0	''
40·00 E.- '' 10............	21	25	6	'' 21, '13.	44·2	''
40·00 S.- '' 10	21	25	6	'' 22, '13.	25 55·8	''
20·00 W.-¼ sec. cor. E. by sec. 33.....	21	25	6	Sept. 3, '13.	26 55·8	''
At NE cor. sec. 22	21	25	6	Sept. 4, '13	27 45·0	C. H. Taggart.
20·00 S.- '' 17....	21	25	6	'' 17, '13	26 36·4	''
40·00 E.- '' 31............	21	25	6	'' 22, '13	21·5	''
20·00 E.- '' 31............	21	25	6	'' 22, '13	07·5	''
15·00 N.-NW '' 6............	21	25	6	'' 30, '13	38·2	''
40·41 W.-NE '' 2	5	26	6	June 4, '13	25 13·5	W. J. Johnston.
At '' 3....	5	26	6	'' 5, '13	24 55·4	''
20·00 E.- '' 3............	5	26	6	'' 7, '13	25 18·4	''
At SE cor. Lot. 2	5	26	6	'' 10, '13	26·4	''
40·00 S.-NE cor. sec. 22............	5	26	6	'' 13, '13	37·5	''
67·00 S.- '' 22............	5	26	6	'' 16, '13	31·2	''
45·00 N.- '' 22............	55	26	6	'' 18, '13	41·4	''
22·00 S.- '' 27.... ...	5	26	6	'' 19, '13	50·9	''
45·00 W.- '' 27	5	26	.6	'' 20, '13	45·7	''
53·00 W.- '' 27............	5	26	6	'' 21, '13	31·6	''
49·40 N.- '' 27............	5	26	6	'' 23, '13	24·8	''
35·49 W.- '' 34	5	26	6	July 7, '13	26 13·4	''
10·00 W.-NE cor. Lot 873 sec. 34.....	5	26	3	'' 11, '13	24 54·7	''
At NE cor. sec. 28.....	5	26	6	Aug. 11, '13	25 38·5	''
At NW cor. of Yale I. R. 8..........	6	26	6	'' 9, '13	23·9	''
At NE cor. sec. 21	6	26	6	'' 13, '13	34·7	''
20·50 N.- '' 21	6	26	6	'' 15, '13	26 14·1	''
35·00 E.-NW cor SW ¼ sec. 27........	6	26	6	'' 16, '13	25 46·9	''
25·00 W.-NE cor. sec. 15...........	6	26	6	'' 19, '13	26 14·0	''
70·00 S.- '' 3............	6	26	6	June 24, '13	25 47·6	''
26·10 S.- '' 3	6	26	6	'' 25, '13	51·5	''
18·00 N.- '' 3	6	26	6	'' 30, '13	44·4	''
40·00 N.- '' 3............	6	26	6	July 2, '13	35·2	''
At '' 10............	6	26	6	'' 3, '13	27·6	''
40·25 N.- '' 10............	6	26	6	'' 4, '13	36·6	''
40·00 N.- '' 15............	6	26	6	'' 15, '13	14·9	''
35·00 S.- '' 27...	6	26	6	'' 17, '13	48·9	''
40·00 N.- '' 27............	6	26	6	July 19, '13	25 15·8	''
40·40 E.- '' 3............	6	26	6	'' 24, '13	14·2	''
20·00 W.- '' 3	6	26	6	'' 28, '13	17·0	''
8·60 W.- '' 3...	6	26	6	'' 29, '13	11·1	''
At SE cor. of Yale I. R. No. 11, sec. 3.	6	26	6	'' 31, '13	24·6	''
At NE cor. sec. 9.............	6	26	6	Aug. 2, '13	30 2	''
At '' 4....	6	26	6	'' 4, '13	25·2	''
40·00 S.-NW cor. of Yale I. R. No. 11.	6	26	6	'' 6, '13	38·2	''
At SE cor. sec. 3	7	26	6	'' 22, '13	26 04·9	''
22·00 N.-NE cor. NW ¼ sec. 3.........	7	26	6	'' 26, '13	13·0	''
30·00 S.-NW cor. Lot 48...............	7	26	6	'' 27, '13	23·4 .	''
5·00 E.-SW '' 48...............	7	26	6	'' 28, '13	28·8	''
25·00 W.-NE cor. sec. 14............	7	26	6	'' 30, '13	38·3	''
65·00 S.- '' 35.............	7	26	6	Sept. 5, '13	30·2	''
36·10 S.- '' 26	7	26	6	'' 6, '13	31·0	''
40·25 S.-NE cor. NW ¼ sec. 24........	7	26	6	'' 10, '13	31·4	''
40·61 W.-NE cor. sec. 13........	7	26	6	'' 11, '13	41·5	''
14·00 W.- '' 13............	7	26	6	'' 15, '13	25·9	''
38·00 W.- '' .36............	7	26	6	'' 17, '13	35·0	''
20·12 S.- '' 2............	7	26	6	'' 20, '13	32·1	''
10·00 N.- '' 11	7	26	6	'' 23, '13	34·0	''
63·00 E.-SW cor. of Yale I. R. No. 3..	7	26	6	'' 27, '13	40·5	''
At NE cor. NW ¼ sec. 14	7	26	6	Oct. 2, '13	44·4	''
39·00 N.-NE cor. sec. 1.............	8	26	6	June 10, '13	25 32·1	A. E. Hunter.
45·00 E.- '' 11.............	8	26	6	'' 14, '13	33·9	''

240

5 GEORGE V., A. 1915

RESULTS OF MAGNETIC OBSERVATIONS—*Continued.*

TABLE I.—DECLINATION OBSERVATIONS—*Continued.*

Place.	Township.	Range.	Meridan.	Date.	Declination.	Observer.
					° ′	
50·00 S.-NE. cor. sec. 1	8	26	6	June 15, '13	24 51·2	A. E. *H*unter.
20·00 W.- " 13	8	26	6	" 17, '13	25 59·0	"
48·00 E.- " 26	8	26	6	July 1, '13	31·1	"
54·30 N.- " 25	8	26	6	" 4, '13	26 15·7	"
67·20 N.- " 35	8	26	6	" 10, '13	21·5	"
20·00 W.- " 35	8	26	6	Aug. 9, '13	18·1	"
65·00 W.-NE cor. sec. 35	8	26	6	Aug. 11, '13	26 13·9	"
23·56 N.- " 2	9	26	6	July 11, '13	21·9	"
56·00 N.- " 2	9	26	6	" 12, '13	10·4	"
75·00 N.- " 2	9	26	6	" 14, '13	16·3	"
10 00 N.- " 14	9	26	6	" 17, '13	35·3	"
50·00 N.- " 14	9	26	6	" 18, '13	49·7	"
20·00 N.- " 3	9	26	6	Aug. 15, '13	02·6	"
40·00 N.- " 3	9	26	6	" 16, '13	00·0	"
63·00 N.- " 3	9	26	6	" 19, '13	09·9	"
33 00 N.- " 10	9	26	6	" 20, '13	07·9	"
41·00 N.- " 15	9	26	6	" 23, '13	12·3	"
15·00 N - " 21	9	26	6	Sept. 11, '13	07·0	"
36·00 N.- " 21	9	26	6	" 12, '13	04·0	"
ᴹᴵᴹAt " 28	9	26	6	" 15, '13	07·8	"
17·20 E.- " 28	9	26	6	" 16, '13	05·4	"
77·00 N.- " 22	9	26	6	" 25, '13	14·1	"
48·00 N.- " 22	9	26	6	" 26, '13	14·6	"
31·00 N.- " 27	9	26	6	" 27, '13	20·0	"
63 00 N.- " 27	9	26	6	" 29, '13	25·2	"
10·00 N.- " 34	9	26	6	" 30, '13	23·8	"
3·50 W.- " 34	9	26	6	Oct. 1, '13	31.4	"
68 00 N.- " 34	9	26	6	" 2, '13	23·6	"
30·00 N.- " 33	9	26	6	" 11, '13	07·8	"
20·00 N.- " 3	10	26	6	" 3, '13	23·6	"
46 00 N.- " 3	10	26	6	" 4, '13	25·0	"
35·00 W.- " 3	10	26	6	" 7, '13	21·2	"
34·00 N.- " 4	10	26	6	" 15, '13	04·6	"
27·00 E.- " 9	10	26	6	" 17, '13	14·2	"
70·00 E.- " 9	10	26	6	" 18, '13	21·9	"
43·00 N.- " 10	10	26	6	" 20, '13	1ᴎ 2	"
36·00 W.- " 4	10	26	6	" 30, '13	25 54·4	·
40·00 E.- " 10	10	26	6	Nov. 1, '13	21·0	"
10·00 S.- " 7	12	26	6	Oct. 25, '13	46·2	A. V. Chase.
35·00 E.- NW " 31	12	26	6	Nov. 8, '13	55·8	"
30·00 S.-NE " 19	12	26	6	" 13, '13	26 20·6	"
At Sta. 9 traverse Left bank of Fraser R	12	26	6	" 18, '13	25 20·6	"
13·00 N.-SE cor. sec. 5	12	26	6	" 20, '13	25 55 0	"
14·50 W.-Wit. P.N. By. Boothroyd I.R. No. 8	13	26	6	Aug. 13, '13	25 40·7	"
44·00 N.-SE cor. sec. 6	15	26	6	Dec. 12, '13	27 13·0	J.A. Calder.
At NE " 31	19	26	6	Nov. 6, '13	25 45·4	C. H. Taggart.
20·00 S.- " 17	20	26	6	Oct. 28, '13	26 11·5	"
At " 19	20	26	6	Nov. 1, '13	08·6	"
5·00 S.- " 8	20	26	6	" 8, '13	09·4	"
50·00 S.- " 7	21	26	6	Oct. 16, '13	18·7	"
13·00 S.- " 29	4	27	6	" 17, '13	24 43·5	W. J. Johnston.
14·00 W.- " 20	4	27	6	" 20, '13	38·7	"
67·00 S.- " 19	4	27	6	" 21, '13	47·2	"
37·00 S.- " 2	5	27	6	June 28, '13	25 07·3	"
30 00 E.- " 15	12	27	6	Sept. 5, '13	23 40·8	A. V. Chase.
At Sta. 60, traverse of N. river	12	27	6	" 9, '13	25 32·2	"
4·00 W.-NE cor. sec. 15	12	27	6	" 10, '13	41 2	"
60·00 W.- " 15	12	27	6	" 12, '13	33·2	"
At Sta. S. 10 traverse S. side of Lake Francis	12	27	6	" 22, '13	36·8	"
44·00 W.-NE cor. sec. 36	13	27	6	July 4, '13	26 15·4	"
40·25 S.- " 13	13	27	6	" 14, '13	25 40·1	"
32 00 N.- " 26	13	27	6	" 21, '13	26 19·5	"

SESSIONAL PAPER No. 25b

RESULTS OF MAGNETIC OBSERVATIONS—*Continued.*

TABLE I.—DECLINATION OBSERVATIONS—*Concluded.*

Place.	Township.	Range.	Meridiam.	Date.	Declination.	Observer.
					° ′	
15·00 N.-SE ,, 1........ ...	13	27	6	Aug. 16, '13	25 37 7	A, V. Chase.
At NE ,, 1	13	27	6	,, 20, '13	19·4	,,
At ¼ cor. N. by. sec. 1................	13	27	6	Nov. 3, '13	36 5	
15'00 N.- ¼ cor. N. by. sec. 12	13	27	6	,, 5, '13	22·8	
At Centre sec. 25	14	27	6	May 30, '13	50·7	
At ,. 12....	14	27	6	June 10, '13	26 13·7	
50·00 N.-NE cor. sec. 27.............	14	27	6	,, 19, '13	21·0	
At ,, 22.............	14	27	6	,, 21, '13	02·9	
60·00 N.- ,, 22.............	14	27	6	,, 17, '13	25 02 8	
56·00 E.- ,, 15	14	27	6	Dec. 1, '13	26 27·0	
At ¼ cor. N. By. sec. 35...............	14	27	6	,, 3, '13	24·5	,,
40·00 W.-NE cor. Lytton I.R. No. 3...	16	27	6	Oct. 1, '13	27 09·3	J. A. Calder.
40·00 W.- ,, ,,	16	27	6	,, 1, '13	09·4	,,
40·00 W.- ,, ,, ...	16	27	6	,, 1, '13	12·0	,,
40·00 E.- ,, ,, ...	16	27	6	,, 1, '13	13·6	,,
40·00 W.- ,, ,, ...	16	27	6	,, 1, '13	18·4	,,
40·00 W.- ,, ,, ...	16	27	6	,, 1, '13	13·3	,,
40·00 E.- ,, ,,	16	27	6	,, 1, '13	09·0	,,
40·00 W.- ,, ,, ...	16	27	6	,, 1, '13	06·8	,,
40·00 W.- ,, ,, ...	16	27	6	,, 1, '13	07·1	,,
42·00 S.- cor. sec. 6	17	27	6	,, 17, '13	26 35·9	,,
4·00 E.-NW ,, 7..............	17	27	6	,, 29, '13	- 06·0	,,
1·00 S.-NE ,, 5..............	18	27	6	Nov. 14, '13	35·0	,,
4·00 W.- ,, 26........ .. .	20	27	6	Oct. 20, '13	25 07·7	C. H. Taggart.
53·00 S.- ,, 27..............	20	27	6	,, 21, '13	26 33·3	,,
10·00 N.- ,, 15........ .	20	27	6	,, 22, '13	23 31·2	,,
20·00 W.SE ,, 32..............	1	28	6	Sept. 30, '13	25 17·0	R. B. McKay.
10·00 W.-NE ,, 2	4	28	6	Oct. 22, '13	24 57·2	W. J. Johnston.
20·00 S.- ,, 11..............	4	28	6	,, 25, '13	50·8	,,
44·45 W.- ,, 12	4	28	6	,, 29, '13	57·2	,,
10·00 W.- ,, 13..............	12	28	6	Sept. 25, '13	25 33·8	A. V. Chase.
20·00 E.- ,, 14..............	12	28	6	,, 26, '13	38·0	,,
At ¼ sec. cor. N. by. sec. 14.......	12	28	6	,, 27, '13	35·1	,,
At Sta. 103, N. of Nahatlatch lake.. .	12	28	6	Oct. 19, '13	16·8	,,
19·00 E.-Centre of sec. 9..	12	28	6	,, 20, '13	19·4	,,
20·00 W.- ,, 10..............	12	28	6	,, 20, '13	44·7	,,
10·00 N.- ,, 10..............	12	28	6	,, 21, '13	48·3	,,
24·70 N.- ¼ sec. cor. N. by. sec. 12.. . .	17	28	6	Nov. 3, '13	25 46·6	J. A. Calder.
40·40 E.-NE cor. sec. 11..............	18	28	6	Dec. 8, '13	27 49·5	,,
31·00 E.- ,, 14..............	18	28	6	,, 8, '13	28 50·3	,,
20·00 S.- ¼ sec. cor. E. by. sec. 33....	1	29	6	Sept. 26, '13	24 31·6	R. B. McKay.
At NE cor. Lot 20, Gr. 2	12		E.C.M	Oct. 28, '12	25 55·4	A. Lighthall.
At NW cor. Langley Townsite.... ..	12		,,	,, 30, '12	26·4	,,
At ¼ cor. S. by. sec. 1...............	19	....	,,	Aug. 22, '13	23 24·5	R. B. McKay.
5·00 E.-¼ cor. W. by. sec. 12..........	19	....	,,	Oct. 16, '13	25 45·5	,,
7·00 E.-NW cor. sec. 19.......... ...	21	....	,,	June 17, '13	32·1	,,
1·00 N.-¼ cor S. by. sec. 7..........	22	....	,,	Aug. 22, '13	23 18·1	,,
7·00 S.-¼ cor E. by. sec. 35..........	22	....	,,	Sept. 19. '13	43·6	,,
At ¼ cor. S. by. sec. 29..............	22	....	,,	Oct. 5, '13	43·5	,,
52·00 S.-NE cor. sec. 27.............	23	....	,,	,, 29, '13	35·2	,,
11·00 W.- ,, T.B. 86, in sec. 14. ..	39	....	W.C.M.	July 3, '13	24 48·6	,,
At NE cor. sec. 11..................	39	....	,,	,, 8, '13	36·5	,,
6·00S.-¼ cor. E. by. sec. 11..	39	....	,,	,, 5, '13	49·1	,,
60·00 S.-NE cor. sec. 20.......... ...	39	....	,,	,, 28, '13	34·9	,,

DEPARTMENT OF THE INTERIOR

5 GEORGE V., A. 1915

RESULTS OF MAGNETIC OBSERVATIONS—Continued.
TABLE II.—INCLINATION AND TOTAL INTENSITY.

Station. Distance in Chains from Nearest Post.	Tp.	Rge.	Mer.	Date	Inclination L.M.T.	Inclination Value.	Total Intensity L.M.T.	Total Intensity Value. c.g.s.	Observer.	Instrument.
37·00 W., 25·00 N.—NE cor. 1 sec. 23	29	19	Pr.	Nov. 17, '13	14·1-15·1	79 12 16	14·5-14·8	0·63537	R. C. Purser	T. S. 62.
" " 23	29	19	Pr.	17, '13	14·8-15·4	12·8	15·1-15·4	0·63543	"	"
" " 23	29	19	Pr.	17, '13	15·4-16·3	12·8	15·8-16·1	0·63540	G. A. Bennett	T. S. 61.
30·00 NE.—NE. cor. sec. 5	18	20	Pr.	June 16, '13	11·1-13·3	78 01·4	10·4-11·0	0·63334	"	"
30·00 NE.— " 5	18	20	Pr.	16, '13	12·7-14·4	01·4	11·7-12·3	0·63138	Blair	"
" 5	18	20	Pr.	16, '13	13·9-15·6	00·6	13·3-13·9	0·63176	Gay	"
12·00 S.—NE cor. sec. 8	18	21	Pr.	16, '13	15·6-17·2	77 59·9	14·4-15·0	0·63213	G. A. Bennett	"
" 3	18	21	Pr.	17, '13	16·8-18·8	78 09·1	15·2-16·7	0·63825	Blair	"
30·00 S.— " 8	18	21	Pr.	17, '13	8·4-10·5	08·1	17·6-18·2	0·63753	Gay	"
" 8	18	21	Pr.	23, '13	10·0-11·6	07·8	9·3-9·9	0·63682	G. A. Bennett	"
15·00 E.— " 6	33	31	Pr.	23, '13	11·3-13·5	08·0	10·6-11·1	0·63779	Blair	T. S. 62.
20·00 S.— " 6	33	31	Pr.	20, '13	15·4-16·6	07·8	12·1-12·7	0·63734	E. J. Wight	T. S. 61.
" 28	19	1	2	20, '13	16·3-17·4	32·7	15·9-16·3	0·63887	Blair Gray	"
" 28	19	1	2	7, '13	14·1-16·0	33·4	16·6-16·9	0·63765	G. A. Bennett	"
" 28	19	1	2	7, '13	15·6-17·9	77 41·7	14·7-15·4	0·63065	Blair	"
" 28	19	1	2	7, '13	17·1-19·4	44·3	16·2-17·0	0·63154	Gay	"
15·00 S.— 28	19	1	2	9, '13	19·0-20·7	46·0	18·0-18·9	0·63048	G. A. Bennett	T. S. 62.
2·00 NE.—¼ M.N. by. sec. 23	19	8	2	Nov. 3, '13	8·5-10·2	43·2	19·5-20·1	0·63026	"	"
12·00 N.—¼ " 11	7	10	2	July 14, '13	9·9-10·9	41·0	9·1-9·6	0·63140	G. A. Bennett	"
12·00 N.—¼ " 11	7	10	2	June 16, '13	7·3-9·6	76 31·9	8·3-8·9	0·62741	Blair Gray	T. S. 61.
9·00 SE.—¼ P.E. by. sec. 21	26	11	2	16, '13	9·1-11·2	34·9	9·8-10·5	0·62581	G. A. Bennett	"
10·50 S., 25·00W.—NE cor. sec. 27	33	11	2	Dec. 13, '13	9·1-10·3	36·1	9·8	0·62833	E. J. Wight	T. S. 62.
" 27	33	11	2	13, '13	9·8-11·1	77 52·2	10·3-10·8	0·62755	"	"
" 27	33	11	2	13, '13	13·8-14·6	78 51·6	14·0-14·3	0·62832	"	"
20·00 W.—NE cor. sec. 13	18	13	2	July 25, '13	14·3-15·2	14·9	14·6-14·9	0·62828	"	"
" 13	33	13	2	25, '13	14·9-15·8	15·1	15·2-15·5	0·62825	Blair Gray	T. S. 61.
8·00 S., 30·00 W.—NE cor. sec. 12	33	13	2	Aug. 26, '13	14·1-16·1	15·1	14·9-15·5	0·62961	E. J. Wight	T. S. 62.
" 12	33	13	2	26, '13	15·6-17·2	77 04·0	16·1-16·6	0·62938	"	"
" 12	33	13	2	26, '13	13·2-14·2	04·8	13·6-13·9	0·62807	"	"
36·00S., 30·00 E.—NW cor. sec. 31	47	14	2	July 27, '13	13·9-14·7	78 11·6	14·2-14·5	0·62810	"	"
" 31	47	14	2	27, '13	14·5-15·3	11·6	14·7-15·1	0·62816	"	"
1·00 SE.—¼ I.P. centre sec. 22	42	16	2	June 7, '13	10·3-11·2	79 00·0	10·7-11·0	0·63177	"	"
48·00 N., 8·00 W.—SE cor. sec. 15	25	27	2	July 5, '13	11·0-11·8	00·6	11·2-11·6	0·63180	"	"
					14·3-16·2	78 35·9	15·1-15·7	0·62891	"	"
					7·4-8·4	77 04·7	7·8-8·1	0·62809	"	"

Station			Date						Observer		Value
48·00 N., 8·00 W.—SE cor. sec. 15	25	27	July	2			05·2	8·4— 8·7	E. J. Wight	T. S. 62	0·62816
" 15	25	27	"	2			05·3	8·8— 9·1	"	"	0·62839
25·00 W., 15·00 S.—NE cor. sec. 21	33	28	Sept.	2			34·1	8·8— 9·1	"	"	0·62907
" 21	33	28	"	2			33·8	9·3— 9·7	"	"	0·62910
25·00W. 15·00 S.-NE cor. sec. 21	17	1	Sept. 1, '13	3			33·5	9·9—10·3	G. A. Bennett	T. S. 61	0·62D8
40·00E.-NE cor. sec. 21	15	1	May 23, '13	3			02·9	18·7—20·2	Blair Gray	"	0·62718
30·00E.-NE " 21	15	2	July 7, 13.	3			58·3	16·2—16·7	"	"	0·62745
20·00N.-NE " 35	15	2	June 30, '13	3			46·3	15·3— 7·4	"	"	0·62191
20·00N.-NE " 35	15	2	" 30, 13	3			44·7	15·7—16·7	"	"	0·62666
30·00N.-NE " 35	30	3	July 1, '13	3			46·3	16·1—18·3	"	"	0·62710
30·00N.- NE " 9	39	3	" 1, 13	3			45·9	9·7—11·4	E. J. Wight	T. S. 62	0·62909
At NE	37	5	June 2, '13	3			14·1	10·9—12·4	"	"	0·62885
At NE	37	5	" 2, 13	3			13·5	12·— 40·3·8	"	"	0·62864
15·00E. 29 00S.-NW cor. sec. 9	25	6	Aug. 14, '13	3			37·2	14·9—15·9	"	"	0·62893
15·00E. 20·00S.-NW cor. sec. 9	42	6	" 14, '13	3			37·1	15·6—16·5	"	"	0·62897
15·00E. 20·00S.-NW cor. sec. 9	53	6	" 14, 13	3			37·0	16·2—17·1	Blair Gray	T. S. 61	0·62488
43· 60. NE cor. sec. 14	53	7	Nov. 21, '13	3			55·6	13·6—14·7	G. A. Bennett	T. S. 62	0·62490
43·00E.-NE " 9	15	7	" 13.	3			57·5	13·7—14·7	E. J. Wight	"	0·62484
20·00W.-NE " 9	15	14	June 27, '13	3			07·8	13·7—14·7	R. C. Purser	"	0·62638
12·00E.¼ sec. cor. N by sec. 9	30	15	" 27, '13	3			16·5	·5—15·0	E. J. Wight	"	0·631l9
5· 00N. ¾·00W.-SE cor. sec. 21	17	16	Nov. 4, '13	3			59·4	·5—10·5	"	"	0·63123
5·00N. 3·00W.-SE " 21	39	18	" 4, '13.	3			39·1	10·3—11·1	"	"	0·63125
5·00N. W.-SE " 21	39	19	Oct. 16, '13.	3			59·0	10·9—11·8	Blair Gray	T. S. 61	0·12M6
15·00W.-NE cor. sec. 13	15	14	May 14,'19	3			15·1	14·7—16·3	E. J. Wight	T. S. 62	0·62147
15·00W.-NE " 13	15	14	" 28, '13.	3			14·9	9·8—11·8	"	"	0·62539
6·50N. 4·50E.-NE cor. sec. 2	30	15	" 28, '13.	3			01·3	8·8—10·9	Blair Gray	T. S. 61	0·62568
6·50N. 4·50E.-NE " 2	17	16	Oct. 17, '13.	3			24·4	10·2—12·1	Blair Gray	T. S. 61	0·62154
15·00N.-NE cor. sec. 25	39	18	May 22, '13.	3			32·2	11·4—12·9	E. J. Wight	T. S. 62	0·62667
10· W.-NE " 17	19	19	July 19, '13.	3			33·5	8·8—11·3	"	"	0·62435
2·00S.-NE " 28	39	23	" 19, '13.	3			34·2	15·0—15·9	"	"	0·62438
2·00S.-NE " 28	45	23	" 9, '13.	3			49·8	14·5—15·5	E. J. Wight	T. S. 62	0·62335
18·00E.¼ P.W. by sec. 16	50	23	" 9, '13.	3			50·1	15·1—16·1	"	"	0·62336
18·00E.¼ P.W. by sec. 16	51	27	Aug. 12, '13.	3			07·9	13·4—14·3	"	"	0·62128
55·00S.-NE cor. sec. 17	17	5	July 4, '13.	4			03·4	7·4— 9·6	"	"	0·62128
15·00N. 43·00W.-SE cor. sec. 3	17	5	Sept. 29, '13.	4			39·1	13·—415·0	Blair Gray	T. S. 61	0·6455
25· 00E. cor. sec. 23	12	6	" 20, '13.	4			39·8	14·5—17·4	G. A. Bennett	"	0·61746
25· 00E. " 23	18	10	" 20, '13.	4			42·2	16·8—17·4	Blair Gray.	"	0·61850
25·00S. NE " 23	33	10	" 23, '13.	4			29·5	15·9—17·5	Blair Gray.	"	0·61512
10·00NW.-NE cor. sec. 36	33	10	" 9, '13.	4			31·6	14·9—15·9	Blair Gray.	"	0·61957
16·00NW.-NE " 36	15	11	Aug. 9, '13.	4			08·2	7·4— 9·4			
8· (0E-NE " 34	15	13	" 7, '13.	4			08·3	6·6— 7·6;	Blair Gray.	T. S. 61	0·61596
10·00W. 28·00N.-SE cor. sec. 19	17	13	" 7, 13.	4			24·2	7·0— 7·9			0·684
10· W. 28·00N.-SE " 19			" 7, '13.	4			24·8	7·3— 8·2	G. A. Bennett	T. S. 62	0·62080
10·00W·28·00N.-SE " 19			Aug. 5, '13.	4			24·9	7·9— 8·8	E. J. Wight	"	0·62080
30·00 E.-NE cor. sec. 24			" 5, '13.	4			08·3	14·1—15·9	Blair Gray.	T. S. 61	0·61515
" 24			July 28, '13	4			08·2	16·1—16·8			0·61l86
10·00 W. " 24			"	4			24·2	9·1—10·9	"		0·6144·2
" 24			"	4			25·0	10·9—11·6	"		0·61335

5 GEORGE V., A. 1915

RESULTS OF MAGNETIC OBSERVATIONS.—*Concluded,*

TABLE II.—INCLINATION AND TOTAL INTENSITY.

STATION. Distance in Chains from Nearest Post.	Tp.	Rge.	Mer.	Date.	INCLINATION. L. M. T.	INCLINATION. Value.	TOTAL INTENSITY. L. M. T.	TOTAL INTENSITY. Value. c.g.s.	Observer.	Instrument
					h h	° '	h h			
20·00 N. NE cor. sec. 10..........	9	16	4	Oct. 15, '13.	13·4—15·6	74 40·1	14·1—14·9	0·61450	G. A. Bennett..	T. S. 61.
10·00 S.- " " 10..........	9	16	4		15·—417·0	40·6	15·9—16·4	0·61468	Blair Gray.....	"
30·00 S., 15·00W.-NE cor. sec. 24.	8	21	4	Sept. 8, '13.	10·7—12·3	33·0	11·2—11·7	0·6187	R. C. Purser...	T. S. 62.
30·00 SW.-NE cor. sec. 9..........	34	21	4	Oct. 23, '13.	13·5—15·2	76 09·1	14·2—14·7	0·61770	Blair Gray.....	T. S. 61.
35·00 S.- " " 1..........	3	25	4	Aug. 16, '13.	14·6—16·3	74 22·1	15·3—15·7	0·61831	G. A. Bennett	"
" " " 11..........	3	25	4	Aug. 5, '13.	15·9—17·7	22·3	16·6—17·2	0·61315	Blair Gray.....	"
55·00 S.- " " 29..........	2	29	4		15·8—17·6	73 52·5	16·6—17·1	0·61438	"	"
60·00 S. SE., " 29..........	20	29	4	Sept. 24, '13.	17·2—18·9	52·2	17·9—18·5	0·61363	"	"
5·00S W.-¼M. E by. sec. 35...	20	29	4	Oct. 2, '13.	14·4—16·2	75 13·3	15·1—15·7	0·61286	G. A. Bennett..	"
	19	4	5	Sept. 25, '13.	15·0—16·7	12·5 74 55·6	15·7—16·2	0·61176 0·61300	Blair Gray.....	"

SESSIONAL PAPER No. 25b

APPENDIX No. 59.

RESULTS OF WATCH TRIALS.

Name.	Number of Watch	Escapement, &c. Balance spring	Mean daily variation of mean daily rate.								Mean Error.	Diff. between m.d.r. and m. of m.d.r. at 65° F.						Mean Error.	M. ch. of r. for 1° F.	Total Marks 0–1000.
			P.U. 65°	P.R. 65°	P.L. 65°	D.U. 40°	D.U. 65°	D.U. 90°	D.D. 65°	P.U. 65°		P.U.	P.R.	P.L.	D.U.	D.D.	P.U.			
Waltham Watch Co.	19001012	D r., g b., l.e., s.o.	0·32	0·48	0·23	0·23	0·57	0·22	0·24	0·30	0·32	−0·18	−1·98	+0·58	+0·58	+0·52	+0·50	0·72	0·09	687·0
"	18091081	"	0·46	0·42	0·09	0·44	0·34	0·42	0·10	0·15	0·30	+0·21	−2·09	−2·17	+1·91	+1·27	+0·85	1·42	0·07	631·0
"	18028560	"	0·28	0·16	0·64	0·41	0·40	6·57	0·37	0·12	0·37	+2·67	−3·13	+2·17	−0·13	−1·37	−0·23	1·62	0·06	577·5
"	18091036	"	0·33	0·18	0·39	0·43	0·55	0·25	0·22	0·16	0·34	−2·08	−2·11	+0·84	+3·02	+1·10	−0·72	1·65	0·08	576·8
"	52	"	0·34	0·26	0·12	0·50	0·48	0·60	0·21	0·25	0·34	+2·67	−4·57	+0·35	−1·15	+0·31	+2·39	1·91	0·08	547·1
"	15	"	0·42	0·12	0·23	0·36	0·29	0·24	0·24	0·22	0·26	+3·67	−2·31	=1·85	−2·75	−0·11	+3·37	2·34	0·10	527·2
"	94	"	0·50	0·44	0·40	0·45	0·39	0·34	0·24	0·30	0·38	+2·35	−1·57	−2·07	+2·09	−1·27	+1·45	1·80	0·12	511·6
Hamilton Watch Co.	688005	"	0·18	0·49	0·15	0·63	0·36	0·46	0·22	0·34	0·35	−0·17	−5·37	+2·35	−2·11	+3·13	+2·17	2·55	0·03	501·9
Waltham Watch Co.	19001065	"	0·56	0·57	0·21	0·33	0·58	0·44	0·14	0·31	0·40	−1·78	−0·62	+3·98	−1·36	+0·54	−3·46	1·96	0·10	496·0
"	18091079	"	0·64	0·21	0·44	0·23	0·96	0·74	0·30	1·10	0·49	−0·07	+2·57	+4·67	+1·01	+1·81	−0·63	1·79	0·09	474·1
"	27	"	0·35	0·50	0·15	0·75	0·76	0·16	0·26	0·44	0·42	−2·04	−2·42	+1·64	+1·42	+1·60	−1·22	2·01	0·14	453·0
"	38	"	0·61	0·85	0·54	0·12	0·84	0·30	0·31	0·19	0·46	−1·86	+4·76	+1·38	+1·38	+3·46	−0·28	1·89	0·13	452·0
"	19091083	"	1·47	0·45	0·39	0·37	0·41	0·27	0·26	0·91	0·57	+0·90	−0·52	−5·52	+1·70	−0·90	−2·78	2·01	0·06	426·3
"	33	"	0·70	1·03	0·42	0·49	0·28	0·28	0·32	0·38	0·48	+3·58	−0·98	−1·78	+0·30	+2·78	+3·25	2·22	0·10	423·6
"	18028541	"	0·60	0·76	0·20	0·28	0·59	0·26	0·13	0·47	0·42	+0·63	−1·00	−1·47	+0·09	−6·93	−1·51	2·40	0·06	416·0
"	18091028	"	1·65	0·43	0·71	0·34	0·39	6·34	0·36	0·33	0·49	+2·41	+1·01	−4·01	+0·49	+1·65	−1·69	1·85	0·09	412·8
"	19001067	"	0·57	1·14	0·31	0·74	0·50	0·56	1·18	0·67	0·67	−1·33	−1·99	+1·21	+1·75	+3·49	−3·02	1·73	0·06	402·7
"	18091046	"	0·36	0·26	0·46	0·31	0·37	6·39	0·27	0·19	0·33	+4·30	−1·34	−0·48	−2·96	+1·30	−0·76	2·09	0·31	385·9
"	82	"	0·56	0·44	0·86	0·26	0·69	0·26	0·41	0·90	0·58	+1·46	−2·96	−2·22	+3·02	−1·48	−1·48	2·06	0·11	381·9
"	74	"	0·94	0·48	0·78	0·64	0·64	0·44	0·13	0·58	0·54	+4·30	−2·62	−3·54	+2·98	+0·96	+0·98	2·05	0·05	377·7
"	45	"	0·20	0·32	1·02	0·66	0·29	0·50	0·57	1·14	0·58	−0·68	−2·48	−2·48	−1·30	−3·44	−0·02	2·39	0·09	354·7
Hamilton Watch Co.	9656920	"	0·64	0·84	0·32	0·40	0·40	0·44	0·41	1·16	0·56	+2·70	−7·38	+5·22	+1·32	+0·88	+0·62	2·68	0·06	301·7
Waltham Watch Co.	18091050	"	0·90	0·54	0·15	0·81	064	0·16	0·41	0·76	0·55	−0·30	−5·96	+1·98	−0·82	−1·98	+6·38	3·02	0·12	281·5

Falls on Sheep River near Rocky Mountain House, Alberta. Taken by L. C. Tilt, B.Sc.F., Forestry Branch.

DEPARTMENT OF THE INTERIOR
DOMINION OF CANADA

HON. W. J. ROCHE, *Minister;* W. W. CORY, *Deputy Minister.*

Irrigation Branch.

E. F. DRAKE, *Superintendent.*

REPORT

OF

Progress of Stream Measurements

(HYDROMETRIC SURVEYS)

FOR

THE CALENDAR YEAR 1914

PREPARED UNDER THE DIRECTION OF

F. H. PETERS, M. Can. Soc. C.E.,

COMMISSIONER OF IRRIGATION.

BY

P. M. SAUDER, M. Can. Soc. C.E., Chief Hydrometric Engineer,
Assisted by G. H. WHYTE and G. R. ELLIOTT, B.A.Sc., A.M. Can. Soc. C.E.

PRINTED BY ORDER OF PARLIAMENT

OTTAWA
PRINTED BY J. de L. TACHE, PRINTER TO THE KING'S MOST
EXCELLENT MAJESTY
1915

[No. 25c—1915.]

CONTENTS

Corrected table on page 59 of 1912 report and page 67 of 1913 report between pages 100 and 101
Corrected table on page 225 of 1913 report between pages...................... .. 282 and 283
Corrected table on page 260 of 1912 report between pages........................ 286 and 287
Corrected table on page 348 of 1912 report between pages........................ 404 and 405
Corrected table on page 318 of 1913 report between pages........................ 404 and 405
Corrected table on page 343 of 1913 report between pages........................ 432 and 433
Corrected table on page 418 of 1912 report between pages........................ 472 and 473
Corrected table on page 380 of 1913 report between pages........................ 472 and 473

ILLUSTRATIONS

To Field Marshal, His Royal Highness Prince Arthur William Patrick Albert, Duke of Connaught and of Strathearn, K.G., K.T., K.P., etc., etc., etc., Governor General and Commander in Chief of the Dominion of Canada.

MAY IT PLEASE YOUR ROYAL HIGHNESS:

The undersigned has the honour to lay before Your Royal Highness the report of the Progress of Stream Measurements for the year 1914.

Respectfully submitted,

W. J. ROCHE,
Minister of the Interior.

OTTAWA, August 14, 1915.

DEPARTMENT OF THE INTERIOR,

OTTAWA, August 14, 1915.

The Honourable W. J. ROCHE, M.D.,
      Minister of the Interior.

SIR:—

    I have the honour to submit the report of Stream Measurements for the year 1914, and to recommend that it be published as the sixth of a series of progress reports.

I have the honour to be, Sir,
      Your obedient servant,

          W. W. CORY,
          Deputy Minister of the Interior.

DEPARTMENT OF THE INTERIOR,
Irrigation Branch,
OTTAWA, August 14, 1915.

W. W. CORY, Esq., C.M.G.,
Deputy Minister of the Interior.

SIR:—

I submit herewith the report of Stream Measurements for the year 1914, submitted by F. H. Peters, C.E., Commissioner of Irrigation, and would recommend that it be published.

Respectfully submitted,

E. F. DRAKE,
Superintendent of Irrigation.

DEPARTMENT OF THE INTERIOR,
IRRIGATION OFFICE,
CALGARY, ALBERTA, July 30, 1915.

E. F. DRAKE, Esq.,
Superintendent of Irrigation,
Department of the Interior,
Ottawa, Canada.

SIR:—

I have the honour to transmit herewith the manuscript of the Report of the Progress of Stream Measurements for the calendar year 1914. This report has been prepared, under my direction, by P. M. Sauder, M. Can. Soc. C.E., Chief Hydrometric Engineer, G. H. Whyte, and G. R. Elliott, B. A. Sc.

I beg to recommend that it be published as the sixth of the series of Reports of Progress of Stream Measurements.

I have the honour to be, Sir,
Your obedient servant,
F. H. PETERS,
Commissioner of Irrigation.

DEPARTMENT OF THE INTERIOR,
IRRIGATION OFFICE,
CALGARY, ALBERTA, July 29, 1915.

F. H. PETERS, Esq., M. Can. Soc. C.E.,
Commissioner of Irrigation,
Department of the Interior,
Calgary, Alberta.

SIR:—

I beg to submit herewith the manuscript of the Report of Progress of Stream Measurements for the calendar year 1914.

Owing to the fact that much of my time has been taken by other duties, most of the work of preparing this report has fallen to my assistants, G. H. Whyte and G. R. Elliott, B.A. Sc. The report gives a brief outline of the methods of obtaining and compiling the data contained therein, but owing to the want of space and time, many of the details had to be omitted. There is given in tabulated form all the records of stream flow during 1914.

I beg to recommend that this report be published as the sixth of the series of Reports of Progress of Stream Measurements.

I have the honour to be, Sir,
Your obedient servant,
P. M. SAUDER,
Chief Hydrometric Engineer.

The methods of carrying on the investigations were similar to those of previous years. Local residents were engaged to observe the gauge heights at regular stations. These observations were recorded in a book supplied by the department, and at the end of each week the observer copied the week's records on a postal card which was forwarded to the Calgary office by the first convenient mail.

District hydrometric engineers made regular visits to the gauging stations, usually once in every three weeks. On these visits they examined the observers' records, made discharge measurements, and collected such information and data as would be of use in making estimates of the daily flow at the station. The results of the discharge measurements and all data collected were forwarded as soon as possible after being completed to the Calgary office, where all reports are copied on regular forms and filed.

During the winter no records were taken at a number of the gauging stations, which made it possible to reduce the field staff and have each engineer spend some time in the office and assist in the final computations and estimates of run-off. As far as possible, the same engineer that did the field work made or checked the office computations, so as to eliminate any chance of error through lack of knowledge of the conditions at the gauging station.

Gauge height-area, gauge height-mean velocity, and gauge height-discharge curves were plotted and rating tables constructed. Tables of discharge measurements, daily gauge

MONTHLY DISCHARGE of Jones Creek at Stearns' Ranch, for 1914.

(Drainage area 5 square miles.)

MONTH.	DISCHARGE IN SECOND-FEET.				RUN-OFF.	
	Maximum.	Minimum.	Mean.	Per Square Mile.	Depth in inches on Drainage Area.	Total in Acre-feet.
April........................	18.20	2.10	6.930	1.380	1.54	412
May.........................	2.30	0.88	1.77	0.354	0.41	109
June........................	2.50	0.34	1.12	0.224	0.25	67
July........................	0.51	0.00	0.126	0.025	0.03	8
August......................	....	....	....	....	....	............a
September.....	....	....	....	....	....	............a
October......	....	....	....	....	....	............a
The period..................	....	....	....	....	2 23	596

(a) Creek dry.

REPORT

OF

PROGRESS OF STREAM MEASUREMENTS FOR THE CALENDAR YEAR 1914.

By P. M. SAUDER, G. H. WHYTE, and G. R. ELLIOTT.

INTRODUCTION.

SCOPE OF WORK.

The chief features of the stream measurement work are the collection of data relating to the flow of surface waters and a study of the conditions affecting this flow. Information is also collected concerning river profiles, the duration and magnitude of floods, irrigation, water-power, storage, seepage, etc., which may be of use in hydrometric studies.

This information is obtained by a series of observations at regular gauging stations which are established at suitable points. The selection of sites for these gauging stations and their maintenance depend largely upon the physical features and needs of the locality. If water is to be used for irrigation purposes the summer flow receives special attention; where it is required for power purposes, it becomes necessary to determine the minimum flow; if water is to be stored, information is obtained regarding the maximum flow. In all cases the duration of the different stages of the streams is recorded. Throughout the country gauging stations are maintained for general statistical purposes, to show the conditions existing through long periods. They are also used as primary stations, and their records in connection with short series of measurements will serve as bases for estimating the flow at other points in the drainage basin.

During the open water season of 1914, records were taken at one hundred and seventy-four (174) regular gauging stations on various streams in Alberta and Saskatchewan, and at sixty-five (65) regular gauging stations on irrigation ditches and canals. Winter records, which are so valuable for power investigations and municipal water supplies, received special attention, and records were secured on almost all the important streams in the two provinces throughout the year.

ORGANIZATION.

The methods of carrying on the investigations were similar to those of previous years. Local residents were engaged to observe the gauge heights at regular stations. These observations were recorded in a book supplied by the department, and at the end of each week the observer copied the week's records on a postal card which was forwarded to the Calgary office by the first convenient mail.

District hydrometric engineers made regular visits to the gauging stations, usually once in every three weeks. On these visits they examined the observers' records, made discharge measurements, and collected such information and data as would be of use in making estimates of the daily flow at the station. The results of the discharge measurements and all data collected were forwarded as soon as possible after being completed to the Calgary office, where all reports are copied on regular forms and filed.

During the winter no records were taken at a number of the gauging stations, which made it possible to reduce the field staff and have each engineer spend some time in the office and assist in the final computations and estimates of run-off. As far as possible, the same engineer that did the field work made or checked the office computations, so as to eliminate any chance of error through lack of knowledge of the conditions at the gauging station.

Gauge height-area, gauge height-mean velocity, and gauge height-discharge curves were plotted and rating tables constructed. Tables of discharge measurements, daily gauge

5 GEORGE V, A. 1915

height and discharge, and monthly discharge were also compiled. These records have been collected and are embodied in this, the Sixth Annual Report of Progress of Stream Measurements.

The organization during 1914 was also similar to the previous year, and the staff consisted of the chief hydrometric engineer, two assistant engineers, one recorder, one computer, and one clerk in the office, and thirteen assistant engineers in the field.

During 1914 the territory was divided for administrative purposes into eleven districts, viz., Banff, Calgary, Macleod, Cardston, Milk River, Western Cypress Hills, Eastern Cypress Hills, Wood Mountain, Saskatoon, Edmonton and Athabaska. In each district there was one engineer, who while in the field employed temporary assistance and was equipped with the necessary gauging and surveying instruments. In Banff, Calgary, Macleod, Saskatoon, Edmonton and Athabaska districts, the engineers travelled by train and hired livery, and stopped at hotels and stopping houses; while in the other districts they were supplied with a team, democrat and camping outfit. One engineer was employed in an investigation of seepage and other losses in irrigation canals. The thirteenth engineer was employed at rating current meters, gauging the streams at Calgary, and other extra work. During the early spring, two of the irrigation inspecting engineers assisted in collecting records of the early spring run-off in the Cypress hills. An extra assistant engineer was employed during the winter of 1913-14 to make a special study of the winter flow of the North Saskatchewan River at Prince Albert, Saskatchewan.

BANFF DISTRICT.

This district included the following regular gauging stations:

Stream	Location	Date Established	
Bath Creek	NE. 32-28-16-5	April	9, 1913
Bow River	SE. 28-28-16-5a	July	18, 1910
Bow River	SE. 35-25-12-5	May	25, 1909
Bow River	NW. 32-24-8-5	March	10, 1912
Cascade River	SE. 19-26-11-5	August	16, 1911
Forty-mile Creek	SW. 2-26-12-5	July	31, 1912
Ghost River	NE. 23-26-6-5	August	17, 1911
Jumpingpound Creek	SE. 30-24-4-5	May	7, 1908
Kananaskis River	SW. 34-24-8-5b	August	31, 1911
Louise Creek	NE. 20-28-16-5	July	5, 1913
Pipestone River	SW. 27-28-16-5	August	31, 1911
Spray River	NW. 25-25-12-5	July	15, 1910
Spray River	SE. 31-22-10-5	July	23, 1914
Spray Lakes overflow	SW. 32-22-10-5	July	24, 1914

Records have been obtained throughout the year on all the above stations excepting those on Bath Creek, Spray River (at Spray Lake), Spray Lake overflow and Jumpingpound Creek; observers were not available in the first three cases, and it was not desired to maintain the last station during the winter months.

Miscellaneous gaugings were made of Beaupré Creek (NE. 15-26-5-5), Big Hill Creek (SW. 10-26-4-5), Bow River (SW. 32-26-14-5), Grand Valley Creek (SW. 24-26-5-5), Healy Creek (SW. 29-25-12-5), Horse Creek (NE. 8-26-4-5), Spencer Creek (SE. 18-26-5-5), Vermillion Creek (SW. 32-26-14-5), Whiteman Creek (NW. 24-24-11-5), and tail-race of the Lake Louise power house.

By means of the storage facilities which the Calgary Power and Transmission Company now has, it can and usually does keep the flow of Bow River at their power plants uniform all winter and prevents the sudden very low flows that used to occur previously under natural conditions.

As much data as possible was collected on the flow of Spray River near the Spray Lakes, and it is expected that this information will be of value in connection with the proposed storage reservoirs at Spray Lakes.

H. C. Ritchie, A.M. Can. Soc. C.E., was in charge of the field work in this district, and the final computations were made by G. R. Elliott, A. Clement, and H. C. Ritchie.

CALGARY DISTRICT.

This district included the following regular gauging stations:

Stream	Location	Date Established	
Bow River	SE. 2-21-19-4c	August	20, 1909
Bow River	NE. 32-21-25-4d	Sept.	, 1909
Boxelder Creek	NE. 2-12-30-3	May	24, 1910
Bullshead Creek	SE. 16-12-5-4	July	26, 1909

a This station was originally located on NE. 28-28-16-5, but was moved to its present position on August 31, 1911.
b This station was originally located on NW. 33-24-8-5, but was moved to its present position on May 13, 1913.
c This station was originally located on Sec. 13-21-19-4, but was moved to its present position in May, 1913.
d This station was originally located on Sec. 31-21-25-4, but was moved to its present position in May, 1913.

Stream	Location	Date Established
E. B. Canadian Pacific Railway Company Canal.	SE. 3-21-18-4	June 6, 1914
N. B. Canadian Pacific Railway Company Canal..	NW. 3-21-18-4	June 6, 1914
Elbow River	NW. 12-23-5-5	Sept. 29, 1914
Findlay & McDougal Ditch.	SW. 31-18-29-4	June 17, 1911
Fish Creek	SW. 26-22-3-5	May 13, 1907
Highwood River	SE. 20-18-2-5	July 27, 1912
Highwood River	NW. 6-19-28-4	May 28, 1908
Highwood River	NW. 17-20-28-4	Oct. 3, 1911
Little Bow Ditch	SW. 6-19-28-4	Aug. 1, 1910
Mackay Creek	NW. 26-11-1-4	July 29, 1909
Pekisko Creek	NW. 8-17-2-5	Oct. 6, 1911
Ross Creek	NW. 31-11-2-4	July 28, 1909
Sevenpersons River	NE. 30-12-5-4	April 27, 1910
Sheep River	NW. 22-20-29-4	May 25, 1908
N.B. Sheep River	SW. 12-21-3-5	May 22, 1908
S.B. Sheep River	SW. 17-20-2-5	May 23, 1908
South Saskatchewan River	NW. 31-12-5-4	May 31, 1911
Stimson Creek	NW. 2-17-2-5a	Oct. 6, 1911

Miscellaneous gaugings were made of the North and South Branches of Fish Creek near Priddis, Lineham's spillway at High River, Pine Creek near De Winton, Tongueflag Creek near High River, and several springs.

It will be noted that this district did not include the Bow and Elbow Rivers at Calgary, and Nose Creek and Canadian Pacific Railway Company Canal near Calgary, but included instead several streams at and east of Medicine Hat, Alberta. Only a few records were obtained at the upper station on Bow River in this district. The new station on the Elbow River was established for the purpose of collecting better data on the possibilities of developing a water power and municipal water supply a few miles above that point.

The Calgary winter district included only Bow River near Bassano, Highwood River and Little Bow Ditch at High River, and Elbow River of the above list. The South Saskatchewan River at Medicine Hat was included in the Macleod district during the winter months.

J. S. Tempest, A.M. Can. Soc. C.E., H. S. Kerby, B.A.Sc., and R. J. McGuinness were in charge of this district for various periods, and H. S. Kerby made the final computations for the annual report.

MACLEOD DISTRICT.

This district included the following regular gauging stations:

Stream	Location	Date Established
Belly River	NW. 1-9-22-4	August 31, 1911
Canyon Creek	NE. 14-6-2-5	July 6, 1910
Castle (Southfork) River	SW. 2-7-1-5	August 5, 1909
Cow Creek	NE. 14-8-2-5	May 26, 1910
Crowsnest River	SW. 12-8-5-5	July 28, 1910
Crowsnest River	NE. 36-7-4-5	July 28, 1910
Crowsnest River	NE. 26-7-2-5	Sept. 7, 1907
McGillivray Creek	SE. 7-8-4-5	July 23, 1913
Mill Creek	SW. 18-6-1-5	July 7, 1910
Mosquito Creek	NE. 30-16-28-4	August 1, 1908
Muddypound Creek	SW. 27-11-28-4	July 27, 1908
Nanton Creek	SE. 19-16-28-4b	August 3, 1908
Oldman River	NE. 34-7-1-5	Sept. 15, 1908
Oldman River	NW. 10-9-26-4	July 12, 1910
Pincher Creek	SW. 23-6-30-4	August 13, 1906
St. Mary River	NE. 26-7-22-4	Oct. 13, 1911
Todd Creek	SW. 19-8-1-5	August 3, 1909
Trout Creek	SE. 33-11-28-4	July 7, 1911
Willow Creek	SE. 26-9-26-4	July 1, 1909

Miscellaneous gaugings were made of Allison Creek (SW. 11-8-5-5), Bellevue Creek (NE. 29-7-3-5), Blairmore Creek (SE. 3-8-4-5), Connelly Creek (SE. 36-7-2-5), Dago Creek (NW. 17-13-2-5), Drum Creek (NW. 18-7-3-5) Ernst Creek (NW. 26-10-3-5), Fortier Springs (SE. 17-7-1-5), Gold Creek (SE. 30-7-3-5), Jim Creek (NE. 6-15-1-5), Lyon Creek (near Blairmore),

a This station was originally located on the SE. 14-17-2-5, but was moved to its present position on July 4th.
b This station was originally located on NW. 20-16-28-4, but was moved to its present location in Sept. 1913.

5 GEORGE V. A. 1915

Nez-Perce Creek (SE. 17-8-4-5), Playle Creek (SW. 32-11-1-5), Summit Creek (SW. 12-8-6-5), York Creek (NW. 34-7-4-5), and several other spring creeks and springs.

As this district has been organized for several years and there have been no extensive developments of the water resources, no changes of any account were made during the past year. Records of the flow of Oldman River have, however, become very valuable in connection with the investigation of the proposed scheme to irrigate a large tract of land lying between Little Bow River and Oldman River.

Winter records were taken of Belly River, Castle River, Crowsnest River (three stations), Oldman River (two stations), St. Mary River and Summit Creek (miscellaneous); Belly and St. Mary Rivers being included in the Cardston district during the winter months.

E. W. W. Hughes and *F. R. Burfield*, A.M.I.C.E., were in charge of field work in this district for short periods until May, when *J. E. Caughey*, B.Sc., was placed in charge for the balance of the year. The final computations were made by *J. E. Caughey*, *W. E. G. Hall*, and *O. H. Hoover*.

CARDSTON DISTRICT.

This district included the following regular gauging stations :

Stream	Location	Date Established
Alberta Railway and *I*rrigation Company Canal...	SE. 21-2-24-4	July 26, 1910
Alberta Railway and *I*rrigation Company Canal...	NW. 28-4-23-4	May 1, 1914
Belly River..................................	*NE*. 5-2-28-4	Nov. 1, 1911
Belly River..................................	SE. 21-6-25-4	May 27, 1909
Boundary Creek..............................	NW. 20-1-26-4	June 18, 1913
Christianson Ditch...........................	SE. 12-3-28-4	Sept. 14, 1911
Crooked Creek..	SW. 22-2-29-4	Sept. 15, 1909
Fidler Brothers Ditch........................ ...	SE. 19-1-26-4	Sept. 13. 1911
Lee Creek....................................	NW. 10-3-25-4	June 28, 1909
Lee Creek	SE. 27-2-26-4	May 5, 1913
Mami Creek ....·	SE. 19-2-27-4	August 13, 1909
N. B. Milk River............................	*NE*. 11-1-23-4*a*	July 21, 1909
N. B. Milk River............................	NE. 18-2-20-4	July 17, 1909
S. B. Milk River.............................	{SW. 29-37 N. 9 W.P.M.} {Montana, U.S.A. }	}April 23, 1913
Pinepound Creek.............................	NE. 29-4-23-4	April 30, 1914
Pothole Creek...............................	*NE*. 1-6-22-4	April 28, 1914
Pothole Creek...............................	NW. 10-5-22-4	April 27, 1914
Rolph Creek.................................	SE. 21-2-24-4	May 17, 1911
St. Mary River..............................	NW. 25-1-25-4	By A.R.I. Co. in 1905
Waterton River..............................	*NE*. 8-2-29-4	Aug. 26, 1908

As more satisfactory records can be obtained on Lee Creek, at the upper station, the lower station at Cardston was abandoned on July 13, 1914.

In 1912 an arrangement was made with the United States Geological Survey by which regular gauging stations on St. Mary and Milk Rivers would be maintained jointly, each bearing half the cost of construction and maintenance. The upper stations on St. Mary River and the North Branch of Milk River were therefore re-located at better sites, and a new station was established on the South Branch of Milk River in the state of Montana. These stations were equipped with automatic recording gauges early in 1913, which have been used since then.

Miscellaneous gaugings were made of North and South Branches of Belly River (Montana), Berta Creek (Waterton Lakes), Blakiston Brook (*NE*. 30-1-29-4), Cottonwood Creek (20-2-29-4), Drywood River (NW. 18-4-29-4), Hellroaring Creek (Waterton Lakes), Oil Creek (SW. 23-1-30-4), Pine Creek (NW. 21-3-29-4), and St. Mary River (SW. 23-3-25-4), J. N. West's Ditch and Yarrow Creek (14-4-29-4). ·

Winter records were taken of Belly River (two stations), Lee Creek, North Branch of Milk River, St. Mary River, and Waterton River.

J. E. Degnan was in charge of the field work in this district until March, and *O. H. Hoover*, B.A.Sc., for the balance of the year. The final computations for the annual report were made by *O. H. Hoover* and *J. E. Degnan*.

MILK RIVER DISTRICT.

This district included the following regular gauging stations:

Stream	Location	Date Established
Deer Creek Cattle Co. West Ditch..............	SW. 36-1-12-4	April 30, 1914
Deer Creek Cattle Co. *E*ast Ditch...............	SW. 36-1-12-4	April 27, 1912
*E*tzikom Coulee...............................	SW. 3-7-19-4	April 16, 1914

a This station was originally located on NE. 13-1-23-4, but was moved to its present position on May 1, 1913.

SESSIONAL PAPER No. 25c

Stream	Location	Date Established	
Hooper and Huckvale South Ditch	NE. 22-4-6-4	May	2, 1912
Hooper and Huckvale North Ditch.	SW. 27-4-6-4	March	7, 1914
Manyberries Creek	SW. 27-4-6-4a	June	17, 1910
Milk River...................................	NE. 21-2-16-4	May	18, 1909
Milk River...................................	SW. 35-1-13-4	August	2, 1909
Milk River...................................	SW. 21-2-8-4	August	5, 1909
Milk River...................................	NE. 6-37 N-9 E.P.M. Montana, U.S.A.b	August	7, 1909
N.B. Milk River.........	SW. 19-2-18-4	July	15, 1909
S.B. Milk River..	NW. 31-1-18-4	July	14, 1909

It was impossible to secure an observer for the gauge on the North Branch of Milk River on the SW. ¼ Sec. 19, Tp. 2, Rge. 18, W. 4th Mer., but discharge measurements were made at every opportunity.

The gauging station in the State of Montana is maintained jointly with the United States Geological Survey. It was equipped with an automatic gauge early in the summer of 1913.

Miscellaneous gaugings were made of Beargulch Creek (Sec. 19-2-9-4), Canal Creek (Sec. 6-4-6-4), Deadhorse Coulee (Sec. 4-2-11-4), Deer Creek (NE. 26, S.W. 36, and SW. 15-1-12-4), Halfbreed Creek (Sec. 28-2-10-4), Irrigation Creek (SW. 36-5-7-4), Kennedy Creek (Sec. 3-1-5-4), Ketchum Creek (4-6-4), Mackie Creek (Sec. 19-2-18-4), Miners Coulee (Sec. 11-2-11-4), and Police Coulee (Sec. 35-1-13-4).

Winter records were taken only at the regular gauging station on Milk River on the NE. ¼ Sec. 21, Tp. 2, Rge. 16, W. 4th Mer., which was included in the Cardston district during the winter months.

J. E. Degnan was in charge of field work in this district and made the final computations for the annual report. During the early spring run-off, H. W. Rowley, B.Sc., made numerous gaugings on Manyberries Creek and the other streams in Pakowki Lake drainage basin.

WESTERN CYPRESS HILLS.

This district included the following regular gauging stations:

Stream	Location	Date Established	
Adams North Ditch............................	NE. 10-9-27-3	May	22, 1914
Adams South Ditch............................	NE. 10-9-27-3	May	22, 1914
Anderson Ditch...............................	SW. 23-6-3-4	Sept.	23, 1911
Battle Creek.................................	NE. 33-5-29-3	June	3, 1909
Battle Creek.................................	NW. 33-5-27-3c	July	5, 1910
Battle Creek.................................	NE. 3-3-27-3	May	11, 1910
Bullshead Creek..............................	NW. 15-9-5-4	Oct.	9, 1911
Cheeseman West Ditch	SW. 12-8-29-3	June	24, 1911
Cheeseman East Ditch	SW. 12-8-29-3	June	24, 1911
Gaff Ditch...................................	SW. 25-5-29-3	July	11, 1911
Gap Creek...................................	SE. 4-10-27-3	April	25, 1909
Gap Creek...................................	NE. 31-11-26-3	May	3, 1910
Gilchrist Bros. Ditch..	SW. 11-5-27-3	Oct.	16, 1911
Grosventre Creek	SE. 27-9-4-4	Oct.	10, 1911
Lindner Ditch................................	NW. 10-6-29-3	July	26, 1910
Lodge Creek.................................	NW. 10-6-3-4	July	22, 1909
Lodge Creek.................................	NE. 25-3-1-4d	August	31, 1912
Lodge Creek.................................	SE. 12-1-29-3	August	13, 1909
E.B. Lodge Creek............................	SE. 1-7-3-4	Oct.	17, 1911
E.B. Mackay Creek...........................	NW. 36-10-1-4	Oct.	13, 1911
W. B. Mackay Creek.........................	NE. 27-10-1-4e	Oct.	12, 1911
Maple Creek.................................	NE. 16-11-26-3	May	9, 1908
Maple Creek	SE. 28-11-26-3	May	4, 1910
Marshall & Gaff Ditch.......................	NE. 33-5-29-3	July	11, 1911
McKinnon Ditch..............................	NW. 20-4-26-3	Oct.	20, 1911
McShane Creek..............................	SW. 3-10-27-3	April	23, 1909
Middle Creek................................	SW. 35-5-1-4	June	21, 1910
Middle Creek................................	SW. 30-5-29-3	July	20, 1909
Middle Creek................................	NE. 4-2-29-3	June	13, 1910
Oxarart Creek..	NE. 20-6-27-3	June	15, 1909
Pollock East Ditch..........................	SW. 17-9-27-3	May	19, 1914
Pollock West Ditch..........................	SW. 17-9-27-3	May	19, 1914

a This station was originally located on SE. 3-5-6-4. but was moved to its present position on May 2, 1912.
b This station was originally located on SE. 3-1-5-4. but was moved to its present position in the spring of 1913.
c This station was originally located on the SW. 2-6-28-3. but was moved to its present position on May 29, 1912.
d This station was originally located on the SW. 23-10-2-4. but was moved to its present position on September 20, 1912.
e This station was originally located on the NE. 36-3-1-4. but was moved to its present position on April 29, 1914.

5 GEORGE V, A. 1915

Stream	Location	Date Established
Richardson Ditch.	SE. 2-5-27-3	Oct. 14, 1911
Ross Creek...	SE. 32-9-3-4a	Oct. 11, 1911
Sage Creek...	NE. 9-1-2-4	August 10, 1909
Sixmile Creek.	SW. 6-7-28-3b	July 22, 1909
Spangler Ditch..................................	SW. 6-7-28-3	July 10, 1911
Starks & Burton Ditch..........................	SE. 17-11-5-4	Oct. 9, 1911
Stirling & Nash Ditch	SE. 22-3-27-3	July 11, 1911
Tenmile Creek..................................	SE. 4-6-29-3	July 21, 1909
White Ditch.......................................	SW. 1-9-27-3	June 15, 1911
Wilson Ditch...	NE. 34-5-28-3	June 21, 1911
Wood & Anderson Ditch.......................	NE. 21-7-29-3	June 20, 1914
Wood & Anderson East Ditch..................	SE. 22-7-29-3	June 20, 1914
Wood & Anderson West Ditch..................	NE. 22-7-29-3	June 20, 1914

At all these stations, with the exception of Sage Creek, some records were obtained, but on a number of the ditches not sufficient data was obtained to enable any computations of daily flow being made.

Miscellaneous gaugings were made of Adams Springs (NW. 32-5-1-4), Battle Creek (Sec. 28-5-28-3), Fourmile Coulee (NW. 14-8-29-3), Gap Creek (NE. 20-8-27-3), Link's Spring (NW. 32-5-1-4), Maple Creek (Sec. 8-10-26-3), and on several other creeks and springs.

No winter records were taken on any of the streams in this district during 1914.

A special effort was made to obtain full information of the spring run-off of this district during 1914, and the district was divided into three sections with an engineer in each. H. D. St. A. Smith (Grad. R.M.C.), was in charge of the Willow Creek section, H. R. Carscallen, B.A.Sc., in charge of the Tenmile section, and R. J. Srigley in charge of the section north of the Cypress Hills, west of Maple Creek. From April to the end of the season H. W. Rowley, B.Sc., was in charge of the whole district, and during the fall also acted as Water-master on Battle Creek, where, due to the low discharge, several questions of water rights came up. Mr. Rowley also made the final computations for the annual report.

The year 1914 was one of the driest on record, and the whole of this district suffered from lack of moisture. Most of the streams dried up for the greater part of their courses, and there was generally a lack of water for domestic and irrigation purposes. Apparently the only solution to a serious problem is the construction of reservoirs to retain the spring run-off until later in the year, when it is of most value.

During 1914, steel was laid on the Weyburn-Lethbridge Branch of the Canadian Pacific Railway as far west as the interprovincial boundary, and when this line is in operation it will make the district more accessible, and probably make it advisable to re-adjust the Eastern and Western Cypress Hills districts.

EASTERN CYPRESS HILLS.

This district included the following regular gauging stations:

Stream	Location	Date Established
Axton Ditch.....................................	NE. 26-7-21-3	July 26, 1913
Barroby Ditch.................................	NE. 33-6-23-3	August 12, 1913
Bear Creek.....................................	SE. 18-11-23-3	June 22, 1908
E.B. Bear Creek.	SE. 21-10-23-3	August 18, 1909
W.B. Bear Creek.....	SW. 32-10-23-3	Sept. 16, 1909
Belanger Creek................................	SW. 30-6-25-3	March 31, 1912
Beveridge Ditch...............................	NW. 18-10-24-3	June 27, 1914
Bolingbroke Ditch............................	NE. 7-7-22-3	August 11, 1913
Bone Creek.....................................	NW. 34-8-22-3	July 2, 1908
Braniff Ditch..	SE. 30-11-23-3	June 22, 1911
Bridge Creek..	SE. 33-10-22-3	April 8, 1911
Bridge Creek..	NW. 12-11-22-3	July 29, 1909
Clark & Thompson Ditch......................	NE. 5-7-21-3	July 19, 1913
F. Cross Ditch.................................	NW. 15-7-22-3	Sept. 9, 1911
A. M. Cross Ditch.............................	SE. 5-8-22-3	August 14, 1913
Cumberland Ditch........	SW. 17-11-24-3	June 27, 1914
Davis Creek....................................	NE. 29-6-25-3	May 24, 1909
Dimmock Bros. Ditch........	SE. 16-11-21-3	Sept. 2, 1914
Drury Ditch	NW. 19-6-25-3	Sept. 2, 1914
Fairwell Creek.................................	NW. 30-6-24-3	June 10, 1909
Fauquier Ditch.................................	NE. 30-10-25-3	June 8, 1914
Fearon Ditch...................................	SW. 6-11-24-3	June 25, 1912
Frenchman River..............................	NW. 16-6-24-3	July 10, 1912

a This station was originally located on the NW. 24-9-3-4. but was moved to its present position on May 15, 1914.
b This station was originally located on the NW. 29-7-28-3. but was moved to its present position on July 4, 1911.

SESSIONAL PAPER No. 25c

Stream	Location	Date Established
Frenchman River	*NE*. 23-6-23-3	July 9, 1912
Frenchman River	SE. 31-6-21-3*a*	July 31, 1908
N.B. Frenchman River	*NE*. 16-7-22-3	July 25, 1908
Hammond Ditch	SW. 16-10-25-3	June 13, 1912
Hawkin Ditch	SE. 26-9-20-3	July 9, 1913
Hay Creek	SW. 29-10-25-3	July 4, 1910
Hay Creek	*NE*. 30-10-25-3	April 22, 1909
Jones Creek	SE. 20-8-20-3	May 15, 1912
Kearney Bros. Ditch	SE. 19-8-23-3	Sept. 6, 1913
Lonepine Creek	NW. 27-7-26-3	July 17, 1909
Mann Ditch	NW. 32-10-22-3	July 1, 1913
E. B. McCarthy, Bertram & Salt Ditch	NW. 29-11-23-3	June 15, 1914
W. B. McCarthy, Bertram & Salt Ditch	NW. 29-11-23-3	June 15, 1914
Moorhead Ditch	SE. 25-10-25-3	June 10, 1911
Morrison Bros. Ditch	SW. 26-6-21-3	August 22, 1911
Needham Bros. Ditch	SW. 30-11-23-3	June 22, 1911
Parker North Ditch	SW. 4-9-20-3	July 15, 1913
Parker South Ditch	SW. 4-9-20-3	July 15, 1913
Pollock *East* Ditch	NW. 22-7-21-3	August 10, 1911
Pollock West Ditch	NW. 22-7-21-3	August 10, 1911
Piapot Creek	*NE*. 18-11-24-3*b*	June 17, 1908
Rose Creek	*NE*. 26-7-22-3	May 1, 1911
Skull Creek	*NE*. 29-10-22-3	April 8, 1911
Skull Creek	NW. 10-11-22-3	June 29, 1908
Stearns Ditch	NW. 20-8-20-3	July 16, 1913
Stearns Ditch	SW. 20-8-20-3	July 16, 1913
Stearns Ditch	SW. 17-8-20-3	July 16, 1913
Strong & Day Ditch	*NE*. 25-6-22-3*c*	July 31, 1908
Sucker Creek	NW. 24-6-26-3	May 26, 1909
Swiftcurrent Creek	SW. 22-7-21-3	May 18, 1909
Swiftcurrent Creek	*NE*. 18-10-19-3	June 15, 1910
Swiftcurrent Creek	NW. 17-10-19-3	May 27, 1910

Miscellaneous gaugings were made on Blacktail Creek (30-6-23-3), Calf Creek (SE. 5-8-22-3), Concrete Coulee (11-7-23-3), Cypress Lake overflow, Doyle Coulee (17-7-23-3), Frenchman River (26-6-21-3), Petrified Coulee (30-6-23-3), Saunders Springs, near Maple Creek, and several other streams and springs.

Artificial controls were constructed in Frenchman River at SE. 31-6-21-3 and *NE*. 23-6-23-3, late in the fall, and should improve the results at these points. A number of permanent weirs were placed on the smaller streams of the district, and it is the intention to continue the use of these devices in the future, as very satisfactory results were obtained.

The Weyburn-Lethbridge Branch of the Canadian Pacific Railway has been completed through the southern part of the district, and will materially assist the development of this territory, and no doubt result in many changes in our work in this district in the future.

The only winter records obtained in this district during 1914 were on Saunders Springs, near Maple Creek.

The year 1914 was noted for its small precipitation throughout this district, and thus the streams were all very low during the year.

The early spring run-off was obtained by two engineers in this district, M. H. French covering the stations south of Cypress Hills and H. O. Brown those north of the hills. F. R. Steinberger was in charge of the whole district from April to August; *E*. W. W. Hughes took charge for the balance of the season and made the final computations for the annual report.

WOOD MOUNTAIN DISTRICT.

This district included the following regular gauging stations:

Stream	Location	Date Established
Bate Creek	NW. 6-6-16-3	April 16, 1914
Bigbreed Creek	SE. 15-2-11-3	March 30, 1914
Bowrey Ditch	{ From Rock Creek (Montana) }	April 30, 1914
Frenchman River	NW. 3-2-11-3	March 28, 1914

a This station was originally located on the NE. 31–6-21–3, but was moved to its present location on August 21, 1914.

b This station was originally located on the SW. 17–11–24–3, but was moved to its present location on May 13, 1909.

c This station was originally located on Sec. 36–6–22–3, but was moved to its present location on April 17, 1911.

No. 25c—2½

5 GEORGE V, A. 1915.

Stream	Location	Date Established
Frenchman River..............................	SE. 27-5-16-3	April 10, 1914
Horse Creek..................	Near Barnard (Montana)	May 1, 1914
Littlebreed Creek	NW. 11-2-11-3	March 31, 1914
McEachran Creek.........................	Near Barnard (Montana)	May 1, 1914
Mule Creek..................	SW. 33-5-17-3	April 15, 1914
Rock Creek	Near Barnard (Montana)	April 30, 1914
Snake Creek..................	SW. 16-4-13-3	April 17, 1914

Miscellaneous gaugings were made of a few small spring creeks and coulees.

This district was established to obtain records of the flow of the Frenchman River and tributaries near the international boundary in connection with the investigations of boundary waters and proposed storage reservoirs. In order to get suitable sites, a few of the stations had to be established in the State of Montana. In connection with the establishment of these stations, cables were erected at three points, viz.: Frenchman River (two stations) and Snake Creek.

E. W. W. Hughes was in charge of the field work in this district, established the stations. and made the final computations for the annual report. From August to November he also had charge of the field work in the Eastern Cypress Hills district, as well as the Wood Mountain district.

SASKATOON DISTRICT.

This district included the following regular gauging stations:

Stream	Location	Date Established
Battle River..................................	NW. 25-43-17-3	May 23, 1914
Battle River..................................	SE. 19-43-16-3	June 17, 1911
Bridge Creek.......	SE. 23-13-19-3	March 29, 1911
Long Creek..................................	SE. 10-2-8-2	June 22, 1911
Moose Mountain Creek......	NE. 15-3-2-2	Sept. 4, 1913
Moosejaw Creek...............................	NE. 24-11-19-2	June 21, 1911
Moosejaw Creek...............................	NW. 16-16-26-2	April 7, 1910
Notukeu Creek................................	NW. 10-11-10-3	August 7, 1914
Qu'Appelle River.............................	NW. 33-19-21-2	May 12, 1911
North Saskatchewan River..................	{ SW. 33 and NE. 29-43-16-3 }	May 16, 1911
North Saskatchewan River...............	{ River Lot No. 76, Prince Albert Settlement }	Oct. 2, 1911
South Saskatchewan River..................	SW. 28-36-5-3	May 27, 1911
Souris River.................................	NE. 11-2-8-2	June 23, 1911
Souris River.................................	NE. 36-2-1-2	June 26, 1911
Souris River.................................	SW. 6-4-26-1	July 20, 1911
Swiftcurrent Creek............................	SW. 12-15-14-3	April 30, 1910
Swiftcurrent Creek............................	NW. 18-15-13-3	May 5, 1913

The station on Notukeu Creek was established to determine the quantity of water available in that locality for domestic and municipal purposes. The ones on Swiftcurrent Creek are maintained for the same purpose, and to make it possible to get accurate records a concrete control and weir were constructed in this stream at the gauge on the SW. ¼ Sec. 12, Tp. 15, Rge. 14, W. 3rd Mer., late in the fall of 1914.

Miscellaneous gaugings were made of Souris River at Weyburn, Little Red River at Prince Albert, Springs near Gull Lake, and elsewhere.

Winter records were obtained at all the regular stations in this district, excepting the upper station on Battle River, Moose Mountain Creek, the upper station on Moosejaw Creek, and the two lower stations on Souris River. The stations west of Moosejaw were included in the Macleod district during the winter of 1914-15.

As intimated elsewhere, a special study was made of the flow of the North Saskatchewan River at Prince Albert during the winter of 1913-14, by W. H. Storey. The gauge was read and recorded three times each day and the discharge was measured three times each week. Besides providing the data required by the Water Power Branch, these records are very valuable on account of their great accuracy for testing the different methods of determining the discharge of an ice-covered stream. A special report on this work was written by Mr. G. H. Whyte, and is attached to this report as an appendix.

F. R. Steinberger, B.E., was in charge of the district except from April to September, when W. H. Storey was in charge. Mr. Storey also made the final computations for the annual. report.

EDMONTON DISTRICT.

This district included the following regular gauging stations:

Stream	Location	Date Established
Athabaska River	SE. 20-66-22-4	Feb. 23, 1913
Battle River	SW. 4-43-25-4	May 7, 1913
Clearwater River..	SE. 16-39-7-5	June 3, 1913
Pigeon Creek	SE. 15-46-28-4	August 7, 1914
Red Deer River	SE. 20-38-27-4	Dec. 2, 1911
North Saskatchewan River	NW. 33-52-24-4	May 14, 1911
North Saskatchewan River	NE. 21-39-7-5	June 2, 1913
Sturgeon River	NW. 28-55-22-4	Dec. 30, 1913
Sturgeon River	{Bet. River Lots 27 and {52 St. Albert Settlement}	Apr 1 23, 1913

Miscellaneous gaugings were made of Blindman River (NW. 15-39-27-4), Brazeau River (19-45-10-5), Buck Creek (SE. 23-47-6-5), Lesser Slave River (Mirror Landing), Nordegg River (SE. 24-45-10-5), and North Saskatchewan River (26-45-9-5 and NW. 2-49-7-5).

A cable and boat station was established on the Athabaska River at Athabaska so that continuous records could be obtained. Cable stations were also established on the North Saskatchewan and Clearwater Rivers at Rocky Mountain House.

All the stations in this district were maintained throughout the winter. Those on the Red Deer, North Saskatchewan and Clearwater Rivers were included in the Calgary district.

Miscellaneous gaugings of Buck Creek, Brazeau River, Nordegg River, North Saskatchewan River (near mouth of Brazeau River), and Pigeon Creek were also made in February and March by J. S. Tempest, who was in charge of the Calgary district at that time.

P. H. Daniells, B.Sc., was in charge of the Edmonton district, except from May to October, when J. M. Paul, B.A., B.E., was in charge. Mr. Paul made the final computations for the annual report.

ATHABASKA DISTRICT.

This district included the following regular gauging stations:

Stream	Location	Date Established
Athabaska River	NW. 15-45-1-6	March 4, 1913
Lobstick River	NE. 30-53-7-5	July 11, 1913
Maligne River	SW. 1-46-1-6	June 17, 1914
McLeod River	NW. 3-54-16-5	May 18, 1914
Miette River	SW. 9-45-1-6	August 23, 1913
Pembina River	SW. 20-53-7-5	Dec. 19, 1913
Rocky River	NW. 13-48-28-5	July 3, 1913
Sturgeon River	SW. 14-54-5-5	April 21, 1914
Sturgeon River. .	SE. 7-55-2-5	April 23, 1914
Sturgeon River	NW. 32-54-26-4	April 22, 1914

Miscellaneous gaugings were made of Athabaska River (NE. 5-51-25-5), Edson River (SE. 16-54-16-5), Embarras River (SW. 5-52-18-5), Fiddle Creek (near Miette Hot Springs), McLeod River (NW. 3-54-16-5), Maligne River (near Jasper), Prairie Creek (NE. 5-51-25-5), Snaring River (NW. 33-46-1-6), Sundance Creek (NW. 4-53-18-5), Stony River (near Hawes), North Saskatchewan River (NW. 2-49-7-5), and Wolf Creek (SW. 3-54-16-5).

Cable stations were constructed on the Pembina and Maligne Rivers during the year, and the ferry cable on the McLeod River used for gauging.

All the above regular and most of the miscellaneous gauging stations were maintained throughout the winter, and were included in the Edmonton district. Due to the fact that the country is not well settled, it is very hard to obtain observers at most points, and thus impossible to maintain regular gauging stations everywhere they are desired.

P. H. Daniells, B.Sc., was in charge of the field work during the year and also made the fina computations for the annual report.

INVESTIGATION OF ABSORPTION LOSSES IN CANALS.

During 1914 the investigations which were commenced in 1913, to determine the absorption and seepage losses in canals, were continued by R. J. McGuinness, who spent the whole of the irrigation season on this work on the canals of the Western Section of the Canadian Pacific Railway Company's irrigation tract near Calgary, and the Alberta Railway and Irrigation Company's irrigation tract near Lethbridge. In this work we received the assistance of the officials of the above companies, and in all 256 measurements were made. ' The

5 GEORGE V. A. 1915

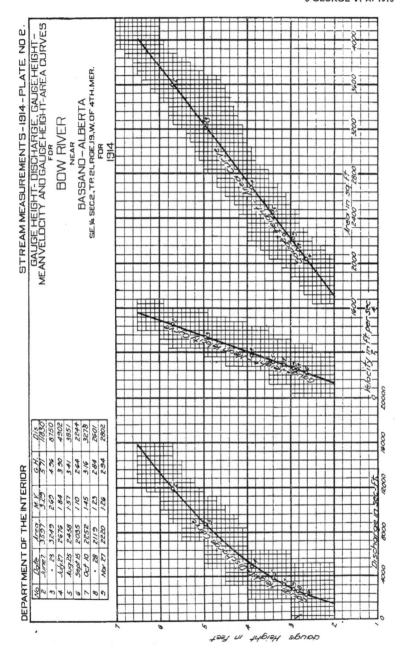

STREAM MEASUREMENTS-1914-PLATE NO 2.

GAUGE HEIGHT-DISCHARGE, GAUGE HEIGHT-
MEAN VELOCITY AND GAUGE HEIGHT-AREA CURVES

FOR

BOW RIVER

NEAR

BASSANO-ALBERTA

SE.¼ SEC.2, TP.21, RGE.19, W. OF 4 TH.MER.

FOR

1914

DEPARTMENT OF THE INTERIOR

No.	Date	Area	M.V.	G.H.	Dis.
2	June 7	3337	3.25	3.71	11830
3	" 23	3249	2.69	4.56	8750
4	July 27	2676	1.84	3.90	4902
5	Aug 25	2458	1.57	3.41	3851
6	Sept 16	2035	1.10	2.64	2244
7	Oct 10	2252	1.45	3.16	3278
8	" 28	2119	1.23	2.84	2601
9	Nov 27	2220	1.26	2.94	2802

SESSIONAL PAPER No. 25c

records obtained are given later in the report, and in addition to the work of measuring the flow of the canals the temperatures of the waters were also obtained. This work is being continued and should produce some valuable data in a year or two.

CURRENT-METER RATING STATION.

The rating station was kept in operation from early in April until the end of November. During this period all the current-meters used in the field were rated at least once, and most of them twice, while a few used on special work were rated three times.

During the season seventy-five current-meters were rated, forty-one for this branch, eleven for the British Columbia Hydrographic Survey, five for the British Columbia Government, twelve for the Manitoba Hydrographic Survey, four for the Department of Public Works of Canada, and two for the Canadian Pacific Railway Company. Each meter was rated in the condition it was received and, with few exceptions, again after being cleaned, adjusted and fitted with a new bearing. Rating tables were prepared for each rating of a meter and blueprints made, which are sent out with the instrument, while the originals are filed for reference in the office.

In addition to the regular work a few experiments on rating meters were carried out. These gave results which will be of assistance in future rating and field work. It is the intention, however, to make further and more extensive investigations before publishing the results.

R. J. Srigley was in charge of the work. He was assisted by Captain Clifford, D.S.O., until he left with the first Canadian Overseas Expeditionary Force in August. For the balance of the season Mr. Srigley rated the current meters without help.

BENCH-MARKS.

When the stream measurement work was first started, the gauges were usually referred to bench-marks on wooden stakes or stumps of trees. These were easily shifted or destroyed, and were not satisfactory. In 1911 an iron bench-mark was adopted by this branch, and now almost all the gauges are either referred to bench-marks on concrete piers or other permanent structures, or to one of these iron bench-marks. Whenever an opportunity is afforded, these are tied to the Canadian Pacific Railway or Dominion Government levels, to determine their elevation above sea level, and they are therefore also a convenient reference for local levelling operations.

Descriptions of the iron bench-marks are given in the Report of the Progress of Stream Measurements for 1911 and 1912.

OFFICE WORK.

As above intimated, the reports of the gauge height observers and the hydrometric engineers are transmitted to the office by mail. These are copied on office forms and filed in a cabinet, which is carefully indexed, and where they can be referred to at any time without trouble. As the engineers complete their computations, the results are entered on convenient forms and filed in the same cabinet.

A cabinet made up of four styles of drawers is used for filing the records. The top section is used for filing the gauge height books of the observers and the current meter notes of the engineers. The gauge height books and current meter notes are filed alphabetically, according to the names of the streams. The next section contains the postal cards sent in by the observers, and these are also filed alphabetically according to the names of the streams. The third section is made up of map drawers, and contains the gauge height-area, gauge height-mean velocity and gauge height-discharge curves, and plotted cross-sections which are filed alphabetically, according to the names of the streams. The same section contains the maps showing the outlines of the drainage basins, filed numerically according to the number of the sectional sheet. The rating curves for the current meters are also filed in this section numerically, according to the office numbers of the meters. The bottom section of the cabinet consists of letter-size pockets, alphabetically arranged for each gauging station. The tables of gauge heights, discharge measurements, daily gauge height and discharge, monthly discharge, a description of the station, and memos of any changes are filed in these pockets. The different rating tables for each meter are also filed numerically in this section, and another drawer contains the daily and monthly reports of the meteorological service.

The copying and filing of the reports of the gauge height observers and the engineers is entrusted to the office recorder. While doing this he carefully examines all records to see that there are no errors, and where there are doubtful or impossible records it is his duty to have the data corrected or ascertain the cause of the unusual condition. He also makes out the pay list for the observers and conducts the correspondence relating to the records.

All computations are checked before being used or published. For this reason, as far as possible, men with some technical education, or students in science, are engaged as helpers. The gaugings are computed by the helper and his work is checked by the engineer. In some instances, where there is a great deal of driving and camping out, the engineer cannot secure a helper who can compute discharges, and in that case he computes the discharges himself, and his computations are checked in the office.

5 GEORGE V, A. 1915

Gaugings of the flow under ice are usually made by using the multiple point method, and vertical velocity curves have to be plotted to determine the mean velocity in the vertical.

The computation by this method is long and tedious and cannot be done by the engineer in the field. There are therefore a great many computations to be made in the office, and the services of a computer are required.

During the year 1914, G. H. Nettleton filled the position of office recorder, and J. B. Gray that of office computer.

The results of the discharge measurements are plotted on cross-section paper by one of the assistant engineers as soon as they are received in the office, and thus a very close check is kept on the records, and errors can be detected at once and in most cases can be rectified. At the same time the records are kept up to date, and demands for provisional estimates can be met at an early date. Important changes in the flow are also detected at once, and instructions are issued without delay to the field men to obtain further gaugings. The first and second assistants to the chief engineer supervise the office and field work by constantly checking and inspecting it, and also do considerable work in the preparation of the annual and special reports.

P. M. Sauder, M. Can. Soc. C.E., occupies the position of chief hydrometric engineer, and G. H. Whyte and G. R. Elliott, B.A.Sc., A.M. Can. Soc. C.E., are respectively the first and second assistants.

CONVENTIONS AND CONFERENCES.

In January, G. H. Whyte attended a conference of the Western District Engineers of the Water Resources Branch of the United States Geological Survey, held at Boise, Idaho. As particulars of this conference were given in the report for 1913, no further space will be given to it here.

On February 20th and 21st, the second annual conference of the hydrometric engineers of this office was held at Calgary, with all but two members of the staff present. A good deal of interest was taken in this, and a number of valuable suggestions made and papers given. It is hoped that we will be able to hold such conferences each year in future, as they enable the men to discuss the different features of the work and to obtain a better idea of the way the office and field work is carried on.

In October, P. M. Sauder and G. R. Elliott attended the International Irrigation Congress held at Calgary. This congress was very successful, but as complete printed reports of it will soon be available no further space will be given to it here.

It is unfortunate that it was not possible to send a representative to the conference of the District Engineers of the Water Resources Branch of the United States Geological Survey, held at Washington, D.C., in December, as this conference is always a great success. Copies of the papers read at this conference have, however, been received, and are very valuable and interesting.

FUTURE WORK.

During 1915, a special effort is being made to again obtain the total spring run-off of the main streams in the Cypress Hills and of Milk River drainage basin. The records obtained in 1914 on these streams are of especial value, and no doubt those of 1915 will be just as valuable, and it may not be found necessary to do early spring work in 1916, although it would be advisable.

The special work in the Wood Mountain district is to be continued during 1915, and will be of value in connection with the International Waterways' Treaty.

The investigations of absorption losses in irrigation canals will be continued during 1915, and will be extended to include other problems in connection with irrigation work.

Parties will be placed on the headwaters of the North Saskatchewan River and in the Peace River district, where scarcely any data regarding the run-off has been collected. In both these districts there are water power sites and records of the flow are required to determine the possibilities. Ordinary transportation facilities are not available in either district. The engineer on the headwaters of the North Saskatchewan River will therefore have to use pack ponies, and the one in Peace River district will probably use boats or canoes.

DEFINITIONS.

The volume of water flowing in a stream is known as run-off or discharge. In expressing it various units are used, depending upon the kind of work for which the data is needed. Those used in this report are " second-feet," " acre-feet," " run-off per square mile " and " run-off in depth in inches " and may be defined as follows:

" Second-foot " is an abbreviation for cubic foot per second, and is the body of water flowing in a stream one foot wide and one foot deep at the rate of one foot per second.

The " acre-foot " is the unit capacity used in connection with storage for irrigation work and is equivalent to 43,560 cubic feet. It is the quantity required to cover an acre to a depth of one foot.

The expression " second-feet per square mile " means the average number of cubic feet of water flowing each second from every square mile of drainage area on the assumption that the run-off is uniformly distributed.

" Depth in inches " means the depth of water in inches that would have covered the drainage area, uniformly distributed, if all the water could have accumulated on the surface. This quantity is used for comparing run-off with rainfall, which quantity is usually given in depth in inches.

It should be noticed that " acre-feet " and " depth in inches " represent the actual quantities of water which are produced during the periods in question, while " second-feet," on the contrary, is merely a rate of flow per second.

EXPLANATION AND USE OF TABLES.

The data obtained and the estimates made therefrom have been compiled in tabulated form, and for each regular gauging station are given, as far as available, the following data:—
1. Description of station.
2. List of discharge measurements.
3. Table of daily gauge heights and discharges.
4. Table of monthly discharges and run-off.

The description of stations gives such general information about the locality and equipment as would enable the reader to find and use the station. *It* also gives, as far as possible, complete history of all the changes that have occurred since the station was established and that might affect the records in any way.

The list of discharge measurements gives the results of all the discharge measurements that have been made at or in the vicinity of the gauging station or have been used in completing the records for the gauging station. *It* gives the date on which the measurement was made, the name of the engineer, the width and area of cross-section, the mean velocity of the current, the gauge height and the discharge in second-feet.

The table of daily gauge heights and discharges given in this report is a combination of two tables kept in the office of the survey, namely, the table of daily gauge heights and the station rating table. The table of daily gauge heights gives the daily fluctuations of the surface of the water above the zero of the gauge, as reported by the observer. During high water, two observations of the gauge were made at some stations, and the gauge height given in the table is the mean of the observation for the day. Where automatic gauges are maintained the records given are the mean stage for the day. The discharge measurements and gauge heights are the base data from which the other tables are computed. The table of daily discharges is the discharge in second-feet, corresponding to the stage of the stream, as given by the station rating table.

In the table of monthly discharge the column headed " maximum " gives the mean flow for the day when the mean gauge height was highest. As the gauge height is the mean for the day, there might have been short periods when the water level and the corresponding discharge were higher than given in this column. Likewise, in the column " minimum," the quantity given is the mean flow for the day when the mean gauge height was lowest. The column headed " mean " is the average flow for each second during the month. The computations for the quantities in the remaining columns have been based upon this mean. The drainage area for each gauging station was marked off on the sectional maps of the department and the area taken off with a planimeter. In many districts, information regarding topographical features is very incomplete, and the computed areas are only approximate. As the surveys of the department are extended and completed, these computations will be checked and, if necessary, corrected.

CONVENIENT EQUIVALENTS.

The following is a list of convenient equivalents for use in hydraulic computations:—

1 cubic foot equals 6.23 British *I*mperial gallons.
1 cubic foot equals 7.48 United States gallons.
1 acre equals 43,560 square feet; equals 4,840 square yards.
1 acre-foot equals 43,560 cubic feet.
1 acre-foot equals 271,472 British *I*mperial gallons.
1 acre-foot equals 325,850 United States gallons.
1 inch deep on 1 square mile equals 2,323,200 cubic feet.
1 inch deep on 1 square mile equals 0.0737 second-feet per year.
1 second-foot equals 6.23 British *I*mperial gallons per second; equals 373.8 gallons per minute; equals 538,272 gallons for one day.
1 second-foot equals 7.48 United States gallons per second; equals 448.8 gallons per minute; equals 646,272 gallons for one day.
1 second-foot equals about 1 acre-inch per hour.
1 second-foot for one day equals 1.983 acre-feet.
1 second-foot for one 28-day month equals 55.54 acre-feet.
1 second-foot for one 29-day month equals 57.52 acre-feet.
1 second-foot for one 30-day month equals 59.50 acre-feet.
1 second-foot for one 31-day month equals 61.49 acre-feet.
1 second-foot for 153 days equals 303.47 acre-feet.
1 second-foot for one year equals 724 acre-feet.

5 GEORGE V, A. 1915

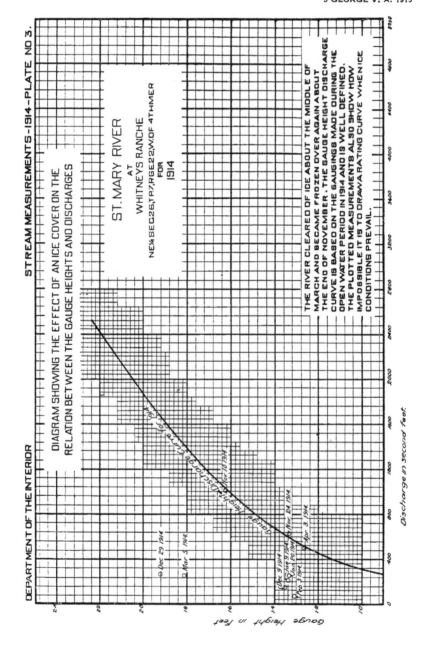

DEPARTMENT OF THE INTERIOR

STREAM MEASUREMENTS—1914—PLATE NO 3.

DIAGRAM SHOWING THE EFFECT OF AN ICE COVER ON THE
RELATION BETWEEN THE GAUGE HEIGHTS AND DISCHARGES

ST. MARY RIVER
AT
WHITNEY'S RANCHE
NE¼ SEC 26,T P.7,RGE 22,W.OF 4TH MER
FOR
1914

THE RIVER CLEARED OF ICE ABOUT THE MIDDLE OF
MARCH AND BECAME FROZEN OVER AGAIN ABOUT
THE END OF NOVEMBER. THE GAUGE HEIGHT DISCHARGE
CURVE IS BASED ON THE GAUGINGS MADE DURING THE
OPEN WATER PERIOD IN 1914 AND IS WELL DEFINED.
THE PLOTTED MEASUREMENTS ALSO SHOW HOW
IMPOSSIBLE IT IS TO DRAW A RATING CURVE WHEN ICE
CONDITIONS PREVAIL.

Gauge Height in feet

Discharge in second feet.

1 second-foot for one 28-day month covers 1 square mile 1.041 inches deep.
1 second-foot for one 29-day month covers 1 square mile 1.079 inches deep.
1 second-foot for one 30-day month covers 1 square mile 1.116 inches deep.
1 second-foot for one 31-day month covers 1 square mile 1.153 inches deep.
1 second-foot for 153 days covers 150 acres 24,278 inches or 2.023 feet deep.
1 second-foot for one year covers 1 square mile 13,572 inches or 1.131 feet deep.
100 British *I*mperial gallons per minute equals 0.268 second-feet.
100 United States gallons per minute equals 0.223 second-feet.
1,000,000 British *I*mperial gallons per day equals 1.86 second-feet.
1,000,000 United States gallons per day equals 1.55 second-feet.
1,000,000 British *I*mperial gallons equals 3.68 acre-feet.
1,000,000 United States gallons equals 3.07 acre-feet.
1,000,000 cubic feet equals 22.95 acre-feet.
1 foot per second equals 0.682 miles per hour.
1 cubic foot of water weighs 62.5 pounds.
1 horse-power equals 550 foot-pounds per second.
1 horse-power equals 746 watts.
1 horse-power equals 1 second-foot falling 8.80 feet.
1⅓ horse power equals 1 kilowatt.
1 British Columbia miner's inch equals 1.68 cubic feet per minute, or 1 second-foot approximately equals 35.7 British Columbia miner's inches.

To calculate water power quickly: $\dfrac{\text{sec. ft. x fall in feet}}{11} = $ net horsepower on water wheel, realizing 80 per cent of the theoretical power.

To find the number of acre-feet required for a certain acreage under the prescribed duty of water of one hundred and fifty acres for each cubic foot of water per second flowing continuously during the irrigation season (153 days), multiply the acreage by 2.02314.

METHODS OF MEASURING STREAM FLOW.

There are three distinct methods of determining the surface flow of streams: (1) by measurements of slope and cross-section and the use of Chezy's and Kutter's formulae; (2) by means of weirs, which include any device or structure that by measuring the depth on a crest or sill of known length and form, the flow of water may be determined; (3) by measuring the velocity of the current and the cross-section. The third method is the one most commonly used by this survey. The second is used when the flow is too small to be accurately determined by the third, while the first is only used in making estimates of the discharge of a stream when the only data available are the cross-section and slope.

SLOPE METHOD OF DETERMINING DISCHARGE.—The slope of a stream, or rather of a section of a stream, is the difference in elevation between the upper and lower ends of the section, commonly called the fall, divided by the distance or the length of the section. Slope sections vary in length from a few hundred feet to several thousand feet, depending largely upon the nature of the stream.

It is difficult to ascertain accurately the slope of the water surface in a stream, since in nearly all streams there are pulsations in the water, causing the surface to rise and fall locally. In most streams the slope of the bottom is far from uniform, and the flow of water in any given section is more or less influenced by the flow in the adjacent section, above or below. For this reason it is a good plan to consider a number of adjacent sections, comprising a considerable length of the stream in one computation, being careful to take into account the diversity of cross-section at various places in the length, and the fact that the slope of the water surface of a stream becomes more uniform during high water and flood stages.

In determining the slope of the surface of a stream, levels are taken of the water surface at each end of the slope section, and referred to some datum or bench-mark. A good plan is to set firmly a stout wooden stake below the water surface at each end of the slope section, and then to drive a nail into the top of each stake, so that the nail-head will exactly coincide with the water surface. The difference in elevation between the two nail-heads, divided by the distance between the stakes, will give the slope.

The wetted perimeter is that portion of a stream channel that is in contact with the water. The form or outline of the wetted perimeter of a stream has an important influence upon the velocity of the current. It is usually determined graphically from the plotted cross-section or may be measured by means of a flexible tape or chain after the flood has subsided.

The hydraulic radius, which is sometimes called the mean radius of the channel below the water surface is found by dividing the area of the cross-section (in sq. ft.) by the length of the wetted perimeter (in feet).

The Chezy formula, which is the fundamental formula for stream discharge, is:

$$Q = A\,V$$

in which $Q =$ the discharge of the stream in sec.-ft.
  $A =$ the area of the cross-section in sq. feet.
  $V =$ the mean velocity of flow, in ft. per sec.

In applying this formula to the determination of stream discharge, the mean velocity of a

5 GEORGE V, A. 1915

stream is considered a function of the slope and of the wetted perimeter of the stream. This may be expressed by formula as follows:

$$V = C \sqrt{rs}$$

in which $r =$ the hydraulic radius of the channel.

          $s =$ the surface slope.

and C is a variable coefficient, depending upon the nature of the channel.

In determining the value of C for any given case it is customary to make use of *K*utter's formula, which is:

$$C = \frac{41.6 + \dfrac{.00281}{s} + \dfrac{1.811}{n}}{1 + \left\{ 41.6 + \dfrac{.00281}{s} \right\} \sqrt{\dfrac{n}{r}}}$$

In this formula r and s have the same significance as in the Chezy formula and the new factor n is called the coefficient of roughness. *I*t is a variable coefficient, and its value is dependent upon the size, shape, slope and degree of roughness of the channel. Tables of values of n are given in various text books, but it is difficult to choose the ccrrect value. *I*t is therefore advisable, whenever possible, to compute the value of n from a measured discharge. As the slope method of determining discharge is seldom employed except to estimate flood discharge, a current meter measurement is very often made at the slope section, during low water. Having determined the mean velocity, slope and hydraulic radius at the time of the metering, the value of C may be found from the formula $V = C \sqrt{rs}$ or $C = \dfrac{V}{\sqrt{rs}}$. Trautwine's Pocket Book for Civil *E*ngineers and other texts contain tables giving the value of n for different values of r, s, and c. From these tables we can interpolate the proper value of n for a particular section of the stream, at low water stage. In most cases this value of n is applicable to high water and flood conditions of the stream also, and is used with values of r and s for the high water or flood cross-section to determine the value of C at the higher stage. Having determined the value of C the computation of the discharge is simple.

The results obtained by the slope method are in general only roughly approximate, owing to the difficulty in obtaining accurate data and the uncertainty of the value of n to be used.

WEIR METHOD OF DETERMINING DISCHARGE.—As yet few permanent weirs have been constructed by this survey, but many regular weir measurements are made on small streams by means of a temporary weir. The weir used consists of a wooden base of 2-inch plank, to which is bolted a rectangular notch of three-eights inch steel with bevelled edges.

In making a measurement by means of a temporary weir, the following directions should be followed as far as possible. The weir should be placed perpendicular and at right angles to the bed of the stream with the crest level. The discharge should be free in so much as the nappe should have sufficient fall to allow air to have free circulation underneath it, and the head or depth on the crest should not exceed one-third of the length. The channel of approach should be several times as wide as the opening and the depth of water in the bay or pond should be at least twice the head on the weir, so as to eliminate velocity of approach and crosscurrents. In choosing a site for a weir, a point should be chosen that will fulfil the above conditions and give a good-sized bay or pond.

To set up a temporary weir, a dam of sods and earth is thrown across the stream, the weir is set in place and the sods are tramped firmly around it to stop all leakage. On a stream with a sandy bed, sods or clay must be placed on the bottom for a few feet upstream to form a mattress to prevent the undermining of the dam.

After the bay has filled up, the head of the water is observed by taking the difference in elevation of the crest of the weir and the elevation of the water surface in the bay at a distance of 4 to 10 feet from the weir, with an engineer's level. Two common methods of getting the elevation of the water surface are: (1) hold the levelling rod on a stone or other solid body under water and subtract the depth of water on the rod from the sight on the rod; (2) drive a pin divided into tenths of feet into the bed of the stream so that an even tenth is level with the surface of the water, then hold the levelling rod on the top of the pin and add the length of pin above the water to the sight on the rod.

When the head of water has been determined, the discharge is computed by using one of the standard formulae which will suit the case. Tables giving the discharges for different heads and lengths of crests are published in many engineering texts.

The formula used by this survey for rectangular sharp-crested weirs is:

$$Q = 3.33 \ (L - .2H) \ H^{3/2} \text{ being a modification of Francis' formula, to allow for}$$
end contractions and elimination of velocity of approach.

in which $Q =$ discharge in sec. ft.; $L =$ length of crest in feet; $H =$ head in feet.

Measurements by means of temporary weirs should be made some distance above or below the gauge. *I*f they are made close to a gauge, the gauge must be read before the weir is placed in the stream, and the pond must be allowed to run off after the weir is removed before the gauge is re-read.

Where permanent weirs are installed, the gauge height observed is that of an auxiliary gauge above the weir, which is kept so that the head of the weir can be read direct. The weir is not usually placed so that it will interfere with the regular station, so that if at any time the weir is destroyed the regular gauge can be read during the period that the weir is out of order.

VELOCITY METHOD OF DETERMINING DISCHARGE.—There are two methods of determining the velocity of flow of a stream, namely, direct and indirect. In the direct method, by which the velocity is determined by means of floats, the liability of error is large, and the results are far from satisfactory. This method is seldom used except for very rough estimates, or when a current meter cannot be used. There are three common kinds of floats, viz.: surface, sub-surface and tube or rod floats. In each the procedure is the same. A straight piece of channel is selected for the run and two cross-sections are taken at some convenient distance apart, usually from 100 to 200 feet. They are then divided into strips by means of a tagged wire. The velocity in each strip is then measured by noting the time taken by the float in traversing the run or distance between the two cross-sections. As the time and distance are both known the velocity can easily be computed. The velocity, whether measured by surface, sub-surface or tube floats, must be multiplied by a coefficient less than unity to reduce to the mean velocity before being used to compute the discharge.

The indirect or current meter method is the most reliable and most widely used method of determining the velocity of the flow of a stream. The meter used by this survey is the Price Patent, manufactured by W. & L. E. Gurley, Troy, N.Y. It consists of six cups attached to a vertical shaft, which revolves on a conical hardened steel point when immersed in moving water. The number of revolutions is indicated electrically. The rating or relation between the velocity of the moving water and the revolutions of the wheel is determined for each meter by drawing it through still water for a given distance at different speeds and noting the number of revolutions for each run. From this data a rating table is prepared which gives the velocity per second of moving water for any number of revolutions in a given time interval.

In making a measurement with a current meter, a number of points, called measuring points, are measured off above and in the plane of the measuring section, at which observations of depth and velocity are taken. These points are spaced equally for those parts of the section where the flow is uniform and smooth, but should be spaced unequally for other parts according to the discretion and judgment of the engineer. In general, the points should not be spaced farther apart than 5 per cent of the distance between piers, nor farther apart than the approximate mean depth of the section at the time of measurement.

The measuring points divide the total cross-section into elementary strips, at each end of which observations of depth and velocity are made. The discharge of any elementary strip is the product of the average of the depths at the ends, the width of the strip, and the average of the mean velocities at the two ends of the strip. The sum of the discharges of the elementary strips is the total discharge of the stream.

The accuracy of a discharge measurement taken at a velocity area station is dependent on two factors, the accuracy with which the area of the cross-section and the mean velocity of the flow normal to that section are measured. The greatest, and the most common errors in measurements of discharge are caused by erroneous soundings. Errors in soundings by weight and line are due to the weight being carried down-stream, or, sometimes, to the bowing of the line. Both these causes make the soundings too great. Errors in soundings with rods are due to the rod not being perpendicular, to the water rising on the rod, and to the rod sinking in the bed. In order to verify the accuracy of soundings made at medium or high stages, they should be compared with those at low water. The mean velocity is also very difficult to measure accurately, because it is constantly changing. It varies not only from the surface to the bottom, but from one bank of the stream to the other, making it necessary to measure it at a number of points.

METHODS OF DETERMINING MEAN VELOCITY.

There are a number of different methods of determining the mean velocity at the ends of these strips, or, as it is commonly called, the mean velocity in a vertical, namely, multiple-point, single-point, and integration. These three principal multiple-point methods in general use are the vertical velocity-curve, three-point and two-point method.

VERTICAL VELOCITY CURVE METHOD OF DETERMINING MEAN VELOCITY.—In this method the centre of the meter is held as close to the surface of the water as possible, being careful to keep it out of reach of all surface disturbances, and then at a number of different depths throughout the vertical. The velocity at each position of the meter is recorded. These observations are then plotted with velocities in feet per second as abscissae and their corresponding depths in feet as ordinates, and a mean curve is drawn through the points. The mean velocity for the vertical is obtained by dividing the area bounded by the curve and its axis by the depth. In the absence of a planimeter for measuring the area, the depth is divided into 5 to 10 equal parts, and the velocities of the centre ordinates of these parts are noted. The mean of these velocities will very closely approximate the mean in the vertical.

It is often more convenient, when the depth is a number of feet and a fraction, as 7.4, to divide the depth into 7 parts of a foot width, and a part of 0.4 foot width. Then the velocity to enter for the narrow part is 0.4 of the velocity at the centre of it.

5 GEORGE V, A. 1915

The vertical velocity curve is useful in studying the manner in which velocities occur in a vertical. From a study of a number of these curves the other shorter methods of determining mean velocity are deduced. On account of the length of time taken to complete a measurement, this method is not used in general routine measurements, except during the winter, for a change of stage is almost sure to occur during a measurement on a large stream which counterbalances the increased accuracy. For this reason its use is limited to the determination of the coefficient to be used in the reduction of values obtained by other methods of measuring velocity to the true value, to the measurements of velocities under new and unusual conditions of flow, and for measurements under ice.

THREE-POINT METHOD OF DETERMINING MEAN VELOCITY.—This method is one of the short methods of obtaining the mean velocity in the vertical and, under some conditions, gives the most accurate results next to the vertical velocity curve method. It has been used almost exclusively by this survey in past years, during the open water period, but recently has been superseded by the two-point method which, under most conditions, gives more accurate results. In the three-point method, the current-meter is held at 0.2, 0.6, and 0.8 depth. The mean is then obtained by dividing by 4 the sum of the velocities at 0.2 and 0.8 depth plus twice the velocity at 0.6 depth.

TWO-POINT METHOD OF DETERMINING MEAN VELOCITY.—In studying the vertical curves made at a number of different points and under varied conditions, it has been found that the mean of the velocities occurring at 0.2 and 0.8 depth gives very nearly the mean velocity in the vertical. Use is made of this fact in the two-point method of determining mean velocity, the meter being held at 0.2 and 0.8 depth in the vertical. This method has been found more accurate than the single point method and the time required for a metering is not very much greater. This method has been found to give, also, a very close approximate to the mean velocity in measurements of ice-covered streams, although these flow under very different conditions from those of open water.

SINGLE-POINT METHOD OF DETERMINING MEAN VELOCITY.—*E*xperiments made under most favourable conditions and extending over a long period have established the point of mean velocity in a vertical at 0.6 of the depth. Therefore the error resulting from the use of the 0.6 depth as the depth of mean velocity is very small, though in some few cases a study of the vertical velocity curve will show the need of a coefficient to reduce the observed velocities to the mean. The variation of the coefficient from unity in individual cases is, however, greater than in the two or three point method, and the general results are not as satisfactory. For that reason this method is not employed very extensively by the survey.

In the other principal single-point method the meter is held near the surface, at from 0.5 to 1 feet below the surface, care being taken to sink the instrument below the influence of wind or waves. The resulting velocities must be multiplied by a coefficient to reduce them to mean velocities. This coefficient as found by a large number of experiments, varies from 0.78 to 0.98, depending upon the depth and speed of the stream. The deeper the stream and the greater the velocity, the larger the coefficient. In flood work coefficients varying from 0.90 to 0.95 should be used. This method is only used when the current is too strong to permit the sinking of the meter to any great depth below the surface of the water. It is often employed at times of flood, or when a stream is carrying a lot of drift wood or ice.

INTEGRATION METHOD OF DETERMINING MEAN VELOCITY.—This method of determining the mean velocity in a vertical consists in moving the meter at a slow uniform speed from the bed of the stream to the surface and return in a vertical direction, the time and revolutions being observed. In travelling through all parts of the vertical the meter is acted upon by each and every thread of velocity from the bed to the surface of the stream, and the resulting observations determine the mean in that vertical.

This method is very useful in checking the results of other methods. *I*t is, however, seldom used by this survey, as the Price meter is not suited to observations by this method, since the vertical motion of the meter causes the wheel to revolve.

GAUGING STATIONS.

The first step is to select a suitable locality for a gauging station. Although apparently simple, this is really a difficult task. Not only must the water be moving in nearly straight lines over a solid bed and between well defined banks, but the place must be accessible at moderate cost, and there must be living near it a competent person who can be engaged to serve as observer. Permanent gauging stations should only be selected after a very thorough reconnaissance. In the irrigation districts and in more thickly populated districts there is more or less diversion of water. This is apt to complicate matters for the hydrometric engineer, for a gauging station above all works may not include all the tributaries of the stream, and it is often necessary to establish gauging stations at several points along the streams, and on tributaries, canals, and pipe lines in order to obtain complete information regarding the water supply in a particular stream.

There are three classes of gauging stations, namely, wading, bridge and cable stations. The wading station can of course only be used in the case of small streams having a maximum depth at its highest stage of three feet or less. The equipment for a wading station is small, consisting usually of a plain staff gauge, graduated to feet and hundredths, and fixed vertically to one of the banks of the stream. For convenience a measuring line, usually a wire with tags.

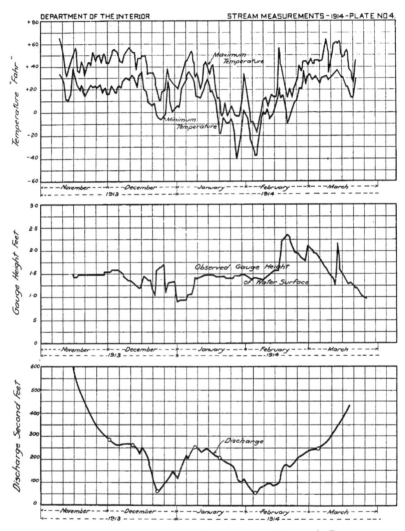

OBSERVATIONS OF GAUGE HEIGHTS ON S⫟ MARY RIVER AT WHITNEY'S RANCH WITH
CORRESPONDING MAXIMUM AND MINIMUM TEMPERATURES AND THE ESTIMATED DAILY
DISCHARGES FOR THE WINTER 1913–1914.

The circles on the discharge graph indicate actual discharge measurements

5 GEORGE V, A. 1915

may be fixed permanently at this section. When taking the reading, the engineer should stand below and to one side of the meter so as not to cause eddies in the water.

Bridge stations, because of their permanency and the freedom of movement allowed the engineer, are much preferred. Very often, however, more particularly in swift currents, the piers materially affect the accuracy of the results. When the gauge cannot be attached to a pier, it is often attached horizontally to the guard-rail or floor of the bridge, and the height of the stream is found by lowering a weight by a chain over a pulley. It is indicated by a marker on the chain. Distances of three, five or ten feet, according to the size of the stream, are marked on the lower chord of the down stream side of the bridge, to serve as a measuring line.

Frequently it is impossible to establish a permanent gauging station at a bridge. In that case the wire cable of a ferry can be utilized, or, if that is not available, a permanent wire cable is stretched across the river. For spans of average length a galvanized wire cable three-fourths of an inch in diameter is safe. It is supported at each bank by means of high struts or by passing it through the crotch of a tree. The cable is run into the ground and anchored securely to a "dead man" buried at least six feet below the surface, or, if convenient, it is anchored to the lower part of the trunk of a tree. A turnbuckle is inserted in the cable between the strut and anchorage to permit tightening the cable when it begins to sag. A permanent measuring line, usually a wire, with tags 5 or 10 feet apart, is stretched across the stream just above the cable. A cage large enough to carry two men and instruments is constructed, and suspended from the cable by means of cast-iron pulleys. The cage is moved from point to point by hand. A stay line, usually quarter-inch guy wire, is stretched across the stream about thirty to forty feet upstream from the cable, and securely fastened. By passing a sash cord through a pulley hung on this stay line the current meter is prevented from being carried down-stream. This type of station has the advantage that it can usually be located at the most desirable point on the stream and is free of piers and other obstructions.

LOW VELOCITY LIMITATIONS.

Owing to the presence of a slight amount of friction in the current meter, a certain definite velocity is required to make the wheel revolve, i.e., to overcome the frictional resistance of the wheel. For this reason the meter is unsuitable for the measurement of low velocities approaching this value. This velocity, which is required to overcome friction, and which is obtained from the meter rating curve, is called the velocity of no flow for the particular meter referred to. It varies in different types of meters, and also slightly in meters of the same type, according to the time the meter is in use, but very seldom exceeds 0.2 foot per second in any meter. From a number of observations the low velocity limit, below which values of velocity are unreliable, is found to be 0.5 foot per second. In many cases at low stages the gauging station on a stream becomes unsuitable for a discharge measurement owing to the mean velocity in the section falling below the safe limit. In such instances, where it is possible to wade the stream, a suitable gauging section may be located within a reasonable distance of the regular station and the discharge measurements made at this point. When a gauging is made at a cross-section other than the regular station, sufficient soundings should be made at the latter at the time of the gauging to develop the cross-section and compute the area. The measurement is thus referred to the regular gauging station, and the mean velocity and area at the regular section are reported and used in the office computations.

OFFICE COMPUTATIONS.

RATING CURVES AND TABLES.—When a series of discharge measurements has been made at a gauging station a rating curve is constructed for that station, showing graphically the discharge corresponding to any stage of the stream within the limits covered by the gaugings. This curve, as it is usually drawn, has as abscissae the discharges in second-feet, and as ordinates the corresponding gauge heights at which the discharges were made. A smooth curve is drawn through the resulting set of points, and from this curve the discharges at any stage within the limits of the curve are taken. Some measurements may be more reliable than others, owing to more or less favourable conditions at different times of gauging, or to other causes. In order to obtain the weight of the different measurements, curves with area and mean velocity, as abscissae, and gauge heights as ordinates, are also drawn. From a study of these curves any discrepancies in a measurement, either in its area or mean velocity, may be detected. Should it be necessary to extend the rating curve beyond the limits of actual discharge measurements, the area and mean velocity curves may be constructed to the stages for which the discharge curve is desired, and the latter found by taking the product of the two curves. The discharge curve under natural conditions of flow is always convex to the gauge height axis. The area curve is either a straight line or is convex to the gauge height axis, except in the case of overhanging banks, when it becomes concave to the axis. The mean velocity curve is always concave to the gauge height axis, except in cases where standing water occurs below the stage of no-flow. In this case the curve will assume a reverse form, starting from the gauge height of zero flow with a curve convex to the gauge height axis and gradually reversing to a curve concave to this axis. In plotting all three curves the horizontal and vertical scales should be chosen that the curves may be used within the limits of accuracy for the work, and in their critical position will make, as nearly as possible, angles of 45 degrees with each axis.

SESSIONAL PAPER No. 25c

The rating curve being constructed, it becomes necessary to prepare a station rating table, giving the discharge at any stage of the stream within the limits of the daily gauge height observations on record. From this rating table the daily discharges corresponding to the daily gauge heights are read and tabulated. The rating table is constructed for tenths, half-tenths, or hundredths of feet, according to the readings of the gauge to which it is to be applied. The discharges for this table are read directly from the rating curve and are then adjusted so that the differences for successive stages shall be either constant or gradually increasing, but never decreasing, unless the station is affected by backwater.

DAILY DISCHARGE, MONTHLY MEAN, AND RUN-OFF.—The rating table being made to cover the range of daily gauge height observations, the next procedure in the computations is to make out a table of daily discharges from this rating table. The daily gauge heights are copied as they were sent in by the observer, and opposite each the corresponding discharge is filled in from the rating table. The monthly discharge is found by totalling the daily discharges for the month in question, and the monthly mean is obtained by dividing this total by the number of days in the month.

The run-off is computed with two different sets of units, depending upon the kind of work for which the data is intended, as follows:

(1) Run-off in inches is the depth to which a plane surface equal in extent to the drainage area would be covered if all the water flowing from it in a given time were conserved and uniformly distributed thereon; it is used for comparing run-off with rainfall, which is usually expressed in depth in inches. The monthly mean run-off in second-feet is divided by the area of the drainage basin in square miles to find the monthly mean run-off per square mile. This result, reduced to run-off in depth in inches for the monthly period, is in the form required.

(2) The run-off in acre-feet is the form of most use in connection with storage. An acre-foot is equivalent to 43,560 cubic feet, and is the quantity of water required to cover an acre to the depth of one foot. The monthly mean run-off in second-feet is used for the computation of run-off in acre-feet. The monthly mean is reduced to cubic feet per month, and this quantity divided by 43,560 gives the run-off in acre-feet.

The run-off of the stream being computed both in depth in inches and in acre-feet for each month, the run-off for the period during which observations of run-off were made is found by the summation of the amounts of run-off for the several months making up this period.

CHANGING CONDITIONS OF CHANNEL.—On streams such as Milk River, whose bed is in a constant state of motion, measurements of discharge should be made every few days, otherwise considerable data relating to changes cannot be obtained. For discharges on days other than those on which measurements are taken, the interpolation method is used. The two methods of interpolation in general use are the Stout and Bolster methods.

The Stout method deals with the correction of the gauge heights. A curve is drawn, using the difference between the actual gauge heights at the time of measurement and the gauge height corresponding to the measured discharge as ordinates, and the corresponding days of the month as abscissae. From an irregular curve drawn through these points corrections for gauge heights can be made for days on which there was no discharge measurement. When the discharge is greater than that given by the curve the correction is positive, and vice-versa. Each daily gauge height is corrected by the amount shown on the correction curve, and the corresponding discharge taken from an approximate rating curve for the station.

The Bolster method deals more particularly with the modification of the discharge. Results of discharge measurements covering a whole year or season are plotted and, though considerably scattered, will define one or more regular curves, called standard curves, the number and position of each indicating the radical changes. Where the river bed changes from day to day, the position of the standard curve also varies and must pass through the points indicating the different days. The points indicating two successive measurements are joined by a line, which for short distances on the cross-section paper is a straight line, and otherwise a curve. This line is divided into a number of equal parts, each indicating an intervening day, the assumption being that as the change during this period is gradual the daily rating must pass through each point or day, as represented by the divisions. A simple and convenient way of making these interpolations and moving the daily rating curve is to make a tracing of the standard curve with a vertical line of reference. By keeping the lines of reference coincident this curve can be shifted into any desired position and the discharge read for any gauge height.

WINTER RECORDS.

FORMATION OF ICE AND ICE CONDITIONS.—Perhaps the greatest difficulties in stream measurements are met with in the early part of the winter, just as the streams are commencing to freeze up. Especially is this true in the swift running streams in or near the mountains. Needle and anchor ice often form in large quantities in rapids and, flowing in masses with the water, make gaugings very difficult and unreliable. Even after a permanent ice cover is obtained at the gauging station this ice will, in some cases, obstruct the channel below the station and cause "backwater."

A further difficulty is that the surface ice usually forms along the edges of the stream for some time before forming in the centre of the channel. At first this may be broken away if the stream is small and open water measurements made, but later it is necessary to take some

5 GEORGE V, A. 1915

observations through holes in the ice along the edge. As the streams get farther away from the mountains their velocity decreases, and fewer rapids occur along their course. There is then less trouble with needle and anchor ice, and a permanent ice cover forms much more quickly.

In many cases the section used during the summer is very unsuitable for making measurements during the winter. *It* may be (a) too wide and shallow or flowing in two channels during the winter, due to low water; (b) partially open, due to swift running water or warm water running in; (c) affected by needle and anchor ice, either by flowing in the water, or causing backwater; (d) located where the snow drifts over the ice to a great depth; (e) that it is likely to have a rough ice cover or pile up with ice, due to swift water and a rough bed; (f) that there is a tendency for ice jams to occur, with consequent backwater, etc.

It is therefore often necessary to choose a new section for winter observations. This should be done before freeze-up, for then the width, depth, uniformity of flow and conditions above and below can be easily noted. The most suitable stations for winter measurements are those which have a long stretch of very smooth, sluggish water above, and a rapid fall below.

DISCHARGE MEASUREMENTS.—In winter as in summer, the daily discharges of a stream are computed from frequent discharge measurements, and daily gauge height observations. The discharge measurements are made through holes in the ice from five to ten or even twenty feet apart, depending upon the size of the stream, and large enough to allow the current meter to pass through freely. The gaugings are made in the same manner as at open sections except that the depth of the stream is taken as the distance from the bottom of the ice to the bed of the stream. The soundings, however, are always referred to the surface of the water in the holes, the distance from the surface of the water to the bottom of the ice being measured and subtracted from the soundings to obtain the depth.

The vertical velocity curve method is usually used for the determination of the mean velocity in the vertical. A curve is plotted for each vertical, and the mean velocity is determined in the usual manner. These curves vary greatly as to form for different kinds and conditions of channel.

The typical curve, however, differs from that obtained from an open water observation in that it is drawn back more at the surface, owing no doubt to greater friction between the ice and the water as compared with the water and the atmosphere. As a result there are two points in the vertical at which the thread of mean velocity occurs under an ice cover. These points are near 0.2 and 0.8 of the total depth below the bottom of the ice, and the mean of the velocities at these two depths will give fairly accurate results, but when close estimates of the discharges are required, and the conditions are not very favourable, the vertical velocity method should be used.

It is found that when all the holes are opened on a small swift stream, there are sometimes vertical pulsations of the water in the holes, which affect the velocity readings. This can usually be avoided by only opening one hole at a time, and filling it in again with ice and snow as soon as the observation is finished. It can also be overcome by inserting a thin sheet of galvanized tin or iron at the bottom of the hole after the meter has been lowered into the water. The meter should always be held near the upstream side of the hole.

In using the meter care must be taken to keep it under the water as much as possible to prevent ice from forming around the bearings. It is a good plan to clean and oil the meter indoors before starting out to make a gauging.

GAUGES AND GAUGE OBSERVATIONS.—The gauge is usually read once each day, the observer noting the elevation of the water as it rises in a hole cut through the ice, the height of the top of the ice, the thickness of the ice, presence of needle or slush ice, snow on top of ice, ice jams, and any sudden changes in temperature. To do this the observers are provided with an ice chisel for chopping holes, and an L-shaped ice scale to measure the thickness of the ice.

A difficulty which arises in obtaining the thickness of the ice is that in a hole kept open for some time the ice wears away around the bottom of the hole, and may make it necessary to cut a new hole near by, or to enlarge the original.

Any form of gauge may be used, but the chain gauge is the most satisfactory, as the staff gauge, being frozen to the ice, heaves with it, and also in cutting away the ice from around it the figures are effaced. The automatic gauge gives trouble with the well freezing over.

ESTIMATES OF DAILY DISCHARGE.—While the run-off, particularly during the winter months, does not vary directly in accordance with the precipitation, the rate at which it reaches the streams is, of course, dependent almost entirely upon the climatic conditions. The climate in the mountains is subject to great extremes, but during the winter almost the entire precipitation is in the form of snow.

There is, therefore, very little surface run-off, and the flow of the streams comes almost entirely from the glaciers, ground waters and lake storage, and except for the losses due to freezing and the slight increases, due to the melting of snow and ice by chinooks (warm winds), the flow in the streams would remain constant or would change gradually.

There are, however, certain local conditions in Western Canada which make it exceptionally difficult to make estimates of the daily discharge during the winter. The gauge height in many cases fluctuates very much, and often sudden rises or drops occur. These rises are often explained by the fact that during very cold spells a great deal of slush, frazil, and anchor ice is formed and chokes up the channel, thus raising the surface of the water, when in reality the discharge is decreasing. Then, again, a chinook causes a sudden rise in temperature and the discharge is often increased, while at the same time the gauge height gradually lowers, evidently because the warmer weather and water have melted out a lot of the ice from the channel and given it a greater carrying capacity.

In order to make reliable estimates of the daily discharge, gaugings must be made at short intervals and the weather conditions and temperatures in the whole of the drainage area above the stations must be very carefully studied.

W. G. Hoyt, District Engineer, Water Resources Branch, U.S. Geological Survey, has made an exhaustive study of methods for estimating the flow when streams are frozen. The various methods described by him in an article in "Engineering News" on April 10, 1913, and Water-Supply Paper 337, published by the United States Geological Survey, in 1913, and modifications of them, are used. The graphic method of interpolation has been found to be generally applicable, but as the precipitation during the winter months has so little effect upon the run-off during that period, it is seldom plotted on the sheets. It is also considered that the extremes and ranges of temperatures are better guides for interpolation than the mean temperatures, and the minimum and maximum temperatures are both plotted and given due consideration rather than the mean temperatures.

The weather conditions and temperatures at the gauging station are not always typical for the whole drainage basin above, and care must therefore be taken to have the meteorological observations made at some other place, or, if necessary, at two or more places. Of course, care must be taken to study all the possible conditions which may affect the estimates.

Plate 4 shows typical conditions and illustrates the graphic method of interpolating the daily discharges.

Additional information on this subject may be found in the appendix of this report.

RATING CURRENT-METERS.

Each meter is rated before being used, in order to determine the relation between the revolutions of the wheel and the velocity of the water. The meter is driven at a uniform rate of speed through still water for a given distance, and the number of revolutions of the whee and the time are recorded. From this data the number of revolutions per second and the corresponding velocity per second are computed. Tests are made for speeds varying from the slowest which will cause the wheel to revolve to several feet per second. The results of these runs, when plotted with revolutions per second as abscissae, and velocity in feet per second as ordinates, locate points that define the meter rating-curve, which for all meters is practically a straight line. From this curve a meter rating table is prepared. Theoretically, the rating for all meters of the same make and type should be the same, but as the result of slight variations in construction and in the bearing of the wheel on the axis at different velocities, the ratings differ.

After a meter has been in use for some time the cups may have received small injuries, or the bearing of the wheel on the axis may have changed owing to unavoidable rough usage. These changes will affect the running of the meter and change its rating. As a consequence, each meter is re-rated at regular intervals and a new rating curve and table prepared.

Descriptions of the rating station, discussions of the methods employed, and the results of ratings, are given in the Reports of Progress of Stream Measurements for the years 1911 and 1912.

5 GEORGE V. A. 1915

ATHABASKA RIVER DRAINAGE BASIN.

General Description.

Athabaska River rises on the eastern slope of Rocky Mountains and flows in a north-easterly direction for about one thousand miles, eventually emptying into Lake Athabaska.

The Athabaska basin forms the most southerly portion of the great Mackenzie system, and the portion dealt with in this report comprises only the headwaters.

Rising in country very similar to the watershed of the other streams of importance in Alberta, it flows out of the mountains and then through foothill country. From the foothills to t e lake the basin consists of stretches of muskeg and uplands, well timbered with spruce and pine.

The general character of the basin is such that the winter precipitation or snow cover is conserved to a great extent, and floods in the early spring are not usual. However, in June, July and August rains and warm winds cause the upper parts of the system to discharge large quantities of the snow water from the higher peaks and glaciers, and when rains of any magnitude occur the invariable result is a flood. The muskeg country is a great source of storage, but, when its capacity is reached, it accelerates rather than retards the run-off.

The main transcontinental lines of the Grand Trunk Pacific and the Canadian Northern Railways cross the upper portion of this drainage basin, and transportation is now a much easier problem than in the past.

Many valuable deposits of coal, limestone and other minerals are found in this basin, and, on account of these as well as the many power possibilities and stretches of timber and pulpwood, it is expected that this country will develop very much during the next few years.

During 1913 a few stations were established in this basin, and a regular hydrometric engineer employed, who made a number of miscellaneous measurements. As the country is settled more stations will be established where necessary, and much better records obtained. A very full description of this drainage is attached as an appendix to the 1913 report.

MIETTE RIVER NEAR JASPER.

Location.—On the SW. ¼ Sec. 9, Tp. 45, Rge. 1, W. 6th Mer., at a traffic bridge about two miles southwest of Jasper, and about one mile from the mouth of the river.

Records available.—From May 23, 1914, to December 31, 1914. Discharge measurements available from February 13, 1913, to December 31, 1914.

Gauge.—Vertical staff, on downstream side of bridge pier about 20 feet from the left bank.

Bench-marks.—Six-inch spike driven in 15-inch spruce tree on the left bank of the river, and about 30 feet east of the gauge; elevation 10.76 feet above the zero of gauge.

Channel.—Three channels at all stages, slightly shifting.

Discharge measurements.—Made from bridge.

Winter flow.—River affected by ice from November to April. Discharge measurements made at a point about 1,000 feet downstream from regular section.

Observer.—Matt. Crevie.

DISCHARGE MEASUREMENTS of Miette River near Jasper, in 1914.

Date.	Engineer.	Width.	Area of Section.	Mean Velocity.	Gauge Height.	Discharge.
		Feet.	*Sq. ft.*	*Ft. per sec.*	*Feet.*	*Sec.-ft.*
Jan. 22	P. H. Daniells,	39	51	0.46	........a	23
Mar. 6	do	47	47	0.56	........a	26
April 16	do	50	82	1.80	........a	148
May 14	do	73	423	1.42	3.60	600
May 23	do	76	522	1.84	4.09	963
June 11	do	76	612	1.81	4.95	1,109
June 26	do	75	548	2.55	4.54	1,177
July 13	do	76	690	2.19	5.49	1,511
July 28	do	71	530	1.57	3.74	832
Aug. 11	do	73	377	1.05	1.80	394
Aug. 22	do	77	385	1.03	1.98	401
Sept. 9	do	72	317	0.83	1.05	263
Sept. 23	do	74	328	0.96	1.11	314
Oct. 10	do	74	280	1.05	1.10	296
Oct. 22	do	74	260	0.54	0.41	140
Oct. 31	do	53	90	1.77	0.56	159
Nov. 13	do	54	109	1.10	0.46	120
Nov. 28	do	48	68	1.22	0.30	82
Dec. 24	do	43	110	0.22	1.06	24

a No gauge.

View of the Car at the Current-meter Rating Station at Calgary, Alberta, showing the
Apparatus for suspending the Current-meter in the Tank.
Taken by H. M. Nelson.

View of the Car at the Current-meter Rating Station at Calgary, Alberta, showing the
Recording Apparatus.   Taken by H. M. Nelson.

SESSIONAL PAPER No. 25c

DAILY GAUGE HEIGHT AND DISCHARGE of Miette River near Jasper, for 1914.

DAY.	May.		June.		July.		August.	
	Gauge Height.	Dis- charge.	Gauge Height.	Dis- charge.	Gauge Height.	Dis- charge.	Gauge Height.	Dis- charge.
	Feet.	*Sec.-ft.*	*Feet.*	*Sec.-ft.*	*Feet.*	*Sec.-ft.*	*Feet.*	*Sec.-ft.*
1	....	....	3.62	742	6.30	1,887	2.90	607
2	....	....	5.40	1,388	6.22	1,852	2.85	595
3	....	....	7.35	2,232	6.27	1,874	2.76	574
4	....	....	7.20	2,152	6.35	1,909	2.62	542
5	....	....	6.60	1,878	6.32	1,896	2.50	516
6	....	....	5.87	1,548	5.87	1,698	2.43	501
7	....	....	5.68	1,490	5.33	1,460	2.32	478
8	....	....	5.43	1,330	5.10	1,360	2.18	450
9	....	....	5.05	1,165	5.22	1,412	1.90	397
10	....	....	4.90	1,097	5.27	1,434	1.85	388
11	....	....	4.95	1,110	5.35	1,469	1.72	365
12	....	....	5.20	1,233	5.37	1,478	1.60	345
13	....	....	6.00	1,595	5.20	1,403	1.67	357
14	....	....	6.95	2,030	5.13	1,373	1.73	367
15	....	....	7.05	2,100	5.05	1,338	1.80	379
16	....	....	7.23	2,198	4.73	1,206	1.89	395
17	....	....	7.60	2,377	4.46	1,100	1.90	397
18	....	....	7.50	2,352	3.98	926	1.85	388
19	....	....	6.90	2,112	3.40	744	1.82	383
20	....	....	5.70	1,600	3.60	803	1.80	379
21	....	....	5.05	1,338	4.35	1,060	1.85	388
22	....	....	4.40	1,078	3.75	850	1.92	401
23	4.09	965a	4.33	1,052	3.68	828	1.65	354
24	3.97	913	4.00	933	3.20	687	1.40	313
25	3.80	785	4.15	987	3.56	791	1.37	308
26	3.64	790	4.55	1,135	3.43	753	1.30	298
27	3.00	605	5.00	1,317	3.55	788	1.40	313
28	2.45	477	5.20	1,403	3.74	847	1.28	295
29	2.05	396	5.40	1,491	3.39	741	1.25	290
30	1.85	355	6.00	1,755	3.24	698	1.22	286
31	2.80	537	....	....	3.12	665	1.18	280

a Station established.

5 GEORGE V, A. 1915

DAILY GAUGE HEIGHT AND DISCHARGE of Miette River near Jasper, for 1914.

DAY	September.		October.		November.		December.	
	Gauge Height.	Dis- charge.	Gauge Height.	Dis- charge.	Gauge Height.	Dis- charge.	Gauge Height.	Dis- charge.
	Feet.	*Sec.-ft.*	*Feet.*	*Sec.-ft.*	*Feet.*	*Sec.-ft.*	*Feet.*	*Sec.-ft.*
1	1.15	276	2.32	528	0.53	188	0.31	70
2	1.10	268	2.03	464	0.49	183	0.16	65
3	1.08	265	1.79	416	0.43	174	0.14	60
4	0.94	246	1.40	350	0.39	169	0.10	56
5	0.88	237	1.32	333	0.36	165	0.09	55
6	0.85	233	1.25	323	0.34	161	0.12	57
7	0.82	229	1.16	307	0.29	156	0.27	58
8	0.86	234	1.10	296	0.24	149	0.22	55
9	0.95	247	1.07	293	0.27	153	0.16	40
10	0.89	243	1.02	285	0.25	150	0.28	35
11	0.85	237	0.78	243	0.32	140b	0.42	33
12	0.82	237	0.84	248	0.39	130	0.46	32
13	0.73	228	0.80	240	0.48	120	0.52	33
14	0.68	223	0.76	228	0.46	114	0.54	33
15	0.63	218	0.74	223	0.52	102	0.55	35
16	0.59	215	0.77	220	0.49	91	0.63	33
17	0.55	208	0.80	218	0.50	97	0.72	35
18	0.87	258	0.83	217	0.52	98	0.76	40
19	1.14	305	0.79	205	0.55	100	0.85	35
20	1.07	298	0.65	183	0.49	103	0.92	30
21	1.05	299	0.52	158	0.43	102	0.88	35
22	1.04	297	0.35	133	0.40	95	0.91	30
23	1.12	315	0.38	135	0.37	91	0.87	27
24	1.08	305	0.44	144	0.36	94	1.12	24
25	1.22	330	0.37	134	0.40	96	1.30	23
26	1.71	411	0.40	138	0.38	98	1.38	18
27	2.83	657	0.33	128	0.34	90	1.35	24
28	2.76	640	0.25	118	0.30	82	1.45	30
29	2.72	627	0.30	125	0.25	78	1.54	35
30	2.78	643	0.47	145	0.00	75	1.30	35
31	....	....	0.55	157	....	....	1.22	40b

b Ice conditions Nov. 11-Dec. 31.

View of Athabaska River near Hinton, Alberta. Taken by G. H. Whyte.

Boat used for making Discharge Measurements of Athabaska River at Athabaska, Alberta.
Taken by G. H. Whyte.

SESSIONAL PAPER No. 25c

MONTHLY DISCHARGE of Miette River near Jasper, for 1914.

(Drainage area 258 square miles.)

MONTH.	DISCHARGE IN SECOND-FEET.				RUN-OFF.	
	Maximum.	Minimum.	Mean.	Per square Mile.	Depth in inches on Drainage Area.	Total in Acre-feet.
May (23-31).............................	965	355	647	2.508	0.84	11,550
June.............................	2,377	742	1,541	5.973	6.66	91,699
July.............................	1,909	665	1,204	4.667	5.38	74,028
August.............................	607	280	398	1.542	1.78	24,472
September.............................	657	208	314	1.217	1.36	18,084
October.............................	528	118	237	0.919	1.06	14,573
November.............................	188	75	121	0.469	0.52	7,200
December.............................	70	18	39	0.151	0.17	2,398
The period.............................	....	....	....	....	17.77	244,604

ATHABASKA RIVER AT JASPER.

Location.—On the NW. ¼ Sec. 15, Tp. 45, Rge. 1, W. of 6th Mer., about one-half mile east of'the Grand Trunk Pacific Station and three-quarters of a mile below the mouth of the Miette River.

Records available.—March 4, 1913, to December 31, 1914.

Gauge.—Vertical staff; datum maintained at 83.81 feet during 1913, and at 83.83 feet during 1914.

Bench-mark.—Permanent iron bench-mark, assumed elevation 100.00 feet.

Channel.—Slightly shifting.

Discharge measurements.—Made from cable car.

Winter flow.—River affected by ice from November to April. Discharge measurements made at a point about 1½ miles below the regular station.

Observer.—Gauge read by G. Thompson from January 1, 1914, to July 19, 1914, and by Matt. Crevie from July 19, 1914, to December 31, 1914.

DISCHARGE MEASUREMENTS of Athabaska River at Jasper, in 1914.

Date.	Engineer.	Width.	Area of Section.	Mean Velocity.	Gauge Height.	Discharge.
		Feet.	*Sq. ft.*	*Ft. per sec.*	*Feet.*	*Sec.-ft.*
Jan. 7.............	P. H. Daniells...............	200	222	2.27	2.98	503
Jan. 23.............	do	275	543	0.80	4.33	434
Feb. 13.............	do	139	144	2.24	4.78	323
Mar. 5.............	do	170	164	2.27	2.38	364
Mar. 31.............	do	140	131	2.42	2.28	317
April 17.............	do	186	229	3.56	3.05	818
May 11.............	do	228	349	3.85	3.76	1,334
May 26.............	do	364	911	4.88	5.84	4,447
June 12.............	do	431	1,384	5.18	7.09	7,167
June 27.............	do	407	1,475	5.67	7.64	8,341
July 14.............	do	434	1,837	8.11	9.08	15,102
July 31.............	do	408	1,486	5.56	7.33	8,273
Aug. 10.............	do	405	954	5.45	6.00	5,205
Aug. 24.............	do	407	1,096	5.10	6.16	5,591
Sept. 12.............	do	262	499	5.90	4.52	2,949
Sept. 24.............	do	250	453	4.61	3.95	2,087
Oct. 7.............	do	248	437	4.92	3.88	2,136
Oct. 21.............	do	243	350	4.35	3.45	1,523
Nov. 13.............	do	188	201	3.61	2.64	726
Nov. 30.............	do	186	243	2.96	2.53	720
Dec. 26.............	do	120	220	2.16	4.24	476

5 GEORGE V, A. 1915

DAILY GAUGE HEIGHT AND DISCHARGE of Athabaska River at Jasper, for 1914.

DAY.	January.		February.		March.		April.		May.		June.	
	Gauge Height.	Dis- charge.	Gauge Height.	Dis- charge.	Gauge Height.	Dis- charge.	Gauge Height.	Dis- charge.	Gauge Height.	Dis- charge.	Gauge Height	Dis- charge.
	Feet.	*Sec.-ft.*	*Feet.*	*Sec.-ft.*	*Feet.*	*Sec.-ft.*	*Feet.*	*Sec.-ft.*	*Feet.*	*Sec.-ft.*	*Feet.*	*Sec.-ft.*
1	4.18	500a	5 33	380	2 83	280	2.28	340	3 20	820	5.54	3,904
2	4.06	516	5 44	368	1.88	338	2.33	360	3.25	875	6 88	6,580
3	3.93	524	5.24	351	1.23	362	2.33	385	3 40	1,040	8.01	9,946
4	3.98	531	5 63	340	0 83	371	2.33	412	3 60	1,260	7.86	9,410
5	3.58	532	5 67	318	2.43	364	2 33	438	3.68	1,348	7.27	7,599
6	3.40	524	5.68	291	2.53	370	2.58	463	3.75	1,430	7.32	7,736
7	3.08	503	5.62	278	2.50	368	2.58	490	3.77	1,454	7.52	8,300
8	2.73	492	5.54	287	2.48	360	2.58	520	3.80	1,490	6.86	6,530
9	3.14	478	5.55	330	2.43	360	2.58	555	3.73	1,406	6.79	6,357
10	3.33	470	5.50	330	2.33	385	2.58	583	3.65	1,315	6.58	5,888
11	2.78	480	5.48	280	2.38	388	2.63	612	3.80	1,490	6.85	6,505
12	2.68	520	5.98	291	2.50	340	2.83	641	3.95	1,670	7.05	7,020
13	2.63	525	4.68	323	2.58	678	2.93	678	4.20	1,970	7.43	8,040
14	2.54	528	3.93	342	2.53	344	3.08	700a	4.43	2,259	8.10	10,260
15	2.48	539	3.73	360	2.48	341	3.13	750	4.70	2,620	8.40	11,420
16	2.60	549	3.71	360	2.45	330	3.23	853	4.78	2,732	8.56	12,040
17	2.68	557	3.78	350	2.43	320	3.10	720	4.85	2,835	8.87	13,360
18	2.77	540	3.78	328	2.42	326	3.05	670	4.73	2,662	8.90	13,440
19	3.83	519	3.78	300	2.41	335	3.00	620	4.60	2,480	8.37	11,120
20	3.96	490	3.68	325	2.48	340	2.95	575	4.67	2,578	7.68	8,640
21	4.13	462	3.68	328	2.50	346	2.80	440	4.70	2,620	7.30	7,540
22	3.98	447	3.68	326	2.58	360	2.80	440	4.76	2,704	6.92	6,480
23	4.33	434	3.68	310	2.78	342	2.90	530	5.60	4,000	6.55	5,640
24	4.43	414	3.73	322	3.08	310	2.90	530	6.10	4,900	6.28	5,260
25	4.48	406	3.78	333	3.38	280	3.00	620	6.25	5,200	6.50	5,520
26	4.53	411	3.76	336	3.03	271	3.00	620	5.65	4,080	7.10	6,880
27	4.58	408	3.73	298	2.60	280	3.00	620	5.30	3,520	7.50	7,920
28	5.83	371	3.67	243	2.48	286	3.05	670	5.11	3,225	7.63	8,400
29	5.88	354	.....	.....	2.38	293	3.05	670	4.67	2,578	7.86	9,280
30	5.53	364	.....	.....	2.33	309	3.10	720	4.58	2,454	8.10	10,260
31	5.48	380	.....	.....	2.28	317	.....	.....	4.78	2,732	.....	.....

a Ice conditions Jan. 1 to Apr. 14.

SESSIONAL PAPER No. 25c

DAILY GAUGE HEIGHT AND DISCHARGE of Athabaska River at Jasper, for 1914.

DAY.	July. Gauge Height.	July. Discharge.	August. Gauge Height.	August. Discharge.	September. Gauge Height.	September. Discharge.	October. Gauge Height.	October. Discharge.	November. Gauge Height.	November. Discharge.	December. Gauge Height.	December. Discharge.
	Feet.	*Sec.-ft.*	*Feet.*	*Sec.-ft.*	*Feet.*	*Sec.-ft.*	*Feet.*	*Sec.-ft.*	*Feet.*	*Sec.-ft.*	*Feet.*	*Sec.-ft.*
1	8.55	12,160	7.32	8,258	5.82	4,876	5.13	3,775	3.12	1,212	2.54	715
2	8.95	14,080	7.50	8,790	5.65	4,590	4.74	3,216	3.10	1,190	2 47	690
3	9.24	15,480	7.67	9,341	5.60	4,510	4.43	2,782	3 06	1,146	2.46	645
4	9.40	16,320	7.80	9,780	5.45	4,270	4.13	2,389	3 02	1,102	2.44	600
5	9.27	15,780	7.68	9,374	5.27	3,992	4.00	2,220	3.05	1,135	2 47	575
6	8.80	13,640	7.40	8,490	5.20	3,880	3.86	2,052	3.03	1,113	2.47	570
7	8.48	12,320	7.10	7,650	5.17	3,835	3.97	2,184	3.00	1,080	3.83	570
8	8.28	11,540	6.55	6,320	5.16	3,820	3.90	2,100	2.97	1,050	4.90	573
9	8.20	11,200	6.15	5,500	5.10	3,730	3.88	2,076	3.01	1,091	6.01	573
10	8.49	12,420	5.70	4,670	4.92	3,468	3.95	2,160	2.94	1,020	5.54	533
11	8.87	14,120	5.78	4,806	4.68	3,132	3.74	1,908	2.90	980	4.75	490
12	9.10	15,200	5.85	4,930	4.56	2,964	3.78	1,956	2.82	908	4.25	488
13	9.00	14,760	6.07	5,343	4.20	2,480	3.70	1,860	2.65	726	5.24	503
14	9.05	14,990	6.45	6,105	4.09	2,337	3.75	1,920	2.70	700*b*	4.04	518
15	8.54	12,716	6.63	6,499	3.94	2,148	3.72	1,884	2.60	675	4.12	515
16	8.11	10,931	6.47	6,147	3.83	2,016	3.94	2,148	2.32	660	4.16	522
17	7.83	9,882	6.38	5,960	3.74	1,908	4.05	2,285	2.54	677	4.20	530
18	7.66	9,308	6.34	5,880	3.97	2,184	3.86	2,052	2.84	690	4.28	530
19	8.31	11,751	6.42	6,042	4.22	2,506	3.74	1,908	2.90	700	4.36	500
20	8.26	11,546	6.40	6,000	3.99	2,208	3.61	1,752	2.87	708	4.43	487
21	8.16	11,136	7.00	7,390	3.85	2,040	3.43	1,553	2.80	710	4.55	500
22	7.81	9,814	7.05	7,520	3.74	1,908	3.25	1,355	2.70	706	4.52	540
23	7.76	9,644	6.94	7,240	3.85	2,040	3.27	1,377	2.73	700	4.45	540
24	7.01	7,416	6.00	5,210	4.01	2,233	3.23	1,333	2.72	696	4.33	520
25	7.21	7,948	6.08	5,362	4.23	2,519	3.17	1,267	2.76	710	4.35	495
26	7.16	7,812	6.10	5,400	4.83	3,342	3.25	1,355	2.84	732	4.25	480
27	7.26	8,088	6.47	6,147	5.61	4,526	3.14	1,234	2.80	732	4.18	500
28	6.81	6,924	6.35	5,900	5.43	4,288	3.04	1,124	2.65	720	4.10	500
29	7.11	7,677	6.12	5,440	5.34	4,094	3.05	1,135	2.59	715	3.85	500
30	7.21	7,948	6.03	5,267	5.23	3,928	3.09	1,179	2.38	723	3.80	508
31	7.15	7,785	5.94	5,096	......	......	3.16	1,256	......	......	3.65	523*b*

b Ice conditions Nov. 14 to Dec. 31.

MONTHLY DISCHARGE of Athabaska River at Jasper, for 1914.

(Drainage area 1,600 square miles.)

MONTH.	DISCHARGE IN SECOND-FEET. Maximum.	Minimum.	Mean.	Per square Mile.	RUN-OFF. Depth in inches on Drainage Area.	Total in Acre-feet.
January	557	354	476	0.298	0.34	29,268
February	380	243	556	0.348	0.36	30,879
March	388	271	334	0.209	0.24	20,537
April	853	340	574	0.359	0.40	34,155
May	5,200	820	2,379	1.488	1.72	146,279
June	13,440	3,904	8,242	5.151	5.75	490,430
July	16,320	6,924	11,366	7.104	8.19	698,892
August	9,780	4,670	6,512	4.070	4.69	400,404
September	4,876	1,908	3,191	1.994	2.22	189,879
October	3,775	1,124	1,897	1.186	1.37	116,637
November	1,212	660	857	0.535	0.60	50,995
December	715	480	540	0.338	0.39	33,203
The year	....	....	....	....	26.27	2,241,558

5 GEORGE V, A. 1915

MALIGNE RIVER NEAR JASPER.

Location.—On the SW. ¼ Sec. 1, Tp. 46, Rge. 1, W. 6th Mer., about 4½ miles northeast of Jasper and about 400 feet from the point where the Maligne enters the Athabaska.

Records available.—Discharge measurements from June 29, 1914, to December 31, 1914.

Drainage area.—448 square miles.

Gauge.—Vertical staff on right bank of river about 250 feet upstream from cable support.

Bench-mark.—Six-inch spike driven in a 15-inch spruce stump on right bank of the river, and about 4 feet north of the gauge, elevation 8.38 feet above zero of gauge.

Channel.—One channel at all stages, fairly permanent.

Discharge measurements.—Made from cable and car.

Winter flow.—Not affected by ice.

Observer.—None.

DISCHARGE MEASUREMENTS of Maligne River near Jasper, in 1914.

Date.	Engineer.	Width.	Area of Section.	Mean Velocity.	Gauge Height.	Discharge.
		Feet.	*Sq. ft.*	*Ft.persec.*	*Feet.*	*Sec.-ft.*
Jan. 26	P. H. Daniells	45	42	2.55	....a	108
Feb. 12	do	32	43	2.05	....a	87
Mar. 4	do	25	40	2.10	....a	84
April 1	do	54	59	1.12	....a	66
April 17	do	57	71	1.32	....a	94
May 12	do	62	109	2.35	....a	256
June 29	do	90	273	6.64	3.50	1,814
July 16	do	90	274	6.64	3.46	1,817
July 30	do	87	261	5.98	3.33	1,561
Aug. 13	do	87	254	4.95	3.86	1,260
Aug. 26	do	87	262	5.58	3.23	1,461
Sept. 11	do	87	251	5.73	3.10	1,440
Sept. 25	do	76	157	3.73	2.01	570
Oct. 8	do	76	150	3.54	1.97	531
Oct. 24	do	73	118	2.68	1.55	316
Nov. 14	do	60	93	1.90	1.07	177
Dec. 24	do	57	73	1.50	0.60	110

a No gauge.

ROCKY RIVER NEAR HAWES.

Location.—On the NW. ¼ Sec. 13, Tp. 48, Rge. 28, W. 5th Mer., about three-quarters of a mile east of Hawes station and about 300 yards from the point where the Rocky enters the Athabaska River.

Records available.—June 9, 1913, to December 31, 1914.

Gauge.—Vertical staff; elevation of zero maintained at 90.91 feet since establishment.

Bench-mark.—On right concrete abutment; assumed elevation 100.00 feet.

Channel.—Shifting.

Winter flow.—River affected by ice from November to April. Discharge measurements made at a point about one mile above station.

Observer.—C. Picarell.

SESSIONAL PAPER No. 25c

DISCHARGE MEASUREMENTS of Rocky River near Hawes, in 1914.

Date.	Engineer.	Width.	Area of Section.	Mean Velocity.	Gauge Height.	Discharge.
		Feet.	*Sq. ft.*	*Ft. per sec.*	*Feet.*	*Sec.-ft.*
Jan. 5	P. H. Daniells	80	82	1.58	4.26	129
Feb. 11	do	38	46	1.47	5.31	67
Mar. 30	do	57	100	0.88	5.01	88
April 15	do	83	70	2.40	4.29	169
May 15	do	115	175	3.72	2.98	651
May 29	do	121	182	2.49	2.88	454
June 18	do	194	460	5.40	4.11	2,488
July 3	do	200	446	5.73	4.01	2,552
July 17	do	149	270	4.06	3.80	1,097
Aug. 3	do	136	184	3.70	3.45	682
Aug. 14	do	128	190	2.65	3.29	503
Sept. 14	do	128	152	2.41	3.08	366
Sept. 28	do	126	176	3.14	3.08	553
Oct. 9	do	126	175	2.61	3.21	456
Oct. 27	do	114	141	1.89	2.80	267
Nov. 16	do	34	35	2.66	4.85	94
Dec. 2	do	53	64	1.56	4.81	100
Dec. 28	do	35	38	2.66	5.76	101

DAILY GAUGE HEIGHT AND DISCHARGE of Rocky River near Hawes, for 1914.

Day.	January. Gauge Height.	January. Discharge.	February. Gauge Height.	February. Discharge.	March. Gauge Height.	March. Discharge.	April. Gauge Height.	April. Discharge.	May. Gauge Height.	May. Discharge.	June. Gauge Height.	June. Discharge.
	Feet.	*Sec.-ft.*	*Feet.*	*Sec.-ft.*	*Feet.*	*Sec.-ft.*	*Feet.*	*Sec.-ft.*	*Feet.*	*Sec.-ft.*	*Feet.*	*Sec.-ft.*
1	4.19	120a	5 29	69	4 80	70	4 93	94	2 07	265	27	719
2	3.99	124	5.19	65	4 87	71	5 08	96	2 18	279	61	1,140
3	3.96	126	4.92	60	4 87	71	5 00	100	2 30	296	.80	1,531
4	4.25	129	5.17	57	4.97	72	5 17	113	2 25	289	86	1,729
5	4.29	129	4.41	53	4 77	72	5 13	118	2 15	277	3 55	1,048
6	4.26	124	5.03	60	4.53	72	5.22	122	2.12	272	3.61	1,140
7	4.29	118	5.13	64	4.91	72	5.24	126	2.14	274	3.95	2,161
8	4.15	113	5.47	68	5.03	72	5.21	134	2.25	289	3.71	1,328
9	3.91	108	5.59	72	5.00	70	5.11	152	2.35	304	3.71	1,328
10	1.79	108	5.37	70	3.36	68	4.85	155	2.53	339	3.78	1,486
11	0.26	110	5.42	67	3.46	72	4.83	156	2.52	336	3.79	1,508
12	4.07	108	4.81	64	4.55	75	4.58	161	2.61	359	3.81	1,564
13	4.13	104	5.13	66	5.11	76	4.25	163	2.68	380	3.87	1,762
14	4.11	100	4.99	68	5.17	74	4.33	166	2.92	476	3.95	2,161
15	4.11	100	5.10	72	5.13	72	4.20	169	2.99	511	4.09	3,253
16	4.16	101	4.67	68	5.15	73	3.18	240a	3.13	780	4.17	3,964
17	4.25	100	4.48	65	4.97	74	2.41	313	3.06	705	4.17	3,964
18	3.59	91	4.43	63	4.97	70	2.14	274	2.93	590	4.09	3,233
19	2.33	86	3.85	62	4.90	66	2.13	273	2.87	550	4.01	2,549
20	2.24	81	3.46	62	4.89	64	2.10	269	2.79	490	3.89	1,828
21	2.26	78	3.77	63	4.97	72	2.02	259	2 80	485	.79	1,508
22	2.28	75	4.01	65	5.13	78	1.99	255	2 91	540	73	1,374
23	2.30	76	4.35	67	5.09	80	2.03	260	.25	810	74	1,496
24	2.32	70	4.68	69	4.97	78	2.01	257	53	1,150	67	1,250
25	2.34	72	4.63	71	4.75	77	1.98	254	3 56	1,170	3 85	1,696
26	4.49	73	4.66	72	4.59	77	1.95	251	3.34	860	3.81	1,564
27	4.97	68	4.81	72	4.64	81	1.93	249	3.16	665	3.79	1,508
28	4.83	62	4.73	68	4.89	86	1.95	251	3.01	535	3.83	1,630
29	5.01	70			5.16	89	1.97	253	2.87	452	3.99	2,401
30	5.13	70			5.03	88	1.99	255	2.79	418	3.95	2,161
31	5.25	77			5.03	92			2.90	466		

a Ice conditions Jan. 1 to April 16.

STREAM MEASUREMENTS, 1914

5 GEORGE V, A. 1915

DAILY GAUGE HEIGHT AND DISCHARGE of Rocky River near Hawes, for 1914.

DAY.	July.		August.		September.		October.		November.		December.	
	Gauge Height.	Dis-charge.	Gauge Height.	Dis-charge.	Gauge Height.	Dis-charge.	Gauge Height.	Dis-charge.	Gauge Height.	Dis-charge.	Gauge Height.	Dis-charge.
	Feet.	*Sec.-ft.*	*Feet.*	*Sec.-ft.*	*Feet.*	*Sec.-ft.*	*Feet.*	*Sec.-ft.*	*Feet.*	*Sec.-ft.*	*Feet.*	*Sec.-ft.*
1..........	3.90	1,861	3.41	620	3.23	471	3 23	625	2.80	270	4.66	101
2..........	4.07	3,077	3.41	620	3.18	438	3.23	605	2.78	264	4 78	100
3..........	4.06	2,989	3.43	640	3.15	420	3.23	582	2.78	264	4 77	98
4..........	4.05	2,901	3 47	680	3.15	420	3.20	540	2.77	261	4.77	96
5..........	4.19	4,150	3.43	640	3.13	408	3.17	505	2.77	261	4.75	94
6..........	4.16	3,800	3.42	630	3.11	396	3.15	480	2.77	261	4.81	96
7..........	4.05	2,890	3.40	610	3.09	385	3.15	460	2.78	264	4.87	98
8..........	4.09	3,253	3.37	583	3.07	375	3.18	460	2.66	232	5.07	99
9..........	4.32	5,290	3.33	547	3.16	426	3.20	456	2.61	222	4.55	97
10..........	4.33	5,290	3.33	547	3.14	414	3.18	438	2.61	222	4.81	94
11..........	4.17	3,700	3.29	513	3.13	408	3.16	426	2.87	187*b*	4.45	94
12..........	4.25	4,300	3.29	513	3.13	408	3.15	420	3.01	151	5.88	96
13..........	4.24	4,000	3.28	506	3.11	396	3.13	408	3.48	127	5.65	98
14..........	4.17	3,070	3.30	520	3.09	370	3.09	385	3.95	114	5.73	100
15..........	4.13	2,500	3.30	520	3.07	380	3.05	365	4.42	100	5.82	103
16..........	3.95	1,500	3.29	513	3.06	390	3.05	365	4.91	94	6.14	106
17..........	3.77	1,060	3.31	529	3.03	395	3.03	355	4.91	98	5.62	108
18..........	3.83	1,203	3.27	499	3.03	410	3.03	355	5.27	104	6.76	108
19..........	3.63	872	3.29	513	3.04	422	3.01	345	5.26	106	6.68	105
20..........	3.79	1,123	3.28	506	3.05	435	2.99	336	5.03	109	6.92	103
21..........	3.68	942	3.29	513	3.05	452	2.97	328	4.93	109	6.94	105
22..........	3.61	844	3.29	513	3.05	472	2.95	320	4.91	106	6.76	106
23..........	3.50	710	3.35	565	3.06	485	2.94	316	4.88	105	6.95	106
24..........	3.40	610	3.33	547	3.10	520	2.93	312	4.71	106	6.92	105
25..........	3.39	601	3.30	520	3.18	590	2.90	300	4.63	110	6.60	104
26..........	3.37	583	3.27	499	3.21	630	2.85	285	4.66	113	6.16	100
27..........	3.35	565	3.27	499	3.27	695	2.83	279	4.75	109	5.32	98
28..........	3.41	620	3.26	492	3.29	732	2.83	279	4.59	104	6.20	100
29..........	3.39	601	3.27	499	3.25	680	2.81	273	4.59	104	6.70	103
30..........	3.37	583	3.27	499	3.23	640	2.81	273	4.72	103	6.14	105
31..........	3.38	592	3.25	485	......	......	2.79	267	......	......	6.86	106

b Ice conditions Nov. 11 to Dec. 31.

MONTHLY DISCHARGE of Rocky River near Hawes, for 1914.

(Drainage area 428 square miles.)

MONTH.	DISCHARGE IN SECOND-FEET.				RUN-OFF.	
	Maximum.	Minimum	Mean.	Per square Mile.	Depth in inches on Drainage Area.	Total in Acre-feet.
January..............................	129	62	96	0.224	0.26	5,903
February.............................	72	53	66	0.154	0.16	3,665
March..........................	92	64	75	0.175	0.20	4,612
April................................	313	94	198	0.463	0.52	11,782
May.................................	1,170	265	504	1.178	1.36	30,990
June..........................	3,964	719	1,866	4.360	4.86	111,034
July...................	5,290	565	2,132	4.981	5.74	131,092
August..............................	680	485	545	1.273	1.47	33,511
September...........................	732	370	469	1.096	1.22	27,907
October.......................... ...	625	267	392	0.916	1.06	24,103
November.......................... ..	270	94	159	0.372	0.42	9,461
December............................	108	94	101	0.236	0.27	6,210
The year.............................	....	....	....	....	17.54	400,270

MCLEOD RIVER NEAR THORNTON.

Location.—On the NW. ¼ Sec. 3, Tp. 54, Rge. 16, W. of 5th Mer., at the Thornton ferry, about one mile downstream from the mouth of Wolf Creek, and about 200 feet south of *E.* Smith's ranch buildings.

Records available.—May 18, 1914, to December 31, 1914; discharge measurements available from September 26, 1913, to December 31, 1914.

Gauge.—Vertical staff, directly under the ferry cable, on the right bank of the river.

Bench-mark.—Spike driven in 4-inch tree on the right bank, about 200 feet downstream from gauge. Elevation 11.52 feet above zero of gauge.

Channel.—One channel at all stages, fairly permanent.

Discharge measurements.—Made from ferry cable and by wading.

Winter flow.—Stream affected by ice from November to April. Discharge measurements made at a point about 1,000 feet above regular station.

Observer.—Edward Smith.

DISCHARGE MEASUREMENTS of McLeod River near Thornton, in 1914.

Date.	Engineer.	Width.	Area of Section.	Mean Velocity.	Gauge Height.	Discharge.
		Feet.	*Sq. ft.*	*Ft. per sec.*	*Feet.*	*Sec.-ft.*
Jan. 2	P. H. Daniells	220	116	.36	........*a*	42.0
Jan. 19	do	200	75	.24	........*a*	18.3
Feb. 7	do	111	81	.21	........*a*	17.0
Mar. 2	do	178	124	.43	........*a*	54.0
Mar. 26	do	221	209	.56	........*a*	117.0
May 18	do	298	781	2.10	2.70	1,640.0
June 3	do	270	525	1.68	1.80	884.0
June 9	do	374	2,555	8.03	10.80	20,500.0*b*
June 19	do	337	1,258	2.91	4.24	3,668.0
July 12	do	322	1,056	2.54	3.50	2,685.0
July 20	do	290	689	1.75	2.31	1,210.0
Aug. 4	do	261	451	1.43	1.46	646.0
Aug. 15	do	262	437	1.40	1.40	611.0
Aug. 29	do	266	486	1.60	1.65	781.0
Sept. 17	do	260	505	1.50	1.70	755.0
Sept. 30	do	262	461	1.39	1.52	642.0
Oct. 15	do	258	418	1.34	1.38	558.0
Oct. 29	do	247	341	1.18	1.09	402.0
Nov. 18	do	240	294	0.73	1.43	215.0
Dec. 5	do	125	179	1.22	1.40	218.0
Dec. 30	do	120	138	0.72	1.12	100.0

a No gauge.
b Estimate.

5 GEORGE V, A. 1915

DAILY GAUGE HEIGHT AND DISCHARGE of McLeod River near Thornton, for 1914.

DAY.	May.		June.		July.		August.	
	Gauge Height.	Dis- charge.	Gauge Height.	Dis- charge.	Gauge Height.	Dis- charge.	Gauge Height.	Dis- charge.
	Feet.	*Sec.-ft.*	*Feet.*	*Sec.-ft.*	*Feet.*	*Sec.-ft.*	*Feet.*	*Sec.-ft.*
1	....	....	1.60	720	5.00	5,220	1.60	720
2	....	....	1.70	790	4.80	4,770	1.50	660
3	....	....	1.80	860	4.50	4,170	1.50	660
4	....	....	2.40	1,360	4.20	3,640	1.40	600
5	....	....	2.30	1,270	4.00	3,320	1.40	600
6	....	....	2.30	1,270	4.00	3,320	1.40	600
7	....	....	7.00	10,400	3.90	3,170	1.30	540
8	....	....	8.00	13,080	3.80	3,020	1.30	540
9	....	....	10.80	20,584	3.60	2,730	1.40	600
10	....	....	9.80	17,904	3.50	2,590	1.40	600
11	....	....	9.00	15,760	3.50	2,590	1.50	660
12	....	....	8.30	13,884	3.60	2,730	1.50	660
13	....	....	7.70	12,276	3.30	2,320	1.40	600
14	....	....	7.10	10,668	3.40	2,450	1.40	600
15	....	....	6.50	9,060	3.10	2,080	1.40	600
16	....	....	5.90	7,460	3.00	1,970	1.30	540
17	....	....	5.30	5,930	2.70	1,640	1.30	540
18	2.70	1,640a	4.70	4,560	2.60	1,540	1.20	480
19	2.50	1,450	4.30	3,810	2.40	1,360	1.20	480
20	2.40	1,360	4.40	3,990	2.30	1,270	1.20	480
21	2.70	1,640	4.40	3,990	2.20	1,180	1.20	480
22	2.70	1,640	5.30	5,930	2.20	1,180	1.20	480
23	2.60	1,540	6.60	9,328	2.10	1,090	1.30	540
24	2.60	1,540	6.30	8,524	2.00	1,010	1.50	660
25	2.70	1,640	6.10	7,988	2.00	1,010	1.70	790
26	2.70	1,640	5.90	7,460	1.90	930	2.00	1,010
27	2.30	1,270	5.70	6,940	1.80	860	1.80	860
28	2.10	1,090	5.50	6,420	1.80	860	1.70	790
29	2.00	1,010	5.30	5,930	1.80	860	1.60	720
30	1.80	860	5.10	5,450	1.70	790	1.50	660
31	1.70	790	....	....	1.70	790	1.40	600

a Station established.

SESSIONAL PAPER No. 25c

DAILY GAUGE HEIGHT AND DISCHARGE of McLeod River near Thornton, for 1914.

DAY.	September.		October.		November.		December.	
	Gauge Height.	Dis-charge.	Gauge Height.	Dis-charge.	Gauge Height.	Dis-charge.	Gauge Height.	Dis-charge.
	Feet.	*Sec.-ft.*	*Feet.*	*Sec.-ft.*	*Feet.*	*Sec.-ft.*	*Feet.*	*Sec.-ft.*
1	1.40	600	1.50	660	1.10	430	1.40	280
2	1.40	600	1.50	660	1.10	430	1.50	262
3	1.30	540	1.50	660	1.00	390	1.50	250
4	1.30	540	1.60	720	1.00	390	1.40	235
5	1.20	480	1.60	720	1.10	430	1.40	220
6	1.20	480	1.60	720	1.10	430	1.40	236
7	1.20	480	1.60	720	1.00	390	1.40	250
8	1.30	540	1.50	660	1.10	430	1.40	256
9	1.40	600	1.50	660	1.20	480	1.40	250
10	2.50	1,450	1.50	660	1.30	540	1.30	235
11	2.40	1,360	1.50	660	1.40	600	1.30	220
12	2.10	1,090	1.50	660	1.20	480	1.30	200
13	2.00	1,010	1.40	600	1.10	430	1.30	200
14	1.80	860	1.40	600	1.20	440b	1.20	220
15	1.80	860	1.40	600	1.20	290	1.20	225
16	1.80	860	1.40	600	1.00	270	1.10	225
17	1.70	790	1.30	540	1.20	208	1.10	233
18	1.70	790	1.30	540	1.40	211	1.10	245
19	1.70	790	1.30	540	1.40	240	1.00	220
20	1.60	720	1.30	540	1.40	260	1.00	180
21	1.60	720	1.20	480	1.40	292	0.90	183
22	1.60	720	1.20	480	1.40	323	0.90	190
23	1.50	660	1.10	430	1.40	320	1.00	136
24	1.50	660	1.10	430	1.50	315	1.00	100
25	1.50	660	1.10	430	1.50	336	1.00	75
26	1.40	600	1.20	480	1.50	342	1.00	95
27	1.40	600	1.20	480	1.50	305	1.10	122
28	1.50	660	1.20	480	1.50	286	1.10	123
29	1.50	660	1.10	430	1.50	309	1.10	112
30	1.50	660	1.10	430	1.40	300	1.10	100
31	....	....	1.10	430	....	....	1.10	120b

b Ice conditions Nov. 14 to Dec. 31.

MONTHLY DISCHARGE of McLeod River near Thornton, for 1914.

(Drainage area 2,507 square miles.)

MONTH.	DISCHARGE IN SECOND-FEET.				RUN-OFF.	
	Maximum.	Minimum.	Mean.	Per square Mile.	Depth in inches on Drainage Area.	Total in Acre-feet.
May (18–31)	1,640	790	1,365	0.544	0.28	37,903
June	20,584	720	7,453	2.973	3.32	443,487
July	5,220	790	2,144	0.855	0.99	131,828
August	1,010	480	624	0.249	0.29	38,368
September	1,450	480	709	0.283	0.32	42,188
October	720	430	571	0.228	0.26	35,109
November	600	208	363	0.145	0.16	21,600
December	280	75	193	0.077	0.09	11,867
The period	....	....	....	....	5.71	762,350

5 GEORGE V, A. 1915

LOBSTICK RIVER NEAR ENTWISTLE.

Location.—On the *NE.* ¼ Sec. 30, Tp. 53, Rge. 7, W. of 5th Mer., about 2½ miles northwest of the village of *Entwistle.*

Records available.—July 11, 1913, to December 31, 1914. Discharge measurements available from February 20, 1913.

Gauge.—Vertical staff; elevation of zero maintained at 96.17 feet during 1913, and 95.44 feet during 1914.

Bench-mark.—Spike driven in 6-inch spruce stump on right bank of the river, and about 20 feet south of the gauge; assumed elevation 100.00 feet.

Channel.—Fairly permanent.

Discharge measurements.—Made from bridge.

Winter flow.—River affected by ice from November to April, and discharge measurements are made at a point about 700 feet downstream from regular section.

Observer.—A. H. Young.

DISCHARGE MEASUREMENTS of Lobstick River near *Entwistle*, in 1914.

Date.	Engineer.	Width.	Area of Section.	Mean Velocity.	Gauge Height.	Discharge.
		Feet.	*Sq. ft.*	*Ft. per sec.*	*Feet.*	*Sec.-ft.*
Feb. 6............	P. H. Daniells ......*........	30	28	1.00	....a	29
Mar. 25............	do	26	33	1.63	....a	54
May 9............	do	36	54	1.83	2.03	99
June 9..	do	71	321	5.57	5.67	1,800b
Oct. 30..	do	38	48	2.30	2.09	111
Nov. 10............	do	33	47	1.90	1.97	89
Nov. 27............	do	25	88	1.08	3.11	92
Dec. 22.......	do	30	33	1.84	3.36	60

a No gauge.
b Estimate.

DAILY GAUGE HEIGHT AND DISCHARGE of Lobstick River near *Entwistle*, for 1914.

DAY.	May.		June.		July.		August.	
	Gauge Height.	Dis-charge.	Gauge Height.	Dis-charge.	Gauge Height.	Dis-charge.	Gauge Height.	Dis-charge.
	Feet.	*Sec.-ft.*	*Feet.*	*Sec.-ft.*	*Feet.*	*Sec.-ft.*	*Feet.*	*Sec.-ft.*
1............	....	.. ...	1.80	60	a......	....	a......	....
2............	....	....	1.76	56	....	....	....	....
3............	....	....	1.76	56	....	....	....	....
4............	... ...	....	2.18	126	....	....	....	....
5............	....	....	2.56	218	....	....	....	....
6............	....	....	3.23	452	....	....	....	....
7............	....	....	4.13	886	....	....	....	....
8............	....	....	4.90	1,350	....	....	....	....
9............	2.03	96	5.67	1,888	....	....	....	....
10............	1.98	87	a	....	....	....	....	....
11............	1.93	80	....	....	....	....	....	....
12............	1.93	80	....	....	....	....	....	....
13............	1.96	84	....	....	....	....	....	....
14............	1.90	75	....	....	....	....	....	....
15............	1.80	60	....	....	....	....	....	....
16............	1.98	87	....	....	....	....	....	....
17............	1.88	72	....	....	....	....	....	....
18............	1.93	80	....	....	....	....	....	....
19............	1.92	78	....	....	....	....	....	....
20............	2.04	98	....	....	....	....	....	....
21............	2.03	96	....	....	....	....	....	....
22............	1.98	87	....	....	....	....	....	....
23............	2.01	92	....	....	....	....	....	....
24............	2.03	96	....	....	....	....	....	....
25............	2.03	96	....	....	....	....	....	....
26............	2.03	96	....	....	....	....	....	....
27............	2.02	94	....	....	....	....	....	....
28............	1.88	72	....	....	....	....	....	....
29............	2.13	116	....	....	....	....	....	....
30............	1.96	84	....	....	....	....	....	....
31............	1.88	72	....	....	....	....	....	....

a No observer from June 10 to Sept. 21.

SESSIONAL PAPER No. 25c

DAILY GAUGE HEIGHT AND DISCHARGE of Lobstick River near Entwistle, for 1914.

DAY.	September.		October.		November.		December.	
	Gauge Height.	Dis- charge.	Gauge Height.	Dis- charge.	Gauge Height.	Dis- charge.	Gauge Height.	Dis- charge.
	Feet.	*Sec.-ft.*	*Feet.*	*Sec.-ft.*	*Feet.*	*Sec.-ft.*	*Feet.*	*Sec.-ft.*
1	......a	....	2.06	102	2.05	100	2.54	78
2	....	....	2.06	102	2.03	96	2.51	76
3	....	....	2.06	102	2.01	92	2.41	74
4	....	....	2.11	112	2.01	92	2.41	73
5	....	....	2.11	112	2.01	92	2.41	71
6	....	....	2.16	122	2.00	90	2.45	69
7	....	....	2.16	122	2.01	92	2.46	69
8	....	....	2.14	118	1.96	84	2.58	69
9	....	....	2.10	110	1.93	80	2.68	70
10	....	....	2.06	102	1.96	89b	2.71	68
11	....	....	2.07	104	1.81	88	2.66	62
12	....	....	2.01	92	1.81	84	2.38	54
13	....	....	2.03	96	1.76	80	2.31	56
14	....	....	2.06	102	1.71	81	2.26	59
15	....	....	2.09	108	1.81	68	2.22	60
16	....	....	2.09	108	1.80	68	2.09	61
17	....	....	2.10	110	2.71	66	2.31	63
18	....	....	2.11	112	2.71	64	2.11	65
19	....	....	2.11	112	2.74	76	2.06	65
20	......a	....	2.10	110	2.76	80	2.04	58
21	2.26	142	2.10	110	2.71	84	2.01	58
22	2.26	142	2.08	106	2.71	89	3.36	60
23	2.25	140	2.07	104	2.71	86	3.36	62
24	2.24	138	2.06	102	2.71	83	3.29	60
25	2.22	134	2.06	102	2.71	83	3.29	52
26	2.21	132	2.06	102	2.68	88	3.26	48
27	2.26	142	2.05	100	2.64	92	c	48
28	2.30	150	2.06	102	2.61	90	c	52
29	2.16	122	2.06	102	2.58	80	c	52
30	2.11	112	2.05	100	2.56	79	c	51
31	....	....	2.05	100	....	....	c	52

a No observer from June 10 to Sept. 21.
b Ice conditions from Nov. 10 to Dec. 31.
c No gauge heights.

MONTHLY DISCHARGE of Lobstick River near Entwistle, for 1914.

(Drainage area 718 square miles.)

MONTH.	DISCHARGE IN SECOND-FEET.				RUN-OFF.	
	Maximum.	Minimum.	Mean.	Per square Mile.	Depth in inches on Drainage Area.	Total in Acre-feet.
May (9–31)	116	60	86	0.120	0.10	3,922
June (1–9)	1,888	56	566	0.788	0.26	10,102
July	....	....	....	....	....	....
August	....	....	....	....	....	....
September (21–30)	150	112	135	0.188	0.07	2,677
October	122	92	106	0.148	0.17	6,518
November	100	64	84	0.117	0.13	4,998
December	78	48	62	0.086	0.10	3,812
The period	....	....	....	....	0.83	32,029

5 GEORGE V, A. 1915

PEMBINA RIVER NEAR ENTWISTLE.

Location.—On the SW. ¼ Sec. 20, Tp. 53, Rge. 7, W. 5th Mer., directly under the Grand Trunk Pacific Railway trestle, about 1½ miles west of the Entwistle station.

Records available.—May 8, 1914, to December 31, 1914. Discharge measurements available from February 20, 1913.

Gauge.—Vertical staff, spiked to pile about 20 feet downstream from the cable and 20 feet from the right bank.

Bench-mark.—Spike driven in 12-inch square pile on the right bank, and about 4 feet west of the cable support; elevation 16 66 feet above zero of gauge.

Channel.—One channel at all stages, fairly permanent.

Discharge measurements.—Made from cable car.

Winter flow.—River affected by ice from November to April. Discharge measurements made at a point about 1,500 feet above regular station.

Observer.—Fred Williams.

DISCHARGE MEASUREMENTS of Pembina River near Entwistle, in 1914.

Date.	Engineer.	Width.	Area of Section.	Mean Velocity.	Gauge Height.	Discharge.
		Feet.	*Sq. ft.*	*Ft. per sec.*	*Feet.*	*Sec.-ft.*
Jan. 17	P. H. Daniells	70	44	0.54	1.25	24.0
Feb. 6	do	46	26	0.40	1.40	104.0
Feb. 27	do	97	44	0.31	1.70	13.6
Mar. 24	do	105	65	0.50	1.85	33.0
April 11	do	150	126	0.77	1.95	97.0
May 9	do	156	756	2.24	3.03	1,694.0
June 9	do	195	2,100	7.29	10.50	15,300.0a
June 10	do	191	1,923	7.05	9.43	13,564.0
June 25	do	177	1,191	4.57	5.64	5,443.0
July 9	do	163	870	2.36	3.35	2,054.0
July 27	do	162	603	0.90	1.95	544.0
Aug. 31	do	134	480	0.57	1.29	275.0
Sept. 19	do	149	543	0.80	1.64	442.0
Oct. 16	do	147	485	0.58	1.32	279.0
Oct. 30	do	143	472	0.48	1.16	227.0
Nov. 10	do	108	137	0.94	0.80	127.0
Nov. 27	do	85	228	0.56	1.41	128.0
Dec. 22	do	83	176	0.25	0.92	44.0

a Estimate.

SESSIONAL PAPER No. 25c

DAILY GAUGE HEIGHT AND DISCHARGE of Pembina River near Entwistle, for 1914.

DAY.	May.		June.		July.		August.	
	Gauge Height.	Dis-charge.	Gauge Height.	Dis-charge.	Gauge Height.	Dis-charge.	Gauge Height.	Dis-charge.
	Feet.	*Sec.-ft.*	*Feet.*	*Sec.-ft.*	*Feet.*	*Sec.-ft.*	*Feet.*	*Sec.-ft.*
1			1.40	310	3.90	2,730	1.80	540
2			1.40	310	3.70	2,470	1.70	480
3			1.40	310	3.40	2,100	1.70	480
4			1.30	270	3.01	1,660	1.60	420
5			2.50	1,150	3.00	1,650	1.40	310
6			2.50	1,150	3.00	1,650	1.40	310
7			3.20	1,860	3.10	1,750	1.40	310
8	3.10	1,750a	7.07	8,190	3.30	1,980	1.40	310
9	3.00	1,650	10.95	17,260	3.50	2,220	1.40	310
10	3.30	1,980	9.45	13,660	3.40	2,100	1.40	310
11	3.50	2,220	8.50	11,380	3.40	2,100	1.40	310
12	3.40	2,100	7.20	8,450	3.30	1,980	1.40	310
13	3.00	1,650	6.70	7,450	3.50	2,220	1.40	310
14	3.00	1,650	5.90	5,880	3.70	2,470	1.40	310
15	2.60	1,250	5.20	4,630	3.50	2,220	1.40	310
16	2.40	1,050	4.80	4,000	3.40	2,100	1.30	270
17	2.30	950	4.50	3,560	3.30	1,980	1.30	270
18	2.40	1,050	4.20	3,140	3.10	1,750	1.30	270
19	2.40	1,050	4.00	2,860	2.80	1,450	1.30	270
20	2.70	1,350	4.10	3,000	2.50	1,150	1.30	270
21	2.70	1,350	4.20	3,140	2.40	1,050	1.30	270
22	2.60	1,250	4.50	3,560	2.30	950	1.30	270
23	2.50	1,150	4.80	4,000	2.30	950	1.30	270
24	2.30	950	6.20	6,450	2.20	850	1.30	270
25	2.10	760	5.60	5,340	2.10	760	1.30	270
26	2.00	680	5.00	4,300	2.00	680	1.30	270
27	1.90	610	4.70	3,850	1.95	645	1.30	270
28	1.80	540	4.50	3,560	1.95	645	1.30	270
29	1.70	480	4.30	3,280	1.95	645	1.30	270
30	1.60	420	4.20	3,140	1.95	645	1.30	270
31	1.50	360			1.90	610	1.30	270

a Ice conditions.

5 GEORGE V. A. 1915

DAILY GAUGE HEIGHT AND DISCHARGE of Pembina River near *Entwistle*, for 1914.

DAY.	September. Gauge Height.	September. Dis- charge.	October. Gauge Height.	October. Dis- charge.	November. Gauge Height.	November. Dis- charge.	December. Gauge Height.	December. Dis- charge.
	Feet.	*Sec.-ft.*	*Feet.*	*Sec.-ft.*	*Feet.*	*Sec.-ft.*	*Feet.*	*Sec.-ft.*
1	1.20	240	1.30	270	1.20	240	1.44	108
2	1.20	240	1.30	270	1.20	240	1.44	104
3	1.10	210	1.30	270	1.20	240	1.44	100
4	1.10	210	1.30	270	1.20	240	1.44	94
5	1.10	210	1.30	270	1.20	240	1.44	85
6	1.10	210	1.40	310	1.20	240	1.40	72
7	1.10	210	1.50	360	1.10	210	1.40	72
8	1.10	210	1.50	360	1.00	180	1.40	72
9	1.30	270	1.50	360	0.90	150	1.40	72
10	1.30	270	1.50	360	0.80	128b	1.40	68
11	1.30	270	1.40	310	1.00	127	1.36	60
12	1.40	310	1.40	310	1.00	127	1.36	53
13	1.40	310	1.40	310	1.00	124	1.36	50
14	1.40	310	1.30	270	1.00	122	1.36	50
15	1.50	360	1.30	270	1.00	119	1.36	52
16	1.50	360	1.30	270	1.10	116	1.32	50
17	1.60	420	1.30	270	1.20	114	1.12	52
18	1.60	420	1.30	270	1.20	112	1.12	52
19	1.65	450	1.30	270	1.20	114	1.12	50
20	1.65	450	1.30	270	1.20	118	1.12	46
21	1.60	420	1.30	270	1.40	120	1.12	43
22	1.50	360	1.20	240	1.40	120	0.90	44
23	1.50	360	1.20	240	1.40	120	0.90	47
24	1.50	360	1.20	240	1.40	120	0.90	46
25	1.50	360	1.20	240	1.50	122	0.90	41
26	1.50	360	1.20	240	1.50	124	0.90	37
27	1.50	360	1.20	240	1.50	128	0.90	36
28	1.50	360	1.20	240	1.48	120	0.90	39
29	1.40	310	1.20	240	1.48	112	0.90	42
30	1.40	310	1.20	240	1.48	110	0.90	44
31			1.20	240			0.90	45b

b Ice conditions.

MONTHLY DISCHARGE of Pembina River near Entwistle, for 1914.

(Drainage area 1,858 square miles.)

MONTH.	DISCHARGE IN SECOND-FEET. Maximum.	DISCHARGE IN SECOND-FEET. Minimum.	DISCHARGE IN SECOND-FEET. Mean.	DISCHARGE IN SECOND-FEET. Per square Mile.	RUN-OFF. Depth in inches on Drainage Area.	RUN-OFF. Total in Acre-feet.
April						
May (8-31)	2,220	360	1,177	0.633	0.56	56,016
June	17,260	270	4,348	2.340	2.61	258,722
July	2,730	610	1,554	0.836	0.96	95,554
August	540	270	311	0.167	0.19	19,123
September	450	210	317	0.171	0.19	18,863
October	360	240	277	0.149	0.17	17,032
November	240	110	150	0.081	0.09	8,926
December	108	36	59	0.032	0.04	3,628
The period					4.81	477,864

ATHABASKA RIVER AT ATHABASKA.

Location.—On the SE. ¼ Sec. 20, Tp. 66, Rge. 22, W. 4th Mer., 400 feet below the ferry cable in the town of Athabaska.

Records available.—March 17, 1914, to December 31, 1914. Discharge measurements only during the winters of 1912-13 and 1913-14.

Drainage area.—29,200 square miles; taken from small scale map and is liable to be in error.

Gauge.—Inclined staff, reading to feet and tenths, located on left bank of river, 300 feet above ferry cable and 100 feet below measuring section. Zero elevation of gauge maintained at 1,635.38 feet since established.

Bench-mark.—On a track spike in a telegraph pole on right bank of river; pole located at foot of Strathcona Street north side of C.N.R. track, and opposite Hudson Bay Co. office; elevation 1,660.60 feet. (Canadian Northern Railway datum.)

Channel.—One slightly shifting channel at all stages.

Discharge measurements.—Made from a boat run on a cable.

Winter flow.—From November to April the river is frozen over, and measurements are made at the regular section.

Observer.—L. J. Cole.

DISCHARGE MEASUREMENTS of Athabaska River at Athabaska, in 1914.

Date.	Engineer.	Width.	Area of Section.	Mean Velocity.	Gauge Height.	Discharge.
		Feet.	*Sq. ft.*	*Ft. per sec.*	*Feet.*	*Sec.-ft.*
Jan. 13	P. H. Daniells	685	2,587	1.31	2.93	3,401
Feb. 3	do	650	2,466	1.16	2.90	2,857
Feb. 24	do	645	2,186	1.21	3.06	2,636
Mar. 18	do	650	2,400	1.31	3.56	3,158
April 3	do	650	2,522	1.28	3.65	3,219
May 12	G. J. Smith and J. M. Paul.	690	4,636	2.59	4.18	12,020
May 30	J. M. Paul	714	5,586	3.14	5.45	17,532
June 23	do	783	11,130	5.55	12.89	61,772
July 9	do	795	10,190	5.19	11.45	52,855
Aug. 5	do	771	6,970	3.37	6.82	22,809
Aug. 21	do	760	5,932	3.04	5.90	18,064
Sept. 4	do	719	5,161	2.86	5.20	14,748
Sept. 23	do	716	5,091	2.75	5.07	14,164
Oct. 15	do	704	4,998	2.50	4.72	12,473
Nov. 6	P. H. Daniells	682	4,138	2.04	3.19	8,449
Dec. 15	do	680	3,508	0.90	3.60	3,146

STREAM MEASUREMENTS, 1914

5 GEORGE V, A. 1915

DAILY GAUGE HEIGHT AND DISCHARGE of Athabaska River at Athabaska, for 1914.

DAY.	March.		April.		May.		June.		July.	
	Gauge Height.	Dis-charge.	Gauge Height.	Dis-charge.	Gauge Height.	Dis-charge.	Gauge Height.	Dis-charge.	Gauge Height.	Dis-charge.
	Feet.	*Sec.-ft.*	*Feet.*	*Sec.-ft.*	*Feet.*	*Sec.-ft.*	*Feet.*	*Sec.-ft.*	*Feet.*	*Sec.-ft.*
1			3.65	3,175	4.20b	12,100	4.55	13,500	11.92	55,656
2			3.60	3,175	4.10b	11,750	4.23	12,220	11.55	53,140
3			3.65	3,220	4.08	11,680	3.98	11,340	11.20	50,760
4			3.65	3,220	3.98	11,340	4.00	11,400	11.00	49,400
5			3.70	3,250	3.95	11,250	4.72	14,180	10.98	49,284
6			3.75	3,300	3.92	11,160	6.05	20,575	11.02	49,536
7			3.75	3,300	4.00	11,400	8.60	35,900	11.15	50,420
8			3.75	3,300	4.08	11,680	9.58	42,560	11.35	51,780
9			3.80	3,300	4.08	11,680	15.10	81,200	11.40	52,120
10			3.80	3,325	4.10	11,750	19.02	108,640	11.00	49,400
11			3.85	3,360	4.12	11,820	18.97	106,300	10.52	46,136
12			3.90	3,400	4.12	11,820	16.82	91,500	10.30	44,640
13			4.05	3,450	4.25	12,300	15.25	80,300	10.18	43,824
14			4.30	3,450	4.37	12,780	14.27	73,350	10.35	44,980
15			4.40	3,400	4.43	13,020	13.84	70,000	10.90	48,720
16			4.70	3,380	4.45	13,100	12.57	60,950	10.92	48,856
17	3.55	3,170a	5.05	3,380	4.50	13,300	12.09	57,300	10.75	47,700
18	3.60	3,150	5.40	3,380	4.48	13,220	12.04	56,472	10.52	46,136
19	3.60	3,150	5.50	3,380	4.62	13,780	12.24	57,832	10.12	43,416
20	3.65	3,175	5.70	3,370	4.78	14,420	12.22	57,696	9.40	38,700
21	3.67b	3,200	5.80b	3,350	4.85	14,725	12.22	57,696	8.80	34,800
22	3.70	3,200	6.00b	3,400	4.75	14,300	12.20	57,560	8.45	32,525
23	3.70	3,200	6.20b	4,500	4.65	13,900	12.75	61,300	8.52	32,980
24	3.70	3,200	5.90b	5,400	4.45	13,100	12.92	62,456	8.65	33,825
25	3.70	3,175	5.60b	6,400	4.32	12,580	14.22	71,296	8.00	29,800
26	3.65	3,150	5.20b	7,550	4.55	13,500	14.60	73,880	7.60	27,400
27	3.60	3,150	5.00b	8,550	4.82	14,590	13.30	65,040	7.32	25,720
28	3.60	3,150	4.60b	9,600	5.35	16,975	12.50	59,600	7.22	25,120
29	3.65	3,150	4.30b	10,880a	5.65	18,450	12.18	57,424	7.18	24,880
30	3.65	3,200	4.25b	12,300	5.40	17,200	12.15	57,220	7.12	24,520
31	3.70	3,200			4.92	15,040			6.95	23,525

a Ice conditions March 17 to April 29; discharge estimated.
b Gauge height interpolated.

SESSIONAL PAPER No. 25c

DAILY GAUGE HEIGHT AND DISCHARGE of Athabaska River at Athabaska, for 1914.

DAY.	August.		September.		October.		November.		December.	
	Gauge Height.	Dis-charge.	Gauge Height.	Dis-charge.	Gauge Height.	Dis-charge.	Gauge Height	Dis-charge.	Gauge Height.	Dis-charge.
	Feet.	*Sec.-ft.*	*Feet.*	*Sec.-ft.*	*Feet.*	*Sec.-ft.*	*Feet.*	*Sec.-ft.*	*Feet.*	*Sec.-ft.*
1	6.95	23,525	5.60	16,400	4.88	13,320	3.35	8,600	5.01	4,000
2	6.72	22,260	5.52	16,040	5.38	15,410	3.35	8,600	4.70	3,820
3	6.55	21,325	5.40	15,500	5.35	15,275	3.35	8,600	4.60	3,680
4	6.62	21,710	5.22	14,690	5.48	15,860	3.40	8,700	4.20	3,600
5	6.82	22,810	5.12	14,280	5.68	16,800	3.30	8,500	4.35	3,790
6	6.88	23,140	4.88	13,320	5.70	16,900	3.23	8,360	4.25	3,700
7	6.90	23,250	4.82	13,080	5.60	16,400	3.20	8,300	4.25	3,700
8	6.95	23,525	4.95	13,600	5.50	15,950	3.18	8,260	4.05	3,450
9	6.80	22,700	5.12	14,280	5.38	15,410	3.10	8,100	3.80	3,200
10	6.65	21,875	5.08	14,120	5.20	14,600	3.06	8,020	3.80	3,200
11	6.68	22,040	5.14	14,360	5.02	13,880	2.08	7,860a	3.65	2,900
12	6.55	21,325	5.60	16,400	4.92	13,480	2.96	7,000	3.75	2,930
13	6.10	18,900	5.88	17,800	4.88	13,320	2.88	6,050	3.60	2,960
14	5.87	17,750	5.32	15,140	4.78	12,930	2.88	5,100	3.50	3,000
15	5.62	16,500	4.90	13,400	4.68	12,580	2.88	4,200	3.60	3,150
16	5.68	16,800	4.70	12,650	4.62	12,370	2.00	3,900	3.60	3,200
17	5.62	16,500	4.50	11,950	4.52	12,020	1.88	3,600	3.45	3,200
18	5.72	17,000	4.38	11,530	4.40	11,600	2.13	3,600	3.50	3,140
19	5.90	17,900	4.68	12,580	4.35	11,425	4.32	4,000	3.45	3,050
20	5.95	18,150	4.98	13,720	4.35	11,425	5.00	4,310	3.45	3,000
21	5.80	17,400	5.08	14,120	4.25	11,075	5.10	4,400	3.45	3,100
22	5.80	17,400	5.10	14,200	4.25	11,075	4.63	4,220	3.47	3,000
23	5.82	17,500	5.02	13,880	4.25	11,075	4.58	4,200	3.48	3,000
24	5.85	17,650	5.00	13,800	4.15	10,750	4.18	4,000	3.49	2,900
25	5.98	18,300	4.90	13,400	3.98	10,240	5.50	4,400	3.50	2,800
26	6.10	18,900	4.70	12,650	3.75	9,575	5.30	4,380	3.51	2,700
27	6.00	18,400	4.55	12,125	3.60	9,200	5.10	4,100	3.52	2,700
28	5.70	16,900	4.45	11,775	3.60	9,200	5.10	4,000	3.53	2,800
29	5.58	16,310	4.50	11,950	3.52	9,000	5.05	4,000	3.54	2,900
30	5.52	16,040	4.58	12,230	3.48	8,900	4.95	4,000	3.55	2,900
31	5.58	16,310			3.40	8,700			3.56	3,200a

a Ice conditions Nov. 11 to Dec. 31.

MONTHLY DISCHARGE of Athabaska River at Athabaska, for 1914.

(Drainage area 29,200 square miles.)

MONTH.	DISCHARGE IN SECOND-FEET.				RUN-OFF.	
	Maximum.	Minimum	Mean.	Per square Mile.	Depth in inches on Drainage Area.	Total in Acre-feet.
January	3,500	2,900	3,200	0.110	0.13	196,760
February	3,150	2,630	2,902	0.099	0.10	161,168
March	3,300	3,000	3,161	0.108	0.12	194,362
April	12,300	3,175	4,615	0.158	0.18	274,610
May	18,450	11,160	13,216	0.453	0.52	812,592
June	108,040	11,340	56,223	1.925	2.15	3,345,480
July	55,656	23,525	41,280	1.414	1.63	2,538,180
August	23,525	16,040	19,358	0.663	0.76	1,190,296
September	17,800	11,530	13,832	0.474	0.53	823,088
October	16,900	8,700	12,572	0.431	0.50	772,992
November	8,700	3,600	5,845	0.200	0.22	347,800
December	4,000	2,700	3,183	0.109	0.13	195,716
The year					6.97	10,853,044

NOTE.—Discharges for Jan., Feb. and March estimated, as no gauge heights were obtained until March. 17

5 GEORGE V. A. 1915

MISCELLANEOUS DISCHARGE MEASUREMENTS made in Athabaska River drainage basin, in 1914.

Date.	Engineer.	Stream.	Location.	Width.	Area of Section.	Mean Velocity.	Discharge.
				Feet.	Sq. ft.	Ft. per sec.	Sec.-ft.
Jan. 3....	P. H. Daniells...	Athabaska River..	NW. 5-51-25-5..	620.0	1,374.0	0.65	900.0
Feb. 9....	do	do	do	198.0	1,009.0	0.99	998.0
Mar. 27....	do ...	do	do	200.0	930.0	0.95	888.0
June 3....	do ...	Edson River......	NW. 5-54-16-5..	43.0	70.0	0.48	34.0
July 20....	do ...	do	do	43.0	96.0	1.11	107.0
Aug. 4....	do ...	do	do	46.0	72.0	0.43	31.0
Oct. 15....	do ...	do	do	44.0	75.0	0.47	35.0
Jan. 20....	do ...	Embarras River...	SW. 5-52-18-5..	53.0	30.0	0.12	3.7
April 14....	do ...	do	do	260.0	230.0	1.14	262.0
May 16....	do ...	do	do	135.0	211.0	1.81	381.0
June 2....	do ...	do	do	92.0	170.0	0.68	116.0
July 21....	do ...	do	do	125.0	252.0	1.06	267.0
Aug. 18....	do ...	do	do	95.0	162.0	0.84	135.0
Sept. 18....	do ...	do	do	107.0	178.0	0.82	146.0
Oct. 28....	do ...	do	do	94.0	144.0	0.55	80.0
Dec. 4....	do ...	do	do	105.0	130.0	0.53	67.0
Feb. 28....	do ...	do	NW. 6-51-19-5..	48.0	53.0	0.15	7.8
Jan. 4....	do ...	Fiddle Creek..	SE. 15-49-27-5..	13.0	7.6	0.92	7.1
Feb. 10....	do ...	do	do	18.5	6.7	0.98	6.6
Mar. 29....	do ...	do	do	15.0	5.0	0.97	4.6
May 30....	do ...	do	do	52.0	34.0	2.09	70.0
July 4....	do ...	do	SE. 15-49-27-5..	116.0	96.0	3.28	313.0
Aug. 14....	do ...	do	do	51.0	32.0	1.58	51.0
Sept. 15....	do ...	do	do	55.0	34.0	1.90	64.0
Sept. 29....	do ...	do	do	62.0	44.0	2.48	105.0
Oct. 26....	do ...	do	do	45.0	27.0	1.52	41.0
Nov. 17....	do ...	do	do	31.0	22.0	0.84	18.1
Dec. 3....	do ...	do	do	22.0	11.1	0.57	6.3
Dec 29....	do ...	do	do	26.0	12.2	0.75	9.2
Oct. 9....	J. M. Paul......	Lesser Slave River.	22-71-1-5	217.0	980.0	4.42	4,342.0
Sept. 8....	do ...	do	do	212.0	922.0	3.15	2,905.0
Oct. 10....	do ...	do	6-73-5-5	194.0	1,346.0	1.70	2,285.0
May 12....	P. H. Daniells..	Maligne River....	Above Canyon..	24.0	19.5	1.05	20.0
May 27....	do ...	do	do ..	41.0	36.0	1.58	57.0
June 15....	do ...	do	do ..	32.0	57.0	3.47	199.0
June 29....	do ...	do	do ..	30.0	51.0	5.49	281.0
July 16....	do ...	do	do ..	35.0	67.0	5.65	377.0
Aug. 13....	do ...	do	do ..	24.0	33.0	2.11	70.0
Aug. 25....	do ...	do	do ..	24.0	29.0	1.95	57.0
Sept. 11....	do ...	do	do ..	24.0	26.0	1.78	45.0
Sept. 25....	do ...	do	do ..	25.0	21.0	0.95	20.0
Oct. 8....	do ...	do	do ..	24.0	24.0	1.05	25.0
Oct. 24....	do ...	do	do ..	23.0	21.0	1.00	21.0
Jan. 20....	do ...	McLeod River....	NW. 5-52-18-5..	32.0	24.0	0.20	4.8
July 13....	do ...	Prairie Creek.....	NE. 5-51-25-5..	24.0	28.0	1.50	43.0
Jan. 27....	do ...	Snaring River.....	NW. 33-46-1-6..	67.0	91.0	0.47	43.0
Mar. 7....	do ...	do	do	35.0	14.0	1.32	18.5
April 18....	do ...	do	do	45.0	65.0	0.70	46.0
May 13....	do ...	do	do	226.0	232.0	3.51	812.0
May 28....	do ...	do	do	141.0	205.0	3.63	747.0
June 13....	do ...	do	do	190.0	381.0	5.95	2,268.0
June 30....	do ...	do	do	214.0	416.0	5.56	2,319.0
July 15....	do ...	do	do	199.0	408.0	5.65	2,307.0
July 29....	do ...	do	do	136.0	230.0	4.42	1,018.0
Aug. 12....	do ...	do	do	236.0	286.0	2.46	707.0
Aug. 27....	do ...	do	do	236.0	261.0	2.29	597.0
Sept. 10....	do ...	do	do	101.0	117.0	2.88	338.0
Sept. 26....	do ...	do	do	257.0	299.0	3.07	918.0
Oct. 13....	do ...	do	do	92.0	102.0	2.91	296.0
Oct. 23....	do ...	do	do	67.0	98.0	1.91	187.0
Dec. 1....	do ...	do	do	60.0	114.0	0.72	83.0
Mar. 28....	do ...	Spring..	SW. 2-51-26-5..	....	....	....	0.0131
Jan. 5....	do ...	Stony River......	SE. 35-46-1-6...	55.0	144.0	1.28	185.0
Jan. 21....	do ...	do	do	42.0	91.0	2.01	187.0
Feb. 11....	do ...	do	do	64.0	64.0	2.07	133.0
Mar. 3....	do ...	do	do	82.0	100.0	1.71	171.0
Mar. 30....	do ...	do	do	82.0	107.0	1.62	174.0
May 29....	do ...	do	do	97.0	439.0	2.53	1,112.0
Dec. 28....	do ...	do	do	53.0	87.0	1.49	128.0
June 1....	do ...	Sundance Creek...	NW. 3-53-18-5..	26.0	28.0	0.80	22.0
July 10....	do ...	do	do	27.0	41.0	3.07	126.0
Aug. 17....	do ...	do	do	23.0	26.0	1.11	31.0
Sept. 16....	do ...	do	do	21.0	23.0	1.68	39.0
Oct. 14 ...	do ...	do	do	27.0	28.0	1.18	33.0
July 20....	do ...	Wolf Creek......	SW. 3-54-16-5..	55.0	60.0	3.16	188.0
Sept. 22....	do ...	do	do	38.0	34.0	1.35	56.0

NORTH SASKATCHEWAN RIVER DRAINAGE BASIN.

General Description.

The North Saskatchewan River draws its principal water supply from the eastern slope of the Rocky Mountains. The basin is bounded on the south by those of the Red Deer and South Saskatchewan Rivers, and on the north by those of the Athabaska and Churchill Rivers. The general trend of the stream from its source to where it joins the South Saskatchewan, a few miles below the city of Prince Albert, and forms the Saskatchewan River, is easterly.

The basin of the river easily divides itself into five parts or divisions, each of which requires a separate description for a clear understanding of the conditions of run-off.

The first, or upper section, consists of the eastern slope of the Rocky Mountains. While this part of the basin is not the greatest in area, it supplies the greater part of the run-off. In glaciers, and the perpetual snows of the higher peaks, innumerable small streams rise which form the main stream and its larger tributaries. These streams have well defined rocky valleys and considerable fall. The upper regions of this section are not well wooded, and allow a rapid run-off of melting snow and rain.

East of this first section is a division consisting of the foothills, which are, for the most part, well covered with forest and vegetable growth, forming probably the largest in area of the five sections. Here also is a very large source of supply for the stream, but due to its cover, a more regulated supply than in the first section. In this section the main stream is joined by the Clearwater and Brazeau Rivers, two of the most important tributaries of the whole basin. The streams in this section flow through deep valleys with fairly permanent beds and medium slopes.

From a little west of the city of Edmonton to the mouth of the Vermilion River the country is of a park-like nature, with large stretches of prairie. This section is small in area and has not a very large run-off. The principal tributaries are the Sturgeon and Vermilion Rivers, the first of which drains in from the wooded country of the north, the latter from the prairie sections of the south. The main stream is in a well defined valley with large flats along its course and a more or less permanent bed with a small slope.

Below the third section to a little above the city of Prince Albert is a division which has little drainage into the river. It consists of prairie uplands for the most part, with small patches of timber to the north. The stream widens out into shallow reaches, full of shifting sand bars, and has very little slope. The valley, while still well defined, is also much wider. In this section the main stream is fed by the Battle River, which has its source at the outlet of Battle Lake, and flows eastward through park land and prairie sections south of the main river, until it empties into the latter at the town of Battleford.

The east division is one in which the river, with a greater slope and more permanent bed, narrows considerably, as does also the valley. The run-off in this division is mostly from the north, which consists of well-wooded country drained by a number of small streams.

During 1913, stations were established on the Sturgeon River at St. Albert and Fort Saskatchewan, and on the Battle River at Ponoka. Cables were erected on the main river and the Clearwater River near Rocky Mountain House in 1913, records being obtained at these points during 1914.

A description of flood conditions in this basin may be found on page 30 and 31 in the Report of the Progress of Stream Measurements for 1912.

CLEARWATER RIVER NEAR ROCKY MOUNTAIN HOUSE.

Location.—On the SE. ¼ Sec. 16, Tp. 39, Rge. 7, W. 5th Mer., on G. Fletcher's farm, three miles southwest of Rocky Mountain House.

Records available.—January 1, 1914, to December 31, 1914.

Gauge.—Chain, located on left bank of river 10 feet below cable, and graduated to feet and tenths; length of chain from bottom of weight to marker is 15.28 feet. Zero elevation of gauge maintained at 3,105.04 feet since established.

Bench-mark.—On nails in poplar stump directly in front of cable tower on right bank; elevation 3,120.00 feet above mean sea level. (Department of Public Works of Canada datum.)

Channel.—One permanent channel at low water and probably two in high stages.

Discharge measurements.—Made from cable car.

Winter flow.—From November to April river is frozen over, and measurements are made at the cable section.

Observer.—G. Fletcher.

5 GEORGE V, A. 1915

DISCHARGE MEASUREMENTS of Clearwater River near Rocky Mountain House, in 1914.

Date.	Engineer.	Width.	Area of Section.	Mean Velocity.	Gauge Height.	Discharge.
		Feet.	*Sq. ft.*	*Ft. per sec.*	*Feet.*	*Sec.-ft.*
Jan. 3	J. S. Tempest	133	295	0.44	2.82	129
Mar. 7	do	128	437	0.59	3.65	256
April 25	do	182	510	0.85	1.89	435
May 19	G. J. Smith and J. M. Paul	190	627	1.43	2.48	898
June 9	J. M. Paul	197	864	2.62	3.79	2,261
June 24	Dept. of Public Works, Canada	192	694	1.74	2.80	1,204
June 29	J. M. Paul	193	744	1.86	3.00	1,385
July 20	do	190	696	1.58	2.69	1,102
Aug. 8	Dept. of Public Works, Canada	190	626	1.46	2.50	912
Aug. 12	J. M. Paul	186	622	1.28	2.30	798
Aug. 27	do	184	592	1.11	2.13	657
Sept. 14	do	186	605	1.19	2.20	718
Sept. 29	do	183	557	1.07	2.10	595
Oct. 10	Dept. of Public Works, Canada	189	607	1.40	2.41	853
Oct. 20	J. M. Paul	185	550	1.07	2.10	589
Nov. 5	H. S. Kerby	180	473	0.88	1.80	417
Dec. 3	R. J. McGuinness	180	410	0.62	2.14	256
Dec. 19	do	163	344	0.46	2.18	158

DAILY GAUGE HEIGHT AND DISCHARGE of Clearwater River near Rocky Mountain House, for 1914.

DAY.	January.		February.		March.		April.		May.		June.	
	Gauge Height.	Dis- charge	Gauge Height.	Dis- charge.	Gauge Height.	Dis- charge.	Gauge Height.	Dis- charge.	Gauge Height.	Dis- charge.	Gauge Height.	Dis- charge.
	Feet.	*Sec.-ft.*	*Feet.*	*Sec.-ft.*	*Feet.*	*Sec.-ft.*	*Feet.*	*Sec.-ft.*	*Feet.*	*Sec.-ft.*	*Feet.*	*Sec.-ft.*
1	2.72	128a	3.59	205	3.49	234	3.55	240	1.79	388	1.75	360
2	2.72	128	3.60	210	3.41	220	3.55	240	1.69	324	1.74	354
3	2.71	129	3.57	193	3.41	220	3.55	240	1.71	336	1.88	451
4	3.15	164	3.46	175	3.51	235	3.65	270	2.39	842	2.35	810
5	3.30	198	3.36	160	3.61	246	3.70	270	2.29	762	2.51	944
6	3.69	230	3.45	190	3.71	260	4.00	300	2.19	682	2.92	1,313
7	3.78	235	3.39	175	3.67	256	4.00	300	2.14	642	2.98	1,367
8	3.77	235	3.34	160	3.67	257	3.95	290	2.04	563	3.80	2,280
9	3.82	240	3.47	200	3.60	247	3.95	290	2.34	802	3.65	2,095
10	3.81	240	3.43	190	3.55	240	4.00	300	2.69	1,106	3.01	1,395
11	3.51	203	3.42	190	3.50	230	4.10	320	2.79	1,196	3.00	1,385
12	3.37	180	3.51	207	3.70	260	4.20	320	2.64	1,061	3.00	1,385
13	3.69	215	3.51	207	3.70	260	4.20	320	2.61	1,034	3.00	1,385
14	3.60	202	3.55	216	3.83	265	4.20	320	2.30	770	3.00	1,385
15	3.68	215	3.55	216	3.70	260	4.10	300	2.29	762	3.00	1,385
16	3.63	210	3.49	210	3.60	240	4.10	300a	2.29	762	3.03	1,415
17	3.62	210	3.48	210	3.70	260	4.10	310b	2.34	802	3.06	1,445
18	3.56	200	3.48	210	3.60	240	4.00	330	2.44	882	3.50	1,805
19	3.56	200	3.42	200	3.60	240	3.80	350	2.48	917	3.50	1,915
20	3.55	200	3.27	180	3.60	240	3.80	370	2.47	908	3.50	1,915
21	3.45	180	3.06	160	3.50	220	3.60	400	2.46	899	3.60	2,035
22	3.44	180	3.10	165	3.60	237	2.60	420	2.40	850	3.00	1,915
23	3.33	160	3.35	200	3.75	270	2.10	440	2.24	722	3.00	1,385
24	3.33	160	3.34	200	3.70	260	2.10	450b	2.22	714	2.79	1,196
25	3.32	160	3.44	215	3.55	240	1.89	458	2.22	706	2.80	1,205
26	3.42	180	3.48	225	3.10	170	1.84	423	2.21	698	2.80	1,205
27	3.31	162	3.47	225	3.00	150	1.84	423	2.25	730	3.00	1,385
28	3.25	150	3.47	225	3.00	150	1.79	388	2.24	722	3.00	1,385
29	3.60	200	....	....	3.10	167	1.79	388	2.08	594	3.00	1,385
30	3.59	200	....	....	3.20	185	1.79	388	1.97	514	3.00	1,385
31	3.59	200	....	....	3.50	230	....	....	1.86	437	....	....

a Ice conditions Jan. 1 to April 16.
b Ice breaking up April 17 to April 24; discharges during this period interpolated.

DAILY GAUGE HEIGHT AND DISCHARGE of Clearwater River near Rocky Mountain House, for 1914.

DAY.	July.		August.		September.		October.		November.		December.	
	Gauge Height.	Dis-charge.	Gauge Height.	Dis-charge.	Gauge Height.	Dis-charge.	Gauge Height.	Dis-charge	Gauge Height.	Dis-charge.	Gauge Height.	Dis-charge.
	Feet.	*Sec.-ft.*	*Feet.*	*Sec.-ft.*	*Feet.*	*Sec.-ft.*	*Feet.*	*Sec.-ft.*	*Feet.*	*Sec.-ft.*	*Feet.*	*Sec.-ft.*
1	3.08	1,465	2.45	890	2.17	666	2.05	570	1.80	395	2.10	269
2	3.06	1,445	2.50	935	2.10	610	2.00	535	1.85	430	2.00	262
3	3.02	1,405	2.45	890	2.05	570	2.00	535	1.85	430	2.00	256
4	3.15	1,535	2.40	850	2.02	549	2.00	535	1.85	430	2.00	256
5	3.50	1,915	2.45	890	2.05	570	2.10	610	1.80	395	2.00	256
6	3.50	1,915	2.50	935	2.05	570	2.05	570	1.82	409	2.00	256
7	3.50	1,915	2.60	1,025	2.12	626	2.00	535	1.82	409	2.00	240
8	3.42	1,827	2.60	1,025	2.22	706	2.00	535	1.90	465	1.90	185
9	3.25	1,640	2.50	935	2.32	786	2.15	650	1.95	500	1.90	185
10	3.20	1,585	2.45	890	2.22	706	2.40	850	2.00	535	1.90	188
11	3.20	1,585	2.40	850	2.28	754	2.40	850	2.00	535	2.00	204
12	3.20	1,585	2.30	770	2.38	834	2.32	786	2.00	535	1.90	192
13	3.20	1,585	2.25	730	2.38	834	2.25	730	2.10	515*b*	1.80	150
14	3.30	1,695	2.20	690	2.18	674	2.20	690	2.18	502	1.80	146
15	3.45	1,860	2.28	754	2.10	610	2.20	690	2.30	480*b*	1.80	143
16	3.30	1,695	2.30	770	2.10	610	2.20	690	2.65	455*a*	1.70	131
17	3.20	1,585	2.28	754	2.05	570	2.20	690	2.70	438	1.70	125
18	3.20	1,585	2.30	770	2.00	535	2.15	650	2.90	428	1.90	138
19	3.00	1,385	2.30	770	2.00	535	2.15	650	3.05	425	2.08	158
20	2.72	1,133	2.22	706	2.06	578	2.10	610	3.02	424	2.08	178
21	3.00	1,385	2.20	690	2.10	610	2.10	610	3.00	422	2.08	180
22	2.88	1,277	2.20	690	2.05	570	2.10	610	2.75	418	2.08	182
23	2.75	1,160	2.28	754	2.00	535	2.10	610	2.60	409	2.08	182
24	2.65	1,070	2.25	730	2.00	535	2.05	570	2.60	393	2.08	182
25	2.50	935	2.25	730	1.95	500	2.00	535	2.60	369	2.09	182
26	2.62	1,043	2.20	690	1.90	465	2.00	535	2.60	355	2.09	180
27	2.50	935	2.10	610	1.90	465	1.95	500	2.40	352	1.99	165
28	2.45	890	2.11	618	1.98	521	1.95	500	2.30	342	1.99	136
29	2.42	866	2.12	626	2.10	610	1.90	465	2.30	317	2.09	135
30	2.40	850	2.10	610	2.10	610	1.80	395	2.30	280	2.09	140
31	2.38	834	2.20	690	......	......	1.80	395	......	......	2.10	155*a*

a Ice conditions Nov. 16 to Dec. 31.
b Ice forming Nov. 13 to Nov. 15; discharges during this period interpolated.

MONTHLY DISCHARGE of Clearwater River near Rocky Mountain House, for 1914.

(Drainage area 850 square miles.)

MONTH.	DISCHARGE IN SECOND-FEET.				RUN-OFF.	
	Maximum.	Minimum.	Mean.	Per square Mile.	Depth in inches on Drainage Area.	Total in Acre-feet.
January	240	128	190	0.224	0.26	11,683
February	225	160	197	0.232	0.24	10,941
March	270	150	232	0.273	0.31	14,265
April	458	240	449	0.528	0.59	26,717
May	1,196	324	746	0.878	1.01	45,870
June	2,280	354	1,376	1.620	1.81	81,880
July	1,915	834	1,406	1.650	1.90	86,453
August	1,025	610	783	0.921	1.06	48,145
September	834	465	610	0.718	0.80	36,298
October	850	395	603	0.709	0.82	37,077
November	535	280	426	0.501	0.56	25,349
December	269	125	185	0.218	0.25	11,375
The year	......	......	......	......	9.61	436,053

5 GEORGE V. A. 1915

NORTH SASKATCHEWAN RIVER NEAR ROCKY MOUNTAIN HOUSE.

Location.—On the *NE.* ¼ Sec. 21, Tp. 39, Rge. 7, W. 5th Mer., one-quarter of a mile below the railway bridge and one mile west of Rocky Mountain House.

Records available.—June 2, 1913, to December 31, 1914.

Gauge.—Inclined staff, graduated to feet and tenths, located on left bank of river 600 feet above cable. Zero elevation from June 2 to October 23, 1913, maintained at 3,108.39 feet. Zero elevation maintained at 3,108.42 feet since October 23, 1913.

Bench-mark.—Stump on left bank at ferry cable; elevation 3127.74 feet above mean sea level. (Department of Public Works of Canada datum.)

Channel.—One permanent channel at all stages.

Discharge measurements.—Made from cable located about 600 feet below the gauge.

Winter flow.—From November to April river is frozen over, and measurements are made at the cable section.

DISCHARGE MEASUREMENTS of North Saskatchewan River near Rocky Mountain House, in 1914.

Date.	Engineer.	Width.	Area of Section.	Mean Velocity.	Gauge Height.	Discharge.
		Feet.	*Sq. ft.*	*Ft. per sec.*	*Feet.*	*Sec.-ft.*
Jan. 5	J. S. Tempest	320	809	1.10	5.70	886
Mar. 8	do	330	444	1.82	5.65	806
April 27	do	421	749	2.28	4.01	1,709
May 18	G. J. Smith and J. M. Paul	434	1,277	3.82	5.74	4,878
June 6	J. M. Paul	441	1,954	5.22	7.35	10,206
June 25	Dept. of Public Works, Canada	437	1,584	4.50	6.45	7,135
June 29	J. M. Paul	444	2,035	5.10	7.48	10,387
July 21	do	465	2,486	5.66	8.51	14,070
Aug. 7	Dept. of Public Works, Canada	441	2,001	5.41	7.58	10,812
Aug. 11	J. M. Paul	438	1,634	4.20	6.50	6,864
Aug. 28	do	439	1,788	4.40	6.82	7,876
Sept. 14	do	434	1,279	3.28	5.45	4,193
Sept. 28	do	434	1,328	3.60	5.73	4,784
Oct. 9	Dept. of Public Works, Canada	433	1,240	3.86	5.61	4,788
Oct. 19	J. M. Paul	431	1,046	3.00	5.04	3,137
Nov. 6	H. S. Kerby	415	720	2.40	4.41	1,728
Dec. 2	R. J. McGuinness	410	915	0.96	5.98	878
Dec. 20	do	417	720	1.17	6.32	843

DAILY GAUGE HEIGHT AND DISCHARGE of North Saskatchewan River near Rocky Mountain House, for 1914.

DAY.	January.		February.		March.		April.		May.		June.	
	Gauge Height.	Dis-charge.	Gauge Height.	Dis-charge.	Gauge Height.	Dis-charge.	Gauge Height.	Dis-charge.	Gauge Height.	Dis-charge.	Gauge Height.	Dis-charge.
	Feet.	*Sec.-ft.*	*Feet.*	*Sec.-ft.*	*Feet.*	*Sec.-ft.*	*Feet.*	*Sec.-ft.*	*Feet.*	*Sec.-ft.*	*Feet.*	*Sec.-ft.*
1	5.7	885a	5.4	740	5.7	810	5.60	920	4.17	1,894	5.55	4,350
2	5.7	885	5.3	720	5.7	825	5.60	930	4.50	2,350	6.35	6,440
3	5.6	870	5.3	720	5.7	840	5.70	936	4.90	3,000	7.20	9,150
4	5.7	885	5.3	720	5.8	820	5.70	944	5.30	3,800	8.15	12,680
5	5.7	885	5.3	714	5.7	840	5.80	950	5.12	3,410	7.95	11,920
6	5.8	900	5.3	707	5.5	830	5.80	925	5.07	3,310	7.70	10,970
7	5.9	920	5.1	700	5.6	818	5.90	900	4.65	2,570	9.55	18,000
8	5.8	920	5.1	680	5.6	806	5.70	900	4.67	2,602	8.15	12,680
9	5.6	880	5.1	660	5.7	800	5.80	910	5.20	3,580	7.40	9,870
10	5.4	840	5.0	655	5.7	816	5.80	920	5.40	4,020	7.15	8,980
11	5.6	860	5.0	650	5.6	830	5.90	950	5.70	4,690	7.05	8,640
12	5.4	840	5.0	650	5.6	820	5.80	920	5.55	4,350	7.30	9,510
13	5.7	870	5.2	708	5.7	840	5.80	920	5.77	4,862	7.40	9,870
14	6.0	900	5.2	760	5.8	860	5.80	920	5.50	4,240	7.75	11,160
15	6.2	910	5.3	790	5.8	840	5.80	930	5.65	4,570	8.15	12,680
16	6.3	910	5.3	790	5.7	857	5.80	930	6.00	5,460	8.80	15,150
17	6.2	900	5.4	740	5.7	870	5.80	930	5.90	5,200	9.05	16,100
18	6.1	880	5.4	700	5.7	870	5.90	940	5.75	4,810	9.05	16,100
19	6.1	860	5.2	730	5.7	896	5.90	950	5.75	4,810	8.80	15,150
20	6.0	860	5.3	650	5.7	920	5.90	960a	5.60	4,460	8.30	13,250
21	6.0	860	5.3	650	5.7	930	5.80	1,060b	5.50	4,240	7.55	10,410
22	6.0	837	5.3	730	5.7	940	5.80	1,170	5.45	4,130	7.30	9,510
23	5.9	815	5.4	785	5.7	940	7.80	1,280	5.55	4,350	7.00	8,470
24	5.6	800	5.5	830	5.6	920	5.50	1,390	6.00	5,460	6.70	7,490
25	5.6	800	5.5	820	5.5	900	5.20	1,500b	6.30	6,300	6.57	7,074
26	5.5	800	5.6	810	5.5	900	4.00	1,690	6.05	5,600	7.15	8,980
27	5.5	780	5.6	810	5.3	870	4.00	1,690	5.75	4,810	7.30	9,510
28	5.3	755	5.7	790	5.2	850	3.95	1,630	5.40	4,020	7.25	9,330
29	5.3	720			5.4	870	4.00	1,690	5.25	3,690	7.45	10,050
30	5.4	720			5.5	890	4.05	1,750	5.05	3,270	7.65	10,780
31	5.4	740			5.6	920			5.10	3,370		

a Ice conditions Jan. 1 to April 20.
b Ice breaking up April 21 to April 25; discharges during this period interpolated.

5 GEORGE V, A. 1915

DAILY GAUGE HEIGHT AND DISCHARGE of North Saskatchewan River near Rocky Mountain House, for 1914.

Day.	July.		August.		September.		October.		November.		December.	
	Gauge Height.	Dis-charge	Gauge Height.	Dis-charge	Gauge Height.	Dis-charge	Gauge Height.	Dis-charge	Gauge Height.	Dis-charge	Gauge Height.	Dis-charge.
	Feet.	*Sec.-ft.*	*Feet.*	*Sec.-ft.*	*Feet.*	*Sec.-ft.*	*Feet.*	*Sec.-ft.*	*Feet.*	*Sec.-ft.*	*Feet.*	*Sec.-ft.*
1........	8.60	14,390	7 70	10,970	6 45	6,720	5.30	3,800	4.48	2,322	6.40	955
2........	8.75	14,960	7 85	11,540	6 25	6,160	5.37	3,954	4.45	2,280	5.90	905
3........	8.95	15,720	7.95	11,920	6 50	6,860	5.35	3,910	4.46	2,294	5.75	850
4........	9.00	15,910	8 12	12,566	6.47	6,776	5 30	3,800	4.42	2,238	5.80	825
5........	9.20	16,670	7 95	11,920	6.55	7,010	5.17	3,514	4.42	2,238	5.60	818
6........	9.22	16,746	7.40	9,870	6 55	7,010	5.10	3,370	4.40	2,210	5.65	818
7........	9.00	15,910	7.75	11,160	6 12	5,796	5.10	3,370	4.38	2,182	5.45	818
8........	8.85	15,340	7.70	10,970	6 20	6,020	5.07	3,310	4.32	2,098	5.30	815
9........	8 65	14,580	7.10	8,810	6.55	7,010	5.12	3,410	4.38	2,182	5.15	803
10........	8.40	13,630	6.75	7,650	5.95	5,330	5.40	4,020	4.48	2,322	5.40	802
11........	8.50	14,010	6.55	7,010	5.77	4,862	5.55	4,350	4.38	2,182	5.40	810
12........	8.60	14,390	6.75	7,650	5.95	5,330	5.45	4,130	4.32	2,098	5.45	814
13........	9.00	15,910	6.72	7,554	5.75	4,810	5.20	3,580	4.25	2,000	5.50	816
14........	9.15	16,480	6.85	7,970	5.45	4,130	5.10	3,370	9.00	1,700b	5.70	825
15........	9.07	16,176	6.85	7,970	5.35	3,910	5.07	3,310	9.30	1,480a	5.90	832
16........	8.80	15,150	7.15	8,980	5.55	4,350	5.02	3,216	9.40	1,474	5.90	826
17........	8.00	12,110	7.15	8,980	5.15	3,470	5.00	3,180	9.40	1,485	5.60	826
18........	7.65	10,780	7.02	8,538	5.12	3,410	5.07	3,310	9.50	1,514	5.80	830
19........	7.87	11,616	6.85	7,970	5.25	3,690	5.02	3,216	9.45	1,526	6.20	837
20........	8.25	13,060	7.00	8,470	5.20	3,580	4.92	3,036	9.30	1,529	6.30	843
21........	8.40	13,630	7.15	8,980	5.15	3,470	4.90	3,000	9.30	1,502	6.70	860
22........	7.50	10,230	7.10	8,810	5.20	3,580	4.75	2,730	9.10	1,475	6.70	878
23........	7.07	8,708	7.17	9,048	5.05	3,270	4.72	2,682	8.90	1,433	6.65	890
24........	7.10	8,810	7.00	8,470	4.95	3,090	4 67	2,602	8.40	1,398	6.60	893
25........	7.17	9,048	6.60	7,170	5.05	3,270	4.55	2,420	8.35	1,328	6.50	892
26........	7.25	9,330	6.55	7,010	5.22	3,624	4.55	2,420	7.90	1,300	6.35	885
27........	7.10	8,810	6.62	7,234	5.40	4,020	4.58	2,462	7.60	1,250	6.35	875
28........	7.05	8,640	6.75	7,650	5.65	4,570	4.52	2,378	7.45	1,254	6.45	870
29........	7.52	10,302	6.92	8,198	5.55	4,350	4.50	2,350	7.60	1,270	6.50	876
30........	7.30	9,510	6.80	7,810	5.25	3,690	4.48	2,322	7.30	1,040	6.40	882
31........	7.37	9,762	6.72	7,554	....	....	4.45	2,280	....	....	6.35	880a

a Ice conditions Nov. 15 to Dec. 31.
b Ice forming Nov. 14; discharge for this date interpolated.

MONTHLY DISCHARGE of North Saskatchewan River near Rocky Mountain House, for 1914.

(Drainage area 4,030 square miles.)

MONTH.	DISCHARGE IN SECOND-FEET.				RUN-OFF.	
	Maximum.	Minimum.	Mean.	Per square Mile.	Depth in inches on Drainage Area.	Total in Acre-feet.
January........................	920	720	848	0.210	0.24	52,141
February.......................	830	650	729	0.181	0.19	40,487
March.........................	940	800	862	0.214	0.25	53,002
April..........................	1,750	900	1,114	0.276	0.31	66,286
May...........................	6,300	1,894	4,104	1.020	1.18	252,343
June...........................	18,000	4,350	10,808	2.680	2.99	643,080
July...........................	16,746	8,640	12,914	3.200	3.69	794,059
August.........................	12,566	7,010	8,916	2.210	2.55	548,222
September......................	7,010	3,090	4,772	1.180	1.32	283,950
October........................	4,350	2,280	3,187	0.791	0.91	195,964
November......................	2,322	1,040	1,753	0.435	0.48	104,310
December......................	955	802	850	0.211	0.24	52,264
The year.......................	....	....	....	....	14.35	3,086,108

SESSIONAL PAPER No. 25c

DAILY GAUGE HEIGHT AND DISCHARGE of North Saskatchewan River near Rocky Mountain House, for 1913.

DAY.	June.		July.		August.	
	Gauge Height.	Dis-charge.	Gauge Height.	Dis-charge.	Gauge Height.	Dis-charge.
	Feet.	*Sec.-ft.*	*Feet.*	*Sec.-ft.*	*Feet.*	*Sec.-ft.*
1			8.65	14,580	7.65	10,780
2	7.60	10,590	8.70	14,770	8.30	13,250
3	7.50	10,230	8.20	12,870	8.60	14,390
4	7.55	10,410	8.75	14,960	8.90	15,530
5	7.55	10,410	8.25	13,060	9.00	15,910
6	7.50	10,230	7.05	8,640	8.85	15,340
7	7.20	9,150	7.50	10,230	8.90	15,530
8	7.55	10,410	9.15	16,480	8.55	14,200
9	8.55	14,210	8.00	12,110	9.85	19,140
10	9.00	15,910	7.75	11,160	10.35	21,040
11	9.35	17,240	7.90	11,730	9.80	18,950
12	9.05	16,100	7.80	11,350	9.85	19,140
13	8.80	15,150	7.50	10,230	10.80	22,750
14	8.65	14,580	8.05	12,300	10.30	20,850
15	8.20	12,870	7.50	10,230	9.60	18,190
16	7.25	9,330	7.05	8,640	8.65	14,580
17	7.20	9,150	6.95	8,300	8.10	12,490
18	7.35	9,690	7.05	8,640	7.70	10,970
19	7.45	10,050	7.40	9,870	7.40	9,870
20	7.75	11,160	8.25	13,060	7.00	8,470
21	9.25	16,860	8.85	15,340	6.65	7,330
22	8.30	13,250	9.90	19,330	7.05	8,640
23	7.75	11,160	10.35	21,040	6.70	7,490
24	7.55	10,410	9.90	19,330	7.30	9,510
25	7.65	10,780	9.80	18,950	7.65	10,780
26	8.55	14,200	9.75	18,760	7.65	10,780
27	8.25	13,060	9.20	16,670	7.80	11,350
28	8.40	13,630	8.85	15,340	7.65	10,780
29	8.45	13,820	8.80	15,150	7.30	9,510
30	8.50	14,010	8.30	13,250	7.65	10,780
31			7.65	10,780	7.90	11,730

5 GEORGE V, A. 1915

DAILY GAUGE HEIGHT AND DISCHARGE of North Saskatchewan River near Rocky Mountain House, for 1913.

DAY.	September.		October.		November.		December.	
	Gauge Height.	Dis- charge.	Gauge Height.	Dis- charge.	Gauge Height.	Dis- charge.	Gauge Height.	Dis- charge.
	Feet.	*Sec.-ft.*	*Feet.*	*Sec.-ft.*	*Feet.*	*Sec.-ft.*	*Feet.*	*Sec.-ft.*
1	7.90	11,730	5.60	4,460	4.40	2,210	3.90	1,580
2	7.05	8,640	5.50	4,240	4.50	2,350	4.00	1,690
3	7.45	10,050	5.75	4,810	4.30	2,070	4.10	1,810
4	7.45	10,050	5.65	4,570	4.50	2,350	4.00	1,690
5	7.90	11,730	5.50	4,240	4.20	1,930	3.90	1,580
6	7.45	10,050	5.40	4,020	4.10	1,810	3.70	1,390
7	6.75	7,650	5.25	3,690	4.30	2,070	3.80	1,480
8	7.45	10,050	5.20	3,580	4.20	1,930	4.00	1,690
9	7.30	9,510	5.10	3,370	4.20	1,930	4.00	1,690
10	6.70	7,490	5.10	3,370	4.30	2,070	4.20	1,930
11	6.85	7,970	5.00	3,180	4.30	2,070	4.70	2,650
12	6.65	7,330	5.00	3,180	4.20	1,930	4.40	2,210
13	6.55	7,010	5.00	3,180	4.10	1,810	4.30	2,070
14	6.75	7,650	4.80	2,820	3.90	1,580	4.70	2,650
15	6.65	7,330	4.90	3,000	4.10	1,810	4.80	2,820
16	6.50	6,860	5.00	3,180	4.20	1,930	5.20	3,580
17	6.35	6,440	4.90	3,000	4.30	2,070	5.10	2,870a
18	6.45	6,720	4.85	2,910	4.30	2,070	5.20	2,480
19	6.65	7,330	4.75	2,730	4.10	1,810	4.70	1,850
20	6.45	6,720	4.70	2,650	4.00	1,690	4.60	1,190a
21	6.30	6,300	4.60	2,490	4.00	1,690	5.80	865b
22	6.20	6,020	4.50	2,350	3.70	1,390	5.60	840
23	6.25	6,160	4.55	2,420	3.90	1,580	5.40	850
24	6.15	5,880	4.60	2,490	4.00	1,690	5.50	830
25	6.05	5,600	4.50	2,350	4.30	2,070	5.30	830
26	5.90	5,200	4.50	2,350	4.40	2,210	5.60	872
27	5.80	4,940	4.50	2,350	4.30	2,070	5.70	920
28	5.70	4,690	4.50	2,350	4.00	1,690	5.90	920
29	5.60	4,460	4.50	2,350	3.80	1,480	5.80	910
30	5.80	4,940	4.40	2,210	3.70	1,390	5.80	910
31			4.40	2,210			5.60	870b

a Ice forming Dec. 17 to Dec. 20; discharges interpolated during this period.
b Ice conditions Dec. 21 to Dec. 31.

MONTHLY DISCHARGE of North Saskatchewan River near Rocky Mountain House, for 1913.

(Drainage area 4,030 square miles.)

MONTH.	DISCHARGES IN SECOND-FEET.				RUN-OFF.	
	Maximum	Minimum	Mean.	Per square Mile.	Depth in inches on Drainage Area.	Total in Acre-feet.
June (2-30)	17,240	9,150	12,347	3.060	3.30	710,226
July	21,040	8,300	13,456	3.340	3.85	827,400
August	22,750	7,330	13,550	3.360	3.87	833,150
September	11,730	4,460	7,417	1.840	2.05	441,343
October	4,810	2,210	3,100	0.769	0.89	190,612
November	2,350	1,390	1,892	0.469	0.52	112,580
December	3,580	830	1,630	0.404	0.47	100,220
The period					14.95	3,215,531

STURGEON RIVER AT MCDONALD'S RANCH.

Location.—On the SW. ¼ Sec. 14, Tp. 54, Rge. 5, W. 5th Mer., at ford near McDonald's ranch, 300 feet below mouth of creek passing under Canadian Northern Railway trestle at mile 54.

Records available.—April 21, 1914, to November 1, 1914.

Gauge.—Vertical staff, on left bank of river about 50 feet downstream from ford.

Bench-mark.—Six-inch spike driven in a 12-inch poplar tree, on left bank of stream, 10 feet downstream from gauge. Elevation 9.68 feet above zero of gauge.

Channel.—One channel at all stages, shifting.

Discharge measurements.—Made by wading.

Winter flow.—Gauge height observations discontinued on November 1st. One discharge measurement made under winter conditions.

Observer.—H. H. Jones.

Remarks.—Relation between gauge height and discharge changed during summer because of a growth of weeds in the river.

DISCHARGE MEASUREMENTS of Sturgeon River at McDonald's Ranch, in 1914.

Date.	Engineer.	Width.	Area of Section.	Mean Velocity.	Gauge Height.	Discharge.
		Feet.	*Sq. ft.*	*Ft. per sec.*	*Feet.*	*Sec.-ft.*
April 21............	P. H. Daniells.............	29	17.4	0.78	2.54	13.6
May 22............	do	29	16.0	0.62	2.50	10.0
June 9............	do	55	134.0	1.51	5.28	204.0
June 24............	do	49	101.0	1.27	5.18	128.0
July 8............	do	46	111.0	1.01	5.10	112.0
July 25............	do	44	95.0	0.80	5.20	76.0
Aug. 8............	do	42	83.0	0.54	4.90	45.0
Aug. 21............	do	45	76.0	0.53	4.75	40.0
Sept. 1............	do	46	74.0	0.62	4.28	46.0
Oct. 6............	do	40	54.0	0.91	3.60	49.0
Oct. 17............	do	37	52.0	0.75	3.45	39.0
Dec. 21............	do	30	22.0	0.66	3.08	14.1

STREAM MEASUREMENTS, 1914

5 GEORGE V. A. 1915

DAILY GAUGE HEIGHT AND DISCHARGE of Sturgeon River at McDonald's Ranch, for 1914.

DAY.	April.		May.		June.		July.	
	Gauge Height.	Dis-charge.	Gauge Height.	Dis-charge.	Gauge Height.	Dis-charge.	Gauge Height.	Dis-charge.
	Feet.	*Sec.-ft.*	*Feet.*	*Sec.-ft.*	*Feet.*	*Sec.-ft.*	*Feet.*	*Sec.-ft.*
1........	....	....	2.50	11.0	2.50	11.0	5.31	139
2........	....	....	2.50	11.0	2.50	11.0	5.30	138
3........	....	....	2.50	11.0	2.56	12.2	5.30	137
4........	....	....	2.50	11.0	2.75	16.8	5.30	136
5........	....	....	2.50	11.0	3.48	42.0	5.30	135
6........	....	....	2.50	11.0	3.76	55.0	5.30	135
7........	....	....	2.50	11.0	4.14	79.0	5.32	136
8........	....	....	2.50	11.0	5.95	297.0	5.31	134
9........	....	....	2.50	11.0	5.28	203.0	5.26	126
10.......	....	....	2.50	11.0	5.18	186.0	5.24	121
11.......	....	....	2.50	11.0	5.18	184.0	5.20	114
12.......	....	....	2.50	11.0	5.08	166.0	5.20	111
13.......	....	....	2.40	9.0	4.98	148.0	5.22	108
14.......	....	....	2.40	9.0	4.93	140.0	5.25	110
15.......	....	....	2.40	9.0	4.92	134.0	5.23	106
16.......	....	....	2.40	9.0	4.90	130.0	5.22	102
17.......	....	....	2.40	9.0	4.87	122.0	5.20	98
18.......	....	....	2.40	9.0	4.87	118.0	5.20	94
19.......	....	....	2.50	11.0	4.87	115.0	5.20	92
20.......	....	....	2.50	11.0	4.87	111.0	5.21	90
21.......	2.60	13.0a	2.50	11.0	4.89	110.0	5.21	88
22.......	2.50	11.0	2.50	11.0	4.92	109.0	5.20	84
23.......	2.50	11.0	2.51	11.2	4.91	105.0	5.20	81
24.......	2.50	11.0	2.52	11.4	4.93	103.0	5.20	79
25.......	2.60	13.0	2.52	11.4	5.30	141.0	5.20	76
26.......	2.50	11.0	2.51	11.2	5.33	144.0	5.20	75
27.......	2.50	11.0	2.51	11.2	5.33	144.0	5.20	74
28.......	2.50	11.0	2.52	11.4	5.32	142.0	5.20	73
29.......	2.50	11.0	2.51	11.2	5.32	141.0	5.20	72
30.......	2.50	11.0	2.51	11.2	5.31	139.0	5.19	71
31.......	....	....	2.50	11.0	....	....	5.20	70

a Station established.

SESSIONAL PAPER No. 25c

DAILY GAUGE HEIGHT AND DISCHARGE of Sturgeon River at McDonald's Ranch, for 1914.

DAY.	August.		September.		October.	
	Gauge Height.	Dis- charge.	Gauge Height.	Dis- charge.	Gauge Height.	Dis- charge.
	Feet.	*Sec.-ft.*	*Feet.*	*Sec.-ft.*	*Feet.*	*Sec.-ft.*
1	5.15	67	4.28	46	3.80	52
2	5.15	65	4.25	46	3.80	53
3	5.14	63	4.24	46	3.78	53
4	5.12	61	4.21	46	3.76	54
5	5.20	65	4.19	46	3.74	54
6	5.20	63	4.10	42	3.70	52
7	5.15	59	4.10	43	3.68	51
8	5.15	58	4.20	49	3.64	49
9	5.18	60	4.30	55	3.61	48
10	5.10	56	4.20	51	3.61	48
11	5.04	52	4.20	52	3.60	47
12	5.02	52	4.20	53	3.60	47
13	5.00	51	4.18	53	3.57	46
14	4.96	49	4.14	52	3.54	45
15	4.94	48	4.10	51	3.50	43
16	4.94	48	4.10	52	3.48	42
17	4.90	47	4.10	53	3.46	41
18	4.85	45	4.10	54	3.44	41
19	4.80	42	4.20	60	3.42	40
20	4.74	40	4.10	56	3.40	39
21	4.70	38	4.10	57	3.30	35
22	4.67	39	4.08	57	3.30	35
23	4.67	42	4.08	58	3.30	35
24	4.68	45	4.05	57	3.30	35
25	4.64	45	4.00	56	3.30	35
26	4.60	45	3.92	53	3.30	35
27	4.55	46	3.92	53	3.30	35
28	4.51	47	3.90	54	3.30	35
29	4.45	47	3.86	52	3.30	35
30	4.40	47	3.80	51	3.30	35
31	4.34	46	....	....	3.20	31

MONTHLY DISCHARGE of Sturgeon River at McDonald's Ranch, for 1914.

(Drainage area 100 square miles.)

MONTH.	DISCHARGE IN SECOND-FEET.				RUN-OFF.	
	Maximum.	Minimum.	Mean.	Per square Mile.	Depth in inches on Drainage Area.	Total in Acre-feet.
April (21–30)	13.0	11.0	11.4	0.114	0.04	226
May	11.4	9.0	10.7	0.107	0.12	658
June	297.0	11.0	119.0	1.190	1.33	7,081
July	139.0	70.0	103.0	1.030	1.19	6,333
August	67.0	38.0	51.0	0.510	0.59	3,136
September	60.0	42.0	52.0	0.520	0.58	3,094
October	54.0	31.0	43.0	0.430	0.50	2,644
The period	....	....	....	....	4.35	23,172

5 GEORGE V, A. 1915

STURGEON RIVER NEAR ONOWAY.

Location.—On the SE. ¼ of Sec. 7, Tp. 55, Rge. 2, W. of 5th Mer., at a highway bridge about 3 miles northwest of Onoway, near Trek's ranch.

Records available.—April 23, 1914, to November 1, 1914.

Gauge.—Vertical staff, spiked to pile near centre of downstream side of bridge.

Bench-mark.—Six-inch spike driven in pile on downstream side of east abutment. *E*levation 4.84 feet above zero of gauge.

Channel.—One channel at all stages, permanent.

Discharge measurements.—Made from bridge.

Winter flow.—Gauge height observations discontinued on November 1st. One discharge measurement made under ice conditions.

Observer.—J. Calnan.

Remarks.—Relation of gauge height to discharge changed during summer because of a growth of weeds in the river.

DISCHARGE MEASUREMENTS of Sturgeon River near Onoway, in 1914.

Date.	Engineer.	Width.	Area of Section.	Mean Velocity.	Gauge Height.	Discharge.
		Feet.	*Sq. ft.*	*Ft. per sec.*	*Feet.*	*Sec.-ft.*
April 23........ ..	P. H. Daniells............	34	54	1.10	2.06	60
May 21............	do	33	64 .	0.85	2.02	46
June 6............	do	36	69	1.35	2.43	93
June 23............	do	37	86	1.70	2.79	147
July 7............	do	37	79	1.26	2.70	100
July 24............	do	35	64	0.90	2.42	58
Aug. 7............	do	36	69	0.69	2.64	48
Aug. 20	do	36	72	0.56	2.53	41
Sept. 4............	do	36	66	0.63	2.46	42
Sept. 22............	do	36	68	0.85	2.48	57
Oct. 3............	do	36	69	0.95	2.48	66
Oct. 20............	do	36	64	1.04	2.39	67
Dec. 19	do	20	23	2.10	2.92	49

SESSIONAL PAPER No. 25c

DAILY GAUGE HEIGHT AND DISCHARGE of Sturgeon River near Onoway, for 1914.

Date.	April.		May.		June.		July.	
	Gauge Height.	Dis-charge.	Gauge Height.	Dis-charge.	Gauge Height.	Dis-charge.	Gauge Height.	Dis-charge.
	Feet.	*Sec.-ft.*	*Feet.*	*Sec.-ft.*	*Feet.*	*Sec.-ft.*	*Feet.*	*Sec.-ft.*
1			2.00	50	2.00	50	2.70	113
2			2.00	50	2.00	50	2.70	111
3			2.00	50	2.00	50	2.70	108
4			2.00	50	2.00	50	2.60	93
5			2.00	50	2.30	74	2.60	91
6			2.00	50	2.40	84	2.60	89
7			2.00	50	3.00	202	2.70	100
8			2.01	51	3.00	202	2.70	100
9			2.01	51	3.83	481	2.70	99
10			2.01	51	3.2ɔ	267	2.70	99
11			2.01	51	3.00	202	2.70	99
12			2.01	51	2.70	128	2.60	86
13			2.01	51	2.70	128	2.60	85
14			2.01	51	2.70	128	2.60	84
15			2.01	51	2.60	111	2.60	83
16			2.01	51	2.60	111	2.60	82
17			2.01	51	2.60	111	2.50	72
18			2.01	51	2.60	111	2.45	67
19			2.01	51	2.70	128	2.40	62
20			2.01	51	2.70	128	2.45	65
21			2.00	50	2.70	128	2.45	64
22			2.00	50	2.70	128	2.45	63
23	2.00	50a	2.00	50	2.80	149	2.40	58
24	2.00	50	2.00	50	2.70	126	2.40	57
25	2.00	50	2.00	50	2.70	124	2.40	55
26	2.00	50	2.00	50	2.70	122	2.40	53
27	2.00	50	2.00	50	2.70	121	2.40	51
28	2.00	50	2.00	50	2.70	117	2.40	50
29	2.00	50	2.00	50	2.70	117	2.40	48
30	2.00	50	2.00	50	2.70	115	2.40	46
31			2.00	50			2.50	51

a Station established.

·5 GEORGE V, A. 1915

DAILY GAUGE HEIGHT AND DISCHARGE of Sturgeon River near Onoway, for 1914.

DAY.	August.		September.		October.	
	Gauge Height.	Dis-charge.	Gauge Height.	Dis-charge.	Gauge Height.	Dis-charge.
	Feet.	*Sec.-ft.*	*Feet.*	*Sec.-ft.*	*Feet.*	*Sec.-ft.*
1	2.50	49	2.50	44	2.50	66
2	2.50	47	2.50	44	2.50	67
3	2.60	52	2.50	45	2.50	68
4	2.60	51	2.50	45	2.50	69
5	2.60	49	2.50	46	2.50	70
6	2.60	47	2.50	47	2.50	71
7	2.60	46	2.50	48	2.50	72
8	2.60	46	2.50	49	2.50	73
9	2.60	46	2.60	56	2.50	74
10	2.60	46	2.60	57	2.50	76
11	2.60	46	2.60	58	2.50	77
12	2.60	46	2.60	59	2.50	78
13	2.60	46	2.60	59	2.50	80
14	2.60	46	2.50	53	2.50	81
15	2.60	46	2.50	54	2.50	82
16	2.60	46	2.50	55	2.50	83
17	2.60	46	2.50	56	2.50	85
18	2.60	46	2.50	56	2.50	86
19	2.60	46	2.50	57	2.50	87
20	2.60	46	2.50	57	2.40	78
21	2.60	47	2.50	58	2.40	84
22	2.60	47	2.50	58	2.40	84
23	2.60	48	2.50	59	2.40	84
24	2.50	41	2.50	60	2.40	84
25	2.50	41	2.50	61	2.40	84
26	2.50	42	2.50	62	2.40	84
27	2.50	42	2.50	63	2.30	74
28	2.50	42	2.50	64	2.30	74
29	2.50	43	2.50	65	2.30	74
30	2.50	43	2.50	65	2.30	74
31	2.50	43	....	....	2.30	74

MONTHLY DISCHARGE of Sturgeon River near Onoway, for 1914.

(Drainage area 241 square miles.)

MONTH.	DISCHARGE IN SECOND-*FEET.*				RUN-OFF.	
	Maximum.	Minimum	Mean.	Per square Mile.	Depth in inches on Drainage Area.	Total in Acre-feet.
April (23–30)	50	50	50	0.207	0.06	793
May	51	50	50	0.207	0.24	3,074
June	481	50	135	0.560	0.62	8,033
July	113	46	77	0.320	0.37	4,734
August	52	41	46	0.191	0.22	2,828
September	65	44	55	0.228	0.25	3,273
October	87	66	77	0.320	0.37	4,734
The period	....	....	....	....	2.13	27,469

STURGEON RIVER NEAR VILLENEUVE.

Location.—On the NW. ¼ Sec. 32, Tp. 54, Rge. 26, W. 4th Mer., at the highway bridge near Majeau's ranch, about 2½ miles north of Villeneuve and about 3 miles west of Ray.

Records available.—April 22, 1914, to October 31, 1914.

Gauge.—Vertical staff, spiked to upstream end of the pier near the right bank; elevation 88.97 feet.

Bench-mark.—Spike driven in 12-inch pile in the east abutment of bridge; assumed elevation 100.00 feet.

Channel.—Straight for about 25 feet on either side of section. Gravel bed covered with clay and sand, fairly permanent. Two channels at high stages, one channel at low stages.

Discharge measurements.—Made from bridge.

Winter flow.—Gauge height observations discontinued on November 1st. One discharge measurement made under winter conditions.

Observer.—V. Majeau.

DISCHARGE MEASUREMENTS of Sturgeon River near Villeneuve, in 1914.

Date.	Engineer.	Width.	Area of Section.	Mean Velocity.	Gauge Height.	Discharge.
		Feet.	*Sq. ft.*	*Ft. per sec.*	*Feet.*	*Sec.-ft.*
April 22	P. H. Daniels	48	194	0.51	3.55	101
May 20	do	55	169	0.46	2.91	78
June 5	do	47	246	1.07	4.50	263
June 22	do	61	377	1.60	6.94	632
July 6	do	56	284	1.39	5.65	396
July 23	do	45	209	0.89	4.00	184
Aug. 6	do	44	170	0.61	3.03	87
Aug. 19	do	43	162	0.46	2.98	74
Sept. 3	do	43	152	0.40	2.68	61
Sept. 21	do	44	174	0.58	3.20	102
Oct. 2	do	44	178	0.63	3.24	113
Oct. 19	do	44	185	0.61	3.30	113
Dec. 18	do	63	85	0.68	3.59	58

STREAM MEASUREMENTS, 1914

5 GEORGE V, A. 1915

DAILY GAUGE HEIGHT AND DISCHARGE of Sturgeon River near Villeneuve, for 1914.

DAY.	April.		May.		June.		July.	
	Gauge Height.	Dis-charge.	Gauge Height.	Dis-charge.	Gauge Height.	Dis-charge.	Gauge Height.	Dis-charge.
	Feet.	*Sec.-ft.*	*Feet.*	*Sec.-ft.*	*Feet.*	*Sec.-ft.*	*Feet.*	*Sec.-ft.*
1	......	......	3.00	85	2.60	52	6.90	625
2	......	......	3.00	85	2.60	52	6.30	517
3	......	......	2.90	86	2.50	44	5.90	449
4	......	......	2.90	76	2.60	52	5.60	400
5	......	......	3.00	85	4.30	224	5.50	384
6	......	......	3.00	85	5.45	376	5.60	400
7	......	......	3.00	85	6.50	553	5.70	416
8	......	......	3.00	85	8.25	867	5.80	432
9	......	......	3.00	85	10.30	1,237a	5.90	449
10	......	......	2.90	76	11.10	1,381a	5.90	449
11	......	......	2.90	76	11.20	1,399a	5.70	416
12	......	......	2.80	68	11.40	1,435a	5.60	400
13	......	......	2.70	60	11.20	1,399a	5.50	384
14	......	......	2.70	60	11.00	1,363a	5.50	384
15	......	......	2.70	60	10.30	1,237	5.70	416
16	......	......	2.70	60	9.70	1,129	6.10	483
17	......	......	2.70	60	9.00	1,003	6.00	466
18	......	......	2.70	60	8.40	895	5.60	400
19	......	......	2.70	60	7.90	805	4.70	273
20	......	......	2.80	68	7.10	661	4.40	236
21	......	......	3.00	85	7.10	661	4.20	212
22	3.40	124	3.10	94	6.90	625	4.10	200
23	3.10	94	3.20	104	7.30	697	4.00	188
24	3.10	94	3.20	104	7.70	769	3.90	177
25	3.10	94	3.10	94	8.00	823	3.80	166
26	3.10	94	3.00	85	8.30	877	3.70	155
27	3.10	94	2.90	76	8.40	895	3.60	144
28	3.00	85	2.80	68	8.40	895	3.50	134
29	3.00	85	2.80	68	8.00	823	3.40	124
30	3.00	85	2.70	60	7.50	733	3.40	124
31	......	......	2.70	60	......	......	3.40	124

a Gauge height interpolated.

SESSIONAL PAPER No. 25c

DAILY GAUGE HEIGHT AND DISCHARGE of Sturgeon River near Villeneuve, for 1914.

DAY.	August.		September.		October.	
	Gauge Height.	Dis- charge.	Gauge Height.	Dis- charge.	Gau e Height.	Dis- charge.
	Feet.	Sec.-ft.	Feet.	Sec.-ft.	Feet.	Sec.-ft.
1	3.35	119	2.70	60	3.30	114
2	3.30	114	2.70	60	3.20	104
3	3.30	114	2.70	60	3.30	114
4	3.20	104	2.70	60	3.30	114
5	3.10	94	2.70	60	3.30	114
6	3.10	94	2.60	52	3.40	124
7	3.10	94	2.60	52	3.50	134
8	3.00	85	.2.70	60	3.50	134
9	3.00	85	2.90	76	3.50	134
10	3.10	94	3.00	85	3.50	134
11	3.10	94	3.00	85	3.50	134
12	3.10	94	3.10	94	3.40	124
13	3.00	85	3.10	94	3.40	124
14	3.00	85	3.00	85	3.30	114
15	3.00	85	3.00	85	3.30	114
16	3.00	85	3.00	85	3.30	114
17	3.00	85	3.00	85	3.30	114
18	3.00	85	3.00	85	3.30	114
19	3.00	85	3.00	85	3.30	114
20	3.00	85	3.10	94	3.30	114
21	2.90	76	3.20	104	3.30	114
22	2.90	6	3.20	104	3.20	104
23	2.90	76	3.20	104	3.20	104
24	2.90	76	3.30	114	3.20	104
25	2.90	76	3.30	114	3.10	94
26	2.90	76	3.30	114	3.10	94
27	2.90	76	3.30	114	3.10	94
28	2.90	76	3.30	114	3.00	85
29	2.80	68	3.30	114	3.00	85
30	2.80	68	3.30	114	3.00	85
31	2.70	60	....	....	3.00	85

MONTHLY DISCHARGE of Sturgeon River near Villeneuve, for 1914.

(Drainage area 506 square miles.)

MONTH.	DISCHARGE IN SECOND-FEET.				RUN-OF	
	Maximum.	Minimum	Mean.	Per square Mile.	Depth in inches on Drainage Area.	Total in Acre-feet.
April (22–30)	124	85	94	0.186	0.06	1,678
May	104	60	76	0.150	0.17	4,673
June	1,435	44	799	1.579	1.76	47,544
July	625	124	327	0.646	0.74	20,106
August	119	60	86	0.170	0.20	5,288
September	114	52	87	0.172	0.19	5,177
October	134	85	111	0.219	0.25	6,825
The period	....	....	....	....	3.37	91,291

5 GEORGE V, A. 1915

STURGEON RIVER AT ST. ALBERT.

Location.—Between river lots 27 and 52, St. Albert Settlement, at the steel traffic bridge in the town of St. Albert.

Records available.—April 23, 1913, to December 31, 1914.

Gauge.—Vertical staff, fastened to timber cribbing on right bank of river, and on upstream side of bridge; elevation of zero maintained at 90.23 since establishment.

Bench-mark.—Marked with white paint on the cement sill of the east basement window of the St. Albert hotel; assumed elevation 100.00 feet.

Channel.—One channel, with considerable growth of vegetation, at all stages.

Discharge measurements.—Made from bridge.

Winter flow.—From November to April river is frozen over, and measurements are made at a point about one-quarter of a mile below the bridge.

Observer.—C. Pelletier.

DISCHARGE MEASUREMENTS of Sturgeon River at St. Albert, in 1914.

Date.	Engineer.	Width.	Area of Section.	Mean Velocity.	Gauge Height.	Discharge.
		Feet.	*Sq. ft.*	*Ft. per sec.*	*Feet.*	*Sec.·ft.*
Jan. 16............	P. H. Daniells............	82a	62.4	0.37	2.05	23
Jan. 30............	do	75a	53.0	0.45	2.12	24
Feb. 14............	do	73a	49.3	0.46	2.03	22
Mar. 16............	do	79a	69.8	0.51	3.01	36
April 9............	do	83a	128.0	0.50	3.37	63
April 25............	do	86	224.0	0.98	2.53	220
April 30............	G. J. Smith and J. M. Paul...	86	199.0	0.99	2.24	196
May 25............	J. M. Paul.................	86	143.0	0.67	1.50	96
June 15............	do	86	752.0	2.11	8.14	1,587
July 4............	do	86	645.0	1.56	6.99	1,005
July 24............	do	86	430.0	1.33	4.51	571
Aug. 19............	do	82	178.0	0.75	1.67	134
Sept. 2............	do	80	153.0	0.61	1.32	94
Sept. 21............	do	82	163.0	0.60	1.46	98
Oct. 6............	do	82	180.0	0.72	1.71	130
Nov. 4............	P. H. Daniells	88	184.0	0.71	1.61	130
Nov. 21............	do	77a	178.0	0.52	1.92	93
Dec. 10............	do	91a	111.0	0.66	1.92	73

a Measured below regular station.

DAILY GAUGE HEIGHT AND DISCHARGE of Sturgeon River at St. Albert, for 1914.

DAY.	January.		February.		March.		April.		May.		June.	
	Gauge Height.	Dis- charge	Gauge Height	Dis- charge.	Gauge Height.	Dis- charge	Gauge Height.	Dis- charge.	Gauge Height.	Dis- charge.	Gauge Height	Dis- charge.
	Feet.	*Sec.-ft.*	*Feet.*	*Sec.-ft.*	*Feet.*	*Sec.-ft.*	*Feet.*	*Sec.-ft.*	*Feet.*	*Sec.-ft.*	*Feet.*	*Sec.-ft.*
1..........	2.00	32a	2 12	24	2.87	28	3 51	51	2.25	190	1 20	84
2..........	2.01	32	2.10	22	2 88	31	3.51	54	2.25	190	1.06	74
3..........	2.01	32	2.09	21	2 88	34	3.50	54	2 15	178	1.11	78
4..........	2.00	33	2 09	20	2 89	34	3.49	54	2 25	190	1 22	86
5..........	2.00	33	2 09c	16	2.89	33	3.47	56	2.22	186	1.71	131
6..........	2.01	34	2.13	17	2.90	32	3.45	57	2.12	174	1.78	138
7..........	2.01	38	2.17	18	2.90	34	3.43	59	2.11	173	2.34	201
8..........	2.01	30	2.23	18	2.90	33	3.41	61	2.07	168	3.09	302
9..........	2.01	22	2.27	18	2.92	31	3.40	63	2.00	160	3.94	436
10.........	2.02	23	2.29	20	2.92	30	3.39	67	1.95	155	4.90	614
11.........	2.01	24	2.33	22	2.92	31	3.37	71	1.86	146	6.00	852
12.........	2.01	18	2.20	22	2.92	32	3.42	76	1.84	144	6.92	1,094
13.........	2.03	20	2.07c	22	2.93	33	3.43	80a	1.80	140	7.40	1,228
14.........	2.03	22	2.03	22	2.95	34	3.47	160b	1.70	130	7.90	1,378
15	2.03	24	2.80	24	2.95	35	3.61	290b	1.73	133	8.07	1,432
16	2.03	23	2.82	30	2.96	36	3.55	372	1.68	128	8.24	1,487
17.........	2.04	22	2.82	27	3.55	37	3.22	321	1.62	122	8.24	1,487
18.........	2.07	21	2.82	24	3.55	38	3.10	303	1.56	116	8.25	1,490
19	2.08	20	2.82	20	3.55	36	3.01	290	1.54	114	8.25	1,490
20.........	2.10	19	2.82	20	3.55	38	2.92	277	1.61	121	8.10	1,442
21..... ...	2.11	18	2.82	20	3.55	40	2.87	270	1.43	103	7.96	1,397
22.........	2.11	17	2.82	20	3.55	41	2.75	253	1.47	107	7.94	1,391
23..... ...	2.10	16	2.82	21	3.55	42	2.67	242	1.47	107	7.80	1,346
24.........	2.10	17	2.83	22	3.55	42	2.62	235	1.47	107	7.73	1,325
25.........	2.11	18	2.87	23	3.55	42	2.55	226	1.50	110	7.65	1,301
26.........	2.11	19	2.87	25	3.54	42	2.43	212	1.60	120	7.60	1,286
27.........	2.11	20	2.87	26	3.54	42	2.23	188	1.45	105	7.64	1,298
28.........	2.11	19	2.87	27	3.54	43	2.22	186	1.59	119	7.62	1,292
29.........	2.11	18	......	......	3.54	44	2.16	179	1.56	116	7.54	1,269
30	2.11	24	......	......	3.53	46	2.20	184	1.44	104	7.53	1,266
31.........	2.11	26	......	......	3.52	48	......	......	1.31	93	......	......

a Ice conditions from Jan. 1 to April 13.
b Ice breaking up April 14 and 15; discharges for these days interpolated.
c Gauge heights interpolated Feb. 5 to Feb. 13.

STREAM MEASUREMENTS, 1914

5 GEORGE V, A. 1915

DAILY GAUGE HEIGHT AND DISCHARGE of Sturgeon River at St. Albert, for 1914.

DAY.	July. Gauge Height.	July. Discharge	August. Gauge Height.	August. Discharge	September. Gauge Height	September. Discharge	October. Gauge Height.	October. Discharge	November. Gauge Height.	November. Discharge.	December. Gauge Height.	December. Discharge.
	Feet.	Sec.-ft.	Feet.	Sec.-ft.	Feet.	Sec.-ft.	Feet.	Sec.-ft.	Feet.	Sec.-ft.	Feet.	Sec.-ft.
1	7.45	1,242	3.24	324	1.34	95	1.61	121	1.67	127	2.02	84
2	7.34	1,211	3.04	294	1.29	91	1.61	121	1.65	125	2.07	82
3	7.20	1,172	3.00	288	1.24	87	1.65	125	1.65	125	1.91	80
4	7.05	1,130	2.88	271	1.19	83	1.64	124	1.64	124	1.97	74
5	6.89	1,085	2.74	252	1.26	89	1.70	130	1.60	120	1.99	68
6	6.76	1,049	2.51	221	1.20	84	1.74	134	1.61	121	2.01	69
7	6.60	1,006	2.50	220	1.16	81	1.75	135	1.62	122	2.02	70
8	6.50	980	2.41	209	1.21	85	1.75	135	1.62	122	1.97	72
9	6.35	941	2.34	201	1.40	100	1.75	135	1.65	125	2.02	74
10	6.28	923	2.20	184	1.35	96	1.75	135	1.62	122	1.97	73
11	6.12	882	2.14	177	1.34	95	1.78	138	1.63	123	1.97	65
12	6.04	862	2.05	166	1.35	96	1.77	137	1.66	126	1.98	65
13	5.93	836	2.00	160	1.35	96	1.79	139	2.05	117b	1.97	68
14	5.87	822	1.92	152	1.48	108	1.80	140	2.01	106b	1.95	70
15	5.81	808	1.90	150	1.46	106	1.80	140	2.00	104a	1.94	72
16	5.64	771	1.85	145	1.40	100	1.75	135	1.90	102	1.92	74
17	5.52	744	1.79	139	1.35	96	1.80	140	1.90	100	1.92	76
18	5.39	716	1.74	134	1.35	96	1.80	140	1.90	102	1.96	74
19	5.19	672	1.67	127	1.45	105	1.79	139	1.90	104	1.96	69
20	5.11	656	1.62	122	1.46	106	1.79	139	1.90	106	1.93	64
21	5.04	642	1.56	116	1.46	106	1.79	139	1.88	93	1.95	66
22	4.86	606	1.54	114	1.50	110	1.76	136	1.88	88	1.94	66
23	4.64	564	1.52	112	1.50	110	1.76	136	1.88	88	1.93	64
24	4.51	539	1.51	111	1.51	111	1.74	134	1.88	86	1.97	62
25	4.34	507	1.48	108	1.51	111	1.72	132	1.88	82	1.97	57
26	4.11	466	1.46	106	1.53	113	1.70	130	1.88	78	1.97	53
27	3.93	434	1.45	105	1.57	117	1.70	130	1.89	79	2.02	50
28	3.80	412	1.45	105	1.60	120	1.69	129	1.89	80	2.02	53
29	3.70	396	1.42	102	1.60	120	1.68	128	1.88	82	2.02	56
30	3.50	364	1.39	99	1.61	121	1.68	128	1.89	83	2.02	56
31	3.40	348	1.40	100	......	......	1.69	129	......	......	2.02	58a

a Ice conditions Nov. 15 to Dec. 31.
b Ice forming Nov. 13 and 14; discharges interpolated.

MONTHLY DISCHARGE of Sturgeon River at St. Albert, for 1914.

(Drainage area 1,010 square miles.)

MONTH.	DISCHARGE IN SECOND-FEET. Maximum.	Minimum.	Mean.	Per square Mile.	RUN-OFF. Depth in inches on Drainage Area.	Total in Acre-feet.
January	38	16	24	0.024	0.03	1,476
February	30	16	22	0.022	0.02	1,222
March	48	28	37	0.037	0.04	2,275
April	372	51	166	0.164	0.18	9,878
May	190	93	137	0.136	0.16	8,424
June	1,490	74	956	0.946	1.06	56,886
July	1,242	348	767	0.759	0.88	47,161
August	324	99	165	0.163	0.19	10,145
September	121	81	101	0.100	0.11	6,010
October	140	121	133	0.132	0.15	8,178
November	127	78	105	0.104	0.12	6,248
December	84	50	67	0.066	0.08	4,120
The year	....	....	....	....	3.02	162,023

STURGEON RIVER NEAR FORT SASKATCHEWAN.

Location.—On the NW. ¼ Sec. 28, Tp. 55, Rge. 22, W. 4th Mer., at the steel traffic bridge about five miles north of Fort Saskatchewan and 1½ miles from the mouth of the river.

Records available.—January 1, 1914, to December 31, 1914. Discharge measurements only during 1913.

Gauge.—Vertical staff, fastened to pile near right bank of river; elevation of zero maintained at 87.52 feet since establishment.

Bench-mark.—Marked with white paint on top of the downstream side of the left abutment; assumed elevation 100.00 feet.

Channel.—One permanent channel at all stages.

Discharge measurements.—Made from downstream side of bridge.

Winter flow.—From November to April river is frozen over, and measurements are made at the regular station or a point about one-quarter of a mile above the mouth of the river.

Observer.—A. McDougall.

Remarks.—Owing to the ice being flooded it is sometimes not possible to make winter measurements at the regular station.

DISCHARGE MEASUREMENTS of Sturgeon River near Fort Saskatchewan, in 1914.

Date.	Engineer.	Width.	Area of Section.	Mean Velocity.	Gauge Height.	Discharge.
		Feet.	*Sq. ft.*	*Ft. per sec.*	*Feet.*	*Sec.-ft.*
Jan. 15	P. H. Daniells	41	86.3	0.37	4.00	32
Jan. 31	do	32a	51.3	0.47	4.70	24
Feb. 17	do	37a	56.6	0.52	5.35	30
Mar. 14	do	32a	49.8	0.74	5.14	36
April 8	do	30	30.0	2.14	6.13	64
April 29	do	51	148.0	1.24	3.27	184
May 1	G. J. Smith and J. M. Paul	52	151.0	1.30	3.41	196
May 26	J. M. Paul	53	130.0	0.78	2.97	101
June 16	do	78	386.0	3.74	5.79	1,442
July 3	do	78	361.0	3.87	5.63	1,376
July 25	do	78	245.0	2.56	4.29	627
Aug. 18	do	65	164.0	1.03	3.25	176
Aug. 31	do	64	154.0	0.76	3.06	117
Sept. 19	do	64	148.0	0.78	3.07	115
Oct. 3	do	65	149.0	0.91	3.16	135
Nov. 3	P. H. Daniells	65	152.0	0.95	3.14	143
Nov. 25	do	65	140.0	0.76	3.36	106
Dec. 9		59	100.0	0.73	3.50	73

a Measured below regular station.

5 GEORGE V, A. 1915

DAILY GAUGE HEIGHT AND DISCHARGE of Sturgeon River near Fort Saskatchewan, for 1914.

DAY.	January.		February.		March.		April.		May.		June.	
	Gauge Height.	Dis-charge.	Gauge Height.	Dis-charge.	Gauge Height.	Dis-charge.	Gauge Height.	Dis-charge.	Gauge Height.	Dis-charge.	Gauge Height.	Dis-charge.
	Feet.	*Sec-ft.*	*Feet.*	*Sec.-ft.*	*Feet.*	*Sec.-ft.*	*Feet.*	*Sec.-ft.*	*Feet.*	*Sec.-ft.*	*Feet.*	*Sec.-ft.*
1.........	3.70	37a	4.70	26	5.16	33	5.78	51	3.36	193	2.84	86
2.........	3.70	37	4.60	24	5.27	34	5.79	54	3.35	190	2.84	86
3.........	3.70	38	4.50	22	5.35	36	5.90	54	3.43	218	2.84	86
4.........	3.80	38	4.30	19	5.20	35	6.02	54	3.42	215	2.99	105
5.........	3.60	39	4.30	16	5.11	35	6.03	57	3.30	173	3.24	155
6.........	3.70	40	4.50	18	5.03	34	6.04	59	3.29	170	3.49	242
7.........	3.80	46	4.70	20	5.04	36	6.06	62	3.28	167	3.69	331
8.........	3.80	36	5.00	20	4.96	34	6.07	64	3.26	161	3.99	475
9.........	3.80	26	5.20	20	4.97	32	6.16	68	3.25	158	4.64	808
10	3.80	28	5.30	23	4.98	33	5.95	71	3.23	153	4.84	916
11..... ..	3.80	30	5.50	26	5.00	34	6.14	74	3.22	150	5.04	1,024
12.........	3.90	22	5.10	24	5.01	35	6.03	78	3.21	148	5.04	1,024
13.........	3.90	28	5.20	24	5.02	36	5.92	82	3.09	121	5.19	1,108
14.........	4.00	36	5.00	22	5.14	37	5.71	170	3.08	119	5.39	1,224
15.........	4.00	32	4.80	20	5.15	37	5.50	300	3.06	116	5.59	1,340
16.........	3.80	30	5.60	38	5.06	38	5.29	380	3.05	114	5.78	1,450
17.........	3.90	26	5.30	30	5.08	36	5.18	340a	3.04	112	5.88	1,508
18..... ..	4.10	24	5.11	27	5.19	37	5.47	320b	3.02	109	5.98	1,566
19.........	4.30	23	4.83	24	5.30	38	5.56	300	3.01	108	6.08	1,624
20.........	4.20	21	4.74	23	5.52	39	5.45	290	2.99	105	6.08	1,624
21.........	4.10	20	4.65	22	5.73	40	5.54	280	2.98	103	6.08	1,624
22.....	4.10	18	4.37	22	5.64	41	5.33	270	2.97	102	6.43	1,827
23..... ..	4.20	16	4.47	22	5.66	42	4.92	258	2.95	99	6.28	1,740
24.........	4.30	17	4.69	23	5.77	42	4.81	250b	2.94	98	6.18	1,682
25.........	4.40	18	4.91	29	5.58	42	3.50	246	2.94	98	6.08	1,624
26	4.60	20	5.02	30	5.30	42	3.49	242	2.94	98	6.08	1,624
27..... ..	4.70	22	5.03	31	5.71	42	3.48	238	2.94	98	5.98	1,566
28.........	4.80	20	5.05	32	5.42	43	3.47	234	2.94	98	5.98	1,566
29.........	4.80	18	......	......	5.44	45	3.42	215	2.94	98	5.88	1,508
30.........	4.80	21	......	......	5.55	46	3.47	234	2.94	98	5.88	1,508
31	4.70	24	......	......	5.76	49	......	......	2.84	86	......	......

a Ice conditions Jan. 1 to April 17.
b Ice breaking up April 18 to April 24; discharges interpolated during this period.

SESSIONAL PAPER No. 25c

DAILY GAUGE HEIGHT AND DISCHARGE of Sturgeon River near Fort Saskatchewan, for 1914.

DAY.	July.		August.		September.		October.		November.		December.	
	Gauge Height.	Dis-charge.	Gauge Height.	Dis-charge.	Gauge Height	Dis-charge	Gauge Height.	Dis-charge	Gauge Height.	Dis-charge.	Gauge Height.	Dis-charge.
	Feet.	*Sec.-ft.*	*Feet.*	*Sec.-ft.*	*Feet.*	*Sec.-ft.*	*Feet.*	*Sec.-ft.*	*Feet.*	*Sec.-ft.*	*Feet.*	*Sec.-ft.*
1...........	5.78	1,450	3.90	432	3.10	123	3.10	123	3.16	135	3.50	80
2...........	5.73	1,421	3.90	432	3.00	106	3.20	145	3.16	135	3.50	83
3...........	5.68	1,392	3.80	384	3.00	106	3.20	145	3.16	135	3.50	84
4...........	5.53	1,305	3.75	360	3.00	106	3.19	143	3.19	143	3.50	84
5...........	5.48	1,276	3.70	336	3.00	106	3.19	143	3.19	143	3.40	82
6...........	5.68	1,392	3.65	312	3.00	106	3.19	143	3.19	143	3.40	80
7...........	5.28	1,160	3.60	290	3.00	106	3.19	143	3.19	143	3.50	76
8...........	5.18	1,103	3.50	246	3.00	106	3.19	143	3.19	143	3.50	75
9...........	5.18	1,103	3.50	246	3.00	106	3.19	143	3.32	180	3.50	73
10...........	5.08	1,047	3.50	246	3.00	106	3.19	143	3.29	170	3.50	69
11...........	5.08	1,047	3.50	246	3.10	123	3.19	143	3.38	200	3.50	64
12...........	4.98	991	3.40	207	3.10	123	3.18	140	3.28	167	3.50	64
13...........	4.98	991	3.40	207	3.10	123	3.18	140	3.28	167	3.50	65
14	4.88	937	3.40	207	3.10	123	3.18	140	3.38	120*b*	3.50	67
15...........	4.88	937	3.35	190	3.10	123	3.18	140	3.48	93	3.50	69
16...........	4.78	883	3.30	173	3.10	123	3.18	140	3.57	89	3.50	71
17...........	4.78	883	3.30	173	3.10	123	3.18	140	3.57	86	3.50	72
18...........	4.68	829	3.20	145	3.00	106	3.18	140	3.37	86*b*	3.50	72
19...........	4.68	829	3.20	145	3.10	123	3.18	140	3.37	86*a*	3.50	72
20...........	4.58	776	3.20	145	3.10	123	3.17	138	3.37	90	3.50	71
21...........	4.48	724	3.20	145	3.10	123	3.17	138	3.26	98	3.50	68
22...........	·4.48	724	3.20	145	3.10	123	3.17	138	3.26	102	3.50	69
23...........	4.48	724	3.20	145	3.10	123	3.17	138	3.36	104	3.50	66
24	4.38	672	3.10	123	3.10	123	3.17	138	3.36	106	3.40	56
25...........	4.29	625	3.10	123	3.10	123	3.17	138	3.30	106	3.40	54
26...........	4.20	580	3.10	123	3.10	123	3.17	138	3.30	105	3.40	53
27...........	4.20	580	3.10	123	3.10	123	3.17	138	3.40	103	3.50	52
28...........	4.10	530	3.10	123	3.10	123	3.16	135	3.40	96	3.50	55
29...........	4.05	505	3.10	123	3.10	123	3.16	135	3.40	76	3.50	60
30...........	4.00	480	3.10	123	3.10	123	3.16	135	3.50	76	3.60	61
31...........	4.00	480	3.10	123	......	......	3.16	135	......	......	3.60	60*a*

a Ice conditions Nov. 19 to Dec. 31.
b Ice forming Nov. 14 to Nov. 18; discharges interpolated during this period.

MONTHLY DISCHARGE of Sturgeon River near Fort Saskatchewan, for 1914.

(Drainage area 1,330 square miles.)

MONTH.	DISCHARGE IN SECOND-FEET.				RUN-OFF.	
	Maximum.	Minimum.	Mean.	Per square Mile.	Depth in inches on Drainage Area.	Total in Acre-feet.
January..............................	46	16	27	0.020	0.02	1,660
February.............................	38	16	24	0.018	0.02	1,333
March................................	49	32	38	0.029	0.03	2,336
April................................	380	51	180	0.135	0.15	10,711
May.................................	218	86	132	0.099	0.11	8,116
June.................................	1,827	86	1,102	0.828	0.92	65,573
July.................................	1,450	480	915	0.688	0.79	56,261
August...............................	432	123	211	0.159	0.18	12,974
September............................	123	106	117	0.088	0.10	6,962
October..............................	145	123	139	0.104	0.12	8,547
November............................	200	76	121	0.091	0.10	7,200
December............................	84	52	69	0.052	0.06	4,243
The year.............................	....	....	....	....	2.60	185,916

5 GEORGE V, A. 1915

NORTH SASKATCHEWAN RIVER AT EDMONTON.

Location.—On the NW. ¼ Sec. 33, Tp. 52, Rge. 24, W. 4th Mer., at the low-level traffic and railway bridge in the city of Edmonton.

Records available.—May 1, 1911, to December 31, 1914.

Gauge.—Two vertical staff gauges at this station, a low-level one reading from 0 to 10 feet, and a high-level one reading from 10 to 34 feet. The high-level gauge is spiked to a timber pier a short distance above the mill of the Edmonton Lumber Company, the low-level being attached to a pier about 75 feet above the other and 200 feet from the right bank of the river. Zero elevation of low-level gauge maintained at 1,991.73 feet during 1911. Zero elevation of low-level gauge maintained at 1,991 09 feet during 1912-14. Zero elevation of high-level gauge maintained at 1,995 67 feet during 1911-12. Zero elevation of high-level gauge maintained at 1,991 09 feet during 1913-14.

Bench-mark.—Permanent iron bench-mark under stay line to stack of mill and about 50 fee downstream from high-level gauge; elevation 2,025.04 feet. (Public Works of Canada datum.)

Channel.—One slightly shifting channel at all stages.

Discharge measurements.—Made from downstream side of bridge with rope, weights and stay line.

Floods.—Largest flood within memory took place in August, 1899, followed by another one, not quite so large, in 1900. On both occasions considerable damage was done, but no actual figures are available.

Winter flow.—From November to April the river is frozen over, and measurements are made at a point about one-half mile below the bridge.

Maximum flow.—In August, 1899, gauge height was 35.45 feet, and the estimated discharge 180,000 sec.-feet.

Minimum flow.—The lowest recorded flow of the stream at this point took place December 24-27, 1913, when the discharge was measured and found to be 650 sec.-feet.

Observer.—Edmonton Lumber Company (per W. H. Schneider).

DISCHARGE MEASUREMENTS of North Saskatchewan River at Edmonton, in 1914.

Date.	Engineer.	Width.	Area of Section.	Mean Velocity.	Gauge Height.	Discharge.
		Feet.	*Sq. ft.*	*Ft. per sec.*	*Feet.*	*Sec.-ft.*
Jan. 8	P. H. Daniells	455	1,695	0.80	7.96	1,358
Jan. 28	do	445	1,539	0.62	7.83	969
Feb. 18	do	337a	1,671	0.54	8.46	834
Mar. 20	do	377	1,255	1.01	7.90	1,279
April 6	do	389	1,324	0.83	7.80	1,142
April 27	do	411	2,354	1.87	9.19	4,424
May 4	G. J. Smith and J. M. Paul	492	3,255	2.53	10.90	8,233
May 23	J. M. Paul	536	3,746	2.44	10.95	9,143
June 12	do	582	6,773	4.68	16.30	31,875
July 6	do	578	6,343	3.94	15.55	24,976
July 23	do	562	4,964	3.29	13.18	16,342
Aug. 17	do	553	3,759	2.87	11.48	10,773
Sept. 1	do	550	3,543	2.65	10.98	9,406
Sept. 18	do	408	2,623	2.02	9.30	5,298
Oct. 2	do	408	2,523	2.01	9.27	5,081
Nov. 4	P. H. Daniells	382	1,890	1.60	8.14	3,025
Nov. 26	do	385a	2,200	1.06	8.35	2,322
Dec. 8	do	238a	1,745	0.45	7.30	782

a Measured below regular station.

SESSIONAL PAPER No. 25c

DAILY GAUGE HEIGHT AND DISCHARGE of North Saskatchewan River at Edmonton, for 1914.

DAY.	January.		February.		March.		April.		May.		June.	
	Gauge Height.	Discharge	Gauge Height.	Discharge	Gauge Height.	Discharge	Gauge Height.	Discharge	Gauge Height.	Discharge.	Gauge Height.	Discharge.
	Feet.	Sec.-ft.	Feet.	Sec.-ft.	Feet.	Sec.-ft.	Feet.	Sec.-ft.	Feet.	Sec.-ft.	Feet.	Sec.-ft.
1	7.20	1,280a	7.90	1,075	8.40	975	7 60	1,250	8.90	3,950	9.90	6,520
2	7.30	1,300	7.90	1,075	8 40	1,045	7 60	1,075	8.90	3,950	9.60	5,840
3	7.70	1,325	8 00	1,000	8 40	1,125	7.60	1,200	9 40	4,860	9.40	5,440
4	7.70	1,360	8 00	1,000	8.40	1,100	7 70	1,200	10 10	6,330	10.40	7,810
5	7.70	1,400	8 00	1,000	8.40	1,125	7.80	1,225	13.10	15,000c	13.40	17,120
6	7.60	1,450	8.00	800	8.20	1,100	7.80	1,185	12 40	12,780	14.80	22,200
7	7.80	1,450	8.00	812	8.20	1,075	8 00	1,145	11 60	10,300	16 00	26,760
8	7.90	1,400	8.00	825	8.20	1,050	8.00	1,160	11.30	9,650	23.10	57,780
9	8.00	1,360	8.00	875	8.10	1,025	8.10	1,175	10.90	8,480	24 00	61,740
10	8.10	1,360	8.00	925	8.00	1,000	8.20	1,200	11.00	8,800	21,60	51,180
11	8.10	1,285	8.00	925	7.90	1,050	8.20	1,200	11.70	10,820	19.60	42,380
12	8.10	1,200	8.00	925	8.00	1,100	8.50	1,250	12.10	12,080	16 80	30,060
13	8.00	1,190	8.00	925	8.00	1,050	8 50	1,250a	11 60	10,610	16 10	27,150
14	7.90	1,175	8.00	960	8.00	1,125	8.60	1,275b	11.10	9,260	15 60	25,240
15	7.80	1,175	8.00	1,000	7.90	1,200	8 90	1,890	10.80	8,400	15.00	22,960
16	7.80	1,175	8.00	1,025	7.80	1,150	8.70	2,300	10.90	8,800	15.10	23,340
17	7.90	1,175	8.00	975	7.90	1,150	8.70	2,380	11.00	9,140	15.40	24,480
18	8.00	1,200	8.40	900	7.90	1,125	9 10	3,570	11.40	10,250	16 00	26,760
19	8.00	1,225	8.40	835	7.90	1,175	9 60	4,390	11.00	9,200	16 00	26,760
20	8.00	1,225	8.40	835	7.90	1,125	10.00	5,200b	10.90	8,950	15.90	26,380
21	8.00	1,185	8.40	800	7.90	1,280	1 .10	6,330	11.10	9,500	15.00	22,960
22	8.00	1,135	8.40	885	7.90	1,300	1 .10	6,330	11.30	10,090c	14.70	21,820
23	8.00	1,095	8.40	975	7.90	1,300	1 20	6,570	10 90	9,110	14.60	21,440
24	8.00	1,050	8.40	1,035	7.90	1,300	10 00	6,110	11.00	9,370	14.40	20,680
25	8.00	1,050	8.40	1,100	7.90	1,100	9.70	5,460	11.00	9,370	14.80	22,200
26	8.00	1,075	8.40	1,075	7.90	1,075	.50	5,060	11.40	10,510	14 00	19,230
27	7.90	1,100	8.40	1,050	7.90	1,100	.20	4,460	11.30	10,210	13.90	18,870
28	7.80	1,100	8.40	1,050	7.90	1,137	.20	4,460	11.00	9,370	13.80	18,510
29	7.80	968			7.80	1,175	00	4,090	10.60	8,330	13.60	17,800
30	7.80	1,075			7.70	1,250	9 00	4,090	10.00	6,770	13.40	17,120
31	7.90	1,075			7.60	1,275			10.00	6,770		

a Ice conditions Jan. 1 to April 13.
b Ice breaking up April 14 to April 20; discharges during this period interpolated.
c Shifting conditions May 5 to May 22.

5 GEORGE V, A. 1915.

DAILY GAUGE HEIGHT AND DISCHARGE of North Saskatchewan River at Edmonton, for 1914..

Day.	July.		August.		September.		October.		November.		December.	
	Gauge Height.	Dis-charge	Gauge Height.	Dis-charge	Gauge Height.	Dis-charge.	Gauge Height.	Dis-charge	Gauge Height.	Dis-charge	Gauge Height.	Dis-charge.
	Feet.	Sec.-ft.	Feet.	Sec.-ft.	Feet.	Sec.-ft.	Feet.	Sec.-ft.	Feet.	Sec.-ft.	Feet.	Sec.-ft.
1..........	14.00	19,230	11 90	12,090	11.00	9,370	9.40	5,440	8.10	2,970	8.70	2,350
2..........	14.40	20,680	12.00	12,410	10.80	8,850	9 20	5,040	8.10	2,970	8.30	2,080
3..........	14.70	21,820	12.50	14,060	10.70	8,590	9.20	5,040	8 10	2,970	8.10	1,850
4..........	14.90	22,580	12.30	13,380	10.60	8,330	9.20	5,040	8.10	2,970	8.30	1,900
5..........	15.20	23,720	12 60	14,400	10.40	7,810	9.20	5,040	8.10	2,970	8.10	1,750
6..........	15 60	25,240	12 60	14,400	10 40	7,810	9.20	5,040	8.10	2,970	7.90	1,500
7..........	15.70	25,620	12 60	14,400	10.30	7,550	9.10	4,840	8.00	2,830	7.30	770
8..........	15 70	25,620	12.00	12,410	10.30	7,550	9.10	4,840	8.00	2,830	7.40	782
9..........	15.10	23,340	12.30	13,380	10 20	7,290	9.30	5,240	7.90	2,690	7.40	790
10..........	15.00	22,960	12.00	12,410	10 50	8,070	9.20	5,040	7.70	2,410	7.40	800
11..........	14.70	21,820	11.50	10,810	10.50	8,070	9.30	5,240	8.10	2,500b	7.40	800
12.......... .	14.50	21,060	11.00	9,370	10.40	7,810	9 50	5,640	8.00	2,460	7.40	800
13..........	14.20	19,950	10.90	9,110	10.30	7,550	9.60	5,840	8.00	2,450	7.30	755
14..........	14.60	21,440	10.90	9,110	10 20	7,290	9.40	5,440	8.00	2,450	7.20	710
15..........	15.20	23,720	11.00	9,370	10.00	6,770	9.20	5,040	7.90	2,400	7.10	700
16..........	15.20	23,720	11.20	9,920	9 80	6,280	9.10	4,840	7.80	2,320a	7.30	700
17..........	15.00	22,960	11.40	10,510	9.50	5,640	9.00	4,640	7.40	2,145	7.40	765
18..........	14 80	22,200	11 50	10,810	9.30	5,240	9 00	4,640	7.30	2,050	7.40	800
19..........	14.00	19,230	11.40	10,510	9.40	5,440	8.90	4,440	7.40	2,090	7.30	770
20..........	13.60	17,800	11.20	9,920	9.20	5,040	8 90	4,440	7.40	2,100	7.30	750
21..........	13.00	15,760	11.10	9,640	9.10	4,840	8 90	4,440	7.40	2,100	7.30	770
22..........	13 80	18,510	11.50	10,810	9.10	4,840	8.90	4,440	8.00	2,175	7.60	900
23..........'	12.20	13,050	11.80	11,770	9.10	4,840	8.70	4,045	8.30	2,250	7.60	930
24..........	12 00	12,410	11.60	11,130	9.10	4,840	8.60	3,855	8.50	2,315	7.65	1,000
25..........	12.00	12,410	11.60	11,130	9.00	4,640	8.50	3,670	8.70	2,400	7.70	1,035
26..........	11.80	11,770	11.30	10,210	8.80	4,240	8.50	3,670	8.35	2,322	7.80	1,070
27..........	11.70	11,450	11 00	9,370	9.00	4,640	8.40	3,490	8.30	2,150	7.80	1,100
28..........	11.60	11,130	11 00	9,370	9.00	4,640	8 30	3,310	8.40	2,335	7.90	1,210
29..........	11.60	11,130	10.80	8,850	9.20	5,040	8 30	3,310	8.70	2,340	8.00	1,330
30..........	11.60	11,130	11 00	9,370	9.60	5,840	8.20	3,130	8.60	2,250	8.00	1,350
31..........	11.90	12,090	11 10	9,640	......	....	8 20	3,130	......	....	8.00	1,340a

a Ice conditions Nov. 16 to Dec. 31.
b Ice forming Nov. 11 to Nov. 15; discharges during this period interpolated.

MONTHLY DISCHARGE of North Saskatchewan River at Edmonton, for 1914.

(Drainage area 10,620 square miles.)

MONTH.	DISCHARGE IN SECOND-FEET.				RUN OFF.	
	Maximum.	Minimum.	Mean.	Per square Mile.	Depth in inches on Drainage Area.	Total in Acre-feet.
January............................	1,450	968	1,213	0.114	0.13	74,583
February...........................	1,100	800	952	0.000	0.09	52,871
March..............................	1,300	975	1,134	0.107	0.12	69,728
April...............................	6,570	1,075	2,430	0.229	0.26	144,600
May................................	15,000	3,950	9,064	0.854	0.98	557,324
June...............................	61,740	5,440	24,618	2.320	2.59	1,464,880
July...............................	25,620	11,130	18,889	1.780	2.05	1,161,429
August.............................	14,400	9,110	11,099	1.040	1.20	682,439
September....................	9,370	4,240	6,492	0.611	0.68	386,300
October............................	5,840	3,130	4,558	0.429	0.49	280,258
November..........................	2,970	2,050	2,473	0.233	0.26	147,157
December..........................	2,350	700	1,102	0.104	0.12	67,762
The year	....	....	....	....	8.97	5,089,331

PIGEON CREEK AT PIGEON LAKE.

Location.—On SE. ¼ Sec. 15, Tp. 46, Rge. 28, W. 4th Mer., at the traffic bridge near outlet of Pigeon Lake, and on the trail from Wetaskiwin to Westerose post office.

Records available.—Discharge measurements only, made during 1912, 1913 and 1914.

Gauge.—Vertical staff, spiked to a post in creek on downstream side of bridge.

Bench-mark.—On a spike in a pile at the southwest corner of the bridge; elevation of bench-mark, 6.64 feet above zero of the gauge.

Channel.—Permanent sand and gravel.

Discharge measurements.—Made by wading near the bridge.

Winter flow.—The creek is partly open all winter, and measurements are made by wading.

Artificial control.—Dam at outlet of lake fitted with two gates and a fishway.

Remarks.—The gauge was established in 1914, but, owing to the construction of the dam, the creek was dry during the months of July, August, September and part of October. As it was difficult to secure a satisfactory observer, no gauge heights were obtained when the creek was opened in October.

DISCHARGE MEASUREMENTS of Pigeon Creek at Pigeon Lake, in 1914.

Date.	Engineer.	Width.	Area of Section.	Mean Velocity.	Gauge Height.	Discharge.
		Feet.	*Sq. ft.*	*Ft. per sec.*	*Feet.*	*Sec.-ft.*
Jan. 28	J. S. Tempest	11.0	6.55	0.82	........a	9.1
Mar. 13	do	13.0	8.25	1.38	........a	11.4
July 13	J. M. Paul	30.0	48.40	1.39	4.61	67.0
Aug. 7	do				2.65	Nil b
Oct. 23	do	14.8	5.71	0.73	2.82	4.2
Dec. 12	P. H. Daniells	18.0	9.80	1.26	3.06	12.4

a No gauge.
b Water standing in pools.

BATTLE RIVER AT PONOKA.

Location.—On the SW. ¼ Sec. 4, Tp. 43, Rge. 25, W. 4th Mer., at the steel traffic bridge 300 yards southeast of the C.P.R. depot in the town of Ponoka.

Records available.—May 7, 1913, to December 31, 1914.

Gauge.—Vertical staff; elevation of zero maintained at 88.31 since establishment.

Bench-mark.—Permanent iron bench-mark located beside outside pile on upstream side of left abutment; assumed elevation, 100.00.

Channel.—Slightly shifting.

Discharge measurements.—Made by wading at a point 300 feet upstream.

Winter flow.—From November to April river is frozen over, and measurements are made at a point 300 feet upstream from bridge.

Observer.—G. R. Edwards.

5 GEORGE V, A. 1915

DISCHARGE MEASUREMENTS of Battle River at Ponoka, in 1914.

Date.	Engineer.	Width.	Area of Section.	Mean Velocity.	Gauge Height.	Discharge.
		Feet.	*Sq. ft.*	*Ft. per sec.*	*Feet.*	*Sec.-ft.*
Jan. 10............	P. H. Daniells...............	15.5a	10.0	0.78	2.51	7.8
Feb. 16............	do	23.0a	23.0	0.64	3.16	14.7
Mar. 23............	do	21.0a	26.8	1.12	3.34	31.0
April 28............	do	68.0	203.0	0.73	3.57	149.0
May 15............	G. J. Smith and J. M. Paul...	70.0	253.0	0.87	4.12	221.0
June 3............	J. M. Paul................	64.0	178.0	0.58	3.04	103.0
June 25............	do	82.5	596.0	1.22	7.04	727.0
July 11............	do	69.0	342.0	0.56	3.93	192.0
Aug. 10............	do	64.0	246.4	0.12	2.65	30.0
Aug. 22............	do	62.0	231.0	0.01	2.34	3.6
Sept. 11............	do	68.0	266.0	0.25	2.85	66.0
Sept. 25............	do	65.5	239.0	0.15	2.55	35.0
Oct. 16............	do	67.0	258.0	0.24	2.84	62.0
Nov. 5............	P. H. Daniells...............	66.0	237.0	0.20	2.61	46.0
Nov. 20............	do	23.0a	20.8	1.34	2.51	28.0
Dec. 11............	do	22.0a	26.8	1.26	2.76	34.0

a Measured above regular section.

DAILY GAUGE HEIGHT AND DISCHARGE of Battle River at Ponoka, for 1914.

DAY.	March.		April.		May.		June.		July.	
	Gauge Height.	Dis-charge.	Gauge Height.	Dis-charge.	Gauge Height.	Dis-charge.	Gauge Height.	Dis-charge.	Gauge Height.	Dis-charge.
	Feet.	*Sec.-ft.*	*Feet.*	*Sec.-ft.*	*Feet.*	*Sec.-ft.*	*Feet.*	*Sec.-ft.*	*Feet.*	*Sec.-ft.*
1................	....	....	3.08	28	3.27	108	3.08	87	6.03	533
2................	....	....	3.07	28	3.26	107	3.05	84	5.65	468
3................	....	....	3.09	28	4.86	337	3.02	80	5.26	402
4................	....	....	3.13	29	7.54	803	3.12	91	4.97	354
5................	....	....	4.00	30	8.37	953	4.41	265	4.74	317
6................	....	....	3.97	32	8.99	1,064	5.37	421	4.57	290
7................	....	....	4.65	33	10.04	1,253	6.62	638	4.50	279
8................	....	....	5.02	34	9.76	1,203	8.55	985	4.35	255
9................	....	....	5.13	36	8.66	1,005	10.79	1,388	4.18	229
10................	....	....	5.18	37	6.82	674	13.99	1,964	4.04	209
11................	....	....	5.25	38	5.58	457	13.62	1,898	3.93	193
12................	3.32	27a	5.27	39	5.06	369	13.01	1,788	3.87	185
13................	3.34	31	5.29	40a	4.64	301	12.65	1,723	3.85	182
14................	3.36	30	5.36	51b	4.47	274	10.90	1,408	3.86	183
15................	3.35	30	5.40	60	4.11	218	9.67	1,187	4.08	214
16................	3.42	30	5.23	72	4.07	213	8.05	895	4.08	214
17................	3.47	29	5.08	83	4.02	206	6.67	647	3.97	199
18................	3.43	29	4.60	91	3.88	186	6.68	648	3.76	169
19................	3.36	28	4.30	99	3.77	171	6.69	650	3.67	157
20................	3.25	27	4.20	104	3.78	172	6.76	663	3.56	143
21................	3.26	27	3.94	120	3.82	178	6.75	661	3.44	129
22................	3.28	31	3.90	136	3.76	169	6.78	666	3.32	114
23................	3.26	31	3.73	148	3.70	161	7.00	706	3.23	104
24................	3.27	31	3.54	161b	3.57	144	7.15	733	3.10	89
25................	3.20	30	3.79	174	3.52	138	7.05	715	3.07	86
26................	3.12	28	3.75	168	3.46	131	6.88	684	3.07	86
27................	3.08	27	3.69	160	3.46	131	6.93	693	3.03	81
28................	3.12	28	3.59	147	3.37	120	6.99	704	2.98	76
29................	3.12	29	3.47	132	3.31	113	6.83	675	2.94	72
30................	3.12	29	3.37	120	3.27	108	6.56	627	2.91	69
31................	3.08	28	....	....	3.23	104	...,.....	....	2.88	66

a Ice conditions March 12 to April 13.
b Ice breaking up April 14 to 24; discharges estimated.

SESSIONAL PAPER No. 25c

DAILY GAUGE HEIGHT AND DISCHARGE of Battle River at Ponoka, for 1914.

DAY.	August.		September.		October.		November.		December.	
	Gauge Height.	Dis- charge.	Gauge Height.	Dis- charge.	Gauge Height.	Dis- charge.	Gauge Height.	Dis- charge.	Gauge Height.	Dis- charge.
	Feet.	*Sec.-ft.*	*Feet.*	*Sec.-ft.*	*Feet.*	*Sec.-ft.*	*Feet.*	*Sec.-ft.*	*. Feet.*	*Sec.-ft.*
1..............	2.82	60.0	2.29	15.3	2.45	28	2.60	40	2.72	32
2..............	2.76	54.0	2.27	13.9	2.53	34	2.55	36	2.71	31
3..............	2.71	50.0	2.25	12.5	2.55	36	2.58	38	2.68	31
4..............	2.65	44.0	2.23	11.1	2.64	44	2.57	38	2.65	31
5..............	2.61	41.0	2.21	9.7	2.71	50	2.57	46b	2.68	31
6..............	2.57	· 38.0	2.20	9.0	3.03	81	2.61	46	2.70	32
7..............	2.52	34.0	2.23	11.1	3.05	84	2.57	46	2.68	32
8..............	2.50	32.0	2.29	15.3	3.00	78	2.57	42	2.74	33
9..............	2.53	34.0	2.40	24.0	3.02	80	2.63	39	2.76	34
10.......... ..	2.66	45.0	2.55	36.0	3.03	81	2.57	35	2.74	34
11..............	2.81	59.0	2.78	56.0	3.02	80	2.64	32	2.80	34
12..............	2.76	54.0	2.79	57.0	2.96	74	2.52	29b	2.78	34
13..............	2.70	49.0	2.76	54.0	2.89	67	2.56	28a	2.78	34
14.	2.69	48.0	2.72	51.0	2.85	63	2.56	28	2.77	34
15..............	2.67	46.0	2.70	49.0	2.82	60	2.54	27	2.78	34
16............ .	2.62	42.0	2.67	46.0	2.83	61	2.54	27	2.78	34
17..............	2.60	40.0	2.65	44.0	2.82	60	2.56	28	2.77	34
18..............	2.63	43.0	2.62	42.0	2.80	58	2.61	29	2.78	34
19..............	2.60	40.0	2.60	40.0	2.75	54	2.56	28	2.76	33
20.........	2.55	36.0	2.60	40.0	2.70	49	2.57	28	2.77	34
21..............	2.50	32.0	2.64	44.0	2.67	46	2.60	28	2.77	34
22..............	2.33	18.4	2.60	40.0	2.65	44	2.56	28	2.83	35
23..............	2.33	18.4	2.59	39.0	2.63	43	2.61	30	2.87	33
24..............	2.33	18.4	2.55	36.0	2.63 ·	43	2.59	29	2.89	32
25	2.32	17.6	2.55	36.0	2.62	42	2.59	29	2.90	31
26..............	2.32	17.6	2.52	34.0	2.61	41	2.58	29	2.94	30
27..............	2.35	20.0	2.49	31.0	2.61	41	2.62	29	2.94	31
28..............	2.33	18.4	2.46	29.0	2.61	41	2.62	30	2.96	32
29..............	2.32	17.6	2.45	28.0	2.61	41	2.66	31	2.96	32
30..............	2.34	19.2	2 45	28.0	2.63	43	2.73	32	2.96	32
31..............	2.31	16.8	....	....	2.65	44	....	....	3.01	32a

a Ice conditions Nov. 13 to Dec. 31.
b Ice forming Nov. 5 to 12; discharges estimated.

MONTHLY DISCHARGE of Battle River at Ponoka, for 1914.

(Drainage area 670 square miles.)

MONTH.	DISCHARGE IN SECOND-FEET.				RUN-OFF.	
	Maximum.	Minimum.	Mean.	Per square Mile.	Depth in inches on Drainage Area.	Total in Acre-feet.
January.............................	14	6.1	9.7	0.014	0.02	596
February............................	15	5.0	11.0	0.016	0.02	611
March...............................	31	12.1	25.0	0.037	0.04	1,537
April................................	174	28.0	82.0	0.122	0.14	4,879
May.................................	1,253	104.0	373.0	0.557	0.64	22,935
June...............................	1,964	80.0	812.0	1.210	1.35	48,317
July...............................	533	66.0	198.0	0.296	0.34	12,175
August..............................	60	16.8	36.0	0.054	0.06	2,214
September...........................	57	9.0	33.0	0.049	0.06	1,964
October.............................	84	28.0	54.0	0.081	0.09	3,320
November............................	46	27.0	33.0	0.049	0.06	1,964
December............................	35	30.0	33.0	0.049	0.06	2,029
The year...........................	....	....	....	....	2.88	102,541

NOTE.—Discharges for Jan., Feb. and March estimated, as no gauge heights Were obtained previous to March 12 -

BATTLE RIVER AT BATTLEFORD (UPPER STATION).

Location.—On NW. ¼ Sec. 25, Tp. 43, Rge. 17, W. 3rd. Mer., at the traffic bridge about one-half mile west of the Canadian Northern Railway station at Battleford.

Records available.—May 23, 1914, to October 31, 1914.

Gauge.—Chain gauge at chainage 200 feet on bridge; gauge zero maintained at elevation 83.89 feet.

Bench-mark.—On top of abutment, downstream side of west end of bridge; assumed elevation, 100.00 feet.

Channel.—Permanent.

Discharge measurements.—From bridge.

Winter flow.—No winter observations have been taken, as the lower station is maintained.

Observer.—H. Saunders.

Remarks.—This station was established to obtain records of gauge height not affected by backwater from the North Saskatchewan River, and during 1914 proved very satisfactory.

DISCHARGE MEASUREMENTS of Battle River at Battleford (Upper Station), in 1914.

Date.	Engineer.	Width.	Area of Section.	Mean Velocity.	Gauge Height.	Discharge.
		Feet.	*Sq. ft.*	*Ft. per sec.*	*Feet.*	*Sec.-ft.*
June 21	W. H. Storey.......... ...	206	1035	2.76	7.37	2,860
July 22.	do	199	560	2.64	5.40	1,475
Aug. 18........ ..	do	121	226	2.1	3.38	475
Oct 15...........	F. R. Steinberger..........	192	348	2.12	4.10	737

DAILY GAUGE HEIGHT AND DISCHARGE of Battle River at Battleford (Upper Station),
· for 1914.

DAY.	May.		June.		July.		August.		September.		October.	
	Gauge Height.	Dis-charge.	Gauge Height.	Dis-charge	Gauge Height.	Dis-charge	Gauge Height.	Dis-charge.	Gauge Height.	Dis-charge.	Gauge Height.	Dis-charge.
	Feet.	*Sec.-ft.*	*Feet.*	*Sec.-ft.*	*Feet.*	*Sec.-ft.*	*Feet.*	*Sec.-ft.*	*Feet.*	*Sec.-ft.*	*Feet.*	*Sec.-ft.*
1.........	......	......	4.55	956	7.35	2,842	4.42	889	3.19	414	3 07	381
2.........	......	......	4.45	905	7.33	2,828	4.36	859	3 13	398	3 05	375
3.........	......	......	4.45	905	7.30	2,806	4 28	821	3.12	395	3 03	370
4.........	......	......	4.43	894	7.28	2,792	4 25	807	3 11	392	3 09	386
5.........	......	......	4.34	850	7.24	2,763	4.14	756	3.10	389	3 28	440
6.........	......	......	4.24	801	7.20	2,734	4.06	721	3.14	400	3.31	449
7.........	......	......	4.14	756	7.14	2,691	3.98	687	3.17	409	3.46	495
8.........	......	......	4.12	747	7.08	2,648	3.95	674	3.16	406	3.45	492
9.........	......	......	4.08	729	6.99	2,583	3.86	638	3.17	409	3.43	486
10.........	......	......	4.01	699	6.89	2,511	3.81	619	3.15	403	3.49	505
11	......	......	4.58	972	6.75	2,411	3.80	615	3.13	398	3.48	502
12.........	......	......	4.49	925	6.72	2,389	3.77	604	3.15	403	3.50	539
13...... ...	......	......	4.57	967	6.61	2,311	3.72	585	3.14	400	4.16	765
14...... ..	......	......	4.82	1,107	6.49	2,226	3.69	574	3.10	389	4.18	774
15..... ...	......	......	5.18	1,329	6.36	2,133	3.64	556	3.12	395	4.10	738
16.........	......	......	5.45	1,504	6.24	2,048	3.62	549	3.12	395a	3.93	666
17.........	......	......	5.43	1,491	6.13	1,971	3.59	539	3.11	392	3.87	642
18.........	......	......	5.38	1,458	6.02	1,894	3.51	511	3.11	392	3.70	578
19.........	......	......	5.53	1,557	5.89	1,803	3.49	505	3.10	389	3.58	535
20	......	......	5.60	1,604	5.81	1,748	3.44	489	3.11	392	3.56	528
21.........	......	......	5.68	1,658	5.67	1,651	3.41	479	3.10	389	3.52	515
22.........	......	......	5.96	1,852	5.47	1,517	3.40	476	3.10	389	3.47	498
23.........	5.67	1,652	6.37	2,141	5.36	1,445	3.49	505	3.10	389	3.42	482
24.........	5.58	1,591	6.79	2,439	5.28	1,393	3.40	476	3.09	386	3.37	467
25.	5.54	1,564	7.39	2,871	5.14	1,303	3.35	461	3.09	386	3.35	461
26.........	5.35	1,438	7.50	2,950	5.02	1,228	3.36	464	3.09	386	3.37	467
27	5.38	1,458	7.39	2,871	4.91	1,160	3.34	458	3.09	386	3.34	458
28..	5.14	1,304	7 36	2,849	4.77	1,078	3.27	437	3.08	384	3.31	449
29.........	4.93	1,172	7.35	2,842	4.66	1,016	3.26	434	3.08	384b	3.29	443
30	4.95	1,184	7.38	2,864	4.58	972	3.24	430	3.08	384	3.32	452
31.........	4.55	956	......	......	4.51	935	3.23	426	......	......	3.30	446c

a to *b* Interpolated. Observer ill.
c Observations discontinued from Oct. 31. ·

SESSIONAL PAPER No. 25c

MONTHLY DISCHARGE of Battle River at Battleford (Upper Station), for 1914.

(Drainage area 11,850 square miles.)

MONTH.	DISCHARGE IN SECOND-FEET.				RUN-OFF.	
	Maximum.	Minimum.	Mean.	Per square Mile.	Depth in inches on Drainage Area.	Total in Acre-feet.
May (23–31)	1,652	956	1,369	0.116	0.0390	24,428
June.................................	2,950	699	1,550	0.131	0.1460	92,230
July.................................	2,842	935	1,995	0.170	0.1960	122,660
August...............................	889	426	582	0.049	0.0560	35,786
September.................	414	384	394	0.033	0.0370	23,445
October..............................	774	370	509	0.043	0:0499	31,297
The period.......	....	....	....	....	0.5239	329,846

BATTLE RIVER AT BATTLEFORD (LOWER STATION).

Location.—On SE. ¼ Sec. 19, Tp. 43, Rge. 16, W. 3rd Mer.
Records available.—June 17, 1911, to December 31, 1914.
Gauge.—Vertical staff. Zero of gauge was maintained at 71.95 feet during 1911-12.
Chain.—Zero of gauge was maintained at 72.53 feet during 1913-14.
Bench-mark.—On top of left abutment on outer downstream corner; assumed elevation,. 100.00 feet.
Channel.—Sand, which is subject to shift. River also is liable to backwater effect from. North Saskatchewan River.
Discharge measurements.—From bridge at gauge.
Observer.—C. J. Johnson.

DISCHARGE MEASUREMENTS of Battle River at Battleford (Lower Station), in 1914.

Date.	Engineer.	Width.	Area of Section.	Mean Velocity.	Gauge Height.	Discharge.
		Feet.	*Sq. ft.*	*Ft. per sec.*	*Feet.*	*Sec.-ft.*
Jan. 8............	F. R. Steinberger......... .	67.0	91.5	0.28	4.34	26.0
Jan. 29............	do	88.0	48.8	0.60	4.50	29.3
Feb. 16–17........	do	36.0	58.4	0.34	4.80	19.9
Mar 6............	do	31.0	54.6	0.38	4.79	21.0
April 14............	do	134.0	184.0	0.83	4.62	171.0
May 21............	W. H. Storey.......	198.0	658.0	2.71	6.04	1,858.0
June 26	do ....*a*	....	....	....	7.42	2,859.0
July 22............	do ....*a*	....	....	....	6.00	1,475.0
Aug. 18............	do ....*a*	....	....	....	4.28	475.0
Oct. 15............	F. R. Steinberger...........*a*	....	....	....	4.89	737.0
Nov. 28............	do	101.0	186.0	0.99	4.41	184.0
Dec. 15............	do	109.0	184.9	1.07	4.53	197.0

a Measurements made at upper station.

5 GEORGE V, A. 1915

DAILY GAUGE HEIGHT AND DISCHARGE of Battle River at Battleford (Lower Station),
for 1914.

DAY.	January.		February.		March.		April.		May.		June.	
	Gauge Height	Dis-charge	Gauge Height.	Dis-charge.	Gauge Height.	Dis-charge.	Gauge Height.	Dis-charge	Gauge Height.	Dis-charge	Gauge Height.	Dis-charge.
	Feet.	Sec.-ft.	Feet.	Sec.-ft.	Feet.	Sec.-ft.	Feet.	Sec.-ft.	Feet.	Sec.-ft.	Feet.	Sec.-ft.
1	4.15	39c	4 54	24	4.96	21	4.67	37	4.95	1,000	5.09	1,020
2	4.17	38	4.57	23	4 91	21	4.66	40	4.97	1,015	5.04	990
3	4.17	37	4.57	23	4.93	21	4.66	45	4.99	1,035	5.02	970
4	4.20	35	4.59	22	5 07	21	4.65	50	4.94	1,000	4.96	930
5	4.21	33	4.59	22	4.87	21	4.66	57	4.83	935	4.86	870
6	4.24	30	4.60	21	4.91	21	4.66	64	4.77	900	4.84	855
7	4.29	28	4.61	21	4.90	21	4.67	73	4.70	855	4.81	835
8	4.33	26	4.64	21	4.88	22	4.67	82	4.61	805	4.76	785
9	4.33	24	4.66	21	4.86	22	4.67	95	4.80	910	4.72	770
10	4.35	24	4.66	21	4.86	22	4.70	108	5.37	1,290	⁓ 4.72	760
11	4.35	25	4.69	21	4.85	22	4.65	123	6.16	1,970	7.88	3,630
12	4.37	27	4.70	21	4.76	22	4.65	138	6.14	1,950	7.32	2,950
13	4.39d	29	4.72	20	4.74	22	4.65	154	6.02	1,840	6.28	1,840
14	4.40	30	4.74	20	4.70	22	4.63	171	6 00	1,820	5.67	1,320
15	4.41	30	4.80	20	4.65	22	4.61	200a	6.00	1,820	5.50	1,160
16	4.41	30	4.73	20	4.57	21	4.56	300	6.00	1,820	5.79	1,395
17	4.41	29	4.80	20	4.61	21	4.55	400	6.00	1,820	5.96	1,520
18	4.42	28	4.80	20	4.57	20	4.51	500	6.00	1,820	5.76	1,350
19	4.44	28	4.84	20	4.51	21	4.41	600	5.98	1,795	5.76	1,340
20	4.45	27	4.84	20	4.54	21	3.85	700	6.04	1,840	5.80	1,360
21	4.46	26	4.86	21	4.45	21	3.96	800	6.06	1,858	5.96	1,480
22	4.47	26	4.87	21	4.45	21	5.03	1,071bc	5.98	1,800	6.16	1,620
23	4.48d	26	4.87	21	4.47	21	5.00	1,040	5.89	1,710	6.40	1,840
24	4.49	27	4.86	21	4.57	21	4.91	998	5.82	1,640	6.68	2,100
25	4.50	28	4.87	21	4.58	21	4.60	805	5.74	1,560	7.11	2,530
26	4.50	28	4.88	21	4.58	22	4.50	755	5.68	1,500	7.44	2,859
27	4.50	29	4.93	21	4.70	23	4.75	890	5.55	1,380	7.38	2,827
28	4.51	29	4.95	21	4.71	25	5.01	1,045	5.43	1,290	7.36	2,805
29	4.50	29	......	......	4.76	27	4.98	1,030	5.26	1,160	7.39	2,839
30	4.53	28	......	......	4.80	30	4.95	1,005	5.18	1,100	7.40	2,850
31	4.54	26	......	......	4.71	33	......	......	5.12	1,055	......	......

a to b Ice broken up and going out.
c Ice conditions Jan. 1 to April 22.
d Gauge heights interpolated Jan. 13–23.

SESSIONAL PAPER No. 25c

DAILY GAUGE HEIGHT AND DISCHARGE of Battle River at Battleford (Lower Station), for 1914.

DAY.	July.		August.		September.		October.		November.		December.	
	Gauge Height.	Dis- charge	Gauge Height.	Dis- charge.	Gauge Height.	Dis- charge	Gauge Height.	Dis- charge	Gauge Height.	Dis- charge	Gauge Height.	Dis- charge.
	Feet.	Sec.-ft.	Feet.	Sec.-ft.	Feet.	Sec.-ft.	Feet.	Sec.-ft.	Feet.	Sec.-ft.	Feet.	Sec.-ft
1	7.42	2,873	4 96	770	4.12	417	3 91	348	4.16	431	4.46	190
2	7.40	2,850	4.92	750	4.10	410	3.94	357	4.16	431	4 48	189
3	7.39	2,839	4.87	725	4.08	403	3.96	363	4.14	424	4.51	188
4	7.39	2,839	4 84	710	4.07	400	4.15	427	4.11	414	4 51	187
5	7.35	2,793	4.80	690	4 06	396	4.23	455	4.11	413	4.51	186
6	7.31	2,748	4.74	663	4.05	392	4.30	480	4.10	410	4.52	186
7	7.26	2,693	4.69	640	4.16	431	4.32	487	4.16	431	4.52	187
8	7.22	2,649	4.64	618	4.15	427	4.30	480	4.18	438	4.52	191
9	7.17	2,594	4.58	591	4.12	417	4.30	480	4.13	420	4.53	194
10	7.08	2,495	4.55	578	4.08	403	4.30	480	4.10	410	4.53	194
11	7.02	2,429	4.51	560	4.05	392	4.34	494	4.06	396	4.53	194
12	6.93	2,332	4.47	543	4.08	403	4.39	512	4.05	392	4.54	195
13	6.83	2,226	4.44	531	4.35	497	4.81	695	4.00	375	4.56	195
14	6.73	2,125	4.46	539	4.41	519	4.94	760	3.98	300c	4.56	196
15	6.62	2,019	4.47	543	4.39	512	4.89	735	4.00	240	4.53	197
16	6.54	1,943	4.42	523	4.40	515	4.74	663	4.03	175	4.53	199
17	6.42	1,829	4.34	494	4.34	494	4.62	609	4.03	167	4.53	204
18	6.32	1,738	4.28	473	4.25	463	4.52	564	4.08	171	4.53	204
19	6.22	1,652	4.28	473	4.18	438	4.47	543	4.17	178	4.52	193
20	6.14	1,584	4.34	494	4.14	424	4.42	523	4.23	185	4.52	178
21	6.03	1,494	4.30	480	4.12	417	4.39	511	4.30	192	4.52	156
22	5.96	1,438	4.27	469	4.10	410	4.35	497	4.34	186	4.52	138
23	5.86	1,358	4.25	463	4.06	396	4.32	487	4.37	180	4.52	117
24	5.74	1,265	4.24	459	4.03	385	4.30	480	4.40	185	4.52	100
25	5.62	1,179	4.22	452	4.02	382	4.24	459	4.46	190	4.52	93
26	5.52	1,109	4.20	445	4.02	382	4.20	445	4.43	184	4.52	96
27	5.38	1,018	4.20	445	3.98	369	4.20	445	4.41	176	4.52	108
28	5.24	934	4.18	438	3.94	357	4.19	441	4.41	184	4.51	109
29	5.14	874	4.16	431	3.93	354	4.19	441	4.41	189	4.51	104
30	5.06	826	4.14	424	3.92	351	4.18	438	4.41	191	4.51	106
31	5.00	790	4.13	420			4.16	431			4.54	117c

c Ice conditions Nov. 14 to Dec. 31.

MONTHLY DISCHARGE of Battle River at Battleford (Lower Station), for 1914.

(Drainage area 11,850 square miles.)

MONTH.	DISCHARGE IN SECOND-FEET.				RUN-OFF.	
	Maximum.	Minimum.	Mean.	Per square Mile.	Depth in inches on Drainage Area.	Total in Acre-feet.
January	39	24	29	0.0024	0.003	1,783
February	24	20	21	0.0018	0.002	1,166
March	33	20	22	0.0019	0.002	1,353
April	1,071	37	446	0.0376	0.040	26,539
May	1,970	805	1,429	0.1210	0.140	87,868
June	3,630	760	1,680	0.1420	0.160	99,970
July	2,873	790	1,920	0.1620	0.190	118,060
August	770	420	543	0.0458	0.050	33,388
September	519	351	419	0.0345	0.040	24,932
October	760	348	501	0.0423	0.050	30,805
November	438	167	289	0.0244	0.030	17,197
December	204	93	164	0.0140	0.020	10,084
The year					0.727	453,145

5 GEORGE V, A. 1915

NORTH SASKATCHEWAN RIVER AT BATTLEFORD.

Location.—North channel: SW. ¼ Sec. 33, Tp. 43, Rge. 16, W. 3rd Mer.   South channel:
NE. ¼ Sec. 29, Tp. 43, Rge. 16, W. 3rd. Mer.

Records available.—May 16, 1911, to December 31, 1914.

Gauges.—North channel: Chain; elevation of zero maintained at 1,512.30 feet since establishment.   South channel: Chain; elevation of zero maintained at 1,511.88 feet since establishment.

Bench-marks.—North channel: On downstream side of left abutment; elevation 1,525.66 feet
above mean sea level (Department of Public Works, Canada).   South channel: Permanent
iron bench-mark on right bank; elevation, 1,530.72 feet above mean sea level (Department of
Public Works, Canada).

Channel.—Shifts considerably at high stages.

Discharge measurements.—From bridge.

Observer.—Harold W. Fisher.

DISCHARGE MEASUREMENTS of North Channel of North Saskatchewan River,
at Battleford, in 1914.

Date.	Engineer.	Width.	Area of Section.	Mean Velocity.	Gauge Height.	Discharge.
		Feet.	*Sq. ft.*	*Ft. per sec.*	*Feet.*	*Sec.-ft.*
Jan. 7	F. R. Steinberger	201	719	0.18	2.60	130
Jan. 24–26	do	196	671	0.29	3.29	194
Feb. 13	do	185	502	0.21	3.36	108
Mar. 4	do	180	535	0.37	3.62	194
April 10–11	do	565	783	0.66	3.54	515
May 22	W. H. Storey	748	2,212	2.19	4.36	4,848
June 27–29	do	1,132	5,773	2.95	7.58	17,062
July 23	do	985	3,924	2.74	6.05	10,778
Aug. 24	do	793	2,345	2.50	4.83	5,885
Oct. 16	F. R. Steinberger	592	1,444	1.57	3.50	2,267
Nov. 26	do	214	831	0.93	2.73	776
Dec. 16	do	208	666	0.36	2.25	241

SESSIONAL PAPER No. 25c

DAILY GAUGE HEIGHT AND DISCHARGE of North Channel of North Saskatchewan River at Battleford, for 1914.

DAY.	January.		February.		March.		April.		May.		June.	
	Gauge Height.	Dis-charge.	Gauge Height.	Dis-charge	Gauge Height.	Dis-charge	Gauge Height.	Dis-charge	Gauge Height.	Dis-charge.	Gauge Height.	Dis-charge.
	Feet.	*Sec.-ft.*	*Feet.*	*Sec.-ft.*	*Feet.*	*Sec.-ft.*	*Feet.*	*Sec.-ft.*	*Feet.*	*Sec.-ft.*	*Feet.*	*Sec.-ft.*
1	2.97	360a	3.31	175	3.61	195	67	220	4.17	3,973	4.84	6,062
2	2.94	340	3 26	170	3.57	195	.68	245	3.94	3,328	4.54	5,098
3	2.91	315	3 25	165	3.56	195	.67	275	3.66	2,618	4.15	3,784
4	2.87	270	3 22	160	3 59	195	.64	310	3.54	2,384	3.89	3,196
5	2.77	210	3.22	150	3.63	195	3.67	345	3.64	2,602	3.78	2,932
6	2.64	150	3.22	145	3.63	195	3.68	375	3.59	2,489	3.38	2,074
7	2.61	130	3.21	135	3.62	190	3.68	400	3.57	2,447	4.14	3,886
8	2.56	125	3.21	130	3.59	190	3.66	435	3.97	3,402	4.71	5,642
9	2.51	120	3.21	120	3.59	190	3.66	470	6.31	11,672	6.94	14,362
10	2.38	120	3.16	115	3.58	190	3.65	505	6.04	10,564	11.09	36,024
11	2.36	120	3.16	110	3.59	190	3.59	515	5.73	9,320	11.99	37,404
12	2.36	125	3.31	110	3.62	195	3.59	600b	5.24	7,464	11.09	33,264
13	2.39	130	3.34	110	3.60	200	3.58	700	5.14	7,104	10.74	31,654
14	2.46	140	3.39	120	3.57	200	3.56	800	5.02	6,672	9.74	27,054
15	2.61	150	3.46	145	3.57	200	3.47	900	4.87	6,161	8.92	23,282
16	2.76	160	3.54	170	3.57	200	3.29	1,000	5.24	7,464	8.39	20,844
17	2.89	170	3.54	180	3.57	190	3.24	1,100	5 09	6,924	8.22	20,062
18	2.86	180	3.54	180	3.57	185	3.16	1,200	4.96	6,464	8.04	19,234
19	2.83	185	3.54	180	3.59	175	2.99	1,400b	4.89	6,227	7.84	18,314
20	2.81	190	3.54	180	3.56	160	2.96	1,600a	4 76	5,802	7.67	17,548
21	2.81	190	3.54	180	3.56	150	3.20	1,770	4.53	5,258	7.59	17,196
22	2.86	195	3.56	180	3.56	150	3.29	1,714	4.63	5,386	7.94	18,774
23	2.88	195	3.56	180	3.57	150	3.49	2,281	4.84	6,062	8.17	19,832
24	2.98	195	3.61	185	3.59	150	3.94	3,324	4.69	5,578	7.94	18,774
25	3.25	190	3.64	190	3.59	155	4.35	4,510	4.58	5,226	7.74	17,860
26	3.25	190	3.61	190	3.59	160	.79	9,560	4.78	5,866	7.70	17,680
27	3.26	190	3.62	190	3.58	165	.31	7,716	4 69	5,578	7.63	17,372
28	3.26	190	3.62	195	3.59	170	.13	7,068	4 60	5,290	7.45	16,580
29	3.29	185			3.63	180	.83	6,029	4.54	5,098	7.32	16,008
30	3.32	185			3.63	190	5.49	4,939	4.45	4,676	7.08	14,964
31	3.35	180			3.63	200			4.44	4,784		

a Ice conditions Jan. 1 to April 20.
b to b Estimated.

5 GEORGE V, A. 1915

DAILY GAUGE HEIGHT AND DISCHARGE of North Channel of North Saskatchewan River at Battleford, for 1914.

DAY.	July.		August.		September.		October.		November.		December.	
	Gauge Height.	Dis-charge	Gauge Height.	Dis-charge	Gauge Height.	Dis-charge	Gauge Height.	Dis-charge	Gauge Height.	Dis-charge	Gauge Height.	Dis-charge.
	Feet.	Sec.-ft.	Feet.	Sec.-ft.	Feet.	Sec.-ft.	Feet.	Sec.-ft.	Feet.	Sec.-ft.	Feet.	Sec.-ft.
1	7.14	15,242	5 01	6,636	4 48	4,908	2.95	1,415	2.87	1,314	2.81	746
2	7.42	16,448	5 16	7,176	4.31	4,390	2.99	1,467	2.88	1,326	2.84	738
3	7 34	16,096	5.04	6,744	4 23	4,150	3.01	1,494	2.85	1,290	2.84	732
4	7.23	15,612	4.99	6,566	4 33	4,450	3 23	1,818	2.80	1,230	2.98	745
5	5.96	10,240	4.94	6,396	4.23	4,150	3 41	2,129	2.70	1,120	2.99	745
6	6 10	10,810	4.89	6,227	4.11	3,799	3.49	2,281	2.70	1,120	2 84	738
7	7.20	15,480	4.99	6,566	4 03	3,567	3.51	2,321	2 65	1,070	2.84	660
8	7.37	16,228	5.08	6,888	3.98	3,428	3 53	2,363	2 60	1,020	2.79	610
9	7 60	17,240	5.18	7,248	3 90	3,220	3 49	2,281	2.55	970	2.74	540
10	7.76	17,950	5 57	8,683	3.90	3,220	3.44	2,186	2 50	920	2.67	480
11	7 87	18,452	5 43	8,151	3.88	3,172	3.38	2,074	2.50	920	2.49	426
12	7 93	18,728	5.23	7,428	3 85	3,100	3.33	1,984	2.45	880	2.43	380
13	7.84	18,314	5.20	7,320	3 87	3,148	3 28	1,898	2.43	864	2.39	340
14	6 93	14,319	5.08	6,888	3 87	3,148	3.26	1,866	2.40	840	2.34	300
15	6.50	12,470	5.07	6,852	3.95	3,350	3.45	2,205	2.40	840	2.34	260
16	6.51	12,513	5.02	6,672	4 06	3,654	3.45	2,205	2 37	816	2.29	241
17	6.63	13,029	4.38	4,600	4 08	3,712	3.55	2,405	2 35	800	2.14	270
18	6.94	14,362	4 37	4,570	3 79	2,956	3.56	2,426	2.35	800	2.12	380
19	6 90	14,190	4.33	4,450	3.65	2,625	3.48	2,262	2 35	800	2.09	340
20	7.18	15,394	4.32	4,420	3.52	2,342	3 28	1,898	2.55	970	2.04	300
21	7 14	15,222	4 61	5,322	3.42	2,148	3 36	2,038	2.57	990	2.00	280
22	6 85	13,975	4.78	5,866	3.32	1,966	3 26	1,866	2.60	1,020	1.99	260
23	6 10	10,810	4.80	5,930	3.22	1,802	3.15	1,695	2 65	1,070	1.96	250
24	5 80	9,600	4.76	5,802	3.16	1,710	3 10	1,620	2.70	1,020a	1.94	240
25	5 76	9,440	4 46	4,846	3.12	1,650	3.02	1,508	2.75	975	1 91	145
26	5 73	9,400	4.51	5,002	3.10	1,620	3.00	1,480	2.76	776	1.92	152
27	5.86	9,840	4.56	5,162	3 05	1,550	2.98	1,454	2.76	790	1.89	180
28	5 35	7,860	4.57	5,194	3.04	1,536	2 95	1,415	2 76	816	1.91	188
29	5.10	6,960	4 62	5,354	3 08	1,592	2 93	1,389	2.78	892	1.94	180
30	4.95	6,430	4 66	5,482	2.94	1,402	2.90	1,350	2.80	770	1.99	180
31	5.03	6,708	4 58	5,226			2.90	1,350			2.00	200a

a Ice conditions Nov. 24 to Dec. 31.

MONTHLY DISCHARGE of North Channel of North Saskatchewan River at Battleford, for 1914.

MONTH.	DISCHARGE IN SECOND-FEET.			RUN-OFF.
	Maximum.	Minimum.	Mean.	Total in Acre-feet.
January	360	120	186	11,437
February	195	110	158	8,775
March	200	150	182	11,191
April	9,560	220	444	26,420
May	11,672	2,384	5,609	344,888
June	37,404	2,074	16,892	1,002,428
July	18,728	6,430	13,205	811,910
August	8,683	4,420	6,118	376,178
September	4,908	1,402	2,916	173,514
October	2,426	1,350	1,876	115,352
November	1,326	770	968	57,600
December	746	145	394	24,226
The year				2,963,919

DISCHARGE MEASUREMENTS of South Channel of North Saskatchewan River at Battleford, in 1914.

Date.	Engineer.	Width.	Area of Section.	Mean Velocity.	Gauge Height.	Discharge.
		Feet.	*Sq. ft.*	*Ft. per Sec.*	*Feet.*	*Sec.-ft.*
Jan. 8...............	F. R. Steinberger............	318	915	0.85	3.42	780
Jan. 27-28...........	do	281	978	1.19	4.05	1,172
Feb. 14-16...........	do	270	871	1.21	4.33	1,055
Mar. 5..............	do	267	765	1.52	4.49	1,167
April 11-12..........	do	309	837	1.15	4.08	959
May 23.............	W. H. Storey...............	466	2,418	2.75	5.54	6,649
June 29.............	do	506	4,670	3.22	8.42	15,031
July 24.............	do	496	4,584	2.19	7.17	10,060
Aug. 25.............	do	457	3,795	1.78	5.64	6,749
Oct. 17.............	F. R. Steinberger............	452	3,356	1.62	4.95	5,425
Nov. 27.............	do	142	1,128	1.40	3.85	1,580
Dec. 17.............	do	137	960	1.33	3.90	1,279

DAILY GAUGE HEIGHT AND DISCHARGE of South Channel of North Saskatchewan River at Battleford, for 1914.

DAY.	January. Gauge Height.	January. Discharge.	February. Gauge Height.	February. Discharge.	March. Gauge Height.	March. Discharge.	April. Gauge Height.	April. Discharge.	May. Gauge Height.	May. Discharge.	June. Gauge Height.	June. Discharge.
	Feet.	*Sec.-ft.*	*Feet.*	*Sec.-ft.*	*Feet.*	*Sec.-ft.*	*Feet.*	*Sec.-ft.*	*Feet.*	*Sec.-ft.*	*Feet.*	*Sec.-ft.*
1..........	3.66	1,700a	4 24	1,000	4.51	1,120	4.51	1,010	5 10	5,700	5 80	7,140
2..........	3.66	1,550	4.20	945	4.51	1,160	4.49	1,000	4.87	5,279	5.52	6,542
3..........	3.65	1,420	4.15	920	4.52	1,165	4.43	990	4 59	4,814	5 17	5,833
4..........	3.62	1,280	4.14	900	4.52	1,165	4.39	980	4.45	4,595	5 05	5,605
5..........	3.56	1,160	4.24	895	4.47	1,165	4.39	975	4.50	4,670	4.97	5,456
6..........	3.51	1,020	4.21	890	4.47	1,165	4.29	970	4.55	4,750	4.55	4,750
7..........	3.41	900	4.16	890	4.45	1,160	4.29	960	4.52	4,702	5.20	5,890
8..........	3.35	780	4.11	895	4.45	1,150	4.27	960	5.05	5,605	5.85	7,250
9..........	3.33	730	4.06	900	4.43	1,130	4.24	955	6.90	9,880	7.75	12,295
10..........	3.25	720	4.08	910	4.43	1,125	4.19	955	6.63	9,288	12.30	25,930
11..........	3.25	705	4.08	940	4.48	1,135	4.11	955	6.35	8,455	12.60	26,830
12..........	3.25	705	4.12	980	4.53	1,150	4.14	960	6.00	7,590	11.75	24,280
13..........	3.27	715	4.22	1,020	4.53	1,150	4.15	980	5.92	7,406	11.00	22,030
14..........	3.34	745	4.28	1,045	4.53	1,150	4.15	955b	5.80	7,140	10.38	20,170
15..........	3.45	800	4.34	1,050	4.54	1,150	4.05	1,010	5.65	6,815	9.76	18,310
16..........	3.67	890	4.42	1,050	4.53	1,150	4.05	1,400	5.95	7,475	9.34	17,050
17..........	3.80	960	4.35	1,045	4.53	1,150	4.00	2,100	5.80	7,140	9.17	16,540
18..........	3.75	940	4.35	1,030	4.53	1,150	3.92	2,800	5.70	6,920	8.97	15,940
19..........	3.70	925	4.35	980	4.48	1,145	3.68	3,300	5.60	6,710	8.76	15,310
20..........	3.70	925	4.37	960	4.39	1,130	3.71	3,622ab	5.52	6,542	8.51	14,560
21..........	3.75	930	4.37	955	4.36	1,110	4.09	4,107	5.30	6,090	8.44	14,350
22..........	3.76	940	4.37	955	4.38	1,090	4.17	4,211	5.56	6,626	8.85	15,550
23..........	3.80	950	4.42	965	4.39	1,080	4.35	4,450	5.76	7,052	9.09	16,300
24..........	3.84	975	4.47	975	4.39	1,065	4.95	5,420	5.60	6,710	8.86	15,610
25..........	3.88	1,020	4.50	1,000	4.41	1,060	5.30	6,090	5.56	6,626	8.70	15,130
26..........	3.92	1,100	4.50	1,035	4.44	1,055	6.70	9,340	5.62	6,752	8.50	14,530
27..........	3.94	1,165	4.52	1,060	4.44	1,055	6.18	8,030	5.57	6,647	8.30	13,930
28..........	3.99	1,175	4.52	1,090	4.43	1,050	6.00	7,590	5.50	6,500	8.30	13,930
29..........	4.04	1,175	......	......	4.44	1,045	5.70	6,920	5.47	6,437	8.38	14,170
30..........	4.05	1,150	......	......	4.49	1,035	5.41	6,311	5.45	6,395	8.12	13,390
31..........	4.10	1,070	......	......	4.54	1,025	......	......	5.45	6,395	......	......

a Ice conditions Jan. 1 to April 20.
b to b Estimated.

5 GEORGE V, A. 1915

DAILY GAUGE HEIGHT AND DISCHARGE of South Channel of North Saskatchewan River at Battleford, for 1914.

DAY.	July.		August.		September.		October.		November.		December.	
	Feet.	Sec.-ft.	Feet.	Sec.-ft.	Feet.	Sec.-ft.	Feet.	Sec.-ft.	Feet.	Sec.-ft.	Feet.	Sec.-ft.
1...........	8.20	13,630	6.35	8,455	5 66	6,836	4 60	4,830	4.20	4,250	4.16	1,515
2...........	8.35	14,080	6.50	8,830	5 51	6,521	4.63	4,878	4.19	4,237	4.19	1,508
3...........	8 29	13,900	6 00	7,590	5.40	6,290	4.70	4,990	4.19	4,237	4.19	1,504
4...........	8 20	13,630	6 01	7,614	5.45	6,395	4 80	5,160	4.10	4,120	4.31	1,500
5...........	7.91	12,760	6 05	7,710	5.37	6,230	4.91	5,348	4.05	4,055	4.31	1,495
6...........	8.10	13,330	6.06	7,734	5.35	6,190	4.95	5,420	4.02	4,016	4.26	1,485
7...........	8.30	13,930	6.17	8,005	5.25	5,990	4.95	5,420	4.00	3,990	4.26	1,470
8...........	8.47	14,440	6.25	8,205	5.20	5,890	4.96	5,438	3.90	3,860	4.21	1,450
9...........	8.70	15,130	6.35	8,455	5.15	5,795	4.92	5,366	3.85	3,795	4.19	1,430
10...........	8.80	15,430	6.50	8,830	5.20	5,890	4.90	5,330	3.70	3,610	4.16	1,410
11...........	8.85	15,580	6.35	8,455	5.20	5,890	4.79	5,143	3.58	3,466	4.11	1,390
12...........	8.90	15,730	6.25	8,205	5.25	5,990	4.70	4,990	3.55	3,430	4.09	1,370
13...........	8.81	15,460	6.22	8,130	5.20	5,890	4.68	4,958	3.51	3,382	4.09	1,345
14.......	8.11	13,360	6.25	8,205	5.18	5,852	4.65	4,910	3.45	3,315	4.11	1,310
15...........	7.78	12,382	6.27	8,255	5.25	5,990	4.62	4,862	3.45	3,315	4.11	1,290
16	7.80	12,440	6.21	8,105	5.37	6,230	5.01	5,529	3.42	3,282	4.09	1,275
17...........	7.97	12,940	5.57	6,647	5.39	6,270	5.11	5,719	3.40	3,260	4.03	1,279
18...........	8.40	14,230	5.55	6,605	5.14	5,776	5.12	5,738	3.42	3,282	4.01	1,315
19...........	8.33	14,020	5.50	6,500	5.00	5,510	5.04	5,586	3.45	3,315	3.97	1,318
20...........	8.17	13,540	5.43	6,353	4.87	5,279	4.84	5,228	3.55	3,430	3.93	1,290
21...........	8.10	13,330	5.70	6,920	4.80	5,160	4.92	5,366	3.60	3,490	3.91	1,260
22...........	7.78	12,382	5.92	7,406	4.73	5,041	4.82	5,194	3.65	3,550	3.87	1,240
23...........	7.25	10,845	5.85	7,250	4.71	5,007	4.81	5,177	3.70	3,010a	3.86	1,190
24...........	7.13	10,504	5.78	7,096	4.68	4,958	4.66	4,926	3.75	2,760	3.81	1,150
25...........	7.11	10,448	5.60	6,710	4.65	4,910	4.60	4,830	3.80	2,430	3.79	1,120
26...........	7.10	10,420	5.65	6,815	4.65	4,910	4.50	4,670	3.85	1,890	3.80	1,118
27...........	7.14	10,532	5.70	6,920	4.63	4,878	4.42	4,550	3.87	1,580	3.81	1,116
28...........	6.77	9,529	5.73	6,986	4.63	4,878	4.36	4,464	3.90	1,480	3.81	1,120
29...........	6.51	8,855	5.78	7,096	4.65	4,910	4.30	4,380	4.00	1,562	3.83	1,140
30...........	6.32	8,380	5.82	7,184	4.60	4,830	4.27	4,341	4.05	1,530	3.86	1,250
31...........	6.40	8,580	5.74	7,008	......	....	4.25	4,315	......	......	3.86	1,400a

    a Ice conditions Nov. 23 to Dec. 31.

MONTHLY DISCHARGE of South Channel of North Saskatchewan River at Battleford, for 1914.

MONTH.	DISCHARGE IN SECOND-FEET.			RUN-OFF.
	Maximum.	Minimum.	Mean.	Total in Acre-feet.
January..	1,700	705	1,007	61,916
February...	1,090	890	974	54,093
March..	1,165	1,025	1,117	68,684
April..	9,340	955	3,012	179,228
May...	9,880	4,595	6,571	404,590
June..	26,830	4,750	17,488	1,040,592
July..	15,730	8,380	12,702	781,022
August..	8,830	6,353	7,557	464,664
September.......................................	6,836	4,830	5,673	337,567
October...	5,738	4,315	5,066	311,496
November.......................................	4,250	1,480	3,231	192,259
December..	1,515	1,116	1,324	81,408
The year	....	....	....	3,977,519

MONTHLY DISCHARGE of North Saskatchewan River at Battleford, for 1914.

(Drainage area 27,100a square miles.)

MONTH.	DISCHARGE IN SECOND-FEET.				RUN-OFF.	
	Maximum.	Minimum	Mean.	Per square Mile.	Depth in inches on Drainage Area.	Total in Acre-feet.
January........................	2,060	825	1,193	0.044	0.05	73,353
February........................	1,285	1,020	1,132	0.042	0.04	62,868
March............................	1,360	1,215	1,299	0.048	0.06	79,875
April..........................	18,900	1,230	3,456	0.127	0.14	205,648
May............................	21,552	6,979	12,180	0.450	0.52	749,478
June............................	64,234	6,824	31,046	1.146	1.28	1,844,668
July............................	34,458	14,810	25,907	0.956	1.10	1,592,932
August..........................	17,513	10,773	13,675	0.505	0.58	840,842
September....	11,744	6,232	8,589	0.317	0.35	511,081
October........	8,164	5,665	6,942	0.256	0.30	426,848
November........................	5,564	2,296	4,199	0.155	0.17	249,839
December...	2,261	1,265	1,718	0.064	0.07	105,634
The Year.....	....	....	....	....	4.66	6,743,086

a The drainage area given in this table is only approximate. It must be remembered that the greater part of the run-off at this station is derived from the eastern slope of the Rocky Mountains and must not be used to base estimates of run-off on other streams in the same territory.

NORTH SASKATCHEWAN RIVER AT PRINCE ALBERT.

Location.—At the Canadian Northern Railway and traffic bridge on river lot 76, Prince Albert Settlement.

Records available.—October 2, 1911, to December 31, 1914.

Gauge.—Chain length 40.314 feet; elevation of zero maintained at 1,370.397 feet since establishment.

Bench-mark.—Brass bolt on top of the right abutment Canadian Northern Railway bridge, downstream side, marked P.W.D. B.M. 47. The elevation of this bench-mark is 1,403 502 feet above sea-level, established by Canadian Geodetic Surveys, 1913, and equals an assumed elevation by the Public Works Department in 1911 of 1,489.202 feet.

Channel.—Permanent.

Discharge measurements.—From bridge to gauge.

Winter flow.—Affected by ice.

Maximum flow.—During the floods of August, 1899, the river reached a gauge height of 25.9 feet, which would give a discharge of 160,000 sec.-ft.

Minimum flow.—On January 19, 1914, the lowest recorded discharge took place, when the flow was 850 sec.-ft.

Observer.—W. Moodie.

STREAM MEASUREMENTS, 1914

5 GEORGE V, A. 1915

DISCHARGE MEASUREMENTS of North Saskatchewan River at Prince Albert, in 1914.

Date.	Engineer.	Width.	Area of Section.	Mean Velocity.	Gauge Height.	Discharge.
		Feet.	*Sq. ft.*	*Ft. per sec.*	*Feet.*	*Sec.-ft.*
Jan. 2.............	W. H. Storey.............	600	2,616	0.56	3.90	1,454
Jan. 5.............	do	600	2,520	0.50	3.78	1,249
Jan. 9.............	do	600	2,520	0.50	3.68	1,272
Jan. 12–13	do	600	2,392	0.43	3.50	1,020
Jan. 19.............	do	600	2,260	0.38	3.41	850
Jan. 21.............	do	600	2,414	0.47	3.75	1,132
Jan. 23	do	600	2,430	0.48	3.84	1,174
Jan. 26	do	600	2,486	0.63	4.05	1,565
Jan. 28.............	do	600	2,440	0.63	4.06	1,529
Jan. 29.............	do	600	2,440	0.57	4.03	1,383
Jan. 30.............	do	600	2,394	0.59	4.00	1,420
Feb. 2.............	do	600	2,370	0.53	4.00	1,252
Feb. 4.............	do	600	2,394	0.54	4.06	1,290
Feb. 6.............	do	600	2,322	0.62	4.06	1,433
Feb. 9.............	do	600	2,278	0.51	4.01	1,165
Feb. 11.............	do	600	2,250	0.52	4.00	1,159
Feb. 12.............	do	600	2,250	0.48	4.01	1,086
Feb. 13.............	do	600	2,222	0.49	4.00	1,097
Feb. 16.............	do	600	2,202	0.49	4.02	1,077
Feb. 18	do	600	2,142	0.52	4.06	1,112
Feb. 20	do	600	2,152	0.52	4.15	1,120
Feb. 23.............	do	600	2,166	0.56	4.19	1,203
Feb. 25.............	do	600	2,138	0.56	4.21	1,200
Feb. 27.............	do	600	2,138	0.57	4.23	1,212
Mar. 2.............	do	600	2,138	0.58	4.26	1,244
Mar. 4.............	do	600	2,080	0.59	4.24	1,229
Mar. 6.............	do	600	2,080	0.60	4.29	1,237
Mar. 9.............	do	600	2,140	0.58	4.36	1,232
Mar. 11.............	do	600	2,114	0.59	4.32	1,245
Mar. 13.............	do	600	2,064	0.60	4.30	1,234
Mar. 16.............	do	600	2,110	0.60	4.29	1,277
Mar. 18.............	do	600	2,130	0.62	4.30	1,331
Mar. 20.............	do	600	2,114	0.64	4.34	1,353
Mar. 23.............	do	600	2,124	0.64	4.40	1,370
Mar. 25.............	do	600	2,106	0.65	4.37	1,361
Mar. 27.............	do	600	2,100	0.64	4.40	1,354
Mar. 30.............	do	600	2,150	0.64	4.49	1,370
April 1.............	do	600	2,154	0.65	4.46	1,402
April 3.............	do	600	2,174	0.67	4.51	1,453
April 6.............	do	600	2,184	0.68	4.54	1,492
April 8.............	do	600	2,242	0.68	4.60	1,524
April 10.............	do	600	2,248	0.72	4.61	1,617
April 13.............	do	600	2,358	0.78	4.70	1,839
April 15.............	do	600	2,514	0.81	4.73	2,036
April 16.............	do	605	2,635	0.88	4.86	2,319a
April 17.............	do	640	2,827	0.96	4.91	2,713a
April 18.............	do	660	3,223	1.07	4.97	3,448a
April 19.............	do	680	3,495	1.20	5.05	4,194a
April 20.............	do	772	4,445	1.75	5.87	7,778a
April 21.............	do	805	4,958	1.90	6.52	9,420a
April 22.............	do	775	4,475	1.75	5.91	7,831a
April 22–23.........	do	755	4,166	1.66	5.50	6,908
April 23.............	do	740	3,269	1.67	4.65	5,557a
April 23–24.........	do	732	3,232	1.69	4.60	5,466
May 25–27.........	do	820	6,164	2.45	6.88	15,130
June 24–25.........	do	864	8,669	4.38	11.10	37,939
July 20	do	856	7,294	3.67	9.54	27,144
Aug. 14–15.........	do	837	5,836	2.85	7.45	16,622
Sept. 10–11.........	do	805	4,754	2.39	6.17	11,372
Oct. 10–12.........	F. R. Steinberger............	790	4,087	1.97	5.41	8,040
Nov. 21–23.........	do	607	3,012	0.68	3.95	2,040
Dec. 10–12.........	do	632	2,353	1.48	4.75	3,494

a Estimated.

SESSIONAL PAPER No. 25c

DAILY GAUGE HEIGHT AND DISCHARGE of North Saskatchewan River at Prince Albert, for 1914.

DAY.	January.		February.		March.		April.		May.		June.	
	Gauge Height.	Dis- charge	Gauge Height.	Dis- charge	Gauge Height.	Dis- charge	Gauge Height.	Dis- charge	Gauge Height.	Dis- charge	Gauge Height	Dis- charge.
	Feet.	Sec.-ft.	Feet.	Sec.-ft.	Feet.	Sec -ft.	Feet.	Sec.-ft.	Feet.	Sec.-ft.	Feet.	Sec.-ft.
1...........	3 92a	1,420	3.95	1,265	4 23	1,230	4.46	1,402	6.98	14,588	6.39	11,958
2...........	3 90	1,454	4 00	1,252	4.26	1,244	4.49	1,430	6 76	13,580	6.24	11,334
3...........	3 86	1,390	4 03	1,270	4.27	1,235	4.51	1,453	6 66	13,134	6.42	12,086
4...........	3 84	1,340	4 06	1,290	4.27	1,229	4 53	1,465	6 23	11,293	6.66	13,134
5...........	3.78	1,249	4.06	1,380	4.27	1,235	4 54	1,480	5.92	10,076	6.60	12,870
6...........	3 74	1,230	4.07	1,433	4.29	1,237	4 55	1,492	5.75	9,445	6 29	11,539
7...........	3.74	1,250	4.03	1,350	4 33	1,235	4.57	1,510	5.61	8,936	6.12	10,850
8...........	3 72	1,265	4 03	1,190	4.36	1,233	4 60	1,524	5 50	8,550	5 98	10,304
9...........	3.67	1,272	4 01	1,165	4 36	1,232	4.60	1,595	5 58	8,830	5 63	9,008
10...........	3 61	1,190	4.00	1,160	4 34	1,235	4 62	1,617	5.49	8,516	5.62	8,972
11	3 59	1,150	4 00	1,159	4 32	1,245	4 65	1,690	5.60	8,900	5.60	8,900
12...........	3.52	1,070	4 01	1,086	4.32	1,240	4.68	1,770	6.25	11,375	10 69	35,196
13...........	3.47	1,020	4 00	1,097	4.30	1,234	4 70	1,839	7 59	17,520	13.84	57,752
14	3.48	1,010	3.99	1,095	4 31	1,250	4.72	1,925	7 68	17,978	14 55	63,290
15..	3 46	1,000	3 99	1,085	4 32	1,270	4.75	2,036	7.42	16,678	13.55	55,515
16...........	3 39	965	4 02	1,077	4 29	1,277	4 86	2,319f	7 18	15,526	12 60	48,430
17	3 34	920	4.03	1,085	4 28	1,295	4 91	2,713	6 83	13,898	12 00	44,100
18...........	3 33	870	4.06	1,112	4 30	1,331	4 97b	3,448	6 85	13,990	11 45	40,245
19...........	3 41	850	4 05	1,115	4 33	1,345	5 05c	4,194	7 10	15,150	11 64	41,560
20...........	3 68	1,020	4 15	1,120	4 34	1,353	5 84	7,778	7 38	16,484	11.17	38,349
21	3.75	1,132	4.14	1,145	4.37	1,360	6.50	9,420	7 28	16,004	10.90	36,560
22...........	3 80	1,155	4.17	1,165	4.40	1,370	5 89d	7,831g	7 08	15,056	10 67	35,068
23...........	3 84	1,174	4.19	1,203	4.40	1,370	4 68	5,902	6 90	14,220	10 88	36,430
24...........	3 94	1,250	4.21	1,202	4 35	1,340	4 58	5,614	6 77	13,625	11.07	37,682
25...........	4 01	1,400	4 21	1,200	4 38	1,361	4 85	6,415	6 69	13,266	11.14	38,148
26...........	4 04	1,565	4 21	1,205	4 38	1,355	5 14	7,342	6 93	14,358	11.12	38,014
27...........	4 04	1,560	4 23	1,212	4.40	1,354	5 22	7,606	6 87	14,082	10 90	36,560
28...........	4 06	1,529	4.22	1,202	4.43	1,355	5 34	8,006	7 04	14,868	10.78	35,780
29...........	4 03	1,383	......	......	4 48	1,360	6 36	11,832	6 83	13,898	10 69	35,196
30...........	4 00	1,420	......	......	4.49	1,370	7 25	15,860	6 76	13,580	10.75	35,585
31...........	3 95	1,360	......	......	4 49	1,380	......	......	6 60	12,870	......	......

a to b Ice conditions.
c Ice commenced to move.
d Stream clear of ice.
f to g Estimated.

5 GEORGE V, A. 1915

DAILY GAUGE HEIGHT AND DISCHARGE of North Saskatchewan River at Prince Albert, for 1914.—*Concluded.*

DAY.	July.		August.		September.		October.		November.		December.	
	Gauge Height.	Dis-charge.	Gauge Height.	Dis-charge.	Gauge Height.	Dis-charge	Gauge Height.	Dis-charge.	Gauge Height.	Dis-charge	Gauge Height.	Dis-charge.
	Feet.	*Sec.-ft.*	*Feet.*	*Sec.-ft.*	*Feet.*	*Sec.-ft.*	*Feet.*	*Sec.-ft.*	*Feet.*	*Sec.-ft.*	*Feet.*	*Sec.-ft.*
1	10.72	35,390	7.44	16,776	6 76	13,580	5.01	6,922	4.89	6,539	4.30	2,930
2	10.37	33,161	7.32	16,196	6 68	13,222	5.02	6,954	4.86	6,446	4 35	3,000
3	10.14	31,718	7.27	15,956	6.44	12,172	4.95	6,730	4.79	6,230	4.22	2,940
4	10 25	32,405	7 22	15,716	6.27	11,457	4.98	6,826	4.73	6,050	4.18	2,770
5	10.34	32,972	7 04	14,868	6.16	11,010	5.20	7,540	4.68	5,902	4.12	2,660
6	10.22	32,216	6.99	14,634	6.18	11,090	5.20	7,540	4.60	5,670	4.14	2,670
7	10.18	31,966	7.16	15,432	6 28	11,498	5.29	7,837	4.59	5,642	4.15	2,780
8	10 02	30,974	7.11	15,197	6.30	11,580	5.35	8,040	4.59	5,642	4.41	3,000
9	10 06	31,222	7.04	14,868	6 25	11,375	5.51	8,585	4.54	5,502	4.57	3,250
10	10.22	32,216	7.15	15,385	6 24	11,334	5.50	8,550	4.45	5,255	4.70	3,400
11	10 44	33,602	7.38	16,484	6 06	10,614	5.42	8,278	4.45	5,255a	4.75	3,500
12	10 67	35,068	7.57	17,420	5.94	10,152	5.35	8,040	4.30	4,860	4.75	3,490
13	10.76	35,650	7.54	17,270	5.94	10,152	5.35	8,040	4.48	4,336	4.75	3,450
14	10.71	35,325	7.56	17,370	6.16	11,010	5 37	8,108	4.42c	3,600	4.72	3,310
15	10 31	32,783	7.37	16,436	6.36	11,832	5 34	8,006	4.35c	2,750	4.65	3,170
16	10.04	31,098	7.29	16,052	6.30	11,580	5.34	8,006	4.28c	2,100	4.57	3,210
17	9.89	30,169	7.30	16,100	6.14	10,930	5 34	8,006	4.22c	1,670	4.52	3,370
18	9.55	28,115	6.95	14,450	6.10	10,770	5.44	8,346	4.16	1,730	4.35	3,060
19	9 43	27,407	6.69	13,266	6.18	11,090	5.54	8,690	4.10	1,850	4.35	3,000
20	9.55	28,115	6 43	12,129	6.06	10,614	5.60	8,900	4.09	2,000	4.23	2,750
21	9.90	30,230	6.31	11,622	5 87	9,889	5.61	8,936	4.00	2,140	4.11	2,450
22	9.97	30,664	6.30	11,580	5.77	9,519	5.54	8,690	3.96	2,040	4.05	2,100
23	9.86	29,986	6.38	11,916	5.63	9,008	5 41	8,244	3.90	1,890	4.00	1,920
24	9 53	27,997	6.56	12,694	5.53	8,655	5.30	7,870	4.10	2,030	3.95	1,750
25	9.03	25,108	6.74	13,490	5.41	8,244	5.20	7,540	4.10	2,170	3.90	1,610
26	8.57	22,601	6.86	14,036	5.30	7,870	5.10	7,210	4.05	2,350	3.85	1,340
27	8.34	21,388	6.75	13,535	5.20	7,540	5.07	7,114	4.15	2,470	3.85	1,190
28	8.32	21,284	6.51	12,474	5.12	7,276	5.00	6,890	4.20	2,570	3 75	1,050
29	8.56	22,548	6.44	12,172	5 06	7,082	4 98	6,826	4.25	2,680	3.75	1,090
30	8 30	21,180	6.51	12,474	5.03	6,986	4.96	6,762	4.30	2,700	3.65	1,130
31	7.80	18,590	6.64	13,046	......	....	4.92	6,634	......	....	3.65	1,200b

a to *b* Ice conditions.
c Gauge height interpolated.

MONTHLY DISCHARGE of North Saskatchewan River at Prince Albert, for 1914.

(Drainage area 59,900*a* square miles.)

MONTH.	DISCHARGE IN SECOND-FEET.				RUN-OFF.	
	Maximum.	Minimum.	Mean.	Per square Mile.	Depth in inches on Drainage Area.	Total in Acre-feet.
January	1,565	850	1,221	0.0204	0.02	75,072
February	1,433	1,077	1,191	0.0199	0.02	66,146
March	1,380	1,229	1,295	0.0216	0.02	79,627
April	15,860	1,402	4,350	0.0726	0.08	258,840
May	17,978	8,516	13,235	0.2210	0.26	813,770
June	63,290	8,900	30,347	0.5066	0.57	1,805,773
July	35,650	18,590	29,456	0.4918	0.52	1,811,172
August	17,420	11,580	14,550	0.2430	0.28	894,650
September	13,580	6,986	10,304	0.1720	0.19	613,136
October	8,936	6,634	7,763	0.1296	0.15	477,326
November	6,539	1,670	3,736	0.0624	0.07	222,310
December	3,500	1,050	2,533	0.0423	0.05	155,746
The year	....	....	....	....	2.23	7,273,568

a The drainage area given in this table is only approximate. It must be remembered that the greater part of the run-off at this station is derived from the eastern slope of the Rocky Mountains, and must not be used to base estimates of run-off on other streams in the same territory.

MISCELLANEOUS DISCHARGE MEASUREMENTS made in North Saskatchewan River drainage basin, in 1914.

Date.	Engineer.	Stream.	Location.	Width.	Area of Section.	Mean Velocity.	Dis- charge.
				Feet.	*Sq. feet.*	*Ft. per sec.*	*Sec.-ft.*
Feb. 3....	J. S. Tempest...	Brazeau River....	*a*19–45–10–5.....	165	158	1.40	222.0
Mar. 18..	do	do	SE. 24–45–10–5.	173	209	1.36	285.0
Mar. 19 ..	do	do	do	163	214	1.32	283 0
Mar. 23....	do	Buck Creek.......	SE. 23–47–6–5...	28	16	0.43	7.0
Nov. 24....	F. R. Steinberger	Little Red River...	49–27–2........	29	25	1.01	25 0
Feb. 3....	J. S. Tempest...	Nordegg River....	*a*SE. 24–45–10–5..	10	5	0.90	4.5
Mar. 18....	do	do	do	50	37	1.18	44.0
Mar. 19....	do	do	do	50	41	1.14	47.0
Feb. 4....	do	North Saskatche- wan River......	*a*SW. 26–45–9–5...	315	828	0.90	746.0
Mar. 20....	do	do	do	270	652	1.29	840.0
Mar. 21....	do	do	do	270	650	1.28	831.0
Mar. 25....	do	do	NW. 2–49–7–5...	113	462	2.86	1,324.0
Mar. 26....	do	do	do	113	457	2.44	1,124.0
Sept. 7....	P. H. Daniells...	do	do	380	2,148	3.70	7,950.0

a Approximate locations.

SOUTH SASKATCHEWAN RIVER DRAINAGE BASIN.

General Description.

The upper portion of this drainage basin will be dealt with in the descriptions of the drainage basins of Bow, Little Bow, Oldman, Waterton, Belly, and St. Mary Rivers. These streams are all conjoined at a point known as the Grand Forks, to form the South Saskatchewan River. From the Grand Forks the river flows in a north and easterly direction to its junction with the North Saskatchewan River, a short distance east of the city of Prince Albert. From this point onward the stream takes the name of the Saskatchewan River.

After the confluence of the Bow and Belly Rivers the stream receives comparatively little drainage, the principal tributaries being the Red Deer River, draining that portion of the basin between the North and the South Saskatchewan Rivers, and Sevenpersons River and Swiftcurrent Creek emptying into the main stream from the south. Descriptions of the drainage basin of all these streams are given elsewhere in this report.

The drainage basin of this stream is quite similar to that of all such streams which have their source in the mountains and flow across the prairies. The upper part of the basin has considerable fall, with rock and gravel formation and a good growth of timber. In contrast to this, the prairie section of the basin is sparsely wooded, except along the banks of the stream, and the rock formation changes to earth; also the stream is more apt to change its channel, especially in times of flood. The high water occurs in the hot months of summer, and is caused by the melting of the snow fields in the mountains. The low water occurs in the winter months when there is no melting snow to augment the stream flow.

In addition to the gauging stations on the tributaries, which are taken up in detail elsewhere in this report, there are two stations on the main stream. These stations are located at the cities of Medicine Hat and Saskatoon.

Up to the present the chief value of this stream has been as a source of municipal water supply. There are no irrigation schemes or water power developments on the main stream. The cities of Medicine Hat and Saskatoon derive their water supply from this stream. The South Saskatchewan is also being considered as a possible source of supply for the cities of Moosejaw and Regina. In this connection, surveys were carried out during 1913 by this Department and also by the Provincial Government.

SOUTH SASKATCHEWAN AT MEDICINE HAT.

Location.—On the NW. ¼ Sec. 31, Tp. 12, Rge. 5, W. 4th Mer., at the traffic bridge in the city of Medicine Hat.

Records available.—From May 31, 1911, to December 31, 1914.

Gauge.—Chain gauge. Elevation of zero of gauge (79.78) unchanged since establishment.

Bench-mark.—Permanent iron bench-mark; assumed elevation 100.00 feet.

Channel.—Shifting.

Discharge measurements.—Made from traffic bridge.

Observer.—E. King.

No. 25c—7½

5 GEORGE V, A. 1915

DISCHARGE MEASUREMENTS of South Saskatchewan River at Medicine Hat, in 1914.

Date.	Engineer.	Width.	Area of Section.	Mean Velocity.	Gauge Height.	Discharge.
		Feet.	*Sq. ft.*	*Ft. per sec.*	*Feet.*	*Sec.-ft.*
Jan. 9............ ...	R. Palmer..	540	2,287	1.48	3.30	3,396
Jan. 23............	do	490	1,728	1.02	2.30	1,767
Feb. 11-12.	E. W. W. Hughes	414	2,080	0.69	2.58	1,447
Mar. 3............ ..	do	387	2,340	0.80	2.85	1,981
Mar. 18............	F. R. Burfield	511	3,186	1.94	3.10	6,184
April 22............	H. D. St. A. Smith.........	656	3,562	1.84	3.24	6,554
May 13........ ..	H. S. Kerby............. .	590	4,857	2.42	5.06	11,793
June 8............	do	746	5,576	3.56	7.51	19,485
June 30...... ..	do	735	5,241	3.20	6.09	16,612
July 29...... ..	do	505	3,696	2.15	3.81	7,953
Aug. 26	do	510	3,664	1.93	3.70	7,076
Sept. 17...... ..	do	425	2,902	1.24	2.35	3,616
Oct. 13...... ..	do	590	3,743	2.10	3.89	7,885
Oct. 30...... . .	do	495	3,560	1.90	3.53	6,780
Nov. 11............	J. Coughey...............	513	3,618	1.78	3.54	6,577
Nov. 23............	do	347	3,203	1.61	3.20	5,162
Dec. 16............	do	443	2,548	0.55	2.40	1,392

DAILY GAUGE HEIGHT AND DISCHARGE of South Saskatchewan River at Medicine Hat,
for 1914.

DAY.	January.		February.		March.		April.		May.		June.	
	Gauge Height.	Dis-charge	Gauge Height.	Dis-charge	Gauge Height.	Dis-charge.	Gauge Height.	Dis-charge	Gauge Height.	Dis-charge.	Gauge Height.	Dis-charge.
	Feet.	*Sec.-ft.*	*Feet.*	*Sec.-ft*	*Feet.*	*Sec.-ft.*	*Feet.*	*Sec.-ft.*	*Feet.*	*Sec.-ft.*	*Feet.*	*Sec.-ft.*
1............	1.55	2,900b	2.26	1,530	2.79	1,860	2.34	4,300	3 81	8,180	5.35	14,125
2............	1.85	3,100	2 23	1,420	2.82	1,900	2.33	4,275	3 90	8,450	5.79	16,250
3............	1.90	3,250	2.30	1,330	2.84	1,981	2.31	4,225	3 34	6,800	5.20	13,450
4............	2.30	3,400	2 26	1,310	2.99	2,080	1.54	2,760	4.53	10,655	6.22	18,400
5............	3.20	3,500	2 41	1,360	3.44	2,500	1.54	2,760	5.28	15,250		
6............	3.25	3,580	2.38	1,460	3.39	2,620	2.68	5,150	5.02	12,640	7.34	24,200
7............	3.50	3,580	2.51	1,470	3.19	2,690	2.16	3,920	5.07	12,865	7.60	25,500
8............	3.46	3,540	2.48	1,470	2.85	3,000	1.52	2,730	4.99	12,460	7.54	25,000
9............	3.25	3,396	2.61	1,570	2.79	3,120	1.96	3,520	4.89	12,060	7.49	24,600
10	3.10	3,240	2.78	1,620	2.92	3,300	3.16	6,350	4.62	10,970	7.25	23,150
11	3.00	3,000	2.68	1,510	2.99	3,600	2.80	5,450	4.38	10,130	6.59	19,300
12.	2.85	2,740	2.47	1,490	3.70	3,800	2.70	5,200	5.16	13,270	6.32	17,750
13	2.80	2,970	2.43	1,570	3.20	4,300	2.73	5,275	5.25	13,675	5.97	16,000
14	2.65	2,860	2.63	1,670	3.00	4,600	2.10	3,800	5.02	12,640	5.80	15,200
15..	2.10	2,910	2.63	1,800	2.60	4,900	2.60	4,950	5.24	13,810	5.79	15,155
16............	3.00	2,820	2.83	1,800	2.00	5,150	2.96	5,850	5.16	13,270	6.73	19,800
17	2.60	2,600	2.53	1,600	3.00	5,600	3.28	6,650	5.56	15,100	7.05	21,400
18............	2.80	2,400	2.88	1,560	2.80	6,184	3.29	6,675	5.90	16,800	7.24	22,350
19....	2.70	2,360	2.23	1,570	1.65	5,000	3.36	6,850	6.20	18,390	7.50	23,650
20............	2.70	2,260	2.18	1,580	1.50	4,900	2.87	5,625	6.57	20,150	7.76	24,950
21	2.75	2,080	2.28	1,600	1.25	4,800	2.70	5,200	6.54	20,000	7.86	25,450
22............	2.20	1,940	2.29	1,600	1.35a	4,700	3.13	6,275	6.61	20,350	7.38	23,050
23............	2.30	1,767	2.52	1,610	1.45a	4,750	3.91	8,480	6.30	18,800	7.40	23,150
24............	2.15	1,740	2.54	1,650	1.55a	4,800	3.60	7,550	6.31	18,850	7.11	21,700
25	2.17	1,720	2.64	1,700	1.65a	4,900	3.62	7,610	6.03	17,450	6.75	19,900
26	2.20	1,670	2.84	1,760	1.75a	4,800	3.55	7,400	5.97	17,150	6.21	17,200
27........ ...	2.20	1,590	2.84	1,720	1.85a	4,750	3.62	7,610	6.36	19,100	6.03	16,300
28	2.18	1,480	2.89	1,810	1.95a	4,700	3.80	8,150	6.28	18,700	6.20	17,150
29............	2.15	1,490	......	......	2.05a	4,600	3.87	8,360	6.45	19,550	6.47	18,500
30.	2.20	1,530	......	......	2.15a	4,500	4.11	9,185	6.09	17,750	6.18	17,050
31.	2.25	1,540	......	... ...	2.25a	4,300b	......	......	5.97	17,100	......	......

a Gauge height interpolated.
b Ice conditions Jan. 1 to Mar. 31.

SESSIONAL PAPER No. 25c

DAILY GAUGE HEIGHT AND DISCHARGE of South Saskatchewan River at Medicine Hat, for 1914.
—*Concluded.*

DAY.	July. Gauge Height.	July. Dis- charge	August. Gauge Height.	August. Dis- charge	September. Gauge Height.	September. Dis- charge	October. Gauge Height.	October. Dis- charge	November. Gauge Height.	November. Dis- charge	December. Gauge Height.	December. Dis- charge.
	Feet.	*Sec.-ft.*	*Feet.*	*Sec.-ft.*	*Feet.*	*Sec.-ft.*	*Feet.*	*Sec.-ft.*	*Feet.*	*Sec.-ft.*	*Feet.*	*Sec.-ft.*
1	6.07	16,500	3.70	7,100	3.15	5,625	2.89	4,975	3.46	6,400	2 99	4,300
2	5.81	15,245	3.60	6,800	3.04	5,350	2.93	5,075	3.25	5,875	2.58	4,025
3	5.79	15,155	3.56	6,680	3.04	5,375	2.95	5,125	3.35	6,125	2 36	3,700
4	5.69	14,705	3.52	6,560	3.02	5,300	2.81	4,775	3.20	5,750	1.02	3,400
5	5.96	15,950	3.62	6,860	3.00	5,250	3.01	5,275	3.12	5,550	1.40	3,200
6	6.16	16,950	3.56	6,680	2.90	5,000	3.17	5,675	3.34	6,100	1.26	3,100
7	6.34	17,850	3.52	6,560	2.78	4,700	3.52	6,560	3.48	6,450	0.58	2,775
8	6.69	19,600	3.52	6,560	2.85	4,875	3.53	6,740	3.57	6,710	0.79	2,475
9	6.69	19,600	3.72	7,160	2.81	4,775	3.33	6,075	3.53	6,590	1.13	2,250
10	6.47	18,500	3.46	6,400	2.76	4,650	3.38	6,200	3.62	6,860	1.20	2,050
11	6.24	17,350	3.52	6,560	2.72	4,550	3.95	7,875	3.50	6,500	1.50	1,850
12	6.07	16,500	3.59	6,770	2.71	4,525	3.10	5,500	3.34	6,100	1.56	1,680
13	5.94	15,850	3.59	6,770	2.68	4,450	3.66	6,980	3.52	6,560a	1.68	1,500
14	5.79	15,155	3.42	6,300	2.36	3,650	3.63	6,890	3.21	6,100	2.03	1,420
15	5.63	14,435	3.27	5,925	1.86	2,420	3.64	6,920	3.29	5,200	2.25	1,380
16	5.75	14,975	2.94	5,100	2.62	4,300	3.48	6,450	2.69	4,100	2.32	1,392
17	5.80	15,200	3.28	5,950	2.34	3,600	3.76	7,280	2.35	4,175	2.30	1,425
18	5.81	15,245	3.12	5,550	2.45	3,875	4.47	9,695	1.79	4,600	2.52	1,500
19	5.77	15,065	3.41	6,275	2.38	3,700	4.91	11,340	1.60	5,000	2.56	1,580
20	5.60	14,300	3.65	6,950	2.25	3,375	5.25	12,725	2.34	5,100	2.64	1,670
21	6.07	16,500	3.73	7,190	2.47	3,925	5.14	12,260	4.79	5,150	2.73	1,725
22	5.81	15,245	3.90	7,700	2.30	3,500	4.88	11,220	2.95	5,160	2.88	1,790
23	4.68	10,430	3.74	7,220	2.36	3,650	4.83	11,020	3.21	5,162	2.98	1,790
24	4.94	11,460	3.72	7,160	2.57	4,175	4.53	9,905	3.21	5,160	3.08	1,760
25	4.73	10,620	3.42	6,300	2.93	5,075	4.37	9,345	4.94	5,125	3.12	1,750
26	4.53	9,905	3.75	7,250	3.07	5,425	4.05	8,225	4.23	5,110	3.13	1,830
27	3.97	7,945	3.62	6,860	3.00	5,250	3.95	7,875	3.20	5,110	3.11	2,015
28	4.06	8,260	3.62	6,860	2.79	4,725	3.84	7,520	3.08	5,100	3.23	2,350
29	4.12	8,470	3.45	6,375	2.85	4,875	3.56	6,680	3.12	5,000	3.26	2,600
30	3.87	7,610	3.33	6,075	2.76	4,650	3.62	6,560	2.86	4,750	3.39	2,700
31	3.74	7,220	3.22	5,800	......	......	3.52	6,560	......	......	3.45	2,775a

a Ice conditions Nov. 13 to Dec. 31.

MONTHLY DISCHARGE of South Saskatchewan River at Medicine Hat, for 1914.

(Drainage area 22,700 square miles.)

MONTH.	DISCHARGE IN SECOND-FEET. Maximum.	Minimum.	Mean.	Per square Mile.	RUN-OFF. Depth in inches on Drainage Area.	Total in Acre-feet.
January	3,580	1,480	2,547	0.112	0.13	156,608
February	1,810	1,310	1,576	0.069	0.07	87,527
March	6,184	1,860	4,022	0.177	0.20	247,304
April	9,185	2,730	5,754	0.253	0.28	342,386
May	20,350	6,800	14,679	0.647	0.75	902,576
June	25,500	13,450	19,831	0.874	0.98	1,180,026
July	19,600	7,220	14,122	0.622	0.72	868,342
August	7,700	5,100	6,590	0.290	0.33	405,200
September	5,625	2,420	4,486	0.198	0.22	266,934
October	12,725	4,775	7,600	0.335	0.39	467,306
November	6,860	4,100	5,556	0.245	0.27	330,605
December	4,300	1,380	2,251	0.099	0.11	138,410
The year	......	......	......	......	4.45	5,393,224

5 GEORGE V, A. 1915

SOUTH SASKATCHEWAN RIVER AT SASKATOON.

Location.—On SW. ¼ Sec. 28, Tp. 36, Rge. 5, W. 3rd Mer., at the Canadian Northern Railway bridge in the city of Saskatoon.

Records available.—May 27, 1911, to December 31, 1914.

Gauge.—Chain. *E*levation of zero maintained at 1,527.59 feet since establishment.

Bench-mark.—Painted mark on side of downstream end of left abutment; elevation 1,553.35 feet, referred to a waterworks bench-mark of the city of Saskatoon on top of hydrant 300 feet northeast, elevation 1,571.31 feet.

Channel.—Permanent.

Discharge measurements.—From bridge.

Observer.—A. B. Hay.

DISCHARGE MEASUREMENTS of South Saskatchewan River at Saskatoon, in 1914.

Date.	Engineer.	Width.	Area of Section.	Mean Velocity.	Gauge Height.	Discharge.
		Feet.	*Sq. ft.*	*Ft. per sec.*	*Feet.*	*Sec.-ft.*
Jan. 12............	F. R. Steinberger...........	685	2,136	1.10	4.05	2,343
Jan. 30-31, Feb. 2....	do	682	1,994	1.18	4.23	2,352
Feb. 18, 19, 20.......	do	661	1,800	1.11	3.92	1,996
Mar. 9, 10, 11........	do	649	1,961	1.44	4.43	2,931
April 16-17.........	do	509	3,043	1.78	5.16	8,450
April 28-30.........	W. H. Storey	570	3,321	2.56	5.08	8,511
June 5, 6............	do	712	5,088	4.47	7.80	22,646
July 2	do	751	6,047	4.80	8.85	28,990
July 17	do	724	5,425	4.18	8.21	22,762
Aug. 12-13...........	do	532	3,289	2.83	4.90	9,332
Sept. 8, 9...........	do	507	3,030	2.76	4.40	8,370
Oct. 20-21...........	F. R. Steinberger...........	564	3,127	2.83	5.09	8,854
Dec. 2-3.............	do	677	3,118	2.14	5.42	6,662
Dec. 18, 19, 21.......	do	588	1,358	1.46	3.19	1,979

DAILY GAUGE HEIGHT AND DISCHARGE of South Saskatchewan River at Saskatoon, for 1914.

DAY.	January.		February.		March.		April.		May.		June.	
	Gauge Height.	Dis- charge.	Gauge Height.	Dis- charge.	Gauge Height.	Dis- charge.	Gauge Height.	Dis- charge.	Gauge Height.	Dis- charge.	Gauge Height.	Dis- charge.
	Feet.	Sec.-ft.	Feet.	Sec.-ft.	Feet.	Sec.-ft.	Feet.	Sec.-ft.	Feet.	Sec.-ft.	Feet.	Sec.-ft.
1	4.09	3,160a	4.15	2,370	4.15	2,200	6.34	3,620	5.48	9,970	7.38	20,130
2	4.21	3,150	4.15	2,350	4.17	2,300	6.12	3,650	5.37	9,545	7.40	20,250
3	4.26	3,200	4.16	2,330	4.19	2,370	6.16	3,690	5.20	8,950	7 57	21,270
4	4.33	3,250	4.12	2,300	4.19	2,460	6.04	3,740	5.20	8,950	7.72	22,170
5	4.35	3,250	4.14	2,280	4.25	2,580	5.86	3,800	5.10	8,600	7.82	22,770
6	4.13	3,240	4.15	2,290	4.30	2,660	5.64	3,850	5.00	8,300	7.54	21,090
7	4.06	3,170	4.13	2,300	4.38	2,740	5.44	3,940	5.20	8,950	7.42	20,370
8	4.11	3,150	4.10	2,300	4.40	2,800	5.29	4,150	5.25	9,125	7.02	17,970
9	4.17	3,150	4.09	2,280	4.42	2,870	5.18	4,650	5.08	8,540	7.02	17,970
10	4.11	3,080	4.09	2,250	4.48	2,930	5.47	5,050	4.92	8,060	6.77	16,585
11	4.08	2,670	4.08	2,200	4.38	2,920	6.22	5,550	4.70	7,500	7 02	17,970
12	4.05	2,340	4.08	2,160	4.21	2,880	6.64	6,150	5.05	8,450	7.87	23,070
13	4.00	2,320	4.08	2,130	4.26	2,780	8.57	6,690	5.65	10,675	8.87	29,124
14	3.96	2,320	4.08	2,090	4.28	2,770	10.31	7,100	6.08	12,790	9.17	31,011
15	4.08	2,350	4.05	2,050	4.34	2,810	7.70	7,600	6.22	13,560	8.93	29,499
16	4.23	2,400	4.07	2,030	4.40	2,870	5.69	8,500a	6.30	14,000	.92	29,436
17	4.23	2,470	4.09	2,010	4.52	3,000	4.81	7,775	6.40	14,550	52	26,970
18	4.25	2,480	4.02	2,000	4.66	3,160	4.70	7,500	6.27	13,835	.54	27,090
19	4.29	2,440	3.93	1,996	4.75	3,320	4.40	6,900	6.59	15,595	57	27,270
20	4.28	2,420	3.91	1,950	4.83	3,420	4.32	6,780	6.74	16,420	8.55	27,150
21	4.32	2,470	3.85	1,890	4.90	3,470	4.25	6,675	6.62	15,760	8.33	25,830
22	4.45	2,530	3.83	1,860	4.96	3,460	4.40	6,900	6.66	15,980	8.62	27,574
23	4.68	2,610	3.84	1,870	5.07	3,450	4.55	7,200	6.60	15,650	9.26	31,578
24	4.77	2,620	3.95	1,900	5.38	3,430	4.80	7,750	6.81	16,805	9.53	33,229
25	4.71	2,610	4.04	2,000	5.80	3,400	4.90	8,000	7.06	18,210	9.74	34,616
26	4.61	2,590	3.93	2,120	5.98	3,400	5.08	8,540	7.42	20,370	9.82	35,128
27	4.50	2,550	3.96	2,160	6.12	3,450	5.14	8,740	7.78	22,530	9.81	35,064
28	4.43	2,480	4.00	2,170	6.00	3,500	4.98	8,240	7.91	23,370	9.67	34,168
29	4.30	2,450	......	......	6.14	3,560	4.83	7,825	7.91	23,370	9.45	32,775
30	4.22	2,430	......	......	6.33	3,600	5.22	9,020	7.58	21,330	9.34	32,082
31	4.14	2,420	......	......	6.52	3,630	......	......	7.43	20,430	......	.....

a Ice conditions Jan. 1 to April 16.

5 GEORGE V, A. 1915

DAILY GAUGE HEIGHT AND DISCHARGE of South Saskatchewan River at Saskatoon, for 1914.
—*Concluded.*

DAY.	July.		August.		September.		October.		November.		December.	
	Gauge Height.	Dis-charge	Gauge Height.	Dis-charge.	Gauge Height.	Dis-charge	Gauge Height.	Dis-charge	Gauge Height.	Dis-charge.	Gauge Height.	Dis-charge.
	Feet.	*Sec.-ft.*	*Feet.*	*Sec.-ft.*	*Feet.*	*Sec.-ft.*	*Feet.*	*Sec.-ft.*	*Feet.*	*Sec.-ft.*	*Feet.*	*Sec.-ft.*
1..........	8.91	28,752	6 28	14,160	4.98	9,550	3 65	7,077	6.10	13,350	4 86	6,560
2..........	8.70	28,070	6.12	13,440	4 91	9,375	3 70	7,150	5 88	12,420	5 15	6,640
3..........	8.26	25,410	5 73	11,837	4 83	9,192	4.00	7,600	5 68	11,655	5.75	6,600
4..........	8 20	25,050	5.54	11,165	4.78	9,080	4 40	8,300	5.50	11,025	6.52	6,320
5..........	8 32	25,770	5 43	10,815	4 68	8,860	4.37	8,240	5 30	10,425	6.68	5,880
6..........	8.14	24,690	5.27	10,343	4 52	8,540	4.35	8,200	5.15	10,012	6.10	5,480
7..........	8.03	24,030	5 19	10,123	4.46	8,420	4.36	8,220	5.10	9,875	5.35	5,100
8..........	7.92	23,370	5.10	9,875	4.45	8,400	4.39	8,280	5 06	9,765	4 92	4,700
9..........	7 85	22,950	4.94	9,450	4.33	8,160	4.40	8,300	4 88	9,305	4 72	4,280
10........ ..	7.77	22,470	4.84	9,215	4.27	8,048	4.57	8,640	4.72	8,945	4 50	3,800
11..........	7.76	22,410	4.88	9,305	4.20	7,925	4.62	8,740	4.65	8,800	4.20	3,400
12..........	8.00	23,850	4.88	9,305	4.13	7,802	4.58	8,660	4.62	8,740	4.00	2,920
13..........	8.34	25,890	4.90	9,350	4.09	7,735	4.62	8,740	4.50	8,500	3.90	2,590
14...	8.67	27,884	4.83	9,192	4.05	7,675	4.80	9,125	4.00	7,600	3.60	2,200
15......	8.69	28,008	4.84	9,215	4.13	7,802	5.13	9,957	3.12	6,328	3.45	1,900
16..........	8.58	27,330	4.90	9,350	4.21	7,942	5 19	10,123	2.85	5,970	3.25	1,860
17..........	8.17	24,870	4.90	9,350	4.24	7,995	5 05	9,737	2 72	5,300a	3.25	2,020
18..........	8.10	24,450	4.77	9,057	4.18	7,895	5.10	9,875	3.65	5,550	3.20	2,240
19..........	7.90	23,250	4.82	9,170	4.12	7,785	5 25	10,287	4.65	6,070	3.20	1,980
20..........	7.79	22,590	4.89	9,328	4.10	7,750	5 00	9,600	5.64	6,620	3.25	1,900
21.	7.46	20,610	4.80	9,125	4.02	7,630	5.11	9,902	5.50	7,100	3.22	1,750
22..........	7.43	20,430	4.64	8,780	3.94	7,510	5.23	10,232	5.20	7,070	3.28	1,700
23..........	7.44	20,490	4.50	8,500	3.82	7,330	5 36	10,605	5 20	7,000	3.25	1,650
24..........	7.50	20,850	4.44	8,380	3.67	7,106	5 58	11,305	5 45	7,000	3.25	1,570
25..........	7.52	20,970	4.53	8,560	3.61	7,020	5 83	12,220	5.42	6,900	3.32	1,580
26..........	7.34	19,830	4.66	8,820	3.67	7,106	6 14	13,350	5.48	6,700	3.45	1,700
27..........	7.08	18,353	4.74	8,990	3.70	7,150	6.46	15,010	5.30	6,380	3.60	1,870
28..........	6.76	16,540	4.85	9,237	3.72	7,180	6.73	16,382	5.36	6,720	3.65	2,040
29..........	6.46	15,000	5.00	9,600	3.75	7,225	6 72	16,330	5 08	6,980	3.70	2,150
30..........	6.40	14,725	5.10	9,875	3.70	7,150	6.47	15,057	4.85	6,420	3.75	2,250
31..........	6.38	14,630	5.04	9,710	......	......	6.32	14,345	... ...	......	3.80	2,700a

a Ice conditions Nov. 17 to Dec. 31.

MONTHLY DISCHARGE of South Saskatchewan River at Saskatoon, for 1914.

(Drainage area 64,500a square miles.)

MONTH.	DISCHARGE IN SECOND-*FEET.*				RUN-OFF.	
	Maximum.	Minimum.	Mean.	Per square Mile.	Depth in inches on Drainage Area.	Total in Acre-feet.
January..........................	3,250	2,320	2,702	0.042	0.05	166,140
February.........................	2,370	1,860	2,130	0.033	0.03	118,290
March............................	3,630	2,200	3,038	0.047	0.05	186,798
April.............................	9,020	3,620	6,319	0.098	0.11	376,010
May..............................	23,370	7,500	13,876	0.215	0.25	853,212
June.............................	35,128	16,585	26,375	0.409	0.46	1,569,425
July.............................	28,752	14,630	22,694	0.352	0.41	1,395,428
August...........................	14,160	8,380	9,762	0.151	0.17	600,242
September........................	9,550	7,020	7,945	0.123	0.14	472,760
October..........................	16,382	7,077	10,315	0.160	0.18	634,230
November........................	13,350	5,300	8,151	0.126	0.14	485,019
December........................	6,640	1,570	3,204	0.050	0.06	197,006
The year.........................	....	....	....	....	2,05	7,054,560

a The drainage area given in this table is only approximate. It must be remembered that the greater part of the run-off at this station is derived from the eastern slope of the Rocky Mountains, and must not be used to base estimates of run-off on other streams in the same territory.

SESSIONAL PAPER No. 25c

RED DEER RIVER DRAINAGE BASIN.

General Description.

The Red Deer River rises in the Sawback Range of the Rockies in the northern portion of the Rocky Mountain Park, near the boundary between the provinces of Alberta and British Columbia. *I*t flows eastward for about 40 miles, then northeastward for 70 or 80 miles to a point near Red Deer, Alberta. From here the river flows in a southeasterly and easterly direction to its junction with the South Saskatchewan River just east of the 4th Mer., in Tp. 22, Rge. 28, W. 3rd Mer. *I*t has a length of approximately 400 miles.

The valley of the Red Deer is wide and deep, the banks being very rough and cut up with a large number of deep coulees, draining into the river. Near its source the basin is well timbered, and a good growth of timber is found along its banks for some distance out into the prairie. Seams of coal well suited for domestic use are found in the valley, and form the principal source of fuel supply for the settlers along the stream in the prairie section.

The river carries a considerable supply of water at all times of the year, but the volume is subject to sudden variations, due to the melting of snow in the mountains and to heavy summer rains.

Of the tributaries of the Red Deer, the most important are Panther River, near its head, Little Red Deer and Medicine Rivers entering in Tp. 36, Rge. 1, W. 5th Mer., and Rosebud River emptying into it in Tp. 28, Rge. 19, W. 4th Mer. In addition, there are numerous small streams draining into the main river in the western portion of the basin. From the mouth of the Rosebud River eastward there is very little drainage into the river.

Very little hydrometric work has been done in this basin as yet. A gauging station was established on the Red Deer River near *I*nnisfail in 1910, but an observer could not be secured, and only periodic discharge measurements were obtained at this station. In December, 1911, another station was established at the town of Red Deer, and continuous records have been obtained since then. Of the tributaries of the Red Deer River, Berry and Blood *I*ndian Creeks are the only ones which have been given any attention. These small creeks, which drain into the river in the prairie section, have a few small irrigation rights registered against them. Gauging stations were established on them in 1911, but owing to the high cost of obtaining data they were abandoned in 1913.

RED DEER RIVER AT RED DEER.

Location.—On the SE. ¼ Sec. 20, Tp. 38, Rge. 27, W. 4th Mer., at the steel traffic bridge in the town of Red Deer.

Records available.—January 1, 1912, to December 31, 1914.

Gauge.—Chain. Length of chain from bottom of weight to marker is 29.52 feet. Zero elevation of gauge maintained at 84.40 feet since established.

Bench-mark.—Marked with white paint on northwest face of north abutment; assumed elevation, 100.00 feet.

Channel.—Slightly shifting.

Discharge measurements.—Made from bridge.

Winter flow.—From November to *A*pril river is frozen over, and measurements are made at a point about one-half mile below the bridge.

Observer.—C. H. Snell.

Observer.—W. Austin.

STREAM MEASUREMENTS, 1914

5 GEORGE V, A. 1915

DISCHARGE MEASUREMENTS of Red Deer River at Red Deer, in 1914.

Date.	Engineer.	Width.	Area of Section.	Mean Velocity.	Gauge Height.	Discharge.
		Feet.	Sq. ft.	Ft. per sec.	Feet.	Sec.-ft.
Jan. 20............	J. S. Tempest............	190a	319	0.96	4.89	309
Feb. 24............	do	180a	284	1.04	5.03	306
Mar. 3	do	193a	298	1.18	5.04	351
Mar. 31.....	do	257a	365	1.11	4.88	404
April 23	do	356	673	2.27	4.26	1,532
April 28............	G. J. Smith and J. M. Paul..	239	612	2.00	3.90	1,224
May 21	J. M. Paul............	268	754	2.52	4.46	1,902
June 9............	G. R. Elliott	337	1,157	3.54	5.89	4,093
July 2............	J. M. Paul............	333	1,023	3.20	5.36	3,274
July 16............	do	324	939	2.83	5.00	2,655
Aug. 13............	do	243	603	1.96	3.90	1,186
Aug. 25............	do	239	613	1.95	3.88	1,195
Sept. 12............	do	239	630	1.87	3.90	1,180
Oct. 1............	do	236	552	1.85	3.74	1,024
Oct. 17............	do	243	682	2.26	4.29	1,544
Nov. 9............	H. S. Kerby....	225	524	1.36	3.45	715
Dec. 1.	R. J. McGuinness............	272a	547	1.26	4.51	690
Dec. 18............	do	249a	313	0.88	3.63	274

a Measured below regular station.

DAILY GAUGE HEIGHT AND DISCHARGE of Red Deer River at Red Deer, for 1914.

DAY.	January.		February.		March.		April.		May.		June.	
	Gauge Height.	Dis-charge	Gauge Height.	Dis-charge	Gauge Height.	Dis-charge	Gauge Height.	Dis-charge	Gauge Height.	Dis-charge	Gauge Height.	Dis-charge
	Feet.	Sec.-ft.	Feet.	Sec.-ft.	Feet.	Sec.-ft.	Feet.	Sec.-ft.	Feet.	Sec.-ft.	Feet.	Sec.-ft.
1..........	4.28	195a	4.89	302	5.06	338	4.97	406	3.81	1,110	4.00	1,300
2..........	4.42	210	4.93	296	5.01	345	4.97	407	3.91	1,210	4.22	1,544
3..........	4.47	220	4.91	289	5.02	351	4.97	408	4.16	1,472	4.52	1,921
4..........	4.54	235	4.96	280	5.04	357	4.97	410	4.40	1,765	5.26	3,087
5..........	4.63	250	4.96	271	5.07	360	5.14	409	4.66	2,114	5.44	3,402
6..........	4.67	260	4.99	270	5.08	365	5.33	404	4.87	2,442	5.06	2,747
7..........	4.67	266	4.95	270	5.03	361	5.58	399	4.90	2,490	5.04	2,714
8..........	4.79	286	4.90	275	4.99	355	5.94	394	4.84	2,394	6.44	5,349
9..........	4.80	290	4.97	282	5.06	362	6.17	390	4.74	2,234	5.94	4,340
10	4.74b	285	4.95	290	5.05	361	6.11	390	4.64	2,086	5.86	4,180
11..........	4.68b	280	4.95	280	5.04	358	5.88	390	4.56	1,974	5.92	4,300
12	4.61	276	4.95	283	5.03	355	5.83	410	4.46	1,843	6.20	4,860
13..........	4.64	279	4.95	286	5.00	350	5.38	450	4.40	1,765	6.37	5,202
14..........	4.67	281	4.98	292	5.01	355	5.04	490	4.26	1,592	6.54	5,559
15	4.69	286	4.99	300	5.13	372	5.40	471	4.30	1,640	6.51	5,496
16..........	4.77	295	4.99	307	5.19	397	5.58	450	4.63	2,072	6.37	5,202
17....	4.75	294	4.99	315	5.29	419	4.85	890	5.10	2,815	6.26	4,980
18..........	4.72	291	5.00	315	5.29	425	4.73	1,280	4.82	2,362	6.04	4,540
19..........	4.80b	300	5.02	307	5.24	420	4.77	1,750a	4.62	2,058	5.82	4,103
20	4.89	309	4.94	295	5.21	415	4.76	2,266	4.51	1,908	5.66	3,799
21.... ...	4.84	301	5.05	315	5.07	401	4.46	1,843	4.47	1,856	5.48	3,474
22	4.85	303	5.07	314	5.11	404	4.33	1,676	4.42	1,791	5.32	3,189
23..........	4.79	290	4.99	305	5.19	410	4.24	1,568	4.48	1,869	5.11	2,832
24..........	4.77	288	5.03	306	5.11	400	4.23	1,556	4.54	1,947	4.97	2,602
25..........	4.77	288	5.03	310	5.11	395	4.15	1,460	4.59	2,016	4.97	2,602
26	4.77	287	5.08	320	5.02	392	4.05	1,350	4.88	2,458	5.22	3,019
27..........	4.82	294	5.08	325	4.87	386	3.97	1,270	4.57	1,988	5.41	3,348
28..........	4.71	281	5.08	330	4.83	381	3.90	1,200	4.35	1,700	5.54	3,582
29..........	4.85	290	......	......	4.85	388	3.84	1,140	4.20	1,520	5.46	3,438
30	4.89	305	......	......	4.88	398	3.84	1,140	4.07	1,370	5.41	3,348
31..........	4.88	304	......	......	4.95	404	......	......	3.98	1,280	......	......

a Ice conditions Jan. 1 to April 19.
b Gauge heights interpolated.

Monthly Discharge of Red Deer River at Red Deer, for 1912-13.

(Drainage area 4,500 square miles.)

MONTH.	DISCHARGE IN SECOND-FEET.				RUN-OFF.	
	Maximum.	Minimum	Mean.	Per square Mile.	Depth in inches on Drainage Area.	Total in Acre-feet.
1912.						
January	264	222	238	0.053	0.06	14,635
February	313	248	274	0.061	0.06	15,764
March	1,425	246	401	0.089	0.10	22,270
April	2,698	1,290	1,919	0.426	0.48	114,190
May	7,040	1,705	3,954	0.879	1.01	243,124
June	13,532	1,450	3,953	0.878	0.98	235,220
July	19,043	3,232	10,091	2.240	2.58	620,448
August	7,010	3,340	4,985	1.110	1.28	306,515
September	8,744	2,908	4,532	1.010	1.13	269,070
October	4,353	1,585	2,721	0.605	0.70	167,311
November	1,765	560	1,290	0.287	0.32	76,760
December	867	434	545	0.121	0.14	33,511
The year	....	....	....	....	8.84	2,119,418
1913.						
January	436	373	417	0.093	0.11	25,640
February	431	360	396	0.088	0.09	21,993
March	440	370	410	0.091	0.10	25,210
April	10,236	460	3,887	0.864	0.96	231,292
May	9,477	1,262	4,101	0.911	1.05	252,160
June	13,500	2,648	4,946	1.100	1.23	294,308
July	11,960	3,251	5,242	1.160	1.34	322,318
August	5,482	2,153	3,284	0.730	0.84	201,925
September	2,044	1,280	1,787	0.397	0.44	106,334
October	1,441	900	1,223	0.272	0.31	75,200
November	1,080	585	825	0.183	0.20	49,091
December	555	105	327	0.073	0.08	20,106
The year	....	....	....	....	6.75	1,625,577

NOTE.—These tables are inserted in this report to correct tables published on page 59 of the report for 1912 and page 67 of the report for 1913. The drainage area, discharges in second-feet per square mile, and run-off in depth in inches on the drainage area were incorrect, but the balance of the tables were correct as then published.

SESSIONAL PAPER No. 25c

DAILY GAUGE HEIGHT AND DISCHARGE of Red Deer River at Red Deer, for 1914.—*Concluded.*

DAY.	July.		August.		September.		October.		November.		December.	
	Gauge Height.	Dis-charge.	Gauge Height.	Dis-charge.	Gauge Height.	Dis-charge.	Gauge Height.	Dis-charge.	Gauge Height.	Dis-charge.	Gauge Height.	Dis-charge.
	Feet.	*Sec.-ft.*	*Feet.*	*Sec.-ft.*	*Feet.*	*Sec.-ft.*	*Feet.*	*Sec.-ft.*	*Feet.*	*Sec.-ft.*	*Feet.*	*Sec.-ft.*
1	5.38	3,294	4.14	1,448	3.84	1,140	3.75	1,050	3.69	996	4.44	690
2	5.35	3,240	4.20	1,520	3.74	1,041	3.74	1,041	3.67	978	4.27	612
3	5.30	3,155	4.22	1,544	3.72	1,023	3.76	1,060	3.66	969	4.11	555
4	5.33	3,206	4.18	1,496	3.72	1,023	3.82	1,120	3.62	933	4.02	490
5	5.36	3,258	4.19	1,508	3.73	1,032	3.90	1,200	3.56	879	3.90	420
6	5.32	3,189	4.14	1,448	3.70	1,005	3.94	1,240	3.60	915	3.81	380
7	5.36	3,258	4.13	1,436	3.69	996	3.92	1,220	3.50	760a	3.70	300
8	5.30	3,155	4.18	1,496	3.72	1,023	3.93	1,230	3.37	660	3.67	280
9	5.14	2,883	4.11	1,412	3.92	1,220	4.24	1,568	3.54	715	3.68	280
10	4.98	2,618	4.06	1,360	3.82	1,120	4.94	2,554	3.59	740	3.59	240
11	4.90	2,490	4.04	1,340	3.75	1,050	5.03	2,698	3.52	720	3.47	200
12	4.89	2,474	3.96	1,260	3.95	1,250	4.80	2,330	3.58	740	3.48	210
13	4.88	2,458	3.94	1,240	4.05	1,350	4.64	2,086	3.51	720	3.49	210
14	4.99	2,634	3.93	1,230	3.91	1,210	4.51	1,908	5.39	720	3.45	200
15	5.04	2,714	3.96	1,260	3.85	1,150	4.40	1,765	4.80	720	3.46	215
16	5.06	2,650	3.98	1,280	3.82	1,120	4.32	1,664	4.39	730	3.48	227
17	4.81	2,346	3.98	1,280	3.78	1,080	4.29	1,628	4.63	760	3.50	240
18	4.61	2,044	4.04	1,340	3.74	1,041	4.26	1,592	4.58	740	3.63	274
19	4.53	1,934	4.00	1,300	3.71	1,014	4.19	1,508	4.91	770	3.65	300
20	4.50	1,895	3.92	1,220	3.75	1,050	4.14	1,448	5.09	800	3.60	280
21	4.68	2,142	3.93	1,230	3.87	1,170	4.07	1,370	5.10	800	3.70	288
22	4.58	2,002	3.97	1,270	3.83	1,130	4.01	1,310	5.03	785	3.77	298
23	4.34	1,688	4.01	1,310	3.79	1,090	3.95	1,250	4.93	765	3.82	307
24	4.29	1,628	3.98	1,280	3.76	1,060	3.88	1,180	4.83	742	3.85	320
25	4.22	1,544	3.90	1,200	3.72	1,023	3.87	1,170	4.77	720	3.86	330
26	4.22	1,544	3.86	1,160	3.74	1,041	3.83	1,130	4.96	760	3.88	340
27	4.22	1,544	3.82	1,120	3.78	1,080	3.83	1,130	4.85	752	3.87	340
28	4.17	1,484	3.84	1,140	3.82	1,120	3.79	1,090	4.72	745	3.89	335
29	4.22	1,544	3.84	1,140	3.88	1,180	3.75	1,050	4.66	735	3.89	320
30	4.14	1,448	3.86	1,160	3.80	1,100	3.70	1,005	4.61	720	3.85	338
31	4.12	1,424	3.84	1,140	......	......	3.72	1,023	......	......	3.89	338a

a Ice conditions Nov. 7 to Dec. 31.

MONTHLY DISCHARGE of Red Deer River at Red Deer, for 1914.

(Drainage area 4.500 square miles.)

MONTH.	DISCHARGE IN SECOND-FEET.				RUN-OFF.	
	Maximum.	Minimum	Mean.	Per square Mile.	Depth in inches on Drainage Area.	Total in Acre-feet.
January	309	195	278	0.062	0.07	17,094
February	330	270	298	0.066	0.07	16,550
March	425	338	380	0.084	0.10	23,365
April	2,266	390	902	0.200	0.22	53,673
May	2,815	1,110	1,908	0.424	0.49	117,317
June	5,559	1,300	3,669	0.815	0.91	218,321
July	3,294	1,424	2,351	0.522	0.60	144,561
August	1,544	1,120	1,309	0.291	0.34	80,488
September	1,350	996	1,098	0.244	0.27	65,335
October	2,698	1,005	1,439	0.320	0.37	88,479
November	996	715	783	0.174	0.19	46,592
December	690	200	328	0.073	0.08	20,168
The year	......	......	......	......	3.71	891,943

5 GEORGE V, A. 1915

MISCELLANEOUS DISCHARGE MEASUREMENTS made in Red Deer drainage basin, in 1914.

Date.	Engineer.	Stream.	Location.	Width.	Area of Section.	Mean Velocity.	Discharge.
				Feet.	*Sq. ft.*	*Feet per sec.*	*Sec.-ft.*
Jan. 7....	J. S. Tempest...	Blindman River...	NW. 15-39-27-4.	31	27.6	0.44	12.1
Jan. 21....	do	do	do	28	19.2	0.72	13.8
Feb. 25....	do	do	do	30	23.3	0.94	22.0
Mar. 4....	do	do	do	30	28.7	0.84	24.0
April 24....	do	do	do	97	324.0	0.55	178.0
May 16....	J. M. Paul......	do	do	98	307.0	0.60	184.0
June 11....	do	do	do	122	947.0	2.93	2,779.0
June 27....	do	do	do	102	438.0	1.21	529.0
July 15....	do	do	do	100	322.0	0.52	166.0
Aug. 14....	do	do	do	98	283.0	0.21	59.0
Aug. 24....	do	do	do	98	261.0	0.16	41.0
Sept. 17....	do	do	do	62	114.0	0.83	95.0
Sept. 26....	do	do	do	62	116.0	0.58	68.0
Oct. 17....	do	do	do	61	122.0	0.77	94.0
Nov. 7....	H. S. Kerby....	do	do	58	93.0	0.27	25.0
Dec. 5....	R.J. McGuinness	do	do	59	143.0	0.17	24.0

BOW RIVER DRAINAGE BASIN.

General Description.

Bow River rises in Lakes Bow and Hector, which are situated in the Rocky Mountains Park, north of the main line of the Canadian Pacific Railway and just east of the Great Divide, and whose elevations are 6,420 and 5,694 feet, respectively, above mean sea level. It flows in a south and easterly direction to the city of Calgary, where it takes a big bend to the south, and then continues in a south and easterly direction to its junction with Belly River at the Grand Forks. Below this point the united stream is known as the South Saskatchewan River.

Bow River has a large number of tributaries in the western portion of its course. Of these the principal are Cascade and Ghost Rivers, draining the northern portion of the basin, and Spray, Kananaskis, Elbow, Sheep, and Highwood Rivers draining the southern portion. Below the mouth of Highwood River very little drainage reaches Bow River, and in consequence it depends for its supply almost wholly upon the run-off from the mountains and foothills. As a result, Bow River possesses a normally steady flow throughout the year, but is subject to sudden freshets caused by melting snow and heavy rains in the mountains. The minimum flow occurs in the frozen season, when there is little run-off from the snowfields in the western part of the drainage basin.

The valley of the Bow is deep and well defined throughout its course. In the mountain section it is comparatively narrow and very heavily timbered, while the bed is stony and the banks high and rocky. The nature of the valley changes gradually until, when it reaches the prairie, it is wide, of a clay formation, and devoid of trees, the bed consisting for the most part of gravel. The water is clear and pure.

A large quantity of water is diverted from the Bow River for irrigation purposes. The two chief users are the Department of Natural Resources, Canadian Pacific Railway Company, and the Southern Alberta Land Company.

The Department of Natural Resources diverts water at two points, one just east of the city of Calgary and the other three miles southwest of Bassano. The first system has been in operation for several years and distributes water over the Western Section of the Irrigation block, which extends east as far as Gleichen. The works at Bassano comprise a very large earth fill dam and concrete spillway, which were completed in 1913. This system is to serve the Eastern Section of the Irrigation block, which extends east from Bassano. In all, it is proposed to irrigate about 1,000,000 acres of land.

The Southern Alberta Land Company have a dam and reservoir near Namaka. These works were practically completed in 1913. It is proposed to irrigate by this system about 300,000 acres.

There are many favourable sites for power development on the Bow River, but only one company has up to the present developed power. The Calgary Power Company has two plants; one is at Kananaskis Falls, at the junction of the Kananaskis and Bow Rivers, and two miles east of Kananaskis station; the other is at Horseshoe Falls, one mile below. The latter plant has been in operation for some years, and has a capacity of 19,500 horse power. The dam at Kananaskis Falls was completed in 1913, and this plant has a rated capacity of 11,600 horsepower. All the power developed is used by the city of Calgary.

The city of Calgary takes its domestic water supply from Elbow River. The intake is about twelve miles southwest of Calgary, above which point the course of the river is through a wild and unsettled country, where there is no possibility of human contamination.

For information regarding floods in this drainage basin see 1913 report.

SESSIONAL PAPER No. 25c

BATH CREEK NEAR LAKE LOUISE.

Location.—On the *NE.* ¼ Sec. 32, Tp. 28, Rge. 16, W. 5th Mer., and one and one-quarter miles west of Lake Louise station, near the mouth of the stream.

Records available.—May 25 to September 20, 1913; discharge measurements only, in 1914.

Gauge.—Vertical staff. Elevation of zero maintained at 89.59 feet during 1913. Elevation of zero maintained at 90.54 feet during 1914.

Bench-marks.—Downstream corner of right concrete abutment, assumed elevation 100.00 feet.

Channel.—Gravel, shifting.

Discharge measurements.—Made by wading.

Observer.—None obtainable in 1914.

DISCHARGE MEASUREMENTS of Bath Creek near Lake Louise, in 1914.

Date.	Engineer.	Width.	Area of Section.	Mean Velocity.	Gauge Height.	Discharge.
		Feet.	*Sq. ft.*	*Ft. per sec.*	*Feet.*	*Sec.-ft.*
Jan. 16........	H. C. Ritchie..............	25.5	13.1	0.98	1.05	12.8
Jan. 30	do	25.0	12.4	0.99	0.99	12.3
Feb. 14	do	25.0	12.4	1.00	1.00	12.4
Feb. 27..........	do	25.3	11.2	0.78	0.96	8.7
Mar. 12..........	do	25.6	11.7	0.87	0.95	10.2
Mar. 25	do	25.8	11.6	0.88	0.98	10.2
April 9	do	25.5	13.0	1.08	1.05	14.1
April 23..........	do	27.0	14.6	1.30	1.10	19.0
May 8..........	do	27.5	16.9	1.62	1.22	27.0
May 23	do	29.0	21.4	2.04	1.41	44.0
June 19..........	do	42.0	49.8	4.25	2.54	212.0
July 3..........	do	42.5	54.1	4.40	2.59	237.0
July 17..........	do	40.5	51.1	4.17	2.40	213.0
July 31	do	40.5	51.1	4.17	2.40	213.0
Aug. 13	do	40.0	38.2	3.66	2.00	140.0
Aug. 27..........	do	41.5	42.5	4.10	2.12	174.0
Sept. 17........ ...	do	30.4	23.3	2.04	1.50	47.0
Sept. 30	do	31.5	26.7	2.52	1.67	67.0
Oct. 16	do	28.7	19.0	1.66	1.28	32.0
Oct. 28..........	do	28.7	18.3	1.61	1.25	29.0
Nov. 12..........	do	28.8	18.7	1.61	1.20	30.0
Nov. 26	do	28.0	15.8	1.44	1.15	23.0
Dec. 10	do	27.6	14.8	1.41	1.10	21.0
Dec. 23	do	26.0	12.7	1.11	1.00	14.0

BOW RIVER AT LAKE LOUISE.

Location.—On the SE. ¼ Sec. 28, Tp. 28, Rge. 16, W. 5th Mer., one-half mile east of Lake Louise station, at the junction of the Bow and Pipestone Rivers.

Records available.—January 1, 1911, to December 31, 1914. In 1910, discharge measurements only.

Gauge.—Chain; elevation of zero maintained at 4,931.72 feet since establishment. Previous to September 1, 1911, gauge at old station was used.

Bench-mark.—Permanent iron bench-mark on the left bank; elevation 4,942.82 feet above mean sea level (Canadian Pacific Railway).

Channel.—Gravel and boulders.

Discharge measurements.—Made from cable and car at low water by wading.

Observer.—E. Braund.

5 GEORGE V, A. 1915

DISCHARGE MEASUREMENTS of Bow River at Lake Louise, in 1914.

Date.	Engineer.	Width.	Area of Section.	Mean Velocity.	Gauge Height.	Discharge.
		Feet.	*Sq. ft.*	*Ft. per sec.*	*Feet.*	*Sec.-ft.*
Jan. 16	H. C. Ritchie	74.5	81.4	0.78	6.85	64
Jan. 30	do	74.0	74.4	0.86	6.39	64
Feb. 14	do	74.0	71.8	0.86	5.07	62
Feb. 27	do	72.5	67.3	0.66	4.83	44
Mar. 12	do	74.0	74.0	0.76	7.51	56
Mar. 25	do	74.5	79.0	0.78	4.96	62
April 8	do	53.0	52.8	1.00	4.88	53
April 22	do	45.0	40.5	1.35	4.39	55
May 7	do	52.0	87.2	2.28	5.53	199
May 20	do	66.5	138.0	3.12	6.25	431
June 5	do	74.0	238.5	5.11	7.62	1,219
June 18	do	75.0	298.0	5.69	8.38	1,698
July 2	do	74.0	244.0	5.36	7.89	1,309
July 17	do	74.0	250.0	5.55	7.66	1,390
Aug. 1	do	74.0	218.0	5.33	7.34	1,162
Aug. 12	do	69.5	168.0	4.70	6.66	788
Aug. 26	do	69.0	159.0	3.99	6.58	733
Sept. 17	do	56.0	79.2	2.75	5.40	218
Sept. 29	do	62.0	105.0	2.92	5.82	307
Oct. 15	do	57.0	82.5	2.23	5.40	184
Oct. 27	do	48.0	61.5	1.98	4.99	122
Nov. 11	do	46.5	58.6	1.88	4.94	110
Nov. 25	do	42.0	55.2	1.63	4.86	90
Dec. 9	do	42.0	42.1	1.38	6.40	58
Dec. 23	do	44.0	43.8	1.40	6.20	62

DAILY GAUGE HEIGHT AND DISCHARGE of Bow River at Lake Louise, for 1914.

DAY.	January.		February.		March.		April.		May.		June.	
	Gauge Height.	Discharge.	Gauge Height	Discharge	Gauge Height.	Discharge.	Gauge Height.	Discharge	Gauge Height	Discharge.	Gauge Height.	Discharge.
	Feet.	*Sec.-ft.*	*Feet.*	*Sec.-ft.*	*Feet.*	*Sec.-ft.*	*Feet.*	*Sec.-ft.*	*Feet.*	*Sec.-ft.*	*Feet.*	*Sec.-ft.*
1	7.51	68c	6 38	66	4 93	45	4.73	51	5.34	156	6 39	488
2	7.57	68	6 11	65	5 27	46	4.51	51	5 65	230	6 77	671
3	7.54	68	6 24	64	5 25	47	4.47	52	5 84	284	7.46	1,067
4	7.41	68	5 93	56	5 21	48	4.32	52	5 60	216	7.94	1,384
5	7.60	68	6 68	48	6 56	49	4.58	52	5 44	177	7 64	1,182
6	7.67	68	6.47	49	6.63	50	4.39	52	5.44	177	7.56	1,130
7	....b	68	5.92	50	5.47	51	4.37	53	5.49	189	7.59	1,150
8		68	5.44	52	5.40	52	4.98	53	5.55	203	7.25	940
9		66	5.25	54	6.32	54	4.35	53	5.81	275	7.01	802
10		64	5.18	56	7.17	55	4.33	53	5.79	269	6.85	714
11		64	5.12	57	7.57	56	4.33a	54	5.88	297	6.91	747
12		65	5.10	59	7.51	56	4.36a	54c	5.94	316	7.05	824
13		66	5.09	61	6.09	56	4.37a	54	6.06	358	7.24	934
14		65	5.07	62	6.03	57	4.43a	56	6.15	391	7.49	1,086
15	....b	64	5.02	62	6.09	58	4.51a	60	6.39	488	7.84	1,315
16	6.84	64	4.87	61	5.92	58	4.43a	56	6.53	551	8.05	1,461
17	6.82	63	4.92	60	6.23	58	4.41a	55	6.52	547	8.23	1,590
18	6.68	62	4.92	52	5.89	59	4.49a	59	6.44	510	8.32	1,656
19	6.62	61	4.89	40	6.21	60	4.48a	58	6.35	471	8.14	1,525
20	6.62	60	4.96	40	6.26	60	4.43a	56	6.25	430	7.83	1,308
21	6.51	57	4.96	41	5.93	61	4.38a	54	6.24	426	7.56	1,130
22	6.67	56	4.82	41	4.60	62	4.40	55	6.24	426	7.24	934
23	6.38	54	4.86	42	4.46	62	4.52	60	6.31	454	6.95	769
24	7.02	53	4.86	42	4.43	62	4.59	64	6.45	514	6.76	666
25	7.01	52	4.88	42	4.96	62	4.56	62	6.64	605	6.79	682
26	6.72	52	4.94	44	5.68	60	4.64	67	6.52	547	7.00	796
27	6.68	52	4.83	44	5.89	50	4.60	64	6.26	434	7.00	763
28	6.62	52	5.13	44	5.08	50	4.63	66	6.23	422	7.00	796
29	6.50	55			4.89	50	4.86	84	6.11	376	7.14	875
30	6.39	64			4.93	50	5.04	106	6.24	426	7.39	1,024
31	6.43	66			4.58	50			6.14	387		

a Gauge height interpolated.
b Ice flooded.
c Ice conditions Jan. 1 to April 12.

SESSIONAL PAPER No. 25c

DAILY GAUGE HEIGHT AND DISCHARGE of Bow River at Lake Louise, for 1914.—*Concluded.*

DAY.	July.		August.		September.		October.		November.		December.	
	Gauge Height.	Dis-charge	Gauge Height.	Dis-charge.	Gauge Height.	Dis-charge.	Gauge Height.	Dis-charge.	Gauge Height.	Dis-charge.	Gauge Height.	Dis-charge
	Feet.	*Sec.-ft.*	*Feet.*	*Sec.-ft.*	*Feet.*	*Sec.-ft.*	*Feet.*	*Sec.-ft.*	*Feet.*	*Sec.-ft.*	*Feet.*	*Sec.-ft.*
1	7.57	1,135	7.33	1,167	6.48	687	5.84	309	5.01	121	4.61	79
2	7.87	1,336	7.46	1,252	6.46	677	5 82	302	4.96	115	4.84	78
3	8.15	1,533	7.44	1,239	6.46	677	5.74	278	4.99	119	4.84	77
4	8.26	1,612	7 47	1,259	6.58	738	5.63	246	5.00	120	4.93	75
5	8.32	1,656	7.25	1,116	6 47	682	5.55	223	5.00	120	4.85	73
6	8.28	1,626	7.27	1,128	6.33	616	5.54	222	5.00	120	4.61	69
7	8.16	1,539	7.30	1,147	6.34	620	5.55	225	4.95	114	5.25	65
8	8.04	1,480	7.04	990	6.35	625	5.84	309	5.00	120	6.05	61
9	7.95	1,428	6.80	855	6.20	558	5.76	284	4.94	113	6.44	58
10	7.95	1,455	6.69	796	6.00	475	5.67	258	4.90	108	6.55	56
11	7.96	1,475	6.64	769	5.90	430	5.59	235	4.94	113	6.63	54
12	8.24	1,684	6.64	709	5.86	408	5.54	222	4.89	107	6.67	51
13	8.51	1,900	6.69	796	5.75	360	5.49	210	4.84	102	6.69	50
14	8.43	1,864	6.78	844	5.64	324	5.45	201	4.84	102	6.69	50
15	8.50	1,940	6.84	877	5.55	288	5.41	191	4.62	85	6.66	51
16	7.96	1,564	6.85	883	5.43	245	5.40	189	4.54	82	6.64	52
17	7.66	1,388	6.82	866	5.39	215	5.36	181	4.66	83*a*	6.53	52
18	7.54	1,306	6.66	780	5.55	258	5.37	183	4.69	84	6.53	54
19	7.65	1,381	6.74	823	5.82	338	5.34	176	4.86	86	6.65	55
20	7.93	1,579	6.83	871	5.64	278	5.34	176	5.06	87	6.64	56
21	7.54	1,306	6.94	933	5.54	245	5.24	157	5.28	88	6.55	58
22	7.20	1,085	6.94	933	5.45	220	5.14	140	5.34	88	6.43	60
23	7.00	967	6.80	855	5.43	210	5.10	134	4.94	89	6.20	61
24	7.00	967	6.66	780	5.44	210	5.06	128	4.86	90	6.05	62
25	7.09	1,019	6.60	748	5.46	214	5.07	130	4.88	90	5.60	62
26	7.03	984	6.62	759	5.63	256	5.04	126	4.86	87	5.40	59
27	6.96	944	6.64	769	6.04	385	4.99	119	4.99	84	5.05	59
28	6.99	961	6.68	790	5.89	330	4.95	114	5.01	83	4.90	59
29	6.97	950	6.68	790	5.80	296	4.95	114	4.78	82	......	59
30	7.00	967	6.61	753	5.75	281	4.95	114	4.65	80	......	60
31	7.22	1,097	6.60	748	......	......	5.00	120	......	......	......	60*a*

a Ice conditions Nov. 17 to Dec. 31.

MONTHLY DISCHARGE of Bow River at Lake Louise, for 1914.

(Drainage area 166 square miles.)

MONTH.	DISCHARGE IN SECOND-FEET.				RUN-OFF.	
	Maximum.	Minimum.	Mean.	Per square Mile.	Depth in inches on Drainage Area.	Total in Acre-feet.
January	68	52	62.0	0.374	0.43	3,812
February	66	40	51.9	0.312	0.32	2,882
March	62	45	55.0	0.332	0.38	3,382
April	106	51	58.9	0.354	0.40	3,505
May	605	156	373.0	2.250	2.59	22,935
June	1,656	488	1,013.0	6.100	6.81	60,280
July	1,940	944	1,725.0	10.000	11.99	106,060
August	1,259	748	906.0	5.460	6.30	55,708
September	738	210	405.0	2.440	2.72	24,099
October	309	114	194.0	1.170	1.35	11,929
November	121	80	98.7	0.595	0.66	5,873
December	79	50	60.5	0.364	0.42	3,720
The year	......	......	......	......	34 37	304,185

5 GEORGE V, A. 1915

PIPESTONE RIVER AT LAKE LOUISE.

Location.—On the SW. ¼ Sec. 27, Tp. 28, Rge. 16, W. 5th Mer., one-half mile east of Lake Louise station, at junction of the Bow and Pipestone Rivers.

Records available.—September. 1, 1911, to October 31, 1911. January 1, 1912, to December 31, 1914.

Gauge.—Chain; elevation of zero maintained at 4,934.08 feet since establishment.

Bench-mark.—Iron spike in tree on left bank; elevation, 4,943.77 feet above mean sea level, (Canadian Pacific Railway).

Channel.—Gravel and boulders.

Discharge measurements.—Made from cable and car; at low water by wading.

Observer.—E. Braund.

DISCHARGE MEASUREMENTS of Pipestone River at Lake Louise, in 1914.

Date.	Engineer.	Width.	Area of Section.	Mean Velocity.	Gauge Height.	Discharge.
		Feet.	*Sq. ft.*	*Ft. per sec.*	*Feet.*	*Sec.-ft.*
Jan. 14	H. C. Ritchie.	36.0	38.6	1.23	4.90	48
Jan. 31	do	36.0	33.5	0.95	4.68	32
Feb. 9	do	35.0	28.5	1.05	4.41	30
Feb. 28	do	37.0	30.0	0.86	4.15	26
Mar. 11.	do	35.0	27.5	1.16	5.54	30
Mar. 24	do	41.0	30.0	1.00	4.02	30
April 8.	do	36.0	25.4	0.99	3.93	25
April 22.	do	41.0	30.8	1.30	4.04	40
May 7.	do	57.0	62.8	1.90	4.57	119
May 20	do	69.0	94.9	2.77	5.10	263
June 5.	do	76.2	149.8	5.48	5.86	821
June 18.	do	78.0	180.0	6.38	6.21	1,149
July 2.	do	76.0	163.0	5.96	6.08	971
July 17.	do	75.0	122.0	4.26	5.47	519
Aug. 1	do	73.5	111.0	4.03	5.41	459
Aug. 12	do	65.0	88.4	3.29	5.03	291
Aug. 26	do	64.0	81.8	3.07	4.92	251
Sept. 17.	do	57.5	57.5	2.12	4.50	122
Sept. 29	do	63.5	81.1	2.72	4.86	221
Oct. 15	do	61.0	69.2	1.94	4.70	132
Oct. 27.	do	56.0	52.2	1.59	4.39	83
Nov. 11.	do ·.	47.5	50.4	1.36	4.40	69
Nov. 25.	do	. . . .	. . . .	. . . . .	. . . . .	. . . . *a*
Dec. 22.	do	48.0	41.3	0.97	5.94	40

a Ice jam.

SESSIONAL PAPER No. 25c

DAILY GAUGE HEIGHT AND DISCHARGE of Pipestone River at Lake Louise, for 1914.

DAY.	January. Gauge Height.	January. Dis-charge	February. Gauge Height.	February. Dis-charge	March. Gauge Height.	March. Dis-charge	April. Gauge Height.	April. Dis-charge	May. Gauge Height.	May. Dis-charge.	June. Gauge Height.	June. Dis-charge.
	Feet.	Sec.-ft.	Feet.	Sec.-ft.	Feet.	Sec.-ft.	Feet.	Sec.-ft.	Feet.	Sec.-ft.	Feet.	Sec.-ft.
1	6.09	33a	4.65	35	4.15	26	4.15	26	4 68	150	5.38	441
2	6.14	34	4 43	34	4 21	28	4.16	28	4.91	232	5.64	610
3	6.09	35	4 45	30	4.12	28	4 11	30a	4.98	258	5.99	899
4	5.96	36	4 40	24	4.13	28	3.98	29	4.75	179	6.13	1.028
5	5.84	37	4 37	22	4.24	27	3 95	27	4 65	150	5 85	778
6	5.89	38	4.40	22	4.16	26	3.95	27	4.56	126	5.74	687
7	5.54	40	4.43	24	4.05	28	3.95	27	4.57	128	5.76	704
8	5.45	41	4.43	28	4.06	30	3.94	26	4.65	150	5.55	546
9	5.23	42	4.41	30	4.66	32	3.92	25	4.87	218	5.44	476
10	5.05	44	4.36	31	5.40	31	3.92	25	4.82	201	5.40	452
11	5.26	45	4.35	31	5.54	30	3.94	26	4.85	211	5.45	482
12	5.28	46	4.33	30	4.83	32	4.00	31	4.96	250	5.69	648
13	5.02	47	4.33	30	4.22	33	3.98	29	5.09	302	5.73	679
14	4.89	48	4.30	30	4.20	34	3.98	29	5.14	324	5.84	770
15	4.82	48	4.26	30	4.06	33	3.98	29	5.34	420	6.06	963
16	4.72	49	4.23	30	4.14	32	4.02	33	5.36	431	6.15	1,048
17	4.65	50	4.21	30	4.24	30	4.00	31	5.36	431	6.22	1,114
18	4.65	50	4.27	29	4.19	28	3.95	27	5.27	384	6.20	1,095
19	4.61	46	4.24	29	4.23	29	4.02	33	5.18	341	6.04	945
20	4.56	40	4.20	28	4.20	30	3.98	29	5.10	306	5.83	761
21	4.50	36	4.23	28	4.20	31	3.94	26	5.10	306	5.70	655
22	4.55	39	4.25	28	3.98	34	3.99	30	5.14	324	5.52	526
23	4.46	36	4.25	28	3.98	33	4.11	42	5.25	374	5.39	447
24	4.44	32	4.17	28	4.04	30	4.19	53	5.36	431	5.30	399
25	4.44	30	4.16	22	4.24	27	4.15	47	5.45	482	5.36	431
26	4.51	33	4.15	26	4.32	24	4.15	47	5.36	431	5.49	506
27	4.50	32	4.12	26	4.30	24	4.20	54	5.15	328	5.45	482
28	4.50	30	4.14	26	4.26	24	4.18	51	5.04	281	5.52	526
29	4.45	28	......	......	4.25	24	4.34	78	4.96	250	5.65	618
30	4.54	30	......	......	4.24	25	4.48	107	5.10	306	5.84	770
1	4.67	32	......	......	4.20	25	......	......	5.12	315	......	......

a Ice conditions Jan. 1 to April 3.

5 GEORGE V, A. 1915

DAILY GAUGE HEIGHT AND DISCHARGE of Pipestone River at Lake Louise, for 1914.— *Concluded*

DAY.	July.		August.		September.		October.		November.		December.	
	Gauge Height.	Dis- charge.	Gauge Height	Dis- charge.	Gauge Height.	Dis- charge	Gauge Height.	Dis- charge	Gauge Height.	Dis- charge.	Gauge Height.	Dis- charge.
	Feet.	*Sec.-ft.*	*Feet.*	*Sec.-ft.*	*Feet.*	*Sec.-ft.*	*Feet.*	*Sec.-ft.*	*Feet.*	*Sec.-ft.*	*Feet.*	*Sec.-ft.*
1	5.90	820	5.41	458	4.77	185	4.89	225	4.44	97	5.73	40
2	6.04	945	5.38	441	4.77	185	4.86	214	4.41	91	5.84	46
3	6.14	1,038	5.37	436	4.80	194	4.78	188	4 38	85	5.82	41
4	6.06	963	5.40	452	4.84	208	4.73	172	4.41	91	5.75	36
5	6.04	945	5.22	360	4 79	191	4.70	163	4.43	96	5.74	34
6	6.02	926	5.24	370	4.74	175	4.72	169	4.42	93	5.80	33
7	5.95	864	5.28	390	4.74	175	4.72	169	4.35	80	5.72	32
8	5.82	753	5.12	315	4.79	191	5.12	315	4.40	78a	5.72	30
9	5.73	679	5.03	277	4.72	169	4.95	246	4.39	75	5.84	29
10	5.72	671	5.02	273	4.63	144	4.88	221	4.38	72	5.93	28
11	5.72	671	4.94	243	4.63	144	4.76	182	4.42	69	5.90	28
12	5.83	761	4.94	243	4.64	147	4.73	172	4.38	66	5.88	29
13	6.09	991	4.99	261	4.62	141	4.73	172	4.35	60	5.91	30
14	6.00	908	5.06	290	4.59	134	4.72	169	4.32	56	5.90	29
15	5.97	882	5.07	294	4.56	126	4.68	158	4.03	34	5.84	28
16	5.61	588	5.07	294	4.53	119	4.66	152	4.12	30	5.81	29
17	5.47	494	5.03	277	4.52	116	4.63	144	4.71	30	5.81	32
18	5.44	476	4.96	250	4.65	150	4.65	150	5.32	31	6.41	30
19	5.56	553	5.01	269	4.83	204	4.64	147	5.65	33	6.56	31
20	5.70	655	5.01	269	4.66	152	4.62	141	5.72	37	5.85	32
21	5.45	482	5.04	281	4.61	139	4.51	113	5.74	41	5.92	37
22	5.25	374	5.00	265	4.57	129	4.42	93	5.79	47	5.94	40
23	5.19	346	4.99	261	4.57	129	4.41	91	5.80	51	6.00	46
24	5.24	370	4.92	235	4.62	141	4.41	91	5.80	53	6.03	44
25	5.33	415	4.90	228	4.68	157	4.47	104	5.77	54	5.88	42
26	5.25	374	4.90	228	4.84	208	4.43	96	5.65	50	5.86	40
27	5 25	374	4.91	232	5.12	315	4.39	87	5.70	49	5.63	41
28	5.25	374	4.93	239	4.92	235	4.34	78	5.72	50	5.58	42
29	5.24	370	4.90	228	4.84	208	4.33	76	5.55	45	5.63	43
30	5.25	374	4.85	211	4.80	194	4.33	76	5.54	42	5.63	44
31	5.32	410	4.83	204	......	......	4.42	93	......	......	5.70	45a

a Ice conditions Nov. 8 to Dec. 31.

MONTHLY DISCHARGE of Pipestone River at Lake Louise, for 1914.

(Drainage area 139 square miles.)

MONTH.	DISCHARGE IN SECOND-*FEET*.				RUN-OFF.	
	Maximum.	Minimum.	Mean.	Per square Mile.	Depth in inches on Drainage Area.	Total in Acre-feet.
January	50	28	39	0.280	0.32	2,398
February	35	22	28	0.203	0.21	1,566
March	34	24	29	0.208	0.24	1,777
April	107	25	37	0.264	0.29	2,184
May	482	126	291	2.100	2.42	17,803
June	1,114	441	683	4.910	5.48	40,641
July	1,038	346	640	4.600	5.30	39,352
August	458	204	293	2.100	2.42	18,016
September	315	116	170	1.220	1.36	10,116
October	315	76	151	1.080	1.24	9,285
November	97	30	60	0.428	0.48	3,540
December	46	28	36	0.257	0.30	2,201
The year	......	......	......	....	20 06	148,969

LOUISE CREEK.

Location.—On the *NE.* ¼ Sec. 20, Tp. 28, Rge. 16, W. 5th Mer., at the Chateau Lake Louise, 500 feet from the lake itself.

Records available.—July 11, 1913, to December 31, 1914.

Gauge.—Vertical staff; elevation of zero 93.72 feet since establishment.

Bench-marks.—Spikes in tree; assumed elevation 100.00 feet.

Channel.—Loose gravel, steep slope.

Discharge measurements.—Made by wading.

Diversions.—The penstock of the Lake Louise power plant takes water from the lake, and this quantity must be added to the discharge of Louise Creek to obtain the total run-off from the lake.

Observers.—James Laing, Sam Farquhar, and David Greig.

DISCHARGE MEASUREMENTS of Louise Creek near Lake Louise, in 1914.

Date.	Engineer.	Width.	Area of Section.	Mean Velocity.	Gauge Height.	Discharge.
		Feet.	*Sq. ft.*	*Ft. per sec.*	*Feet.*	*Sec.-ft.*
Jan. 29	H. C. Ritchie	7.7	2.96	0.85	0.73	2.50
Feb. 25	do	7.6	2.46	0.38	0.39	0.94
May 22	do	14.0	8.20	1.91	1.08	15.70
June 19	do	23.0	19.80	3.00	1.70	60.00
July 2	do	18.0	18.60	3.34	1.73	62.00
July 16	do	21.0	23.80	3.89	1.95	93.00
July 31	do	25.5	26.80	3.85	1.96	103.00
Aug. 13	do	24.2	18.80	1.72	1.72	64.00
Aug. 26	do	24.0	18.80	1.70	1.70	58.00
Sept. 18	do	15.9	9.91	1.26	1.26	22.00
Sept. 29	do	15.7	10.20	1.27	1.27	23.00
Oct. 15	do	15.0	7.20	1.09	1.09	11.40
Oct. 27	do	9.0	2.00	0.75	0.75	1.03
Nov. 11	do	13.5	5.38	1.04	1.04	8.60
Nov. 25	do	10.0	4.70	0.97	0.97	5.70
Dec. 9	do	10.0	4.15	0.94	0.94	3.80
Dec. 24	do	9.0	3.90	0.66	0.66	3.70

STREAM MEASUREMENTS, 1914

5 GEORGE V, A. 1915

DAILY GAUGE HEIGHT AND DISCHARGE of Louise Creek near Lake Louise, for 1914.

DAY.	January.		February.		March.		April.		May.		June.	
	Gauge Height.	Dis-charge.	Gauge Height.	Dis-charge.	Gauge Height.	Dis-charge.	Gauge Height.	Dis-charge.	Gauge Height.	Dis-charge.	Gauge Height.	Dis-charge.
	Feet.	*Sec.-ft.*	*Feet.*	*Sec.-ft.*	*Feet.*	*Sec.-ft.*	*Feet.*	*Sec.-ft.*	*Feet.*	*Sec.-ft.*	*Feet.*	*Sec.-ft.*
1............	1.08	3.5	0.62	2.00	0.41	0.80	0.33	0.20	0.43	0.70	1.14	18
2............	1.08	3.5	0.63	1.98	0.40	0.80	0.33	0.20	0.42	0.60	1.19	20
3............	1.07	3.5	0.65	1.96	0.40	0.75	0.31	0.20	0.45	0.90	1.25	23
4............	1.07	3.5	0.63	1.94	0.40	0.70	0.30	0.20	0.47	1.10	1.37	30
5............	1.07	3.5	0.69	1.92	0.41	0.70	0.31	0.20	0.48	1.20	1.42	34
6............	1.07	3.5	0.68	1.90	0.42	0.65	0.32	0.20	0.50	1.40	1.47	38
7............	1.07	3.5	0.69	1.90	0.42	0.60	0.33	0.19	0.51	1.53	1.50	40
8............	1.07	3.5	0.56	1.90	0.42	0.60	0.32	0.19	0.53	1.79	1.47	38
9............	1.08	3.5	0.52	1.80	0.41	0.55	0.32	0.19	0.54	1.92	1.41	33
10.	1.08	3.5	0.50	1.80	0.41	0.50	0.32	0.19	0.55	2.00	1.37	30
11....	1.08	3.5	0.48	1.70	0.41	0.50	0.32	0.18	0.56	2.20	1.40	32
12.... .	1.08	3.5	0.47	1.63	0.41	0.45	0.32	0.18	0.59	2.60	1.45	36
13........	1.08	3.5	0.47	1.63	0.40	0.40	0.32	0.18	0.62	3.00	1.43	34
14	1.08	3.5	0.47	1.50	0.39	0.40	0.32	0.18	0.65	3.50	1.49	39
15..........	1.07	3.5	0.47	1.40	0.39	0.35	0.32	0.18	0.84	7.70	1.57	46
16..........	1.05	3.4	0.47	1.30	0.39	0.30	0.32	0.17	1.05	14.60	1.60	49
17.... .	1.03	3.4	0.47	1.20	0.40	0.30	0.32	0.17	1.13	17.90	1.65	54
18. .	1.01	3.1	0.42	1.10	0.41	0.30	0.32	0.17	1.20	21.00	1.67	57
19.... ...	0.97	3.3	0.41	1.10	0.41	0.30	0.35	0.17	1.18	20.00	1.70	60
20..........	0.93	3.1	0.51	1.10	0.41	0.30	0.35	0.17	1.15	18.80	1.68	58
21.	0.86	3.0	0.46	1.05	0.40	0.30	0.34	0.16	1.13	17.90	1.65	54
22.... . .	0.82	3.0	0.41	1.00	0.39	0.25	0.35	0.20	1.10	16.50	1.55	44
23........ .	0.79	2.9	0.40	1.00	0.39	0.24	0.37	0.28	1.10	16.50	1.47	38
24........ .	0.76	2.8	0.40	0.96	0.39	0.23	0.36	0.24	1.13	17.90	1.49	39
25........ .	0.76	2.8	0.39	0.94	0.39	0.22	0.36	0.24	1.15	18.80	1.50	40
26..........	0.74	2.7	0.40	0.90	0.39	0.21	0.37	0.28	1.16	19.30	1.45	36
27..........	0.72	2.6	0.41	0.90	0.38	0.20	0.36	0.24	1.16	19.30	1.42	34
28..........	0.73	2.6	0.42	0.85	0.35	0.20	0.38	0.32	1.12	17.40	1.50	40
29..........	0.70	2.5	....	....	0.36	0.20	0.42	0.60	1.09	16.10	1.56	45
30..........	0.69	2.5	....	....	0.36	0.20	0.43	0.70	1.05	14.60	1.63	52
31........	0.66	2.2			0.34	0.20			1.09	16.10	....	.....

NOTE.—No measurement was made in March or April, and discharge for these months is only approximate.

SESSIONAL PAPER No. 25c

DAILY GAUGE HEIGHT AND DISCHARGE of Louise Creek near Lake Louise, for 1914.—*Concluded.*

DAY.	July.		August.		September.		October.		November.		December.	
	Gauge Height.	Dis-charge	Gauge Height.	Dis-charge	Gauge Height.	Dis-charge	Gauge Height	charge	Gauge Height.	Dis-charge.	Gauge Height.	Dis-charge.
	Feet.	*Sec.-ft.*	*Feet.*	*Sec.-ft.*	*Feet.*	*Sec.-ft.*	*Feet.*	*Sec.-ft.*	*Feet*	*Sec.-ft.*	*Feet.*	*Sec.-ft.*
1	1.66	56	2 06	111	1 65	53	1.28	23.00	0.84	2 4	0 97	5.1
2	1.76	67	2 02	1ᴏ5	1.62	50	1 25	22.00	1.12	8.5	0.96	4.8
3	1.81	74	1 98	99	1.56	44	1 22	19 20	0 85	2.7	0.96	4.6
4	1.91	89	1 97	97	1 56	44	1.20	17 90	0.86	3.2	0.96	4.6
5	1.94	93	1.95	95	1 54	43	1.18	17.00	0 92	4 1	0.96	4.4
6	1.96	96	1.93	91	1.54	42	1.16	15.70	0 95	4.8	0.96	4.4
7	1.94	93	1.88	84	1.52	40	1.16	15.70	0.96	5.3	0.95	4.1
8	1.91	89	1.84	78	1.52	40	1.20	17 00	1 00	6.4	0.94	3.9
9	1.90	87	1.74	65	1.46	35	1.20	17 00	1 04	7.7	0.94	3.7
10	1.88	84	1.70	60	1.42	32	1 16	14.90	1 04	8.2	0.94	4.1
11	1.90	87	1.72	62	1.40	30	1 15	14 60	1 04	8.5	0.92	4.1
12	2.04	108	1.74	65	1.38	28	1 14	13 80	1 04	8.5	0.90	4.1
13	2.16	126	1.74	65	1.35	26	1 14	13 80	1 05	8.8	0.85	3.5
14	2.15	125	1.76	67	1.32	25	1 11	12.30	1 05	8.8	0.84	3.7
15	2.07	112	1.78	70	1.29	22	1 09	11.60	1 04	8.5	0.84	4.1
16	1.94	93	1.81	74	1.26	20	1 08	10.90	1 04	8.4	0.84	4.4
17	1.94	93	1.84	78	1.25	19	1.10	11 30	1 04	8.4	0.81	4.2
18	1.95	95	1.74	65	1.25	19	1.09	10 60	1 02	7.7	0.78	4.1
19	1.98	99	1.74	65	1.35	27	1 10	10.60	1.00	6.9	0.73	3.5
20	2.08	114	1.76	67	1.30	24	1 07	9 30	1 00	6.9	0.70	4.4
21	1.94	93	1.80	72	1.26	22	1.05	8.50	1.00	6.6	0.87	7.4
22	1.86	81	1.86	81	1.25	22	1.05	8.00	0.99	6.4	0.85	7.4
23	1.85	80	1.78	70	1.25	22	......	Nil *a*	0.99	6.4	0.82	7.1
24	1.84	78	1.71	61	1.24	21	......	Nil	0.99	6.4	0.74	5.3
25	1.84	78	1.66	56	1.22	20	......	Nil	0.97	5.7	0.63	3.2
26	1.81	74	1.65	55	1.26	22	......	Nil	0.98	5.9	0.64	3.4
27	1.79	71	1.6S	58	1.34	26	0.75	1.10	0.97	5.5	0.62	3.0
28	1.76	67	1.76	67	1.32	25	0.76	1.20	0.98	5.7	0.62	3.0
29	1.78	70	1.76	67	1.26	22	0.78	1.53	0.99	5.7	0.60	2.7
30	1.85	80	1.74	65	1.26	22	0.80	1.80	0.98	5.5	0.58	2.4
31	1.95	95	1.73	64	......	......	0.82	2.20	......	......	0.56	2.2

a Water dammed back at lake.

MONTHLY DISCHARGE of Louise Creek near Lake Louise, for 1914.

(Drainage area 11 square miles)

MONTH.	DISCHARGE IN SECOND-FEET.				RUN-OFF.	
	Maximum.	Minimum.	Mean.	Per square Mile.	Depth in inches on Drainage Area.	Total in Acre-feet.
January	3.50	2.20	3.20	0.288	0.33	195
February	2.00	0.85	1.44	0.131	0.14	80
March	0.80	0.20	0.41	0.037	0.04	25
April	0.70	0.16	0.27	0.021	0.02	14
May	21.00	0.60	10.20	0.927	1.07	627
June	60.00	18.00	40.00	3.610	4.03	2,362
July	126.00	56.00	89.00	8.050	9.28	5,448
August	111.00	55.00	74.00	6.700	7.72	4,538
September	53.00	19.00	30.00	2.690	3.00	1,761
October	23.00	Nil	10.40	0.946	1.09	640
November	8.80	2.40	6.50	0.589	0.66	386
December	7.4ᴏ	2.22	4.20	0.384	0.44	259
The year	......	......	......	......	27.82	16,335

5 GEORGE V, A. 1915

DISCHARGE MEASUREMENTS of Tail Race of Chateau Lake Louise Power Plant near Lake Louise, in 1914.

Date.	Engineer.	Width.	Area of Section.	Mean Velocity.	Discharge.
		Feet.	*Sq. ft.*	*Ft. per sec.*	*Sec.-ft.*
Jan. 29............	H. C. Ritchie........................	4.3	1.19	1.56	1.86
Feb. 25............	do	5.0	1.40	1.10	1.54
Feb. 25............	do	6.4	5.69	2.63	15.00*a*
Feb. 25............	do	6.4	5.65	2.73	15.40*a*
April 24............	do	6.5	3.53	1.66	5.90
May 22............	do	5.3	3.09	1.98	6.10
June 19............	do				9.10
July 2............	do	5.7	4.10	2.67	11.00
July 16	do	2.8	4.34	2.44	10.60
July 31.........	do	2.8	4.34	2.46	10.70
Aug. 13.	do	2.6	4.29	2.28	9.80
Aug. 26...........	do	2.7	4.34	2.27	9.80
Sept. 18...........	do	2.5	4.50	2.02	9.10
Sept. 29...........	do	2.5	3.88	1.99	7.70
Oct. 15...........	do	2.5	3.88	2.09	7.80
Oct. 27...........	do	2.5	3.88	1.99	7.70
Nov. 11...........	do	2.5	4.12	2.17	9.00
Nov. 25...........	do	2.5	4.25	2.20	9.30
Dec. 9.	do	2.5	3.00	1.07	3.20
Dec. 24........	do	2.5	3.55	1.60	5.70

a Turbine test.

FORTYMILE CREEK NEAR BANFF.

Location.—On the SW. ¼ Sec. 2, Tp. 26, Rge. 12, W. 5th Mer., near the Canadian Pacific Railway station at Banff and one mile from the mouth of the stream.

Records available.—August 1, 1912, to December 31, 1914.

Gauge.—Vertical staff; elevation of zero 91.06 feet since establishment.

Bench-mark.—On right abutment of bridge; elevation assumed, 100.00 feet.

Channel.—Clay and gravel.

Discharge measurements.—Made from bridge.

Observer.—Peter Peterson.

DISCHARGE MEASUREMENTS of Fortymile Creek at Banff, in 1914.

Date.	Engineer.	Width.	Area of Section.	Mean Velocity.	Gauge Height.	Discharge.
		Feet.	*Sq. ft.*	*Ft. per sec.*	*Feet.*	*Sec.-ft.*
Jan. 3............	H. C. Ritchie...	25.0	34.60	0.73	2.51	25
Jan. 15	do	24.0	32.60	0.81	2.51	26
Jan. 27..........	do	23.0	30.20	0.46	2.95	14
Feb. 13....	do	25.0	34.60	0.79	2.51	27
Feb. 28..........	do	24.5	32.00	0.79	2.41	25
Mar. 13..........	do	24.5	32.50	0.90	2.42	29
Mar. 28..........	do	24.5	39.70	0.60	2.67	24
April 4..........	do	24.5	30.05	0.81	2.40	24
April 18........ .	do	25.0	33.10	0.90	2.49	29
May 5..........	do	27.2	50.90	1.54	3.05	79
May 19	do	32.5	67.80	2.46	3.62	167
June 2	do	32.5	84.25	2.64	4.04	223
June 16...	do	32.5	135.58	3.28	5.64	146
June 29..........	do	32.5	91.37	2.60	4.26	237
July 14	do	32.5	99.75	2.27	4.54	226
July 27..........	do	30.5	59.60	2.06	3.35	123
Aug. 11	do	28.5	51.30	1.76	3.04	91
Aug. 24..........	do	27.5	47.60	1.60	2.99	76
Sept. 15...	do	27.5	43.60	1.42	2.78	62
Oct. 1..........	do	28.3	48.60	1.68	2.93	81
Oct. 13....	do	28.0	47.60	1.56	2.94	75
Oct. 31..........	do	28.0	44.80	1.30	2.75	58
Nov. 9..........	do	27.0	44.40	1.18	2.75	52
Nov. 24..........	do	26.5	41.25	0.93	2.64	38
Dec. 8..........	do	25.5	35.03	0.60	2.40	21
Dec. 28.	do	24.5	35.70	0.78	2.50	28

SESSIONAL PAPER No. 25c

DAILY GAUGE HEIGHT AND DISCHARGE of Fortymile Creek at Banff, for 1914.

DAY.	January.		February.		March.		April.		May.		June.	
	Gauge Height.	Dis-charge.	Gauge Height.	Dis-charge	Gauge Height.	Dis-charge.	Gauge Height.	Dis-charge.	Gauge Height.	Dis-charge.	Gauge Height.	Dis-charge.
	Feet.	*Sec.-ft.*	*Feet.*	*Sec.-ft.*	*Feet.*	*Sec.-ft.*	*Feet.*	*Sec.-ft.*	*Feet.*	*Sec.-ft.*	*Feet.*	*Sec.-ft.*
1...........	2.09	25.0a	2.60	22	2.49	25	2.36	20	2.80	60	3.80	183
2...........	2.09	25.0	2.78	21	2.48	26	2.36	20	2.87	67	4.36	262
3...........	2.65	25.0	2.71	18	2.49	26	2.37	21	2.98	79	5.11	369
4...........	2.65	25.0	2.62	16	2.49	26	2.39	22	3.03	85	5.36	406
5...........	2.66	25.0	2.62	15	2.50	27	2.41	24	2.95	76	5.10	368
6...........	2.67	26.0	2.72	15	2.42	27	2.42	25	2.91	71	5.85	476
7...........	2.68	26.0	2.78	16	2.44	27	2.42	25	2.87	67	4.70	312
8...........	2.67	26.0	2.82	17	2.45	28	2.43	25	2.96	77	4.40	269
9...........	2.66	26.0	2.90	20	2.43	28	2.43	25	2.97	78	4.25	247
10...........	2.65	26.0	2.90	24	2.45	28	2.43	25	2.98	79	4.05	218
11	2.65	26.0	2.90	26	2.43	29	2.44	26	3.00	81	4.20	215
12...........	2.63	26.0	2.60	27	2.43	29	2.45	27	3.00	81	4.20	240
13...........	2.62	26.0	2.53	27	2.45	29	2.46	28	3.20	105	4.30	254
14...........	2.59	26.0	2.53	27	2.45	30	2.46	28	3.30	117	4.80	326
15...........	2.50	26.0	2.54	27	2.44	30	2.46	28	3.65	162	5.20	382
16...........	2.58	26.0	2.55	26	2.45	30	2.47	29	3.75	176	5.60	440
17...........	2.58	26.0	2.55	24	2.44	30	2.47	29	3.68	166	5.90	483
18...........	2.57	26.0	2.52	22	2.45	30	2.48	29	3.62	159	5.70	454
19...........	2.56	26.0	2.50	23	2.44	31	2.49	30	3.55	149	5.60	440
20...........	2.85	25.0	2.49	23	2.43	31	2.52	33	3.55	149	5.20	382
21...........	2.78	24.0	2.48	23	2.44	31	2.52	33	3.45	136	4.93	344
22...........	2.61	23.0	2.48	23	2.44	31	2.51	32	3.45	136	4.25	247
23...........	2.42	21.0	2.48	24	2.43	31	2.52	33	3.58	153	4.15	232
24...........	2.25	18.5	2.48	24	2.41	31	2.53	34	3.71	170	4.15	232
25...........	2.15	16.0	2.47	24	2.63	·30	2.55	35	3.90	197	4.20	240
26...........	2.15	14.0	2.49	24	2.65	28	2.55	35	3.83	187	4.15	232
27...........	2.90	13.9	2.44	25	2.41	25	2.55	35	3.65	162	4.10	225
28...........	2.90	15.0	2.41	25	2.40	24	2.56	36	3.60	156	4.15	232
29...........	2.92	16.5	......	......	2.45	24	2.57	37	3.45	136	4.25	236
30...........	2.98	18.0	......	......	2.38	24	2.65	45	3.35	123	4.35	246
31...........	2.65	20.0	......	......	2.37	22a	......	......	3.45	136	......	......

a Ice conditions Jan. 1 to March 31.

5 GEORGE V, A. 1915

DAILY GAUGE HEIGHT AND DISCHARGE of Fortymile Creek at Banff, for 1914.—*Concluded.*

DAY.	July.		August.		September.		October.		November.		December.	
	Gauge Height.	Dis-charge.	Gauge Height.	Dis-charge.	Gauge Height.	Dis-charge.	Gauge Height.	Dis-charge	Gauge Height.	Dis-charge.	Gauge Height.	Dis-charge.
	Feet.	Sec.-ft.	Feet.	Sec.-ft.	Feet.	Sec.-ft.	Feet.	Sec.-ft.	Feet.	Sec.-ft.	Feet.	Sec.-ft.
1	4.72	295	3.23	109	2.70	50	2.85	65	2.75	55	2.50	36.0
2	4.90	317	3.23	109	2.68	48	2.83	63	2.75	55	2.46	33.0
3	5.15	350	3.23	109	2.68	48	2.83	63	2.75	55	2.65	38.0
4	5.25	360	3.24	110	2.67	47	2.84	64	2.75	55	2.45	30.0
5	5.15	343	3.16	100	2.66	46	2.85	65	2.75	55	2.44	27.0
6	5.15	339	3.16	100	2.64	44	2.83	63	2.76	56	2.44	24.0
7	4.98	311	3.17	101	2.62	42	2.81	61	2.75	55	2.40	23.0
8	4.65	260	3.14	98	2.64	44	2.81	61	2.74	54	2.40	21.0
9	4.46	230	3.13	97	2.66	46	2.89	69	2.73	53	2.68	20.0
10	4.46	226	3.05	87	2.64	44	2.90	70	2.74	54	2.51	19.0
11	4.38	210	3.02	83	2.75	55	2.87	67	2.73	53	2.75	18.0
12	4.45	218	3.00	81	2.75	55	2.85	65	2.74	54	2.67	17.5
13	4.53	228	3.00	81	2.74	54	2.82	62	2.75	55	2.70	17.0
14	4.45	213	3.01	82	2.78	58	2.85	65	2.73	53	2.70	17.0
15	4.40	211	2.99	80	2.69	49	2.87	67	2.45	27	2.85	17.0
16	4.05	167	3.00	81	2.65	45	2.90	70	2.40	23	2.95	17.5
17	3.85	143	2.93	73	2.65	45	2.93	73	2.41	24	3.00	18.0
18	3.75	134	2.90	70	2.67	47	2.94	74	2.44	26	3.05	18.0
19	3.75	139	2.87	67	2.73	53	2.92	72	2.51	32	3.10	19.0
20	3.85	158	2.85	65	2.75	55	2.87	67	2.51	32	3.00	22.0
21	3.70	142	2.84	64	2.75	55	2.86	66	2.50	31	2.67	24.0
22	3.65	141	2.82	62	2.77	57	2.85	65	2.65	28a	2.50	24.0
23	3.60	138	2.81	61	2.75	55	2.83	63	2.64	38	2.49	25.0
24	3.55	136	2.99	80	2.76	56	2.81	61	2.65	38	2.51	26.0
25	3.50	134	2.75	55	2.80	60	2.80	60	2.65	38	2.58	26.0
26	3.35	117	2.74	54	2.83	63	2.79	59	2.65	38	2.56	27.0
27	3.33	123	2.75	55	2.87	67	2.78	58	2.64	38	2.55	27.0
28	3.31	118	2.75	55	2.92	72	2.76	56	2.64	38	2.50	28.0
29	3.26	112	2.73	53	2.86	66	2.75	55	2.64	38	2.50	29.0
30	3.24	110	2.71	51	2.85	65	2.75	55	2.60	38	2.49	29.0
31	3.23	109	2.72	52	......	......	2.75	55	......	......	2.49	30.0a

a Ice conditions Nov. 22 to Dec. 31.

MONTHLY DISCHARGE of Fortymile Creek at Banff, for 1914.

MONTH.	DISCHARGE IN SECOND-*FEET.*				RUN-OFF.	
	Maximum.	Minimum	Mean.	Per square Mile.	Depth in inches on Drainage Area.	Total in Acre-feet.
January	26	13.9	23.0	0.365	0.42	1,414
February	27	15.0	22.4	0.356	0.37	1,244
March	31	22.0	28.0	0.445	0.51	1,722
April	45	20.0	29.1	0.462	0.51	1,732
May	197	60.0	122.0	1.940	2.24	7,501
June	483	183.0	306.0	4.850	5.41	18,208
July	360	109.0	201.0	3.190	3.68	12,359
August	110	51.0	78.2	1.240	1.43	4,808
September	72	42.0	53.0	0.841	0.94	3,154
October	74	55.0	63.8	1.020	1.18	3,923
November	56	23.0	43.3	0.687	0.77	2,576
December	38	17.0	24.1	0.383	0.44	1,482
The year	......	......	......	......	17.90	60,123

BOW RIVER AT BANFF.

Location.—On the SE. ¼ Sec. 35, Tp. 25, Rge. 12, W. 5th Mer., at the highway bridge at Banff.

Records available.—May 25, 1909, to November 11, 1909. April 26, 1910, to December 31, 1914.

Gauge.—Vertical staff; elevation of zero maintained at 92.36 feet during 1909-12; 93.53 feet during 1913; and 93.38 feet during 1914.

Bench-mark.—Permanent iron bench-mark on the right bank; assumed elevation, 100.00 feet.

Channel.—Gravel and boulders, deep hole with backwater near right bank.

Discharge measurements.—Made from bridge.

Winter flow.—This station is entirely free from the backwater effect of ice, and one discharge curve is used throughout the year.

Observer.—N. B. Sanson.

DISCHARGE MEASUREMENTS of Bow River at Banff, in 1914.

Date.	Engineer.	Width.	Area of Section.	Mean Velocity.	Gauge Height.	Discharge.
		Feet.	*Sq. ft.*	*Ft. per sec.*	*Feet.*	*Sec.-ft.*
Jan. 12	H. C. Ritchie	54.0	173	2.27	0.71	393
Jan. 26	do	54.0	162	2.15	0.60	349
Feb. 10	do	54.0	159	2.12	0.57	338
Feb. 23	do	53.5	153	1.88	0.43	289
Mar. 9	do	75.6	169	1.62	0.29	274
Mar. 21	do	79.0	167	1.64	0.30	273
April 3	do	83.5	173	1.79	0.44	309
April 21	do	121.0	494	0.82	0.70	407
May 6	do	232.0	703	1.34	1.38	941
May 21	do	292.0	929	2.12	2.10	1,975
June 3	do	319.0	1,356	3.80	3.46	5,152
June 17	do	320.5	1,602	4.59	4.15	7,349
July 15	do	320.5	1,466	4.10	3.83	6,015
July 29	do	309.0	1,097	2.78	2.62	3,055
Aug. 14	do	306.0	1,017	2.49	2.35	2,528
Aug. 28	do	297.0	981	2.26	2.24	2,221
Sept. 19	do	289.0	890	1.87	1.92	1,662
Oct. 2	do	292.0	886	1.73	1.94	1,535
Oct. 17	do	274.0	794	1.47	1.62	1,169
Oct. 26	do	246.0	721	1.18	1.35	854
Nov. 10	do	236.0	673	1.06	1.15	710
Nov. 27	do	172.0	601	1.03	0.99	616
Dec. 12	do	72.0	172	1.71	0.47	293
Dec. 21	do	54.5	174	2.03	0.63	353

5 GEORGE V, A. 1915

DAILY GAUGE HEIGHT AND DISCHARGE of Bow River, at Banff, for 1914.

DAY.	January.		February.		March.		April.		May.		June.	
	Gauge Height.	Dis- charge.	Gauge Height.	Dis- charge.	Gauge Height.	Dis- charge.	Gauge Height.	Dis- charge	Gauge Height.	Dis- charge.	Gauge Height.	Dis- charge.
	Feet.	Sec.-ft.	Feet.	Sec.-ft.	Feet.	Sec.-ft.	Feet.	Sec.-ft.	Feet.	Sec.-ft.	Feet.	Sec.-ft.
1............	0.64	386	0.51a	324	0.37	289	0.35	285	1.39	915	2.40	2,580
2............	0.64	386	0.49	318	0.37	289	0.35	285	1.68	1,273	2.75	3,360
3............	0.64	386	0.46	310	0.38	291	0.43	303	2.00	1,780	3.43	5,081
4............	0.67a	390	0.49	318	0.37	289	0.44	305	1.93	1,661	3.88	6,352
5............	0.69	395	0.47	312	0.37	289	0.46	310	1.74	1,360	3.40	5,000
6............	0.71	400	0.47	312	0.37	289	0.51	324	1.67	1,259	3.42	5,054
7............	0.66	379	0.47	312	0.36	287	0.50	320	1.32	841	3.43	5,081
8............	0.63	377	0.52	327	0.37	289	0.53	330	1.37	893	3.23	4,548
9............	0.60	355	0.57	344	0.37	289	0.55	338	1.59	1,153	2.95	3,840
10	0.51	324	0.57	344	0.25	268	0.55	338	1.67	1,259	2.84	3,576
11...........	0.70	395	0.56	341	0.29	274	0.58	348	1.68	1,273	2.95	3,840
12...........	0.62	363	0.56	341	0.27	270	0.73	410	1.72	1,330	3.13	4,288
13...........	0.64	371	0.57	344	0.28	272	0.76	425	1.83	1,498	3.30	4,730
14...........	0.62	363	0.55	338	0.29a	273	0.80	445	1.97	1,729	3.53	5,354
15...........	0.61	359	0.54	334	0.30a	275	0.75	410	2.28	2,329	3.79	6,091
16...........	0.62	363	0.53	330	0.31a	277	0.80	445	2.48	2,748	4.05	6,850
17...........	0.58	348	0.48	315	0.32a	279	0.77	430	2.43	2,643	4.19	7,270
18...........	0.57a	344	0.48	315	0.33a	281	0.74	415	2.32	2,412	4.29	7,570
19...........	0.56	341	0.47	312	0.34a	283	0.67	383	2.25	2,267	4.19	7,270
20...........	0.45	308	0.39	293	0.35a	285	0.78	435	2.16	2,087	3.89	6,381
21...... ...	0.57	344	0.41	298	0.40	295	0.73	410	2.08	1,932	3.64	5,662
22.	0.52	327	0.43	303	0.44	305	0.69	391	2.10	1,970	3.34	4,838
23...........	0.47	313	0.37	289	0.45	308	0.71	400	2.20	2,165	3.07	4,135
24...........	0.41	298	0.40	295	0.40	295	0.85	475	2.38	2,538	2.85	3,600
25.	0.60a	355	0.35	285	0.16	258	0.85	475	2.55	2,900	2.95	3,840
26...........	0.48	315	0.40	295	0.08	255	0.82	457	2.46	2,706	3.12	4,262
27...........	0.45	308	0.39	293	0.28	272	0.79	440	2.30	2,370	3.02	4,010
28...........	0.43	303	0.37	289	0.36	287	0.85	475	2.20	2,165	3.08	4,160
29...........	0.48	315	......	......	0.49	318	0.92	519	2.08	1,932	3.14	4,314
30...........	0.48	315	......	......	0.43	303	1.09	642	2.02	1,818	3.30	4,730
31...........	0.53	330	......	......	0.41	298	......	......	2.13	2,028	......	......

a Gauge height interpolated.

SESSIONAL PAPER No. 25c

DAILY GAUGE HEIGHT AND DISCHARGE of Bow River at Banff, for 1914.—*Concluded.*

DAY.	July.		August.		September.		October.		November.		December.	
	Gauge Height.	Dis-charge	Gauge Height.	Dis-charge	Gauge Height.	Dis charge	Gauge Height.	Dis-charge	Gauge Height.	Dis-charge	Gauge Height.	Dis-charge.
	Feet.	*Sec.-ft.*	*Feet.*	*Sec.-ft.*	*Feet.*	*Sec.-ft.*	*Feet.*	*Sec.-ft.*	*Feet.*	*Sec.-ft.*	*Feet.*	*Sec.-ft.*
1	3.54	5,382	2.71	3,264	2.07	1,913	1.84	1,514	1.24	766	0.63	367
2	3.77	6,033	2.82	3,528	2 03	1,837	1.94	1,678	1.27	793	0.78	435
3	3.97	6,613	2.79	3,456	2.02	1,818	1.89	1,594	1.26	784	0.79	440
4	4.12	7,060	2.83	3,552	2.05	1,875	1.82	1,482	1.24	766	0.69	391
5	4.07	6,910	2.69	3,217	2.04	1,856	1.75	1,375	1.25	775	0.63	367
6	4.04	6,820	2.68	3,194	1.93	1,661	1.74	1,360	1.22	748	0.30a	275
7	3.91	6,439	2.68	3,194	1.94	1,678	1.73	1,345	1.12	666	0.00	253
8	3.76	6,004	2.63	3,079	1.94	1,678	1.87	1,562	1.20	730	0.49	318
9	3.63	5,634	2.40	2,580	1.90	1,610	1.97	1,729	1.18	714	0.38	291
10	3.58	5,494	2.34	2,454	1.78	1,420	1.90	1,610	1.14	682	0.37	289
11	3.57	5,466	2.30	2,370	1.79	1,435	1.84	1,514	1.14	682	0.38	291
12	3.62	5,606	2.26	2,288	1.81	1,466	1.76	1,390	1.13	674	0.47	312
13	3.82	6,178	2.29	2,350	1.73	1,345	1.74	1,360	1.03	597	0.46	310
14	3.77	6,033	2.33	2,433	1.65	1,233	1.68	1,273	0.80	445	0.52	327
15	3.82	6,178	2.36	2,496	1.60	1,165	1.65	1,233	0.75	420	0.55	338
16	3.51	5,298	2.34	2,454	1.53	1,078	1.63	1,205	0.50	320	0.55	338
17	3.28	4,678	2.45	2,685	1.50	1,040	1.62	1,192	0.00	253	0.57	344
18	3.16	4,366	2.32	2,412	1.53	1,078	1.64	1,219	0.00	253	0.57	344
19	3.11	4,236	2.30	2,370	1.90	1,610	1.63	1,205	0.00	253	0.58	348
20	3.23	4,548	2.31	2,391	1.81	1,466	1.60	1,165	0.99	568	0.60a	355
21	3.16	4,366	2.35	2,475	1.70	1,300	1.54	1,090	1.01	583	0.63	367
22	2.88	3,672	2.45	2,685	1.63	1,205	1.48	1,017	0.97	554	0.65	375
23	2.67	3,171	2.33	2,433	1.60	1,165	1.41	936	0.94	533	0.69	391
24	2.66	3,148	2.27	2,308	1.62	1,192	1.41	936	0.96	547	0.71	400
25	2.64	3,102	2.21	2,186	1.66	1,246	1.38	904	1.02	590	0.74	415
26	2.66	3,148	2.18	2,126	1.76	1,390	1.35	872	1.06	620	0.75	420
27	2.59	2,988	2.18	2,126	2.05	1,875	1.33	852	1.00	575	0.74a	415
28	2.64	3,102	2.18	2,126	2.01	1,799	1.32	841	0.96	547	0.72	405
29	2.58	2,966	2.20a	2,165	1.80	1,450	1.27	793	0.94	533	0.72a	405
30	2.58	2,966	2.22	2,206	1.91	1,627	1.25	775	0.82	457	0.72a	405
31	2.64	3,102	2.14	2,048	......	......	1.25	775	......	......	0.72a	405

a Gauge height interpolated.

MONTHLY DISCHARGE of Bow River at Banff, for 1914.

(Drainage area 893 square miles.)

MONTH.	DISCHARGE IN SECOND-FEET.				RUN-OFF.	
	Maximum.	Minimum.	Mean.	Per square Mile.	Depth in inches on Drainage Area.	Total in Acre-feet.
January	400	298	350	0.392	0.45	21,521
February	344	285	315	0.353	0.37	17,494
March	318	255	285	0.320	0.37	17,524
April	642	285	399	0.447	0.50	23,742
May	2,900	841	1,846	2.070	2.39	113,506
June	7,570	2,580	4,922	5.510	6.15	292,880
July	7,060	2,966	4,861	5.440	6.27	298,890
August	3,552	2,048	2,602	2.910	3.36	159,980
September	1,913	1,040	1,484	1.660	1.85	88,310
October	1,729	775	1,219	1.370	1.58	74,950
November	793	253	581	0.651	0.73	34,572
December	440	253	359	0.402	0.46	22,074
The year	....	....	....	....	24.48	1,165,443

5 GEORGE V, A. 1915

SPRAY RIVER AT SPRAY LAKES.

Location.—On the SE. ¼ Sec. 31, Tp. 22, Rge. 10, W. 5th Mer.
Records available.—July 23, 1914, to October 27, 1914.
Gauge.—Chain gauge on right bank.
Bench-mark.—On tree; elevation 11.48 feet above the zero of the gauge.
Channel.—Hard bottom; current very swift.
Discharge measurements.—Made by wading.
Observer.—Louis Mumford.
Remarks.—Not sufficient discharge measurements have been made to accurately determine the daily discharge; from July 23 to October 27 the discharge varied between 800 and 200 sec.-ft.

DISCHARGE MEASUREMENTS of Spray River at Spray Lakes, in 1914.

Date.	Engineer.	Width.	Area of Section.	Mean Velocity.	Gauge Height.	Discharge.
		Feet.	*Sq. ft.*	*Ft. per sec.*	*Feet.*	*Sec.-ft.*
July 24............	H. C. Ritchie........	116.0	200	3.95	6.16	787
Sept. 1............	do	76.0	118	2.28	5.74	270

SPRAY LAKES OVERFLOW AT SPRAY LAKES.

Location.—On the SW. ¼ Sec. 32, Tp. 22, Rge. 10, W. 5th Mer.
Records available.—July 23, 1914, to October 27, 1914.
Gauge.—Vertical staff at left bank.
Bench-mark.—On tree; elevation 4.98 feet above the zero of the gauge.
Channel.—Clean gravel and sand.
Discharge measurements.—Made by wading.
Observer.—Louis Mumford.
Remarks.—Not sufficient discharge measurements have been made to accurately determine the daily discharge; from July 23 to October 27 the discharge varied between 105 and 47 sec.-ft.

DISCHARGE MEASUREMENTS of Spray Lakes Overflow at Spray Lakes, in 1914.

Date.	Engineer.	Width.	Area of Section.	Mean Velocity.	Gauge Height.	Discharge.
		Feet.	*Sq. ft.*	*Ft. per sec.*	*Feet.*	*Sec.-ft.*
July 24............	H. C. Ritchie..	37.5	36.0	2.78	1.54	100
Sept. 1............	do	35.0	27.4	1.83	1.04	50

SPRAY RIVER NEAR BANFF.

Location.—On the S.W. ¼ Sec. 25, Tp. 25, Rge. 12, W. 5th Mer., at the highway bridge near the Canadian Pacific Railway Banff Springs Hotel, near the junction of the stream with the Bow River.
Records available.—July 15, 1910, to December 31, 1914.
Gauge.—Chain on left bank; elevation of zero maintained at 93.29 feet during 1910-11. Elevation of zero maintained at 88.71 feet during 1912-14.
Bench-mark.—Permanent iron bench-mark on the left bank; assumed elevation, 100.00 feet.
Channel.—Gravel, large boulders at left bank.
Discharge measurements.—Made from bridge.
Observer.—N. B. Sanson.

SESSIONAL PAPER No. 25c

DISCHARGE MEASUREMENTS of Spray River near Banff, in 1914.

Date.	Engineer.	Width.	Area of Section.	Mean Velocity.	Gauge Height.	Discharge.
		Feet.	*Sq. ft.*	*Ft. per sec.*	*Feet.*	*Sec.-ft.*
Jan. 15............	H. C. Ritchie.........	27.5	63.9	3.63	5.200	232
Jan. 28	do	26.5	63.1	2.37	5.220	150
Feb. 11..	do	23.5	59.4	2.96	5.200	176
Feb. 24............	do	25.0	54.0	3.05	4.960	165
Mar. 7............	do	24.5	49.5	3.49	4.730	173
Mar. 26	do	25.0	47.5	2.65	4.690	126
April 4	do	37.5	51.0	3.30	4.680	168
April 17..........	do	37.5	52.0	3.52	4.750	183
May 4..........	do	114.0	109.0	4.43	5.500	484
May 19..........	do	117.5	191.3	5.26	6.150	1,006
June 2..........	do	118.5	227.1	5.83	6.420	1,325
June 16..........	do	122.0	327.0	7.97	7.220	2,605
June 29..........	do	118.5	228.0	6.55	6.540	1,494
July 27..........	do	118.0	193.0	5.48	6.205	1,059
Aug. 11	do	118.0	169.0	4.92	6.000	832
Aug. 24	do	116.0	145.0	4.41	5.720	640
Sept. 16..........	do	108.0	105.0	3.81	5.395	401
Sept. 28....	do	116.0	135.0	4.17	5.670	563
Oct. 23	do	125.0	116.0	3.93	5.580	491
Nov. 9....	do	104.0	101.0	3.84	5.330	390
Nov. 23............	do	52.5	81.2	3.83	5.100	311
Dec. 7	do ·	34.5	90.3	2.62	5.620	236

DAILY GAUGE HEIGHT AND DISCHARGE of Spray River near Banff, for 1914.

DAY.	January. Gauge Height.	January. Dis- charge	February. Gauge Height.	February. Dis- charge	March. Gauge Height	March. Dis- charge	April. Gauge Height.	April. Dis- charge	May. Gauge Height.	May. Dis- charge	June. Gauge Height.	June. Dis- charge.
	Feet.	*Sec.-ft.*	*Feet.*	*Sec.-ft.*	*Feet.*	*Sec.-ft.*	*Feet.*	*Sec.-ft.*	*Feet.*	*Sec.-ft*	*Feet.*	*Sec.-ft.*
1............	5.25	195a	......	178	......	169	4 76	186	5.12	290	6.19	1,039
2............	5.43	194	4 85	183	4 77	170	4 72	176	5 36	394	6.40	1,300
3............	5.49	194	4.85	177	4 75	170	4 63	158	5.43	430	6 93	2,110
4............	......	202	4 84	168	4.74	171	4 66	164	5 50	468	7.27	2,684
5............	5 53	208	4 90	160	4 64	172	4 64	160	5 47	452	7.10	2,395
6............	5.32	214	4.84	150	4.65	172	4.63	158	5.42	425	6.90	2,060
7............	5.20	220	4.95	142	4.73	173	4.60	152	5.40	414	6.80	1,900
8............	5.19	227	......	164	......	174	4.60	152	5.49	467	6.70	1,745
9............	5.08	220	5.18	174	4.76	175	4.61	154	5.58	516	6.60	1,590
10.	5.02	214	5.10	170	4.63	176	4.60	152	5.62	541	6.51	1,455
11.	......	220	5.19	176	4.66	176	4.60	152	5.65	562	6.47	1,398
12............	......	224	5.08	174	4.73	177	4.63	158	5.66	568	6.58	1,560
13............	5.27	231	5.00	172	4.74	178	4.66	164	5.73	617	6.74	1,807
14............	5.12	224	4.96	168	4.71	176	4.71	174	5.84	702	6.90	2,060
15...	5.25	232	... ...	169	......	177	4.70	172	6.04	880	7.05	2,310
16............	5.03	208	4.98	170	4.72	178	4.75	184	6.12	962	7.22	2,599
17.	4.99	202	4.92	166	4.70	176	4.74	180	6.18	1,028	7.30	2,735
18............	......	205	4.93	168	4.71	176	4.73	178	6.23	1,086	7.40	2,905
19............	5.21	208	4.89	165	4.71	176	4.78	190	6.16	1,006	7.48	3,041
20............	4.91	180	4.75	160	4.77	180	4.83	203	6.13	973	7.35	2,820
21............	4.99	181	4.75	160	4.76	180	4.76	186	6.04	880	7.10	2,395
22.	5.03	182	......	161	......	170	4.76	186	6.07	910	6.84	1,964
23.	5.01	188	4.85	162	4.56	160	4.78	190	6.09	930	6.64	1,652
24............	5.19	178	4.96	165	4.56	152	4.80	195	6.16	1,006	6.52	1,470
25.	......	170	4.81	166	4.59	140	4.82	200	6.32	1,196	6.56	1,530
26.....	5.26	162	4.80	167	4.65	126	4.82	200	6.32	1,196	6.54	1,500
27............	5.00	156	4.77	168	4.86	134	4.83	203	6.21	1,062	6.52	1,470
28............	5.25	150	4.74	168	4.86	143	4.85	208	6.10	940	6.54	1,500
29............	5.25	153	......	......	......	150	4.89	218	6.08	920	6.57	1,545
30............	5.10	159	......	......	4.71	160	4.96	238	6.00	840	6.68	1,714
31............	5.05	166	......	......	4.69	170a	......	......	......	......	......	......

a Ice conditions Jan. 1 to March 31.

5 GEORGE V, A. 1915

DAILY GAUGE HEIGHT AND DISCHARGE of Spray River near Banff, for 1914.—*Concluded.*

DAY.	July.		August.		September.		October.		November.		December.	
	Gauge Height.	Dis-charge.	Gauge Height.	Dis-charge.	Gauge Height.	Dis-charge.	Gauge Height.	Dis-charge	Gauge Height.	Dis-charge	Gauge Height.	Dis-charge.
	Feet.	*Sec.-ft.*	*Feet.*	*Sec.-ft.*	*Feet.*	*Sec.-ft.*	*Feet.*	*Sec.-ft.*	*Feet.*	*Sec.-ft.*	*Feet.*	*Sec.-ft.*
1........	6.86	1,996	6.18	1,028	5.63	548	5.61	535	5.46	446	4.86	211
2........	6.90	2,060	6.17	1,017	5.62	541	5.59	522	5.46	446	5.10	216b
3........	7.06	2,327	6.15	995	5.54	492	5.59	522	5.44	436	5.13	225
4........	7.20	2,565	6.12	962	5.55	498	5.59	522	5.42	425	5.22	233
5........	7.15	2,480	6.10	940	5.56	504	5.59	522	5.42	425	5.25	238
6........	7.10	2,395	6.10	940	5.54	492	5.56	504	5.37	399	......	240
7........	7.00	2,225	6.10	940	5.51	474	5.57	510	5.36	394	5.69	236
8........	7.03	2,276	6.08	920	5.51	474	5.74	625	5.35	389	5.84	230
9........	6.90	2,060	6.05	890	5.50	468	5.72	610	5.34	385	5.88	220
10........	6.92	2,093	6.04	880	5.44	436	5.69	588	5.31	370	6.00	200
11........	6.85	1,980	6.02	860	5.51	474	5.66	568	5.30	365	6.18	175
12........	6.90	2,060	6.00	840	5.48	458	5.63	548	5.29	361	6.20	150
13........	6.95	2,142	5.97	813	5.45	441	5.58	516	5.27	351	......	153
14........	7.00	2,225	5.92	768	5.43	430	5.58	516	5.16	305	6.36	160
15........	6.95	2,142	5.87	726	5.43	430	5.61	535	5.08	276	......a	155
16........	6.89	2,044	5.87	726	5.39	409	5.69	588	4.99	247	......	150
17........	6.60	1,590	5.86	718	5.39	409	5.74	625	5.06	269	......	158
18........	6.54	1,500	5.84	702	5.39	409	5.74	625	5.13	293	......	165
19........	6.52	1,470	5.82	686	5.66	568	5.74	625	5.18	312	......	155
20........	6.53	1,485	5.80	670	5.61	535	5.69	588	5.16	305	......	158
21........	6.52	1,470	5.79	662	5.56	504	5.67	575	5.19	316	......	160
22........	6.51	1,455	5.79	662	5.58	516	5.61	535	5.10	282	......	165
23........	6.29	1,158	5.78	655	5.51	474	5.58	516	5.13	293	......	175
24........	6.29	1,158	5.78	655	5.53	486	5.56	504	5.13	293	......	165
25........	6.28	1,146	5.76	640	5.57	510	5.54	492	5.12	288	......	160
26........	6.24	1,098	5.76	640	5.63	548	5.51	474	5.11	286	......	160
27........	6.21	1,062	5.74	625	5.65	562	5.50	468	5.06	269	......	165
28........	6.20	1,050	5.74	625	5.67	575	5.46	446	5.10	282	......	170
29........	6.20	1,050	5.74	610	5.64	555	5.43	430	5.07	253	......	175
30........	6.18	1,028	5.68	582	5.60	528	5.45	441	4.92	227	......	180
31........	6.18	1,028	5.65	562	......	......	5.47	452	......	......		190b

a Ice jam.
b Ice conditions Dec. 2 to 31.

MONTHLY DISCHARGE of Spray River near Banff, for 1914.

(Drainage area 301 square miles.)

MONTH.	DISCHARGE IN SECOND-*FEET.*				RUN-OFF.	
	Maximum.	Minimum	Mean.	Per square Mile.	Depth in inches on Drainage Area.	Total in Acre-feet.
January.............................	231	150	196	0.651	0.75	12,052
February............................	183	142	167	0.555	0.58	9,275
March..............................	180	126	167	0.555	0.64	10,268
April...............................	238	152	180	0.598	0.67	10,711
May................................	1,196	290	755	2.510	2.89	46,423
June................................	3,041	1,039	1,942	6.450	7.20	115,560
July................................	2,565	1,028	1,736	5.770	6.65	106,740
August.............................	1,028	562	772	2.560	2.95	47,468
September..........................	575	409	491	1.630	1.82	29,217
October............................	625	430	533	1.770	2.04	32,773
November...........................	446	227	333	1.110	1.24	19,815
December...........................	240	150	183	0.608	0.70	11,252
The year..........................	....	....	....	....	28.13	451,554

CASCADE RIVER AT BANKHEAD.

Location.—On the SE. ¼ Sec. 19, Tp. 26, Rge. 11, W. 5th Mer., at the Bankhead Mines.
Records available.—August 16, 1911, to December 31, 1914.
Gauge.—Vertical staff; elevation of zero maintained at 93.49 feet since establishment.
Bench-mark.—Tree stump on left bank; assumed elevation, 100.00 feet.
Channel.—Coarse gravel.
Discharge measurements.—Made from foot bridge; bridge replaced October 30 by one 50 feet downstream.
Artificial control.—This station is two and one-half miles below the reservoir of the Calgary Power Company at Lake Minnewanka, and the flow of the stream is controlled by the gates.
Observer.—J. B. Mackinlay.

DISCHARGE MEASUREMENTS of Cascade River at Bankhead, in 1914.

Date.	Engineer.	Width.	Area of Section.	Mean Velocity.	Gauge Height.	Discharge.
		Feet.	*Sq. ft.*	*Ft. per sec.*	*Feet.*	*Sec.-ft.*
Jan. 2	H. C. Ritchie	52.5	126.0	2.71	2.52	341.0
Jan. 13	do	52.0	104.0	1.99	2.10	207.0
Jan. 28	do	52.0	143.0	1.08	3.25	155.0
Feb. 28	do	52.0	81.8	1.09	1.59	89.0
Mar. 10	do	52.0	79.2	1.05	1.58	83.0
Mar. 27	do	52.0	95.6	1.57	1.90	150.0
April 6	do	52.0	90.2	1.45	1.76	131.0
April 25	do	34.0	51.6	0.35	1.10	18.0
May 5	do	50.0	128.0	3.26	2.65	415.0
May 18	do	32.5	45.7	0.14	0.95	6.8
June 1	do	32.0	43.7	0.16	0.90	7.1
June 15	do	54.0	183.8	5.68	3.72	1,044.0
July 28	do	45.0	66.5	3.45	1.46	230.0
Aug. 10	do	45.0	76.0	4.01	1.72	305.0
Aug. 24	do	43.7	49.3	2.26	1.07	111.0
Sept. 12	do	32.0	30.2	1.60	0.65	49.0
Oct. 1	do	43.3	48.0	2.89	1.20	139.0
Oct. 14	do	45.0	62.8	3.09	1.48	194.0
Oct. 30	do	43.0a	68.2	2.66	1.51	181.0
Nov. 14	do	43.0	62.6	2.48	1.30	156.0
Nov. 24	do	43.5	70.6	2.96	1.46	209.0
Dec. 11	do	42.3	60.3	2.66	1.25	161.0
Dec. 30	do	41.8	56.4	2.36	1.15	133.0

a Measurements on and after October 30 made at new bridge 50 feet downstream.

STREAM MEASUREMENTS, 1914

5 GEORGE V, A. 1915

DAILY GAUGE HEIGHT AND DISCHARGE of Cascade River at Bankhead, for 1914.

DAY.	January.		February.		March.		April.		May.		June.	
	Gauge Height.	Dis-charge	Gauge Height.	Dis-charge.	Gauge Height.	Dis-charge.	Gauge Height.	Dis-charge	Gauge Height.	Dis-charge.	Gauge Height.	Dis-charge.
	Feet.	Sec.-ft.	Feet.	Sec.-ft.	Feet.	Sec.-ft.	Feet.	Sec.-ft.	Feet.	Sec.-ft.	Feet.	Sec.-ft.
1............	2.60	372	2.19	180	1.55	79	1.82	133.0	0.84	2 6	0.91	5.1
2............	2.52	340	2 55	180	1.54	77	1 81	130.0	0.97	9 2	0.93	6.8
3............	2.47	322	3.35	167	1.54	77	1.78	124.0	1.21	29.0	2.30	275.0
4............	2.42	310	3 52	142	1.54	77	1.78	124 0	1.23	32.0	3.65	997.0
5............	2.38	290	3.58	126	1 56	81	1.79	126.0	2.65	414.0	4.28	1,400.0
6............	2.34	284	3.81	108	1.58	84	1.76	120 0	2.56	376.0	4.12	1,298.0
7............	2.30	273	3.59	88	1.55	79	1.76	120.0	2.50	351 0	4.06	1,259.0
8............	2.27	263	3.25	70	1.56	81	1.76	120 0	2 45	331.0	4.00	1,221.0
9............	2.26	259	3.23	70	1.55	79	1.75	117.0	2.48	343.0	3.85	1,125.0
10...	2.21	242	3.04	72	1.58	84	1.75	117.0	2.46	335.0	3.75	1,061.0
11............	2.17	230	2.90	74	1.58	84	1.73	113.0	2.42	320 0	3.68	1,016.0
12.	2.14	220	2.53	75	1.56	81	1.73	113.0	2 40	312 0	2.97	571.0
13............	2.10	207	2.29	77	1.56	81	1.73	113.0	1.93	159 0	3.08	636.0
14.... ...	2.10	207	1.90	77	1.57	83	1 73	113.0	1.10	18 0	3.19	704.0
15............	2.06	197	1.72	79b	1.58	84	1.73	113.0	1.10	18 0	4.03	1,240.0
16............	2.04	195	1.57	81	1.58	84	1.73	113 0	0.98	9.8	4.19	1,343.0
17............	2.08	202	1.53	75	1.62	92	1.73	113.0	1.00	11.0	4.10	1,285.0
18............	2.00	180	1.52	74	1.61	90	1 72	111.0	1.01	11.1	4.05	1,253.0
19.	1.99	177	1.50	70	1.61	90	1 74	115 0	0.96	8.6	3.90	1,157.0
20.........	2.05	177	1.55	72	1.63	94	1.76	120.0	2.43	324.0	3.70	1,029.0
21........ ·..	2.18	172	1.68	72	1.61	90	1.76	120.0	2.44	328.0	3.55	980.0
22............	1.96	167	1.62	73	1.61	90	0.97	9.2	0 89	5.0	3.30	870.0
23............	2.21	164	1.55 ·	75	1.61	90	0 97	9 2	0.89	5 0	3.18	840.0
24............	2.61	162	1.53	75	1.64	96	1.03	13.0	0.88	4 2	3.10	835.0
25............	2.40	159	1.54	77	1.86	142	1.06	15.2	0.88	4 2	3.00	820.0
26............	2.56	157	1.55	79	1.95	164	1.15a	23.0	0.94	7.4	2.90	805.0
27............	2.90a	157	1.51	74	1.90	151	1.24	33.0	0.95	8.0	2.88	835.0
28............	3.25	155	1.91	86	1.89	149	1.26	35.0	0.90	5.0 ·	2.80	820.0
29............	3.67	159b	....	....	1.86	142	1.31	41.0	0.90	5.0	2.43	642.0
30............	3.50	164	....	....	1.84	137	1.35	47.0	0.89	5.0	1.90	381.0
31............	3.25	170	....	....	1.83	135	....	....	0.90	5.0	....	....

a Gauge height interpolated.
b Ice conditions Jan. 29 to Feb. 15.

SESSIONAL PAPER No. 25c

DAILY GAUGE HEIGHT AND DISCHARGE of Cascade River at Bankhead, for 1914.

DAY.	July.		August.		September.		October.		November.		December.	
	Gauge Height.	Discharge.	Gauge Height.	Discharge.	Gauge Height.	Discharge.	Gauge Height.	Discharge.	Gauge Height.	Discharge.	Gauge Height.	Discharge
	Feet.	Sec.-ft.	Feet.	Sec -ft.	Feet.	Sec.-ft.	Feet.	Sec.-ft.	Feet.	Sec.-ft.	Feet.	Sec -ft.
1	2.25	548	0.65	47	0 65	47	1.20	137	1.48	218	1 38	187
2	2.26	553	0.65	47	0 65	47	0.92	82	1.48	218	1.35	177
3	2.38	615	1.66	282	0 65	47	1 07	109	1.54	238	1.33	172
4	2.58	726	1 68	289	0.67	49	1.13	122	1 47	214	1 34	175
5	2.72	806	1.71	301	0.71	53	1.16	128	1.53	234	1 32	169
6	2.80	852	1.76	322	0.95	87	1.23	145	1.49	221	1.30	163
7	2.80	852	1.71	301	0.98	93	1.28	160	1.48	218	1.29	160
8	2.05	450	1.71	301	0.65	47	1.38	186	1.40	192	1.28	158
9	2.50	681	1.74	313	0.64	47	1.34	175	1.40	192	1.27	155
10	3.07	1,014	1.72	305	0.64	47	1.36	180	1.39	189	1.25	150
11	3.04	995	1.73	309	0.64	47	1.43	202	1.42	198	1.25	150
12	3.00	971	1.74	313	0.63	46	1.45	208	1.43	202	1.25	150
13	2.95	941	1.70	297	0.71	53	1.43	202	1.44	205	1.23	145
14	2.95	941	1.70	297	0.75	58	1.48	218	1.30	163	1.23	145
15	2.71	800	1.20	137	0.84	70	1.46	211	1.65	278	1.41	195
16	2.76	829	1.28	159	0.90	79	1.52	231	1.54	238	1.99	422
17	2.65	765	1.35	177	0.93	84	1.56	245	1.74	313	1.34	175
18	2.55	709	1.38	188	0.69	51	1.59	254	1.66	288	1.34	175
19	2.53	698	0.50	36	0.76	59	1.59	254	1.66	288	1.22	142
20	2.54	703	0.50	36	0.85	72	1.59	254	1.64	274	1.20	137
21	2.47	664	0.55	40	0.93	84	1.59	254	1.59	254	1.17	130
22	2.43	642	0.67	49	0.78	62	1.60	259	1.52	231	1.14	124
23	1.74	313	0.80	64	0.84	70	1.57	248	1.51	228	1.14	124
24	1.76	322	0.89	77	0.89	77	1.58	252	1.46	211	1.17	130
25	1.78	330	1.07	109	0.98	93	1.59	254	1.46	211	1.16	128
26	1.81	342	1.04	104	0.49	36	1.55	242	1.46	211	1.14	124
27	1.80	338	1.17	130	0.60	43	1.55	242	1.46	211	1.15	126
28	1.80	338	0.76	59	1.57	248	1.55	242	1.44	205	1.15	126
29	1.47	214	0.95	87	1.50	224	1.50	224	1.42	198	1.15	126
30	1.48	218	1.05	106	1.05	106	1.50	224	1.40	192	1.15	126
31	1.47	214	0.68	50	......	......	1.51	228	......	......	1.14	124

MONTHLY DISCHARGE of Cascade River at Bankhead, for 1914.

(Drainage area 248 square miles)

MONTH.	DISCHARGE IN SECOND-FEET.				RUN-OFF.	
	Maximum.	Minimum.	Mean.	Per square Mile.	Depth in inches on Drainage Area.	Total in Acre-feet.
January	372	155.0	217	0.875	1.01	13,343
February	180	70.0	92	0.370	0.38	5,093
March	164	77.0	98	0.396	0.46	6,044
April	133	9.2	90	0.364	0.41	5,379
May	414	2.6	122	0.492	0.57	7,501
June	1,400	5.1	89	3.590	4.00	52,958
July	1,014	214.0	625	2.520	2.90	38,430
August	322	36.0	172	0.694	0.80	10,576
September	248	36.0	74	0.299	0.33	4,415
October	259	82.0	206	0.831	0.96	12,666
November	313	163.0	224	0.903	1.01	13,329
December	422	124.0	158	0.637	0.73	9,715
The year					13.56	179,449

No 25c—9

5 GEORGE V, A. 1915

BOW RIVER NEAR KANANASKIS.

Location.—On the NW. ¼ Sec. 32, Tp. 24, Rge. 8, W. 5th Mer., at the Canadian Pacific Railway bridge, one mile above the Kananaskis Falls dam of the Calgary Power Company.

Records available.—March 10, 1912, to December 31, 1914. Records obtained at Morley, ten miles downstream, from May 25, 1910, to November 30, 1911.

Gauge.—Chain; elevation of zero maintained at 90.84 feet since establishment.

Bench-mark.—On side of east pier; assumed elevation, 100.00 feet.

Channel.—Solid rock, fairly uniform.

Discharge measurements.—Made from bridge; at very low stages by wading.

Observer.—The Calgary Power Company.

DISCHARGE MEASUREMENTS of Bow River near Kananaskis, in 1914.

Date.	Engineer.	Width.	Area of Section.	Mean Velocity.	Gauge Height.	Discharge.
		Feet.	*Sq. ft.*	*Ft. per sec.*	*Feet.*	*Sec.-ft.*
Jan. 6	H. C. Ritchie	293	478	2.41	3.97	1,155
Jan. 20–21	do	310	592	1.05	4.80	624
Feb. 3	do	263	315	2.26	4.00	710
Feb. 7	do	293	327	2.19	3.65	718
Mar. 3	do	283	297	2.09	2.16	620
Mar. 17	do	357	424	1.58	2.42	670
Mar. 31	do	360	431	1.59	2.43	688
April 14	do	350	314	2.74	1.91	860
April 29	do	352	321	2.76	1.88	885
May 12	do	375	535	4.22	2.42	2,256
May 27	do	399	724	5.57	2.91	4,032
June 9	do	412	1,004	6.86	3.65	6,888
June 23	do	414	1,072	7.35	3.81	7,878
July 7	do	420	1,230	8.01	4.25	9,844
Aug. 4	do	402	784	6.21	3.12	4,870
Sept. 8	do	385	569	4.33	2.46	2,465
Sept. 22	do	380	499	3.76	2.37	1,873
Oct. 7	do	380	505	3.85	2.38	1,943
Oct. 19	do	383	546	3.98	2.42	2,172
Nov. 3	do	377	478	3.43	2.24	1,641
Dec. 1	do	358	461	2.14	2.33	986
Dec. 15	do	241	350	1.24	3.46	433

SESSIONAL PAPER No. 25c

DAILY GAUGE HEIGHT AND DISCHARGE of Bow River near Kananaskis, for 1914.

DAY.	January.		February.		March.		April.		May.		June.	
	Gauge Height.	Dis-charge.	Gauge Height.	Dis-charge.	Gauge Height.	Dis-charge	Gauge Height.	Dis-charge.	Gauge Height.	Dis-charge	Gauge Height.	Dis-charge.
	Feet.	*Sec.-ft.*	*Feet.*	*Sec.-ft.*	*Feet.*	*Sec.-ft.*	*Feet.*	*Sec.-ft.*	*Feet.*	*Sec.-ft.*	*Feet.*	*Sec.-ft.*
1	5.36	1,260a	4.36	740	2.41	605	2.46	700	2 04	1,168	2 62	2,872
2	5.54	1,240	4.21	730	2.15	610	2 45	705	2.04	1,168	2 71	3,198
3	5.47	1,220	4.00	710	2 25	620	2.26	710	2.25	1,675	3.11	4,781
4	4.92	1,200	4.10	660	2.10	625	2 25	720	2.25	1,675	3.90	8,260
5	4.52	1,170	3 73	590	2 20	630	2 47	730	2 40	2,120	3.90	8,260
6	3.96	1,155	3.90	580	2.10	640	2.36	740	2.45	2,285	3.91	8,306
7	3.56	1,130	3.89	580	2.36	650	2.39	745	2.35	1,965	3.71	7,386
8	3.35	1,100	3.95	600	2.26	660	2.30	750	2.36	1,996	3.70	7,340
9	3.32	1,070	3.89	640	2.30	665	2.31	760	2.43	2,219	3.65	7,115
10	3.39	1,040	3.92	680	2.20	675	2.40	770	2.43	2,219	3.30	5,570
11	4.02	1,000	3.95	700	2.30	680	2.25	790	2.35	1,965	3.32	5,656
12	4.12	960	3.94	720	2.25	675	1.95	815	2.38	2,058	3.33	5,699
13	4.55	910	3.94	730	3.05	655	1.94	840	2.45	2,285	3.27	5,444
14	4.74	860	3.84	740	3.54	640	1.91	860a	2.43	2,219	3.55	6,665
15	4.89	810	3.95	740	3.42	645	1.91	900	2.42	2,186	3.75	7,570
16	4.90	760	3.84	735	3.05	655	1.92	920	2.42	2,186	4.25	9,870
17	5.00	720	3.60	720	2.70	670	1.90	880	2.66	3,016	4.35	10,330
18	4.97	680	3.59	680	2.40	680	1.95	980	2.69	3,124	4.37	10,422
19	4.90	650	3.41	620	2.61	700	1.85	790	2.73	3,274	4.30	10,100
20	4.80	625	3.35	560	2.33	710	1.90	880	2.76	3,388	4.20	9,640
21	4.80	620	3.37	560	2.30	720	1.91	900	2.73	3,274	3.95	8,490
22	4.95	615	3.35	565	2.32	730	1.85	790	2.60	2,800	3.85	8,030
23	4.94	610	3.40	570	2.46	740	1.80	700	2.65	2,980	3.75	7,570
24	5.03	605	3.44	575	2.35	740	1.86	808	2.67	3,052	3.36	5,828
25	4.95	600	3.70	580	2.37	730	1.88	844	2.83	3,657	3.35	5,785
26	5.00	600	3.30	585	2.41	710	1.91	900	2.95	4,130	3.32	5,656
27	4.60	600	3.00	595	2.91	660	1.85	790	2.90	3,930	3.29	5,528
28	4.65	620	2.70	600	3.04	640	1.89	862	2.80	3,540	3.22	5,234
29	4.65	680			2.90	655	1.85	790	2.75	3,350	3.35	5,785
30	5.02	760			2.40	670	1.90	880	2.55	2,625	3.30	5,570
31	4.60 .	760			2.40	690			2.53	2,555		

a Ice conditions Jan. 1 to April 14.

STREAM MEASUREMENTS, 1914

5 GEORGE V, A. 1915

DAILY GAUGE HEIGHT AND DISCHARGE of Bow River near Kananaskis, for 1914.—*Concluded.*

DAY.	July.		August.		September.		October.		November.		December.	
	Gauge Height.	Dis-charge.	Gauge Height.	Dis-charge	Gauge Height.	Dis-charge.	Gauge Height.	Dis-charge.	Gauge Height.	Dis-charge.	Gauge Height.	Dis-charge
	Feet.	*Sec.-ft.*	*Feet.*	*Sec.-ft.*	*Feet.*	*Sec.-ft.*	*Feet.*	*Sec.-ft.*	*Feet.*	*Sec.-ft.*	*Feet.*	*Sec.-ft.*
1	3.39	5,957	3.00	4,330	2.46	2,318	2.50	2,450	2.25	1,675	2.40	990
2	3.80	7,800	2.98	4,250	2.45	2,285	2.52	2,520	2.23	1,621	2.71	960
3	3.89	8,214	3.05	4,535	2.47	2,351	2.52	2,520	2.24	1,648	2.92	930
4	4.04	8,904	3.12	4,822	2.45	2,285	2.50	2,450	2.21	1,567	3.00	900
5	4.21	9,686	3.14	4,904	2.47	2,351	2.50	2,450	2.20	1,540	2.84	860
6	4.28	10,008	3.10	4,740	2.45	2,285	2.46	2,318	2.20	1,540	3.02	810
7	4.31	10,146	3.15	4,945	2.42	2,186	2.38	2,058	2.15	1,420	3.26	760
8	4.01	8,766	3.11	4,781	2.44	2,252	2.43	2,219	2.16	1,444	3.45	720
9	3.92	8,352	3.12	4,622	2.50	2,450	2.55	2,625	2.15	1,420	3.80	670
10	3.89	8,214	2.90	3,930	2.35	1,965	2.50	2,450	2.20	1,540	3.29	620
11	3.87	8,122	2.89	3,891	2.36	1,996	2.47	2,351	2.16	1,444	3.85	580
12	3.90	8,260	2.79	3,502	2.43	2,219	2.44	2,252	2.14	1,396	3.75	550
13	3.91	8,306	2.71	3,198	2.35	1,975	2.46	2,318	2.13	1,372	3.56	480
14	3.94	8,444	2.76	3,388	2.38	2,058	2.40	2,120	2.00	1,080	3.64	430
15	3.95	8,490	2.78	3,464	2.43	2,219	2.37	2,027	2.23	960a	3.57	420
16	3.97	8,582	2.72	3,236	2.42	2,186	2.35	1,975	2.80	860	3.46	420
17	3.72	7,432	2.74	3,312	2.40	2,120	2.40	2,120	3.64	865	3.38	430
18	3.47	6,308	2.71	3,198	2.32	1,872	2.41	2,153	4.28	870	3.37	440
19	3.41	6,044	2.68	3,088	2.31	1,841	2.42	2,186	3.63	880	3.26	450
20	3.36	5,828	2.66	3,016	2.34	1,934	2.45	2,285	3.43	900	3.39	500
21	3.48	6,352	2.62	2,872	2.32	1,872	2.40	2,120	2.81	920	3.38	580
22	3.44	6,176	2.60	2,800	2.37	2,027	2.33	1,903	2.25	970	3.41	610
23	3.29	5,528	2.66	3,016	2.38	2,058	2.33	1,903	2.10	1,020	3.33	630
24	3.10	4,740	2.70	3,160	2.38	2,058	2.32	1,872	2.05	1,050	3.31	650
25	3.03	4,453	2.69	3,124	2.37	2,027	2.40	2,120	2.10	1,090	3.30	660
26	3.06	4,576	2.60	2,800	2.34	1,934	2.38	2,058	2.11	1,110	3.44	670
27	3.05	4,535	2.58	2,730	2.35	1,975	2.34	1,934	2.02	1,110	3.42	670
28	3.02	4,412	2.52	2,520	2.43	2,219	2.33	1,903	2.05	1,110	3.40	640
29	3.04	4,494	2.50	2,450	2.47	2,351	2.31	1,841	2.09	1,080	3.40	610
30	3.00	4,330	2.47	2,351	2.49	2,417	2.27	1,729	2.25	1,050	3.41	650
31	2.97	4,210	2.49	2,417	......	......	2.27	1,729	......	......	3.64	700a

a Ice conditions Nov. 15 to Dec. 31.

MONTHLY DISCHARGE of Bow River near Kananaskis, for 1914.

(Drainage area 1,646 square miles.)

MONTH.	DISCHARGE IN SECOND-FEET.				RUN-OFF.	
	Maximum	Minimum	Mean	Per square Mile.	Depth in inches on Drainage Area.	Total in Acre-feet.
January	1,260	600	859	0.521	0.60	52,818
February	740	560	646	0.393	0.41	35,877
March	740	605	670	0.407	0.47	41,197
April	920	700	808	0.490	0.55	48,079
May	4,130	1,168	2,583	1.570	1.81	158,820
June	10,422	2,872	6,932	4.200	4.69	412,480
July	10,146	4,210	6,957	4.230	4.88	427,770
August	4,945	2,351	3,528	2.140	2.47	216,930
September	2,450	1,841	2,136	1.300	1.45	127,100
October	2,625	1,729	2,128	1.290	1.49	130,850
November	1,675	860	1,218	0.740	0.83	72,480
December	990	420	645	0.392	0.45	39,660
The year	....	....	....	....	20 10	1,764,061

KANANASKIS RIVER NEAR KANANASKIS.

Location.—On the SW. ¼ Sec. 34, Tp. 24, Rge. 8, W. 5th Mer., one and one-half miles above the junction with the Bow River.

Records available.—September 1, 1911, to November 11, 1911.   January 1, 1912, to December 31, 1914.

Gauge.—Chain; elevation of zero maintained at 88.17 feet since April 20, 1912.   Previous to April 20, 1912, gauge readings are at old station one and one-half miles downstream.

Bench-mark.—Permanent iron bench-mark; assumed elevation, 100.00 feet.

Channel.—Gravel, very uniform.

Discharge measurements.—From cable and car.

Observer.—The Calgary Power Company.

DISCHARGE MEASUREMENTS of Kananaskis River near Kananaskis, in 1914.

Date.	Engineer.	Width.	Area of Section.	Mean Velocity.	Gauge Height.	Discharge.
		Feet.	*Sq. ft.*	*Ft. per sec.*	*Feet.*	*Sec.-ft.*
Jan. 7	H. C. Ritchie	100	117.0	1.11	6.14	206
Jan. 20	do	105	210.0	0.46	6.68	96
Feb. 16	do	36	73.1	2.18	9.46	159
Mar. 2	do	43	50.3	3.54	7.00	178
Mar. 16	do	97	177.0	0.80	4.72	144
April 1	do	97	132.0	1.05	4.67	139
April 13	do	100	186.0	0.93	4.76	172
April 30	do	104	209.0	1.15	5.02	231
May 11	do	114	244.0	2.02	5.55	492
May 26	do	120	333.3	3.44	6.26	1,147
June 8	do	123	384.7	4.33	6.69	1,666
June 22	do	120	417.0	4.68	6.62	1,951
July 8	do	125	432.0	4.82	6.70	2,086
July 20	do	123	392.0	4.03	6.42	1,580
Aug. 5	do	120	352.0	3.40	6.06	1,197
Aug. 17	do	121	329.0	3.06	5.89	1,008
Sept. 9	do	116	294.0	2.40	5.61	707
Sept. 21	do	116	286.0	2.22	5.56	635
Oct. 6	do	115	274.0	1.99	5.45	548
Oct. 20	do	115	282.0	2.12	5.55	598
Nov. 2	do	113	254.0	1.64	5.26	416
Nov. 30	do	107	224.0	1.16	5.00	260
Dec. 14	do	30	111.0	2.00	6.99	219

5 **GEORGE V, A. 1915**

DAILY GAUGE HEIGHT AND DISCHARGE of Kananaskis River near Kananaskis, for 1914.

DAY.	January.		February.		March.		April.		May.		June.	
	Gauge Height.	Discharge	Gauge Height.	Discharge	Gauge Height.	Discharge	Gauge Height.	Discharge	Gauge Height.	Discharge	Gauge Height.	Discharge
	Feet.	*Sec.-ft.*	*Feet.*	*Sec.-ft.*	*Feet.*	*Sec.-ft.*	*Feet.*	*Sec.-ft.*	*Feet.*	*Sec.-ft.*	*Feet.*	*Sec.-ft.*
1	6.87	.204a	8.46	125	7.20	180	4.65	139	5.06	249	6.23	1,104
2	6.56	204	7.72	100	7.05	178	4.66	141	5.24	322	6.50	1,430
3	6.47	205	7.75	90	6.75	173	4.66	141	5.35	375	6.90	1,930
4	6.39	205	7.81	82	6.50	170	4.66	141	5.36	380	7.05	2,117
5	6.31	205	9.72	75	6.82	175	4.69	146	5.35	375	7.05	2,117
6	6.25	206	9.76	77	6 40	166	4.70	148	5.31	355	6.85	1,867
7	6.24	206	9.74	95	6.30	167	4.69	146	5.30	350	6.80	1,805
8		202	9 81	130	6.35	169	4.69	146	5.32	360	6.69	1,673
9	6.16	195	10.20	155	6.16	165	4.68	144	5.42	412	6.23	1,130
10	6.19	180	10.10	155	6.14	165	4.70	148	5.53	480	6.17	1,090
11	5.72	145	10 00	153	6.15	165	4.75	158	5.54	486	6.17	1,110
12	5.73	143	10.10	150	6.14	165	4.74	156	5.54	486	6.28	1,250
13	6.10	158	10.15	151	6.10	164	4.75	158	5.60	525	6.38	1,400
14	6.15	162	9.99	153	5.78	163	4.74	156	5.67	577	6.50	1,570
15	6.18	160	9.74	157	5 01	150	4.76	160	5.97	830	6.60	1,720
16	5.95	140	9.27	159	4.65	144	4.80	169	5.97	830	6.70	1,880
17	5.76	125	9.10	161	4.63	142	4.78	164	6.12	982	6.78	2,100
18	5.44	115	9.00	164	4.62	140	4.79	167	6.15	1,015	6.95	2,260
19	6.36	105	8.84	160	4.62	140	4.84	179	6.16	1,026	7.00	2,370
20	6.70	96	8.44	160	4.66	140	4.82	174	6.16	1,026	6.75	2,070
21	8.54	94	8.75	170	4.65	142	4.83	177	6.01	870	6.65	1,960
22	8.35	88	8.10	162	4.66	142	4.84	179	6.02	880	6.65	2,000
23	9.34	83	8.20	167	4.70	143	4.89	192	6.01	870	6.45	1,720
24		81	8.91	175	4.68	143	4.88	190	6.16	1,026	6.25	1,445
25	9.96	81	7.40	170	6.45	135	4.87	187	6.20	1,070	6.27	1,471
26	8.80	81	7.10	165	8.19	127	4.93	205	6.26	1,139	6.23	1,419
27	9.02	81	7.10	165	7.95	135	4.95	211	6.28	1,162	6.20	1,380
28	8.70	88	7.90	180	7.54	138	4.94	208	6.21	1,082	6.15	1,315
29	8.20	110			7.21	138	4.96	214	6.15	1,015	6.20	1,380
30	9.25	140			6.60	137	4.99	224	6.00	860	6.29	1,497
31	8.02	115			5.10	137a			6.10	960		

a Ice conditions Jan. 1 to March 31.

DAILY GAUGE HEIGHT AND DISCHARGE of Kananaskis River near Kananaskis, for 1914.

DAY.	July.		August.		September.		October.		November.		December.	
	Gauge Height.	Dis- charge	Gauge Height.	Dis- charge	Gauge Height.	Dis- charge.	Gauge Height.	Dis- charge	Gauge Height.	Dis- charge.	Gauge Height.	Dis- charge.
	Feet.	*Sec.-ft.*	*Feet.*	*Sec.-ft.*	*Feet.*	*Sec.-ft.*	*Feet.*	*Sec.-ft.*	*Feet.*	*Sec.-ft.*	*Feet.*	*Sec.-ft.*
1	6.34	1,566	6.03	1,159	5 62	700	5.42	526	5.25	405	4 92	228
2	6.47	1,748	6.01	1,133	5.63	710	5.41	518	5.25	405	5 03	275
3	6.53	1,832	6.02b	1,146	5.64	720	5.39	503	5.26	412	4.98	252
4	6.60	1,930	6.03b	1,159	5 64	720	5.40	510	5.23	391	4 98	252
5	6.65	2,000	6.05	1,185	5.61	690	5.44	542	5.23	391	4.98	232
6	6.71	2,084	6.02	1,146	5.60	680	5.44	542	5.21	377	4.97	248
7	6.77	2,168	6.00	1,120	5.54	626	5.40	510	5.19	364	5.29	245c
8	6.73	2,112	6.03	1,159	5.55	635	5.39	503	5.17	352	6.04	241
9	6.70	2,070	6.06	1,198	5.60	680	5.55	635	5.19	364	7.58	237
10	6.66	2,014	6.01	1,133	5.52	608	5.48	574	5.16	346	7.71	232
11	6.64	1,986	5.96	1,072	5.50	590	5.44	542	5.16	346	8.54	227
12	6.60	1,930	5.93	1,036	5.51	599	5.40	510	5.15	340	8.51	224
13	6.59	1,916	5.89	989	5.48	574	5.37	489	5.13	328	7.22	220
14	6.63	1,972	5.86	956	5.42	526	5.52	608	5 08	300	6.99	218
15	6.70	2,070	5.82	912	5.42	526	5.54	626	5.00b	260	6.76	210
16	6.68	2,042	5.80	890	5.40	510	5.60	680	5 00b	260	6.58	195
17	6.58	1,902	5.86	956	5.37	489	5.62	700	5.00b	260	7.45	210
18	6.49	1,776	5.88	978	5.37	489	5.61	690	5.00b	260	6.98	200
19	6.47	1,748	5.86	956	5.50	590	5.57	653	5.00b	260	6.70	180
20	6.38	1,622	5.82	912	5.49	582	5.57	653	4.98	252	6.77	175
21	6.44	1,706	5.80	890	5.48	574	5.46	558	5.04	280	6.86	180
22	6.37	1,608	5.70	780	5.52	608	5.45	550	5.04	280	6.94	185
23	6.25	1,445	5.72	802	5.46	558	5.40	510	5.01	265	7.35	188
24	6.16	1,328	5.76	846	5.45	550	5.46	558	5.01	265	6.90	180
25	6.10	1,250	5.74	824	5.44	542	5.38	496	5.02	270	6.69	150
26	6.08	1,224	5.70	780	5.46	558	5.33	461	5.01	265	6.48	125
27	6.03	1,159	5.66	740	5.50	590	5.31	447	5.00	260	6.47	123
28	6.01	1,133	5.62	700	5.51	599	5.30	440	5.00	260	6.44	121
29	6.04	1,172	5.68	760	5.49	582	5.28	426	5.00	260	6.28	115
30	6.01	1,133	5.66	740	5.46	558	5.28	426	4.98	252	6.04	110
31	5.98	1,096	5.64	720	......	......	5.28	426	......	......	6.20	120c

b Gauge height interpolated.
c Ice conditions Dec. 7 to 31.

MONTHLY DISCHARGE of Kananaskis River near Kananaskis, for 1914.

(Drainage area 398 square miles.)

MONTH.	DISCHARGE IN SECOND-FEET.				RUN-OFF.	
	Maximum.	Minimum	Mean.	Per square Mile.	Depth in inches on Drainage Area.	Total in Acre-feet.
January	206	81	142	0.356	0.41	8,731
February	180	75	143	0.360	0.37	7,942
March	180	127	153	0.384	0.44	9,408
April	224	139	169	0.425	0.47	10,056
May	1,139	249	722	1.810	2.09	44,394
June	2,370	1,090	1,653	4.150	4.63	98,360
July	2,168	1,096	1,701	4.280	4.93	104,590
August	1,198	700	961	2.420	2.79	59,090
September	720	489	599	1.500	1.67	35,643
October	700	426	542	1.360	1.57	33,326
November	412	252	311	0.780	0.87	18,506
December	275	110	197	0.495	0.57	12,113
The year	....	....	....	....	20.81	442,159

5 GEORGE V, A. 1915

GHOST RIVER AT GILLIES' RANCH.

Location.—On the NE. ¼ Sec. 23, Tp. 26, Rge. 6, W. 5th Mer., one mile above the junction with the Bow River.

Records available.—August 17, 1911, to November 11, 1911. January 1, 1912, to December 31, 1914.

Gauge.—Chain on left bank; 1911–13 elevation of zero, 91.15 feet; 1914 elevation of zero, 89.22 feet.

Bench-mark.—Stone on left bank; assumed elevation, 100.00 feet.

Channel.—Shifting gravel.

Discharge measurements.—Made by wading; at very high stages measurements made at highway bridge, one mile downstream.

Observer.—Miss *E.* Gillies.

DISCHARGE MEASUREMENTS of Ghost River at Gillies' Ranch, in 1914.

Date.	Engineer.	Width.	Area of Section.	Mean Velocity.	Gauge Height.	Discharge.
		Feet.	*Sq. ft.*	*Ft. per sec.*	*Feet.*	*Sec.-ft.*
Jan. 9	H. C. Ritchie	41.0	59.6	2.34	3.68	139
Feb. 5	do	30.0	37.0	2.46	4.14	91
Mar. 5	do	35.0	32.5	3.88	3.50	126
Mar. 19	do	30.0	28.5	3.80	4.00	108
April 2	do	32.0	36.8	2.50	4.63	92
April 16	do	74.5	56.2	3.24	3.25	182
April 28	do	74.0	47.0	2.82	3.20	132
May 14	do	75.0	60.6	2.88	3.19	174
June 11	do	77.5	79.9	3.16	3.47	252
June 25	do	79.0	89.3	3.60	3.74	321
July 9	do	77.0	87.6	3.42	3.65	300
Aug. 6	do	76.0	76.4	3.14	3.50	240
Aug. 20	do	76.0	75.8	3.25	3.54	246
Sept. 10	do	75.5	67.7	2.84	3.42	192
Sept. 24	do	75.6	75.4	2.90	3.48	219
Oct. 8	do	76.0	78.7	3.08	3.50	243
Oct. 21	do	75.7	74.7	2.86	3.45	214
Nov. 5	do	75.6	70.8	2.73	3.37	194
Nov. 19	do	57.0	68.4	2.98	3.46	204
Dec. 3	do	56.0	70.6	2.02	3.47	142
Dec. 17	do	44.0	80.6	1.25	3.70	101

SESSIONAL PAPER No. 25c

DAILY GAUGE HEIGHT AND DISCHARGE of Ghost River at Gillies' Ranch, for 1914.

DAY.	January.		February.		March.		April.		May.		June.	
	Gauge Height.	Dis-charge.	Gauge Height.	Dis-charge.	Gauge Height.	Dis-charge	Gauge Height.	Dis-charge.	Gauge Height.	Dis-charge	Gauge Height.	Dis-charge.
	Feet.	*Sec.-ft.*	*Feet.*	*Sec.-ft.*	*Feet.*	*Sec.-ft.*	*Feet.*	*Sec.-ft.*	*Feet.*	*Sec.-ft.*	*Feet.*	*Sec.-ft.*
1.........	3.92	167a	4.85	98.	3.82	120	3.70	93	3.31	171	3.19	175
2.........	3.95	168	4.34	97	.80	123	4.58	92	3.39	196	3.10	151
3.........	4.30	172	4.20	96	.80	126	4.45	95	3.29	171	3.36	221
4.........	4.50	174	4.20	93	.80	128	4.56	98	3.25	163	3.30	205
5.........	4.10	160	3.93	91	3.49	126	5 58	102	3.30	180	3.29	202
6.........	3.95	150	4.65	91	.65	121	5.48	108	3.19	152	3.24	189
7.........	3.80	144	4.60	92.	.80	126	5.46	118	3.29	182	3.34	216
8.........	3.65	138	3.85	94	.70	121	4.80	130	3.29	185	3.80	340
9.........	3.72	139	4.45	100	60	114	3.12	146a	3.32	196	3.43	240
10.........	3.72	139	4.10	104	3 34	110	3.11	143	3.37	208	3.44	243
11.........	3.63	134	3.82	102	3.80	115	3.11	143	3.35	210	3.47	251
12.........	3.60	132	4.10	110	4.00	118	3.15	154	3.36	215	3.50	259
13.........	3.65	134	4.05	108	4.19	116	3.20	168	3.30	202	3.83	348
14.........	3.65	134	3.98	107	4.25	113	3.30	196	3.22	183	3.56	275
15.........	3.56	128	4.10	122	4.25	111	3.36	212	3.32	210	3.69	310
16.........	3.49	124	4.08	120	4.90	110	3.25	182	3.22	183	3.68	308
17.........	3.50	125	4.08	118	4.01	110	3.20	165	3.15	163	3.70	313
18.........	3.52	126	4.05	114	3.96	108	3.20	162	3.15	163	3.76	329
19... (...	3.50	125	3.95	110	3.94	108	3.21	161	3.10	151	3.76	329
20.........	3.47	124	3.92	106	3.75	110	3.19	153	3.15	163	3.79	337
21.........	3.49	120	3.90	105	3.80	109	3.19	150	3.10	151	3.50	259
22.........	3.55	115	3.95	104	3.76	114	3.19	147	3.15	163	3.47	251
23.........	3.52	112	3.95	110	3.94	116	3.21	148	3.15	163	3.42	237
24.........	3.49	104	3.95	115	3.62	112	3.22	148	3.25	192	3.41	235
25.........	4.35	96	4.00	118	3.55	109	3.19	138	3.15	163	3.74	324
26.........	5.05	95	4.00	116	4.87	106	3.20	138	3.05	138	3.56	275
27.........	5.06	94	3.84	124	4.03	103	3.20	135	3.05	138	3.73	321
28.........	5.05	94	3.82	120	5.76	101	3.25	146	3.00	124	3.70	313
29.........	5.00	97	......	......	4.05	99	3.25	150	2.96	113	3.65	300
30.........	5.00	103	......	......	4.12	97	3.30	166	2.96	113	3.60	286
31.........	4.85	101	......	......	5.75	95	......	......	3.09	148	......	......

a Ice conditions Jan. 1 to April 9.

5 GEORGE V, A. 1915

DAILY GAUGE HEIGHT AND DISCHARGE of Ghost River at Gillies' Ranch, for 1914.—*Concluded.*

DAY.	July.		August.		September.		October.		November.		December.	
	Gauge Height.	Dis-charge	Gauge Height.	Dis-charge	Gauge Height.	Dis-charge.	Gauge Height.	Dis-charge.	Gauge Height.	Dis-charge.	Gauge Height.	Dis-charge
	Feet.	*Sec.-ft.*	*Feet.*	*Sec.-ft.*	*Feet.*	*Sec.-ft.*	*Feet.*	*Sec.-ft.*	*Feet.*	*Sec.-ft.*	*Feet.*	*Sec.-ft.*
1..........	3.54	270	3.54	250	3.44	205	3.43	215	3.39	199	3.37	163
2..........	3.53	267	3.54	250	3.44	205	3.42	216	3.39	199	3.37	152
3..........	3.53	267	3.53	251	3.44	204	3.41	212	3.36	191	3.47	142
4..........	3.52	264	3.54	250	3.43	201	3.43	220	3.37	193	3.48	135
5..........	3.75	327	3.56	256	3.43	200	3.44	224	3.39	199	3.48	129
6..........	3.83	348	3.56	256	3.43	199	3.42	219	3.38	195	3.57	121
7..........	3.66	302	3.54	251	3.43	198	3.41	218	3.38	195	3.57	115
8..........	3.56	275	3.50	240	3.44	199	3.50	243	3.38	192	3.60	110
9..........	3.65	300	3.54	250	3.43	195	3.60	268	3.35	183	3.65	105
10........	3.63	293	3.56	254	3.42	191	3.80	320	3.30	169	3.54	101
11.	3.63	292	3.54	249	3.43	193	3.60	265	3.30	168	3.80	98
12........	3.63	291	3.54	248	3.43	194	3.60	264	3.33	175	3.87	98
13........	3.65	295	3.54	248	3.42	196	3.53	246	3.34	176	3.87	99
14........	3.68	302	3.54	247	3.42	195	3.54	249	3.33	172	3.95	100
15........	3.69	303	3.54	247	3.43	198	3.54	247	3.36	180	3.84	100
16...	3.56	268	3.56	251	3.45	203	3.55	248	3.36	178	3.94	101
17........	3.57	269	3.60	262	3.46	206	3.60	259	3.55	231	3.70	101
18........	3.55	263	3.60	261	3.66	261	3.49	229	3.55	230	4.00	102
19....	3.55	262	3.55	249	3.49	216	3.49	227	3.48	210	4.50	102
20........	3.55	261	3.54	245	3.46	209	3.49	225	3.30	200	4.68	103
21........	3.56	262	3.54	245	3.44	205	3.45	214	3.30	200	5.11	106
22........	3.56	261	3.56	248	3.43	202	3.43	209	3.30	200	5.12	109
23........	3.60	271	3.55	245	3.43	203	3.40	201	3.30	200	5.10	112
24........	3.60	270	3.54	241	3.48	219	3.41	203	3.32	200*a*	5.05	112
25........	3.60	275	3.53	237	3.46	215	3.40	201	3.49	200	......	112
26....	3.58	270	3.53	236	3.46	216	3.41	203	3.49	200	5.04	110
27........	3.55	261	3.49	225	3.45	215	3.40	201	3.46	200	5.00	111
28...	3.55	260	3.47	218	3.44	214	3.40	201	3.46	200	5.02	112
29........	3.54	257	3.47	217	3.44	215	3.40	201	3.39	196	5.00	114
30....	3.54	257	3.47	216	3.43	214	3.39	199	3.38	180	4.85	114
31........	3.54	256	3.43	204	......	......	3.39	199	......	......	4.75	112*a*

a Ice conditions Nov. 24 to Dec. 31.

MONTHLY DISCHARGE of Ghost River at Gillies' Ranch, for 1914.

(Drainage area 378 square miles.)

MONTH.	DISCHARGE IN SECOND-FEET.				RUN-OFF.	
	Maximum.	Minimum	Mean.	Per square Mile.	Depth in inches on Drainage Area.	Total in Acre-feet.
January.......	174	94	128	0.339	0.39	7,870
February....	124	91	107	0.284	0.29	5,942
March....	128	95	113	0.299	0.34	6,948
April.	212	92	143	0.378	0.42	8,509
May.	215	113	169	0.447	0.52	10,391
June	348	151	268	0.710	0.79	15,947
July......	348	256	278	0.735	0.85	17,094
August	262	204	243	0.643	0.74	14,941
September...	261	191	206	0.545	0.61	12,258
October.	320	199	227	0.600	0.69	13,958
November	231	168	194	0.513	0.57	11,544
December.....	163	98	113	0.299	0.34	6,948
The year..	....	....	....	....	6.55	125,402

Location.—On the SE. ¼ Sec. 30, Tp. 24, Rge. 4, W. 5th Mer., at Jumping Pound post office.
Records available.—April 19, 1908, to October 31, 1914.   Discharge measurements only,
June, 1906.
Gauge.—Vertical staff, attached to bridge pile; elevation of zero has been maintained
at 89.82 feet since establishment.
Bench-mark —Permanent iron bench-mark on right bank; assumed elevation, 100.00 feet.
Channel.—Gravel and clay.
Discharge measurements.—At high water, made from highway bridge; at ordinary stages,
by wading, downstream.
Winter flow.—No winter records have been obtained.
Observer.—John Bateman.

DISCHARGE MEASUREMENTS of Jumpingpound Creek near Jumping Pound, in 1914.

Date.	Engineer.	Width.	Area of Section.	Mean Velocity.	Gauge Height.	Discharge.
		Feet.	*Sq. ft.*	*Ft. per sec.*	*Feet.*	*Sec.-ft.*
April 27.............	H. C. Ritchie	50.0	54.0	0.89	2.16	48.0
May 15.............	do	52.7	64.5	1.04	2.25	67.0
June 12........ . ..	do	52.0	65.5	1.05	2.25	69.0
June 26	do	56.5	76.3	1.46	2.40	111.0
July 10.............	do	50.3	55.1	0.75	2.14	42.0
Aug. 7.............	do	27.5	30.9	0.39	1.91	12.0
Aug. 21	do	28.0	30.9	0.36	1.90	11.0
Sept. 11.... , ...	do	20.0	26.8	0.35	1.84	9.4
Sept. 25............	do	27.5	30.7	0.35	1.85	10.7
Oct. 9.............	do	31.0	36.6	0.73	2.04	27.0
Oct. 22.............	do	33.5	38.8	1.16	2.12	45.0

5 GEORGE V, A. 1915

DAILY GAUGE HEIGHT AND DISCHARGE of Jumpingpound Creek, near Jumping Pound, for 1914.

DAY.	April.		May.		June.	
	Gauge Height.	Dis- charge.	Gauge Height.	Dis- charge.	Gauge Height.	Dis- charge.
	Feet.	Sec.-ft.	Feet.	Sec.-ft.	Feet.	Sec.-ft.
1			2.12	39	2.14	42
2			2.12	39	2.14	42
3			2.15	44	2.15	44
4	2.90	345	2.15	44	2.19	53
5	3.00	410	2.16	46	2.25	67
6	3.06	456	2.14	42	2.40	111
7	2.92	358	2.14	42	2.40	111
8	2.79	282	2.14	42	2.35	96
9	2.75	261	2.13	40	2.35	96
10	2.75	261	2.19	53	2.36	99
11	2.74	256	2.20	55	2.25	67
12	2.65	212	2.20	55	2.35	96
13	2.55	168	2.20	55	2.36	99
14	2.30	80	2.20	55	2.40	111
15	2.25	67	2.20	55	2.35	96
16	2.24	65	2.25	67	2.30	80
17	2.20	55	2.23	67	2.29	78
18	2.18	51	2.25	67	2.29	78
19	2.16	46	2.26	70	2.26	70
20	2.16	46	2.26	70	2.21	57
21	2.14	42	2.25	67	2.17	48
22	2.12	39	2.27	73	2.15	44
23	2.20	55	2.29	78	2.14	42
24	2.19	53	2.28	75	2.14	42
25	2.18	51	2.27	72	2.18	51
26	2.17	48	2.26	70	2.20	55
27	2.15	44	2.25	67	2.22	60
28	2.14	42	2.24	65	2.26	70
29	2.14	42	2.22	60	2.20	55
30	2.13	40	2.20	55	2.18	51
31			2.16	46		

SESSIONAL PAPER No. 25c

DAILY GAUGE HEIGHT AND DISCHARGE of Jumpingpound Creek near Jumping Pound, for 1914.

DAY.	July. Gauge Height.	July. Dis-charge.	August. Gauge Height.	August. Dis-charge.	September. Gauge Height.	September. Dis-charge.	October. Gauge Height.	October. Dis-charge.
	Feet.	*Sec.-ft.*	*Feet.*	*Sec.-ft.*	*Feet.*	*Sec.-ft.*	*Feet.*	*Sec.-ft.*
1	2.15	44.0	1.93	14.4	1.88	11.0	1.82	8.6
2	2.14	42.0	1.92	13.6	1.87	10.5	1.81	8.3
3	2.16	46.0	1.91	12.8	1.85	9.5	1.84	9.2
4	2.18	51.0	1.90	12.0	1.86	10.0	1.86	10.0
5	2.20	55.0	1.89	11.5	1.86	10.0	1.90	12.0
6	2.20	55.0	1.96	17.0	1.85	9.5	1.94	15.2
7	2.40	111.0	1.99	20.0	1.85	9.5	1.95	16.0
8	2.28	75.0	1.99	20.0	1.87	10.5	1.95	16.0
9	2.27	73.0	2.00	21.0	1.86	10.0	2.04	26.0
10	2.27	73.0	2.08	32.0	1.85	9.5	2.02	22.0
11	2.25	67.0	2.10	35.0	1.84	9.2	2.01	22.0
12	2.20	55.0	2.06	29.0	1.87	10.5	2.00	21.0
13	2.22	60.0	2.05	27.0	1.90	12.0	1.98	19.0
14	2.19	53.0	2.01	22.0	1.95	16.0	1.95	16.0
15	2.13	40.0	2.00	21.0	1.98	19.0	2.00	21.0
16	2.08	32.0	2.00	21.0	1.98	19.0	2.07	30.0
17	2.08	32.0	1.98	19.0	1.95	16.0	2.15	44.0
18	2.06	29.0	2.01	22.0	1.95	16.0	2.00	21.0
19	2.05	27.0	2.00	21.0	1.94	15.2	2.25	67.0
20	2.04	26.0	1.99	20.0 *	1.94	15.2	2.26	70.0
21	2.03	25.0	2.00	21.0	1.92	13.6	2.12	39.0
22	2.02	23.0	2.00	21.0	1.90	12.0	2.14	42.0
23	2.00	21.0	1.91	12.8	1.88	11.0	2.11	37.0
24	1.99	20.0	1.92	13.6	1.86	10.0	2.09	33.0
25	1.95	16.0	1.92	13.6	1.85	9.5	2.08	32.0
26	1.98	19.0	1.93	13.4	1.85	9.5	2.07	30.0
27	1.96	17.0	1.93	14.4	1.84	9.2	2.06	29.0
28	1.95	16.0	1.92	13.6	1.83	8.9	2.05	27.0
29	1.95	16.0	1.91	12.8	1.83	8.9	2.02	23.0
30	1.94	15.2	1.90	12.0	1.82	8.6	2.00	21.0
31	1.93	14.4	1.89	11.5	....	....	1.98*a*	19.0

a Gauge height interpolated.

MONTHLY DISCHARGE of Jumpingpound Creek near Jumping Pound, for 1914.

(Drainage area 188 square miles.)

MONTH.	DISCHARGE IN SECOND-FEET. Maximum.	Minimum.	Mean.	Per square Mile.	RUN-OFF. Depth in inches on Drainage Area.	Total in Acre-feet.
April (4 to 30)	456.0	39.0	143.0	0.761	0.77	7,658
May	78.0	39.0	57.3	0.305	0.35	3,523
June	111.0	42.0	70.4	0.374	0.42	4,189
July	111.0	14.4	40.3	0.214	0.25	2,478
August	35.0	11.5	18.5	0.098	0.11	1,137
September	19.0	8.6	11.6	0.062	0.07	690
October	70.0	8.3	26.0	0.138	0.16	1,599
The period	....	....	....	....	2.13	21,274

5 GEORGE V, A. 1915

BOW RIVER AT CALGARY.

Location.—On NE. ¼ Sec. 15, Tp. 24, Rge. 1, W. 5th Mer., at Langevin traffic bridge on Fourth Street East, in the city of Calgary.

Records available.—May 5, 1908, to December 31, 1914; at this location since 1912.

Gauges.—(1) Standard chain type, on Langevin bridge; elevation of zero 82.59 feet during 1912-14.   (2) Gurley automatic, on Langevin bridge; elevation of zero 82.59 feet during 1914.

Bench-mark.—Permanent iron bench-mark near intersection of Second and Third avenues east; assumed elevation, 100.00 feet.

Channel.—Composed of coarse gravel; may shift in flood stages.

Discharge measurements.—Made from the downstream side of bridge.

Observer.—C. A. Lang.

DISCHARGE MEASUREMENTS of Bow River at Calgary, in 1914.

Date.	Engineer.	Width.	Area of Section.	Mean Velocity.	Gauge Height.	Discharge.
		Feet.	*Sq. ft.*	*Ft. per sec.*	*Feet.*	*Sec.-ft.*
Jan. 3	Hughes and Hoover	303	846	1.34	4.77	1,318
Jan. 9	J. S. Tempest	282	733	1.39	4.18	1,019
Jan. 14	do	284	853	1.30	4.89	1,149
Jan. 23	do	286	904	0.94	5.09	853
Jan. 29	R. J. Srigley	272	841	1.20	5.62	1,017
Feb. 14	J. S. Tempest	271	747	1.30	5.56	974
Feb. 19	do	256	714	1.41	5.44	1,010
Feb. 27	do	276	712	1.25	5.24	892
Mar. 10	R. J. Srigley	268	646	1.55	5.04	1,003
April 2	J. S. Tempest	247	818	1.41	4.58	1,155
May 8	Whyte and Kerby	245	910	2.30	4.34a	2,096
May 27	R. J. Srigley	306	1,415	3.60	5.54a	5,096
June 8	do	318	1,871	5.35	6.96a	10,014
June 18	do	325	2,211	6.44	8.02a	14,242
July 21	do	316	1,800	4.68	6.68a	8,425
Aug. 12	do	300	1,374	3.43	5.45a	4,716
Sept. 14	do	293	1,163	2.50	4.78a	2,907
Oct. 16	do	294	1,194	2.61	4.83a	3,118
Nov. 12	H. S. Kerby	280	943	2.02	4.19a	1,910
Dec. 16	Srigley and Rowley	254	773	1.24	4.01	958

a Automatic gauge heights.

SESSIONAL PAPER No. 25c

DAILY GAUGE HEIGHT AND DISCHARGE of Bow River at Calgary, for 1914.

Day.	January.		February.		March.		April.		May.		June.	
	Gauge Height.	Dis-charge	Gauge Height.	Dis-charge	Gauge Height.	Dis-charge	Gauge Height.	Dis-charge	Gauge Height.	Dis-charge	Gauge Height.	Dis-charge
	Feet.	Sec.-ft.	Feet.	Sec.-ft.	Feet.	Sec.-ft.	Feet.	Sec.-ft.	Feet.	Sec.-ft.	Feet.	Sec.-ft.
1	4.66ad	1,500	......	1,055	5.34	898	4.36	1,150	4.91	1,990	5.53	4,560
2	4.50	1,440	......	1,005	5.23	916	4.47	1,155	4.19	1,895	6.02	6,470
3	4.75	1,318	......	925	......	928	4.54	1,160	4.39	2,155	6.51	8,640
4	4.68	1,270	....	885	......	938	4.58	1,162	4.58	2,500	7.52	12,090
5	4.72	1,210	....	855	......	945	4.61	1,160	4.43	2,360	7.45	11,300
6	4.46	1,110	5.20	845	......	955	4.65	1,200e	4.38	2,170	7.42	11,840
7	4.48	1,095	5.11	856	4.45	965	4.42a	1,240	4.25	2,125	7.28	11,040
8	4.42	1,025	5.30	885	4.52	975	......	1,560	4.40	2,300	6.57	9,880
9	4.33	1,019	5.29	680	5.02	990	......	1,710e	4.59	2,560	6.54	8,840
10	4.70	1,000	5.10	850	4.99	1,003	4.166d	1,840	4.74	2,860	6.47	8,045
11	....	998	5.22	955	5.02	1,010	4.06	1,790	4.79	2,980	6.52	8,220
12	4.98	1,060	5.30	962	4.96	1,020	4.15	1,825	4.77	2,840	6.64	8,640
13	5.12	1,140	5.30	968	4.94	1,030	4.18	1,870	4.87	3,175	6.94	9,760
14	4.90	1,142	5.56	974	4.78	1,040	4.15	1,825	5.02	3,560	7.28	11,040
15	5.01	1,146	5.45	1,029	4.78	1,048	4.12	1,780	5.23	4,060	7.65	12,025
16	5.04	1,110	5.56	1,026	4.81	1,055	3.97	1,620	5.44	4,720	7.94	13,930
17	5.09	1,085	5.43	1,065	4.63	1,064	3.79	1,436	5.52	4,990	8.00	14,200
18	5.13	1,054	....	1,030	4.55	1,072	3.80	1,560	5.53	4,990	8.02	14,200
19	5.12	1,025	5.48	1,010	4.59	1,080	3.78	1,490	5.51	4,930	7.50	14,155
20	......	975	5.28	990	4.35	1,088	3.73	1,465	5.27	4,510	7.92	12,840
21	......	925	5.20	965	4.40	1,094	3.78	1,490	5.26	4,490	7.66	12,670
22	......	895	5.51	945	4.44	1,096	3.74	1,470	5.32	4,360	7.23	10,920
23	......	853	5.28	920	4.47	1,095	3.80	1,500	5.28	4,540	6.73	9,120
24	......	825	5.49	890	4.41	1,085	3.79	1,496	5.55	5,050	6.54	8,560
25	......	805	......	882	4.31	1,065	3.80	1,500	5.69	5,470	6.60	8,500
26	......	900	5.38	884	4.29	1,054	3.83	1,515	5.65	5,350	6.59	8,465
27	......	860	5.25	892	4.46	1,054	3.75	1,475	5.56	5,090	6.49	8,115
28	......	820	5.38	898	4.52	1,070	3.77	1,455	5.39	4,570	6.51	8,155
29	......	1,017	......	...	....	1,120	3.76	1,450	5.27	4,219	6.54	8,200
30	......	1,045	......	...	4.60	1,125	3.89	1,500	5.19	3,975	6.61	8,585
31	......	1,065	......	...	4.43	1,144	....	......	5.28	4,180	....	...

a Jan. 1 to April 7 and Dec. 6 to 31—observers' records.
b April 10 to Dec. 5—automatic gauge records.
c Gauge heights interpolated.
d Jan. 1 to April 10 and Dec. 1 to 31—ice conditions.
e April 6 to 9—discharge estimated.

5 GEORGE V, A: 1915

DAILY GAUGE HEIGHT AND DISCHARGE of Bow River at Calgary, for 1914.—Concluded.

DAY.	July.		August.		September.		October.		November.		December.	
	Gauge Height.	Dis- charge	Gauge Height.	Dis- charge	Gauge Height.	Dis- charge.	Gauge Height.	Dis- charge	Gauge Height.	Dis- charge.	Gauge Height.	Dis- charge.
	Feet.	*Sec.-ft.*	*Feet.*	*Sec.-ft.*	*Feet.*	*Sec.-ft.*	*Feet.*	*Sec.-ft.*	*Feet.*	*Sec.-ft.*	*Feet.*	*Sec.-ft.*
1	6.93	9,720	5.72	5,560	5.11	3,775	4.81	3,025	4.30	2,050	3.98d	1,720
2	7.30	11,200	5.75	5,650	4.94	3,350	4.79	2,980	4.28	2,020	3.81	1,640
3	7.57	12,280	5.82	5,860	4.92	3,300	4.79c	2,980	4.29	2,035	3.78	1,540
4	7.82	13,390	5.82	5,860	4.90	3,250	4.78c	2,960	4.22	1,930	3.76	1,460
5	7.74c	13,030	5.87	6,010	4.86	3,150	4.78	2,960	4.04	1,690	3.74b	1,400
6	7.66c	12,670	5.81	5,830	4.90	3,250	4.76	2,920	3.98	1,630	3.72a	1,340
7	7.58c	12,320	5.81	5,830	4.86	3,150	4.71	2,820	3.90c	1,550	3.73	1,260
8	7.50c	12,000	5.81	5,830	4.84	3,100	4.87	3,175	3.82c	1,510	3.72	1,160
9	7.40	11,600	5.75	5,650	4.84	3,100	4.98	3,450	3.74	1,470	3.70	1,100
10	7.40	11,600	5.66	5,380	4.79	2,980	4.78	2,960	3.80	1,500	4.02	1,040
11	7.35	11,400	5.54	5,020	4.73	2,860	4.80	3,000	3.90	1,550	3.79	990
12	7.31	11,240	5.45	4,750	4.77	2,940	4.84	3,100	4.16	1,840	4.05	940
13	7.35	11,400	5.36	4,480	4.76	2,920	4.86	3,150	3.99	1,640	4.34	920
14	7.50	12,000	5.36	4,480	4.70	2,800	4.86	3,150	3.97	1,620	4.82	925
15	7.56	12,240	5.36	4,480	4.64	2,680	4.85	3,125	3.97	1,620	4.16	935
16	7.55	12,200	5.36	4,480	4.58	2,560	4.83	3,075	3.97	1,620	4.05	958
17	7.27	11,080	5.41	4,630	4.57	2,540	4.79	2,980	4.00	1,650	4.25	960
18	6.82	9,280	5.44	4,720	4.56	2,520	4.73	2,860	4.03c	1,680	4.28	970
19	6.58	8,430	5.38	4,540	4.55	2,500	4.70	2,800	4.07c	1,720	4.62	980
20	6.52	8,220	5.33	4,390	4.69	2,780	4.64	2,680	4.11c	1,765	4.56	990
21	6.67	8,745	5.26	4,180	4.76	2,920	4.57	2,540	4.15c	1,825	4.38	995
22	6.54	8,290	5.27	4,210	4.71	2,820	4.57	2,540	4.19c	1,885	4.75	1,000
23	6.26	7,310	5.33	4,390	4.64	2,680	4.54	2,480	4.22	1,930	4.87	1,000
24	6.07	6,645	5.32	4,300	4.59	2,580	4.51	2,420	4.27	2,005	4.97	1,005
25	5.96	6,280	5.23	4,090	4.57	2,540	4.51	2,420	4.38	2,170	5.06	1,010
26	5.89	6,070	5.15	3,875	4.60	2,600	4.48	2,360	4.23	1,945	4.99	1,020
27	5.83	5,890	5.10	3,750	4.67	2,740	4.50	2,400	4.18	1,870	5.01	1,025
28	5.79	5,770	5.10	3,750	4.78	2,960	4.41	2,220	4.14	1,810	5.06	1,030
29	5.74	5,620	5.10	3,750	4.90	3,250	4.40	2,200	4.10	1,750	5.19	1,035
30	5.73	5,590	5.09	3,725	4.88	3,200	4.34	2,110	4.08	1,730	5.00	1,040
31	5.70	5,500	5.10	3,750	......	......	4.33	2,095	......	......	4.99a	1,045

a Jan. 1 to April 7 and Dec. 6 to 31—observers' records.
b April 10 to Dec. 5—automatic gauge records.
c Gauge heights interpolated.
d Jan. 1 to April 10 and Dec. 1 to 31—ice conditions.

MONTHLY DISCHARGE of Bow River at Calgary, for 1914.

(Drainage area 3,113 square miles.)

MONTH.	DISCHARGE IN SECOND-FEET.				RUN-OFF.	
	Maximum.	Minimum	Mean.	Per square Mile.	Depth in inches on Drainage Area.	Total in Acre-feet.
January	1,560	800	1,054	0.339	0.39	64,808
February	1,055	845	945	0.304	0.32	52,483
March	1,144	908	1,034	0.332	0.38	63,578
April	1,870	1,150	1,498	0.481	0.54	89,140
May	5,470	1,660	3,700	1.190	1.37	227,500
June	14,200	4,990	10,208	3.280	3.66	607,380
July	13,390	5,500	9,645	3.100	3.57	593,050
August	6,010	3,725	4,750	1.530	1.76	292,070
September	3,775	2,500	2,926	0.940	1.05	174,110
October	3,450	2,095	2,772	0.890	1.03	170,444
November	2,170	1,470	1,767	0.568	0.63	105,143
December	1,720	920	1,111	0.357	0.41	68,312
The year	......	......	......	......	15 11	2,508,018

SESSIONAL PAPER No. 25c

ELBOW RIVER AT FULLERTON'S RANCH.

Location.—On the NW. ¼ Sec. 12, Tp. 23, Rge. 5, W. 5th Mer., about 600 feet from Jake Fullerton's ranch, 35 miles southwest of Calgary.
Records available.—September 29, 1914, to December 31, 1914.
Gauge.—Vertical staff; elevation of zero maintained at 90.83 feet since establishment.
Bench-mark.—Tree-stump about 50 feet southeast of gauge; assumed elevation, 100 00 feet.
Channel.—Fairly permanent.
Discharge measurements.—Made by wading, about 800 feet downstream, from gauge.
Observer.—Jake Fullerton.

DISCHARGE MEASUREMENTS of Elbow River at Fullerton's Ranch, in 1914.

Date.	Engineer.	Width.	Area of Section.	Mean Velocity.	Gauge Height.	Discharge.
		Feet.	*Sq. ft.*	*Ft. per sec.*	*Feet.*	*Sec.-ft.*
Sept. 11	H. S. Kerby	71.0	86.8	2.17	1.30	188
Sept. 29	do	71.0	96.4	2.39	1.43	230
Nov. 19	do	69.0	95.6	2.57	1.35	245
Dec. 29	R. J. McGuinness	100.0	89.0	1.39	2.75	123

DAILY GAUGE HEIGHT AND DISCHARGE of Elbow River at Fullerton's Ranch, for 1914.

DAY.	September.		October.		November.		December.	
	Gauge Height.	Dis-charge.	Gauge Height.	Dis-charge.	Gauge Height.	Dis-charge.	Gauge Height.	Dis-charge.
	Feet.	*Sec.-ft.*	*Feet.*	*Sec.-ft.*	*Feet.*	*Sec.-ft.*	*Feet.*	*Sec.-ft.*
1			1.43	232	1.50	275	1.35	230
2			1.43	233	1.49	272	1.36	215
3			1.44	236	1.49	272	1.36	197
4			1.45	240	1.48	272	1.37	176
5			1.45	242	1.47	269	1.40	157
6			1.45	243	1.47	271	1.50	135
7			1.46	245	1.46	267	1.65	120
8			1.47	246	1.47	270	1.69	105
9			1.47	248	1.46	270	1.68	97
10			1.47	250	1.45	266	1.70	90
11			1.47	252	1.45	268	1.70	85
12			1.48	254	1.44	266	2.30	85
13			1.48	256	1.44	266	2.35	86
14			1.49	258	1.44	267	2.90	88
15			1.49	260	1.35	243	3.80	90
16			2.00	404	1.33	238	3.80	93
17			2.02	410	1.35	244	3.55	96
18			2.02	412	1.34	243	3.32	98
19			1.82	354	1.31	234c	3.32	102
20			1.64	304	1.30	245	3.32	104
21			1.60	294	1.30	245	3.32	106
22			1.58	290	1.30a	245	3.27	108
23			1.57	287	1.30a	245	3.17	112
24			1.55	283	1.30a	245	3.07	114
25			1.55	283	1.30a	245	3.07	115
26			1.54	282	1.30a	245	3.07	117
27			1.54	283	1.30a	245	3.07	120
28			1.54	284	1.30	245	3.07	122
29	1.43	230	1.53	281	1.30	243	2.62	123
30	1.43	232c	1.53	282	1.35	240b	2.57	126
31			1.53	284			2.53	128b

a Gauge heights interpolated.
b to *b* Ice conditions.
c to *c* Shifting conditions.

No. 25c—10

5 GEORGE V, A. 1915

MONTHLY DISCHARGE of Elbow River at Fullerton's Ranch, for 1914.

(Drainage area 254 square miles.)

MONTH.	DISCHARGE IN SECOND-FEET.				RUN-OFF.	
	Maximum.	Minimum	Mean.	Per square Mile.	Depth in inches on Drainage Area.	Total in Acre-feet.
September (29-30)	232	230	231	0.909	0.068	916
October	412	232	281	1.110	1.280	17,278
November	275	234	255	1.000	1.120	15,174
December	230	85	121	0.476	0.550	7,440
The period					3.018	40,808

ELBOW RIVER AT CALGARY.

Location.—On SW. ¼ Sec. 14, Tp. 24, Rge. 1, W. 5th Mer.
Records available.—May 8, 1908, to December 31, 1914.
Gauge.—Standard chain on Twelfth ave. bridge; elevation of zero, 3,404.82 feet during 1912-14.
Bench-marks.—(1) Permanent iron bench-mark near cable station; elevation, 3,423.85 feet above mean sea level (Geodetic Surveys of Canada). (2) Corner of wing wall of left abutment of traffic bridge; elevation, 3,420.07 feet above mean sea level (Geodetic Surveys of Canada).
Channel.—Composed of gravel and boulders, liable to shift and affected by back water from the Bow River during flood stages of that stream.
Discharge measurements.—Made from cable car, or in low stages by wading.
Winter flow.—Open water conditions prevail at station.
Diversions.—City of Calgary water supply intake twelve miles upstream from station.
Observer.—Mrs. I. S. White.

DISCHARGE MEASUREMENTS of Elbow River at Calgary, in 1914.

Date.	Engineer.	Width.	Area of Section.	Mean Velocity.	Gauge Height.	Discharge.
		Feet.	*Sq. ft.*	*Ft. per sec.*	*Feet.*	*Sec.-ft.*
Jan. 8	J. S. Tempest	69.0	75.8	2.08	1.93	157
Jan. 15	do	65.0	65.8	1.94	1.87	128
Jan. 19	do	66.0	63.2	1.69	1.85	97
Jan. 24	do	63.0	52.0	1.45	1.68	75
Feb. 3	R. J. Srigley	120.0	204.0	0.50	1.90	101
Feb. 16	J. S. Tempest	58.4	65.0	1.94	1.86	126
Feb. 23	do	57.0	60.2	1.74	1.86	104
Mar. 9	R. J. Srigley	63.0	45.6	2.42	1.84	110
April 4	J. S. Tempest	72.0	77.6	2.48	1.93	192
May 9	R. J. Srigley	131.0	262.0	0.91	1.96	238
May 30	do	131.0	307.0	1.32	2.28	406
June 26	do	139.0	396.0	1.81	2.65	716
July 11	do	134.0	340.0	1.44	2.46	489
Aug. 13	do	129.0	277.0	0.89	1.93	248
Sept. 16	do	128.0	259.0	0.78	1.92	202
Oct. 22	do	136.0	323.0	1.22	2.25	395
Nov. 11	H. S. Kerby	128.0	260.0	0.84	2.02	219
Nov. 18	do	120.0	244.0	0.73	1.98	179
Dec. 12	R. J. McGuinness	123.0	196.0	0.52	1.88	102
Dec. 28	do	130.0	217.0	0.71	1.77	154

SESSIONAL PAPER No. 25c

DAILY GAUGE HEIGHT AND DISCHARGE of *E*lbow River at Calgary, for 1914.

DAY.	January.		February.		March.		April.		May.		June.	
	Gauge Height.	Dis-charge.	Gauge Height.	Dis-charge.	Gauge Height.	Dis-charge.	Gauge Height.	Dis-charge.	Gauge Height.	Dis-charge	Gauge Height.	Dis-charge
	Feet.	*Sec.-ft.*	*Feet.*	*Sec.-ft.*	*Feet.*	*Sec.-ft.*	*Feet.*	*Sec.-ft.*	*Feet.*	*Sec.-ft.*	*Feet.*	*Sec.-ft*
1............	1.73	104a	1.94	92	1.84	109	1.80	145	2 05	280	2.44	520
2............	1.66	119	1.82	97	1.84	109	1.88	156	2.12	322	2 55	606
3............	1.68	128	1.90	101	1.81	110	2.02	186	2.13	328	2 70	730
4............	1.70	141	1 89	102	1 81	110	1.93	192b	2 15	340	2 84	822
5............	1.72	156	1.88	100	1.81	110	2.06	260	2.08	300	2.74	752
6............	1.89	159	1.87	98	1.84	110	2.19	334	2.05	284	2.65	684
7............	1.88	159	1.90	98	1.84	110	2.10	280	2.01	252	2.80	794
8............	1.87	157	2.06	100	1.84	110	2.02	240	1.97	232	2.56	624
9............	1.84	155	1.82	103	1.84	110	2.07	266	1.96	238	2.47	558
10.	1.72	153	1.75	108	1.79	111	1.96	210	2.14	338	2.44	540
11............	1.95	148	1.82	112	1.83	112	2.14	↘310	2 15	344	2.39	504
12............	1.65	148	1.82	116	1.84	113	2 22	360	2.10	314	2.38	498
13............	1.66	144	1.82	119	1.88	114	2.24	372	2 09	308	2.52	602
14...	1.82	136	1.88	122	1.89	115	2.16	326	2.19	370	2.81	812
15............	1.83	128	1.88	125	2.14	115	2.06	270	2.19	370	2.82	822
16............	1.82	121	1.89	126	2.06	115	2.16	326	2.18	362	2.90	878
17............	1.84	114	1.90	127	2.05	115	2.14	318	2.36	484	2.99	944
18............	2.03	106	1.86	127	1.84	114	2.05	266	2.36	484	3.11	1,020
19............	1.86	97	1.84	125	1.82	114	1.97	224	2.49	576	3.09	1,014
20............	1.70	94	1.84	119	1.78	113	2.10	298	2.46	556	3.01	962
21............	1.70	93	1.90	110	1.76	112	1.92	200	2.41	514	2.77	796
22............	1.66	87	2.06	105	1.86	112	1.89	190	2.37	486	2.60	674
23....	1.68	80	1.86	104	1.82	111	1.96	224	2.35	468	2.50	604
24............	1.68	75	1.86	104	1.76	111	1.96	224	2.32	446	2.37	412
25............	1.68	75	1.98	105	1.74	111	2.02	258	2.40	500	2.51	614
26............	1.70	76	1.81	106	1.61	112	2.09	302	2.46	542	2.67	730
27............	1.70	78	1.80	107	1.61	113	1.96	230	2.47	546	2.53	624
28............	1.69	80	1.81	108	1.61	115	1.89	196	2.32	440	2.45	560
29............	1.66	81	....	....	1.61	119	1.94	222	2.30	422	2.39	510
30............	1.63	82	....	....	1.70	122	2.01	258	2.28	408	2.41	520
31............	1.64	85	....	....	1.84	130	....	....	2.32	436	....	....

a to *b* Ice conditions.

STREAM MEASUREMENTS, 1914

5 GEORGE V, A. 1915

DAILY GAUGE HEIGHT AND DISCHARGE of Elbow River at Calgary, for 1914.—Concluded.

DAY.	July.		August.		September.		October.		November.		December.	
	Gauge Height.	Dis-charge.	Gauge Height.	Dis-charge.	Gauge Height.	Dis-charge.	Gauge Height.	Dis-charge.	Gauge Height.	Dis-charge.	Gauge Height.	Dis-charge.
	Feet.	Sec.-ft.	Feet.	Sec.-ft.	Feet.	Sec.-ft.	Feet.	Sec.-ft.	Feet.	Sec.-ft.	Feet.	Sec.-ft.
1	2.44	532	1.98	254	1.85	186	1.97	236	2.00	234	1.91	125
2	2.47	548	1.97	250	1.85	186	1.97	236	1.95	208	1.91	124
3	2.47	542	1.97	254	1.86	190	2.02	262	1.93	196	1.87	123
4	2.48	544	1.96	250	1.84	178	2.06	284	1.93	194	1.83	117
5	2.67	678	1.95	248	1.89	200	2.10	306	1.93	192	1.80	112
6	2.84	796	1.93	238	1.87	192	2.11	316	1.94	194	1.79	109
7	2.70	686	1.96	256	1.85	180	2.06	284	1.94	192	1.78	110
8	2.58	594	1.89	222	1.90	200	2.01	256	1.94	190	1.78	110
9	2.51	538	1.97	264	1.85	180	2.10	306	1.94	188	1.78	100
10	2.47	502	2.21	414	1.85	176	2.19	364	1.97	198	1.82	100
11	2.46	490	2.05	314	1.85	176	2.15	338	2.01	214	1.86	101
12	2.42	464	1.98	274	1.84	172	2.13	324	1.99	202	1.87	102
13	2.43	476	1.93	248	1.84	168	2.06	296	1.95	182	1.77	104
14	2.50	528	1.94	250	1.85	172	2.04	272	1.92	166	1.62	106
15	2.51	542	1.95	256	1.87	182	2.21	372	1.90	156	1.56	106
16	2.52	554	1.91	234	1.91	198	2.22	378	1.86	138	1.55	104
17	2.43	492	2.15	370	1.86	178	2.24	390	1.94	166	1.55	108
18	2.32	418	2.06	314	1.86	178	2.26	402	1.89	179	1.54	112
19	2.25	374	2.09	330	1.86	178	2.30	430	1.98	172	1.52	110
20	2.17	328	2.01	280	1.90	198	2.35	464	2.02	179	1.61	114
21	2.21	356	1.92	232	1.94	216	2.36	472	2.12	170	1.70	120
22	2.26	392	1.85	200	1.97	232	2.32	442	2.01	162	1.75	125
23	2.18	346	1.94	240	1.94	218	2.26	398	1.96	154	1.81	130
24	2.14	326	1.95	244	1.96	228	2.24	386	1.97	151	1.86	136
25	2.11	310	1.95	244	1.96	228	2.21	364	1.98	149	1.93	142
26	2.10	306	1.95	240	1.96	228	2.19	352	1.96	146	1.96	149
27	2.10	308	1.91	220	1.98	240	2.17	336	1.94	142	2.01	158
28	2.06	290	1.89	210	1.97	236	2.14	318	1.92	138	1.89	153
29	2.03	274	1.84	184	1.97	236	2.07	276	1.92	134	1.89	149
30	1.99	256	1.83	180	1.97	236	2.12	302	1.91	130	1.78	144
31	1.98	252	1.84	184	......	......	2.06	268	......	......	1.80	143

MONTHLY DISCHARGE of Elbow River at Calgary, for 1914.

(Drainage area 474 square miles.)

MONTH.	DISCHARGE IN SECOND-FEET.				RUN-OFF.	
	Maximum	Minimum	Mean.	Per square Mile.	Depth in inches on Drainage Area.	Total in Acre-feet.
January	159	75	115	0.242	0.27	7,071
February	127	92	110	0.231	0.24	6,109
March	130	109	113	0.238	0.27	6,948
April	372	145	255	0.538	0.60	15,174
May	576	232	396	0.836	0.96	24,349
June	1,020	412	691	1.458	1.63	41,117
July	796	252	453	0.956	1.10	27,854
August	414	180	255	0.538	0.62	15,679
September	240	168	199	0.420	0.47	11,841
October	472	236	336	0.709	0.81	20,660
November	234	130	174	0.367	0.41	10,354
December	158	100	121	0.255	0.29	7,440
The year	....	....	....	....	7.69	194,596

SESSIONAL PAPER No. 25c

NOSE CREEK AT CALGARY.

Location.—On the NW. ¼ Sec. 13, Tp. 24, Rge. 1, W. 5th Mer., at the traffic bridge about one and one-half miles east of the centre of the city, and about one-quarter mile above the junction of Nose Creek with Bow River.

Records available.—April 24, 1911, to October 31, 1914.

Gauge.—Vertical staff; the elevation of zero of gauge maintained at 92.83 feet during 1911-12; 92.81 feet during 1913-14.

Bench-mark.—Permanent iron bench-mark; assumed elevation, 100 00 feet.

Channel.—Probably permanent.

Discharge measurements.—Made from the bridge or by wading.

Winter flow.—Observations discontinued through winter months.

Artificial control.—The regulation of the new C.P.R. dam in the Bow River about three-quarters of a mile downstream from station might affect this station.

Observer.—C. A. Lang.

DISCHARGE MEASUREMENTS of Nose Creek at Calgary, in 1914.

Date.	Engineer.	Width	Area of Section.	Mean Velocity.	Gauge Height.	Discharge.
		Feet.	*Sq. ft.*	*Ft. per sec.*	*Feet.*	*Sec.-ft.*
April . . . 7.	J. S. Tempest.	14.3	8.49	1.83	2.04	15.60
May 1.	G. H. Whyte and H. S. Kerby.	23.8	16.20	0.70	1.74	12.20
June 1.	R. J. Srigley.	19.6	11.70	0.59	1.64	6.92
June 27.	do	23.4	14.24	1.69	1.84	24.12
July 22.	do	21.5	8.20	0.86	1.66	7.02
Aug. 20.	do	17.8	5.83	0.76	1.60	4.44
Sept. 14	do	19.1	6.72	0.86	1.63	5.77
Oct. 22.	do	21.2	8.52	1.03	1.70	8.76

DAILY GAUGE HEIGHT AND DISCHARGE of Nose Creek at Calgary, for 1914.

DAY.	May.		June.		July.		August.		September.		October.	
	Gauge Height.	Dis-charge.	Gauge Height.	Dis-charge.	Gauge Height.	Dis-charge.	Gauge Height.	Dis-charge.	Gauge Height.	Dis-charge.	Gauge Height.	Dis-charge.
	Feet.	*Sec.-ft.*	*Feet.*	*Sec.-ft.*	*Feet.*	*Sec.-ft.*	*Feet.*	*Sec.-ft.*	*Feet.*	*Sec.-ft.*	*Feet.*	*Sec.-ft.*
1.	. . . . . .	. . . . . .	1.66	7.0	1.72	10.9	1.58	4.1	1.55	3.4	1.63	5.7
2.	. . . . . .	. . . . . .	1.66	7.0	1.67	7.6	1.58	4.1	1.55	3.4	1.63	5.7
3.	. . . . . .	. . . . . .	1.66	7.0	1.66	7.0	1.58	4.1	1.55	3.4	1.63	5.7
4.	. . . . . .	. . . . . .	1.65	6.4	1.64	6.0	1.56	3.6	1.55	3.4	1.66	7.0
5.	. . . . . .	. . . . . .	1.66	7.0	1.66	7.0	1.54	3.2	1.55	3.4	1.70	9.3
6.	. . . . . .	. . . . . .	1.70	9.3	1.78	16.7	1.50	2.6	1.55	3.4	1.76	14.4
7.	1.71	10.1	1.70	9.3	1.74	12.5	1.58	4.1	1.55	3.4	1.77	15.5
8	1.71	10.1	1.71	10.1	1.71	10.1	1.60	4.6	1.67	7.6	1.77	15.5
9.	1.71	10.1	1.71	10.1	1.66	7.0	1.63a	5.7	1.64	6.0	1.77	15.5
10.	1.70	9.3	1.74	12.5	1.66	7.0	1.66	7.0	1.60	4.6	1.77	15.5
11.	1.70	9.3	1.75	13.3	1.64	6.0	1.65	6.4	1.70	9.3	1.75	13.3
12.	1.70	9.3	1.79	17.8	1.64	6.0	1.63	5.6	1.64	6.0	1.75	13.3
13.	1.70	9.3	1.81	20.2	1.68	8.1	1.61	5.0	1.64	6.0	1.75	13.3
14.	1.70	9.3	1.83	22.9	1.70	9.3	1.59	4.4	1.64	6.0	1.73	11.7
15.	1.70	9.3	1.82	21.5	1.69	8.7	1.57	3.9	1.63	5.7	1.73	11.7
16.	1.70	9.3	1.82	21.5	1.70	9.3	1.60	4.6	1.63	5.7	1.73	11.7
17.	1.70	9.3	1.85	25.5	1.70	9.3	1.64	6.0	1.67	7.6	1.75	13.3
18.	1.70	9.3	1.91	33.9	1.69	8.7	1.60	4.6	1.67	7.6	1.75	13.3
19.	1.71	10.1	2.01	48.3	1.67	7.6	1.58	4.1	1.65	6.4	1.75	13.3
20.	1.72	10.9	1.86	26.9	1.67	7.6	1.58	4.1	1.62	5.3	1.74	12.5
21.	1.73	11.7	1.70	9.3	1.71	10.1	1.57	3.9	1.62	5.3	1.74	12.5
22.	1.76	14.4	1.66	7.0	1.71	10.1	1.55	3.4	1.64	6.0	1.70	9.3
23.	1.76	14.4	1.66	7.0	1.65	6.4	1.54	3.2	1.64	6.0	1.68	8.1
24.	1.76	14.4	1.66	7.0	1.64	6.0	1.65	6.4	1.64	6.0	1.66	7.0
25.	1.72	10.9	1.69	8.7	1.64	6.0	1.64	6.0	1.64	6.0	1.66	7.0
26.	1.70	9.3	1.81	20.2	1.62	5.3	1.61	5.0	1.64	6.0	1.66	7.0
27.	1.69	8.7	1.81	20.2	1.62	5.3	1.57	3.9	1.64a	6.0	1.66	7.0
28.	1.69	8.7	1.78a	16.7	1.62	5.3	1.56	3.6	1.64	6.0	1.65	6.4
29.	1.68	8.1	1.76	14.4	1.60	4.6	1.56	3.6	1.63	5.7	1.65	6.4
30.	1.66	7.0	1.76	14.4	1.57	3.9	1.56	3.6	1.63	5.7	1.65	6.4
31.	1.66	7.0	. . . . . .	. . . . . .	1.58	4.1	1.56	3.6	. . . . . .	. . . . . .	1.65	6.4

a Gauge height interpolated.

5 GEORGE V, A. 1915

MONTHLY DISCHARGE of Nose Creek at Calgary, for 1914.

(Drainage area 319 square miles.)

MONTH.	DISCHARGE IN SECOND-FEET.				RUN-OFF.	
	Maximum.	Minimum	Mean.	Per square Mile.	Depth in inches on Drainage Area.	Total in Acre-feet.
May (7–31)	14.4	7.0	9.9	0.031	0.04	608
June..	48.0	7.0	15.5	0.048	0.05	916
July.....................	16.7	4.1	7.7	0.024	0.03	474
August.........................	7.0	3.2	4.4	0.014	0.02	270
September.....	9.3	3.4	5.5	0.017	0.02	327
October......	15.5	5.7	10.3	0.032	0.04	633
The period.	....	....	....	....	0 20	3,228

CANADIAN PACIFIC RAILWAY COMPANY CANAL AT OGDEN.

Location.—On the NE. ¼ Sec. 21, Tp. 23, Rge. 29, W. 4th Mer., at bridge No. 3, six miles from headgates.

Records available.—May 1, 1911, to October 8, 1914. At bridge No. 2, two miles upstream, May 8, 1908, to October 9, 1910.

Gauge.—Vertical staff, in stilling box; also automatic two-day gauge.

Bench-mark.—Iron post on left bank on upstream side of traffic bridge; elevation, 13.35 feet above the zero of the gauge.

Discharge Measurements.—Made from bridge constructed by the Canadian Pacific Railway Company for this purpose.

Observer.—A. Hatcher, for the Canadian Pacific Railway Company.

Remarks.—Previous to July 1 and after September 21, daily gauge readings were not obtained at the regular station, and therefore records at the headgates were used for these periods. The computations have been made in co-operation with the Canadian Pacific Railway Company.

DISCHARGE MEASUREMENTS of Canadian Pacific Railway Company Canal at Headgates, in 1914.

Date.	Engineer.	Width.	Area of Section.	Mean Velocity.	Gauge Height.	Discharge.
		Feet.	*Sq. ft.*	*Ft. per sec.*	*Feet.*	*Sec.-ft.*
June 10...	C. L. Dodge (C.P.R.)........	70.1	148	2.30	2.51	342
June 19.......... ...	do	74.0	234	3.10	4.06	727
June 20	R. J. Srigley.............	66.5	169	2.36	2.70	399
July 18.	C. L. Dodge (C.P.R.)	....	....	....	1.74	202

DISCHARGE MEASUREMENTS of Canadian Pacific Railway Company Canal at Ogden, in 1914.

Date.	Engineer.	Width.	Area of Section.	Mean Velocity.	Gauge Height.	Discharge.
		Feet.	*Sq. ft.*	*Ft. per sec.*	*Feet.*	*Sec.-ft.*
May 7	C. H. Whyte and H. S. Kerby.	50.0	93.7	0.81	1.33	78
May 29	R. J. Srigley...............	60.0	196.0	1.62	3.12	318
June 12.............	do	59.0	183.0	1.91	2.97	350
June 19...	do	65.0	294.0	2.52	4.46	741
July 24	do	56.5	145.0	1.30	2.30	189
Aug. 21......... ..	do	61.0	217.0	1.65	3.45	337

SESSIONAL PAPER No. 25c

DAILY GAUGE HEIGHT AND DISCHARGE of Canadian Pacific Railway Company Canal
at Ogden, for 1914.

DAY.	April.		May.		June.		July.		August.		September	
	Gauge Height.	Dis- charge.	Gauge Height.	Dis- charge	Gauge Height.	Dis- charge.	Gauge Height.	Dis- charge	Gauge Height.	Dis- charge.	Gauge Height.	Dis- charge.
	Feet.	*Sec.-ft.*	*Feet.*	*Sec.-ft.*	*Feet.*	*Sec.-ft.*	*Feet.*	*Sec.-ft.*	*Feet.*	*Sec.-ft.*	*Feet.*	*Sec.-ft.*
1.			0.60	50	2.10	266	3 15	311	3 17	315	3.23	325
2.			0.80	74	2.10	266	3.20	320	3.18	317	3.19	318
3.			0.90	86	4.10	738	3.20	320	3.18	317	3.20	320
4.			0.90	86	4.35	812	3 25	325	3.19	318	3.23	325
5.			0.90	86	3.50	582	3 31	339	3.24	327	3 22	323
6.			1.90	230	2.85	421	3.35	346	3.40	355	3.24	327
7.			0.90	86	2.85	421	3.40	355	3.65	400	3.40	355
8.			0.90	86	4.45	829	2.95	279	3.68	405	3.65	400
9.			1.40	150	3.85	673	2.69	241	3.67	404	3.75	418
10.			1.85	222	2.90	434	2.64	234	3.65	400	3.70	409
11.			1.90	230	2.44	332	3.45	364	3.68	405	3.55	382
12.			2.00	248	2.42	328	3.45	364	3.55	382	3.56	384
13.			1.80	214	2.45	334	3.47	368	3.51	375	3.59	389
14.			1.50	166	2.55	355	3.40	355	3.53	378	3.52	377
15.			1.50	166	2.45	334	3.40	355	3.50	373	3.50	373
16.			1.50	166	2.55	355	2.35	193	3.48	369	3.37	350
17.			1.50	166	2.62	370	2.32	190	3.47	368	3.45	364
18.			1.50	166	2.60	366	2.29	186	3.45	364	4.30	528
19.	1.00	98a	1.50	166	2.80	412	2.30	187	3.44	362	4.50	575
20.	1.00	98	1.90	230	2.70	388	2.38	196	3.43	360	4.09	622
21.	1.60	182	1.90	230	2.64	375	2.32	190	3.42	359	4.16	501
22.	2.25	295	1.80	214	2.60	366	2.27	183	3.42	358	0.60	50a
23.	2.25	295	1.80	214	2.40	324	2.25	180	3.46	366	0.60	50
24.	1.80	214	1.80	214	4.00	710	2.25	180	3.45	364	0.60	50
25.	1.00	98	1.90	230	3.50	582	2.23	178	3.40	355	0.60	50
26.	0.70	62	1.90	230	3.00	458	2.23	178	3.40	355	0.60	50
27.	1.90	230	1.90	230	3.15	494	2.32	190	3.40	355	0.60	50
28.	0.60	50	1.90	230	3.15	494	3.44	362	3.40	355	0.60	50
29.	0.60	50	2.30	304	3.10	482	3.20	320	3.30	337	0.60	50
30.	0.60	50	2.30	304	2.80	412a	3.15	312	3.31	339	3.70	631a
31.			2.30	304			3.16	313	3.32	341		

a Records from April 19 to June 30 and Sept. 22 to Sept. 30 were taken at the headgates.

MONTHLY DISCHARGE of Canadian Pacific Railway Company Canal at Ogden, for 1914.

MONTH.	DISCHARGE IN SECOND-FEET.			RUN-OFF.
	Maximum.	Minimum.	Mean.	Total in Acre-feet.
April (19-30)	295	50	143	3,403
May	304	50	186	11,437
June	829	266	457	27,193
July	368	178	271	16,663
August	405	315	361	22,197
September	631	50	313	18,625
The period				99,518

CANADIAN PACIFIC RAILWAY COMPANY CANALS, WESTERN SECTION, IRRIGATION BLOCK.

Main Canal *A*, which feeds the various secondary canals and distributaries of the Western Section, diverts water from the Bow River on the SE. ¼ Sec. 13, Tp. 24, Rge. 1, W. 5th Mer., at the city of Calgary.

The discharge measurements published herewith were made during investigations to determine absorption losses in the canals, conducted by this department in conjunction with the Canadian Pacific Railway Company, during 1913 and 1914.

5 GEORGE, V. A. 1915

DISCHARGE MEASUREMENTS of Secondary Canal A, in 1913-14.

Date.		Location	Engineer.	Width.	Area of Section.	Mean Velocity.	Gauge Height.	Discharge.
				Feet.	*Sq. ft.*	*Ft. per sec.*	*Feet.*	*Sec.-ft.*
1913 Sept.	18......	NE. 3-24-28-4...	G. R. Elliott....	61.7	206.0	1.84	3.40	379a
1913 Sept.	22......	NW. 2-24-28-4...	do	36.5	104.0	2.12	3.55	221
1914 June	5......	do	R.J. McGuinness & G. H. Whyte	39.0	127.0	1.91	4.00	242
1914 Aug.	27......	do ..	R.J.McGuinness	38.1	105.0	1.89	3.32	199
1914 June	6......	SE. 4-23-27-4 ...	R.J. McGuinness & G. H. Whyte	39.5	129.0	2.17	3.95	280
1914 Aug.	28	do ..	R.J. McGuinness	38.1	100.0	1.79	3.30	179
1913 Sept.	25......	SW. 31-22-26-4...	G. R. Elliott....	34.5	100.0	2.21	3.30	221
1914 June	15......	do ..	R. J.McGuinness	34.5	72.5	1.80	2.40	131
1914 Aug.	29......	do ..	do ..	33.2	71.6	1.83	2.80	131
1914 June	15......	SE. 21-22-26-4...	do ..	27.3	60.1	2.08	2.40	126
1914 Aug.	29......	do ..	do ..	28.5	63.3	2.12	2.38	134
1914 June	15......	NE. 35-22-26-4...	do ..	32.0	69.1	1.63	2.50	112
1914 Aug.	29......	do ..	do ..	32.0	72.6	1.66	2.58	121
1913 Sept.	25......	NE. 7-23-25-4 ...	G. R. Elliott....	32.5	....	....	2.50	154
1914 June	15......	do ..	R.J. McGuinness	29.0	60.6	1.77	2.00	107
1914 Aug.	31......	do ..	do ..	28.3	63.6	1.82	2.68	116
1914 Aug.	31......	NW. 15-24-25-4..	do ..	29.3	61.4	1.76	2.50	108

a Measurement on Main Canal A.

DISCHARGE MEASUREMENTS of Distributaries from Secondary Canal A, in 1913-14.

Date.		Location.	Engineer.	Width.	Area of Section.	Mean Velocity.	Gauge Height.	Discharge.
				Feet.	*Sq. ft.*	*Ft. per sec.*	*Feet.*	*Sec.-ft.*
1914 Aug.	28......	SW. 31-23-27-4...	R.J. McGuinness	3.5	4.07	0.54	....	2.20
1913 Sept.	25......	SE. 5-23-27-4 ..	G. R. Elliott....	14.0	-12.80	1.00	1.20	12.80
1914 June	5......	do ..	R.J. McGuinness & G. H. Whyte	10.7	4.55	0.77	0.67	3.50
1914 Aug.	28......	do ..	R.J. McGuinness	6.0	2.29	0.90	0.60	2.20
1914 June	6......	SW. 31-22-26-4..	R.J. McGuinness & G. H. Whyte	27.7	38.80	2.11	2.75	82.00a
1914 Aug.	29......	do ..	R.J. McGuinness	26.0	24.00	2.42	2.18	53.00a
1914 Aug.	20......	NW. 16-22-26-4..	do ..	3.5	1.95	1.51	....	3.00
1913 Sept.	25......	NE. 16-22-26-4..	G. R. Elliott....	6.5	6.21	1.05	0.72	6.50
1914 Aug.	29......	do ..	R.J.McGuinness	....	....	....	....	0.40
1914 Aug.	29......	NE. 26-22-26-4..	do ..	9.0	5.12	1.06	....	5.40
1914 Aug.	31......	NW. 7-23-25-4...	do ..	....	....	....	....	0.42
1914 Aug.	31......	SW. 21-23-25-4..	do ..	5.9	1.86	2.69	0.23	5.00
1914 Aug.	31......	SE. 33-23-25-4..	do ..	5.0	2.20	0.99	0.52	2.20
1914 Aug.	31......	NE. 9-24-25-4....	do ..	3.6	1.08	0.92	0.30	0.99
1914 Aug.	31......	NW. 15-24-25-4..	do ..	3.0	1.80	1.22	0.82	2.20

a Spillway.

DISCHARGE MEASUREMENTS of North Secondary Canal A, in 1913-14.

Date.		Location.	Engineer.	Width.	Area of Section.	Mean Velocity.	Gauge Height.	Discharge.
				Feet.	*Sq. ft.*	*Ft. per sec.*	*Feet.*	*Sec.-ft.*
1913 Sept.	26......	NE. 22-24-25-4...	G. R. Elliott.. ..	15.4	12.90	1.70	1.55	22.0
1914 June	8......	do	R.J. McGuinness	16.5	29.90	1.70	1.90	51.0
1914 Aug.	8......	do ..	do ..	15.2	22.10	1.74	1.34	38.0
1914 June	4......	NE. 26-24-25-4...	R.J. McGuinness & G. H. Whyte	12.5	15.50	1.55	1.70	24.0
1914 Aug.	8......	do ..	R.J. McGuinness	12.3	18.80	1.86	1.80	35.0
1914 Aug.	8......	NW. 25-24-25-4..	do ..	12.7	13.50	1.71	1.30	23.0
1914 Aug.	8......	do ..	do ..	12.4	12.00	1.54	1.01	10.4
1914 June	24......	NE. 36-23-24-4 .	do ..	.0	6.40	1.41	0.80	9.0
1914 Aug.	10......	do ..	do ..	3.0	6.72	1.55	0.80	10.4

SESSIONAL PAPER No. 25c

DISCHARGE MEASUREMENTS of Distributaries from North Secondary Canal *A*, in 1914.

Date.	Location.	Engineer.	Width.	Area of Section.	Mean Velocity.	Gauge Height.	Discharge
			Feet.	*Sq. ft.*	*Ft. per sec.*	*Feet.*	*Sec.-ft.*
1914 Aug. 10......	NE. 29-24-24-4...	R.J.McGuinness.	3.2	2.16	1.35	....	2.90
1914 Aug. 10......	SE. 22-24-24-4...	do	2.3	1.21	1.50	....	1.82
1914 Aug. 10......	SE. 12-24-24-4...	do	2.0	0.24	0.58	....	0.14

DISCHARGE MEASUREMENTS of South Secondary Canal *A*, in 1913-14.

Date.	Location.	Engineer.	Width.	Area of Section.	Mean Velocity.	Gauge Height.	Discharge.
			Feet.	*Sq. ft.*	*Ft. per sec.*	*Feet.*	*Sec.-ft.*
1913 Sept. 26.,....	SE. 22-24-25-4...	G. R. Elliott...	27.0	57.6	2.23	2.55	·129.0
1914 June 8......	do	R.J. McGuinness	26.0	51.4	1.81	2.40	93.0
1914 Aug. 20......	do	do	25.5	45.2	1.68	2.04	76.0
1914 June 23......	SW. 15-24-24-4...	do	25.5	55.4	1.89	2.40	105.0
1914 Aug. 20......	do	do	26.3	47.6	1.51	2.30	72.0
1914 June 24......	SW. 25-23-24-4...	do	25.0	44.8	1.96	2.10	88.0
1914 Aug. 21......	do	do	23.7	42.4	1.70	1.75	72.0
1913 Sept. 26......	SW. 2-23-23-4...	G. R. Elliott ...	24.0	51.0	1.88	2.75	96.0
1914 June 7......	do	R.J. McGuinness	24.0	56.4	1.86	3.10	105.0
1914 Aug. 22......	do	do	21.5	42.8	1.50	2.61	64.0
1914 June 27......	NE. 34-22-23-4...	do	21.7	48.1	1.64	2.30	79.0
1914 Aug. 26......	do	do	20.0	34.1	1.44	1.60	49.0
1914 June 26.....	NW. 31-22-22-4..	do	11.0	9.5	1.27	1.00	12.0

DISCHARGE MEASUREMENTS of Gleichen Distributary B from South Secondary Canal *A*, in 1914

Date.	Location.	Engineer.	Width.	Area of Section.	Mean Velocity.	Gauge Height.	Discharge.
			Feet.	*Sq. ft.*	*Ft. per sec.*	*Feet.*	*Sec.-ft.*
1914 June 26	SW. 5-23-22-4 ...	R.J. McGuinness	13.3	18.00	1.64	1.80	30.0
1914 Aug. 24......	do	do	12.7	14.60	1.38	1.50	20.0
1914 June 26......	NW. 9-23-22-4...	do	3.0	2.80	2.54	1.20	7.1a
1914 June 29......	SE. 1-23-22-4....	do	12.2	12.40	1.22	1.40	15.2
1914 Aug. 24......	do	do	12.0	13.80	1.40	1.49	19.4
1914 June 29......	NE. 33-22-21-4...	do	8.0	6.80	1.44	0.90	9.8
1914 Aug. 24......	do	do	9.3	12.00	1.44	1.29	17.3

a Spillway.

DISCHARGE MEASUREMENTS of Gleichen Distributary C from South Secondary Canal *A*, in 1913-14.

Date.	Location.	Engineer.	Width.	Area of Section.	Mean Velocity.	Gauge Height.	Discharge.
			Feet.	*Sq. ft.*	*Ft. per sec.*	*Feet.*	*Sec.-ft.*
1913 Sept. 26......	NW. 31-22-22-4..	G. R. Elliott....	11.2	11.30	1.53	1.05	17.30
1914 Aug. 25......	do	R.J. McGuinness	10.0	8.24	1.21	0.90	10.10
1914 June 29......	SW. 25-22-22-4...	do	....	....	....	0.40	1.06a
1914 Aug. 25......	do	do	....	....	....	0.75	2.20a
1914 June 29......	SW. 25-22-22-4..	do	7.0	5.20	1.00	1.20	5.20
1914 Aug. 25....	do	do	7.2	6.34	1.09	1.28	7.00

a Spillway.

5 GEORGE V, A. 1915

DISCHARGE MEASUREMENTS of Gleichen Distributary D from South Secondary Canal *A*, in 1913-14.

Date.	Location.	Engineer.	Width.	Area of Section.	Mean Velocity.	Gauge Height.	Discharge
			Feet.	*Sq. ft.*	*Ft. per sec.*	*Feet.*	*Sec.-ft.*
1913 Sept. 26......	SE. 2-23-23-4..	G. R. Elliott .	9 8	10.80	1.68	1.60	18.10
1914 June 27......	do ..	R J. McGuinness	8 6	10.00	1.63	1.70	16.40
1914 Aug. 22......	do	do ..	9 3	11.20	1.45	1.60	16.20
1914 June 26......	SW. 14-23-23-4..	do ..	6 4	6.32	1.51	1.60	9.60
1914 June 29......	WS. 14-23-23-4..	do ..	8 0	9.48	1.55	1.82	14.60
1914 Aug. 22......	NE. 10-23-23-4...	do ..	3 6	1.69	0.35	....	0.60*b*
1914 Aug. 22......	SE. 25-23-23-4...	do ..	10 9	8.46	1.63	0.68	13.80

a SpillWay.
b Lateral.

DISCHARGE MEASUREMENTS of Minor Distributaries from South Secondary Canal A, in 1913-14

Date.	Location.	Engineer.	Width.	Area of Section.	Mean Velocity.	Gauge Height.	Discharge
			Feet.	*Sq. ft.*	*Ft. per sec.*	*Feet.*	*Sec.-ft.*
1914 Aug. 20.....	SE. 14-24-25-4...	R.J. McGuinness	....	....	....	....	0.33
1914 Aug. 20.....	NW. 7-24-24-4 ..	do ..	....	....	....	....	0.11
1914 Aug. 20.....	SW. 20-24-24-4..	do ..	....	....	....	....	0.06
1914 Aug. 21.....	SE. 4-24-24-4...	do ..	....	....	....	....	0.06
1914 Aug. 21.....	NE. 33-23-23-4	do ..	....	....	....	....	0.06
1914 Aug. 21.....	NE. 33-23-23-4 .	do ..	....	....	....	....	0.26
1914 Aug. 21.....	SW. 26-23-23-4..	do ..	....	....	....	....	0.17
1914 Aug. 21.....	NW. 24-23-23-4..	do ..	....	....	....	....	0.83
1914 Aug. 21.....	SE. 20-23-23-4..	do ..	....	....	....	....	0.36
1913 Sept. 26.....	NE. 34-22-23-4..	G. R. Elliott...	9.0	7.00	1.01	1.51	7.10*b*
1914 June 27.....	do	R.J. McGuinness	8.1	5.25	1.03	1.40	5.40*b*
1914 Aug. 22.....	NE. 10-23-23-4...	do ..	3.6	1.69	0.36	....	0.60
1913 Sept. 26.....	SE. 2-23-23-4....	G. R. Elliott....	8.3	8.96	1.88	0.65	16.80*a*
1914 June 26.....	SW. 7-23-22-4 ...	R.J. McGuinness	11.0	19.00	1.93	1.90	37.00*a*
1914 Aug. 22.....	do ..	do .	11.0	18.30	1.09	1.89	20.00*a*

a Mennenite spillWay.
b Distributary E.

DISCHARGE MEASUREMENTS of North Secondary Canal B, in 1913-14.

Date.	Location.	Engineer.	Width.	Area of Section.	Mean Velocity.	Gauge Height.	Discharge.
			Feet.	*Sq. ft.*	*Ft. per sec.*	*Feet.*	*Sec.-ft.*
1914 June 5	SE. 36-24-28-4.	R.J. McGuinness & G. H. Whyte	36.5	58.4	1.66	1.81	97*a*
1913 Sept. 15	SW. 7-25-26-4 ...	G. R. Elliott....	....	....	....	3.72	260
1914 June 10......	do	R.J. McGuinness	22.0	32.0	2.25	2.20	72
1914 Sept. 3......	do .	do ..	20.7	23.8	1.47	1.78	35
1914 June 5......	NE. 6-25-25-4 .	do ..	24.2	25.6	1.64	1.50	42
1914 Sept. 1......	do ..	do ..	24.4	20.4	1.57	1.20	32
1913 Sept. 16.....	SE. 33-24-24-4..	G. R. Elliott ...	33.8	97.1	2.56	3.80	248
1914 June 19......	do ..	R.J. McGuinness	23.3	47.0	1.02	1.80	48
1914 Sept. 1......	do ..	do ..	23.5	47.8	0.82	1.38	39

a Measurement on Secondary Canal B above North and South branches.

SESSIONAL PAPER No. 25c

DISCHARGE MEASUREMENTS of Spillways, etc., from North Secondary Canal B, in 1913-14.

Date.	Location.	Engineer.	Width.	Area of Section.	Mean Velocity.	Gauge Height.	Discharge.
			Feet.	*Sq. ft.*	*Ft. per sec.*	*Feet.*	*Sec.-ft.*
1913 Sept. 15......	NW. 36-24-27-4..	G. R. Elliott....	13 0	36.10	2.16	0.98	78.00a
1914 June 10......	do	R.J. McGuinness	7 3	2.02	0.46	0.65	0.92
1914 Sept. 2	do	do	8.1	3.43	0.55	0.89	1.90
1914 June 8	NE. 36-21-26-4..	do	4.3	1.69	0.84	0.40	1.42c
1914 June 30......	NW. 1-25-25-4...	do	13 6	7.15	1.24	1.09	8.80
1914 June 30......	do	do	16 6	19.80	1.88	1.90	37.00
1914 Sept. 1....	do	do	11 5	5.71	0.94	0.86	5.50
1914 Sept. 1	SW. 1-25-25-4 ..	do	9.0	16.90	0.92	....	15.60b

a Runs into North secondary B from South secondary B.
b Runs into North secondary B from North secondary A.
c South branch of Serviceberry Creek.

DISCHARGE MEASUREMENTS of Glenrose Distributary from North Secondary Canal B, in 1913-14.

Date.	Location.	Engineer.	Width.	Area of Section.	Mean Velocity.	Gauge Height.	Discharge.
			Feet.	*Sq. ft.*	*Ft. per sec.*	*Feet.*	*Sec.-ft.*
1913 Sept. 16......	SW. 3-25-24-4 ..	G. R. Elliott ...	11.2	43.00	1.09	3.34	47.0
1914 June 19......	do	R.J. McGuinness	14.3	27.10	0.74	2.40	20.0
1914 Aug. 13....	do	do	16.9	29.80	0.77	2.52	23.0
1913 Sept. 17....	SW. 18-25-23-4.	G. R. Elliott...	9.6	13.40	1.94	1.80	26.0
1914 June 19....	do	R.J. McGuinness	8.4	6.36	1.24	0.75	7.6
1914 Aug. 13....	do	do	10.3	12.40	1.53	1.51	19.9
1914 June 19	SE. 24-25-24-4..	do	8.7	7.81	0.96	1.60	7.5
1914 Aug. 13......	do	do	9.7	10.80	1.15	1.90	12.4

DISCHARGE MEASUREMENTS of North Crowfoot Distributary from North Secondary Canal B, in 1914.

Date.	Location.	Engineer.	Width.	Area of Section.	Mean Velocity.	Gauge Height.	Discharge.
			Feet.	*Sq. ft.*	*Ft. per sec.*	*Feet.*	*Sec.-ft.*
1914 June 19... .	NW. 34-24-24-4..	R.J. McGuinness	29 0	74.80	0.56	2.80	42.0a
1914 Aug. 12......	do	do	15.7	13.40	1.13	0.88	15.1
1914 June 23......	NW. 30-24-22-4.	do	10 5	15.40	1.96	1.40	30.0
1914 Aug. 12......	do	do	5.6	5.30	2.40	0.90	13.4
1914 June 23......	SW. 31-24-22-4..	do	7.9	11.00	1.93	1.60	21.0b
1914 Aug. 12......	do	do	7.0	3.59	1.22	0.46	4.4b

a Measured above division of North and South Crowfoot.
b Spillway.

DISCHARGE MEASUREMENTS of South Crowfoot Distributary from North Secondary Canal B, in 1914.

Date.	Location.	Engineer.	Width.	Area of Section.	Mean Velocity.	Gauge Height.	Discharge.
			Feet.	*Sq. ft.*	*Ft. per sec.*	*Feet.*	*Sec.-ft.*
1914 June 19.....	NW. 27-24-24-4.	R.J. McGuinness	16.0	14.40	1.25	1.10	19.0
1914 Aug. 11......	do	do	10.5	10.40	1.68	0.92	17.5
1914 June 23	SE. 13-24-24-4..	do	7.0	5.20	0.79	0.80	4.4
1914 Aug. 11......	do	do	9.0	11.10	1.76	1.48	19.6
1914 June 24	SE. 9-24-23-4...	do	6.7	2.65	0.69	0.70	2.0
1914 Aug. 11......	do	do	8 3	8.44	1.26	1.48	10.6

5 GEORGE V, A. 1915

DISCHARGE MEASUREMENTS of Laterals from Crowfoot Distributaries, in 1913-14.

Date.	Location.	Engineer.	Width.	Area of Section.	Mean Velocity.	Gauge Height.	Discharge.
			Feet.	*Sq. ft.*	*Ft. per sec.*	*Feet.*	*Sec.-ft.*
1914 June 19......	NW. 27-24-24-4	R.J. McGuinness	7.3	4.67	1.00	0.40	4.70
1914 Aug. 11......	do	do					0.23
1914 Aug. 11......	SE. 9-24-23-4..	do	5.8	3.81	1.29	....	4.92a
1913 Sept. 17......	NW. 30-24-22-4	G. R. Elliott....	12.0	10.80	1.63	0.90	17.60
1914 June 23......	do	R.J. McGuinness	5.2	4.12	2.29	0.80	9.40
1913 Sept. 17......	SW. 16-24-22-4	G. R. Elliott....	6.5	5.71	1.21	....	6.90
1913 Sept. 17......	NW. 9-24-22-4.	do	8.0	3.54	0.68	....	2.40

a Spillway.

DISCHARGE MEASUREMENTS of South Secondary Canal B, in 1913-14.

Date.	Location.	Engineer.	Width.	Area of Section.	Mean Velocity.	Gauge Height.	Discharge.
			Feet.	*Sq. ft.*	*Ft. per sec.*	*Feet.*	*Sec. ft.*
1913 Sept. 15......	NW. 33-24-27-4.	G. R. Elliott. ..	20.6	41.10	2.48	2.18	102.00
1914 June 5......	do	R.J McGuinness & G. H. Whyte	19.0	14.40	1.05	0.70	15.10
1914 Sept. 2......	do	R.J. McGuinness	18.5	16.90	0.96	0.88	16.30
1913 Sept. 15......	NW. 12-24-27-4.	G. R. Elliott....	12.0	20.90	2.06	2.40	43.20
1914 June 12......	do	R.J. McGuinness	18.2	18.80	0.76	1.70	14.30
1914 Sept. 2......	do	do	18.7	16.40	0.91	1.69	15.00
1914 June 12......	SW. 29-24-26-4	do	8.3	6.42	1.42	0.80	9.10
1913 Sept. 25......	NE. 15-24-26-4.	G. R. Elliott...	8.6	8.19	1.45	....	11.90
1914 June 13......	do	R.J. McGuinness	8.3	5.11	1.33	1.20	6.80
1914 Sept. 2......	do	do	6.2	3.89	0.92	1.08	3.60
1914 June 13......	SW. 23-24-26-4	do	5.5	3.65	1.04	0.80	3.80
1914 Sept. 2......	do	do	3.9	1.27	1.27	0.30	1.09

DISCHARGE MEASUREMENTS of Spillways from South Secondary Canal B, in 1913-14.

Date.	Location.	Engineer.	Width.	Area of Section.	Mean Velocity.	Gauge Height.	Discharge.
			Feet.	*Sq. ft.*	*Ft. per sec.*	*Feet.*	*Sec.-ft.*
1913 Sept. 15......	SW. 13-24-27-4.	G. R. Elliott ...	14.5	21.60	2.64	2.10	57.00
1914 June 12......	do	R.J. McGuinness	6.0	2.86	0.86	0.40	2.50
1914 Sept. 2......	do	do	6.8	3.94	0.89	0.44	3.50
1913 Sept. 25......	SW. 29-24-26-4.	G. R. Elliott. ..	2.8	3.72	2.63	1.25	9.80a
1914 Sept. 2......	do	R.J. McGuinness	2.8	1.26	1.04	0.69	1.31a

a Spill into North Secondary B Canal.

DISCHARGE MEASUREMENTS of Secondary Canal C, in 1913-14.

Date.	Location.	Engineer.	Width.	Area of Section.	Mean Velocity.	Gauge Height.	Discharge.
			Feet.	*Sq. ft.*	*Ft. per sec.*	*Feet.*	*Sec.-ft.*
1913 Sept. 15......	NE. 36-24-28-4.	G. R. Elliott....	37.0	34.3	1.20	1.36	41
1913 Sept. 19......	do	do	43.5	112.0	2.46	3.06	276
1914 June 5......	do	R.J. McGuinness & G. H. Whyte	43.5	98.3	1.99	2.75	195
1914 Aug. 5......	do	R.J. McGuinness	42.0	66.0	1.66	1.99	109

SESSIONAL PAPER No. 25c

DISCHARGE MEASUREMENTS of West Secondary Canal C, in 1913-14.

Date.	Location.	Engineer.	Width.	Area of Section.	Mean Velocity.	Gauge Height.	Discharge.
			Feet.	*Sq. ft.*	*Ft. per sec.*	*Feet.*	*Sec.-ft.*
1913 Sept. 24......	SW. 30-25-27-4	G. R. Elliott ..	19.4	32.80	2.01	2.10	66.0
1914 June 12......	do ..	R.J. McGuinness	18.0	25.40	1.74	1.50	44.0
1914 Aug. 5......	do .	do .	16 8	14.80	1.26	0.81	18.7
1913 Sept. 24......	NW. 19-27-27-4.	G. R. Elliott ..	6.9	21.60	2.82	3.18	61.0
1914 June 11......	do	R.J. McGuinness	12 0	23.00	1.92	2.80	44.0
1914 Aug. 6......	do ..	do ..	11 9	11.00	1.06	1.47	11.7
1914 Aug. 6......	SW. 29-27-27-4	do .	7 0	3.66	1.14	0.51	4.2

DISCHARGE MEASUREMENTS of Distributaries from West Secondary Canal C, in 1914.

Date.	Location.	Engineer.	Width.	Area of Section.	Mean Velocity.	Gauge Height.	Discharge.
			Feet.	*Sq. ft.*	*Ft. per sec.*	*Feet.*	*Sec.-ft.*
1914 Aug. 5......	SE. 30-25-27-4..	R.J. McGuinness	4 8	2.06	0.38	....	0.78
1914 Aug. 6......	NE. 5-26-27-4 ..	do	5.8	2.46	0.98	0.53	2.41
1914 Aug. 6......	SE. 30-26-27-4.	do ..	4 4	2.22	0.37	....	0.82
1914 Aug. 6......	NE. 5-27-27-4 ..	do ..	5 0	7.30	0.27	....	2.00
1914 June 11......	SW. 29-27-27-4 .	do ..	7 0	3.00	0.92	0 70	2.80

DISCHARGE MEASUREMENTS of East Secondary Canal C, in 1913-14.

Date.	Location.	Engineer.	Width.	Area of Section.	Mean Velocity.	Gauge Height.	Discharge.
			Feet.	*Sq. ft.*	*Ft. per sec.*	*Feet.*	*Sec.-ft.*
1914 Aug. 5	SW. 30-25-27-4.	R.J. McGuinness	26 6	26.0	2.20	....	57.0
1913 Sept. 19......	NW. 16-26-26-4.	G. R. Elliott....	16 7	57.6.	5.01	3.30	289.0
1914 June 10......	do ..	R.J. McGuinness	38 7	40.8	1.41	0.80	58.0
1914 Sept. 3......	do ..	do ..	38 5	43.7	1.49	0.87	65.0
1913 Sept. 19......	SW. 27-26-26-4 .	G. R. Elliott .	31.1	103.0	2.35	3.70	242.0
1914 June 11......	do ..	R.J. McGuinness	26 6	27.1	1.40	1.20	38.0
1914 Sept. 3......	do ..	do ..	28 7	36.5	1.44	1.53	54.0
1913 Sept. 20......	SE. 34-26-25-4.	G. R. Elliott....	37.6	106.0	1.91	3.90	203.0
1914 June 16......	do ..	R.J. McGuinness	27.5	35.8	1.05	2.00	38.0
1914 Sept. 4......	do ..	do ..	25 0	34.6	1.07	1.36	37.0
1914 June 17......	SW. 25-26-25-4 .	R.J. McGuinness	22 -3	28.0	0.90	1.60	25.0
1914 Sept. 5......	do ..	do ..	22.6	28.4	1.16	1.81	33.0
1913 Sept. 20......	NE. 18-26-24-4.	G. R. Elliott....	31 3	105.0	1.89	4.10	198.0
1914 June 17......	do .	R.J. McGuinness	20 5	19.1	1.29	1.10	25.0
1914 Sept. 5......	do ..	do ..	19 6	25.6	1.34	1.24	34.0
1913 Sept. 20......	NE. 16-26-24-4.	G. R. Elliott .	21.5	50.5	2.54	3.12	128.0
1914 June 18......	do ..	R.J. McGuinness	15 1	16.6	1.36	1.40	22.0
1914 Sept. 5......	do ..	do ..	15.6	19.8	1.55	1.60	31.0
1914 Sept. 7......	do ..	do ..	15 -0	16.6	1.47	1.41	24.0
1914 June 18......	NW. 30-26-23-4.	do ..	8 0	8.5	2.18	1.50	18.6
1914 Sept. 7......	do ..	do ..	14 2	16.6	1.27	1.31	21.0
1913 Sept. 23......	SE. 31-26-23-4.	G. R. Elliott .	12 0	14.4	1.88	1.49	27.0
1914 June 18,.....	do ..	R.J. McGuinness	9 8	10.4	1.71	....	17.9

5 GEORGE V, A. 1915

DISCHARGE MEASUREMENTS of Distributaries from East Secondary Canal C, in 1913-14.

Date.	Location.	Engineer.	Width.	Area of Section.	Mean Velocity.	Gauge Height.	Discharge.
			Feet.	Sq. ft.	Ft. per sec.	Feet.	Sec.-ft.
1914 June 10. ...	NW. 30-25-26-4..	R.J. McGuinness	43.4	53.20	0.64	1.20	34.00a
1914 Sept. 3......	do	do	12.5	4.38	0.20	0.20	0.87a
1914 June 10......	NW. 22-26-26-4..	do	6.8	4.25	0.91	0.40	3.90
1913 Sept. 19......	SE. 28-26-26-4 .	G. R. Elliott....	11.5	11.80	2.54	0.90	30.00
1914 Sept. 3......	NW. 27-26-26-4..	R.J. McGuinness	7.0	5.24	0.84	0.49	4.40
1914 Sept. 3......	SW. 27-26-26-4..	do	6.3	3.80	1.08	0.18	3.40
1914 Sept. 4......	SE. 35-26-26-4...	do	4.6	3.22	1.59	....	5.10
1914 June 16......	NE. 34-26-25-4..	do	15.2	6.44	1.22	1.30	7.90b
1914 Aug. 14......	do	do	12.0	5.23	0.78	1.19	4.10b
1914 Sept. 4......	do	do	13.8	6.22	1.02	1.31	6.40b
1914 Aug. 15......	SE. 1-27-25-4...	do	4.0	1.44	1.00	....	1.45b
1914 Aug. 15......	NW. 36-26-25-4..	do	....	....	....	....	0.08b
1914 June 17......	SE. 33-26-24-4...	do	3.7	1.32	1.31	0.50	1.71b
1914 Aug. 15......	do	do	2.5	0.55	0.53	0.10	0.29b
1914 June 17......	NE. 23-26-25-4..	do	8.0	6.20	1.84	0.90	11.40
1914 Sept. 5......	do	do	8.1	5.07	0.98	0.66	5.00
1914 Sept. 5......	SW. 17-26-24-4..	do	4.0	1.30	0.88	....	1.15

a Spillway.
b Lateral F Swastika.

FISH CREEK NEAR PRIDDIS.

Location.—On SW. ¼ Sec. 26, Tp. 22, Rge. 3, W. 5th Mer., at the Percival ra..h, which is about one mile north of Priddis post office.

Records available.—May 13, 1907, to October 31, 1914.

Gauge.—Vertical staff; elevation of zero maintained at 91.24 feet during 1907-10; 90.81 feet during 1911-14.

Bench-mark.—Permanent iron bench-mark; assumed elevation, 100 00 feet.

Channel.—Not liable to shift except in extreme high water.

Discharge measurements.—By wading, or from traffic bridge about one mile upstream.

Winter flow.—Observations discontinued during winter months.

Observer.—Fred Percival.

DISCHARGE MEASUREMENTS of Fish Creek near Priddis, in 1914.

Date.	Engineer.	Width.	Area of Section.	Mean Velocity.	Gauge Height.	Discharge.
		Feet.	Sq. ft.	Ft. per sec.	Feet.	Sec.-ft.
April 8............	J. S. Tempest............	53	38.6	1.220	5.38	47.30
May 22............	G. H. Whyte & H. S. Kerby	38	29.1	1.450	1.48	42.10
June 18..	H. S. Kerby...............	35	29.5	0.953	1.31	28.10
July 8............	do	38	41.6	1.110	1.52	46.30
Aug. 7............	do	....	....	....	0.55	1.05a
Sept. 3............	do	....	....	....	0.60	1.93a
Sept. 23............	do	26	16.3	0.341	0.78	4.80
Oct. 21............	do	34	26.4	0.760	1.23	20.10

a Weir measurement.

SESSIONAL PAPER No. 25c

DAILY GAUGE HEIGHT AND DISCHARGE of Fish Creek near Priddis, for 1914.

DAY.	March.		April.		May.		June.	
	Gauge Height.	Dis-charge.	Gauge Height.	Dis-charge.	Gauge Height.	Dis-charge.	Gauge Height.	Dis-charge.
	Feet.	*Sec.-ft.*	*Feet.*	*Sec.-ft.*	*Feet.*	*Sec.-ft.*	*Feet.*	*Sec.-ft.*
1	....	....	6.20	....	1.20	20.0	1.10	15.2
2	....	....	6.21	....	1.20	20.0	1.11	15.7
3	....	....	6.22	....	1.20	20.0	1.11	15.7
4	....	....	6.10	....	1.35	31.0	1.11	15.7
5	....	....	6.13	....	1.35	31.0	1.13	16.6
6	....	....	6.15	... .	1.34	30.0	1.16	18.1
7	....	....	5.99	....	1.34	30.0	1.40	35.0
8	....	....	5.15	47.0*a*	1.34	30.0	1.42	36.0
9	....	....	4.45	43.0	1.18	19.2	1.47	41.0
10	....	....	4.45	43.0	1.24	23.0	1.31	28.0
11	....	....	4.44	42.0	1.40	35.0	1.50	43.0
12	....	....	4.47	44.0	1.33	29.0	1.41	35.0
13	....	....	4.47	44.0	1.29	26.0	1.56	49.0
14	....	....	4.19	39.0	1.28	25.0	1.71	66.0
15	6.20	....*a*	3.84	35.0	1.24	23.0	1.63	57.0
16	6.05	....	3.84	35.0	1.23	22.0	1.47	41.0
17	5.89	....	4.03	38.0	1.23	22.0	1.47	41.0
18	5.80	....	3.68	33.0	1.18	19.2	1.46	40.0
19	5.81	....	3.37	28.0	1.25	23.0	1.44	38.0
20	5.82	....	2.78	26.0	1.42	36.0	1.21	21.0
21	5.82	....	2.70	25.0*a*	1.62	55.0	1.12	16.2
22	5.82	....	1.26	24.0	1.59	52.0	1.11	15.7
23	5.82	....	1.35	31.0	1.43	37.0	1.10	15.2
24	5.80	....	1.34	30.0	1.49	42.0	1.10	15.2
25	5.80	....	1.44	38.0	1.32	28.0	1.19	19.7
26	5.81	....	1.44	38.0	1.31	28.0	2.01	110.0
27	5.80	....	1.44	38.0	1.20	20.0	1.91	94.0
28	5.81	....	1.44	38.0	1.29	26.0	1.75	71.0
29	5.82	....	1.23	22.0	1.16	18.1	1.55	48.0
30	5.79	....	1.22	21.0	1.13	16.6	1.45	39.0
31	5.80	....	....	....	1.10	15.2	....	....

a Ice conditions March 15 to April 21—discharge estimated April 8 to 21. Not sufficient data to compute daily discharge from March 15 to April 8.

5 GEORGE V, A. 1915

DAILY GAUGE HEIGHT AND DISCHARGE of Fish Creek near Priddis, for 1914.—*Concluded.*

DAY.	July.		August.		September.		October.	
	Gauge Height.	Dis-charge.	Gauge Height.	Dis-charge.	Gauge Height.	Dis-charge.	Gauge Height.	Dis-charge.
	Feet.	*Sec.-ft.*	*Feet.*	*Sec.-ft.*	*Feet.*	*Sec.-ft.*	*Feet.*	*Sec.-ft.*
1	1.34	30.0	0.63	1.7	0.61	1.6	0.72	2.5
2	1.23	22.0	0.63	1.7	0.60	1.5	0.73	2.6
3	1.23	22.0	0.54	1.2	0.60	1.5	0.73	2.6
4	·1.23	22.0	0.57	1.3	0.60	1.5	0.74	2.8
5	1.29	26.0	0.63	1.7	0.60	1.5	0.98	9.9
6	1.30	27.0	0.62	1.6	0.60	1.5	0.99	10.2
7	1.82	81.0	0.66	1.9	0.59	1.4	1.05	12.8
8	1.59	52.0	0.54	1.2	0.70	2.1	1.06	13.3
9	1.56	49.0	0.54	1.2	0.72	2.5	1.14	17.1
10	1.52	45.0	1.20	20.2	0.72	2.5	1.14	17.1
11	1.18	19.2	1.09	14.7	0.66	1.9	1.25	23.0
12	1.10	15.2	1.10	15.2	0.66	1.9	1.25	23.0
13	1.03	11.9	0.90	7.2	0.86	5.9	1.25	23.0
14	1.06	13.3	0.90	7.2	0.86	5.9	1.24	23.0
15	1.05	12.8	0.76	3.2	0.85	5.6	1.28	26.0
16	1.03	11.9	0.75	3.0	0.85	5.6	1.28	26.0
17	0.98	9.9	0.94	8.5	0.85	5.6	1.31	28.0
18	0.92	7.8	0.98	9.9	0.85	5.6	1.38	33.0
19	0.87	6.2	0.97	9.5	0.85	5.6	1.27	25.0
20	0.87	6.2	0.86	5.9	0.84	5.3	1.26	24.0
21	0.89	6.9	0.85	5.6	0.84	5.3	1.26	24.0
22	0.93	8.2	0.85	5.6	0.84	5.3	1.24	23.0
23	0.88	6.6	0.85	5.6	0.84	5.3	1.24	23.0
24	0.86	5.9	0.84	5.3	0.77	3.5	1.10	15.2
25	0.78	3.7	0.77	3.5	0.77	3.5	1.10	15.2
26	0.78	2.7	0.75	3.0	0.77	3.5	1.10	15.2
27	0.73	2.6	0.75	3.0	0.77	3.5	1.10	15.2
28	0.68	2.0	0.70	2.1	0.77	3.5	1.10	15.2
29	0.68	2.0	0.68	2.0	0.68	2.0	1.03	11.9
30	0.68	2.0	0.68	2.0	0.68	2.0	1.04	12.4
31	0.63	1.7	0.68	2.0	....	....	1.04	12.4

MONTHLY DISCHARGE of Fish Creek near Priddis, for 1914.

(Drainage area 109 square miles.)

MONTH.	DISCHARGE IN SECOND-FEET.				RUN-OFF.	
	Maximum.	Minimum	Mean.	Per square Mile.	Depth in inches on Drainage Area.	Total in Acre-feet.
April (7-30)	47.0	21.00	35.0	0.321	0.275	1,591
May	55.0	15.20	28.0	0.257	0.295	1,722
June	110.0	15.20	37.0	0.340	0.413	2,202
July	81.0	1.70	17.3	0.159	0.183	1,064
August	20.2	1.20	5.1	0.047	0.054	314
September	5.9	1.40	3.5	0.032	0.036	208
October	33.0	2.50	17.0	0.136	0.180	1,045
The period	....	....	....	....	1.436	8,146

NORTH BRANCH OF SHEEP RIVER NEAR MILLARVILLE.

Location.—On SW. ¼ Sec. 12, Tp. 21, Rge. 3, W. 5th Mer., at Malcolm T. Miller's ranch, about one and one-half miles east of Millarville post office.

Records available.—May 22, 1908, to October 31, 1914.

Gauge.—Vertical staff; elevation of zero of gauge 3,740.00 feet during 1908-10; 3,738.73 feet during 1911-14.

Bench-mark.—Permanent iron bench-mark; elevation 3,821 40 feet (Dominion Western Railway datum); located 36 feet southwest of the *NE.* corner of Sec. 2, Tp. 21, Rge. 3, W. 5th Mer., and about 300 feet west of the gauge.

Discharge measurements.—Made at the traffic bridge about one mile downstream on the road allowance on the east boundary of Sec. 12, or at a wading section, 200 feet downstream from the gauge.

Winter flow.—Observations not taken during winter months.

Diversions.—The headgates of Malcolm T. Miller's irrigation ditch are about 2 miles above station; to date this ditch has not been used.

Observer.—Malcolm T. Miller.

DISCHARGE MEASUREMENTS of North Branch of Sheep River near Millarville, in 1914.

Date.	Engineer.	Width.	Area of Section.	Mean Velocity.	Gauge Height.	Discharge.
		Feet.	*Sq. ft.*	*Ft. per sec.*	*Feet.*	*Sec.-ft.*
April 7	J. S. Tempest	73	47.8	0.524	3.10	25.0
April 8	do	58	62.1	3.290	2.70	20.4
May 22	G. H. Whyte and H. S. Kerby	38	45.5	3.140	3.01	143.0
June 18	H. S. Kerby	34	33.6	2.721	2.78	91.0
July 7	do	35	32.4	2.564	2.74	83.0
Aug. 7	do	24	10.0	0.329	1.95	3.3
Sept. 3	do	19	11.0	0.412	2.00	4.5
Oct. 27	do	25	15.0	0.733	2.15	11.0
Sept. 20	do	35	35.8	2.508	2.85	90.0

No. 25c—11.

5 GEORGE V. A. 1915

DAILY GAUGE HEIGHT AND DISCHARGE of North Branch of Sheep River near Millarville, for 1914.

DAY.	April.		May.		June.		July.	
	Gauge Height.	Dis-charge.	Gauge Height.	Dis-charge.	Gauge Height.	Dis-charge.	Gauge Height.	Dis-charge.
	Feet.	*Sec.-ft.*	*Feet.*	*Sec.-ft.*	*Feet.*	*Sec.-ft.*	*Feet.*	*Sec.-ft.*
1			2.74	85	2.72	82	2.76	89.0
2			2.88	113	2.72	82	2.68	74.0
3			2.93	124	2.72	82	2.63	66.0
4			2.82	100	2.72	82	2.63	66.0
5			2.73	83	2.72	82	2.63	66.0
6			2.73	83	2.74	85	2.76	89.0
7			2.63	66	2.82	100	2.74	85.0
8	2.70	20a	2.68	74	2.72	82	2.59	59.0
9	2.75	50	2.74	85	2.72	82	2.56	55.0
10	2.90	70a	2.96	130	2.72	82	2.46	41.0
11	2.78	92	2.94	126	2.72	82	2.39	33.0
12	2.95	128	2.94	126	2.76	89	2.37	31.0
13	2.85	106	3.03	147	2.92	121	2.44	39.0
14	2.79	94	3.01	142	3.47	283	2.46	41.0
15	2.70	78	3.07	157	2.92	121	2.39	33.0
16	2.83	102	3.04	150	2.92	121	2.37	31.0
17	2.70	78	3.04	150	2.82	100	2.29	23.0
18	2.70	78	2.99	138	2.78	92	2.29	23.0
19	2.64	67	3.02	145	2.73	83	2.24	19.2
20	2.69	76	3.04	150	2.68	74	2.19	15.4
21	2.39	33	3.05	152	2.68	74	2.21	16.8
22	2.36	30	3.02	145	2.59	59	2.12	11.2
23	2.62	64	3.01	142	2.52	49	2.12	11.2
24	2.78	92	3.01	142	2.52	49	2.12	11.2
25	2.74	85	3.01	142	2.73	83	2.09	9.4
26	2.59	59	2.97	133	2.93	124	2.09	9.4
27	2.56	55	2.87	110	3.03	147	2.07	8.2
28	2.59	59	2.84	104	2.92	121	2.07	8.2
29	2.58	57	2.82	100	2.86	108	2.02	5.8
30	2.54	52	2.82	100	2.81	98	2.02	5.8
31			2.72	82			1.98	1.8

a Ice conditions to April 11—discharge estimated.

SESSIONAL PAPER No. 25c

DAILY GAUGE HEIGHT AND DISCHARGE of North Branch of Sheep River near Millarville, for 1914.

DAY.	August.		September.		October.	
	Gauge Height.	Dis-charge.	Gauge Height.	Dis-charge.	Gauge Height.	Dis-charge.
	Feet.	*Sec.-ft.*	*Feet.*	*Sec.-ft.*	*Feet.*	*Sec.-ft.*
1	1.94	2.8	2.02	5.8	2.15	13.0
2	1.94	2.8	1.99	4.6	2.15	13.0
3	1.94	2.8	2.00	5.0	2.15	13.0
4	1.94	2.8	2.00	5.0	2.23	13.0
5	1.94	2.8	2.00	5.0	2.30	24.0
6	1.94	2.8	2.00	5.0	2.30	24.0
7	1.97	3.8	1.98	4.2	2.30	24.0
8	1.94	2.8	2.01	5.4	2.38	32.0
9	2.09	9.4	2.01	5.4	2.42	36.0
10	2.09	9.4	2.00	5.0	2.55	53.0
11	2.04	6.6	2.00	5.0	2.50	46.0
12	2.02	5.8	2.05	7.0	2.40	34.0
13	2.01	5.4	2.05	7.0	2.50	46.0
14	2.01	5.4	2.05	7.0	2.42	36.0
15	1.99	4.6	2.07	8.2	2.58	58.0
16	1.99	4.6	2.07	8.2	2.82	100.0
17	2.09	9.4	2.10	10.0	2.95	128.0
18	2.15	13.0	2.10	10.0	2.95	128.0
19	2.11	10.6	2.10	10.0	2.92	121.0
20	2.09	9.4	2.08	8.8	2.85	106.0
21	2.09	9.4	2.19	15.4	2.77	91.0
22	2.07	8.2	2.15	13.0	2.70	78.0
23	2.11	10.6	2.12	11.2	2.65	69.0
24	2.14	12.4	2.10	10.0	2.65	69.0
25	2.14	12.4	2.10	10.0	2.63	66.0
26	2.14	12.4	2.10	10.0	2.63	66.0
27	2.14	12.4	2.10	10.0	2.58	58.0
28	2.09	9.4	2.10	10.0	2.55	53.0
29	2.07	8.2	2.10	10.0	2.53	50.0
30	2.07	8.2	2.10	10.0	2.53	50.0
31	2.04	6.6	....	....	2.50	46.0

MONTHLY DISCHARGE of North Branch of Sheep River near Millarville, for 1914.

(Drainage area 199 square miles.)

MONTH.	DISCHARGE IN SECOND-FEET.				RUN-OFF.	
	Maximum.	Minimum	Mean.	Per square Mile.	Depth in inches on Drainage Area.	Total in Acre-feet.
April (8-30)	128.0	20.0	71.0	0.357	0.30	3,238
May	157.0	66.0	120.0	0.603	0.69	7,378
June	283.0	49.0	97.0	0.487	0.54	5,772
July	89.0	1.8	35.0	0.176	0.20	2,152
August	13.0	2.8	7.3	0.037	0.04	449
September	15.4	4.2	8.0	0.040	0.04	492
October	128.0	13.0	56.0	0.281	0.31	3,443
The period	....	....	....	....	2.12	22,924

5 GEORGE V, A. 1915

SOUTH BRANCH OF SHEEP RIVER NEAR BLACK DIAMOND.

Location.—On steel highway bridge on road allowance west of the SW. ¼ Sec. 17, Tp. 20, Rge. 2, W. 5th Mer., about one-half mile from Black Diamond post office.

Records available.—From May 23, 1908, to October 31, 1914.

Gauge.—Standard chain gauge; elevation of zero of gauge 93.66 feet, unchanged since established.

Bench-mark.—Permanent iron bench-mark; assumed elevation, 100.00 feet.

Channel.—Permanent.

Discharge measurements.—Made from traffic bridge or by wading.

Winter flow.—No observations taken during winter months.

Observer.—H. A. Arnold.

DISCHARGE MEASUREMENTS of South Branch of Sheep River near Black Diamond, in 1914.

Date.	Engineer.	Width.	Area of Section.	Mean Velocity.	Gauge Height.	Discharge.
		Feet.	*Sq. ft.*	*Ft. per sec.*	*Feet.*	*Sec.-ft.*
April 7	J. S. Tempest	28	27.4	2.26	0.82	62
May 21	G. H. Whyte and H. S. Kerby	79	126.0	2.51	1.41	317
June 17	H. S. Kerby	80	166.5	3.13	1.82	522
July 6	do	80	175.5	3.19	1.95	540
Aug. 6	do	73	72.3	1.24	0.81	90
Sept. 2	do	72	65.2	1.13	0.74	74
Sept. 22	do	74	82.5	1.48	0.96	123
Oct. 20	do	78	108.0	1.90	1.18	206

DAILY GAUGE HEIGHT AND DISCHARGE of South Branch of Sheep River near Black Diamond, for 1914.

DAY.	March.		April.		May.		June.	
	Gauge Height.	Dis-charge.	Gauge Height.	Dis-charge.	Gauge Height.	Dis-charge.	Gauge Height.	Dis-charge.
	Feet.	*Sec.-ft.*	*Feet.*	*Sec.-ft.*	*Feet.*	*Sec.-ft.*	*Feet.*	*Sec.-ft.*
1			1.90	40	1.10	174	1.56	377
2			1.70	43	1.30	250	1.76	492
3			1.40	48	1.20	210	2.00	653
4			1.30	51	1.10	174	2.04	683
5			1.55	56	1.02	147	1.76	492
6			1.32	59	0.95	124	1.67	439
7			1.20	62	0.92	116	1.77	498
8			1.10	80b	1.03	150	1.66	433
9			0.90	110	1.30	250	1.57	383
10			0.92	116	1.40	295	1.46	325
11			0.90	110	1.34	268	1.47	330
12			1.05	157	1.34	268	1.52	356
13			1.00	140	1.34	268	1.62	410
14			1.05	157	1.50	345	1.77	498
15	1.70	b	1.05	157	1.75	486	1.82	529
16	1.70		1.10	174	1.70	456	1.84	542
17	1.70		1.05	157	1.55	372	1.84	542
18	1.70		1.00	140	1.55	372	1.86	555
19	1.70		0.90	110	1.65	427	1.75	486
20	1.70		1.00	140	1.55	372	1.64	421
21	1.70		0.80	85	1.52	356	1.48	335
22	1.70		0.80	85	1.55	372	1.36	277
23	1.70		0.95	124	1.62a	410	1.34	268
24	1.68a		1.10	174	1.68a	444	1.17	197
25	1.65a		1.00	140	1.72	468	1.45	320
26	1.62a		0.85	97	1.65	427	1.43	310
27	1.60		0.90	110	1.52	356	1.57	383
28	1.60		0.84	95	1.47	330	1.49	340
29	1.42		0.85	97	1.41	300	1.42	305
30	1.60		1.00	140	1.56	377	1.30	250
31	1.50				1.33	263		

a Gauge heights interpolated.

b Ice conditions March 15 to April 8—discharge estimated. April 1 to 8—insufficient data to estimate discharge previous to April 1.

SESSIONAL PAPER No. 25c

DAILY GAUGE HEIGHT AND DISCHARGE of South Branch of Sheep River near Black Diamond, for 1914.—*Concluded.*

DAY.	July. Gauge Height.	July. Dis-charge.	August. Gauge Height.	August. Dis-charge.	September. Gauge Height	September. Dis-charge.	October. Gauge Height.	October. Dis-charge.
	Feet.	*Sec.-ft.*	*Feet.*	*Sec.-ft.*	*Feet.*	*Sec.-ft.*	*Feet.*	*Sec.-ft*
1	1.26	234	0.86	100	0.77	79	0.99a	137
2	1.26	234	0.86	100	0.75	75	1.00	140
3	1.22	218	0.83	92	0.74	73	0.97	130
4	1.20	210	0.80	85	0.74	73	1.10	174
5	1.28	242	0.80	85	0.71	67	1.00	140
6	1.70	456	0.83a	92	0.71	67	0.90	110
7	1.60	399	0.86a	100	0.71	67	0.92	116
8	1.50	345	0.89a	107	0.76	77	0.98	134
9	1.44	315	0.93a	118	0.71	67	1.02	147
10	1.35	272	0.96	127	0.69	63	1.02	147
11	1.31	254	0.88	105	0.72	69	1.01a	143
12	1.30	250	0.88	105	0.78	81	0.99a	137
13	1.30	250	0.83	92	0.77	79	0.98	134
14	1.30	250	0.80	85	0.77	79	1.05	157
15	1.27	238	0.78	81	0.80	85	1.15	192
16	1.20	210	0.87	102	0.82a	90	1.40	295
17	1.10	174	0.96	127	0.85	97	1.37	281
18	1.07	164	0.98	134	0.90	110	1.32	259
19	1.09	171	0.98	134	1.25	230	1.25	230
20	1.09	171	0.96	127	1.10	174	1.18	203
21	1.09	171	0.89	107	1.02	147	1.10	174
22	0.99	137	0.89	107	1.00	140	1.08	167
23	0.98	134	0.96	127	0.98	134	1.00	140
24	0.97	130	0.92	116	0.98	134	1.00	140
25	0.96	127	0.91	113	0.98	134	1.00	140
26	0.94	121	0.89	107	0.98	134	0.98	134
27	0.89	107	0.86	100	1.05	157	0.93	118
28	0.89	107	0.86	100	1.02	147	0.92	116
29	0.89	107	0.81	87	0.98	134	0.92	116
30	0.86a	100	0.81	87	0.99a	137	0.93	118
31	0.86a	100	0.79	83	....	....	0.91	113

a Gauge heights interpolated.

MONTHLY DISCHARGE of South Branch of Sheep River near Black Diamond, for 1914.

(Drainage area 248 square miles.)

MONTH.	DISCHARGE IN SECOND-FEET. Maximum.	Minimum.	Mean.	Per square Mile.	RUN-OFF. Depth in inches on Drainage Area.	Total in Acre-feet.
April	174	40	108	0.436	0.49	6,426
May	486	116	310	1.250	1.44	19,061
June	683	197	414	1.670	1.86	24,635
July	456	100	206	0.831	0.96	12,666
August	134	81	104	0.420	0.48	6,395
September	230	63	107	0.432	0.48	6,367
October	295	110	157	0.633	0.73	9,054
The period	....	....	....	....	6.44	85,204

5 GEORGE V, A. 1915

SHEEP RIVER NEAR OKOTOKS.

Location.—On the NW. ¼ Sec. 22, Tp. 20, Rge. 29, W. 4th Mer., at the Canadian Pacific Railway Company's bridge about one mile southeast of Okotoks.

Records available.—From May 7, 1909, to October 31, 1914.

Gauge.—Staff. High water staff gauge is imbedded in the cement on centre pier. The elevation of the zero of the gauge was maintained at 3,420.09 feet during 1909-10; 3,418.12 feet during 1911; 3,417.12 feet during 1912-14.

Bench-mark.—Top of the left abutment at southwest corner; elevation, 3,431.57 feet above mean sea level (C.P.R. datum).

Channel.—Shifting.

Discharge measurements.—From bridge or by wading.

Winter flow.—Observations discontinued during winter months.

Artificial control.—Gas pipes crossing river below gauging section form good control.

Observer.—Miss M. B. Henderson.

DISCHARGE MEASUREMENTS of Sheep River near Okotoks, in 1914.

Date.	Engineer.	Width.	Area of Section.	Mean Velocity.	Gauge Height.	Discharge.
		Feet.	*Sq. ft.*	*Ft. per sec.*	*Feet.*	*Sec.-ft.*
April 9	J. S. Tempest	51	57.6	2.69	2.40	156
May 20	H. S. Kerby	98	369.0	1.89	3.09	696
June 16	do	98	378.8	1.85	3.34	699
July 10	do	143	264.0	1.42	2.75	374
Aug. 10	do	85	135.0	1.04	2.42	140
Sept. 1	do	86	129.0	0.78	2.28	100
Sept. 21	do	87	131.0	1.20	2.52	157
Oct. 17	do	97	342.0	1.02	2.90	351

DAILY GAUGE HEIGHT AND DISCHARGE of Sheep River near Okotoks, for 1914.

DAY.	April.		May.		June.	
	Gauge Height.	Dis- charge.	Gauge Height.	Dis- charge.	Gauge Height.	Dis- charge.
	Feet.	*Sec.-ft.*	*Feet.*	*Sec.-ft.*	*Feet.*	*Sec.-ft.*
1			2.63a	276	2.87	382
2			2.78	397	3.11	602
3			2.83	442	3.32	804
4	2.54	217	2.68	313	3.37	854
5	3.04	646	2.58a	242	3.17	636
6	2.93	537	2.49	187	3.17	628
7	2.71	337	2.48	182	3.37	820
8	2.53	211	2.53	211	3.11	550
9	2.53	217	2.68	313	3.01	446
10	2.60	254	2.88	489	2.93	362
11	2.49	187	2.87	479	2.93	354
12	2.53	211	2.90a	508	3.01	430
13	2.62	269	2.93	537	3.08	492
14	2.53	211	2.98	586	3.27	646
15	2.53	211	3.18	789	3.35	710
16	2.58	242	3.18	789	3.32	682
17	2.49a	187	3.18	789	3.25	620
18	2.45	167	3.18	789	3.20	584
19	2.44	162	3.18	789	3.16	556
20	2.47	177	3.09	696	3.06	470
21	2.38	135	3.09	692	2.96	390
22	2.38	135	3.06	652	2.92	360
23	2.37	131	3.05	632	2.77	252
24	2.61	261	3.08	652	2.76	252
25	2.53	211	3.08a	650	3.06	502
26	2.48	182	3.07	624	3.37	838
27	2.48	182	3.07	610	3.28	756
28	2.43	157	2.92	460	3.28	768
29	2.42	152	2.82	360	3.11	606
30	2.48	182	2.89a	414	3.04	552
31			2.95	464		

a Gauge height interpolated.

DAILY GAUGE HEIGHT AND DISCHARGE of Sheep River near Okotoks, for 1914.—*Concluded.*

DAY.	July.		August.		September.		October.	
	Gauge Height.	Dis-charge.	Gauge Height.	Dis-charge.	Gauge Height.	Dis-charge.	Gauge Height.	Dis-charge.
	Feet.	*Sec.-ft.*	*Feet.*	*Sec.-ft.*	*Feet.*	*Sec.-ft.*	*Feet.*	*Sec.-ft.*
1	2.99	512	2.33	117	2.28	100	2.45	135
2	2.98	512	2.32	114	2.25	92	2.45a	135
3	2.97	514	2.31	110	2.25	92	2.45	135
4	2.95	500	2.30	106	2.24	88	2.48a	145
5	3.05	608	2.29	103	2.23	84	2.50	152
6	3.20	772	2.29	103	2.23	82	2.47	141
7	3.07a	648	2.31	110	2.24	84	2.47a	141
8	2.95	540	2.30	106	2.26	86	2.47	141
9	2.86	464	2.37a	131	2.24	82	2.58	182
10	2.81	424	2.45	167	2.23	80	2.60	190
11	2.79	405	2.36	128	2.24	80	2.55	171
12	2.78a	397	2.35	124	2.30	92	2.53a	163
13	2.77	388	2.35	124	2.25	80	2.50	152
14	2.76	380	2.31	110	2.25	78	2.50	152
15	2.73	353	2.33	117	2.30a	88	2.65	212
16	2.65	291	2.35	124	2.32a	90	2.84	311
17	2.61	261	2.40	142	2.35	98	2.95	385
18	2.54	217	2.45	167	2.33	92	3.03	443
19	2.54	217	2.44	162	2.42a	116	3.05	458
20	2.53	211	2.40	142	2.55	172	2.85	319
21	2.52	204	2.37	131	2.50	152	2.82a	300
22	2.48	182	2.41a	147	2.45	135	2.80	288
23	2.46	172	2.45	167	2.44a	132	2.80	288
24	2.44	162	2.41	147	2.43	129	2.65	212
25	2.41	147	2.40	142	2.44a	132	2.63a	203
26	2.40	142	2.37	131	2.45	135	2.60	190
27	2.35	124	2.36a	128	2.47	141	2.55	171
28	2.35	124	2.35	124	2.45	135	2.55	171
29	2.35	124	2.33a	117	2.45a	135	2.55	171
30	2.35	124	2.30	106	2.45	135	2.51	156
31	2.34	120	2.30	106	....	....	2.49	149

a Gauge height interpolated.

MONTHLY DISCHARGE of Sheep River near Okotoks, for 1914

(Drainage area 632 square miles.)

MONTH.	DISCHARGE IN SECOND-FEET.				RUN-OFF.	
	Maximum.	Minimum.	Mean.	Per square Mile.	Depth in inches on Drainage Area.	Total in Acre-feet.
April (4–30)	646	131	228	0.361	0.36	12,188
May	789	182	517	0.818	0.94	31,789
June	854	252	563	0.890	0.99	33,501
July	772	120	330	0.522	0.60	20,290
August	167	103	128	0.203	0.23	7,870
September	172	78	108	0.171	0.19	6,426
October	458	135	212	0.335	0.39	13,035
The period	....	....	....	....	3.70	125,099

HIGHWOOD RIVER AT BROWN'S RANCH.

Location.—On SE. ¼ Sec. 20, Tp. 18, Rge. 2, W. 5th Mer., at B. F. Brown's ranch, about eight miles north of Pekisko and five miles west of Longview post office.

Records available.—July 27, 1912, to October 31, 1914.

Gauge.—Vertical staff; elevation of zero of gauge maintained at 93.90 feet during 1912; 91.97 feet during 1913-14.

5 GEORGE V, A. 1915

Bench-mark.—Permanent iron bench-mark; assumed elevation, 100.00 feet.
Channel.—Shifts during floods.
Discharge measurements.—Made from the traffic bridge one and one-half miles down-stream, or by wading near bridge.
Winter flow.—Observations discontinued during winter months.
Observer.—B. F. Brown.

DISCHARGE MEASUREMENTS of Highwood River at Brown's Ranch, in 1914.

Date.	Engineer.	Width.	Area of Section.	Mean Velocity.	Gauge Height.	Discharge.
		Feet.	*Sq. ft.*	*Ft. per sec.*	*Feet.*	*Sec.-ft.*
April 12 . . .	J. S. Tempest	128	103.0	2.64	1.40	271
May 27	H. S. Kerby	178	340.0	3.29	1.65	1,118
June 22	do	159	286.0	3.15	2.05	910*a*
July 19	do	158	171.0	2.53	1.18	434
Aug. 17	do	120	93.5	2.05	0.77	188
Sept. 5	do	119	77.5	1.85	0.62	144
Sept. 24	do	120	95.5	2.00	0.75	191
Oct. 24	do	120	117.0	2.33	0.95	272

a Measurement affected by a log jam.

DAILY GAUGE HEIGHT AND DISCHARGE of Highwood River at Brown's Ranch, for 1914.

Day.	April.		May.		June.		July.	
	Gauge Height.	Dis-charge.	Gauge Height.	Dis-charge.	Gauge Height.	Dis-charge.	Gauge Height.	Dis-charge.
	Feet.	*Sec.-ft.*	*Feet.*	*Sec.-ft.*	*Feet.*	*Sec.-ft.*	*Feet.*	*Sec.-ft.*
1	. . . .	. . . .	1.00	310	2.02	1,850	1.85*c*	1,510
2	. . . . . .	. . . . . .	1.25	510	2.32	2,450	2.05	1,910
3	. . . . . .	. . . . . .	1.40	690	2.42	2,650	1.95	1,110
4	. .	. . . . . .	1.35	625	2.37	2,550	1.80	1,410
5	. . . .	. . . .	1.15	420	2.27	2,350	1.75	1,310
6	. . . . . .	. . . . . .	1.05	345	2.17	2,150	1.65	1,115
7	. . . . . .	. . . . . .	1.00	310	2.15	2,110	1.45	760
8	. .	. . . . . .	1.15	420	2.00	1,810	1.40	690
9	. . . . . .	. . . . . .	1.33	601	1.85	1,510	1.38	664
10	. . . .	. .	1.35	625	1.80	1,410	1.35	625
11	. . . . . .	. . . . . .	1.20	465	1.85	1,510	1.30	565
12	1.40	271*a*	1.22	478	1.90	1,610	1.30	565
13	1.00	230	1.35	625	1.92	1,650	1.28	543
14	1.05	220	1.50	840	2.47*b*	1,310	1.25	510
15	0.80	195*a*	1.70	1,210	2.52	1,210	1.25	510
16	0.75	180	1.70	1,210	2.75	1,510	1.20	465
17	0.73	174	1.68	1,172	2.95	1,610	1.02	324
18	0.70	165	1.70	1,210	3.00	1,610	1.15	420
19	0.65	150	1.74	1,290	2.65	1,210	1.15*c*	420
20	0.75	180	1.75	1,310	2.22	1,020	1.15	420
21	0.60	140	1.73	1,270	2.28	1,020	1.14	412
22	0.60	140	1.70	1,210	2.05	930	1.10	380
23	0.75	180	1.70	1,210	1.93	930	1.05	345
24	0.70	165	1.73	1,270	2.00	1,020	1.00	310
25	0.80	200	1.85	1,510	2.25	1,210	1.00	310
26	0.80	200	1.80	1,410	2.40	1,410	0.95	280
27	0.75	180	1.75	1,310	2.55*b*	1,610	0.95	280
28	0.75	180	1.60	1,020	2.00	1,810	0.92	262
29	0.80	200	1.47	792	2.05	1,910	0.90	250
30	0.85	225	1.42	718	2.00	1,810	0.88	240
31	. . . . . .	. . . . . .	1.67	1,153	. . . . . .	. . . . . .	0.85	225

a Ice conditions April 12 to 15—discharge estimated.
b Log jam June 14 to 27—discharge estimated.
c Logs took gauge out July 1—gauge height estimated by observer.

SESSIONAL PAPER No. 25c

DAILY GAUGE HEIGHT AND DISCHARGE of Highwood River at Brown's Ranch, for 1914.
—*Concluded.*

DAY.	August.		September.		October.	
	Gauge Height.	Dis- charge.	Gauge Height.	Dis- charge.	Gauge Height.	Dis- charge.
	Feet.	*Sec.-ft.*	*Feet.*	*Sec.-ft.*	*Feet.*	*Sec.-ft.*
1	0.85	225	0.65	150	0.75	180
2	0.84	220	0 65	150	0.80	200
3	0.82	210	0.65	150	0.85	225
4	0.85	225	0.64	148	0.88	240
5	0.85	225	0.65	150	0.90	250
6	0.85	225	0.65	150	0.86	230
7	0.85	225	0.63	146	0.85	225
8	0.85	225	0.65	150	0 85	225
9	0.86	230	0.65	150	0.87	235
10	0.85	225	0.65	150	0.90	250
11	0.85	225	0.67	156	0.87	235
12	0.80	200	0.68	159	0.85	225
13	0.79	196	0.70	165	0.85	225
14	0.75	180	0.68	159	0.85	225
15	0.75	180	0.65	150	0.87	235
16	0.76	184	0.66	153	0.90	250
17	0.75	180	0.70	165	1.15	420
18	0.75	180	0.75	180	1.20	465
19	0.80	200	0.80	200	1.15	420
20	0.77	188	0.85	225	1.15	420
21	0.75	180	0.85	225	1.14	412
22	0.75	180	0.83	215	1.10	380
23	0.75	180	0.80	200	0.98	298
24	0.76	184	0.75	180	0.95	280
25	0.75	180	0.74	177	0.94	274
26	0.73	174	0.73	174	0.90	250
27	0.73	174	0.80	200	0.90	250
28	0.75	180	0.80	200	0.88	240
29	0.72	171	0.80	200	0.87	235
30	0.70	165	0.77	188	0.87	235
31	0.67	156	....	....	0.85	225

MONTHLY DISCHARGE of Highwood River at Brown's Ranch, for 1914.

(Drainage area 421 square miles.)

MONTH.	DISCHARGE IN SECOND-FEET.				RUN-OFF.	
	Maximum.	Minimum.	Mean.	Per square Mile.	Depth in inches on Drainage Area.	Total in Acre-feet.
April (12–30)	271	140	188	0.446	0.325	7,093
May	1,510	310	888	2.110	2.433	54,601
June	2,650	930	1,632	3.880	4.329	97,110
July	1,910	225	617	1.466	1.690	37,938
August	230	156	196	0.466	0.537	12,052
September	225	146	172	0.409	0.456	10,235
October	465	180	273	0.648	0.747	16,786
The period	....	....	....	....	10.517	235,815

PEKISKO CREEK AT PEKISKO.

Location.—On the NW. ¼ Sec. 8, Tp. 17, Rge. 2, W. 5th Mer., at George Lane's Bar U ranch, and about twenty-five miles southwest of High River.

Records available.—October 6, 1911, to October 31, 1914.

Gauge.—Vertical staff; elevation of zero of gauge is 93.90 feet, unchanged since establishment.

Bench-mark.—Permanent iron bench-mark; assumed elevation, 100.00 feet.

5 GEORGE V, A. 1915

Channel.—Fairly permanent.
Discharge measurements.—Made from a small suspension footbridge or by wading.
Winter flow.—Observations not taken during winter months.
Diversions.—The headgates of George Lane's irrigation ditch are about one and one-half miles upstream from station. Ditch flowing continuously from July 22, 1914, to August 14, 1914.
Observer.—F. R. Pike.

DISCHARGE MEASUREMENTS of Pekisko Creek at Pekisko, in 1914.

Date.	Engineer..	Width.	Area of Section.	Mean Velocity.	Gauge Height.	Discharge.
		Feet.	*Sq. ft.*	*Ft. per sec.*	*Feet.*	*Sec.-ft.*
April 12..	J. S. Tempest........... ...	50	118.0	0.58	1.54	69.0
May 26	H. S. Kerby..............	48	109.0	0.55	1.57	60.0
June 21..........	do	46	36.0	1.06	1.37	38.0
July 17..........	do	41	36.3	0.42	1.20	15.2
Aug. 15	do	17	6.7	0.70	0.98	4.7
Sept. 7..........	do	17	8.8	0.52	1.00	4.6
Sept. 25..........	do	20	9.6	0.70	1.08	6.7
Oct. 24..........	do	51	44.2	0.72	1.45	32.0

DAILY GAUGE HEIGHT AND DISCHARGE of Pekisko Creek at Pekisko, for 1914.

DAY.	April.		May.		June.		July.	
	Gauge Height.	Dis-charge.	Gauge Height.	Dis-charge.	Gauge Height.	Dis-charge.	Gauge Height.	Dis-charge.
	Feet.	*Sec.-ft.*	*Feet.*	*Sec.-ft.*	*Feet.*	*Sec.-ft.*	*Feet.*	*Sec.-ft.*
1...............................			1.60	72	1.48	53	1.60	72.0
2...............................			1.61	74	1.46	50	1.52	59.0
3...............................			1.66	82	1.46	50	1.46	50.0
4...............................			1.60	72	1.48	53	1.41	42.0
5...............................			1.50	56	1.49	54	1.45	48.0
6...............................			1.46	50	1.52	59	1.44	46.0
7...............................	1.55	64	1.50	56	1.53	61	1.40	40.0
8...............................	1.38	37	1.50	56	1.51	57	1.36	34.0
9...............................	1.35	33	1.60	72	1.44	46	1.35	33.0
10...............................	1.32	29	1.66	82	1.44	46	1.33	30.0
11...............................	1.36	34	1.63	77	1.48	53	1.31	27.0
12...............................	1.52	59	1.64	78	1.50	56	1.28	24.0
13...............................	1.54	62	1.63	77	1.47	51	1.28	24.0
14...............................	1.48	53	1.63	77	1.51	57	1.24	19.0
15...............................	1.44	46	1.65	80	1.49	54	1.23	18.0
16...............................	1.46	50	1.64	78	1.44	46	1.20	15.0
17...............................	1.36	34	1.63	77	1.42	43	1.18	13.4
18...............................	1.33	30	1.63	77	1.40	40	1.18	13.4
19...............................	1.29	25	1.63	77	1.38	37	1.17	12.6
20...............................	1.37	36	1.65	80	1.38	37	1.16	12.6
21...............................	1.37	36	1.65	80	1.36	34	1.15	11.0
22...............................	1.37	36	1.64	78	1.37	36	1.10	7.7
23...............................	1.40	40	1.63	77	1.35	33	1.08	6.9
24...............................	1.58	68	1.62	75	1.36	34	0.98	4.5
25...............................	1.53	61	1.61	74	1.66	82	0.94	4.1
26...............................	1.48	53	1.59	70	1.88	117	0.94	4.1
27...............................	1.45	48	1.56	66	1.88	117	0.93	4.0
28...............................	1.46	50	1.55	64	1.80	104	0.95	4.2
29...............................	1.50	56	1.52	59	1.74	93	0.96	4.3
30...............................	1.47	51	1.50	56	1.67	83	0.97	4.4
31...............................			1.48	53			0.94	4.1

SESSIONAL PAPER No. 25c

DAILY GAUGE HEIGHT AND DISCHARGE of Pekisko Creek at Pekisko, for 1914.—*Concluded.*

DAY.	August.		September.		October.	
	Gauge Height.	Dis- charge.	Gauge Height.	Dis- charge.	Gauge Height.	Dis- charge.
	Feet.	*Sec.-ft.*	*Feet.*	*Sec.-ft.*	*Feet.*	*Sec.-ft.*
1	0.94	4.1	0.98	4.5	1.15	11.0
2	0.92	3.9	0.98	4.5	1.16	11.8
3	0.90	3.8	0.97	4.4	1.18	13.4
4	0.93	4.0	0.96	4.3	1.21	16.0
5	0.91	3.9	0.98	4.5	1.23	18.0
6	0.91	3.9	0.98	4.5	1.23	18.0
7	0.95	4.2	0.98	4.5	1.25	20.0
8	0.94	4.1	1.05	5.7	1.27	22.0
9	0.94	4.1	1.05	5.7	1.29	25.0*c*
10	1.08	6.9	1.05	5.7	1.31	26.0
11	1.0)	4.7	1.02	5.1	1.33	28.0
12	0.98	4.5	1.05	5.7	1.35	30.0
13	0.96	4.3	1.05	5.7	1.40	36.0
14	0.95	4.2	1.06	6.1	1.46	44.0
15	0.98	4.5	1.07	6.5	1.71	80.0
16	1.00	4.7	1.08	6.9	1.86	109.0
17	1.08	6.9	1.10	7.7	1.86	108.0
18	1.08	6.9	1.10	7.7	1.82	100.0
19	1.06	6.1	1.10	7.7	1.76	88.0
20	1.02	5.1	1.11	8.4	1.66	72.0
21	1.00	4.7	1.10	7.7	1.59	58.0
22	1.01	4.9	1.08	6.9	1.55	50.0
23	1.06	6.1	1.08	6.9	1.50	41.0
24	1.06	6.1	1.05	5.7	1.46	36.0*a*
25	1.06	6.1	1.08	6.9	1.44	31.0
26	1.03	5.3	1.09	7.3	1.41	27.0
27	1.00	4.7	1.11	8.4	1.38	23.0
28	1.00	4.7	1.13	9.7	1.37	22.0
29	1.00	4.7	1.13	9.7	1.35	19.0
30	1.00	4.7	1.15	11.0	1.32	16.0
31	1.00	4.7	....	....	1.31	15.0

a Shifting conditions from Oct. 9 to 24.

MONTHLY DISCHARGE of Pekisko Creek at Pekisko, for 1914.

(Drainage area 99 square miles.)

MONTH.	DISCHARGE IN SECOND-FEET.				RUN-OFF.	
	Maximum.	Minimum	Mean.	Per square Mile.	Depth in inches on Drainage Area.	Total in Acre-feet.
April (7–30)	68.0	25.0	45.0	0.450	0.40	2,141
May	82.0	50.0	71.0	0.718	0.83	4,366
June	117.0	33.0	58.0	0.586	0.65	3,451
July	72.0	4.1	22.0	0.224	0.26	1,352
August	6.9	3.8	5.0	0.051	0.06	307
September	11.0	4.3	6.5	0.066	0.07	387
October	109.0	11.0	39.0	0.394	0.45	2,398
The period	....	....	....	....	2.72	14,402

5 GEORGE V, A. 1915

STIMSON CREEK NEAR PEKISKO.

Location.—On the NW. ¼ Sec. 2, Tp. 17, Rge. 2, W. 5th Mer., at *E. R.* Baker's ranch, about three miles east of Pekisko post office.

Records available.—From October 6th, 1911, to October 31, 1914.

Gauge.—Staff; elevation of zero of gauge maintained at 90.20 feet since establishment.

Bench-mark.—Permanent iron bench-mark; assumed elevation 100.00 feet.

Channel.—Fairly permanent.

Discharge measurements.—By wading or from bridge.

Winter flow.—No observations taken during winter months.

Observer.—E. R. Baker.

DISCHARGE MEASUREMENTS of Stimson Creek near Pekisko, in 1914.

Date.	Engineer.	Width.	Area of Section.	Mean Velocity.	Gauge Height.	Discharge.
		Feet.	*Sq. ft.*	*Ft. per sec.*	*Feet.*	*Sec.-ft.*
April 11............	J. S. Tempest.............	39.5	23.6	1.68	......*b*	39.8
June 21............	H. S. Kerby.............	30.0	25.2	0.32	1.34	7.6
July 15............	do	19.0	6.0	0.37	1.36	2.2
Aug. 14............	do				0.94	Nil *a*
Sept. 7............	do				0.65	Nil *a*
Sept. 25............	do				1.02	Nil *a*
Oct. 23............	do	19.0	8.7	0.58	1.33	5.0

a Water standing in pools.
b Gauge height not read.

DAILY GAUGE HEIGHT AND DISCHARGE of Stimson Creek near Pekisko, for 1914.

	June.		July.		August.		September.		October.	
DAY.	Gauge Height.	Dis-charge.	Gauge Height.	Dis-charge.	Gauge Height.	Dis-charge.	Gauge Height.	Dis-charge.	Gauge Height.	Dis-charge.
	Feet.	*Sec.-ft.*	*Feet.*	*Sec.-ft.*	*Feet.*	*Sec.-ft.*	*Feet.*	*Sec.-ft.*	*Feet.*	*Sec.-ft.*
1................	1.71	26.0	1.49	12.0	1.03	Nil	0.66	Nil	1.14	0.40
2................	1.69	24.0	1.40	7.0	1.02	"	0.67	"	1.13	0.30
3................	1.65	22.0	1.45	9.0	1.02	"	0.67	"	1.04	Nil
4................	1.60	18.0	1.42	7.5	1.00	"	0.67	"	1.03	"
5................	1.59	17.4	1.45	8.5	0.98	"	0.66	"	1.35	4.80
6................	1.60	18.0	1.54	13.0	0.97	"	0.67	"	1.42	7.50
7................	1.57	16.0	1.54	13.0	0.97	"	0.67	"	1.42	7.50
8................	1.62	19.4	1.51	11.0	0.97	"	0.67	"	1.42	7.50
9................	1.59	17.4	1.47	8.5	0.92	"	0.67	"	1.32	3.70
10................	1.62	19.4	1.42	6.5	0.98	"	0.67	"	1.42	7.50
11................	1.62	19.4	1.41	5.0	1.02	"	0.71	"	1.52	12.80
12................	1.64	21.0	1.39	4.5	1.01	"	0.70	"	1.52	12.80
13................	1.66	22.0	1.37	3.5	0.99	"	0.70	"	1.32	12.80
14................	1.70	25.0*a*	1.32	2.0	0.96	"	0.71	"	....	....
15................	1.74	30.0	1.35	2.3	0.94	"	0.70	"	....	....
16................	1.69	27.0	1.38	3.0	0.92	"	0.71	"	....	....
17................	1.69	28.0	1.36	3.0	1.02	"	0.67	"	....	....
18................	1.66	26.0	1.34	3.0	1.05	"	0.67	"	....	....
19................	1.64	26.0	1.28	2.0	1.05	"	0.67	"	....	....
20................	1.50	16.0	1.27	2.0	1.02	"	0.66	"	....	....
21................	1.34	7.6	1.26	2.0	1.02	"	0.70	"	....	....
22................	1.25	4.2	1.22	2.2*a*	1.04	"	0.70	"	....	....
23................	1.44	15.2	1.19	0.9	1.02	"	0.70	"	....	....
24................	1.45	13.0	1.17	0.7	1.02	"	0.71	"	....	....
25................	1.60	25.0	1.14	0.4	1.00	"	1.12	0.20	....	....
26................	2.43	148.0	1.12	0.2	0.97	*a*	1.12	0.20	....	....
27................	2.06	78.0	1.09	Nil	0.97	"	1.12	0.20	....	....
28................	1.80	40.0	1.07	"	0.95	"	1.15	0.50	....	....
29................	1.73	30.0	1.05	"	0.95	"	1.15	0.50	....	....
30................	1.65	23.0	1.05	"	0.97	"	1.30	3.00	....	....
31................	....	....	1.04	"	0.91	"			....	....

a to *a* Shifting conditions.

MONTHLY DISCHARGE of Stimson Creek near Pekisko, for 1914.

(Drainage area 78 square miles.)

MONTH.	DISCHARGE IN SECOND-FEET.				RUN-OFF.	
	Maximum.	Minimum	Mean.	Per square Mile.	Depth in inches on Drainage Area.	Total in Acre-feet.
June..	148.0	4.2	27.00	0.346	0.39	1,607
July.............................	13.0	0.0	4.30	0.055	0.06	264
August.............................						Nil.
September	3.0	0.0	1.05	0.013	0.01	62
October (1-13)............	12.8	0.0	6.00	0.077	0.04	155
The period					0.50	2,088

FINDLAY AND MCDOUGAL DITCH FROM HIGHWOOD RIVER.

Location.—On SW. ¼ Sec. 31, Tp. 18, Rge. 29, W. 4th Mer., about four and one-half miles west of the town of High River.
Records available.—June 17, 1911, to October 25, 1914.
Gauge.—Vertical staff on left bank; elevation of zero of gauge 99.25 feet, unchanged since establishment.
Bench-mark.—Permanent iron bench-mark; assumed elevation, 100.00 feet.
Channel.—Soft mud, liable to shift.
Discharge measurements.—By wading.
Winter flow.—Ditch closed off at freeze-up.
Artificial control.—Discharge at station may be controlled by means of the headgates about one-quarter mile above station.
Observer.—No observations of daily gauge height during 1914.

DISCHARGE MEASUREMENTS of Findlay-McDougal Ditch from Highwood River, in 1914.

Date.	Engineer.	Width.	Area of Section.	Mean Velocity.	Gauge Height.	Discharge.
		Feet.	Sq. ft.	Ft. per sec.	Feet.	Sec.-ft.
June 22............	H. S. Kerby...............	9.0	4.0	1.24	1.35	5.00
Aug. 18............	do	8.0	5.1	0.79	1.46	4.00
Sept. 5....	do	6.0	2.9	0.58	1.10	1.70
Sept. 24............	do	8.0	4.4	0.76	1.28	3.30

LITTLE BOW DITCH AT HIGH RIVER.

Location.—On the SW. ¼ Sec. 6, Tp. 19, Rge. 28, W. 4th Mer., about 100 feet from the power station and pumping plant of the town of High River.
Records available.—August 1, 1910, to December 31, 1914.
Gauge.—Staff; elevation of zero of gauge maintained at 91.06 feet during 1910-11; 92.06 feet during 1912-14.
Bench-mark.—Permanent iron bench-mark; assumed elevation, 100.00 feet.
Channel.—Fairly permanent.
Discharge measurements.—Made by wading.
Winter flow.—Continuous records kept during winter.
Artificial control.—Formed by headgates of ditch about one mile above station.
Observer.—Philip Weinard.

5 GEORGE V, A. 1915

Discharge Measurements of Little Bow Ditch at High River, in 1914.

Date.	Engineer.	Width.	Area of Section.	Mean Velocity.	Gauge Height.	Discharge.
		Feet.	*Sq. ft.*	*Ft. per sec.*	*Feet.*	*Sec.-ft.*
Jan. 13..........	J. S. Tempest	12.5	10.1	2.12	0.93	22.00
Feb. 17..........	do	12.7	17.6	0.93	1.65	16.40
Feb. 28..........	do	13.3	12.8	1.54	1.01	19.90
April 10..........	do	13.0	8.8	1.63	0.66	14.10
April 26..........	do				0.38	0.02a
May 4..........	do					Nil.
May 28..........	do	17.7	24.6	1.07	1.15	26.20
June 22..........	H. S. Kerby	17.5	24.5	1.19	1.04	29.20
July 13..........	do	16.0	19.8	0.86	0.75	17.20
Aug. 11..........	do	17.0	20.6	0.88	0.82	18.20
Sept. 8..........	do	16.0	16.9	0.73	0.55	12.40
Sept. 25..........	do	16.0	15.2	0.67	0.55	10.20
Oct. 22..........	do	15.0	13.6	0.63	0.45	8.58
Nov. 13..........	do	16.0	13.9	0.63	0.45	8.84
Dec. 10..........	R. J. McGuinness.	13.9	13.4	0.63	0.61	8.37

a Weir measurement.

Daily Gauge Height and Discharge of Little Bow Ditch at High River, for 1914.

DAY.	January.		February.		March.		April.		May.		June.	
	Gauge Height	Dis-charge	Gauge Height.	Dis-charge.	Gauge Height.	Dis-charge	Gauge Height	Dis-charge	Gauge Height	Dis-charge	Gauge Height.	Dis-charge.
	Feet.	*Sec.-ft.*	*Feet.*	*Sec.-ft.*	*Feet.*	*Sec.-ft.*	*Feet.*	*Sec.-ft.*	*Feet.*	*Sec.-ft.*	*Feet.*	*Sec.-ft.*
1..........	0.94	11.6a	1.44	14.0	0 95	16.5	0.74	15 9a	0.88	20 0	1 18	30
2..........	1.15	12.8	1.32	9.5	0 95	18 0	1 05	26 0	0 99	23 0	1 25	32
3..........	1.00	12.2	1.50	12.0	1 00	16 7	0.85	19 1	1.05	26.0	1 40	38
4..........	0.95	11.7	1.30	13.0	0.92	16 8	0 84	18.8	1.00	24 0	1 53	44
5..........	1.00	11.0	1.30	10.0	0 90	17 0	0.95	22 0	0 95	22 0	1.30	34
6..........	0.98	11.0	1.00	8.2	1 00	17 0	0 95	22 0	0.94	22 0	1.21	31
7..........	0.92	10.8	1.30	8.4	0.77	16 0	0 90	21.0	0 90	21 0	1.20	31
8..........	0.90	10.9	1.30	9.2	0.80	16 2	0 76	16 5	0.80	17.6	1.11	28
9..........	0.83	11.0	1.45	10.8	0 95	17 0	0 70	14 8	0 92	21 0	1 06	26
10. ...	2.00	11.0	1.44	12.0	0 95	17.1	0 75	16 2	1 08	27.0	1 04	25
11.	1.43	11.0	1.62	12.4	0.75	15.0	0.75	16 2	1 04	25 0	1.20	31
12..........	1.37	12.4	1.65	13.0	0.98	16.0	0.75	16 2	0 97	23 0	1 05	26
13 . . .	0.90	22.0	1.75	14.0	1.05	17.0	0.75	16 2	1 00	24 0	1.05	26
14..........	0.90	18.6	1.60	15.0	1.05	17.0	0.72	15.4	1 05	26 0	1.15	29
15..........	0.90	13.4	1.64	15.5	1.10	17.0	0.71	15 1	1.15	29 0	1 15	29
16.	0.83	12.5	1.67	16.0	1 15	17 0	0 77	16 8	1 20	31 0	1.14	28
17..........	0.90	12.2	1.63	16.6	1 10	17 0	0 75	16 2	1.24	32 0	1.18	30
18. .	0.94	12.0	1.60	17.0	1 00	16 6	0.74	15.9	1.24	32 0	1 19	30
19..	1.68	11.5	1.50	17.3	0.97	18 4	0 73	15 6	1 24	32 0	1 15	29
20 ..	1.75	11.4	1.55	17.4	1 04	16 4	0 75	16 2	1.20	31 0	1 43	40
21..........	1.24	11.0	1.30	16.9	1 45	16.2	0 75	16.2	1 20	31 0	1.06	26
22..........	0.94	10.5	1.45	16.5	0 80	16.2	0 75	16 2	1.17	30 0	1 35	36
23..........	1.05	11.0	1.40	17.6	0 75	16 0	0 75	16.2	1.18	30.0	0 95	22
24	1.16	12.0	1.34	18.2	0 75	15 0	0 79	17 3	1 19	30 0	0.89	20
25 . .	1.15	13.0	1.40	18.8	0 72	14 2	0 80	17.6	1 25	32 0	1 00	24
26 .	1.25	13.8	1.37	19.1	0 70	14 9	0 80	17.6	1 24	32.0	1.10	27
27..........	1.45	12.8	1.00	19.4	0 90	16 6	0 84	18.8	1 20	31 0	1.00	24
28	1.36	11.6	1.15	19.6	0 95	16.7	0 81	17 9	1 17	30.0	0 93	22
29 ..	1.30	11.0			0.85	16 8	0 84	18.8	1 10	27 0	0 92	21
30.. . .	1.30	13.0			0 74	16.8	0 84	18.8	1.06	26 0	0.94	22
31. .	1.57	15.0			0.74	16 8			1 09	27.0		

a Ice conditions Jan. 1 to April 1.

DAILY GAUGE HEIGHT AND DISCHARGE of Little Bow Ditch at High River, for 1914.—*Concluded.*

DAY.	July.		August.		September.		October.		November.		December.	
	Gauge Height.	Dis- charge.	Gauge Height.	Dis- charge.	Gauge Height.	Dis- charge.	Gauge Height.	Dis- charge	Gauge Height.	Dis- charge	Gauge Height.	Dis- charge.
	Feet.	*Sec.-ft.*	*Feet.*	*Sec.-ft.*	*Feet.*	*Sec.-ft.*	*Feet.*	*Sec.-ft.*	*Feet.*	*Sec.-ft.*	*Feet.*	*Sec.-ft.*
1..........	0.90	21.0	0.94	22.0	0 55	11.0	0 54	10.8	0.42	8.2	0.35	12.3
2..........	0.90	21.0	0.94	22 0	0 54	10.8	0.54	10.8	0.41	8.0	0.32	11.3
3..........	0.90	21.0	0.90	21 0	0.50	9 8	0 54	10.8	0.42	8.2	0.28	10.5
4..........	0.90	21.0	0.84	18 8	0.53	10 5	0 61	12.5	0.42	8.2	0.36	9.8
5..........	0.95	22.0	0.85	19.1	0 50	9 8	0 65	13.5	0.46	9.0	0.36	9.3
6..........	1.05	26.0	0.84	18 8	0.50	9 8	0.54	10.8	0.41	8.0	0.35	9.0
7..........	1.04	25.0	0.90	21.0	0 52	10 2	0 55	11.0	0.90	21.0	0.29	8.7
8..........	1.10	27.0	0.83	18.5	0 52	10 2	0 51	10.0	0.54	10.8	0.43	8.5
9..........	0.83	18.5	0.83	18.5	0 54	10.8	0 55	11.0	0.42	8.2	0.56	8.5
10.... ...	0.91	21.0	0.85	19.1	0 54	10 8	0 55	11.0	0.40	7.8	0.63	8.4
11..........	0.94	22.0	0.81	17 9	0 57	11 5	0 55	11.0	0.40	7.8	0.61	8.4
12.....	0.79	17.3	0.75	16 2	0.57	11.5	0.51	10.0	0.40	7.8	0.81	8.6
13....	0.76	16.5	0.75	16 2	0 53	10 5	0 51	10.0	0.35	6.8	0.86	9.2
14..........	0.74	15.9	0.69	14 6	0 55	11 0	0 51	10.0	0.54	10.8	0.83	9.7
15.........	0.66	13.8	0.67	14 0	0 55	11 0	0 51	10.0	0.62	12.7	0.80	9.9
16..........	0.60	12.2	0.65	13.5	0.55	11 0	0 51	10.0	0.55	11.0	0.73	9.8
17...	0.59	11.9	0.66	13.8	0.55	11 0	0 56	11.2	0.60	12.2	0.60	9.6
18..........	0.58	11.7	0.66	13.8	0 54	10.8	0.56	11.2	0.82	13.2*a*	0.57	9.4
19..........	1.70	51.0	0.65	13.5	0 54	10 8	0 55	11.0	0.85	13.8	0.55	9.0
20..........	1.33	36.0	0.60	12.2	0 54	10 8	0 55	11.0	0.80	14.3	0.51	8.8
21....	1.33	36.0	0.60	12.2	0.54	10.8	0.47	9.2	0.67	14.3	0.46	8.5
22..........	1.33	36.0	0.58	11.7	0.55	11.0	0.47	9.2	0.62	13.8	0.36	8.0
23..........	1.11	28.0	0.55	11.0	0.55	11.0	0.46	9.0	0.56	13.4	0.41	7.8
24.....	1.10	27.0	0.56	11.2	0.54	10.8	0.44	8.6	0.55	13.5	0.35	7.7
25..... ...	1.05	26.0	0.58	11.7	0.55	11.0	0.44	8.6	0.64	14.0	0.35	7.6
26.....	1.00	24.0	0.55	11.0	0.55	11.0	0.44	8.6	0.54	14.1	0.36	7.6
27..........	1.00	24.0	0.55	11.0	0.55	11.0	0.44	8.6	0.54	13.8	0.36	7.6
28..........	0.98	23.0	0.55	11.0	0.56	11.2	0.43	8.4	0.44	13.4	0.36	7.9
29..........	0.96	23.0	0.55	11.0	0.55	11.0	0.44	8.6	0.56	13.5	0.36	7.9
30..........	0.95	22.0	0.55	11.0	0.54	10.8	0.44	8.6	0.56	13.5	0 40	7.6
31..........	0.95	22.0	0.55	11.0	....	....	0.44	8.6	....	....	0.35	7.4*a*

a Ice conditions Nov. 18 to Dec. 31.

MONTHLY DISCHARGE of Little Bow Ditch at High River, for 1914.

MONTH.	DISCHARGE IN SECOND-FEET.			RUN-OFF.
	Maximum.	Minimum.	Mean.	Total in Acre-feet.
January..	22.0	10.5	12.4	762
February...	19.6	8.2	14.6	811
March..	18.0	14.2	16.4	1,008
April...	26.0	14.8	17.6	1,047
May..	32.0	17.6	27.0	1,660
June..	44.0	20.0	29.0	1,726
July..	51.0	11.7	23.0	1,414
August...	22.0	11.0	15.1	928
September..	11.5	9.8	10.7	637
October..	13.5	8.4	10.1	621
November	21.0	6.8	11.5	684
December...	12.3	7.4	8.8	541
The year...	....	....	....	11,839

HIGHWOOD RIVER AT HIGH RIVER.

Location.—On the NW. ¼ Sec. 6, Tp. 19, Rge. 28, W. 4th Mer., at the new steel traffic bridge in the town of High River.

Records available.—May 28, 1908, to December 31, 1914.

Gauge.—Chain gauge; elevation of zero of gauge maintained at 3,381.66 feet during 1908-13; 3,379.74 feet during 1914.

18........... 1.95
19........... 1.94
20........... 1.92

SESSIONAL PAPER N₁ 25c

DAILY GAUGE HEIGHT AND DISCHARGE of Highwood River at High River, for 1914.—*Concluded.*

DAY.	July.		August.		September.		October.		November.		December.	
	Gauge Height.	Dis-charge.	Gauge Height.	Dis-charge.	Gauge Height.	Dis-charge.	Gauge Height.	Dis-charge.	Gauge Height.	Dis-charge.	Gauge Height.	Dis-charge.
	Feet.	*Sec.-ft.*	*Feet.*	*Sec.-ft.*	*Feet.*	*Sec.-ft.*	*Feet.*	*Sec.-ft.*	*Feet.*	*Sec.-ft.*	*Feet.*	*Sec.-ft.*
1	3.23	8	3.97	196	3 79	143	3.71	127	4.01	210	3 54	113
2	3.22	84	3.92	181	3.79	143	3.71	127	4.04	225	3.42	102
3	3.21	84	3.92	181	3.77	139	3.76	137	4.05	230	3.36	104
4	3.21	84	3.99	202	3.77	139	4.01	210	4.01	210	3.58	108
5	3.24	85	3.93	184	3.66	119	4.11	210	4.01	210	3.51	101
6	3.28	92	3.91	178	3.65	118	4.06	235	4.05	230	3.08	96
7	3.23	87	3.96	193	3.70	125	4.01	210	3.87	166	3.26	83
8	3.11	74	3.96	193	3.80	145	4.06	235	3.92	181	2.97	61
9	3.01	64	3.96	193	3.76	137	4.05	230	3.96	193	3.25	51
10	2.93	56	4.02	215	3.76	137	4.10	255	4.01	210	3.29	51
11	2.91	57	3.96	193	3.80	145	4.01	210	4.01	210	3.25	54
12	2.88	85	3.96	193	3.65	117	4.05	230	4.00	205	3.20	59
13	2.84	84	3.92	181	3.78	141	4.01	210	3.64	116	3.35	61
14	4.73a	73	3.87	166	3.75	135	4.00	205	3.64	116	3.39	62
15	4.63	63	3.87	166	3.67	121	4.10	255	3.49	100	3.50	65
16	4.58	92	3.82	151	3.77	139	4.29	368	3.40	98b	3.57	71
17	4.48	84	3.92	181	3.73	131	4.52	548	3.31	96	3.53	76
18	4.40	80	3.92	181	3.75	135	4.57	593	3.48	104	3.52	80
19	4.40	80	3.92	181	3.64	116	4.57	593	3.72	120	3.52	82
20	4.30	75	3.92	181	4.03	220	4.47	506	3.85	139	3.60	84
21	4.35	82	3.87	166	3.82	151	4.43	474	3.81	150	3.53	85
22	4.30	75	3.87	166	3.73	131	4.31	383	3.90	152	3.58	86
23	4.26	77	3.86	163	3.77	139	4.29	368	3.76	152	3.57	87
24	4.21	72	3.87	166	3.77	139	4.24	333	3.86	154	3.60	88
25	4.20	65	3.87	166	3.77	139	4.19	300	4.13	200	3.64	89
26	4.16	65	3.78	141	3.82	151	4.15	280	4.00	178	3.63	90
27	4.10	65	3.77	139	3.82	151	4.14	275	4.03	174	3.64	90
28	4.10	65	3.73	131	3.78	141	4.10	255	3.96	168	3.63	90
29	4.06	65	3.78	141	3.86	163	4.10	255	3.75	132	3.61	91
30	4.06	65	3.78	141	3.86	163	4.05	230	3.74	124	3.60	92
31	4.06	65	3.79	143	......	......	4.05	230	......	......	3.64	93b

a Gauge read at ne station from July 14.
b Ice conditions No 16 to Dec. 31.

MONTHLY DISCHARGE of Highwood River at High River, for 1914.

(Drainage area 746 square miles.)

MONTH	DISCHARGE IN SECOND-FEET.				RUN-OFF.	
	Maximum.	Minimum.	Mean.	Per square Mile.	Depth in inches on Drainage Area.	Total in Acre-feet.
January	85	46	69	0.092	0.11	4,243
February	60	43	51	0.068	0.07	2,832
March	92	60	66	0.088	0.10	4,058
April	365	107	264	0.354	0.40	15,709
May	1,272	365	880	.1.180	1.36	54,109
June	1,921	744	1,209	1.620	1.81	71,940
July	922	235	550	0.737	0.85	33,818
August	215	131	173	0.232	0.27	10,637
September	220	116	140	0.188	0.21	8,331
October	593	127	293	0.393	0.45	18,016
November	230	96	165	0.221	0.25	9,818
December	113	51	825	0.110	0.13	5,042
The year	......	......	......	......	6.01	238,553

5 GEORGE V. A. 1915

Bench-mark.—Permanent iron bench-mark 128 feet N. 60° *E.* from SE. corner of stream face of right abutment; elevation, 3,389.60 feet above mean sea level (Canadian Pacific Railway Company).

Channel.—Fairly permanent.

Discharge measurements.—From bridge.

Diversions.—The Little Bow Ditch diverts water about two miles above the station.

Observer.—Philip Weinard.

DISCHARGE MEASUREMENTS of Highwood River at High River, in 1914.

Date.	Engineer.	Width.	Area of Section.	Mean Velocity.	Gauge Height.	Discharge.
		Feet.	*Sq. ft.*	*Ft. per sec.*	*Feet.*	*Sec.-ft.*
Jan. 13............	J. S. Tempest	23.5	19.2	4.27	1.88	82
Feb. 17..	do	34.5	27.9	1.88	2.18	52
Feb. 28.... ..	do	37.0	36.3	1.64	2.14	60
April 10..	do	135.0	414.0	0.65	2.20	271
May 26....	H. S. Kerby.	139.0	524.0	1.98	3.42	1,041
June 20........ ..	do	142.0	629.8	2.13	3.63	1,336
July 14...... .. .	do	137.0	342.0	1.82	4.60	620a
Aug. 11..	do	117.0	254.0	0.92	4.05	222
Sept. 9..........	do	110.0	225.0	0.57	3.73	128
Sept. 26	do	112.0	237.0	0.72	3.86	171
Oct. 22	do	120.0	280.0	1.16	4.22	325
Nov. 13..	do	....	....	....	3.67	.... b
Dec. 9............	R. J. McGuinness.	75.0	155.0	0.33	3.25	51

a Station moved to present position on July 14.
b Unable to measure on account of slush ice.

DAILY GAUGE HEIGHT AND DISCHARGE of Highwood River at High River, for 1914.

DAY.	January.		February.		March.		April.		May.		June.	
	Gauge Height.	Dis- charge.	Gauge Height.	Dis- charge.	Gauge Height.	Dis- charge.	Gauge Height.	Dis- charge.	Gauge Height.	Dis- charge.	Gauge Height.	Dis- charge.
	Feet.	*Sec.-ft.*	*Feet.*	*Sec.-ft.*	*Feet.*	*Sec.-ft.*	*Feet.*	*Sec.-ft.*	*Feet.*	*Sec.-ft.*	*Feet.*	*Sec.-ft.*
1............	1.77	78a	2.04	52	2.13	60	1.93	107	2.49	365	3.40	1,040
2............	1.90	80	2.07	50	2 14	60	2.21	119	2.80	540	3.62	1,272
3............	1.96	83	1.99	47	2.14	60	2.14	131	3.12	778	4.01	1,701
4............	1.96	84	2 02	45	2.16	60	2.35	141	3.07	736	4.21	1,921
5............	2.16	85	2.15	43	2.13	61	2.48	156	2.95	645	3.92	1,602
6............	2.14	84	2.17	44	2.10	61	2.70	171	2.81	547	3.79	1,459
7............	2.11	83	2.17	44	2.10	61	2.38	186	2.78	528	3.79	1,459
8............	2.10	81	2.18	45	2.10	61	2.10	204	2.68	468	3.62	1,272
9............	1.98	80	2.20	47	2.08	61	2.18	225a	2.80	540	3.47	1,110
10............	1.87	78	2.20	49	2.05	60	2.18	233	3.17	823	3.29	931
11............	1.86	79	2.23	50	2.04	62	2.23	252	3.20	850	3.32	960
12............	1.90	81	2.25	49	2.14	65	2.32	288	3.02	696	3.36	1,000
13............	1.94	82	2.28	50	2.23	69	2.43	335	3.02	696	3.37	1,010
14............	1.96	83	2.27	57	2.50	71	2.46	350	3.12	778	3.64	1,294
15............	1.99	83	2.25	57	2.48	71	2.33	292	3.32	960	3.68	1,338
16............	1.98	82	2.21	56	2.25	70	2.42	330	3.42	1,060	3.73	1,393
17............	1.95	77	2.16	52	2.15	69	2.42	330	3 49	1,130	3.82	1,492
18............	1.95	69	2.14	50	2.04	68	2.43	335	3 52	1,162	3.82	1,492
19............	1.94	62	2.14	49	1.83	67	2.27	268	3.53	1,173	3.77	1,437
20............	1.92	59	2.07	49	1.91	66	2.25	260	3.47	1,110	3.63	1,283
21..·..........	1.90	56	2.08	49	1.90	65	2.27	268	3 48	1,120		
22............	1.90	55	2.10	50	1.87	66	2.29	276	3.42	1,060	3 48	1,120
23............	1.89	54	2.13	52	1.87	66	2.22	248	3.39	1,030	3.30	940
24............	1.87	53	2.16	54	1.84	64	2.49	365	3.40	1,040	3.18	832
25............	1.85	51	2.17	58	1.79	62	2.47	355	3.45	1,090	3.08	744
26............	1.84	49	2.19	60	1.76	61	2.47	355	3.60	1,250	3.16	814
27............	1.85	47	2.20	60	1.75	62	2.46	350	3 62	1,272	3.64	1,294
28............	1.86	46	2.13	60	1.73	66	2.41	325	3.57	1,217	3.51	1,151
29............	2.06	47	......	......	1.78	71	2.41	325	3.42	1,060	3.39	1,030
30............	2.06	50	......	......	1.83	81	2.41	325	3 31	950	3.33	970
31............	2.04	52	......	......	1.86	92	......	......	3.20	850	3.25	895
									3 22	868		

a Ice conditions Jan. 1 to April 9.

SESSIONAL PAPER No. 25c

DAILY GAUGE HEIGHT AND DISCHARGE of Highwood River at High River, for 1914.—*Concluded.*

DAY.	July.		August.		September.		October.		November.		December.	
	Gauge Height.	Dis-charge	Gauge Height.	Dis-charge	Gauge Height.	Dis-charge.	Gauge Height.	Dis-charge	Gauge Height.	Dis-charge.	Gauge Height.	Dis-charge.
	Feet.	*Sec.-ft.*	*Feet.*	*Sec.-ft.*	*Feet.*	*Sec.-ft.*	*Feet.*	*Sec.-ft.*	*Feet*	*Sec -ft.*	*Feet.*	*Sec.-ft.*
1	3.23	877	3.97	196	3.79	143	3.71	127	4.01	210	3 54	113
2	3.22	868	3 92	181	3.79	143	3.71	127	4.04	225	3.42	102
3	3.21	859	3.92	181	3 77	139	3.76	137	4.05	230	3 36	104
4	3.21	859	3.99	202	3.77	139	4.01	210	4.01	210	3 58	108
5	3.24	886	3.93	184	3.66	119	4.11	210	4.01	210	3.51	101
6	3.28	922	3.91	178	3.65	118	4.06	235	4.05	230	3.08	96
7	3.23	877	3.96	193	3.70	125	4.01	210	3.87	166	3.26	83
8	3.11	769	3.96	193	3.80	145	4.06	235	3.92	181	2.97	61
9	3.01	688	3.96	193	3.76	137	4.05	230	3.96	193	3.25	51
10	2.93	631	4.02	215	3.76	137	4.10	255	4.01	210	3.29	51
11	2.91	617	3.96	193	3.80	145	4.01	210	4.01	210	3.25	54
12	2.88	596	3.96	193	3.65	117	4.05	230	4.00	205	3.20	59
13	2.84	568	3.92	181	3.78	141	4.01	210	3.64	116	3.35	61
14	4.73a	753	3.87	166	3.75	135	4.00	205	3.64	116	3.39	62
15	4.63	650	3.87	166	3.67	121	4.10	255	3.49	100	3.50	65
16	4.58	602	3.82	151	3.77	139	4.29	368	3.40	98b	3.57	71
17	4.48	514	3.92	181	3.73	131	4.52	548	3.31	96	3.53	76
18	4.40	450	3.92	181	3.75	135	4.57	593	3.48	104	3.52	80
19	4.40	450	3.92	181	3.64	116	4.57	593	3.72	120	3.52	82
20	4.30	375	3.92	181	4.03	220	4.47	506	3.85	139	3.60	84
21	4.35	412	3.87	166	3.82	151	4.43	474	3.81	150	3.53	85
22	4.30	375	3.87	166	3.73	131	4.31	383	3.90	152	3.58	86
23	4.26	347	3.86	163	3.77	139	4.29	368	3.76	152	3.57	87
24	4.21	312	3.87	166	3.77	139	4.24	333	3.86	154	3.60	88
25	4.20	305	3.87	166	3.77	139	4.19	300	4.13	200	3.64	89
26	4.16	285	3.78	141	3.82	151	4.15	280	4.00	178	3.63	90
27	4.10	255	3.77	139	3.82	151	4.14	275	4.03	174	3.64	90
28	4.10	255	3.73	131	3.78	141	4.10	255	3.96	168	3.63	90
29	4.06	235	3.78	141	3.86	163	4.05	255	3.75	132	3.61	91
30	4.06	235	3.78	141	3.86	163	4.05	230	3.74	124	3.60	92
31	4.06	235	3.79	143			4.05	230			3.64	93b

a Gauge read at new station from July 14.
b Ice conditions Nov. 16 to Dec. 31.

MONTHLY DISCHARGE of Highwood River at High River, for 1914.

(Drainage area 746 square miles.)

MONTH.	DISCHARGE IN SECOND-FEET.				RUN-OFF.	
	Maximum.	Minimum.	Mean.	Per square Mile.	Depth in inches on Drainage Area.	Total in Acre-feet.
January	85	46	69	0.092	0.11	4,243
February	60	43	51	0.068	0.07	2,832
March	92	60	66	0.088	0.10	4,058
April	365	107	264	0.354	0.40	15,709
May	1,272	365	880	.1.180	1.36	54,109
June	1,921	744	1,209	1.620	1.81	71,940
July	922	235	550	0.737	0.85	33,818
August	215	131	173	0.232	0.27	10,637
September	220	116	140	0.188	0.21	8,331
October	593	127	293	0.393	0.45	18,016
November	230	96	165	0.221	0.25	9,818
December	113	51	825	0.110	0.13	5,042
The year					6.01	238,553

5 GEORGE V, A. 1915

HIGHWOOD RIVER NEAR ALDERSYDE.

Location.—On NW. ¼ Sec. 17, Tp. 20, Rge. 28, W. 4th Mer., at L. W. Barret's ranch, about three miles *NE.* of Aldersyde.

Records available.—From October 3, 1911, to October 31, 1914.

Gauge.—Standard chain gauge; elevation of zero of the gauge is 90.64 feet, unchanged since establishment.

Bench-mark.—Permanent iron bench-mark; assumed elevation, 100.00 feet.

Channel.—Large stones and boulders in and near section.

Discharge measurements.—From traffic bridge or by wading.

Winter flow.—No observations taken during winter months.

Observer.—L. W. Barret.

DISCHARGE MEASUREMENTS of Highwood River, near Aldersyde, in 1914.

Date.	Engineer.	Width.	Area of Section.	Mean Velocity.	Gauge Height.	Discharge.
		Feet.	*Sq. ft.*	*Ft. per sec.*	*Feet.*	*Sec.-ft.*
April 9.............	J. S. Tempest...............	90	182	1.16	1.79	211
May 25.............	H. S. Kerby...............	175	359	3.18	2.32	1,141
June 16.............	do	180	418	3.36	2.63	1,415
July 10.............	do	155	283	2.69	1.95	762
Aug. 10.............	do	125	156	1.32	1.17	220
Sept. 1.............	do	85	98	1.36	0.96	132
Sept. 21.............	do	111	126	1.51	1.15	189
Oct. 16.............	do	132	193	1.64	1.45	344

DAILY GAUGE HEIGHT AND DISCHARGE of Highwood River near Aldersyde, for 1914.

DAY.	March.		April.		May.		June.	
	Gauge Height.	Dis-charge.	Gauge Height.	Dis-charge.	Gauge Height.	Dis-charge.	Gauge Height.	Dis-charge.
	Feet.	*Sec.-ft.*	*Feet.*	*Sec.-ft.*	*Feet.*	*Sec.-ft.*	*Feet.*	*Sec.-ft.*
1......................	....	....	1.85	150	1.37	302	2.13	919
2......................	....	....	2.07	160	1.77	572	2.33	1,140
3......................	....	....	2.12	163	1.97	758	2.48	1,325
4......................	....	....	2.05	160	2.02	807	3.08	2,135
5......................	....	....	2.32	180	1.97	758	2.86	1,830
6......................	....	....	3.07	230	1.79	589	2.62	1,509
7......................	....	....	3.20	240	1.67	492	2.63	1,522
8......................	....	....	2.56	202	1.62	455	2.58	1,455
9......................	....	....	2.26	211*a*	1.71	523	2.50	1,350
10......................	....	....	1.60	441	2.02	807	2.36	1,176
11......................	....	....	1.31	270	2.09	878	2.23	1,026
12......................	....	....	1.26	245	2.02	807	2.23	1,026
13......................	....	....	1.46	352	1.88	671	2.30	1,105
14......................	....	....	1.42	329	2.01	797	2.38	1,201
15......................	2.55	......*a*	1.36	296	2.07	857	2.51	1,363
16......................	2.54	....	1.34	286	2.32	1,129	2.56	1,428
17......................	2.52	....	1.36	296	2.29	1,094	2.58	1,455
18......................	2.45	....	1.35	291	2.35	1,164	2.60	1,482
19......................	2.29	....	1.28	255	2.37	1,188	2.63	1,522
20......................	2.23	....	1.29	200	2.32	1,129	2.53	1,389
21......................	1.94	....	1.20	217	2.33	1,140	2.49	1,337
22......................	1.99	....	1.16	201	2.30	1,105	2.47	1,312
23......................	1.92	....	1.21	222	2.28	1,083	2.27	1,071
24......................	1.88	....	1.31	270	2.21	1,004	2.15	940
25......................	1.87	....	1.48	364	2.30	1,105	2.12	909
26......................	1.86	....	1.46	352	2.43	1,262	2.57	1,442
27......................	1.85	....	1.36	296	2.31	1,117	2.47	1,312
28......................	1.84	....	1.39	313	2.30	1,105	2.32	1,129
29......................	1.83	....	1.37	302	2.21	1,004	2.30	1,105
30......................	1.82	....	1.38	307	2.08	868	2.27	1,071
31......................	1.84	....	....	....	2.06	847	....	....

a Ice conditions March 15 to April 9. Discharge estimated April 1 to 9.

SESSIONAL PAPER No. 25c

DAILY GAUGE HEIGHT AND DISCHARGE of Highwood River near Aldersyde, for 1914.
—*Concluded.*

DAY.	July.		August.		September.		October.	
	Gauge Height.	Dis- charge.	Gauge Height.	Dis- charge.	Gauge Height.	Dis- charge.	Gauge Height.	Dis- charge.
	Feet.	*Sec.-ft.*	*Feet.*	*Sec.-ft.*	*Feet.*	*Sec.-ft.*	*Feet.*	*Sec.-ft.*
1	2.25	1,048	1.25	240	0.90	118	1.14	193
2	2.22	1,015	1.22	226	0.89	116	1.15	197
3	2.21	1,004	1.21	222	0.87	111	1.16	201
4	2.18	972	1.20	217	0.88	113	1.20	217
5	2.21	1,004	1.21	222	0.87	111	1.22	226
6	2.26	1,059	1.19	213	0.89	116	1.25	240
7	2.21	1,004	1.19	213	0.90	118	1.26	245
8	2.14	930	1.20	217	0.92	123	1.28	255
9	2.09	878	1.22	226	0.94	128	1.28	255
10	2.09	878	1.25	240	0.93	126	1.30	265
11	2.00	787	1.22	226	0.93a	126	1.27	250
12	1.93	719	1.18	209	0.92	123	1.24	235
13	1.90	690	1.10	178	0.95	131	1.25	240
14	1.92	709	1.05	160	1.00	145	1.27	250
15	1.89	681	1.03	154	1.02	151	1.27	250
16	1.87	662	1.00	145	1.03	154	1.45	346
17	1.87	662	1.40	318	1.03	154	1.66	485
18	1.74	547	1.10	178	1.05	160	1.74	547
19	1.68	500	1.08	171	1.02	151	1.75	555
20	1.64	470	1.06	164	1.09	174	1.65	477
21	1.60	441	1.05	160	1.10	178	1.59	434
22	1.56	414	1.05a	160	1.09	174	1.53	395
23	1.51	382	1.05	160	1.09a	174	1.46	352
24	1.48	364	1.07	167	1.10	178	1.41	324
25	1.43	335	1.04	157	1.10a	178	1.39	313
26	1.41a	324	1.03	154	1.10	178	1.36	296
27	1.39a	313	1.00	145	1.12	186	1.32	275
28	1.36	296	0.98	140	1.15	197	1.32	275
29	1.34	286	0.97	137	1.13	189	1.30	265
30	1.32	275	0.98	140	1.14	193	1.28	255
31	1.26	245	0.96a	134	....	....	1.26	245

a Gauge height interpolated.

MONTHLY DISCHARGE of Highwood River near Aldersyde, for 1914.

(Drainage area 883 square miles.)

MONTH.	DISCHARGE IN SECOND-FEET.				RUN-OFF.	
	Maximum.	Minimum.	Mean.	Per square Mile.	Depth in inches in Drainage Area.	Total in Acre-feet.
April	441	150	262	0.297	0.33	15,590
May	1,262	302	884	1.000	1.15	54,355
June	2,135	909	1,300	1.473	1.64	77,355
July	1,059	245	642	0.727	0.84	39,475
August	318	134	187	0.212	0.24	11,498
September	197	111	149	0.169	0.19	8,866
October	555	193	302	0.342	0.39	18,569
The period	....	....	....	....	4.78	225,702

STREAM MEASUREMENTS, 1914

5 GEORGE V. A. 1915

BOW RIVER NEAR NAMAKA.

Location.—On the *NE.* ¼ Sec. 32, Tp. 21, Rge. 25, W. 4th Mer., about one-half mile below the Southern Alberta Land Company's dam.

Records available.—From September, 1909, to October, 1910. From May 13, 1913, to August 22, 1914.

Gauge.—Inclined staff; elevation of zero of gauge is 2,952.00 feet, unchanged since establishment.

Bench-mark.—Permanent iron bench-mark; elevation, 2,962.92 feet above mean sea level (C.P.R. datum); located about 25 feet *NE.* of cable tower on the right bank.

Channel.—Permanent.

Discharge measurements.—By means of cable and car.

Winter flow.—No observations during the winter.

Artificial control.—Opening or closing gates on Southern Alberta Land Company's canal will affect discharge at station.

Diversions.—Southern Alberta Land Company's headgates for their main canal are about one-half mile upstream.

Co-operation.—The Southern Alberta Land Company supplied the gauge heights and also took some discharge measurements.

DISCHARGE MEASUREMENTS of Bow River near Namaka, in 1914.

Date.	Engineer.	Width.	Area of Section.	Mean Velocity.	Gauge Height.	Discharge.
		Feet.	*Sq. ft.*	*Ft. per sec.*	*Feet.*	*Sec.-ft.*
April 22............	J. S. Tempest.............	291	1,279	1.54	55.48	1,960
April 18............	T. H. Hatch (S.A.L. Co.)....	337	1,293	2.38	56.20	3,080
May 6............	do	339	1,292	2.54	56.30	3,292
May 9............	H. S. Kerby.................	340	1,276	2.42	56.35	3,088
May 22............	T. H. Hatch (S.A.L. Co.)....	349	1,719	3.59	57.60	6,174
June 3............	H. S. Kerby.................	352	1,784	4.02	58.00	7,107
June 26............	do	357	2,178	4.45	59.00	9,696
June 22............	T. H. Hatch (S.A.L. Co.)....	366	2,443	4.90	59.35	12,030
July 4............	do	366	2,305	4.77	59.15	11,243
July 7............	do	364	2,508	5.44	59.65	13,691
July 25............	H. S. Kerby.................	350	1,812	3.42	57.70	6,184
July 29............	T. H. Hatch (S.A.L. Co.)....	349	1,681	3.32	57.45	5,584
Aug. 22............	H. S. Kerby.................	343	1,463	2.63	56.80	3,862
Oct. 3............	do	333	1,345	2.25	56.50	3,030

SESSIONAL PAPER No. 25c

DAILY GAUGE HEIGHT AND DISCHARGE of Bow River near Namaka, for 1914.

DAY.	April.		May.		June.		July.		August.	
	Gauge Height.	Dis-charge.	Gauge Height.	Dis-charge.	Gauge Height.	Dis-charge.	Gauge Height.	Dis-charge.	Gauge Height.	Dis-charge.
	Feet.	*Sec.-ft.*	*Feet.*	*Sec.-ft.*	*Feet.*	*Sec.-ft.*	*Feet.*	*Sec.-ft.*	*Feet.*	*Sec.-ft.*
1			5.60	2,050	7.90a	6,750	8.60	9,050	7.30	5,050
2			5.90	2,425	7.95a	6,900	8.70	9,400	7.30	5,050
3			6.00	2,550	8.00	7,050	8.80	9,750	7.35	5,175
4			6.00	2,550	8.60	9,050	9.20	11,300	7.40	5,300
5			6.50	3,325	9.20	11,300	9.40	12,110	7.45	5,425
6			6.40	3,150	9.50	12,500	9.70	13,400	7.45	5,425
7			6.50	3,325	9.20	11,300	9.70	13,400	7.30	5,050
8			6.30	3,000	9.10	10,900	9.50	12,500	7.35	5,175
9			6.30	3,000	8.90	10,100	9.20	11,300	7.40	5,300
10			6.50	3,325	8.80	9,750	9.10	10,900	7.40	5,300
11			6.90	4,125	8.70	9,400	9.00	10,500	7.20	4,800
12			6.60	3,500	8.60	9,050	8.90	10,100	7.10	4,575
13			6.70	3,700	8.80	9,750	8.00	7,050	7.00	4,350
14			6.90	4,125	9.80	13,850	9.00	10,500	6.95	4,237
15			7.00	4,350	9.90	14,300	9.10	10,900	6.95	4,237
16			7.00	4,350	10.10	15,200	9.20	11,300	6.90	4,125
17	6.28	2,970	7.50	5,550	10.20	15,650	9.00	10,500	7.00	4,350
18	5.98	2,525	7.70	6,150	10.10	15,200	8.60	9,050	7.10	4,575
19	5.78	2,275	7.70	6,150	9.90	14,300	8.40	8,350	7.05	4,162
20	5.68	2,150	7.60	5,850	9.70	13,400	8.20	7,650	6.95	4,237
21	5.58	2,030	7.60	5,850	9.60	12,950	8.40	8,350	6.85	4,012
22	5.48	1,930	7.50	5,550	9.40	12,100	8.40	8,350	6.85b	4,012
23	5.48	1,930	7.50	5,550	9.20	11,300	8.10	7,350		
24	5.48	1,930	7.50a	5,550	9.00	10,500	7.85	6,600		
25	5.68	2,150	7.55a	5,700	9.00	10,500	7.70	6,150		
26	5.68	2,150	7.60a	5,850	9.00	10,500	7.67	6,060		
27	5.78	2,275	7.65a	6,000	9.00	10,500	7.55	5,700		
28	5.78	2,275	7.70a	6,150	8.60	9,050	7.35	5,175		
29	5.58	2,030	7.75a	6,300	8.20	7,650	7.40	5,300		
30	5.60	2,050	7.80a	6,450	8.20	7,650	7.40	5,300		
31			7.85a	6,600			7.35	5,175		

a Gauge heights interpolated.
b Observations discontinued Aug. 22.
NOTE.—Add 2,950.00 to gauge heights to get elevation above sea level.

MONTHLY DISCHARGE of Bow River near Namaka, for 1914.

(Drainage area 6,208 square miles.)

MONTH.	DISCHARGE IN SECOND-FEET.				RUN-OFF.	
	Maximum.	Minimum.	Mean.	Per square Mile.	Depth in inches on Drainage Area.	Total in Acre-feet
April (17-30)	2,970	1,930	2,191	0.353	0.183	60,732
May	6,600	2,050	4,584	0.738	0.851	281,858
June	15,650	6,750	10,947	1.763	1.967	651,400
July	13,400	5,175	8,984	1.447	1.668	552,410
August (1-22)	5,425	4,012	4,724	0.761	0.622	206,077
The period					5.291	1,752,477

5 GEORGE V, A. 1915

BOW RIVER NEAR BASSANO.

Location.—On SE. ¼ of Sec. 2, Tp. 21, Rge. 19, W. 4th Mer., about one-half mile down-stream from Canadian Pacific Railway Company's dam, and about three miles southwest of the town of Bassano.

Records available.—August 20, 1909, to December 31, 1914.

Gauge.—Staff; elevation of zero of gauge 2,519.43 feet during 1909-10; 2,517.90 feet during 1911-12; 2,513.60 feet during 1913; 2,510.68 feet during 1914.

Bench-mark.—Permanent iron bench-mark; elevation 2,524.29 feet above mean sea level (Canadian Pacific Railway Company).

Channel.—Permanent.

Discharge measurements.—By cable and car.

Winter flow.—Records taken during winter season.

Artificial control.—Formed by Canadian Pacific Railway Company's dam one-half mile upstream.

Diversions.—Eastern section of Canadian Pacific Railway Company's Irrigation Canal diverts water about one-half mile upstream.

Co-operation.—Gauge heights supplied by Canadian Pacific Railway Company.

DISCHARGE MEASUREMENTS of Bow River near Bassano, in 1914.

Date.	Engineer.	Width.	Area of Section.	Mean Velocity.	Gauge Height.	Discharge.
		Feet.	*Sq. ft.*	*Ft. per sec.*	*Feet.*	*Sec.-ft.*
May 12...........	H. S. Kerby...............	574	2,603	1.57	3.26	4,081
June 7...........	do	590	3,597	3.29	5.71	11,830
June 23...........	do	590	3,249	2.69	4.96	8,750
July 27...........	do	560	2,676	1.84	3.90	4,902
Aug. 25. . . .	do	557	2,458	1.57	3.41	3,851
Sept. 15...........	do	512	2,035	1.10	2.64	2,244
Oct. 10...........	do	545	2,252	1.45	3.16	3,278
Oct. 28...........	do	532	2,119	1.23	2.84	2,601
Nov. 27...........	R. McGuinness........ . . .	565	2,220	1.26	2.94	2,802
Dec. 15	do	500	1,487	0.43	1.73	640

SESSIONAL PAPER No. 25c

DAILY GAUGE HEIGHT AND DISCHARGE of Bow River near Bassano, for 1914.

DAY.	June.		July.		August.		September.	
	Gauge Height.	Dis-charge.	Gauge Height.	Dis-charge.	Gauge Height.	Dis-charge.	Gauge Height.	Dis-charge.
	Feet.	*Sec.-ft.*	*Feet.*	*Sec.-ft.*	*Feet.*	*Sec.-ft.*	*Feet.*	*Sec.-ft.*
1	5.96	12,740	4.86	8,360	3.79	4,820	3.66	4,450
2	5.66	11,540	4.86	8,360	3.79	4,820	3.56	4,200
3	5.26	9,940	4.86	8,360	3.78	4,790	3.56	4,200
4	5.46	10,740	5.06	9,140	3.78	4,790	3.56	4,200
5	5.46	10,740	5.46	10,740	3.78	4,790	3.56	4,200
6	5.86	12,340	5.66	11,540	3.67	4,475	2.46	1,940
7	5.86	12,340	6.06	13,140	3.67	4,475	2.46	1,940
8	5.66	11,540	6.06	13,140	3.67	4,475	2.46	1,940
9	5.46	10,740	5.66	11,540	3.67	4,475	2.66	2,240
10	5.46	10,740	5.46	10,740	3.66	4,450	2.66	2,240
11	5.66	11,540	5.26	9,940	3.66	4,450	2.66	2,240
12	5.96	12,740	5.27	9,980	3.76	4,730	2.45	1,925
13	5.86	12,340	5.27	9,980	3.86	5,030	2.25	1,625
14	5.86	12,340	5.07	9,180	3.86	5,030	2.45	1,925
15	6.16	13,540	5.27	9,980	3.86	5,030	2.65	2,225
16	6.06	13,140	5.47	10,780	3.96	5,330	2.65	2,225
17	6.16	13,540	5.48	10,820	3.96	5,330	3.05	3,000
18	6.26	13,940	4.88	8,430	3.96	5,330	3.25	3,425
19	6.36	14,340	4.88	8,430	3.86	5,030	3.05	3,000
20	6.06	13,140	4.68	7,730	3.76	4,730	3.05	3,000
21	5.86	12,340	4.68	7,730	3.66	4,450	2.86	2,620
22	5.86	12,340	4.79	8,115	3.66	4,450	2.66	2,240
23	6.16	13,540	4.69	7,765	3.66	4,450	2.46	1,940
24	6.16	13,540	4.79	8,115	3.66	4,450	2.66	2,240
25	6.16	13,540	4.29	6,365	3.76	4,730	2.86	2,620
26	5.86	12,340	4.09	5,720	3.76	4,730	3.06	3,020
27	5.46	10,740	4.00	5,450	3.46	3,950	3.06	3,020
28	5.66	11,540	4.10	5,750	3.46	3,950	3.06	3,020
29	4.86	8,360	3.80	4,850	3.46	3,950	3.06	3,020
30	4.86	8,360	3.80	4,850	3.66	4,450	2.86	2,620
31	....	....	3.79	4,820	3.66	4,450	....	....

5 GEORGE V. A. 1915

DAILY GAUGE HEIGHT AND DISCHARGE of Bow River near Bassano, for 1914.—*Concluded.*

DAY.	October.		November.		December.	
	Gauge Height.	Dis- charge.	Gauge Height.	Dis- charge.	Gauge Height.	Dis- charge.
	Feet.	*Sec.-ft.*	*Feet.*	*Sec.-ft.*	*Feet.*	*Sec.-ft.*
1	3.06	3,020	2.66	2,240	2.62	2,180
2	2.86	2,620	2.56	2,090	2.42	1,880
3	2.86	2,620	2.46	1,940	2.22	1,580
4	3.06	3,020	2.66	2,240	2.22	1,580
5	2.86	2,620	2.66	2,240	2.02	1,370
6	2.86	2,620	2.66	2,240	1.81	1,150
7	2.86	2,620	1.96	1,310	1.76	1,000
8	2.86	2,620	1.96	1,310	1.56	800
9	2.86	2,620	2.66	2,240	1.46	700
10	3.66	4,450	2.46	1,940	1.36	620
11	3.46	3,950	2.68	2,270	1.36	550
12	3.06	3,020	2.68	2,270	1.46	550
13	2.86	2,620	2.58	2,120	1.56	580
14	3.26	3,450	2.48	1,970	1.56	600
15	3.00	3,020	2.52*a*	2,030	1.66	640
16	3.26	3,450	2.55*a*	2,075	1.76	800
17	3.46	3,950	2.58*a*	2,120	1.66	750
18	3.66	4,450	2.62*a*	2,180	1.90	1,000
19	3.66	4,450	2.66*a*	2,240	1.90	1,000
20	3.46	3,950	2.70*a*	2,300	1.80	950
21	3.36	3,700	2.73*a*	2,360	1.80	950
22	3.26	3,450	2.76*a*	2,420	1.90	1,000
23	3.06	3,020	2.80*a*	2,500	1.90	1,000
24	2.86	2,620	2.83*a*	2,560	1.80	950
25	3.06	3,020	2.86*a*	2,620	1.80	950
26	3.06	3,020	2.88*a*	2,660	1.90	1,000
27	3.06	3,020	2.92	2,740	1.90	1,000
28	2.86	2,620	2.92	2,740	2.10	1,100
29	2.96	2,820	2.82	2,540	2.10	1,150
30	2.76	2,420	2.72	2,340	2.10	1,150
31	2.76	2,420	....	....	2.40	1,300

a Gauge height interpolated.

MONTHLY DISCHARGE of Bow River near Bassano, for 1914.

(Drainage area 7,613 square miles.)

MONTH.	DISCHARGE IN SECOND-FEET.				RUN-OFF.	
	Maximum.	Minimum.	Mean.	Per square Mile.	Depth in inches on Drainage Area.	Total in Acre-feet.
June	14,340	8,360	12,021	1.579	1.76	715,310
July	13,140	4,820	8,705	1.143	1.32	533,250
August	5,330	3,950	4,658	0.612	0.71	286,408
September	4,450	1,625	2,750	0.361	0.40	163,640
October	4,450	2,420	3,138	0.412	0.48	192,948
November	2,740	1,310	2,228	0.293	0.33	132,572
December	2,180	550	1,027	0.135	0.16	63,150
The period	....	....	....	....	5.16	2,089,278

NORTH BRANCH OF CANADIAN PACIFIC RAILWAY COMPANY CANAL NEAR BASSANO.

Location.—On NW. ¼ Sec. 3, Tp. 21, Rge. 18, W. 4th Mer., about five miles southeast of the town of Bassano, and about three and one-half miles east of the Bassano dam.
Records available.—From May 1, 1914, to October 31, 1914.
Gauge.—Hand gauge read from mark on bridge.

SESSIONAL PAPER No. 25c

Bench-mark.—Top of left abutment of gauging bridge; assumed elevation, 100.00 feet.
Channel.—Permanent concrete channel.
Discharge measurements.—From gauging bridge or by wading underneath.
Winter flow.—Ditch closed off at freeze-up.
Artificial control.—Discharge at station may be controlled by means of the headgates about 400 feet above the station.
Co-operation.—Gauge heights supplied by Canadian Pacific Railway Company.

DISCHARGE MEASUREMENTS of North Branch of Canadian Pacific Railway Company Canal near Bassano, in 1914.

Date.	Engineer.	Width.	Area of Section.	Mean Velocity.	Gauge Height.	Discharge.
		Feet.	*Sq. ft.*	*Ft. per sec.*	*Feet.*	*Sec.-ft.*
June 5	H. S. Kerby	33	30.9	1.09	1.07	34
June 28	do	35	34.8	1.46	1.50	64
July 28	do	34	37.8	1.44	1.30	54
Aug. 24	do					......a
Sept. 14	do					......a
Oct. 10	do					......a
Oct. 29	do	33	27.0	1.15	0.95	31

a Headgates closed; canal dry.

DAILY GAUGE HEIGHT AND DISCHARGE of North Branch of Canadian Pacific Railway Company Canal near Bassano, for 1914.

DAY.	May.		June.		July.		August.		September.		October.	
	Gauge Height.	Dis-charge.	Gauge Height.	Dis-charge.	Gauge Height.	Dis-charge.	Gauge Height.	Dis-charge.	Gauge Height.	Dis-charge.	Gauge Height.	Dis-charge.
	Feet.	*Sec.-ft.*	*Feet.*	*Sec.-ft.*	*Feet.*	*Sec.-ft.*	*Feet.*	*Sec.-ft.*	*Feet.*	*Sec.-ft.*	*Feet.*	*Sec.-ft.*
1	1.0	33	1.5	65	1.5	65	1.4	58			1.5	65
2	1.0.	33	1.6	73	1.2	45	2.7	169			1.5	65
3	1.0	33	1.6	73	1.2	45	1.6	73			......	....a
4	1.0	33	1.6	73	1.2	45	1.6	73				
5	1.0	33	1.4	58	1.2	45	1.6	73				
6	0.5	12	1.9	97	1.2	45	1.6	73				
7	......	....a	1.9	97	1.2	45	1.6	73				
8			1.9	97	1.2	45	1.6	73				
9			1.9	97	1.2	45	1.6	73				
10	......	....a	1.9	97	1.2	45	1.6	73				
11	1.0	33	1.9	97	1.4	58	1.6	73				
12	1.0	33	1.9	97	1.4	58	1.6	73	......	....a		
13	1.0	33	1.9	97	1.4	58	1.6	73	0.3	6		
14	1.0	33	1.9	97	1.4	58	1.6	73	0.3	6		
15	1.3	51	1.9	97	1.4	58	1.6	73	1.0	33		
16	1.3	51	1.9	97	1.4	58	......	....a	1.0	33		
17	1.3	51	1.9	97	1.4	58			1.0	33		
18	1.3	51	1.9	97	1.4	58			1.0	33		
19	1.3	51	1.9	97	1.4	58			1.0	33		
20	1.3	51	1.9	97	1.4	58			1.3	51		
21	1.3	51	1.8	89	1.4	58			1.3	51		
22	1.3	51	1.8	89	1.4	58			1.5	65		
23	1.3	51	1.8	89	1.4	58			1.5	65	......	....a
24	1.3	51	1.8	89	1.4	58			1.5	65	1.0	33
25	1.3	51	1.5	65	1.4	58			1.5	65	1.0	33
26	1.5	65	1 0	33	1.4	58			1.5	65	1.0	33
27	1.5	65	1.0	33	1.4	58			1.5	65	1.0	33
28	1.5	65	1.5	65	1.4	58			1.5	65	1.0	33
29	1.5	65	1.5	65	1.4	58			1.5	65	1.0	33
30	1.5	65	1.5	65	1.4	58			1.5	65	1.0	33
31	1.5	65	......	......	1.4	58					1.0	33

a Headgates closed from May 6 to 11; from Aug. 15 to Sept. 13; and from Oct. 2 to 24.

5 GEORGE V. A. 1915

MONTHLY DISCHARGE of North Branch Canadian Pacific Railway Company's Canal near
Bassano, for 1914.

MONTH.	DISCHARGE IN SECOND-FEET.			RUN-OFF.
	Maximum.	Minimum.	Mean.	Total in Acre-feet.
May..	65	....	41	2,520
June...	97	33	83	4,939
July...	65	45	54	3,320
August..	169	....	38	2,336
September.	65	....	29	1,726
October...	65	....	13	799
The period...	....	....	....	15,640

EAST BRANCH OF CANADIAN PACIFIC RAILWAY COMPANY CANAL NEAR BASSANO.

Location.—On SE. ¼ Sec. 3, Tp. 21, Rge. 18, W. 4th Mer., about 400 feet from headgates
of *E*ast Branch and about three and one-half miles east of the Bassano dam.
Records available.—May 28, 1914, to November 1, 1914.
Gauge.—Head gauge read from mark on bridge.
Bench-mark.—Top of left abutment of gauging bridge; assumed elevation, 100.00 feet.
Channel.—Permanent concrete channel.
Discharge measurements.—From gauging bridge or by wading underneath.
Winter flow.—Ditch closed off at freeze-up.
Artificial control.—Discharge may be controlled by means of the headgates about 250 feet
above station.
Co-operation.—Gauge heights supplied by the Canadian Pacific Railway Company.

DISCHARGE MEASUREMENTS of *E*ast Branch of Canadian Pacific Railway Company Canal
near Bassano, in 1914.

Date.	Engineer.	Width.	Area of Section.	Mean Velocity.	Gauge Height.	Discharge.
		Feet.	*Sq. ft.*	*Ft. per sec.*	*Feet.*	*Sec.-ft.*
June 5............	H. S. Kerby................	69	40.4	0.76	0.59	29
June 28............	do	73	92.6	1.21	1.40	112
July 28............	do	76	163.0	1.48	2.30	242
Aug. 24............	do	......	......	......	......	a
Sept. 16............	do	75	102.0	1.14	1.45	116
Oct. 10............	do	73	70.6	1.10	1.05	78
Oct. 29............	do	82	254.0	1.91	3.40	486

a Headgates closed; canal dry.

SESSIONAL PAPER No. 25c

DAILY GAUGE HEIGHT AND DISCHARGE of *E*ast Branch of Canadian Pacific Railway
Company Canal near Bassano, for 1914.

DAY.	May.		June.		July.	
	Gauge Height.	Dis-charge.	Gauge Height.	Dis-charge.	Gauge Height.	Dis-charge.
	Feet.	*Sec.-ft.*	*Feet.*	*Sec.-ft.*	*Feet.*	*Sec.-ft.*
1			1.5	122	1.0	68
2			1.5	122	1.5	122
3			1.3	98	1.7	148
4			0.9	59	2.0	192
5			0.9	59	2.0	192
6			1.2	88	2.0	192
7			1.2	88	2.2	224
8			0.6	34	2.4	260
9			0.6	34	2.5	280
10			0.6	34	2.5	280
11			0.6	34	2.5	280
12			1.0	68	2.5	280
13			1.0	68	2.5	280
14			1.0	68	2.5	280
15			1.0	68	2.5	280
16			1.0	68	2.5	280
17			1.0	68	2.5	280
18			1.9	177	2.5	280
19			1.9	177	2.5	280
20			1.0	68	2.5	280
21			1.0	68	2.5	280
22			0.8	50	2.5	280
23			1.4	110	2.5	280
24			1.6	134	2.5	280
25			1.5	122	2.5	280
26			1.5	122	2.5	280
27			1.5	122	2.5	280
28	0.9	59	1.5	122	2.5	280
29	1.2	88	1.5	122	2.5	280
30	1.2	88	1.5	122	2.5	280
31	1.5	122			2.5	280

5 GEORGE V, A. 1915

DAILY GAUGE HEIGHT AND DISCHARGE of *E*ast Branch of Canadian Pacific Railway Company Canal near Bassano, for 1914.—*Concluded.*

DAY.	August.		September.		October.		November.	
	Gauge Height.	Dis-charge.	Gauge Height.	Dis-charge.	Gauge Height.	Dis-charge.	Gauge Height.	Dis-charge.
	Feet.	*Sec.-ft.*	*Feet.*	*Sec.-ft.*	*Feet.*	*Sec.-ft.*	*Feet.*	*Sec.-ft.*
1	2.8	342	.....	......	3.0	388	3.5	512
2	2.8	342	.....	......	3.0	388	2.0	192
3	2.8	342	......	......	3.0	388	1.6	134
4	2.8	342	......	......	1.5	122	1.6	134
5	2.8	342	......	......	1.5	122	1.6	134
6	2.8	342	......	......	1.3	98	1.6	134
7	2.8	342	....	*a*	1.0	68	1.0	68
8	2.8	342	0.3	14	1.0	68	1.0	68
9	2.8	342	0.3	14	1.0	68	1.0	68
10	2.8	342	1.0	68	1.0	68	0.5	27
11	2.8	342	1.5	123	1.0	68	0.5	27
12	2.8	342	2.0	192	1.0	68	....	.... *a*
13	2.8	342	2.0	192	1.0	68	....	....
14	2.8	342	2.4	260	1.0	68	....	....
15	2 8	342	2.5	280	1.0	68	....	....
16	....	....*a*	2.5	280	1.0	68	....	....
17	....	....	2.5	280	1.0	68	....	....
18	....	....	2.5	280	1.0	68	....	....
19	....	....	2.5	280	1.5	122	....	....
20	....	....	2.5	280	2.0	192	....	....
21	....	....	3.0	388	3.0	388	....	....
22	....	....	3.0	388	3.5	512	....	....
23	....	....	3.0	388	3.5	512	....	....
24	....	....	3.0	388	3.5	512	....	....
25	....	....	3.0	388	3.5	512	....	....
26	....	....	3.0	388	3.5	512	....	....
27	....	....	3.0	388	3.5	512	....	....
28	....	....	3 0	388	3 5	512	....	....
29	....	....	3.0	388	3.5	512	....	....
30	....	....	3.0	388	3.5	512	....	....
31	....	....	....	....	3.5	512		

a Headgates closed; canal dry.

MONTHLY DISCHARGE of *E*ast Branch of Canadian Pacific Railway Company Canal near Bassano, for 1914.

MONTH.	DISCHARGE IN SECOND-FEET.			RUN-OFF.
	Maximum.	Minimum.	Mean.	Total in Acre-feet.
May (28–31)	122	59	89	706
June	177	34	90	5,355
July	280	68	253	15,556
August	342	0	165	10,145
September	385	0	214	12,734
October	512	68	263	16,171
November	512	0	50	2,975
The period	....	....	....	63,642

SESSIONAL PAPER No. 25c

MISCELLANEOUS DISCHARGE MEASUREMENTS made in Bow River drainage basin, in 1914.

Date.	Engineer.	Stream.	Location.	Width.	Area of Section.	Mean Velocity.	Discharge.
				Feet.	*Sq. ft.*	*Ft. per sec.*	*Sec.-ft.*
May 14....	H. C. Ritchie..	Beaupré Creek..	SE. 15-26-5-5.				0.50a
June 11....	do	do	do	4.5	1.33	2.08	2.80
July 9...	do	do	do	4.5	0.85	0.72	0.61
Aug. 6....	do	do	do				Nil b
Aug. 20....	do	do	do				Nil b
Sept. 10....	do	do	do				Nil b
Sept. 24....	do	do	do				Nil b
Oct. 8....	do	do	do				Nil b
Oct. 21...	do	do	do				Nil b
May 14...	do	Bighill Creek.	SW. 10-26-4-5..	11.8	4.87	1.45	7.10
June 11...	do	do	do	12.5	7.05	1.59	11.20
Aug. 6...	do	do	do	11.3	4.05	0.94	3.80
Aug. 20...	do	do	do	11.5	4.55	1.19	5.40
Sept. 10...	do	do	do	11.3	4.87	1.07	5.20
Sept. 24...	do	do	do	12.0	5.10	1.14	5.80
Oct. 8...	do	do	do	12.0	5.40	1.20	6.40
Oct. 21..	do	do	do	12.2	5.74	1.28	7.30
May 15...	do	Chiniki Creek..	Morley Indian Reserve....	6.8	1.38	0.88	1.22
July 10....	do	do	do	4.7	1.64	0.68	1.12
April 8....	J. S. Tempest ..	Fish Creek........ (North Branch)	SE. 22-22-3-5	58.6	38.60	0.79	30.50
Oct. 21....	H. S. Kerby ..	do	26-22-3-5.	37.0	23.90	0.30	6.80
April 8....	J. S. Tempest...	Fish Creek........ (South Branch)	SE. 22-22-3-5..	28.0	23.10	1.49	34.00
July 8...	H. S. Kerby..	do	NE. 22-22-3-5	32.0	30.80	0.88	27.00
July 8...	do	do	do	40.0	30.20	0.62	18.80
Oct. 21...	do	do	26-22-3-5.	3.3	26.90	0.55	14.80
May 14...	H. C. Ritchie...	Grand Valley Creek	SW. 24-26-5-5	5.3	1.55	0.97	1.50
June 11...	do	do	do	11.0	3.85	1.80	6.30
July 9...	do	do	do	5.5	1.45	1.28	1.86
Aug. 6...	do	do	do				Nil c
Aug. 20...	do	do	do				0.50
Sept. 10...	do	do	do				1.00a
Sept. 24...	do	do	do				1.00a
Oct. 8...	do	do	do				1.00a
Oct. 21...	do	do	do	5.2	1.43	0.99	1.41
May 14...	do	Horse Creek..	NE. 8-26-4-5.				0.75
June 11...	do	do	do	10.0	5.10	0.50	2.60
July 9...	do	do	do				0.25
Aug. 6...	do	do	do				Nil c
Aug. 20...	do	do	do				Nil c
Sept. 10...	do	do	do				Nil b
Sept. 24...	do	do	do				Nil b
Oct. 8...	do	do	do				Nil b
Oct. 21...	do	do	do				Nil b
July 9....	H. S. Kerby...	Pine Creek....	10-22-1-5				0.28
Aug. 8...	do	do					Nil c
Oct. 21...	do	do					Nil c
May 14...	H. C. Ritchie...	Spencer Creek..	SE. 18-26-5-5..	7.5	2.27	1.12	2.60
June 11.	do	do	do	7.0	2.25	1.20	2.70
July 9...	do	do	do	7.0	1.90	1.24	2.40
Aug. 6...	do	do	do	7.3	1.99	1.07	2.10
Aug. 20...	do	do	do	7.3	1.99	1.06	2.10
Sept. 10...	do	do	do	7.3	1.87	0.92	1.73
Sept. 24...	do	do	do	7.4	2.14	1.15	2.40
Oct. 8...	do	do	do	7.6	2.16	1.24	2.70
Oct. 21...	do	do	do	7.0	1.80	0.94	1.69
April 7...	J. S. Tempest.	Spring Creek....	NE. 15-20-2-5	5.0	2.20	0.68	1.50
June 11...	R. H. Goodchild	do	4-26-2-5				0.06
July 15...	H. S. Kerby...	do	do				Nil
Aug. 13...	do	do	do				Nil
Aug. 18...	do	Tongueflag Creek..	Near Finlay's Ranch......				0.05
Sept. 26 .	H. C. Ritchie..	Whiteman's Creek.	Canmore (above intake of Coal Co.)...	12.1	9.92	0.61	6.00
Sept. 26...	do	do	Canmore (near foot of falls)..	4.3	3.73	1.56	5.80
Sept. 26...	do	do	Canmore (near creek mouth).	5.2	2.94	1.89	5.60
Nov. 21...	do	do	NW. 24-24-11-5..	10.1	12.20	0.52	6.30
Dec. 5 ..	do	do	do	9.8	12.50	0.55	6.80
Dec. 29 .	do	do	do	10.0	7.40	0.73	5.40

a Estimated.
b Creek dry.
c Water standing in pools.

LITTLE BOW RIVER DRAINAGE BASIN.

General Description.

The source of Little Bow River is a spring in the town of High River in Sec. 6, Tp. 19, Rge. 28, W. 4th Mer. From here it flows in a southeasterly direction for 100 miles and empties into the Belly River. In the first few miles, the natural flow is dependent entirely on a number of small springs and coulees which are dry most of the year, but later is augmented by the flow from Mosquito Creek, which drains the south and westerly part of the drainage basin.

There is a comparatively large flow in this stream during the spring freshets, but during summer it would under natural conditions dry up. There are a large number of ranchers and settlers on this stream, and it is very important that there should be a good flow for domestic and stock watering purposes. For this reason the Provincial Government has constructed a canal, and diverts water from Highwood River into Little Bow River whenever required.

MOSQUITO CREEK NEAR NANTON.

Location.—On the NE. ¼ Sec. 30, Tp. 16, Rge. 28, W. 4th Mer., about four miles from Nanton.

Records available.—August 1st, 1908, to October 31st, 1914. Discharge measurements from 1906.

Gauge.—Vertical staff; elevation of zero maintained at 89.22 feet during 1908-12, and at 89.47 feet during 1913-14.

Bench-marks.—Permanent iron bench-mark.

Channel.—Liable to shift.

Discharge measurements.—Made from the bridge at flood stages; by wading during low water.

Winter flow.—Station not maintained during the winter.

Observer.—Wm. Monkman.

DISCHARGE MEASUREMENTS of Mosquito Creek near Nanton, in 1914.

Date.	Engineer.	Width.	Area of Section.	Mean Velocity.	Gauge Height.	Discharge.
		Feet.	*Sq. ft.*	*Ft.per sec.*	*Feet.*	*Sec.-ft.*
April 2	F. R. Burfield	51.0	45.80	1.84	3.35	84.00
April 21	J. E. Caughey	25.0	19.60	0.76	2.38	14.90
May 7	do	17.0	7.70	1.13	2.21	8.70
May 28	do	12.0	5.40	0.67	2.11	3.60
June 19	do	10.0	2.50	0.26	1.90	0.66
July 2	do	10.0	3.30	0.43	2 02	1.39
July 18	do				1.78	1.39
July 31	do				Dry	Nil *a*
Aug. 17	do				"	"
Sept. 17	do				"	"
Sept. 28	do				"	"
Oct. 20	do	16.0	7.20	0 82	2.11	6.00

a Water standing in pools.

SESSIONAL PAPER No. 25c

DAILY GAUGE HEIGHT AND DISCHARGE of Mosquito Creek near Nanton, for 1914.

DAY.	April.		May.		June.	
	Gauge Height.	Dis- charge.	Gauge Height.	Dis- charge.	Gauge Height.	Dis- charge.
	Feet.	*Sec.-ft.*	*Feet.*	*Sec.-ft.*	*Feet.*	*Sec.-ft.*
1	2.80	42.0	2.28	10.0	2.08	3.00
2	3.35	84.0	2.29	10.4	2.07	2.80
3	3.30	80.0	2.28	10.0	2.07	2.80
4	3.39	87.0	2.27	9.5	2.05	2.40
5	3.29	79.0	2.26	9.1	2.01	1.60
6	3.18	70.0	2.24	8.3	2.05	2.40
7	3.33	82.0	2.22	7.4	2.01	1.60
8	3.33	82.0	2.24	8.3	1.99	1.30
9	3.37	86.0	2.26	9.1	1.98	1.20
10	3.36	85.0	2.54	25.0	1.99	1.30
11	3.21	73.0	2.49	21.0	2.01	1.60
12	3.15	68.0	2.47	20.0	1.99	1.30
13	3.05	61.0	2.41	16.6	1.98	1.20
14	2.88	48.0	2.39	15.5	1.99	1.30
15	2.75	38.0	2.34	12.9	2.01	1.60
16	2.68	34.0	2.38	15.0	1.98	1.20
17	2.62	30.0	2.35	13.4	1.97	1.10
18	2.41	16.6	2.35	13.4	1.96	1.00
19	2.40	16.0	2.35	13.4	1.97	1.10
20	2.40	16.0	2.34	12.9	1.93	0.70
21	2.38	15.0	2.33	12.4	1.94	0.80
22	2.36	13.9	2.30	10.8	1.92	0.60
23	2.36	13.9	2.25	8.7	1.90	0.40
24	2.35	13.4	2.23	7.9	1.87	0.28
25	2.35	13.4	2.20	6.6	1.90	0.40
26	2.35	13.4	2.15	5.0	2.32	11.80
27	2.33	12.4	2.11	3.7	2.37	14.40
28	2.29	10.4	2.11	3.7	2.37	14.40
29	2.32	11.8	2.09	3.2	2.22	7.40
30	2.30	10.8	2.07	2.8	2.12	4.00
31	....	....	2.07	2.8	....	....

5 GEORGE V, A. 1915

DAILY GAUGE HEIGHT AND DISCHARGE of Mosquito Creek near Nanton, for 1914.—*Concluded.*

DAY.	July.		August.		September.		October.	
	Gauge Height.	Dis-charge	Gauge Height.	Dis-charge.	Gauge Height.	Dis-charge.	Gauge Height.	Dis-charge.
	Feet.	Sec.-ft.	Feet.	Sec.-ft.	Feet.	Sec.-ft.	Feet.	Sec.-ft.
1	2.10	3.40	Dry.	Nil.	Dry.	Nil.	Dry.	Nil.
2	2.04	2.20	"	"	"	"	"	"
3	1.97	1.10	"	"	"	"	"	"
4	1.97	1.10	"	"	"	"	"	"
5	1.94	0.80	"	"	"	"	"	"
6	1.92	0.60	"	"	"	"	"	"
7	1.97	1.10	"	"	"	"	2.32	14.7
8	1.94	0.80	"	"	"	"	2.33	15.2
9	1.94	0.80	"	"	"	"	2.35	16.3
10	1.95	0.90	"	"	"	"	2.37	17.4
11	1.94	0.80	"	"	"	"	2.38	17.9
12	1.92	0.60	"	"	"	"	2.40	19.0
13	1.91	0.50	"	"	"	"	2.38	17.9
14	1.89	0.36	"	"	"	"	2.37	17.4
15	1.87	0.28	"	"	"	"	2.33	15.2
16	1.85	0.20	"	"	"	"	2.32	14.7
17	1.80	Nil.	"	"	"	"	2.27	12.2
18	1.80	"	"	"	"	"	2.23	10.4
19	Dry.	"	"	"	"	"	2.17	8.0
20	"	"	"	"	"	"	2.11	6.0
21	"	"	"	"	"	"	2.10	5.6
22	"	"	"	"	"	"	2.05	4.4
23	"	"	"	"	"	"	2.05	4.4
24	"	"	"	"	"	"	2.00	3.2
25	"	"	"	"	"	"	2.02	3.7
26	"	"	"	"	"	"	2.02	3.7
27	"	"	"	"	"	"	2.05	4.4
28	"	"	"	"	"	"	2.00	3.2
29	"	"	"	"	"	"	2.05	4.4
30	"	"	"	"	"	"	2.00	3.2
31	"	"	"	"	....	....	2.00	3.2

MONTHLY DISCHARGE of Mosquito Creek near Nanton, for 1914.

(Drainage area 186 square miles.)

MONTH.	DISCHARGE IN SECOND-FEET.				RUN OFF.	
	Maximum	Minimum	Mean.	Per square Mile.	Depth in inches on Drainage Area.	Total in Acre-feet.
April	87.0	10.40	43.500	0.234	0.260	2,588
May	25.0	2.80	10.600	0.057	0.066	652
June	14.4	0.28	2.900	0.016	0.018	173
July	3.4	Nil.	0.501	0.003	0.004	31
August	....	....	....	....	....	Nil.
September	....	....	....	....	....	Nil.
October	19.0	Nil.	7.930	0.043	0.050	488
The period	....	....	....	....	0.398	3,932

NANTON CREEK NEAR NANTON.

Location.—On the SE. ¼ Sec. 19, Tp. 16, Rge. 28, W. 4th Mer., at highway bridge.

Records available.—August 3, 1908, to October 31, 1914.

Gauge.—Vertical staff; zero of gauge maintained at 82.18 feet during 1908-11; 82.57 feet during 1912; 93.33 feet during 1913; 92 31 feet during 1914.

SESSIONAL PAPER No. 25c

Bench-mark.—Permanent iron bench-mark.
Channel.—Not liable to shift.
Discharge measurements.—Made upstream by wading.
Observer.—W. Monkman.

DISCHARGE MEASUREMENTS of Nanton Creek near Nanton, in 1914.

Date.	Engineer.	Width.	Area of Section.	Mean Velocity.	Gauge Height.	Discharge.
		Feet.	*Sq. ft.*	*Ft. per sec.*	*Feet.*	*Sec.-ft.*
April 2	F. R. Burfield	14.5	16.50	0.67	3.91	10.90
April 21	J. E. Caughey	11.0	5.88	0.81	1.96	4.80
May 7	do	10.0	3.99	0.61	1.84	2.40
May 28	do	10.5	2.49	0.44	1.73	1.09
June 19	do	5.0	0.90	0.20	1.62	0.18
July 2	do	6.0	2.10	0.34	1.72	0.71
July 18	do				1.57	0.01
July 31	do				Dry.	Nil.
Aug. 17	do				"	"
Sept. 17	do				1.65	0 76
Sept. 28	do				Dry.	Nil.
Oct. 20	do	6.0	1.90	0.90	1.75	1.71

DAILY GAUGE HEIGHT AND DISCHARGE of Nanton Creek near Nanton, for 1914.

DAY.	April.		May.		June.	
	Gauge Height.	Dis- charge.	Gauge Height.	Dis- charge	Gauge Height.	Dis- charge.
	Feet.	*Sec.-ft.*	*Feet.*	*Sec.-ft.*	*Feet.*	*Sec.-ft.*
1			1.92	3.90	1.69	0.59
2	3.65	10.9a	1.90	3.50	1.68	0.52
3	3.67	11.2	1.90	3.50	1.65	0.46
4	3.40	20.0a	1.89	3.30	1.65	0.32
5	3.05	29.0	1.88	3.10	1.66	0.39
6	3.00	28.0	1.88	3.10	1.65	0.32
7	3.00	28.0	1.89	3.30	1.63	0.23
8	3.00	28.0	1.85	2.60	1.65	0.32
9	3.00	28.0	2.05	6.80	1.63	0.23
10	2.94	26.0	2.00	5.70	1.61	0.14
11	2.90	26.0	1.98	5.30	1.61	0.14
12	2.90	26.0	1.96	4.80	1.60	0.10
13	2.60	18.9	1.92	3.90	1.62	0.19
14	2.42	14.9	1.92	3.90	1.61	0.14
15	2.38	14.1	1.92	3.90	1.61	0.14
16	2.03	6.4	1.91	3.70	1.64	0.28
17	2.00	5.7	1.91	3.70	1.62	0.19
18	1.94	4.4	1.92	3.90	1.65	0.32
19	1.94	4.4	1.91	3.70	1.62	0.19
20	1.96	4.8	1.92	3.90	1.61	0.14
21	1.96	4.8	1.90	3.50	1.61	0.14
22	1.94	4.4	1.85	2.60	1.60	0.10
23	1.94	4.4	1.82	2.10	1.60	0.10
24	1.93	4.2	1.80	1.80	1.59	0.07
25	1.93	4.2	1.75	1.16	1.59	0.07
26	1.90	3.5	1.70	0.66	1.82	2.10
27	1.91	3.7	1.71	0.76	1.91	3.70
28	1.90	3.5	1.73	0.96	1.88	3.10
29	1.91	3.7	1.71	0.76	1.84	2.40
30	1.91	3.7	1.70	0.66	1.82	2.10
31			1.70	0.66		

a to *a* Ice conditions.

5 GEORGE V, A. 1915

DAILY GAUGE HEIGHT AND DISCHARGE of Nanton Creek near Nanton, for 1914.
—Concluded.

DAY.	July.		August.		September.		October.	
	Gauge Height.	Dis-charge.	Gauge Height.	Dis-charge.	Gauge Height.	Dis-charge.	Gauge Height.	Dis-charge.
	Feet.	Sec.-ft.	Feet.	Sec.-ft.	Feet.	Sec.-ft.	Feet.	Sec.-ft.
1	1.82	2.10	.Dry.	Nil.	Dry.	Nil.	Dry.	Nil.
2	1.87	2.90	"	"	"	"	"	"
3	1.82	2.10	"	"	"	"	"	"
4	1.81	2.00	"	"	"	"	"	"
5	1.84	2.40	"	"	"	"	"	"
6	1.82	2.10	"	"	"	"	"	"
7	1.81	2.00	"	"	"	"	2.35	13.40
8	1.77	1.42	"	"	"	"	2.38	14.10
9	1.74	1.06	"	"	"	"	2.32	12.70
10	1.70	0.66	"	"	"	"	2.30	12.30
11	1.64	0.28	1.70	0.66	"	"	2.25	11.20
12	1.62	0.19	1.68	0.52	"	"	2.23	10.80
13	1.60	0.10	1.65	0.32	"	"	2.17	9.40
14	1.59	0.07	1.63	0.23	"	"	2.10	7.90
15	1.58	0.04	1.58	0.04	"	"	2.08	7.50
16	1.57	0.01	1.57	0.01	"	"	2.04	6.60
17	1.57	0.01	1.70	0.66	1.63	0.23	2.01	5.90
18	1.57	0.01	1.68	0.52	1.62	0.19	1.90	3.50
19	Dry.	Nil.	1.65	0.32	1.60	0.10	1.83	2.30
20	"	"	1.64	0.28	1.58	0.04	1.75	1.16
21	"	"	1.63	0.23	1.57	0.01	1.75	1.16
22	"	"	1.61	0.14	Dry.	Nil.	1.73	0.96
23	"	"	1.60	0.10	"	"	1.72	0.86
24	"	"	1.60	0.10	"	"	1.72	0.86
25	"	"	1.59	0.07	"	"	1.71	0.76
26	"	"	1.59	0.07	"	"	1.71	0.76
27	"	"	1.58	0.04	"	"	1.70	0.66
28	"	"	1.57	0.01	"	"	1.70	0.66
29	"	"	1.56	....	"	"	1.70	0.66
30	"	"	Dry.	Nil.	"	"	1.69	0.59
31	"	"	"	"	....	....	1.69	0.59

MONTHLY DISCHARGE of Nanton Creek near Nanton, for 1914.

(Drainage area 46 square miles.)

MONTH.	DISCHARGE IN SECOND-FEET.				RUN-OFF.	
	Maximum.	Minimum	Mean.	Per square Mile.	Depth in inches on Drainage Area.	Total in Acre-feet.
April	29.00	3.50	12.90	0.280	0.31	768
May	6.80	0.66	3.10	0.067	0.08	191
June	3.70	0.07	0.64	0.014	0.02	38
July	2.90	Nil.	0.63	0.014	0.02	39
August	0.66	"	0.14	0.003	0.00	9
September	0.23	"	0.02	0.000	0.00	1
October	14.10	"	4.10	0.089	0.10	252
The period	....	....	....	....	0.53	1,298

SESSIONAL PAPER No. 25c

MISCELLANEOUS DISCHARGE MEASUREMENTS made in Little Bow River drainage basin, in 1914.

Date.	Engineer.	Stream.	Location.	Width.	Area of Section.	Mean Velocity.	Discharge.
				Feet.	*Sq. ft.*	*Ft. per sec.*	*Sec.-ft.*
April 11	J. S. Tempest .	Spring Creek......	NE. 10-17-1-5..	....	.. ..	.. ....	0.25
April 11	do	do	.............a	4.7	2 66	0.47	1.27
July 16....	H. S. Kerby....	do	NE. 10-17-1-5.	....	....	....	0.21
Aug. 14....	do	do	do	....	....	....	0.14
Oct. 23....	do	do	do	....	....	....	0.34
June 18....	R. H. Goodchild	Springhill Creek. .	SE. 11-16-29-4..	....	....	....	0.30

a Combined springs below McMillan's ranch.

OLDMAN RIVER DRAINAGE BASIN.

General Description.

Oldman River, one of the principal tributaries of the South Saskatchewan River, is formed in the Livingstone Range of the Rocky Mountains by the junction of four small rivers, viz., Livingstone, Northwest Branch, West Branch and Racehorse Creek; and flows in a south and easterly direction to near Cowley, where it is joined by the Crowsnest and Southfork Rivers. Between Cowley and Kipp, where it empties into the Belly River, the Oldman River is augmented by several creeks, its course being easterly and northerly. It drains the area bounded on the north by the parallel of latitude through $59° 20'$; on the south by the parallel of latitude through $49° 20'$; and on the west by the Great Divide, this area being estimated to contain about 2,235 square miles, with topography varying from mountains to rolling prairie.

The bed of the river is of rock and gravel and has a large fall, with consequent swift water interspersed with falls and rapids, but it changes to quicksand and mud after reaching the prairie region, where the current is more sluggish.

The flow of this river, draining as it does mountain ranges with peaks extending above the snow line, is subject to great changes, caused by melting snow and heavy summer rains in the mountains. Floods occur regularly during the latter part of May and the early part of June. From this time on the flow is normally steady, but gradually decreases until the minimum is reached during January and February.

The precipitation throughout the basin is quite large. Consequently, though the region is almost entirely under cultivation where practicable, there is little need of irrigation. Owing to the depth of the valley and its steep, rocky banks, irrigation from this river would be expensive, if not impossible, but there are many excellent power sites at its falls and rapids. Up to the present, however, no power has been developed on this river, but investigations with that end in view are being made.

SUMMIT CREEK AT CROWSNEST.

Location.—On the SE. ¼ Sec. 12, Tp. 8, Rge. 6, W. 5th Mer., about 1,000 feet upstream from the Canadian Pacific Railway Company's concrete dam.

Records available.—Discharge measurements only are available from February 21, 1912, to December 31, 1914.

Gauge.—Vertical staff, nailed to a tree on the right bank.

Bench-mark.—Spruce stump on the right bank, about 30 feet downstream from the gauge; elevation, 5.94 feet above the zero of the gauge.

Channel.—Fairly permanent, with a bed of fine gravel.

Discharge measurements.—Made by wading in high water, and by means of a 24-inch weir in low stages.

Winter flow.—Discharge measurements are continued throughout the winter.

Observer.—No gauge height records are obtained at this station.

5 GEORGE V, A. 1915

DISCHARGE MEASUREMENTS of Summit Creek near Crowsnest, in 1914.

Date.	Engineer.	Width.	Area of Section.	Mean Velocity.	Gauge Height.	Discharge.
		Feet.	*Sq. ft.*	*Ft. per sec.*	*Feet.*	*Sec.-ft.*
Feb. 16	E. W. W. Hughes..........	5.5	1.13	0.24	1.65	0.27
Mar. 5...........	do	6.0	1.20	0.24	1.53	0.29
Mar. 23..........	F. R. Burfield	5.5	1.30	0.34	1.62	0.44
April 10..........	J. E. Caughey	6.5	1.96	0.49	1.70	0.97
April 25..........	do	10.5	6.05	1.42	2.08	8.60
May 14..........	do	10.0	11.20	1.61	2.35	18.40
June 16..........	do	7.0	2.70	1.08	1.87	2.90
June 24..........	do	7.0	2.50	0.78	1.79	1.95
July 9..........	do	6.0	1.80	0.59	....	1.06
July 24	do	....	....	....	....	0.63a
Aug. 8..........	do	....	....	....	....	0.31a
Aug. 22..........	do	....	....	....	....	0.53a
Sept. 2..........	do	....	....	....	....	0.29a
Sept. 23..........	do	....	....	....	1.65	0.82a
Oct. 8..........	do	....	....	....	1.65	0.36a
Oct. 31..........	do	....	....	....	1.70	0.71a
Nov. 16........ ..	do	....	....	....	1.79	0.86a
Dec. 5..........	do	....	....	....	1.74	0.53a
Dec. 29..........	do	....	....	....	1.61	0.18a

a Weir measurements.

DISCHARGE MEASUREMENTS of Allison Creek near Sentinel, in 1914.

(SW. 11-8-5-5.)

Date.	Engineer.	Width.	Area of Section.	Mean Velocity.	Gauge Height.	Discharge.
		Feet.	*Sq. ft.*	*Ft. per sec.*	*Feet.*	*Sec.-ft.*
Mar. 20	F. R. Burfield.	13.5	5.90	1.38	1.35	7.9
April 9.... .	J. E. Caughey....	14.5	7.00	1.26	1.12	8.8
April 24....... .	do	14.5	8.00	1.40	1.52	11.2
June 15..........	do	15.5	13.08	2.94	2.05	38.4
July 9..........	do	16.0	11.40	2.36	1.70	27.0
Aug. 7..........	do	15.0	9.75	1.91	....	18.6
Sept. 4..........	do	15.0	9.15	1.60	1.60	14.6
Sept. 22..........	do	14.0	8.70	1.95	1.65	16.9

CROWSNEST RIVER NEAR COLEMAN.

Location.—On SW. ¼ Sec. 12, Tp. 8, Rge. 5, W. 5th Mer., near Prudent Le Gal's house.

Records available.—June 13, 1910, to December 31, 1914.

Gauge.—Vertical staff; zero of gauge maintained at 92.12 feet during 1910-12; 92.73 feet during 1913-14.

Bench-mark.—Permanent iron bench-mark located on left bank at the station; assumed elevation, 100.00 feet.

Channel.—Composed of gravel, and slightly shifting.

Discharge measurements.—Made from a wooden bridge during high water, and by wading during low stages at a point about one mile below the gauge.

Winter flow.—Discharge measurements continued during the winter season.

Observer.—Prudent Le Gal.

SESSIONAL PAPER No. 25c

DISCHARGE MEASUREMENTS of Crowsnest River near Coleman, in 1914.

Date.	Engineer.	Width.	Area of Section.	Mean Velocity.	Gauge Height.	Discharge.
		Feet.	*Sq. ft.*	*Ft. per sec.*	*Feet.*	*Sec.-ft.*
Jan. 19	R. Palmer	43.0	25.6	1.44	1.50	37
Feb. 7	do	42.0	28.2	1.39	2.28	39
Mar. 7	E. W. W. Hughes	32.0	25.8	1.21	1.50	31
Mar. 20	F. R. Burfield	35.0	27.2	1.41	1.51	38
April 8	J. E. Caughey	36.0	31.4	1.60	1.67	50
April 24	do	42.0	49.2	2.75	2.28	135
May 13	do	47.0	65.5	3.24	2.85	213
June 15	do	54.0	81.0	3.30	3.25	268
June 23	do	30.0	64.2	2.99	2.70	192
July 9	do	54.0	74.8	3.37	2.85	252
July 23	do	48.0	49.8	2.82	2.25	140
Aug. 7	do	27.0	44.7	2.15	2.09	96
Aug. 21	do	30.0	57.0	2.40	2.35	137
Sept. 4	do	36.0	35.7	2.29	1.85	82
Sept. 22	do	38.0	40.8	2.72	2.05	111
Oct. 7	do	36.0	38.7	2.42	2.00	94
Oct. 27	do	38.0	42.6	2.73	2.05	116
Nov. 14	do	36.0	40.2	2.30	1.95	93
Dec. 4	do	34.0	37.2	2.04	1.94	76
Dec. 28	do	29.0	28.9	1.81	2.24	52

DAILY GAUGE HEIGHT AND DISCHARGE of Crowsnest River near Coleman, for 1914.

DAY.	January. Gauge Height.	January. Discharge.	February. Gauge Height.	February. Discharge.	March. Gauge Height.	March. Discharge.	April. Gauge Height.	April. Discharge.	May. Gauge Height.	May. Discharge.	June. Gauge Height.	June. Discharge.
	Feet.	*Sec.-ft.*	*Feet.*	*Sec.-ft.*	*Feet.*	*Sec.-ft.*	*Feet.*	*Sec.-ft.*	*Feet.*	*Sec.-ft.*	*Feet.*	*Sec.-ft.*
1	1.69	58a	1 93	33	1 55	30	1.52	36	3.04	243	3.39	292
2	1.65	56	1 87	31	1 63	31	1.60	46	3.25	272	3 47	303
3	1.63	55	1.99	32	1.66	32	1.63	50	3.45	300	3 62	324
4	1.57	53	2 12	34	1 61	31	1.67	55	3.70	335	3.71	336
5	1.59	54	2.20	35	1 61	31	1.72	62	3.70	335	3 49	306
6	1.69	55	2.25	37	1.63	31	1.67	55	3.70	335	3.28	276
7	1.69	55	2.28	39	1.53	31	1.67	55	3.60	321	3.08	248
8	1.64	53	2.33	40	1.53	34b	1.67	55	3.64	327	3.06	245
9	1.64	53	2.18	40	1.53	37	1.67	55	3.64	327	2.80	209
10	2.09	50	2.09	39	1.55	40	1.70	59	2.81	210	2.77	205
11	2.09	46	2.06	39	1.56	41	1.75	66	2.91	224	2.81	210
12	2.01	43	2.02	39	1.51	34	1.77	68	2.80	209	2.79	208
13	1.54	40	1.76	35	1.66	54	1.85	78	2.85	216	3.85	356
14	1.54	39	1.65	32	1.68	56	1.90	85	2.98	234	3.50	307
15	1.54	38	1.65	32	1.65	52	1.92	88	3.03	241	3.25	272
16	1.57	37	1.60	31	1.63	50	1.95	92	3.13	255	3.29	278
17	1.49	36	1.60	31	1.60	46	2.00	98	3.19	264	3.26	273
18	1.49	36	1.50	30	1.63	50	2.00	98	3.25	272	3.25	272
19	2.07	37	1.50	30	1.63	50	2.00	98	3.30	279	3.25	272
20	2.50	37	1.45	28	1.54	38	2.15	118	3.40	293	3.16	259
21	2.59	38	1.45	28	1.59	45	2.15	118	3.98	374	3.07	247
22	2.59	38	1.49	29	1.59	45	2.20	125	3.66	329	2.92	226
23	1.70	38	1.55	30	1.62	49	2.25	132	3.54	313	2.70	192c
24	1.73	38	1.55	30	1.79	71	2.28	136	3.54	313	2.80	210
25	2.13	37	1.57	30	1.81	73	2.28	136	3.42	296	3.05	245
26	2.20	33	1.54	30	1.77	68	2.28	136	3.29	278	3.15	261
27	2.09	30	1.55	30	1.68	56	2.28	136	3.97	373	3.10	256
28	1.80	30	1.55	30	1.58	43	3.00	237	3.26	273	2.95	238
29	2.29	33			1.52	36	3.00	237	3.12	254	2.95	240
30	2.19	37			1.55	40	3.00	237	3.25	272	3.05	256d
31	2.02	35			1.55	40			3.07	247		

a to b Ice conditions.
c to d Shifting conditions.

5 GEORGE V, A. 1915

DAILY GAUGE HEIGHT AND DISCHARGE of Crowsnest River near Coleman, for 1914.
—*Concluded.*

DAY.	July.		August.		September.		October.		November.		December.	
	Gauge Height.	Dis-charge.	Gauge Height.	Dis-charge.	Gauge Height.	Dis-charge	Gauge Height.	Dis-charge.	Gauge Height.	Dis-charge.	Gauge Height.	Dis-charge.
	Feet.	*Sec.-ft.*	*Feet.*	*Sec.-ft.*	*Feet.*	*Sec.-ft.*	*Feet.*	*Sec.-ft.*	*Feet.*	*Sec.-ft.*	*Feet.*	*Sec.-ft.*
1	3.02	255c	2.21	121	1.85	80	2.00	98	1.95	100	2.50	84
2	3.02	258	2.21	120	1.85	80	2.00	98	2.00	107	2.55	80
3	3.00	257	2.18	114	1.85	81	1.95	90	1.98	103	1.75	77
4	3.05	266	2.14	107	1.85	82	2.10	111	2.00	105	1.94	76
5	3.05	268	2.10	101	1.85	82	2.10	110	2.10	119	1.49	74
6	2.95	257	2.06	94	1.85	82	2.05	101	2.00	105	1.50	71
7	2.90	253	2.09	96	1.85	83	2.00	94	1.98	101	2.13	69
8	2.90	255	2.02	88	1.90	89	2.04	101	1.95	97	2.52	67
9	2.85	252	2.00	85	1.87	87	2.04	101	1.95	96	2.85	64
10	2.80	244	1.95	78	1.72	65	2.00	97	1.95	96	2.85	60
11	2.77	237	1.95	78	1.65	56	2.00	97	1.95	95	2.65	58
12	2.75	232	1.95	79	1.65	56	2.15	117	2.00	102	2.34	56
13	2.75	230	1.95	80	1.65	56	2.32	142	2.00	101	2.05	54
14	2.75	228	1.95	80	1.65	56	2.43	158	1.95	93d	2.05	52
15	2.71	220	1.95	80	1.84	82	2.49	166	1.95	90a	2.12	52
16	2.66	211	1.91	75	1.83	82	2.52	171	2.45	91	2.35	52
17	2.62	203	2.25	122	1.85	84	2.60	182	2.40	92	2.60	52
18	2.57	195	2.66	178	1.82	80	2.53	175	2.30	94	2.65	53
19	2.55	190	2.66	179	1.82	80	2.70	197	2.15	95	2.68	53
20	2.53	185	2.55	164	2.01	105	2.62	188	1.98	97	2.70	53
21	2.50	179	2.35	137	1.99	102	2.44	165	1.85	98	2.74	54
22	2.50	176	2.35	138	2.05	111	2.31	147	1.85	99	2.71	53
23	2.25	140	2.26	127	1.98	100	2.28	144	1.85	100	2.68	53
24	2.25	138	2.24	125	2.00	103	2.25	141	1.85	100	2.68	52
25	2.25	137	2.22	123	2.05	109	2.10	121	1.85	100	2.52	52
26	2.25	136	2.21	123	2.09	114	2.10	122	1.85	100	2.52	52
27	2.25	134	2.21	123	2.15	122	2.05	116	1.85	98	2.50	52
28	2.25	133	2.11	111	2.09	113	2.10	122	1.85	96	2.24	52
29	2.30	138	2.02	100	2.03	104	2.05	115	1.85	93	2.41	52
30	2.26	131	1.85	77	2.00	99	2.00	108	1.85	89	2.30	52
31	2.25	128	1.85	79	......	......	1.93	98	......	......	2.05	53b

a to *b* Ice conditions.
c to *d* Shifting conditions.

MONTHLY DISCHARGE of Crowsnest River near Coleman, for 1914.

(Drainage area 70 square miles.)

MONTH.	DISCHARGE IN SECOND-FEET.				RUN-OFF.	
	Maximum.	Minimum.	Mean.	Per square Mile.	Depth in inches on Drainage Area.	Total in Acre-feet.
January	58	30	42	0.600	0.69	2,582
February	40	28	33	0.471	0.49	1,833
March	73	30	44	0.629	0.72	2,705
April	237	36	102	1.460	1.63	6,069
May	374	209	284	4.010	4.62	17,464
June	356	192	261	3.730	4.16	15,531
July	268	128	202	2.880	3.32	12,420
August	179	75	109	1.560	1.80	6,702
September	122	56	88	1.260	1.41	5,236
October	197	90	129	1.840	2.12	9,732
November	119	89	98	1.400	1.56	5,831
December	84	52	59	0.843	0.97	3,628
The year					23 49	89,733

MCGILLIVRAY CREEK, NEAR COLEMAN.

Location.—On SE. ¼ Sec. 7, Tp. 8, Rge. 4, W. 5th Mer., about 150 feet north of C.P.Ry. Co.'s culvert across the creek.

Records available.—January 9, 1913, to October 31, 1914.

Gauge.—Vertical staff.

SESSIONAL PAPER No. 25c

Bench-mark.—Stump on left bank about 50 feet downstream from the gauge; elevation, 2.99 feet above zero of the gauge.
Channel.—Gravel, and slightly shifting.
Discharge measurements.—Made by wading during low stages, and from a foot bridge during high water.
Winter flow.—Discharge measurements are not made during the winter season.
Observer.—Mrs. H. G. Perdue.

DISCHARGE MEASUREMENTS of McGillivray Creek near Coleman, in 1914.

Date.	Engineer.	Width.	Area of Section.	Mean Velocity.	Gauge Height.	Discharge.
		Feet.	*Sq. ft.*	*Ft. per sec.*	*Feet.*	*Sec.-ft.*
Mar. 7	E. W. W. Hughes	13.0	5.02	0.38	0.95	1.90
Mar. 20	F. R. Burfield	15.5	5.76	0.47	0.95	2.70
April 8	J. E. Caughey	16.0	7.35	0.75	1.23	5.50
April 24	do	20.0	19.70	2.30	1.85	45.00
May 13	do	20.0	19.70	2.65	1.85	52.00
June 15	do	19.0	15.00	2.34	1.70	35.00
June 23	do	18.0	12.20	2.10	1.50	26.00
July 9	do	17.0	9.80	1.76	1.40	17.30
July 23	do	17.0	7.85	1.19	1.25	9.40
Aug. 7	do	10.0	5.80	1.26	1.18	7.30
Aug. 21	do	9.0	6.30	0.82	1.25	5.20
Sept. 4	do	9.0	5.50	0.73	1.20	4.00
Sept. 22	do	11.0	8.75	1.10	1.35	9.70
Oct. 7	do	10.0	7.50	0.87	1.30	6.60
Oct. 27	do	11.0	8.90	1.50	1.42	13.30

DAILY GAUGE HEIGHT AND DISCHARGE of McGillivray Creek near Coleman, for 1914.

DAY.	April. Gauge Height.	April. Dis-charge.	May. Gauge Height.	May. Dis-charge.	June. Gauge Height.	June. Dis-charge.
	Feet.	*Sec.-ft.*	*Feet.*	*Sec.-ft.*	*Feet.*	*Sec.-ft.*
1			2.04	63.0	1.82	46.0
2			2.05	64.0	1.91	53.0
3			2.11	69.0	1.96	57.0
4			1.91	53.0	1.95	56.0
5			1.78	42.0	1.82	46.0
6			1.71	37.0	1.75	40.0
7			1.65	32.0	1.64	32.0
8	1.23	8.9	1.76	41.0	1.65	32.0
9	1.23	8.9	2.00	60.0	1.61	30.0
10	1.21	8.2	2.00	60.0	1.55	26.0
11	1.25	9.6	1.85	48.0	1.55	26.0
12	1.41	16.8	1.82	46.0	1.64	32.0
13	1.48	21.0	1.83	46.0	1.64	32.0
14	1.55	26.0	1.88	50.0	1.65	32.0
15	1.62	30.0	2.02	62.0	1.65	32.0
16	1.71	37.0	2.08	66.0	1.68	35.0
17	1.72	38.0	2.04	63.0	1.68	35.0
18	1.61	30.0	2.05	64.0	1.68	35.0
19	1.89	51.0	2.01	61.0	1.64	32.0
20	1.98	58.0	1.88	50.0	1.63	31.0
21	1.82	46.0	1.83	46.0	1.50	22.0
22	1.81	45.0	1.82	46.0	1.50	22.0
23	1.94	55.0	1.81	45.0	1.51	23.0
24	1.85	48.0	1.86	49.0	1.46	19.7
25	1.75	40.0	1.91	53.0	1.50	22.0
26	1.72	38.0	1.83	46.0	1.46	19.7
27	1.66	33.0	1.85	48.0	1.55	26.0
28	1.65	32.0	1.71	37.0	1.55	26.0
29	1.61	30.0	1.65	32.0	1.55	26.0
30	1.64	32.0	1.65	32.0	1.54	25.0
31			1.82	46.0		

5 GEORGE V, A. 1915

DAILY GAUGE HEIGHT AND DISCHARGE of McGillivray Creek near Coleman, for 1914.
—*Concluded.*

DAY.	July.		August.		September.		October.	
	Gauge Height.	Dis- charge.	Gauge Height.	Dis- charge.	Gauge Height.	Dis- charge.	Gauge Height.	Dis- charge.
	Feet.	*Sec.-ft.*	*Feet.*	*Sec.-ft.*	*Feet.*	*Sec.-ft.*	*Feet.*	*Sec.-ft.*
1	1.52	23.0	1.20	7.8	1.23	4.6	1.26	5.6
2	1.50	22.0	1.18	7.2	1.23	4.6	1.26	5.6
3	1.50	22.0	1.18	7.2	1.23	4.6	1.28	6.3
4	1.50	22.0	1.18	7.2	1.21	3.9	1.28	6.3
5	1.47	20.0	1.18	7.2	1.21	3.9	1.28	6.3
6	1.46	19.7	1.18	7.2	1.21	3.9	1.30	7.0
7	1.44	18.5	1.18	7.2	1.21	3.9	1.30	7.0
8	1.42	17.4	1.18	7.2	1.21	3.9	1.32	8.0
9	1.40	16.2	1.17	7.0	1.21	3.9	1.32	8.0
10	1.38	15.2	1.17	7.0	1.18	3.2	1.32	8.0
11	1.38	15.2	1.17	7.0	1.18	3.2	1.32	8.0
12	1.35	13.8	1.17	7.0	1.18	3.2	1.35	9.5
13	1.35	13.8	1.15	6.4	1.18	3.2	1.35	9.5
14	1.33	12.8	1.15	6.4	1.18	3.2	1.54	21.0
15	1.35	13.8	1.15	6.4	1.26	5.6	1.66	29.0
16	1.33	12.8	1.15	6.4a	1.26	5.6	1.85	44.0
17	1.32	12.4	1.35	9.5	1.26	5.6	1.80	40.0
18	1.30	11.4	1.35	9.5	1.35	9.5	1.68	31.0
19	1.30	11.4	1.30	7.0	1.35	9.5	1.65	28.0
20	1.28	10.7	1.30	7.0	1.35	9.5	1.58	24.0
21	1.28	10.7	1.25	5.3	1.35	9.5	1.55	22.0
22	1.27	10.3	1.25	5.3	1.35	9.5	1.51	18.7
23	1.25	9.6	1.31	7.5	1.33	8.5	1.48	16.8
24	1.25	9.6	1.31	7.5	1.33	8.5	1.46	15.8
25	1.25	9.6	1.28	6.3	1.32	8.0	1.45	15.0
26	1.22	8.5	1.28	6.3	1.32	8.0	1.45	15.0
27	1.22	8.5	1.25	5.3	1.30	7.0	1.44	14.4
28	1.21	8.2	1.25	5.3	1.30	7.0	1.42	13.2
29	1.21	8.2	1.25	5.3	1.30	7.0	1.41	12.6
30	1.21	8.2	1.24	5.0	1.28	6.3	1.41	12.6
31	1.20	7.8	1.24	5.0	....	....	1.41	12.6b

a to *b* Changed conditions.

MONTHLY DISCHARGE of McGillivray Creek near Coleman, for 1914.

(Drainage area 16 square miles)

MONTH.	DISCHARGE IN SECOND-FEET.				RUN-OFF.	
	Maximum.	Minimum.	Mean.	Per square Mile.	Depth in inches on Drainage Area.	Total in Acre-feet.
April (8–30)	58.0	8.2	32.0	2.00	1.71	1,460
May	69.0	32.0	50.0	3.12	3.58	3,074
June	57.0	19.7	32.0	2.00	2.23	1,904
July	23.0	7.8	13.6	0.85	0.98	842
August	9.5	5.0	6.7	0.42	0.48	412
September	9.5	3.2	5.9	0.37	0.41	363
October	44.0	5.6	15.5	0.97	1.12	953
The period	....	....	....	....	10.51	9,008

CROWSNEST RIVER, NEAR FRANK.

Location.—On the *NE.* ¼ Sec. 36, Tp. 7, Rge. 4, W. 5th Mer., at the traffic bridge.
Records available.—June 13, 1910, to December 31, 1914.
Gauge.—Vertical staff.
Bench-mark.—A stump on the left bank about 4 feet from the gauge; elevation, 9.43 feet above the zero of the gauge.

Channel.—Gravel, and fairly permanent.
Discharge measurements.—Made from traffic bridge during high water, and by wading in low stages.
Observer.—I. Wilson.

DISCHARGE MEASUREMENTS of Crowsnest River near Frank, in 1914.

Date.	Engineer.	Width.	Area of Section.	Mean Velocity.	Gauge Height.	Discharge.
		Feet.	*Sq. ft.*	*Ft. per sec.*	*Feet.*	*Sec.-ft.*
Jan. 17	R. Palmer	52.0	49.8	1.36	3.91	68
Feb. 6	do	51.0	35.6	1.36	3.97	50
Feb. 17	E. W. W. Hughes	50.0	33.7	1.31	4.04	44
Mar. 6	do	49.5	38.6	1.17	3.95	45
Mar. 21	F. R. Burfield	49.5	42.3	1.21	4.05	51
April 9	J. E. Caughey	53.0	56.8	1.64	4.27	93
April 25	do	67.0	113.0	3.40	5.20	384
May 12	do	69.0	126.0	3.57	5.35	451
June 13	do	66.0	107.3	3.38	5.15	363
June 22	do	66.0	103.3	2.99	5.10	309
July 8	do	67.0	96.6	3.19	5.00	301
July 22	do	57.0	79.0	2.41	4.65	192
Aug. 6	do	60.0	65.0	1.88	4.43	122
Aug. 20	do	65.0	84.5	2.56	4.73	216
Sept. 3	do	51.0	59.8	1.72	4.33	103
Sept. 21	do	65.0	82.5	2.12	4.60	175
Oct. 6	do	51.0	70.0	1.86	4.50	130
Oct. 26	do	65.0	86.8	2.47	4.74	214
Nov. 12	do	60.0	81.5	2.49	4.70	204
Dec. 4	do	54.0	60.0	1.80	4.35	108
Dec. 28	do	52.0	55.5	1.65	4.30	92

DAILY GAUGE HEIGHT AND DISCHARGE of Crowsnest River near Frank, for 1914.

DAY.	January.		February.		March.		April.		May.		June.	
	Gauge Height.	Dis-charge	Gauge Height.	Dis-charge	Gauge Height	Dis-charge.	Gauge Height.	Dis-charge.	Gauge Height.	Dis-charge.	Gauge Height.	Dis-charge.
	Feet.	*Sec.-ft.*	*Feet.*	*Sec.-ft.*	*Feet.*	*Sec.-ft.*	*Feet.*	*Sec.-ft.*	*Feet.*	*Sec.-ft.*	*Feet.*	*Sec.-ft.*
1	4.00	49	4.01	50	4.01	50	4.05	56	5.25	402	5.25	402
2	4.02	52	3.99	48	4.01	50	4.05	56	5.53	521	5.40	465
3	4.05	56	3.99	48	4.01	50	4.05	56	5.75	616	5.40	551
4	4.07	58	3.99	48	3.99	48	4.10	62	5.55	530	5.63	564
5	4.17	74	3.97	46	3.97	46	4.25	89	5.35	444	5.55	530
6	4.32	103	3.97	46	3.94	42	4.28	95	5.25	402	5.40	465
7	4.40	121	3.96	45	3.94	42	4.25	89	5.15	362	5.25	402
8	4.30	99	3.97	46	4.01	50	4.25	89	5.25	402	5.20	382
9	4.32	103	3.97	46	4.03	53	4.27	93	5.50	508	5.10	343
10	4.17	74	3.98	47	3.99	48	4.30	99	5.55	530	5.00	306
11	4.17	74	4.01	50	3.96	45	4.35	110	5.40	465	5.00	306
12	4.14	69	4.01	50	4.01	50	4.50	145	5.40	465	5.05	324
13	4.15	70	4.01	50	4.06	57	4.70	201	5.43	478	5.15	362
14	4.16	72	4.01	50	4.11	64	4.93	281	5.50	508	5.22	394
15	4.16	72	4.01	50	4.09	61	5.10	343	5.65	572	5.23	394
16	4.15	70	4.01	50	4.06	57	5.13	355	5.65	572	5.23	394
17	4.16	72	4.02	52	4.06	57	5.05	324	5.65	572	5.25	402
18	4.15	70	4.02	52	4.13	67	4.90	270	5.63	564	5.28	414
19	4.12	65	4.01	50	4.11	64	5.33	444	5.60	551	5.25	402
20	4.02	52	4.01	50	3.96	45	5.33	435	5.55	530	5.23	394
21	3.97	46	4.01	50	4.01	50	5.10	343	5.45	486	5.17	370
22	3.97	46	4.01	50	4.05	56	5.07	332	5.45	486	5.08	336
23	3.97	46	4.01	50	4.05	56	5.10	343	5.45	486	5.15	295
24	3.95	44	4.01	50	4.00	49	5.25	402	5.60	551	4.90	270
25	3.97	46	4.01	50	3.95	44	5.18	374	5.55	530	5.20	382
26	3.98	47	3.99	48	3.95	44	5.14	359	5.50	508	5.33	435
27	4.00	49	3.98	47	4.00	49	5.10	343	5.35	444	5.22	390
28	3.98	47	3.99	48	4.03	53	5.07	332	5.30	422	5.15	362
29	3.98	47			4.05	56	5.00	306	5.20	382	5.15	362
30	3.98	47			4.05	56	5.05	324	5.15	362	5.15	362
31	4.00	49			4.05	56			5.15	362		

5 GEORGE V. A. 1915

DAILY GAUGE HEIGHT AND DISCHARGE of Crowsnest River near Frank, for 1914.—*Concluded.*

DAY.	July.		August.		September.		October.		November.		December.	
	Gauge Height.	Dis- charge.	Gauge Height	Dis- charge.	Gauge Height.	Dis- charge.	Gauge Height.	Dis- charge	Gauge Height.	Dis- charge.	Gauge Height.	Dis- charge.
	Feet.	*Sec.ft.*	*Feet.*	*Sec.-ft.*	*Feet.*	*Sec.ft.*	*Feet.*	*Sec.ft.*	*Feet.*	*Sec.ft.*	*Feet.*	*Sec.-ft.*
1............	5.10	343	4 45	133	4.36	112	4.45	133	4.65	186	4.52	150
2............	5.08	336	4 44	131	4.35	110	4.45	133	4.70	201	4.52	150
3............	5.08	336	4.43	128	4 33	106	4.50	145	4.73	211	4.47	138
4............	5.10	343	4.43	128	4.33	106	4.54	155	4.70	201	4.42	126
5............	5.13	355	4 42	126	4.32	103	4 54	155	4.72	208	4.40	121
6............	5.08	336	4.41	123	4.32	103	4.52	150	4.75	218	4.38	117
7............	5.00	306	4.40	121	4.31	101	4.50	145	4.73	211	4.30	99
8............	4.95	288	4.40	121	4.30	99	4.49	143	4.70	201	4.25	89
9............	4.95	288	4.38	117	4.30	99	4.52	150	4.67	192	4.22	83
10........ ..	4.93	281	4.36	112	4.28	95	4.55	158	4.65	186	4.19	77
11........ ..	4.90	270	4.35	110	4.27	93	4.55	158	4.68	195	4.14	69
12............	4.90	270	4.35	110	4.25	89	4.55	158	4.66	189	4.17	74
13............	4.93	281	4.34	108	4.25	89	4.70	201	4.63	180	4.23	85
14............	4.90	270	4.32	103	4.20	79	4.85	252	4.60	171	4.25	89
15............	4.85	252	4.30	99	4.33	106	5.05	324	4.35	110	4.25	89
16............	4.80	235	4.30	99	4.35	110	5.20	382	4.32	103	4.23	85
17....	4.75	218	4.65	186	4.34	108	5.25	402	4.30	99	4.22	83
18............	4.70	201	4.80	235	4.40	121	5.15	362	4.35	110	4.22	83
19....	4.67	192	4.77	225	4.60	171	5.10	343	4.40	121	4.24	87
20............	4.65	186	4.70	201	4.62	177	5.05	324	4.53	153	4.24	87
21............	4.65	186	4.60	171	4.58	166	4.95	288	4.55	158	4.25	89
22............	4.60	171	4.53	153	4.55	158	4.90	270	4.55	158	4.27	93
23............	4.65	186	4.65	186	4.53	153	4.85	252	4.55	158	4.27	93
24............	4.55	158	4.60	171	4.53	153	4.82	242	4.57	163	4.28	95
25............	4.53	153	4.55	158	4.53	153	4.75	218	4.60	171	4.29	97
26............	4.52	150	4.50	145	4.54	155	4.72	208	4.63	180	4.29	97
27............	4.52	150	4.47	138	4.55	158	4.70	201	4.63	180	4.30	99
28............	4.50	145	4.45	133	4.54	155	4.68	195	4.60	171	4.30	99
29............	4.50	145	4.43	128	4.50	145	4.65	186	4.57	163	4.30	99
30............	4.48	140	4.40	121	4.47	138	4.65	186	4.52	150	4.30	99
31...	4.46	135	4.38	117	......	....	4.63	180	....	....	4.29	97

MONTHLY DISCHARGE of Crowsnest River near Frank, for 1914.

(Drainage area 168 square miles.)

MONTH.	DISCHARGE IN SECOND-*FEET.*				RUN-OFF.	
	Maximum.	Minimum	Mean.	Per square Mile.	Depth in inches on Drainage Area.	Total in Acre-feet.
January....	121	44	64	0.382	0.44	3,948
February..	52	45	49	0.290	0.30	2,710
March...	67	42	52	0.310	0.36	3,204
April.....	444	56	238	1.420	1.58	14,180
May	616	362	484	2.880	3.32	29,778
June....	564	270	392	2.340	2.61	23,344
July....	343	135	236	1.400	1.61	14,511
August	235	99	140	0.833	0.96	8,608
September ..	177	79	124	0.738	0.82	7,379
October	402	133	219	1.300	1.50	13,466
November ...	218	99	170	1.010	1.13	10,116
December..	150	69	98	0.583	0.67	6,026
The year..........................	....	....	....	....	15.30	137,270

Gauging Station on Crowsnest River near Frank, Alberta. Taken by G. H. Whyte.

Gauging Station on Crowsnest at Lundbreck, Alberta. Taken by G. H. Whyte.

Location.—On the N.E. ¼ Sec. 26, Tp. 7, Rge. 2, W. 5th Mer., at the traffic bridge just north of Lundbreck.

Records available.—September 7, 1907, to December 31, 1914.

Gauge.—Chain on downstream side of the traffic bridge about 75 feet upstream from the old staff gauge; elevation of zero of staff gauge maintained at 91.82 feet during 1912-13; 90.86 feet during 1914.

Bench-mark.—Permanent bench-mark cut in the left wing-wall on the downstream side; assumed elevation, 100.00 feet.

Channel.—Rocky formation and fairly permanent.

Discharge measurements.—Made from the traffic bridge during high water, and by wading in low stages.

Winter flow.—Discharge measurements are continued during the winter season.

Observer.—Ed. Marlow.

DISCHARGE MEASUREMENTS of Crowsnest River near Lundbreck, in 1914.

Date.	Engineer.	Width.	Area of Section.	Mean Velocity.	Gauge Height.	Discharge.
		Feet.	*Sq. ft.*	*Ft. per sec.*	*Feet.*	*Sec.-ft.*
Jan. 19	R. Palmer	54.0	67.0	1.12	2.40	75
Jan. 30	do	50.0	77.0	0.97	2.95	75
Feb. 18	E. W. W. Hughes	65.0	65.5	0.99	3.01	65
Mar. 10	F. R. Burfield	55.0	69.2	1.01	2.66	70
Mar. 26	do	60.0	133.0	0.90	2.78	121
April 11	J. E. Caughey	55.0	82.5	1.82	2.03	150
April 27	do	65.0	134.0	3.33	3.02	447
May 19	do	68.0	171.0	4.31	3.45	738
June 6	do	66.0	146.6	3.90	3.26	571
June 26	do	66.0	155.9	3.61	3.20	562
July 13	do	62.0	107.8	2.65	2.50	285
July 28	do	57.0	90.8	2.02	2.20	183
Aug. 13	do	55.0	84.0	1.75	1.90	147
Aug. 24	do	60.0	106.0	2.42	2.39	256
Sept. 12	do	55.0	80.5	1.68	1.87	135
Sept. 25	do	57.0	97.9	2.20	2.12	215
Oct. 14	do	60.0	117.0	2.74	2.52	321
Nov. 3	do	60.0	108.0	2.72	2.45	294
Nov. 19	do	55.0	92.0	2.00	2.30	184
Dec. 10	do	55.0	89.5	1.19	2.30	107
Dec. 30	do	68.0	96.0	1.52	3.16	146

STREAM MEASUREMENTS, 1914

5 GEORGE V, A. 1915

DAILY GAUGE HEIGHT AND DISCHARGE of Crowsnest River near Lundbreck, for 1914.

DAY.	January.		February.		March.		April.		May.		June.	
	Gauge Height.	Dis-charge.	Gauge Height.	Dis-charge	Gauge Height.	Dis-charge.	Gauge Height.	Dis-charge.	Gauge Height.	Dis-charge.	Gauge Height.	Dis-charge.
	Feet.	*Sec.-ft.*	*Feet.*	*Sec.-ft.*	*Feet.*	*Sec.-ft.*	*Feet.*	*Sec.-ft.*	*Feet.*	*Sec.-ft.*	*Feet.*	*Sec.-ft.*
1.........	2.81	95a	2 96	76	2.96	71	1.82	126	3.15	528	3.00	460
2.........	2.76	96	2 86	74	2.96	71	1.82	126	3.30	600	3.05	482
3.........	2.74	97	2.86	72	2.96	70	1.77	119	3.75	855	3.32	610
4.........	2.71	97	2.76	70	2.96	70	1.84	129	3.55	735	3.31	605
5.........	2.76	98	2.71	70	2.76	69	1.95	146	3.45	678	3.28	590
6.........	2.76	98	2.76	74	2.71	69	2.09	172	3.10	505	3.18	541
7.........	2.80	97	2.86	75	2.76	69	2.03	161	3.10	505	3.00	460
8.........	2.79	96	2.96	75	2.91	70	1.97	150	3.10	505	2.80	375
9.........	2.66	94	2.86	75	2.91	70	1.99	153	3.35	625	2.81	379
10....... .	2.60	92	2.86	75	2.66	70	2.01	157	3.45	678	2.75	357
11.........	2.61	92	2.91	76	2.61	71	2.03	161	2.40	244	2.70	339
12.........	2.56	92	2.91	78	2.71	74	2.28	212	3.35	625	2.70	339
13...	2.66	90	2.86	78	1.66	76	2.54	286	3.30	600	2.85	395
14.... .. .	2.46	88	2.91	76	1.61	78	2.79	371	3.35	625	2.95	438
15.	2.61	84	2.88	74	1.60	84	2.79	371	3.40	650	2.96	442
16.	2.41	82	2.86	71	1.51	90	3.09	500	3.40	650	3.00	460
17.	2.41	80	2.81	66	1.51	95	3.04	478	3.35	625	3.02	469
18...	2.66	78	3.01	65	1.57	99	2.80	375	3.50	705	3.00	460
19.	2.76	75	2.81	65	1.52	104	2.75	357	3.40	650	3.00	460
20.	2.86	75	2.76	66	1.52	110	3.35	625	3.40	650	2.95	438
21.	2.96	75	2.88	70	1.52	113	3.00	460	3.40	650	2.88	407
22.........	3.11	74	2.76	72	1.47	115	2.95	438	3.20	550	2.80	375
23.	2.96	74	2.96	73	1.52	117	3.00	460	3.20	550	2.70	339
24.........	2.82	73	2.96	74	1.52	119	3.30	600	3.40	650	2.68	332
25...... .	2.96	72	3.01	74	1.57	120	3.10	505	3.40	650	2.80	375
26.	3.01	72	2 91	73	2.77	121	3.10	505	3.30	600	3.15	528
27.	3.06	72	2.96	72	2.52	121	3.05	482	3.23	565	3.00	460
28.	3.01	72	2.94	71	2.17	118	3.00	460	3.05	482	2.90	415
29... . ..	2.86	73	......	......	2.07	110	2.95	438	3.00	460	2.90	415
30.	3.01	73	......	......	1.87	104	3.00	460	2.90	415	2.85	395
31.........	2.96	76	......	......	1.57	98b	......	......	3.00	460	......	......

a to *b* Ice conditions.

SESSIONAL PAPER No. 25c

DAILY GAUGE HEIGHT AND DISCHARGE of Crowsnest River near Lundbreck, for 1914.

DAY.	July. Gauge Height.	July. Dis- charge.	August. Gauge Height.	August. Dis- charge	September. Gauge Height.	September. Dis- charge.	October. Gauge Height.	October. Dis- charge.	November. Gauge Height.	November. Dis- charge	December. Gauge Height.	December. Dis- charge
	Feet.	*Sec.-ft.*	*Feet.*	*Sec.-ft.*	*Feet.*	*Sec.-ft.*	*Feet.*	*Sec.-ft.*	*Feet.*	*Sec.-ft*	*Feet.*	*Sec.-ft.*
1	2.85	395	2 10	174	2 00	155	2.10	210	2 35	270	2.40	154
2	2.80	375	2 11	176	2.00	155	2.07	204	2 35	270	2.35	149
3	2.78	368	2 10	174	1 95	146	2 07	204	2.45	300	2.25	143
4	2.78	368	2.06	166	1.93	143	2 10	210	2.40	284	2.25	138
5	2.76	361	2 06	166	1.91	140	2 18	228	2.50	315	2.25	130
6	2.76	361	2.05	164	1.90	138	2.10	210	2.48	309	2.28	125
7	2.74	353	2.05	164	1.90	138	2.10	210	2.40	284	2.30	120
8	2.65	322	2.05	164	1.94	145	2.12	214	2.35	270	2.26	114
9	2.65	322	2.05	164	1.90	138	2.15	221	2.36	273	2.16	108
10	2.60	305	2.04	163	1.88	135	2.20	232	2.30	257	2.20	107
11	2.55	290	2.00	155	1.85	130	2.20	232	2.30	257	2.45	106
12	2.52	280	2.00	155	1.87	134	2.20	232	2.30	257	2.85	106
13	2.50	274	1.90	138	1.85	130	2.28	252	2.30	257	3.45	106
14	2.50	274	1.86	132	1.85	130	2.52	322	2.25	244	4.05	106
15	2.51	277	1.85	130	1.90	138	2.90	465	2.05	200	4.00	107
16	2.48	268	1.85	130	1.90	138	3.05	530	2.05	200	4.00	107
17	2.45	259	2.10	174	1.90	140c	3.15	580	2.10	180a	3.95	108
18	2.40	244	2.40	244	2.00	164	2.95	485	2.25	182	3.85	109
19	2.40	244	2.40	244	2.16	202	2.90	465	2.26	184	3.70	111
20	2.36	233	2.35	230	2.20	215	2.80	425	2.20	186	3.65	112
21	2.35	230	2.25	206	2.20	220	2.80	425	2.35	187	3.50	114
22	2.30	217	2.18	190	2.15	212	2.70	385	2 30	187	3.50	117
23	2.28	212	2.26	208	2.10	204	2.55	332	2 30	187	3.40	120
24	2.24	203	2.40	244	2.10	207	2.53	326	2 33	186	3.20	124
25	2.24	203	2.30	217	2.12	215d	2 45	300	2.38	183	3.30	128
26	2.26	208	2.15	184	2.15	221	2.47	306	2.40	178	3.28	134
27	2.26	208	2.12	178	2.10	210	2.45	300	2.38	169	3.25	138
28	2.20	194	2.10	174	2.10	210	2.40	284	2.40	164	3.20	141
29	2.18	190	2.05	164	2.10	210	2.40	284	2.36	161	3.23	144
30	2.15	184	2.05	164	2.05	200	2.35	270	2.25	158	3.27	146
31	2.15	184	2.00	155	.....	.....	2.35	270	.....	.....	3.25	147b

a to *b* Ice conditions.
c to *d* Shifting conditions.

MONTHLY DISCHARGE of Crowsnest River near Lundbreck, for 1914.

(Drainage area 276 square miles.)

MONTH.	DISCHARGE IN SECOND-FEET. Maximum.	Minimum.	Mean.	Per square Mile.	RUN-OFF. Depth in inches on Drainage Area.	Total in Acre-feet.
January	98	72	84	0.30	0.35	5,165
February	78	65	72	0.26	0.27	3,999
March	121	69	91	0.33	0.38	5,595
April	625	119	333	1.21	1.35	19,815
May	855	244	589	2.13	2.46	36,216
June	610	332	438	1.59	1.77	26,063
July	395	184	271	0.98	1.13	16,663
August	244	130	177	0.64	0.74	10,883
September	221	130	169	0.61	0.68	10,056
October	580	204	310	1.12	1.29	19,061
November	315	158	225	0.82	0.91	13,388
December	154	106	123	0.44	0.51	7,563
The year	.....	.....	.....	.....	11.84	174,467

5 GEORGE V. A. 1915

CONNELLY CREEK NEAR LUNDBRECK.

Location.—On SE. ¼ Sec. 36, Tp. 7, Rge. 2, W. 5th Mer., on the north side of Crowsnest River, about half way between Lundbreck and Cowley.

Records.—Discharge measurements only are available from August 20, 1908, to December 31, 1914.

Gauge.—Vertical staff, nailed to a tree on the left bank.

Bench-mark.—The head of a bolt driven vertically in a notch cut in a leaning tree, on the left bank; elevation, 3.93 feet above the zero of the gauge.

Discharge measurements.—Made by wading in high water, and by means of an 18-inch weir in low stages.

Winter flow.—Discharge measurements are not made during the winter season.

Observer.—Gauge height records are available from August 1, 1909, to October 31, 1909; since then there has been no observer at this station.

DISCHARGE MEASUREMENTS of Connelly Creek near Lundbreck, in 1914.

Date.	Engineer.	Width.	Area of Section.	Mean Velocity.	Gauge Height.	Discharge.
		Feet.	*Sq. ft.*	*Ft. per sec.*	*Feet.*	*Sec.-ft.*
Mar. 26	F. R. Burfield	4.0	3.43	0.41	....	1.40
April 11	J. E. Caughey	11.5	8.11	1.14	2.57	9.20
April 27	do	11.5	6.07	0.72	....	4.40
May 19	do	11.0	6.37	0.84	....	5.30
June 6	do	11.5	5.90	0.60	....	3.60
June 23	do	12.5	9.42	1.97	....	18.60
July 13	do	11.0	5.05	0.38	4.35	1.92
July 28	do	5.0	1.40	0.34	....	0.48
Aug. 13	do					0.76a
Aug. 24	do	11.5	7.15	0.94	2.45	0.67
Sept. 12	do				2.20	0.65a
Sept. 25	do				2.30	0.36a
Oct. 14	do	12.0	7.70	1.27	2.46	9.80
Nov. 3	do	10.0	5.10	0.55	2.34	2.80

a Weir measurements.

COW CREEK NEAR COWLEY.

Location.—On NE. ¼ Sec. 14, Tp. 8, Rge. 2, W. 5th Mer., at John Ross' ranch, five miles north of Lundbreck station.

Records available.—August 20, 1908, to December 31, 1914.

Gauge.—Vertical staff; zero elevation maintained at 94.53 feet during 1912-14.

Bench-mark.—Permanent iron bench-mark; assumed elevation, 100.00 feet.

Channel.—Clay and rocks, fairly permanent.

Discharge measurements.—Made from a foot bridge during high water, and by wading in low stages.

Winter flow.—Discharge measurements are not made during the winter season.

Observer.—Wm. Mackay.

SESSIONAL PAPER No. 25c

DISCHARGE MEASUREMENTS of Cow Creek near Cowley, in 1914.

Date.	Engineer.	Width.	Area of Section.	Mean Velocity.	Gauge Height.	Discharge.
		Feet.	*Sq. ft.*	*Ft. per sec.*	*Feet.*	*Sec.-ft.*
Mar. 27......	F. R. Burfield.	8.5	14.0	0.37	3.06	5.20
April 11.........	J. E. Caughey...........	8.0	11.0	1.89	2.52	21.00
April 27......	do	8.5	9.1	0.98	2.14	9.00
May 19...	do	8.7	11.6	1.33	2.35	15.50
June 6...........	do	8.5	10.5	1.10	2.22	11.50
June 26...........	do	8.0	13.0	1.72	2.54	22.00
July 13...........	do	8.0	6.7	0.72	1.89	4.80
July 28.....	do	8.5	5.8	0.44	1.74	2.60
Aug. 13.... .	do	8.0	5.0	0.36	1.68	1.78
Aug. 24	do	8.5	7.0	0.59	1.85	4.10
Sept. 12....	do	8.5	4.8	0.34	1.69	1.60
Sept. 25....	do	5.5	1.9	0.74	1.67	1.43
Oct. 14...........	do	7.0	6.9	1.44	2.15	9.90
Nov. 3...........	do	6.0	4.0	0.82	1.86	3.20

DAILY GAUGE HEIGHT AND DISCHARGE of Cow Creek near Cowley, for 1914.

DAY.	March.		April.		May.		June.	
	Gauge Height.	Dis-charge.	Gauge Height.	Dis-charge.	Gauge Height.	Dis-charge.	Gauge Height.	Dis-charge.
	Feet.	*Sec.-ft.*	*Feet.*	*Sec.-ft.*	*Feet.*	*Sec.-ft.*	*Feet.*	*Sec.-ft.*
1............			2.27	12.7	2.23	11.5	2.16	9.7
2............			2.71	13.0	2.19	10.5	2.15	9.5
3............			2.71	13.0	2.20	10.7	2.14	9.3
4............			2.74	18.0	2.30	13.5	2.14	9.3
5............			3.60	14.0	2.30	13.5	2.18	10.2
6............			3.31	16.0	2.27	12.7	2.22	11.3
7............			2.82	18.0	2.25	12.1	2.19	10.5
8............			2.72	20.0	2.23	11.5	2.12	8.8
9............			2.65	23.0	2.30	13.5	2.09	8.1
10............			2.62	24.8b	2.27	12.7	2.09	8.1
11............			2.44	18.0	2.31	13.8	2.08	7.9
12............			3.10	45.0	2.29	13.2	2.08	7.9
13............			2.80	32.0	2.35	15.1	2.29	13.2
14............			2.50	20.0	2.30	13.5	2.15	9.5
15............	3 40	2.00a	2.43	17.7	2.29	13.2	2.11	8.5
16............	3.10	2.30	2.38	16.1	2.30	13.5	2.08	7.9
17............	2.91	2.60	2.24	11.8	2.30	13.5	2.06	7.5
18............	3.00	2.80	2.13	9.0	2.30	13.5	1.99	6.0
19............	2.98	3.00	2.30	13.5	2.35	15.1	1.98	5.8
20............	2.95	3.30	2.95	38.0	2.40	16.7	1.97	5.7
21............	3.39	3.70	2.30	13.5	2.36	15.4	1.96	5.5
22............	2.60	4.00	2.29	13.2	2.35	15.1	1.94	5.1
23............	2.68	4.20	2.24	11.8	2.34	14.8	1.94	5.1
24............	3.19	4.50	2.21	11.0	2.30	13.5	1.95	5.3
25............	2.70	4.80	2.18	10.2	2.28	12.9	2.61	24.0
26............	3.50	5.00	2.15	9.5	2.27	12.7	2.89	36.0
27............	2.94	5.20	2.14	9.3	2.26	12.4	2.17	10.0
28............	2.51	7.00	2.26	12.4	2.29	13.2	2.09	8.1
29............	2.48	9.00	2.35	15.1	2.25	12.1	2.14	9.3
30............	2.31	11.00	2.29	13.2	2.20	10.7	2.12	8.8
31............	2.29	13.20	....	....	2.22	11.3	....	....

a to *b* Discharge estimated—ice conditions.

STREAM MEASUREMENTS, 1914

5 GEORGE V, A. 1915

DAILY GAUGE HEIGHT AND DISCHARGE of Cow Creek near Cowley, for 1914.
—Concluded.

DAY.	July.		August.		September.		October.	
	Gauge Height.	Dis- charge.	Gauge Height.	Dis- charge.	Gauge Height.	Dis- charge.	Gauge Height.	Dis- charge.
	Feet.	*Sec.-ft.*	*Feet.*	*Sec.-ft.*	*Feet.*	*Sec.-ft.*	*Feet.*	*Sec.-ft.*
1	2.09	8.1	1.71	1.83	1.68	1.52	1.68	1.52
2	2.06	7.5	1.69	1.61	1.68	1.52	1.69	1.61
3	2.00	6.2	1.69	1.61	1.67	1.43	1.69	1.61
4	1.99	6.0	1.66	1.34	1.66	1.34	1.75	2.40
5	2.09	8.1	1.65	1.25	1.68	1.52	1.87	4.00
6	2.05	7.2	1.64	1.16	1.68	1.52	1.90	4.40
7	1.99	6.0	1.64	1.16	1.66	1.34	1.70	1.70
8	1.97	5.7	1.67	1.43	1.71	1.83	1.90	4.40
9	1.95	5.3	1.69	1.61	1.70	1.70	1.87	4.00
10	1.94	5.1	1.73	2.10	1.69	1.61	1.87	4.00
11	1.93	4.9	1.69	1.61	1.69	1.61	1.81	3.10
12	1.91	4.6	1.69	1.61	1.70	1.70	2.01	6.40
13	1.90	4.4	1.69	1.61	1.70	1.70	2.19	10.50
14	1.90	4.4	1.66	1.34	1.70	1.70	2.19	10.50
15	1.90	4.4	1.62	0.98	1.73	2.10	1.90	4.40
16	1.89	4.3	1.60	0.80	1.75	2.40	1.88	4.10
17	1.87	4.0	1.70	1.70	1.81	3.10	1.86	3.80
18	1.83	3.4	1.91	4.60	1.81	3.10	1.84	3.60
19	1.79	2.9	1.79	2.90	1.75	2.40	1.82	3.30
20	1.79	2.9	1.69	1.61	1.78	2.70	1.82	3.30
21	1.79	2.9	1.69	1.61	1.71	1.83	1.81	3.10
22	1.78	2.7	1.68	1.52	1.71	1.83	1.82	3.30
23	1.78	2.7	1.94	5.10	1.68	1.52	1.82	3.30
24	1.78	2.7	1.94	5.10	1.68	1.52	1.85	3.70
25	1.76	2.5	1.79	2.90	1.68	1.52	1.82	3.30
26	1.76	2.5	1.70	1.70	1.67	1.43	1.82	3.30
27	1.75	2.4	1.69	1.61	1.67	1.43	1.83	3.40
28	1.74	2.2	1.68	1.52	1.68	1.52	1.84	3.60
29	1.74	2.2	1.68	1.52	1.68	1.52	1.84	3.60
30	1.74	2.2	1.65	1.25	1.68	1.52	1.83	3.40
31	1.74	2.2	1.67	1.43			1.84	3.60

MONTHLY DISCHARGE of Cow Creek near Cowley, for 1914.

(Drainage area 29 square miles.)

MONTH.	DISCHARGE IN SECOND-FEET.				RUN-OFF.	
	Maximum.	Minimum.	Mean.	Per square Mile.	Depth in inches on Drainage Area.	Total in Acre-feet.
March (15-31)	13.2	2.00	5.20	0.179	0.113	175
April	45.0	9.00	17.10	0.589	0.657	1,018
May	16.7	10.50	13.10	0.452	0.521	806
June	36.0	5.10	9.70	0.334	0.373	577
July	8.1	2.20	4.30	0.145	0.171	264
August	5.1	0.80	1.91	0.066	0.076	117
September	3.1	1.34	1.75	0.061	0.068	106
October	10.5	1.52	3.90	0.136	0.157	240
The period					2.136	3.303

ELTON DITCH FROM TODD CREEK.

Location.—On SW. ¼ Sec. 19, Tp. 8, Rge. 1, W. 5th Mer., on *E*lton's ranch, seven miles north of Cowley.

Records available.—June 6, 1914, to September 25, 1914.

Gauge.—Vertical staff.

Bench-mark.—Two spikes in a post 150 feet south of the gauge; elevation, 1.66 feet above the zero of the gauge.

Channel.—Clay, and fairly permanent.

Discharge measurements.—Made by wading.

Observer.—Cecil *E*lton.

DISCHARGE MEASUREMENTS of *E*lton Ditch from Todd Creek, in 1914.

Date.	Engineer.	Width.	Area of Section.	Mean Velocity.	Gauge Height.	Discharge.
		Feet.	*Sq. ft.*	*Ft. per sec.*	*Feet.*	*Sec.-ft.*
June 6	J. E. Caughey	2.5	1.28	0.55	2.24	0.71
June 26	do	3.0	2.19	0.55	2.40	1.20
Sept. 25	do			........*a*	2.02	0.04

a Weir measurement.

DAILY GAUGE HEIGHT AND DISCHARGE of *E*lton Ditch from Todd Creek, for 1914.

DAY.	May.		June.	
	Gauge Height.	Discharge.	Gauge Height.	Discharge.
	Feet.	*Sec.-ft.*	*Feet.*	*Sec.-ft.*
1			2.30	0.89
2			2.30	0.89
3			2.29	0.86
4			2.31	0.92
5			2.32	0.95
6			2.34	1.01
7			2.34	1.01
8			2.34	1.01
9			2.32	0.95
10			2.32	0.95
11			2.32	0.95
12			2.31	0.92
13			2.32	0.95
14	2.25	0.74	2.32	0.95
15	2.25	0.74	2.32	0.95
16	2.24	0.71	2.31	0.92
17	2.24	0.71	2.31	0.92
18	2.24	0.71	2.31	0.92
19	2.25	0.74	2.30	0.89
20	2.28	0.83	2.30	0.89
21	2.29	0.86	2.29	0.86
22	2.29	0.86	2.29	0.86
23	2.30	0.89	2.29	0.86
24	2.30*a*	0.89	2.28	0.83
25	2.30*a*	0.89	2.33	0.98
26	2.30	0.89	2.37	1.10
27	2.34	1.01		
28	2.34	1.01	2.32	0.95
29	2.31	0.92	2.33	0.98
30	2.32	0.95		
31	2.31	0.92		

a Gauge height interpolated.

No. 25c—14

5 GEORGE V, A. 1915

MONTHLY DISCHARGE of *E*lton Ditch from Todd Creek, for 1914.

MONTH.	DISCHARGE IN SECOND-*FEET*.				RUN-OFF.	
	Maximum.	Minimum.	Mean.	Per square Mile.	Depth in inches on Drainage Area.	Total in Acre-feet.
May (14-31)............................	1.01	0.71	0.843	....	....	30
June (1-29)............................	1.10	0.83	0.933	....	....	52
The period............................	....	....	....	....	....	82

TODD CREEK AT ELTON'S RANCH.

Location.—On SW. ¼ Sec. 19, Tp. 8, Rge. 1, W. 5th Mer., near Cecil *E*lton's house, seven miles north of Cowley.

Records available.—August 20, 1908, to December 31, 1914.

Gauge.—Vertical staff; elevation of zero maintained at 93.30 feet during 1909-1911; 93.02 feet during 1912-14.

Bench-mark.—Permanent iron bench-mark; assumed elevation, 100.00 feet.

Channel.—Sand and gravel, and quite permanent.

Discharge measurements.—These are made from a foot bridge during high water, and by wading during low stages.

Winter flow.—No discharge measurements are made during the winter season.

Observer.—Cecil *E*lton.

DISCHARGE MEASUREMENTS of Todd Creek at Elton's Ranch, in 1914.

Date.	Engineer.	Width.	Area of Section.	Mean Velocity.	Gauge Height.	Discharge.
		Feet.	*Sec.-ft.*	*Ft. per sec.*	*Feet.*	*Sec.-ft.*
March 27.	F. R. Burfield..	6.5	6.60	1.02	4.47	6.70
April 11..:.........	J. E. Caughey..............	18.0	23.10	1.41	3.95	33.00
April 27............	do	18.0	15.10	1.20	2.91	18.20
May 19.......... .	do	18.3	17.00	1.39	2.98	24.00
June 6..........	do	18.0	17.50	1.44	3.01	25.00
June 26..........	do	19.0	35.40	1.80	3.50	64.00
July 3..........	do	18.0	12.15	0.92	2.75	11.50
July 28..........	do	18.0	8.60	0.70	2.64	6.00
Aug. 13..........	do	18.0	8.00	0.61	2.60	4.90
Aug. 24..........	do	17.5	15.05	1.02	2.86	15.40
Sept. 12..........	do	18.0	9.70	0.60	2.64	6.00
Sept. 25..........	do	18.0	9.50	0.62	2.64	5.90
Oct. 14..... ...	do	18.0	13.80	1.14	2.85	15.80
Nov. 3......	do	18.0	10.60	0.87	2.72	9.30

SESSIONAL PAPER No. 25c

DAILY GAUGE HEIGHT AND DISCHARGE of Todd Creek at *Elton's* Ranch, for 1914.

DAY.	March.		April.		May.		June.	
	Gauge Height.	Dis- charge.	Gauge Height.	Dis- charge.	Gauge Height.	Dis- charge.	Gauge Height.	Dis- charge.
	Feet.	*Sec.-ft.*	*Feet.*	*Sec.-ft.*	*Feet.*	*Sec.-ft.*	*Feet.*	*Sec.-ft.*
1			3.98	16.5	2.98	23.0	2.93	20.0
2			3.98	18.0	2.94	20.0	2.93	20.0
3			4.13	19.5	2.96	22.0	2.90	18.0
4			4.28	20.0	3.03	26.0	2.93	20.0
5			5.06	23.0	3.01	25.0	2.99	23.0
6			5.18	25.0	3.00	24.0	3.01	25.0
7			4.85	27.0	2.94	20.0	2.98	23.0
8			4.27	28.5	2.94	20.0	2.95	21.0
9			4.08	30.0	3.00	24.0	2.92	19.2
10			4.08	31.0	2.98	23.0	2.91	18.6
11			3.88	33.0	3.01	25.0	2.91	18.6
12			3.86	36.5	2.98	23.0	2.90	18.0
13			3.95	40.0	3.00	24.0	2.92	19.2
14			3.43	44.0	2.99	23.0	2.94	20.0
15			3.34	47.0	2.96	22.0	2.89	17.4
16	4.29	2.0*a*	3.34	50.0*b*	2.94	20.0	2.87	16.5
17	4.17	2.6	3.13	33.0	2.94	20.0	2.84	14.7
18	4.00	3.2	3.04	27.0	2.96	22.0	2.84	14.7
19	3.97	3.7	3.00	24.0	2.98	23.0	2.81	13.0
20	3.93	3.9	3.30	46.0	3.02	25.0	2.78	11.6
21	3.88	4.4	3.04	27.0	3.05	27.0	2.77	11.2
22	4.00	5.0	3.12	32.0	3.02	25.0	2.78	11.6
23	3.88	5.4	3.06	28.0	3.00	24.0	2.77	11.2
24	3.99	5.8	3.04	27.0	3.00	24.0	2.76	10.7
25	4.17	6.1	3.00	24.0	3.02	25.0	2.98	23.0
26	4.28	6.4	2.94	20.0	3.00	24.0	3.45	60.0
27	4.46	6.7	2.92	19.2	3.00	24.0	3.20	38.0
28	4.53	8.8	2.94	20.0	3.00	24.0	3.00	24.0
29	4.15	10.9	3.07	29.0	2.99	23.0	2.94	20.0
30	4.10	13.0	3.00	24.0	2.97	22.0	2.91	18.6
31	4.08	15.5			2.94	20.0		

a to *b* Discharge estimated—ice conditions.

STREAM MEASUREMENTS, 1914

5 GEORGE V. A. 1915

DAILY GAUGE HEIGHT AND DISCHARGE of Todd Creek at *Elton's* Ranch, for 1914.
—Concluded.

DAY.	July.		August.		September.		October.	
	Gauge Height.	Dis-charge.	Gauge Height.	Dis-charge.	Gauge Height.	Dis-charge.	Gauge Height.	Dis-charge.
	Feet.	*Sec.-ft.*	*Feet.*	*Sec.-ft.*	*Feet.*	*Sec.-ft.*	*Feet.*	*Sec.-ft.*
1	2.88	16.9	2.58	4.5	2.60	5.0	2.60	5.0
2	2.86	15.8	2.55	3.7	2.59	4.8	2.62	5.6
3	2.86	15.8	2.56	4.0	2.60	5.0	2.64	6.2
4	2.85	15.2	2.56	4.0	2.60	5.0	2.70	8.0
5	2.89	17.4	2.55	3.7	2.59	4.8	2.70	8.0
6	2.86	15.8	2.57	4.3	2.59	4.8	2.71	8.4
7	2.84	14.7	2.57	4.3	2.60	5.0	2.70	8.0
8	2.81	13.0	2.57	4.3	2.64	6.2	2.69	7.7
9	2.80	12.5	2.59	4.8	2.64	6.2	2.72	8.9
10	2.78	11.6	2.65	6.5	2.64	6.2	2.73	9.4
11	2.79	12.0	2.58	4.5	2.63	5.9	2.74	9.8
12	2.79	12.0	2.58	4.5	2.64	6.2	2.74	9.8
13	2.79	12.0	2.59	4.8	2.63	5.9	2.74	9.8
14	2.73	9.4	2.56	4.0	2.62	5.6	2.83	14.2
15	2.72	8.9	2.55	3.7	2.62	5.6	2.96	22.0
16	2.72	8.9	2.54	3.5	2.64	6.2	2.91	18.6
17	2.70	8.0	2.61	5.3	2.67	7.1	2.85	15.2
18	2.72	8.9	2.79	12.0	2.70	8.0	2.76	10.7
19	2.70	8.0	2.76	10.7	2.67	7.1	2.74	9.8
20	2.68	7.4	2.69	7.7	2.66	6.8	2.73	9.4
21	2.68	7.4	2.69	7.7	2.64	6.2	2.73	9.4
22	2.67	7.1	2.67	7.1	2.64	6.2	2.72	8.9
23	2.65	6.5	2.72	8.9	2.64	6.2	2.70	8.0
24	2.64	6.2	2.81	13.0	2.63	5.9	2.71	8.4
25	2.64	6.2	2.73	9.4	2.62	5.6	2.71	8.4
26	2.63	5.9	2.69	7.7	2.62	5.6	2.70	8.0
27	2.62	5.6	2.66	6.8	2.58	4.5	2.70	8.0
28	2.64	6.2	2.64	6.2	2.58	4.5	2.72	8.9
29	2.62	5.6	2.63	5.9	2.60	5.0	2.72	8.9
30	2.61	5.3	2.64	6.2	2.60	5.0	2.71	8.4
31	2.58	4.5	2.62	5.6	....	....	2.70	8.0

MONTHLY DISCHARGE of Todd Creek at *Elton's* Ranch, for 1914.
(Drainage area 57 square miles).

MONTH.	DISCHARGE IN SECOND-FEET.				RUN-OFF.	
	Maximum.	Minimum	Mean.	Per square Mile.	Depth in inches on Drainage Area.	Total in Acre-feet.
March (16–31)	15.5	2.0	6.5	0.114	0.068	206
April	50.0	16.5	29.0	0.509	0.568	1,726
May	27.0	20.0	23.0	0.404	0.466	1,414
June	38.0	10.7	20.0	0.351	0.392	1,190
July	17.4	4.5	10.0	0.175	0.202	615
August	13.0	3.5	6.1	0.107	0.123	375
September	8.0	4.5	5.7	0.100	0.111	339
October	22.0	5.0	9.6	0.168	0.187	590
The period	....	....	....	....	2.12	6,455

OLDMAN RIVER NEAR COWLEY.

Location.—On the N*E.* ¼ Sec. 34, Tp. 7, Rge. 1, W. 5th Mer.

Records available.—June 17, 1908, to December 31, 1914; one discharge measurement in 1907.

Gauge.—Vertical staff; elevation of zero maintained at 92.08 feet since establishment.

Bench-mark.—Permanent iron bench-mark on right bank; assumed elevation, 100.00 feet.

Channel.—Rock and gravel.

Discharge measurements.—Made by means of cable and car; at low water by wading.

Observer.—Archie McKay.

SESSIONAL PAPER No. 25c

DISCHARGE MEASUREMENTS of Oldman River near Cowley, in 1914.

Date.	Engineer.	Width.	Area of Section.	Mean Velocity.	Gauge Height.	Discharge.
		Feet.	*Sq.ft.*	*Ft. per sec.*	*Feet.*	*Sec.-ft.*
Jan. 15	R. Palmer	80	95.0	1.290	2.18	123
Jan. 31	do	90	78.0	1.100	2.28	86
Feb. 19	E. W. W. Hughes	83	83.6	1.130	2.41	95
March 11	F. R. Burfield	174	105.0	0.807	1.75	85
March 27	do	135	108.0	1.090	1.62	118
April 14	J. E. Caughey	180	220.0	2.460	2.23	541
April 29	do	185	248.0	2.410	2.32	597
May 14	do	188	378.0	3.586	3.02	1,354
June 2	do	192	405.5	3.850	3.23	1,561
June 24	do	190	285.5	2.706	2.60	773
July 10	do	180	264.0	2.640	2.45	696
July 25	do	175	174.0	1.850	2.04	323
Aug. 12	do	145	146.0	1.620	1.80	237
Aug. 26	do	155	149.0	1.720	1.83	257
Sept. 7	do	140	130.0	1.300	1.67	170
Sept. 24	do	150	146.0	1.540	1.80	226
Oct. 8	do	145	179.0	1.460	1.85	260
Nov. 2	do	175	218.0	2.190	2.18	477
Nov. 17	do	180	303.0	1.230	2.98	374
Dec. 10	do	120	159.5	0.800	2.75	127
Dec. 29	do	180	156.0	1.080	3.66	168

DAILY GAUGE HEIGHT AND DISCHARGE of Oldman River near Cowley, for 1914.

DAY.	January.		February.		March.		April.		May.		June.	
	Gauge Height.	Dis-charge.	Gauge Height.	Dis-charge.	Gauge Height.	Dis-charge.	Gauge Height.	Dis-charge.	Gauge Height.	Dis-charge.	Gauge Height	Dis-charge.
	Feet.	*Sec.-ft.*	*Feet.*	*Sec.-ft.*	*Feet.*	*Sec.-ft.*	*Feet.*	*Sec.-ft.*	*Feet.*	*Sec.-ft.*	*Feet.*	*Sec.-ft.*
1	1.94	160a	2.26	85	2.36	87	1.54	148	2.15	455	2.98	1,266
2	1.98	159	2.25	85	2.31	86	1.52	155	3.50	1,960	3.24	1,602
3	2.02	158	2.28	85	2.28	86	1.57	162	3.15	1,485	3.38	1,792
4	2.02	157	2.29	85	2.26	84	1.59	169	2.95	1,230	3.54	2,016
5	2.04	156	2.30	86	2.23	84	1.63	173a	2.85	1,115	3.32	1,708
6	2.08	153	2.30	87	2.18	84	1.68	172	2.75	1,005	3.18	1,524
7	2.08	151	2.30	87	2.18	84	1.63	152	2.57	810	3.10	1,420
8	2.10	149	2.30	87	2.08	84	1.58	133	2.60	840	2.98	1,266
9	2.10	146	2.31	87	2.03	84	1.64	156	3.02	1,316	2.82	1,082
10	2.11	143	2.31	88	1.88	84	1.64	156	3.14	1,472	2.75	1,005
11	2.13	140	2.33	90	1.75	84	1.69	176	2.95	1,230	2.75	1,005
12	2.14	136	2.35	91	1.84	85	1.74	200	2.85	1,115	2.75	1,005
13	2.14	133	2.36	92	1.84	86	1.79	225	2.93	1,206	2.85	1,115
14	2.16	129	2.35	94	1.85	86	2.25	530	2.97	1,254	3.05	1,355
15	2.18	123	2.34	96	1.87	86	2.24	422	3.25	1,615	3.05	1,355
16	2.18	120	2.35	97	1.88	87	2.22	506	.31	1,694	3.07	1,381
17	2.16	116	2.36	98	1.80	89	2.19	483	.37	1,778	3.09	1,407
18	2.18	112	2.39	98	1.75	90	2.16	462	.36	1,764	3.07	1,381
19	2.21	109	2.39	95	1.70	92	2.14	448	.27	1,641	3.00	1,290
20	2.21	105	2.39	95	1.65	95	2.09	413	3.25	1,615	2.95	1,230
21	2.21	102	2.37	93	1.60	98	2.18	476	3.13	1,459	2.85	1,115
22	2.19	100	2.37	92	1.60	100	2.32	586	3.06	1,368	2.78	1,038
23	2.19	98	2.37	90	1.61	102	2.26	538	3.02	1,316	2.61	851
24	2.19	96	2.39	90	1.61	106	2.25	530	3.19	1,537	2.60	840
25	2.20	94	2.41	89	1.59	110	2.19	483	3.32	1,708	2.74	994
26	2.22	92	2.42	88	1.57	114	2.29	562	3.19	1,537	3.08	1,394
27	2.23	90	2.42	87	1.56	118	2.32	586	3.10	1,420	2.99	1,278
28	2.25	90	2.40	87	1.56	123	2.36	618	3.00	1,290	2.98	1,266
29	2.26	89			1.56	128	2.39	642	2.97	1,254	2.92	1,194
30	2.26	88			1.56	135	2.45	695	2.82	1,082	2.82	1,082
31	2.27	86			1.54	142			2.88	1,148		

a to a Ice conditions.

5 GEORGE V, A. 1915

DAILY GAUGE HEIGHT AND DISCHARGE of Oldman River near Cowley, for 1914.—*Concluded.*

. DAY.	July.		August.		September.		October.		November.		December.	
	Gauge Height.	Dis- charge.	Gauge Height.	Dis- charge	Gauge Height.	Dis- charge.	Gauge Height.	Dis- charge.	Gauge Height.	Dis- charge.	Gauge Height.	Dis- charge.
	Feet.	*Sec.-ft.*	*Feet.*	*Sec.-ft.*	*Feet.*	*Sec.-ft.*	*Feet.*	*Sec.-ft.*	*Feet.*	*Sec.-ft.*	*Feet.*	*Sec.-ft.*
1............	2.75	1,005	1.91	296	1.72	190	1.74	200	2.12	434	1.98	280
2............	2 75	1,005	1.90	290	1.70	180	1.74	200	2.13	441	2.07	250
3............	2.74	994	1.90	290	1.70	180	1.78	220	2.14	448	2.40	212
4............	2.70	950	1.88	278	1.68	172	1.84	254	2.14	448	2.38	172
5............	2.72	972	1.86	266	1.68	172	1.85	260	2.14	448	2.36	153
6............	2.68	928	1.85	260	1.67	168	1.86	266	2.08	406	2.50	142
7............	2.62	862	1.85	260	1.66	164	1.86	266	2.09	413	2.90	135
8............	2.61	851	1.88	278	1.73	195	1.88	278	2.09	413	2.92	130
9............	2.51	750	1.90	290	1.70	180	1.90	290	2.00	350	2.93	128
10...:.	2.48	722	1.90	290	1.70	180	1.90	290	2.03	371	2.93	127
11...... ...	2.40	650	1.88	278	1.70	180	1.92	302	1.98	338	2.84	128
12..........	2.39	642	1.80	230	1.70	180	1.92	302	2.00	350	2.44	129
13....	2.38	634	1.78	220	1.70	180	1.92	302	2.04	378	3.25	129
14..........	2.36	618	1.76	210	1.68	172	1.94	314	1.86	266	3.55	130
15....... .	2.31	578	1.76	210	1.71	185	2.04	378	1.84	254	3.36	131
16..........	2.31	578	1.75	205	1.70	180	2.25	530	2.30	340a	3.33	132
17..........	2.26	538	1.85	260	1.70	180	2.75	1,005	2.18	374	3.27	134
18..........	2.20	490	2.20	490	1.73	195	2.78	1,038	2.06	380	3.77	136
19	2.18	476	1.99	344	1.76	210	2.72	972	2.00	385	3.18	138
20..........	2.15	455	1.98	338	1.86	266	2.58	820	2.14	388	3.26	141
21..........	2.15	455	1.92	302	1.90	290	2.40	650	2.12	389	3.59	143
22.	2.12	434	1.86	266	1.84	254	2.32	586	2.02	388	3.63	146
23..........	2.10	420	1.90	290	1.88	278	2.30	570	2.00	386	3.60	149
24..........	2.06	392	1.92	302	1.80	230	2.24	522	2.02	382	3.41	152
25..........	2.05	385	1.90	290	1.80	230	2.20	490	2.10	379	3.41	155
26..........	2.02	364	1.86	266	1.79	225	2.16	462	2.11	370	3.49	158
27..........	2.00	350	1.81	236	1.79	225	2.14	448	2.16	359	3.52	161
28..........	1.96	326	1.77	215	1.78	220	2.12	434	2.03	343	3.42	164
29..........	1.94	314	1.76	210	1.76	210	2.10	420	2.03	324	3.64	168
30....	1.94	314	1.78	220	1.74	200	2.10	420	2.03	304	3.62	172
31..........	1.90	290	1.75	205	....	....	2.10	420	....	....	3.53	175a

a to *a* Ice conditions.

MONTHLY DISCHARGE of Oldman River near Cowley, for 1914.

(Drainage area 800 square miles.)

MONTH.	DISCHARGE IN SECOND-FEET.				RUN-OFF.	
	Maximum.	Minimum.	Mean.	Per square Mile.	Depth in inches on Drainage Area.	Total in Acre-feet.
January............	160	86	122	0.152	0.18	7,501
February....	98	85	90	0.112	0.12	4,998
March............	142	84	97	0.121	0.14	5,964
April.......................... ...	695	133	372	0.465	0.52	22,136
May...........................	1,960	455	1,346	1.680	1.94	82,743
June..	2,016	840	1,275	1.590	1.77	75,850
July.....	1,005	290	605	0.756	0.87	37,200
August........	490	205	270	0.338	0.39	16,602
September.....	290	164	202	0.252	0 28	12,020
October....	1,038	200	449	0.561	0.65	27,608
November.................	448	254	375	0.469	0.52	22,314
December.....	280	127	155	0.194	0.22	9,531
The year.........	....	....	....	....	7.60	324,467

Gauging Station on Oldman River near Cowley, Alberta.　Taken by G. H. Whyte.

Gauging Station on Oldman River near Macleod, Alberta.　Taken by G. H. Whyte.

CANYON CREEK NEAR MOUNTAIN MILL.

Location.—On the NE. ¼ Sec. 14, Tp. 6, Rge. 2, W. 5th Mer.
Records available.—April 10, 1911, to October 31, 1914. Discharge measurements from 1910.
Gauge.—Vertical staff.
Bench-mark.—Spike in tree on left bank; elevation, 14.49 feet above zero of gauge.
Channel.—Clean gravel and rock.
Discharge measurements.—During high stages made at traffic bridge one-half mile upstream; at ordinary stages by wading below the gauge.
Winter flow.—Station not maintained during the winter.
Observer.—G. Biron.

DISCHARGE MEASUREMENTS of Canyon Creek near Mountain Mill, in 1914.

Date.	Engineer.	Width.	Area of Section.	Mean Velocity.	Gauge Height.	Discharge.
		Feet.	*Sq. ft.*	*Ft. per sec.*	*Feet.*	*Sec.-ft.*
Mar. 1............	F. R. Burfield.............	5.0	4.65	0.535	4.34	2.5
April 15............	J. E. Caughey.............	22.5	23.00	1.750	4.97	40.2
April 30............	do	22.5	19.30	1.520	4.79	29.5
May 18............	do	22.0	17.30	1.310	4.67	22.7
June 8............	do	20.0	12.70	0.933	4.48	11.8
June 27............	do	22.0	16.00	1.200	4.61	19.2
July 14............	do	18.0	8.20	0.821	4.22	6.7
July 29............	do ·	8.0	4.20	0.690	4.05	2.9
Aug. 10............	do	5.0	2.36	1.090	4.03	2.5
Aug. 27............	do	5.0	2.30	1.390	4.10	3.2
Sept. 11............	do	5.0	2.20	1.210	4.05	2.7
Sept. 24............	do	5.0	2.30	1.340	4.05	3.1
Oct. 15............	do	11.0	11.60	2.660	4.77	31.0
Nov. 5............	do	9.0	6.50	2.010	4.51	13.1

DAILY GAUGE HEIGHT AND DISCHARGE of Canyon Creek near Mountain Mill, for 1914.

DAY.	March.		April.		May.		June.	
	Gauge Height.	Discharge.	Gauge Height.	Discharge.	Gauge Height.	Discharge.	Gauge Height.	Discharge.
	Feet.	*Sec.-ft.*	*Feet.*	*Sec.-ft.*	*Feet.*	*Sec.-ft.*	*Feet.*	*Sec.-ft.*
1....................	....	....	4.37	4.4	4.77	28.0	4.49	14.6
2....................	....	....	4.28	3.1	4.78	28.0	4.47	13.8
3....................	....	....	4.27	3.3	4.80	29.0	4.44	12.8
4....................	....	....	4.28	3.8	4.83	31.0	4.44	12.8
5....................	....	....	4.32	5.1	4.84	31.0	4.44	12.8
6....................	....	....	4.34	5.9	4.79	28.0	4.47	13.8
7....................	....	....	4.36	6.9	4.77	28.0	4.45	13.2
8....................	....	....	4.36	7.4	4.75	26.0	4.40	11.4
9....................	....	....	4.40	9.0	4.76	27.0	4.41	11.8
10....................	....	....	4.51	13.2	4.77	28.0	4.38	10.8
11....................	....	....	4.52	14.2	4.77	28.0	4.38	10.8
12....................	....	....	4.84	30.0a	4.80	29.0	4.34	9.6
13....................	....	....	4.84	31.0	4.79	28.0	4.38	10.8
14....................	....	....	4.89	34.0	4.76	27.0	4.53	16.1
15....................	....	....	4.93	37.0	4.73	26.0	4.51	15.3
16....................	....	....	4.90	35.0	4.71	24.0	4.47	13.8
17....................	3.99	1.00a	4.86	33.0	4.70	24.0	4.41	11.8
18....................	4.06	1.00	4.83	31.0	4.67	22.0	4.35	9.9
19....................	4.07	1.00	4.81	30.0	4.67	22.0	4.33	9.3
20....................	4.13	1.00	5.03	45.0	4.65	22.0	4.32	9.0
21....................	4.14	1.00	4.93	37.0	4.64	21.0	4.29	8.2
22....................	4.24	1.00	4.94	38.0	4.62	20.0	4.29	8.2
23....................	4.25	1.00	4.89	34.0	4.61	20.0	4.26	7.4
24....................	4.47	4.80	4.90	35.0	4.60	19.0	4.27	7.6
25....................	4.22	1.10	4.85	32.0	4.61	20.0	4.54	16.5
26....................	4.28	1.50	4.82	30.0	4.48	14.2	4.82	30.0
27....................	4.43	4.00	4.80	29.0	4.56	17.4	4.61	19.5
28....................	4.35	2.60	4.79	28.0	4.58	18.2	4.52	15.7
29....................	4.35	3.00	4.82	30.0	4.52	15.7	4.36	10.2
30....................	4.35	3.30	4.73	28.0	4.52	15.7	4.43	12.4
31....................	4.36	3.80	....	....	4.51	15.3	....	....

a to a Ice conditions.

5 GEORGE V, A. 1915

DAILY GAUGE HEIGHT AND DISCHARGE of Canyon Creek near Mountain Mill, for 1914.

—Concluded.

DAY.	July.		August.		September.		October.	
	Gauge Height.	Dis- charge.	Gauge Height.	Dis- charge.	Gauge Height.	Dis- charge.	Gauge Height.	Dis- charge.
	Feet.	*Sec.-ft.*	*Feet.*	*Sec.-ft.*	*Feet.*	*Sec.-ft.*	*Feet.*	*Sec.-ft.*
1	4.41	11.8	4.01	2.30	4.08	3.5	4.10	3.8
2	4.38	10.8	3.97	1.60	4.08	3.5	4.12	4.2
3	4.34	9.6	3.97	1.60	4.07	3.3	4.15	4.8
4	4.31	8.7	3.96	1.50	4.05	3.0	4.19	5.7
5	4.36	10.2	3.95	1.40	4.06	3.1	4.16	5.1
6	4.32	9.0	3.95	1.40	4.05	3.0	4.16	5.1
7	4.31	8.7	3.95	1.40	4.05	3.0	4.20	5.9
8	4.28	7.9	3.95	1.40	4.10	3.8	4.17	5.3
9	4.25	7.2	4.00	2.10	4.06	3.1	4.20	5.9
10	4.24	6.9	4.04	2.80	4.06	3.1	4.24	6.9
11	4.24	6.9	3.98	1.80	4.05	3.0	4.23	6.6
12	4.22	6.4	3.99	2.00	4.06	3.1	4.24	6.9
13	4.22	6.4	4.02	2.40	4.08	3.5	4.28	7.9
14	4.22	6.4	3.95	1.40	4.06	3.1	4.48	14.2
15	4.21	6.2	3.95	1.40	4.11	4.0	4.77	28.0
16	4.19	5.7	3.94	1.20	4.10	3.8	4.89	34.0
17	4.18	5.5	4.30	8.40	4.11	4.0	4.87	33.0
18	4.18	5.5	4.25	7.20	4.08	3.5	4.88	34.0
19	4.15	4.8	4.11	4.00	4.06	3.1	4.80	29.0
20	4.13	4.4	4.06	3.10	4.08	3.5	4.74	26.0
21	4.12	4.2	4.10	3.80	4.10	3.8	4.70	24.0
22	4.12	4.2	4.05	3.00	4.09	3.6	4.64	21.0
23	4.11	4.0	4.22	6.40	4.09	3.6	4.51	15.3
24	4.10	3.8	4.18	5.50	4.08	3.5	4.59	18.6
25	4.09	3.6	4.16	5.10	4.07	3.3	4.57	17.8
26	4.08	3.5	4.12	4.20	4.06	3.1	4.56	17.4
27	4.07	3.3	4.10	3.80	4.07	3.3	4.54	16.5
28	4.05	3.0	4.10	3.80	4.09	3.6	4.54	16.5
29	4.04	2.8	4.10	3.80	4.10	3.8	4.52	15.7
30	4.03	2.6	4.09	3.60	4.09	3.6	4.50	14.9
31	4.03	2.6	4.09	3.60	....	....	4.49	14.6

MONTHLY DISCHARGE of Canyon Creek near Mountain Mill, for 1914.

(Drainage area 27 square miles.)

MONTH.	DISCHARGE IN SECOND-FEET.				RUN-OFF.	
	Maximum.	Minimum	Mean.	Per square Mile.	Depth in inches on Drainage Area.	Total in Acre-feet.
March (17-31)	4.8	1.00	2.1	0.078	0.04	62
April	45.0	3.10	23.0	0.852	0.95	1,369
May	31.0	14.20	24.0	0.889	1.02	1,476
June	30.0	7.40	12.7	0.470	0.52	756
July	11.8	2.60	6.0	0.222	0.26	369
August	8.4	1.20	3.1	0.115	0.13	191
September	4.0	3.00	3.4	0.126	0.14	202
October	34.0	3.80	15.0	0.556	0.64	922
The period	....	....	....	....	3.70	5,347

MILL CREEK NEAR MOUNTAIN MILL.

Location.—On the SW. ¼ Sec. 18, Tp. 6, Rge. 1, W. 5th Mer.
Records available.—July 7, 1910, to October 31, 1914.
Gauge.—Vertical staff; elevation of zero maintained at 93.41 feet since establishment.
Bench-mark.—Permanent iron bench-mark; assumed elevation, 100 00 feet.
Channel.—Coarse gravel.
Discharge measurements.—By wading at ordinary stages, and from bridge at flood stages.
Winter flow.—Station not maintained during the winter.
Observer.—K. B. Parsons.

DISCHARGE MEASUREMENTS of Mill Creek near Mountain Mill, in 1914.

Date.	Engineer.	Width.	Area of Section.	Mean Velocity.	Gauge Height.	Discharge.
		Feet.	*Sq. ft.*	*Ft. per sec.*	*Feet.*	*Sec.-ft.*
Mar. 28	F. R. Burfield	14	12.5	1.78	.....*a*	22
April 15	J E. Caughey	44	48.0	2.79	2.20	134
April 30	do	43	49.2	2.86	2.25	141
April 18	do	59	88.1	3.49	2.77	307
June 8	do	45	50.4	3.11	2.37	156
June 27	do	48	64.5	3.71	2.66	239
July 14	do	42	39.0	2.47	2.07	96
July 29	do	36	25.5	1.67	1.85	42
Aug. 10	do	36	23.6	1.33	1.75	31
Aug. 27	do	39	30.2	2.02	1.95	61
Sept. 11	do	36	24.0	1.57	1.78	38
Sept. 24	do	39	30.6	2.00	1.93	62
Nov. 5	do	44	42.4	2.49	2.15	106

a Solid ice about the gauge.

DAILY GAUGE HEIGHT AND DISCHARGE of Mill Creek near Mountain Mill, for 1914.

DAY.	April.		May.		June.	
	Gauge Height.	Dis-charge.	Gauge Height.	Dis-charge.	Gauge Height.	Dis-charge.
	Feet.	*Sec.-ft.*	*Feet.*	*Sec.-ft.*	*Feet.*	*Sec.-ft.*
1			2.42	179	2.53	211
2			2.55	217	2.71	267
3			2.56	220	2.92	336
4			2.61	235	2.93	339
5			2.59	229	2.85	312
6			2.49	199	2.60	232
7			2.45	188	2.42	179
8			2.45	188	2.37	165
9			2.57	223	2.26	136
10			2.74	277	2.24	130
11			2.70	264	2.22	125
12			2.62	238	2.45	188
13	2.13	104	2.60	232	2.62	238
14	2.14	106	2.73	274	2.85	312
15	2.19	118	2.78	290	2.54	214
16	2.16	111	2.83	306	2.55	217
17	2.05	86	2.83	306	2.53	211
18	2.01	77	2.74	277	2.57	223
19	2.09	95	2.69	261	2.44	185
20	2.38	168	2.63	242	2.37	165
21	2.33	154	2.61	235	2.32	151
22	2.23	128	2.58	226	2.28	141
23	2.30	146	2.56	220	2.22	125
24	2.35	160	2.53	211	2.17	113
25	2.35	160	2.50	202	2.24	130
26	2.36	162	2.49	199	2.95	346
27	2.36	162	2.46	190	2.66	251
28	2.38	168	2.41	176	2.55	217
29	2.25	133	2.38	168	2.48	196
30	2.27	138	2.34	157	2.45	188
31			2.44	185		

5 GEORGE V, A. 1915

DAILY GAUGE HEIGHT AND DISCHARGE of Mill Creek near Mountain Mill, for 1914.
—*Concluded.*

DAY.	July.		August.		September.		October.		November.	
	Gauge Height.	Dis-charge.	Gauge Height.	Dis-charge.	Gauge Height.	Dis-charge.	Gauge Height.	Dis-charge.	Gauge Height.	Dis-charge.
	Feet.	*Sec.-ft.*	*Feet.*	*Sec.-ft.*	*Feet.*	*Sec.-ft.*	*Feet.*	*Sec.-ft.*	*Feet.*	*Sec.-ft.*
1	2.35	160	1.77	35	1.85	48	1.87	51	2.15	108
2	2.34	157	1.75	32	1.85	48	1.89	54	2.15	108
3	2.27	138	1.74	31	1.85	48	1.89	54	2.30	146
4	2.26	136	1.74	31	1.85	48	1.93	62	....	....
5	2.25	133	1.73	30	1.85	48	1.95	66		
6	2.25	133	1.73	30	1.85	48	1.86	49		
7	2.23	128	1.72	29	1.85	48	1.84	46		
8	2.16	111	1.72	29	1.85	48	1.90	56		
9	2.15	108	1.71	27	1.83	44	1.95	66		
10	2.12	102	1.75	32	1.80	39	2.00	75		
11	2.10	97	1.74	31	1.78	36	2.00	75		
12	2.07	90	1.80	39	1.77	35	1.96	67		
13	2.07	90	1.80	39	1.76	34	2.04	84		
14	2.06	88	1.71	27	1.75	32	2.78	290		
15	2.04	84	1.71	27	1.83	44	3.08	389		
16	2.03	82	2.26	136	1.85	48	3.12	403		
17	2.02	79	2.45	188	1.85	48	3.15	413		
18	2.01	77	2.20	120	1.87	51	2.90	329		
19	1.99	73	2.10	97	1.90	56	2.70	264		
20	1.97	69	2.00	75	1.92	60	2.60	232		
21	1.94	64	2.10	97	1.94	64	2.50	202		
22	1.91	58	2.08	93	1.95	66	2.40	173		
23	1.90	56	2.10	97	1.94	64	2.35	160		
24	1.90	56	2.00	75	1.94	64	2.30	146		
25	1.88	53	1.97	69	1.92	60	2.30	146		
26	1.87	51	1.95	66	1.87	51	2.30	146		
27	1.86	49	1.95	66	1.85	48	2.30	146		
28	1.85	48	1.95	66	1.83	44	2.23	128		
29	1.83	44	1.91	58	1.82	42	3.15	413		
30	1.82	42	1.90	56	1.81	41	2.15	108		
31	1.80	39	1.89	54	....	....	2.22	125		

MONTHLY DISCHARGE of Mill Creek near Mountain Mill, for 1914.
(Drainage area 64 square miles.)

MONTH.	DISCHARGE IN SECOND-FEET.				RUN-OFF.	
	Maximum.	Minimum.	Mean.	Per square Mile.	Depth in inches on Drainage Area.	Total in Acre-feet.
April (13-30)	168	77	132	2.06	1.38	4,713
May	306	157	226	3.53	4.07	13,896
June	346	113	208	3.25	3.63	12,377
July	160	39	87	1.36	1.57	5,349
August	188	27	61	0.95	1.10	3,751
September	66	32	48	0.75	0.84	2,856
October	413	46	162	2.53	2.92	9,961
November (1-3)	146	108	121	1.89	0.21	720
The period	....	....	....	....	15.72	53,623

CASTLE (SOUTH FORK) RIVER NEAR COWLEY.

Location.—On the SW. ¼ Sec. 2, Tp. 7, Rge. 1, W. 5th Mer., at G. W. Buchanan's ranch.
Records available.—August 5, 1909, to December 31 1914. Discharge measurements from 1908.
Gauge.—Vertical staff; elevation of zero maintained at 92.34 feet since establishment.
Bench-mark.—Permanent iron bench-mark; assumed elevation, 100.00 feet.
Channel.—Coarse gravel, and not liable to shift.
Discharge measurements.—Made from the bridge at all stages.
Observer.—G. W. Buchanan.

SESSIONAL PAPER No. 25c

DISCHARGE MEASUREMENTS of Castle (South fork) River near Cowley, in 1914.

Date.	Engineer.	Width.	Area of Section.	Mean Velocity.	Gauge Height.	Discharge.
		Feet.	Sq. ft.	Ft. per sec.	Feet.	Sec.-ft.
Jan. 16	R. Palmer	80	176	0.966	3.20	171
Feb. 25	E. W. W. Hughes	74	301	0.658	3.43	198
Mar. 12	F. R. Burfield	75	142	0.885	2.90	126
Mar. 25	do				3.90	a
April 13	J. E. Caughey	100	225	2.480	2.69	557
May 1	do	150	317	3.300	3.21	1,047
May 15	do	213	518	4.420	4.00	2,287
June 3	do	207	565	4.790	4.46	2,769
June 29	do	125	342	3.420	3.40	1,168
July 11	do	110	256	2.760	2.85	705
July 27	do	78	106	3.218	2.31	340
Aug. 11	do	59	79	2.750	2.09	217
Aug. 25	do	102	217	2.360	2.53	512
Sept. 10	do	60	101	2.630	2.14	266
Sept. 26	do	98	197	2.120	2.43	419
Oct. 16	do	174	437	4.030	3.92	1,760
Nov. 4	do	105	275	2.840	2.95	781
Nov. 18	do	77	146	3.830	2.75	556
Dec. 9	do	50	86	2.660	4.75	218
Dec. 31	do	84	256	1.150	3.58	305

a On March 25 impossible to measure stream due to ice jam below gauge.

DAILY GAUGE HEIGHT AND DISCHARGE of Castle (South fork) River near Cowley, for 1914.

DAY.	January.		February.		March.		April.		May.		June.	
	Gauge Height.	Dis-charge.	Gauge Height.	Dis-charge.	Gauge Height.	Dis-charge.	Gauge Height.	Dis-charge.	Gauge Height.	Dis-charge.	Gauge Height.	Dis-charge.
	Feet.	Sec.-ft.	Feet.	Sec.-ft.	Feet.	Sec.-ft.	Feet.	Sec.-ft.	Feet.	Sec.-ft.	Feet.	Sec.-ft.
1	2.68	114a	2.72	88	2.80	190	2.78	646	3.21	1,010	3.85	1,835
1	2.67	123	2.65	94	2.75	184	2.85	695	3.59	1,457	4.15	2,292
3	2.60	132	2 70	102	2.71	177	2.90	730	4.14	2,277	4.45	2,770
4	2.60	147	2.75	112	2.70	169	2.91	738	3.99	2,045	4.55	2,930
5	2.70	162	2.80	121	2.68	163	3.16	960	3.64	1,526	4.00	2,060
6	2.85	170	2.85	130	2.70	155	3.16	960	3.49	1,327	3.80	1,760
7	2.75	180	2.85	137	2.67	149	3.07	873	3.44	1,262	3.55	1,405
8	2.65	183	2.85	144	2.65	144	3.15	950	3.39	1,199	3.50	1,340
9	2.63	185	2.90	151	2.60	139	3.15	950	3.65	1,540	3.25	1,050
10	2.63	186	2.90	157	2.53	134	3.18	980	3.70	1,610	3.25	1,050
11	2.60	185	2.95	163	2.40	131	3.13	1,030	3.75	1,685	3.20	1,000
12	2.65	184	2.97	167	2.35	127	3.08	882	3.70	1,610	3.20	1,000
13	2.65	182	2.95	172	2.30	123	2.84	688	3.70	1,610	3.50	1,340
14	2.67	179	2.95	176	2.25	120	2.79	653	3.80	1,760	3.90	1,910
15	2.65	176	3.00	180	2.15	117	2.89	723	3.95	1,985	3.85	1,835
16	2.60	171	3.03	183	2.08	114	2.94	762	4.15	2,292	3.70	1,610
17	2.59	168	3.05	186	2.00	113	2.94	762	4.25	2,450	3.80	1,760
18	2.57	162	3.00	188	1.90	110	2.88	716	4.35	2,610	3.80	1,760
19	2.50	155	2.96	192	1.88	108	3.14	940	4.25	2,450	3.80	1,760
20	2.45	148	2.95	193	1.85	107	3.54	1,392	4.00	2,060	3.80	1,760
21	2.50	140	2.99	195	1.87	105	3.39	1,199	3.90	1,910	3.45	1,275
22	2.55	128	3.00	196	1.85	105	3.34	1,144	3.80	1,760	3.30	1,100
23	2.60	118	2.99	197	1.85	106	3.21	1,010	3.75	1,685	3.19	990
24	2.68	108	2.98	198	1.80	107	3.24	1,040	4.10	2,215	3.09	891
25	2.70	95	2.88	199	3.28	109	3.29	1,090	4.25	2,450	3.44	1,262
26	2.75	88	2.93	198	3.25	112	3.24	1,040	3.95	1,985	3.69	1,596
27	2.70	83	2.90	195	3.30	115	3.19	990	3.75	1,685	3.54	1,392
28	2.70	82	2.85	193	3.23	120	3.14	940	3.70	1,610	3.44	1,262
29	2.70	82			3.20	128	3.09	891	3.50	1,340	3.39	1,199
30	2.72	83			3.15	250	3.04	846	3.50	1,340	3.34	1,144
31	2.75	84			2.90	450a			3.60	1,470		

a to a Ice conditions.

5 GEORGE V. A. 1915

DAILY GAUGE HEIGHT AND DISCHARGE of Castle (South fork) River near Cowley, for 1914.
—Concluded.

DAY.	July.		August.		September.		October.		November.		December.	
	Gauge Height.	Dis- charge.	Gauge Height	Dis- charge.	Gauge Height.	Dis- charge.	Gauge Height.	Dis- charge.	Gauge Height.	Dis- charge.	Gauge Height.	Dis- charge.
	Feet.	*Sec.-ft.*	*Feet.*	*Sec.-ft.*	*Feet.*	*Sec.-ft.*	*Feet.*	*Sec.-ft.*	*Feet.*	*Sec.-ft.*	*Feet.*	*Sec.-ft.*
1...........	3.24	1,040	2.10	250	2.20	300	2.30	350	2.88	716	2.55	490
2...........	3.19	990	2 10	250	2.15	275	2.30	350	2.98	794	2.55	490
3...........	3.14	940	2 15	275	2.10	250	2.30	350	2.97	786	2.40	400
4...........	3.09	891	2.13	265	2.10	250	2 30	350	2.95	770	2.30	350
5...........	3.04	846	2.13	265	2.10	250	2.33	365	3.02	828	2.35	375
6...........	3.04	846	2.10	250	2.10	250	2.35	375	3.00	810	2.40	400
7...........	2.97	786	2.10	250	2.10	250	2.35	375	2.95	770	2.45	430
8...........	2.94	762	2.10	250	2.13	265	2.42	412	2.90	730	3.00	226b
9...........	2.94	762	2.10	250	2.10	250	2.40	400	2.85	695	4.70	218
10........	2.89	723	2.10	250	2.10	250	2.45	430	2.83	681	3.99	218
11...........	2.85	695	2.10	250	2.10	250	2.45	430	2.80	660	3.69	220
12...........	2.80	660	2.10	250	2.10	250	2.48	448	2.75	625	3.69	223
13...........	2.78	646	2.10	250	2.10	250	2.48	448	2.70	590	3.51	226
14...........	2.75	625	2.05	230	2.10	250	3.20	1,000	2.65	555	3.64	231
15...........	2.75	625	2.03	222	2.10	250	3.45	1,275	2.65	555a	3.79	235
16...........	2.78	646	2.00	210	2.10	250	3.80	1,760	2.60	555	3.44	240
17...........	2.62	534	2.50	460	2.10	250	4.00	2,060	2.78	556	3.59	245
18...........	2.58	508	3.00	810	2.10	250	4.05	2,138	2.75	556	3.34	250
19...........	2.50	460	2.75	625	2.16	280	3.95	1,985	2.70	540	3.59	256
20...........	2.50	460	2.55	490	2.25	325	3.95	1,985	2.65	522a	3.64	262
21...........	2.45	430	2.50	460	2.60	520	3.78	1,730	2.60	510	3.73	269
22...........	2.45	430	2.45	430	2.53	478	3.73	1,655	2.55	490	3.81	274
23...........	2.40	400	2.55	490	2.45	430	3.58	1,444	2.52	472	3.78	280
24...........	2.40	400	2.60	520	2.45	430	3.45	1,275	2.48	448	3.83	286
25...........	2.35	375	2.53	478	2.43	418	3.30	1,100	2.55	490	3.88	293
26........	2.31	355	2.43	418	2.40	400	3.15	950	2.55	490	3.81	297
27........	2.31	355	2.40	400	2.35	375	2.98	794	2.55	490	3.96	300
28...........	2.29	345	2.35	375	2.35	375	2.85	695	2.55	490	3.88	303
29........	2.25	325	2.28	340	2.30	350	2.85	695	2.55	490	3.80	305
30...........	2.25	325	2.25	325	2.30	350	2.80	660	2.55	490	3.75	305
31...........	2.20	300	2.25	325	......	......	2.80	660	......	......	3.56	305b

a to a Ice conditions.
b to b Ice conditions.

MONTHLY DISCHARGE of Castle (South fork) River, near Cowley, for 1914.

(Drainage area 348 square miles.)

MONTH.	DISCHARGE IN SECOND-*FEET.*				RUN-OFF.	
	Maximum	Minimum	Mean.	Per square Mile.	Depth in inches on Drainage Area.	Total in Acre-feet.
January.............................	186	82	141	0.405	0.47	8,670
February............................	199	88	164	0.471	0.49	9,108
March...............................	450	105	145	0.416	0.48	8,916
April.......	1,392	646	907	2.610	2.91	53,970
May.................................	2,610	1,010	1,781	5.120	5.90	109,483
June.......	2,930	891	1,545	4.440	4.95	91,912
July.........	1,040	300	596	1.710	1.97	36,647
August.	810	210	352	1.010	1.16	21,644
September....	520	250	311	0.894	1.00	18,506
October...	2,138	350	934	2.680	3.09	57,429
November.	828	448	605	1.740	1.94	36,000
December.......	490	218	297	0.853	0.98	18,262
The year.............................	....	....	....	....	25 34	470,547

SESSIONAL PAPER No. 25c

PINCHER CREEK AT PINCHER CREEK.

Location.—On the SW. ¼ Sec. 23, Tp. 6, Rge. 30, W. 4th Mer., in the town of Pincher Creek.
Records available.—April 1, 1910, to October 31, 1914. Discharge measurements from 1906.
Gauge.—Vertical staff; elevation of zero maintained at 86.35 feet since establishment.
Bench-mark.—On right concrete abutment of bridge; assumed elevation, 100.00 feet.
Channel.—Rock, gravel and gumbo.
Discharge measurements.—From bridge and by wading.
Winter flow.—Station not maintained during the winter.
Observer.—Hugh Bertles.

DISCHARGE MEASUREMENTS of Pincher Creek at Pincher Creek, in 1914.

Date.	Engineer.	Width.	Area of Section.	Mean Velocity.	Gauge Height.	Discharge.
		Feet.	Sq. ft.	Ft. per sec.	Feet.	Sec.-ft.
Mar. 30	F. R Burfield	28	13.0	1.030	2.36	13.3
April 16	J. E. Caughey	46	43.0	2.070	2.83	89.0
May 1	do	45	40.7	1.870	2.74	76.0
May 15	do	51	53.6	2.534	3.00	136.0
June 3	do	48	46.9	2.010	2.85	94.0
June 29	do	46	41.0	1.863	2.76	76.0
July 11	do	36	22.2	1.145	2.35	25.0
July 27	do	26	12.4	0.767	2.14	9.5
Aug. 13	do	24	10.0	0.702	2.05	7.0
Aug. 25	do	46	30.3	1.240	2.45	38.0
Sept. 10	do	26	13.4	0.980	2.15	13.1
Sept. 26	do	37	19.4	1.290	2.29	25.0
Nov. 4	do	38	24.3	1.620	2.50	39.0

DAILY GAUGE HEIGHT AND DISCHARGE of Pincher Creek at Pincher Creek, for 1914.

DAY.	March.		April.		May.		June.	
	Gauge Height.	Dis-charge.	Gauge Height.	Dis-charge.	Gauge Height.	Dis-charge.	Gauge Height.	Dis-charge.
	Feet.	Sec.-ft.	Feet.	Sec.-ft.	Feet.	Sec.-ft.	Feet.	Sec.-ft.
1			2.18	7.0	2.70	68	2.65	60
2			2.17	7.0	2.85	96	2.68	65
3			2.16	7.2	2.93	116	2.78	82
4			2.22	9.6	2.90	108	2.85	96
5			2.66	50.0	2.80	85	2.80	85
6			2.62	46.0	2.80	85	2.75	76
7			2.57	43.0	2.80	85	2.65	60
8			2.44	30.0	2.80	85	2.60	53
9			2.57	46.0	2.95	122	2.54	45
10			2.57	48.0a	3.20	198	2.54	45
11			2.64	59.0	3.00	136	2.52	43
12	2.76	52.0a	2.75	76.0	2.95	122	2.53	44
13	2.73	48.0	2.75	76.0	2.93	116	2.55	46
14	2.60	33.0	2.75	76.0	2.95	122	2.86	99
15	2.45	19.6	2.75	76.0	2.96	125	2.80	85
16	2.27	8.5	2.75	76.0	2.98	130	2.79	83
17	2.25	8.0	2.65	60.0	2.96	125	2.67	64
18	2.42	17.5	2.60	53.0	2.94	119	2.66	62
19	2.29	9.6	2.64	59.0	2.91	111	2.66	62
20	2.27	8.5	2.92	114.0	2.88	103	2.62	56
21	2.32	11.2	2.78	82.0	2.84	94	2.57	49
22	2.22	7.2	2.78	82.0	2.80	85	2.53	44
23	2.27	8.5	2.75	76.0	2.77	80	2.52	43
24	2.22	7.2	2.80	85.0	2.82	90	2.52	43
25	2.32	11.2	2.75	76.0	2.84	94	3.04	148
26		11.6b	2.75	76.0	2.80	85	2.98	130
27		12.1	2.65	60.0	2.75	76	2.82	90
28		12.5	2.70	68.0	2.70	68	2.77	80
29		13.0b	2.65	60.0	2.65	60	2.72	71
30	2.36	13.4	2.65	60.0	2.62	56	2.67	64
31	2.57	31.0			2.63	58		

a to a Ice conditions.
b to b Discharges interpolated.

5 GEORGE V, A. 1915

DAILY GAUGE HEIGHT AND DISCHARGE of Pincher Creek at Pincher Creek, for 1914.
—Concluded.

DAY.	July.		August.		September.		October.	
	Gauge Height.	Dis- charge.	Gauge Height.	Dis- charge.	Gauge Height.	Dis- charge.	Gauge Height.	Dis- charge.
	Feet.	*Sec.-ft.*	*Feet.*	*Sec.-ft.*	*Feet.*	*Sec.-ft.*	*Feet.*	*Sec.-ft.*
1	2.62	56.0	2.07	7.8	2.26	18.2	2.25	17.5
2	2.62	56.0	2.05	7.2	2.26	18.2	2.25	17.5
3	2.62	56.0	2.03	6.8	2.24	16.8	2.35	26.0
4	2.62	56.0	2.02	6.5	2.21	14.7	2.35	26.0
5	2.72	71.0	2.01	6.2	2.21	14.7	2.35	26.0
6	2.67	64.0	2.01	6.2	2.21	14.7	2.35	26.0
7	2.62	56.0	2.01	6.2	2.21	14.7	2.33	26.0
8	2.45	35.0	2.01	6.2	2.24	16.8	2.35	26.0
9	2.40	30.0	2.08	8.0	2.21	14.7	2.50	40.0
10	2.39	29.0	2.06	7.5	2.15	11.2	2.50	40.0
11	2.36	26.0	2.04	7.0	2.15	11.2	2.50	40.0
12	2.35	26.0	2.08	8.0	2.20	14.0	2.45	35.0
13	2.37	27.0	2.06	7.5	2.18	12.9	2.43	33.0
14	2.37	27.0	2.04	7.0	2.15	11.2	3.22	204.0
15	2.36	26.0	2.01	6.2	2.25	17.5	3.23	207.0
16	2.32	23.0	2.01	6.2	2.25	17.5	3.25	214.0
17	2.30	21.0	2.37	27.0	2.25	17.5	3.25	214.0
18	2.27	18.9	2.97	128.0	2.30	21.0	3.10	167.0
19	2.25	17.5	2.55	46.0	2.35	26.0	3.00	136.0
20	2.23	16.1	2.47	37.0	2.35	26.0	2.95	122.0
21	2.22	15.4	2.41	31.0	2.35	26.0	2.85	96.0
22	2.22	15.4	2.36	26.0	2.35	26.0	2.75	76.0
23	2.21	14.7	2.51	41.0	2.32	23.0	2.68	65.0
24	2.21	14.7	2.43	33.0	2.30	21.0	2.65	65.0
25	2.20	14.0	2.43	33.0	2.30	21.0	2.60	53.0
26	2.17	12.4	2.37	27.0	2.30	21.0	2.57	49.0
27	2.15	11.2	2.35	26.0	2.28	19.6	2.53	44.0
28	2.14	10.7	2.35	26.0	2.25	17.5	2.50	40.0
29	2.12	9.6	2.29	20.0	2.25	17.5	2.50	40.0
30	2.12	9.6	2.29	20.0	2.25	17.5	2.47	37.0
31	2.10	8.5	2.29	20.0	....	....	2.45	35.0

MONTHLY DISCHARGE of Pincher Creek at Pincher Creek, for 1914.

(Drainage area 50 square miles.)

MONTH.	DISCHARGE IN SECOND-FEET.				RUN-OFF.	
	Maximum.	Minimum	Mean.	Per square Mile.	Depth in inches on Drainage Area.	Total in Acre-feet.
March (12-31)	52	7.2	17.2	0.344	0.26	682
April	114	7.0	58.0	1.160	1.29	3,451
May	198	56.0	100.0	2.000	2.31	6,149
June	148	43.0	69.0	1.380	1.54	4,106
July	71	8.5	28.0	0.560	0.65	1,722
August	128	6.2	21.0	0.420	0.48	1,291
September	26	11.2	18.0	0.360	0.40	1,071
October	214	17.5	73.0	1.460	1.68	4,489
The period	....	....	....	....	8.61	22,961

SESSIONAL PAPER No. 25c

OLDMAN RIVER NEAR MACLEOD.

Location.—On the NW. ¼ Sec. 10, Tp. 9, Rge. 26, W. 4th Mer., at the traffic bridge.
Records available.—July 10, 1910, to December 31, 1914.
Gauge.—Vertical staff; zero of gauge maintained at 91.47 feet during 1913; 87.67 feet during 1910, 1911, 1912 and 1914.
Bench-mark.—Permanent bench-mark established on concrete pier; assumed elevation, 100 00 feet.
Channel.—Shifts slightly.
Discharge measurements.—Above from bridge.
Winter flow.—Records are obtained during the winter season 600 feet below the bridge.
Observer.—Mrs. W. A. Jackson.

DISCHARGE MEASUREMENTS of Oldman River near Macleod, in 1914.

Date.	Engineer.	Width.	Area of Section.	Mean Velocity.	Gauge Height.	Discharge.
		Feet.	*Sq. ft.*	*Ft. per sec.*	*Feet.*	*Sec.-ft.*
Jan. 20	R. Palmer	105.0	362.0	0.74	4.45	267
Feb. 14	E. W. W. Hughes	96.0	216.0	1.04	3.90	224
Feb. 28	do	95.0	238.0	1.21	3.75	288
Mar. 14	F. R. Burfield	87.0	239.0	1.81	2.95	433
Mar. 31	do	95.0	272.0	1.84	2.68	499
April 17	J. E. Caughey	115.0	510.0	4.57	4.66	2,329
May 5	do	251.0	889.0	4.43	5.73	3,939
May 21	do	250.0	1,006.0	4.73	6.22	4,765
June 16	do	247.0	871.5	4.31	5.65	3,760
June 30	do	118.0	555.3	5.30	5.18	2,941
July 15	do	106.0	417.0	3.43	4.15	1,428
July 30	do	95.0	317.0	2.28	3.12	724
Aug. 15	do	96.0	278.0	1.74	2.70	484
Aug. 28	do	98.0	326.0	2.50	3.20	813
Sept. 14	do	94.0	287.0	1.87	2.75	537
Sept. 29	do	97.0	321.0	2.45	2.86	787
Oct. 17	do	249.0	826.0	4.90	5.64	4,056
Nov. 6	do	106.0	437.0	3.82	4.24	1,669
Nov. 20	do	96.0	371.0	3.00	3.65	1,112
Dec. 11	do				4.83	.... *a*

a Impossible to gauge on account of frazil ice.

5 GEORGE V, A. 1915

DAILY GAUGE HEIGHT AND DISCHARGE of Oldman River near Macleod, for 1914.

DAY.	January.		February.		March.		April.		May.		June.	
	Gauge Height	Dis-charge.	Gauge Height.	Dis-charge.	Gauge Height.	Dis-charge	Gauge Height.	Dis-charge.	Gauge Height.	Dis-charge.	Gauge Height.	Dis-charge.
	Feet.	Sec.-ft.	Feet.	Sec.-ft.	Feet.	Sec.-ft.	Feet.	Sec.-ft.	Feet.	Sec.-ft.	Feet.	Sec.-ft.
1...........	3.00	300a	4.56	201	3.75	298	2.60	440	4.80	2,350	5.65	3,765
2...........	3.00	302	4.51	202	3.75	306	2.59	435	5.40	3,290	5.80	4,060
3...........	3.00	306	4.46	204	3.70	313	2.57	425	6.10	4,700	6.35	5,280
4...........	3.20	313	4.41	206	3.67	323	2.57	425	6 00	4,480	6.47	5,568
5...........	3.40	322	4 36	208	3.65	333	3.00	660	5.72	3,900	6.60	5,880
6...........	3.40	332	4.32	210	3.60	343	3.40	920	5.45	3,385	6.00	4,480
7...........	3.60	338	4.22	212	3.55	354	3.20	780	5.24	3,018	5.90	4,260
8...........	4.00	342	4.12	214	3.55	366	3.17	762	5.20	2,950	5.50	3,480
9...........	4.20	344	4.07	216	3.80	380	3.09	714	5.10	2,790	5.30	3,120
10...........	4.40	345	4.02	218	3.65	392	3.03	678	5.35	3,205	5.20	2,950
11...........	4.50	343	4.02	219	3.35	402	3.09	714	5.95	4,370	5.10	2,790
12...........	4.60	340	3.97	221	3.40	414	3.19	774	5.65	3,765	5.00	2,630
13...........	4.70	335	3.92	223	3.25	424	3.99	1,410	5.65	3,765	5.20	2,950
14...........	4.60	328	3.90	226	3.20	433	4.19	1,610	5.65	3,765	5.50	3,480
15...........	4.55	319	3.90	229	2.95	436a	4.34	1,774	5.75	3,960	5.70	3,860
16...........	4.50	310	3.87	233	2.60	440	4.39	1,829	6.25	5,045	5.70	3,860
17...........	4.45	300	3.87	236	2.80	540	4.69	2,197	6.40	5,400	5.75	3,960
18...........	4.30	290	3.82	240	2.80	540	4.44	1,888	6.45	5,520	5.80	4,060
19...........	4.20	280	3.81	244	2.65	465	4.24	1,664	6.40	5,400	5.75	3,960
20...........	4.45	269	3.71	247	2.60	440	4.74	2,266	6.35	5,280	5.70	3,860
21...........	4.50	258	3.76	252	2.57	425	5.09	2,774	6.24	5,022	5.55	3,575
22...........	4.55	246	3.71	256	2.55	415	4.79	2,336	5.90	4,260	5.30	3,120
23...........	4.55	233	3.61	263	2.65	465	4.79	2,336	5.85	4,160	5.18	2,918
24...........	4.60	224	3.60	267	2.70	490	5.29	3,103	5 93	4,326	5.00	2,630
25...........	4.60	218	3.65	273	2.55	415	5.49	3,461	6.18	4,884	5.00	2,630
26...........	4.60	212	3.68	277	2.20	220	4.80	2,350	6.17	4,861	5.80	4,060
27...........	4.60	208	3.71	284	2.25	260	4.75	2,280	5.60	4,480	5.60	3,670
28...........	4.61	204	3.75	290	2.50	390	4.70	2,210	5.85	4,160	5.40	3,290
29...........	4.61	202	....	....	2.60	440	4.55	2,020	5.50	3,670	5.15	2,870
30...........	4.61	201	....	....	2.70	490	4.50	1,960	5.52	3,518	5.00	2,630
31...........	4.61	200	....	....	2.68	480	....	....	5.50	3,480	....	....

a to a Ice conditions.

SESSIONAL PAPER No. 25c

DAILY GAUGE HEIGHT AND DISCHARGE of Oldman River near Macleod, for 1914.

DAY.	July.		August.		September.		October.		November.		December.	
	Gauge Height	Dis-charge	Gauge Height.	Dis-charge.	Gauge Height	Dis-charge	Gauge Height.	Dis-charge	Gauge Height.	Dis-charge.	Gauge Height.	Dis-charge.
	Feet.	*Sec.-ft.*	*Feet.*	*Sec.-ft.*	*Feet.*	*Sec.-ft.*	*Feet.*	*Sec.-ft.*	*Feet.*	*Sec.-ft.*	*Feet.*	*Sec.-ft.*
1	4.90	2,490	3.04	684	2.95	630	3.04	684	4.02	1,440	3.50	946
2	4.85	2,420	3.00	660	2.90	600	3.00	660	4.02	1,440	3.45	890
3	4.83	2,392	3.00	660	2.88	588	3.00	660	4.17	1,590	3.40	820
4	4.80	2,350	2.98	648	2.86	576	3.10	720	4.17	1,590	3.35	740
5	4.80	2,350	2.95	630	2.82	552	3 20	780	4.12	1,540	3.30	670
6	4.75	2,280	2.90	600	2.79	535	3.30	850	4.10	1,520	2.10	590
7	4.70	2,210	2.87	582	2.76	520	3.35	885	4.09	1,510	2.20	520
8	4.60	2,080	2.83	558	3.01	666	3.37	899	4.07	1,490	2.60	463
9	4.50	1,960	2.80	540	2.92	612	3.39	913	4.05	1,470	2.40	430
10	4.40	1,840	3.00	660	2.82	552	3.40	920	4.02	1,440	3.70	415
11	4.32	1,752	2.90	600	2.80	540	3.42	934	3.99	1,410	4.90	408
12	4.20	1,620	2.90	600	2.77	525	3.45	955	3.91	1,330	4.90	403
13	4.15	1,570	2.90	600	2.72	500	3.60	1,070	3.86	1,290b	4.80	407
14	4.15	1,570	2.85	570	2.80	540	3.70	1,150	3.81	1,245	4.90	410
15	4.10	1,520	2.75	515	2.85	570	4.50	1,960	3.51	1,200	5.00	413
16	4.00	1,420	2.60	440	2.87	582	5.20	2,950	3.70	1,145	5.10	415
17	3.90	1,320	2.75	515	2.90	600	5.60	3,670	2.40	1,120	5.00	420
18	3.83	1,257	3.40	920	3.10	720	5.80	4,060	3.00	1,116	4.90	425
19	3.80	1,230	4.15	1,570	3.30	850	5.50	3,480	3.70	1,112	4.80	428
20	3.76	1,198	3.90	1,320	3.50	990	5.30	3,120	3.65	1,113	4.80	433
21	3.73	1,174	3.60	1,070	3.45	955	5.05	2,710	4.40	1,122	4.80	437
22	3.70	1,150	3.35	885	3.40	920	4.90	2,490	3.70	1,140	4.80	443
23	3.60	1,070	3.50	990	3.35	885	4.71	2,224	3.60	1,156	4.80	448
24	3.55	1,030	3.70	1,150	3.25	815	4.51	1,972	3.60	1,163	4.80	450
25	3.40	920	3.60	1,070	3.17	762	4.36	1,796	3.65	1,162	4.80	455
26	3.35	885	3.47	969	3.15	750	4.31	1,741	3.75	1,150	4.70	460
27	3.27	829	3.35	885	3.13	738	4.21	1,631	3.75	1,138	4.60	463
28	3.18	768	3.20	780	3.13	738	4.11	1,530	3.70	1,105	4.50	468
29	3.15	750	3.20	780	3.10	720	4.06	1,480	3.60	1,060	4.40	470
30	3.12	732	3.05	690	3.05	690	4.03	1,450	3.55	1,000	4.28	475
31	3.08	708	3.00	660	......	......	4.02	1,440	......	......	4.20	478b

b to b Ice conditions.

MONTHLY DISCHARGE of Oldman River near Macleod, for 1914.

(Drainage area 2,255 square miles.)

MONTH.	DISCHARGE IN SECOND-FEET.				RUN-OFF.	
	Maximum.	Minimum.	Mean.	Per square Mile.	Depth in inches on Drainage Area.	Total in Acre-feet.
January	345	200	283	0.125	0.14	17,401
February	290	201	235	0.104	0.11	13,051
March	540	220	401	0.178	0.20	24,657
April	3,461	425	1,573	0.698	0.78	93,600
May	5,520	2,350	4,102	1.820	2.11	252,222
June	5,880	2,630	3,655	1.620	1.81	217,220
July	2,490	708	1,511	0.670	0.77	92,911
August	1,570	440	768	0.340	0.39	47,222
September	990	500	674	0.299	0.33	40,106
October	4,060	660	1,670	0.740	0.85	102,680
November	1,590	1,000	1,277	0.566	0.63	75,990
December	946	403	506	0.224	0.26	31,1
The year	......	......	......	......	8 38	1,00

5 GEORGE V, A. 1915

WILLOW CREEK NEAR MACLEOD.

Location.—On the SE. ¼ Sec. 26, Tp. 9, Rge. 26, W. 4th Mer.
Records available.—July 1, 1909, to October 31, 1914.
Gauge.—Vertical staff; zero of gauge maintained at 90 84 feet during 1910-14.
Bench-mark.—Permanent iron bench-mark located 39 feet northwest of the gauge.
Channel.—Consists of clean gravel, and is not liable to shift.
Discharge measurements.—Made from the bridge during flood stages, and by wading at low stages.
Observer.—J. R. McLean.

DISCHARGE MEASUREMENTS of Willow Creek near Macleod, in 1914.

Date.	Engineer.	Width.	Area of Section.	Mean Velocity.	Gauge Height.	Discharge.
		Feet.	*Sq. ft.*	*Ft. per sec.*	*Feet.*	*Sec.-ft.*
March 19..........	F. R. Burfield..............	31	90.2	1.12	2.31	101
April 6..........	J. E. Caughey........... ...	96	195.0	2.30	3.65	448
April 18..........	do	81	133.0	1.62	2.80	216
May 4..........	do	74	118.0	1.57	2.70	185
May 20..........	do	70	110.0	1.51	2.65	168
June 16..........	do	70	107.0	1.44	2.55	154
June 30..........	do	78	124.8	1.73	2.93	216
July 15..........	do	48	71.3	0.92	2.06	65
July 30..........	do	38	52.2	0.34	1.55	20
Aug. 15..........	do	40	53.8	0.51	1.65	27
Aug. 28..........	do	39	53.4	0.53	1.67	28
Sept. 14..........	do	24	20.4	1.08	1.56	22
Sept. 29..........	do	24	22.0	1.25	1.65	27
Oct. 17	do	68	116.0	1.64	2.77	190
Nov. 6	do	30	36.7	2.66	2.23	98

DAILY GAUGE HEIGHT AND DISCHARGE of Willow Creek near Macleod, for 1914.

DAY.	March.		April.		May.		June.	
	Gauge Height.	Dis- charge.	Gauge Height.	Dis- charge.	Gauge Height.	Dis- charge.	Gauge Height.	Dis- charge.
	Feet.	*Sec.-ft.*	*Feet.*	*Sec.-ft.*	*Feet.*	*Sec.-ft.*	*Feet.*	*Sec.-ft.*
1....................................			2.91	236	2.47	132	2.35	109
2....................................			2.96	249	2.50	138	2.35	109
3....................................			2.85	220	2.50	138	2.30	100
4....................................			2.58	156	2.50	138	2.28	97
5....................................			2.95	246	2.70	183	2.28	97
6....................................			3.65	448	2.65	172	2.25	92
7....................................			3.20	316	2.50	138	2.25	92
8....................................			2.75	195	2.50	138	2.25	92
9....................................			2.68	178	2.65	172	2.23	89
10....................................			2.60	160	2.65	172	2.23	89
11....................................			2.57	153	2.70	183	2.20	84
12....................................			2.52	142	2.74	193	2.20	84
13....................................			2.60	160	2.70	183	2.20	84
14....................................			2.76	197	2.64	169	2.18	81
15....................................			2.83	215	2.65	172	2.45	128
16....................................			2.70	183	2.64	169	2.54	147
17....................................			2.80	207	2.64	169	2.54	147
18....................................			2.76	197	2.64	169	2.50	138
19....................................	2.31	102	2.65	172	2.65	172	2.46	130
20....................................	2.20	84	2.60	160	2.65	172	2.40	118
21....................................	2.15	77	2.52	142	2.65	172	2.35	109
22....................................	2.08	68	2.40	118	2.65	172	2.20	84
23....................................	1.92	50	2.40	118	2.65	172	2.12	73
24....................................	1.82	41	2.45	128	2.60	160	2.20	84
25....................................	1.87	45	2.47	132	2.50	138	2.50	138
26....................................	1.94	52	2.47	132	2.50	138	3.10	288
27....................................	1.96	54	2.45	128	2.47	132	3.65	448
28....................................	2.04	63	2.43	124	2.44	126	3.60	433
29....................................	1.99	57	2.45	128	2.42	122	3.50	403
30....................................	2.10	70	2.45	128	2.40	118	3.40	373
31....................................	2.15	77			2.40	118		

SESSIONAL PAPER No. 25c

DAILY GAUGE HEIGHT AND DISCHARGE of Willow Creek near Macleod, for 1914.—*Concluded.*

DAY.	July. Gauge Height.	July. Dis-charge.	August. Gauge Height.	August. Dis-charge.	September. Gauge Height.	September. Dis-charge.	October. Gauge Height.	October. Dis-charge.
	Feet.	*Sec.-ft.*	*Feet.*	*Sec.-ft.*	*Feet.*	*Sec.-ft.*	*Feet.*	*Sec.-ft.*
1	3.35	358	1.53	19.8	1.50	18.0	1.45	15.5
2	3.20	316	1.50	18.0	1.50	18.0	1.45	15.5
3	3.16	305	1.50	18.0	1.48	17.0	1.45	15.5
4	3.09	285	1.48	17.0	1.45	15.5	1.45	15.5
5	2.40	118	1.45	15.5	1.45	15.5	1.45	15.5
6	2.35	109	1.43	14.5	1.45	15.5	1.50	18.0
7	2.33	105	1.40	13.0	1.45	15.5	1.53	19.8
8	2.30	100	1.38	12.2	1.43	14.5	1.60	24.0
9	2.25	92	1.35	11.0	1.43	14.5	1.65	28.0
10	2.23	89	1.70	31.0	1.40	13.0	2.05	64.0
11	2.20	84	1.80	39.0	1.40	13.0	2.60	160.0
12	2.17	80	1.86	44.0	1.40	13.0	2.65	172.0
13	2.17	80	1.79	38.0	1.40	13.0	2.65	172.0
14	2.15	77	1.72	33.0	1.38	12.2	2.65	172.0
15	2.10	70	1.64	27.0	1.46	16.0	2.65	172.0
16	2.05	64	1.59	23.0	1.58	23.0	2.80	207.0
17	2.05	64	1.59	23.0	1.65	28.0	2.96	249.0
18	2.00	58	1.59	23.0	1.70	31.0	3.00	260.0
19	1.90	48	1.74	34.0	1.75	35.0	3.10	288.0
20	1.75	35	2.05	64.0	1.75	35.0	3.00	260.0
21	1.75	35	1.75	35.0	1.70	31.0	2.80	207.0
22	1.75	35	1.75	35.0	1.78	37.0	2.80	207.0
23	1.75	35	1.80	39.0	1.78	37.0	2.74	193.0
24	1.60	24	2.23	89.0	1.75	35.0	2.56	151.0
25	1.60	24	2.10	70.0	1.73	33.0	2.53	145.0
26	1.55	21	1.95	53.0	1.60	24.0	2.40	118.0
27	1.55	21	1.82	41.0	1.60	24.0	2.38	114.0
28	1.55	21	1.68	30.0	1.55	21.0	2.35	109.0
29	1.55	21	1.60	24.0	1.53	19.8	2.35	109.0
30	1.55	21	1.53	19.8	1.45	15.5	2.30	100.0
31	1.55	21	1.50	18.0	....	....	2.25	92.0

MONTHLY DISCHARGE of Willow Creek near Macleod, for 1914.

(Drainage area 1,013 square miles.)

MONTH.	DISCHARGE IN SECOND-FEET. Maximum.	Minimum.	Mean.	Per square Mile.	RUN-OFF. Depth in inches on Drainage Area.	Total in Acre-feet.
March (19–31)	102	41.0	65	0.064	0.03	1,676
April	448	118.0	182	0.180	0.20	10,830
May	193	118.0	156	0.154	0.18	9,592
June	448	73.0	151	0.149	0.17	8,985
July	358	21.0	91	0.090	0.10	5,595
August	89	11.0	31	0.031	0.03	1,906
September	37	12.2	22	0.022	0.02	1,309
October	288	15.5	125	0.123	0.14	7,686
The period	....	....	....	....	0.87	47,579

5 GEORGE V, A. 1915

MUDDYPOUND CREEK AT HART'S RANCH.

Location.—On the SW. ¼ Sec. 27, Tp. 11, Rge. 28, W. 4th Mer., at the foot bridge on L. O. Hart's ranch.

Records available.—July 27, 1908, to October 31, 1914.

Gauge.—Vertical staff; zero of gauge maintained at 91.06 feet during 1908-1911; 90.06 feet during 1912-1914.

Bench-mark.—Permanent iron bench-mark 35 feet northeast of gauge; assumed elevation, 100.00 feet.

Channel.—Not liable to shift.

Discharge measurements.—Made from bridge at high water, and by wading at low water.

Observer.—Mrs. M. *E.* Hart.

DISCHARGE MEASUREMENTS of Muddypound Creek at Hart's Ranch, in 1914.

Date.	Engineer.	Width.	Area of Section.	Mean Velocity.	Gauge Height.	Discharge.
		Feet.	*Sq. ft.*	*Ft. per sec.*	*Feet.*	*Sec.-ft.*
April 1	F. R. Burfield	7.5	4.24	1.91	2.73	8.30
April 20	J. E. Caughey	8.0	4.00	1.32	2.23	5.30
May 6	do	6.5	2.58	0.86	2.11	2.20
May 27	do	5.5	1.45	0.61	2.02	0.88
June 18	do	3.5	0.65	0.35	1.95	0.23
July 3	do	3.5	0.65	0.38	1.95	0.25
July 17	do				1.80	Nil.
July 31	do				Dry.	"
Aug. 17	do				"	"
Sept. 16	do	5.0	1.70	0.56	2.02	0.95
Sept. 28	do				1.95	0.15
Oct. 19	do	6.0	2.30	1.31	2.12	3.00

DAILY GAUGE HEIGHT AND DISCHARGE of Muddypound Creek at Hart's Ranch, for 1914.

DAY.	April.		May.		June.	
	Gauge Height.	Dis-charge.	Gauge Height.	Dis-charge.	Gauge Height.	Dis-charge.
	Feet.	*Sec.-ft.*	*Feet.*	*Sec.-ft.*	*Feet.*	*Sec.-ft.*
1	2.69	21.0	2.09	1.85	2.00	0.65
2	2.60	17.7	2.09	1.85	2.00	0.65
3	2.48	13.6	2.09	1.85	2.00	0.65
4	2.38	10.2	2.09	1.85	2.00	0.65
5	2.48	13.6	2.10	2.00	1.90	0.65
6	2.38	10.2	2.11	2.20	1.90	0.05
7	2.30	7.5	2.11	2.20	1.90	0.05
8	2.24	5.5	2.11	2.20	1.90	0.05
9	2.25	5.8	2.10	2.00	1.90	0.05
10	2.26	6.1	2.10	2.00	1.90	0.05
11	2.28	6.8	2.10	2.00	1.90	0.05
12	2.28	6.8	2.10	2.00	2.00	0.65
13	2.28	6.8	2.10	2.00	2.00	0.65
14	2.26	6.1	2.10	2.00	2.00	0.65
15	2.25	5.8	2.10	2.00	2.00	0.65
16	2.23	5.2	2.09	1.85	1.90	0.05
17	2.23	5.2	2.09	1.85	1.80	0.01
18	2.21	4.7	2.09	1.85	1.60	....
19	2.21	4.7	2.09	1.85	1.50	....
20	2.23	5.2	2.09	1.85	1.40	....
21	2.23	5.2	2.09	1.85	1.30	....
22	2.22	5.0	2.09	1.85	Dry.	Nil.
23	2.21	4.7	2.08	1.70	"	"
24	2.20	4.4	2.08	1.70	1.80	0.01
25	2.19	4.1	2.07	1.55	2.48	13.60
26	2.18	3.8	2.06	1.40	2.22	5.00
27	2.17	3.6	2.05	1.25	2.10	2.00
28	2.15	3.0	2.05	1.25	2.05	1.25
29	2.14	2.8	2.03	1.01	2.03	1.01
30	2.12	2.4	2.00	0.65	2.01	0.77
31	....	....	2.00	0.65	....	....

DAILY GAUGE HEIGHT AND DISCHARGE of Muddypound Creek, at Hart's Ranch, for 1914.
—*Concluded.*

DAY.	July.		August.		September.		October.	
	Gauge Height.	Dis-charge.	Gauge Height.	Dis-charge.	Gauge Height.	Dis-charge.	Gauge Height.	Dis-charge.
	Feet.	*Sec.-ft.*	*Feet.*	*Sec.-ft.*	*Feet.*	*Sec.-ft.*	*Feet.*	*Sec.-ft.*
1	2.00	0.65	Dry.	Nil.	1.80	·0.01	1.80	0.01
2	1.95	0.25	"	"	1.80	0.01	1.78	0.01
3	1.87	0.04	"	"	1.75	0.00	1.85	0.03
4	1.84	0.03	"	"	....	....	2.05	1.25
5	2.00	0.65	"	"	....	....	2.13	2.60
6	1.90	0.05	"	"	1.80	0.01	2.20	4.40
7	1.80	0.01	"	"	1.90	0.05	2.25	5.80
8	1.79	0.01	"	"	1.85	0.03	2.30	7.50
9	1.75	0.00	"	"	1.85	0.03	2.35	9.20
10	1.50	....	"	"	1.80	0.01	2.25	5.80
11	Dry.	Nil.	"	"	1.75	0.00	2.20	4.40
12	"	"	"	"	1.80	0.01	2.15	3.00
13	"	"	"	"	1.95	0.25	2.25	5.80
14	1.75	0.00	"	"	2.00	0.65	2.30	7.50
15	1.75	0.00	"	"	2.00	0.65	2.35	9.20
16	1.75	0.00	"	"	2.02	0.89	2.36	9.50
17	1.75	0.00	"	"	2.02	0.89	2.35	9.20
18	Dry.	Nil.	2.05	1.25	2.03	1.01	2.33	8.50
19	"	"	2.00	0.65	2.02	0.89	2.25	5.80
20	"	"	1.80	0.01	2.02	0.89	2.21	4.70
21	"	"	Dry.	Nil.	2.01	0.77	2.20	4.40
22	"	"	"	"	2.00	0.65	2.10	2.00
23	"	"	2.00	0.65	2.00	0.65	2.10	2.00
24	"	"	2.18	3.80	1.09	....	2.10	2.00
25	"	"	2.00	0.65	1.08	....	2.10	2.00
26	"	"	1.90	0.05	1.75	0.00	2.10	2.00
27	"	"	1.80	0.01	1.09	....	2.10	2.00
28	"	"	1.80	0.01	1.09	....	2.10	2.00
29	"	"	1.80	0.01	1.85	0.03	2.10	2.00
30	"	"	1.75	0.00	1.80	0.01	2.10	2.00
31	"	"	1.75	0.00	....	....	2.10	2.00

MONTHLY DISCHARGE of Muddypound Creek at Hart's Ranch, for 1914.

(Drainage area 44 square miles.)

MONTH.	DISCHARGE IN SECOND-*FEET.*				RUN-OFF.	
	Maximum.	Minimum	Mean.	Per square Mile.	Depth in inches on Drainage Area.	Total in Acre-feet.
April	21.00	2.40	6.90	0.157	0.180	411
May	2.20	0.65	1.75	0.040	0.050	108
June	13.60	0.01	1.00	0.023	0.020	60
July	0.65	Nil.	0.05	0.001	0.001	3
August	3.80	"	0.23	0.005	0.006	14
September	1.01	"	0.28	0.006	0.007	17
October	9.50	0.01	4.10	0.093	0.110	252
The period	....	....	....	....	0 374	865

TROUT CREEK AT LOCKWOOD'S RANCH.

Location.—On SE. ¼ Sec. 32, Tp. 11, Rge. 28, W. 4th Mer.
Records available.—July 7, 1911, to October 31, 1914.
Gauge.—Vertical staff; elevation 90.30 feet during 1911; 92.19 feet during 1912-14.
Bench-mark.—Permanent iron bench-mark; assumed elevation, 100.00 feet.
Channel.—Composed of gravel.
Discharge measurements.—Made by wading.
Winter flow.—Station not maintained during the winter.
Observer.—Mrs. G. P. Stewart.

5 GEORGE V, A. 1915

DISCHARGE MEASUREMENTS of Trout Creek at Lockwood's Ranch, in 1914.

Date.	Engineer.	Width.	Area of Section.	Mean Velocity.	Gauge Height.	Discharge.
		Feet.	*Sq. ft.*	*Ft. per sec.*	*Feet.*	*Sec.-ft.*
April 1	F. R. Burfield	43.0	25.4	1.60	4.34	41.0
April 20	J. E. Caughey...........	26.0	16.2	1.04	2.93	16.8
May 6	do	26.0	16.8	1.18	3.03	19.8
May 27	do	26.0	17.2	1.10	3.08	18.9
June 18	do	22.0	12.6	1.06	2.80	13.4
July 3	do	28.0	21.7	0.96	3.26	21.0
July 17	do	26.0	17.0	0.84	3.10	14.2
July 31	do	22.0	12.0	0.79	2.85	9.6
Aug. 17	do	24.0	14.4	0.79	2.95	11.4
Sept. 16	do	23.0	12.4	0.63	2.92	7.9
Sept. 28	do	24.0	13.6	0.37	2.95	5.0
Oct. 19	do	24.0	18.1	0.60	3.29	11.9

DAILY GAUGE HEIGHT AND DISCHARGE of Trout Creek at Lockwood's Ranch, for 1914.

DAY.	April.		May.		June.	
	Gauge Height.	Dis-charge.	Gauge Height.	Dis-charge.	Gauge Height.	Dis-charge.
	Feet.	*Sec.-ft.*	*Feet.*	*Sec.-ft.*	*Feet.*	*Sec.-ft.*
1.........	4.34	41.0	2.91	16.7	2.95	16.0
2.........	4.34	41.0	2.90	16.3	2.95	16.0
3.........	4.32	41.0	3.02	19.5	2.95	16.0
4.........	4.32	42.0	3.05	20.5	2.94	15.8
5.........	4.40	42.0	3.00	19.0	3.02	18.0
6.........	4.36	42.0	3.04	19.8	3.00	17.5
7.........	4.33	43.0	3.04	19.8	2.96	16.6
8.........	4.30	43.0	3.04	19.7	2.95	16.4
9.........	4.27	43.0	3.06	20.0	2.93	16.0
10.........	4.17	44.0	3.06	20.0	2.87	14.6
11.........	3.89	44.0	3.06	20.0	2.96	16.7
12.........	3.97	47.0	3.06	19.8	2.96	16.7
13.........	4.10	50.0	3.04	19.8	2.98	17.4
14.........	4.03	48.0	3.04	19.6	3.02	18.5
15.........	4.08	50.0	3.05	19.6	2.95	16.7
16.........	4.00	48.0	3.06	19.7	2.84	14.2
17.........	3.88	44.0	3.06	19.8	2.82	13.7
18.........	3.87	44.0	3.06	19.8	2.80	13.3
19.........	3.40*a*	30.0	3.08	20.0	2.78	13.4
20.........	2.92	16.8*b*	3.14	22.0	2.77	12.7
21.........	2.90	16.0	3.14	22.0	2.76	12.6
22.........	2.88	16.0	3.09	20.0	2.75	12.5
23.........	2.88	15.6	3.09	20.0	2.77	12.7
24.........	2.91	16.5	3.05	18.0	2.77	12.7
25.........	2.95	17.5	3.04	18.7	3.82	42.0
26.........	2.92	17.0	3.04	18.4	3.38	26.0
27.........	2.92	16.8	3.04	18.9	3.12	18.7
28.........	2.96	17.8	3.04	17.8	3.14	18.8
29.........	2.96	17.8	3.04	17.8	3.12	18.0
30.........	2.93	17.0	3.01	17.2	3.14	18.2*c*
31.........	....	....	2.98	16.7	....	....

a Gauge height interpolated.
b to *c* Shifting conditions.

DAILY GAUGE HEIGHT AND DISCHARGE of Trout Creek at Lockwood's Ranch, for 1914.
—*Concluded.*

DAY.	July.		August.		September.		October.	
	Gauge Height.	Dis-charge.	Gauge Height.	Dis-charge.	Gauge Height.	Dis-charge.	Gauge Height.	Dis-charge.
	Feet.	*Sec.-ft.*	*Feet.*	*Sec.-ft.*	*Feet.*	*Sec.-ft.*	*Feet.*	*Sec.-ft.*
1	3.28	22.0a	2.85	9.6	2.79	6.2	3.00	6.0
2	3.28	21.0	2.85	9.6	2.79	6.2	3.00	6.0
3	3.25	21.0b	2.83	9.3	2.78	6.0	3.02	6.3
4	3.25	19.8	2.82	8.9	2.80	6.0	3.13	8.4
5	3.30	21.0	2.80	8.5	2.79	5.8	3.24	10.7
6	3.30	21.0	2.80	8.5	2.80	5.9	3.12	8.1
7	3.26	20.0	2.80	8.5	2.80	5.9	3.10	7.8
8	3.21	18.7	2.84	9.4	2.84	6.7	3.14	8.6
9	3.21	18.7	2.84	9.4	2.78	5.3	3.11	8.0
10	3.18	17.8	3.28	22.0	2.75	4.6	3.36	13.7
11	3.15	17.0	2.97	12.9	2.74	4.6	3.30	12.1
12	3.15	17.0	2.94	11.7	2.90	7.2	3.28	11.6
13	3.22	19.0	2.89	11.0	2.90	7.2	3.40	14.8
14	3.22	19.0	2.85	9.6	2.86	6.6	3.46	16.0
15	3.12	16.2	2.85	9.6	2.94	8.3	3.39	14.5
16	3.10	15.7	2.84	9.4	2.96	8.8	3.36	13.7
17	3.09	15.4	2.90	10.7c	2.94	7.5	3.36	13.7
18	3.09	15.4	3.07	13.2	2.89	6.6	3.34	13.1
19	3.06	14.7	2.92	10.5	2.90	6.5	3.34	13.1
20	3.04	14.1	2.86	8.7	2.89	5.9	3.32	12.6
21	3.03	13.9	2.84	8.7	2.86	5.0	3.30	12.1
22	3.01	13.4	2.83	8.2	2.85	4.6	3.24	10.7
23	2.99	12.9	3.28	19.5	2.85	4.3	3.24	10.7
24	2.95	11.9	3.14	15.4	2.85	4.0	3.22	10.2
25	2.95	11.9	2.93	10.0	2.84	3.8	3.22	10.2
26	2.94	11.7	2.86	8.3	2.86	4.0	3.21	10.0
27	2.96	12.2	2.84	7.8	2.98	5.8d	3.18	9.4
28	3.01	13.4	2.82	7.2	2.96	5.3	3.18	9.4
29	2.94	11.7	2.80	6.8	2.95	5.1	3.20	9.8
30	2.90	10.7	2.80	6.6	2.96	5.3	3.20	0.8
31	2.88	10.2	2.80	6.6	....	....	3.22	10.2

a to *b* and *c* to *d* Shifting conditions.

MONTHLY DISCHARGE of Trout Creek at Lockwood's Ranch, for 1914.

(Drainage area 164 square miles.)

MONTH.	DISCHARGE IN SECOND-FEET.				RUN-OFF.	
	Maximum.	Minimum	Mean.	Per square Mile.	Depth in inches on Drainage Area.	Total in Acre-feet.
April	50.0	15.6	33.70	0.206	0.23	2,005
May	22.0	16.3	19.30	0.117	0.13	1,187
June	42.0	12.5	16.90	0.103	0.11	1,006
July	22.0	10.2	16.10	0.098	0.11	990
August	22.0	6.6	10.20	0.062	0.07	627
September	8.8	3.8	5.83	0.036	0.04	347
October	16.0	6.0	10.70	0.065	0.07	658
The period	....	....	....	....	0.76	6,820

5 GEORGE V, A. 1915

Miscellaneous Discharge Measurements made in Oldman River drainage basin, in 1914.

Date.	Engineer.	Stream.	Location.	Width.	Area of Section.	Mean Velocity.	Discharge.
				Feet.	*Sq. ft.*	*Ft. per sec.*	*Sec.-ft.*
April 8.....	J. E. Caughey...	Bellevue Creek....	NE. 29-7-3-5...	4.0	0.64	1.00	0.6400
April 24....	do	do	do	2.4	0.88	1.10	0.9700
June 13....	do	do	do	1.4	0.36	1.36	0.4900
July 8...	do	do	do	1.7	0.51	1.22	0.6200
Aug. 6....	do	do	do	3.0	0.90	1.01	0.9100
Aug. 20....	do	do	do .a	....	....	....	0.6790
Sept. 3....	do	do	do .a				0.6610
Sept. 21....	do	do	do .a				0.6040
Oct. 6....	do	do	do .a				0.8360
Oct. 26....	do	do	do .a				0.7560
Mar. 23....	F. R. Burfield...	Blairmore Creek...	SE. 3-8-4-5......	6.0	3.50	0.76	2.7000
April 9....	J. E. Caughey..	do	do	11.0	7.80	1.23	9.6000
April 25...	do	do	do	21.5	22.60	2.92	66.0000
May 12...	do	do	do	20.5	21.38	2.90	62.0000
June 13....	do	do	do	21.0	13.55	1.94	26.0000
June 22....	do	do	do	11.0	6.54	1.39	9.1000
July 8...	do	do	do	9.0	4.70	1.10	5.2000
July 22....	do	do	do	8.0	3.70	1.00	3.7000
Aug. 6....	do	do	do	9.0	2.90	0.58	1.6800
Aug. 20....	do	do	do	9.0	4.30	0.95	4.1000
Sept. 3....	do	do	do	9.0	3.60	0.76	2.7000
Sept. 21....	do	do	do	10.0	6.10	1.28	7.8000
Oct. 6....	do	do	do	9.0	5.60	1.30	7.3000
Oct. 26....	do	do	do	12.0	9.85	2.08	21.0000
April 1....	do	Brocket Springs...	NE. 6-7-28-4..			....b	...0.0046
July 14....	R. H. Goodchild	Chaffin Creek....	NE. 6-13-2-5..			....a	0.2200
July 14....	do	Dago Creek....	NW. 17-13-2-5..			....a	1.2390
Aug. 14....	do	do	do			....a	1.2400
Jan. 17....	R. Palmer.....	Drum Creek......	NW. 18-7-3-5...	8.0	2.80	0.55	1.5500
Feb. 6....	do	do	do	8.0	2.31	0.51	1.1800
Feb. 16....	E. W. W. Hughes	do	do	7.5	3.07	0.53	1.6200
Mar. 6....	do	do	do	7.5	2.86	0.52	1.4900
Mar. 20....	F. R. Burfield...	do	do	6.5	2.22	0.72	1.5900
April 8....	J. E. Caughey..	do	do	4.5	2.05	1.07	2.2000
April 24....	do	do	do	8.0	8.90	1.77	15.8000
May 12....	do	do	do	12.0	8.00	1.75	14.0000
June 13....	do	do	do	8.5	2.95	1.75	5.2000
June 22....	do	do	do	8.0	2.20	1.50	3.3000
July 8...	do	do	do	9.0	2.30	1.48	3.4000
July 22....	do	do	do	8.0	2.35	1.06	2.5000
Aug. 6....	do	do	do	7.0	2.30	0.96	2.2000
Aug. 20....	do	do	do	6.0	2.10	1.22	2.6000
Sept. 3....	do	do	do	7.0	2.80	0.98	2.8000
Sept. 21....	do	do	do	5.0	2.20	1.43	3.1000
Oct. 6....	do	do	do	7.0	3.00	0.97	2.9000
Oct. 26....	do	do	do	9.0	4.80	1.26	6.0000
Nov. 12....	do	do	do	9.0	3.50	1.26	4.4000
Dec. 4....	do	do	do	8.0	3.30	1.05	3.5000
Dec. 28....	do	do	do	8.0	2.90	0.93	2.7000
Aug. 31....	R. H. Goodchild.	Ernst Creek......	NW. 26-10-3-5..			....a	0.9190
Feb. 18....	E. W. W. Hughes	Fortier N. Spring..	SE. 17-7-1-5....	c	6895	....e	0.0128
Mar. 10....	F. R. Burfield...	do	do		2995	....	0.0056
Mar. 24....	do	do	do		2578	....	0.0048
April 14....	J. E. Caughey...	do	do		2260	....	0.0042
April 29....	do	do	do		2045	....	0.0038
May 16...	do	do	do		2420	....	0.0045
June 2....	do	do	do		646	....	0.0012
July 25....	do	do	do		1346	....	0.0025
Aug. 12....	do	do	do		2207	....	0.0041
Sept. 9....	do	do	do		7934	....	0.0147
Sept. 24....	do	do	do		2476	....	0.0046
Oct. 15....	do	do	do		5436	....	0.0101
Nov. 2....	do	do	do		4090	....	0.0076
Nov. 19....	do	do	do		3337	....	0.0062
Dec. 9....	do	do	do		3660	....	0.0068
Dec. 29....	do	do	do		4200	....	0.0078
Feb. 18....	E. W. W. Hughes	Fortier S. Spring..	SE. 17-7-1-5 ..		969	....	0.0018
Mar. 10....	F. R. Burfield...	do	do		969	....	0.0018
Mar. 24....	do	do	do		969	....	0.0018
April 14....	J.E. Caughey...	do	do		1900	....	0.0035
April 29....	do	do	do		2110	....	0.0039
May 16...	do	do	do		1728	....	0.0032
June 2....	do	do	do		1045	....	0.0019
July 10....	do	do	do		915	....	0.0017
July 25....	do	do	do		700	....	0.0013
Aug. 12....	do	do	do		753	....	0.0014
Aug. 26....	do	do	do		915	....	0.0017
Sept. 9....	do	do	do		1076	....	0.0020
Sept. 24....	do	do	do	....d	915	....f	0.0017

a Weir measurements.
c to d Imperial gals. per 24 hours.
e to f Discharge determined by standard measures.

SESSIONAL PAPER No. 25c

MISCELLANEOUS DISCHARGE MEASUREMENTS made in Oldman River drainage basin in 1914.
—*Concluded.*

Date.	Engineer.	Stream.	Location.	Width.	Area of Section.	Mean Velocity.	Discharge.
				Feet.	*Sq. ft.*	*Ft per sec.*	*Sec.-ft.*
Oct. 15....	J. E. Caughey ..	Fortier S. Spring ..	SE. 17-7-1-5. .	.... *c*	915	..... *e*	0.0017
Nov. 19....	do	do	do ...	......	1291	....	0.0024
Dec. 9....	do	do	do ...	......	1844	....	0.0034
Dec. 29....	do	do	do ...	.... *d*	3014	.... *f*	0.0056
Mar. 21 ...	F. R. Burfield...	Gold Creek.......	SE. 30-7-3-5...	19.5	14.05	0.91	12.7000
April 8....	J. E. Caughey...	do	do ...	21.5	15.60	0.90	14.1000
April 24....	do ...	do	do ...	22.0	23.40	1.83	43.0000
May 12....	do ...	do	do ...	22.0	26.60	2.21	59.0000
June 13....	do ...	do	do ...	21.4	21.45	1.77	38.0000
June 22....	do ...	do	do ...	26.0	21.20	1.32	28.0000
July 8....	do ...	do	do ...	22.0	20.80	1.42	30.0000
July 22....	do ...	do	do ...	20.0	17.40	1.36	24.0000
Aug. 6 ...	do ...	do	do ...	20.0	16.40	1.11	18.2000
Aug. 20....	do ...	do	do ...	22.0	20.40	1.29	26.0000
Sept. 3....	do ...	do	do ...	22.0	18.40	1.23	23.0000
Sept. 21....	do ...	do	do ...	21.0	18.40	1.13	21.0000
Oct. 6....	do ...	do	do ...	21.0	18.70	1.06	19.8000
Mar. 23....	F. R. Burfield...	Lyon Creek.......	SE. 35-7-4-5..	5.0	1.39	0.52	0.7200
April 9....	J. E. Caughey...	do	do ...	13.5	7.97	0.93	7.4000
April 25....	do ...	do	do ...	26.0	21.40	3.24	69.0000
June 13....	do ...	do	do ...	8.0	3.90	1.74	6.8000
July 8....	do ...	do	do ...	7.0	2.63	0.76	2.0000
July 22....	do ...	do	do ...	......	....	....	Nil.
Aug. 6....	do ...	do	do ...	......	....	....	Nil.
Aug. 21....	do ...	do	do ...	11.0	7.80	0.61	4.7000
Sept. 4 ...	do ...	do	do ...	......	....	....	Nil.
Sept. 22....	do ...	do	do ...	9.0	4.20	1.46	6.1000
Oct. 5....	do ...	do	do ...	13.0	10.60	0.67	7.1000
Oct. 26 .	do ...	do	do ...	15.0	13.60	1.22	16.6000
Mar. 7....	E. W. W. Hughes	Nez-Perce Creek..	SE. 17-8-4-5...	3.0	1.30	1.00	1.3000
Mar. 20....	F. R. Burfield...	do ..	do ...	4.5	2.24	0.34	0.7600
April 8....	J. E. Caughey...	do ..	do ...	7.0	2.25	0.94	2.1000
April 24....	do ...	do ..	do ...	14.0	12.30	1.97	24.0000
May 13....	do ...	do ..	do ...	14.2	13.04	2.17	28.0000
June 15..	do ...	do ..	do ...	13.2	6.59	0.96	6.4000
June 23....	do ...	do ..	do ...	12.0	6.30	0.81	5.1000
July 9....	do ...	do ..	do ...	12.5	4.23	0.98	4.1000
July 23....	do ...	do ..	do ...	5.0	1.30	1.30	1.6900
Aug. 7...	do ...	do ..	do ...	4.0	1.21	1.16	1.4100
Aug. 21...	do ...	do ..	do ...	5.0	1.90	0.91	1.7300
Sept. 4....	do ...	do ..	do ...	4.0	1.00	1.17	1.1700
Sept. 22....	do ...	do ..	do ...	6.0	3.10	1.23	3.8000
Oct. 7...	do ...	do ..	do ...	6.0	2.60	0.89	2.3000
July 6....	R. H. Goodchild.	Spring Creek..	NE. 9-5-1-5 .	......	....	.......*a*	0.0510
July 15. ..	do ...	do ..	SW. 30-13-2-5..	......	....	.......*a*	0.3540
July 16....	do ...	do ..	NE. 23-13-2-5..	......	....	.......*a*	0.1030
July 16....	do ...	do ..	SE. 23-13-2-5..	......	....	.......*a*	0.2220
July 20....	do ...	Spring	NE. 13-14-30-4	......	....	.......*a*	0.0500
Mar. 23 . .	F. R. Burfield...	York Creek......	NW. 30-7-4-5..	6.0	4.17	0.69	2.8000
April 9....	J. E. Caughey...	do	do ...	9.5	6.97	1.72	12.0000
April 25....	do ...	do	do ...	22.0	20.30	2.30	47.0000
May 12 ..	do ...	do	do ...	23.0	22.25	2.54	57.0000
June 13....	do ...	do	do ...	22.0	20.50	2.08	43.0000
June 22....	do ...	do	do ...	20.0	16.90	1.82	31.0000
July 8....	do ...	do	do ...	21.0	15.00	1.68	25.0000
July 22....	do ...	do	do ...	20.0	12.40	1.29	16.1000
Aug. 6....	do ...	do	do ...	8.0	4.30	1.34	5.8000
Aug. 20....	do ...	do	do ...	20.0	11.20	1.19	13.4000
Sept. 3....	do ...	do	do ...	7.0	4.40	0.96	4.2000
Sept. 21....	do ...	do	do ...	16.0	16.30	1.43	23.0000
Oct. 26....	do ...	do	do ...	26.0	18.00	1.08	19.4000

a Weir measurements.
b Capacity measurement.
c to *d* Imperial gals. per 24 hours.
e to *f* Discharge determined by standard measures.

5 GEORGE V, A. 1915

WATERTON RIVER DRAINAGE BASIN.

General Description.

Waterton River rises in the northwestern portion of the state of Montana, on the eastern slope of the Rocky Mountains. It flows in a northerly direction and, passing through a chain of lakes near the international boundary, known as Waterton Lakes, it continues in a north and easterly direction and finally empties into Belly River, near Stand Off, Alta.

The topography of the basin is of a varied character, ranging from the mountainous regions of Montana to the rolling prairie of southern Alberta. The tributaries are mostly in the upper portion of the basin, near the international boundary and from the west side.

There is a large snowfall in the upper portion of the basin, and the melting of this, combined with heavy rains, often causes big floods on this river in the early summer. Thereafter the river steadily decreases in volume, until the minimum is reached about mid-winter.

Waterton Lakes offer a very favourable site for a storage reservoir, approximately fourteen miles long and one mile wide. The steep, rocky banks of the narrows is an ideal site for the construction of a dam. The flow could be more than doubled during the summer months and used for irrigation purposes, or a power project could easily be developed.

WATERTON RIVER AT WATERTON MILLS.

Location.—On the *NE.* ¼ Sec. 8, Tp. 2, Rge. 29, W. 4th Mer., near Waterton Mills.
Records available.—August 26, 1908, to December 31, 1914.
Gauge.—Vertical staff; zero of gauge maintained at 4,153.07 feet during 1908-12; 4,152.87 feet during 1913-14.
Bench-mark.—Permanent iron bench-mark, located within six feet of the gauge; elevation, 4,152.87 feet above mean sea level (*Irrigation* Surveys datum).
Channel.—Composed of rocks, stone and gravel; not liable to shift.
Discharge measurements.—Made from a cable car at ordinary stages, and by wading at very low stages.
Winter flow.—The high velocity prevents a complete ice cover at the gauge during the winter, and open water measurements are obtained.
Observer.—H. H. Hanson.
Remarks.—In view of obtaining more accurate measurements, the cable was moved from the *NE.* ¼ Sec. 8, Tp. 2, Rge. 29, W. 4th Mer., to SW. ¼ Sec. 21, Tp. 2, Rge. 29, W. 4th Mer., in November, 1914. The channel at this point is straight for about 300 feet above and 300 feet below the cable. The bed of the stream consists of small stones and gravel, and is not liable to shift.

DISCHARGE MEASUREMENTS of Waterton River at Waterton Mills, in 1914.

Date.	Engineer.	Width.	Area of Section.	Mean Velocity.	Gauge Height.	Discharge.
		Feet.	*Sq. ft.*	*Ft. per sec.*	*Feet.*	*Sec.-ft.*
Jan. 4	J. E. Degnan	104	105.0	1.34	2.28	141
Jan 15	do	152	135.0	1.35	2.53	183
Jan. 28	do	55	81.8	1.93	2.53	158
Feb. 13	do	51	80.0	1.79	2.32	144
Mar. 8	do	102	99.8	1.12	2.20	111
Apr. 3	O. H. Hoover	45	80.9	1.68	2.56	135
Apr. 16	do	283	297.0	1.80	3.17	536
May 7	do	293	501.0	3.00	3.92	1,506
May 28	do	294	596.0	3.21	4.23	1,913
June 16	do	296	633.0	3.76	4.35	2,383
July 6	do	289	491.4	2.69	3.87	1,322
Aug. 1	do	281	266.0	1.62	3.07	431
Aug. 22	do	286	309.0	1.84	3.23	568
Sept. 12	do	212	187.0	1.34	2.76	252
Nov. 5	do	144	446.0	1.70	3.54	741
Nov. 19	do	136	365.0	1.42	3.36	502
Dec. 2	do	136	340.0	1.14	3.12	378
Dec. 21	do.	130	203.0	0.86	2.61	174

SESSIONAL PAPER No. 25c

DAILY GAUGE HEIGHT AND DISCHARGE of Waterton River at Waterton Mills, for 1914.

Day.	January.		February.		March.		April.		May.		June.	
	Gauge Height.	Discharge	Gauge Height.	Discharge.	Gauge Height.	Discharge	Gauge Height.	Discharge.	Gauge Height.	Discharge.	Gauge Height.	Discharge.
	Feet.	*Sec.-ft.*	*Feet.*	*Sec.-ft.*	*Feet.*	*Sec.-ft.*	*Feet.*	*Sec.-ft.*	*Feet.*	*Sec.-ft.*	*Feet.*	*Sec.-ft.*
1	2.23	116	2.48	165	2.23	116	2.57	189	3.64	1,012	4 13	1,830
2	2.22	114	2.47	163	2.30	129	2.56	186	3.73	1,135	4.32	2,212
3	2.26	122	2.46	161	2.46	161	2.57	189	4.03	1,637	4.53	2,666
4	2.29	127	2.42	152	2.45	158	2.58	192	4.06	1,694	4.64	2,908
5	2.32	133	2.39	146	2 43	154	2.64	211	4.08	1,732	4.63	2,886
6	2.65	131*a*	2.36	140	2.30	129	2.69	227	4.05	1,675	4 52	2,644
7	2.30	129	2.36	140	2.18	109	2.70	230	4 03	1,637	4.34	2,254
8	2.27	124	2.38	144	2.19	110	2.71	234	3.88	1,368	4.35	2,275
9	2.34	137	2.39	146	2.16	106	2.74	247	3 94	1,472	4.20	1,970
10	2.40	148	2.41	150	2.17	107	2.76	256	4 03	1,637	3.96	1,508
11	2.49	167	2.39	146	2.18	109	2.80	273	4 05	1,675	3.86	1,336
12	2.65	214	2.36	140	2.18	109	2.90	323	4.06	1,694	3.81	1,256
13	2.63	208	2.32	133	2.19	110	3.01	392	4.11	1,790	4.05	1,675
14	2.58	192	2.33	135	2.25	120	3.15	488	4.19	1,950	4 33	2,233
15	2.53	178	2.34	137	2.33	135	3.23	551	4 17	1,910	4 36	2,296
16	2.52	175	2.36	140	2.31	131	3.17	503	4.30	2,170	4 36	2,296
17	2.51	172	2.31	131	2.29	127	3.31	620	4.40	2,380	4.35	2,275
18	2.50	169	2.28	125	2.28	125	3.38	690	4.43	2,446	4.51	2,622
19	2.49	167	2.25	120	2.29	127	3.43	746	4.45	2,490	4.43	2,446
20	2.48	165	2.23	116	2.30	129	3.50	830	4.43	2,446	4.36	2,296
21	2.50	169	2.22	115	2.33	135	.61	973	4 37	2,317	4.30	2,170
22	2.53	178	2.24	118	2.32	133	.65	1,025	4.33	2,233	4.32	2,212
23	2.52	175	2.26	122	2.33	135	.69	1,077	4.30	2,170	4.05	1,675
24	2.51	172	2.28	125	2.35	138	.72	1,120	4 35	2,275	3.95	1,490
25	2.51	172	2.29	127	2.37	142	3.73	1,135	4.43	2,446	3.93	1,454
26	2.52	175	2.18	109	2.36	140	.72	1,120	4.41	2,402	3.92	1,436
27	2.52	175	2.18	109	2.34	137	.72	1,120	4.32	2,212	3.91	1,418
28	2.52	175	2.19	110	2.37	142	.70	1,090	4.24	2,050	3.89	1,384
29	2.51	172			2.41	150	68	1,064	4.15	1,870	3.88	1,368
30	2.50	169			2.43	154	3.65	1,025	4 06	1,694	3.84	1,304
31	2.49	167			2.42	152			4.05	1,675		

a Ice jam—discharge estimated.

DAILY GAUGE HEIGHT AND DISCHARGE of Waterton River at Waterton Mills, for 1914.
—*Concluded.*

Day.	July. Gauge Height.	July. Dis-charge.	August. Gauge Height.	August. Dis-charge.	September. Gauge Height.	September. Dis-charge.	October. Gauge Height.	October. Dis-charge.	November a Gauge Height	November a Dis-charge.	December.a Gauge Height.	December.a Dis-charge
	Feet.	Sec.-ft.	Feet.	Sec.-ft.	Feet.	Sec.-ft.	Feet.	Sec.-ft.	Feet.	Sec.-ft.	Feet.	Sec.-ft.
1	3.83	1,288	3 08	439	3.12	467	3.18	510	3 38	690	2.58	156
2	3 85	1,320	3 06	425	3.04	412	3 20	525	3 35	630	3 14	385
3	3 84	1,304	3 05	419	2.96	360	3 25	568	3.46	710	3.02	318
4	3 81	1,256	3 04	412	2.97	366	3.30	610	3.51	734	3.30	503
5	3 86	1,336	3 03	405	2.92	335	3.24	559	3.54	734	3.00	308
6	3.87	1,352	3.01	392	2.89	318	3.32	630	3.61	806	2.95	288
7	3.84	1,304	2.99	379	2.88	313	3.31	620	3.59	782	2.88	256
8	3.81	1,256	2.96	360	2.88	313	3.27	585	3.56	734	2.85	243
9	3.78	1,210	2.93	342	2.92	335	3.29	602	3.52	806	2.82	230
10	3.74	1,150	2.94	348	2.88	313	3.26	576	3.50	660	2.79	224
11	3.70	1,090	2.91	329	2.85	298	3.26	576	3.45	610	2.76	214
12	3.65	1,025	2.90	323	2.76	256	3.27	585	3.43	585	2.73	204
13	3.61	973	2.89	318	2.78	264	3.30	610	3.44	593	2.79	224
14	3.64	1,012	2.87	308	2.80	273	3.34	650	3.55	690	2.73	208
15	3.58	934	2.86	303	2.78	264	3.53	869	3.37	525	2.69	195
16	3.55	895	2.85	298	2.80	273	3 68	1,064	3.35	503	2.51	130
17	3.52	856	2.99	379	2.83	288	3.83	1,288	3.32	481	2.40	129
18	3.50	830	3.18	510	2.83	288	3.93	1,454	3.30	459	2.30	113
19	3.48	806	3.23	551	2.90	323	3 92	1,436	3 35	496	2.21	101
20	3.47	794	3.23	551	3.02	398	3.92	1,436	3.27	445	2.12	93
21	3.46	782	3.23	551	3.13	474	3.90	1,400	3.19	392	2.55	161
22	3.33	640	3.23	551	3.16	496	3.85	1,320	3.14	366	2.55	163
23	3.30	610	3.20	525	3.20	525	3.78	1,210	3.09	335	2.54	163
24	3.27	585	3.22	542	3.22	542	3 71	1,105	3.15	373	2.49	154
25	3.24	559	3.21	534	3.23	551	3 64	1,012	3 18	398	2.47	152
26	3.20	525	3.19	518	3.24	559	3.57	921	3.02	303	2.45	150
27	3.17	503	3.17	503	3.26	576	3.50	830	3.02	303	2.46	154
28	3.13	474	3.12	467	3.26	576	3.47	794	3.02	308	2.42	148
29	3.12	467	3.11	459	3.23	551	3.44	758	3.02	308	2.40	146
30	3.11	459	3.09	445	3.20	525	3.41	722	3.05	323	2.44	156
31	3.09	445	3.12	467	......	......	3.39	700	......	......	2.43	154

a Slight ice conditions during November and December.

MONTHLY DISCHARGE of Waterton River at Waterton Mills, for 1914.

(Drainage area 214 square miles.)

MONTH.	DISCHARGE IN SECOND-FEET. Maximum.	Minimum.	Mean.	Per square Mile.	RUN-OFF. Depth in inches on Drainage Area.	Total in Acre-feet.
January	214	114	161	0.752	0.87	9,900
February	165	109	134	0.626	0.65	7,442
March	161	106	131	0.612	0.70	8,055
April	1,135	186	611	2.850	3.18	36,357
May	2,490	1,012	1,913	8.940	10.31	117,626
June	2,908	1,256	1,993	9.310	10.39	118,589
July	1,352	445	905	4.230	4.88	55,646
August	551	298	431	2.010	2.32	26,501
September	576	256	394	1.840	2.05	23,445
October	1,454	510	856	4.000	4.61	52,633
November	806	303	536	2.500	2.79	31,804
December	503	93	201	0.939	1.08	12,359
The year	....	....	....	....	43.83	300,447

SESSIONAL PAPER No. 25c

CROOKED CREEK NEAR WATERTON MILLS.

Location.—On the SW. ¼ Sec. 22, Tp. 2, Rge. 29, W. 4th Mer.
Records available.—September 15, 1909, to October 31, 1914.
Gauge.—Vertical staff; zero of gauge maintained at 89.48 feet during 1913-14.   For previous gauge data, refer to previous reports.
Bench-mark.—Permanent iron bench-mark located on the left bank, 25 feet from the gauge; assumed elevation, 100.00 feet.
Channel.—Consists of sand, gravel and small stones; not liable to shift.
Discharge measurements.—Made by wading.
Winter flow.—No records are kept after October 31.
Observer.—Frank Rowe.

DISCHARGE MEASUREMENTS of Crooked Creek near Waterton Mills, in 1914.

Date.	Engineer.	Width.	Area of Section.	Mean Velocity.	Gauge Height.	Discharge.
		Feet.	*Sq. ft.*	*Ft. per sec.*	*Feet.*	*Sec.-ft.*
April 2	O. H. Hoover	12.6	11.40	1.34	2.90	15.4
April 15	do	16.9	22.00	1.58	2.26	35.0
May 8............	do	17.6	24.60	1.70	2.36	42.0
May 29............	do	16.8	20.40	1.67	2.15	28.0
June 18..	do	16.5	17.80	1.24	2.05	22.0
Aug. 25............	do	9.2	4.67	2.17	1.78	10.1
Sept. 11	do	6.4	1.88	1.71	1.55	3.2
Sept. 26	do	7.2	2.69	1.78	1.66	4.8
Nov. 5.......	do	16.8	17.50	0.94	2.01	16.5

DAILY GAUGE HEIGHT AND DISCHARGE of Crooked Creek near Waterton Mills, for 1914.

DAY.	April.		May.		June.	
	Gauge Height.	Dis-charge.	Gauge Height.	Dis-charge.	Gauge Height.	Dis-charge.
	Feet.	*Sec.-ft.*	*Feet.*	*Sec.-ft.*	*Feet.*	*Sec.-ft.*
1............	....	....	1.99	18.7	2.07	23.0
2............	....	....	2.00	19.2	2.10	25.0
3............	....	....	2.05	22.0	2.11	26.0
4............	....	....	2.21	32.0	2.09	24.0
5............	....	....	2.29	37.0	2.15	28.0
6............	...	....	2.34	41.0	2.17	29.0
7............	....	....	2.35	42.0	2.11	26.0
8............	1.71	7.3	2.35	42.0	2.04	22.0
9............	1.80	10.4	2.37	43.0	2.00	19.2
10............	1.77	9.3	2.65	63.0	1.97	17.8
11............	1.83	11.6	2.51	53.0	1.93	15.8
12............	2.07	23.0	2.34	41.0	1.90	14.4
13............	2.12	26.0	2.29	37.0	2.37	43.0
14............	2.05	22.0	2.24	34.0	2.54	55.0
15............	2.00	19.2	2.24	34.0	2.39	44.0
16............	2.21	32.0	2.24	34.0	2.28	37.0
17............	2.05	22.0	2.24	34.0	2.10	25.0
18............	2.01	19.8	2.24	34.0	2.05	22.0
19............	2.06	23.0	2.24	34.0	2.02	20.0
20............	2.32	39.0	2.34	41.0	1.98	18.2
21............	2.25	35.0	2.34	41.0	1.94	16.3
22............	2.19	30.0	2.28	37.0	1.93	15.8
23............	2.14	27.0	2.25	35.0	1.91	14.9
24............	2.15	28.0	2.23	33.0	1.99	18.7
25............	2.05	22.0	2.23	33.0	2.35	42.0
26............	2.03	21.0	2.22	32.0	2.40	45.0
27............	2.00	19.2	2.19	30.0	2.23	33.0
28............	2.10	25.0	2.16	29.0	2.10	25.0
29............	2.06	23.0	2.14	27.0	2.11	26.0
30............	2.01	19.8	2.11	26.0	2.09	24.0
31............	....	....	2.09	24.0	....	....

5 GEORGE V, A. 1915

DAILY GAUGE HEIGHT AND DISCHARGE of Crooked Creek near Waterton Mills, for 1914.
—*Concluded.*

DAY.	July.		August.		September.		October.	
	Gauge Height.	Dis-charge.	Gauge Height.	Dis-charge.	Gauge Height.	Dis-charge.	Gauge Height.	Dis-charge.
	Feet.	*Sec.-ft.*	*Feet.*	*Sec.-ft.*	*Feet.*	*Sec.-ft.*	*Feet.*	*Sec.-ft.*
1	1.99	18.7	1.53	2.8	1.59	4.1	1.67	6.2
2	1.98	18.2	1.52	2.6	1.58	3.9	1.69	6.7
3	1.89	14.0	1.50	2.2	1.58	3.9	1.89	14.0
4	1.86	12.8	1.47	1.8	1.56	3.5	1.84	12.0
5	2.02	20.0	1.47	1.8	1.56	3.5	1.77	9.3
6	1.95	16.8	1.49	2.0	1.56	3.5	1.89	14.0
7	1.89	14.0	1.49	2.0	1.56	3.5	1.82	11.2
8	1.85	12.4	1.49	2.0	1.68	6.5	1.90	14.4
9	1.82	11.2	1.51	2.4	1.67	6.2	1.95	16.8
10	1.80	10.4	1.58	3.9	1.67	6.2	1.89	14.0
11	1.79	10.1	1.53	2.8	1.55	3.2	1.84	12.0
12	1.86	12.8	1.51	2.4	1.58	3.9	1.95	16.8
13	1.74	8.3	1.49	2.0	1.63	5.0	2.77	71.0
14	1.76	9.0	1.47	1.8	1.69	6.7	2.78	72.0
15	1.71	7.3	1.46	1.6	1.70	7.0	2.81	74.0
16	1.71	7.3	1.46	1.6	1.73	8.0	2.86	77.0
17	1.69	6.7	1.70	7.0	1.86	12.8	2.77	71.0
18	1.67	6.2	1.96	17.3	1.71	7.3	2.65	63.0
19	1.64	5.4	1.74	8.4	1.69	6.7	2.50	52.0
20	1.63	5.1	1.73	8.0	1.74	8.3	2.50	52.0
21	1.61	4.6	1.68	6.5	1.76	9.0	2.24	34.0
22	1.61	4.6	1.64	5.4	1.73	8.0	2.26	35.0
23	1.61	4.6	1.64	5.4	1.68	6.5	2.09	24.0
24	1.60	4.3	1.79	10.1	1.68	6.5	2.07	23.0
25	1.59	4.1	1.78	9.7	1.68	6.5	2.04	22.0
26	1.57	3.7	1.68	6.5	1.67	6.2	2.02	20.0
27	1.56	3.5	1.66	5.9	1.67	6.2	2.00	19.2
28	1.55	3.2	1.64	5.4	1.66	5.9	1.98	18.2
29	1.55	3.2	1.64	5.4	1.66	5.9	1.96	17.3
30	1.55	3.2	1.58	3.9	1.68	6.5	1.93	15.8
31	1.54	3.0	1.60	4.3	....	....	1.92	15.4

MONTHLY DISCHARGE of Crooked Creek near Waterton Mills, for 1914.

(Drainage area 26 square miles.)

MONTH.	DISCHARGE IN SECOND-FEET.				RUN-OFF.	
	Maximum.	Minimum.	Mean.	Per square Mile.	Depth in inches on Drainage Area.	Total in Acre-feet.
April (8–30)	39.0	7.30	22.0	0.846	0.72	1,004
May	63.0	18.70	35.0	1.350	1.56	2,152
June	55.0	14.40	26.0	1.000	1.12	1,547
July	20.0	3.00	8.7	0.335	0.39	535
August	17.3	1.60	4.7	0.181	0.21	289
September	12.8	3.20	6.0	0.231	0.26	357
October	77.0	6.20	30.0	1.150	1.33	1,845
The period	....	....	....	....	5.59	7,729

MISCELLANEOUS DISCHARGE MEASUREMENTS made in Waterton River drainage basin, in 1914.

Date.	Engineer.	Stream.	Location.	Width.	Area of Section.	Mean Velocity.	Discharge.
				Feet.	*Sq. ft.*	*Ft. per sec.*	*Sec.-ft.*
Aug. 24....	O. H. Hoover...	Berta Creek......	Waterton Lakes.	7.8	5.06	1.44	7.3
June 17....	do ...	Blakiston Brook...	NE. 30-1-29-4..	27.9	64.28	5.88	378.0
July 4....	do ...	do	do ..	40.8	59.30	3.32	197.0
Aug. 3....	do ...	do	SE. 30-1-20-4...	28.0	20.70	2.10	43.0
Aug. 22...	do ...	do	Waterton Lakes.	34.0	39.50	3.31	131.0
Sept. 11....	do ...	do	do ..	27.7	26.10	1.60	42.0
Aug. 4...	do ...	Cottonwood Creek.	20-2-29-4.......	23.5	7.14	0.77	5.5
Aug. 4..	do ...	do N. Br.	29-2-29-4.......	8.6	2.43	0.97	2.4
Aug. 4...	do ...	Foothill Creek....	11-5-29-4.......	17.4	18.00	1.19	21.0
Aug. 24...	do ...	Hellroaring Creek..	Waterton Lake.	18.2	8.17	1.28	10.4
June 17...	do ...	Oil Creek.......	NE. 30-1-29-4..	65.0	80.20	2.93	235.0
July 4...	do ...	do	do ..	48.0	64.50	2.17	140.0
Aug. 3...	do ...	do	NW. 23-1-30-4.	22.0	24.70	1.62	40.0
Aug. 24...	do ...	do	Waterton Lake.	32.3	45.30	1.42	66.0
Aug. 4...	do ...	Pine Creek.......	33-3-29-4.......	11.4	8.55	1.10	9.4
Aug. 4...	do ...	Yarrow Creek.....	14-4-29-4.......	29.6	20.20	1.20	24.0

BELLY RIVER DRAINAGE BASIN.

General Description.

Belly River rises near Chief Mountain, in northern Montana. The main stream is augmented on the United States side of the boundary line by Middle Fork, and on the Canadian side by North Fork. From the junction with North Fork, in Sec. 21, Tp. 1, Rge. 28, W. 4th Mer., the river flows in a winding northeasterly course until it is joined by Oldman River in Sec. 27, Tp. 9, Rge. 23, W. 4th Mer., where it turns southeasterly, and after making a loop, flows in a north and easterly direction until it joins Bow River in Sec. 27, Tp. 11, Rge. 13, W. 4th Mer., and forms the South Saskatchewan River.

The topography of the basin is of the most varied character, ranging from the mountainous regions of Montana and the rolling prairie and foothills at the boundary to the level prairie which extends from Lethbridge to the junction with the Bow River. The upper tributaries drain a forested region; the main stream flows through a deep valley with many clumps of large whitewood on its banks.

There is an abundant snowfall in the upper portion of the basin, but the precipitation diminishes into semi-arid conditions near Lethbridge. At first, Belly River is a comparatively clear stream, but soon after crossing the boundary line it gradually becomes turbid, especially at the times of high water. The greater portion of the sediment is caused by the washing away of banks and cutting of new channels. Freshets caused by melting snow and heavy rains are frequent in the summer. The maximum flow usually occurs in June or July, and after that the flow gradually decreases until it reaches the minimum in January or February.

As yet very little use has been made of the water in this basin. In the upper regions, where water could easily be diverted, it is not required for irrigation purposes, and farther downstream it would be an expensive undertaking.

There are a couple of small private irrigation schemes diverting water from this river, and the city of Lethbridge receives its domestic supply from the same source.

The Alberta Railway and Irrigation Company have located and may construct a canal from Belly River to supply their irrigation system, if St. Mary River is found deficient. A survey and estimate of the cost of this proposed canal were made by the government during 1912, and a copy of the report may be seen in the report of the Commissioner of Irrigation for 1912. There are also a number of feasible power sites in the upper regions which will no doubt be developed when there is a market.

BELLY RIVER NEAR MOUNTAIN VIEW.

Location.—On the NE. ¼ Sec. 5, Tp. 2, Rge. 28, W. 4th Mer., at John West's ranch.
Records available.—November 1, 1911, to December 31, 1914.
Gauge.—Vertical staff; zero of gauge maintained at 4,344.90 feet during 1911-14.
Bench-mark.—Permanent iron bench-mark, located on the right bank at the station; elevation 4,356.74 above mean sea level (Irrigation Surveys datum).
Channel.—Composed of gravel and sand; not liable to shift on account of the rocky control about 200 feet downstream.
Discharge measurements.—Made from a cable car for all open water measurements.
Winter flow.—Winter records are obtained about 100 feet above the cable.
Observer.—J. N. West.

STREAM MEASUREMENTS, 1914

5 GEORGE V, A. 1915

DISCHARGE MEASUREMENTS of Belly River near Mountain View, in 1914.

Date.	Engineer.	Width.	Area of Section.	Mean Velocity.	Gauge Height.	Discharge.
		Feet.	*Sq. ft.*	*Ft. per sec.*	*Feet.*	*Sec.-ft.*
Jan. 5.............	J. E. Degnan...............	55.0	102.0	0.93	2.21	95
Jan. 16.............	do	55.0	102.0	0.82	1.98	84
Jan. 30.............	do	54.0	67.7	0.74	1.90	50
Feb. 12.............	do	55.0	91.0	0.76	2.52	69
Mar. 9.............	do	54.0	91.7	0.65	1.81	59
April 1.............	O. H. Hoover...	47.4	60.3	1.25	1.66	75
April 15.............	do	86.0	214.0	1.09	2.20	233
May 8.............	do	92.0	256.0	1.89	2.73	485
May 27.............	do	96.0	305.0	2.65	3.24	808
June 15....	do	99.0	341.0	3.64	3.69	1,243
July 7.............	do	96.0	295.0	2.52	3.18	744
July 28.............	do	88.0	229.0	1.48	2.47	339
Aug. 19.............	do	90.0	242.0	1.69	2.63	411
Sept. 10.	do	83.5	195.0	0.86	2.04	168
Oct. 21.............	do	92.0	266.0	1.90	2.80	506
Nov. 20.............	do	83.0	204.0	0.93	2.13	191
Dec. 2.............	do	84.0	204.0	0.82	2.12	168
Dec. 22.............	do	56.0	142.6	0.64	2.42	92

DAILY GAUGE HEIGHT AND DISCHARGE of Belly River near Mountain View, for 1914.

DAY.	January.		February.		March.		April.		May.		June.	
	Gauge Height.	Dis-charge.	Gauge Height.	Dis-charge.	Gauge Height.	Dis-charge	Gauge Height.	Dis-charge.	Gauge Height.	Dis-charge.	Gauge Height.	Dis-charge.
	Feet.	*Sec.-ft.*	*Feet.*	*Sec.-ft.*	*Feet.*	*Sec.-ft.*	*Feet.*	*Sec.-ft.*	*Feet.*	*Sec.-ft.*	*Feet.*	*Sec.-ft.*
1...........	2.12	93a	1.93	56	1.70	65	1.75	75	2.60	400	3.40	958
2...........	2.12	91	2.04	56	1.80	64	1.63	76	2.90	582	3.55	1,082
3...........	2.08	91	2.05	55	1.90	63	1.63	77	3.31	884	3.76	1,260
4...........	2.12	93	2.04	53	2.00	62	1.66	78	3.20	798	3.75	1,251
5...........	2.16	95	2.05	54	1.80	62	1.79	79	3.00	652	3.65	1,166
6...........	2.00	96	2.15	58	1.80	61	1.79	78	2.92	596	3.44	991
7...........	2.13	94	2.30	62	1.90	60	1.74	78	2.81	523	3.10	724
8...........	2.14	92	2.40	66	1.80	59	1.75	78	2.73	463	3.02	666
9...........	2.08	89	2.40	66	1.83	59	1.79	81	2.93	603	2.90	582
10...........	2.07	87	2.42	67	1.60	60	1.83	100a	2.97	631	2.74	479
11...........	2.07	86	2.40	68	1.70	61	1.89	126	3.00	652	2.74	479
12...........	2.10	88	2.52	69	1.85	62	1.94	141	3.05b	688	2.75	486
13...........	2.00	88	2.53	70	1.90	63	2.06	176	3.10b	724	3.80	1,294
14...........	2.02	86	2.15	71	1.90	64	2.14	204	3.16	768	3.89	1,370
15....	2.00	85	2.10	72	1.85	65	2.19	221	3.12	739	3.69	1,200
16...........	1.98	84	2.05	72	1.90	65	2.35	283	3.35	917	3.52	1,057
17...........	2.00	82	2.05	72	1.90	65	2.40	304	3.61	1,132	3.54	1,074
18...........	2.05	80	2.00	71	1.93	65	2.35	283	3.63	1,150	3.56	1,090
19...........	2.00	78	2.00	70	1.75	65	2.45	327	3.56	1,090	3.52	1,057
20...........	1.95	74	1.95	69	1.80	66	2.60	400	3.47	1,015	3.50	1,040
21...........	1.95	71	2.00	67	1.65	67	2.70	455	3.44	991	3.15	761
22...........	2.04	66	1.95	65	1.70	68	2.65	428	3.22	814	3.10	724
23...........	2.07	61	1.90	63	1.67	68	2.66	433	3.16	768	3.05	688
24...........	2.08	58	2.00	63	1.65	67	2.74	479	3.36	925	3.08	710
25...........	2.25	56	1.84	64	1.57	67	2.73	473	3.52	1,057	3.05	688
26...........	2.25	61	1.70	65	1.90	67	2.70	455	3.47	1,015	3.00	652
27...........	2.27	64	1.70	66	2.00	68	2.62	411	3.52	1,057	2.95	617
28...........	2.34	62	1.60	67	1.95	69	2.65	428	3.18	783	2.94	610
29...........	2.35	60	......	......	1.85	73	2.60	400	3.04	681	2.98	638
30...........	1.91	50	......	......	1.82	75	2.55	375	3.00	652	3.00	652
31...........	1.93	52	......	......	1.72	75	......	......	3.40	958	......	......

a to a Ice conditions.
b Gauge height interpolated.

SESSIONAL PAPER No. 25c

DAILY GAUGE HEIGHT AND DISCHARGE of Belly River near Mountain View, for 1914.
—*Concluded.*

DAY.	July.		August.		September.		October.		November		December	
	Gauge Height.	Dis- charge	Gauge Height.	Dis- charge.	Gauge Height.	Dis- charge.	Gauge Height	Dis- charge.	Gauge Height.	Dis- charge	Gauge Height.	Dis- charge.
	Feet.	*Sec.-ft.*	*Feet.*	*Sec.-ft.*	*Feet.*	*Sec.-ft.*	*Feet.*	*Sec.-ft.*	*Feet*	*Sec.-ft.*	*Feet.*	*Sec.-ft.*
1...........	2.96	624	2.47	336	2.10	190	2.25	243	2 36	287	2 16	175
2...........	3.00	652	2.47	336	2.05	174	2.24	239	2.40	304	2.01	168
3...........	3.04	681	2 46	332	2.04	171	2.43	318	2.61	406	2.10	165
4...........	3.10	724	2.46	332	2.03	168	2 40	304	2 62	411	2.10	162
5...........	3.20	798	2 48	341	2.03	168	2.39	300	2 64	422	2 08	153
6...........	3.20	798	2.42	313	2.02	164	2.37	291	2.67	438	2.07	141
7...........	3.19	791	2.42	313	2.02	164	2.36	287	2.60	490	2.10	132
8...........	3.14	754	2.36	287	2.02	164	2.33	275	2.51	355	2.36	124
9...........	3.09	717	2.28	254	2.01*a*	161	2.34	279	2.43	318	2.45	121
10....	3.05	688	2.23	243	2.01	161	2.30	262	2.43	318	2.58	119
11...........	2.96	624	2.23	235	2.01	161	2.27	251	2.44	322	2.64	117
12	2.96	624	2.20	224	2.02	164	2.21	228	2.44*b*	313	2.75	115
13... ᵧ	2.95	617	2.20	224	2.01	161	2.26	247	2.37	282	2.76	116
14...........	2.96	624	2.18	217	2.01	161	2.53	365	2.35	270	2.77	115
15...........	2.90	582	2.18	217	2.03	168	2.97	631	2.19	253	2.78	110
16...	2.86	556	2.17	214	2.04	171	3.15	761	2.10	243	2.78	101
17...........	2.81	523	2.20	224	2.06	177	3.26	845	2.30	247	2.64	103
18..	2.70	455	2.70	455	2.20	224	3.13	746	2.20	240	2.48	100
19...........	2.66	433	2.63	416	2.44	322	3.05	688	2.15	223	2.45	94
20...........	2.65	428	2.55	375	2.56	380	2.98	638	2.12	207	2.45	87
21...	2.60	400	2.48	341	2.60	400	2.80	516	2.11	193	2.47	89
22...........	2.57	385	2.40	304	2.50	350	2.70	455	2.11	187	2.47	92
23...........	2.55	375	2.36	287	2.46	332	2.57	385	2.12	190	2.44	98
24..	2.53	365	2.36	287	2.44	322	2.50	350	2.12	198	2.42	102
25...........	2.50	350	2.36	287	2.43	318	2.44	322	2.15*c*	207	2.38	100
26...........	2.48	341	2.30	262	2.42	313	2.40	304	2.10	190	2.35	95
27...........	2.48	341	2.25	243	2.40	304	2.35	283	2.07	180	2.17	90
28...........	2.47	336	2.24	239	2.40	304	2.32	270	2.09	187	2.20	86
29........	2.48	341	2.24	239	2.36	287	2.30	262	2.08*d*	184	2.11	81
30...........	2.47	336	2.18	217	2.31	266	2.28	254	2.13	179	2.27*d*	77
31...........	2.46	332	2.14	204	....		2.30	262	....		2 12	77

a Gauge height interpolated.
b to c Ice conditions.
d to d Ice conditions.

MONTHLY DISCHARGE of Belly River near Mountain View, for 1914.

(Drainage area 121 square miles.)

MONTH.	DISCHARGE IN SECOND-FEET				RUN-OFF.	
	Maximum.	Minimum.	Mean.	Per square Mile.	Depth in inches on Drainage Area.	Total in Acre-feet.
January..........................	96	52	78	0.645	0.744	4,796
February..........................	72	53	65	0.537	0.559	3,610
March..........................	75	59	65	0.537	0.619	3,997
April..........................	479	75	253	2.090	0.233	15,055
May..........................	1,150	400	797	6.590	7.600	49,006
June..........................	1,370	479	868	7.170	8.000	51,650
July..........................	798	332	535	4.420	5.100	32,896
August..........................	455	204	284	2.350	2.710	17,462
September.......	400	161	232	1.920	2.140	13,805
October....	845	228	383	3.170	3.660	23,550
November..........................	438	179	272	2.250	2.510	16,185
December.......	175	77	113	0.934	1.080	6,948
The year..........................	....	....	....	....	34 955	238,960

5 GEORGE V, A. 1915

MAMI CREEK NEAR MOUNTAIN VIEW.

Location.—On the NE. ¼ Sec. 18, Tp. 2, Rge. 27, W. 4th Mer.
Records available.—August 13, 1909, to October 31, 1914.
Gauge.—Vertical staff; zero of gauge maintained at 93.06 feet during 1909-14.
Bench-marks.—Permanent iron bench-mark; assumed elevation, 100.00 feet.
Channel.—Composed of stones covered with sand and gravel; not liable to shift.
Discharge measurements.—Made by wading.
Winter flow.—Records are discontinued after October 31.
Observer.—C. H. Findlay.

DISCHARGE MEASUREMENTS of Mami Creek near Mountain View, in 1914.

Date.	Engineer.	Width.	Area of Section.	Mean Velocity.	Gauge Height.	Discharge.
		Feet.	*Sq. ft.*	*Ft. per sec.*	*Feet.*	*Sec.-ft.*
April 1...........	O. H. Hoover............	5.6	2.13	1.20	3.41	2.60
May 9...........	do	14.0	9.73	2.05	2.42	19.90
May 30...........	do	11.3	5.07	1.67	2.14	6.20
June 13...........	do	12.0	6.28	1.30	2.25	8.20
July 3...........	do	9.3	2.85	0.78	2.00	2.20
Aug. 1...........	do	....	....	........*a*	1.82	0.23
Aug. 21...........	do	....	....	........*a*	1.90	0.60
Sept. 10...........	do	....	....	........*a*	1.85	0.35
Sept. 29...........	do	....	....	........*a*	1.86	0.45
Oct. 21...........	do	12.7	6.81	1.42	2.22	9.70
Nov. 6...........	do	11.6	5.07	0.99	2.13	5.00

a Weir measurement.

DAILY GAUGE HEIGHT AND DISCHARGE of Mami Creek near Mountain View, for 1914.

DAY.	April.		May.		June.	
	Gauge Height.	Dis-charge.	Gauge Height.	Dis-charge.	Gauge Height.	Dis-charge.
	Feet.	*Sec.-ft.*	*Feet.*	*Sec.-ft.*	*Feet.*	*Sec.-ft.*
1...........	....	....	2.19	7.0	2.13	5.0
2...........	....	....	2.20	7.4	2.13	5.0
3...........	....	....	2.21	7.8	2.13	5.0
4...........	....	....	2.23	8.7	2.14	5.3
5...........	....	....	2.29	11.5	2.14	5.3
6...........	....	....	2.37	16.4	2.18	6.7
7...........	....	....	2.44	21.3	2.16	6.0
8...........	....	....	2.41	19.2	2.14	5.3
9...........	....	....	2.42	19.9	2.14	5.3
10...........	....	....	2.48	24.0	2.14	5.3
11...........	....	....	2.50	26.0	2.12	4.8
12...........	....	....	2.40	18.5	2.10	4.2
13...........	....	....	2.36	15.7	2.12	4.8
14...........	....	....	2.35	15.0	2.16	6.0
15...........	....	....	2.32	13.2	2.18	6.7
16...........	....	....	2.29	11.5	2.16	6.0
17...........	2.24	9.1	2.26	10.0	2.14	5.3
18...........	2.24	9.1	2.23	8.7	2.13	5.0
19...........	2.30	12.0	2.23	8.7	2.13	5.0
20...........	2.35	15.0	2.35	15.0	2.13	5.0
21...........	2.31	12.6	2.30	12.0	2.11	4.5
22...........	2.29	11.5	2.28	11.0	2.09	3.9
23...........	2.24	9.1	2.27	10.5	2.08	3.7
24...........	2.22	8.2	2.26	10.0	2.08	3.7
25...........	2.22	8.2	2.25	9.5	2.13	5.0
26...........	2.20	7.4	2.24	9.1	2.29	11.5
27...........	2.20	7.4	2.18	6.7	2.27	10.5
28...........	2.22	8.2	2.16	6.0	2.25	9.5
29...........	2.23	8.7	2.16	6.0	2.20	7.4
30...........	2.21	7.8	2.14	5.3	2.15	5.6
31...........	....	....	2.13	5.0	....	....

SESSIONAL PAPER No. 25c

DAILY GAUGE HEIGHT AND DISCHARGE of Mami Creek near Mountain View, for 1914.
—*Concluded.*

DAY.	July.		August.		September.		October.	
	Gauge Height.	Dis-charge.	Gauge Height.	Dis-charge.	Gauge Height.	Dis-charge.	Gauge Height.	Dis-charge.
	Feet.	*Sec.-ft.*	*Feet.*	*Sec.-ft.*	*Feet.*	*Sec.-ft.*	*Feet.*	*Sec.-ft.*
1	2.10	4.20	1.96	1.36	1.91	0.80	1.88	0.58
2	2.08	3.70	1.90	0.70	1.90	0.70	1.90	0.70
3	2.08	3.70	1.83	0.32	1.88	0.58	1.90	0.70
4	2.08	3.70	1.81	0.24	1.90	0.70	1.93	1.00
5	2.10	4.20	1.80	0.20	1.90	0.70	1.98	1.68
6	2.09	3.90	1.79	0.18	1.90	0.70	2.08	3.70
7	2.08	3.70	1.78	0.16	1.98	1.68	2.08	3.70
8	2.08	3.70	1.80	0.20	2.00	2.00	2.08	3.70
9	2.00	2.00	1.88	0.58	2.00	2.00	2.08	3.70
10	2.00	2.00	1.88	0.58	1.96	1.36	2.08	3.70
11	1.99	1.84	1.88	0.58	1.96	1.36	2.08	3.70
12	1.99	1.84	1.88	0.58	1.98	1.68	2.08	3.70
13	1.99	1.84	1.87	0.52	2.00	2.00	2.08	3.70
14	2.00	2.00	1.86	0.46	1.96	1.36	2.13	5.00
15	2.00	2.00	1.85	0.40	1.98	1.68	2.15	5.60
16	2.00	2.00	1.84	0.36	1.99	1.84	2.18	6.70
17	2.00	2.00	2.01	2.20	1.99	1.84	2.20	7.40
18	2.00	2.00	2.02	2.40	1.99	1.84	2.23	8.70
19	2.00	2.00	2.04	2.70	1.99	1.84	2.25	9.50
20	2.00	2.00	1.98	1.68	1.99	1.84	2.28	11.00
21	2.00	2.00	1.95	1.20	1.98	1.68	2.26	10.00
22	2.00	2.00	1.90	0.70	1.98	1.68	2.23	8.70
23	2.00	2.00	2.03	2.50	1.96	1.36	2.20	7.40
24	2.00	2.00	2.02	2.40	1.93	1.00	2.18	6.70
25	2.00	2.00	2.00	2.00	1.90	0.70	2.17	6.30
26	2.00	2.00	1.97	1.52	1.89	0.64	2.16	6.00
27	1.99	1.84	1.90	0.70	1.88	0.58	2.15	5.60
28	1.99	1.84	1.89	0.64	1.88	0.58	2.14	5.30
29	1.98	1.68	1.89	0.64	1.88	0.58	2.14	5.30
30	1.97	1.52	1.89	0.64	1.88	0.58	2.14	5.30
31	1.96	1.36	1.89	0.64	....	....	2.14	5.30

MONTHLY DISCHARGE of Mami Creek near Mountain View, for 1914.

(Drainage area 22 square miles).

MONTH.	DISCHARGE IN SECOND-FEET.				RUN-OFF.	
	Maximum.	Minimum.	Mean.	Per square Mile.	Depth in inches on Drainage Area.	Total in Acre-feet.
April (17–30)	15.0	7.40	9.60	0.436	0.23	266
May	26.0	5.00	12.10	0.550	0.63	744
June	11.5	3.70	5.70	0.259	0.29	339
July	4.2	1.36	2.40	0.110	0.13	148
August	2.7	0.16	0.97	0.044	0.05	60
September	2.0	0.58	1.38	0.063	0.07	82
October	11.0	0.58	5.20	0.236	0.27	320
The period	....	....	....	....	1.67	1,959

5 GEORGE V, A. 1915

CHRISTIANSON DITCH NEAR MOUNTAIN VIEW.

Location.—On the SE. ¼ Sec. 12, Tp. 3, Rge. 28, W. 4th Mer.
Records available.—May 17, 1913, to July 1, 1913.   One discharge measurement only in 1914.
Gauge.—Plain staff; elevation of zero 96.04 feet.
Bench-mark.—Wooden stake, left bank; assumed elevation, 100.00 feet.
Observer.—No observations in 1914.

DISCHARGE MEASUREMENTS of Christianson Ditch near Mountain View, in 1914.

Date.	Engineer.	Width.	Area of Section.	Mean Velocity.	Gauge Height.	Discharge.
		Feet.	*Sq. ft.*	*Ft. per sec.*	*Feet.*	*Sec.-ft.*
June 18........	O. H. Hoover..	5.5	3 41	0.57	1.62	1.94

BELLY RIVER NEAR STAND OFF.

Location.—On the SE. ¼ Sec. 21, Tp. 6, Rge. 25, W. 4th Mer., near Stand Off.
Records available.—May 27, 1909, to December 31, 1914.
Gauge.—Chain gauge from bank; zero of gauge maintained at 92.51 feet during 1909-12; 91.82 feet during 1913; 90.82 feet during 1914.
Bench-mark.—Permanent iron bench-mark; assumed elevation, 100.00 feet.
Channel.—Composed of clean gravel and small stones; not liable to shift.
Discharge measurements.—Made by wading at low stages, and from the traffic bridge on the NE. ¼ Sec. 21, Tp. 6, Rge. 25, W. 4th Mer., at high stages.
Winter flow.—Measurements through the ice are made at a point 150 feet below the chain gauge.
Observer.—George Pearson.

DISCHARGE MEASUREMENTS of Belly River near Stand Off, in 1914.

Date.	Engineer.	Width.	Area of Section.	Mean Velocity.	Gauge Height.	Discharge.
		Feet.	*Sq. ft.*	*Ft. per sec.*	*Feet.*	*Sec.-ft.*
Jan. 26............	R. Palmer.........	35.0	65.2	0.93	1.44	58
Feb. 26............	E. W. W. Hughes...........	41.0	58.1	1.06	2.33	61
March 13............	F. R. Burfield..............	53.0	64.2	1.67	1.60	107
March 28............	O. H. Hoover	47.0	91.3	1.03	2.25	94
April 13............	do	72.0	106.0	2.15	2.50	228
May 5............	do	92.0	261.0	3.29	3.50	858
May 21............	do	92.3	280.0	3.44	3.70	964
June 11............	do	85.7	202.5	2.78	3.13	563
July 9	do	90.9	233.0	3.45	3.39	701
Aug. 6............	do	86.0	167.0	2.11	2.79	352
Aug. 31............	do	74.0	111.0	2.15	2.57	238
Sept. 14............	do	67.5	94.5	1.66	2.37	157
Nov. 16............	do	88.0	153.0	1.04	2.84	159
Dec. 5............	do	86.0	103.0	0.72	2.88	74
Dec. 18............	do	34.0	40.1	1.83	1.35	73

SESSIONAL PAPER No. 25c

DAILY GAUGE HEIGHT AND DISCHARGE of Belly River near Stand Off, for 1914.

DAY.	January.		February.		March.		April.		May.		June.	
	Gauge Height.	Dis- charge	Gauge Height	Dis- charge.	Gauge Height.	Dis- charge	Gauge Height	Dis- charge	Gauge Height	Dis- charge.	Gauge Height	Dis- charge.
	Feet.	*Sec.-ft.*	*Feet.*	*Sec.-ft.*	*Feet.*	*Sec.-ft.*	*Feet.*	*Sec.-ft.*	*Feet.*	*Sec.-ft.*	*Feet.*	*Sec.-ft*
1	1.89	143	1.19	59	2.09	63	2.45	188	3.08	526	3.49	798
2	1.89	144	1.19	52	2 09	64	2.45	188	3.15	569	3.55	843
3	1.89	145	1.19	43	2 04	64	2 35	146	3.41	740	3.80	1,043
4	1.89	147	1 21	38	1.97	65	2 25	108	3.65	921	4 15	1,338
5		145	1.22	31	1.94	68	2 28	119	4.45	1,604	4.10	1,295
6		140	1.24	29	1.88	72	2.30	126	4 00	1,210	3.90	1,126
7		132	1.19	36	1.83	77	2.30	126	3.50	805	3.66	929
8		122	1.19	44	1.73	83	2.32	134	3 00	478	3 55	843
9		113	1.29	49		83	2.34	142	3.15	569	3.31	672
10		110	1.29	50		83	2.35	146	3 46	776	3.16	573
11		107	1.29	46		87	2.39	163	3.50	805	3.11	544
12		105	1.41	46		94	2.39	163	3.35	699	3.15	569
13		106	1.94	51		107	2.60	258	3.15	569	3.15	569
14		106	2.32	55		115	2.70	310	3.16	575	4.15	1,338
15		105	2.33	60	2.15	114	2.85	392	3.55	843	4.05	1,252
16		103	2.29	67	2.20	112	2.89	414	3 66	929	3 96	1,176
17		98	2.29	63	2.20	111	2.90	420	3.75	1,002	3.81	1,051
18		88		57	2.25	109	2.90	420	3.95	1,168	3 95	1,168
19		72		53	2.25	107	3.00	478	3.86	1,093	3.81	1,051
20		55		47	2.25	106	3.11	544	3.76	1,010	3 79	1,035
21		45	2.29	41	2.30	105	3.20	600	3.70	961	3.67	937
22		51	2.32	42	2.30	103	3.21	606	3.60	881	3.56	851
23		55	2.29	45	2.30	101	3.20	600	3.62	897	3.42	747
24		55	2.30	48	2.25	98	3.18	588	3.62	897	3.39	726
25		57	2.30	53		95	3.15	569	3.89	1,118	3.36	706
26	1.44	58	2.33	61		92	3.15	569	3.89	1,118	3.36	706
27	1.44	56	2.25	62		93	3.15	569	3 76	1,010	3.34	692
28	1.44	48	2.10	62	2.45	94	3.13	557	3.65	921	3 34	692
29	1.19	47			2.45	120	3.10	538	3.58	866	3.34	692
30	1.19	58			2.50	165	3.08	526	3.41	740	3.34	692
31	1.19	65			2.47	180			3.40	733		

5 GEORGE V, A. 1915

DAILY GAUGE HEIGHT AND DISCHARGE of Belly River near Stand Off, for 1914.—*Concluded.*

DAY.	July.		August.		September.		October.		November.		December.	
	Gauge Height.	Dis- charge	Gauge Height.	Dis- charge	Gauge Height.	Dis- charge	Gauge Height.	Dis- charge.	Gauge Height.	Dis- charge	Gauge Height	Dis- charge.
	Feet.	Sec.-ft.	Feet.	Sec.-ft.	Feet.	Sec.-ft.	Feet.	Sec.-ft.	Feet.	Sec.-ft.	Feet.	Sec.-ft.
1	3.32	679	2.79	359	2 50	210	2.76	342	2 86	398	3.18	137
2	3.32	679	2.79	359	2.50	210	2.76	342	2 98	466	3 08	122
3	3.32	679	2.79	359	2 49	206	2.76	342	2 96	455	2.98	97
4	3.38	719	2.79	359	2 49	206	2.76	342	2 96	455	......	83
5	3.46	776	2.77	348	2 48	201	2.77	348	2 96	455	......	74
6	3.58	866	2.75	337	2.46	193	2.77	348	2.92	432	2.88	72
7	3.56	850	2.73	326	2.45	189	2.78	353	2.87	403	2.71	72
8	3.44	762	2.69	305	2.44	184	2.74	332	2.83	381	2.61	72
9	3.39	726	2.65	284	2.42	176	2.73	326	2.78	353	2.53	73
10	3.36	706	2.65	284	2.40	167	2.68	300	2.78	353	2.47	74
11	3.33	685	2.60	258	2.39	163	2.66	289	2.73	326	2.38	75
12	3.28	652	2.60	258	2.37	155	2.72	321	2.71	315	2.32	79
13	3.25	632	2.58	248	2.36	151	2.80	364	2.63	274a	......	75
14	3.12	550	2.57	244	2.36	151	2.85	392	2.78	235	......	75
15	3.10	538	2.55	234	2.40	167	2.90	420	3.13	178	......	75
16	3.08	526	2.53	224	2.45	189	3.50	805	2.98	159	......	76
17	3.05	508	2.76	342	2.50	210	3.70	961	2.98	155	......	75
18	3.05	508	2.76	342	2.52	220	3.60	881	2.98	151	1.31	73
19	3.03	496	3.00	478	2.56	239	3.60	881	2.93	148	1.55	71
20	3.02	490	3.05	508	2.75	337	3.39	726	2.90	145	1.65	72
21	3.00	478	2.95	449	2.85	392	3.30	665	2.84	142	1.65	74
22	3.00	478	2.90	420	2.90	420	3.18	588	2.77	135	1.65	75
23	2.98	466	2.82	375	2.90	420	3.00	478	2.71	130	1.65	75
24	2 97	462	2.79	359	2.85	392	2.94	443	2.71	126	1.65	72
25	2.96	455	2.75	337	2.83	381	2.90	420	2.68	123	1.65	68
26	2.94	443	2.70	310	2.80	364	2.80	364	2.68	122	1.65	66
27	2.93	437	2.60	258	2.78	353	2.75	337	2.68	121	1.60	70
28	2.85	392	2.58	248	2.76	342	2.73	326	2.68	122	1.60	72
29	2.79	359	2.57	244	2.76	342	2.70	310	3.32	127	1.60	74
30	2.79	359	2.57	244	2.76	342	2.68	300	3.33	138	1.63	75
31	2.79	359	2.55	234	......	......	2.67	294	......	......	1.65	77a

a to *a* Ice conditions.

MONTHLY DISCHARGE of Belly River near Stand Off, for 1914.

(Drainage area 461 square miles.)

MONTH.	DISCHARGE IN SECOND-FEET.				RUN-OFF.	
	Maximum	Minimum	Mean.	Per square Mile	Depth in inches on Drainage Area.	Total in Acre-feet.
January	147	45	93	0.202	0.23	5,718
February	67	29	50	0.108	0.11	2,777
March	180	63	98	0.213	0.25	6,026
April	606	108	357	0.774	0.86	21,243
May	1,604	478	872	1.890	2.18	53,617
June	1,338	544	888	1.930	2.15	52,840
July	866	359	571	1.240	1.43	35,109
August	508	224	320	0.604	0.80	19,676
September	420	151	256	0.555	0.62	15,233
October	961	289	450	0.976	1.12	27,609
November	466	121	251	0.544	0.61	14,936
December	137	66	78	0.169	0.19	4,796
The year	....	....	....	....	10 55	259,639

SESSIONAL PAPER No. 25c

BELLY RIVER NEAR LETHBRIDGE.

Location.—On the NW. ¼ Sec. 1, Tp. 9, Rge. 22, W. 4th Mer.
Records available.—August 31, 1911, to December 31, 1914.
Gauge.—Chain gauge located on traffic bridge; zero of gauge maintained at 87.82 feet during 1911-12; 85.70 feet during 1913-14.
Bench-mark.—Top of arrow marked with white paint on the right abutment; assumed elevation, 100.00 feet.
Discharge measurements.—Made from downstream side of the traffic bridge.
Winter flow.—Obtained through the ice one-half mile below the traffic bridge.
Observer.—Wm. Bedster.

DISCHARGE MEASUREMENTS of Belly River near Lethbridge, in 1914.

Date.	Engineer.	Width.	Area of Section.	Mean Velocity.	Gauge Height.	Discharge.
		Feet.	*Sq. ft.*	*Ft. per sec.*	*Feet.*	*Sec.-ft.*
Jan. 10	J. E. Degnan	195	583	1.22	2.75	708
Jan. 21	do	193	511	1.30	2.49	654
Feb. 3	do	188	503	1.33	2.85	618
Feb. 18	do	180	561	1.09	2.77	605
March 4	do	189	742	1.40	2.99	1,043
April 4	J. E. Caughey	325	1,271	1.28	2.58	1,623
March 22	do	367	2,026	2.57	4.76	5,209
May 9	do	380	2,467	2.65	5.34	6,536
May 29	do	415	2,789	3.01	6.20	8,401
June 19	do	424	2,952	3.04	6.37	8,965
July 6	do	373	2,347	2.48	5.20	5,807
July 20	do	353	1,740	1.73	3.70	3,013
Aug. 3	do	336	1,498	1.44	3.01	2,149
Aug. 18	do	300	1,380	1.18	2.65	1,569
Aug. 31	do	231	1,376	1.33	2.80	1,833
Sept. 17	do	292	1,242	1.08	2.40	1,343
Sept. 30	do	339	1,513	1.36	3.06	2,072
Oct. 22	do	370	2,290	2.46	5.23	5,639
Nov. 11	O. H. Hoover	361	1,876	1.91	3.96	3,579
Nov. 25	do	356	1,745	1.84	3.68	3,213
Dec. 10	do	315	1,181	0.61	2.56	720
Dec. 28	do	175	831	1.58	4.39	1,316

STREAM MEASUREMENTS, 1914

5 GEORGE V. A. 1915

DAILY GAUGE HEIGHT AND DISCHARGE of Belly River near Lethbridge, for 1914.

DAY.	January.		February.		March.		April.		May.		June.	
	Gauge Height.	Dis-charge.	Gauge Height.	Dis-charge.	Gauge Height.	Dis-charge	Gauge Height.	Dis-charge	Gauge Height.	Dis-charge.	Gauge Height.	Dis-charge.
	Feet.	Sec.-ft.	Feet.	Sec. ft.	Feet.	Sec.-ft.	Feet.	Sec.-ft.	Feet.	Sec.-ft.	Feet.	Sec.-ft.
1	2.55	620a	......	630	2 97	898	2 35	1,585	4 60	4,880	5.71	6,947
2	2.55	625	......	620	2 97	954	2.49	1,508	4 75	5,200	6.08	8,028
3	2.45	600	2.86	618	2 89	962	2 55	1,585	4.95	5,645	6.52	9,514
4	2.90	732	2.73	605	3.10	1,043	2 45	1,460	5.95	8,285	7.01	11,442
5	2.85	720	2.70	594	2 90	1,075	2.52	1,546	6.19	9,085	7.22	12,324
6	2.89	730	2.63	586	2 69	1,106	2 62	1,676	5 95	8,285	7.00	11,400
7	2.93	740	2.59	580	2 60	1,132	3 22	2,488	5 72	7,598	6.55	9,625
8	2.87	730	2.57	570	2 53	1,158	3 11	2,334	5 36	6,630	6.25	8,575
9	......	720	2.56	562	2 28	1,181	2 79	1,897	5 34	6,536b	5.75	7,055
10	2.80	708	2.53	560	2 35	1,207	2 75	1,845	5 43	6,760	5.55	6,530
11	2.67	681	2.63	562	3.27	1,222	2 78	1,884	6 14	8,840	5.35	6,030
12	2.66	680	2.70	565	2.25	1,260	2 54	1,572	6 15	8,840	5.23	5,749
13	2.69	685	2.74	570	2 28	1,298	3 00	2,180	6 00	8,320	5.16	5,592
14	2.67	690	2.71	577	2 35	1,330	3.50	2,900	5 78	7,640	5.33	5,982
15	2.71	694	2.91	583	2 45	1,370	3 76	3,322	6 04	8,400	6.54	9,588
16	2.79	700	......	590	2 65	1,417	3 90	3,560	6 34	9,400	6.35	8,910
17	2.72	680	......	598	2 55	1,393a	4 22	4,136	6 74	10,880	6.30	8,740
18	2.77	692	2.77	605	2 37	1,364	4.20	4,100	6 94	11,680	6.33	8,842
19	2.67	680	2.79	610	2.35	1,340	4 13	3,974	6 91	11,520	6.37	8,978
20	2.61	662	2.87	618	2 31	1,292	4 00	3,740	6.86	11,240	6.35	8,910
21	2.55	654	2.90	630	2 22	1,184	4 86	5,442	6 77	10,840	6.16	8,282
22	2.45	646	2.95	643	2 14	1,088	4.77	5,244	6 53	9,840	6.02	7,842
23	2.36	644	2.89	645	2 11	1,052	4.76	5,222	6 41	9,340	5.78	7,136
24	2.35	639	2.90	662	2 21	1,172	4 72	5,134	6.30	8,960	5.35	6,030
25	2.45	635	2.93	686	2 09	1,029	4.77	5,244	6 60	10,000	5.30	5,910
26	2.54	628	3.00	732	2.07	1,007	4.97	5,691	6 80	10,740	5.41	6,175
27	2.55	624	3.03	783	1.39	290	4 87	5,464	6 62	10,040	5.91	7,510
28	2.55	612	3.00	840	1.48	380	4 81	5,332	6 34	8,920	6.04	7,904
29	2.67	602	......	......	1 67	570	4 77	5,244	6 04	8,401b	5.45	6,275
30	2.85	615	......	......	2.47	1,484	4.68	5,048	5 80	7,190	5.35	6,030
31	3.00	638	......	......	2.51	1,533	......	......	5.67	6,842	......	......

a to a Ice conditions.
b to b Shifting conditions.

SESSIONAL PAPER No. 25c

DAILY GAUGE HEIGHT AND DISCHARGE of Belly River near Lethbridge, for 1914.

DAY.	July.		August.		September.		October.		November.		December.	
	Gauge Height	Dis- charge	Gauge Height.	Dis- charge	Gauge Height.	Dis- charge	Gauge Height.	Dis- charge	Gauge Height.	Dis- charge	Gauge Height.	Dis- charge
	Feet.	*Sec.-ft.*	*Feet.*	*Sec.-ft.*	*Feet.*	*Sec.-ft.*	*Feet.*	*Sec.-ft*	*Feet.*	*Sec.-ft.*	*Feet*	*Sec.-ft.*
1..........	5.22	5,726	2.90	1,920	2 69	1,668	2.95	1,980	3.91	3,305	3 00	2,040
2..........	5.13	5,526	3 05	2,105	2.62	1,584	2 90	1,920	3.92	3,320	2.80	1,800
3..........	5 00	5,240	3 01	2,053	2 58	1,538	2 79	1,788	3.91	3,350	2 63	1,596
4..........	5.00	5,240	2.82	1,824	2.53	1,483	3 11c	2,183	4 03	3,188	2 80	1,800
5..........	5.10 ·	5,460	2.70	1,680	2.46	1,406	3 43c	2,622	4 13	3,648	2.74	1,728a
6..........	5 20	5,680	2 62	1,584	2.38	1,318	3.75	3,070	4.21	3,777	2.49b	1,370
7..........	5.25	5,795	2.53	1,483	2.39	1,320	4.25	3,845	4.28	3,896	1.86	1,060
8..........	5.13	5,526	2.40	1,340	2.42	1,362	3.55	2,790	4.26	3,862	1.82	870
9..........	4.88	4,900	2.57	1,527	2.52	1,472	3.53	2,762	4.14	3,664	1.83	760
10..........	4.80	4,830	2.71	1,692	2.38	1,318	3.50	2,720	4.14	3,664	2.56	720
11..........	4.80	4,830	2.59	1,549	2.38	1,318	3.54	2,776	3.96	3,380	2.50	708
12.	4.53	4,334	2.50	1,450	2.36	1,296	3.61	2,874	3.88	3,260	2.50	704
13..........	4.40	4,100	2.41	1,351	2.32	1,252	3.53	2,762	3.90	3,290	2.95	715
14...	4.45	4,190	2.36	1,296	2.33	1,263	3.52	2,748	3.98	3,410	2.53	730
15..........	4.35	4,015	2.25	1,175	2.34	1,274	4.00	3,410	3.08	2,144	2.63	752
16..........	4.33	3,981	2.20	1,120	2.29	1,219	5 13	5,526	2 80	1,800	4.005	794
17..........	4.30	3,930	2.55	1,505	2.42	1,362	5 75	7,055	2 70	1,680	4.00	835
18..........	4.00	3,440	2.64	1,608	2.37	1,307	5 92	7,540	3.08	2,144	3.98	840
19..........	3.88	3,260	3.78	3,112	2.36	1,296	6 05	7,935	3.25	2,370	3.95	840
20..........	3.70	3,000	3.74	3,056	2.50	1,430	5 75	7,055	3.62	2,888	3.90	858
21..........	3.55	2,790	3.49	2,706	2.79	1,788	5.65	6,790	3.80	3,140	4.00	900
22..........	2.50	2,720	3.36	2,524	3.08	2,144	5.25	5,795	3.65	2,930	4.06	960
23..........	3.43	2,622	3.33	2,482	3.33	2,482	4 95	5,135	3.63	2,902	4.65	993
24..........	3.30	2,440	3.31	2,454	3.15	2,235	4.75	4,735	3.64	2,916	4.03	998
25..........	3.18	2,274	3.33	2,482	3.09	2,157	4.56	4,388	3.70	3,000	4.01	1,000
26..........	3.07	2,131	3.31	2,454	3.05	2,105	4.39	4,083	3.60	2,860	4.27	1,025
27..........	3.05	2,105	3.21	2,314	3.01	2,053	4.19	3,744	3.51	2,734	4.32	1,260
28..........	2.96	1,992	3.15	2,235	2.95	1,980	4.15	3,680	3.40	2,580	4.17	1,316
29..........	2.90	1,920	2.93	1,956	2.96	1,992	4.08	3,568	3.22	2,328	4.15	1,320
30..........	2.86	1,872	2.85	1,860	2 99	2,028	3.93	3,335	3.07	2,131	4.13	1,315
31..........	2.82	1,824	2.73	1,716	....	....	3.93	3,335	....	....	4.00	1,305a

a to *a* Ice conditions.
b to *b* Gauge height of top of ice.
c Gauge height interpolated.

MONTHLY DISCHARGE of Belly River near Lethbridge, for 1914.

(Drainage area 6,764 square miles.)

MONTH.	DISCHARGE IN SECOND-FEET.				RUN-OFF.	
	Maximum.	Minimum.	Mean.	Per square Mile.	Depth in inches on Drainage Area.	Total in Acre-feet.
January............................	740	602	671	0.099	0.11	41,258
February...........................	840	560	622	0.092	0.10	34,544
March..............................	1,484	290	1,122	0.166	0.19	68,992
April..............................	5,691	1,460	3,412	0.505	0.56	203,028
May................................	11,680	4,880	8,606	1.270	1.46	529,162
June...............................	12,324	5,592	7,928	1.170	1.30	471,750
July...............................	5,795	1,824	3,799	0.562	0.65	233,589
August	3,112	1,120	1,923	0.284	0.33	118,243
September..........................	2,482	1,219	1,616	0.239	0.27	96,160
October............................	7,935	1,788	3,999	0.591	0.68	245,889
November...........................	3,896	1,680	2,995	0.443	0.49	178,215
December...	2,040	704	1,094	0.162	0.19	67,268
The year............................	....	....	....	....	6.33	2,288,098

5 GEORGE V, A. 1915

MISCELLANEOUS DISCHARGE MEASUREMENTS made in Belly River drainage basin, in 1914.

Date.	Engineer.	Stream.	Location.	Width.	Area of Section.	Mean Velocity.	Discharge
				Feet.	*Sq. ft.*	*Ft. per sec.*	*Sec.-ft.*
Oct. 23....	O. H. Hoover...	North Branch of Belly River	16-1-28-4......	67.3	53.80	1.43	77 00
Oct. 23.....	do ...	West Branch of Belly River.. ...	Glacier Nat.Park	48.8	50.20	3.01	151.00
Oct. 23....	do ...	South Branch of Belly River	do	54.0	59.80	1.99	119.00
June 15....	do ...	J. N West's ditch	NW. 2-2-28-4..	4.0	2.45	0.63	1.55

ST. MARY RIVER DRAINAGE BASIN.

General Description.

St. Mary River, an important tributary of the Belly River and thus indirectly of the South Saskatchewan River, heads in northern Montana on the eastern slope of the main range of the Rocky Mountains. It starts from the great Blackfoot glacier and receives affluents from numerous lesser glaciers. These streams unite within a short distance from their source and flow into Upper St. Mary Lake. Below this lake and in close proximity is Lower St. Mary Lake, the aggregate lengths of the two being about 22 miles. The river flows out of the lower lake at an elevation of 4,460 feet above mean sea level, and takes a northerly course through the foothills to the international boundary. From the boundary it flows in a north and easterly direction through a rolling country, finally emptying into the Belly River near Lethbridge, Alta.

The basin is bounded on the south by the Rocky Mountains, on the west by the watershed between Belly and St. Mary Rivers, and on the east by the watershed between Milk and St. Mary Rivers. The upper portion of the basin is heavily timbered, and receives its precipitation mostly in the shape of snowfall; the lower and major portion is totally devoid of tree growth and has a small precipitation.

The river flows through a very deep valley having steep banks, making the diversion of water from this stream for irrigation an expensive undertaking. In Canada the Alberta Railway and Irrigation Company has water rights on this river. The headgates of their canal is at Kimball, five miles north of the boundary, and they already have 231 miles of ditch constructed, which irrigates land surrounding Lethbridge.

As this is an international river, discharge measurements are taken on it by the H drometric Surveys branches of both the Canadian and American Governments. The hydrometric engineers of both countries use a common gauging station near Kimball.

FIDLER BROTHERS' DITCH FROM BOUNDARY CREEK.

Location.—On the SE. ¼ Sec. 19, Tp. 1, Rge. 26, W. 4th Mer.
Records available.—September 13, 1911, to July 13, 1914.
Gauge.—Vertical staff.
Bench-mark.—Wooden plug on the left bank, eight feet west of the gauge; elevation, 3 90 feet above zero of the gauge.
Channel.—Consists of sand and clay.
Discharge measurements.—Made by current meter.
Observer.—Jos. Fidler.

DISCHARGE MEASUREMENTS of Fidler Brothers' Ditch from Boundary Creek, in 1914.

Date.	Engineer.	Width.	Area of Section.	Mean Velocity.	Gauge Height.	Discharge.
		Feet.	*Sq. ft.*	*Ft. per sec.*	*Feet.*	*Sec.-ft.*
June 12.	O. H. Hoover..............	4.6	2.00	1.32	1.51	2 6
July 2.............	do	4.8	2.03	1.23	1.46	2.5

SESSIONAL PAPER No. 25c

DAILY GAUGE HEIGHT AND DISCHARGE of Fidler Brothers' Ditch from Boundary Creek, for 1914.

DAY.	June.		July.	
	Gauge Height.	Dis- charge.	Gauge Height.	Dis- charge.
	Feet.	*Sec.-ft.*	*Feet.*	*Sec.-ft.*
1	....	....	1.45	2.4
2	....	....	1.46	2.5
3	1.50	2.6	1.46	2.5
4	1.50	2.6	1.47	2.5
5	1.49	2.6	1.47	2.5
6	1.49	2.6	1.49	2.6
7	1.49	2.6	1.48	2.5
8	1.48	2.5	1.47	2.5
9	1.48	2.5	1.45	2.4
10	1.47	2.5	1.44	2.4
11	1.46	2.5	1.43	2.4
12	1.44	2.4	1.44	2.4
13	1.59	2.9	1.45	2.4
14	1.49	2.6	....	....
15	1.40	2.2	....	....
16				
17				
18				
19				
20				
21				
22				
23				
24				
25				
26				
27				
28				
29				
30				
31				

MONTHLY DISCHARGE of Fidler Brothers' Ditch from Boundary Creek, for 1914.

MONTH.	DISCHARGE IN SECOND-FEET.				RUN-OFF.	
	Maximum.	Minimum.	Mean.	Per square Mile.	Depth in inches on Drainage Area.	Total in Acre-feet.
June (3-15)	2.9	2.2	2.5	....	....	64
July (1-13)	2.6	2.4	2.5	....	....	64
The period	....	....	....	....	....	128

BOUNDARY CREEK AT FIDLER BROTHERS' RANCH.

Location.—On the NW. ¼ Sec. 20, Tp. 1, Rge. 26, W. 4th Mer.
Records available.—June 18, 1913, to October 31, 1914.
Gauge.—Vertical staff; zero of gauge maintained at 96 98 feet during 1913; 95.06 feet during 1914.
Bench-mark.—Permanent iron bench-mark located 25 feet from edge of left bank, and 20 feet downstream from the gauge.
Channel.—Consists of fine gravel, stone and clay; not liable to shift.
Discharge measurements.—Made by wading.
Winter flow.—Records are discontinued during the winter season.
Observer.—James Fidler.

5 GEORGE V, A. 1915

DISCHARGE MEASUREMENTS of Boundary Creek at Fidler Brothers' Ranch, in 1914.

Date.	Engineer.	Width.	Area of Section.	Mean Velocity.	Gauge Height.	Discharge.
		Feet.	*Sq. ft.*	*Ft. per sec.*	*Feet.*	*Sec.-ft.*
Mar. 31.....	O. H. Hoover.	12.8	9.96	1.34	2.56	13.4
April 14.......... ..	do	14.5	13.10	1.44	1.82	18.9
May 6............	do	12.8	21.80	1.01	1.86	22.0
May 26	do	12.2	19.40	0.68	1.72	13.2
June 12............	do	11.3	5.62	0.90	1.51	5.1
July 2............	do	11.0	5.44	0.76	1.49	4.1
July 27.....	do	11.0	4.80	0.58	1.42	2.8
Aug. 18.....	do	12.0	9.25	0.69	1.60	6.4
Sept. 25.....	do	11.4	5.41	0.56	1.51	3.0
Nov. 6............	do	12.0	8.98	1.09	1.66	9.8

DAILY GAUGE HEIGHT AND DISCHARGE of Boundary Creek at Fidler Brothers' Ranch, for 1914.

DAY.	April.		May.		June.	
	Gauge Height.	Dis-charge.	Gauge Height.	Dis-charge.	Gauge Height.	Dis-charge.
	Feet.	*Sec.-ft.*	*Feet.*	*Sec.-ft.*	*Feet.*	*Sec.-ft.*
1..........	2.00	35.0	1.78	16.3	1.67	10.5
2..........	1.51	4.9	1.78	16.3	1.60	7.7
3..........	0.56	Nil.	1.76	15.1	1.54	5.7
4..........	0.53	"	1.78	16.3	1.58	7.0
5..........	0.65	"	1.79	16.9	1.66	10.1
6..........	0.53	"	1.85	21.0	1.67	10.5
7..........	1.86	22.0	1.86	22.0	1.65	9.6
8..........	1.96	31.0	1.92	27.0	1.64	9.2
9..........	1.92	27.0	1.94	29.0	1.63	8.8
10..........	1.77	15.7	1.87	23.0	1.60	7.7
11..........	1.75	14.5	1.86	22.0	1.59	7.4
12..........	1.74	14.0	1.84	20.0	1.58	7.0
13..........	1.78	16.3	1.83	20.0	1.57	6.7
14..........	1.80	17.5	1.82	19.0	1.57	6.7
15..........	1.81	18.2	1.80	17.5	1.59	7.4
16..........	1.81	18.2	1.79	16.9	1.71	12.4
17..........	1.75	14.5	1.78	16.3	1.69	11.4
18..........	1.72	12.9	1.76	15.1	1.66	10.1
19..........	1.70	11.9	1.76	15.1	1.55	6.0
20	1.70	11.9	1.78	16.3	1.55	6.0
21..........	1.74	14.0	1.80	17.5	1.54	5.7
22..........	1.78	16.3	1.78	16.3	1.55	6.0
23..........	1.76	15.1	1.76	15.1	1.57	6.7
24..........	1.74	14.0	1.76	15.1	1.58	7.0
25..........	1.70	11.9	1.74	14.0	1.64	9.2
26..........	1.70	11.9	1.74	14.0	1.74	14.0
27..........	1.69	11.4	1.72	12.9	1.73	13.5
28..........	1.70	11.9	1.70	11.9	1.64	9.2
29..........	1.70	11.9	1.70	11.9	1.64	9.2
30..........	1.69	11.4	1.69	11.4	1.64	9.2
31..........	....	....	1.68	11.0	....	....

DAILY GAUGE HEIGHT AND DISCHARGE of Boundary Creek at Fidler Brothers' Ranch, for 1914.

DAY.	July.		August.		September.		October.	
	Gauge Height.	Dis-charge.	Gauge Height.	Dis-charge.	Gauge Height.	Dis-charge.	Gauge Height.	Dis-charge.
	Feet.	*Sec.-ft.*	*Feet.*	*Sec.-ft.*	*Feet.*	*Sec.-ft.*	*Feet.*	*Sec.-ft.*
1	1.42	2.8	1.40	2.1	1.53	3.8	1.51	3.2
2	1.42	2.8	1.39	2.0	1.53	3.8	1.52	3.6
3	1.48	4.1	1.39	1.9	1.52	3.4	1.52	3.6
4	1.46	3.6	1.38	1.8	1.51	3.1	1.53	3.9
5	1.48	4.1	1.38	1.7	1.51	3.1	1.53	4.0
6	1.48	4.1	1.38	1.7	1.52	3.4	1.53	4.0
7	1.49	4.4	1.37	1.5	1.52	3.4	1.54	4.3
8	1.49	4.4	1.37	1.5	1.53	3.8	1.54	4.3
9	1.48	4.1	1.38	1.6	1.53	3.8	1.55	4.7
10	1.46	3.6	1.39	1.7	1.52	3.4	1.57	5.4
11	1.46	3.6	1.39	1.7	1.52	3.4	1.60	6.6
12	1.44	3.2	1.39	1.7	1.54	4.1	1.72	12.6
13	1.46	3.6	1.40	1.8	1.55	4.4	1.76	15.3
14	1.68	11.0	1.40	1 8	1.54	4.1	1.77	16.0
15	1.50	4.6	1.39	1.6	1.55	4.4	1.78	16.8
16	1.45	3.4	1.39	1.6	1.54	4.1	1.75	14.7
17	1.49	4.4	1.67	8.7a	1.54	4.1	1.76	15.4
18	1.48	4.1	1.66	8.6	1.54	4.1	1.78	16.8
19	1.48	4.1	1.56	4.8	1.54	4.1	1.78	16.8
20	1.48	4.1	1.56	4.8	1.54	4.1	1.79	17.6
21	1.47	3.9	1.55	4.4	1.54	4.1	1.80	18.4
22	1.47	3.9	1.55	4.4	1.53	3.8	1.81	19.2
23	1.46	3.6	1.53	3.8	1.53	3.8	1.82	20.0
24	1.46	3.6	1.56	4.8	1.53	3.8	1.79	17.7
25	1.46	3.6	1.55	4.4	1.53	3.6	1.78	17.0
26	1.45	3.4	1.54	4.1	1.52	3.4b	1.78	17.0
27	1.45	3.4	1.54	4.1	1.52	3.5	1.77	16.4
28	1.44	3.1a	1.53	3.8	1.52	3.5	1.76	15.8
29	1.43	2.8	1.53	3.8	1.52	3.5	1.76	15.8
30	1.42	2.6	1.52	3.4	1.51	3.2	1.75	15.5
31	1.41	2.4	1.52	3.4	......	....	1.75	15.5b

a to *a* Shifting conditions.
b to *b* Shifting conditions.

MONTHLY DISCHARGE of Boundary Creek at Fidler Brothers' Ranch, for 1914.

(Drainage area 48 square miles.)

MONTH.	DISCHARGE IN SECOND-FEET.				RUN-OFF.	
	Maximum.	Minimum.	Mean	Per square Mile.	Depth in inches on Drainage Area.	Total in Acre-feet.
April (1–30)	35.0	0.0	13.8	0.288	0.32	821
May	29.0	11.0	17.2	0.358	0.41	1,058
June	14.0	5.7	8.6	0.179	0.20	512
July	11.0	2.4	3.9	0.081	0.09	240
August	8 7	1.5	3.2	0.067	0.08	197
September	4.4	3.1	3.7	0.077	0.09	220
October (1 31)	20.0	3.2	12.2	0.254	0.29	750
The period	....	....	....	....	1.48	3.798

5 GEORGE V, A. 1915

ST. MARY RIVER NEAR KIMBALL.

Location.—Cable station on the SW. ¼ Sec. 25, Tp. 1, Rge. 25, W. 4th Mer., about 2,000 feet above the *A*lberta Railway and *I*rrigation Company's Dam.

Records available.—April 13, 1908, to December 31, 1914.

Gauges.—Priez automatic stage recorder housed in a concrete shelter, about 3,000 feet above the cable station; zero of auto. gauge maintained at 88.75 feet during 1913-14. Vertical staff at summer cable station; zero of staff maintained at 85.84 feet during 1914. Chain gauge at winter station located at the bridge on the SW. ¼ Sec. 1, Tp. 2, Rge. 25, W. 4th Mer.; zero of chain gauge maintained at 86 97 feet during 1914.

Bench-marks.—At auto. gauge: a spike on the downstream side of the concrete shelter; assumed elevation, 100.00 feet. *A*t summer station: a permanent iron bench-mark; assumed elevation, 100 00 feet. At winter station: a permanent iron bench-mark; assumed elevation, 100 00 feet; located 131 feet *NE*. of the right abutment of the bridge.

Channel.—Consists of sand and gravel; liable to slight shifting conditions.

Discharge measurements.—Made from a cable car.

Winter flow.—Difficulty is often experienced in obtaining accurate discharges during the winter months on account of slush ice and the formation of more than one layer of ice. Measurements of this season are obtained at the SW. ¼ Sec. 1, Tp. 2, Rge. 25, W. 4th Mer.

Diversions.—Alberta Railway and *I*rrigation Company's Canal, capacity about 700 sec.-ft., below the station about one mile.

Observer.—J. M. Dunn.

Remarks.—The station is maintained in co-operation with the stream measurement work carried out by United States Geological Surveys.

DISCHARGE MEASUREMENTS of St. Mary River near Kimball, in 1914.

Date.	Engineer.	Width.	Area of Section.	Mean Velocity.	Gauge Height.	Discharge.
		Feet.	*Sq. ft.*	*Ft. per sec.*	*Feet.*	*Sec.-ft.*
Jan. 12	J. E. Degnan	42	134	1.60	3.61a	214
Jan. 23	do	97	144	0.57	3.20	82
Feb. 11	do	37	56	1.71	5.40	96
Feb. 26	do	40	60	1.96	5.50	119
Mar. 13	W. A. Burton	58	93	2.45	5.11	229
Mar. 25	O. H. Hoover	120	86	1.16	4.34	100
April 7	do	95	168	1.76	2.59b	295
April 20	do	223	413	2.20	3.00c	910
May 13	do	229	591	3.30	4.10	1,952
May 23	W. A. Lamb (U.S.G.S.)	230	611	4.11	4.53	2,510
June 2	O. H. Hoover	228	639	4.25	4.63	2,718
June 21	W. A. Lamb (U.S.G.S.)	229	605	4.03	4.53	2,440
June 23	O. H. Hoover	228	546	3.75	4.19	2,049
July 15	do	226	490	3.25	3.77	1,591
July 21	W. A. Lamb (U.S.G.S.)	226	414	2.87	3.40	1,190
Aug. 11	O. H. Hoover	197	299	2.18	2.71	654
Sept. 2	do	189	278	2.11	2.56	588
Sept. 5	do	186	266	1.99	2.49	529
Sept. 10	W. A. Lamb (U.S.G.S.)	183	259	1.84	2.46	477
Sept. 18	O. H. Hoover	181	251	1.88	2.36	470
Sept. 22	do	206	328	2.45	2.97	806
Oct. 1	do	196	304	2.30	2.78	700
Oct. 10	do	198	309	2.27	2.80	700
Oct. 16	do	224	380	2.73	3.18	1,036
Nov. 12	do	201	321	2.44	2.89c	791
Nov. 26	do	178	234	1.81	2.30d	422
Dec. 14	do	65	100	2.67	2.37d	267

a to *b* Gauge heights from Winter gauge.
c to *c* Gauge heights from automatic gauge.
d Gauge heights from Winter gauge.

SESSIONAL PAPER No. 25c

DAILY GAUGE HEIGHT AND DISCHARGE of St. Mary River near Kimball, for 1914.

DAY.	January.		February.		March.		April.		May.		June.	
	Gauge Height.	Dis- charge.	Gauge Height.	Dis- charge	Gauge Height.	Dis- charge	Gauge Height.	Dis- charge.	Gauge Height.	Dis- charge.	Gauge Height.	Dis- charge.
	Feet.	*Sec.-ft.*	*Feet.*	*Sec.-ft.*	*Feet.*	*Sec.-ft.*	*Feet.*	*Sec.-ft.*	*Feet.*	*Sec.-ft.*	*Feet.*	*Sec.-ft.*
1	2.29a	85	......	81	......	128	3.99	265	3.28	1,092	4.38	2,314
2	2.30	94	3.62	78	5.25	139	3.94	275	3.73	1,543	4.59	2,587
3	2.35	103	3.42	73	5.25	148	3.94	288	4.20	2,085	4.83	2,899
4	......	114	......	71	5.20	157	3.84	312	4.10	1,965	5.00	3,120
5	2.70	123	5.42	70	5.20	168	3.84	290	3.93	1,764	4.98	3,094
6	2.75	135	5.42	73	5.20	177	2.94	265	3.85	1,675	4.88	2,964
7	2.85	146	5.47	78	5.18	186	2.64	295	3.84	1,664	4.70	2,730
8	2.82	159	......	82	......	197	2.59	320	3.86	1,686	4.48	2,444
9	2.85	172	......	87	......	207	2.59	343	3.88	1,708	4.30	2,210
10	3.00	183	......	90	5.15	215	2.59	362	4.10	1,965	4.08	1,941
11	3.30	198	5.40	96	5.15	222	2.54a	364	4 17	2,049	3.95	1,788
12	3.70	215	5.40	97	5.15	226	2.18b	366	4.09	1,953	3.92	1,753
13	3 40	195	5.40	98	5.12	229	2.33	440	4.10	1,965	4.25	2,148
14	3.25	182	5.40	98	5.11	230	2.47	510	4 17	2,049	4.50	2,470
15	3.25	175	......	100	5.11	228	2.55	555	4.31	2,223	4.45	2,405
16	3.25	165	5.50	105	5.10	220	2.68	633	4.50	2,470	4.38	2,314
17	3.25	156	5.60	111	5.05	205	2.68	633	4.67	2,691	4.42	2,366
18	......	143	5.60	118	5.05	190	2.63	603	4.73	2,769	4.51	2,483
19	3.30	138	5.85	122	5.00	190	2.76	684	4.75	2,795	4.60	2,600
20	3.25	128	5.90	127	5.00	182	3.00	855	4.78	2,834	4.62	2,626
21	3.25	115	......	130	5.00	178	3.12	952	4.76	2,808	4.55	2,535
22	......	97	......	127	......	185	3.10	935	4.65	2,665	4.48	2,444
23	3.20	82	6.00	122	......	189	3.15	978	4 58	2,574	4.21	2,098
24	3.40	81	5.50	119	......	160	3.23	1,047	4.60	2,600	4 05	1,905
25	......	85	5.45	117	4.34	100	3.23	1,047	4.77	2,841	3.98	1,822
26	......	85	5.50	119	.....	98	3.28	1,092	4.78	2,834	3.97	1,810
27	3.55	78	5.40	120	......	102	3.28	1,092	4.62	2,626	3.95	1,788
28	3.55	77	5.35	123	......	170	3.32	1,129	4 53	2,509	3.94	1,776
29	......	82	......	......	3.85	202	3.28	1,092	4 43	2,379	3.92	1,753
30	3.60	85	......	......	3.95	222	3.26	1,074	4.29	2,198	3.91	1,742
31	3.65	84	......	......	3.95	248	......	......	4.28	2,185	......	......

a Gauge heights to April 11 are readings on Winter gauge-rod.
b Gauge heights April 12 to Dec. 4 recorded by auto gauge.

5 GEORGE V, A. 1915

DAILY GAUGE HEIGHT AND DISCHARGE of St. Mary River near Kimball, for 1914.—*Concluded.*

DAY.	July. Gauge Height.	July. Dis- charge	August. Gauge Height.	August. Dis- charge	September. Gauge Height.	September. Dis- charge	October. Gauge Height.	October. Dis- charge	November. Gauge Height.	November. Dis- charge	December. Gauge Height.	December. Dis- charge
	Feet.	*Sec.-ft.*	*Feet.*	*Sec.-ft.*	*Feet.*	*Sec.-ft.*	*Feet.*	*Sec.-ft.*	*Feet.*	*Sec.-ft.*	*Feet.*	*Sec.-ft.*
1..........	3.86	1,686	2 97	832	2 64	609	2 77	690	2.70	645	2.42	367d
2..........	3.85	1,675	2 94	810	2.57	567	2 83	731	2.77	691	2.17	362
3..........	3.89	1,719	2 94	810	2.52	537	2 86	752	2.92	795	2.18	366
4..........	3.92	1,753	2.96	825	2 50	525	2.91	788	3.08	919	2.07	316
5..........	4.02	1,869	2.93	802	2 47	510	2 93	802	3.11	944	3.29c	310
6..........	4.11	1,977	2.92	795	2.46	505	2.90	780	3.19	1,012	3.29	302
7..........	4.12	1,989	2.94	810	2.47	510	2.87	759	3.19	1,012	3.24	290
8..........	4.06	1,917	2.88	766	2.45	500	2.82	724	3.19	1,012	3.19	277
9..........	4.03	1,881	2.82	724	2.44	495	2.81	717	3.09	927	3.59	272
10.	4.00	1,845	2.78	697	2.42	485	2.80	710	2.98	840	3.39	272
11..........	3.97	1,810	2.68	633	2.39	470	2.78	697	2.95	818	3.59	273
12..........	3.92	1,753	2.67	627	2.37	460	2.74	671	2.90	780	......	269
13..........	3.87	1,697	2.64	609	2.34	445	2.75	678	2.93	802	......	267
14...... ..	3.87	1,697	2.61	591	2.31	430	2.82	724	2.90	780	3.41	267
15...... ..	3.81	1,631	2.57	567	2.27	410	2.97	832	2.90	780	3.61	260
16..........	3.72	1,532	2.53	543	2.31	430	3.20	1,020	2.99	848	3.95	250
17..	3.62	1,426	2.74	671	2.36	455	3.40	1,205	2.90	780	3.95	239
18.... ..	3.58	1,385	2.97	832	2.36	455	3.45	1,255	2.83	731	......	238
19.... .	3.46	1,265	2.98	840	2.48	515	3.38	1,186	2.83	731	5.90	239
20.. .	3.43	1,235	2.94	810	2.68	633	3.31	1,120	2.78	697	5.30	233
21...... ..	3.42	1,225	2.87	759	2.89	773	3.24	1,056	2.74	671	5.30	223
22...	3.35	1,158	2.84	738	2.95	818	3.19	1,012	2.52	537	5.35	219
23..........	3.24	1,056	2.85	745	2.92	795	3.14	969	2.34	445	5.40	221
24...... ..	3.18	1,003	2.90	780	2.91	788	3.07	911	2.32	435	5.45	221
25..........	3.13	960	2.86	752	2.82	724	2.99	848	2.34	445	......	216
26..... ...	3.07	911	2.82	724	2.80	710	2.94	810	2.31	430	5.40	207
27...	3.02	871	2.75	678	2.90	780	2.90	780	2.26	405	5.35	200
28.	3.00	855	2.72	658	2.86	752	2.85	745	2.23	390	4.95	193
29..........	3.00	855	2.68	633	2.82	724	2.82	724	2.20	375	4.55	188
30..... ...	3.00	855	2.65	615	2.80	710	2.76	684	2.79	371d	5.30	185
31..........	2.98	840	2.64	609	......	.. ..	2.75	678	......	......	5.27c	183

c to *c* Gauge heights from staff gauge at SW. 1-2-25-4.
d Discharge estimated.

MONTHLY DISCHARGE of St. Mary River near Kimball, for 1914.

(Drainage area 472 square miles.)

MONTH	DISCHARGE IN SECOND-FEET. Maximum.	Minimum	Mean.	Per square Mile.	RUN-OFF. Depth in inches on Drainage Area.	Total in Acre-feet.
January............................	215	77	128	0.271	0.31	7,870
February	130	70	101	0.214	0.22	5,609
March............................	248	98	184	0.390	0.43	11,314
April............................	1,129	265	637	1.350	1.51	37,904
May	2,834	1,092	2,230	4.725	5.43	137,120
June	3,120	1,742	2,331	4.939	5.51	138,700
July	1,989	840	1,430	3.030	3.49	87,930
August	840	543	719	1.523	1.76	44,210
September	818	410	584	1.237	1.38	34,750
October	1,255	671	841	1.782	2.05	51,711
November	1,012	375	702	1.488	1.66	41,772
December	367	183	256	0.542	0.62	15,741
The year	....	....	....	....	24.40	614,631

ALBERTA RAILWAY AND IRRIGATION COMPANY CANAL NEAR KIMBALL.

Location.—On the SE. ¼ Sec. 21, Tp. 2, Rge. 24, W. 4th Mer., at the flume over Rolph Creek.
Records available.—July 26, 1910, to October 6, 1914.
Gauge.—Vertical staff; datum unchanged.
Channel.—Smooth plank flume, 768 feet long.
Discharge measurements.—Made from a foot bridge spanning the flume at a point about midway from the ends.
Artificial control.—The discharge is controlled by headgates at Kimball, about six miles above the flume.
Observer.—J. M. Dunn.
Remarks.—A new flume was built just to the right, to replace the old structure, during October, November and December. It is 27 feet wide and 8 feet deep. A vertical metal staff is countersunk in the left side of this flume about midway from the ends for future gauge height records.

DISCHARGE MEASUREMENTS of Alberta Railway and Irrigation Company Canal near Kimball, for 1914.

Date.	Engineer.	Width.	Area of Section.	Mean Velocity.	Gauge Height.	Discharge.
		Feet.	*Sq. ft.*	*Ft. per sec.*	*Feet.*	*Sec.-ft.*
May 14	O. H. Hoover.	27.2	83.8	5.98	2.92	502
June 3	do	27.2	102.5	6.50	3.62	666
June 23	do	27.2	108.1	6.81	3.83	736
June 27	do	27.2	105.4	6.68	3.75	705
July 16	do	27.2	104.0	6.49	3.69	672
July 16	do	27.2	103.6	6.49	3.69	672
July 22	do	27.2	101.0	6.39	3.61	644
Aug. 12	do	27.2	87.9	5.93	3.18	521
Aug. 14	do	27.2	85.7	5.91	3.10	507
Aug. 27	do	27.2	87.7	5.93	3.16	520
Sept. 2	do	27.2	83.8	5.78	3.02	483
Sept. 9	do	27.2	73.4	5.36	2.67	394
Sept. 17	do	27.2	72.3	5.22	2.64	378
Sept. 20	do	27.2	37.6	2.83	1.31	107
Sept. 20	do	27.2	27.1	2.18	0.93	59
Sept. 20	do	27.2	21.0	1.81	0.75	38
Sept. 21	do	27.2	57.4	4.35	2.10	250
Sept. 21	do	27.2	64.5	4.86	2.36	313
Oct. 1	do	27.2	71.2	5.13	2.56	365

No. 25c—17

5 GEORGE V, A. 1915

DAILY GAUGE HEIGHT AND DISCHARGE of *A*lberta Railway and *I*rrigation Company Canal near Kimball, for 1914.

DAY.	April.		May.		June.	
	Gauge Height.	Dis-charge.	Gauge Height.	Dis-charge.	Gauge Height.	Dis-charge.
	Feet.	*Sec. ft.*	*Feet.*	*Sec. ft.*	*Feet.*	*Sec. ft.*
1			2.23	283	3.52	627
2			2.25	288	3.52	627
3			2.58	365	3.62	658
4			2.60	370	3.75	700
5			2.60	370	3.75	700
6			2.58	365	3.75	700
7			2.70	395	3.74	697
8			2.75	408	3.72	691
9			2.76	411	3.74	697
10			2.77	413	3.76	704
11			2.77	413	3.75	700
12			2.77	413	3.75	700
13			2.90	448	3.74	697
14			2.92	453	3.75	700
15			2.91	451	3.75	700
16			2.93	456	3.75	700
17			2.93	456	3.75	700
18			2.93	456	3.75	700
19			2.91	451	3.75	700
20			2.90	448	3.75	700
21			3.12	509	3.79	714
22			3.00	475	3.80	717
23			3.12	509	3.83	727
24			3.20	531	3.90	717
25			3.20	531	3.82	724
26			3.20	531	3.75	700
27			3.20	531	3.75	700
28			3.19	528	3.75	700
29	2.23*a*	283	3.45	606	3.75	700
30	2.23	283	3.40	590	3.70	684
31			3.48	615		

a Gates opened.

DAILY GAUGE HEIGHT AND DISCHARGE of Alberta Railway and Irrigation Company Canal near Kimball, for 1914.

DAY.	July.		August.		September.		October.	
	Gauge Height.	Dis charge.	Gauge Height.	Dis- charge.	Gauge Height.	Dis- charge.	Gauge Height.	Dis- charge.
	Feet.	*Sec.-ft.*	*Feet.*	*Sec.-ft.*	*Feet.*	*Sec.-ft.*	*Feet.*	*Sec.-ft.*
1	3.68	678	3.46	609	3.00	475	2.50	346
2	3.70	684	3.46	609	3.01	478	2.50	346
3	3.70	684	3.45	606	3.02	481	2.50	346
4	3.70	684	3.45	606	3.01	478	2.65	382
5	3.70	684	3.42	596	3.00	475	2.20	276
6	3.68	678	3.42	596	2.75	408	2.20	276b
7	3.70	684	3.42	596	2.65	382	....	....
8	3.70	684	3.38	584	2.65	382	....	....
9	3.70	684	3.32	566	2.68	390	....	....
10	3.70	684	3.28	556	2.65	382	....	....
11	3.69	681	3.25	545	2.55	358	....	....
12	3.69	681	3.18	525	2.50	346	....	....
13	3.70	684	3.15	517	2.50	346	....	....
14	3.69	681	3.12	509	2.45	334	....	....
15	3.70	684	3.08	497	2.40	322	....	....
16	3.69	681	3.05	489	2.42	327	....	....
17	3.70	684	3.35	575	2.55	358	....	....
18	3.69	681	2.95	462	2.54	356	....	....
19	3.69	681	3.08	497	2.55	358	....	....
20	3.70	684	3.08	497	1.40	122	....	....
21	3.70	684	3.16	520	2.56	360	....	....
22	3.61	655	3.25	545	2.50	346	....	....
23	3.59	649	3.25	545	2.50	346	....	....
24	3.59	649	3.25	545	2.50	346	....	....
25	3.58	646	3.15	517	2.50	346	....	....
26	3.57	643	3.15	517	2.50	346	....	....
27	3.52	627	3.15	517	2.50	346	....	....
28	3.48	615	3.15	517	2.50	346	....	....
29	3.47	612	3.15	517	2.50	346	....	....
30	3.47	612	3.15	517	2.50	346	....	....
31	3.46	609	3.15	517	....	....	....	....

b Headgates closed for season.

MONTHLY DISCHARGE of Alberta Railway and Irrigation Company Canal near Kimball, for 1914.

MONTH.	DISCHARGE IN SECOND-FEET.			RUN-OFF.
	Maximum.	Minimum	Mean.	Total in Acre-feet.
April (29-30)	283	283	283	1,122
May	615	283	454	27,915
June	727	627	696	41,415
July	684	609	666	40,951
August	609	462	542	33,326
September	481	122	368	21,898
October (1-6)	382	276	329	3,911
The period	....	....	....	170,538

ALBERTA RAILWAY AND IRRIGATION COMPANY CANALS.

The main canal of the Alberta Railway and Irrigation Company diverts water from the St. Mary River on the SE. ¼ Sec. 36, Tp. 1, Rge. 25, W. 4th Mer.

The discharge measurements published herewith were made during investigations to determine absorption losses, conducted by this department during 1913 and 1914.

5 GEORGE V, A. 1915

DISCHARGE MEASUREMENTS of Main Canal near Kimball, in 1914.

(SE. 21-2-24-4.)

Date.	Engineer.	Width.	Area of Section.	Mean Velocity.	Gauge Height.	Discharge.
		Feet.	*Sq. ft.*	*Ft. per sec.*	*Feet.*	*Sec.-ft.*
1914.						
July 11............	R. J. McGuinness..........	27.2	103.3	6.22	3.69	642
July 13...........	do	48.0	241.9	2.72	3.70	659a

a Measurement at NE. 36-1-25-4.

DISCHARGE MEASUREMENTS of Pinepound Spillway at Spring Coulee, in 1914.

(NE. 29-4-23-4.)

Date.	Engineer.	Width.	Area of Section.	Mean Velocity.	Gauge Height.	Discharge.
		Feet.	*Sq. ft.*	*Ft. per sec.*	*Feet.*	*Sec.-ft.*
1914.						
July 15............	R. J. McGuinness..........	24.0	14.0	0.89	2.90	12.6

DISCHARGE MEASUREMENTS of Main Canal at Spring Coulee, in 1914.

(NW. 28-4-23-4.)

Date.	Engineer.	Width.	Area of Section.	Mean Velocity.	Gauge Height.	Discharge.
		Feet.	*Sq. ft.*	*Ft. per sec.*	*Feet.*	*Sec.-ft.*
1914.						
July 15............	R. J. McGuinness..........	50.5	146.6	4.07	4.69	597

DISCHARGE MEASUREMENTS of Magrath Lateral near Headgates, in 1913-14.

(SW. 9-5-22-4.)

Date.	Engineer.	Width.	Area of Section.	Mean Velocity.	Gauge Height.	Discharge.
		Feet.	*Sq. ft.*	*Ft. per sec.*	*Feet.*	*Sec.-ft.*
1913.						
July 24............	G. D. Walters.............	9.5	12.3	1.37	2.10	16.8
Aug. 14............	do	9.0	3.0	0.67	1.14	2.0
Aug. 27............	do	9.5	9.6	0.97	1.72	9.4
Aug. 27....... ...	do	9.5	9.6	0.98	1.72	9.5
Aug. 28............	G. R. Elliott.............	9.7	11.9	0.88	1.72	10.4
Aug. 29...........	R. J. Srigley..............	10.4	11.1	0.70	1.72	7.7
Aug. 29............	do	9.6	8.5	1.10	....	9.4a
Sept. 1............	do	9.4	8.7	1.00	1.64	8.7
Sept. 2............	G. R. Elliott.............	9.8	10.4	0.74	1.64	7.7
Sept. 3............	R. J. Srigley..............	9.4	8.6	1.00	1.58	-8.6
Sept. 3............	do	10.1	5.7	1.41	2.40	8.1b
Sept. 3............	do	9.3	7.1	1.13	....	8.1a
1914.						
July 16......... ..	R. J. McGuinness..........	12.2	14.4	2.09	2.65	30.0
July 16............	do	12.0	13.8	1.25	2.65	17.3
Sept. 22............	do	7.6	9.1	1.09	1.20	9.9
Sept. 23............	do	7.6	9.3	1.14	1.22	10.6
Sept. 24.....	do	7.6	9.3	1.15	1.22	10.7
Sept. 25............	do	7.6	7.6	0.89	1.00	6.8
Sept. 26	do	7.6	7.6	0.91	1.00	7.0
Sept. 30............	do	7.6	10.6	1.28	1.40	13.6
Sept. 30............	do	7.6	10.6	1.26	1.40	13.3
Sept. 30............	do	7.6	10.6	1.25	1.40	13.3
Sept. 30	do	7.6	10.6	1.27	1.40	13.5
Oct. 1............	do	7.6	11.0	1.33	1.45	14.6
Oct. 2............	do	7.6	8.7	0.92	1.15	8.0

a Measurement one mile doWnstream.
b Measurement at headgates.

DISCHARGE MEASUREMENTS of Distributaries from Magrath Lateral, in 1914.

Date.	Location.	Engineer.	Width.	Area of Section.	Mean Velocity.	Gauge Height.	Dis-charge.
			Feet.	*Sq. ft.*	*Ft. per sec*	*Feet.*	*Sec.-ft.*
1914.							
July 18........	SW. 21–5–22–4	R. J. McGuinness..	....	....	....	....	2.20
July 18........	SE. 20–5–22–4	do	....	....	....	....	1.79
July 18........	NE. 20–5–22–4.........	do	....	....	....	....	0.39
July 18	NE. 20–5–22–4.........	do	....	....	....	....	6.23
July 18........	SE. 29–5–22–4...	do	....	....	....	....	1.77
July 18........	NW. 32–5–22–4.........	do	....	....	....	....	1.29
July 18........	SE. 6–6–22–4............	do	....	....	....	....	1.71*a*

a Magrath Lateral.

DISCHARGE MEASUREMENTS of Pothole Creek at Magrath, in 1913-14.

(SE. 26–5–22–4.)

Date.	Engineer.	Width.	Area of Section.	Mean Velocity.	Gauge Height.	Discharge.
		Feet.	*Sq. ft.*	*Ft. per sec.*	*Feet.*	*Sec.-ft.*
1913.						
July 24	G. D. Walters..............	33.0	31.7	1.73	1.30	55
Aug. 14............	do	54.0	42.7	1.95	1.33	83
Aug. 27............	do	54.0	69.6	3.06	1.88	213
Aug. 27............	do	54.5	69.7	2.81	1.87	196
Aug. 28............	G. R. Elliott..............	54.5	76.0	2.94	1.82	223
Sept. 1............	R. J. Srigley..............	54.5	62.6	2.11	1.58	132
Sept. 2............	G. R. Elliott..............	54.5	62.5	2.14	1.56	134
Sept. 3............	R. J. Srigley..............	53.5	63.1	2.06	1.55	130
Sept. 4............	do	54.6	53.2	1.75	1.37	94
Sept. 5............	G. R. Elliott	55.4	52.5	1.84	1.36	97
1914.						
July 17............	R. J. McGuinness...........	52.0	49.4	2.28	....	108
July 17............	do	49.0	48.6	2.08	....	101*a*

a Measurement at NE. 17–7–21–4.

DISCHARGE MEASUREMENTS of Main Canal at Flume No. 2, in 1913-14.

(SW. 25–5–22–4.)

Date.	Engineer.	Width.	Area of Section.	Mean Velocity.	Gauge Height.	Discharge.
		Feet.	*Sq. ft.*	*Ft. per sec.*	*Feet.*	*Sec.-ft.*
1913.						
June 24............	G. D. Walters..............	22.0	67.0	4.09	2.93	275
Aug. 14............	do	22.0	67.2	4.16	2.94	280
Aug. 26............	R. J. Srigley..............	22.0	66.1	4.12	2.89	272
Aug. 26............	G. R. Elliott..............	22.0	66.4	4.11	2.90	273
Aug. 27............	G. D. Walters..............	22.0	64.8	4.02	2.83	260
Aug. 27............	do	22.0	65.1	3.84	2.84	260
Aug. 28............	G. R. Elliott..............	22.0	63.5	4.11	2.77	261
Aug. 30............	do	22.0	47.0	3.43	2.02	161
Sept. 1............	R. J. Srigley..............	22.0	58.2	3.82	2.53	223
Sept. 2............	G. R. Elliott..............	22.0	57.2	3.91	2.49	224
Sept. 3............	R. J. Srigley..............	22.0	57.1	3.66	2.47	219
Sept. 4............	do	22.0	62.6	4.02	2.73	251
Sept. 5............	G. R. Elliott..............	22.0	63.3	4.03	2.77	255
1914.						
July 16............	R. J. McGuinness...........	22.4	85.8	5.34	3.75	458
Sept. 19............	do	22.2	56.3	4.34	2.28	244
Sept. 21............	do	22.2	25.7	2.51	0.97	64
Sept. 22............	do	22.2	64.1	4.31	2.66	277
Sept. 23............	do	22.2	64.4	4.24	2.65	273
Sept. 24............	do	22.2	63.2	4.35	2.60	275
Sept. 25............	do	22.2	63.2	4.37	2.60	277
Sept. 30............	do	22.2	64.4	4.35	2.65	280
Oct. 1............	do	22.2	65.5	4.35	2.70	285
Oct. 2............	do	22.2	67.7	4.39	2.80	298

5 GEORGE V. A. 1915

DISCHARGE MEASUREMENTS of Main Canal at Welling, in 1913-14.

(NE. 5–6–21–4.)

Date.	Engineer.	Width.	Area of Section.	Mean Velocity.	Gauge Height.	Discharge.
		Feet.	*Sq. ft.*	*Ft. per sec.*	*Feet.*	*Sec.-ft.*
1913						
July 28.............	G. D. Walters..............	44.2	127.2	2.18	2.40	278
Aug. 14.............	do	30.2	134.4	2.17	2.66	292
Aug. 27.............	G. R. Elliott...............	47.3	180.9	1.85	2.60	332
Aug. 28.............	R. J. Srigley...... :	45.0	121.7	2.06	2.56	250
Aug. 28.............	do	45.0	118.0	2.09	2.09	248
Aug. 30.............	G. R. Elliott.......	44.8	114.7	2.06	2.44	243
Sept. 1.............	do	43.5	110.8	1.97	2.36	214
Sept. 2.............	R. J. Srigley......	44.0	109.6	1.89	2.34	208
Sept. 3.............	G. R. Elliott.......	44.2	112.1	1.78	2.36	206
Sept. 4.............	do	46.0	125.3	2.17	2.63	252
Sept. 5.............	R. J. Srigley...............	45.5	119.5	2.09	2.62	250
Oct. 6.............	G. D. Walters...	44.0	132.1	2.11	2.64	278
1914						
July 18.............	R. J. McGuinness	46.0	162.4	2.92	3.16	445
Sept. 21.............	do	37.7	46.6	1.03	0.71	48
Sept. 22.............	do	46.7	116.5	2.22	2.55	258

DISCHARGE MEASUREMENTS of Raymond Lateral at Headgates, in 1913-14.

(SE. 5–6–21–4.)

Date.	Engineer.	Width.	Area of Section.	Mean Velocity.	Gauge Height.	Discharge.
		Feet.	*Sq. ft.*	*Ft. per sec.*	*Feet.*	*Sec.-ft.*
1913.						
July 28	G. D. Walters	12.0	16.8	2.96	1.40	50.0
Aug. 15...... ..	do	12.0	13.2	2.90	1.10	38.0
Aug. 27	G. R. Elliott	12.0	12.6	2.95	1.05	37.0
Aug. 28.............	R. J. Srigley	12.0	12.0	2.99	1.00	36.0
Aug. 29.............	G. R. Elliott	12.0	9.1	3.04	0.76	28.0
Aug. 29.............	do	16.4	18.6	1.35	....	25.0a
Aug. 30	R. J. Srigley......	12.0	7.8	3.02	0.65	24.0
Sept. 1.............	G. R. Elliott...............	12.0	7.2	3.06	0.60	22.0
Sept. 2.............	R. J. Srigley...............	12.0	7.2	3.05	0.60	22.0
Sept. 3.............	G. D. Walters..............	12.0	7.7	3.02	0.64	23.0
Sept. 3.............	do	16.0	18.2	1.26	....	23.0a
Sept. 5.............	R. J. Srigley	12.0	14.4	3.03	1.20	44.0
1914.						
July 18	R. J. McGuinness	12.0	24.2	2.91	2.05	71.0
July 25......	do	12.0	24.6	2.80	2.05	70.0
July 25.............	do	5.6	14.0	2.82	....	39.0a
Sept. 21.............	do	12.0	6.2	1.53	0.50	9.6
Sept. 21	do	12.0	12.1	2.04	0.99	25.0
Sept. 22...	do	12.0	24.2	2.63	2.00	64.0
Sept. 23	do	12.0	18.5	2.27	1.52	42.0
Sept. 23..	do	12.0	18.2	2.38	1.50	43.0
Sept. 24.............	do	12.0	15.5	2.07	1.27	32.0
Sept. 24.............	do	12.0	10.0	1.81	0.81	18.0
Sept. 25.............	do	12.0	22.4	2.63	1.85	59.0
Oct. 2.............	do	12.0	21.8	2.60	1.80	57.0

a Measurement one mile doWnstream.

SESSIONAL PAPER No. 25c

DISCHARGE MEASUREMENTS of Distributaries from Raymond Lateral, in 1914.

Date.	Location.	Engineer.	Width.	Area of Section.	Mean Velocity.	Gauge Height.	Dis- charge.
			Feet.	*Sq. ft.*	*Ft. per sec.*	*Feet.*	*Sec.-ft.*
1914.							
July 25......	NE. 4–6–21–4...........	R. J. McGuinness...	3.9	3.9	1.26	....	4.90
July 25......	NW. 2–6–21–4..........	do ...	3.4	3.1	1.22	....	3.80
July 25......	NE. 2–6–21–4..........	do ...	3.0	1.7	0.88	....	1.49
July 25......	NW. 1–6–21–4..........	do ...	4.5	3.6	0.83	....	3.00
July 25......	SE. 12–6–21–4.........	do ...	2.1	1.7	1.71	....	2.80
July 25......	SW. 7–6–20–4..........	do ...	3.0	1.7	1.17	....	1.98
July 25....	SW. 7–6–20–4....	do ...	3.7	2.2	1.50	....	3.30
July 25......	SE. 7–6–20–4..........	do ...	6.0	3.1	0.82	....	2.50
July 25......	SE. 7–6–20–4..........	do ...	3.7	3.8	0.42	....	1.61
July 25	SE. 8–6–20–4..........	do ...	2.0	1.0	0.82	....	0.82
July 27......	SE. 9–6–20–4..........	do ...	2.9	1.4	1.06	....	1.51
July 27......	NW. 10–6–20–4	do ...	3.4	1.1	0.55	....	0.60
July 27......	SE. 15–6–20–4	do ...	3.0	1.3	0.98	....	1.25
July 27......	SW. 14–6–20–4........	do ...	3.5	2.8	2.90	....	8.10
July 27......	SW. 14–6–20–4........	do ...	3.3	1.4	0.82	....	1.15
July 27.....	SE. 14–6–20–4.........	do ...	3.3	4.8	1.04	....	5.00
July 27.....	SW. 13–6–20–4........	do ...	3.7	2.6	1.17	....	3.03
July 27.....	NW. 7–6–19–4.........	do ...	3.5	2.2	1.05	....	2.20
July 27.....	NW. 8–6–19–4.........	do ...	3.0	1.4	1.07	....	1.47
July 27.... ..	NE. 8–6–19–4..........	·do ...	6.0	8.4	1.31	....	11.30*a*

a Raymond Lateral.

DISCHARGE MEASUREMENTS of Main Canal at NW. 36-6-21-4, in 1913-14.

Date.	Engineer.	Width.	Area of Section.	Mean Velocity.	Gauge Height.	Discharge.
		Feet.	*Sq. ft.*	*Ft. per sec.*	*Feet.*	*Sec.-ft.*
1913.						
July 28	G. D. Walters.	47.0	83.5	2.09	1.84	175
Aug. 15..........	do	51.0	116.6	1.99	2.18	233
Aug. 27	G. R. Elliott...............	50.8	110.0	1.89	2.17	207
Aug. 28..........	G. D. Walters.....	51.5	114.2	1.95	2.16	209
Aug. 28...	do	51.5	109.3	2.02	2.15	221
Aug. 30..........	R. J. Srigley................	52.3	106.8	1.66	1.96	177
Sept. 2	do	52.0	100.9	1.80	2.02	181
Sept. 4..........	G. R. Elliott.........	50.3	123.5	1.74	2.12	202
Sept. 5..........	R. J. Srigley.............. .	55.7	119.5	1.86	2.15	221
Oct. 6	G. D. Walters.....	49.0	119.1	1.89	2.10	225
1914.						
July 20............	R. J. McGuinness	59.0	156.3	2.52	2.78	396

DISCHARGE MEASUREMENTS of Big Chin Canal at Headgates, in 1914.

(SW. 18-8-20-4.)

Date.	Engineer.	Width.	Area of Section.	Mean Velocity.	Gauge Height.	Discharge.
		Feet.	*Sq. ft.*	*Ft. per sec.*	*Feet.*	*Sec.-ft.*
July 21............	R. J. McGuinness...........	30.2	56.1	2.82	2.28	158
Sept. 28............	do	29.9	39.2	1.48	1.37	58
Sept. 29............	do	28.3	23.8	1.26	0.98	30

5 GEORGE V. A. 1915

DISCHARGE MEASUREMENTS of Main Canal at Big Chin Gates, in 1914.

(SE. 13–8–21–4.)

Date.	Engineer.	Width.	Area of Section.	Mean Velocity.	Gauge Height.	Discharge.
		Feet.	*Sq. ft.*	*Ft. per sec.*	*Feet.*	*Sec.-ft.*
July 21............	R. J. McGuinness...........	32.0	130.4	2.77	....	361a
July 22............	do	25.8	90.0	2.10	3.20	201
Sept. 28	do	25.7	67.0	1.91	2.70	128
Sept. 29............	do	25.0	41.8	0.89	1.69	37

a Measurement at NW. 7-8-20-4.

DISCHARGE MEASUREMENTS of Distributaries from Main Canal, in 1914.

Date.	Location.	Engineer.	Width.	Area of Section.	Mean Velocity.	Gauge Height.	Discharge.
			Feet.	*Sq. ft.*	*Ft. per sec.*	*Feet.*	*Sec.-ft.*
1914.							
July 22............	NW. 7-8-20-4....	R. J. McGuinness	6.0	2.7	1.09	....	3.00
July 22............	SW. 7-8-20-4....	do	3.5	2.7	1.19	....	3.20
July 22............	NE. 6-8-20-4 ...	do	3.0	1.6	1.50	....	2.40
July 22............	NE. 31-7-20-4...	do	2.1	0.8	0.70	....	0.54
July 22............	NE. 36-7-21-4...	do	4.8	4.3	1.92	....	8.40

ROLPH CREEK NEAR KIMBALL.

Location.—On the SE. ¼ Sec. 21, Tp. 2, Rge. 24, W. 4th Mer.
Records available.—May 17, 1911, to October 31, 1914.
Gauge.—Vertical staff; zero of gauge maintained at 93.41 feet during 1913-14.
Bench-mark.—Permanent iron bench-mark located on the left bank 100 feet downstream; assumed elevation, 100.00 feet.
Channel.—Consists of sand, gravel and stone; likely to shift.
Discharge measurements.—Made by wading.
Observer.—J. M. Dunn.

DISCHARGE MEASUREMENTS of Rolph Creek near Kimball, in 1914.

Date.	Engineer.	Width.	Area of Section.	Mean Velocity.	Gauge Height.	Discharge.
		Feet.	*Sq. ft.*	*Ft. per sec.*	*Feet.*	*Sec.-ft.*
April 11............	O. H. Hoover...............	11.7	7.50	2.12	1.07	15.90
April 21............	do	8.1	3.65	1.31	0.63	4.80
May 14............	do	8.4	4.16	1.21	0.64	5.00
June 3............	do	3.8	0.83	0.35	0.49	0.30
June 23............	do	........a	....	....	0.57	0.21
July 16	do	........a	....	....	0.60	0.38
Aug. 12............	do	........a	....	....	0.60	0.13
Sept. 21............	do	........a	....	....	0.65	0.05
Oct. 17....	do	20.3	20.70	1.98	1.44	41.00

a Weir measurement.

DAILY GAUGE HEIGHT AND DISCHARGE of Rolph Creek near Kimball, for 1914.

DAY.	April.		May.		June.	
	Gauge Height.	Dis- charge.	Gauge Height.	Dis- charge.	Gauge Height.	Dis- charge.
	Feet.	*Sec.-ft.*	*Feet.*	*Sec.-ft.*	*Feet.*	*Sec.-ft.*
1	1.56	55.0	0.60	4.30	0.45	Nil.
2	1.55	54.0	0.60	4.30	0.47	0.10
3	1.53a	51.0	0.60	4.30	0.50	0.30
4	1.51	49.0	0.60	4.30	0.50	0.40
5	1.44a	42.0	0.65	5.20	0.50	0.35
6	1.38a	36.0	0.70	6.20	0.50	0.30
7	1.31a	30.0	0.75	7.20	0.50	0.20
8	1.25a	26.0	0.85	9.50	0.49	Nil.
9	1.18a	21.0	0.85	9.50	0.48	"
10	1.11	17.7	0.85	9.50	0.47	"
11	1.07	16.1	0.85	9.50	0.47	"
12	1.07a	16.1	0.70	6.20	0.47	"
13	1.06a	15.7	0.67	5.60	0.47	"
14	1.06	15.7	0.64	5.10	0.48	"
15	0.99a	13.2	0.63b	4.70	0.47	"
16	0.92a	11.3	0.60	4.10	0.47	"
17	0.85	9.5	0.60	4.00	0.47	"
18	0.80a	8.3	0.60	3.90	0.47	"
19	0.75a	7.2	0.60	3.80	0.47	"
20	0.70a	6.2	0.60	3.70	0.47	"
21	0.65	5.2	0.57	3.00	0.50a	"
22	0.64a	5.1	0.55	2.60	0.53a	"
23	0.63a	4.9	0.55	2.50	0.57	0.21
24	0.62	4.7	0.53	2.00	0.54a	Nil.
25	0.62a	4.7	0.53	1.90	0.52a	"
26	0.61a	4.5	0.50	1.20	0.50	"
27	0.61a	4.5	0.48	0.75	0.50	"
28	0.60	4.3	0.47	0.45	0.50	"
29	0.62	4.7	0.45	0.10	0.50	"
30	0.60	4.3	0.45	Nil.	Dry.b	"
31	....	....	0.45	"	....	....

a Gauge height interpolated.
b to b Shifting conditions May 15 to Sept. 21.

5 GEORGE V, A. 1915

DAILY GAUGE HEIGHT AND DISCHARGE of Rolph Creek near Kimball, for 1914.—*Concluded.*

DAY.	July.		August.		September.		October.	
	Gauge Height.	Dis- charge.	Gauge Height.	Dis- charge.	Gauge Height.	Dis- charge.	Gauge Height.	Dis- charge.
	Feet.	*Sec.-ft.*	*Feet.*	*Sec.-ft.*	*Feet.*	*Sec.-ft.*	*Feet.*	*Sec.-ft.*
1	Dry.b	Nil.	0.55	Nil.	0.67	0.85	0.71a	1.93
2	"	"	0.55	"	0.67	0.77	0.73a	2.60
3	"	"	0.58	"	0.65	0.69	0.75a	3.20
4	"	"	0.60	0.25	0.67	0.61	0.77a	3.90
5	0.50	"	0.60	0.23	0.65	0.53	0.80	4.90
6	0.50	"	0.60	0.22	0.65	0.45	0.80	4.90
7	0.50	"	0.60	0.21	0.65	0.43	0.85	6.60
8	0.50	"	0.60	0.19	0.65	0.41	0.90a	8.20
9	0.50	"	0.60	0.17	0.65	0.39	0.95a	10.10
10	0.54a	"	0.60	0.16	0.65	0.37	1.00a	12.00
11	0.56a	"	0.60	0.14	0.65	0.35	1.05a	14.10
12	0.58a	0.10	0.60	0.13	0.65	0.33	1.10a	16.20
13	0.60	0.45	0.60	0.46	0.70	0.31	1.15a	19.10
14	0.60	0.43	0.60	0.79	0.68	0.29	1.20	22.00
15	0.60	0.40	0.60	1.12	0.66	0.27	1.19a	21.00
16	0.60	0.38	0.60	1.45	0.65	0.25	1.18	21.00
17	0.60	0.36	0.70	1.80	0.65	0.21	1.15	19.10
18	0.60	0.34	0.67	1.60	0.65	0.17	1.15	19.10
19	0.60	0.32	0.67	1.40	0.65	0.13	1.14	18.50
20	0.60	0.30	0.65	1.20	0.65a	0.09	1.12	17.40
21	0.55	Nil.	0.65	1.00	0.65b	0.05	1.10	16.20
22	0.55	"	0.65	0.80	0.65	0.05	1.10	16.20
23	0.55	"	0.65	0.76	0.65	0.05	1.08	15.40
24	0.55	"	0.65	0.72	0.65	0.05	1.05	14.10
25	0.55	"	0.65	0.68	0.65	0.05	1.05	12.00
26	0.55	"	0.65	0.64	0.65	0.05	1.00	12.00
27	0.50	"	0.65	0.60	0.65	0.05	0.90	8.20
28	0.50	"	0.65	0.65	0.65	0.05	0.85	6.60
29	0.50	"	0.65	0.70	0.67a	0.67	0.80	4.90
30	0.50	"	0.65	0.75	0.69a	1.29	0.75	3.20
31	0.50	"	0.67	0.80	....	....	0.70	1.60

a Gauge height interpolated.
b to b Shifting conditions May 15 to Sept. 21.

MONTHLY DISCHARGE of Rolph Creek near Kimball, for 1914.
(Drainage area 74 square miles.)

MONTH.	DISCHARGE IN SECOND-FEET.				RUN-OFF.	
	Maximum.	Minimum	Mean.	Per square Mile.	Depth in inches on Drainage Area.	Total in Acre-feet.
April	55.00	4.30	18.30	0.247	0.280	1,089
May	9.50	0.00	4.20	0.057	0.060	258
June	0.40	0.00	0.06	0.001	0.001	4
July	0.45	0.00	0.10	0.001	0.001	6
August	1.80	0.00	0.73	0.010	0.010	45
September	1.29	0.05	0.34	0.005	0.006	20
October	22.00	1.60	11.50	0.155	0.018	707
The period	....	....	....	....	0.376	2,129

LEE CREEK AT LAYTON'S RANCH.

Location.—SE. ¼ Sec. 27, Tp. 2, Rge. 26, W. 4th Mer., at B. Layton's ranch.
Records available.—May 25, 1913, to January 31, 1914.
Gauge.—Vertical staff; zero of gauge maintained at elevation 88 14 feet during 1913-14.
Bench-mark.—Permanent iron bench-mark; assumed elevation, 100 00 feet; located on the left bank about 300 feet below the gauge.
Channel.—Straight and quite uniform, with a flat rock bed; not liable to shift.
Discharge measurements.—Made by wading at all ordinary stages, and from temporary cable at very high stages.
Winter flow.—Obtained through the ice 610 feet below the gauge.
Observer.—B. Layton.

SESSIONAL PAPER No. 25c

DISCHARGE MEASUREMENTS of Lee Creek at Layton's Ranch, in 1914.

Date.	Engineer.	Width.	Area of Section.	Mean Velocity.	Gauge Height.	Discharge.
		Feet.	*Sq. ft.*	*Ft. per sec.*	*Feet.*	*Sec.-ft.*
Jan. 3............	J. E. Degnan.............	18.0	10.80	0.66	2.60	7.2
Jan. 14	do	18.0	11.30	2.12	2.44	24.0
Jan. 27........	do	16.0	9.12	1.12	3.03	10.2
Feb. 7...........	do	13.0	8.60	0.81	2.37	6.9
Feb. 28	do	14.0	7.40	1.10	3.90	8.2
Mar. 7..........	do	10.1	10.20	1.52	3.60	16.5
Mar. 30.........	O. H. Hoover.............	43.1	27.10	0.98	2.88	26.0
April 17........	do	54.0	48.30	1.89	2.17	92.0
May 9.........	do	65.4	78.20	2.50	2.43	195.0
May 12.........	do	77.8	64.50	2.16	2.31	139.0
May 25	do	78.5	64.10	1.96	2.30	125.0
June 19.........	do	48.5	37.20	2.00	2.13	75.0
July 8..........	do	32.0	24.70	1.73	1.95	43.0
July 25.........	do	23.3	12.40	1.47	1.70	18.3
Aug. 8.......	do	19.7	8.34	1.18	1.58	9.9
Aug. 26.........	do	25.5	17.00	1.43	1.79	24.0
Sept. 10.........	do	20.1	9.24	1.28	1.62	11.8
Sept. 29	do	20.0	9.62	1.23	1.63	11.8
Oct. 20.........	do	57.7	57.80	1.97	2.27	114.0
Nov. 21.........	do	61.0	63.80	0.88	2.24	56.0
Nov. 30	do	21.0	11.20	1.19	1.67	13.3
Dec. 23.........	do	20.5	12.00	1.66	2.31	19.9

DAILY GAUGE HEIGHT AND DISCHARGE of Lee Creek at Layton's Ranch, for 1914.

DAY.	January.		February.		March.		April.		May.		June.	
	Gauge Height.	Dis-charge	Gauge Height.	Dis-charge	Gauge Height.	Dis-charge.	Gauge Height.	Dis-charge.	Gauge Height.	Dis-charge	Gauge Height	Dis-charge.
	Feet.	*Sec.-ft.*	*Feet.*	*Sec.-ft.*	*Feet.*	*Sec.-ft.*	*Feet.*	*Sec.-ft.*	*Feet.*	*Sec.-ft.*	*Feet.*	*Sec.-ft.*
1..........	2 94	7 2b		11.6	3.93	9.5	2.98	31	2 13	76	2 28	122
2.........	2.57	7.2	2.64	11.9	3.93	11.2	2.64a	34	2.19	92	2 27	118
3.........	2.58	7.2		11.6	3.88a	12.6	2.30	38	2.28	122	2 27	118
4.........	2.55	9 0	2 51	10 0	3.83	13.9	2.23	41	2 34	149	2 26	115
5.........	2.74	12.2	2.44	8 0	3.73a	15.0	2.21a	44	2.37	165	2.23	104
6.........	2 69	18 0	2.36	6.6	3.63	16.0	2.19b	47	2.35	154	2.21	98
7.........	2.68	20 0	2.35	6.9	3.60	16.5	1.99	49	2.33	144	2.20	94
8.........	2.63	21.0	2 38	8 0	3.58	16.9	1.98a	47	2.31	134	2.18	89
9.........		21 0	2.39	10.6	3.50a	16.8	1.96	44	2 35	154	2.16	84
10.......	2.56	21.0	2 40	11.8	3.43	16.8	2.01	52	2 33a	144	2 14	79
11.........		21.0	2.41	11.3	3.43a	17.2	2.09	67	2.31	134	2.14	79
12.........	2.48	21 0		11 1	3.43	18.6	2.03a	56	2.30	129	2.14	79
13.........		23 0	2.42	12 0	3.26a	21.0	1.97	46	2.32	139	2.13a	76
14.........	2.42	24 0	2 54	13.2	3.09a	23.0	2.02	54	2.31	134	2.13	76
15.........		24.0	2.60	13.9	2.93	24.0	2.25	112	2.29	126	2.12	74
16.........	2.56	24.0	2 67	13 8	2.91a	25.0	2.24a	108	2.27	118	2.12	74
17.......		22 0	2.74	12.7	2.89	25.0	2.22	101	2.26a	115	2.12a	74
18.........	2 66	19 5		10.2	2.83	26.0	2.14	79	2.25	112	2.13	76
19.........	2 71	16.5	2.91	7.2	2.78	26.0	2.22	101	2.25	112	2.13	76
20.........	2.76	14.3		5 6	2.80a	26.0	2.35	154	2.26	115	2.13	76
21.........		13.9	3.10	5.2	2.83	25.0	2.37	163	2.26	115	2.14	79
22.........	2.85	13.8	3.23	5.5	2.87	25.0	2.34a	149	2.27	118	2.15	82
23.........		13.6		5.7	2.88a	25.0	2.32	139	2.28	122	2.15	82
24.........	2.95	13.0	3.47	6.0	2.89	24.0	2.28	122	2.29a	126	2.25	112
25.........		12.1		6.4	2.95	23.0	2.26a	115	2.30	129	2.30	129
26.........	2.99	11.2	3.67	6.9	2.99a	23.0	2.24a	108	2.31	134	2.34	149
27.........	3.01	10.2	3.77	7.3	3.03	23.0	2.23	104	2.30	129	2.30	129
28.........		9.1	3.88	8.2	2.97a	24.0	2.20	94	2.29	126	2.25	112
29.........	2.89	8.6			2.90a	25.0	2.17a	86	2.28	122	2.15	82
30.........	2.81	9.2			2.83	26.0	2.14	79	2.28	122	2.11	72
31.........	2.73	10.3			2.96	28.0			2.28a	122		

a Gauge height interpolated.
b to b Ice conditions.

5 GEORGE V, A. 1915

DAILY GAUGE HEIGHT AND DISCHARGE of Lee Creek at Layton's Ranch, for 1914.
—Concluded.

DAY.	July.		August.		September.		October.		November.		December.	
	Gauge Height.	Dis-charge.	Gauge Height.	Dis-charge.	Gauge Height.	Dis-charge.	Gauge Height.	Dis-charge	Gauge Height.	Dis-charge.	Gauge Height.	Dis-charge.
	Feet.	*Sec.-ft.*	*Feet.*	*Sec.-ft.*	*Feet.*	*Sec.-ft.*	*Feet.*	*Sec.-ft.*	*Feet.*	*Sec.-ft.*	*Feet.*	*Sec.-ft.*
1	2.06	61.0	1.62	12.2	1.63a	12.8	1.63	12.8	2.02	54.0	2.19	13.8
2	2.02	54.0	1.62	12.2	1.63	12.8	1.63	12.8	2.04	58.0	2.24	14.0
3	1.98	47.0	1.61	11.6	1.62	12.2	1.64	13.4	2.05	60.0	2.21	14.0
4	1.96	44.0	1.61	11.6	1.62	12.2	1.66	14.6	2.06	61.0	2.16	13.3
5	1.98	47.0	1.60	11.0	1.66	14.6	1.70	17.0	2.06	61.0	2.19a	13.2
6	1.97a	46.0	1.60	11.0	1.69	16.4	1.74	20.0	2.07	63.0	2.22	13.5
7	1.96a	44.0	1.60	11.0	1.71	17.8	1.78	23.0	2.08	65.0	2.21	14.0
8	1.95	43.0	1.60	11.0	1.70	17.0	1.82	27.0	2.08	65.0	2.21	14.1
9	1.96a	44.0	1.63	12.8	1.70	17.0	1.88	34.0	2.10	69.0	2.23	14.1
10	1.97a	46.0	1.64	13.4	1.68	15.8	1.92	39.0	2.10	69.0	2.26	14.0
11	1.97	46.0	1.65	14.0	1.68	15.8	1.95	43.0	2.12	74.0	2.29	14.3
12	1.96	44.0	1.63	12.8	1.77	23.0	1.97	46.0	2.14	79.0	2.29	15.2
13	1.95	43.0	1.60	11.0	1.76	22.0	1.99	49.0	2.18	89.0	2.30a	15.9
14	1.94	42.0	1.58	10.0	1.75	21.0	2.19	92.0	2.20	94.0b	2.30	16.0
15	1.93	40.0	1.56	9.0	1.80	25.0	2.29	126.0	2.20	90.0	2.30	16.0
16	1.92	39.0	1.55	8.5	1.78	23.0	2.40	178.0	2.20a	86.0	2.31	16.7
17	1.90	36.0	2.06	61.0	1.76	22.0	2.36	158.0	2.20	80.0	2.31	17.8
18	1.89	35.0	1.95	43.0	1.75	21.0	2.32	139.0	2.20	74.0	2.31	17.2
19	1.87	33.0	1.90	36.0	1.74	20.0	2.30	129.0	2.21	67.0	2.31	16.8
20	1.85	30.0	1.85	30.0	1.72	18.6	2.27	118.0	2.22	62.0	2.30a	18.0
21	1.82	27.0	1.78	23.0	1.70	17.0	2.20	94.0	2.24	56.0	2.30	19.1
22	1.79	24.0	1.72	18.6	1.68	15.8	2.11	72.0	2.22	51.0	2.31	19.8
23	1.76	22.0	2.02	54.0	1.66	14.6	2.09	67.0	2.22	44.0	2.33	19.9
24	1.74	20.0	1.98	47.0	1.66	14.6	2.08	65.0	2.20	38.0	2.33	19.7
25	1.70	17.0	1.90	36.0	1.65	14.0	2.07	63.0	2.15	32.0	2.36a	18.3
26	1.68	15.8	1.76	22.0	1.65	14.0	2.06	61.0	2.00	35.0	2.38	17.5
27	1.66	14.6	1.70	17.0	1.64	13.4	2.05	60.0	1.95	43.0	2.41	18.0
28	1.65	14.0	1.66	14.6	1.64	13.4	2.04	58.0	1.92	39.0	2.43	18.6
29	1.64	13.4	1.64	13.4	1.63	12.8	2.04	58.0	2.00	21.0	2.48	19.4
30	1.63	12.8	1.62	12.2	1.63	12.8	2.03	56.0	2.07	13.3	2.51	19.7
31	1.63	12.8	1.62a	12.2	......	......	2.02	54.0	......	......	2.54	20.0b

a Gauge height interpolated.
b to *b* Ice conditions.

MONTHLY DISCHARGE of Lee Creek at Layton's Ranch, for 1914.
(Drainage area 92 square miles.)

MONTH.	DISCHARGE IN SECOND-*FEET.*				RUN-OFF.	
	Maximum.	Minimum.	Mean.	Per square Mile.	Depth in inches on Drainage Area.	Total in Acre-feet.
January	24.0	7.2	15.4	0.167	0.19	947
February	13.9	5.2	9.2	0.100	0.10	511
March	26.0	9.5	21.0	0.228	0.26	1,291
April	163.0	31.0	82.0	0.891	0.99	4,879
May	163.0	76.0	127.0	1.380	1.59	7,809
June	149.0	72.0	94.0	1.020	1.14	5,593
July	61.0	12.8	34.0	0.370	0.43	2,091
August	61.0	8.5	20.0	0.217	0.25	1,230
September	25.0	12.2	16.7	0.182	0.20	994
October	178.0	12.8	65.0	0.707	0.82	3,997
November	94.0	13.3	60.0	0.652	0.73	3,570
December	20.0	13.2	16.5	0.179	0.21	1,014
The year	......	......	......	......	6.91	33,926

LEE CREEK AT CARDSTON.

Location.—On the NW. ¼ Sec. 10, Tp. 3, Rge. 25, W. 4th Mer.
Records available.—June 28, 1909, to July 13, 1914.
Gauge.—Vertical staff; zero of gauge maintained at 87.91 feet during 1913-14. For previous gauge data see previous reports.

Bench-mark.—Permanent iron bench-mark.
Discharge measurements.—Made by wading.
Winter flow.—Records are discontinued during the frozen season.
Observer.—O. Williams.
Remarks.—Daily records were discontinued at this station on July 13, 1914, and the station abandoned in favour of the station at Layton's ranch. (See Lee Creek at Layton's ranch.)

DISCHARGE MEASUREMENTS of Lee Creek at Cardston, in 1914.

Date.	Engineer.	Width.	Area of Section.	Mean Velocity.	Gauge Height.	Discharge.
		Feet.	*Sq. ft.*	*Ft. per sec.*	*Feet.*	*Sec.-ft.*
Mar. 21	O. H. Hoover......	19.0	25.6	1.51	1.37	39.0
April 4........... ..	do	28.3	36.7	1.93	1.47	71.0
April 18...........	do	29.9	42.9	1.90	1.38	82.0
May 4...........	do	69.0	63.9	2.11	1.56	135.0
May 22	do	69.0	58.7	2.00	1.52	117.0
June 8...........	do	29.3	43.1	1.71	1.36	74.0
June 20	do	29.0	42.5	1.70	1.35	72.0
July 1...........	do	24.5	29.3	1.86	1.28	55.0
July 11...........	do	27.7	34.0	0.99	1.15	34.0
Aug. 6...........	do	21.0	13.4	0.69	0.90	9.2
Sept. 1...........	do	14.8	12.0	1.15	1.05	13.9
Sept. 30...........	W. A. Burton	15.9	12.6	1.04	1.03	13.0
Oct. 7...........	O. H. Hoover.	17.7	18.1	1.87	1.17	33.8
Oct. 19...........	do	69.5	63.4	2.27	1.59	144.0
Nov. 7...........	do	42.0	30.5	1.82	1.29	55.8

DAILY GAUGE HEIGHT AND DISCHARGE of Lee Creek at Cardston, for 1914.

DAY.	March.		April.		May.		June.		July.	
	Gauge Height.	Dis-charge.	Gauge Height.	Dis-charge.	Gauge Height.	Dis-charge.	Gauge Height.	Dis-charge.	Gauge Height.	Dis-charge.
	Feet.	*Sec.-ft.*	*Feet.*	*Sec.-ft.*	*Feet.*	*Sec.-ft.*	*Feet.*	*Sec.-ft.*	*Feet.*	*Sec.-ft.*
1.............	....	....	1.43	60	1.49	110	1.44	95	1.28	56
2.............	....	....	1.35	44	1.55	130	1.44	95	1.35	71
3.............	....	....	1.19	22	1.55	130	1.55	130	1.33	67
4.............	....	....	1.47	71*b*	1.54	127	1.49	110	1.32	64
5.............	....	....	1.37	56	1.55	130	1.45	98	1.29	58
6.............	....	....	1.32	50	1.55	130	1.45	98	1.25	50
7.............	....	....	1.26	42	1.55	130	1.44	95	1.23	46
8.............	....	....	1.35	64	1.60	148	1.37	56	1.19	38
9.............	....	....	1.35	69	1.70	186	1.34	69	1.19	38
10.............	....	....	1.24	48	1.71	190	1.34	69	1.13	30
11.............	....	....	1.38	79	1.65	166	1.34	69	1.12	28
12.............	....	....	1.45	98	1.65	166	1.33	67	1.13	30
13.............	....	....	1.50	113	1.65	166	1.51	116	1.11*a*	27
14.............	....	....	1.50	113	1.64	162	1.60	148	....	....
15.............	....	....	1.55	130	1.63	159	1.46	101	....	....
16.............	....	....	1.50	113	1.60	148	1.45	98	....	....
17.............	....	....	1.45	98	1.58	141	1.43	92	....	....
18.............	....	....	1.41	87	1.55	130	1.40	84	....	....
19.............	....	....	1.38	79	1.55	130	1.35	71	....	....
20.............	....	....	1.64	162	1.56	134	1.34	69	....	....
21.............	1.39	39*b*	1.45	98	1.54	127	1.32	64	....	....
22.............	1.35	35	1.47	104	1.52	120	1.30	60	....	....
23.............	1.26	25	1.49	110	1.51	116	1.26	52	....	....
24.............	1.76	144	1.54	127	1.52	120	1.26	52	....	....
25.............	1.69	123	1.49	110	1.50	113	1.50	113	....	....
26.............	1.64	107	1.45	98	1.48	107	1.54	127	.... ..	....
27.............	1.91	212	1.41	87	1.46	101	1.36	74	....	....
28.............	1.86	190	1.42	90	1.45	98	1.32	64	....	....
29.............	1.92	221	1.41	87	1.44	95	1.32	64	....	....
30.............	1.75	152	1.40	84	1.43	92	1.32	64	....	....
31.............	1.43	60	....	....	1.43	92	....	....	....	....

a Station abandoned.
b Ice conditions March 21 to April 4.

5 GEORGE V, A. 1915

MONTHLY DISCHARGE of Lee Creek at Cardston, for 1914.

(Drainage area 118 square miles)

MONTH.	DISCHARGE IN SECOND-FEET.				RUN-OFF.	
	Maximum	Minimum	Mean.	Per square Mile.	Depth in inches on Drainage Area.	Total in Acre-feet.
March (21-31).........................	221	25	119	1.010	0.41	2,596
April................................	162	22	86	0.729	0.81	5,117
May.................................	190	92	132	1.120	1.29	8,116
June................................	148	52	86	0.729	0.81	5,117
July (1-13)...........................	71	27	46	0.390	0.19	1,186
The period...........	....	....	....	....	3.51	22,132

PINEPOUND CREEK AT PACKARD'S FARM.

Location.—On the *NE.* ¼ Sec. 29, Tp. 4, Rge. 24, W. 4th Mer.
Records available.—April 30, 1914, to October 31, 1914.
Gauge.—Vertical staff; zero of gauge maintained at elevation of 90.66 feet during 1914.
Bench-mark.—Temporary iron bench-mark located 70 feet northeast of the staff gauge on the right bank; assumed elevation, 100.00 feet.
Channel.—Composed of sand, gravel, and small stones; not liable to shift on account of the good control located about 100 feet below the gauge.
Discharge measurements.—Made by wading.
Winter flow.—Station discontinued during winter season.
Observer.—Earl O. Packard.

DISCHARGE MEASUREMENTS of Pinepound Creek at Packard's Farm, in 1914.

Date.	Engineer.	Width.	Area of Section.	Mean Velocity.	Gauge Height.	Discharge.
		Feet.	*Sq. ft.*	*Ft. per sec.*	*Feet.*	*Sec.-ft.*
April 30............	O. H. Hoover..............	60.4	73.40	2.98	3.73	218.0
May 1............	do	37.7	36.50	2.42	3.36	88.0
May 20............	do	35.3	31.40	1.64	3.26	52.0
June 10............	do	34.3	22.52	1.76	3.12	40.0
June 30............	do	15.8	12.80	1.25	2.92	16.0
July 14............	do	24.0	12.90	1.02	2.90	13.1
July 24............	do	15.5	12.36	0.88	2.84	10.9
Aug. 7............	do	16.9	9.52	0.71	2.74	6.7
Aug. 15............	do	17.2	8.94	0.61	2.73	5.5
Aug. 28............	do	17.5	8.66	0.62	2.72	5.4
Sept. 16............	do	14.0	4.43	0.96	2.71	4.3
Sept. 24............	do	14.2	4.58	0.98	2.70	4.4
Oct. 2............	do	14.7	4.94	0.93	2.71	4.6

SESSIONAL PAPER No. 25c

DAILY GAUGE HEIGHT AND DISCHARGE of Pinepound Creek at Packard's Farm, for 1914.

DAY.	April.		May.		June.		July.	
	Gauge Height.	Dis- charge.	Gauge Height	Dis- charge.	Gauge Height.	Dis- charge.	Gauge Height.	Dis- charge.
	Feet.	*Sec.-ft.*	*Feet.*	*Sec.-ft.*	*Feet.*	*Sec.-ft.*	*Feet.*	*Sec.-ft.*
1	....	....	3.45	114.0	3.18	50.0	2.86	12.4
2	....	....	3.46	117.0	3.20	53.0	2.87	13.0
3	....	....	3.22	57.0	3.19	51.0	2.87	13.0
4	....	....	3.25	63.0	3.24	61.0	2.89	14.4
5	....	....	3.22	57.0	3.15	45.0	2.88	13.7
6	....	....	3.20	53.0	3.15	45.0	2.88	13.7
7	....	....	2.85	11.7	3.15	45.0	2.87	13.0
8	....	....	2.84	11.1	3.14	43.0	2.87	13.0
9	....	....	2.83	10.5	3.13	42.0	2.88	13.7
10	....	....	2.84	11.1	3.12	40.0	2.88	13.7
11	....	....	2.82	9.8	3.11	39.0	2.89	14.4
12	....	....	2.79	8.2	3.11	39.0	2.89	14.4
13	....	....	2.78	8.0	3.12	40.0	2.90	15.0
14	....	....	2.87	13.0	3.10	37.0	2.90	15.0
15	....	....	3.29	72.0	3.11	39.0	2.90	15.0
16	....	....	3.29	72.0	3.11	39.0	2.90	15.0
17	....	....	3.17	48.0	3.11	39.0	2.90	15.0
18	....	....	3.17	48.0	3.10	37.0	2.91	15.1
19	....	....	3.17	48.0	3.10	37.0	2.87	13.0
20	....	....	3.16	47.0	2.95	19.5	2.90	15.0
21	....	....	3.16	47.0	2.92	16.8	2.90	15.0
22	....	....	3.18	50.0	2.93	17.7	2.90	15.0
23	....	....	3.17	48.0	2.92	16.8	2.88	13.7
24	....	....	3.18	50.0	2.91	15.1	2.85	11.8
25	....	....	3.19	51.0	2.91	15.1	2.85	11.8
26	....	....	3.16	47.0	2.88	13.7	2.84	11.1
27	....	....	3.17	48.0	2.88	13.7	2.83	10.5
28	....	....	3.17	48.0	2.90	15.0	2.82	9.8
29	....	....	3.16	47.0	2.90	15.0	3.40	99.0
30	3.73	219	3.19	51.0	2.92	16.8	2.85	11.7
31	....	....	3.20	53.0	....	....	2.75	6.0

STREAM MEASUREMENTS, 1914

5 GEORGE V, A. 1915

DAILY GAUGE HEIGHT AND DISCHARGE of Pinepound Creek at Packard's Farm, for 1914.
—*Concluded.*

	August.		September.		October.	
DAY.	Gauge Height.	Dis- charge.	Gauge Height.	Dis- charge.	Gauge Height.	Dis- charge.
	Feet.	*Sec.-ft.*	*Feet.*	*Sec.-ft.*	*Feet.*	*Sec.-ft.*
1	2.75	6.0	2.75	6.0	2.71	4.8
2	2.75	6.0	2.74	5.7	2.71	4.8
3	2.75	6.0	2.74	5.7	2.73	5.4
4	2.75	6.0	2.74	5.7	3.50	129.0
5	2.74	5.7	2.74	5.7	3.51	133.0
6	2.74	5.7	2.74	5.7	2.81	9.2
7	2.74	5.7	2.73	5.4	2.79	8.0
8	2.74	5.7	2.73	5.4	2.77	7.0
9	2.75	6.0	2.73	5.4	2.78	7.5
10	2.74	5.7	2.74	5.7	2.70	4.5
11	2.73	5.4	2.74	5.7	2.70	4.5
12	2.74	5.7	2.74	5.7	2.66	3.3
13	2.73	5.4	2.73	5.4	2.65	3.0
14	2.73	5.4	2.73	5.4	2.65	3.0
15	2.72	5.1	2.74	5.7	2.68	3.9
16	2.73	5.4	2.74	5.7	2.80	8.5
17	2.73	5.4	2.71	4.8	2.82	9.8
18	2.74	5.7	2.71	4.8	2.82	9.8
19	2.73	5.4	2.71	4.8	2.86	12.4
20	2.73	5.4	2.71	4.8	2.80	8.5
21	2.73	5.4	2.71	4.8	2.76	6.5
22	2.73	5.4	2.71	4.8	2.70	4.5
23	2.73	5.4	2.71	4.8	2.65	3.0
24	2.73	5.4	2.70	4.5	2.64	2.8
25	2.74	5.7	2.70	4.5	2.64	2.8
26	2.73	5.4	2.71	4.8	2.64	2.8
27	2.73	5.4	2.71	4.8	2.63	2.6
28	2.73	5.4	2.71	4.8	2.62	2.4
29	2.73	5.4	2.70	4.5	2.62	2.4
30	2.74	5.7	2.71	4.8	2.60	2.0
31	2.75	6.0	....	....	2.60	2.0

MONTHLY DISCHARGE of Pinepound Creek at Packard's Farm, for 1914.

(Drainage area *a* square miles.)

	DISCHARGE IN SECOND-FEET.				RUN-OFF.	
MONTH.	Maximum.	Minimum.	Mean.	Per square Mile.	Depth in inches on Drainage Area.	Total in Acre-feet.
April (30)	219	....	219.0	....	....	434
May	117	8.0	45.8	....	....	2,816
June	61	13.7	33.2	....	....	1,975
July	99	6.0	16.0	....	....	984
August	6	5.1	5.6	....	....	344
September	6	4.5	5.2	....	....	310
October (1–31)	133	2.0	13.3	....	....	818
The period	....	....	....	....	....	7,681

a Owing to the fact that the greater portion of the discharge is waste water from the Alberta Railway and Irrigation Company's Canal the drainage area has not been taken out.

ALBERTA RAILWAY AND IRRIGATION COMPANY CANAL AT SPRING COULEE.

Location.—On the NW. ¼ Sec. 28, Tp. 4, Rge. 23, W. 4th Mer.
Records available.—May 1, 1914, to August 31, 1914.
Gauge.—Vertical staff; zero of gauge maintained at elevation 94.38 feet during 1914.
Bench-mark.—Top of a large boulder inset in the right bank 10 feet from the gauge;
assumed elevation, 100 00 feet.

SESSIONAL PAPER No. 25c

Channel.—Straight for 300 feet above and 150 feet below the cable. The banks are steep and high, and the stream bed consists of sand, clay and small stones, liable to shift.

Discharge measurements.—Made from a temporary cable structure located 150 feet below the gauge.

Observer.—E. M. Eby.

Remarks.—Records may be obtained only during the irrigating season.

DISCHARGE MEASUREMENTS of Alberta Railway and Irrigation Company Canal at Spring Coulee, in 1914.

Date.	Engineer.	Width.	Area of Section.	Mean Velocity.	Gauge Height.	Discharge.
		Feet.	Sq. ft.	Ft. per sec.	Feet.	Sec.-ft.
May 1	O. H. Hoover	41.0	68.6	2.88	2.92	197
May 20	W. A. Burton	37.5	108.0	3.77	3.77	405
July 14	O. H. Hoover	51.2	138.0	4.50	4.69	623
July 24	do	50.9	139.0	4.43	4.66	615
Aug. 7	do	50.0	130.0	4.19	4.42	548
Aug. 15	do	49.5	121.0	4.01	4.15	487
Aug. 28	do	50.0	124.0	4.10	4.20	511
Sept. 16	do	47.5	89.8	3.30	3.47	296
Sept. 24	do	48.0	103.0	3.57	3.65	368
Oct. 2	do	49.5	103.0	3.45	3.72	357

DAILY GAUGE HEIGHT AND DISCHARGE of Alberta Railway and Irrigation Company Canal at Spring Coulee, for 1914.

DAY.	May.		June.	
	Gauge Height.	Dis-charge.	Gauge Height.	Dis-charge.
	Feet.	Sec.-ft.	Feet.	Sec.-ft.
1	2.92	196	4.10	469
2	2.97	207	4.12	474
3	3.36	292	4.20	495
4	3.49	321	4.32	526
5	3.95	430	4.38	542
6	3.48	319	4.60	590
7	3.80	394	4.62	604
8	3.92	423	4.64	609
9	3.91	420	4.70	625
10	3.87	411	4.63	607
11	3.89	416	4.69	622
12	3.87	411	4.68	620
13	3.91	420	4.69	622
14	3.89	416	4.67	617
15	3.92	423	4.71	628
16	3.91	420	4.73	633
17	3.93	426	4.71	628
18	3.93	426	4.70	625
19	3.93	426	4.69	622
20	3.96	433	4.72	630
21	3.95	430	4.71	628
22	3.91	420	4.69	622
23	3.95	430	4.72	630
24	3.98	438	4.72	630
25	3.97	436	4.70	625
26	3.96	433	4.71	628
27	3.98	438	4.70	625
28	3.98	438	4.72	630
29	4.02	448	4.73	633
30	4.05	456	4.74	635
31	4.08	464		

STREAM MEASUREMENTS, 1914

5 GEORGE V, A. 1915

DAILY GAUGE HEIGHT AND DISCHARGE of *A*lberta Railway and *I*rrigation Company Canal at Spring Coulee, for 1914.—*Concluded.*

	July.		August. .	
DAY.	Gauge Height.	Dis-charge.	Gauge Height.	Dis-charge.
	Feet.	*Sec.-ft.*	*Feet.*	*Sec.-ft.*
1	4.75	638	4.29	518
2	4.73	633	4.32	526
3	4.74	635	4.34a	531
4	4.74	635	4.36	537
5	4.72	630	4.38	542
6	4.73	633	4.40b	547
7	4.74	635	4.42	552
8	4.73	633	4.34c	531
9	4.71	628	4.26d	511
10	4.69	622	4.18	490
11	4.70	625	4.14	479
12	4.74	635	4.16	485
13	4.73	633	4.16	485
14	4.72	630	4.18	490
15	4.73	633	4.15	482
16	4.73	633	4.16	485
17	4.69	622	4.20	495
18	4.71	628	4.13	477
19	4.70	625	4.13	477
20	4.71	628	4.17	487
21	4.72	630	4.15	482
22	4.72	630	4.18	490
23	4.71	628	4.10	469
24	4.66	615	4.12	474
25	4.67	617	4.09	466
26	4.70	625	4.11	472
27	4.62	604	4.12	474
28	4.68	620	4.14	479
29	4.53	581	4.07	461
30	4.51	576	4.10	469
31	4.43	555	4.09	466

a to *b* Gauge heights interpolated.
c to *d* Gauge heights interpolated.

MONTHLY DISCHARGE of *A*lberta Railway and *I*rrigation Company Canal at Spring Coulee, for 1914.

	DISCHARGE IN SECOND-FEET.				RUN-OFF.	
MONTH.	Maximum	Minimum	Mean.	Per square Mile.	Depth in inches on Drainage Area.	Total in Acre-feet.
May	464	196	402	....	....	24,718
June	635	469	603	....	....	35,881
July	638	555	622	....	....	38,245
August	552	461	494	....	....	30,375
The period	....	....	....	....	....	129,219

POTHOLE CREEK NEAR MAGRATH (UPPER STATION).

Location.—On the NW. ¼ Sec. 10, Tp. 5, Rge. 22, W. 4th Mer., three and one-half miles southwest of Magrath.

Records available.—April 27, 1914, to October 9, 1914.

Gauge.—Vertical staff; zero of gauge maintained at elevation 93.70 feet during 1914.

Bench-mark.—Temporary iron bench-mark, located on the left bank 70 feet directly across the stream from the staff gauge; assumed elevation, 100 00 feet.

Channel.—Straight for about 100 feet above and 50 feet below gauge, composed of fine gravel and stones, and liable to shift during floods.

Discharge measurements.—Made by wading.

Winter flow.—Station discontinued during winter season.

Observer.—L. A. Harrison.

DISCHARGE MEASUREMENTS of Pothole Creek near Magrath (Upper Station), in 1914.

Date.	Engineer.	Width.	Area of Section.	Mean Velocity.	Gauge Height.	Discharge.
		Feet.	*Sq. ft.*	*Ft. per sec.*	*Feet.*	*Sec.-ft.*
April 27	O. H. Hoover...............	8.2	2.75	0.730	0.90	2.01
May 20	do	7.8	1.75	0.446	0.80	0.78
June 9...........	do	....	....	....	....	Nil.a
June 29	do	....	....	....	....	"
July 13	do	....	....	....	....	"
Sept. 16...........	do	....	....	....	....	"

a Water standing in pools.

DAILY GAUGE HEIGHT AND DISCHARGE of Pothole Creek near Magrath (Upper Station), for 1914.

DAY.	April.		May.		June.	
	Gauge Height.	Dis-charge.	Gauge Height.	Dis-charge.	Gauge Height.	Dis-charge.
	Feet.	*Sec.-ft.*	*Feet.*	*Sec.-ft.*	*Feet.*	*Sec.-ft.*
1........	....	....	0.85	1.28	0.60	0.01
2........	....	....	0.85	1.28	0.60	0.01
3........	....	....	0.92	2.40	0.60	0.01
4........	....	....	0.95	2.90	0.58	Nil.
5........	....	....	1.10	5.60	0.56	"
6........	....	....	1.05	4.70	0.54	"
7........	....	....	1.00	3.80	0.52	"
8........	....	....	1.06	4.90	0.48	"
9........	....	....	1.03	4.30	0.47	"
10........	....	....	1.00	3.80	....	......a
11........	....	....	0.95	2.90	... ...	....
12........	....	....	0.93	2.50	....	....
13........	....	....	0.90	2.00	....	....
14........	....	....	0.86	1.42	....	....
15........	....	....	0.86	1.42	....	....
16........	....	....	0.84	1.18	....	....
17........	....	....	0.82	0.98	....	....
18........	....	....	0.80	0.79	....	....
19........	....	....	0.80	0.79	....	....
20........	....	....	0.80	0.79	....	....
21........	....	....	0.80	0.79	....	....
22........	....	....	0.80	0.79	....	....
23........	....	....	0.78	0.65	....	....
24........	....	....	0.77	0.59	....	....
25........	....	....	0.78	0.65	....	....
26........	....	....	0.78	0.65	....	....
27........	0.90	2.00	0.75	0.45	....	....
28........	0.90	2.00	0.70	0.23	....	....
29........	0.90	2.00	0.68	0.17	....	....
30........	0.90	2.00	0.67	0.15	....	....
31........	....	....	0.66	0.12	....	....

a No flow after June 9.

No. 25c—18½

5 GEORGE V, A. 1915

MONTHLY DISCHARGE of Pothole Creek near Magrath (Upper Station), for 1914.

(Drainage area 162 square miles.)

MONTH.	DISCHARGE IN SECOND-*FEET.*				RUN-OFF.	
	Maximum.	Minimum	Mean.	Per square Mile.	Depth in inches on Drainage Area.	Total in Acre-feet.
April (27–30)........................	2.00	2.00	2.00	0.012	0.002	16
May.............................	5.60	0.12	1.77	0.011	0.012	109
June	0.01	0.00	....	....	....	Nil.
July.............................	....	....	....	....	....	"
August	....	....	....	....	....	"
September.........................	....	....	....	....	....	"
October (1–9)	....	....	....	....	....	"
The period.........................	....	....	....	....	0 014	125

POTHOLE CREEK NEAR MAGRATH (LOWER STATION).

Location.—On the *NE.* ¼ Sec. 1, Tp. 6, Rge. 22, W. 4th Mer., three miles northeast of Magrath.

Records available.—April 28, 1914, to October 31, 1914.

Gauge.—Vertical staff; zero of gauge maintained at elevation of 93.90 feet from *April* 28th to July 13th. Gauge moved 336 feet downstream on July 13th; zero of gauge maintained at elevation of 94.47 feet from July 13th.

Bench-marks.—(1) Temporary iron bench-mark, assumed elevation 100.00 feet, located on the left bank directly across stream from the staff from April 28th to July 13th. (2) Temporary iron bench-mark, assumed elevation 100.00 feet, located on the left bank 50 feet from the staff.

Channel.—Composed of sand, gravel and clay; liable to shift during floods.

Discharge measurements.—Made by wading.

Floods.—Caused by overflow from Alberta Railway and *I*rrigation Company Canal.

Winter flow.—Stream discontinued during winter season.

Observer.—R. Hyden.

DISCHARGE MEASUREMENTS of Pothole Creek near Magrath (Lower Station), in 1914.

Date.	Engineer.	Width.	Area of Section.	Mean Velocity.	Gauge Height.	Discharge.
		Feet.	*Sq. ft.*	*Ft. per sec.*	*Feet.*	*Sec.-ft.*
April 28............	O. H. Hoover..............	14.7	3.06	0.64	0.90	1.97
May 20............	do	44.0	34.30	2.04	1.81	70.00
June 9............	do	44.3	41.20	2.34	1.95	94.00
June 29............	do	47.0	40.60	1.94	2.17	79.00
July 13*a*........ .	do	51.0	57.00	2.32	1.93	132.00
July 24............ .	do	50.0	52.80	2.79	1.86	148.00
Aug. 7............	do	51.0	46.80	2.92	1.74	114.00
Aug. 15............	do	46.5	34.90	1.89	1.47	66.00
Aug. 28............	do	59.0	72.00	3.22	2.14	232.00
Sept. 16............	do	47.0	39.40	2.02	1.43	80.00
Sept. 24............	W. A. Burton..............	44.0	33.50	1.83	1.33	61.00

a Station moved doWnstream on July 13.

SESSIONAL PAPER No. 25c

DAILY GAUGE HEIGHT AND DISCHARGE of Pothole Creek near Magrath (Lower Station), for 1914.

DAY.	April.		May.		June.		July.	
	Gauge Height.	Dis- charge.	Gauge Height.	Dis- charge.	Gauge Height.	Dis- charge.	Gauge Height.	Dis- charge.
	Feet.	*Sec.-ft.*	*Feet.*	*Sec.-ft.*	*Feet.*	*Sec.-ft.*	*Feet.*	*Sec.-ft.*
1			2.44	213	2.24	163	2.35	125
2			2.31	180	1.95	95	2.30	113
3			2.00	105	1.85	76	2.29	111
4			2.15	140	1.98	101	2.30	113
5			2.20	153	2.00	105	2.35	125
6			2.05	117	2.10	128	2.45	150
7			2.25	165	3.30	428	2.40	138
8			2.25	165	2.50	228	2.40	138
9			2.35	190	1.95	95	2.45	150
10			2.34	188	2.05	114	4.25	600
11			2.34	188	3.80	549	2.45	150
12			2.30	178	3.95	580	2.53	170
13			1.98	101	4.25	611	1.93a	132
14			2.30	178	4.20	636	1.85	120
15			1.33	21	2.55	220	1.80	112
16			2.13	136	4.32	660	1.95	146
17			2.13	136	4.29	649	1.90	139
18			1.60	44	2.85	285	1.90	141
19			1.58	42	2.35	156	2.00	164
20			1.80	68	2.55	203	1.95	156
21			1.50	34	4.20	612	1.90	145
22			1.72	58	2.35	146	1.90	149
23			1.90	85	2.35	142	2.00	172
24			1.84	75	2.45	164	1.83	145
25			1.85	76	2.35	135	1.85	140
26			1.85	76	2.25	107	1.85	136
27			2.00	105	2.25	103	1.85	140
28	0.90	2.00	1.80	68	2.20	88	1.85	140
29	0.90	2.00	1.60	44	2.17	78	1.50	70
30	0.88	1.60	3.48	473	2.23	108	1.85	140
31			3.50	478			1.80	130

a Gauge moved 336 feet downstream on July 13.

5 GEORGE V, A. 1915

DAILY GAUGE HEIGHT AND DISCHARGE of Pothole Creek near Magrath (Lower Station), for 1914.—*Concluded.*

DAY.	August.		September.		October.	
	Gauge Height.	Dis- charge.	Gauge Height.	Dis- charge.	Gauge Height.	Dis- charge.
	Feet.	*Sec.-ft.*	*Feet*	*Sec.-ft.*	*Feet.*	*Sec.-ft.*
1	1.80	130	2.00	200	1.30	56
2	3.50	519	2.00	200	1.30	56
3	3.50	519	2.00	200	1.30	56
4	2.00	174	2.00	200	3.15	465
5	1.95	161	2.00	200	4.00	660
6	1.95	161	2.00	200	2.00	200
7	1.95	161	2.00	200	1.50	92
8	1.90	152	1.95	189	1.50	92
9	1.70	109	1.93	185	1.30	56
10	1.60	89	1.95	189	Dry.	Nil.
11	1.60	89	1.90	178	"	"
12	1.59	87	1.95	189	"	"
13	1.60	89	2.00	200	"	"
14	1.60	89	1.90	178	"	"
15	1.55	80	1.65	123	1.30	56
16	1.50	74	1.60	112	1.30	56
17	1.50	76	1.57	106	1.30	56
18	1.50	78	1.55	102	1.30	56
19	1.50	80	1.55	102	1.20	40
20	1.50	82	1.60	112	1.10	27
21	1.53	91	1.50	92	0.90	4
22	1.50	87	1.30	56	......a	....
23	2.00	195	1.30	56	....	....
24	2.30	267	1.30	56	....	....
25	2.20	242	1.30	56	....	....
26	2.00	197	1.50	92	....	....
27	2.50	315	1.30	56	....	....
28	2.45	304	1.30	56	....	....
29	2.40	292	1.33	61	....	....
30	2.40	292	1.30	56	....	....
31	2.00	200	....	....	....	....

a Dry after Oct. 21.

MONTHLY DISCHARGE of Pothole Creek near Magrath (Lower Station), for 1914.

(Drainage area, *a* square miles.)

MONTH.	DISCHARGE IN SECOND-FEET.			RUN-OFF.
	Maximum.	Minimum	Mean.	Total in Acre-feet.
April (28-30)	2.0	1.6	1.87	11
May	478.0	21.0	138.00	8,485
June	660.0	76.0	259.00	15,412
July	600.0	70.0	152.00	9,346
August	519.0	74.0	177.00	10,883
September	200.0	56.0	133.00	7,914
October	660.0	0.0	65.00	3,997
The period	....	....	....	56,048

a Owing to the greater part of the discharge being Waste Water from the Alberta Railway and Irrigation Company Canal, the drainage area has not been taken out.

SESSIONAL PAPER No. 25c

ST. MARY RIVER AT WHITNEY'S RANCH.

Location.—On the N.E. ¼ Sec. 26, Tp. 7, Rge. 22, W. 4th Mer.
Records available.—October 13, 1911, to December 31, 1914.
Gauge.—Vertical staff; zero of gauge maintained at 87.55 feet during 1911; 89.13 feet during 1912; 89.15 feet during 1913; 88.15 feet during 1914.
Bench-mark.—Permanent iron bench-mark; assumed elevation, 100.00 feet; located near Mr. Whitney's house.
Channel.—Consists of gravel, and is liable to shift.
Discharge measurements.—Made from a cable car located about 2,000 feet downstream from the gauge.
Winter flow.—Obtained through the ice 240 feet downstream from the cable.
Observer.—W. D. Whitney.

DISCHARGE MEASUREMENTS of St. Mary River at Whitney's Ranch, in 1914.

Date.	Engineer.	Width.	Area of Section.	Mean Velocity.	Gauge Height.	Discharge.
		Feet.	*Sq. ft.*	*Ft. per sec.*	*Feet.*	*Sec.-ft.*
Jan. 9	J. E. Degnan	75	89.0	2.83	1.43	252
Jan. 20	do	85	99.5	2.06	1.43	204
Feb. 5	do	110	66.2	0.87	1.41	57
Mar. 5	do	135	250.0	0.99	1.91	248
April 3	J. E. Caughey	185	242.0	2.04	1.36	496
April 23	do	236	370.0	2.92	1.73	1,080
May 11	do	265	502.0	3.66	2.12	1,841
May 30	do	268	523.6	3.65	2.09	1,912
June 20	do	303	547.0	3.80	2.14	2,083
July 7	do	245	422.0	3.17	1.89	1,341
July 21	do	195	298.0	2.25	1.52	671
Aug. 4	do	190	261.0	2.21	1.43	577
Aug. 19	do	190	256.0	2.27	1.41	579
Sept. 1	do	180	175.0	2.06	1.15	360
Sept. 19	do	85	104.0	2.08	1.00	218
Oct. 1	do	185	217.0	2.12	1.30	459
Oct. 21	do	243	442.0	3.20	1.86	1,415
Nov. 10	O. H. Hoover	223	357.0	2.82	1.72	1,006
Nov. 24	do	190	267.0	2.33	1.43	622
Dec. 9	do	129	339.0	0.44	1.46	148
Dec. 29	do	100	132.0	1.79	2.02	236

5 GEORGE V, A. 1915

DAILY GAUGE HEIGHT AND DISCHARGE of St. Mary River at Whitney's Ranch, for 1914.

DAY.	January. Gauge Height	January. Dis-charge	February. Gauge Height	February. Dis-charge.	March. Gauge Height.	March. Dis-charge.	April. Gauge Height.	April. Dis-charge	May. Gauge Height.	May. Dis-charge	June. Gauge Height	June. Dis-charge.
	Feet.	*Sec.-ft.*	*Feet.*	*Sec.-ft.*	*Feet.*	*Sec.-ft.*	*Feet.*	*Sec.-ft.*	*Feet.*	*Sec-ft.*	*Feet.*	*Sec.-ft.*
1...........	0.89	115b	1.46	108	2.11	235	1 44	608	1.96	1,538	2.09	1,855
2...........	0.91	142	1.44	83	2 06	238	1.45	620	1.99	1,607	2 09	1,855
3...........	0.93	171	1.42	58	2 01	242	1.46	632	1.99	1,607	2.09	1,855
4...........	0.93	196	1.37	56	1.93	248	1.50	680	1 99	1,607	2.09	1,855
5...........	0.93	220	1.41	57	1.92	248	1.35	510	2 02	1,680	2 09	1,855
6...........	1 03	200	1.40	63	1.88	254	1.39	550	1.98	1,584	2.14	1,980
7...........	1.05	230	1.40	68	1.75	263	1.37	530	1.95	1,515	2.12	1,930
8...........	1.07	243	1.39	82	1.65	272	1.43	596	1.95	1,515	2.09	1,855
9...........	1.44	252	1.38	88	1.62	280	1.33	490	1.92	1,446	2.09	1,855
10.	1.38	214	1.41	94	1.50	290	1.25	415	2.01	1,655	2.12	1,930
11...........	1.42	232	1.45	96	1.43	302	1.22	388	2.12	1,930	2:13	1,955
12...........	1.44	230	1.47	85	1.37	313	1.24	406	2.04	1,730	2.09	1,855
13...........	1.46	239	1.51	83	1.22	327	1.32	480	2.02	1,680	2.09	1,855
14....	1.46	245	1.56	87	2.16	342a	1.38	540	2.02	1,680	2.07	1,805
15...........	1.46	240	1.56	93	1.60	356	1.46	632	2.01	1,655	2.09	1,855
16...........	1.48	232	1.56	108	1.49	373	1.51	694	2.01	1,655	2.09	1,855
17....	1.48	222	2.21	155	1.44	391	1.53	722	2.09	1,855	2.14	1,980
18...........	1.45	215	2.26	176	......	408b	1.60	820	2.09	1,855	2.14	1,980
19...........	1.43	208	2.34	178	1.27	433	1.64	888	2.14	1,980	2.14	1,980
20...........	1.43	204	2.35	168	1.30	460	1.68	956	2.19	2,105	2.17	2,055
21......	1.43	190	2.31	167	1.28	442	1.71	1,009	2.22	2,184	2.14	1,980
22...........	1.45	187	2.11	176	1.18	356	1.72	1,028	2.24	2,238	2.09	1,855
23...........	1.40	184	1.96	194	1.16	342	1.73	1,047	2.24	2,238	2.05	1,755
24...........	1.40	180	1.94	203	1.06	272	1.74	1,066	2.29	2,373	1.94	1,492
25...........	1.40	177	1.92	212	0.96	202	1.79	1,161	2.29	2,373	1.94	1,492
26....... ..	1.40	168	1.84	218	0.95	195	1.79	1,161	2.24	2,238	1.94	1,492
27....	1.45	140	1.81	224	1.16	342	1.82	1,224	2.19	2,105	1.94	1,492
28...........	1.45	100	1.77	230	1.23	397	1.83	1,246	2.14	1,980	1.89	1,378
29...........	1.47	99	......	......	1.30	460	1.90	1,400	2.13	1,955	1.89	1,378
30...........	1.48	102	......	......	1.38	540	1.93	1,469	2.13	1,955	1.89	1,378
31...........	1.48	112	......	......	1.43	596	......	......	2.09	1.855	......	......

a Ice jam.
b Ice conditions Jan. 1 to March 18.

SESSIONAL PAPER No. 25c

DAILY GAUGE HEIGHT AND DISCHARGE of St. Mary River at Whitney's Ranch, for 1914.

DAY.	July.		August.		September.		October.		November.		December.	
	Gauge Height	Dis-charge	Gauge Height.	Dis-charge	Gauge Height	Dis-charge	Gauge Height.	Dis-charge.	Gauge Height.	Dis-charge	Gauge Height.	Dis-charge.
	Feet.	Sec.-ft.	Feet.	Sec.-ft.	Feet.	Sec.-ft.	Feet.	Sec.-ft.	Feet.	Sec.-ft.	Feet.	Sec.-ft.
1............	1.84	1,264	1.19	363	1.15	335	1 30	460	1 60	820	1.45	370
2............	1.79	1,161	1 19	363	1 15	335	1 30	460	1.60	820	1.50	320
3............	1.74	1,066	1.49	668	1 09	293	1.30	460	1.65	905	1.55	285
4............	1.74	1,066	1.49	668	1 09	293	1.40	560	1.65	905	1.60	250
5............	1.74	1,066	1 34	500	1 09	293	1.40	560	1 65	905	1.65	220
6............	1.79	1,161	1.29	451	1.09	293	1.45	620	1.65	905	1.65	195
7............	1.70	1,161	1.19	363	1.04	258	1.50	680	1.65	905	1.70	175
8............	1.94	1,492	1.17	349	1.04	258	1.50	680	1.72	1,028	1.75	160
9............	1.94	1,492	1.09	293	1.04	258	1.65	905	1.75	1,085	1.75	148
10...... ...	1.99	1,607	1.09	293	1.05	265	1.75	1,085	1.75	1,085	1.70	133
11............	2.03	1,705	1.04	258	1.10	300	1.90	1,400	1.75	1,085	1.70	130
12............	1.94	1,492	0.99	223	1.10	300	1.90	1,400	1.80	1,180	1 80	135
13............	1.84	1,268	0.99	223	1.05	265	1.90	1,400	1.80	1,180	1.80	140
14............	1.79	1,161	0.94	188	1.05	265	1.90	1,400	1.82	1,224	1.80	142
15............	1.79	1,161	0.89	154	1.05	265	1.94	1,492	1.85	1,165c	1.80	148
16............	1.79	1,161	0.89	154	1.05	265	1.94	1,492	1.85	1,115	1.80	153
17......... .	1.74	1,066	0.89	154	1.01	237	1.94	1,492	1.82	1,065	1.90	162
18............	1.74	1,066	0.89	154	1.00	230	2.00	1,630	1.85	1,015	1.90	170
19......... .	1.74	1,066	1.41	572	1.00	230	2.00	1,630	1.85	970	1.90	176
20............	1.69	973	1.35	510	1.05	265	1.93	1,515	1.85	955	1.85	185
21............	1.59	806	1.30	460	1.05	265	1.88	1,356	1.85	975c	1.85	195
22............	1.49	668	1.30	460	1.10	300	1.83	1,246	1.70	990	1.85	212
23............	1.49	668	1.35	510	1.15	335	1.80	1,180	1.60	820	1.85	227
24............	1.46	632	1.40	560	1.15	335	1.80	1,180	1.34	500	1.85	233
25............	1.46	632	1.37	530	1.25	415	1.75	1,085	1.34	500	1.85	234
26............	1.34	500	1.37	530	1.30	460	1.75	1,085	1.40	560	1.85	230
27............	1.34	500	1.30	460	1.30	460	1.75	1,085	1.40	560	1.95	229
28............	1.32	480	1.30	460	1.35	510	1.70	990	1.40	560	2.05	230
29............	1.29	451	1.24	406	1.35	510	1.65	905	1.35	480	2.02	236
30............	1.24	406	1.19	363	1.30	460	1.60	820	1.35	417d	2.00	236
31............	1.19	363	1.15	335	....	....	1.60	820	....	....	2.05	236d

c to c Ice conditions.
d to d Ice conditions.

MONTHLY DISCHARGE of St. Mary River at Whitney's Ranch, for 1914.

(Drainage area 1,406 square miles.)

MONTH.	DISCHARGE IN SECOND-FEET.				RUN-OFF.	
	Maximum.	Minimum.	Mean.	Per square Mile.	Depth in inches on Drainage Area.	Total in Acre-feet.
January................................	252	99	191	0.136	0.16	11,744
February...............................	230	56	129	0.092	0.10	7,164
March.................................	596	236	336	0.239	0.28	20,660
April..................................	1,469	388	799	0.568	0.63	47,544
May...................................	2,373	1,446	1,851	1.320	1.52	113,812
June...................................	2,055	1,378	1,790	1.270	1.42	106,510
July...................................	1,705	363	992	0.706	0.81	60,996
August.................................	668	154	386	0.274	0.32	23,734
September..............................	510	230	318	0.226	0.25	18,922
October................................	1,630	460	1,067	0.759	0.88	65,607
November..............................	1,224	417	889	0.632	0.70	52,899
December..............................	370	130	203	0.144	0.17	12,482
The year..............................	....	....	....	....	7.24	542,074

5 GEORGE V, A. 1915

MISCELLANEOUS DISCHARGE MEASUREMENTS made in St. Mary River drainage basin, in 1914.

Date.	Engineer.	Stream.	Location.	Width.	Area of Section.	Mean Velocity.	Discharge.
				Feet.	*Sq. ft.*	*Ft. per sec.*	*Sec.-ft.*
May 23...	O. H. Hoover...	St. Mary River...	SW. 23-3-25-4..	97.6	409	5.58	2,282
Aug. 8...	do	do ...	do	64.0	212	1.04	222

MILK RIVER DRAINAGE BASIN.

General Description.

Milk River rises on the eastern slope of the foothills in the Blackfoot Indian Reserve in the United States. Its headwaters run down in two main streams which are known, after entering Canada, as the north and south branches. The north branch runs in a north-easterly direction through the Blackfoot Reserve for a distance of about 15 miles, and then enters Canada near the quarter-mound on the south side of Section 3, Township 1, Range 23, West of the 4th Meridian. From the international boundary the stream continues in a north-easterly direction for about nine miles, when it bends to the east and runs in an easterly direction through the second tier of townships to its junction with the south branch at the centre of Section 20, Township 2, Range 18, West of the 4th Meridian.

The south branch runs to the south and east of, and parallels the north branch for a distance of about 48 miles, as the crow flies, through the Blackfoot Reserve, and then enters Canada near the quarter-mound on the south side of Section 1, Township 1, Range 20, West of the 4th Meridian. From the international boundary it runs in a north-easterly direction to its junction with the north branch. From the junction of the two branches Milk River runs in an easterly direction through the second tier of townships in Canada to the east boundary of Range 7. From this point the river runs in a south-easterly direction to its first point of crossing the international boundary into the United States. This first point of crossing is near the quarter-mound on the south side of Section 3, Township 1, Range 5, West of the 4th Meridian. From this point the river meanders in an easterly direction through Canada and United States to a point on the international boundary about 900 feet west of the east boundary of Section 1, Township 1, Range 5, West of the 4th Meridian, where it finally crosses into the United States. This point is known as the "Eastern Crossing." The length of the course of Milk River in Canada from the western crossing of the north branch to the eastern crossing is 215 3 miles. The length of the course of the south branch in Canada is 24.7 miles.

Throughout its course in Canada from the western crossing of the north branch to the eastern crossing, Milk River runs through a well-defined valley bordered on each side by a range of hills. The whole of its watershed in Canada is bald prairie land. The river receives a number of small tributary creeks along its course, all of which discharge a considerable volume of water during the spring freshets; usually they all dry up by about July 1 and have no considerable discharge again until late in the fall, when some of them have a small flow for perhaps a month before the freeze-up.

The general conditions of flow in the river are such as are typical of all rivers which have a watershed devoid of tree growth; that is, it is subject to extreme floods during the freshet period and to correspondingly low flow during the summer months. From its headwaters to the eastern crossing the total area of the watershed of Milk River is 2,464 square miles. Of this total amount, 1,615 square miles are in Canada and 849 square miles in the United States.

NORTH BRANCH OF MILK RIVER AT PETERS' RANCH.

Location.—NE. ¼ Sec. 11, Tp. 1, Rge. 23, W. 4th Mer.
Records available.—July 21, 1909, to December 31, 1914.
Gauges.—Stevens automatic gauge used during open water. Vertical staff used during ice conditions. Zero of gauge maintained at elevation 4,089.57 feet during 1913-14.
Bench-mark.—Permanent iron bench-mark; elevation, 4,095.99 feet above mean sea level (*Irrigation surveys 1914 datum*).
Channel.—Slightly curved at the gauge, and generally winding stream bed consists of clay, gravel and small stone, not liable to shift.
Discharge measurements.—Made by wading at low stages, and from a cable car two miles below at flood periods.
Winter flow.—Obtained through the ice 750 feet below the gauge.
Observer.—Wm. Wheeler.
Remarks.—Location of station and gauge data prior to 1913 may be obtained in previous reports.

DISCHARGE MEASUREMENTS of North Branch of Milk River at Peters' Ranch, in 1914.

Date.	Engineer.	Width.	Area of Section.	Mean Velocity.	Gauge Height.	Discharge.
		Feet.	*Sq. ft.*	*Ft. per sec.*	*Feet.*	*Sec.-ft.*
Jan. 13	J. E. Degnan	18	12.3	1.34	2.00	16.5
Jan. 24	do	15	9.0	1.36	2.55	12.3
Feb. 10	do	17	7.6	1.81	3.42	13.5
Feb. 27	do	17	12.5	1.29	2.93	16.2
Mar. 14	W. A. Burton	17	18.6	2.30	2.25	43.0
Mar. 27	O. H. Hoover	19	17.6	1.37	1.97	24.0
April 8	do	28	28.4	1.50	1.96	43.0
April 22	do	19	25.4	0.99	1.77	25.0
May 15	do	21	18.4	1.35	1.75	25.0
May 24	W. A. Lamb (U.S.G.S.)	29	19.0	1.26	1.75	24.0
June 5	O. H. Hoover	23	17.9	1.30	1.72	23.0
June 21	W. A. Lamb (U.S.G.S.)	23	14.0	1.11	1.64	15.6
June 24	O. H. Hoover	22	17.5	0.95	1.63	16.5
June 25	do	27	23.4	1.34	1.84	31.0
June 25	do	23	20.2	1.12	1.71	23.0
July 17	do	21	17.0	0.80	1.58	13.6
July 21	do	21	16.0	0.75	1.56	12.0
July 22	W. A. Lamb (U.S.G.S.)	17	12.0	0.95	1.54	11.4
Aug. 12	O. H. Hoover	22	17.0	0.80	1.57	13.5
Sept. 3	do	22	17.0	0.81	1.59	14.1
Sept. 7	G.H.Whyte and O.H Hoover.	22	16.9	0.82	1.58	13.8
Sept. 10	W. A. Lamb (U.S.G.S)	21	12.8	1.03	1.60	13.2
Sept. 18	O. H. Hoover	22	17.8	0.84	1.61	14.9
Oct. 14	do	37	47.6	2.13	2.40	101.0
Oct. 15	do	33	40.7	2.71	2.42	110.0
Nov. 13	do	23	21.5	1.21	1.78	26.0
Nov. 27	do	28	24.9	1.38	1.89	31.0
Dec. 15	do	22	14.3	1.10	2.12	15.7

STREAM MEASUREMENTS, 1914

5 GEORGE V, A. 1915

DAILY GAUGE HEIGHT AND DISCHARGE of North Branch of Milk River at Peters' Ranch, for 1914.

DAY.	January.		February.		March.		April.		May.		June.	
	Gauge Height.	Dis- charge	Gauge Height.	Dis- charge	Gauge Height.	Dis- charge	Gauge Height.	Dis- charge	Gauge Height.	Dis- charge	Gauge Height.	Dis- charge.
	Feet.	*Sec.-ft.*	*Feet.*	*Sec.-ft.*	*Feet.*	*Sec.-ft.*	*Feet.*	*Sec.-ft.*	*Feet.*	*Sec.-ft.*	*Feet.*	*Sec.-ft.*
1...........	2.30	14.0a	2.98	13.3	3.14	16.8	3.10	34.0	1.78	26.0	1.63	16.0
2...........	2.28	13.4	3.08	12.7	3.24	17.3	2.59	33.0a	1.77	26.0	1.64	16.6
3...........	2.31	13.8	3.10	12 0	2.84	18 3	2 52	35 0b	1.78	26.0	1.65	17.2
4...........	2.16	14.2	3.09	11.5	2.66	19 4	3.18	197.0c	1.87	34 0	1.67	18.5
5...........	2.28	15.2	3.07	11.2	2.49	21.0	4.48	517.0	1.88	35.0	1.72	22.0
6...........	2.77	18.0	3.43	11.8	2.43	22.0	3.31d	282.0	2 04	52 0	1.73	23.0
7...........	2 25	17.8	3.54	12.3	2 42	22 0	2 01d	48 0	1.97	44 0	1.70	20.0
8...........	2.11	16.9	3 55	13.1	2.39	22 0	1.96d	43.0	1.90	37.0	1.69	19.8
9...........	2 07	16.2	3.52	13 6	2.90	21.0	1.95d	42.0	1.87	34 0	1.67	18.5
10.........	2 06	15.3	3.79	13.5	3 04	20.0	1.94d	41.0	1.82	30 0	1.65	17.2
11.........	2 07	15.3	3.54	13.3	2 04	42.0	1.93d	40.0	1.79	27.0	1.65	17.2
12....	2 09	16 2	....	12.7	2 08	42 0	1.92d	39 0	1.76	25.0	1.65	17.2
13.........	2.08	16.5	....	13 0	2.38	42.0	1 91d	38 0	1.78	26 0	1.75	24.0
14.........	2.11	16.4	3.99	13.5	2.39	43.0	1.90	37 0	1.76	25.0	1.77	26.0
15.........	2.13	16.4	4.01	14.0	2.39	42 0	1.88	35.0	1.76	25 0	1.70	20.0
16.........	2.12	16.2	3.97	14 0	2.14	43.0	1.81e	29.0	1.74	23.0	1.67	18.5
17.........	2.15	16.2	3.91	13.9	2.10	43.0	1.75e	24.0	1.72	22.0	1.67	18.5
18.........	2.17	15.8	3.82	13.8	2.14	40.0	1.69	19.8	1.71	21.0	1.63	16.0
19.........	2.24	15.3	3.84	13.7	2.29	37.0	1.76	25.0	1.71	21.0	1.60	14.3
20.........	2.31	14 7	3.83	13.4	2.09	37.0	1.85	32.0	1.78	26.0	1.61	14.9
21........	2.38	14.2	3 83	13.2	2 08	35.0	1.75	24.0	1.80	28 0	1.62	15.5
22.........	2 45	13.7	3.72	13.0	2.18	38 0	1.62	15.5	1.74	23.0	1.62	15.5
23	2.52	13.0	3.79	13.7	2.64	38 0	1.77f	26.0	1.73	23.0	1.62	15.5
24.........	2.47	12.3	....	15 0	2.34	32 0	1.77	26.0	1.74	23.0	1.63	16.0
25....	2 45	12.4	2 67	16.0	1 68	24 0	1.77	26 0	1.72	22 0	1.75	24.0
26........ ..	2.85	13.1	2.73	16.2	....	24.0	1.76	25.0	1.68	19.2	1.77	26.0
27.........	2.93	14 0	3.07	16.2	2.11	24 0	1.76	25.0	1.66	17.9	1.65	17.2
28.........	2.96	12 7	3.04	16.4	2.09	25.0	1.77	26.0	1.65	17.2	1.62	15.5
29.........	2.68	13.2	....	....	2.08	27.0	1.81	29.0	1.63	16.0	1.60	14.3
30.........	2.59	14 0	....	....	2.10	31.0	1.80	28.0	1.63	16.0	1.62f	15.5
31.........	3.00	13.7	....	....	2.88	34.0	....	....	1.63	16.0	....	....

a to *a* Ice conditions.
b Discharge estimated.
c Slope measurement.
d Gauge heights interpolated from gauge height of April 8.
e Gauge heights interpolated.
f to *f* Gauge heights from automatic gauge.

SESSIONAL PAPER No. 25c

DAILY GAUGE HEIGHT AND DISCHARGE of North Branch of Milk River at Peter's Ranch, for 1914.

DAY.	July.		August.		September.		October.		November.		December.	
	Gauge Height.	Dis-charge.	Gauge Height.	Dis-charge	Gauge Height.	Dis-charge	Gauge Height.	Dis-charge.	Gauge Height.	Dis-charge.	Gauge Height.	Dis-charge.
	Feet.	*Sec.-ft.*	*Feet.*	*Sec.-ft.*	*Feet.*	*Sec.-ft.*	*Feet.*	*Sec.-ft.*	*Feet.*	*Sec.-ft.*	*Feet.*	*Sec.-ft.*
1	1.61	14.9	1.59	13.8	1.61	14.9	1 61	14.9	1.82	30.0	1.74	23.0
2	1.59	13.8	1.59	13.8	1.60	14.3	1.67	18.5	1.80	28 0	1.82	30 0
3	1.60	14.3	1.57	12.8	1.60	14 3	1.71	21.0	1.81	29 0	1.78	26 0
4	1.58	13.3	1.55	11.9	1 59	13.8	1.70	20 0	1.80	28 0	1.70	20.0
5	1.66	17.9	1.56	12.4	1.59	13 8	1.74	23.0	1.79	27.0	1.79	27.0
6	1.67	18.5	1.54	11.5	1.58	13.3	1.84	31.0	1.75	24 0	1.79	27.0
7	1.65	17.2	1.53	11.1	1.59	13.8	1 90	37 0	1.73	23 0	1 84	31 0
8	1.62	15.5	1.53	11.1	1 62	15 5	1.81	29.0	1.71	21.0	1 85	32 0
9	1.61	14.9	1.55	11.9	1 61	14.9	1.72	22 0	1.70	20.0	2 01g	28 0
10	1.61	14.9	1.57	12 8	1 58	13.3	1.74	23.0	1.68	19.2	2 05	24.0
11	1.62	15.5	1.56	12.4	1.56	12.4	1.73	22.0	1.69	19.8	2.11	22.0
12	1.63	16.0	1.56	12.4	1.63	16.0	1.70	20.0	1.70	20 0	......	21.0
13	1.63	16.0	1.59	13.8	1.66	17.9	1.74	23.0	1.72	22.0	2.14	22 0
14	1.63	16.0	1.56	12.4	1.61	14.9	2.19	71.0	1.76	25.0	......	22 0
15	1.62	15.5	1.55	11.9	1.58	13.3	2.52	125.0	1.76	25.0	2.12	15.7
16	1.64	16.6	1.55	11.9	1.59	13.8	2.43	108.0	1.78	26 0	2.11	15 8
17	1.62	15.5	1.75	24.0	1.60	14.3	2 27	82.0	1.83	30 0	......	16 1
18	1.58	13.3	1.84	31 0	1.61	14 9	2.15	66 0	1.83	30 0	2 13	16 2
19	1.58	13.3	1.68	19 2	1.61	14.9	2.04	52.0	1.85	32.0	2.13	16.4
20	1.58	13.3	1.63	16.0	1.61	14.9	2 00	47.0	1.86	33 0	2 15	16 5
21	1.58	13.3	1.61	14.9	1.61	14.9	1.91	38 0	1.85	32 0	2 17	16 5
22	1.57	12.8	1.60	14.3	1.62	15.5	1.89	36 0	1.81	29.0	2.16	16.2
23	1.59	13.8	1.63	16 0	1.63	16 0	1.88	35.0	1.79	27 0	2 17	15.9
24	1.60	14.3	1.76	25 0	1 63	16.0	1.86	33.0	1.77	26.0	.....	15 6
25	1.60	14.3	1.69	19.8	1.64	16.6	1.84	31.0	1.87	34.0	2.19	15 3
26	1.59	13.8	1.66	17.9	1.62	15 5	1.82	30.0	1.90	37.0	2.17	15.2
27	1.60	14.3	1.63	16 0	1.61	14.9	1.81	29 0	1.93	40 0	2 18	15 2
28	1.59	13.8	1.61	14.9	1.60	14.3	1.81	29 0	1.85	32.0	2 22	15.4
29	1.60	14.3	1.60	14.3	1.61	14 9	1 81	29.0	2.40	103.0	2 20	15 5
30	1.60	14.3	1.61	14.9	1.61	14.9	1 81	29 0	2.00	47.0	2.23	15 6
31	1.58	13.3	1.60	14.3	......	......	1.82	30.0	......	......	2.26g	15.5

g to *g* Gauge heights from staff gauge; ice conditions.

MONTHLY DISCHARGE of North Branch of Milk River at Peters' Ranch, for 1914.

(Drainage area 101 square miles.)

MONTH.	DISCHARGE IN SECOND-FEET.				RUN-OFF.	
	Maximum.	Minimum.	Mean.	Per square Mile.	Depth in inches on Drainage Area.	Total in Acre-feet.
January	18.0	12.3	14.8	0.147	0.17	910
February	16.4	11.2	13.6	0.135	0.14	755
March	43.0	16.8	30.4	0.301	0.35	1,869
April	517.0	15.5	61.4	0.608	0.68	3,654
May	52.0	16.0	26.0	0.257	0.30	1,599
June	26.0	14.3	18.3	0.181	0.20	1,089
July	18.5	12.8	14.8	0.147	0.17	910
August	31.0	11.1	15.2	0.150	0.17	935
September	17.9	12.4	14.8	0.147	0.16	881
October	125.0	14.9	38.9	0.385	0.44	2,392
November	103.0	19.2	30.6	0.303	0.34	1,821
December	32.0	15.2	20.1	0.199	0.23	1,236
The year	....	....	....	....	3.35	18,051

5 GEORGE V, A. 1915

NORTH BRANCH OF MILK RIVER AT KNIGHT'S RANCH.

Location.—On the *NE.* ¼ Sec. 18, Tp. 2, Rge. 20, W. 4th Mer.
Records available.—July 17, 1909, to August 25, 1914.
Gauge.—Vertical staff; zero of gauge maintained at 90.72 feet during 1909; 90.70 feet during 1910-14.
Bench-mark.—Permanent iron bench-mark; assumed elevation, 100.00 feet.
Channel.—Composed of clay, gravel and boulders.
Discharge measurements.—Made by wading at low stages, and from a cable car at flood stages.
Winter flow.—Records are discontinued during the winter.
Observer.—E. Whitney.
Remarks.—Records were not obtained after August 25 on account of no observer being available.

DISCHARGE MEASUREMENTS of North Branch of Milk River at Knight's Ranch, in 1914.

Date.	Engineer.	Width.	Area of Section.	Mean Velocity.	Gauge Height.	Discharge.
		Feet.	*Sq. ft.*	*Ft. per sec.*	*Feet.*	*Sec.-ft.*
April 9	O. H. Hoover	40.1	50.8	2.02	1.61	70.0
April 24	do	41.5	40.8	0.78	1.15	32.0
May 18	do	29.0	26.5	1.03	1.11	27.0
June 6	do	28.5	28.5	0.94	1.09	27.0
July 20	do	14.8	8.6	1.52	0.90	13.0

DAILY GAUGE HEIGHT AND DISCHARGE of North Branch of Milk River at Knight's Ranch, for 1914.

DAY.	July.		August.	
	Gauge Height.	Dis-charge.	Gauge Height.	Dis-charge.
	Feet.	*Sec.-ft.*	*Feet.*	*Sec.-ft.*
1	1.05	24.0	0.85	10.0
2	1.05	24.0	0.85	10.0
3	1.04	23.0	0.85	10.0
4	1.03	22.0	0.85	10.0
5	1.05	24.0	0.83	8.8
6	1.03	22.0	0.80	7.0
7	1.00	20.0	0.85	10.0
8	0.95	16.5	0.85	10.0
9	0.95	16.5	0.95	16.5
10	0.95	16.5	0.98	18.6
11	0.95	16.5	0.98	18.6
12	0.94	15.8	0.95	16.5
13	0.98	18.6	0.90	13.0
14	1.00	20.0	0.90	13.0
15	0.95	16.5	0.85	10.0
16	0.95	16.5	0.85	10.0
17	0.94	15.8	1.30	43.0
18	0.94	15.8	1.35	48.0
19	0.94	15.8	1.30	43.0
20	0.92	14.4	1.25	39.0
21	0.90	13.0	1.20	35.0
22	0.88	11.8	0.95	16.5
23	0.88	11.8	1.20	35.0
24	0.88	11.8	1.25	39.0
25	0.88	11.8	1.25	39.0
26	0.88	11.8	......	......
27	0.88	11.8	......	......
28	0.85	10.0	......	......
29	0.85	10.0	......	......
30	0.85	10.0	......	......
31	0.85	10.0	......	......

SESSIONAL PAPER No. 25c

MONTHLY DISCHARGE of North Branch of Milk River at Knight's Ranch, for 1914.

(Drainage area 239 square miles.)

MONTH.	DISCHARGE IN SECOND-*FEET*.				RUN-OFF.	
	Maximum.	Minimum.	Mean.	Per square Mile.	Depth in inches on Drainage Area.	Total in Acre-feet.
July.................................	24	10.0	16.1	0.067	0.077	990
August (1–25).................	48	7.0	19.8	0.083	0.077	982
The period........................ ..	....	....	....	....	0.154	1,972

NORTH BRANCH OF MILK RIVER NEAR MACKIE'S RANCH.

Location.—SW. ¼ Sec. 19, Tp. 2, Rge. 18, W. 4th Mer., about four miles north of the Mackie ranch buildings.

Records available.—July 8, 1909, to November 14, 1910. Discharge measurements only were taken during 1911-14.

Gauge.—Vertical staff; elevation of zero 91 50 feet since establishment.

Bench-mark.—Permanent iron bench-mark; assumed elevation, 100 00 feet.

Channel.—Sand, gravel and rock; control probably permanent.

Discharge measurements.—During low water by wading; during high water from a cable car.

DISCHARGE MEASUREMENTS of North Branch of Milk River near Mackie's Ranch, in 1914.

Date.	Engineer.	Width.	Area of Section.	Mean Velocity.	Gauge Height.	Discharge.
		Feet.	*Sq. ft.*	*Ft. per sec.*	*Feet.*	*Sec.-ft.*
May 6............	J. E. Degnan..............	25.5	34.2	1.38	1.92	47.0
May 21............	do	26.5	35.3	0.96	1.80	33.0
June 26............	do	29.0	20.5	1.26	1.70	26.0
July 21............	do	21.0	10.8	0.99	1.50	10.7
Aug. 6	do	18.0	8.2	0.92	1.47	7.6
Aug. 23...	do	23.0	11.5	1.18	1.57	13.5
Sept. 11.. .,......	F. R. Steinberger	23.2	12.8	1.20	1.60	15.4
Oct. 14.. .,......	J. E. Degnan..............	29.0	19.5	1.81	1.83	35.4
Oct. 26	do	24.0	21.8	1.77	1.84	38.5

NOTE.—Measurements all taken above regular section.

SOUTH BRANCH OF MILK RIVER AT CROFF'S RANCH.

Location.—On the SW. ¼ Sec. 29, Tp. 37N, Rge. 9, W. Prin. Mer., Montana, U.S.A.

Records available.—April 13, 1913, to November 8, 1914.

Gauge.—Stevens continuous automatic; elevation of zero maintained at 87 08 feet since establishment.

Bench-mark.—Iron pipe; assumed elevation, 100 00 feet.

Channel.—Gravel.

Discharge measurements.—During high stages by means of cable and car; during ordinary stages by wading.

Remarks.—This station is maintained in conjunction with the United States Geological Survey.

5 GEORGE V, A. 1915

DISCHARGE MEASUREMENTS of South Branch of Milk River at Croff's Ranch, in 1914.

Date.	Engineer.	Width	Area of Section.	Mean Velocity.	Gauge Height.	Discharge.
		Feet.	*Sq. ft.*	*Ft. per sec.*	*Feet.*	*Sec.-ft.*
Mar. 15.......... ...	W. A. Lamb (U.S.G.S.) .. .	57.0	37.00	1.89	3.010	70.0
April 10....	O. H. Hoover..............	74.0	92.90	3.02	3.990	280.0
April 23.....	do	62.2	74.30	1.75	3.280	130.0
May 16	do	42.0	42.60	2.74	3.150	117.0
June 5............	do	36.3	34.40	2.41	2.980	83.0
June 21.....	W. A. Lamb (U.S.G.S.)	34.0	18.90	2.00	2.720	38.0
June 26	O. H. Hoover..............	38.0	38.70	2.52	3.080	98.0
July 18............	do	25.5	14.50	1.14	2.500	16.6
July 22............	W. A. Lamb (U.S.G.S.)..	14.0	6.80	1.47	2.410	10.0
Aug. 13............	O. H. Hoover..............	15.8	9.36	1.16	2.430	10.8
Sept. 4............	do	14.8	9.33	1.33	2.440	12.4
Sept. 10............	W. A. Lamb (U.S.G.S.)..	12.0	8.60	1.84	2.510	15.8
Sept. 19............	O. H. Hoover..............	20.0	12.60	1.80	2.570	23.0
Oct. 15............	do	73.6	69.10	2.42	3.385	167.0
Nov. 8............	W. A. Lamb (U.S.G.S.)......	39.0	25.00	1.72	2.740	43.0
Dec. 18	B. E. Jones, (U.S.G.S.)......	12.0	9.80	1.52	2.480	14.9

DAILY GAUGE HEIGHT AND DISCHARGE of South Branch of Milk River at Croff's Ranch, for 1914.

DAY.	March.		April.		May.		June.	
	Gauge Height.	Dis-charge.	Gauge Height.	Dis-charge.	Gauge Height.	Dis-charge.	Gauge Height.	Dis-charge.
	Feet.	*Sec.-ft.*	*Feet.*	*Sec.-ft.*	*Feet.*	*Sec.-ft.*	*Feet.*	*Sec.-ft.*
1....................................	....	....	3.18	116	.. ...b	....	2.88	63
2....................................	....	....		128	......	....	2.88	63
3....................................	.. ....	.....	....	140	.... ..	....	2.90	66
4....................................	....	....	3.37	153	.... ..	....	2.91	68
5....................................	......	. ..	4.21	381	......	....	2.95	74
6....................................	... ..	......	4.35	429	......	....	3.01	85
7....................................	......	......	3.84	266	.... ..	....	3.00	83
8....................................	....	......	3.67	222	.... ..	....	2.90	66
9....................................	....	......	3.90	283	.. ..	. ..	2.85	58
10....................................	....	......	3.89	280	. .	. ..	2.81	52
11....................................	......	... ..	3.90	283	......	....	2.81	52
12....................................	... ..	.. ..	4.52	488	......	....	2.78	47
13....................................	......	.. ..	4.47	470	......	....	2.89	64
14....................................	. 00	......	3.98	307	......	. ....	3.22	124
15....................................	3 00	83	3.76	245	.... b	. ...	3.16	112
16....................................	2.95	74	3.80	255	3.15	110	3.01	85
17....................................	2.99	81	3.64	214	3.15	110	2.90	66
18....................................	3.00	83	3.39	157	3.12	105	2.83	55
19....................................	2.97	78	3.25	130	3.10	101	2.77	46
20....................................	3.00	83	3.53	188	3.14	109	2.74	42
21....................................	2.94	73	3.60	204	3.25	130	2.72	39
22....................................	2.92	69	3.37	153	3.18	116	2.69	35
23....................................	3.03	88	3.28	135	3.09	99	2.71	37
24....................................	3.11	103	3.43	166	3.03	88	2.72	39
25....................................	3.05	92	3.46	172	3.01	85	2.86	60
26....................................	3.06	94	.....a	....	2.99	81	3.05	92
27....................................	3.06	94	....	....	2.98	80	2.96	76
28....................................	3.07	96	....	....	2.95	74	2.83	55
29....................................	3.06	94	....	....	2.93	71	2.79	49
30....................................	3.04	90	.....a	....	2.91	68	2.75	43
31....................................	2.99	81	....	....	2.89	64	....	....

a to *a* No gauge heights obtained and estimated; mean discharge is 130 sec.-ft.
b to *b* No gauge heights obtained and estimated; mean discharge is 148 sec.-ft.

MONTHLY DISCHARGE of South Branch of Milk River at Croff's Ranch, for 1913.

(Drainage area 288 square miles.)

MONTH.	DISCHARGE IN SECOND-FEET.				RUN-OFF.	
	Maximum.	Minimum.	Mean.	Per square Mile.	Depth in inches on Drainage Area.	Total in Acre-feet.
April (13-30).........................	864	211.0	479.0	1.660	1.11	17,101
May.................................	494	194.0	311.0	1.080	1.24	19,123
June................................	386	104.0	196.0	0.680	0.76	11,663
July................................	173	50.0	79.0	0.274	0.32	4,858
August..............................	104	22.0	44.0	0.152	0.18	2,705
September...........................	40	15.2	22.7	0.079	0.09	1,351
October.............................	131	22.0	52.2	0.182	0.21	3,210
November............................	50	20.0	31.2	0.108	0.12	1,856
December............................	37	15.0	19.5	0.068	0.08	1,199
The period..........................	....	....	....	....	4.11	63,066

NOTE.—This table is inserted in this report to correct a table on page 225 of the 1913 report. Corrections have been made to discharge in sec.-ft. per square mile and depth in inches on drainage area to correspond with a corrected drainage area.

SESSIONAL PAPER No. 25c

DAILY GAUGE HEIGHT AND DISCHARGE of South Branch of Milk River at Croff's Ranch, for 1914.—*Concluded.*

DAY.	July.		August.		September.		October.		November.	
	Gauge Height	Dis-charge.	Gauge Height.	Dis-charge.	Gauge Height.	Dis-charge.	Gauge Height.	Dis-charge.	Gauge Height.	Dis-charge.
	Feet.	*Sec.-ft.*	*Feet.*	*Sec.-ft.*	*Feet.*	*Sec.-ft.*	*Feet.*	*Sec.-ft.*	*Feet.*	*Sec.-ft.*
1..............	2.71	37.0	2.35	7.0	2.47	14.0	2.43	11	2.65	30
2..............	2.65	30.0	2.34	6.6	2.48	15.0	2.49	15	2.64	29
3..............	2.62	27.0	2.33	6.2	2.43	11.0	2.58	23	2.67	33
4..............	2.59	24.0	2.28	4.6	2.46	13.0	......a	37	2.76	44
5..............	2.63	28.0	2.28	4.6	2.47	14.0	....	42	2.79	49
6..............	2.69	35.0	2.27	4.4	2.46	13.0	....	51	2.73	40
7..............	2.67	33.0	2.27	4.4	2.46	13.0	....	25	2.70	36
8..............	2.59	24.0	2.27	4.4	2.48	15.0	....	22	2.71	37
9..............	2.56	21.0	2.34	6.6	2.53	19.0	....	23	....	....
10.............	2.54	20.0	2.41	9.7	2.51	17.0	....	26	....	....
11.............	2.54	20.0	2.45	12.0	2.51	17.0	....	54	....	....
12.............	2.54	20.0	2.45	12.0	2.55	20.0	......a	53	....	....
13.............	2.52	18.0	2.40	9.0	2.60	25.0	......a	68	....	....
14.............	2.50	16.0	2.38	8.2	2.59	24.0	3.03	88	....	....
15.............	2.50	16.0	2.33	6.2	2.59	24.0	3.47	174	....	....
16.............	2.49	15.0	2.29	4.8	2.60	25.0	3.67	222	....	....
17.............	2.50	16.0	2.45	12.0	2.58	23.0	3.61	206	....	....
18.............	2.50	16.0	2.71	37.0	2.59	24.0	3.48	177	....	....
19.............	2.49	15.0	2.78	47.0	2.57	22.0	3.22	124	....	....
20.............	2.46	13.0	2.59	24.0	2.54	20.0	3.08	97	....	....
21.............	2.43	11.0	2.51	17.0	2.53	19.0	2.94	73	....	....
22.............	2.42	10.0	2.46	13.0	2.51	17.0	2.85	58	....	....
23.............	2.40	9.0	2.47	14.0	2.49	15.0	2.79	49	....	....
24.............	2.39	8.6	2.60	25.0	2.48	15.0	2.75	43	....	....
25.............	2.40	9.0	2.69	35.0	2.47	14.0	2.72	39	....	....
26.............	2.38	8.2	2.63	28.0	2.46	13.0	2.71	37	....	....
27.............	2.36	7.4	2.57	22.0	2.42	10.0	2.68	34	....	....
28.............	2.34	6.6	2.52	18.0	2.42	10.0	2.66	32	....	....
29.............	2.35	7.0	2.49	15.0	2.41	9.7	2.64	29	....	....
30.............	2.35	7.0	2.49	15.0	2.40	9.0	2.65	30	....	....
31.............	2.35	7.0	2.48	15.0	....	....	2.66	32	....	....

a to *a* No gauge heights obtained; discharges estimated.

MONTHLY DISCHARGE of South Branch of Milk River at Croff's Ranch, for 1914.

(Drainage area 288 square miles.)

MONTH.	DISCHARGE IN SECOND-FEET.				RUN-OFF.	
	Maximum.	Minimum	Mean.	Per square Mile.	Depth in inches on Drainage Area.	Total in Acre-feet.
March (15-31)..	103	69.0	85.6	0.297	0.19	2,887
April...............................	488	116.0	220.5	0.762	0.85	13,120
May................................	140	64.0	119.7	0.415	0.48	7,360
June...............................	124	35.0	63.2	0.220	0.24	3,761
July...............................	37	6.6	17.2	0.060	0.07	1,058
August.............................	47	4.4	14.4	0.500	0.06	885
September	25	9.0	16.6	0.058	0.06	988
October	222	11.0	64.3	0.223	0.26	3,954
November..........................	........a	....	36.0	0.125	0.14	2,142
December..........................	........a	....	18.0	0.062	0.71	1,107
The period..................	....	....	....	....	3.06	37,262

a Gauge heights for the first eight days in November were obtained, but it is estimated that the mean flow for the months of November and December was as above shown.

5 GEORGE V, A. 1915

SOUTH BRANCH OF MILK RIVER AT MACKIE'S RANCH.

Location.—On the NW. ¼ Sec. 31, Tp. 1, Rge. 18, W. 4th Mer.
Records available.—July 14, 1909, to October 31, 1914.
Gauge.—Vertical staff; maintained at original elevation of 86 60 feet.
Bench-mark.—Permanent iron bench-mark; assumed elevation, 100 00 feet.
Channel.—Permanent.
Discharge measurements.—Made by wading 100 feet below the gauge at low stages, or from a cable and car at the gauge during high stages. The initial point for sounding is the face of a cedar post located on left bank.
Floods.—Highest water of recent years was in June, 1908.
Winter flow.—Station not maintained during the winter.
Observer.—Mrs. F. Cathro and Mrs. J. D. Levvix.

DISCHARGE MEASUREMENTS of South Branch of Milk River Creek at Mackie's Ranch, in 1914.

Date.	Engineer.	Width.	Area of Section.	Mean Velocity.	Gauge Height.	Discharge.
		Feet.	*Sq ft.*	*Ft. per sec.*	*Feet.*	*Sec.-ft.*
April 8............	J. E. Degnan	86.0	139.3	1.67	3.38	232.0
May 6............	do	89.0	95.8	1.60	2.97	154.0
May 21............	do	84.0	77.6	1.45	2.78	113.0
June 7............	do	79.0	62.4	1.24	2.54	77.0
June 25	do	68.0	42.8	1.14	2.34	49.0
July 21....	do	22.0	8.2	0.99	1.82	8.1
Aug. 23.	do	29.0	14.4	1.28	1.97	18.3
Aug. 5.	do				1.55	Nil.
Sept. 11......... ...	F. R. Steinberger	24.6	9.4	0.97	1.86	9.1
Oct. 14......... ...	J. E. Degnan............	84.0	63.4	1.28	2.59	81.0
Oct. 26..	do	71.0	44.0	0.99	2.35	44.0

DAILY GAUGE HEIGHT AND DISCHARGE of South Branch of Milk River at Mackie's Ranch, for 1914.

DAY.	March.		April.		May.		June.	
	Gauge Height.	Dis-charge.	Gauge Height.	Dis-charge.	Gauge Height.	Dis-charge.	Gauge Height.	Dis-charge.
	Feet.	*Sec.-ft.*	*Feet.*	*Sec.-ft.*	*Feet.*	*Sec.-ft.*	*Feet.*	*Sec.-ft.*
1..........	....	....	2.98	....	....	....	2.47	64
2..........	....	....	4.01	....	....	....	2.45	61
3..........	....	....	3.95a	....	....	....	2.44 .	60
4..........	....	....	3.69	341b	....	....	2.44	60
5..........	....	....	3.42	246	....	....	2.46	62
6..........	....	....	3.94	436	2.97	156	2.50	68
7..........	....	....	3.57	298	....	....	2.54	74
8..........	....	....	3.43	249	....	....	2.55	76
9..........	....	....	3.37	250	....	....	2.46	62
10..........	....	....	3.23	227	....	....	2.45	61
11..........	....	....	....	....	....	....	2.39	54
12..........	....	....	....	....	....	....	2.37	51
13..........	....	....	....	....	....	....	2.44	60
14..........	3.24a	....	....	....	....	....	2.43	59
15..........	3.36	....	....	....	....	....	2.86	131
16..........	3.38	....	....	....	....	....	2.70	100
17..........	3.38	....	....	....	....	....	2.55	76
18..........	3.36	....	....	....	....	....	2.45	61
19..........	3.36	....	....	....	....	....	2.36	50
20..........	3.30	....	....	....	2.73	105	2.30	43
21..........	3.30	....	....	....	2.78	115	2.26	39
22..........	3.60	....	....	....	2.90	140	2.16	30
23..........	3.61	....	....	....	2.80	119	2.20	33
24..........	3.50	....	....	....	2.74	107	2.18	31
25..........	3.39	....	....	....	2.70	100	2.33	47
26..........	3.31	....	....	....	2.65	92	2.33	47
27..........	2.99	....	....	....	2.63	89	2.54	74
28..........	2.82	....	....	....	2.59	82	2.50	68
29..........	2.91	....	....	....	2.56	78	2.36	50
30..........	2.87	....	....	....	2.54	74	2.30	43
31..........	2.92	....	....	....	2.50	68	....	....

a Gauge heights affected by ice.
b Discharge for April low; control affected by ice.

Gauging Station on the North Branch of Milk River near Mackie's Ranch.
Taken by G. H. Whyte.

Gauging Station on Milk River at Milk River, Alberta. Taken by G. H. Whyte.

SESSIONAL PAPER No. 25c

DAILY GAUGE HEIGHT AND DISCHARGE of South Branch of Milk River at Mackie's Ranch, for 1914.—*Concluded.*

DAY.	July.		August.		September.		October.	
	Gauge Height.	Dis- charge.	Gauge Height.	Dis- charge.	Gauge Height.	Dis- charge.	Gauge Height.	Dis- charge.
	Feet.	*Sec.-ft.*	*Feet.*	*Sec.-ft.*	*Feet.*	*Sec.-ft.*	*Feet.*	*Sec.-ft.*
1	2.27	40.0	1.60	1.0	1.89	9.6	1.83	7.2
2	2.20	33.0	1.61	1.2	1.88	9.2	1.93	11.8
3	2.17	31.0	1.57	0.4	1.86	8.4	2.08	23.0
4	2.13	27.0	1.58	0.6	1.81	6.4	2.26	39.0
5	2.13	27.0	1.55	Nil.	1.85	8.0	2.31	44.0
6	2.10	25.0	1.51	"	1.85	8.0	2.39	54.0
7	2.14	28.0	1.47	"	1.81	6.4	2.11	26.0
8	2.16	30.0	1.45	"	1.84	7.6	2.06	22.0
9	2.13	27.0	1.48	"	1.84	7.6	2.08	23.0
10	2.06	22.0	1.52	"	1.83	7.2	2.11	26.0
11	2.04	20.0	1.55	"	1.87	8.8	2.38	53.0
12	2.00	17.0	1.57	0.6	1.94	12.4	2.37	51.0
13	1.99	16.2	1.55	Nil.	1.94	12.4	2.48	65.0
14	1.98	15.4	1.55	"	1.92	11.2	2.58	81.0
15	2.00	17.0	1.49	"	2.01	17.8	2.71	102.0
16	1.95	13.0	1.48	"	2.03	19.4	3.18	212.0
17	1.92	11.2	1.50	"	2.00	17.0	3.19	215.0
18	1.89	9.6	2.21	34.0	1.97	14.6	3.08	184.0
19	1.88	9.2	2.14	28.0	2.00	17.0	2.96	153.0
20	1.87	8.8	2.26	39.0	2.01	17.8	2.78	115.0
21	1.81	6.4	2.15	29.0	2.03	19.4	2.67	95.0
22	1.80	6.0	2.03	19.4	1.97	14.6	2.70	100.0
23	1.73	4.8	1.97	14.6	1.96	13.8	2.56	78.0
24	1.74	3.8	1.99	16.2	1.95	13.0	2.49	67.0
25	1.73	3.6	2.00	17.0	1.93	11.8	2.37	51.0
26	1.71	3.2	2.04	20.0	1.90	10.0	2.35	49.0
27	1.70	3.0	2.15	29.0	1.88	9.2	2.32	45.0
28	1.68	2.6	2.09	24.0	1.87	8.8	2.31	44.0
29	1.65	2.0	2.00	17.0	1.86	8.4	2.30	43.0
30	1.60	1.0	1.99	16.2	1.84	7.6	2.28	41.0
31	1.58	0.6	1.92	11.2	....	....	2.26	39.0

MONTHLY DISCHARGE of South Branch of Milk River at Mackie's Ranch, for 1914. (Drainage area 504 square miles.)

MONTH.	DISCHARGE IN SECOND-FEET.				RUN-OFF.	
	Maximum.	Minimum	Mean.	Per square Mile.	Depth in inches on Drainage Area.	Total in Acre-feet.
April (4–10)	436.0	227.0	292.0	0.579	0.15	4,060
May (6) (20–31)	156.0	68.0	102.0	0.202	0.10	2,608
June	131.0	30.0	60.0	0.119	0.13	3,570
July	40.0	0.6	15.0	0.030	0.04	922
August	39.0	Nil.	10.3	0.020	0.02	633
September	19.4	6.4	11.4	0.023	0.03	678
October	215.0	7.2	70.0	0.139	0.16	4,304
The period	....	....	....	....	0.63	16,775

MILK RIVER AT MILK RIVER.

Location.—On the *NE.* ¼ Sec. 21, Tp. 2, Rge. 16, W. 4th Mer.

Records available.—July 1, 1909, to December 31, 1914.

Gauge.—Vertical staff; maintained at the original elevation of 3,403.39 feet since establishment.

Bench-mark.—Permanent iron bench-mark; elevation, 3,412.42 feet above mean sea level (Geodetic Survey of Canada).

Channel.—The stream flows in one channel at all stages; bed consists of sand and fine gravel, and shifts during flood conditions.

Discharge measurements.—At low stages made by wading; at high stages from the traffic bridge 100 feet above the gauge.

Observer.—Dan O'Connell.

No. 25c—19½

5 GEORGE V, A. 1915

DISCHARGE MEASUREMENTS of Milk River at Milk River, in 1914.

Date.	Engineer.	Width.	Area of Section.	Mean Velocity.	Gauge Height.	Discharge.
		Feet.	Sq. ft.	Ft. per sec.	Feet.	Sec.-ft.
Jan. 19............	J. E. Degnan..	27.0	21.30	1.530	2.050	33.00
Jan. 31...	do	20.0	7.23	1.560	1.920	11.30
Feb. 16...	do	11.0	4.24	0.800	2.420	3.38
Mar. 3..........	do	26.0	18.60	2.310	3.270	43.00
April 6..........	do	130.0	345.00	2.440	3.475	844.00
April 11	do	91.0	164.00	2.120	2.420	349.00
April 14	do	129.0	240.00	2.370	2.820	569.00
May 5..........	do	74.0	93.90	2.300	2.010	216.00
May 7..........	do	92.0	113.00	1.960	2.020	222.00
May 19	do	90.0	93.00	1.350	1.630	125.00
May 23	do	91.0	117.20	1.420	1.840	166.00
June 6..........	do	49.0	61.25	1.410	1.420	86.00
June 8..........	do	52.0	65.75	1.450	1.480	95.00
June 23	do	50.0	49.90	0.830	1.120	42.00
June 27..........	do	53.0	62.30	1.110	1.340	69.00
July 20..........	do	46.0	35.65	0.500	0.820	18.00
July 23	do	27.0	16.20	0.980	0.780	15.90
Aug. 4..........	do	11.0	5.60	0.990	0.590	5.40
Aug. 7..........	do	12.0	5.60	0.940	0.600	5.18
Aug. 22..........	do	50.0	42.00	1.050	1.140	44.10
Aug. 24..........	do	49.0	34.40	0.990	1.110	34.00
Sept. 14..........	F. R. Steinberger	48.0	30.40	0.940	1.000	29.00
Sept. 10..........	do	47.0	25.80	0.800	0.870	20.00
Oct. 10..... ...	J. E. Degnan.............	51.0	62.70	1.110	1.450	69.00
Oct. 12.	do	54.0	65.20	1.400	1.530	92.00
Oct. 25..........	do	54.5	66.90	1.350	1.560	91.00
Nov. 9..........	O. H. Hoover	50.5	60.50	1.490	1.450	91.00
Nov. 23 .. .	do	51.5	53.50	1.080	1.600	58.00
Dec. 8..........	do	52.0	41.60	0.695	1.540	29.00
Dec. 24..........	do	49.5	29.80	0.660	2 090	19.60

DAILY GAUGE HEIGHT AND DISCHARGE of Milk River at Milk River, for 1914.

DAY.	January.		February.		March.		April.		May.		June.	
	Gauge Height.	Dis-charge.	Gauge Height.	Dis-charge	Gauge Height.	Dis-charge.	Gauge Height.	Dis-charge.	Gauge Height.	Dis-charge	Gauge Height.	Dis-charge.
	Feet.	Sec.-ft.	Feet.	Sec.-ft.	Feet.	Sec.-ft.	Feet.	Sec.-ft.	Feet.	Sec.-ft.	Feet.	Sec.-ft.
1..........	1.85	20 0a⁻	1.93	10 7	3.20	38	2.63	242	1 78	157	1.35	72
2..........	1 94	22 0	1 97	9 2	3.14	40	3.00	278	1.84	172	1 34	70
3..........	1.86	20 0	2 20	7 0	3.27	43	2.65	314a	1.85	175	1 30	64
4..........	1 95	21 0	2 20	7.3	3.25	45	2.40	349	1 85	175	1.30	64
5..........	2.00	22.0	1.80	7 8	3.24	46	2.40	349	2 00	215	1.32	68
6..........	2.00	23.0	1.70	6.3	3.14	47	3.50	912	1.90	188	1.42	84
7..........	2.04	24.0	1.80	4.4	3.25	48	2.98	614	2.00	215	1.44	87
8..........	2.10	25.0	1.80	2.0	3.22	50	2.50	388	2.10	245	1.48	94
9..........	2.10	24.0	1.75	1.0	3.23	51	2.30	311	2.02	221	1.40	80
10..........	1.95	24.0	2.03	2.2	3.10	47	2.70	475	1.95	201	1.35	72
11..........	2.04	24.0	2.30	4.0	2.98	46	2.50	388	1.90	188	1.30	64
12..........	2.06	25.0	2.55	5.8	2.95	45	2.50	388	1.85	175	1.30	64
13..........	2.06	26.0	2.65	7.0	2.95	47	3.20	734	1.80	162	1.35	72
14..........	2.10	26.0	2.67	7.5	2.98	53	2.90	572	1.70	139	1.35	72
15..........	2.00	27.0	2.45	4.0	2.95	59	2.45	368	1.68	135	1.40	80
16........	2.00	28 0	2 42	3 4	2.70	65	2.20	277	1.64	126	1.73	146
17..........	2 03	29.0	2 40	4 0	3.00	71	2.20	277	1.62	122	1.50	98
18..........	2.00	30.0	2 50	5 2	3.10	77	2.10	245	1.62	122	1.36	74
19.	2 05	33 0	2.50	7 5	3.08	83	1.90	188	1.63	124	1.30	64
20	2.10	34 0	2 65	10.0	2.80	89	1.80	162	1.70	139	1.25	57
21..........	2.10	35 0	2 75	13.0	2.40	131	1.76	152	1.70	139	1.15	44
22..........	1.95	32 0	2.65	12 0	2.25	173	2.05	230	1.80	162	1.12	41
23..........	1.95	30 0	2 55	11 0	2.00	215	1.85	175	1.75	150	1.14	43
24..........	1 95	28 0	2 63	15 0	2.45	192	1.75	150	1.65	128	1.15	44
25..........	1.95	28 0	2.67	18 0	2.47	109	1.85	175	1.60	118	1.24	56
26..........	1.80	26.0	2 85	23 0	3.10	146	1.93	196	1.56	110	1.30	64
27..........	1.86	23 0	3 00	29 0	3.10	123	1.80	162	1.50	98	1.32	67
28..........	1 96	29 0	3.20	34.0	2.95	100	1.75	150	1.50	98	1.51	100
29..........	1 95	21 0	......	......	2.60	136	1.75	150	1.48	94	1.39	78
30.	1.94	18 5	......	......	2.50	171	1.70	139	1.44	87	1.26	58
31..........	1 94	11.3	......	......	2.50	207	......	......	1.40	80	......	......

a Ice conditions Jan. 1 to April 3.

MONTHLY DISCHARGE of Milk River at Milk River, for 1912.

(Drainage area 1,077 square miles.)

MONTH.	DISCHARGE IN SECOND-FEET.				RUN-OFF.	
	Maximum.	Minimum.	Mean.	Per square Mile.	Depth in inches on Drainage Area.	Total in Acre-feet.
January	53	12	37.7	0.035	0.04	2,318
February	88	66	77.3	0.072	0.08	4,446
March (1-28)	852	52	144.0	0.134	0.14	7,997
April (3-30)	1,504	229	496.0	0.460	0.48	27,546
May	1,104	187	293.0	0.272	0.31	18,016
June	214	56	105.0	0.097	0.11	6,248
July	214	60	126.0	0.117	0.13	7,747
August	94	48	61.6	0.057	0.07	3,788
September	91	47	64.7	0.060	0.07	3,850
October	103	59	81.1	0.075	0.09	4,987
The period	....	....	....	....	....	86,943

NOTE.—This table is inserted to correct a table appearing on page 260 of the 1912 report. A correction has been made in the acre-feet for March and in the total acre-feet. The remainder of the table is as previously published.

SESSIONAL PAPER No. 25c

DAILY GAUGE HEIGHT AND DISCHARGE of Milk River at Milk River, for 1914.—*Concluded.*

DAY.	July.		August.		September.		October.		November.		December.	
	Gauge Height	Dis- charge.	Gauge Height.	Dis- charge	Gauge Height.	Dis- charge.	Gauge Height.	Dis- charge.	Gauge Height.	Dis- charge	Gauge Height.	Dis- charge.
	Feet.	*Sec.-ft.*	*Feet.*	*Sec.-ft.*	*Feet.*	*Sec.-ft.*	*Feet.*	*Sec.-ft.*	*Feet.*	*Sec.-ft.*	*Feet.*	*Sec.-ft.*
1	1.21	53.0	0 62	6.8	0.97	29.0	0.90	21	1.40	72	1.25	57.0
2	1.17	48 0	0 61	6 3	0.94	26.0	0.95	24	1.42	76	1.60	54 0
3	1.13	44 0	0 60	5 8	0.92	25.0	1.09	38	1 44	80	1.85	43.0
4	1.10	40 0	0.58	4 9	0.90	24.0	1.52a	83	1 44	81	1.65	37.0
5	1 12	43.0	0 59	5 4	0.90	24.0	1.95	184	1 45	84	1.60	34.0
6	1 07	38.0	0.56	4 0	0.89	23.0	2.14	240	1.50	95	1.60	31.0
7	1.05	36.0	0 56	4.0	0.90	24.0	1.71	124	1.58	114	1.61	30.0
8	1 06	37.0	0 59	5.4	0.98	30.0	1.51	81	1.48	92	1.56	29.0
9	1.07	38 0	0 61	6 3	0.89	23.0	1.50	79	1.45	91	1.70	28.0
10	1 05	36.0	0.69	10 3	0.90	24.0	1.40	61	1.42	84	1.71	28.0
11	1.02	33 0	0.68	9 8	0.89	23.0	1.40	61	1.35	72	1.74	28.0
12	0 98a	30 0	0 70	10 8	0.97	29.0	1.51	81	1.34	70	1.74	28.0
13	0 95	27 0	0 69	10.3	1.00	32.0	1.55	89	1.40	80	1.74	30.0
14	0 90	24 0	0 67	9.2	1.00	32.0	1.58	96	1.65	74a	1.79	28.0
15	0.92	25.0	0.66	8 7	1.04	35.0	1.75	134	1.27	66	1.76	26.0
16	0.95	27.0	0.80	16 7	1.05	36.0	2.55	393	1.35	62	1.77	25.0
17	0 93	26.0	0 77	14 9	1.04	35.0	2.54	389	1.39	57	1.82	23.0
18	0 87	21 0	0.76	14.3	1.01	32.0	2.37	320	1.43	57	1.82	22.0
19	0 85	20 0	1 17	48 0	1.00	32.0	2.24	274	1.40	58	1.82	21.0
20	0.83	18 7	1.19	50 0	1.00	32.0	2.07	218	1.46	59	1.87	20.0
21	0 79	16.1	1 12	43 0	1.00	32.0	2.00	198	1.52	58	1.84	21.0
22	0.77	14.9	1 13	44.0	0.98	30.0	1.79	144	1.64	58	1.95	22.0
23	0 75	13.7	1.13	44 0	0.98	30.0	1.67	115	1.64	58	1.95	21.0
24	0 73	12 5	1 09	40 0	0.97	29 0	1.60	100	1.64	60	1.80	19.6
25	0.71	11.4	1 05	36.0	0.95	27.0	1.54	87	1.70	100	1.80	19.5
26	0.67	9.2	1.05	36.0	0.95	27.0	1.54	87	1.68	138	1.98	20.0
27	0.61	6.3	1.07	38.0	0.91	24.0	1.50	82	1.75	150	2.00	21.0
28	0.65	8.2	1.13	44.0	0.91	24.0	1.49	82	1.62	122	2.10	23.0
29	0.65	8.2	1.05	36.0	0.90	24.0	1.47	78	1.45	89	2.14	25.0
30	0.62	6.8	1.02	33.0	0.90	24.0	1.44	76	1.05	34	2.05	26.0
31	0.64	7.7	0.98	30.0	......	......	1.43	76	......	......	2.00	28.0a

a Ice conditions Nov. 14 to Dec. 31.

MONTHLY DISCHARGE of Milk River at Milk River, for 1914.

(Drainage area 1,104 square miles.)

MONTH.	DISCHARGE IN SECOND-FEET.				RUN-OFF.	
	Maximum.	Minimum.	Mean.	Per square Mile.	Depth in inches on Drainage Area.	Total in Acre-feet.
January	35	11.3	25.0	0.023	0.030	1,537
February	34	1.0	9.7	0.009	0.010	538
March	215	38.0	92.0	0.083	0.100	5,657
April	912	139.0	317.0	0.287	0.320	18,863
May	245	80.0	150.0	0.136	0.160	9,223
June	146	41.0	71.0	0.065	0.070	4,225
July	53	6.3	25.0	0.023	0.030	1,537
August	50	4.0	22.0	0.020	0.020	1,353
September	36	23.0	28.0	0.025	0.030	1,666
October	240	21.0	133.0	0.120	0.140	8,178
November	150	34.0	79.7	0.072	0.080	4,742
December	57	19.5	28.0	0.025	0.029	1,722
The year	......	......	......	......	1 019	59,241

5 GEORGE V, A. 1915

MILK RIVER AT WRITING-ON-STONE POLICE DETACHMENT.

Location.—On SW. ¼ Sec. 35, Tp. 1, Rge. 13, W. 4th Mer.
Records available.—August 2, 1909, to October 31, 1914.
Gauge.—Vertical staff; maintained at the original elevation of 86.13 feet.
Bench-mark.—Permanent iron bench-mark; assumed elevation, 100.00 feet.
Channel.—Composed of sand, and shifts in changes of stage.
Discharge measurements.—Made from a cable and car during high water, and at low stages by wading.
Observer.—A. P. White.

DISCHARGE MEASUREMENTS of Milk River at Writing-on-Stone Police Detachment, in 1914.

Date.	Engineer.	Width.	Area of Section.	Mean Velocity.	Gauge Height.	Discharge.
		Feet.	*Sq. ft.*	*Ft. per sec.*	*Feet.*	*Sec.-ft.*
April 3............	J. E. Degnan.............	126.0a	162.00	2.03	2.89	330.0
April 20............	do	61.0	84.20	2.14	2.43	180.0
May 1............	do	73.0	90.00	1.80	2.24	162.0
May 10............	do	97.0a	116.00	1.94	2.51	225.0
May 18............	do	72.0	72.50	1.77	2.07	128.0
May 23............	do	75.5	93.45	1.82	2.30	170.0
June 2............	do	71.0	61.90	1.38	1.93	85.0
June 9............	do	70.0	62.10	1.50	1.91	93.0
June 22............	do	69.0	48.75	1.29	1.78	63.0
July 2............	do	53.0	42.30	1.45	1.80	61.0
July 15............	do	30.0	21.15	1.20	1.53	26.0
July 24............	do	24.0	14.05	0.99	1.39	13.6
Aug. 1............	do	18.5	6.97	0.75	1.24	5.2
Aug. 8............	do	18.0	5.05	0.49	1.16	2.5
Aug. 19............	do	65.0	24.80	0.76	1.42	18.7
Aug. 25............	F. R. Steinberger..........	56.0b	35.30	1.20	1.67	42.0
Sept. 5............	do	52.0	23.60	0.87	1.52	20.5
Sept. 16............	J. E. Degnan.............	69.0	37.30	0.84	1.65	32.0
Oct. 2............	do	50.0	22.20	0.91	1.51	20.4
Oct. 16............	do	74.0	86.00	1.68	2.26	143.0
Oct. 23............	do	80.0	91.60	1.59	2.32	146.0

a Taken at regular section.
b Taken above regular section.
All other measurements taken below regular section.

View of Milk River near Writing-on-Stone Police Detachment. Taken by G. H. Whyte.

View of Sandstone Formation in Milk River Valley near Writing-on-Stone
Police Detachment. Taken by G. H. Whyte.

SESSIONAL PAPER No. 25c

DAILY GAUGE HEIGHT AND DISCHARGE of Milk River at Writing-on-Stone Police Detachment, for 1914.

DAY.	March.		April.		May.		June.	
	Gauge Height.	Dis-charge.	Gauge Height.	Dis-charge.	Gauge Height.	Dis-charge.	Gauge Height.	Dis-charge.
	Feet.	Sec.-ft	Feet.	Sec.-ft.	Feet.	Sec.-ft.	Feet.	Sec.-ft.
1			2.27	166	2.24	159	1.97	96
2			2.74	288	2.32	178	1.93	88
3			3.02a	369	2.34	183	1.84	70
4			3.02	371	2.33	180	1.84	70
5			2.84	316	2.42	203	1.84	70
6			2.74	285	2.46	214	1.87	76
7			3.43	532	2.42	203	1.89	80
8			3.38	507	2.40	198	1.92	86
9			3.06	378	2.80	305	1.94	90
10			2.86	312	2.50	224	1.97	96
11			3.21	430	2.45	211	1.92	86
12			3.20	422	2.40	198	1.92	86
13			3.01	352	2.34	183	2.00	103
14			3.69	637	2.25	161	1.95	92
15			3.16	401	2.15	137	1.99	101
16			2.92	320	2.18	144	2.13	132
17			2.76	272	2.10	125	2.23	156
18	2.14	135	2.71	258	2.09	123	2.05	114
19	2.11	127	2.57	218	2.05	114	1.93	88
20	2.15	137	2.48	193	2.12	130	1.90	82
21	2.04	112	2.39	172	2.15	137	1.88	78
22	2.36	188	2.32	158	2.18	144	1.78	60
23	2.58	245	2.61	235	2.22	154	1.74	53
24	2.48	219	2.39	180	2.18	144	1.74	53
25	1.99	101	2.39	183	2.14	135	1.78	60
26	1.91	84	2.52	220	2.08	121	1.73	52
27	1.92	86	2.48	210	2.08	121	1.82	67
28	2.69	274	2.38	188	2.05	114	1.90	82
29	2.67	269	2.27	163	2.02	107	1.97	96
30	2.34	183	2.22b	155	2.00	103	1.95	92
31	2.09	123			1.97	96		

a to b Shifting conditions April 3 to April 30.

DAILY GAUGE HEIGHT AND DISCHARGE of Milk River at Writing-on-Stone Police Detachment, for 1914.—*Concluded.*

DAY.	July.		August.		September.		October.	
	Gauge Height.	Dis-charge.	Gauge Height.	Dis-charge.	Gauge Height.	Dis-charge.	Gauge Height.	Dis-charge.
	Feet.	*Sec.-ft.*	*Feet.*	*Sec.-ft.*	*Feet.*	*Sec.-ft.*	*Feet.*	*Sec.-ft.*
1	1.88	78.0	1.24	5.2	1.58	28.0	1.53	22
2	1.80	63.0	1.22	4.5	1.55	24.0	1.53	22
3	1.76	56.0	1.22	4.5	1.55	24.0	1.58	26
4	1.76	56.0	1.20	3.8	1.55	23.0	1.65	33
5	1.72	49.0	1.19	3.5	1.53b	21.0	1.82	54
6	1.70	46.0	1.17	2.8	1.51	20.0	1.67	35
7	1.67	42.0	1.16	2.5	1.50	19.3	1.94	71
8	1.67	42.0	1.15	2.2	1.55	23.0	2.15	112
9	1.67	42.0	1.18	3.2	1.57	25.0	2.03	87
10	1.66	41.0	1.23	4.9	1.55	23.0	2.00	82
11	1.67	42.0	1.35	11.0	1.53	22.0	2.01	84
12	1.60	33.0	1.28	7.0	1.52	21.0	1.97	77
13	1.54	27.0	1.28	7.0	1.60	28.0	2.03	87
14	1.54	27.0	1.29	7.5	1.62	30.0	2.05	91
15	1.57	30.0	1.29	7.5	1.64	32.0	2.08	97
16	1.55	28.0	1.29	7.5	1.64	32.0	2.15	112
17	1.55	28.0	1.27	6.6	1.64	32.0	2.76	277
18	1.53	26.0	1.48	21.0	1.64	32.0	2.93	334
19	1.50	23.0	1.40	14.2	1.64	32.0	2.84	303
20	1.48	21.0	1.41	15.0	1.63	31.0	2.73	268
21	1.48	21.0	1.38	12.9	1.62	30.0	2.62	234
22	1.48	21.0	1.65	39.0	1.60	28.0	2.45	186
23	1.37	12.3	1.70	46.0	1.60	28.0	2.35	159
24	1.35	11.0	1.71	48.0	1.60	28.0	2.24	133
25	1.35	11.0	1.69a	46.0	1.58	26.0	2.15	112
26	1.35	11.0	1.65	39.0	1.55	23.0	2.10	101
27	1.33	9.8	1.60	33.0	1.54	22.0	2.07	95
28	1.28	7.0	1.60	32.0	1.54	22.0	2.05	91
29	1.28	7.0	1.63	35.0	1.53	22.0	2.04	89
30	1.25	5.6	1.63	35.0	1.53	22.0	2.00	82
31	1.24	5.2	1.60	31.0	....	....	2.00	82

a to *b* Shifting conditions Aug. 25 to Sept. 5.

MONTHLY DISCHARGE of Milk River at Writing-on-Stone Police Detachment, for 1914.

(Drainage area 1,516 square miles.)

MONTH.	DISCHARGE IN SECOND-*FEET*.				RUN-OFF.	
	Maximum	Minimum	Mean.	Per square Mile.	Depth in inches on Drainage Area.	Total in Acre-feet.
March (18-31)	274	84.0	163.0	0.105	0.06	4,530
April	637	155.0	296.0	0.191	0.21	17,613
May	305	96.0	160.0	0.103	0.12	9,838
June	156	52.0	85.0	0.055	0.06	5,058
July	78	5.2	30.0	0.019	0.02	1,845
August	48	2.2	17.4	0.111	0.01	1,070
September	32	19.3	26.0	0.017	0.02	1,547
October	334	22.0	117.0	0.076	0.09	7,194
The period	....	....	....	....	0.59	48,695

MILK RIVER AT PENDANT D'OREILLE POLICE DETACHMENT.

Location.—On SW. ¼ Sec. 21, Tp. 2, Rge. 8, W. 4th Mer.
Records available.—August 5, 1909, to October 31, 1914.
Gauge.—Vertical staff; elevation of zero 82 45 feet since establishment.
Bench-mark.—Permanent iron bench-mark; assumed elevation, 100.00 feet.
Channel.—Composed of sand, and shifts in change of stage.
Discharge measurements.—Made from a cable and car during high water; at low stages by wading.
Observers.—E. N. Bird, F. E. Torpey, and R. G. Lipton.

SESSIONAL PAPER No. 25c

DISCHARGE MEASUREMENTS of Milk River at Pendant d'Oreille Police Detachment, in 1914.

Date.	Engineer.	Width.	Area of Section.	Mean Velocity.	Gauge Height.	Discharge.
		Feet.	*Sq. ft.*	*Ft. per sec.*	*Feet.*	*Sec.-ft.*
Mar. 20	J. E. Degnan	39a	52.60	1.08	2.70	57.0
Mar. 31..........	do	175	158.00	1.57	3.29	249.0
April 11..........	H. W. Rowley........ ..	175a	217.00	1.80	3.60	392.0
April 22..........	J. E. Degnan....	80	116.00	1.80	3.13	209.0
April 27..........	do	69a	99.80	1.67	3.07	166.0
May 12..........	do	102b	107.00	1.49	3.26	159.0
May 15	do	127	127.00	1.40	3.14	177.0
May 26..........	do	130	109.50	1.32	3.09	145.0
May 29..........	do	127	87.40	1.23	2.97	108.0
June 11..........	do	125	75.60	1.17	2.91	88.0
June 17..........	do	129	76.60	1.17	2.88	89.0
July 6..........	do	106	48.95	0.88	2.64	43.0
July 12..........	do	43a	35.20	0.77	2.50	27.0
July 27..........	do	18a	5.20	0.50	2.14	2.6
July 30..........	do	20a	5.20	0.48	2.14	2.4
Aug. 11..........	do	....	....	....	....	Nil.
Aug. 18..........	do	....	....	....	....	Nil.
Aug. 27..........	F. R. Steinberger...	43a	25.50	1.13	2.55	29.0
Sept. 2..........	do	39a	23.10	1.08	2.48	25.0
Sept. 3..........	do	37a	21.60	0.92	2.44	19.7
Sept. 21..........	J. E. Degnan...........	41a	26.10	0.88	2.51	23.0
Sept. 28..........	do	40a	22.30	0.72	2.45	16.2
Oct. 18..........	do	171	206.00	1.65	3.59	341.0
Oct. 20..........	do	171	194.00	1.69	3.58	328.0

a Measured below regular station.
b Measured above regular station.

DAILY GAUGE HEIGHT AND DISCHARGE of Milk River at Pendant d'Oreille Police Detachment, for 1914.

DAY.	March.		April.		May.		June.	
	Gauge Height.	Dis-charge.	Gauge Height.	Dis-charge.	Gauge Height.	Dis-charge.	Gauge Height.	Dis-charge.
	Feet.	*Sec.-ft.*	*Feet.*	*Sec.-ft.*	*Feet.*	*Sec.-ft.*	*Feet.*	*Sec.-ft.*
1..................................	..... .	....	3.26	211	2.98	119	2.88	86
2..................................	....	....	3.25	206	3.00	119	2.88	86
3..................................	....	....	3.35	252	3.04	127	2.84	77
4..................................	....	....	3.65	421	3.07	132	2.81	70
5..................................	....	....	3.64	415	3.10	137	2.77	62
6..................................	....	....	3.68	440	3.15	150	2.96	106
7..................................	....	....	3.94	618	3.25	182	3.00	117
8..................................	....	....	4.13	767	3.24	171	2.87	84
9..................................	....	....	3.82	531	3.27	180	2.84	77
10..................................	....	....	3.66	427	3.34	201	2.86	81
11..................................	....	....	3.60a	390	3.30	180	2.91	93
12..................................	... ...	....	3.72	475	3.27	163	2.94	101
13..................................	....	....	3.74	498	3.20	158	2.88	86
14..................................	....	....	3.70	481	3.15	160	2.88	86
15..................................	3.35	252	3.97	684	3.10	162	2.84	77
16..................................	3.29	224	3.80	565	3.10	160	2.88	86
17..................................	3.23	198	3.58	427	3.08	150	2.87	84
18..................................	3.27	215	3.45	354	3.04	136	3.05	133
19..................................	3.23	198	3.42	346	3.04	135	2.98	111
20..................................	2.72	53	3.32	294	3.08	148	2.81	70
21..................................	2.94	101	3.20	235	3.04	134	2.84	77
22..................................	3.26	211	3.14	210	3.05	138	2.84	77
23..................................	3.28	220	3.08	184	3.08	146	2.80	68
24..................................	3.17	175	3.30	280	3.14	164	2.72	53
25..................................	2.61	37	3.20	226	3.13	160	2.84	77
26..................................	3.20	186	3.04	158	3.10b	150	2.81	70
27..................................	2.83	75	3.06	163	3.04	130	2.77	62
28..................................	2.77	62	3.14	187	3.00	117	2.70	50
29..................................	2.86	81	3.08	160	2.94	101	2.75	58
30..................................	3.54	354	3.01	133	2.92	96	2.85	79
31..................................	3.37	262	....	....	2.91	93	....	....

a to b Shifting conditions April 11 to May 26.

5 GEORGE V. A. 1915

DAILY GAUGE HEIGHT AND DISCHARGE of Milk River at Pendant d'Oreille Police Detachment, for 1914.—*Concluded.*

DAY.	July.		August.		September.		October.	
	Gauge Height.	Dis- charge.	Gauge Height.	Dis- charge.	Gauge Height.	Dis- charge.	Gauge Height.	Dis- charge.
	Feet.	*Sec.-ft.*	*Feet.*	*Sec.-ft.*	*Feet.*	*Sec.-ft.*	*Feet.*	*Sec.-ft.*
1	2.91	93.0	2.10	2.5	2.55	30.0	2.41	16.8
2	2.74	56.0	2.03	0.6	2.48	23.0	2.45	20.0
3	2.76	60.0	2.03	0.6	2.44	19.2	2.50	25.0
4	2.80	68.0	2.02	0.4	2.43	18.4	2.85	79.0
5	2.70	50.0	2.01	0.2	2.43	18.4	2.87	84.0
6	2.65	43.0	2.00	Nil.	2.44	19.2	2.90	91.0
7	2.64	42.0	....	"	2.44	19.2	2.92	96.0
8	2.58	34.0	....	"	2.46	21.0	2.95	103.0
9	2.50	25.0	....	"	2.42	17.6	3.05	133.0
10	2.52	27.0	....	"	2.45	20.0	2.98	111.0
11	2.50	25.0	....	"	2.45	20.0	2.95	103.0
12	2.50	25.0	....	"	2.45	20.0	2.93	98.0
13	2.49	24.0	....	"	2.43	18.4	2.87	84.0
14	2.44	19.2	....	"	2.65	43.0	2.95	103.0
15	2.42	17.6	....	"	2.58	34.0	2.98	111.0
16	2.42	17.6	....	"	2.64	42.0	3.11	126.0
17	2.42	17.6	....	"	2.53	28.0	3.25	174.0
18	2.42	17.6	2.12	3.1	2.45	20.0	3.73	419.0
19	2.42a	17.6	2.25	7.0	2.46	21.0	3.83	486.0
20	2.42a	17.6	2.37	13.6	2.46	21.0	3.56	319.0
21	2.42	17.6	2.30	9.0	2.48	23.0	3.56a	286.0
22	2.42	17.6	2.40	16.0	2.48	23.0	3.43	244.0
23	2.45	20.0	2.40	16.0	2.50	25.0	3.40	236.0
24	2.42	17.6	2.70	50.0	2.51	26.0	3.39	232.0
25	2.24	6.7	2.72	53.0	2.53	28.0	3.36	219.0
26	2.19	5.2	2.60	36.0	2.48	23.0	3.33	207.0
27	2.14	3.7	2.55	30.0	2.45	20.0	3.28	186.0
28	2.14	3.7	2.50	25.0	2.44	19.2	3.13	132.0
29	2.14	3.7	2.50	25.0	2.43	18.4	3.03	103.0
30	2.13	3.4	2.51	26.0	2.43	18.4	2.98	92.0
31	2.12	3.1	2.55	30.0	....	....	2.93	81.0

a Gauge height interpolated.

MONTHLY DISCHARGE of Milk River at Pendant d'Oreille Police Detachment, for 1914.

(Drainage area 2,169 square miles.)

MONTH.	DISCHARGE IN SECOND-FEET.				RUN-OFF.	
	Maximum.	Minimum.	Mean.	Per square Mile.	Depth in inches on Drainage Area.	Total in Acre-feet.
March (15–31)	354	37.0	171.0	0.079	0.050	5,760
April	767	133.0	358.0	0.165	0.180	21,302
May	201	93.0	145.0	0.067	0.077	8,916
June	133	50.0	81.0	0.037	0.041	4,820
July	93	3.1	26.0	0.012	0.014	1,599
August	53	Nil.	11.1	0.005	0.006	682
September	43	17.6	23.0	0.011	0.012	1,360
October	486	16.8	155.0	0.071	0.082	9,531
The period	....	....	....	....	0.462	53,979

'MILK RIVER AT SPENCER'S LOWER RANCH.

Location.—South of SE. ¼ Sec. 3, Tp. 1, Rge. 5, W. 4th Mer.
Records available.—August 7, 1909, to December 31, 1914.
Gauge.—Gurley automatic water stage register, installed in a wooden shelter 300 feet south of the international boundary, with a staff gauge inside the stilling box and another outside at the mouth of the intake pipe. Gauges are maintained at an elevation of 82.94 feet.
Bench-mark.—Permanent iron bench-mark; assumed elevation, 100.00 feet; located 1,300 feet upstream from the boundary line on the left bank.
Channel.—Composed of gravel, rock and quicksand, and is subject to shifting conditions.
Discharge measurements.—Made by wading at low stages, and by a cable car structure at high stages.
Winter flow.—From December to April the stream is frozen over, and no records of value are obtained.
Observer.—Frank Galloway.
Co-operation.—This station is maintained in conjunction with the United States Geological Survey.

DISCHARGE MEASUREMENTS of Milk River at Spencer's Lower Ranch, in 1914.

Date.	Engineer.	Width.	Area of Section.	Mean Velocity.	Gauge Height.	Discharge.
		Feet.	*Sq. ft.*	*Ft. per sec.*	*Feet.*	*Sec.-ft.*
Mar. 21....	W. A. Lamb (U.S.G.S.).......	46.0	60.0	1.30	3.30	78.0
Mar. 22............	J. E Degnan.........	80.0	83.0	1.36	3.25	113.0
Mar. 23............	do	92.0	109.0	1.86	3.64	203.0
April 23............	do	70.0	92.2	2.00	3.56	185.0
May 1............	B. E. Jones (U.S.G.S.).......	48.5	94.0	1.63	3.53	153.0
May 27............	J. E. Degnan	49.0	63.3	1.89	3.85	120.0
May 29............	B. F. Jones (U.S.G.S.).......	67.0	72.0	1.89	3.27	112.0
June 16............	J. E. Degnan.	44.0	49.8	1.20	3.16	85.0
June 24............	B. E. Jones (U.S.G.S.).	48.5	37.0	1.54	2.94	57.0
July 8............	J. E. Degnan.............	46.0	34.4	1.15	2.83	40.0
July 14............	B. E. Jones (U.S.G.S.)	38.5	39.0	1.03	2.92	40.0
July 14	do do	38.5	38.0	1.05	2.91	40.0
July 28......... ...	J. E. Degnan..............	8.0	2.45	0.83	2.31	2.0
Aug. 13............	do	....	....	....	....	Nil.
Sept. 1............	F. R. Steinberger.	34.0	14.8	1.06	2.60	15.6
Sept. 4............	W. A. Lamb (U.S.G.S.)......	33.0	15.9	1.10	2.57	17.5
Sept. 23	J. E. Degnan......	35.0	18.1	1.01	2.64	18.3
Oct. 19.... ..	G. H. Whyte and J. E. Degnan.	134.0	180.0	2.50	4.13	449.0
Oct. 30	B. E. Jones (U.S.G.S.)	38.0	58.0	1.76	3.31	102.0
Dec. 21......... ..	do do	31.0a	28.8	0.62	2.97	17.9

NOTE.—Gauge height 2 10 = zero flow.
a Ice conditions.

STREAM MEASUREMENTS, 1914

5 GEORGE V, A. 1915

DAILY GAUGE HEIGHT AND DISCHARGE of Milk River at Spencer's Lower Ranch, for 1914.

DAY.	January.		February.		March.		April.		May.		June.	
	Gauge Height.	Dis-charge.	Gauge Height.	Dis-charge.	Gauge Height.	Dis-charge.	Gauge Height.	Dis-charge.	Gauge Height.	Dis-charge	Gauge Height.	Dis-charge
	Feet.	*Sec.-ft.*	*Feet.*	*Sec.-ft.*	*Feet.*	*Sec.-ft.*	*Feet.*	*Sec.-ft.*	*Feet.*	*Sec.-ft.*	*Feet.*	*Sec.-ft.*
1............	....a	....	3.60	....	4.15	....	4.47c	639	.51	148	.18	90
2............	......	....	3.60	....	4.25	....	4.63c	729	.48	140	19	92
3............	......	....	3.60	....	4.30	....	4.79c	818	.48	140	20	94
4............	....a	....	....a	....	4.35	....	4.95c	908	.51	148	.15	85
5............	3.62	....	......	....	5.11	....	5.12	1,003	3.56	161	3.14	83
6............	3.67	....	......	....	5.24	....	4.98	925	3.58	171	3.53	171
7............	4.00	....	......	....	5.28	....	4.88	869	3.62	184	3.41	138
8............	3.73	....	......	....	5.10	....	5.13	1,009	3.69	208	3.27	108
9............	3.80	....	......	....	5.10	....	5.23	1,065	3.72	220	3.16	87
10	3.90	....	......	....	5.13	....	5.13	1,009	3.67	205	3.10	77
11............	3.98	....	.....	....	5.20	....	4.13	449	.79	254	.12	80
12............	4.10	....	......	....	5.06	....	3.98	366	79	254	.35	124
13....	4.10	....	......	....	5.04	....	3.99	371	.72	224	46	151
14	4.10	....	......	....	....b	....	4.00	376	.58d	177	.59	191
15...	4.10	....	......	....	......	....	4.24	510	3.55	167	3 38	131
16	4.10	....	......	....	......	....	4.37	583	3.50	153	3.16	87
17.	4.07	....	......	....	......	....	4.17	471	3.48	148	3.14	83
18....	4.05	....	......	....	......	....	3.96	355	3.45	140	3.13	82
19	4.05	....	......	....	......	....	3.81	282	3.46	145	3.16	87
20....	4.03	....	......	....	b	....	3.90	325	3.47	148	3.27	108
21....	4.00	....	......	....	3.30	78	3.83	291	3.45	143	3.15	85
22	4.00	....	......	....	3.25	104	3.68	224	3.44	140	3.07	72
23...........	3.98	....	......	....	3.75	254	3.58	187	3.44	143	3.02	65
24	3.90	....	......	....	3.80	277	3.54	171e	3.42c	138	2.95	55
25 ..	3.86	....	......	....	3.92c	335	3.76	250	3.40	133	3.08	74
26 .	3.80	....	......	....	4.05	404	3.60	184	38	128e	3.85	300
27............	3.75	....	......	....	3.93	340	3.51	156	.35d	124	3 22	98
28............	3.72	....	....a	....	4.34	566	3.52	156	30	114	3.02	65
29.	3.69	....	......	....	3.09	371	3.62	184	27	108	3 01	63
30	3.65	....	......	....	4.15c	460	3.57	167	.24	102	2.98	59
31....	3.60	....	......	....	4.31c	550	....	....	3.22	98	......	......

a Frozen to bottom.
b Old gauge used at upper section.
c Gauge height interpolated.
d Staff gauge readings from May 14 to 27 inclusive.
e Shifting conditions April 24 to May 26.

SESSIONAL PAPER No. 25c

DAILY GAUGE HEIGHT AND DISCHARGE of Milk River at Spencer's Lower Ranch, for 1914.

DAY.	July. Gauge Height.	July. Dis- charge.	August. Gauge Height.	August. Dis- charge	September. Gauge Height.	September. Dis- charge.	October. Gauge Height.	October. Dis- charge	November. Gauge Height.	November. Dis- charge	December. Gauge Height.	December. Dis- charge.
	Feet.	Sec.-ft.	Feet.	Sec.-ft.	Feet.	Sec.-ft.	Feet.	Sec.-ft.	Feet.	Sec.-ft.	Feet.	Sec.-ft.
1	2.99	61.0	2.25	1 00	2.61	17.8	2.51	10 7	3 22	98	3.27	35.0
2	3 05	69.0	2.17	0.35	2.64	20.0	2.53	12 1	3.19	92	3 39	36.0
3	3.00	62 0	2 10	Nil	2.64	20.0	2.56	14 2	3 16	87	3.52	34.0
4	2 91	49 0	... .	"	2.59	16.3	2.82	38.0	3.14	83		30.0
5	2 85	42.0	.....	"	2.55	13.5	3.24	102 0	3.12	80	3.30	26 0
6	2.83	40.0	.. ..	"	2.53	12.1	3.44	145.0	3.12	80	3.28	24.0
7	2.82	38.0	.....	"	2.50	10.0	3.56	180.0	3.11	79	3.25	23.0
8	2.82	38.0	. .	"	2.47	8.5	3.68	224.0	3.10	77	3.34	23.0
9	2.79	35.0	... ...	"	2.45	7.5	3.59	191.0	3.10	77	3.34	23.0
10	2.77	33.0	......	"	2.43	6.7	3.60	194.0	3.11	79	3.29	24.0
11	2.74	30.0	... ...	"	2.42	6.3	3.55	177.0	3.12	80	3.29	24.0
12	2.71	27.0	......	"	2.50	10.0	3.44	145.0	3.12	80	3.30	25.0
13	2.88	41.0f	......	"	3.34	122.0	3.33	120.0	3.12	80	3.30	25.0
14	3.16	74.0	......	"	3.14	83.0	3.31	116.0	3.17	89	3.25	27.0
15	2.77	25.0	......	"	2.84	41.0	3.27	108.0	3.14g	83	3.27	21.0
16	2.72	21 0		"	2.73	29.0	3.29	112.0	3.04	68	3.27	21.0
17	2.65	15 6	1.96	"	2.71	27.0	3.38	131.0	3.85	63	3.31	20.0
18	2.61	13.5	2 70	26.0	2.71	27.0	3.59	191.0	3.05	60	3.30	17.0
19	2.59	12.1	2 36	3 9	2.65	21.0	4.13	449.0	3.15	56	3.28	15.0
20	2.58	12.1	2.24	0 9	2.63	19.4	4.05	404.0	3.14	52	3.27	15.0
21	2.57	11.4	2.18	0.4	2.64	20.0	3.97	360.0	3.10	46	3.27	17.0
22	2 56	11.4	2 09	Nil	2.63	19.4	3.88	315.0	3.15	39	3.25	19.0
23	2 54	10.0	2.10	"	2.64	20.0	3.79	272.0	3.13	37	3.25	17.0
24	2.52	9.5	2 87	44 0	2.64	20.0	3.68	224.0	3.10	36	3.25	14.0
25	2.49	8 0	2.68	24 0	2.62	18.6	3.60	194.0	3.41	37	3.24	10.0
26	2.45	6.7	2.69	25.0	2.62	18.6	3.51	164.0	3.50	40	3.29	9.0
27	2.35	3.2f	2.69	25.0	2.59	16.3	3.43	143.0	3.47	45	3.31	10.0
28	2.32	2.6	2.67	23.0	2.58	15.6	3.37	128.0	3.43	45	3.26	11.0
29	2.30	2.0	2.64	20.0	2.56	14.2	3.32	118.0	3.39	44	3.29	10.0
30	2.27	1.4	2.60	17.0	2.53	12.1	3.28	110.0	3.10	40	3.30	11.0
31	2.24	0.9	2.59	16.3	......	......	3.25	104.0			3.30	11.0

f to *f* Shifting conditions.
g Automatic gauge to Nov. 16; staff gauge after Nov. 16.

MONTHLY DISCHARGE of Milk River at Spencer's Lower Ranch, for 1914.

(Drainage area 2,514 square miles.)

MONTH.	DISCHARGE IN SECOND-FEET. Maximum.	DISCHARGE IN SECOND-FEET. Minimum	DISCHARGE IN SECOND-FEET. Mean.	DISCHARGE IN SECOND-FEET. Per square Mile.	RUN-OFF. Depth in inches on Drainage Area.	RUN-OFF. Total in Acre-feet.
March (21–31)	566	78.0	340.0	0.135	0.055	7,416
April	1,065	156.0	501.0	0.199	0.222	29,812
May	254	98.0	158.0	0.063	0.073	9,715
June	300	55.0	103.0	0.041	0.046	6,129
July	74	0.9	26.0	0.010	0.012	1,599
August	44	0.0	7.3	0.003	0.003	449
September	122	6.3	23.0	0.009	0.010	1,369
October	449	10.7	168.0	0.067	0.077	10,330
November	98	36.0	65.0	0.026	0.029	3,868
December	36	9.0	20.0	0.008	0.009	1,230
The period	....	....	....	....	0 536	71,917

5 GEORGE V, A. 1915.

STUDY OF CONDITIONS OF RUN-OFF in watershed of Milk River from its headwaters to its eastern crossing from Canada.
Sec. 3, Tp. 1, Rge. 5, W. 4th Mer.

STATION. For Period Aug. 1 to Oct. 31, 1914.	AREA OF WATERSHED IN SQUARE MILES.						RUN-OFF IN AC. FT.		RUN-OFF PER SQ. MILE IN AC. FT.	
	Additional to last Station.			Total for Station.			Additional to last Station.	Total for Station.	For additional Area.	For total Area.
	Canada.	U.S.A.	Total.	Canada.	U.S.A.	Total.				
Peters' Ranch (N.Br.), NE. 11-1-23-4	....	....	....	10	91	101	....	4,208	....	96
Mackie's Ranch (S.Br.) NW. 31-1-18-4	....	....	....	90	414	504	....	5,615	....	11.14
Milk River .... NE. 21-2-16-4	477	22	499	577	527	1,104	+ 1,374a	11,197	2.75	10.14
Writing-on-Stone .... SW. 35-1-13-4	340	102	442	917	629	1,546	− 1,386	9,811	0.00	6.34
Pendant d'Oreille .... SW. 21-2-8-4	468	155	623	1,385	784	2,169	+ 1,771a	11,582	2.84	5.35
Spencer's Lower Ranch .... SE. 3-1-5-4	242	103	345	1,627	887	2,514	+ 566a	12,148	1.65	4.83

a Heavy fall of snow and rain in the month of October resulted in an abnormal run-off and increase of discharge instead of the usual loss between stations during this period.

SESSIONAL PAPER No. 25c

DEER CREEK CATTLE COMPANY EAST DITCH FROM DEER CREEK.

Location.—On the SW. ¼ Sec. 36, Tp. 1, Rge. 12, W. 4th Mer.
Records available.—April 1, 1912, to November 23, 1912. Discharge measurements only during 1914.
Gauge.—Vertical staff; elevation of zero maintained at 93.49 feet since establishment.
Bench-mark.—Post on left bank; assumed elevation, 100.00 feet.
Discharge measurements.—Made by wading or with a weir.
Observer.—None obtainable in 1914.
Remarks.—The Deer Creek Cattle Company diverts all the water from Deer Creek through their two ditches, except in flood stages.

DISCHARGE MEASUREMENTS of Deer Creek Cattle Company East Ditch from Deer Creek, in 1914.

Date.	Engineer.	Width.	Area of Section.	Mean Velocity.	Gauge Height.	Discharge.
		Feet.	*Sq. ft.*	*Ft. per sec.*	*Feet.*	*Sec.-ft.*
Oct. 17	J. E. Degnan	6.8	4.85	1.03	2.40	5.0
Oct. 21	do	6.0	3.40	1.17	2.35	4.0

DEER CREEK CATTLE COMPANY WEST DITCH FROM DEER CREEK.

Location.—On the SW. ¼ Sec. 36, Tp. 1, Rge. 12, W. 4th Mer.
Records available.—Discharge measurements during 1914.
Gauge.—Vertical staff; elevation, 100.50 feet.
Bench-mark.—Bench-mark at east ditch station.
Discharge measurements.—By wading or with a weir.
Observer.—None obtainable in 1914.

DISCHARGE MEASUREMENTS of Deer Creek Cattle Company West Ditch from Deer Creek, in 1914.

Date.	Engineer.	Width.	Area of Section.	Mean Velocity.	Gauge Height.	Discharge.
		Feet.	*Sq. ft.*	*Ft. per sec.*	*Feet.*	*Sec.-ft.*
April 30	J. E Degnan				3.23	0.118
June 20	do				3.30	0.118

NOTE.—The above are weir measurements.

MISCELLANEOUS DISCHARGE MEASUREMENTS made in Milk River drainage basin, in 1914.
(Deer Creek Seepage.)

Date.	Engineer.	Stream.	Location.	Width.	Area of Section.	Mean Velocity.	Discharge.
				Feet.	*Sq. ft.*	*Ft. per sec.*	*Sec.-ft.*
April 30	J. E. Degnan	Deer Creek	SW. 15-1-12-4				0.47
June 1	do	do	do				0.08
June 2	do	do	do				0.12
June 20	do	do	do				0.61
June 21	do	do	do				1.19
Aug. 25	F. R. Steinberger	do	do				Nil.
Sept. 4	do	do	do				Nil.
Sept. 17	J. E. Degnan	do	SE. 5-1-12-4				0.38
Sept. 17	do	do	SW. 15-1-12-4				0.03
Oct. 1	do	do	SE. 5-1-12-4				0.39
Oct. 1	do	do	NW. 4-1-12-4				0.34
Oct. 1	do	do	NE. 9-1-12-4				0.16
Oct. 1	do	do	SW. 15-1-12-4	*a*			0.17
Oct. 1	do	do	do	*b*			0.05
Oct. 1	do	do	NW. 15-1-12-4				Nil.
Oct. 17	do	do	SW. 36-1-12-4	9.8	16.5	1.36	22.3

a Measured at south line.
b Measured at north line.

5 GEORGE V, A. 1915

Miscellaneous Discharge Measurements made in Milk River drainage basin, in 1914.

Date.	Engineer.	Stream.	Location.	Width.	Area of Section.	Mean Velocity.	Dis-charge.
				Feet.	Sq. ft.	Ft. per sec.	Sec.-ft.
May 30 ...	J. E. Degnan.....	Bear Gulch Creek.	Sec. 19-2-9-4.....	....	....	....	Nil.
June 10 ...	do	do	do ..	....	....	....	"
June 18 ...	do	do	do ..	....	....	....	"
July 4 ...	do	do	do ..	....	....	....	"
July 25 ...	do	do	do ..	....	....	....	"
Sept. 19 ...	do	do	do ..	....	....	....	"
Sept. 29 ...	do	do	do ..	....	....	....	"
Oct. 17 ...	do	do	do ..	10.5	5.37	2.00	10.8
Oct. 21 ..	do	do	do ..	5.5	2.90	1.31	3.8
April 13 ...	H. W. Rowley....	Dead Horse Coulee	Sec. 4-2-11-4.....	....	....	....	Nil.
April 28 ...	J. E. Degnan.....	do	do	....	....	....	"
May 30 ...	do	do	do	....	....	....	"
June 10 ...	do	do	do	....	....	....	"
June 18 ...	do	do	do	....	....	....	"
July 4 ...	do	do	do	....	....	....	"
July 25 ...	do	do	do	....	....	....	"
Sept. 19 ...	do	do	do	....	....	....	"
Sept. 29 ...	do	do	do	....	....	....	"
Oct. 17 ...	do	do	do	7.0	4.90	1.40	6.80
Oct. 21 ...	do	do	do	3.3	0.90	0.88	0.79
April 13 ...	H. W. Rowley....	Halfbreed Creek...	SW. 28-2-10-4 ...	8.0	5.33	0.76	4.00
April 28 ...	J. E. Degnan.....	do	do	7.0	2.70	0.69	1.71
May 30 ...	do	do	do	....	....	....	Nil.
June 10 ...	do	do	do	....	....	....	"
June 18 ...	do	do	do	8.0	6.50	0.81	5.30
July 4 ...	do	do	do	....	....	....	Nil.
July 25 ...	do	do	do	....	....	....	"
Sept. 19 ...	do	do	do	....	....	....	"
Sept. 29 ...	do	do	do	....	....	....	"
Oct. 17 ...	do	do	do	29.5	18.9	1.92	36.0
Oct. 21 ...	do	do	do	25.0	13.0	0.85	11.0
June 26 ...	do	Mackie Creek.....	SW. 19-2-18-4 ...	....	12" Weir	....	0.10
Sept. 11 ..	F. R. Steinberger..	do	do	....	....	....	Nil.
Oct. 14 ...	J. E. Degnan.....	do	do	4.5	0.67	0.52	0.35
Oct. 26 ...	do	do	do	3.0	0.50	0.64	0.32
Aug. 18 ...	do	Milk River.......	NW. 20-2-8-4....	17.0	4.25	0.62	2.60
April 13 ...	H. W. Rowley....	Miners Coulee....	SW. 10-2-11-4 ...	5.0	1.90	0.74	1.41
April 28 ...	J. E. Degnan.....	do	do	....	15" Weir	....	0.07
May 30 ...	do	do	do	....	....	....	Nil.
June 10 ..	do	do	do	....	....	....	"
June 18 ...	do	do	do	....	....	....	"
July 4 ...	do	do	do	....	....	....	"
July 25 ...	do	do	do	....	....	....	"
Sept. 19 ...	do	do	do	....	....	....	"
Sept. 29 ...	do	do	do	....	....	....	"
Oct. 17 ...	do	do	do	18.0	16.20	1.64	26.60
Oct. 21 ...	do	do	do	11.5	6.05	1.10	6.64
May 1 ...	do	Police Creek.....	SW. 35-1-13-4 ...	3.0	0.78	0.45	0.35
June 9 ...	do	do	do	....	....	....	Nil.
Sept. 16 ...	do	do	do	....	....	....	"
Oct. 2 ...	do	do	do	....	....	....	"
Oct. 16 ...	do	do	do	7.5	8.35	0.96	8.03
April 11 ...	do	Red Creek.......	Sec. 18-1-15-4....	....	....	....	Nil.
July 28 ...	do	do	do	....	....	....	"
July 21 ...	do	do	do	....	12" Weir	....	0.11
Sept. 30 ...	do	Spring Creek.....	SE. 3-1-12-4......	....	12" Weir	....	0.13
Sept. 17 ...	do	do	do	....	....	....	
Oct. 22 ...	do	do	NE. 11-1-12-4 ...	1.4	0.69	0.41	0.28

PAKOWKI *LAKE* DRAINAGE BAS*IN*.

General Description.

The drainage into Pakowki Lake comes from three different directions: from the west by way of *E*tzikom Coulee, from the southeast through Canal and *K*etchum Creeks, and from the northeast through Manyberries and Irrigation Creeks. The streams within this drainage basin are very similar in their general characteristics, all having narrow, deep and well-defined valleys, with spare growth of brush along the bottoms, and draining a sandy and very unproductive soil. The drainage consists almost entirely of the spring run-off, the soil being so devoid of moisture as to take care of any ordinary rainfall, except during periods of exceptional heavy rains. Most of the land drained by Canal Creek is gumbo; at its source the land is broken and unproductive, locally known as "bad lands," and any ordinary rain will start the creek to flow.

Two gauging stations have been established in this drainage basin, one on Manyberries Creek at Hooper and Huckvale's ranch. Several measurements of the spring run-off were made in 1914. On April 16, 1914, a station was established on *E*tzikom Coulee. Owing to the very dry season very little data were collected.

Messrs. Hooper and Huckvale have constructed efficient irrigation works, and divert water from Manyberries Creek to irrigate 2,760 acres of hay meadow.

ETZIKOM COULEE NEAR STIRLING.

Location.—On road allowance between SW. ¼ Sec. 3 and SE. ¼ Sec. 4, Tp. 7, Rge. 19, W. 4th Mer., at the highway bridge one mile north and east of Stirling.

Records available.—May 1, 1914, to October 31, 1914.

Drainage area.—The run-off of this coulee during 1914 was practically all overflow of the Alberta Railway and *I*rrigation Company's irrigation ditch, with the exception of the period from October 4 to 31, when there was some run-off from melting snow.

Gauge.—Vertical staff, fastened to bridge pile on the upstream side; elevation of zero of gauge maintained at 93.43 feet.

Bench-mark.—The head of a spike driven into the northeast corner of the bridge abutment; assumed elevation, 100.00 feet.

Channel.—Composed of clay, and liable to be affected by the growth of weeds in the bed.

Discharge measurements.—Made from the bridge, by wading or with a weir.

Observer.—F. Adler.

DISCHARGE MEASUREMENTS of *E*tzikom Coulee near Stirling, in 1914.

Date.	Engineer.	Width.	Area of Section.	Mean Velocity.	Gauge Height.	Discharge.
		Feet.	*Sq. ft.*	*Ft. per sec.*	*Feet.*	*Sec.-ft.*
April 16	J. E. Degnan	....	....	....	1.50	0.03b
May 4...........	do	....	....	....	....	Nil.
May 22...........	do	2.5	0.72	0.40	1.47	0.29a
June 4...........	do	....	....	....	....	Nil.
July 16	do	6.0	1.60	0.49	1.93	0.79a
Oct. 12...........	do	....	....	....	1.70	0.25b

a Measured below bridge.
b Discharge estimated.

No. 25c—20

5 GEORGE V, A. 1915

DAILY GAUGE HEIGHT AND DISCHARGE of *E*tzikom Coulee near Stirling, for 1914.

DAY.	May.		June.		July.		August.		September.		October.	
	Gauge Height.	Dis-charge	Gauge Height.	Dis-charge	Gauge Height.	Dis-charge	Gauge Height.	Dis-charge	Gauge Height.	Dis-charge	Gauge Height.	Dis-charge.
	Feet.	*Sec.-ft.*	*Feet.*	*Sec.-ft.*	*Feet.*	*Sec.-ft.*	*Feet.*	*Sec.-ft.*	*Feet.*	*Sec.-ft.*	*Feet.*	*Sec.-ft.*
1	Dry.	Nil.	Dry.	Nil.	Dry.	Nil.	Dry.	Nil.	2.90	5.90	2.00	1.00
2	"	"	"	"	"	"	"	"	2 87	5.70	1.60	0.15
3	"	"	"	"	"	"	"	"	2.85	5.50	1 80	0.55
4	"	"	"	"	"	"	"	"	2.66	4.20	1.83	0.61
5	"	"	"	"	"	"	"	"	2.50	3.20	1.97	0.91
6	2.98	6.50	"	"	"	"	"	"	2.53	3.50	2 00	1.00
7	2.05	1.15	2.25	1 90	"	"	"	"	2.55	3.50	2.12	1 38
8	1 65	0.25	1.82	0.59	"	"	"	"	2.56	3.60	2.00	1.00
9	2.65	4.10	1.55	0.10	1.76	0.47	"	"	2.62a	3.90	1.93	0.81
10	2.31	2.10	2.00	1.00	2.20	1.70	2.85	5.50	2.67	4.20	1.80	0.55
11	1.96	0.88	1.76	0.47	1.90	0.75	1.76	0.47	2.70	4.40	1.72	0 39
12	1.70	0.35	Dry.	Nil.	1.78	0.51	1.60	0.15	2.72	4.60	1.70	0.35
13	1 68	0.31	"	"	1 60	0.15	Dry.	Nil.	2.68	4.30	1.74	0.43
14	1.58	0 13	"	"	Dry.	Nil.	"	"	2.39	2.50	1.78	0 51
15	1.60	0.15	"	"	"	"	"	"	2.70	4.40	1.80	0.55
16	1.66	0.27	"	"	2.50	3.20	1.85	0.65	2.25	1.90	1.71	0 37
17	1.72	0.39	"	"	2 00	1.00	1.90	0.75	2.28	2 00	1.68	0 31
18	1.70	0.35	"	"	1.90	0.75	2.00	1.00	2.30	2.10	1.62	0 19
19	1.68	0.31	"	"	1.62	0.19	2.30	2.10	2.30	2.10	1.60	0 15
20	1.66	0.27	"	"	1.51	0 06	2.70	4.40	2.32	2.20	1.58	0.13
21	1.53	0.08	"	"	Dry.	Nil.	3.00	6.70	2.20	1.70	1.52	0.07
22	1.50	0.05	"	"	"	"	3.25	8.90	2.10	1.30	1 50	0 05
23	Dry.	Nil.	"	"	"	"	3.50	11.50	2.50	3.20	Dry.	Nil.
24	"	"	"	"	"	"	3.70	14.10	1.70	0.35	"	"
25	"	"	"	"	"	"	3.40	10.40	1.62	0.19	"	"
26	"	"	"	"	"	"	3.36	10.00	Dry.	Nil.	"	"
27	"	"	2.20	1.70	"	"	2.91	6.00	"	"	"	"
28	"	"	1.57	0.12	"	"	2.00	1.00	2 21	1.74	"	"
29	"	"	1.51	0.06	"	"	1.98	0.94	2.90	5.90	"	"
30	"	"	Dry.	Nil.	"	"	2 85	5.50	3.26	9.20	"	"
31	"	"	"	"	"	"	2.87	5.70	"	"	"	"

a Gauge height interpolated.

MONTHLY DISCHARGE of *E*tzikom Coulee near Stirling, in 1914.

(Drainage area 203 square miles.)

MONTH.	DISCHARGE IN SECOND-FEET.				RUN-OFF.	
	Maximum.	Minimum	Mean.	Per square Mile	Depth in inches on Drainage Area.	Total in Acre-feet.
May	6.50	0.00	0.57	....	....	35
June	1.90	0.00	0.20	....	....	12
July	3.20	0.00	0.28	....	....	17
August	14.10	0.00	3.10	....	....	191
September	9.20	0.00	3.20	....	....	190
October	1.38	0.00	0.37	....	....	23

NOTE.—This water is overflow of the A. R. & I. irrigation ditch near Stirling.

MANYBERRIES CREEK AT HOOPER AND HUCKVALE'S RANCH.

Location.—On the SW. ¼ Sec. 27, Tp. 4, Rge. 6, W. 4th Mer.
Records available.—April 1, 1911, to October 31, 1914.
Drainage area.—142 square miles.
Gauge.—Vertical staff; maintained at the original elevation of 87.00 feet.
Bench-mark.—Permanent iron bench-mark; assumed elevation, 100.00 feet.
Channel.—The stream flows in one channel except in very high stages; bed consists of sand, clay and gravel.

Discharge measurements.—At low stages, made by wading; at high stages, a portable cable and cable car is used.

Diversions.—Hooper and Huckvale's north ditch diverts water about one-half mile above this station, and the south ditch about one-half mile below.

Observer.—Sidney Hooper.

Remarks.—Hooper and Huckvale's north ditch is included in the run-off at this station.

DISCHARGE MEASUREMENTS of Manyberries Creek at Hooper and Huckvale's Ranch, in 1914.

Date.	Engineer.	Width.	Area of Section.	Mean Velocity.	Gauge Height.	Discharge.
		Feet.	*Sq. ft.*	*Ft. per sec.*	*Feet.*	*Sec.-ft.*
Mar. 31........ ..	H. W. Rowley..	15.0	18.70	0 78	3.60	14.50a
Mar. 31..	do	....	....	....	5.29	93.00b
April 8.	do	12.0	6.20	1.70	2.48	10.50
April 9	do	6.0	1.50	0.70	1.96	1.05
April 9.	do	8.0	3.60	1.92	2.30	6.90
April 19............	H. R. Carscallen.....	3.2	0.63	0.45	1.74	0.30
April 27............	J. E. Degnan...............	....	....	....	1.66	0.05
June 12........ ..	do	....	....	....	....	Nil.
July 10.....	do	....	....	....	....	"
Aug. 14	do	....	....	....	....	"
Aug. 28............	F. R. Steinberger.	....	....	....	....	"
Sept. 24............	J. E. Degnan...............	....	....	....	....	"

a Measurement affected by ice.
b Measured one mile and one-half upstream.

DAILY GAUGE HEIGHT AND DISCHARGE of Manyberries Creek at Hooper and Huckvale's Ranch, for 1914.

DAY.	March.		April.		May.		June.	
	Gauge Height.	Dis- charge.	Gauge Height.	Dis- charge.	Gauge Height.	Dis- charge.	Gauge Height.	Dis- charge.
	Feet.	*Sec.-ft.*	*Feet.*	*Sec.-ft.*	*Feet.*	*Sec.-ft.*	*Feet.*	*Sec.-ft.*
1	.... .	....	5.00	84.00	Dry.	Nil.	Dry.	Nil.
2			4.74	76.00	"	"	"	"
3	. ...	....	3.96	51.00	"	"	"	"
4	....	....	4.30	62.00	"	"	"	"
5		....	4.96	83.00	"	"	"	"
6	2.92	22.00	4.74	76.00	" .	"	3.81	47.0
7	2.27	6.40	3.22	30.00	"	"	3.75	45.0
8	2.30	6.90	2.28	6.50	"	"	1.90	1.4
9	2.84	19.50	2.17	4.70	"	"	Dry.	Nil.
10	3.09	26.00	2.02	2.70	"	"	"	"
11	2.44	9.70	2.06	3.20	"	"	"	"
12	2.58	12.90	1.92	1.58	"	"	"	"
13	4.08	55.00	2.69	15.60	"	"	"	"
14	5.00	84.00	3.04	25.00	"	"	"	"
15	3.49	38.00	3.04	25.00	"	"	"	"
16	3.25	31.00	2.46	10.10	"	"	"	"
17	3.05	25.00	2.19	5.00	"	"	"	"
18	2.92	22.00	2.11	3.80	"	"	"	"
19	2.14	4.30	1.76	0.46	"	"	"	"
20	2.13	4.10	1.62	Nil.	"	"	"	"
21	2.04	3.00	1.54	"	"	"	"	"
22	1.89	1.32	1.54	"	"	"	"	"
23	1.82	0.82	Dry.	"	"	"	"	"
24	1.79	0.64	"	"	"	"	"	"
25	Dry.	Nil.	"	"	"	"	"	"
26	"	"	"	"	"	"	"	"
27	"	"	1.66	0.04	"	"	2.01	2.6
28	"	"	Dry.	Nil.	"	"	Dry.	Nil.
29	" ..		"	"	"	"	"	"
30	1.93	1.67	"	"	"	"	"	"
31	4.46	67.00	......	....	"	"	....	....

5 GEORGE V, A. 1915

DAILY GAUGE HEIGHT AND DISCHARGE of Manyberries Creek at Hooper and Huckvale's Ranch, for 1914.—*Concluded.*

DAY.	July.		August.		September.		October.	
	Gauge Height.	Dis-charge.	Gauge Height.	Dis-charge.	Gauge Height.	Dis-charge.	Gauge Height.	Dis-charge.
	Feet.	*Sec.-ft.*	*Feet.*	*Sec.-ft.*	*Feet.*	*Sec.-ft.*	*Feet.*	*Sec.-ft.*
1	Dry.	Nil.	Dry.	Nil.	Dry.	Nil.	Dry.	Nil.
2	"	"	"	"	"	"	"	"
3	"	"	"	"	"	"	"	"
4	"	"	"	"	"	"	"	"
5	"	"	"	"	"	"	"	"
6	"	"	"	"	"	"	"	"
7	"	"	"	"	"	"	"	"
8	"	"	"	"	"	"	3.86	48.0
9	"	"	"	"	"	"	4.95	82.0
10	"	"	"	"	"	"	2.94	22.0
11	"	"	"	"	"	"	1.75	0.4
12	"	"	"	"	"	"	Dry.	Nil.
13	"	"	"	"	"	"	"	"
14	"	"	"	"	"	"	"	"
15	"	"	"	"	"	"	"	"
16	"	"	"	"	"	"	"	"
17	"	"	"	"	"	"	"	"
18	"	"	"	"	"	"	"	"
19	"	"	"	"	"	"	"	"
20	"	"	"	"	"	"	"	"
21	"	"	"	"	"	"	"	"
22	"	"	"	"	"	"	"	"
23	"	"	"	"	"	"	"	"
24	"	"	"	"	"	"	"	"
25	"	"	"	"	"	"	"	"
26	"	"	"	"	"	"	"	"
27	"	"	"	"	"	"	"	"
28	"	"	"	"	"	"	"	"
29	"	"	"	"	"	"	"	"
30	"	"	"	"	"	"	"	"
31	"	"	"	"	....	....	"	"

MONTHLY DISCHARGE of Manyberries Creek at Hooper and Huckvale's Ranch, for 1914.

(Drainage area 142 square miles.)

MONTH.	DISCHARGE IN SECOND-FEET.				RUN-OFF.	
	Maximum.	Minimum.	Mean.	Per square Mile.	Depth in inches on Drainage Area.	Total in Acre-feet.
March (6–31)	114.0	0.62	28.00	0.197	0.190	1,444
April	87.0	0.00	23.00	0.162	0.181	1,360
May	....	....	....	....	....	....
June	64.0	0.00	4.70	0 033	0.040	280
July	....	....	....	....	....	....
August	8.6	0.00	0.43	0.003	0.004	26
September	12.1	0.00	0.58	0.004	0.004	34
October	113.0	0.00	8.50	0.060	0.070	523
The period	....	....	....	....	0.488	3,676

NOTE.—This table includes Hooper and Huckvale's north ditch to get the total flow of the creek.

HOOPER AND HUCKVALE NORTH DITCH FROM MANYBERRIES CREEK.

Location.—On SW. ¼ Sec. 27, Tp. 4, Rge. 6, W. 4th Mer.
Records available.—May 2, 1912, to October 31, 1914.
Gauge.—Vertical staff; maintained at the original elevation of 93.35 feet.
Bench-mark.—On the northwest corner of the foundation of the ranch house; assumed elevation, 100.00 feet.
Channel.—One channel at all stages; the bed is composed of clay.
Discharge measurements.—At all stages, with a current-meter, by wading.
Observer.—Sidney Hooper.
Remarks.—1913 discharge taken from the 1914 discharge table.

DISCHARGE MEASUREMENTS of Hooper and Huckvale North Ditch from Manyberries Creek, in 1914.

Date.	Engineer.	Width.	Area of Section.	Mean Velocity.	Gauge Height.	Discharge.
		Feet.	*Sq. ft.*	*Ft. per sec.*	*Feet.*	*Sec.-ft.*
Mar. 21............	H. W. Rowley.............	9.0	10.20	0.68	2.24	7.00
April 6	do	9.5	12.80	0.92	2.45	11.80
April 6	do	10.0	15.70	1.22	2.68	19.10
April 6..........	do	11.4	18.80	1.49	2.95	28.00
April 6..........	do	11.5	19.80	1.55	2.99	31.00
April 6..........	do	7.0	2.10	0.57	1.78	1.19
April 27.........	J. E. Degnan.............	6.0	1.50	0.83	1.84	1.24
July 10......... ..	do	....	....	....	....	Nil.
Sept. 24..........	do	....	....	....	....	

DAILY GAUGE HEIGHT AND DISCHARGE of Hooper and Huckvale North Ditch from Manyberries Creek, for 1914.

DAY.	March.		April.		May.		June.	
	Gauge Height.	Dis-charge.	Gauge Height.	Dis-charge.	Gauge Height.	Dis-charge.	Gauge Height.	Dis-charge.
	Feet.	*Sec.-ft.*	*Feet.*	*Sec.-ft.*	*Feet.*	*Sec.-ft.*	*Feet.*	*Sec.-ft.*
1...................................	....	....	1.60	Nil.	....	....	....	....
2...................................	....	....	1.62	0.08	....	....	....	....
3...................................	....	....	1.62	0.08	....	....	....	....
4...................................	....	....	1.64	0.16	....	....	....	....
5...................................	....	....	2.04	3.80	....	....	....	....
6...................................	2.90c	27.00	2.42	11.00	....	....	2.46b	12.1
7...................................	2.55	14.80	2.46	12.10	....	....	2.69	19.5
8...................................	2.36	9.50	2.38	10.00	....	....	2.27	7.5
9...................................	2.47	12.40	2.30	8.20	....	....	1.98	3.0
10...................................	2.14	5.20	2.32	8.60	....	....	1.88	1.9
11...................................	2.70	19.80	2.35	9.30	....	....	1.60c	Nil.
12...................................	2.78	23.00	2.34	9.10	....	....	....	....
13...................................	2.89	26.00	2.08	4.30	....	....	....	....
14...................................	2.98	30.00	2.12	4.90	....	....	....	....
15...................................	2.76	22.00	2.05	3.90	....	....	....	....
16...................................	2.37	9.80	2.14	5.20	....	....	....	....
17...................................	2.36	9.50	2.28	7.80	....	....	....	....
18...................................	2.34	9.10	2.22	6.60	....	....	....	....
19...................................	2.52	13.80	2.15	5.30	....	....	....	....
20...................................	2.44	11.50	2.08	4.30	....	....	....	....
21...................................	2.04	3.80	2.08	4.30	....	....	....	....
22...................................	2.25	7.10	2.05	3.90	....	....	....	....
23...................................	2.10	4.60	1.98a	3.00	....	....	....	....
24...................................	2.18	5.80	1.90	2.10	....	....	....	....
25...................................	2.25	7.10	1.85	1.60	....	....	....	....
26...................................	1.87	1.80	1.83	1.44	....	....	....	....
27...................................	1.86	1.70	1.84	1.52	....	....	....	....
28...................................	1.80	1.20	1.60c	Nil.	....	....	....	....
29...................................	1.72	0.62	....	....	....	....	....	....
30...................................	1.78	1.04	....	....	....	....	....	....
31...................................	1.60	Nil.	....	....	....	....	....	....

a Gauge height interpolated.
b Headgate open.
c Headgate closed.

5 GEORGE V, A. 1915

DAILY GAUGE HEIGHT AND DISCHARGE of Hooper and Huckvale North Ditch from Manyberries Creek, for 1914.—*Concluded.*

DAY.	August.		September.		October.	
	Gauge Height.	Dis- charge.	Gauge Height.	Dis- charge.	Gauge Height.	Dis- charge.
	Feet.	*Sec.-ft.*	*Feet.*	*Sec.-ft.*	*Feet.*	*Sec.-ft.*
1						
2						
3						
4						
5						
6						
7						
8					2.80b	23.00
9						31.00a
10						24.00a
11						17.00a
12						10.00a
13					1.98	3.00
14			2.46b	12.10	1.86	1.70
15			2.09	4.50	1.76	0.88
16			1.74	0.74	1.61	0.04
17			1.56c	Nil.	1.59c	Nil.
18						
19						
20						
21						
22						
23						
24						
25						
26						
27	2.32b	8.6				
28	2.10c	4.6				
29						
30						
31						

a Discharge estimated.
b Headgate open.
c Headgate closed.

MONTHLY DISCHARGE of Hooper and Huckvale North Ditch from Manyberries Creek, for 1914

MONTH.	DISCHARGE IN SECOND-FEET.			RUN-OFF
	Maximum.	Minimum.	Mean.	Total in Acre-feet.
March (6–31)	30.0	0.0	10.70	552
April	12.1	0.0	4.40	262
May				Nil.
June	19.5	0.0	1.47	87
July				Nil.
August	8.6	0.0	0.43	26
September	12.1	0.0	0.58	34
October	31.0	0.0	3.60	221
The period				1,182

SESSIONAL PAPER No. 25c

DAILY GAUGE HEIGHT AND DISCHARGE of Hooper and Huckvale North Ditch
from Manyberries Creek, for 1913.

DAY.	March.		April.		May.	
	Gauge Height.	Dis-charge.	Gauge Height.	Dis-charge.	Gauge Height.	Dis-charge.
	Feet.	*Sec.-ft.*	*Feet.*	*Sec.-ft.*	*Feet.*	*Sec.-ft.*
1	......	......	3.76	58.0	1.96	2.70
2	......	......	3.36	44.0	1.95	2.60
3	......	......	3.23	39.0	1.98	3.00
4	......	......	3.30	41.0	2.00	3.20
5	......	......	3.28	41.0	1.95	2.60
6	......	......	3.64	54.0	1.95	2.60
7	2.48a	12.60	3.42	46.0	1.95	2.60
8	2.94	28.00	3.33	42.0	1.94	2.50
9	3.60	52.00	3.26	40.0	1.88	1.90
10	3.24	39.00	3.17	37.0	1.87	1.80
11	3.04	32.00	3.09	34.0	1.83	1.44
12	2.84	25.00	3.20	38.0	1.78	1.04
13	2.58	15.70	3.21	38.0	1.75	0.80
14	2.78	23.00	3.08	33.0	2.62	17.10
15	2.66	18.40	2.88	26.0	2.40	10.50
16	2.10	4.60	2.87	26.0	2.42	11.00
17	1.98	3.00	2.84	25.0	2.20	6.20
18	1.74	0.70	2.70	19.8	1.89	2.00
19	1.60	0.00	2.52	13.8	1.86	1.70
20	2.20b	6.20	2.61	16.7	1.83	1.44
21	......	......	2.52	13.8	1.76	0.88
22	......	......	2.41	10.8	1.75	0.80
23	......	......	2.32	8.6	1.74	0.74
24	......	......	2.24	6.9	1.73	0.68
25	......	......	2.21	6.4	1.69	0.44
26	......	......	2.10	4.6	1.64	0.16
27	......	......	1.95	2.6	1.65	0.20
28	......	......	1.92	2.3	1.65	0.20
29	2.23a	6.70	1.89	2.0	1.64	0.16
30	3.62	53.00	1.95	2.6	1.62	0.08
31	3.92	64.00	......	......	1.54b	0.00

a Headgate opened.
b Headgate closed.

MONTHLY DISCHARGE of Hooper and Huckvale North Ditch from Manyberries Creek,
for 1913.

MONTH.	DISCHARGE IN SECOND-FEET.			RUN-OFF.
	Maximum.	Minimum	Mean.	Total in Acre-feet.
March	64.0	0.0	12.40	762
April	58.0	2.0	26.00	1,547
May	17.1	0.0	2.70	166
The period	....	....	....	2,475

HOOPER AND HUCKVALE SOUTH DITCH FROM MANYBERRIES CREEK.

Location.—On N E. ¼ Sec. 22, Tp. 4, Rge. 6, W. 4th Mer.
Records available.—March 31, 1914, to October 31, 1914.
Gauge.—Vertical staff; maintained at the original elevation of 93.07 feet.
Bench-mark.—The head of a spike driven in the top of a 4″ x 4″ post at the dam, about 70 feet north of gauge rod; assumed elevation, 100.00 feet.
Channel.—The channel is narrow and the banks high; the bed is composed of clay, with a silt and sand wash from the creek.
Discharge measurements.—Measurements are made with a current-meter, by wading.
Diversions.—The water through this ditch is diverted from Manyberries Creek.
Observer.—Sidney Hooper.

MONTHLY DISCHARGE   North.   h from Manyberries Creek, for 1

	DISCHARGE IN SECOND-FEET.			RUN-
	Maximum.	Minimum	Mean.	Total Acre
March 6-31... ..	0 6	0 0	10.70	
April..	12 1	0 0	4.40	
May...	0		1.47	
June...		0 0		
July...	6	0 0	0.43	
August	12 1	0 0	0.58	
September............. ..				
October............ . ..				
The period.....				

DAILY GAUGE HEIGHT AND DISCHARGE
from Manyberries

tachment, for 1911.

	RUN-OFF.	
	Depth in inches on Drainage Area.	Total in Acre-feet.
	0.02	171
	. . . .	0
	. . . .	0
	0.06	560
	. . . .	0
	0.18	1,761
	0.09	855
	0.35	3,347

Detachment, for 1912.

		RUN-OFF.	
	are .	Depth in inches on Drainage Area.	Total in Acre-feet.
	57	0.40	3,999
	25	0.03	286
	22	0.02	243a
	. . . .	0 45	4,528

se Police Detachment,

		RUN-OFF.	
	c square Mile.	Depth in inches on Drainage Area.	Total in Acre-feet.
	0.348	0.39	3,898
	0.072	0.08	830a
	. . . .	0.47	4,728

5 GEORGE V, A. 1915

DISCHARGE MEASUREMENTS of Hooper and Huckvale South Ditch from Manyberries Creek, in 1914.

Date.	Engineer.	Width.	Area of Section.	Mean Velocity.	Gauge Height.	Discharge.
		Feet.	*Sq. ft.*	*Ft. per sec.*	*Feet.*	*Sec.-ft.*
April 4............	H. W. Rowley............	9.0	14.90	1.01	2.73	15.10
April 7	do	9.0	11.20	0.83	2.32	9.30
April 9......... ...	do	2.5	0.70	0.70	1.12	0.49
April 9	do	3.5	1.45	0.83	1.30	1.21
Sept. 24.......	J. E. Degnan.............	....	....	....	....	Nil.

DAILY GAUGE HEIGHT AND DISCHARGE of Hooper and Huckvale South Ditch from Manyberries Creek, for 1914.

DAY.	March.		April.		May.		June.	
	Gauge Height.	Dis-charge.	Gauge Height.	Dis-charge.	Gauge Height.	Dis-charge.	Gauge Height.	Dis-charge.
	Feet.	*Sec.-ft.*	*Feet.*	*Sec.-ft.*	*Feet.*	*Sec.-ft.*	*Feet.*	*Sec.-ft.*
1...	....	....	3.00a	19.5	....	....	....	....
2...	....	....	3.60a	30.0	....	....	....	....
3...	....	....	3.60a	30.0	....	....	....	....
4...	....	....	2.73	15.2	....	....	....	....
5...	....	....	2.59b	13.1	....	....	....	....
6...	....	....	2.45b	11.1	....	....	....	....
7...	....	....	2.32	9.4	....	....	2.87c	17.30
8...	....	....	1.82b	4.4	....	....	1.74	3.80
9...	....	....	1.30d	1.2	....	....	1.04d	0.28
10...	....	....	....	....	....	....	....	....
11...	....	....	....	....	....	....	....	....
12...	....	....	....	....	....	....	....	....
13...	....	....	....	....	....	....	....	....
14...	....	....	....	....	....	....	....	....
15...	....	....	....	....	....	....	....	....
16...	....	....	....	....	....	....	....	....
17...	....	....	....	....	....	....	....	....
18...	....	....	....	....	....	....	....	....
19...	....	....	....	....	....	....	....	....
20...	....	....	....	....	....	....	....	....
21...	....	....	....	....	....	....	....	....
22...	....	....	....	....	....	....	....	....
23...	....	....	....	....	....	....	....	....
24...	....	....	....	....	....	....	....	....
25...	....	....	....	....	....	....	....	....
26...	....	....	....	....	....	....	....	....
27...	....	....	....	....	....	....	1.28cd	1.12
28...	....	....	....	....	....	....	....	....
29...	....	....	....	....	....	....	....	....
30...	....	....	....	....	....	....	....	....
31...	2.00a	5.9c	....	....	....	....	....	....

a Gauge heights obtained from marks on bank.
b Gauge height interpolated.
c Headgate open.
d Headgate closed.

SESSIONAL PAPER No. 25c

DAILY GAUGE HEIGHT AND DISCHARGE of Hooper and Huckvale South Ditch
from Manyberries Creek, for 1914.

DAY.	July.		August.		September.		October.	
	Gauge Height.	Dis-charge.	Gauge Height.	Dis-charge.	Gauge Height.	Dis-charge.	Gauge Height.	Dis-charge.
	Feet.	*Sec.-ft.*	*Feet.*	*Sec.-ft.*	*Feet.*	*Sec.-ft.*	*Feet.*	*Sec.-ft.*
1								
2								
3								
4								
5								
6								
7								
8								2.46b	11.2
9							3.05	20.0
10								12.0a
11								20.0a
12							c	
13								
14								
15								
16								
17								
18								
19								
20								
21								
22								
23								
24								
25								
26								
27								
23								
29								
30								
31								

a Discharge estimated.
e Headgate opened.
c Headgate closed.

MONTHLY DISCHARGE of Hooper and Huckvale South Ditch from Manyberries Creek, for 1914.

MONTH.	DISCHARGE IN SECOND-FEET.			RUN-OFF.
	Maximum	Minimum	Mean.	Total in Acre-feet.
March (31)	5.9	5.9	5.90	12
April	30.0	0.0	4.50	268
May				Nil.
June	17.3	0.0	0.77	46
July				Nil.
August				"
September				"
October	20.0	0.0	1.46	90
The period				416

5 GEORGE V, A. 1915

MISCELLANEOUS DISCHARGE MEASUREMENTS made in Pakowki Lake drainage basin, in 1914.

Date.	Engineer.	Stream.	Location.	Width.	Area of Section.	Mean Velocity.	Dis-charge.
				Feet.	*Sq. ft.*	*Ft. per sec.*	*Sec.-ft.*
Mar. 21....	H. W. Rowley....	Canal Creek.....	SW. ¼ 6-4-6-4.. ..	2.6	5.98	0.69	4.10
Mar. 28....	do	do	do				Nil.
April 3 ...	do	do	do	8.5	8.63	0.54	4.60
April 11...	do	do	do				Nil.
April 27....	J. E. Degnan....	do	do				"
June 15....	do	do	Sec. 28-3-6-4. ..	6.0	3.30	0.81	2.70
July 8....	do	do	do				Nil.
Aug. 14....	do	do	do				"
Sept. 24....	do	do	do				"
April 2....	H. W. Rowley....	Irrigation Creek...	SW. 36-5-7-4.....	12.5	7.80	1.12	8.70
April 8....	do	do	do	3.8	1.25	0.78	0.98
Mar. 21....	do	Ketchum Creek...	SW. 14-4-6-4.....				2.00a
Mar. 28....	do	do	do				Nil.
Mar. 31....	do	do	SE. 15-4-6-4.....				2.67
April 3....	do	do	SW. 36-4-7-4.....	15.0	11.6	0.97	11.20
April 11...	do	do	SE. 16-4-6-4.....				Nil.
April 7....	do	do	do	15 "	Weir.		0.25
April 27....	J. E. Degnan.....	do	do				Nil.
June 15....	do	do	do				"
July 8....	do	do	do				"
Aug. 14....	do	do	do				"
Sept. 24....	do	do	do				"

a Estimated.

SAGE CREEK DRAINAGE BASIN.

General Description.

Sage Creek is a small and unimportant stream, which rises in Township 5, Range 4, West of the 4th Meridian, and flows southerly, crossing the international boundary in Range 2.

The stream has no definite or permanent source of supply, and derives its discharge principally from the melting of snow, which accumulates in numerous coulees during the winter months. The period of flow, therefore, is in general confined to the spring months, while the melting snow is passing off. Very heavy rains sometimes cause a flow, but, the drainage area being absolutely devoid of tree growth, the run-off is very rapid.

After entering the United States, Sage Creek spreads out over a large, dry lake, which has no outlet. This lake is about ten miles long and averages one and a half miles in width, and lies close to the boundary. The lake is bounded on the south by a low range of hills, and at some time has held two or three feet of water at its deepest parts. Since 1908 there has been no water in the lake.

SAGE CREEK AT WILD HORSE POLICE DETACHMENT.

Location.—On the *NE.* ¼ Sec. 9, Tp. 1, Rge. 2, W. 4th Mer., near Wild Horse police detachment.

Records available.—Estimated discharge records are available for 1910-13.

Gauge.—Vertical staff; zero of gauge maintained at 93.36 feet since establishment.

Bench-mark.—Permanent iron bench-mark; assumed elevation, 100.00 feet.

Discharge measurements.—Made by wading or with a weir.

Channel.—Composed of hard clay and well grassed over; practically permanent.

Observer.—No records of gauge heights were obtained in 1914, although there was a flow for about a week in the fall.

ESTIMATED MONTHLY DISCHARGE of Sage Creek near Wild Horse Police Detachment, for 1910.

(Drainage area 188 square miles.)

MONTH.	DISCHARGE IN SECOND-FEET.				RUN-OFF.	
	Maximum.	Minimum	Mean.	Per square Mile.	Depth in inches on Drainage Area.	Total in Acre-feet.
March (17-31).	89.0	3.3	42.1	0 224	0.12	1,252
April................................	2.8	Nil.	....	....	....	..........a
The period.............................	....	....	....	....	0.12	1,252

a No flow after April.

SESSIONAL PAPER No. 25c

ESTIMATED MONTHLY DISCHARGE of Sage Creek near Wild Horse Police Detachment, for 1911.

(Drainage area 188 square miles.)

MONTH.	DISCHARGE IN SECOND-FEET.				RUN-OFF.	
	Maximum.	Minimum	Mean.	Per square Mile.	Depth in inches on Drainage Area.	Total in Acre-feet.
April	10.5	Nil.	2.88	0.015	0.02	171
May						0
June						0
July	59	Nil.	9.10	0.049	0.06	560
August						0
September	172	Nil.	29.60	0.158	0.18	1,761
October	50	"	13.90	0.074	0.09	855
The period					0.35	3,347

ESTIMATED MONTHLY DISCHARGE of Sage Creek near Wild Horse Police Detachment, for 1912.

(Drainage area 188 square miles.)

MONTH.	DISCHARGE IN SECOND-FEET.				RUN-OFF.	
	Maximum.	Minimum.	Mean.	Per square Mile.	Depth in inches on Drainage Area.	Total in Acre-feet.
April	170.0	6.5	67.20	0.357	0.40	3,999
May	11.5	Nil.	4.65	0.025	0.03	286
June	17.5	"	4.08	0.022	0.02	243a
The period					0.45	4,528

a No flow after June.

ESTIMATED MONTHLY DISCHARGE of Sage Creek near Wild Horse Police Detachment, for 1913.

(Drainage area 188 square miles.)

MONTH.	DISCHARGE IN SECOND-FEET.				RUN-OFF.	
	Maximum	Minimum.	Mean.	Per square Mile.	Depth in inches on Drainage Area.	Total in Acre-feet.
April	142.0	7.2	65.5	0.348	0.39	3,898
May	8.0	0.5	13.5	0.072	0.08	830a
The period					0.47	4,728

a No flow after May.

5 GEORGE V, A. 1915

LODGE CREEK DRAINAGE BASIN.

General Description.

Lodge Creek, which rises in Township 7, Range 3, West of the 4th Meridian, flows in a southerly direction for about twelve miles, then turns southeastward, crosses the international boundary in Section 4, Township 1, Range 28, West of the 3rd Meridian, and eventually empties into Milk River at Chinook, Montana. Its principal tributary is Middle Creek, which joins it in Section 4, Township 2, Range 29, West of the 3rd Meridian.

Near its head the valley is very deep and narrow, but it broadens out considerably lower down, giving rise to large flats and meadows. The upper part of the drainage basin is cut up to a great extent by deep coulees, which drain into the creek. This part of the creek is thickly covered with brush along the banks, but lower down it is totally devoid of tree growth. The valley is rather unproductive, owing to the absence of moisture, but a few good hay meadows have been developed along its course through the storage of the flood waters, and their application to the soil by irrigation. As is the case with many of the streams in this locality, the flow in Lodge Creek is not continuous throughout the year, the creek being dry, with the exception of pools of standing water, during the greater part of the summer months. At flood stages the creek carries a considerable amount of water, and as a result its channel is wide and well defined throughout the whole length of its course.

Three stations have been established on the main stream—at Willow Creek police detachment, near the international boundary; at Hartt's ranch, near the head of the creek; and about midway between these last two at Hester's ranch, near the 4th Meridian. Descriptions of these stations are given below.

EAST BRANCH OF LODGE CREEK AT ENGLISH'S RANCH.

Location.—On the SE. ¼ Sec. 1, Tp. 7, Rge. 3, W. 4th Mer., at James English's ranch.
Records available.—October 7, 1911, to October 31, 1914.
Gauge.—Vertical staff; elevation of zero maintained at 95.38 feet during 1911; 94.43 feet during 1912; 95.35 feet during 1913-14.
Bench-mark.—Permanent iron bench-mark; assumed elevation, 100.00 feet.
Channel.—Not likely to shift except during floods.
Discharge measurements.—Made by wading, or with weir.
Winter flow.—Station discontinued during winter season.
Diversions.—Water is diverted for irrigation, about three miles above this station, by James English.
Observer.—Mrs. Annie English.

DISCHARGE MEASUREMENTS of East Branch of Lodge Creek at English's Ranch, in 1914.

Date.	Engineer.	Width.	Area of Section.	Mean Velocity.	Gauge Height.	Discharge.
		Feet.	*Sq. ft.*	*Ft. per sec.*	*Feet.*	*Sec.-ft.*
May 18	H. W. Rowley	.a			1.05	0.81
June 15	do	.a			0.98	0.16
July 6	do				Dry.	Nil.
July 24	do				"	"
Sept. 25	do				"	"
Oct. 20	do	.a			1.12	1.26

a Weir measurement.

SESSIONAL PAPER No. 25c

DAILY GAUGE HEIGHT AND DISCHARGE of *E*ast Branch of Lodge Creek at *E*nglish's Ranch, for 1914.

DAY.	April.		May.		June.	
	Gauge Height.	Dis- charge.	Gauge Height.	Dis- charge.	Gauge Height.	Dis. charge.
	Feet.	*Sec.-ft.*	*Feet.*	*Sec.-ft.*	*Feet.*	*Sec.-ft.*
1	2.40	26.0	1.16	1.90	0.98	0.18
2	2.50	28.0	1.16	1.90	0.98	0.18
3	2.60	30.0	1.14	1.62	1.00	0.28
4	2.78	34.0	1.14	1.62	1.00	0.28
5	2.72	32.0	1.10	1.16	1.02	0.44
6	2.77	33.0	1.15	1.74	1.00	0.28
7	1.90	16.2	1.17	2.00	1.02	0.44
8	1.48	7.5	1.23	2.90	1.06	0.78
9	1.46	7.3	1.80	14.20	1.06	0.78
10	1.52	8.6	1.68	11.80	1.10	1.16
11	1.58	9.8	1.50	8.20	1.16	1.89
12	2.23	23.0	1.40	6.20	1.18	2.15
13	2.30	24.0	1.35	5.20	1.20	2.40
14	1.74	13.0	1.28	3.80	1.18	2.15
15	1.90	16.2	1.15	1.74	1.17	2.00
16	1.80	14.2	1.10	1.16	1.15	1.74
17	1.72	12.6	1.10	1.16	1.13	1.51
18	1.70	12.2	1.05	0.68	1.10	1.16
19	1.65	11.2	1.05	0.68	1.10	1.16
20	1.55	9.2	1.03	0.52	1.08	0.97
21	1.50	8.2	1.00	0.28	1.00	0.28
22	1.45	7.2	1.00	0.28	1.00	0.28
23	1.40	6.2	1.00	0.28	0.98	0.18
24	1.38	5.5	0.95	0.04	0.98	0.18
25	1.30	4.2	0.95	0.04	1.00	0.28
26	1.25	3.2	0.95	0.04	1.00	0.28
27	1.23	2.9	0.95	0.04	0.98	0.18
28	1.23	2.9	0.95	0.04	0.95	0.04
29	1.20	2.4	0.95	0.04	0.95	0.04
30	1.16	1.9	0.95	0.04	0.95	0.04
31	....	....	0.95	0.04	....	......

5 GEORGE V, A. 1915

DAILY GAUGE HEIGHT AND DISCHARGE of East Branch of Lodge Creek at English's Ranch, for 1914.—*Concluded.*

DAY.	July.		August.		September.		October.	
	Gauge Height.	Dis- charge.	Gauge Height.	Dis- charge.	Gauge Height.	Dis- charge.	Gauge Height.	Dis- charge.
	Feet.	*Sec.-ft.*	*Feet.*	*Sec.-ft.*	*Feet.*	*Sec.-ft.*	*Feet.*	*Sec.-ft.*
1	0.93	Nil	Dry	Nil	Dry	Nil	Dry	Nil
2	0.90	"	"	"	"	"	"	"
3	0.85	"	"	"	"	"	"	"
4	0.80	"	"	"	"	"	"	"
5	Dry.	"	"	"	"	"	"	"
6	"	"	"	"	"	"	"	"
7	"	"	"	"	"	"	"	"
8	"	"	"	"	"	"	"	"
9	"	"	"	"	"	"	"	"
10	"	"	"	"	"	"	"	"
11	"	"	"	"	"	"	"	"
12	"	"	"	"	"	"	"	"
13	"	"	"	"	"	"	"	"
14	"	"	"	"	"	"	1.75	13.20
15	"	"	"	"	"	"	1.75	13.20
16	"	"	"	"	"	"	1.73	12.80
17	"	"	"	"	"	"	1.70	12.20
18	"	"	"	"	"	"	1.65	11.20
19	"	"	"	"	"	"	1.60	10.20
20	"	"	"	"	"	"	1.50	8.20
21	"	"	"	"	"	"	1.40	6.20
22	"	"	"	"	"	"	1.30	4.20
23	"	"	"	"	"	"	1.20	2.40
24	"	"	"	"	"	"	1.10	1.16
25	"	"	"	"	"	"	1.00	0.28
26	"	"	"	"	"	"	0.90	Nil.
27	"	"	"	"	"	"	0.90	"
28	"	"	"	"	"	"	0.88	"
29	"	"	"	"	"	"	0.88	"
30	"	"	"	"	"	"	0.88	"
31	"	"	"	"	"	"	0.88	"

MONTHLY DISCHARGE of East Branch of Lodge Creek at English's Ranch, for 1914.

(Drainage area 16 square miles.)

MONTH.	DISCHARGE IN SECOND-FEET.				RUN-OFF.	
	Maximum.	Minimum	Mean.	Per square Mile.	Depth in inches on Drainage Area.	Total in Acre-feet.
April	34.00	1.90	13.80	0.860	0.960	821
May	14.20	0.04	2.30	0.144	0.170	141
June	2.40	0.04	0.79	0.049	0.060	47
July						Nil.
August						"
September						"
October	13.20	0.00	3.07	0.191	0.220	189
The period					1.410	1,198

ANDERSON DITCH FROM EAST BRANCH OF LODGE CREEK.

Location.—On the SW. ¼ Sec. 23, Tp. 6, Rge. 3, W. 4th Mer., at the intake of Robert Anderson's ditch near Thelma.

Records available.—For the irrigation seasons of 1912-14.

Gauge.—Vertical staff; zero of gauge maintained at an elevation of 98.63 feet during 1912; 98.64 feet during 1913-14.

Bench-mark.—Wooden stake; assumed elevation, 100.00 feet.

Discharge measurements.—Made by wading, or with a weir.

Observer.—Robt. Anderson.

Remarks.—No water was diverted for irrigation during 1914.

LODGE CREEK AT HARTT'S RANCH.

Location.—On the NW. ¼ Sec. 10, Tp. 6, Rge. 3, W. 4th Mer., at *Ed.* Hartt's ranch.

Records available.—July 22, 1909, to October 31, 1914.

Gauge.—Vertical staff; elevation of zero maintained at 86.36 feet during 1911-12; 83.33 feet during 1913-14.

Bench-mark.—Permanent iron bench-mark; assumed elevation, 100.00 feet.

Channel.—Covered with a heavy growth of willow brush.

Discharge measurements.—Made by wading, or with a weir.

Winter flow.—Station discontinued during winter season.

Artificial control.—There are several small beaver dams near this station.

Diversions.—Water is diverted for irrigation above this station by *Ed.* Hartt and Anderson Brothers.

Observer.—Mrs. Clara B. Hartt.

DISCHARGE MEASUREMENTS of Lodge Creek at Hartt's Ranch, in 1914.

Date.	Engineer.	Width.	Area of Section.	Mean Velocity.	Gauge Height.	Discharge.
		Feet.	*Sq. ft.*	*Ft. per sec.*	*Feet.*	*Sec.-ft.*
April 16	H. R. Carscallen	10.7	39	1 08	5.04	42.00
May 18	H. W. Rowley				1.66	0.98
June 16	do				1.59	0.65
July 6	do				Dry.	Nil.
July 30	do				"	"
Aug. 25	do				"	"
Sept. 25	do				"	"
Oct. 21	do				1.85	0.32

DAILY GAUGE HEIGHT AND DISCHARGE of Lodge Creek at Hartt's Ranch, for 1914.

DAY.	March.		April.		May.		June.	
	Gauge Height.	Dis-charge.	Gauge Height.	Dis-charge.	Gauge Height.	Dis-charge.	Gauge Height.	Dis-charge.
	Feet.	*Sec.-ft.*	*Feet.*	*Sec.-ft.*	*Feet.*	*Sec.-ft.*	*Feet.*	*Sec.-ft.*
1			3.55	15.6	1.84a	1.55	1.00	Nil.
2			6.70	93.0	1.84a	1.55	1.10	"
3			6.20	77.0	1.84a	1.55	1.50	0.32
4			6.88	100.0	1.84	1.55	1.65	0.84
5			7.95	140.0	2.20	3.10	1.66	0.88
6			7.28	115.0	2.15	2.80	2.30	3.70
7			5.10	45.0	2.30	3.70	1.95	1.98
8			5.15	46.0	2.46	4.70	1.95	1.98
9			4.85	38.0	3.85	19.80	1.90	1.78
10			4.88	39.0	3.83	19.40	2.30	3.70
11			4 66	34.0	3.00	9.40	2.25	3.40
12			5 39	56.0	2.15	5.00	1.60	0.66
13			5 75	63.0	2.15	2.80	2.15	2.80
14	6 75	95 00	5.70	61.0	2.05	2.38	1.75	1.21
15	7 80	134 00	5 45	58.0	1.90	1.78	1.59	0.62
16	5.55	62.00	5.10	45.0	1.85	1.59	1.55	0.48
17	4.72	35.00	5.18	47.0	1.75	1.21	1.50	0.32
18	3.70	17.60	4.80	37.0	1.70	1.02	1.50	0.32
19	3.00	9.40	3.98	22.0	1.55	0.48	1.50	0.32
20	3.00	9.40	3.27	12.3	1.55	0.48	1.40	0.08
21	3.00	9.40	3.13a	10.7	1.55	0.48	Dry.	Nil.
22	3.00	9.40	3.00	9.4	1.55	0.48	"	"
23	3.00	9.40	3.15	11.0	1.55	0.48	"	"
24	3.00	9.40	3.25	12.1	1.53	0.42	"	"
25	3.00	9.40	2.90	8.4	1.53	0.42	"	"
26	3.00	9.40	2.50	5.00	1.50	0.32	"	"
27	3.00	9.40	2.40	4.30	1.21	Nil.	"	"
28	3.00	9.40	1.84	1.55	1.10	"	"	"
29	3.00	9.40	1.84	1.55	1.00	"	"	"
30	3.00	9.40	1.84	1.55	1.00	"	"	"
31	3.40	13.80			0.90	"		

a Gauge heights interpolated.

5 GEORGE V. A. 1915

DAILY GAUGE HEIGHT AND DISCHARGE of Lodge Creek at Hartt's Ranch, for 1914.—*Concluded*.

DAY.	July.		August.		September.		October.	
	Gauge Height.	Dis-charge.	Gauge Height.	Dis-charge.	Gauge Height.	Dis-charge.	Gauge Height.	Dis-charge.
	Feet.	Sec.-ft.	Feet.	Sec.-ft.	Feet.	Sec.-ft.	Feet.	Sec.-ft.
1	Dry.	Nil.	Dry.	Nil.	Dry.	Nil.	Dry.	Nil.
2	"	"	"	"	"	"	"	"
3	"	"	"	"	"	"	"	"
4	"	"	"	"	"	"	"	"
5	"	"	"	"	"	"	"	"
6	"	"	"	"	"	"	1.80	1.40
7	"	"	"	"	"	"	3.75	18.30
8	"	"	"	"	"	"	2.75	7.00
9	"	"	"	"	"	"	2.25	3.40
10	"	"	"	"	"	"	2.00	2.20
11	"	"	"	"	"	"	1.75	1.21
12	"	"	"	"	"	"	1.70	1.02
13	"	"	"	"	"	"	1.60	0.66
14	"	"	"	"	"	"	1.56	0.52
15	"	"	"	"	"	"	1.55	0.48
16	"	"	"	"	"	"	2.12	2.70
17	"	"	"	"	"	"	2.30	3.70
18	"	"	"	"	"	"	2.25	3.40
19	"	"	"	"	"	"	2.20	3.10
20	"	"	"	"	"	"	2.05	2.40
21	"	"	"	"	"	"	1.85	1.59
22	"	"	"	"	"	"	1.65	0.84
23	"	"	"	"	"	"	1.45	0.18
24	"	"	"	"	"	"	1.40	0.08
25	"	"	"	"	"	"	1.35	0.02
26	"	"	"	"	"	"	Dry.	Nil.
27	"	"	"	"	"	"	"	"
28	"	"	"	"	"	"	"	"
29	"	"	"	"	"	"	"	"
30	"	"	"	"	"	"	"	"
31	"	"	"	"	....	....	"	"

MONTHLY DISCHARGE of Lodge Creek at Hartt's Ranch, for 1914.

(Drainage area 80 square miles.)

MONTH.	DISCHARGE IN SECOND-FEET.				RUN-OFF.	
	Maximum.	Minimum	Mean.	Per square Mile.	Depth in inches on Drainage Area.	Total in Acre-feet.
March (14–31)	134.00	9.40	26.00	0.3250	0.220	932
April	140.00	1.55	40.00	0.5000	0.560	2,380
May	19.80	0.00	2.80	0.0350	0.040	172
June	3.70	0.00	0.83	0.0100	0.011	49
July	....	....	....	....	....	Nil.
August	....	....	....	....	....	"
September	....	....	....	....	....	....
October	18 30	0.00	1.74	0 0215	0 025	107
The period	....	....	....	....	0.860	3,640

SESSIONAL PAPER No. 25c

LODGE CREEK AT HESTER'S RANCH.

Location.—On the *NE.* ¼ Sec. 25, Tp. 3, Rge. 1, W. 4th Mer., at Hester Brothers' ranch. This station was moved from the *NE.* ¼ Sec. 36, Tp. 3, Rge. 1, W. 4th Mer., on April 29, 1914.

Records available.—August 31, 1912, to October 31, 1914.

Gauge.—Vertical staff; elevation of zero of gauge at original station (records from August 31, 1912, to April 28, 1914), 87.29 feet. At new station, from April 28, 1914, to October 31, 1914, elevation of zero of gauge 89.31 feet.

Bench-mark.—Permanent iron bench-mark; assumed elevation, 100.00 feet. Located 6¼ feet west of the I.P. stake, and 387 feet southwest of Hester's house.

Channel.—Practically permanent.

Discharge measurements.—Made by wading, or with a weir.

Winter flow.—Station discontinued during winter season.

Artificial control.—There are many small beaver dams across the creek near this station, both above the station and below, but as the channel is narrow they do not store much water, and have very little effect upon the flow of the creek.

Diversions.—Geo. Legg and Jas. Mitchell use water for irrigation between this station and the station at Hartt's ranch.

Observer.—Miss Marcia Hester.

DISCHARGE MEASUREMENTS of Lodge Creek at Hester's Ranch, in 1914.

Date.	Engineer.	Width.	Area of Section.	Mean Velocity.	Gauge Height.	Discharge.
		Feet.	*Sq. ft.*	*Ft. per sec.*	*Feet.*	*Sec.-ft.*
April 29..........	H. W. Rowley.........	22	9 2	.77	1.76	7.10
June 17..........	do	......a	....	....	1.51	2.40
July 15..........	do	......a	....	....	1.20	Nil.
Aug. 26..........	do	......a	....	....	Dry.	"
Sept. 26	do	......a	....	....	"	"
Oct. 24..........	do	......a	....	....	1.21	"

a Weir measurement.

DAILY GAUGE HEIGHT AND DISCHARGE of Lodge Creek at Hester's Ranch, for 1914.

DAY.	March.		April.		May.		June.	
	Gauge Height.	Dis-charge.	Gauge Height.	Dis-charge.	Gauge Height.	Dis-charge.	Gauge Height.	Dis-charge.
	Feet.	*Sec.-ft.*	*Feet.*	*Sec.-ft.*	*Feet.*	*Sec.-ft.*	*Feet.*	*Sec.-ft.*
1............	....	....	2.80	106.0	1.66	4.80	1.09	Nil.
2............	....	....	2.30	72.0	1.66	4.80	1.08	"
3............	....	....	2.55	88.0	1.60	3.70	1.08	"
4............	....	....	2.75	102.0	1.62	4.10	1.10	"
5............	....	....	3.00	120.0	1.63	4.20	1.10	"
6............	....	....	3.40	148.0	1.60	3.70	1.10	"
7............	....	....	3.00	120.0	1.61	3.90	1.10	"
8............	....	....	2.50	85.0	1.61	3.90	1.11	"
9............	....	....	2.18	65.0	1.65	4.60	1.14	"
10............	....	....	1.99	53.0	1.76	7.10	1.14	"
11............	....	....	1.73	40.0	1.85	9.40	1.16	"
12............	....	....	1.33	23.0	2.30	21.00	1.16	"
13............	....	....	1.86	46.0	2.35	22.00	1.36	0.78
14............	....	....	3.10	127.0	2.33	22.00	1.45	1.60
15............	....	....	3.17	132.0	1.65	4.60	2.10	15.90
16............	1.06a	14.5	3.11	128.0	1.63	4.20	' 1.97	12.50
17............	1.06	14.5	2.99	119.0	1.50	2.20	1.47	1.84
18............	2.07	58.0	1.96	52.0	1.49	2.10	1.35	0.70
19............	2.04	56.0	1.77	42.0	1.45	1.60	1.27	0.18
20............	1.97	52.0	1.60	34.0	1.35	0.70	1.25	0.10
21............	1.28	21.0	1.49	29.0	1.32	0.46	1.19	Nil.
22............	0.70	6.0	1.30	22.0	1.30	0.30	1.15	"
23............	0.13	Nil.	1.30	22.0	1.30	0.30	1.10	"
24............	0.12	"	1.25	20.0	1.28	0.22	1.10	"
25............	0.11	"	1.20	18.5	1.26	0.14	1.10	"
26............	0.11	"	0.90	10.2	1.25	0.10	1.10	"
27............	0.10	"	0.75	7.0	1.21	0.02	1.10	"
28............	0.10	"	0.70b	6.0	1.16	Nil.	1.16	"
29............	0.11	"	1.76	7.1	1.10	"	1.21	0.02
30............	0.11	"	1.76	7.1	1.09	"	1.25	0.10
31............	1.90	48.0	....	....	1.09	"	....	....

a to *b* Gauge heights and discharge at upper station NE. 36-3-1-4.

No. 25c.—21

5 GEORGE V, A. 1915

DAILY GAUGE HEIGHT AND DISCHARGE of Lodge Creek at Hester's Ranch, for 1914.
—Concluded.

DAY.	July.		August.		September.		October.	
	Gauge Height.	Discharge.	Gauge Height.	Discharge.	Gauge Height.	Discharge.	Gauge Height.	Discharge.
	Feet.	*Sec.-ft.*	*Feet.*	*Sec.-ft.*	*Feet.*	*Sec.-ft.*	*Feet.*	*Sec.-ft.*
1	1.25	0.10	Dry	Nil	Dry	Nil	Dry	Nil
2	1.25	0.10	"	"	"	"	"	"
3	1.24	0.08	"	"	"	"	"	"
4	1.24	0.08	"	"	"	"	"	"
5	1.24	0.08	"	"	"	"	"	"
6	1.23	0.06	"	"	"	"	"	"
7	1.23	0.06	"	"	"	"	"	"
8	1.23	0.06	"	"	"	"	"	"
9	1.22	0.04	"	"	"	"	2.60	29.00
10	1.22	0.04	"	"	"	"	2.50	26.00
11	1.21	0.02	"	"	"	"	2.10	15.90
12	1.21	0.02	"	"	"	"	2.00	13.30
13	1.21	0.02	"	"	"	"	1.95	12.00
14	1.20	Nil	"	"	"	"	1.80	8.10
15	1.20	"	"	"	"	"	1.75	6.80
16	1.20	"	"	"	"	"	1.60	3.70
17	1.20	"	"	"	"	"	1.50	2.20
18	1.19	"	"	"	"	"	1.40	1.10
19	1.18	"	"	"	"	"	1.30	0.30
20	1.18	"	"	"	"	"	1.28	0.22
21	1.16	"	"	"	"	"	1.24	0.08
22	1.14	"	"	"	"	"	1.22	0.04
23	1.13	"	"	"	"	"	1.21	0.02
24	1.09	"	"	"	"	"	1.21	0.02
25	1.06	"	"	"	"	"	1.19	Nil
26	1.06	"	"	"	"	"	1.16	"
27	1.06	"	"	"	"	"	1.10	"
28	1.06	"	"	"	"	"	1.08	"
29	1.06	"	"	"	"	"	1.06	"
30	1.06	"	"	"	"	"	1.02	"
31	1.06	"	"	"	"	"	1.00	"

MONTHLY DISCHARGE of Lodge Creek at Hester's Ranch, for 1914.

(Drainage area 223 square miles.)

MONTH.	DISCHARGE IN SECOND-*FEET*.				RUN-OFF.	
	Maximum.	Minimum.	Mean.	Per square Mile.	Depth in inches on Drainage Area.	Total in Acre-feet.
March (16–31)	58.00	0.00	16.90	0.0760	0.0450	535
April	148.00	6.00	62.00	0.2780	0.3100	3,689
May	22.00	0.00	4.40	0.1970	0.0230	270
June	15.90	0.00	1.13	0.0050	0.0060	67
July	0.10	0.00	0.02	0.0001	0.0001	2
August						Nil
September						
October	29.00	0.00	3.80	0.0170	0.0200	236
The period					0.4000	4,799

MIDDLE CREEK AT MACKINNON'S RANCH.

Location.—On the SW. ¼ Sec. 35, Tp. 5, Rge. 1, W. 4th Mer., at Angus MacKinnon's ranch.
Records available.—From June 21, 1910, to October 31, 1914.
Gauge.—Vertical staff; zero of gauge maintained at 91.49 feet during 1910-11; 91.57 feet during 1912; 91.47 feet during 1913-14.
Bench-mark.—Permanent iron bench-mark; assumed elevation, 100.00 feet.
Channel.—Practically permanent.
Winter flow.—Station discontinued during winter season.
Observer.—A. D. MacKinnon.

DISCHARGE MEASUREMENTS of Middle Creek at MacKinnon's Ranch, in 1914.

Date.	Engineer.	Width.	Area of Section.	Mean Velocity.	Gauge Height.	Discharge.
		Feet.	*Sq. ft.*	*Ft. per sec.*	*Feet.*	*Sec.-ft.*
Mar. 23	H. R. Carscallen	4.90	1.17	0.71	2.14	0.83
April 28	H. W. Rowley	9.00	3.00	0.99	1.10	2.98
May 19	do	........a	.......a	....	0.81	0.98
June 16	do	........a	.......a	....	0.60	0.71
July 7	do	........a	.......a	....	0.55	0.47
July 31	do	........a	.......a	....	0.60	0.24
Aug. 26	do	........a	.......a	....	0.54	0.19
Sept. 26	do	........a	.......a	....	0.79	0.20
Oct. 22	do	........a	.......a	....	0.58	0.35

a Weir measurement.

DAILY GAUGE HEIGHT AND DISCHARGE of Middle Creek at MacKinnon's Ranch, for 1914.

DAY.	March.		April.		May.		June.	
	Gauge Height.	Discharge.	Gauge Height.	Discharge.	Gauge Height.	Discharge.	Gauge Height.	Discharge.
	Feet.	*Sec.-ft.*	*Feet.*	*Sec.-ft.*	*Feet.*	*Sec.-ft.*	*Feet.*	*Sec.-ft.*
1			4.04	67.00	0.83	1.21	0.58	0.37
2			3.85	62.00	0.75	0.85	0.58	0.37
3			3.95	64.00	0.62	0.45	0.58	0.37
4			3.96	64.00	0.67	0.58	0.58	0.37
5			4.66	82.00	0.67	0.58	0.58	0.37
6			4.83	88.00	0.65	0.52	0.90	1.60
7			3.17	44.00	0.64	0.50	0.78	0.97
8			3.28	47.00	0.64	0.50	0.65	0.52
9			3.48	52.00	0.65	0.52	0.62	0.45
10			2.68	31.00	0.60	0.40	0.62	0.45
11			2.84	36.00	1.85	12.00	0.63	0.48
12			3.32b	48.00	1.30	4.70	0.65	0.52
13			3.79	60.00	0.86	1.38	0.75	0.85
14			3.21	46.00	0.65	0.52	0.70	0.65
15			3.26	47.00	0.77	0.93	0.65	0.52
16	3.64	57	3.07b	42.00	0.75	0.85	0.60	0.40
17	2.79	34	2.88	37.00	0.67	0.58	0.59	0.38
18	3.29	48	2.71	32.00	0.66	0.55	0.59	0.38
19	......a	....	2.50	27.00	0.66	0.55	0.59	0.38
20			2.09	16.80	0.66	0.55	0.58	0.37
21			2.73	33.00	0.65	0.52	0.58	0.37
22			2.03	15.50	0.65	0.52	0.58	0.37
23			1.80	11.20	0.64	0.50	0.58	0.37
24			1.85	12.00	0.64	0.50	0.58	0.37
25			2.06	16.10	0.64	0.50	0.65	0.52
26			1.80	11.20	0.64	0.50	0.62	0.45
27			1.30	4.70	0.64	0.50	0.62	0.45
28			1.20	3.80	0.62	0.45	0.60	0.40
29			1.03	2.40	0.61	0.42	0.60	0.40
30			0.92	1.72	0.60	0.40	0.59	0.38
31	......a	....			0.58	0.37		

a to *a* Frozen—no gauge height records.
b Gauge height interpolated.

STREAM MEASUREMENTS, 1914

5 GEORGE V, A. 1915

DAILY GAUGE HEIGHT AND DISCHARGE of Middle Creek at MacKinnon's Ranch, for 1914.
—*Concluded.*

	July.		August.		September.		October.	
	Gauge Height.	Dis-charge.	Gauge Height.	Dis-charge.	Gauge Height.	Dis-charge.	Gauge Height.	Dis-charge.
	Feet.	*Sec.-ft.*	*Feet.*	*Sec.-ft.*	*Feet.*	*Sec.-ft.*	*Feet.*	*Sec.-ft.*
1	0.57	0.36	0.54	0.31	0.50	0.25	0.50	0.25
2	0.56	0.34	0.54	0.31	0.50	0.25	0.50	0.25
3	0.55	0.33	0.54	0.31	0.50	0.25	0.63	0.48
4	0.55	0.33	0.54	0.31	0.50	0.25	0.59	0.38
5	0.55	0.33	0.54	0.31	0.51	0.26	0.65	0.52
6	0.55	0.33	0.54	0.31	0.51	0.26	0.65	0.52
7	0.58	0.37	0.54	0.31	0.51	0.26	0.65	0.52
8	0.58	0.37	0.54	0.31	0.51	0.26	1.30	4.70
9	0.58	0.37	0.62	0.45	0.51	0.26	0.66	0.55
10	0.75	0.85	0.62	0.45	0.51	0.26	0.65	0.52
11	0.75	0.85	0.62	0.45	0.51	0.26	0.63	0.48
12	0.75	0.85	0.61	0.42	0.51	0.26	0.61	0.42
13	0.75	0.85	0.61	0.42	0.51	0.26	0.60	0.40
14	0.75	0.85	0.61	0.42	0.52	0.28	0.59	0.38
15	0.75	0.85	0.61	0.42	0.52	0.28	0.59	0.38
16	0.75	0.85	0.61	0.42	0.52*a*	0.28	0.58	0.37
17	0.74	0.81	0.61	0.42	0.52	0.28	0.58	0.37
18	0.74	0.81	0.61	0.42	0.52	0.28	0.58	0.37
19	0.74	0.81	0.61	0.42	0.52	0.28	0.58	0.37
20	0.74	0.81	0.61	0.42	0.51	0.26	0.58	0.37
21	0.74	0.81	0.61	0.42	0.53	0.29	0.59	0.38
22	0.74	0.81	0.61	0.42	0.51	0.26	0.59	0.38
23	0.74	0.81	0.59	0.38	0.54	0.31	0.59	0.38
24	0.74	0.81	0.55	0.33	0.56	0.34	0.59	0.38
25	0.71	0.69	0.56	0.34	0.58	0.37	0.59	0.38
26	0.71	0.69	0.52	0.28	0.59*a*	0.38	0.59	0.38
27	0.71	0.69	0.51	0.26	0.55	0.33	0.59	0.38
28	0.71	0.69	0.50	0.25	0.50	0.25	0.59	0.38
29	0.71	0.69	0.50	0.25	0.50	0.25	0.59	0.38
30	0.58	0.37	0.50	0.25	0.50	0.25	0.59	0.38
31	0.54	0.31	0.50	0.25	....	....	0.59	0.38

a to *a* Gauge heights affected by beaver dam; correction applied.

MONTHLY DISCHARGE of Middle Creek at MacKinnon's Ranch, for 1914.

(Drainage area 121 square miles.)

MONTH.	DISCHARGE IN SECOND-FEET.				RUN-OFF.	
	Maximum.	Minimum	Mean.	Per square Mile.	Depth in inches on Drainage Area.	Total in Acre-feet.
March (16–18)	57.00	34.00	46.00	0.382	0.040	275
April	88.00	1.72	37.00	0.304	0.340	2,202
May	12.00	0.37	1.09	0.009	0.010	67
June	1.60	0.37	4.90	0.004	0.004	29
July	0.85	0.31	0.64	0.005	0.006	39
August	0.45	0.25	0.36	0.003	0.003	22
September	0.38	0.25	0.28	0.002	0.003	16
October	4.70	0.25	0.54	0.004	0.005	33
The period	....	....	....	....	0.410	2,683

MIDDLE CREEK AT ROSS' RANCH.

Location.—On the SW. ¼ Sec. 30, Tp. 5, Rge. 29, W. 3rd Mer., at Maurice Ross' ranch.

Records available.—From July 20, 1909, to October 31, 1914.

Gauge.—Vertical staff; zero of gauge maintained at 3,291.61 feet during 1909-10; 3,290.99 feet during 1911; 3,290 98 feet during 1912-14.

Bench-mark.—Permanent iron bench-mark; elevation, 3,297.37 feet above sea level (*Irrigation Surveys*).

SESSIONAL PAPER No. 25c

Channel.—Practically permanent.
Discharge measurements.—Made by wading or with a weir.
Winter flow.—Station discontinued during winter season.
Artificial control.—The flow at this station is regulated to some extent by two dams, one at W. X. Wright's and the other at MacKinnon's ranch.
Diversions.—Water is diverted for irrigation above this station by W. X. Wright and Angus MacKinnon.
Observer.—Mrs. W. M. Ross.

DISCHARGE MEASUREMENTS of Middle Creek at Ross' Ranch, in 1914.

Date.	Engineer.	Width.	Area of Section.	Mean Velocity.	Gauge Height.	Discharge.
		Feet.	*Sq. ft.*	*Ft. per sec.*	*Feet.*	*Sec.-ft.*
Mar. 23	H. R. Carscallen	14.5	7.02	0.43	0.88	3.00
April 4	do	14.3	8.60	0.68	1.06	5.90
April 7	do	32.0	42.00	1.42	2.42	60.00
April 8	do	38.0	80.20	1.83	3.46	147.00
April 11	do	29.5	28.80	1.41	1.99	40.00
April 24	do	11.1	8.03	1.37	1.21	11.00
April 27	H. W. Rowley	10.5	5.68	0.80	1.01	4.60
June 5	do	. . . . .a	. . . .	. . . .	0.71	0.53
July 9	do	. . . . .a	. . . .	. . . .	0.67	0.31
Sept. 2	do	. . . .a	. . . .	. . . .	0.65	0.25
Oct. 5	do	. . . . . .a	. . . .	. . . .	0.66	0.52
Oct. 22	do	. . . . . . .a	. . . .	. . . .	0.62	0.29

a Weir measurement.

DAILY GAUGE HEIGHT AND DISCHARGE of Middle Creek at Ross' Ranch, for 1914.

DAY.	March.		April.		May.		June.	
	Gauge Height.	Dis- charge.	Gauge Height.	Dis- charge.	Gauge Height.	Dis- charge.	Gauge Height.	Dis- charge.
	Feet.	*Sec.-ft.*	*Feet.*	*Sec.-ft.*	*Feet.*	*Sec.-ft.*	*Feet.*	*Sec.-ft.*
1	. . . .	. . . .	1 00a	4.70	.70	0.56	0.66	0.34
2	. . . .	. . . .	1 50a	19 00	.66	0.34	0.66	0.34
3	. . . .	. . . .	2.46	66.00	0.70	0.56	0.66	0.34
4	. . . .	. . . .	1.26	11.00	.70	0.56	0.66	0.34
5	. . . .	. . . .	1.33	13.30	.69	0.51	0.67	0.39
6	. . . .	. . . .	2.57	73.00	.66	0.34	0.69	0.51
7	. . . .	. . . . . .	2.26	54 00	.66	0.34	0.70	0.56
8	. . . .	. . . .	3.37	139.00	0.66	0.34	0.69	0.51
9	. . . . .	. . . .	2.74	85.00	.66	0.34	0.66	0.34
10	. . . .	. . . . .	1.94	37.00	.66	0.34	0.66	0.34
11	. . . .	. . . . .	1.93	36 00	.66	0.34	0.70	0.56
12	. . . .	. . . .	1.87	33.00	.66	0.34	0.70	0.56
13	. . . .	. . . .	1.97	38.00	0.66	0.34	0.74	0.85
14	. . . . . .	. . . .	2.98	103.00	.66	0.34	0.74	0.85
15	1.79	30.00	3.20	123.00	.66	0.34	0.69	0.51
16	1.77a	29.00	3.03	108.00	.66	0.34	0.66	0.34
17	1.73a	27.00	2.88	95.00	.66	0.34	0.66	0.34
18	1.70a	26.00	2.59	74 00	0.66	0.34	0.66	0.34
19	1.66a	25.00	2.16	48.00	.66	0.34	0.66	0.34
20	1.62a	23.00	1.63	24 00	.66	0.34	0.66	0.34
21	1.58	22.00	0.97	4.10	0.66	0.34	0.66	0.34
22	0.89	2.80	0.98	4.30	0.66	0.34	0.66	0.34
23	0.87	2.40	1.28	11.70	0.66	0.34	0.66	0.34
24	0.78	1.25	1.21	9.60	0.68	0.45	0.66	0.34
25	0.75a	0.94	1.20	9.30	0.66	0.34	0.69	0.51
26	0.75a	0.94	0.90	2.90	0.66	0.34	0.68	0.45
27	0.75a	0.94	0.88	2.60	0.66	0.34	0.66	0.34
28	0.80a	1.46	0.84	2.00	0.66	0.34	0.66	0.34
29	0.80a	1.46	0.79	1.36	0.66	0.34	0.66	0.34
30	0.90a	2.90	0.74	0.86	0.66	0.34	0.66	0.34
31	1.00a	4.70	. . . .	. . . .	0.66	0.34	. . . .	. . . .

a Gauge height interpolated.

5 GEORGE V, A. 1915

DAILY GAUGE HEIGHT AND DISCHARGE of Middle Creek at Ross' Ranch, for 1914.—*Concluded.*

DAY.	July.		August.		September.		October.	
	Gauge Height.	Dis- charge.	Gauge Height.	Dis- charge.	Gauge Height.	Dis- charge.	Gauge Height.	Dis- charge.
	Feet.	*Sec.-ft.*	*Feet.*	*Sec.-ft.*	*Feet.*	*Sec.-ft.*	*Feet.*	*Sec.-ft.*
1	0.66	0.34	0.63	0.22	0.64	0.25	0.63	0.22
2	0.66	0.34	0.61	0.15	0.64	0.25	0.63	0.22
3	0.66	0.34	0.61	0.15	0.64	0.25	0.64	0.25
4	0.66	0.34	0.61	0.15	0.64	0.25	0.68	0.45
5	0.66	0.34	0.62	0.18	0.64	0.25	0.69	0.51
6	0.66	0.34	0.62	0.18	0.64	0.25	0.68	0.45
7	0.66	0.34	0.62	0.18	0.64	0.25	0.65	0.29
8	0.66	0.34	0.62	0.18	0.64	0.25	0.72	0.67
9	0.66	0.34	0.62	0.18	0.64	0.25	0.66	0.34
10	0.66	0.34	0.62	0.18	0.64	0.25	0.65	0.29
11	0.66	0.34	0.63	0.22	0.65	0.29	0.64	0.25
12	0.66	0.34	0.63	0.22	0.66	0.34	0.63	0.22
13	0.66	0.34	0.63	0.22	0.67	0.39	0.63	0.22
14	0.66	0.34	0.63	0.22	0.66	0.34	0.63	0.22
15	0.66	0.34	0.63	0.22	0.65	0.29	0.63	0.22
16	0.66	0.34	0.63	0.22	0.65	0.29	0.63	0.22
17	0.66	0.34	0.64	0.25	0.65	0.29	0.63	0.22
18	0.66	0.34	0.64	0.25	0.64	0.25	0.63	0.22
19	0.65	0.29	0.66	0.34	0.64	0.25	0.63	0.22
20	0.65	0.29	0.65	0.29	0.64	0.25	0.63	0.22
21	0.64	0.25	0.64	0.25	0.64	0.25	0.63	0.22
22	0.62	0.18	0.64	0.25	0.63	0.22	0.66	0.34
23	0.62	0.18	0.64	0.25	0.63	0.22	0.70	0.56
24	0.60	0.11	0.64	0.25	0.63	0.22	0.70	0.56
25	0.60	0.11	0.66	0.34	0.63	0.22	0.70	0.56
26	0.60	0.11	0.64	0.25	0.63	0.22	0.70	0.56
27	0.60	0.11	0.64	0.25	0.63	0.22	0.70	0.56
28	0.60	0.11	0.64	0.25	0.63	0.22	0.70	0.56
29	0.63	0.22	0.64	0.25	0.63	0.22	0.70	0.56
30	0.66	0.34	0.64	0.25	0.63	0.22	0.70	0.56
31	0.64	0.25	0.64	0.25	....	....	0.70	0.56

MONTHLY DISCHARGE of Middle Creek at Ross' Ranch, for 1914.

(Drainage area 162 square miles.)

MONTH.	DISCHARGE IN SECOND-*FEET*.				RUN-OFF.	
	Maximum.	Minimum	Mean.	Per square Mile.	Depth in inches on Drainage Area.	Total in Acre-feet.
March (15–31)	30.00	0.94	11.90	0.0735	0.050	400
April	139.00	0.86	41.00	0.2540	0.280	2,446
May	0.56	0.34	0.37	0.0023	0.003	23
June	0.85	0.34	0.42	0.0026	0.003	25
July	0.34	0.11	0.28	0.0017	0.002	17
August	0.34	0.15	0.23	0.0014	0.002	14
September	0.39	0.22	0.26	0.0016	0.002	15
October	0.67	0.22	0.37	0.0023	0.003	23
The period	....	....	....	....	0.34	2,963

SESSIONAL PAPER No. 25c

MIDDLE CREEK AT HAMMOND'S RANCH.

Location.—On the N*E*. ¼ Sec. 4, Tp. 2, Rge. 29, W. 3rd Mer., at D. *A.* Hammond's ranch.
Records available.—June 13, 1910, to October 31, 1914.
Gauge.—Vertical staff; elevation of zero of gauge 87.48 feet during 1910; 87.60 feet during 1911-14.
Bench-mark.—Permanent iron bench-mark; assumed elevation, 100.00 feet.
Channel.—Slightly shifting during high water stages.
Discharge measurements.—Made by wading or with a weir.
Winter flow.—Station discontinued during winter season.
Diversions.—Water is diverted above this station by Mr. Lynch, Mr. Peachy and Mr. Jahn.
Observer.—Mrs. D. *A.* Hammond.

DISCHARGE MEASUREMENTS of Middle Creek at Hammond's Ranch, in 1914.

Date.	Engineer.	Width.	Area of Section.	Mean Velocity.	Gauge Height.	Discharge.
		Feet.	*Sq. ft.*	*Ft. per sec.*	*Feet.*	*Sec.-ft.*
Mar. 18............	H. D. St. A. Smith..........	21.0	40.5	0.59	3.17	24.00
Mar. 21...,.......	do	11.0	6.5	1.32	2.32	8.70
Mar. 30............	do	10.0	6.9	0.75	2.07	5.20
April 3............	do	22.0	26.4	1.45	3.14	38.40
April 9............	do	27.0	111.0	1.17	4.44	129.00
April 10............	do	24.0	118.0	1.19	4.58	141.00
April 13............	do	23.0	29.4	1.62	3.29	48.00
April 24............	H. W. Rowley............	9.5*b*	4.7	1.89	2.06	9.00
May 21............	do	.......*a*	....	....	1.49	0.10
May 25............	do	.......*a*	....	....	1.46	0.06
June 17............	do	....	....	....	1.29	Nil.
July 15............	do	....	....	....	Dry.	"
Aug. 26............	do	....	....	....	"	"
Oct. 26............	do	....	....	....	1.05	"

a Weir measurement.
b Measurement made below gauge.

DAILY GAUGE HEIGHT AND DISCHARGE of Middle Creek at Hammond's Ranch, for 1914.

DAY.	March.		April.		May.		June.	
	Gauge Height.	Dis-charge.	Gauge Height.	Dis-charge.	Gauge Height.	Dis-charge.	Gauge Height.	Dis-charge.
	Feet.	*Sec.-ft.*	*Feet.*	*Sec.-ft.*	*Feet.*	*Sec.-ft.*	*Feet.*	*Sec.-ft.*
1................................	....	....	3.12	41.0	1.91	5.20	.....*a*	Nil.
2................................	....	....	3.82	78.0	1.86	4.36	.....*a*	"
3................................	....	....	3.17	40.0	1.82	3.80	.....*a*	"
4................................	....	....	2.92	30.0	1.79	3.40	1.44	0.02
5................................	....	....	3.02	35.0	1.73	2.70	1.44	0.02
6................................	....	....	3.37	52.0	1.70	2.30	1.41	Nil.
7................................	....	....	2.92	33.0	1.67	2.00	1.39	"
8................................	....	....	3.57	64.0	1.67	2.00	1.39	"
9................................	....	....	4.44	129.0	1.65	1.80	1.39	"
10................................	....	....	4.57	140.0	1.64	1.70	1.37	"
11................................	....	....	3.32	50.0	1.62	1.50	1.37	"
12................................	....	....	3.39	54.0	1.61	1.40	.....*a*	"
13................................	4.12	40.0	3.31	50.0	1.59	1.20	.....*a*	"
14................................	5.12	58.0	3.21	45.0	1.58	1.10	.....*a*	"
15................................	5.12	58.0	4.16	106.0	1.57	1.00	.....*a*	"
16................................	4.62	50.0	4.26	114.0	1.56	0.90	.....*a*	"
17................................	4.12	40.0	4.31	118.0	1.53	0.64	1.29	"
18................................	3.17	24.0	4.21	110.0	1.52	0.56	.....*a*	"
19................................	3.02	22.0	4.06	98.0	1.50	0.40	.....*a*	"
20................................	2.72	16.0	3.76	76.0	1.48	0.26	.....*a*	"
21................................	2.32	8.7	3.47	58.0	1.48	0.26	.....*a*	"
22................................	2.12	5.5	3.17	43.0	1.41	Nil.	.....*a*	"
23................................	2.07	4.5	2.87	31.0	1.41	"	.....*a*	"
24................................	2.07	4.5	2.62	23.0	1.40	"	.....*a*	"
25................................	2.02	3.8	2.32	13.9	1.40	"	.....*a*	"
26................................	2.02	3.8	2.22	11.5	1.40	"	.....*a*	"
27................................	2.02	3.8	2.22	11.5	1.39	"	.....*a*	"
28................................	2.00	3.2	2.17	10.4	1.39	"	.....*a*	"
29................................	1.97	3.0	2.12	9.4	1.39	"	.....*a*	"
30................................	1.97	3.0	1.99	6.8	1.38	"	.....*a*	"
31................................	2.92	31.0	....	....	1.38	"	....	....

a Water in pools.

5 GEORGE V, A. 1915

DAILY GAUGE HEIGHT AND DISCHARGE of Middle Creek at Hammond's Ranch, for 1914.
—*Concluded.*

DAY.	July.		August.		September.		October.	
	Gauge Height.	Dis-charge.	Gauge Height.	Dis-charge.	Gauge Height.	Dis-charge.	Gauge Height.	Dis-charge.
	Feet.	Sec.-ft.	Feet.	Sec.-ft.	Feet.	Sec.-ft.	Feet.	Sec.-ft.
1	Dry.	Nil.	Dry.	Nil.	Dry.	Nil.	Dry.	Nil.
2	"	"	"	"	"	"	"	"
3	"	"	"	"	"	"	"	"
4	"	"	"	"	"	"	2.35	14.70
5	"	"	"	"	"	"	2.40	16.10
6	"	"	"	"	"	"	2.40	16.10
7	"	"	"	"	"	"	2.42	16.70
8	"	"	"	"	"	"	2.40	16.10
9	"	"	"	"	"	"	2.38	15.50
10	"	"	"	"	"	"	2.35	14.70
11	"	"	"	"	"	"	2.30	13.40
12	"	"	"	"	"	"	2.30	13.40
13	"	"	"	"	"	"	2.20	11.10
14	"	"	"	"	"	"	2.20	11.10
15	"	"	"	"	"	"	2.10	9.00
16	"	"	"	"	"	"	2.05	8.00
17	"	"	"	"	"	"	2.05	8.00
18	"	"	"	"	"	"	1.90	5.00
19	"	"	"	"	"	"	1.75	2.90
20	"	"	"	"	"	"	1.62	1.50
21	"	"	"	"	"	"	1.60	1.30
22	"	"	"	"	"	"	1.55	0.80
23	"	"	"	"	"	"	1.48	0.26
24	"	"	"	"	"	"	1.40	Nil.
25	"	"	"	"	"	"	1.40	"
26	"	"	"	"	"	"	Dry.	"
27	"	"	"	"	"	"	"	"
28	"	"	"	"	"	"	"	"
29	"	"	"	"	"	"	"	"
30	"	"	"	"	"	"	"	"
31	"	"	"	"	....	....	"	"

MONTHLY DISCHARGE of Middle Creek at Hammond's Ranch, for 1914.

(Drainage area 316 square miles.)

MONTH.	DISCHARGE IN SECOND-FEET.				RUN-OFF.	
	Maximum.	Minimum.	Mean.	Per square Mile.	Depth in inches on Drainage Area.	Total in Acre-feet.
March (13-31)	58.00	3.00	20.00	0.0633	0.050	759
April	140.00	6.80	56.00	0.1770	0.200	3,332
May	5.20	0.00	1.24	0.0039	0.004	76
June	0.00	0.00	0.00	0.0000	0.000	Nil.
July	....	....	....	....	....	..
August	....	....	....	....	....	..
September	....	....	....	....	....	..
October	16 70	0.00	6.30	0.0200	0 020	388
The period	....	....	....	....	0 274	4,555

LODGE CREEK AT WILLOW CREEK POLICE DETACHMENT.

Location.—On the SE. ¼ Sec. 12, Tp. 1, Rge. 29, W. 3rd Mer., at the Willow Creek R.N.W.M.P. detachment.

Records available.—From April 25, 1910, to October 31, 1914.

Gauge.—Vertical staff; zero of gauge maintained at 2,722.98 feet during 1910; 2.721.18 feet during 1911; 2,721 06 feet during 1912-14.

SESSIONAL PAPER No. 25c

Bench-mark.—Permanent iron bench-mark located on the right bank at the cable support; elevation, 2,734.02 feet above mean sea level (*International Boundary Survey*).
Channel.—Practically permanent.
Discharge measurements.—Made at station from cable car by wading or with a weir.
Winter flow.—Station discontinued during winter season.
Observer.—Chas. Hayes.

DISCHARGE MEASUREMENTS of Lodge Creek at Willow Creek Police Detachment, in 1914.

Date.	Engineer.	Width.	Area of Section.	Mean Velocity.	Gauge Height.	Discharge.
		Feet.	*Sq. ft.*	*Ft. per sec.*	*Feet.*	*Sec.-ft.*
Mar. 16	H. D. St. A. Smith	86.0	212.0	2.64	5.25	559.00
Mar. 18.	do	48.0	81.2	2.52	3.73	204.00
Mar. 21.	do	27.0	30.2	2.13	2.73	64.00
May 30	do	9.5	5.9	2.15	1.68	12.70
April 1	do	19.0	21.6	0.80	1.93	17.20
April 3.	do	43.0	63.0	3.59	3.88	225.00
April 8	do	46.0	61.2	3.59	3.89	220.00
April 7	do	55.0	123.0	2.95	4.53	363.00
April 30	H. W. Rowley.	21.0	13.0	1.56	2.05	20.00
May 21	do	4.5	2.6	1.03	1.47	2.60
May 23	do	4.5	2.1	1.00	1.40	2.10
June 18	do	. . . .	. . . .	. . . .	1.00	Nil.
July 13	do	. . . .	. . . .	. . . .	Dry.	"
Aug. 10	do	. . . .	. . . .	. . . .	"	"
Aug. 27.	do	. . . .	. . . .	. . . .	"	"
Sept. 28	do	. . . .	. . . .	. . . .	"	"
Oct. 26	do	. . . .*a*	. . . .	. . . .	1.25	0.66
Oct. 31.	do	. . . .*a*	. . . .	. . . .	1.18	0.31

a Weir measurement.

DAILY GAUGE HEIGHT AND DISCHARGE of Lodge Creek at Willow Creek Police Detachment, for 1914.

DAY.	March.		April.		May.		June.	
	Gauge Geight.	Dis-charge.	Gauge Height.	Dis-charge.	Gauge Height.	Dis-charge.	Gauge Height.	Dis-charge.
	Feet.	*Sec.-ft.*	*Feet.*	*Sec.-ft.*	*Feet.*	*Sec.-ft.*	*Feet.*	*Sec.-ft.*
1.	. . . .	. . . .	3.15	112	1.84	13.60	1.14	0.22
2.	. . . .	. . . .	3.24	123	1.80	12.00	1.12	0.16
3.	. . . .	. . . .	4.46	347	1.74	10.60	1.10	0.10
4.	. . . .	. . . .	3.60	175	1.71	9.40	1.12	0.16
5.	. . . .	. . . .	3.57	170	1.69	8.70	1.11	0.13
6.	. . . .	. . . .	3.99	244	1.72	9.80	1.16	0.28
7.	. . . .	. . . .	4.51	360	1.66	7.80	1.17	0.31
8.	. . . .	. . . .	3.87	221	1.60	6.00	1.13	0.19
9.	. . . .	. . . .	3.33	135	1.65	7.50	1.11	0.13
10.	. . . .	. . . .	3.77	203	1.52	4.30	1.08	0.08
11.	. . . .	. . . .	3.21	119	1.51	4.10	1.08	0.08
12.	. . . .	. . . .	2.77	72	1.50	3.90	1.09	0.09
13.	. . . .	. . . .	2.90	85	1.48	3.60	1.12	0.16
14.	. . . .	. . . .	3.07	103	1.65	7.50	1.12	0.16
15.	3.35	138.0	3.25	124	1.85	14.00	1.10	0.10
16.	5.23	554.0	3.85	217	1.85	14.00	1.08	0.08
17.	5.03	496.0	3.64	181	1.68	8.40	1.04	0.04
18.	3.70	191.0	3.56	169	1.61	6.30	1.02	0.02
19.	3.16	113.0	3.12	108	1.53	4.50	0.97	Nil.
20.	2.65	62.0	2.86	81	1.46	3.30	0.94	"
21.	2.67	63.0	2.67	63	1.48	3.60	0.96	"
22.	2.48	48.0	2.53	51	1.43	2.80	0.95	"
23.	2.41	43.0	2.42	43	1.40	2.30	0.90	"
24.	2.20	30.0	2.34	38	1.40	2.30	0.86	"
25.	1.84	13.6	2.24	32	1.39	2.20	0.90	"
26.	1.73	10.2	2.10	25	1.35	1.70	0.95	"
27.	1.71	9.4	2.10	25	1.30	1.10	0.88	"
28.	1.61	6.3	2.12	26	1.27	0.89	0.90	"
29.	1.67	8.1	2.12	26	1.22	0.54	0.89	"
30.	1.70	9.0	2.06	23	1.20	0.40	0.88	"
31.	1.85	14.0	. . . .	. . . .	1.16	0.28	. . . .	. . . .

5 GEORGE V, A. 1915

DAILY GAUGE HEIGHT AND DISCHARGE of Lodge Creek at Willow Creek Police Detachment, for 1914.—*Concluded.*

DAY.	July.		August.		September.		October.	
	Gauge Height.	Dis-charge.	Gauge Height.	Dis-charge.	Gauge Height.	Dis-charge.	Gauge Height.	Dis-charge.
	Feet.	Sec.-ft.	Feet.	Sec.-ft.	Feet.	Sec.-ft.	Feet.	Sec.-ft.
1	0.84	Nil.	Dry.	Nil.	Dry.	Nil.	Dry.	Nil.
2	0.82	"	"	"	"	"	"	"
3	0.74	"	"	"	"	"	"	"
4	0.69	"	"	"	"	"	"	"
5	0.64	"	"	"	"	"	1.18	0.34
6	0.60	"	"	"	"	"	1.20	0.40
7	0.52	"	"	"	"	"	1.12	0.16
8	0.46	"	"	"	"	"	1.70	9.00
9	0.40	"	"	"	"	"	3.72	194.00
10	Dry.	"	"	"	"	"	3.35	138.00
11	"	"	"	"	"	"	2.90	85.00
12	"	"	"	"	"	"	2.40	42.00
13	"	"	"	"	"	"	2.00	20.00
14	"	"	"	"	"	"	1.88	15.20
15	"	"	"	"	"	"	1.78	12.20
16	"	"	"	"	"	"	1.70	9.00
17	"	"	"	"	"	"	1.68	8.40
18	"	"	"	"	"	"	1.60	6.00
19	"	"	"	"	"	"	1.60	6.00
20	"	"	"	"	"	"	1.52	4.30
21	"	"	"	"	"	"	1.42	2.60
22	"	"	"	"	"	"	1.42	2.60
23	"	"	"	"	"	"	1.30	1.10
24	"	"	"	"	"	"	1.28	0.96
25	"	"	"	"	"	"	1.26	0.82
26	"	"	"	"	"	"	1.25	0.75
27	"	"	"	"	"	"	1.24	0.68
28	"	"	"	"	"	"	1.21	0.47
29	"	"	"	"	"	"	1.20	0.40
30	"	"	"	"	"	"	1.19	0.37
31	"	"	"	"	"	"	1.18	0.34

MONTHLY DISCHARGE of Lodge Creek at Willow Creek Police Detachment, for 1914.

(Drainage area 824 square miles.)

MONTH.	DISCHARGE IN SECOND-FEET.				RUN-OFF.	
	Maximum.	Minimum.	Mean.	Per square Mile.	Depth in inches on Drainage Area.	Total in Acre-feet.
March (15-31)	554.00	6.30	106.00	0.1290	0.0800	3,587
April	360.00	23.00	123.00	0.1490	0.1700	7,319
May	14.00	0.28	5.70	0.0069	0.0080	350
June	0.31	Nil.	0.08	0.0001	0.0001	5
July	0.00	"	Nil.	Nil.	Nil.	Nil.
August	0.00	"	"	"	"	"
September	0.00	"	"	"	"	"
October	194.00	"	18.10	0.0220	0.0200	1,113
The period	....	....	....	....	0.28	12,374

MISCELLANEOUS DISCHARGE MEASUREMENTS made in Lodge Creek drainage basin, in 1914.

Date.	Engineer.	Stream.	Location.	Discharge.	
				Imperial gallons per 24 hours.	*Sec.-ft.*
Oct. 21....	H. W. Rowley......	Adams' Spring.....	NW. 32-5-1-4.........	290	0.00054
May 19...	do	Links' Spring......	NW. 32-5-1-4..	922	0.00172
June 16...	do	do	do	443	0.00082
July 7...	do	do	do	702	0.00132
July 31...	do	do	do	939	0.00175
Aug. 25...	do	do	do	934	0.00174
Sept. 25 ...	do	do	do	897	0.00167
Oct. 21....	do	do	do	910	0.00169

BATTLE CREEK DRAINAGE BASIN.

General Description.

Battle Creek rises in Township 8, Range 2, West of the 4th Meridian, and flows in an easterly direction for about eight miles, where it crosses the 4th Meridian, then turns in a southeasterly direction and crosses the international boundary in Section 3, Township 1, Range 26, West of the 3rd Meridian, eventually emptying into Milk River near Chinook, Montana. As is characteristic of the streams in this locality, the valley is narrow and deep near the source and gradually broadens out into large flats and meadows. These large flats are first noticed in the vicinity of Battle Creek P.O. Near the head of the stream the valley is well wooded with fair-sized timber, but this diminishes to a growth of willow brush along the banks and finally disappears altogether.

The chief tributaries of Battle Creek are Tenmile Creek, joining it in Section 4, Township 6, Range 29, West of the 3rd Meridian, and Sixmile Coulee, joining it in Section 21, Township 6, Range 29, West of the 3rd Meridian. Stations have been established on both of these streams.

There are three stations on Battle Creek, at the following places: Nash's ranch, Wilkes' ranch, and Tenmile police detachment.

Although it will be several years before it reaches its fullest development, the irrigation of the flats along the creek is increasing every year. This, it is expected, will result in a more uniform flow in the creek, as a certain amount of the water diverted by the irrigation ditches will be returned to the creek through seepage.

The principal irrigation schemes taking water from Battle Creek are: Marshall and Gaff's and W. S. Wilson's, near Tenmile police detachment; Richardson's and McKinnon's near Kelvinhurst; Gilchrist's, and Stirling and Nash's near Consul.

SPANGLER DITCH FROM SIXMILE COULEE.

Location.—On the SW. ¼ Sec. 6, Tp. 7, Rge. 28, W. 3rd Mer., at Spangler's ranch.

Records available.—For the irrigation seasons of 1912-14.

Gauge.—Vertical staff; zero of gauge has been maintained at 96.57 feet since establishment.

Bench-mark.—The top of the I.P. stake; assumed elevation, 100.00 feet.

Channel.—Composed of soft clay.

Discharge measurements.—Made by wading or with a weir.

Observer.—J. M. Spangler.

DISCHARGE MEASUREMENTS of Spangler Ditch from Sixmile Coulee, in 1914.

Date.	Engineer.	Width.	Area of Section.	Mean Velocity.	Gauge Height.	Discharge.
		Feet.	*Sq. ft.*	*Ft. per sec.*	*Feet.*	*Sec.-ft.*
May 28............	H. W. Rowley..............	5.0	1.50	0.63	1.49	0.95
June 23............	do	5.0	1.40	0.48	1.44	0.58
Nov. 4............	do	........a	....	....	1.39	0.36

a Weir measurement.

5 GEORGE V, A. 1915

DAILY GAUGE HEIGHT AND DISCHARGE of Spangler Ditch from Sixmile Coulee, for 1914.

	May.		June.		July.	
DAY.	Gauge Height.	Dis-charge.	Gauge Height.	Dis-charge.	Gauge Height.	Dis-charge.
	Feet.	*Sec.-ft.*	*Feet.*	*Sec.-ft.*	*Feet.*	*Sec.-ft.*
1			1.58	1.91	1.43	0.54
2			1.55	1.55	1.39	0.35
3			1.58	1.91	1.35	0.23
4	1.55a	1 55	1.70	3.60	1.32c	0.15
5	b	Nil.	1.75	4.40		
6	b	"	1.79	5.00		
7	1.54	1.45	1.75	4.40		
8	1.53	1.35	1.74	4.20		
9	1.59c	2.00	1.73	4.10		
10			1.72	4.00		
11			1.72	4 00		
12			1.74c	4.20		
13						
14						
15						
16						
17						
18						
19						
20						
21	1.59a	2.00				
22	1.59	2.00	1.55a	1.55		
23	1.61	2.30	1.45	0.64		
24	1.60	2.20	1.37	0.30		
25	1.54	1.45	1.45	0.64		
26	1.47	0.80	1.60	2.20		
27	1.49	0.96	1.55	1.55		
28	1.49	0.96	1.52	1.24		
29	1.49	0.96	1.50	1.04		
30	1.47	0.80	1.47	0.80		
31	1.48	0.88				

a Headgate opened.
b Ditch filled with snow.
c Headgate closed.

MONTHLY DISCHARGE of Spangler Ditch from Sixmile Coulee, for 1914.

	DISCHARGE IN SECOND-FEET.				RUN-OFF.	
MONTH.	Maximum	Minimum	Mean.	Per square Mile.	Depth in inches on Drainage Area.	Total in Acre-feet.
May { 4-9 / 21-31 }	2.30	0.00	1.28			43
June { 1-12 / 22-30 }	5.00	0.30	2.50			105
July (1-4)	0.54	0.15	0.32			2
The period						150

SIXMILE COULEE AT SPANGLER'S RANCH.

Location.—On the SW. ¼ Sec. 6, Tp. 7, Rge. 28, W. 3rd Mer., near Mr. Spangler's house. The present station is 850 feet north of the former station established July 4, 1911.

Records available.—At former station, 850 feet downstream· from July 3, 1911, to November 7, 1911. At present station—April 13, 1912, to October 31, 1914.

Gauge.—Vertical staff; zero of gauge maintained at 90 68 feet (original station), during 1911; 96.73 feet during 1912-14.

Bench-mark.—Permanent iron bench-mark located on the left bank 850 feet below gauge rod.

Channel.—Practically permanent.

Discharge measurements.—Made by wading or with weir.

Winter flow.—Station discontinued during winter season.

Diversions.—Water is diverted by J. M. Spangler for irrigation one-half mile above.

Observer.—D. B. Spangler.

DISCHARGE MEASUREMENTS of Sixmile Coulee at Spangler's Ranch, in 1914.

Date.	Engineer.	Width.	Area of Section.	Mean Velocity.	Gauge Height.	Discharge.
		Feet.	*Sq. ft.*	*Ft. per sec.*	*Feet.*	*Sec.-ft.*
June 5	H. W. Rowley	...a			1.56	0.18
June 23	do	. a			1.65	0.45
July 16	do				1.40	Nil.
July 20	do				1.55	"
Aug. 1	do				0.73	"
Aug. 11	do				Dry.	"
Sept. 3	do				0.47	"
Nov. 4	do	.. a			1.57	0.08

a Weir measurement.

DAILY GAUGE HEIGHT AND DISCHARGE of Sixmile Coulee at Spangler's Ranch, for 1914.

DAY.	March.		April.		May.		June.	
	Gauge Height.	Dis-charge.	Gauge Height.	Dis-charge.	Gauge Height.	Dis-charge.	Gauge Height.	Dis-charge.
	Feet.	*Sec.-ft.*	*Feet.*	*Sec.-ft.*	*Feet.*	*Sec.-ft.*	*Feet.*	*Sec.-ft.*
1					2.03	4.00	1.55	0.10
2					2.01	3.10	1.57	0.14
3			c		2.00	3.60	1.60	0.20
4			4.05		1.97	3.20	1.60	0.20
5			4.87		1.95	3.00	1.60	0.20
6			4.81		2.10	5.00	1.65	0.40
7			4.25		1.97	3.20	1.64	0.36
8			4.13		1.94	2.90	1.64	0.36
9			3.67	.	2.41	10.50	1.62	0.28
10			3.47b	. .	2.23	7.10	1.60	0.20
11			3.33	29.0	2.23	7.10	1.59	0.18
12			3.49	32.0	2.19	6.40	1.61	0.24
13			4.00	42.0	2.15	5.80	2.15	5.80
14			4.07	43.0	2.11	5.20	2.30	8.40
15	4.07a		3.89	40.0	2.07	4.60	2.20	6.60
16	3.55		3.72	36.0	2.01	3.70	2.15	5.80
17	3.40		3.43	31.0	2.02	3.90	2.05	4.30
18	3.28		3.27	27.0	2.01	3.70	2.00	3.60
19	2.85		3.05	23.0	2.00	3.60	1.90	2.40
20	c		2.86	19.5	2.00	3.60	1.75	1.00
21			2.44	11.1	1.87	2.10	1.73	0.88
22			2.44	11.1	1.87	2.10	1.65	0.40
23			2.41	10.5	1.86	2.00	1.56	0.12
24			2.31	8.6	1.91	2.50	1.52	0.05
25			2.23	7.1	1.88	2.20	1.53	0.07
26			2.21	6.8	1.84	1.80	1.82	1.60
27			2.17	6.1	1.55	0.10	1.76	1.08
28			2.13	5.5	1.54	0.08	1.70	0.70
29			2.11	5.2	1.54	0.08	1.69	0.64
30			2.09	4.9	1.55	0.10	1.68	0.58
31					1.53	0.07		

a to *b* Gauge heights affected by ice; not sufficient data to estimate discharge.
c Frozen solid.

5 GEORGE V, A. 1915

DAILY GAUGE HEIGHT AND DISCHARGE of Sixmile Coulee at Spangler's Ranch, for 1914.
—*Concluded.*

DAY.	July.		August.		September.		October.	
	Gauge Height.	Dis-charge.	Gauge Height.	Dis-charge.	Gauge Height.	Dis-charge.	Gauge Height.	Dis-charge.
	Feet.	Sec.-ft.	Feet.	Sec.-ft.	Feet.	Sec.-ft.	Feet.	Sec.-ft.
1	1.64	0.36	0.75	Nil.	.0.45	Nil.	0.86	Nil.
2	1.61	0.24	0.71	"	0.43	"	0.87	"
3	1.56	0.12	0.69	"	0.39	"	0.89	"
4	1.50	0.10	0.65	"	0.37	"	1.27	"
5	1.50	0.10	0.59	"	0.35	"	1.47	0.01
6	1.50	0.10	0.55	"	Dry.	"	1.51	0.04
7	1.50	0.10	0.52	"	"	"	1.57	0.14
8	1.48	0.01	0.51	"	"	"	1.90	2.40
9	1.47	0.01	0.51	"	"	"	2.03	4.00
10	1.47	0.01	0.53	"	"	"	1.95	3.00
11	1.52	0.05	0.53	"	"	"	1.90	2.40
12	1.47	0.01	0.53	"	"	"	1.85	1.90
13	1.45	Nil.	0.51	"	0.75	"	1.80	1.40
14	1.42	"	0.48	"	0.81	"	1.77	1.16
15	1.40	"	0.45	"	0.85	"	1.73	0.88
16	1.38	"	0.43	"	0.85	"	1.70	0.70
17	1.42	"	0.40	"	0.86	"	1.68	0.58
18	1.29	"	0.45	"	0.87	"	1.66	0.46
19	1.25	"	0.50	"	0.87	"	1.65	0.40
20	1.20	"	0.47	"	0.88	"	1.64	0.36
21	1.17	"	0.45	"	0.88	"	1.63	0.32
22	1.15	"	0.43	"	0.87	"	1.61	0.24
23	1.13	"	0.40	"	0.87	"	1.60	0.20
24	1.06	"	0.50	"	0.86	"	1.60	0.20
25	1.00	"	0.52	"	0.86	"	1.59	0.18
26	0.97	"	0.52	"	0.85	"	1.57	0.14
27	0.92	"	0.51	"	0.85	"	1.56	0.12
28	0.88	"	0.50	"	0.85	"	1.55	0.10
29	0.84	"	0.47	"	0.85	"	1.55	0.10
30	0.79	"	0.46	"	0.86	"	1.54	0.08
31	0.77	"	0.46	"	....	....	1.53	0.07

MONTHLY DISCHARGE of Sixmile Coulee at Spangler's Ranch, for 1914.

(Drainage area 42 square miles.)

MONTH.	DISCHARGE IN SECOND-FEET.				RUN-OFF.	
	Maximum.	Minimum.	Mean.	Per square Mile.	Depth in inches on Drainage Area.	Total in Acre-feet.
March...........................a	......	......	......	......	......	......
April (11-30)..............a	43.00	4.90	20.00	0.47600	0.350	791.0
May............................	10.50	0.07	3.40	0.08140	0.094	209.0
June...........................	8.40	0.05	1.57	0.03730	0.042	93.0
July...........................	0.36	0.00	0.04	0.00095	0.001	2.5
August........................	0.00	0.00	0.00	0.00000	0.000	0.0
September.....................	0.00	0.00	0.00	0.00000	0.000	0.0
October.......................	4.00	0.00	0.71	0.01700	0.020	44.0
The period....................	......	......	......	......	0.510	1,140.0

a Ice conditions Mar. 15 to April 10; insufficient data to compute discharge.

SESSIONAL PAPER No. 25c

LINDNER DITCH FROM BATTLE CREEK.

Location.—On the NW. ¼ Sec. 10, Tp. 6, Rge. 29, W. 3rd Mer., near Tenmile police detachment.

Records available.—For the irrigation seasons of 1910-14.

Gauge.—Vertical staff.

Channel.—Composed of gravel and clay loam.

Discharge measurements.—Made with a 42-inch weir, which is permanently installed in the ditch.

Observer.—Phil. Lindner.

Remarks.—This is a weir station, consisting of a 42-inch sharp-crested weir with complete end contractions. The elevation of the crest of the weir was kept at a gauge height of 1.04 feet during 1914.

DAILY GAUGE HEIGHT AND DISCHARGE of Lindner Ditch from Battle Creek, for 1914.

DAY.	April.		May.		June.		July.	
	Gauge Height.	Dis-charge.	Gauge Height.	Dis-charge.	Gauge Height.	Dis-charge.	Gauge Height.	Dis-charge.
	Feet.	*Sec.-ft.*	*Feet.*	*Sec.-ft.*	*Feet.*	*Sec.-ft.*	*Feet.*	*Sec.-ft.*
1			1.70	6.00	1.28	1.34		
2			1.70	6.00	1.30	1.53		
3			1.70	6.00	1.30	1.53		
4			1.70	6.00	1.30	1.53		
5			1.75b	6.70	1.36	2.10	1.40a	2.50
6					1.37	2.20	1.40	2.50
7					1.38	2.30	1.40	2.50
8					1.38	2.30	1.40	2.50
9					1.40	2.50	1.40	2.50
10					1.40b	2.50	1.38	2.30
11							1.36	2.10
12							1.35	2.00
13							1.35	2.00
14							1.35	2.00
15							1.35b	2.00
16								
17			1.53a	3.90				
18			1.53	3.90				
19			1.53	3.90				
20			1.53	3.90				
21			1.53	3.90				
22			1.53	3.90				
23			1.53	3.90				
24			1.40	2.50				
25			1.40	2.50				
26			1.40	2.50				
27			1.38	2.30				
28			1.32	1.71				
29			1.30	1.53				
30	1.70a	6.00	1.29	1.44				
31			1.27	1.26				

a Headgate opened.
b Headgate closed.

MONTHLY DISCHARGE of Lindner Ditch from Battle Creek, for 1914.

MONTH.	DISCHARGE IN SECOND-*FEET.*				RUN-OFF.	
	Maximum	Minimum	Mean.	Per square Mile.	Depth in inches on Drainage Area.	Total in Acre-feet.
April (30)	6.00	6.00	6.00			12
May { 1-5 }{ 17-31}	6.70	1.26	3.70			146
June (1-10)	2.50	1.34	1.98			39
July (5-15)	2.50	2.00	2.30			49
The period						246

5 GEORGE V, A. 1915

TENMILE CREEK AT TENMILE POLICE DETACHMENT.

Location.—On the SE. ¼ Sec. 4, Tp. 6, Rge. 29, W. 3rd. Mer., near the Tenmile R.N.W.M.P. detachment. The original station about 500 feet above the junction of Tenmile Creek with Battle Creek was moved about 1,000 feet farther upstream on September 14, 1914.

Records available.—At original location of station—July 21, 1909, to September 14, 1914. At the new location of the station—September 14, 1914, to October 31, 1914.

Gauge.—Vertical staff; zero of gauge maintained at 93 38 feet during 1909-11; 91.72 feet during 1912; 89.24 feet during 1913; 90.83 feet March 15 to September 14, 1914. Zero of gauge (new station) maintained at 99.76 feet from September 14 to October 31, 1914.

Bench-mark.—Permanent iron bench-mark, assumed elevation 100.00 feet, located on the left bank at the original station, which is 6.70 feet above the permanent iron bench-mark at the highway bridge over Battle Creek.

Channel.—Practically permanent.

Discharge measurements.—Made by wading or with weir.

Winter flow.—Station discontinued during winter season.

Artificial control.—A large beaver dam in Battle Creek, just below the mouth of Tenmile Creek, has a noticeable effect on the gauge heights at the original station but, as the gauge station is about 8 feet higher, the gauge readings at this station are not likely to be affected.

Observer.—R. W. Shafer, March to August. W. H. Tudgay, September and October.

DISCHARGE MEASUREMENTS of Tenmile Creek at Tenmile Police Detachment, in 1914.

Date.	Engineer.	Width.	Area of Section.	Mean Velocity.	Gauge Height.	Discharge.
		Feet.	*Sq. ft.*	*Ft. per sec.*	*Feet.*	*Sec.-ft.*
April 25............	H. R. Carscallen	... .*a*	....	....	1.80	0.88
April 27....	H. W. Rowley...............	.......*a*	....	....	1.77	0.79
May 4...	do	3.50	1 27	0.24	1.65	0.31
May 28...... ..	do	....	....	....	1.62	0.27
June 5...........	do	.......*a*	....	....	1.62	0.25
June 22	do	.......*a*	....	....	1.60	0.32
July 9...........	do	.......*a*	....	....	1.58	0.16
Aug. 1...........	do	.......*a*	....	....	1.58	0.17
Aug. 6...........	do	.......*a*	....	....	1.57	0.13
Sept. 2..	do	.......*a*	....	....	1.67	0.15
Sept. 14...	do	.......*a*	....	....	1.98	0.23
Sept. 15*b*........	do	.......*a*	....	....	0.59*c*	0.12
Oct. 5*b*........	do	.......*a*	....	....	0.60*c*	0.15
Oct. 23*b*........	do	.......*a*	....	....	0.59*c*	0.10
Nov. 2*b*........	do	.......*a*	....	....	0.59*c*	0.11

a Weir measurement.
b Measurement made at upper station.
c Gauge reading from rod at upper station.

SESSIONAL PAPER No. 25c

DAILY GAUGE HEIGHT AND DISCHARGE of Tenmile Creek at Tenmile Police Detachment,
for 1914.

DAY.	March.		April.		May.		June.	
	Gauge Height.	Dis-charge.	Gauge Height.	Dis-charge.	Gauge Height.	Dis-charge.	Gauge Height.	Dis-charge.
	Feet.	*Sec.-ft.*	*Feet.*	*Sec.-ft.*	*Feet.*	*Sec.-ft.*	*Feet.*	*Sec.-ft.*
1	....	....	1.62	0.25	1.69	0.47	1.63	0.28
2	....	....	1.60	0.20	1.68	0.43	1.63	0.28
3	....	....	1.59	0.18	1.67	0.40	1.63	0.28
4	....	....	1.62	0.25	1.67	0.40	1.61	0.23
5	....	....	2.34	3.80	1.69	0.47	1.61	0.23
6	....	....	2.28	3.50	1.67	0.40	1.71	0.54
7	....	....	2.18	2.90	1.67	0.40	1.62	0.25
8	....	....	2.19	3.00	1.67	0.40	1.60	0.20
9	....	....	2.22	3.20	1.69	0.47	1.59	0.18
10	....	....	2.02	2.00	1.69	0.47	1.60	0.20
11	....	....	2.15	2.80	1.72	0.57	1.60	0.20
12	....	....	2.13	2.70	1.68	0.43	1.61	0.23
13	....	....	2.63	5.50	1.67	0.40	1.60	0.20
14	....	....	2.85	6.70	1.68	0.43	1.62	0.25
15	....	....	2.75	6.10	1.67	0.40	1.62	0.25
16	1.91	1.44	2.45	4.50	1.69	0.47	1.61	0.23
17	1.62	0.25	2.22	3.20	1.69	0.47	1.61	0.23
18	1.62	0.25	2.06	2.30	1.70	0.50	1.58	0.16
19	1.62	0.25	1.98	1.80	1.70	0.50	1.58	0.16
20	1.53	0.07	1.96	1.72	1.67	0.40	1.58	0.16
21	1.53	0.07	1.89	1.34	1.67	0.40	1.58	0.16
22	1.53	0.07	1.81	0.95	1.69	0.47	1.59	0.18
23	1.53	0.07	1.78	0.81	1.67	0.40	1.59	0.18
24	1.55	0.09	1.77	0.77	1.67	0.40	1.58	0.16
25	1.55	0.09	1.80	0.90	1.66	0.36	1.60	0.20
26	1.55	0.09	1.78	0.81	1.66	0.36	1.59	0.18
27	1.55	0.09	1.77	0.77	1.63	0.28	1.59	0.18
28	1.58	0.16	1.63	0.28	1.62	0.25	1.60	0.20
29	1.58	0.16	1.75	0.68	1.61	0.23	1.62	0.25
30	1.57	0.13	1.71	0.54	1.61	0.23	1.61	0.23
31	1.71	0.54	....	....	1.62	0.25	....	....

5 GEORGE V, A. 1915

DAILY GAUGE HEIGHT AND DISCHARGE of Tenmile Creek at Tenmile Police Detachment, for 1914.

DAY.	July.		August.		September.		October.	
	Gauge Height.	Dis- charge.	Gauge Height.	Dis- charge.	Gauge Height.	Dis- charge.	Gauge Height.	Dis- charge.
	Feet.	*Sec.-ft.*	*Feet.*	*Sec.-ft.*	*Fee..*	*Sec.-ft.*	*Feet.*	*Sec.-ft.*
1	1.60	0.20	1.56	0.11	1.68	0.16	0.61	0.17
2	1.59	0.18	1.58	0.16	1.68	0.16	0.61	0.17
3	1.59	0.18	1.59	0.18	1.69	0.16	0.63	0.23
4	1.60	0.20	1.56	0.11	1.70	0.16	0.63	0.23
5	1.59	0.18	1.59	0.18	1.70	0.16	0.60	0.14
6	1.59	0.18	1.58	0.13	1.70	0.16	0.61	0.17
7	1.57	0.13	1.57	0.13	1.69	0.16	0.62	0.20
8	1.56	0.11	1.59	0.14	1.70	0.16	0.62 .	0.20
9	1.59	0.18	1.61	0.14	1.70	0.16	0.61	0.17
10	1.59	0.18	1.62	0.14	1.70	0.16	0.61	0.17
	1.59	0.18	1.59	0.14	1.70	0.16	0.60	0.14
12	1.58	0.16	1.60	0.14	1.71	0.17	0.60	0.14
13	1.58	0.16	1.61	0.14	1.87	0.21	0.60	0.14
14	1.56	0.11	1.60	0.14	0.60*a*	0.14	0.60	0.14
15	1.59	0.18	1.61	0.14	0.59	0.11	0.59	0.11
10	1.60	0.20	1.61	0/14	0.59	0.11	0.59	0.11
17	1.57	0.13	1.60	0.14	0.59	0.11	0.59	0.11
18	1.54	0.08	1.64	0.15	0.59	0.11	0.59	0.11
19	1.59	0.18	1.65	0.15	0.61	0.17	0.59	0.11
20	1.57	0.13	1.68	0.16	0.62	0.20	0.59	0.11
21	1.57	0.13	1.64	0.15	0.62	0.20	0.60	0.14
22	1.56	0.11	1.64	0.15	0.62	0.20	0.59	0.11
23	1.56	0.11	1.64	0.15	0.62	0.20	0.59	0.11
24	1.58	0.16	1.66	0.15	0.62	0.20	0.59	0.11
25	1.55	0.09	1.66	0.15	0.61	0.17	0.59	0.11
26	1.56	0.11	1.67	0.16	0.61	0.17	0.59	0.11
27	1.56	0.11	1.69	0.16	0.61	0.17	0.59	0.11
28	1.57	0.13	1.69	0.16	0.61	0.17	0.59	0.11
29	1.56	0.11	1.70	0.16	0.61	0.17	0.59	0.11
30	1.58	0.16	1.69	0.16	0.61	0.17	0.59	0.11
31	1.56	0.11	1.69	0.16	....	....	0.59*b*	0.11

a b Gauge heights taken from new gauge 1,000 ft. upstream.

MONTHLY DISCHARGE of Tenmile Creek at Tenmile Police Detachment, for 1914.

(Drainage area 24 square miles.)

MONTH.	DISCHARGE IN SECOND-FEET.				RUN-OFF.	
	Maximum	Minimum	Mean.	Per square Mile.	Depth in inches on Drainage Area.	Total in Acre-feet.
March (16-31)	1.44	0.07	0.24	0.0100	0.006	7.6
April	6.70	0.18	2.00	0.0890	0.099	127.0
May	0.57	0.23	0.40	0.0170	0.020	24.8
June	0.54	0.16	0.22	0.0093	0.010	13.3
July	0.20	0.08	0.15	0.0062	0.007	9.1
August	0.18	0.11	0.15	0.0062	0.007	9.1
September	0.21	0.11	0.16	0.0068	0.008	9.7
October	0.23	0.11	0.14	0.0058	0.007	8.6
The period	....	....	....	....	0 164	209 0

BATTLE CREEK AT TENMILE POLICE DETACHMENT.

Location.—On the NE. ¼ Sec. 33, Tp. 5, Rge. 29, W. 3rd Mer., at the highway bridge about one quarter mile south of Tenmile R.N.W.M.P. detachment and 300 yards north of the new Battle Creek post office.

Records available.—From June 3, 1909, to October 31, 1914.

Gauge.—Chain gauge, fastened to the guard rail on the downstream side of bridge. Zero of gauge maintained at 86.97 feet, length of chain (from marker to bottom of weight) 19.10 feet, during 1909-10. Zero of gauge maintained at 86.87 feet, length of chain 19.10 feet, during 1911. Zero of gauge maintained at 86.84 feet, length of chain 19.11 feet, during 1912-14.

Bench-mark.—Permanent iron bench-mark; assumed elevation, 100.00 feet.

Channel.—Practically permanent, but might shift during extreme floods. Weeds in the channel affect the gauge heights at times during midsummer season.

Discharge measurements.—Made from downstream side of bridge during high water, and by wading or with weir some distance below during low water flow.

Winter flow.—Station discontinued during winter season.

Artificial control.—There are several large beaver dams above this station which have a tendency to keep the creek running at this point after the creek goes dry farther up towards its source in the Cypress Hills.

Diversions.—Lindner Brothers divert water for irrigation about two miles above.

Observer.—R. W. Shafer, March to August; W. H. Tudgay, September and October.

DISCHARGE MEASUREMENTS of Battle Creek at Tenmile Police Detachment, in 1914.

Date.	Engineer.	Width.	Area of Section.	Mean Velocity.	Gauge Height.	Discharge.
		Feet.	*Sq. ft.*	*Ft. per sec.*	*Feet.*	*Sec.-ft.*
Mar. 19	H. R. Carscallen	27.0	94.1	0.35	4.40	33.00
Mar. 21	do	26.5	65.9	0.34	3.37	22.00
Mar. 31	do	32.5	24.0	0.77	2.88	18.40
April 4	do	33.7	30.1	1.25	3.12	38.00
April 6	do	47.2	86.0	1.50	4.49	129.00
April 7	do	30.5	97.1	1.08	4.30	105.00
April 11	do	41.0	46.8	1.40	3.53	66.00
April 13	do	41.5	168.0	1.54	5.96	258.00
April 14	do	47.0	224.0	1.75	7.18	391.00
April 15	do	44.0	195.0	1.70	6.50	332.00
April 23	do	40.4	43.0	1.50	3.47	65.00
April 24	do	40.6	44.8	1.55	3.50	69.00
April 27	H. W. Rowley.	32.0*b*	30.6	1.83	3.28	56.00
May 4	do	28.5*b*	21.4	1.59	2.97	34.00
May 28	do	24.0*b*	14.9	1.46	2.74	22.00
June 5	do	29.5*b*	19.1	1.18	2.79	22.00
June 22	do	14.0*b*	9.3	1.51	2.65	14.30
July 9	do	9.0*b*	3.5	0.82	2.31	2.90
Aug. 1	do	......*a*			2.23	1.71
Aug. 9	do	......*a*			2.20	1.11
Aug. 11	do				2.23	1.49
Sept. 2	do				2.33	3.00
Sept. 14	do	39.0*b*	36.8	0.94	3.20	36.00
Sept. 15	do	37.5*b*	31.1	0.75	2.90	23.00
Oct. 3	do	32.0*b*	18.2	0.50	2.54	9.00
Oct. 6	do	36.2*b*	25.6	0.74	2.78	19.10
Oct. 23	do	36.5*b*	28.0	0.77	2.78	22.00
Nov. 3	do	33.0*b*	20.7	0.71	2.65	14.70

a Weir measurements.
b Not taken at bridge section

5 GEORGE V, A. 1915

DAILY GAUGE HEIGHT AND DISCHARGE of Battle Creek at Tenmile Police Detachment, for 1914.

DAY	March.		April,		May.		June.	
	Gauge Height.	Dis- charge.	Gauge Height.	Dis- charge.	Gauge Height.	Dis- charge.	Gauge Height.	Dis- charge.
	Feet.	*Sec.-ft.*	*Feet.*	*Sec.-ft.*	*Feet.*	*Sec.-ft.*	*Feet.*	*Sec.-ft.*
1			2.75	18.6	2.96	30.4	2.68	15.0
2			2.75	18.6	2.98	32.0	2.72	17.0
3			2.87	25.0	2.97	31.0	2.73	17.6
4			3.06	37.0	2.99	32.0	2.83	23.0
5			3.35	56.0	3.14	42.0	2.76	19.1
6			3.33	55.0	3.05	36.0	2.83	23.0
7			4.15	116.0	3.01	33.0	2.86	25.0
8			3.96	101.0	3.06	37.0	2.86	25.0
9			3.74	84.0	3.53	69.0	2.78	20.0
10			3.57	71.0	3.56	71.0	2.74	18.1
11			3.76	86.0	3.53	69.0	2.71	16.5
12			4.33	130.0	3.30	53.0	2.74	18.1
13			6.64	337.0	3.19	45.0	2.97	31.0
14			7.59	432.0	3.14	42.0	3.15	42.0
15			7.26	399.0	3.05	36.0	3.12	40.0
16	5.51	47a	6.50	323.0	3.06	37.0	2.91	27.0
17	4.84	39a	4.99	186.0	2.99	32.0	2.85	24.0
18	3.83	27a	4.09	112.0	2.98	30.0	2.74	18.1
19	3.96	28a	3.90	97.0	2.96	30.0	2.69	15.5
20	3.51	24a	3.85	93.0	2.96	30.0	2.65	13.4
21	3.44	23a	3.68	80.0	2.91	27.0	2.62	12.0
22	3.16	21a	3.44	62.0	2.87	25.0	2.62	12.0
23	3.01	20a	3.46	64.0	2.87	25.0	2.59	10.7
24	3.01	20a	3.50	66.0	2.88	26.0	2.55	9.1
25	3.11	21a	3.39	58.0	2.86	25.0	2.69	15.5
26	3.22	22a	3.39	58.0	2.83	23.0	2.71	16.5
27	3.04	20a	3.28	51.0	2.78	20.0	2.75	18.6
28	3.04	20a	3.20	46.0	2.73	17.6	2.69	15.5
29	3.00	20a	3.15	42.0	2.71	16.5	2.63	12.5
30	2.88	19a	3.01	33.0	2.70	16.0	2.59	10.7
31	2.88	19a			2.68	15.0		

a Ice conditions—discharge estimated.

SESSIONAL PAPER No. 25c

DAILY GAUGE HEIGHT AND DISCHARGE of Battle Creek at Tenmile Police Detachment, for 1914.—*Concluded.*

DAY.	July. Gauge Height.	July. Dis-charge.	August. Gauge Height.	August. Dis-charge.	September. Gauge Height.	September. Dis-charge.	October. Gauge Height.	October. Dis-charge.
	Feet.	*Sec.-ft.*	*Feet.*	*Sec.-ft.*	*Feet.*	*Sec.-ft.*	*Feet.*	*Sec.-ft.*
1	2.59	10.70	2.22	1.32	2.32	3.0	2.46	6.3
2	2.55	9.10	2.24	1.64	2.33	3.1	2.46	6.3
3	2.50	7.50	2.22	1.32	2.33	3.1	2.46	6.3
4	2.46	6.30	2.18	0.80	2.33	3.1	2.82	22.0
5	2.36	3.70	2.21	1.16	2.33	3.1	2.86	25.0
6	2.33	3.10	2.20	1.00	2.33	3.1	2.78	20.0
7	2.33	3.10	2.20	1.00	2.32	3.0	2.77	19.6
8	2.28	2.30	2.23	1.48	2.32	3.0	3.02	34.0
9	2.28	2.30	2.25	1.80	2.33	3.1	3.43	62.0
10	2.28	2.30	2.25	1.80	2.33	3.1	3.32	54.0
11	2.28	2.30	2.23	1.48	2.32	3.0	3.20	46.0
12	2.22	1.30	2.24	1.64	2.36	3.7	3.07	37.0
13	2.23	1.50	2.23	1.48	2.61	11.6	2.97	31.0
14	2.22	1.30	2.23	1.48	3.19	45.0	2.88	26.0
15	2.22	1.30	2.22	1.32	2.93	29.0	3.12	40.0
16	2.22	1.30	2.24	1.64	2.82	22.0	3.25	49.0
17	2.73	1.60	2.22	1.32	2.73	17.6	3.21	46.0
18	2.26	2.00	2.25	1.80	2.68	15.0	3.02	34.0
19	2.29	2.40	2.24	1.64	2.65	13.4	2.93	29.0
20	2.29	2.40	2.25	1.80	2.64	12.9	2.88	26.0
21	2.25	1.80	2.22	1.32	2.63	12.5	2.83	23.0
22	2.22	1.32	2.22	1.32	2.58	10.3	2.79	22.0
23	2.24	1.64	2.24	1.64	2.55	9.1	2.78	20.0
24	2.22	1.32	2.32	3.00	2.54	8.8	2.74	18.1
25	2.22	1.32	2.26	1.96	2.52	8.1	2.74	18.1
26	2.24	1.64	2.24	1.64	2.48	6.9	2.74	18.1
27	2.21	1.16	2.34	3.30	2.45	6.0	2.70	16.0
28	2.21	1.16	2.34	3.30	2.45	6.0	2.65	13.4
29	2.22	1.32	2.34	3.30	2.45	6.0	2.69	15.5
30	2.21	1.16	2.33	3.10	2.45	6.0	2.69	15.5
31	2.21	1.16	2.33	3.10	....	....	2.68	15.0

MONTHLY DISCHARGE of Battle Creek at Tenmile Police Detachment, for 1914.

(Drainage area 210 square miles.)

MONTH.	DISCHARGE IN SECOND-FEET. Maximum.	Minimum	Mean.	Per square Mile.	RUN-OFF. Depth in inches on Drainage Area.	Total in Acre-feet.
March (16-31) *a*	47.00	19.00	24.00	0.116	0.070	773
April	432.00	18.60	111.00	0.530	0.591	6,605
May	71.00	15.00	34.00	0.162	0.187	2,091
June	42.00	9.10	19.40	0.092	0.103	1,154
July	10.70	1.16	2.67	0.013	0.015	164
August	3.30	0.80	1.80	0.009	0.010	111
September	45.00	0.30	9.45	0.045	0.050	562
October	62.00	6.30	26.30	0.125	0.144	1,617
The period	....	....	....	....	1 170	13,077

a Ice conditions during March; discharge estimated.

5 GEORGE V, A. 1915

GAFF DITCH FROM BATTLE CREEK.

Location.—On the SW. ¼ Sec. 25, Tp. 5, Rge. 29, W. 3rd Mer., about one-half mile from Mr. Gaff's house near Tenmile police detachment.

Records available.—For the irrigation seasons of 1912-14.

Gauge.—Vertical staff; the zero of the gauge has been maintained at 96.90 feet since establishment.

Bench-mark.—The top of a wooden stake on the right bank; assumed elevation, 100.00 feet.

Channel.—Composed of sandy loam and somewhat grown over with grass and weeds.

Discharge measurements.—Made by wading or with a weir.

Observer.—W. D. Gaff.

DISCHARGE MEASUREMENTS of Gaff Ditch from Battle Creek, in 1914.

Date.	Engineer.	Width.	Area of Section.	Mean Velocity.	Gauge Height.	Discharge.
		Feet.	*Sq. ft.*	*Ft. per sec.*	*Feet.*	*Sec.-ft.*
May 27............	H. W. Rowley..............	9.00	12.6	1.06	1.83	13.5
June 22..	do	9.00	11.2	0.94	1.73	10.6
Oct. 23...	do	7.70	4.4	0.71	0.83	3.2
Oct. 23......... ...	do	7.50	4.4	0.69	0.83	3.1

DAILY GAUGE HEIGHT AND DISCHARGE of Gaff Ditch from Battle Creek, in 1914.

DAY.	May.		June.		July.	
	Gauge Height.	Discharge.	Gauge Height.	Discharge.	Gauge Height.	Discharge.
	Feet.	*Sec.-ft.*	*Feet.*	*Sec.-ft.*	*Feet.*	*Sec.-ft.*
1..........	....	....	1.75	12.20	1.42	8.00
2..........	....	....	1.67	11.00	1.42	8.00
3..........	....	....	1.75	12.20	1.29	6.70
4..........	....	....	1.67	11.00	....	....
5..........	....	....	1.87	14.10	....	....
6..........	....	....	1.83	13.50	....	....
7..........	....	....	1.83	13.50	....	....
8..........	....	....	1.83	13.50	....	....
9..........	....	....	1.83	13.50	....	....
10.........	....	....	1.92	14.80	....	....
11.........	....	....	1.83	13.50	....	....
12.........	....	....	1.79	12.80	....	....
13.........	....	....	1.92	14.80	....	....
14.........	1.33	7.10	1.92	14.80	....	....
15.........	1.50	9.00	1.92	14.80	....	....
16.........	1.50	9.00	1.92	14.80	....	....
17.........	1.60	10.30	1.83	13.50	....	....
18.........	1.85	13.80	1.75	12.20	....	....
19.........	1.96	15.40	1.83	13.50	....	....
20.........	1.92	14.80	1.92	14.80	....	....
21.........	2.04	16.70	1.83	13.50	....	....
22.........	1.92	14.80	1.75	12.20	....	....
23.........	1.87	14.10	1.67	10.00	....	....
24.........	1.75	12.20	1.50	9.00	....	....
25.........	1.50	9.00	1.50	9.00	....	....
26.........	1.42	8.00	2.00	16.10	....	....
27.........	1.83	13.50	2.05	16.70	....	....
28.........	1.75	12.20	1.83	13.50	....	....
29.........	1.67	11.00	1.67	11.00	....	....
30.........	1.50	9.00	1.58	10.00	....	....
31.........	1.50	9.00	....	....	....	....

MONTHLY DISCHARGE of Gaff Ditch from Battle Creek, for 1914.

MONTH.	DISCHARGE IN SECOND-*FEET*.				RUN-OFF.	
	Maximum.	Minimum.	Mean.	Per square Mile.	Depth in inches on Drainage Area.	Total in Acre-feet.
May (14-31)............................	16.70	7.10	11.60	....	....	414
June..................................	16.70	9.00	13.00	....	....	774
July (1-3).............................	8.00	6.70	7.40	....	....	44
The period........	....	....	....	....	....	1,232

WILSON DITCH FROM BATTLE CREEK.

Location.—On the NE. ¼ Sec. 34, Tp. 5, Rge. 28, W. 3rd Mer.
Records available.—Discharge measurements only in 1914.
Gauge.—Plain staff; elevation 96.28 feet.
Bench-mark.—Permanent iron bench-mark on left bank; assumed elevation, 100 00 feet.
Observer.—No observations in 1914.

DISCHARGE MEASUREMENTS of Wilson Ditch from Battle Creek, in 1914.

Date.	Engineer.	Width.	Area of Section.	Mean Velocity.	Gauge Height.	Discharge.
		Feet.	*Sq. ft.*	*Ft. per sec.*	*Feet.*	*Sec.-ft.*
June 20.............	H. W. Rowley...............	....	....	....	0.88	0.53
May 27.............	do	6.5	2.23	1.01	1.13	2.20

BATTLE CREEK AT WILKES' RANCH.

Location.—On the NW. ¼ Sec. 33, Tp. 5, Rge. 27, W. 3rd Mer., at R. W. Wilkes' ranch, 12 miles east of the Tenmile R.N.W.M.P. detachment.
Records available.—From May 1, 1912, to October 31, 1914. From July 5, 1910, to November 7, 1911, a station was maintained at W. S..Wilson's ranch, six miles above.
Gauge.—Vertical staff; zero of gauge maintained at 89.86 feet during 1912; 90 01 feet during 1913-14.
Bench-mark.—Permanent iron bench-mark; assumed elevation, 100.00 feet; located on the left bank 750 feet below the gauge.
Channel.—Composed of sand and slightly shifting.
Discharge measurements.—Made by wading.
Winter flow.—Station discontinued during winter season.
Diversions.—Water is diverted above this station for irrigation purposes by Mrs. L. A. Marshall, J. A. Gaff, Lindner Brothers, W. S. Wilson, and F. W. Henry.
Observer.—Mrs. Bertha Wilkes.

5 GEORGE V, A. 1915

DISCHARGE MEASUREMENTS of Battle Creek at Wilkes' Ranch, in 1914.

Date.	Engineer.	Width.	Area of Section.	Mean Velocity.	Gauge Height.	Discharge.
		Feet.	*Sq. ft.*	*Ft. per sec.*	*Feet.*	*Sec.-ft.*
May 2............	H W. RoWley.. . .	26.0	30.80	1.35	2.25	42.00
May 26............	do	11.5	6.90	0.85	1.66	5.80
June 20............	do	9.5	3.60	1.21	1.44	4.40
July 10............	do	7.0	2.10	0.81	1.34	1.71
Aug. 8.... . .	do	.......*a*	....	....	1.29	0.43
Sept. 1....... ..	do	....*a*	....	....	1.36	2.10
Oct. 1............	do	11.5*b*	7.42	0.92	1.49	6.80
Nov. 2............	do	26.0*b*	16.75	1.17	1.78	19.60

a Weir measurement.
b Measurement made beloW regular section.

DAILY GAUGE HEIGHT AND DISCHARGE of Battle Creek at Wilkes' Ranch, for 1914.

DAY.	April.		May.		June.	
	Gauge Height.	Dis-charge.	Gauge Height.	Dis-charge.	Gauge Height.	Dis-charge.
	Feet.	*Sec.-ft.*	*Feet.*	*Sec.-ft.*	*Feet.*	*Sec.-ft.*
1................	....	....	....*b*	... ...	1.45	4.9
2................	....	....	2.25	42.0	1.43	4.3
3................	....	....	2.25	42.0	1.37	2.5
4................	....	....	2.25	42.0	1.36	2.3
5................	....	....	2.27	43.0	1.49	6.2
6................	4.75	....*a*	2.29	44.0	1.58	9.3
7................	5.34	....	2.29	44.0	1.68	13.2
8................	5.40	....	2.29	44.0	1.70	14.0
9................	5.09	....	2.34	47.0	1.62	10.8
10................	4.39	....	2.45	54.0	1.50	6.5
11................	4.63	....	2.60	64.0	1.44	4.6
12................	4.73	....	2.62	65.0	1.44	4.6
13................	4.69	....	2.36	49.0	1.42	3.9
14................	5.95	....*a*	2.19	38.0	1.47	5.5
15................	....*b*	....	2.13	35.0	1.48	5.9
16................	....	....	2.07	31.0	1.49	6.2
17................	....	....	2.04	30.0	1.53	7.5
18................	....	....	1.95	25.0	1.51	6.8
19................	....	....	1.87	21.0	1.44	4.6
20................	....	....	1.78	17.2	1.41	3.6
21................	....	....	1.74	15.6	1.41	3.6
22................	....	....	1.71	14.4	1.41	3.6
23................	....	....	1.65	12.0	1.43	4.3
24................	....	....	1.68	13.2	1.43	4.3
25................	....	....	1.68	13.2	1.43	4.3
26................	....	....	1.66	12.4	1.40	3.3
27................	....	....	1.53	7.5	1.40	3.3
28................	....	....	1.52	7.2	1.40	3.3
29................	....	....	1.50	6.5	1.38	2.8
30................	....	....	1.48	5.9	1.38	2.8
31................	....	....	1.45	4.9	....	....

a Ice conditions; not sufficient data to estimate discharge.
b to *b* Gauge taken out by ice April 15; replaced May 2.

SESSIONAL PAPER No. 25c

DAILY GAUGE HEIGHT AND DISCHARGE of Battle Creek at Wilkes' Ranch, for 1914.
—*Concluded.*

DAY.	July.		August.		September.		October.	
	Gauge Height.	Discharge.	Gauge Height.	Discharge.	Gauge Height.	Discharge.	Gauge Height.	Discharge.
	Feet.	*Sec.-ft.*	*Feet.*	*Sec.-ft.*	*Feet.*	*Sec.-ft.*	*Feet.*	*Sec.-ft.*
1	1.36	2.30	Dry.	Nil.	1.36	2.3	1.57	8.9
2	1.36	2.30	"	"	1.36	2.3	1.61	10.4
3	1.34	1.76	1.21	0.06	1.35	2.0	1.64	11.6
4	1.34	1.76	1.21	0.06	1.35	2.0	1.72	14.8
5	1.34	1.76	1.21	0.06	1.35	2.0	1.78	17.2
6	1.34	1.76	1.21	0.06	1.35	2.0	1.81	18.4
7	1.34	1.76	1.21	0.06	1.35	2.0	1.83	19.2
8	1.32	1.28	1.21	0.06	1.35	2.0	1.83	19.2
9	1.30	0.80	1.21	0.06	1.35	2.0	1.85	20.0
10	1.30	0.80	1.24	0.24	1.35	2.0	1.89	22.0
11	1.30	0.80	1.24	0.24	1.35	2.0	1.92	24.0
12	1.28	0.60	1.24	0.24	1.76	16.4	1.96	26.0
13	1.28	0.60	1.26	0.40	1.76	16.4	2.01	28.0
14	1.24	0.24	1.26	0.40	1.89	22.0	2.06	31.0
15	1.23	0.18	1.26	0.40	1.89	22.0	2.06	31.0
16	1.21	0.06	1.26	0.40	1.89	22.0	2.09	32.0
17	1.21	0.06	1.30	0.80	1.89	22.0	2.10	32.0
18	1.21	0.06	1.32	1.28	1.88	22.0	1.98	26.0
19	1.21	0.06	1.35	2.00	1.88	22.0	1.98	26.0
20	1.21	0.06	1.35	2.00	1.86	20.0	1.94	24.0
21	1.20	Nil.	1.37	2.50	1.86	20.0	1.94	24.0
22	1.20	"	1.37	2.50	1.86	20.0	1.88	22.0
23	Dry.	"	1.37	2.50	1.81	18.4	1.84	20.0
24	"	"	1.37	2.50	1.81	18.4	1.71	14.4
25	"	"	1.37	2.50	1.79	17.6	1.71	14.4
26	"	"	1.37	2.50	1.79	17.6	1.71	14.4
27	"	"	1.37	2.50	1.78	17.2	1.68	13.2
28	"	"	1.37	2.50	1.78	17.2	1.68	13.2
29	"	"	1.37	2.50	1.73	15.2	1.65	12.0
30	"	"	1.37	2.50	1.54	7.8	1.65	12.0
31	"	"	1.36	2.30	....	....	1.65	12.0

MONTHLY DISCHARGE of Battle Creek at Wilkes' Ranch, for 1914.

(Drainage area 310 square miles.)

MONTH.	DISCHARGE IN SECOND-FEET.				RUN-OFF.	
	Maximum.	Minimum.	Mean.	Per square Mile.	Depth in inches on Drainage Area.	Total in Acre-feet.
April	....	....	....	0.4090	0.4560	7,535a
May (2-31)	65.00	4.90	29.70	0.0958	0.1060	1,767
June	14.00	2.30	5.43	0.0175	0.0200	323
July	2.30	0.00	0.61	0.0020	0.0020	38
August	2.50	0.00	1.16	0.0037	0.0040	71
September	22.00	2.00	12.60	0.0406	0.0450	750
October	32.00	8.90	19.80	0.0640	0.0740	1,218
The period	....	....	....	....	0.7070	11,702

a Estimated from stations at Tenmile police detachment and at Nash's ranch.

5 GEORGE V, A. 1915

GILCHRIST BROTHERS' DITCH FROM BATTLE CREEK.

Location.—On the SW. ¼ Sec. 11, Tp. 5, Rge. 27, W. 3rd Mer., at the intake of Gilchrist Brothers' ditch near Consul.

Records available.—For the irrigation season of 1914.

Gauge.—Vertical staff; the zero of the gauge has remained unchanged at 96.92 feet since establishment.

Bench-mark.—The top of a post at the lower end of the flume; assumed elevation, 100.00 feet.

Dischar ge measurements.—Made with a meter in the flume, or with a weir just below the flume.

Observer.—W. F. Gilchrist.

DISCHARGE MEASUREMENTS of Gilchrist Brothers' Ditch from Battle Creek, in 1914.

Date.	Engineer.	Width.	Area of Section.	Mean Velocity.	Gauge Height.	Discharge.
		Feet.	*Sq. ft.*	*Ft. per sec.*	*Feet.*	*Sec.-ft.*
May 26............	H. W. Rowley..............	3.5	1.30	0.65	0.46	0.85
June 20............	do	3.5	2.10	1.00	0.65	2.11
Oct. 1............	do	3.0	1.75	0.70	0.54	1.23

DAILY GAUGE HEIGHT AND DISCHARGE of Gilchrist Brothers' Ditch from Battle Creek, for 1914.

DAY.	May.		June.		July.		August.		September.		October.	
	Gauge Height.	Dis-charge.	Gauge Height.	Dis-charge.	Gauge Height.	Dis-charge.	Gauge Height.	Dis-charge.	Gauge Height.	Dis-charge.	Gauge Height.	Dis-charge.
	Feet.	*Sec.-ft.*	*Feet.*	*Sec.-ft.*	*Feet.*	*Sec.-ft.*	*Feet.*	*Sec.-ft.*	*Feet.*	*Sec.-ft.*	*Feet.*	*Sec.-ft.*
1.........											0.54	1.25
2.........											0.54	1.25
3.........											0.54	1.25
4.........											0.60	1.67
5.........											0.67	2.40
6.........											0.75*b*	3.20
7.........												......
8.........			0.67*a*	2.40							......	......
9.........			0.07	2.40								......
10....... .			0.58	1.52								
11.........			0.58	1.52								
12...... ..			0.79	3.70								
13.........			0.79	3.70								
14.........												
15.........												
16.........												
17.........			0.79	3.70								
18.........			0.91	5.00								
19.........			0.90	4.80								
20.........	......*a*		0.62*b*	1.90					0.75*a*	3.20		
21.........	0.67	2.40							0.75	3.20		
22.........	0.67	2.40							0.71	2.80		
23.........	0.83*b*	4.20							0.67	2.40		
24.........									0.71*b*	2.80		
25.........	0.09*a*	2.60							......			
26.........	0.38	0.59							......			
27.........	0.33*b*	0.49							0.75*a*	3.20		
28.........									0.75	3.20		
29.........									0.75	3.20		
30...... .									0.75	3.20		
31.......												

a Headgate opened.
b Headgate closed.

MONTHLY DISCHARGE of Gilchrist Brothers' Ditch from Battle Creek, for 1914.

MONTH.	DISCHARGE IN SECOND-FEET.				RUN-OFF.	
	Maximum.	Minimum.	Mean.	Per square Mile.	Depth in inches on Drainage Area.	Total in Acre-feet.
May (21-27)................	4.20	0.49	2.10	....	....	25
June.....................	5.00	1.52	3.10	....	....	61
September {20-24}{27-30}..	3.20	2.40	3.00	....	....	54
October (1-6)............	3.20	1.25	1.84	....	....	22
The period...............	....	....	....	....	....	162

RICHARDSON DITCH FROM BATTLE CREEK.

Location.—On the SE. ¼ Sec. 2, Tp. 5, Rge. 27, W. 3rd Mer., near Consul.
Records available.—October 14, 1911, to October 31, 1914.
Gauge.—Vertical staff; the zero of the gauge has been maintained at 99.79 feet since establishment.
Bench-mark.—The top of the quarter-mound stake; assumed elevation, 100.00 feet.
Channel.—Composed of clay loam and overgrown with grass.
Discharge measurements.—Made by wading or with a weir.
Observer.—L. E. Richardson.
Remarks.—This ditch was used for about 20 days in May, but insufficient data were obtained to estimate the discharge.

DISCHARGE MEASUREMENTS of Richardson Ditch from Battle Creek, in 1914.

Date.	Engineer.	Width.	Area of Section.	Mean Velocity.	Gauge Height.	Discharge.
		Feet.	*Sq. ft.*	*Ft. per sec.*	*Feet.*	*Sec.-ft.*
June 20..........	H. W. Rowley..........	....	4.60	0.43	0.46	1.98

STIRLING AND NASH DITCH FROM BATTLE CREEK.

Location.—On the SE. ¼ Sec. 22, Tp. 3, Rge. 27, W. 3rd Mer., at R. J. Stirling's ranch, near Consul.
Records available.—This station was established July 11, 1911. The ditch was used from July 11 to August 17, 1911; from July 3 to August 20, 1912; and from June 28 to July 19, 1913. Sufficient discharge measurements were not made during 1911-13 to estimate the daily discharge; the first daily discharge records available are for 1914.
Gauge.—Vertical staff; the zero of the gauge has been maintained at 94 81 feet since establishment.
Bench-mark.—A wooden stake on the right bank; assumed elevation, 100.00 feet.
Channel.—Uniform and in good condition.
Discharge measurements.—Made by wading or with a weir.
Observer.—R. J. Stirling.

DISCHARGE MEASUREMENTS of Stirling and Nash Ditch from Battle Creek, in 1914.

Date.	Engineer.	Width.	Area of Section.	Mean Velocity.	Gauge Height.	Discharge.
		Feet.	*Sq. ft.*	*Ft. per sec.*	*Feet.*	*Sec.-ft.*
May 1..........	H. W. Rowley..........	9.0	6.30	1.08	1.39	6.80
May 26..........	do	9.5	7.25	1.04	1.51	7.50
June 19..........	do	9.5	6.93	0.91	1.49	6.30

5 GEORGE V, A. 1915

DAILY GAUGE HEIGHT AND DISCHARGE of Stirling and Nash Ditch from Battle Creek, for 1914.

DAY	April.		May.		June.	
	Gauge Height.	Dis-charge.	Gauge Height.	Dis-charge.	Gauge Height.	Dis-charge.
	Feet.	*Sec.-ft.*	*Feet.*	*Sec.-ft.*	*Feet.*	*Sec.-ft.*
1	....	....	1.42	6.10	1.48	7.10
2	....	....	1.42	6.10	1.48	7.10
3	....	....	1.52	7.80	1.48	7.10
4	....	....	1.52	7.80	1.45	6.60
5	....	....	1.52	7.80	1.45	6.60
6	....	....	1.57	8.70	1.44	6.40
7	....	....	1.60	9.20	1.44	6.40
8	....	....	1.68	10.80	1.44	6.40
9	....	....	1.72	11.40	1.44	6.40
10	....	....	1.72	11.40	1.44	6.40
11	....	....	1.72	11.40	1.40	5.80
12	....	....	1.72	11.40	1.40	5.80
13	....	....	1.72	11.40	1.36	5.30
14	....	....	1.72	11.40	1.36	5.30
15	....	....	1.72	11.40	1.36	5.30
16	....	....	1.72	11.40	1.36	5.30
17	....	....	1.70	11.20	1.30	4.50
18	....	....	1.70	11.20	1.30	4.50
19	1.12	2.80	1.70	11.20	1.25	4.00
20	1.32	4.80	1.70	11.20	1.22	3.70
21	1.32	4.80	1.68	10.80	1.22	3.70
22	1.32	4.80	1.68	10.80	1.15	3.00
23	1.32	4.80	1.68	10.80	1.10	2.60
24	1.32	4.80	1.67	10.60	1.08	2.50
25	1.32	4.80	1.67	10.60	1.08	2.50
26	1.37	5.40	1.63	9.80	1.04	2.20
27	1.35	5.10	1.54	8.10	0.96	1.66
28	1.35	5.10	1.50	7.40	0.80	0.85
29	1.37	5.40	1.50	7.40	0.59	0.28
30	1.37	5.40	1.50	7.40	0.40	0.05
31	....	....	1.50	7.40	....	....

MONTHLY DISCHARGE of Stirling and Nash Ditch from Battle Creek, for 1914.

MONTH	DISCHARGE IN SECOND-FEET.			RUN-OFF.
	Maximum.	Minimum.	Mean.	Total in Acre-feet.
April (19-30)	5.40	2.80	4.80	115
May	11.40	6.10	9.70	598
June	7.10	0.05	4.52	269
The period	....	....	....	982

BATTLE CREEK AT NASH'S RANCH.

Location.—On the *NE.* ¼ Sec. 3, Tp. 3, Rge. 27, W. 3rd Mer., at *E. R.* Nash's ranch (Nash-lyn post office).

Records available.—May 11, 1910, to October 31, 1914.

Gauge.—Vertical staff; elevation of zero of gauge 90.23 feet.

Bench-mark.—Permanent iron bench-mark; assumed elevation, 100.00 feet.

Channel.—Slightly shifting.

Discharge measurements.—Made from cable car, by wading, or weir.

Winter flow.—Stations discontinued during winter season.

Diversions.—Water is diverted for irrigation by Jas. McKinnon, Jr., Mrs. S. J. Richardson, Gilchrist Brothers, Stirling and Nash, and L. *E.* Richardson, between this station and the station at Wilkes' ranch.

Observer.—E. R. Nash.

SESSIONAL PAPER No. 25c

DISCHARGE MEASUREMENTS of Battle Creek at Nash's Ranch, in 1914.

Date.	Engineer.	Width.	Area of Section.	Mean Velocity.	Gauge Height.	Discharge.
		Feet.	*Sq. ft.*	*Ft. per sec.*	*Feet.*	*Sec.-ft.*
Mar. 23	H. D. St. A. Smith	39.0	34.6	0.87	2.35	30.00
Mar. 24	do	39.8	35.1	0.77	2.40	27.00
Mar. 28	do	35.0	22.8	0.99	2.56	23.00
April 1	do	55.0	110.0	0.98	4.08	108.00
April 2	do	44.0	78.4	0.91	3.50	72.00
April 6	do	36.0	43.2	1.36	1.87	59.00
April 10	do	40.0	83.7	2.18	2.70	183.00
April 11	do	39.0	65.4	1.34	2.35	88.00
May 1	H. W. Rowley	30.0*a*	32.2	1.61	1.22	52.00
May 26	do	12.0*a*	4.1	0.73	0.43	3.00
June 19	do	6.5*a*	1.6	0.98	0.36	1.58
July 11	do				0.14	Nil.
Aug. 8	do				Dry.	*a*
Aug. 31	do					*a*
Sept. 30	do	24.0*a*	10.8	0.46	0.51	4.90
Oct. 31	do	26.0*a*	12.3	0.80	0.61	9.80

a Measurements made at trail crossing, 400 feet below gauge.

DAILY GAUGE HEIGHT AND DISCHARGE of Battle Creek at Nash's Ranch, for 1914.

DAY.	March.		April.		May.		June.	
	Gauge Height.	Dis-charge.	Gauge Height.	Dis-charge.	Gauge Height.	Dis-charge.	Gauge Height.	Dis-charge.
	Feet.	*Sec.-ft.*	*Feet.*	*Sec.-ft.*	*Feet.*	*Sec.-ft.*	*Feet.*	*Sec.-ft.*
1			4.35	119	1.28	56.00	0.31	0.94
2			3.63	78	1.19	49.00	0.31	0.94
3			2.96	62	1.08	40.00	0.32	1.08
4			2.68	65	0.99	33.00	0.33	1.22
5			2.55	75	0.99	33.00	0.32	1.08
6			2.55		1.03	36.00	0.33	1.22
7			2.54	132	0.99	33.00	0.33	1.22
8			2.55	145	1.09	41.00	0.34	1.36
9			2.33	137	0.99	33.00	0.34	1.36
10			2.56	169	0.99	33.00	0.30	0.80
11			2.57	169	0.99	33.00	0.30	0.80
12			2.15	132	1.37	64.00	0.30	0.80
13			2.32	147	1.39	65.00	0.32	1.08
14	2.65	36	2.86	195	1.18	48.00	0.34	1.36
15	3.60	76	4.85	374	1.08	40.00	0.35	1.50
16	3.53	72	5.21	407	1.06	39.00	0.34	1.36
17	3.05	51	4.15	312	0.98	32.00	0.35	1.50
18	2.98	48	3.53	256	0.85	23.00	0.35	1.50
19	2.85	43	2.73	184	0.75	17.00	0.34	1.36
20	3.45	68	2.28	143	0.70	14.00	0.33	1.22
21	3.05	51	2.07	124	0.63	10.70	0.30	0.80
22	2.80	41	2.00	118	0.57	8.30	0.25	0.50
23	2.45	29	1.82	102	0.52	6.30	0.20	0.20
24	2.40	27	1.69	90	0.47	4.60	0.23	0.38
25	2.55	32	1.56	79	0.47	4.60	0.23	0.38
26	2.68	37	1.58	80	0.44	3.70	0.23	0.38
27	2.55	32	1.55	78	0.40	2.50	0.23	0.38
28	2.56	33	1.50	74	0.30	0.80	0.24	0.44
29	2.48	30	1.40	66	0.33	1.22	0.25	0.50
30	2.44	28	1.29	57	0.32	1.08	0.35	1.50
31	2.60	34			0.30	0.80		

5 GEORGE V, A. 1915

DAILY GAUGE HEIGHT AND DISCHARGE of Battle Creek at Nash's Ranch, for 1914.—*Concluded.*

DAY.	July.		August.		September.		October.	
	Gauge Height.	Dis-charge.	Gauge Height.	Dis-charge.	Gauge Height.	Dis-charge.	Gauge Height.	Dis-charge.
	Feet.	*Sec.-ft.*	*Feet.*	*Sec.-ft.*	*Feet.*	*Sec.-ft.*	*Feet.*	*Sec.-ft.*
1	0.35	1.50	Dry.	Nil.	Dry.	Nil.	0.53	6.7
2	0.34	1.36	"	"	"	"	0.55	7.5
3	0.34	1.36	"	"	"	"	0.45	4.0
4	0.34	1.36	"	"	"	"	0.49	5.2
5	0.30	0.80	"	"	"	"	0.46	4.3
6	0.20	0.20	"	"	"	"	0.76	17.6
7	0.20	0.20	"	"	"	"	0.81	21.0
8	0.15	Nil.	"	"	"	"	0.76	17.6
9	0.14	"	"	"	"	"	0.79	19.4
10	0.15	"	"	"	"	"	0.93	29.0
11	0.16	0.04	"	"	"	"	0.96	31.0
12	0.15	Nil.	"	"	"	"	1.05	38.0
13	0.15	"	"	"	"	"	0.96	31.0
14	0.11	"	"	"	"	"	0.86	24.0
15	0.09	"	"	"	"	"	0.86	24.0
16	0.06	"	"	"	"	"	0.76	17.6
17	0.04	"	"	"	"	"	0.76	17.6
18	0.03	"	"	"	"	"	0.97	32.0
19	Dry.	"	"	"	"	"	0.95	30.0
20	"	"	"	"	"	"	0.85	23.0
21	"	"	"	"	0.63	10.7	0.76	17.6
22	"	"	"	"	0.55	7.5	0.73	15.8
23	"	"	"	"	0.54	7.1	0.71	14.6
24	"	"	"	"	0.60	9.5	0.56	7.9
25	"	"	"	"	0.58	8.7	0.53	6.7
26	"	"	"	"	0.57	8.3	0.49	5.2
27	"	"	"	"	0.55	7.5	0.55	7.5
28	"	"	"	"	0.54	7.1	0.61	9.9
29	"	"	"	"	0.54	7.1	0.65	11.5
30	"	"	"	"	0.53	6.7	0.59	9.1
31	"	"	"	"	....	....	0.61	9.9

MONTHLY DISCHARGE of Battle Creek at Nash's Ranch, for 1914.
(Drainage area 536 square miles.)

MONTH.	DISCHARGE IN SECOND-FEET.				RUN-OFF.	
	Maximum.	Minimum	Mean.	Per square Mile.	Depth in inches on Drainage Area.	Total in Acre-feet.
March (14-31)	76.00	27.00	43.00	0.0800	0.0530	1,523
April	407.00	57.00	142.00	0.2650	0.2960	8,450
May	65.00	0.80	26.00	0.0480	0.0560	1,599
June	1.50	0.20	0.97	0.0018	0.0020	58
July	1.50	0.00	0.22	0.0004	0.0004	14
August	0.00	0.00	0.00	Nil.	Nil.	Nil.
September	10.70	0.00	2.67	0.0050	0.0060	159
October	38.00	4.00	16.60	0.0311	0.0360	1,027
The period	....	....	....	....	0.4490	12,830

MISCELLANEOUS DISCHARGE MEASUREMENTS made in Battle Creek drainage basin, in 1914.

Date.	Engineer.	Stream.	Location.	Width.	Area of Section.	Mean Velocity.	Dis-charge.
				Feet.	*Sq. ft.*	*Ft. per sec.*	*Sec.-ft.*
June 3	H. W. Rowley.	Fourmile Coulee	NW. 14-8-29-3	8.0	3.50	0.76	2.70
July 20	do	do	do	....	....	....	0.37
Aug. 7	do	Battle Creek	Sec. 28-5-28-3	8.5	3.22	0.70	2.20
Sept. 29	do	do	SW. 4-1-26-3	....	....	....	Nil.
Oct. 30	do	do	do	13.5	6.77	1.12	7.60
Sept. 30	do	do	Sec. 16-2-26-3	....	....	....	3.50

FRENCHMAN RIVER DRAINAGE BASIN   345

SESSIONAL PAPER No. 25c

FRENCHMAN RIVER DRAINAGE BASIN.

General Description.

Frenchman River drains the greater portion of southwestern Saskatchewan. It rises in Cypress Lake in Township 6, Range 26, West of the 3rd Meridian, and follows a southeasterly course for some 150 miles, crossing into the United States in Range 10, West of the 3rd Meridian. It eventually finds its way into Milk River near Saco, Montana, and therefore forms a part of the general drainage basin of the Missouri.

Cypress Lake is on the southern slope of Cypress Hills at an elevation of about 3,155 feet above sea level. It occupies what is probably a portion of an abandoned watercourse or channel of an ancient river which joined Battle Creek to the Frenchman River. The water of the lake is fresh, and is supplied by a number of coulees and small streams which head in the hills to the north. The largest of these are Oxarart and Sucker Creeks, both of which have a small, continuous flow.

During dry years Cypress Lake does not overflow, and the whole discharge of the Frenchman River is derived from Belanger, Davis and Fairwell Creeks and the North Branch. From Township 6, Range 23, West of the 3rd Meridian, where the North Branch joins the main stream, there is no appreciable supply to the river while in Canada. Mule Creek, which joins the river in Township 5, Range 17, West of the 3rd Meridian, and Snake Creek in Township 3, Range 13, West of the 3rd Meridian, however, have a small flow.

The country surrounding Cypress Lake is of rolling prairie, much broken by coulees. In many of these there is considerable tree growth, but for the most part the country is devoid of all vegetation other than grasses. All the streams in the upper section of the drainage basin, with the exception of the North Branch, rise on the plateau at the top of the hills. Flowing southward, they break through deep, well-wooded gorges before reaching the lower flats along the river. The North Branch, however, is in a deep valley throughout its entire length. Its feeders, like the western tributaries of the main stream, cut through from the bench to the valley in deep, well-wooded coulees. Below the mouth of the North Branch there is little tree growth. Here and there along the river may be found small growths of shrubs and maple, while up on the hillsides in some of the coulees there are small clumps of poplar covering an acre or so. Most of these coulees are rapidly becoming cleared by the settlers who are taking up the bench lands above the river valley. The benches are well covered with grasses, but the hills and sides of the valley are almost devoid of all vegetation. In the flats along the river, except where irrigated, the chief vegetation consists of sage brush and cactus.

When the Frenchman leaves the lake, it flows through a wide, flat valley as far as the mouth of Fairwell Creek. Most of this land is under proposed or constructed irrigation ditches, covering an area of about 393 acres. Below this point the valley becomes more broken, and narrows considerably, while the side hills become higher. Small portions of this bottom will, no doubt, be brought under irrigation, but as yet little has been done in that direction.

Below the junction of the North Branch the valley becomes rough and rugged, the sides being cut with buttes and deep coulees. Here numerous outcroppings of lignite may be seen, and also a deep seam of light-coloured clay and sand. This seam, which has been bleached almost a pure white, shows at many points along the river's entire course, and is one of the most conspicuous objects in this region. From its colour and nature the river receives its local name of the "Whitemud."

At East End, some miles lower down, the valley again widens out into flats. Here is located the largest irrigation project in the Cypress Hills district. Messrs. Strong and Day have a large dam in the river and a system of ditches and storage reservoirs, by which they irrigate 2,581 acres. Directly above this project there are two smaller schemes covering 200 acres. Just below, Messrs. Morrison Brothers have a dam and ditch which will irrigate 1,595 acres. Their ditch is carried across the river and continued by Messrs. Duncan and Watson, who irrigate 935 acres more.

Below the East End flat none of the flats, which occur at various points along the river, are irrigated as yet. A short distance below the mouth of Snake Creek the river enters bad lands, which continue into the United States.

The mean annual rainfall of this basin is not well established, but it is estimated that it would range from 12 to 16 inches, most of which falls in May, June and July. From November to April the streams are frozen over, and usually there is an abundant snowfall.

During 1914 a number of new stations were established on the lower branches of this stream, and also two on the main stream. These stations were established to obtain the run-off of this lower region and the total discharge of the stream in Canada.

The construction of the Weyburn-Lethbridge branch of the Canadian Pacific Railway through the upper part of the valley has opened up that part of the drainage basin, and the development has been the reason for one or two settlements coming into existence, the most important of which is East End.

OXARART AT WYLIE'S RANCH.

Location.—On the NE. ¼ Sec. 20, Tp. 6, Rge. 27, W. 3rd Mer., at Joseph Wylie's ranch.
Records available.—From June 15, 1909, to October 31, 1914.
Gauge.—Vertical staff; zero of gauge maintained at 3,199 02 feet during 1909-10; 3,199.06 feet during 1911; 3,199 03 feet during 1912-14.
Bench-mark.—Permanent iron bench-mark, located on the right bank at the station; elevation, 3,203 75 feet above mean sea level (*Irrigation Surveys*).
Channel.—Composed of coarse gravel and stone; liable to shift during flood, owing to great fall in stream.
Discharge measurements.—Made by wading or with a weir.
Winter flow.—Station discontinued during winter season.
Observer.—J. C. Wylie.

DISCHARGE MEASUREMENTS of Oxarart Creek at Wylie's Ranch, in 1914.

Date.	Engineer	Width.	Area of Section.	Mean Velocity.	Gauge Height.	Discharge.
		Feet.	*Sq. ft.*	*Ft. per sec.*	*Feet.*	*Sec.-ft.*
March 28	H. R. Carscallen	6.2	3.03	1.50	0.75	0.45
April 10	do	11.4	6.26	1.14	1.18	7.10
May 2	H. W. Rowley	10.0	5.00	0.41	0.95	2.03
May 27	do	7.5	3.13	0.72	0.95	2.26
June 20	do	a			0.93	1.70
July 10	do	a			0.88	1.03
Aug. 7	do	a			0.85	0.63
Sept. 1	do	a			0.86	0.30
Oct. 1	do	a			0.87	0.42
Nov. 3	do	a			0.88	0.39

*a*Weir measurement.

DAILY GAUGE HEIGHT AND DISCHARGE of Oxarart Creek at Wylie's Ranch, for 1914.

DAY.	March.		April.		May.		June.	
	Gauge Height.	Discharge.	Gauge Height.	Discharge.	Gauge Height.	Discharge.	Gauge Height.	Discharge.
	Feet.	*Sec.-ft.*	*Feet.*	*Sec.-ft.*	*Feet.*	*Sec.-ft.*	*Feet.*	*Sec.-ft.*
1			0.75	0.50	1.02	3.40	0.98	2.60
2			0.75	0.45	0.98	2.60	0.98	2.60
3			0.75	0.35	0.95	2.00	0.98	2.60
4			1.12	7.25	0.95	2.00	0.98	2.60
5			1.62	19.50	0.95	2.00	0.98	2.60
6			1 42	14 25	0.95	2.00	0.98	2.60
7			1 05	4.80	1.10	5.10	0.98	2.60
8			1 05	4 50	1 20	7.60	0.98	2.60
9			1.06	4.50b	1.20	7.60	0.98	2.60
10			0 96	2 20	1.00	3.00	0.98	2.60
11			1.02	3.40	1.00	3.00	0.98	2.60
12			1.02	3.40	0.99	2.80	0.98	2.60
13			1.52	15.60	0.99	2.80	0.98	2.60
14			1.51	15.25	0.98	2.60	0.98	2.60
15			1.53	15.80	0.98	2.60	0.95	2.00
16			1.48	14.60	0.98	2.60	0.95	2.00
17			1.39	12.40	0.98	2.60	0.95	2.00
18			1.31	10.40	0.98	2.60	0.95	2.00
19			1.33	10.80	0.98	2.60	0.95	2.00
20			1.28	9.60	0.98	2.60	0.95	2.00
21			1.28	9.60	0.98	2.60	0.95	2.00
22			1.22	8.10	0.98	2.60	0.95	2.00
23			1.23	8.40	0.98	2.60	0.95	2.00
24			1.20	7.60	0.98	2.60	0.95	2.00
25			1.13	5.80	0.98	2.60	0.95	2.00
26			1.07	4.40	0.98	2.60	0.95	2.00
27			1.03	3.60	0.98	2.60	0.95	2.00
28	0.75	0.45a	1.03	3.60	0.98	2.60	0.95	2.00
29	0.76	0.65	1.03	3.60	0.98	2.60	0.95	2.00
30	0.75	0.55	1.03	3.60	0.98	2.60	0.95	2.00
31	0.75	0.55			0.98	2.60		

a to *b* Shifting conditions.

DAILY GAUGE HEIGHT AND DISCHARGE of Oxarart Creek at Wylie's Ranch, for 1914.—*Concluded.*

DAY.	July.		August.		September.		October.	
	Gauge Height.	Dis-charge.	Gauge Height.	Dis-charge.	Gauge Height.	Dis-charge.	Gauge Height.	Dis-charge.
	Feet.	*Sec.-ft.*	*Feet.*	*Sec.-ft.*	*Feet.*	*Sec.-ft.*	*Feet.*	*Sec.-ft.*
1	0.95	2.00	0.82	0.33	0.86	0.30	0.88	0.42
2	0.93	1.75	0.82	0.33	0.86	0.30	0.88	0.43
3	0.93	1.75	0.84	0.52	0.86	0.30	0.88	0.45
4	0.90	1.30	0.84	0.52	0.86	0.31	0.88	0.46
5	0.90	1.30	0.83	0.41	0.86	0.31	0.88	0.48
6	0.90	1.30	0.84	0.52a	0.86	0.31	0.88	0.49
7	0.90	1.30	0.86	0.74	0.86	0.32	0.88	0.50
8	0.90	1.30	0.86	0.74	0.86	0.32	0.99	2.10
9	0.90	1.30	0.86	0.74	0.86	0.33	1.06	3.40
10	0.88	1.00	0.86	0.72	0.86	0.33	1.00	2.30
11	0.88	1.00	0.86	0.70	0.86	0.33	1.06	3.30
12	0.88	1.00	0.86	0.68	0.86	0.34	1.07	3.50
13	0.85	0.63	0.86	0.66	0.86	0.34	0.95	1.40
14	0.84	0.52	0.86	0.64	0.86	0.35	0.93	1.10
15	0.84	0.52	0.86	0.62	0.86	0.35	0.91	0.76
16	0.84	0.52	0.86	0.60	0.86	0.35	0.88	0.45
17	0.84	0.52	0.86	0.58	0.86	0.36	0.87	0.40
18	0.84	0.52	0.86	0.56	0.86	0.36	0.87	0.40
19	0.83	0.41	0.86	0.54	0.86	0.37	0.87	0.40
20	0.82	0.33	0.86	0.52	0.86	0.37	0.87	0.39
21	0.82	0.33	0.86	0.50	0.86	0.37	0.87	0.38
22	0.82	0.33	0.86	0.48	0.86	0.38	0.87	0.37
23	0.82	0.33	0.86	0.46	0.86	0.38	0.87	0.36
24	0.82	0.33	0.86	0.44	0.86	0.38	0.87	0.35
25	0.82	0.33	0.86	0.42	0.86	0.39	0.87	0.34
26	0.82	0.33	0.86	0.40	0.86	0.39	0.87	0.33
27	0.82	0.33	0.86	0.38	0.87	0.40	0.87	0.33
28	0.82	0.33	0.86	0.36	0.87	0.40	0.87	0.32
29	0.81	0.25	0.86	0.34	0.87	0.41	0.87	0.31
30	0.81	0.25	0.86	0.32	0.87	0.41	0.87	0.31
31	0.81	0.25	0.86	0.30	....	....	0.87	0.30b

a to *b* Shifting conditions.

MONTHLY DISCHARGE of Oxarart Creek at Wylie's Ranch, for 1914.

(Drainage area 77 square miles.)

MONTH.	DISCHARGE IN SECOND-FEET.				RUN-OFF.	
	Maximum	Minimum.	Mean.	Per square Mile.	Depth in inches on Drainage Area.	Total in Acre-feet.
March (28–31)	0.65	0.45	0.55	0.0071	0.001	4
April	19.50	0.35	7.60	0.0987	0.110	452
May	7.60	2.00	3.00	0.0390	0.045	184
June	2.60	2.00	2.30	0.0290	0.033	135
July	2.00	0.25	0.76	0.0100	0.010	47
August	0.74	0.30	0.52	0.0070	0.008	32
September	0.41	0.30	0.35	0.0046	0.005	21
October	3.50	0.30	0.86	0.0110	0.013	53
The period	....	....	....	....	0.225	928

No. 25c.—23

5 GEORGE V, A. 1915

SUCKER CREEK AT WHITCOMB AND ZEIGLER'S RANCH.

Location.—On NW. ¼ Sec. 24, Tp. 6, Rge. 26, W. 3rd Mer.
Records available.—May 25, 1909, to October 31, 1914.
Gauge.—Vertical staff. The elevation of the zero of the gauge has been maintained at
3,191.11 feet since April, 1912; the elevation of the old gauge 200 feet below was 3,189.20 feet.
Bench-mark.—Permanent iron bench-mark; elevation, 3,196 25 feet above mean sea level
(*Irrigation* Surveys).
Channel.—Permanent.
Discharge measurements.—Made by meter and weir in low stages.
Winter flow.—This station has not been maintained during the winter.
Observer.—Mrs. P. A. Zeigler and J. D. Gilchrist.

DISCHARGE MEASUREMENTS of Sucker Creek at Whitcomb and Zeigler's Ranch, in 1914.

Date.	Engineer.	Width.	Area of Section.	Mean Velocity.	Gauge Height.	Discharge.
		Feet.	*Sq. ft.*	*Ft. per sec.*	*Feet.*	*Sec.-ft.*
March 15	M. H. French	13.0	21.70	2.10	2.17	45.00
March 21	do	9.0	5.00	0.61	1.18	3.00
May 9	F. R. Steinberger	23.0	19.30	1.03	1.21	20.00
May 27	do	12.0	3.55	0.66	0.80	2.30
June 29	do	12.0	2.85	0.49	0.75	1.42
July 22	do				0.43	0.16a
Aug. 12	do				0.46	0.18a
Aug. 31	E. W. W. Hughes	7.5	1.70	0.68	0.64	1.16
Sept. 21	do	10.5	2.60	0.62	0.73	1.62
Oct. 18	do	10.5	3.00	0.70	0.79	2.10

a Weir measurement.

DAILY GAUGE HEIGHT AND DISCHARGE of Sucker Creek at Whitcomb and Zeigler's Ranch,
for 1914.

DAY.	March.		April.		May.		June.	
	Gauge Height.	Dis- charge.	Gauge Height.	Dis- charge.	Gauge Height.	Dis- charge.	Gauge Height.	Dis- charge.
	Feet.	*Sec.-ft.*	*Feet.*	*Sec.-ft.*	*Feet.*	*Sec.-ft.*	*Feet.*	*Sec.-ft.*
1			1.10	1.7	0.90	4.8	0.77	1.92
2			1.35	7.7	0.90	4.8	0.78	2.10
3			1.45	11.4	0.88	4.2	0.75	1.60
4			1.56	16.2	0.88	4.2	0.75	1.60
5			1.80	28.0	0.89	4.5	0.80	2.40
6			1.89	32.0	0.89	4.5	0.89	4.50
7			2.09	42.0a	0.90	4.8	0.85	3.40
8			1.64	50.0	0.89	4.5	0.80	2.40
9			1.59	47.0	1.27	24.0	0.78	2.10
10			1.45	37.0	1.14	15.6	0.78	2.10
11			1.37	31.0	1.04	10.1	0.78	2.10
12			2.23	92.0	1.01	8.8	0.78	2.10
13			2.13	85.0	0.98	7.5	0.85	3.40
14			1.68	53.0	0.95	6.4	0.85	3.40
15	2.34	54.00a	1.38	32.0	0.90	4.8	0.80	2.40
16	2.17	45.00	1.07	11.6	0.87	4.0	0.79	2.20
17	2.12	43.00	1.37	31.0	0.87	4.0	0.78	2.10
18	2.12	43.00	1.07	11.6	0.86	3.7	0.76	1.76
19	2.12	43.00	1.05	10.6	0.86	3.7	0.74	1.52
20	1.18	3.10	1.05	10.6	0.85	3.4	0.85	3.40
21	1.18	3.10	1.04	10.1	0.84	3.2	0.85	3.40
22	0.86	Nil.	1.06	11.2	0.81	2.6	0.78	2.10
23		" b	1.03c	9.7	0.79	2.2	0.76	1.76
24		"	1.00c	8.3	0.84	3.2	0.75	1.60
25		"	0.97	7.2	0.80	2.4	0.85	3.40
26		"	0.95	6.4	0.78	2.1	0.80	2.40
27		"	0.92	5.4	0.80	2.4	0.78	2.10
28		"	0.91	5.1	0.80	2.4	0.75	1.60
29		" b	0.90	4.8	0.79	2.2	0.75	1.60
30	0.90	0.05	0.90	4.8	0.79	2.2	0.74	1.52
31	0.93	0.10			0.78	2.1		

a to *a* Ice conditions.
b to *b* Channel frozen over.
c Gauge height interpolated.

DAILY GAUGE HEIGHT AND DISCHARGE of Sucker Creek at Whitcomb and Zeigler's Ranch, for 1914.—*Concluded.*

DAY.	July.		August.		September.		October.	
	Gauge Height.	Dis- charge.	Gauge Height.	Dis- charge.	Gauge Height.	Dis- charge.	Gauge Height.	Dis- charge.
	Feet.	*Sec.-ft.*	*Feet.*	*Sec.-ft.*	*Feet.*	*Sec.-ft.*	*Feet.*	*Sec.-ft.*
1	0.73	1.44	0.43	0.13	0.60	0.50	0.72	1.36
2	0.69	1.12	0.43	0.13	0.60	0.50	0.76	1.76
3	0.67	0.96	0.43	0.13	0.60	0.50	0.79	2.20
4	0.65	0.80	0.43	0.13	0.60	0.50	0.98	7.50
5	0.64	0.74	0.43	0.13	0.59	0.47	0.97	7.20
6	0.64	0.74	0.44	0.14	0.58	0.44	0.84	3.20
7	0.54	0.32	0.45	0.15	0.60	0.50	0.87	4.00
8	0.47	0.17	0.45	0.15	0.61	0.56	0.98	7.50
9	0.47	0.17	0.46	0.16	0.60	0.50	0.90	4.80
10	0.46	0.16	0.46	0.16	0.59	0.47	0.88	4.20
11	0.46	0.16	0.46	0.16	0.60	0.50	0.86	3.70
12	0.56	0.38	0.46	0.16	0.69	1.12	0.80	2.40
13	0.49	0.19	0.46	0.16	0.98	7.50	0.80	2.40
14	0.47	0.17	0.46	0.16	0.79	2.20	0.80	2.40
15	0.56	0.38	0.46	0.16	0.67	0.96	0.80	2.40
16	0.46	0.16	0.46	0.16	0.65	0.80	0.80	2.40
17	0.57	0.41	0.48	0.18	0.65	0.80	0.80	2.40
18	0.48	0.18	0.50	0.20	0.66	0.88	0.80	2.40
19	0.49	0.19	0.56	0.38	0.71	1.28	0.78	1.92
20	0.47	0.17	0.54	0.32	0.71	1.28	0.77	1.92
21	0.43	0.13	0.54	0.32	0.71	1.28	0.78	2.10
22	0.43	0.13	0.54	0.32	0.70	1.20	0.77	1.92
23	0.42	0.12	0.57	0.41	0.71	1.28	0.77	1.92
24	0.42	0.12	0.68	1.04	0.71	1.28	0.77	1.92
25	0.43	0.13	0.68	1.04	0.71	1.28	0.77	1.92
26	0.43	0.13	0.67	0.96	0.71	1.28	0.77	1.92
27	0.44	0.14	0.67	0.96	0.71	1.28	0.77	1.92
28	0.42	0.12	0.64	0.74	0.71	1.28	0.79	2.20
29	0.43	0.13	0.61	0.56	0.71	1.28	0.82	2.80
30	0.42	0.12	0.61	0.56	0.71	1.28	0.82	2.80
31	0.42	0.12	0.60	0.50	....	....	0.82	2.80

MONTHLY DISCHARGE of Sucker Creek at Whitcomb and Zeigler's Ranch, for 1914.

(Drainage area 30 square miles.)

MONTH.	DISCHARGE IN SECOND-FEET.				RUN-OFF.	
	Maximum.	Minimum.	Mean.	Per square Mile.	Depth in inches on Drainage Area.	Total in Acre-feet.
March (15–31)	54.00	0.00	13.80	0.460	0.29	464
April	92.00	1.70	24.00	0.793	0.88	1,416
May	24.00	2.10	5.10	0.171	0.20	316
June	4.50	1.52	2.30	0.078	0.09	139
July	1.44	0.12	0.36	0.011	0.01	21
August	1.04	0.13	0.35	0.012	0.01	22
September	7.50	0.44	1.17	0.039	0.04	70
October	7.50	1.36	3.00	0.099	0.11	183
The period	....	....	....	....	1.63	2,631

No. 25c—23½

5 GEORGE V. A. 1915

LONEPINE CREEK AT HEWITT'S RANCH.

Location.—On the NW. ¼ Sec. 27, Tp. 7, Rge. 26, W. 3rd Mer.
Records available.—April 1, 1910, to October 31, 1914.
Gauge.—Vertical staff. The elevation of the zero of the gauge has been maintained at
93 35 feet since establishment. On June 28, 1913, a permanent weir was established, and since
that date records of the discharge have been made by this means. The elevation of the zero
of the gauge and crest of the weir is 96.34 feet.
Bench-mark.—Permanent iron bench-mark; assumed elevation, 100.00 feet.
Discharge measurements.—Made with meter in flood stages, and by permanent weir at other
stages.
Diversions.—Messrs. A. P. McDonald and S.W. Hewitt divert water for irrigation purposes
above the gauge.
Observer.—S. W. Hewitt.

DISCHARGE MEASUREMENTS of Lonepine Creek at Hewitt's Ranch, in 1914.

Date.	Engineer.	Width.	Area of Section.	Mean Velocity.	Gauge Height.	Discharge.
		Feet.	*Sq. ft.*	*Ft. per sec.*	*Feet.*	*Sec.-ft.*
May 11	F. R. Steinberger	. . . .	. . . .	. . . .	0.58	1.57
May 28	do	. . . .	. . . .	. . . .	0.40	0.99
June 23	do	. . . .	. . . .	. . . .	0.22	0.42
June 30	do	. . . .	. . . .	. . . .	0.25	0.50
Aug. 12	do	. . . .	. . . .	. . . .	0.22	0.42
Aug. 31	E. W. W. Hughes	. . . .	. . . .	. . . .	0.21	0.39
Sept. 21	do	. . . .	. . . .	. . . .	0.32	0.72

DAILY GAUGE HEIGHT AND DISCHARGE of Lonepine Creek at Hewitt's Ranch, for 1914.

DAY.	April.		May.		June.	
	Gauge Height.	Dis-charge.	Gauge Height.	Dis-charge.	Gauge Height.	Dis-charge.
	Feet.	*Sec.-ft.*	*Feet.*	*Sec.-ft.*	*Feet.*	*Sec.-ft.*
1	. . . .	. . . .	0.43	1.10	0.29a	0.62
2	. . . .	. . . .	0.42a	1.06	0.30	0.65
3	. . . .	. . . .	0.40a	0.99	0.30a	0.65
4	. . . .	. . . .	0.39	0.96	0.30a	0.65
5	. . . .	. . . .	0.42	1.06	0.30a	0.65
6	. . . .	. . . .	0.39	0.96	0.30	0.65
7	. . . .	. . . .	0.39	0.96	0.27	0.56
8	. . . .	. . . .	0.48	1.28	0.29	0.62
9	. . . .	. . . .	0.48a	1.28	0.28	0.59
10	. . . .	. . . .	0.49	1.31	0.28a	0.59
11	. . . .	. . . .	0.58	1.67	0.29a	0.62
12	. . . .	. . . .	0.58	1.67	0.29a	0.62
13	1.68	6.70	0.58	1.67	0.30a	0.65
14	0.99	3.40	0.58	1.67	0.30	0.65
15	0.97a	3.40	0.58	1.67	0.28a	0.59
16	0.95	3.20	0.57	1.63	0.26a	0.53
17	1.27a	4.30	0.57	1.63	0.24a	0.47
18	1.59	6.10	0.48	1.28	0.22a	0.42
19	0.95	3.20	0.48a	1.28	0.20	0.36
20	0.96a	3.30	0.48a	1.28	0.20	0.36
21	0.96	3.30	0.48	1.28	0.27	0.56
22	0.96	3.30	0.48a	1.28	0.26	0.53
23	0.96	3.30	0.47a	1.24	0.20	0.36
24	0.72a	2.20	0.47	1.24	0.21a	0.39
25	0.47	1.24	0.40	0.99	0.22a	0.42
26	0.46	1.21	0.35	0.82	0.23a	0.44
27	0.46	1.21	0.34a	0.79	0.24a	0.47
28	0.45	1.17	0.32a	0.72	0.24	0.47
29	0.46	1.21	0.30a	0.65	0.23	0.44
30	0.45	1.17	0.29a	0.62	0.25	0.50
31	. . . .	. . . .	0.28	0.59	. . . .	. . . .

a Gauge height interpolated.

DAILY GAUGE HEIGHT AND DISCHARGE of Lonepine Creek at Hewitt's Ranch, for 1914.
—*Concluded.*

DAY.	July.		August.		September.		October.	
	Gauge Height.	Dis-charge.	Gauge Height.	Dis-charge.	Gauge Height.	Dis-charge.	Gauge Height.	Dis-charge.
	Feet.	*Sec.-ft.*	*Feet.*	*Sec.-ft.*	*Feet.*	*Sec.-ft.*	*Feet.*	*Sec.-ft.*
1	0.24a	0.47	0.18a	0.31	0.22	0.42	0.25a	0.50
2	0.23a	0.44	0.22a	0.31	0.22a	0.42	0.25a	0.50
3	0.22a	0.42	0.18	0.31	0.23	0.44	0.25a	0.50
4	0.21a	0.39	0.18	0.31	0.22	0.42	0.40	0.99
5	0.20	0.36	0.19a	0.34	0.24a	0.47	0.37	0.89
6	0.20	0.36	0.20a	0.36	0.26	0.53	0.38	0.92
7	0.20	0.36	0.21a	0.39	0.26a	0.53	0.40a	0.99
8	0.21a	0.39	0.22	0.42	0.26a	0.53	0.43a	1.10
9	0.23a	0.44	0.27	0.56	0.26a	0.53	0.46a	1.21
10	0.25a	0.50	0.25a	0.50	0.26a	0.53	0.48a	1.28
11	0.27a	0.56	0.23a	0.44	0.26a	0.53	0.50	1.35
12	0.28	0.59	0.22	0.42	0.26a	0.53	0.45	1.17
13	0.29	0.62	0.20a	0.36	0.60	1.75	0.40	0.99
14	0.30	0.65	0.19	0.34	0.51	1.39	0.40a	0.99
15	0.28a	0.59	0.19a	0.34	0.40	0.99	0.40a	0.99
16	0.26a	0.53	0.19	0.34	0.40a	0.99	0.40a	0.99
17	0.24a	0.47	0.19	0.34	0.40a	0.99	0.40a	0.99
18	0.22a	0.42	0.19a	0.34	0.40a	0.99	0.40	0.99
19	0.20	0.36	0.34	0.79	0.40a	0.99	0.35	0.82
20	0.22	0.42	0.30a	0.65	0.40	0.99 ·	0.32	0.72
21	0.22a	0.42	0.26a	0.53	0.32	0.72	0.32a	0.72
22	0.22a	0.42	0.22a	0.42	0.31a	0.68	0.32a	0.72
23	0.22	0.42	0.19	0.34	0.30a	0.65	0.32a	0.72
24	0.21a	0.39	0.35	0.82	0.30	0.65	0.32a	0.72
25	0.20a	0.36	0.25	0.50	0.28a	0.59	0.33	0.75
26	0.20	0.36	0.25a	0.50	0.27a	0.56	0.33	0.75
27	0.20	0.36	0.24a	0.47	0.25	0.50	0.33	0.75
28	0.20	0.36	0.24a	0.47	0.25	0.50	0.33a	0.75
29	0.20a	0.36	0.23a	0.44	0.25	0.50	0.33a	0.75
30	0.19a	0.34	0.22	0.42	0.25a	0.50	0.33a	0.75
31	0.19a	0.34	0.21	0.39	....	....	0.33a	0.75

a Gauge height interpolated.

MONTHLY DISCHARGE of Lonepine Creek at Hewitt's Ranch, for 1914.

(Drainage area 8 square miles.)

MONTH.	DISCHARGE IN SECOND-FEET.				RUN-OFF.	
	Maximum.	Minimum.	Mean.	Per square Mile.	Depth in inches on Drainage Area.	Total in Acre-feet.
April (13–30)	6.70	1.17	2.90	0.370	0.25	105
May	1.67	0.59	1.18	0.147	0.17	73
June	0.65	0.36	0.54	0.067	0.08	32
July	0.65	0.34	0.44	0.054	0.06	27
August	0.79	0.31	0.44	0.054	0.06	27
September	1.75	0.42	0.69	0.087	0.10	41
October	1.35	0.50	0.87	0.109	0.13	54
The period	....	....	....	....	0.85	359

5 GEORGE V, A. 1915

BELANGER CREEK AT OAKES' RANCH.

Location.—On the SW. ¼ Sec. 30, Tp. 6, Rge. 25, W. 3rd Mer.
Records available.—April 1, 1912, to April 11, 1914.
Gauge.—Vertical staff; the elevation of the zero of the gauge has been maintained at
3,164.10 feet since establishment.
Bench-mark.—Permanent iron bench-mark; elevation, 3,168.37 feet above mean sea level
(*Irrigation Surveys*).
Channel.—Slightly shifting.
Discharge measurements.—Made with meter.
Winter flow.—This station is not maintained during the winter.
Diversions.—Messrs. R. G. Williamson, T. A. Drury, J. H. G. Bettington, and Dixon and
Stuart divert water for irrigation purposes above the gauge.
Observer.—E. C. R. Harris.

DISCHARGE MEASUREMENTS of Belanger Creek at Oakes' Ranch, in 1914.

Date.	Engineer.	Width.	Area of Section.	Mean Velocity.	Gauge Height.	Discharge.
		Feet.	*Sq. ft.*	*Ft. per sec.*	*Feet.*	*Sec.-ft.*
Mar. 16	M. H. French		39.00	1.80	2.47	70.00a
Mar. 21	do	5.5	3.70	1.40	1.01	5.20
May 9	F. R. Steinberger	10.3	11.30	1.31	0.52	14.80
May 27	do	10.0	9.25	0.78	0.40	7.20
June 29	do	10.0	8.93	0.51	0.28	4.30
July 22	do	7.4	3.26	0.48	0.12	1.56
Aug. 12	do	6.0	2.50	0.53	0.13	1.32
Aug. 31	E. W. W. Hughes	12.5	2.55	0.64	0.19	1.62
Sept. 21	do	12.8	3.38	0.83	0.38b	2.80
Oct. 18	do	13.6	4.11	0.94	0.30b	3.90

a Discharge approximated.
b Gauge heights affected by beaver dams.

DAILY GAUGE HEIGHT AND DISCHARGE of Belanger Creek at Oakes' Ranch, for 1914.

DAY.	March.		April.	
	Gauge Height.	Dis-charge.	Gauge Height.	Dis-charge.
	Feet.	*Sec.-ft.*	*Feet.*	*Sec.-ft.*
1			0.69	0.60a
2				
3			2.72	138.00
4			2.62	133.00
5			2.60	132.00
6				
7			2.57	130.00
8			2.22	110.00
9				
10				
11			1.26	56.00
12			b	
13				
14	2.43	68.00a		
15	2.73	82.00		
16				
17				
18	1.43	24.00		
19				
20				
21	1.01	5.20		
22				
23	0.59	0.30		
24				
25	0.52	0.05		
26	0.44	Nil.		
27				
28	0.42	Nil.		
29				
30				
31				

a to a Ice conditions.
b No observer obtainable after April 11.

DAVIS CREEK AT DRURY'S RANCH.

Location.—On the NE. ¼ Sec. 29, Tp. 6, Rge. 25, W. 3rd Mer.
Records available.—May 24, 1909, to August 31, 1914.
Gauge.—Vertical staff; the elevation of the zero of the gauge has been maintained at 3,176.79 feet since establishment.
Bench-mark.—Permanent iron bench-mark; elevation, 3,183.06 feet above mean sea level (*Irrigation Surveys*).
Channel.—Permanent.
Discharge measurements.—Made with meter and weir at low stages.
Winter flow.—This station is not maintained during the winter.
Diversions.—Mr. B. C. Wright diverts water for irrigation purposes above the gauge.
Observer.—A. Betteley.

DISCHARGE MEASUREMENTS of Davis Creek at Drury's Ranch, in 1914.

Date.	Engineer.	Width.	Area of Section.	Mean Velocity.	Gauge Height.	Discharge.
		Feet.	*Sq. ft.*	*Ft. per sec.*	*Feet.*	*Sec.-ft.*
Mar. 16	M. H. French	20.5	19.90	2.90	1.42	58.00
Mar. 20	do	10.0	3.50	0.26	0.67	0.93
April 8	do	21.0	25.50	2.27	1.38	58.00
April 22	do	14.0	6.48	1.56	0.68	10.10
May 9	F. R. Steinberger	22.1	26.20	0.98	0.93	26.00
May 27	do	14.0	47.50	0.60	0.42	2.80
June 29	do	13.3	3.70	0.41	0.43	1.53
July 22	do	12.5	3.28	0.34	0.34	1.12
Aug. 12	do				0.24	0.57a
Aug. 31	E. W. W. Hughes				0.16	0.06a
Sept. 21	do					Nil.
Oct. 18	do	14.0	4.40	0 52	0.41	2.30

a Weir measurement.

DAILY GAUGE HEIGHT AND DISCHARGE of Davis Creek, at Drury's Ranch, for 1914.

DAY.	March. Gauge Height.	March. Dis-charge.	April. Gauge Height.	April. Dis-charge.	May. Gauge Height.	May. Dis-charge.	June. Gauge Height.	June. Dis-charge.	July. Gauge Height.	July. Dis-charge.	August. Gauge Height.	August. Dis-charge.
	Feet.	*Sec.ft.*	*Feet.*	*Sec.ft.*	*Feet.*	*Sec.-ft.*	*Feet.*	*Sec.ft.*	*Feet.*	*Sec.ft.*	*Feet.*	*Sec.-ft.*
1			0.87	21.0	0.55	5.00	0.39	1.90	0 42	2 30		
2			0.91	23.0	0.53	4.50			0.42b	2 30		
3			1 04	32 0	0.52	4.20			0 41b	2 20		
4			1 07	35.0	0.54	4.80	0.38	1.80	0 40	2 00		
5			1.91b	96.0	0.54	4.80	0.38	1.80	0 39	1.90		
6			2.73	154.0	0.55	5.00			0.39	1.90		
7			2.31	128.0	0.65b	9.00	0.38	1.80	0.39	1.90		
8			2.23	121.0a	0.76	14.60			0.40	2.00		
9			1.25	48.0	0.93	25.00			0.39	1.90		
10	0.58	5.0a	1.25	48.0	0.91	24.00			0.39	1.90		
11	0 59	5.3	1.10	37.0	0.85	20.00	0.37	1.70	0.38	1.80		
12	0 59	5 3	1.57	72 0	0.78b	15.80			0.38	1.80		
13	0.61	6 0	1.92	98.0	0.72	12.50			0.38	1.80		
14	2.67	150 0	1.68	80.0	0.67	10.00			0.39b	1.90		
15	1.78	84 0	1.39	58 0	0.63	8.20			0.39	1.90		
16	1.59	70 0	1.49	66 0	0.61b	7.40			0.43	2.40		
17	1.19	42 0	1.08	36.0	0.59	6.60			0.43	2.40		
18	0 84	17.2	0.95	26.0	0.56b	5.40			0.43b	2.40		
19	0 90	20.0	0.74	13.5	0.53	4.50			0.43	2.40		
20	0.79	4.2	0.73	13.0	0.51b	4.00			0.43	2.40		
21	0.57	1.9	0 75	14.0	0.50	3.80			0 43	2 40		
22	0.62	4.2	0.70	11 5	0.49b	3.60			0 34	1.40	0.20	0.25
23	0 81	13.2	0.74	13.5	0.48b	3.40			0.35	1 50	0.20	0.25
24	0 71	9.4	0.72	12.5	0.46b	3.00			0.34	1.40	0.21	0.32
25	0.85	17.6	0 66	9.5	0.45b				0.33	1.30	0.20	0.25
26	0.61	6.4	0.65	9.0	0.44b	2.80 2.60			0 34	1.40	0.19	0 20
27	0.60	6.2	0.63b	8.2	0.42	2.30			0.35	1 50	0.19	0.20
28	0.56	5.0	0.61	7.4	0.42	2.30			0 33	1.30	0.18	0 15
29	0.56	5.2	0.61	7.4	0.40	2.00	0.43	2.40	0 32	1 20	0.18	0.15
30	0.59	6.2	0.59	6.6	0.40b	2.00	0.43	2.40	0 32b	1.20	0.18	0.15
31	0.59	6.4			0.39	1.90			0.32b	1.20	0.16	0.05

a to *a* Ice conditions.
b Gauge height interpolated.

5 GEORGE V. A. 1915

MONTHLY DISCHARGE of Davis Creek at Drury's Ranch, for 1914.

(Drainage area 45 square miles.)

MONTH.	DISCHARGE IN SECOND-FEET.				RUN-OFF.	
	Maximum	Minimum.	Mean.	Per square Mile.	Depth in inches on Drainage Area.	Total in Acre-feet.
March (10–31)	150.00	1.90	22.00	0.500	0.410	973
April	154.00	6.60	44.00	0.970	1.080	2,588
May	25.00	1.90	7.20	0.160	0.180	446
June	2.40	1.70	1.97	0.044	0.011	27
July	2.40	1.20	1.85	0.041	0.047	114
August (22–31)	0.25	0.05	0.20	0.004	0.001	4
September	b					
October	b					
The period					1.729	4,152

a Discharges computed on June 1, 4, 5, 7, 11, 29 and 30 only.
b No observer obtainable.

FAIRWELL CREEK AT DRURY'S RANCH.

Location.—On the NW. ¼ Sec. 30, Tp. 6, Rge. 24, W. 3rd Mer.
Records available.—June 10, 1909, to October 31, 1914.
Gauge.—Vertical staff; the elevation of the zero of the gauge has been maintained at 95.13 feet since establishment.
Bench-mark.—Permanent iron bench-mark; assumed elevation, 100.00 feet.
Channel.—Slightly shifting, owing to beaver dams.
Discharge measurements.—Made with meter and weir at low periods.
Diversions.—Messrs. Armstrong and Sons, Kearney Bros., and J. Ingram divert water for irrigation purposes above the gauge.
Observer.—A. J. Hart.

DISCHARGE MEASUREMENTS of Fairwell Creek at Drury's Ranch, in 1914.

Date.	Engineer.	Width.	Area of Section.	Mean Velocity.	Gauge Height.	Discharge.
		Feet.	*Sq. ft.*	*Ft. per sec.*	*Feet.*	*Sec.-ft.*
Mar. 16	M. H. French	87.0	131.00	1.70	3.68	223.00
Mar. 20	do	16.0	20.20	0.80	2.65	16.10
April 7	do	90.0	115.00	1.67	3.61	192.00
April 9	do	62.0	65.00	1.24	3.12	80.00
April 22	do	19.3	19.50	1.35	2.72	26.00
May 8	F. R. Steinberger	24.2	30.20	0.79	2.73	24.00
May 26	do	14.0	10.20	0.92	2.48	9.40
June 27	do	11.3	8.71	0.49	2.41	4.30
July 21	do	12.0	3.80	0.67	2.34	2.60
Aug. 11	do	11.5	3.53	0.55	2.30	1.94
Aug. 29	E. W. W. Hughes	9.7	2.56	0.38	2.34	0.98
Sept. 21	do				2.28	0.50*a*

a Weir measurement.

SESSIONAL PAPER No. 25c

DAILY GAUGE HEIGHT AND DISCHARGE of Fairwell Creek at Drury's Ranch, for 1914.

DAY.	March.		April.		May.		June.	
	Gauge Height.	Dis- charge.	Gauge Height.	Dis- charge.	Gauge Height.	Dis- charge.	Gauge Height.	Dis- charge.
	Feet.	*Sec.-ft.*	*Feet.*	*Sec.-ft.*	*Feet.*	*Sec.-ft.*	*Feet.*	*Sec.-ft.*
1	......	....	2.94	50.0	2.59	14.3	2.46a	6.5
2	......	....	3.25	107.0	2.59	14.3	2.46a	6.5
3	......	....	3.51	172.0	2.59	14.3	2.47a	7.0
4	......	....	3.61	198.0	2.59	14.3	2.47a	7.0
5	......	......	3.94	287.0	2.62	16.4	2.47a	7.0
6	......	....	4.00	303.0	2.62	16.4	2.48a	7.5
7	......	......	3.76	238.0	2.64	17.8	2.48	7.5
8	2.27	0.7	3.41	146.0	2.72	24.0	2.48a	7.5
9	2.26	0.6	3.11	78.0	2.75	27.0	2.48	7.5
10	2.28	0.8	3.06	69.0	2.77	29.0	2.50	8.5
11	2.28	0.8	3.26	109.0	2.75	27.0	2.47	7.0
12	2.28	0.8	4.02	308.0	2.66	19.3	2.46	6.5
13	2.29	0.9	3.86	265.0	2.64	17.8	2.45	6.0
14	2.59	14.3	3.45	156.0	2.60	15.0	2.46	6.5
15	3.65	208.0	3.29	116.0	2.60	15.0	2.48	7.5
16	3.69	219.0	3.20	96.0	2.58	13.6	2.46	6.5
17	3.28	114.0	3.05	67.0	2.57	12.9	2.46	6.5
18	2.95	51.0	2.90	44.0	2.57	12.9	2.46	6.5
19	2.81	33.0	2.79	31.0	2.57	12.9	2.46	6.5
20	2.69	22.0	2.82	34.0	2.55	11.5	2.46	6.5
21	2.59	14.3	2.77	29.0	2.55	11.5	2.48	7.5
22	2.52	9.7	2.71	23.0	2.54	10.9	2.48	7.5
23	2.55	11.5	2.71	23.0	2.54	10.9	2.47	7.0
24	2.52	9.7	2.69	22.0	2.55	11.5	2.47	7.0
25	2.32	1.4	2.68	21.0	2.55	11.5	2.46	6.5
26	2.47	7.0	2.63	17.1	2.48	7.5	2.45	6.0
27	2.61	15.7	2.62	16.4	2.46	6.5	2.42	4.8
28	2.65	18.5	2.59	14.3	2.46	6.5	2.42	4.8
29	2.69	22.0	2.60	15.0	2.45	6.0	2.42	4.8
30	2.70	22.5	2.59	14.3	2.45a	6.0	2.42	4.8
31	2.70	22.5	....	....	2.45a	6.0	....	....

a Gauge height interpolated.

5 GEORGE V, A. 1915

DAILY GAUGE HEIGHT AND DISCHARGE of Fairwell Creek at Drury's Ranch, for 1914.

DAY.	July.		August.		September.		October.	
	Gauge Height.	Discharge.	Gauge Height.	Discharge.	Gauge Height.	Discharge.	Gauge Height.	Discharge.
	Feet.	*Sec.-ft.*	*Feet.*	*Sec.-ft.*	*Feet.*	*Sec.-ft.*	*Feet.*	*Sec.-ft.*
1	2.40	4.00	2.33	1.60	2.33	1.60	2.30	1.00
2	2.40	4.00	2.32	1.40	2.31	1.20	2.29	0.90
3	2.40	4.00	2.32	1.40	2.30	1.00	2.34	1.80
4	2.40	4.00	2.30	1.00	2.30	1.00	2.32	1.40
5	2.40	4.00	2.30	1.00	2.30	1.00	2.36	2.40
6	2.40	4.00	2.30	1.00	2.30	1.00	2.34	1.50
7	2.40	4.00	2.30	1.00	2.30	1.00	2.30	1.00
8	2.38	3.20	2.30	1.00	2.30	1.00	2.30	1.00
9	2.38	3.20	2.30	1.00	2.30	1.00	2.30	1.00
10	2.38	3.20	2.30	1.00	2.30	1.00	2.30	1.00
11	2.38	3.20	2.30	1.00	2.29	0.90	2.30	1.00
12	2.36	2.40	2.29	0.90	2.30	1.00	2.30	1.00
13	2.36	2.40	2.29	0.90	2.40	4.00	2.30	1.00
14	2.36	2.40	2.29	0.90	2.36	2.40	2.30	1.00
15	2.36	2.40	2.29	0.90	2.34	1.80	2.30	1.00
16	2.35	2.00	2.30	1.00	2.34	1.80	2.30	1.00
17	2.35	2.00	2.30	1.00	2.32	1.40	2.30	1.00
18	2.35	2.00	2.30	1.00	2.32	1.40	2.28	0.80
19	2.35	2.00	2.30	1.00	2.30	1.00	2.30	1.00
20	2.35	2.00	2.30	1.00	2.28	0.80	2.30	1.00
21	2.34	1.80	2.30	1.00	2.28	0.80	2.30	1.00
22	2.34	1.80	2.30	1.00	2.27	0.70	2.30	1.00
23	2.34	1.80	2.30	1.00	2.27	0.70	2.30	1.00
24	2.34	1.80	2.32	1.40	2.27	0.70	2.30	1.00
25	2.34	1.80	2.34	1.80	2.27	0.70	2.30	1.00
26	2.34	1.80	2.34	1.80	2.27	0.70	2.29	0.90
27	2.34	1.80	2.33	1.60	2.30	1.00	2.29	0.90
28	2.33	1.60	2.33	1.60	2.36	2.40	2.29	0.90
29	2.34	1.80	2.34	1.80	2.28	0.80	2.29	0.90
30	2.33	1.60	2.34	1.80	2.29	0.90	2.29	0.90
31	2.33	1.60	2.34	1.80	....	....	2.29	0.90

MONTHLY DISCHARGE of Fairwell Creek at Drury's Ranch, for 1914.

(Drainage area 125 square miles.)

MONTH.	DISCHARGE IN SECOND-FEET.				RUN-OFF.	
	Maximum.	Minimum.	Mean.	Per square Mile.	Depth in inches on Drainage Area.	Total in Acre-feet.
March (8-31)	219.00	0.60	34.00	0.273	0.244	1,625
April	308.00	14.30	102.00	0.818	0.913	6,070
May	29.00	6.00	14.20	0.113	0.130	873
June	8.50	4.80	6.60	0.053	0.059	395
July	4.00	1.60	2.60	0.020	0.023	158
August	1.80	0.90	1.21	0.010	0.011	74
September	4.00	0.70	1.22	0.010	0.011	73
October	2.40	0.80	1.08	0.008	0.009	66
The period	....	....	....	....	1.400	9,334

FRENCHMAN RIVER AT GORDON'S RANCH.

Location.—On NW. ¼ Sec. 16, Tp. 6, Rge. 24, W. 3rd Mer., at R. N. S. Gordon's ranch near Ravenscrag.

Records available.—May 17, 1913, to October 31, 1914.

Gauge.—Chain gauge; the elevation of the zero of the gauge has been 85.96 feet since establishment.

Bench-mark.—Permanent iron bench-mark; assumed elevation, 100.00 feet.

Channel.—Shifting, caused by sliding banks.

Discharge measurements.—Made by wading or from cable.

Winter flow.—Station not maintained during winter.

Observer.—J. Plant and P. Harradine.

DISCHARGE MEASUREMENTS of Frenchman River at Gordon's Ranch, in 1914.

Date.	Engineer.	Width.	Area of Section.	Mean Velocity.	Gauge Height.	Discharge.
		Feet.	*Sq. ft.*	*Ft. per sec.*	*Feet.*	*Sec.-ft.*
Mar. 17.............	M. H. French...............	129.0	137.00	1.58	6.01	214.00a
Mar. 23.............	do	10.6	9.75	2.18	3.33	21.00a
April 9.............	do •.............	48.0	70.40	3.05	4.56	247.00a
April 21.............	do	28.0	29.10	2.01	2.63	58.00
May 8.............	F. R. Steinberger............	33.0	36.80	1.18	2.33	44.00
May 26.............	do	30.0	22.80	0.87	2.00	19.90
June 27.............	do	31.5	18.30	0.70	1.89	12.80
July 2.............	do	21.5	10.50	0.39	2.02b	4.08
Aug. 8.............	do	16.5	7.75	0.22	2.27b	1.69
Aug. 29.............	E. W. W. Hughes............	16.5	7.42	0.07	2.44b	0.51

a Ice conditions.
b Gauge height affected by beaver dam.

DAILY GAUGE HEIGHT AND DISCHARGE of Frenchman River at Gordon's Ranch, for 1914.

DAY.	March.		April.		May.	
	Gauge Height.	Dis-charge.	Gauge Height.	Dis-charge.	Gauge Height.	Dis-charge.
	Feet.	*Sec.-ft.*	*Feet.*	*Sec.-ft.*	*Feet.*	*Sec.-ft.*
1.................	....	....	....	....	2.32	39
2.................	....	....	....	....	2.29	37
3.................	....	....	....	....	....	....
4.................	....	....	....	....	....	....
5.................	....	....	....	....	....	....
6.................	....	....	8.51	720	....	....
7.................	....	....	7.51	601	....	....
8.................	....	....	....	....	2.32	39
9.................	....	....	4.66	247	....	....
10.................	....	....	3.72	156	2.57	57
11.................	....	....	3.61	145	2.50	52
12.................	....	....	5.41	349	2.40	45
13.................	....	....	....	....	2.24	34
14.................	3.10	98	5.74	389	2.24	34
15.................	7.09	551	5.11	313	2.27	36
16.................	6.01	421	....	....	2.22	32
17.................	5.89	214	....	....	2.20	31
18.................	4.87	286	3.18	105	2.14	27
19.................	4.67	260	2.85	78	2.19	30
20.................	....	....	2.69	65	2.14	27
21.................	....	....	2.63	61	2.14	27
22.................	....	....	2.52	53	....	....
23.................	3.33	21	2.48	51	....	....
24.................	....	....	2.47	50	....	....
25.................	....	....	2.47	50	....	....
26.................	....	....	2.57	57	2.00	19
27.................	....	....	2.47	50	....	....
28.................	....	....	2.46	49	....	....
29.................	....	....	2.45	49	....	....
30.................	....	....	2.36	42	....	....
31.................	....	....	....	....	....	....

NOTE.—Observations of gauge height periodically taken after May 31 of no value on account of beaver dam below the station.

5 GEORGE V, A. 1915

MONTHLY DISCHARGE of Frenchman River at Gordon's Ranch, for 1914.

MONTH.	DISCHARGE IN SECOND-FEET.				RUN-OFF.	
	Maximum	Minimum.	Mean.	Per square Mile.	Depth in inches on Drainage Area.	Total in Acre-feet.
March......	551	21	264	....	....	....
April....	720	42	175	....	....	....
May.................................	57	19	35	....	....	....
The period............................	....	....	....	....	....	....

NOTE.—Repeated hiatus in gauge heights prevents monthly computations.

FRENCHMAN RIVER AT RAVENSCRAG.

Location.—On the NW. ¼ Sec. 19, Tp. 6, Rge. 23, W. 3rd Mer.
Records available.—One measurement—October 17, 1914.
Gauge.—Vertical staff, fastened to pile in the fourth bent from west end of Canadian Pacific Railway bridge; the elevation of the zero of the gauge has been 89.73 feet since establishment.
Bench-mark.—Six-foot spike driven in the second telegraph pole on the west side of the river; assumed elevation, 100 00 feet.
Channel.—Probably permanent.
Discharge measurements.—Made with meter.
Observer.—None.

DISCHARGE MEASUREMENTS of Frenchman River at Ravenscrag, in 1914.

Date.	Engineer.	Width.	Area of Section.	Mean Velocity.	Gauge Height.	Discharge.
		Feet.	*Sq. ft.*	*Ft. per sec.*	*Feet.*	*Sec.-ft.*
Oct 17	E. W. W. Hughes...........	48.0	17 3	0 56	1.14	9.70

ROSE CREEK NEAR EAST END.

Location.—On the NE. ¼ Sec. 26, Tp. 7, Rge. 22, W. 3rd Mer., at B. Rose's ranch.
Records available.—May 1, 1911, to October 31, 1914.
Gauge.—Vertical staff; elevation of the zero of the gauge has been maintained at 91.09 feet since establishment. On June 16, 1913, a permanent weir was established at this station, and records since that date have been kept on the gauge above the weir; the elevation of the crest of the weir and zero of the rod is 92.98 feet.
Bench-mark.—Permanent iron bench-mark; assumed elevation, 100.00 feet.
Discharge measurements.—Made with permanent weir.
Diversions.—Mr. B. E. Rose diverts water for irrigation purposes above the station.
Observer.—B. E. Rose.

DISCHARGE MEASUREMENTS of Rose Creek near East End, in 1914.

Date.	Engineer.	Width.	Area of Section.	Mean Velocity.	Gauge Height.	Discharge.
		Feet.	*Sq. ft.*	*Ft. per sec.*	*Feet.*	*Sec.-ft.*
Mar. 26.............	M. H. French..............	....	....	....	....	0.12
April 29.............	F. R. Steinberger..........	....	....	....	0.16	0.64
May 19.............	do	....	....	....	0.18	0.75
June 11.............	do	....	....	....	0.15	0.58
July 8.............	do	....	....	....	0.10	0.05
Aug. 1.............	do	....	....	....	0.02	Nil.
Aug. 26.............	E. W. W. Hughes..........	....	....	....	0.14	0.07
Sept. 11.............	do	....	....	....	0.11	0.06

NOTE.—Measurements made with permanent weir.

DAILY GAUGE HEIGHT AND DISCHARGE of Rose Creek near East End, for 1914.

DAY.	March.		April.		May.		June.	
	Gauge Height.	Dis- charge.	Gauge Height.	Dis- charge.	Gauge Height.	Dis- charge.	Gauge Height.	Dis- charge.
	Feet.	*Sec.-ft.*	*Feet.*	*Sec.-ft.*	*Feet.*	*Sec.-ft.*	*Feet.*	*Sec.-ft.*
1...........................	....	....	1.07	10.30	0.15	0.58	0.11	0.36
2...........................	....	....	1.04	9.90	0.14	0.52	0.10	0.31
3...........................	....	....	0.81	6.90	0.14	0.52	0.12	0.41
4...........................	....	....	1 11	10 70	0.15	0.58	0.20	0.92
5...........................	....	....	1.18	11.80	0.23	1.08	0.27	1.38
6...........................	....	....	0.95	8.70	0.23	1.08	0.20	0.92
7...........................	....	....	0.59	4.40	0.18	0.75	0.17	0.69
8...........................	....	....	0.40	2.50	0.18	0.75	0.14	0.52
9...........................	....	....	0.33	1.85	0.17	0.69	0.12	0.41
10...........................	....	....	0.32	1.78	0.17	0.69	0.14	0.52
11...........................	....	....	1.12	11.00	0.16	0.63	0.15	0.58
12...........................	....	....	0.99	9.10	0.15	0.58	0.18	0.75
13...........................	0.84	7.30	0.41	2.60	0.15	0.58	0.35	2.00
14...........................	1.19	13.00	0.49	3.30	0.14	0.52	0.31	1.70
15...........................	0.60	4.50	0.39	2.40	0.14	0.52	0.20	0.92
16...........................	0.42	2.64	0.30	1.62	0.14	0.52	0.16	0.63
17...........................	0.30	1.60	0.26	1.30	0.16	0.63	0.14	0.52
18...........................	0.16	0.63	0.24	1.15	0.16	0.63	0.12	0.41
19...........................	0.13	0.47	0.23	1.08	0.17	0.69	0.10	0.31
20...........................	0.12	0.41	0.22	1.01	0.18	0.75	0.10	0.31
21...........................	0.07	0.19	0.22	1.01	0.18	0.75	0.12	0.41
22...........................	0.09*a*	0.27	0.22	1.01	0.18	0.75	0.12	0.41
23...........................	....	....	0.20	0.87	0.18	0.75	0.10	0.31
24...........................	....	....	0.20	0.98	0.22	1.01	0.10	0.31
25...........................	....	....	0.19	0.82	0.17	0.69	0.15	0.58
26...........................	....	....	0.19	0.82	0.15	0.58	0.18	0.75
27...........................	....	....	0.19	0.82	0.14	0.52	0.14	0.52
28...........................	....	....	0.18	0.75	0.14	0.52	0.13	0.47
29...........................	....	....	0.18	0.75	0.12	0.41	0.14	0.52
30...........................	*a*	....	0.18	0.75	0.12	0.41	0.12	0.41
31...........................	0.40	2.50	....	....	0.12	0.41	....	....

a to *a* Channel frozen.

5 GEORGE V. A. 1915

DAILY GAUGE HEIGHT AND DISCHARGE of Rose Creek near East End, for 1914.—*Concluded.*

DAY.	July.		August.		September.		October.	
	Gauge Height.	Dis-charge.	Gauge Height.	Dis-charge.	Gauge Height.	Dis-charge.	Gauge Height.	Dis-charge.
	Feet.	*Sec.-ft.*	*Feet.*	*Sec.-ft.*	*Feet.*	*Sec.-ft.*	*Feet.*	*Sec.-ft.*
1	0.10	0.31	0.04	0.01	0.12	0.06	0.07	0.18
2	0.08	0.23	0.04	0.01	0.11	0.06	0.07	0.18
3	0.07	0.19	0.04	0.01	0.10	0.05	0.08	0.22
4	0.06	0.15	0.03	0.01	0.10	0.05	0.20	0.92
5	0.06	0.15	0.02	Nil	0.12	0.06	0.15	0.58
6	0.06	0.15	0.03	0.01	0.10	0.05	0.20	0.92
7	0.06	0.15	0.04	0.01	0.10	0.05	0.22	1.01
8	0.06	0.15	0.04	0.01	0.12	0.06	0.30	1.62
9	0.18a	0.12	0.08	0.04	0.14	0.08	0.27	1.38
10	0.18	0.12	0.08	0.04	0.12	0.06	0.22	1.01
11	0.16	0.10	0.06	0.02	0.12	0.06	0.16	0.63
12	0.08	0.04	0.06	0.02	0.18a	0.12	0.15	0.58
13	0.07	0.03	0.06	0.02	0.37	2.20	0.15	0.58
14	0.07	0.03	0.04	0.01	0.32	1.77	0.14	0.52
15	0.10	0.05	0.04	0.01	0.22	1.01	0.14	0.52
16	0.10	0.05	0.04	0.01	0.16	0.63	0.14	0.52
17	0.08	0.04	0.10	0.05	0.14	0.52	0.14	0.52
18	0.10	0.05	0.14	0.08	0.10	0.31	0.13	0.47
19	0.06	0.02	0.12	0.06	0.10	0.31	0.13	0.47
20	0.06	0.02	0.08	0.04	0.10	0.31	0.13	0.47
21	0.07	0.03	0.10	0.05	0.09	0.27	0.13	0.47
22	0.06	0.02	0.08	0.04	0.09	0.27	0.13	0.47
23	0.06	0.02	0.12	0.06	0.08	0.22	0.13	0.47
24	0.06	0.02	0.24	0.18	0.08	0.22	0.12	0.41
25	0.06	0.02	0.20	0.14	0.08	0.22	0.13	0.47
26	0.06	0.02	0.13	0.07	0.08	0.22	0.13	0.47
27	0.05	0.02	0.11	0.06	0.08	0.22	0.13	0.47
28	0.02	Nil	0.10	0.05	0.08	0.22	0.12	0.41
29	0.04	0.01	0.11	0.06	0.08	0.22	0.12	0.41
30	0.02	Nil	0.11	0.06	0.07	0.18	0.12	0.41
31	0.02	"	0.12	0.06	....	....	0.12	0.41

a to *a* Crest of weir reduced from 36 inches to 6 inches.

MONTHLY DISCHARGE of Rose Creek near East End, for 1914.

(Drainage area 13 square miles.)

MONTH.	DISCHARGE IN SECOND-FEET.				RUN-OFF.	
	Maximum.	Minimum	Mean.	Per square Mile.	Depth in inches on Drainage Area.	Total in Acre-feet.
March (13–31)	13.00	....	1.76	0.136	0.100	66
April	11.80	0.75	3.70	0.287	0.320	222
May	1.08	0.41	0.65	0.050	0.060	40
June	2.00	0.31	0.64	0.049	0.060	38
July	0.31	....	0.07	0.006	0.007	5
August	0.18	....	0.04	0.003	0.004	3
September	2.20	0.05	0.34	0.026	0.030	20
October	1.62	0.18	0.59	0.045	0.050	36
The period	....	....	....	....	0 631	430

A. M. CROSS DITCH FROM CALF CREEK.

Location.—On SE. ¼ Sec. 5, Tp. 8, Rge. 22, W. 3rd Mer.
Records available.—June 1 to September 13, 1914.
Gauge.—Vertical staff, located about 40 feet from the intake of the ditch; elevation of the zero of the gauge has been maintained at 96.06 feet since establishment.
Bench-mark.—Is a poplar stump on the left bank of the ditch, surrounded by a cairn of stones; assumed elevation, 100.00 feet.
Channel.—Slightly shifting, owing to growth of weeds.
Discharge measurements.—Made with meter.
Observer.—A. M. Cross.

DISCHARGE MEASUREMENTS of A. M. Cross Ditch from Calf Creek, in 1914.

Date.	Engineer.	Width.	Area of Section.	Mean Velocity.	Gauge Height.	Discharge.
		Feet.	*Sq. ft.*	*Ft. per sec.*	*Feet.*	*Sec.-ft.*
June 20............	F. R. Steinberger....... .	5.2	1.99	0.93	1.46	1.87
Aug. 8....	do	4.4	1.60	0.64	1.40	1.03
Aug. 27.............	E. W. W. Hughes	4.4	1.80	0.71	1.25	1.29

DAILY GAUGE HEIGHT AND DISCHARGE of A. M. Cross Ditch from Calf Creek, for 1914.

DAY.	June. Gauge Height.	June. Discharge.	July. Gauge Height.	July. Discharge.	August. Gauge Height.	August. Discharge.	September. Gauge Height.	September. Discharge.
	Feet.	*Sec.-ft.*	*Feet.*	*Sec.-ft.*	*Feet.*	*Sec.-ft.*	*Feet.*	*Sec.-ft.*
1.................................	1.50	2.00	1.50	1.88	1.42	1.19	1.42	1.74
2.................................	1.50	2.00	1.50	1.86	1.38	1.06	1.42	1.74
3.................................	1.67	2.50	1.50	1.84	1.38	1.05	1.42	1.74
4.................................	1.67	2.50	1.50	1.82	1.38	1.04	1.42	1.74
5.................................	1.58	2.20	1.50	1.80	1.38	1.03	1.42	1.74
6.................................	1.50	2.00	1.50	1.79	1.38	1.01	1.42	1.74
7.................................	1.54	2.10	1.50	1.77	1.38	0.99	1.42	1.74
8.................................	1.50	2.00	1.50	1.75	1.38	1.03	1.46	1.87
9.................................	1.50	2.00	1.50	1.73	1.46	1.23	1.46	1.87
10.................................	1.50	2.00	1.50	1.72	1.42	1.17	1.42	1.74
11.................................	1.50	2.00	1.50	1.70	1.38	1.14	1.42	1.74
12.................................	1.58	2.20	1.50	1.68	1.38	1.16	1.50	2.00
13.................................	1.58	2.20	1.50	1.67	1.42	1.26	1.58	2.20
14.................................	......*a*	....	1.50	1.66	1.42	1.28	....	....
15.................................	....	....	1.50	1.64	1.38	1.24	....	....
16.................................	....	....	1.50	1.62	1.38	1.27	....	....
17.................................	....	....	1.50	1.60	1.38	1.30	....	....
18.................................	....	....	1.50	1.58	1.46	1.50	....	....
19.................................	......*a*	....	1.46	1.48	1.42	1.46	....	....
20.................................	1.46	1.87*b*	1.46	1.46	1.42	1.50	....	....
21.................................	1.54	2.10	1.42	1.36	1.42	1.54	....	....
22.................................	1.50	2.00	1.42	1.34	1.42	1.58	....	....
23.................................	1.50	1.98	1.42	1.32	1.42	1.62	....	....
24.................................	1.50	1.96	1.42	1.30	1.46	1.72	....	....
25.................................	1.50	1.94	1.42	1.28	1.46	1.75	....	....
26.................................	1.58	2.20	1.42	1.26	1.42	1.70	....	....
27.................................	1.58	2.10	1.42	1.24	1.42	1.74*b*	....	....
28.................................	1.54	2.00	1.38	1.14	1.42	1.74	....	....
29.................................	1.50	1.92	1.38	1.13	1.42	1.74	....	....
30.................................	1.54	1.98	1.38	1.11	1.42	1.74	....	....
31.................................	....	....	1.42	1.21	1.46	1.87	....	....

a to *a* Headgate closed.
b to *b* Shifting conditions.

5 GEORGE V, A. 1915

MONTHLY DISCHARGE of A. M. Cross Ditch from Calf Creek, for 1914.

MONTH.	DISCHARGE IN SECOND-FEET.			RUN-OFF.
	Maximum.	Minimum	Mean.	Total in Acre-feet.
June..	2.50	1.87	2.10	99
July..	1.88	1.11	1.54	95
August...	1.87	0.99	1.38	85
September (1-13).......................................	2.20	1.74	1.81	47
The period...	....	....	....	326

F. CROSS DITCH FROM NORTH BRANCH OF FRENCHMAN RIVER.

Location.—On NW. ¼ Sec. 15, Tp. 7, Rge. 22, W. 3rd Mer., about 130 feet from the intake of the ditch.

Records available.—June, 1912, and May 16 to June 21, 1914.

Gauge.—Staff, fastened to the left side of the flume; elevation of the zero of the gauge, 94.45 feet.

Bench-mark.—Nut on the northwest corner of the floor of the bridge across the north branch of Frenchman River; assumed elevation, 100 00 feet.

Discharge measurements.—Made by meter at section or by a weir in ditch.

Observer.—Frank Cross.

DISCHARGE MEASUREMENTS of F. Cross Ditch from North Branch of Frenchman River, in 1914.

Date.	Engineer.	Width.	Area of Section.	Mean Velocity.	Gauge Height.	Discharge.
		Feet.	*Sq. ft.*	*Ft. per sec.*	*Feet.*	*Sec.-ft.*
May 19	F. R. Steinberger............	....	....	....	1.48	1.23a
June 17............	do	....	....	....	1.39	0.52a

a Weir measurement.

DAILY GAUGE HEIGHT AND DISCHARGE of F. Cross Ditch from North Branch of Frenchman River, for 1914.

DAY.	May.		June	
	Gauge Height.	Dis-charge.	Gauge Height.	Dis-charge.
	Feet.	*Sec.-ft.*	*Feet.*	*Sec.-ft.*
1	....	.. .	1.33	0.80
2	....	......	1.33	0.78
3	....	.. ..	1.33	0.76
4	... ..	. ... .	1.38	0.80
5	.....	. .	1.42	0.83
6	. ....	. ....	1.42	0.81
7	......	......	1.42	0.78
8	.... .	. ....	1.38	0.72
9	.... .	. . .	1.38	0.70
10	....	. .	1.38	0.67
11	... .	. .	1.38	0.65
12	....	......	1.33	0.58
13	....	.....	1.33	0.57
14	... .	.... .	1.33	0.54
15	....	.....	1.42	0.61
16	1.42	1.17	1.38	0.54
17	1.42	1.17	1.38	0.53
18	1.42	1.17	1.38	0.53
19	1.46	1.23	1.25	0.40
20	1.46	1.21	1.25	0.40
21	1.38	1.07	1.00	0.20
22	1.38	1.05	....	......
23	1.38	1.03	....	......
24	1.38	1.01	....	......
25	1.38	0.99	....	......
26	1.42	1.03	... ...	......
27	1.42	1.01	....	......
28	1.42	0.99	....	......
29	1.42	0.97	....	......
30	1.38	0.90	....	......
31	1.38	0.88	....	......

MONTHLY DISCHARGE of F. Cross Ditch from North Branch of Frenchman River, for 1914.

MONTH.	DISCHARGE IN SECOND-FEET.			RUN-OFF.
	Maximum.	Minimum.	Mean.	Total in Acre-feet.
May (16–31)	1.23	0.88	1.06	33
June (1–21)	0.83	0.20	0.63	26
The period	....	....	....	59

NORTH BRANCH OF FRENCHMAN RIVER AT F. CROSS' RANCH.

Location.—On *NE.* ¼ Sec. 16, Tp. 7, Rge. 22, W. 3rd Mer., at F. Cross' ranch near *East* End.

Records available.—August 1, 1908, to October 31, 1914.

Gauge.—Vertical staff; the elevation of the zero of the gauge was 91.28 feet during 1908-11; 90 27 feet during 1912-14.

Bench-mark.—Permanent iron bench-mark; assumed elevation, 100.00 feet.

Channel.—Sandy and slightly shifting.

Discharge measurements.—Made by wading.

Winter flow.—Station not maintained during winter.

Diversions.—F. Cross, H. Cross, and W. F. McNicol divert water above this station for irrigation. F. Cross and H. Cross were the only ones to divert water during 1914.

Observer.—Frank Cross.

No. 25c.—24

5 GEÒRGE V, A. 1915

DISCHARGE MEASUREMENTS of North Branch of Frenchman River at F. Cross' Ranch, in 1914.

Date.	Engineer.	Width.	Area of Section.	Mean Velocity.	Gauge Height.	Discharge.
		Feet.	Sq. ft.	Ft. per sec.	Feet.	Sec.-ft.
Mar. 18........	M. H. French	10.3	3.86	4.38	4.15	16.9
Mar. 26....	do	6.6	2.48	3.40	....	8.5
April 2.. ..	do	10.0	9.40	7.00	5.05	66.0
April 13..	do	10.4	10.40	6.73	3.62	70.0
April 20...........	do	11.0	8.60	1.52	1.21	13.1
April 29...........	F. R. Steinberger.	12.3	8.43	1.27	1.20	10.7
May 19...........	do	11.5	5.87	1.19	1.08	7.0
June 18...........	do	11.6	4.18	1.00	0.95	4.2
July 20...........	do	12.5	3.85	0 65	0.89	16.5
Aug. 7.. .. .	do	11.7	3.83	0.74	0.91	2.8
Aug. 14	E. W. W. Hughes........	10.6	2.96	0.88	0.95	2.6
Aug. 27...... .	do	11.7	4.92	0.81	1.00	4.1
Sept. 11...........	do	11.7	5.05	0.92	1.00	4.6
Sept. 14..	do .,........	11.9	13.60	1.64	1.44	22.0
Oct. 10....	do	11.7	10.00	1.30	1.20	13.1

DAILY GAUGE HEIGHT AND DISCHARGE of North Branch of Frenchman River at 'F. Cross' Ranch, for 1914.

DAY.	April		May.		June.	
	Gauge Hight.	Dis-charge.	Gauge Height.	Dis-charge.	Gauge Height.	Dis-charge.
	Feet.	Sec.-ft.	Feet.	Sec.-f .	Feet.	Sec.-ft.
1.................	4.95	70.0	1.19	10.7	1.07	6.8
2.................	4.85	66.0	1.21	11.5	1.06	6.5
3.................	4.35	25.0	1.21	11.5	1.00	4.9
4.................	4.85	74.0	1.21	11.5	1.09	7.4
5.................	4.85	88.0	1.29	15.0	1.31	16.0
6.................	4.75	90.0	1.32	16.5	1.20	11.1
7.................	4.75	102.0	1.32	16.5	1.14	9.0
8.................	4.55	96.0	1.32	16.5	1.08	7.1
9.................	4.05	60.0	1.23	12.3	1.02	5.4
10.................	3.75	47.0	1.24	12.7	1.03	5.7
11.................	3.65	49.0	1.24	12.7	1.03	5.7
12.................	3.75	69.0	1.23	12.3	1.07	6.8
13.................	3 55	65.0	1.22	11.9	1.09	7.4
14.................	3 00	37.0	1.22	11.9	1.31	16.0
15.................	2.25a	30.0	1.21	11.5	1.11	8.0
16.................	1.50	26.0	1.20	11.1	1.01	5.2
17.................	1.48	25.0	1.10	7.7	0.99	4.7
18.................	1.35	18.0	1.10	7.7	0.95	3.8
19.................	1.35	18.0	1.09	7.4	0.95	3.8
20.................	1.35	18.0	1.00	4.9	0.95	3.8
21.................	1.35	18.0	0.99	4.7	1.02	5.4
22.................	1.34	17.5	1.00	4.9	1.08	7.1
23.................	1.33	17.0	1.00	4.9	0.96	4.0
24.................	1.32	16.5	1.12	8.3	1.08	7.1
25.................	1.31	16.0	1.11	8.0	1.08	7.1
26.................	1.32	16.5	1.09	7.4	1.11	8.0
27.................	1.32	16.5	1.08	7.1	1.07	6.8
28.................	1.21	11.5	1.05	6.2	1.05	6.2
29.................	1.20	11.1	1.07	6.8	1.04	5.9
30.................	1.21	11.5	1.08	7.1	1.04	5.9
31.................	....	....	1.08	7.1	....	......

a Ice conditions April 1 to 15.

DAILY GAUGE HEIGHT AND DISCHARGE of North Branch of Frenchman River at F. Cross' Ranch, for 1914.—*Concluded.*

DAY.	July.		August.		September.		October.	
	Gauge Height.	Dis- charge.	Gauge Height.	Dis- charge.	Gauge Height.	Dis- charge.	Gauge Height.	Dis- charge.
	Feet.	*Sec.-ft.*	*Feet.*	*Sec.-ft.*	*Feet.*	*Sec.ft.*	*Feet.*	*Sec.-ft*
1	1.02	5.4	0.91	3.0	1.01	5.2	1.04	5.9
2	1.00	4.9	0.92	3.2	1.00	4.9	1.04	5.9
3	0.99	4.7	0.93	3.4	0.98	4.5	1.03	5.7
4	0.97	4.2	0.92	3.2	0.98	4.5	1.15	9.3
5	0.97	4.2	0.92	3.2	0.98	4.5	1.20	11.1
6	0.96	4.0	0.91	3.0	1.00	4.9	1.18	10.4
7	0.94	3.6	0.92	3.2	1.00	4.9	1.12	8.3
8	0.94	3.6	0.91	3.0	1.01	5.2	1.35	18.0
9	0.95	3.8	0.96	4.0	1.06	6.5	1.35	18.0
10	0.95	3.8	1.00	4.9	1.03	5.7	1.20	11.1
11	0.96	4.0	0.97	4.2	1.00	4.9	1.12	8.3
12	0.96	4.0	0.96	4.0	1.05	6.2	1.11	8.0
13	0.97	4.2	0.98	4.5	1.32	16.5	1.11	8.0
14	0.95	3.8	0.96	4.0	1.46	24.0	1.11	8.0
15	0.93	3.4	0.95	3.8	1.32	16.5	1.09	7.4
16	0.93	3.4	0.94	3.6	1.18	10.4	1.08	7.1
17	0.92	3.2	0.94	3.6	1.09	7.4	1.09	7.4
18	0.91	3.0	1.03	5.7	1.04	5.9	1.08	7.1
19	0.91	3.0	1.01	5.2	1.04	5.9	1.09	7.4
20	0.90	2.8	0.99	4.7	1.03	5.7	1.09	7.4
21	0.90	2.8	0.95	3.8	1.03	5.7	1.09	7.4
22	0.90	2.8	0.95	3.8	1.03	5.7	1.10	7.7
23	0.89	2.6	0.96	4.0	1.03	5.7	1.10	7.7
24	0.89	2.6	1.10	7.7	1.03	5.7	1.10	7.7
25	0.91	3.0	1.05	6.2	1.03	5.7	1.10	7.7
26	0.95	3.8	1.03	5.7	1.03	5.7	1.10	7.7
27	0.93	3.4	1.03	5.7	1.04	5.9	1.11	8.0
28	0.92	3.2	1.02	5.4	1.04	5.9	1.12	8.3
29	0.92	3.2	1.02	5.4	1.04	5.9	1.12	8.3
30	0.91	3.0	1.02	5.4	1.04	5.9	1.13	8.7
31	0.90	2.8	1.01	5.2	....	....	1.13	8.7

MONTHLY DISCHARGE of North Branch of Frenchman River at F. Cross' Ranch, for 1914.

(Drainage area 53 square miles.)

MONTH.	DISCHARGE IN SECOND-*FEET.*				RUN-OFF.	
	Maximum.	Minimum	Mean.	Per square Mile.	Depth in inches on Drainage Area.	Total in Acre-feet.
April	102.0	11.1	41.0	0.770	0.86	2,428
May	16.5	4.7	9.9	0.186	0.21	608
June	16.0	3.8	7.0	0.131	0.15	414
July	5.4	2.6	3.6	0.067	0.08	219
August	7.7	3.0	4.4	0.083	0.10	269
September	24.0	4.5	7.1	0.133	0.15	421
October	18.0	5.7	8.6	0.163	0.19	531
The period	....	....	....	....	1.74	4,890

5 GEORGE V. A. 1915

BOLINGBROKE DITCH NEAR EAST END.

Location.—On the *NE.* ¼ Sec. 7, Tp. 7, Rge. 22, W. 3rd Mer.
Records available.—May 27 to June 13, 1914.
Gauge.—Vertical staff, fastened to post on the left bank; elevation of the zero of the gauge maintained at 98.21 feet since establishment.
Bench-mark.—Wooden post, driven in left bank about 20 feet from the gauge; assumed elevation, 100.00 feet.
Discharge measurements.—Made with weir.
Observer.—J. Bolingbroke.

DISCHARGE MEASUREMENTS of Bolingbroke Ditch near *E*ast End, in 1914.

Date.	Engineer.	Width.	Area of Section.	Mean Velocity.	Gauge Height.	Discharge.
		Feet.	*Sq. ft.*	*Ft. per sec.*	*Feet.*	*Sec.-ft.*
June 26............	F. R. Steinberger............	....	....	....	0.42	0.15

DAILY GAUGE HEIGHT AND DISCHARGE of Bolingbroke Ditch near *E*ast End, for 1914.

DAY.	May.		June.	
	Gauge Height.	Dis-charge.	Gauge Height.	Dis-charge.
	Feet.	*Sec.-ft.*	*Feet.*	*Sec.-ft.*
1	....	....	0.28	0.03
2	....	....	0.28	0.03
3	....	....	0.29	0.03
4	....	....	0.33	0.06
5	....	....	0.33	0.06
6	....	....	0.33	0.06
7	....	....	0.31	0.05
8	....	....	0.29	0.03
9	....	....	0.29	0.03
10	....	....	0.29	0.03
11	....	....	..0.33	0.06
12	....	....	0.35	0.07
13	....	....	0.42	0.16
14	....	....	....	....
15	....	....	....	....
16	....	....	....	....
17	....	....	....	....
18	....	....	....	....
19	....	....	....	....
20	....	....	....	....
21	....	....	....	....
22	....	....	....	....
23	....	....	....	....
24	....	....	....	....
25	....	....	....	....
26	....	....	....	....
27	0.27	0.02	....	....
28	0.27	0.02	....	....
29	0.27	0.02	....	....
30	0.27	0.02	....	....
31	0.27	0.02	....	....

MONTHLY DISCHARGE of Bolingbroke Ditch near East End, for 1914.

MONTH.	DISCHARGE IN SECOND-FEET.			RUN-OFF.
	Maximum.	Minimum.	Mean.	Total in Acre-feet.
May (27-31)	0.02	0.02	0.02	0.2
June (1-13)	0.16	0.03	0.05	1.4
The period..	....	....	....	1.6

BARROBY DITCH FROM NORTH BRANCH OF FRENCHMAN RIVER.

Location.—On the SE. ¼ Sec. 33, Tp. 6, Rge. 23, W. 3rd Mer.
Gauge.—Vertical staff, fastened to wall of headgate; elevation of the zero of the gauge has been maintained at 92.10 feet since establishment.
Bench-mark.—Wooden stake, driven in left bank about 30 feet from the gauge; assumed elevation, 100 00 feet.
Discharge measurements.—Made with meter.
Observer.—No observations in 1914.

DISCHARGE MEASUREMENTS of Barroby Ditch from North Branch of Frenchman River, in 1914.

Date.	Engineer.	Width.	Area of Section.	Mean Velocity.	Gauge Height.	Discharge.
		Feet.	*Sq. ft.*	*Ft. per sec.*	*Feet.*	*Sec.-ft.*
June 27..............	F. R. Steinberger............	3.5	3.50	0.52	2.02	1.84
July 20..............	do	3.5	1.75	0.34	0.58	0.53

FRENCHMAN RIVER AT PHILLIPS' RANCH.

Location.—On the NE. ¼ Sec. 23, Tp. 6, Rge. 23, W. 3rd Mer., at A. Phillips' ranch near Ravenscrag.
Records available.—July 9, 1912, to October 31, 1914.
Gauge.—Vertical staff; the elevation of the zero of the gauge has been 90 02 feet since the station was established.
Bench-mark.—Permanent iron bench-mark; assumed elevation, 100.00 feet.
Channel.—Permanent.
Discharge measurements.—Made by wading or from cable.
Winter flow.—Station not maintained during winter.
Artificial control.—A permanent control was established at this station during October, 1914, by which means more accurate records should be obtained at this station.
Observer.—A. A. Phillips.

5 GEORGE V, A. 1915

DISCHARGE MEASUREMENTS of Frenchman River at Phillips' Ranch, in 1914.

Date.	Engineer.	Width.	Area of Section.	Mean Velocity.	Gauge Height.	Discharge.
		Feet.	*Sq. ft.*	*Ft. per sec.*	*Feet.*	*Sec.-ft.*
Mar. 19............	M. H. French..............	47.0	40.0	1.95	3.45	78.0
Mar. 23............	do	31.0	26.0	1.14	3.00	30.0
April 6............	do	55.0	141.0	4.55	4.55	642.0
April 10............	do	45.0	82.0	2.89	3.10	236.0
April 13............	do	45.0	131.0	5.64	4.33	738.0
April 21............	do	38.0	43.0	2.09	1.95	90.0
May 7............	F. R. Steinberger............	45.0	54.0	1.02	1.69	55.0
May 25............	do	44.0	48.0	0.74	1.50	35.0
June 26............	do	43.0	40.0	0.57	1.39	23.0
July 21............	do	22.0	9.7	0.54	1.04	5.2
Aug. 8............	do	15.5	5.7	0.42	0.90	2.4
Aug. 20............	E. W. W. Hughes.........	28.0	13.2	0.48	1.04	6.3
Sept. 15............	do	44.0	48.0	0.78	1.57	37.7
Oct. 16............	do	44.0	43.0	0.48	1.36	24.0

DAILY GAUGE HEIGHT AND DISCHARGE of Frenchman River at Phillips' Ranch, for 1914.

DAY.	March.		April.		May.		June.	
	Gauge Height.	Dis-charge.	Gauge Height.	Dis-charge.	Gauge Height.	Dis-charge.	Gauge Height.	Dis-charge.
	Feet.	*Sec.-ft.*	*Feet.*	*Sec.-ft.*	*Feet.*	*Sec.-ft.*	*Feet.*	*Sec.-ft.*
1....................	....	....	....	45	1.60	43	1.35	20.0
2....................	....	....	....	60	1.58	41	1.34	19.4
3....................	....	....	....	100	1.58	41	1.34	19.4
4....................	....	....	....	250	1.57	40	1.39	23.0
5....................	....	....	4.57	400	1.61	44	1.49	32.0
6....................	....	....	4.52	642	1.63	47	1.46	29.0
7....................	....	....	4.37	520	1.66	50	1.47	30.0
8....................	....	....	3.72	410	1.68	53	1.44	27.0
9....................	....	....	3.42	320	1.84	74	1.39	23.0
10....................	....	....	2.95	236	1.88	79	1.34	19.4
11....................	....	....	2.78	380	1.84	74	1.34	19.4
12....................	....	....	3.65	610	1.79	67	1.42	26.0
13....................	5	....	4.24	738	1.72	57	1.47	30.0
14....................	5	....	3.62	479	1.68	53	1.49	32.0
15....................	45	....	3.42	413	1.62	45	1.49	32.0
16....................	550	....	3.21	351	1.56	39	1.45	28.0
17....................	300	....	2.53	190	1.57	40	1.42	26.0
18....................	150	....	2.26	141	1.54	37	1.31	17.6
19....................	78	....	2.14	119	1.53	36	1.28	15.8
20....................	65	....	1.99	95	1.52	35	1.27	15.2
21....................	60	....	1.92	85	1.50	33	2.05	105.0
22....................	40	....	1.86	76	1.48	31	1.66	50.0
23....................	30	....	1.79	67	1.49	32	1.53	36.0
24....................	30	....	1.76	62	1.59	42	1.44	27.0
25....................	30	....	1.72	57	1.52	35	1.39	23.0
26....................	25	....	1.69	54	1.48	31	1.37	22.0
27....................	20	....	1.65	49	1.41	25	1.38	22.0
28....................	20	....	1.64	48	1.40	24	1.35	20.0
29....................	20	....	1.64	48	1.40	24	1.35	20.0
30....................	25	....	1.61	44	1.40	24	1.34	19.4
31....................	40	....	....	....	1.40	24	....	....

DAILY GAUGE HEIGHT AND DISCHARGE of Frenchman River at Phillips' Ranch, for 1914.
—*Concluded.*

DAY.	July.		August.		September.		October.	
	Gauge Height.	Dis-charge.	Gauge Height.	Dis-charge.	Gauge Height.	Dis-charge.	Gauge Height.	Dis-charge.
	Feet.	*Sec.-ft.*	*Feet.*	*Sec.-ft.*	*Feet.*	*Sec.-ft.*	*Feet.*	*Sec.-ft.*
1	1.32	18.2	1.02	4.60	1.14	9.1	1.15	9.5
2	1.29	16.4	1.00	4.00	1.12	8.3	1.16	9.9
3	1.25	14.0	1.00	4.00	1.12	8.3	1.18	10.7
4	1.21	12.0	0.89	1.95	1.10	7.5	1.24	13.5
5	1.22	12.5	1.00	4.00	1.08	6.7	1.48	31.0
6	1.12	8.3	0.89	1.50	1.07	6.3	1.53	36.0
7	1.16	9.9	0.90	2.00	1.04	5.2	1.56	39.0
8	1.14	9.1	0.90	2.00	1.03	4.9	1.56	39.0
9	1.14	9.1	0.90	2.00	1.02	4.6	1.66	50.0
10	1.14	9.1	0.88	1.90	1.00	4.0	1.59	42.0
11	1.10	7.5	0.88	1.90	1.00	4.0	1.55	38.0
12	1.07	6.3	0.90	2.00	0.98	3.4	1.50	33.0
13	1.04	5.2	0.92	2.20	1.24	13.5	1.48	31.0
14	1.04	5.2	0.94	2.40	1.67	51.0	1.42	26.0
15	1.04	5.2	0.94	2.40	1.57	40.0	1.38	22.0
16	1.02	4.6	0.94	2.40	1.50	33.0	1.36	21.0
17	1.02	4.6	0.95	2.50	1.42	26.0	1.35	20.0
18	1.02	4.6	0.98	3.40	1.30	17.0	1.34	19.4
19	1.02	4.6	0.96	2.80	1.25	14.0	1.34	19.4
20	1.01	4.3	0.96	2.80	1.20	11.5	1.31	17.6
21	1.04	5.2	0.94	2.40	1.20	11.5	1.28	15.8
22	1.01	4.3	0.95	2.50	1.22	12.5	1.26	14.6
23	1.02	4.6	0.98	3.40	1.22	12.5	1.25	14.0
24	1.04	5.2	1.19	11.10	1.24	13.5	1.24	13.5
25	1.01	4.3	1.21	12.00	1.24	13.5	1.26	14.6
26	1.00	4.0	1.18	10.70	1.25	14.0	1.25	14.0
27	1.01	4.3	1.18	10.70	1.26	14.6	1.24	13.5
28	1.01	4.3	1.17	10.30	1.22	12.5	1.25	14.0
29	1.03	4.9	1.19	11.10	1.19	11.1	1.24	13.5
30	1.03	4.9	1.16	9.90	1.16	9.9	1.24	13.5
31	1.01	4.3	1.14	9.10	....	....	1.24	13.5

MONTHLY DISCHARGE of Frenchman River at Phillips' Ranch, for 1914.

(Drainage area 598 square miles.)

MONTH.	DISCHARGE IN SECOND-FEET.				RUN-OFF.	
	Maximum.	Minimum.	Mean.	Per square Mile.	Depth in inches on Drainage Area.	Total in Acre-feet.
March (13–31)	550.0	5.00	81.0	0.135	0.095	3,050
April	738.0	44.00	236.0	0.395	0.441	14,043
May	79.0	24.00	43.0	0.071	0.082	2,619
June	105.0	15.20	28.0	0.046	0.051	1,697
July	18.2	4.00	7.1	0.012	0.014	437
August	12.0	1.50	4.8	0.008	0.009	295
September	51.0	3.40	13.5	0.023	0.026	803
October	50.0	9.50	22.0	0.037	0.043	1,353
The period	....	....	....	....	1.620	24,297

5 GEORGE V. A, 1915

STRONG AND DAY DITCH AT EAST END.

Location.—On the *NE.* ¼ Sec. 25, Tp. 6, Rge. 22, W. 3rd Mer., about one-half mile below the headgate of the ditch.
Records available.—May 9, 1909, to December 31, 1914.
Gauge.—Staff, fastened to a post on right bank.
Bench-marks.—(1) *A* spike on the initial post, which is about six inches above ground, on the left bank of the ditch; elevation, 5 49 feet above the datum of the gauge. (2) The top of a plug, about four inches above ground, on the right bank and about 50 feet downstream from the gauge; elevation, 7.52 feet above the datum of the gauge.
Channel.—Slightly shifting and affected by growth of weeds.
Discharge measurements.—Made by wading.
Observer.—M. L. Krewet.

DISCHARGE MEASUREMENTS of Strong and Day Ditch at *E*ast End, in 1914.

Date.	Engineer.	Width.	Area of Section.	Mean Velocity.	Gauge Height.	Discharge.
		Feet.	*Sq. ft.*	*Ft. per sec.*	*Feet.*	*Sec.-ft.*
May 2....	F. R. Steinberger............	7.3	7.6	0.91	1.00	7.00
May 22............	do	17.3	16.8	1.17	1.61	19.60
June 22............	do	17.1	19.3	0.65	1.64	12.60
July 16............	do	7.3	2.4	0.34	0.60	0.82

DAILY GAUGE HEIGHT AND DISCHARGE of Strong and Day Ditch at *E*ast End,· for 1914.

DAY.	May.		June.		July.	
	Gauge Height.	Dis-charge.	Gauge Height.	Dis-charge	Gauge Height;	Dis-charge.
	Feet.	*Sec.-ft.*	*Feet.*	*Sec.-ft.*	*Feet.*	*Sec.-ft.*
1.......................................	....	....	1.55	15.8	1.80	15.60
2.......................................	1.00	7.0	1.65	17.8	1.80	15.60
3.......................................	1.30a	12.6	1.45	13.2	1.70	13.80
4.......................................	1.50a	17.0	1.55	15.0	1.70	13.80
5.......................................	1.60a	19.2	1.55	14.8	1.70	13.80
6.......................................	1.60a	19.2	1.55	14.6	1.60	12.00
7.......................................	1.60a	19.2	1.65	16.5	1.40	9.00
8.......................................	1.60a	19.2	1.55	14.1	1.30	7.60
9.......................................	1.60a	19.2	1.45	11.8	1.10	5.00
10.......................................	1.60a	19.2	1.55	13.7	1.00	4.00
11.......................................	1.60a	19.2	1.55	13.5	1.00	4.00
12.......................................	1.60a	19.2	1.55	13.2	0.90	3.00
13.......................................	1.60a	19.2	1.55	13.0	0.80	2.10
14.......................................	1.60a	19.2	1.45	10.7	0.70	1.40
15.......................................	1.60a	19.2	1.45	10.5	0.60	0.85
16.......................................	1.60a	19.2	1.55	12.2	0.60	0.85
17.......................................	1.60a	19.2	1.55	12.0	0.51	0.44
18.......................................	1.60a	19.2	1.45	9.8	0.47	0.31
19.......................................	1.60a	19.2	1.55	11.5	0.23	0.00
20.......................................	1.60a	19.2	1.45	9.3	Dry.	Nil.
21.......................................	1.60a	19.2	1.45	9.1	"	"
22.......................................	1.61	19.6	1.64	12.7	"	"
23.......................................	1.60	19.2	1.30	7.6	"	"
24.......................................	1.57	18.1	1.40	9.0	0.40	0.10
25.......................................	1.57	17.9	1.50	10.4	0.35	Nil.
26.......................................	1.55	17.3	1.40	9.0	0.35	"
27.......................................	1.65	19.3	1.50	10.4	0.42	0.16
28.......................................	1.55	16.7	1.50	10.4	0.34	Nil.
29.......................................	1.65	18.9	1.60	12.0	Dry.	"
30.......................................	1.55	16.3	1.60	12.0	"	"
31.......................................	1.65	18.3	....	....	"	"

a Gauge height interpolated.

MONTHLY DISCHARGE of Strong and Day Ditch at East End, for 1914.

MONTH.	DISCHARGE IN SECOND-*FEET.*			RUN-OFF.
	Maximum.	Minimum.	Mean.	Total in Acre-feet.
May (2–31)	19.2	7.00	18.2	1,083
June	17.8	7.60	12.2	726
July	15.6	0.00	4.0	245
The period	....	....	....	2,054

FRENCHMAN RIVER AT EAST END.

Location.—On the *NE.* ¼ Sec. 31, Tp. 6, Rge. 21, W. 3rd Mer., at Strong and Day's highway bridge. Moved August 21 to Canadian Pacific Railway bridge in the SE. ¼ of the same section, about one-half mile east of East End Railway depot, and about three-quarters of a mile below the old gauging station.
Records available.—April 21, 1909, to October 31, 1914.
Gauge.—Chain gauge at the abandoned station. Vertical staff at new station, fastened to the downstream pile of the fourth bent from the west end of the bridge. The elevation of the zero of the gauge is 2,958.84 feet above sea level.
Bench-mark.—On southeast corner of the cap of the first bent from the east abutment of the bridge; elevation, 2,974.92 feet above sea level (Canadian Pacific Railway datum).
Channel.—Permanent.
Discharge measurements.—Made by wading or from bridge.
Winter flow.—Station not maintained in winter.
Artificial control.—A permanent control for the gauge was established during October, one-quarter mile downstream from the bridge.
Diversions.—Messrs. Strong and Day divert water for irrigation purposes about two miles upstream from this station. A small amount returns to the river channel above the gauge.
Observer.—M. L. Krewet and S. B. C. Gooch.

DISCHARGE MEASUREMENTS of Frenchman River at East End, in 1914.

Date.	Engineer.	Width.	Area of Section.	Mean Velocity.	Gauge Height.	Discharge.
		Feet.	*Sq. ft.*	*Ft. per sec.*	*Feet.*	*Sec.-ft.*
April 14	M. H. French	37.5	249.00	2.17	5.66	540.00
April 17	do	59.0	86.40	3.10	4.41	268.00
April 18	do	57.0	55.50	3.44	4.10	191.00
April 20	do	36.0	43.50	2.18	3.64	95.00
May 2	F. R. Steinberger	33.5	30.30	1.23	3.28	37.00
May 22	do	32.6	25.20	0.59	3.25	14.80
June 22	do	39.5	38.80	1.46	3.24	55.00
July 16	do	12.4	5.48	0.80	3.12	4.40
Aug. 4	do	9.2	3.58	0.85	3.06	3.00
Aug. 15	E. W. W. Hughes	22.2	2.23	0.29	3.18	2.10
Aug. 27	do	9.2	2.83	0.64	0.74	1.81*a*
Sept. 17	do	51.0	51.00	0.42	1.34	21.00*a*

a New station.

5 GEORGE V, A. 1915

DAILY GAUGE HEIGHT AND DISCHARGE of Frenchman River at East End, for 1914.

DAY.	March.		April.		May.		June.	
	Gauge Height.	Dis-charge.	Gauge Height.	Dis-charge.	Gauge Height.	Dis-charge.	Gauge Height.	Dis-charge.
	Feet.	*Sec.-ft.*	*Feet.*	*Sec.-ft.*	*Feet.*	*Sec.-ft.*	*Feet.*	*Sec.-ft.*
1				45.0	3.08	18.6	3.21	23.00
2				62.0	3.07	17.9	3.19	22.00
3				105.0	3.06	17.2	3.17	21.00
4				235.0	3.07	17.9	3.07	12.00
5				400.0	3.08	18.6	2.97	6.00
6				500.0	3.07	17.9	3.07	14.00
7				800.0	3.06	17.2	2.91	4.00
8				650.0	3.08	18.6	2.98	8.50
9				475.0	3.09	20.0	3.07	17.50
10				360.0	3.11	22.0	2.89	4.50
11				280.0	3.12	22.0	2.81	2.00
12				260.0a	3.10	21.0	2.69	0.50
13		5a	6 71	889.0a	3.08	18.6	2.81	2.70
14		5	5 58	585.0	3.06	17.2	2.78	2.00
15		45	5 01	431.0	3.02	14.4	2.68	0.75
16		550	4.71	350.0	3.06	17.2	2.78	2.50
17		310	4.56	308.0	3.06	17.2	2.89	9.00
18		170	4.06	180.0	3.09	20.0	2.94	14.00
19		80	3.84	133.0	3.08	18.6	2.87	9.00
20		75	3.61	89.0	3.06	17.2	3.01	23.00
21		50	3.56	80.0	3.07	17.9	3.64	121.00
22		40	3.16	25.0	3.25	15.5	3.25	56.00
23		40	3.36	48.0	3.21	12.0	3.21	24.00b
24		37	3.26	35.0	3.24	15.5	3.31	20.00
25		30	3.16	25.0	3.22	15.5	3.41	12.60
26		22	3.08	18.6	3.21	15.5	3.53	13 00
27		20	3.08	18.6	3.22	17.5	3.60	11.60
28		20	3.08	18.6	3.21	17.5	3.73	9.60
29		20	3.06	17.2	3.21	19.0	3.67	8.00
30		25	3.06	17.2	3.20	19.5	3.63	7.40b
31		40			3.20	20.0		

a Discharge estimated March 13 to April 12.
b Discharge June 23 to 30 computed from station at Phillips' ranch.

DAILY GAUGE HEIGHT AND DISCHARGE of Frenchman River at East End, for 1914.

DAY.	July.		August.		September.		October.	
	Gauge Height.	Dis- charge.	Gauge Height	Dis- charge.	Gauge Height.	Dis- charge.	Gauge Height	Dis- charge.
	Feet.	*Sec.-ft.*	*Feet.*	*Sec.-ft.*	*Feet.*	*Sec.-ft.*	*Feet.*	*Sec.-ft.*
1	2.94	9.0	3.07	3.10	0.80	2.5	1.01	7.8
2	2.91	6.5	3.07	3.10	0.80	2.5	1.02	8.1
3	2.84	3.0	3.07	3.10	0.80	2.5	1.10	10.5
4	2.82	2.0	3.07	3.10	0.80	2.5	1.18	13.2
5	2.79	1.0	3.08	3.40	0.81	2.7	1.30	19.5
6	2.84	2.0	3.08	3.40	0.83	3.1	1.42	26.0
7	2.88	2.5	3.07	3.10	0.83	3.1	1.35	22.0
8	2.93	3.5	3.08	3.40	0.83	3.1	1.45	28.0
9	2.96	4.0	3.09	3.70	0.83	3.1	1.52	32.0
10	2.94	3.0	3.09	3.70	0.83	3.1	1.53	33.0
11	2.87	1.5	3.08	3.40	0.83	3.1	1.42	26.0
12	2.84	1.0	3.08	3.40	0.83	3.1	1.32	20.0
13	2.88	1.9	3.07	3.10	1.14	11.7	1.33	21.0
14	2.95	3.0	3.07	3.10	1.47	29.0	1.35	22.0
15	2.92	3.5	3.07	3.10	1.54	33.0	1.42	26.0
16	2.92c	4.4	3.08	3.40	1.40	25.0	1.62	39.0
17	2.79c	4.3	3.09	3.70	1.34	22.0	1.60	37.0
18	2.75c	9.4	3.11	4.50	1.19	14.6	1.52	32.0
19	3.11	4.5	3.12	5.00	1.13	11.4	1.52	32.0
20	3.14	6.0	3.09	3.70	1.09	10.2	1.52	32.0
21	3.13	5.5	3.07	3.10	1.05	9.0	1.52	32.0
22	3.08	3.4	0.74d	1.78	1.05	9.0	1.51	32.0
23	3.10	4.0	0.78	2.30	1.02	8.1	1.51	32.0
24	3.12	5.0	0.78	2.30	1.00	7.5	1.50	31.0
25	3.10	4.0	0.80	2.50	1.00	7.5	1.50 ·	31.0
26	3.11	4.5	0.82	2.90	1.00	7.5	1.50	31.0
27	3.10	4.0	0.78	2.30	1.00	7.5	1.49	30.0
28	3.09	3.7	0.80	2.50	1.00	7.5	1.49	30.0
29	3.08	3.4	0.80	2.50	1.00	7.5	1.50	31.0
30	3.07	3.1	0.80	2.50	1.00	7.5	1.50	31.0
31	3.07	3.1	0.80	2.50	....	....	1.50	31.0

c Discharge obtained from Weir measurements.
d New station established.

MONTHLY DISCHARGE of Frenchman River at East End, for 1914.

(Drainage area 648 square miles.)

MONTH.	DISCHARGE IN SECOND-FEET.				RUN-OFF.	
	Maximum.	Minimum	Mean.	Per square Mile.	Depth in inches on Drainage Area.	Total in Acre-feet.
March (13-31)	550	5.00	83.0	0.129	0.091	3,141
April	889	17.20	247.0	0.382 -	0.426	14,722
May	41	25.00	36.0	0.028	0.032	2,183
June	130	11.20	28.0	0.025	0.028	1,678
July	25	3.10	7.9	0.006	0.007	484
August	5	1.78	3.1	0.005	0.006	192
September	33	2.50	9.0	0.014	0.016	536
October	39	7.80	27.0	0.041	0.047	1,642
The period	....	....	....	....	0.653	24,578

NOTE.—This table shows the total discharge of the river and Strong and Day's ditch at this point.

5 GEORGE V, A. 1915

MORRISON BROTHERS DITCH FROM FRENCHMAN RIVER.

Location.—On the SW. ¼ Sec. 26, Tp. 6, Rge. 21, W. 3rd Mer., about three miles down-stream from East End.

Records available.—June 12 to August 28, 1913; May 25 to October 30, 1914.

Gauge.—Vertical staff, fastened to a post at the right bank about one-half mile from the headgate; the elevation of the zero of the gauge has been maintained at 97.36 feet since establishment.

Bench-mark.—Top of rock marked B.M. in red, located on the left bank about 300 feet up-stream from the gauge; assumed elevation, 100 00 feet.

Channel.—Slightly grown with weeds.

Discharge measurements.—Made with meter.

Observer.—A. A. Morrison.

DISCHARGE MEASUREMENTS of Morrison Brothers' Ditch from Frenchman River, in 1914.

Date.	Engineer.	Width.	Area of Section.	Mean Velocity.	Gauge Height.	Discharge.
		Feet.	*Sq. ft.*	*Ft. per sec.*	*Feet.*	*Sec.-ft.*
June 22............	F. R. Steinberger...........	11.0	15.60	1.31	1.67	16.10
July 14............	do	7.3	3.31	0.52	0.48	1.73

DAILY GAUGE HEIGHT AND DISCHARGE of Morrison Brothers' Ditch from Frenchman River, for 1914.

DAY.	May.		June.		July.		August.		September.		October.	
	Gauge Height.	Dis-charge.	Gauge Height.	Dis-charge.	Gauge Height.	Dis-charge.	Gauge Height.	Dis-charge.	Gauge Height.	Dis-charge.	Gauge Height.	Dis-charge.
	Feet.	*Sec.-ft.*	*Feet.*	*Sec.-ft.*	*Feet.*	*Sec.-ft.*	*Feet.*	*Sec.-ft.*	*Feet.*	*Sec.-ft.*	*Feet.*	*Sec.-ft.*
1.........	......	......	0.62a	2.70	1.04a	6.8	......	......	......	......	....b	......
2.........	......	......	0.58	2.40	1.00	6.3	......	......	......	......	0.92	5.4
3.........	......	......	0.69a	3.30	0.92	5.4	......	......	......	......	0.92	5.4
4.........	......	......	0.81a	4.40	0.75	3.8	......	......	......	......	0.92a	5.4
5.........	......	......	0.92	5.40	....b	......	......	......	......	......	0.92	5.4
6.........	......	......	0.83	4.60	......	......	......	......	......	......	0.92	5.4
7.........	......	......	0.77a	4.00	......	......	......	......	......	......	0.92	5.4
8.........	......	......	0.71a	3.50	......	......	......	......	......	......	0.92a	5.4
9.........	......	......	0.65a	3.00	......	......	......	......	......	......	0.92	5.4
10......	......	......	0.59a	2.40	......	......	......	......	......	......	0.92	5.4
11.........	......	......	0.55a	2.20	......	......	......	......	......	......	0.92	5.4
12.........	......	......	0.50	1.80	......	......	......	......	......	......	0.87a	4.9
13.........	......	......	1.00	6.30	......	......	......	......	......	......	0.83	4.6
14.........	......	......	1.25a	9.50	......	......	......	......	......	......	0.83	4.6
15.........	......	......	1.50	13.30	......	......	......	......	......	......	0.83a	4.6
16.........	......	......	1.50	13.30	......	......	......	......	......	......	0.75a	3.8
17.........	......	......	1.42	12.00	......	......	......	......	......	......	0.75	3.8
18.........	......	......	1.21a	8.90	......	......	......	......	......	......	0.75	3.8
19.........	......	......	1.00	6.30	......	......	......	......	......	......	0.75a	3.8
20......	......	......	0.83	4.60	......	......	......	......	......	......	0.75a	3.8
21.........	......	......	1.25a	9.50	......	......	......	......	......	......	0.75	3.8
22......	......	......	1.67	16.30	......	......	......	......	......	......	0.75	3.8
23.........	......	......	1.50	13.30	......	......	......	......	......	......	0.75	3.8
24.........	......	......	1.42	12.00	......	......	......	......	......	......	0.75a	3.8
25......	0.83	4.60	1.33	10.60	......	......	......	......	......	......	0.75a	3.8
26.........	0.83	4.60	1.33	10.60	......	......	......	......	......	......	0.75	3.8
27.........	0.83	4.60	1.17	8.40	......	......	......	......	......	......	0.75a	3.8
28.........	0.71a	3.50	1.17	8.40	......	......	......	......	......	......	0 75a	3.8
29.........	0.50	1.80	1.17	8.40	......	......	......	......	......	......	0.75	3.S
30.........	0.50	1.80	1.08	7.30	......	......	......	......	......	......	0.75	3.S
31......	0.67	3.10	......	......	......	......	......	......	......	......	......	......

a Gauge height interpolated.
b to b Headgate closed.

MONTHLY DISCHARGE of Morrison Brothers' Ditch from Frenchman River, for 1914.

MONTH.	DISCHARGE IN SECOND-FEET.			RUN-OFF.
	Maximum.	Minimum.	Mean.	Total in Acre-feet.
May (25-31)..	4.60	1.80	3.40	48
June..	16.3	1.80	7.30	434
July (1-4)..	6.8	3.80	5.60	44
August...	....	....	....	....
September	....	....	....	....
October (2-30)...	5.4	3.80	4.50	257
The period....................................	....	....	....	783

MULE CREEK AT GUNN'S RANCH.

Location.—On SW. ¼ Sec. 33, Tp. 5, Rge. 17, W. 3rd Mer.

Records available.—April 15 to October 31, 1914. Previous records at old station about one-half mile downstream from present site consist of discharge measurements made during 1911, 1912, and 1913.

Gauge.—Vertical staff, fastened to a post on the left bank about 1½ miles south of Mr. Gunn's ranch; the elevation of the zero of the gauge has been maintained at 91.50 feet since establishment.

Bench-mark.—Permanent iron bench-mark, located on the left bank about 30 feet from the gauge; assumed elevation, 100 00 feet.

Discharge measurements.—Made with meter; with weir at low stages.

Channel.—Probably permanent.

Winter flow.—This station is not maintained during the winter.

Diversions.—There is no diversion above this stream.

Observer.—Wm. Gunn, Jr.

DISCHARGE MEASUREMENTS of Mule Creek at Gunn's Ranch, in 1914.

Date.	Engineer.	Width.	Area of Section.	Mean Velocity.	Gauge Height.	Discharge.
		Feet.	*Sq. ft.*	*Ft. per sec.*	*Feet.*	*Sec.-ft.*
April 15.............	E. W. W. Hughes..........	4.1	2 94	0 58	1.98	1.72
April 15.............	do	....	....	....	1.97	1.90a
May 14.............	do	....	....	....	1.29	0.27a
July 21.............	do	....	....	....	1.21	0.06a
Oct. 22.............	do	....	....	....	1.28	0.29a

a Weir measurement.

5 GEORGE V, A. 1915

DAILY GAUGE HEIGHT AND DISCHARGE of Mule Creek at Gunn's Ranch, for 1914.

DAY.	April.		May.		June.	
	Gauge Height.	Dis-charge.	Gauge Height.	Dis-charge.	Gauge Height.	Dis-charge.
	Feet.	*Sec.-ft.*	*Feet.*	*Sec.-ft.*	*Feet.*	*Sec.-ft.*
1	...	......	1.20	0.08	1.24	0.14
2	... ...	......	1.26	0.17	1.25	0.15
3			1.20	0.08	1.33	0.32
4			1.25	0.15	1.58	1.92
5	.. . .	......	1.21	0.09	2.25	2.60
6	... ...	......	1.18	0.06	3.30	5.22
7			1.16	0.04	1.75	1.34
8			1.14	0 03	1.45	0.60
9			1.12	0.02	1.40	0.48
10	... ...	......	1.10	0.01	1.60	0.97
11	... . .	. ...	1.10	0.01	2.00	1.97
12			1.12	0.02	3.50	5.70
13	. ....	......	1.29	0.23	4.00	6.00
14		.....	1.29	0.23	3.00	4.50
15	1 97	1.90	1.27	0.19	1.95	1.84
16	1.95	1.84	1.28	0.21	1.65	1.10
17	1.89	1.70	1.24	0.14	1.43	0.55
18	1.71	1.24	1.25	0.15	1.35	0.36
19	1.65	1.10	1.23	0.12	1.25	0.15
20	1.64	1.07	1.21	0.09	1.35	0.36
21	1.52	0.77	1.24	0.14	1.38	0.43
22	1.43	0.55	1.26	0.17	1.25	0.15
23	1.40	0.48	1.28	0.21	1.20	0.08
24	1.43	0.55	1.30	0.25	1.22	0.10
25	1.33	0.32	1.27	0.19	1.25	0.15
26	1.30	0.25	1.25	0.15	1.45	0.60
27	1.33	0.32	1.25	0.15	1.43	0.55
28	1.20	0.08	1.23	0.12	1.38	0.43
29	1.25	0.15	1.20	0.08	1.35	0.36
30	1.28	0.21	1.23	0.12	1.28	0.21
31	......	......	1.22	0.10	......	......

SESSIONAL PAPER No. 25c

DAILY GAUGE HEIGHT AND DISCHARGE of Mule Creek at Gunn's Ranch, for 1914.

DAY.	July.		August.		September.		October.	
	Gauge Height.	Dis- charge.	Gauge Height.	Dis- charge.	Gauge Height.	Dis- charge.	Gauge Height.	Dis- charge.
	Feet.	*Sec.-ft.*	*Feet.*	*Sec.-ft.*	*Feet.*	*Sec.-ft.*	*Feet.*	*Sec.-ft.*
1	1.35	0.36	1.30	0.25	1.20	0.08	1.16	0.04
2	1.35	0.36	1.26	0.17	1.22	0.10	1.19	0.07
3	1.30	0.25	1.25	0.15	1.21	0.09	1.92	1.77
4	1.32	0.29	1.20	0.08	1.23	0.12	2.16	2.40
5	1.33	0.32	1.24	0.14	1.20	0.08	2.21	2.50
6	1.30	0.25	1.26	0.17	1.16	0.04	2.41	3.00
7	1.30	0.25	1.28	0.21	1.17	0.05	2.16	2.40
8	1.32	0.29	1.23	0.12	1.19	0.07	2.11	2.20
9	1.31	0.27	1.25	0.15	1.20	0.08	2.01	2.00
10	1.75	1.34	1.29	0.23	1.18	0.06	1.95	1.84
11	1.95	1.84	1.27	0.19	1.21	0.09	1.80	1.47
12	1.65	1.10	1.26	0.17	1.19	0.07	1.74	1.32
13	1.40	0.48	1.28	0.21	3.45	5.60	1.54	0.82
14	1.35	0.36	1.26	0.17	2.24	2.60	1.45	0.60
15	1.34	0.34	1.27	0.19	1.54	0.82	1.50	0.72
16	1.32	0.29	1.24	0.14	1.44	0.58	1.38	0.43
17	1.35	0.36	1.23	0.12	1.49	0.70	1.35	0.36
18	1.38	0.43	1.27	0.19	1.49	0.70	1.30	0.25
19	1.34	0.34	1.32	0.29	1.44	0.58	1.27	0.19
20	1.28	0.21	1.28	0.21	1.39	0.46	1.24	0.14
21	1.26	0.17	1.26	0.17	1.33	0.32	1.21	0.09
22	1.28	0.21	1.23	0.12	1.28	0.21	1.28	0.21
23	1.30	0.25	1.22	0.10	1.21	0.09	1.31	0.27
24	1.28	0.21	1.22	0.10	1.17	0.05	1.30	0.25
25	1.25	0.15	1.23	0.12	1.19	0.07	1.30	0.25
26	1.27	0.19	1.21	0.09	1.21	0.09	1.27	0.19
27	1.30	0.25	1.19	0.07	1.23	0.12	1.29	0.23
28	1.24	0.14	1.21	0.09	1.21	0.09	1.25	0.15
29	1.23	0.12	1.17	0.05	1.20	0.08	1.26	0.17
30	1.26	0.17	1.22	0.10	1.18	0.06	1.32	0.29
31	1.28	0.21	1.23	0.12	....	....	1.30	0.25

MONTHLY DISCHARGE of Mule Creek at Gunn's Ranch, for 1914.

(Drainage area 60 square miles.)

MONTH.	DISCHARGE IN SECOND-FEET.				RUN-OFF.	
	Maximum.	Minimum.	Mean.	Per square Mile.	Depth in inches on Drainage Area.	Total in Acre-feet.
April (15–30)	1.90	0.08	0.78	0.013	0.001	25
May	0.25	0.01	0.12	0.002	0.002	8
June	6.00	0.08	1.31	0.022	0.024	78
July	1.84	0.12	0.38	0.006	0.007	23
August	0.29	0.05	0.15	0.002	0.003	9
September	5.60	0.04	0.47	0.008	0.009	28
October	3.00	0.04	0.87	0.014	0.016	53
The period	....	....	....	....	0.062	224

5 GEORGE V, A. 1915

FRENCHMAN RIVER AT " 76 " RANCH.

Location.—On the SE. ¼ Sec. 27, Tp. 5, Rge. 16, W. 3rd Mer., at the " 76 "ranch, near Waldville post office.

Records available.—April 10 to October 31, 1914.

Gauge.—Vertical staff, fastened to post on left bank, about one-quarter mile south of "76" ranch house; the elevation of the zero of the gauge is 87.95 feet.

Bench-mark.—Permanent iron bench-mark, located about five feet west of the sill of the north tower of the cable; assumed elevation, 100.00 feet.

Channel.—Probably permanent.

Discharge measurements.—Made by wading, or from cable.

Floods.—On account of the crooked channel above this station, floods during the spring are caused by ice jams.

Winter flow.—Station not maintained during winter.

Diversions.—Messrs. Morrison Brothers, Duncan and Watson divert water from the stream some 50 miles above the station.

Observer.—Mrs. Raymond A. Cole.

DISCHARGE MEASUREMENTS of Frenchman River at "76" Ranch, in 1914.

Date.	Engineer.	Width.	Area of Section.	Mean Velocity.	Gauge Height.	Discharge.
		Feet.	*Sq. ft.*	*Ft. per sec.*	*Feet.*	*Sec.-ft.*
April 11............	E. W. W. Hughes...........	70.8	189.0	2.00	4.92	378.0
April 11.....	do	71.5	208.0	2.33	4.97	485.0
April 12.............	do	72.0	225.0	2.49	5.04	560.0
April 17.............	do	68.3	209.0	2.00	4.32	418.0
May 13.............	do	59.5	57.1	1.23	2.66	70.0
May 15.............	do	58.1	57.3	1.20	2.80	69.0
July 20	do	16.8	7.4	0.28	1.46	2.1
Oct. 23.............	do	28.5	15.0	1.16	2.00	17.4

DAILY GAUGE HEIGHT AND DISCHARGE of Frenchman River at "76" Ranch, for 1914.

DAY.	April.		May.		June.	
	Gauge Height.	Discharge.	Gauge Height.	Discharge.	Gauge Height.	Discharge.
	Feet.	*Sec.-ft.*	*Feet.*	*Sec.-ft.*	*Feet.*	*Sec.-ft.*
1..................					1.90	13.0
2..................					1.80	9.5
3..................					1.90	13.0
4..................					1.90	13.0
5..................					2.00	17.0
6..................					2.50	48.0
7..................					3.00	107.0
8..................					2.75	74.0
9..................					2.20	27.0
10.................	5.46	741			2.52	50.0
11.................	5.31	699			2.35	36.0
12.................	5.67	800			2.20	27.0
13.................	4.56	489	2.67	65	2.25	30.0
14.................	4.43	452	2.86	87	2.30	33.0
15.................	5.31	699	2.59	57	2.30	33.0
16.................	4.98	606	2.46	45	2.25	30.0
17.................	4.36	433	2.61	59	2.10	21.0
18.................	4.18	382	2.51	49	1.90	13.0
19.................	3.89	301	2.46	45	1.85	11.0
20.................	3.68	247	2.41	41	1.78	8.9
21.................	3.46	194	2.31	34	1.70	6.8
22.................			2.30	33	1.70	6.8
23.................			2.29	32	1.70	6.8
24.................			2.26	31	1.75	8.0
25.................			2.21	28	1.80	9.5
26.................			2.18	26	1.70	6.8
27.................			2.18	26	1.80	9.5
28.................			2.17	25	1.90	13.0
29.................			2.17	25	1.80	9.5
30.................			2.16	25	1.80	9.5
31.................			2.17	25		

Gauging Station on Frenchman River at "76" Ranch. Taken by R. J. Burley.

Gauging Station on Frenchman River at Buzzard's Ranch. Taken by R. J. Burley.

DAILY GAUGE HEIGHT AND DISCHARGE of Frenchman River at "76" Ranch, for 1914.
—*Concluded.*

DAY.	July.		August.		September.		October.	
	Gauge Height.	Dis-charge.	Gauge Height.	Dis-charge.	Gauge Height.	Dis-charge.	Gauge Height.	Dis-charge.
	Feet.	*Sec.-ft.*	*Feet.*	*Sec.-ft.*	*Feet.*	*Sec.-ft.*	*Feet.*	*Sec.-ft.*
1	1.80a	9.50	1.15	0.70	1.05	0.40	1.64	5.3
2	1.80a	9.50	1.16	0.73	1.03	0.36	1.63	5.1
3	1.80	9.50	1.15	0.70	1.02	0.34	1.66	5.8
4	1.81	9.80	1.11	0.58	1.02	0.34	1.75	8.0
5	1.73	8.00	1.11	0.58	0.99	0.28	1.79	9.2
6	1.70	6.80	1.10	0.55	0.95	0.20	1.85	11.0
7	1.78	8.90	1.08	0.49	0.95	0.20	2.10	21.0
8	1.60	4.50	1.08	0.49	0.96	0.22	1.86	11.4
9	1.50	2.80	1.06	0.43	0.92	0.14	1.90	13.0
10	1.48	2.40	1.04	0.38	0.91	0.12	2.10	21.0
11	1.50	2.80	1.02	0.34	0.92	0.14	2.20	27.0
12	1.50	2.80	1.02	0.34	0.95	0.20	2.20	27.0
13	1.46	2.20	1.02	0.34	1.05	0.40	2.15	24.0
14	1.42	1.82	1.01	0.32	1.70	6.80	2.13	23.0
15	1.50	2.80	1.01	0.32	1.68	6.20	2.05	19.0
16	1.48	2.40	1.01	0.32	1.55	3.50	2.02	17.8
17	1.30	1.20	1.00	0.30	1.70	6.80	2.01	17.4
18	1.35	1.45	0.80	Nil.	1.69	6.50	2.00	17.0
19	1.35	1.45	0.80	"	1.90	13.00	1.94	14.6
20	1.51	2.90	0.80	"	1.91	13.40	1.92	13.8
21	1.40	1.70	0.80	"	1.88	12.20	1.87	11.8
22	1.39	1.65	0.81	"	1.86	11.40	1.82	10.1
23	1.25	1.00	0.80	"	1.90	13.00	1.95	15.0
24	1.26	1.04	1.10	0.55	1.86	11.40	1.95	15.0
25	1.23	0.94	1.10	0.55	1.80	9.50	1.92	13.8
26	1.25	1.00	0.90	0.10	1.74	7.80	1.88	12.2
27	1.27	1.08	1.00	0.30	1.68	6.20	1.86	11.4
28	1.27	1.08	1.00	0.30	1.68	6.20	1.86	11.4
29	1.26	1.04	0.82	Nil.	1.65	5.50	1.87	11.8
30	1.23	0.94	0.90	0.10	1.64	5.30	1.89	12.6
31	1.20	0.85	0.90	0.10	....	....	1.90	13.0

a Gauge height interpolated.

MONTHLY DISCHARGE of Frenchman River at "76" Ranch, for 1914.

(Drainage area 1,106 square miles.)

MONTH.	DISCHARGE IN SECOND-FEET.				RUN-OFF.	
	Maximum	Minimum	Mean.	Per square Mile.	Depth in inches on Drainage Area.	Total in Acre-feet.
April (10-21)	800.00	194.00	504.00	0.4560	0.2030	11,983
May (13-31)	87.00	25.00	40.00	0.0360	0.0250	1,503
June	107.00	6.80	23.40	0.0210	0.0230	1,393
July	9.80	0.85	3.40	0.0030	0.0040	210
August	0.73	0.00	0.32	0.0003	0.0004	20
September	13.40	0.12	4.90	0.0040	0.0040	294
October	27.00	5.10	14.50	0.0130	0.0150	891
The period	....	....	....	....	0 2744	16,294

5 GEORGE V, A. 1915

BATE CREEK AT BATE'S RANCH.

Location.—On NW. ¼ Sec. 6, Tp. 6, Rge. 16, W. 3rd Mer., near Nummola post office.
Records available.—April 15 to October 31, 1914.
Gauge.—Vertical staff, fastened to a post on right bank about one-quarter mile from Mr.
Bate's house; the elevation of the zero of the gauge has been 94.87 feet since establishment.
Bench-mark.—Wooden plug, driven in the left bank, 36 feet from the gauge; assumed elevation, 100.00 feet.
Channel.—Probably permanent.
Discharge measurements.—Made with meter and weir.
Diversions.—Mr. Bate diverts water for irrigation purposes above the gauge.
Observer.—A. E. Bate.

DISCHARGE MEASUREMENTS of Bate Creek at Bate's Ranch, in 1914.

Date.	Engineer.	Width.	Area of Section.	Mean Velocity.	Gauge Height.	Discharge.
		Feet.	*Sq. ft.*	*Ft. per sec.*	*Feet.*	*Sec.-ft.*
April 16............	E. W. W. Hughes...........	....	....	....	1.71	1.23
May 14............	do	....	....	....	1.49	0.34
July 21............	do	....	....	....	1.20	Nil.
Oct. 23............	do	....	....	....	1.42	0.15

DAILY GAUGE HEIGHT AND DISCHARGE of Bate Creek at Bate's Ranch, for 1914.

	April.		May.		June.	
DAY.	Gauge Height.	Dis-charge.	Gauge Height.	Dis-charge.	Gauge Height.	Dis-charge.
	Feet.	*Sec.-ft.*	*Feet.*	*Sec.-ft.*	*Fee'.*	*Sec.-ft.*
1.................	....	....	1.62	0.83	1.40	0.11
2.................	....	....	1.61	0.78	1.42	0.15
3.................	....	....	1.56	0.60	1.46	0.25
4.................	....	....	1.53	0.49	1.58	0.67
5.................	....	....	1.52	0.45	1.54	0.52
6.................	....	....	1.51	0.42	1.49	0.35
7.................	....	....	1.50	0.38	1.50	0.38
8.................	....	....	1.47	0.28	1.42	0.15
9.................	....	....	1.48	0.32	1.41	0.13
10................	....	....	1.48	0.32	1.42	0.15
11................	....	....	1.46	0.25	1.43	0.18
12................	....	....	1.45	0.22	1.54	0.52
13....	....	....	1.42	0.15	1.72	1.28
14................	....	....	1.48	0.32	1.56	0.60
15................	1.02	2.37	1.47	0.28	1.48	0.32
16................	1.77	1.53	1.50	0.38	1.46	0.25
17................	1.72	1.28	1.50	0.38	1.44	0.20
18................	1.75	1.42	1.48	0.32	1.42	0.15
19................	1.80	1.70	1.48	0.32	1.40	0.11
20................	1.78	1.59	1.48	0.32	1.40	0.11
21................	1.72	1.28	1.48	0.32	1.44	0.20
22................	1.73	1.32	1.48	0.32	1.41	0.13
23................	1.74	1.37	1.48	0.32	1.40	0.11
24................	1.73	1.32	1.50	0.38	1.38	0.08
25................	1.68	1.09	1.47	0.28	1.46	0.25
26................	1.67	1.05	1.46	0.25	1.45	0.22
27................	1.66	1.00	1.44	0.20	1.43	0.18
28................	1.65	0.96	1.45	0.22	1.40	0.11
29................	1.65	0.96	1.44	0.20	1.45	0.22
30................	1.65	0.96	1.43	0.18	1.42	0.15
31................	....	....	1.42	0.15	....	....

SESSIONAL PAPER No. 25c

DAILY GAUGE HEIGHT AND DISCHARGE of Bate Creek at Bate's Ranch, for 1914.—*Concluded.*

DAY.	July.		August.		September.		October.	
	Gauge Height.	Dis- charge.	Gauge Height.	Dis- charge	Gauge Height.	Dis- charge.	Gauge Height.	Dis- charge.
	Feet.	*Sec.-ft.*	*Feet.*	*Sec.-ft.*	*Feet.*	*Sec.-ft.*	*Feet.*	*Sec.-ft.*
1	1.38	0.08	1.30	0.02	1.37	0.07	1.41	0.13
2	1.38	0.08	1.28	0.02	1.36	0.05	1.42	0.15
3	1.35	0.04	1.20	Nil	1.34	0.04	1.42	0.15
4	1.32	0.03	1.21	"	1.36	0.05	1.46	0.25
5	1.36	0.05	1.17	"	1.36	0.05	1.45	0.22
6	1.36	0.05	1.18	"	1.35	0.04	1.45	0.22
7	1.38	0.08	1.16	"	1.36	0.05	1.50	0.38
8	1.32	0.03	1.21	"	1.39	0.10	1.55	0.56
9	1.36	0.05	1.26	0.01	1.40	0.11	1.46	0.25
10	1.36	0.05	1.25	0.01	1.37	0.07	1.46	0.25
11	1.36	0.05	1.21	Nil	1.36	0.05	1.44	0.20
12	1.31	0.02	1.20	"	1.38	0.08	1.42	0.15
13	1.28	0.02	1.20	"	1.84	1.92	1.42	0.15
14	1.27	0.01	1.15	"	1.55	0.56	1.42	0.15
15	1.30	0.02	1.15	"	1.44	0.20	1.42	0.15
16	1.22	Nil	1.15	"	1.42	0.15	1.42	0.15
17	1.25	0.01	1.20	"	1.40	0.11	1.42	0.15
18	1.20	Nil	1.28	0.02	1.39	0.10	1.42	0.15
19	1.20	"	1.26	0.01	1.40	0.11	1.42	0.15
20	1.22	"	1.30	0.02	1.40	0.11	1.42	0.15
21	1.20	"	1.28	0.02	1.40	0.11	1.42	0.15
22	1.20	"	1.24	0.01	1.40	0.11	1.42	0.15
23	1.20	"	1.30	0.02	1.40	0.11	1.42	0.15
24	1.18	"	1.59	0.70	1.40	0.11	1.43	0.18
25	1.20	"	1.41	0.13	1.40	0.11	1.43	0.18
26	1.21	"	1.36	0.05	1.40	0.11	1.44	0.20
27	1.15	"	1.34	0.04	1.40	0.11	1.43	0.18
28	1.19	"	1.37	0.07	1.40	0.11	1.43	0.18
29	1.16	"	1.34	0.04	1.40	0.11	1.44	0.20
30	1.16	"	1.36	0.05	1.40	0.11	1.43	0.18
31	1.14	"	1.38	0.08	....	....	1.44	0.20

MONTHLY DISCHARGE of Bate Creek at Bate's Ranch, for 1914.

(Drainage area 12 square miles.)

MONTH.	DISCHARGE IN SECOND-FEET.				RUN-OFF.	
	Maximum	Minimum.	Mean.	Per square Mile.	Depth in inches on Drainage Area.	Total in Acre-feet.
April (15–30)	2.40	0.96	1.32	0.110	0.065	42
May	0.83	0.15	0.34	0.029	0.033	21
June	1.28	0.11	0.27	0.023	0.026	16
July	0.08	....	0.02	0.002	0.002	1
August	0.70	....	0.04	0.004	0.005	3
September	1.92	0.04	0.17	0.014	0.016	10
October	0.56	0.13	0.20	0.016	0.018	12
The period	....	....	....	....	0.165	105

5 GEORGE V, A. 1915

SNAKE CREEK NEAR VAL MARIE.

Location.—On SW. ¼ Sec. 16, Tp. 4, Rge. 13, W. 3rd Mer., about one-half mile east of Val Marie post office.

Records available.—April 7 to October 31, 1914.

Gauge.—Vertical staff, fastened to post on right bank; the elevation of the zero of the gauge in its present location has been 87.91 feet since establishment.

Bench-mark.—Permanent iron bench-mark, located three feet north of the east tower of the cable; assumed elevation, 100.00 feet.

Channel.—Permanent.

Discharge measurements.—Made from cable and by weir.

Observer.—Jean Denniel.

DISCHARGE MEASUREMENTS of Snake Creek near Val Marie, in 1914.

Date.	Engineer.	Width	Area of Section.	Mean Velocity.	Gauge Height.	Discharge.
		Feet.	*Sq. ft.*	*Ft. per sec.*	*Feet.*	*Sec.-ft.*
April 7....	E. W. W. Hughes.. .	15.2	33.7	1.19	3.05	40.00
April 19.. . ..	do	13.4	17.1	0 08	1.81	1.35
May 11.	do	....	....	....	1.14	0.32a
May 18	do	....	....	....	1.04	0.20a
June 20............	do	....	....	....	0.52b	0.24a
June 21.	do	....	....	....	0.59	0.35a
June 22............	do	....	....	....	0.60	0.33a
June 23	do	....	....	....	0.58	0.31a
June 24	do	....	....	....	0.52	0.22a
July 11............	do	....	....	....	0.43	0.05a
July 24..	do	....	....	....	0.34	Nil
Oct. 24..	do	....	....	....	0.54	0.26a

a Weir measurement.
b Station moved upstream about one mile June 20.

DAILY GAUGE HEIGHT AND DISCHARGE of Snake Creek near Val Marie, for 1914.

DAY.	April.		May.		June.	
	Gauge Height.	Dis- charge.	Gauge Height.	Dis- charge.	Gauge Height.	Dis- charge.
	Feet.	*Sec -ft.*	*Feet.*	*Sec.-ft.*	*Feet.*	*Sec.-ft.*
1............	. . ..	. . . .	1.20	0.40	....	......
2............	....	......	1.16	0.34	....	......
3............	....	......	1.16	0.34	....	......
4............	....	.*. .	1.14	0.31	....	......
5............	....	. . . .	1.13	0.30	....	......
6............	....	......	1.12	0.28	....	......
7............	3.03	40.00	1.20	0.40	....	......
8............	2.70	29.00	1.24	0.46	....	......
9............	3.67	60.00	1.19	0.38	....	......
10............	6.41	146.00	1.16	0.34	....	......
11............	6.78	158.00	1.14	0.31	....	......
12............	5.16	107.00	......a	......	....	......
13............	3.11	42.00	....	......	....	......
14............	1.98	6.70	....	......	....	......
15............	2.31	17.10	....	......	....	......
16............	3.59	57.00	....	......	....	......
17............	2.49	23.00	....	......	....	......
18............	1.93	5.20	....	......	....	......
19............	1.81	1.58	....	......	......a	......
20............	1.72	1.18	....	......	0.52b	0.21
21............	1.66	1.09	....	......	0.56	0.28
22............	1.61	1.02	....	......	0.60	0.35
23............	1.58	0.97	....	......	0.58	0.31
24............	1.31	0.56	....	......	0.52	0.21
25............	1.31	0.56	....	......	0.60	0.35
26............	1.26	0.49	....	......	0.62	0.39
27............	1.23	0.44	....	......	0.67	0.48
28............	1.29	0.54	....	......	0.60	0.35
29............	1.26	0.49	....	......	0.60	0.35
30............	1.26	0.49	....	......	0.57	0.30
31............	....	......	....	......	....	......

a to a No observer.
b Station moved about one mile upstream.

DAILY GAUGE HEIGHT AND DISCHARGE of Snake Creek near Val Marie, for 1914.

DAY.	July.		August.		September.		October.	
	Gauge Height.	Dis-charge.	Gauge Height.	Dis-charge.	Gauge Height	Dis-charge.	Gauge Height	Dis-charge.
	Feet.	*Sec.-ft.*	*Feet.*	*Sec.-ft.*	*Feet.*	*Sec.-ft.*	*Feet.*	*Sec.-ft.*
1	0.55	0.26	Dry	Nil	0.42	0.04	0.54	0.24
2	0.51	0.19	"	"	0.41	0.03	0.53	0.22
3	0.50	0.17	"	"	0.39	0.02	0.53	0.22
4	0.49	0.15	"	"	0.39	0.02	0.57	0.30
5	0.49	0.15	"	"	0.38	0.01	0.62	0.39
6	0.47	0.12	"	"	0.37	0.01	0.64	0.42
7	0.45	0.08	"	"	0.37	0.01	0.65	0.44
8	0.42	0.04	"	"	0.39	0.02	0.66	0.45
9	0.42	0.04	"	"	0.45	0.08	0.67	0.48
10	0.42	0.04	"	"	0.45	0.08	0.66	0.46
11	0.46	0.10	"	"	0.44	0.07	0.66	0.46
12	0.44	0.07	"	"	0.44	0.07	0.66	0.46
13	0.42	0.04	"	"	0.62	0.39	0.62	0.39
14	0.39	0.02	"	"	0.68	0.49	0.58	0.31
15	0.38	0.01	"	"	0.66	0.46	0.57	0.30
16	0.37	0.01	"	"	0.64	0.42	0.57	0.30
17	0.35	Nil	"	"	0.60	0.35	0.57	0.30
18	0.35	"	"	"	0.59	0.33	0.58	0.31
19	0.35	"	"	"	0.58	0.31	0.60	0.35
20	0.35	"	"	"	0.59	0.33	0.61	0.37
21	0.36	"	"	"	0.58	0.31	0.52	0.21
22	0.34	"	"	"	0.59	0.33	0.54	0.24
23	Dry	"	"	"	0.57	0.30	0.52	0.21
24	"	"	0.40	0.02	0.57	0.30	0.54	0.24
25	"	"	0.45	0.08	0.55	0.26	0.54	0.24
26	"	"	0.41	0.03	0.54	0.24	0.54	0.24
27	"	"	0.40	0.02	0.54	0.24	0.52	0.21
28	"	"	0.40	0.02	0.53	0.22	0.55	0.26
29	"	"	0.40	0.02	0.53	0.22	0.55	0.26
30	"	"	0.39	0.02	0.54	0.24	0.54	0.24
31	"	"	0.43	0.06	....	....	0.55	0.26

MONTHLY DISCHARGE of Snake Creek near Val Marie, for 1914.
(Drainage area 188 square miles.)

MONTH.	DISCHARGE IN SECOND-FEET.				RUN-OFF.	
	Maximum.	Minimum.	Mean.	Per square Mile.	Depth in inches on Drainage Area.	Total in Acre-feet.
April (7-30)	158.00	0.44	29 10	0.15000	0 01300	1,388
May (1-11)	0.46	0.28	0.35	0.00200	0.00080	8
June (20-30)	0.48	0.21	0.32	0.00200	0.00070	7
July	0.26	Nil.	0 05	0.00020	0.00030	3
August	0.08	Nil.	0 01	0.00005	0.00006	1
September	0.49	0.01	0 21	0.00100	0 00100	12
October	0.48	0.21	0.32	0.00200	0.00200	19
The period	....	....	....	....	0.01786	1,438

BIGBREED CREEK NEAR BUZZARD'S RANCH.

Location.—On the SE. ¼ Sec. 15, Tp. 2, Rge. 11, W. 3rd Mer., near Coriander post office.
Records available.—March 30 to October 31, 1914.
Gauge.—Vertical staff, fastened to a post on the left bank about three miles from Mr. Buzzard's house; elevation of the zero of the gauge has been maintained at 92.13 feet since establishment.
Bench-mark.—Permanent iron bench-mark, located on the left bank 36 feet from the gauge; assumed elevation, 100.00 feet.
Channel.—Probably permanent.
Discharge measurements.—Made with meter and weir.
Winter flow.—This station is not maintained during the winter.
Observer.—Geo. A. Brown and A. A. Hendrix.

5 GEORGE V, A. 1915

DISCHARGE MEASUREMENTS of Bigbreed Creek near Buzzard's Ranch, in 1914.

Date.	Engineer.	Width.	Area of Section.	Mean Velocity.	Gauge Height.	Discharge.
		Feet.	*Sq. ft.*	*Ft. per sec.*	*Feet.*	*Sec.-ft.*
April 1............	E. W. W. Hughes...........	26.3	40.4	0.99	3.19	40.00
April 2............	do	19.8	26.6	1.28	2.45	35.00
April 26............	do				0.98	0.87a
May 4............	do				0.89	0.31a
May 21............	do				0.85	0.06a
June 10............	do				0.34	Nil.
June 13............	do	10.3	6.74	0.59	1.12	3.90
June 27............	do				0.14	Nil.
July 3............	do				0.60	"
July 28............	do					"
Oct. 26............	do					"

a Weir measurement.

DAILY GAUGE HEIGHT AND DISCHARGE of Bigbreed Creek near Buzzard's Ranch, for 1914

DAY.	March.		April.		May		June.	
	Gauge Height.	Dis- charge.	Gauge Height.	Dis- charge.	Gauge Height.	Dis- charge.	Gauge Height.	Dis- charge.
	Feet.	*Sec.-ft.*	*Feet.*	*Sec.-ft.*	*Feet.*	*Sec.-ft.*	*Feet.*	*Sec.-ft.*
1..............			3.19	40.00	0.92	0.26	0.45	Nil.
2..............			2.66	36.00	0.92	0.26	0.36	"
3..............			2.55	35.00	0.96	0.64	0.33	"
4..............			2.14	33.00	0.96	0.64	0.32	"
5..............			2.18	33.00	0.95	0.50	0.32	"
6..............			2.16	33.00	0.95	0.50	0.33	"
7..............			2.14a	33.00	0.95	0.50	0.31	"
8..............			1.61	25.00	0.94	0.42	0.30	"
9..............			1.40	14.80	0.94	0.42	0.30	"
10..............			1.35	12.60	0.93	0.34	0.30	"
11..............			1.20	6.40	1.08	2.80	0.31	"
12..............			1.97	43.00	1.06	2.30	0.31	"
13..............			1.97	43.00	0.93	0.34	1.14	4.50
14..............			2.37	63.00	0.93	0.34	1.18	5.80
15..............			1.45	17.10	0.94	0.42	1.09	3.00
16..............			1.36	13.00	0.94	0.42	1.30	10.40
17..............			1.36	13.00	0.88	0.08	1.19	6.10
18..............			1.20	6.40	0.85	0.05	1.05	2.10
19..............			1.10	3.20	0.88	0.08	1.00	1.20
20..............			1.12	3.80	0.85	0.05	0.98	0.92
21..............			1.07	2.50	0.83	0.03	0.96	0.64
22..............			0.99	1.06	0.84	0.04	1.16	5.10
23..............			0.97	0.78	0.83	0.03	0.90	0.10
24..............			0.96	0.64	0.79	Nil.	0.83	0.03
25..............			0.99	1.06	0.75	"	0.88	0.08
26..............			0.98	0.92	0.68	"	0.97	0.78
27..............			0.94	0.42	0.66	"	1.09	3.00
28..............			0.95	0.50	0.62	"	1.12	3.80
29..............			0.94	0.42	0.59	"	1.10	3.20
30..............	1.05a	25	0.93	0.34	0.58	"	0.90	0.10
31..............	2.01	32			0.47	"		

a to *a* Gauge height affected by ice.

SESSIONAL PAPER No. 25c

DAILY GAUGE HEIGHT AND DISCHARGE of Bigbreed Creek near Buzzard's Ranch, for 1914·
—*Concluded.*

	July.		August.		September.		October.	
DAY.	Gauge Height.	Dis-charge.	Gauge Height.	Dis-charge.	Gauge Height.	Dis-charge.	Gauge Height.	Dis-charge.
	Feet.	*Sec.-ft.*	*Feet.*	*Sec.-ft.*	*Feet.*	*Sec.-ft.*	*Feet.*	*Sec.-ft.*
1	0.78	Nil.	Dry.	Nil.	Dry.	Nil.	Dry.	Nil.
2	0.70	"	"	"	"	"	"	"
3	0.69	"	"	"	"	"	"	"
4	0.65	"	"	"	"	"	"	"
5	0.80	"	"	"	"	"	"	"
6	0.72	"	"	"	"	"	"	"
7	0.64	"	"	"	"	"	0.55	"
8	0.57	"	"	"	"	"	0.60	"
9	0.48	"	"	"	"	"	0.45	"
10	0.44	"	"	"	"	"	Dry.	"
11	Dry.	"	"	"	"	"	"	"
12	"	"	"	"	"	"	"	"
13	"	"	"	"	"	"	"	"
14	"	"	"	"	"	"	"	"
15	"	"	"	"	"	"	"	"
16	"	"	"	"	"	"	"	"
17	"	"	"	"	"	"	"	"
18	"	"	"	"	"	"	"	"
19	"	"	"	"	"	"	"	"
20	"	"	"	"	"	"	"	"
21	"	"	"	"	"	"	"	"
22	"	"	"	"	"	"	"	"
23	"	"	"	"	"	"	"	"
24	"	"	"	"	"	"	"	"
25	"	"	"	"	"	"	"	"
26	"	"	"	"	"	"	"	"
27	"	"	"	"	"	"	"	"
28	"	"	"	"	"	"	"	"
29	"	"	"	"	"	"	"	"
30	"	"	"	"	"	"	"	"
31	"	"	"	"	"	"	"	"

MONTHLY DISCHARGE of Bigbreed Creek near Buzzard's Ranch, for 1914.

(Drainage area 83 square miles.)

MONTH.	DISCHARGE IN SECOND-FEET.				RUN-OFF.	
	Maximum.	Minimum.	Mean.	Per square Mile.	Depth in inches on Drainage Area.	Total in Acre-feet.
March (30-31)	32.00	25.00	28.00	0.343	0.026	113
April	63.00	0.34	17.20	0.207	0.231	1,023
May	2.80	0.00	0.37	0.004	0.005	23
June	10.40	0.00	1.70	0.020	0.020	101
July						Nil.
August						"
September						"
October						"
The period					0 282	1,260

5 GEORGE V. A. 1915

FRENCHMAN RIVER AT BUZZARD'S RANCH.

Location.—On the NW. ¼ Sec. 3, Tp. 2, Rge. 11, W. 3rd Mer., at Wm. Buzzard's ranch, near Coriander post office.

Records available.—March 27, 1914, to October 31, 1914.

Gauge.—Vertical staff, fastened to post on left bank about one-half mile upstream from Mr. Buzzard's house; the elevation of the zero of the gauge is 87.50 feet.

Bench-mark.—Permanent iron bench-mark, located about two feet west of the sill of the north tower of the cable; assumed elevation, 100.00 feet.

Channel.—Probably permanent.

Discharge measurements.—Made by wading, or from cable.

Winter flow.—Station not maintained during winter.

Observer.—Geo. *A*. Brown, and A. Hendrix.

DISCHARGE MEASUREMENTS of Frenchman River at Buzzard's Ranch, in 1914.

Date.	Engineer.	Width.	Area of Section.	Mean Velocity.	Gauge Height.	Discharge.
		Feet.	*Sq. ft.*	*Ft. per sec.*	*Feet.*	*S.-ft.*
Mar. 28.............	E. W. W. Hughes......... ..	43.5	39.0	1.73	1.36	68.0*a*
April 1.............	do	46.0	77.1	1.52	2.18	117.0*a*
April 1.............	do	47.9	92.8	1.54	2.54	139.0*a*
April 2.............	do	46.6	72.7	1.80	2.30	131.0*a*
April 26.............	do	44.0	38.1	2.88	1.05	110.0
May 4.............	do	45.9	53.1	1.33	0.88	71.0
May 20......... ...	do	44.8	41.0	1.19	0.79	49.0
June 8.............	do	44.3	32.8	0.58	0.60	18.9
June 10.............	do	43.5	35.8	0.60	0.61	22.0
June 13.............	do	50.0	106.4	3.27	2.48	348.0
June 27.............	do	45.1	37.4	0.60	0.60	19.0
July 3.............	do	45.1	39.3	0.40	0.69	15.6
July 28.............	do	......	......	......	0.10	0.3*b*
October 26.........	do	41.0	30.0	0.60	0.54	17.4

a Ice conditions.
b Discharge estimated.

DAILY GAUGE HEIGHT AND DISCHARGE of Frenchman River at Buzzard's Ranch, for 1914.

DAY.	March.		April.		May.		June.	
	Gauge Height.	Dis-charge.	Gauge Height.	Dis-charge.	Gauge Height.	Dis-charge.	Gauge Height.	Dis-charge.
	Feet.	*Sec.-ft.*	*Feet.*	*Sec.-ft.*	*Feet.*	*Sec.-ft.*	*Feet.*	*Sec.-ft.*
1.................			2.36	128	0.94	76	0.57	20
2.................			2.32	131	0.93	74	0.56	19
3.................			2.65	146	0.90	69	0.55	18
4.................			3.38	515	0.85	60	0.55	18
5.................			4.34	688	0.85	60	0.56	19
6.................			5.78	947	0.85	60	0.56	19
7.................			7.03	1,172	0.84	58	0.67	32
8.................			4.45	708	0.82	55	0.64	28
9.................			3.93	614	0.81	53	0.60	23
10.................			4.72	757	0.80	51	0.61	24
11.................			6.04	994	0.82	55	0.64	28
12.................			6.15	1,014	0.83	56	0.68	33
13.................			5.45	888	0.84	58	2.70	393
14.................			5.33	866*a*	0.84	58	2.00	267
15.................			3.17	478	0.86	62	0.89	67
16.................			4.95	798	0.91	71	0.74	42
17.................			6.03	992	0.90	69	0.72	39
18.................			4.46	710	0.85	60	0.70	36
19.................			3.72	577	0.85	60	0.69	35
20.................			3.07	460	0.79	49	0.64	28
21.................			2.57	370	0.78	48	0.63	27
22.................			2.04	274	0.75	43	0.61	24
23.................			1.73	218	0.74	42	0.59	22
24.................			1.82	235	0.71	37	0.58	21
25.................			1.67	208	0.67	32	0.68	33
26.................			1.05	96	0.67	32	0.85	60
27.................	1.81	95*a*	1.00	87	0.66	30	0.60	23
28.................	1.28	68	0.95	78	0.63	27	0.59	22
29.................	0.98	44	0.95	78	0.61	24	0.57	20
30.................	1.14	53	0.94	76	0.60	23	0.56	19
31.................	1.88	97	....		0.59	22	....	

a March 27 to April 14—ice conditions.

DAILY GAUGE HEIGHT AND DISCHARGE of Frenchman River at Buzzard's Ranch, for 1914.
—*Concluded.*

DAY.	July.		August.		September.		October.	
	Gauge Height.	Dis-charge.	Gauge Height.	Dis-charge.	Gauge Height.	Dis-charge.	Gauge Height.	Dis-charge.
	Feet.	*Sec.-ft.*	*Feet.*	*Sec.-ft.*	*Feet.*	*Sec.-ft.*	*Feet.*	*Sec.-ft.*
1	0.55a	18.00	0.16	0.55	0.11	0.34	0.39	6.1
2	0.55a	18.00	0.26	1.70	0.01	0.03	0.37	5.3
3	0.54a	17.10	0.26	1.70	0.01	0.03	0.35	4.5
4	0.54a	17.10	0.21	0.90	0.01	0.03	0.32	3.3
5	0.53	16.20	0.15	0.50	0.01	0.03	0.30	2.5
6	0.53	16.20	0.10	0.30	0.01	0.03	0.69	35.0
7	0.52	15.30	0.01	0.03	0.01	0.03	0.84	58.0
8	0.50	13.50	0.02	0.06	0.01	0.03	0.80	51.0
9	0.49	12.70	Dry	Nil	0.01	0.03	0.70	36.0
10	0.43	8.30	"	"	Dry	Nil	0.73	40.0
11	0.41	7.10	"	"	"	"	0.75	43.0
12	0.40	6.50	"	"	"	"	0.80	51.0
13	0.39	6.10	"	"	"	"	0.81	53.0
14	0.36	4.90	"	"	0.82	55.00	0.79	49.0
15	0.34	4.10	"	"	0.42	7.70	0.76	45.0
16	0.33	3.70	"	"	0.30	2.50	0.75	43.0
17	0.31	2.90	"	"	0.20	0.75	0.75	43.0
18	0.30	2.50	"	"	0.17	0.60	0.72	39.0
19	0.28	2.10	"	"	0.15	0.50	0.70	36.0
20	0.26	1.70	"	"	0.10	0.30	0.70	36.0
21	0.24	1.35	"	"	0.02	0.06	0.69	35.0
22	0.23	1.20	"	"	0.10	0.30	0.67	32.0
23	0.17	0.60	"	"	0.13	0.42	0.65	29.0
24	0.11	0.34	"	"	0.60	23.00	0.62	25.0
25	0.10	0.30	0.72	39 00	0.55	18.00	0.58	21.0
26	0.10	0.30	0.54	17.10	0.53	16.20	0.56	19.0
27	0.10	0.30	0.72	39.00	0.50	13.50	0.54	17.1
28	0.11	0.34	0.35	4.50	0.47	11.10	0.54	17.1
29	0.10	0.30	0.32	3.30	0.43	8.30	0.53	16.2
30	0.10	0.30	0.30	2.50	0.41	7.10	0.53	16.2
31	0.11	0.34	0.20	0.75	....	....	0.52	15.3

a Gauge height interpolated.

MONTHLY DISCHARGE of Frenchman River at Buzzard's Ranch, for 1914.

(Drainage area 1,778 square miles.)

MONTH.	DISCHARGE IN SECOND-*FEET.*				RUN-OFF.	
	Maximum.	Minimum	Mean.	Per square Mile.	Depth in inches on Drainage Area.	Total in Acre-feet.
March (27–31)	97	44.00	71.0	0.040	0.007	708
April	1,172	76.00	510.0	0.287	0.320	30,347
May	76	22.00	51.0	0.028	0.032	3,124
June	393	18.00	49.0	0.027	0.030	2,892
July	18	0.30	6.4	0.004	0.005	396
August	39	0.00	3.6	0.002	0.002	222
September	55	0.00	5.5	0.003	0.003	329
October	58	2.50	30.0	0.017	0.020	1,833
The period	....	....	....	....	0 419	39,851

5 GEORGE V, A. 1915

LITTLEBREED CREEK NEAB RUZZARD'S RANCH.

Location.—On the NW. ¼ Sec. 11, Tp. 2, Rge. 11, W. 3rd Mer., near Coriander post office.
Records available.—March 28 to October 31, 1914.
Gauge.—Vertical staff, fastened to post on right bank about two miles from Mr. Buzzard's house; elevation of the zero of the gauge has been 92.82 feet since establishment.
Bench-mark.—Permanent iron bench-mark, located on the left bank about 60 feet from the gauge; assumed elevation, 100.00 feet.
Channel.—Probably permanent.
Discharge measurements.—Made by meter, and by weir at low stages.
Winter flow.—This station is not maintained during the winter.
Artificial control.—Mr. Buzzard has a dam about one mile below this station, but the flow at the gauge is not affected by this structure.
Observer.—Geo. A. Brown and A. A. Hendrix.

DISCHARGE MEASUREMENTS of Littlebreed Creek near Buzzard's Ranch, in 1914.

Date.	Engineer.	Width.	Area of Section.	Mean Velocity.	Gauge Height.	Discharge.
		Feet.	*Sq. ft.*	*Ft. per sec.*	*Feet.*	*Sec.-ft.*
Mar. 31............	E. W. W. Hughes...........	7.5	3.17	0.25	1.23	0.80
Mar. 31............	do	12.0	11.20	0.64	1.84	7.20
April 1............	do	19.0	34.60	0.55	3.36	18.70
April 2............	do	130.0	157.00	0.47	4.52	74.00
April 26............	do	....	....	....	0.38	0.02a
May 4............	do	....	....	....	....	Nil
May 20............	do	....	....	....	....	"
June 8............	do	....	....	....	....	"
June 13............	do	12.8	13.20	0.46	1.82	6.10
June 27............	do	5.5	2.63	0.28	0.63	0.74
July 3............	do	....	....	....	....	Nil
July 28............	do	....	....	....	....	"
Oct. 26............	do	....	....	....	....	"

a Weir measurement.

DAILY GAUGE HEIGHT AND DISCHARGE of Littlebreed Creek near Buzzard's Ranch, for 9114.

DAY.	March.		April.		May.		June.	
	Gauge Height.	Discharge.	Gauge Height.	Discharge.	Gauge Height.	Discharge.	Gauge Height.	Discharge.
	Feet.	*Sec.-ft.*	*Feet.*	*Sec.-ft.*	*Feet.*	*Sec.-ft.*	*Feet.*	*Sec.-ft.*
1.........	....	....	3.16a	18 70	Dry	Nil	Dry	Nil
2.........	....	....	4.32	74.00	"	"	"	"
3.........	....	....	3.95	54.00	"	"	"	"
4.........	....	....	3.57	41.00	"	"	"	"
5.........	....	....	3.23	30 00	"	"	"	"
6.........	....	....	3.53	39.00	"	"	"	"
7.........	....	....	2.36	12.50	"	"	"	"
8.........	....	....	2.00	8.30	"	"	"	"
9.........	....	....	1.45	4.00	"	"	"	"
10.........	....	....	1.19	2.70	"	"	"	"
11.........	....	....	1.08	2.20	"	"	"	"
12.........	....	....	1.29	3.10	"	"	"	"
13.........	....	....	1.30	3.20	"	"	1.91	7.40
14.........	....	....	2.31	11.80	"	"	3.08	26.00
15.........	....	....	2.51	14.80	"	"	1.21	2.70
16.........	....	....	2.35	12.40	"	"	1.56	4.70
17.........	....	....	1.28	3.00	"	"	1.02	1.98
18.........	....	....	1.06	2.10	"	"	0.83	1.24
19.........	....	....	0.95	1.70	"	"	0.55	0.40
20.........	....	....	1.04	2.10	"	"	0.51	0.32
21.........	....	....	0.93	1.62	"	"	0.39	0.08
22.........	....	....	0.91	1.54	"	"	0.38	0.06
23.........	....	....	0.83	1.24	"	"	Dry	Nil
24.........	....	....	0.81	1.18	"	"	"	"
25.........	....	....	0.49	0.28	"	"	0.78	1.09
26.........	....	....	0.38	0.06	"	"	1.72	5.80
27.........	....	....	0.31	Nil	"	"	0.63	0.64
28.........	0.98a	0.20	Dry	"	"	"	0.50	0.30
29.........	0.98	0.20	"	"	"	"	0.40	0.10
30.........	1.14	0.50	"	"	"	"	Dry	Nil
31.........	1.53	4.00	... ...	....	"	"	....	....

a to a Ice in channel.

SESSIONAL PAPER No. 25c

DAILY GAUGE HEIGHT AND DISCHARGE of Littlebreed Creek near Buzzard's Ranch, for 1914.
—*Concluded.*

DAY.	July.		August.		September.		October.	
	Gauge Height.	Dis-charge.	Gauge Height.	Dis-charge.	Gauge Height.	Dis-charge.	Gauge Height.	Dis-charge.
	Feet.	*Sec.-ft.*	*Feet.*	*Sec.-ft.*	*Feet.*	*Sec.-ft.*	*Feet.*	*Sec.-ft.*
1	Dry	Nil	Dry	Nil	Dry	Nil	Dry	Nil
2	"	"	"	"	"	"	"	"
3	"	"	"	"	"	"	"	"
4	"	"	"	"	"	"	"	"
5	"	"	"	"	"	"	"	"
6	"	"	"	"	"	"	"	"
7	"	"	"	"	"	"	1.85	6.80
8	"	"	"	"	"	"	1.51	4.40
9	"	"	"	"	"	"	0.75	1.00
10	"	"	"	"	"	"	0.70	0.85
11	"	"	"	"	"	"	0.80	1.15
12	"	"	"	"	"	"	Dry	Nil
13	"	"	"	"	"	"	"	"
14	"	"	"	"	"	"	"	"
15	"	"	"	"	"	"	"	"
16	"	"	"	"	0.85	1.30	"	"
17	"	"	"	"	0.50	0.30	"	"
18	"	"	"	"	Dry	Nil	"	"
19	"	"	"	"	"	"	"	"
20	"	"	"	"	"	"	"	"
21	"	"	"	"	"	"	"	"
22	"	"	"	"	"	"	"	"
23	"	"	"	"	"	"	"	"
24	"	"	"	"	"	"	"	"
25	"	"	0.89	1.46	"	"	"	"
26	"	"	0.65	0.70	"	"	"	"
27	"	"	Dry	Nil	"	"	"	"
28	"	"	"	"	"	"	"	"
29	"	"	"	"	"	"	"	"
30	"	"	"	"	"	"	"	"
31	"	"	"	"	....	....	"	"

MONTHLY DISCHARGE of Littlebreed Creek near Buzzard's Ranch, for 1914.

(Drainage area 61 square miles.)

MONTH.	DISCHARGE IN SECOND-FEET.				RUN-OFF.	
	Maximum.	Minimum	Mean.	Per square Mile.	Depth in inches on Drainage Area.	Total in Acre-feet.
March (28–31)	4.00	0.20	1.22	0.0200	0.001	10
April	74.00	....	11.70	0.1910	0.213	696
May	....	....	....	....	....	Nil.
June	26.00	....	1.76	0 0290	0.032	106
July	....	....	....	....	....	Nil.
August	1.46	....	0.07	0.0010	0.001	4
September	1.30	....	0.05	0.0009	0.001	3
October	6.80	....	0.46	0.0070	0.008	28
The period	....	....	....	....	0 256	847

5 GEORGE V, A. 1915

McEACHRAN CREEK AT McCOY'S RANCH.

Location.—On the SW. ¼ Sec. 6, Tp. 1, Rge. 7, W. 3rd Mer., about 50 feet north of Mr. McCoy's house.

Records available.—May 1 to October 31, 1914.

Gauge.—Staff gauge, fastened to a post in the right bank; elevation of the zero of the gauge has been maintained at 89.50 feet since establishment.

Bench-mark.—Permanent iron bench-mark, located 32 feet southeast of the gauge; assumed elevation, 100.00 feet.

Channel.—Probably permanent.

Discharge measurements.—Made with meter, and by weir at low stages.

Winter flow.—Station not maintained during the winter.

Diversions.—There is no diversion from this stream.

Observer.—Donald McCoy.

DISCHARGE MEASUREMENTS of McEachran Creek at McCoy's Ranch, in 1914.

Date.	Engineer.	Width.	Area of Section.	Mean Velocity.	Gauge Height.	Discharge.
		Feet.	*Sq. ft.*	*Ft. per sec.*	*Feet.*	*Sec.-ft.*
May 1............	E. W. W. Hughes............	....	....	....	0.60	0.54a
June 30..........	do	....	....	....	0.29	........b
July 1............	do	....	....	....	0.28	........b

a Weir measurement.
b Flow too small to measure.

DAILY GAUGE HEIGHT AND DISCHARGE of McEachran Creek at McCoy's Ranch, for 1914.

DAY.	May.		June.		July.	
	Gauge Height.	Dis-charge.	Gauge Height.	Dis-charge.	Gauge Height.	Dis-charge.
	Feet.	*Sec.-ft.*	*Feet.*	*Sec.-ft.*	*Feet.*	*Sec.-ft.*
1...................	0.60	0.54	0.25	0.01	0.28	0.02
2...................	0.60	0.54	0.25	0.01	0.28	0.02
3...................	0.60	0.54	0.25	0.01	0.25	0.01
4...................	0.55	0.37	0.32	0.03	0.25	0.01
5...................	0.55	0.37	0.35	0.04	0.25	0.01
6...................	0.50	0.24	0.35	0.04	0.25	0.01
7...................	0.50	0.24	0.35	0.04	0.25	0.01
8...................	0.50	0.24	0.30	0.02	0.25	0.01
9...................	0.50	0.24	0.30	0.02	0.20	Nil.a
10..................	0.50	0.24	0.30	0.02	0.20	"
11..................	0.50	0.24	0.30	0.02	0.20	"
12..................	0.50	0.24	0.35	0.04	0.20	"
13..................	0.50	0.24	0.40	0.08	0.20	"
14..................	0.50	0.24	0.40	0.08	0.20	"
15..................	0.50	0.24	0.40	0.08	0.10	"
16..................	0.45	0.13	0.40	0.08	0.10	"
17..................	0.45	0.13	0.35	0.04	Dry.a	"
18..................	0.45	0.13	0.35	0.04	"	"
19..................	0.45	0.13	0.35	0.04	"	"
20..................	0.45	0.13	0.35	0.04	"	"
21..................	0.45	0.13	0.35	0.04	"	"
22..................	0.45	0.13	0.30	0.02	"	"
23..................	0.45	0.13	0.30	0.02	"	"
24..................	0.40	0.08	0.30	0.02	"	"
25..................	0.40	0.08	0.30	0.02	"	"
26..................	0.35	0.04	0.30	0.02	"	"
27..................	0.35	0.04	0.30	0.02	"	"
28..................	0.30	0.02	0.30	0.02	"	"
29..................	0.30	0.02	0.30	0.02	"	"
30..................	0.25	0.01	0.29	0.02	"	"
31..................	0.25	0.01	....	....	"	"

a Stream dry from July 10 to Oct. 31.

MONTHLY DISCHARGE of McEachran Creek at McCoy's Ranch, for 1914.

(Drainage area 107 square miles.)

MONTH.	DISCHARGE IN SECOND-FEET.				RUN-OFF.	
	Maximum.	Minimum	Mean.	Per square Mile.	Depth in inches on Drainage Area.	Total in Acre-feet.
May..	0.54	0.01	0.200	0.00200	0 00200	12.0
June..	0.08	0.01	0 030	0.00030	0.00030	2.0
July..	0 02	0.00	0 004	0.00003	0.00003	0.2
The period...........................	....	....	....	....	0.00233	14.2

HORSE CREEK NEAR BARNARD, MONTANA, U.S.A.

Location.—About one mile north of Barnard post office, on United States unsurveyed land, and about one-quarter mile south of the international boundary.

Records available.—May 1 to October 31, 1914.

Gauge.—Staff gauge, fastened to a post on the right bank; the elevation of the zero of the gauge has been maintained at 92.54 feet since establishment.

Bench-mark.—Wooden plug, driven in the left bank 30 feet from the gauge; assumed elevation, 100.00 feet.

Channel.—Probably permanent.

Discharge measurements.—Made by wading, with meter, and by weir at low stages.

Winter flow.—This station is not maintained during the winter.

Observer.—W. J. Harris.

DISCHARGE MEASUREMENTS of Horse Creek near Barnard, Montana, U.S.A., in 1914.

Date.	Engineer.	Width.	Area of Section.	Mean Velocity.	Gauge Height.	Discharge.
		Feet.	*Sq. ft.*	*Ft. per sec.*	*Feet.*	*Sec.-ft.*
May 1............	E. W. W. Hughes.......	4 9	1.38	0.46	0.64	0.63
June 30..........	do	....	....	....	0.50	0.28a
July 1............	do	....	....	....	0.45	0.22a

a Weir measurement.

5 GEORGE V, A. 1915

DAILY GAUGE HEIGHT AND DISCHARGE of Horse Creek near Barnard, Montana, U.S.A., for 1914.

DAY.	May.		June.		July.	
	Gauge Height.	Dis- charge.	Gauge Height.	Dis- charge.	Gauge Height.	Dis- charge.
	Feet.	*Sec.-ft.*	*Feet.*	*Sec.-ft.*	*Feet.*	*Sec.-ft.*
1	0.66	0.69	0.40	0.14	0.46	0.23
2	0.62	0.57	0.40	0.14	0.46	0.23
3	0.54	0.37	0.40	0.14	0.46	0.23
4	0.46	0.23	0.40	0.14	0.45	0.21
5	0.52	0.33	0.56	0.41	0.44	0.20
6	0.53	0.35	0.56	0.41	0.42	0.17
7	0.53	0.35	0.55	0.39	0.40	0.14
8	0.58	0.46	0.54	0.37	0.37	0.11
9	0.52	0.33	0.54	0.37	0.35	0.09
10	0.52	0.33	0.52	0.33	0.34	0.08
11	0.54	0.37	0.51	0.31	0.32	0.07
12	0.54	0.37	0.67	0.73	0.31	0.06
13	0.53	0.35	0.67	0.73	0.31	0.06
14	0.52	0.33	0.67	0.73	0.40	0.14b
15	0.52	0.33	0.67	0.73	Dry.	Nil.
16	0.51	0.31	0.94	1.66	"	"
17	0.51	0.31	0.59	0.49	"	"
18	0.54	0.37	0.56	0.41	"	"
19	0.57	0.44	0.54	0.37	"	"
20	0.52	0.33	0.54	0.37	"	"
21	0.50	0.29	0.52	0.33	"	"
22	0.48	0.26	0.52	0.33	"	"
23	0.48	0.26	0.50	0.29	"	"
24	0.48	0.26	0.50	0.29	"	"
25	0.48	0.26	0.54	0.37	"	"
26	0.46	0.23	0.56	0.41	"	"
27	0.44	0.20	0.56	0.41	"	"
28	0.44	0.20	0.60	0.51	"	"
29	0.42	0.17	0.55a	0.39	"	"
30	0.42	0.17	0.50	0.29	"	"
31	0.40	0.14	....	....	"	......b

a Gauge height interpolated.
b Stream dry from July 14 to Oct. 31.

MONTHLY DISCHARGE of Horse Creek near Barnard, Montana, U.S.A., for 1914.

(Drainage area 71 square miles.)

MONTH.	DISCHARGE IN SECOND-FEET.				RUN-OFF.	
	Maximum	Minimum	Mean.	Per square Mile.	Depth in inches on Drainage Area.	Total in Acre-feet.
May	0.69	0.14	0.32	0.0045	0.005	20
June	1.66	0.14	0.43	0.0061	0.007	26
July	0.23	0.00	0.06	0.0009	0.001	4
August	....	....	....	....	....	Nil.
September	....	....	....	....	....	"
October	....	....	....	....	....	
The period	....	....	....	....	0.013	50

BOWREY DITCH FROM ROCK CREEK, MONTANA, U.S.A.

Location.—In United States unsurveyed territory, near Barnard, Montana.
Records available.—June 1 to August 26, 1914.
Gauge.—Vertical staff; elevation of zero 96.51 feet.
Bench-mark.—Stake on left bank; assumed elevation, 100.00 feet.
Discharge measurements.—By wading.
Observer.—C. W. Bowrey.

SESSIONAL PAPER No. 25c

DISCHARGE MEASUREMENTS of Bowrey Ditch from Rock Creek, Montana, U.S.A., in 1914.

Date.	Engineer.	Width.	Area of Section.	Mean Velocity.	Gauge Height.	Discharge.
		Feet.	*Sq. ft.*	*Ft. per sec.*	*Feet.*	*Sec.-ft.*
April 30............	E. W. W. Hughes...	....	....	....	....	Nil.
June 30............	do	5.5	2.13	0.25	0.70	0.53
July 1............	do	7.6	6.85	0.15	1.45	1.05

DAILY GAUGE HEIGHT AND DISCHARGE of Bowrey Ditch from Rock Creek, Montana, U.S.A. for 1914.

DAY.	June.		July.		August.	
	Gauge Height.	Dis-charge.	Gauge Height.	Dis-charge.	Gauge Height.	Dis-charge.
	Feet.	*Sec.-ft.*	*Feet.*	*Sec.-ft.*	*Feet.*	*Sec.-ft.*
1............	1.29	0.94	1.45	1.06	....	....
2............	1.35	0.99	1.50	1.09	....	....
3............	1.45	1.06	....	....	....	....
4............	1.50	1.09	....	....	....	....
5............	1.50	1.09	....	....	....	....
6............	1.50	1.09	....	....	....	....
7............	1.40	1.02	....	....	....	....
8............	1.45	1.06	....	....	....	....
9............	....	....	....	....	....	....
10............	....	....	....	....	....	....
11............	....	....	....	....	....	....
12............	....	....	....	....	....	....
13............	....	....	....	....	....	....
14............	....	....	....	....	....	....
15............	....	....	....	....	....	....
16............	....	....	....	....	....	....
17............	....	....	....	....	....	....
18............	....	....	....	....	....	....
19............	....	....	....	....	....	....
20............	....	....	....	....	....	....
21............	....	....	....	....	....	....
22............	....	....	....	....	....	....
23............	....	....	....	....	....	....
24............	....	....	....	....	....	....
25............	....	....	....	....	1.70	1.23
26............	....	....	....	....	1.20	0.89
27............	....	....	....	....	....	....
28............	....	....	....	....	....	....
29............	....	....	....	....	....	....
30............	0.70	0.53	....	....	....	....
31............	....	....	....	....	....	....

MONTHLY DISCHARGE of Bowrey Ditch from Rock Creek, Montana, U.S.A., for 1914.

MONTH.	DISCHARGE IN SECOND-FEET.			RUN-OFF.
	Maximum.	Minimum.	Mean.	Total in Acre-feet.
June (1-8 and 30)............................	1.00	0.00	0.98	18
July (1-2)............................	1.09	0.00	1.08	4
August (25-26)............................	1.23	0.00	1.06	4
The period............................	....	....	....	26

ROCK CREEK NEAR BARNARD, MONTANA, U.S.A.

Location.—On United States unsurveyed land, about one mile south of the international boundary.

Records available.—May 1 to October 31, 1914.

Gauge.—Vertical staff, fastened to a post on the right bank about one-half mile downstream from Mr. Bowrey's house; the elevation of the zero of the gauge has been maintained at 91.83 feet since establishment.

Bench-mark.—Permanent iron bench-mark, located 28 feet west of the gauge; assumed elevation, 100.00 feet.

Channel.—Probably permanent.

Discharge measurements.—Made by wading.

Winter flow.—Station not maintained during the winter.

Diversions.—Mr. Chas. Bowrey diverts water for irrigation purposes, about one-quarter mile above the gauge. Records of the discharge of this ditch appear elsewhere in this report, but are included in the monthly computations of this station.

Observer.—Chas. Bowrey.

DISCHARGE MEASUREMENTS of Rock Creek near Barnard, Montana, U.S.A., in 1914.

Date.	Engineer.	Width.	Area of Section.	Mean Velocity.	Gauge Height.	Discharge
		Feet.	*Sq. feet.*	*Ft. per sec.*	*Feet.*	*Sec.-ft.*
April 30	E. W. W. Hughes.	15.1	8.57	1.10	1.01	9.40
June 30.... ...	do	19.1	19.10	0.98	1.02	9.90
July 1 ...	do	8.1	8.10	0.40	0.50	0.87

DAILY GAUGE HEIGHT AND DISCHARGE of Rock Creek near Barnard, Montana, U.S.A., for 1914.

DAY.	May.		June.		July.		August.		September.		October.	
	Gauge Height	Dis-charge	Gauge Height	Dis-charge	Gauge Height.	Dis-charge	Gauge Height	Dis-charge.	Gauge Height.	Dis-charge	Gauge Height.	Dis-charge
	Feet.	*Sec.-ft.*	*Feet.*	*Sec.-ft.*	*Feet*	*Sec.-ft*	*Feet*	*Sec.-ft*	*Feet.*	*Sec.-ft.*	*Feet.*	*Sec.-ft.*
1...........	1 06	11 4	Dry.a	Nil.	0 50a	0 85	Dry a	Nil	0.60	1.55	....	0.50c
2...........	1 06	11 4	" a	" /	1 05b	11 00	" a	"	....	0.50c	....	0.50c
3...........	1 06	11 4	" a	"	0 99	8 70	" a	"	....	0.50c	....	0.50c
4...........	1 05	11 0	" 'a	"	0 95	7 40	1 32d	22 00	....	0.50c	....	0.50c
5...........	1.05	11.0	" a	"	0 94	7.10	1.12	13.80	....	0.50c	0.60	1.55
6....	1.04	10.6	" a	"	0.94	7.10	0 90	6 10	....	0.50c	0.85	5.00
7...........	1.04	10.6	" a	"	....	7.10c	0 65	2 00	....	0.50c	0.95	7.40
8...........	1.04	10.6	" a	"	....	7 10c	0 65	2 00	....	0.50c	2.45	67.00
9......	1.04	10.6	1.30b	21.0	....	7 10c	... ..	1 55c	....	0.50c	1.65	35.00
10 .	1.04	10.6	1.20	17.0	....	7.10c	... ..	1.15c	....	0.50c	....	26.00c
11. . .	1.04	10 6	1 10	13 0	......	7.10c	....	1.00c	....	0.50c	.... .	20.00c
12......	1.04	10 0	1 07	11 8	1 96	47 00	....	0.85c	....	0.50c	....	15.00c
13.. .	1.04	10 6	1 05	11 0	1 90	45 00	....	0.50c	....	0.50c	1.05	11.00
14	1.04	10 6	1.00	9.0	1 30	21.00	....	0.50c	0.70	2.50	0.90	6.10
15 . .	1.03	10 2	1.00	9.0	1 03	10.20	....	0.50c	1.00	9.00	....	
16 .	1 02	9 8	1 03	10 2	1.03	10.20	.... ..	0.60	1.55	0.85	5.00	
17...........	1 02	9 8	1 03	10 2	1.03	10 20	.... ..	0.50c	0.60	1.55	....	4.50c
18...........	1 04	10 6	1.00	9.0	1 03	10.20	....	0.50c	0.60	1.55	....	4.00c
19......	1.04	10.6	0.98	8.4	Dry.a	Nil.	.... ..	0.50c	0.55	1.15	0.75	3.20
20. . .	1 04	10 6	0 99	8 7	" a	"	.... ..	0.50c	0.55	1.15	0.70	2.50
21 ...	Dry.a	Nil.	1.00	9.0	" a	"	....	0.50c	0.55	1.15	0.97	8.00
22...........	1.04d	10.6	1.02	9.8	" a	"	....	0.50c	0.55	1.15	0.70	2.50
23.... ..	....	10.6c	1.00	9.0	" a	"	....	0.50c	0.55	1.15	0.70	2.50
24. . . .	....	10.6c	1.00	9.0	" a	"	....	0.50c	....	0.50c	0.70	2.50
25	....	10.6c	1.02	9.0	" a	"	1.30	21.00	....	0.50c	0.70	2.50
26	....	10.6c	1.00	9.0	" a	"	1.30	21.00	....	0.50c	....	2.50c
27	....	10.6c	0.95	7.4	" a	"	1.15	15.00	....	0.50c	....	2.50c
28	Dry.a	Nil.	0.96	7.7	" a	"	1.05	11.00	....	0.50c	....	2.50c
29	" a	"	0.90	6.1	" a	"	0.85	5.00	....	0.50c	0.70	2.50
30	" a	"	1.00	9.0	" a	"	0.80	4.00	....	0.50c	....	2.50
31	" a	"	....	...	" a	"	0.65	2.00	....	....	....	2.50c

a Sluice in dam closed, reservoir filling.
b Dam broke.
c Discharge estimated.
d Sluice in dam opened.

SESSIONAL PAPER No. 25c

MONTHLY DISCHARGE of Rock Creek near Barnard, Montana, U.S.A., for 1914.

(Drainage area 230 square miles).

MONTH.	DISCHARGE IN SECOND-FEET.				RUN-OFF.	
	Maximum.	Minimum	Mean.	Per square Mile.	Depth in inches on Drainage Area.	Total in Acre-feet
May	11.4	0.00	8.90	0.039	0.045	549
June	21.0	0.94	7.80	0.034	0.038	462
July	47.0	0.00	7.60	0.033	0.038	463
August	22.0	0.00	4.40	0.019	0.022	273
September	2.5	0.50	0.85	0.004	0.004	51
October	67.0	0.50	8.30	0.036	0.042	510
The period					1.89	2,308

NOTE.—This table includes discharge of Bowrey Ditch.

MISCELLANEOUS DISCHARGE MEASUREMENTS made in Frenchman River drainage basin, in 1914.

Date.	Engineer.	Stream.	Location.	Width.	Area of Section.	Mean Velocity.	Dis-charge.
				Feet.	Sq. ft.	Ft. per sec.	Sec ft.
March 17	M. H. French	Backtail Creek	30-6-23-3				Nil.
June 27	F. R. Steinberger	do	do				"
March 17	M. H. French.	Concrete Coulee	2-7-23-3				"
April 7	F. R. Steinberger	do	do	7.10	3.04	0.70	2.20
June 26	do	do	do				0.13
Aug. 7	do	do	do				0.13
June 20	do	Calf Creek	SE. 5-8-22-3				0.14
Sept. 14	E. W. W. Hughes	do	do	8.00	3.25	0.90	2.90
May 7	F. R. Steinberger	Doyle Coulee	SE. 17-7-22-3				0.22
June 26	do	do	do				0.16
July 20	do	do	do				0.09
Aug. 7	do	do	do				0.08
March 25	M. H. French	Frenchman River	25-6-22-3	38.00	30.00	0.92	28.00
March 31	do	do	do	44.00	32.40	1.34	44.00
April 1	do	do	do	44.00	37.20	1.20	45.00
April 3	do	do	do	55.00	67.00	2.51	168.00
April 3	do	do	do	45.00	48.30	1.95	94.00
April 4	do	do	do	55.00	93.40	2.55	238.00
April 5	do	do	do	58.00	102.00	3.89	399.00
April 6	do	do	do	108.00	113.00	4.08	463.00
April 11	do	do	do	56.00	80.80	3.27	265.00
April 14	do	do	do	50.00	75.60	3.43	259.00
May 9	F. R. Steinberger	Overflow of Cypress Lake	SE. 24-6-25-3				0.72
June 29	do	do	do				0.14
July 22	do	do	do				Nil.
Aug. 12	do	do	do				"
June 26	do	Pearse Ditch	2-7-21-3				1.26
May 7	do	Petrified Coulee	7-7-22-3				0.62
June 26	do	do	do				0.14
July 20	do	do	do				0.11
Aug. 7	do	do	do				0.06

·5 GEORGE V, A. 1915

SWIFTCURRENT CREEK DRAINAGE BASIN.

General Description.

Swiftcurrent Creek rises in the eastern slope of the Cypress Hills, follows a northeasterly course for 75 miles, and then a northerly one for about 25 miles, and finally empties into the South Saskatchewan River in Township 20, Range 13, West of the 3rd Meridian.

The only important tributary is Bone Creek, which rises in the Cypress Hills and joins the Swiftcurrent in Township 10, Range 19, West of the 3rd Meridian.

The main stream flows through a valley, 200 to 300 feet deep and a mile wide, to within a few miles of its mouth, where it enters a sandstone gorge about 500 feet deep.

The bench land above the creek is of rolling prairie, broken by innumerable coulees. The soil is a sandy loam. There is very little tree growth along the stream.

The mean annual rainfall at the town of Swift Current is about 15 inches. This increases slightly at the stream's headwaters. The greatest precipitation occurs during the months of May, June, and July. From November to April the stream is frozen over.

There are a number of small irrigation ditches in this drainage basin, and the town of Swift Current and the Canadian Pacific Railway Company take water for domestic and industrial purposes from the creek.

SWIFTCURRENT CREEK AT POLLOCK'S RANCH.

Location.—On the SW. ¼ Sec. 22, Tp. 7, Rge. 21, W. 3rd Mer.

Records available.—May 18, 1909, to October 31, 1914. Two discharge measurements in 1908.

Gauge.—Vertical staff; elevation of zero, 1909-12, maintained at 89.25 feet; 1913-14, maintained at 88.75 feet.

Bench-mark.—Permanent iron bench-mark.

Channel.—Sand and gravel.

Discharge measurements.—At high stages by wading; permanent three-foot weir installed in 1914 for measuring the ordinary flow.

Winter flow.—Station not maintained during the winter.

Observer.—D. H. Pollock.

DISCHARGE MEASUREMENTS of Swiftcurrent Creek at Pollock's Ranch, in 1914.

Date.	Engineer.	Width.	Area of Section.	Mean Velocity.	Gauge Height.	Discharge.
		Feet.	*Sq. ft.*	*Ft. per sec.*	*Feet.*	*Sec.-ft.*
April 4	M. H. French	5.2	2.08	1.69	4.35	3.50
April 15	do	7.0	4.50	0.95	1.85	4.30
April 17	do	3.0	3.05	0.82	1.65	2.50
April 30	F. R. Steinberger	6.3	2.05	0.91	1.39	1.88
May 20	do				1.30	1.45a
June 24	do				1.13	0.61a
July 9	do				1.11	0.43a
Aug. 6	do				1.18	0.66a
Aug. 14	E. W. W. Hughes				1.24	0.75a
Sept. 10	do				1.31	0.83a
Sept. 16	do				1.47	1.44a

a Weir measurement.

SESSIONAL PAPER No. 25c

DAILY GAUGE HEIGHT AND DISCHARGE of Swiftcurrent Creek at Pollock's Ranch, for 1914.

DAY.	April.		May.		June.	
	Gauge Height.	Dis- charge.	Gauge Height.	Dis- charge.	Gauge Height.	Dis- charge.
	Feet.	*Sec.-ft.*	*Feet.*	*Sec.-ft.*	*Feet.*	*Sec.-ft.*
1	4.52	3.00b	1.42	1.95	1.04	0.74
2	4.52	3.00	1.42	1.95	1.05	0.75
3	4.50	3.20	1.41	1.90	1.40	1.65
4	4.50	3.50	1.44	2.00	1.38	1.59
5	4.30	3.60	1.50	2.30	1.30	1.30
6	3.50	3.70	1.44	2.00	1.30	1.30
7	2.50	3.80	1.44	2.00	1.09	0.70
8	2.40	3.90	1.42	1.95	1.10	0.82
9	2.40	4.00	1.42	1.95	1.07	0.78
10	2.30	4.30	1.45	2.10	1.30	1.25
11	1.88	4.60b	1.42	1.95	1.22	1.00
12	1.87a	4.50	1.40	1.86	1.22	0.99
13	1.86a	4.40	1.40	1.86	1.55	2.00
14	1.85a	4.30	1.35	1.69	1.40	1.45
15	1.85	4.30	1.30	1.52	1.30	1.14
16	1.75	3.40	1.34	1.66	1.25	1.00
17	1.65	2.50	1.30	1.52	1.20	0.87
18	1.64	2.50	1.35	1.69	1.18	0.82
19	1.59	2.40	1.30	1.48	1.15	0.70
20	1.55	2.20	1.30	1.45	1.15	0.69
21	1.56	2.30	1.30	1.45	1.19	0.77
22	1.59	2.40	1.30	1.45	1.15	0.64
23	1.56	2.30	1.30	1.45	1.15	0.63
24	1.52	2.20	1.35	1.60	1.15	0.61
25	1.46	1.99	1.30	1.42	1.15	0.61
26	1.45	1.98	1.10	0.90	1.15	0.61
27	1.45	2.00	1.08	0.85	1.15	0.60
28	1.44	1.98	1.05	0.78	1.15	0.60
29	1.43	1.95	1.05	0.78	1.15	0.60
30	1.42	1.90	1.05	0.76	1.15	0.60
31	....	....	1.04	0.74	....	....

a Gauge height interpolated.
b Ice conditions April 1 to 11; discharge estimated.

5 GEORGE V, A. 1915

DAILY GAUGE HEIGHT AND DISCHARGE of Swiftcurrent Creek at Pollock's Ranch, for 1914.
—Concluded.

DAY.	July.		August.		September.		October.	
	Gauge Height.	Dis-charge.	Gauge Height.	Dis-charge.	Gauge Height.	Dis-charge.	Gauge Height.	Dis-charge.
	Feet.	Sec.-ft.	Feet.	Sec.-ft.	Feet.	Sec.-ft.	Feet.	Sec.-ft.
1	1.25	0.85	1.12	0.46	1.36	1.09	0.33	1.22
2	1.25	0.85	1.14	0.51	1.35	1.06	0.34	1.28
3	1.25	0.85	1.15	0.53	1.36	1.09	0.34	1.28
4	1.25	0.85	1.15	0.53	1.36	1.09	0.40	1.62
5	1.24	0.80	1.15	0.53	1.35	1.06	0.41	1.68
6	1.24	0.80	1.18	0.60	1.36	1.09	0.41	1.68
7	1.25	0.80	1.20	0.64	1.36	1.09	0.44	1.86
8	1.10	0.45	1.18	0.60	1.40	1.21	0.95	5.60
9	1.11	0.43	1.17	0.57	1.38	1.15	0.70	3.60
10	1.10	0.42	1.15	0.60	1.36	1.09	0.65	3.30
11	1.09	0.40	1.14	0.60	1.35	1.06	0.50	2.20
12	1.09	0.40	1.14	0.65	1.35	1.06	0.40	1.62
13	1.08	0.39	1.15	0.70	2.10	5.10	0.40	1.62
14	1.20	0.64	1.15	0.75	1.80	3.00	0.39	1.56
15	1.20	0.64	1.14	0.65	1.60	2.00	0.38	1.50
16	1.19	0.62	1.14	0.65	0.37a	1.44	0.37	1.44
17	1.20	0.64	1.16	0.70	0.37	1.44	0.36	1.39
18	1.20	0.64	2.00	4.30	0.36	1.39	0.36	1.39
19	1.19	0.62	1.45	1.40	0.35	1.33	0.36	1.39
20	1.20	0.64	1.40	1.21	0.34	1.28	0.36	1.39
21	1.19	0.62	1.38	1.15	0.33	1.22	0.37	1.44
22	1.18	0.60	1.37	1.12	0.33	1.22	0.37	1.44
23	1.17	0.57	1.40	1.21	0.33	1.22	0.37	1.44
24	1.15	0.53	2.10	5.10	0.33	1.22	0.37	1.44
25	1.15	0.53	2.00	4.30	0.33	1.22	0.37	1.44
26	1.14	0.51	1.80	3.00	0.33	1.22	0.37	1.44
27	1.12	0.46	1.38	1.15	0.32	1.17	0.37	1.44
28	1.12	0.46	1.35	1.06	0.32	1.17	0.37	1.44
29	1.12	0.46	1.35	1.06	0.32	1.17	0.37	1.44
30	1.12	0.46	1.36	1.09	0.32	1.17	0.37	1.44
31	1.14	0.51	1.36	1.09	....	....	0.37a	1.44

a Gauge heights, Sept. 16 to Oct. 31, are heads on 24-inch Weir.

MONTHLY DISCHARGE of Swiftcurrent Creek at Pollock's Ranch, for 1914.

(Drainage area 16 square miles.)

MONTH.	DISCHARGE IN SECOND-FEET.				RUN-OFF.	
	Maximum.	Minimum	Mean.	Per square Mile.	Depth in inches on Drainage Area.	Total in Acre-feet.
April	4.60	1.90	3.070	0.192	0.21	183
May	2.30	0.74	1.580	0.099	0.11	97
June	2.00	0.60	0.937	0.058	0.06	55
July	0.85	0.39	0.595	0.037	0.04	37
August	5.10	0.46	1.240	0.077	0.09	76
September	5.10	1.06	1.400	0.087	0.10	83
October	5.60	1.22	1.760	0.110	0.13	108
The period	....	....	....	....	0.74	639

AXTON DITCH FROM SWIFTCURRENT CREEK.

Location.—On the N E. ¼ Sec. 26, Tp. 7, Rgc. 21, W. 3rd Mer., near South Fork post office.
Records available.—Gauge heights for the period June 10 to July 9, 1914.
Observer.—J. W. E. Axton.
Remarks.—Not sufficient data are available to compute daily discharges.

DAILY GAUGE HEIGHT of Axton Ditch from Swiftcurrent Creek, for 1914.

DAY.	June.		July.	
	Gauge Height.	Dis- charge.	Gauge Height.	Dis- charge.
	Feet.	*Sec.-ft.*	*Feet.*	*Sec.-ft.*
1	....	....	0.60	....
2	....	....	0.58	....
3	....	....	0.58	....
4	....	....	0.58	....
5	....	....	0.56	....
6	....	....	0.56	....
7	....	....	0.56	....
8	....	....	....	....
9	0.54	....	0.48	....
10	0.54	....	....	....
11	0.54	....	....	....
12	0.52	....	....	....
13	0.50	....	....	....
14	0.50	....	....	....
15	0.50	....	....	....
16	....	....	....	....
17	....	....	....	....
18	....	....	....	....
19	....	....	....	....
20	....	....	....	....
21	....	....	....	....
22	....	....	....	....
23	....	....	....	....
24	....	....	....	....
25	0.75	....	....	....
26	0.75	....	....	....
27	0.73	....	....	....
28	0.71	....	....	....
29	0.67	....	....	....
30	0.65	....	....	....
31	....	....	....	....

JONES CREEK AT STEARNS' RANCH.

Location.—On SE. ¼ Sec. 20, Tp. 8, Rge. 20, W. 3rd Mer.
Records available.—May 15, 1912, to October 31, 1914.
Gauge.—Vertical staff; elevation 93.14 feet since establishment
Bench-mark.—Permanent iron bench-mark; assumed elevation, 100 00 feet.
Channel.—Composed of clay and sand.
Discharge measurements.—Made by wading or with a weir.
Winter flow.—Station not maintained during winter.
Observer.—C. E. Stearns.

5 GEORGE V, A. 1915

DISCHARGE MEASUREMENTS of Jones Creek at Stearns' Ranch, in 1914.

Date.	Engineer.	Width.	Area of Section.	Mean Velocity.	Gauge Height.	Discharge.
		Feet.	*Sq. ft.*	*Ft. per sec.*	*Feet.*	*Sec.-ft.*
Mar. 31.............	M. H. French................	....	....	....	2.84	Nil.
April 15.............	do	4.7	6.55	1.03	2.07	6.70
April 30.............	F. R. Steinberger.	4.4	1.65	1.24	0.75	2.00
May 20.............	do	3.9	1.15	1.57	0.62	1.81
June 24.............	do				0.51	0.29*a*
July 11.......... .	do				0.45	0.22*a*
Aug. 6.............	do				Dry.	Nil.
Sept. 10.............	E. W. W. Hughes.				0.50	0 40*a*

a Weir measurement

DAILY GAUGE HEIGHT AND DISCHARGE of Jones Creek at Stearns' Ranch, for 1914.

DAY.	April.		May.		June.	
	Gauge Height.	Dis-charge.	Gauge Height.	Dis-charge.	Gauge Height.	Dis-charge.
	Feet.	*Sec.-ft.*	*Feet.*	*Sec.-ft.*	*Feet.*	*Sec.-ft.*
1.........	4.32	16.2	0.72	1.94	0.42	0.66
2.........	4.80	18.2	0.72	1.95	0.40	0.58
3.........	3.92	14.5	0.72	1.96	0.62	1.40
4.........	3.71*a*	13.6	0.74*a*	2.10	0.73	1.83
5.........	3.50	12.8	0.77	2.20	0.89	2.50
6.........	3.61	13.2	·0.79	2.30	0.82*a*	2.20
7.........	3.39*a*	12.3	0.74	2.10	0.75*a*	1.82
8.........	3.17	11.4	0.71	2.00	0.62	1.26
9.........	2.67	9.3	0.71*a*	2.00	0.59	1.11
10.........	2.17	7.2	0.70	1.99	0.56	0.96
11.........	2.35	7.9	0.69	1.97	0.57	0.98
12.........	2.44	8.3	0.67	1.90	0.70	1.48
13.........	2.30	7.7	0.65	1.82	0.92	2.40
14.........	2.32	7.8	0.64	1.80	0.94	2.40
15.........	1.97	6.3	0.62	1.74	0.78*a*	1.72
16.........	1.72	5.3	0.62	1.75	0.62	1.02
17.........	1.37	3.9	0.62*a*	1.76	0.58*a*	0.82
18.........	1.17	3.1	0.62	1.78	0.55	0.66
19.........	1.14*a*	3.1	0.62	1.79	0.53*a*	0.56
20.........	1.12	3.1	0.62	1.80	0.52	0.50
21.........	1.02	2.7	0.62	1.78	0.57	0.60
22.........	0.96*a*	2.5	0.61	1.72	0.54*a*	0.46
23.........	0.92	2.4	0.62*a*	1.72	0.51	0.34
24.........	0.87	2.2	0.64	1.78	0.58*a*	0.48
25.........	0.84	2.2	0.62	1.68	0.65*a*	0.84
26.........	0.83*a*	2.2	0.60*a*	1.56	0.72	1.12
27.........	0.82	2.2	0.58	1.46	0.65	0.84
28.........	0.80	2.1	0.55	1.30	0.63*a*	0.76
29.........	0.77	2.1	0.54*a*	1.24	0.61	0.68
30.........	0.76	2.1	0.53	1.16	0.58	0.57
31.........	....	....	0.47*a*	0.88	....	....

a Gauge height interpolated.

SESSIONAL PAPER No. 25c

DAILY GAUGE HEIGHT AND DISCHARGE of Jones Creek at Stearns' Ranch, for 1914.
—*Concluded.*

DAY.	July.		August.		September.		October.	
	Gauge Height.	Dis- charge.	Gauge Height.	Dis- charge.	Gauge Height.	Dis- charge.	Gauge Height.	Dis- charge.
	Feet.	*Sec.-ft.*	*Feet.*	*Sec.-ft.*	*Feet.*	*Sec.-ft.*	*Feet.*	*Sec.-ft.*
1	0.56a	0.51	Dry.	Nil.	Dry.	Nil.	Dry.	Nil.
2	0.53a	0.42	"	"	"	"	"	"
3	0.51	0.37	"	"	"	"	"	"
4	0.51	0.37	"	"	"	"	"	"
5	0.48	0.29	"	"	"	"	"	"
6	0.50	0.34	"	"	"	"	"	"
7	0.48a	0.29	"	"	"	"	"	"
8	0.47	0.27	"	"	"	"	"	"
9	0.45	0.22	"	"	"	"	"	"
10	0.45a	0.22	"	"	"	"	"	"
11	0.45	0.22	"	"	"	"	"	"
12	0.40a	0.14	"	"	"	"	"	"
13	0.36	0.09	"	"	"	"	"	"
14	0.32	0.04	"	"	"	"	"	"
15	0.32a	0.04	"	"	"	"	"	"
16	0.31a	0.03	"	"	"	"	"	"
17	0.31	0.03	"	"	"	"	"	"
18	0.30	0.02	"	"	"	"	"	"
19	0.28a	0.01	"	"	"	"	"	"
20	0.26a	Nil.	"	"	"	"	"	"
21	0.24	"	"	"	"	"	"	"
22	0.20a	"	"	"	"	"	"	"
23	0.16	"	"	"	"	"	"	"
24	......	......	"	"	"	"	"	"
25	......	......	"	"	"	"	"	"
26	......	......	"	"	"	"	"	"
27	......	......	"	"	"	"	"	"
28	0.05	"	"	"	"	"	"	"
29	Dry.	"	"	"	"	"	"	"
30	"	"	"	"	"	"	"	"
31	"	"	"	"	"	"	"	"

a Gauge height interpolated.

MONTHLY DISCHARGE of Jones Creek at Stearns' Ranch, for 1914.

(Drainage area 5 square miles.)

MONTH.	DISCHARGE IN SECOND-FEET.				RUN-OFF.	
	Maximum.	Minimum	Mean.	Per square Mile.	Depth in inches on Drainage Area.	Total in Acre-feet.
April	18.20	2.10	6.930	1.380	1.54	412
May	2.30	0.88	17.700	3.540	4.08	1,088
June	2.50	0.34	11.200	2.240	2.50	666
July	0.51	0.00	0.126	0.025	0.03	8
August	......	......	......	......	......	......a
September	......	......	......	......	......	......a
October	......	......	......	......	......	......a
The period	......	......	......	......	8.15	2,174

a Creek dry.

5 GEORGE V, A. 1915

STEARNS DITCH NEAR DOLLARD.

Location.—On the SW. ¼ Sec. 20, Tp. 8, Rge. 20, W. 3rd Mer., 600 feet from headgate of ditch.
Records available.—Discharge measurements only in 1914.
Gauge.—Vertical staff, graduated to feet and inches; elevation, 97.46 feet.
Bench-mark.—Top of stake, marking initial point for soundings; assumed elevation, 100.00 feet.
Discharge measurements.—Made with weir.
Observer.—No observations in 1914.

DISCHARGE MEASUREMENTS of Stearns' Ditch near Dollard, in 1914.

Date.	Engineer.	Width.	Area of Section.	Mean Velocity.	Gauge Height.	Discharge.
		Feet.	*Sq. ft.*	*Ft. per sec.*	*Feet.*	*Sec.-ft.*
April 4	F. R. Steinberger					0.115
April 30	do					0.094

SWIFTCURRENT CREEK AT SINCLAIR'S RANCH (UPPER STATION).

Location.—On the NE. ¼ Sec. 18, Tp. 10, Rge. 19, W. 3rd Mer., above the mouth of Bone Creek.
Records available.—June 15, 1910, to October 31, 1914.
Gauge.—Vertical staff; the elevation of the gauge was maintained at 87.91 feet during 1910-11, and at 87 86 feet during 1912-14.
Bench-mark.—Permanent iron bench-mark: assumed elevation, 100.00 feet.
Channel.—Permanent.
Discharge measurements.—Made with meter, and by weir at low stages.
Winter flow.—This station is not maintained during the winter.
Diversions.—Messrs D. H. Pollock and J. W. E. Axton divert water for irrigation purposes above this station.
Observer.—Mrs. K. Sinclair.
Remarks.—Records at this station are affected by backwater from Bone Creek at certain stages of that stream.

DISCHARGE MEASUREMENTS of Swiftcurrent Creek at Sinclair's Ranch (Upper Station), in 1914.

Date.	Engineer.	Width.	Area of Section.	Mean Velocity.	Gauge Height.	Discharge.
		Feet.	*Sq. ft.*	*Ft. per sec.*	*Feet.*	*Sec.-ft.*
Mar. 28	M. H. French	7.0	3.40	0.43	2.80	1.43
April 16	do	15.0	22.30	1.53	2.18	34.00
May 1	F. R. Steinberger	11.6	5.10	1.55	0.71	7.90
May 20	do	10.9	4.21	1.13	0.55	4.70
June 23	do	9.7	2.34	0.82	0.42	1.93
July 10	do				0.24	0.14*a*
Aug. 5	do					Nil.
Sept. 9	E. W. W. Hughes					
Oct. 2	do	10.0	2.20	1.06	0.44	2.30

a Weir measurement.

SESSIONAL PAPER No. 25c

DAILY GAUGE HEIGHT AND DISCHARGE of Swiftcurrent Creek at Sinclair's Ranch (Upper Station), for 1914.

DAY.	April.		May.		June.	
	Gauge Height.	Dis- charge.	Gauge Height.	Dis- charge.	Gauge Height.	Dis- charge.
	Feet.	*Sec.-ft.*	*Feet.*	*Sec.-ft.*	*Feet.*	*Sec.-ft.*
1	3.50	62.0	0.72	8.20	0.38	1.39
2	3.75	67.0	0.72	8.20	0.38	1.39
3	5.04	96.0	0.71	8.00	0.37	1.26
4	5.25	100.0	0.71	8.00	0.42	1.99
5	5.32	102.0	0.70	7.80	0.66	6.90
6	5.40	104.0	0.69	7.60	0.69	7.60
7	4.90	93.0	0.73	8.90	0.76	9.10
8	4.20	78.0	0.79	9.70	0.70	7.80
9	4.07	75.0	0.80	10.00	0.61	5.90
10	2.90	50.0	0.84	10.80	0.55	4.60
11	2.72	45.0	0.75	8.90	0.45	2.50
12	2.63a	43.0	0.69	7.60	0.47	2.90
13	2.55	42.0	0.60	5.60	0.52	4.00
14	2.37	38.0	0.55	4.60	0.89	11.90
15	2.00	30.0	0.54	4.40	0.85	11.00
16	2.20	34.0	0.52	4.00	0.77	9.30
17	2.00	32.0	0.53	4.20	0.69	7.60
18	1.75	27.0	0.53	4.20	0.62	6.10
19	1.52	24.0	0.54	4.40	0.55	4.60
20	1.48	24.0	0.55	4.60	0.47	2.90
21	1.39	23.0	0.55	4.60	0.46	2.70
22	1.30	21.0	0.55	4.60	0.45	2.50
23	1.25	19.6	0.55	4.60	0.42	1.99
24	1.00	14.2	0.55	4.60	0.40	1.65
25	0.95	13.2	0.54	4.40	0.40	1.65
26	0.89	11.9	0.54	4.40	0.42	1.99
27	0.82	10.4	0.49	3.30	0.43	2.20
28	0.80	10.0	0.45	2.50	0.43	2.20
29	0.78	9.5	0.42	1.99	0.44	2.30
30	0.76	9.1	0.40	1.65	0.45	2.50
31			0.39	1.52		

5 GEORGE V, A. 1915

DAILY GAUGE HEIGHT AND DISCHARGE of Swiftcurrent Creek at Sinclair's Ranch, (Upper Station), for 1914.—*Concluded.*

DAY.	July.		August.		September.		October.	
	Gauge Height.	Dis- charge.	Gauge Height.	Dis- charge.	Gauge Height.	Dis- charge.	Gauge Heigtt.	Dis- charge.
	Feet.	*Sec.-ft.*	*Feet.*	*Sec.-ft.*	*Feet.*	*Sec.-ft.*	*Feet.*	*Sec.-ft.*
1	0.47	2.90	Dry.	Nil.	0.60	5.60	0.33	0.78
2	0.46	2.70	"	"	0.60	5.60	0.39	1.52
3	0.44	2.30	"	"	0.60	5.60	0.42	1.99
4	0.42	1.99	"	"	Dry.	Nil.	0.57	5.00
5	0.40	1.65	"	"	"	"	1.00	14.20
6	0.40	1.65	"	"	"	"	1.80	31.00
7	0.37	1.26	"	"	"	"	1.99	36.00
8	0.33	0.78	"	"	"	"	1.99	36.00
9	0.27	0.27	"	"	"	"	1.87	33.00
10	0.24	0.14	"	"	"	"	1.50	25.00
11	0.22	0.12	"	"	"	"	1.43	24.00
12	0.22	0.12	"	"	0.70	7.80	1.00	14.20
13	0.21	0.11	"	"	0.30	0.45	0.89	11.90
14	0.21	0.11	"	"	1.25	19.60	0.68	7.40
15	0.23	0.13	"	"	1.30	21.00	0.55	4.60
16	0.22	0.12	"	"	1.32	21.00	0.49	3.30
17	0.21	0.11	"	"	1.30	21.00	0.46	2.70
18	0.21	0.11	"	"	1.17	17.90	0.45	2.50
19	0.21	0.11	"	"	1.00	14.20	0.42	1.99
20	0.22	0.12	"	"	0.87	11.40	0.40	1.65
21	0.21	0.11	"	"	0.40	1.65	0.40	1.65
22	0.20	0.10	"	"	0.38	1.39	0.41	1.82
23	0.19	0.09	0.10	"	0.37	1.26	0.43	2.20
24	0.17	0.07	0.12	0.02	0.36	1.13	0.43	2.20
25	0.17	0.07	Dry.	Nil.	0.33	0.78	0.41	1.82
26	0.16	0.06	"	"	0.30	0.45	0.43	2.20
27	0.16	0.06	"	"	0.30	0.45	0.42	1.99
28	0.16	0.06	"	"	0.29	0.39	0.43	2.20
29	0.14	0.04	"	"	0.30	0.45	0.43	2.20
30	0.10	Nil.	0.60	5.60	0.31	0.56	0.45	2.50
31	Dry.	"	0.70	7.80	....	....	0.44	2.30

MONTHLY DISCHARGE of Swiftcurrent Creek at Sinclair's Ranch (Upper Station), for 1914.

(Drainage area 172 square miles.)

MONTH.	DISCHARGE IN SECOND-FEET.				RUN-OFF.	
	Maximum.	Minimum	Mean.	Per square Mile.	Depth in inches on Drainage Area.	Total in Acre-feet.
April	104.0	9.10	44.00	0.253	0.280	2,594
May	10.8	1.52	5.70	0.033	0.040	353
June	11.9	1.26	4.40	0.025	0.030	262
July	2.9	....	0.56	0.003	0.004	35
August	7.8	....	0.43	0.002	0.003	27
September	21.0	....	5.30	0.031	0.040	317
October	36.0	0.78	9.40	0.054	0.060	575
The period	....	....	....	....	0 457	4,163

MONTHLY DISCHARGE of Swiftcurrent Creek at Sinclair's Ranch (Upper Station), for 1912.

(Drainage area 172 square miles.)

MONTH.	DISCHARGE IN SECOND-FEET.				RUN-OFF.	
	Maximum.	Minimum.	Mean.	Per square Mile.	Depth in inches on Drainage Area.	Total in Acre-feet.
June (28-30)........................	3.7	3.20	3.37	0.020c	0.001c	20
July...............................	5.8	1.38	3.99	0.023	0.026	240
August.............................	4.5	1.14	3.24	0.018	0.020	199
September..........................	4.0	2.80	3.43	0.020	0.022	204
October............................	7.9	2.60	4.41	0.026	0.030	271
November (1-15)....................	9.4	3.70	6.50	0.038	0.021	193
The period.........................	....	....	....	....	0.120	1,127

NOTE.—This table is inserted in this report to correct a table on page 348 of the 1912 report. The drainage area and columns marked ''c'' have been corrected.

MONTHLY DISCHARGE of Swiftcurrent Creek at Sinclair's Ranch (Upper Station), for 1913.

(Drainage area 172 square miles.)

MONTH.	DISCHARGE IN SECOND-FEET.				RUN-OFF.	
	Maximum.	Minimum.	Mean.	Per square Mile.	Depth in inches on Drainage Area.	Total in Acre-feet.
April (8-30)........................	252.00	11.00	96.700	0.560c	0.480c	4,411
May...............................	17.00	3.90	12.040	0.070	0.081	740
June...............................	29.00	1.19	8.120	0.047	0.052	483
July...............................	6.80	0.42	2.840	0.016	0.018	175
August.............................	2.50	0.18	0.960	0.006	0.007	59
September..........................	3.80	0.21	0.994	0.006	0.007	59
October............................	8.20	1.81	3.410	0.020	0.023	210
The period.........................	....	....	....	....	0.668	6,137

NOTE.—This table is inserted in this report to correct a table on page 318 of the 1913 report. The drainage area and columns marked ''c'' have been corrected.

BONE CREEK AT LEWIS' RANCH.

Location.—On the NW. ¼ Sec. 34, Tp. 8, Rge. 22, W. 3rd Mer., at Klintonel post office.
Records available.—July 1, 1908, to October 31, 1914.
Gauge.—Vertical staff; the elevation of the zero of the gauge has been maintained at 95.02 feet since establishment.
Bench-mark.—Permanent iron bench-mark; assumed elevation, 100.00 feet.
Channel.—Slightly shifting.
Discharge measurements.—Made with meter, or with weir at low stages.
Winter flow.—This station is not maintained during the winter.
Observer.—C. L. Lewis.

DISCHARGE MEASUREMENTS of Bone Creek at Lewis' Ranch, in 1914.

Date.	Engineer.	Width.	Area of Section.	Mean Velocity.	Gauge Height.	Discharge.
		Feet.	*Sq. ft.*	*Ft. per sec.*	*Feet.*	*Sec -ft.*
April 28............	F. R. Steinberger............	5.7	2.1	0.93	0.20	1.99
May 18............	do	5.8	2.1	0.88	0.21	1.82
June 16............	do	....	....	....	0.17	1.61a
July 8............	do	....	....	....	0.11	0.52a
July 31...	do	....	....	....	0.08	0.44a
Aug. 27............	E. W. W. Hughes...	....	....	....	0.13	0.60a
Sept. 14............	do	6.0	3.2	1.48	0.35	4.70

a Weir measurement.

DAILY GAUGE HEIGHT AND DISCHARGE of Bone Creek at Lewis' Ranch, for 1914.

DAY.	March.		April.		May.		June.	
	Gauge Height.	Dis-charge.	Gauge Height.	Dis-charge.	Gauge Height.	Dis-charge.	Gauge Height.	Dis-charge.
	Feet.	*Sec.-ft.*	*Feet.*	*Sec.-ft.*	*Feet.*	*Sec.-ft.*	*Feet.*	*Sec.-ft.*
1............	....	....	0.50	7.70	0.22	2.10	0.16	1.15
2............	....	....	0.47	7.10	0.22	2.10	0.12	0.66
3............	....	....	0.60	9.70	0.22	2.10	0.12	0.66
4............	....	....	0.32	4.10	0.24	2.50	0.33	4.30
5............	....	....	1.00	17.70	0.47	7.10	0.33	4.30
6............	....	....	1.04	18.50	0.27	3.10	0.23	2.40
7............	....	....	0.73	12.30	0.30	3.70	0.15	1.00
8............	....	....	0.32	4.10	0.30	3.70	0.12	0.66
9............	....	....	0.32	4.10	0.30	3.70	0.12	0.66
10............	....	....	0.28	3.10	0.30	3.70	0.11	0.55
11............	1.95	37.00	0.50	7.70	0.29	3.50	0.11	0.55
12............	1.13	20.00	1.19	22.00	0.27	3.10	0.11	0.55
13............	1.04	18.50	0.56	8.90	0.25	2.70	0.32	4.10
14............	0.92	16.10	0.61	9.90	0.25	2.70	0.16	1.15
15............	0.92	16.10	0.43	6.30	0.25	2.70	0.12	0.66
16............	0.92	16.10	0.34	4.50	0.25	2.70	0.11	0.55
17............	0.30	3.70	0.25	2.70	0.25	2.70	0.11	0.55
18............	0.30	3.70	0.22	2.10	0.25	2.70	0.11	0.55
19............	0.31	3.90	0.21	1.94	0.24	2.50	0.10	0.44
20............	0.65	10.70	0.21	1.94	0.24	2.50	0.10	0.44
21............	0.65	10.70	0.22	2.10	0.25	2.70	0.24	2.50
22............	0.42	6.10	0.22	2.10	0.24	2.50	0.11	0.55
23............	0.25	2.70	0.22	2.10	0.24	2.50	0.10	0.44
24............	0.20	1.75	0.22	2.10	0.22	2.10	0.10	0.44
25............	0.18	1.45	0.22	2.10	0.22	2.10	0.11	0.55
26............	0.15	1.00	0.22	2.10	0.22	2.10	0.12	0.66
27............	0.15	1.00	0.22	2.10	0.21	1.94	0.12	0.66
28............	0.15	1.00	0.22	2.10	0.21a	1.94	0.24	2.50
29............	0.15	1.00	0.22	2.10	0.20	1.75	0.24	2.50
30............	0.16	1.15	0.22	2.10	0.20	1.75	0.23	2.40
31............	0.40	5.70	....	....	0.18	1.45	....	....

5 GEORGE V, A. 1915

DAILY GAUGE HEIGHT AND DISCHARGE of Bone Creek at Lewis' Ranch, for 1914.—*Concluded.*

DAY.	July.		August.		September.		October.	
	Gauge Height.	Dis-charge.	Gauge Height.	Dis-charge.	Gauge Height.	Dis-charge.	Gauge Height.	Dis-charge.
	Feet.	Sec.-ft.	Feet.	Sec.-ft.	Feet.	Sec.-ft.	Feet.	Sec.-ft.
1	0.20	1.75	0.08	0.31	0.12	0.66	0.13	0.77
2	0.18	1.45	0.08	0.31	0.12	0.66	0.13	0.77
3	0.15	1.00	0.08	0.31	0.12	0.66	0.13	0.77
4	0.13	0.77	0.08	0.31	0.12	0.66	0.20	1.75
5	0.12	0.66	0.08	0.31	0.12	0.66	0.27	3.10
6	0.12	0.66	0.08	0.31	0.12	0.66	0.27	3.10
7	0.10	0.44	0.08	0.31	0.12	0.66	0.29	3.50
8	0.10	0.44	0.08	0.31	0.12	0.66	0.31	3.90
9	0.10	0.44	0.09	0.38	0.12	0.66	0.31	3.90
10	0.10	0.44	0.09	0.38	0.12	0.66	0.31	3.90
11	0.10	0.44	0.10	0.44	0.12	0.66	0.29	3.50
12	0.10	0.44	0.10	0.44	0.20	1.75	0.20	1.75
13	0.10	0.44	0.11	0.55	0.45	6.70	0.18	1.45
14	0.10	0.44	0.11	0.55	0.31	3.90	0.18	1.45
15	0.10	0.44	0.11	0.55	0.29	3.50	0.18	1.45
16	0.11	0.55	0.11	0.55	0.15	1.00	0.18	1.45
17	0.10	0.44	0.11	0.55	0.13	0.77	0.18	1.45
18	0.10	0.44	0.11	0.55	0.13	0.77	0.15	1.00
19	0.10	0.44	0.11	0.55	·0.13	0.77	0.15	1.00
20	0.10	0.44	0.11	0.55	0.13	0.77	0.13	0.77
21	0.10	0.44	0.11	0.55	0.13	0.77	0.13	0.77
22	0.10	0.44	0.11	0.55	0.13	0.77	0.12	0.66
23	0.10	0.44	0.12	0.66	0.13	0.77	0.12	0.66
24	0.10	0.44	0.15	1.00	0.13	0.77	0.12	0.66
25	0.10	0.44	0.15	1.00	0.13	0.77	0.12	0.66
26	0.09	0.38	0.15	1.00	0.13	0.77	0.12	0.66
27	0.08	0.31	0.13	0.77	0.13	0.77	0.12	0.66
28	0.08	0.31	0.13	0.77	0.13	0.77	0.12	0.66
29	0.08	0.31	0.13	0.77	0.13	0.77	0.12	0.66
30	0.09	0.38	0.12	0.66	0.13	0.77	0.12	0.66
31	0.09	0.38	0.12	0.66	....	....	0.12	0.66

MONTHLY DISCHARGE of Bone Creek at Lewis' Ranch, for 1914.

(Drainage area 17 square miles.)

MONTH.	DISCHARGE IN SECOND-FEET.				RUN-OFF.	
	Maximum.	Minimum	Mean.	Per square Mile.	Depth in inches on Drainage Area.	Total in Acre-feet.
March (12–31)	37.00	1.00	8.20	0.480	0.36	323
April	18.50	1.94	5.90	0.350	0.39	352
May	7.10	1.45	2.70	0.160	0.18	167
June	4.30	0.44	1.30	0.077	0.08	77
July	1.75	0.31	0.54	0.032	0.04	33
August	1.00	0.31	0.54	0.032	0.04	34
September	6.70	0.66	1.16	0.068	0.08	69
October	3.90	0.66	1.55	0.090	0.10	95
The period	....	....	....	....	1.27	1,150

SESSIONAL PAPER No. 25c

SWIFTCURRENT CREEK AT SINCLAIR'S RANCH (LOWER STATION).

Location.—On the NW. ¼ Sec. 17, Tp. 10, Rge. 19, W. 3rd Mer., and below the mouth of Bone Creek.

Records available.—May 27, 1910, to October 31, 1914.

Gauge.—Chain gauge, attached to floor of highway bridge; the zero of the gauge was maintained at 85 73 feet during 1913-14.

Bench-mark.—Permanent iron bench-mark, located on the right bank about 600 feet upstream from the bridge; assumed elevation, 100.00 feet.

Channel.—Permanent.

Discharge measurements.—Made with meter from bridge or by wading, and with a weir at very low stages.

Winter flow.—This station is not maintained during the frozen season.

Observer.—Mrs. K. Sinclair.

DISCHARGE MEASUREMENTS of Swiftcurrent Creek at Sinclair's Ranch (Lower Station), in 1914.

Date.	Engineer.	Width.	Area of Section.	Mean Velocity.	Gauge Height.	Discharge.
		Feet.	*Sq. ft.*	*Ft. per sec.*	*Feet.*	*Sec.-ft.*
Mar. 28	M. H. French..............	18.0	18.4	0.75	4.22	13.90
April 16............	do	20.0	54.7	1.59	3.80	87.00
May 1............	F. R. Steinberger.	30.7	23.0	1.19	2.25	27.00
May 20............	do	29.3	19.3	0.95	2.01	18.30
June 23............	do	29.0	14.2	0.68	1.73	9.80
July 10............	do	15.5	4.1	0 83	1.40	3.40
Aug. 5............	do	....	......	....	0.99	0.01*a*
Sept. 9............	E. W. W. Hughes....	13.0	4.3	0.99	1.40	4.20
Oct. 2............	do	26.0	14.2	0.97	1.89	13.80

a Weir measurement.

DAILY GAUGE HEIGHT AND DISCHARGE of Swiftcurrent Creek at Sinclair's Ranch (Lower Station), for 1914.

DAY.	April.		May.		June.	
	Gauge Height.	Dis-charge.	Gauge Height.	Dis-charge.	Gauge Height.	Dis-charge.
	Feet.	*Sec.-ft.*	*Feet.*	*Sec.-ft.*	*Feet.*	*Sec.-ft.*
1	4.73	123	2.24	27.0	1.73	9.8
2	4.80	125	2.21	26.0	1.70	9.0
3	5.97	168	2.19	25.0	1.71	9.3
4	6.32	184	2.22	26.0	1.76	10.6
5	6.70	174	2.24	27.0	2.22	26.0
6	7.00	210	2.29	29.0	2.28	28.0
7	6.75	176	2.39	33.0	2.43	34.0
8	6.18	178	2.43	34.0	2.40	33.0
9	5.90	168	2.44	35.0	2.31	30.0
10	4.95	132	2.51	37.0	2.13	23.0
11	5.00	133	2.40	33.0	1.90	14.7
12	4.64	119	2.29	29.0	1.92	15.4
13	4.28	106	2.21	26.0	2.03	19.2
14	4.05	96	2.16	24.0	2.71	45.0
15	3.94	92	2.04	19.5	2.42	34.0
16	3.80	87	1.98	17.4	2.34	31.0
17	3.75	85	1.98	17.4	2.20	25.0
18	3.72	84	2.00	18.1	2.07	21.0
19	3.68	82	2.03	19.2	2.00	18.1
20	3.67	82	2.01	18.5	1.90	14.7
21	3.50	75	2.01	18.5	1.82	12.2
22	3.37	70	2.00	18.1	1.77	10.8
23	2 95	54	1.97	17.0	1.75	10.3
24	2 64	42	1.97	17.0	1.71	9.3
25	2.63	42	1.93	15.7	1.72	9.5
26	2.69	44	1.92	15.4	1.69	8.8
27	2.64	42	1.90	14.7	1.71	9.3
28	2.51	37	1.88	14.1	1.81	11.9
29	2.35	31	1.86	13.4	1.82	12.2
30	2.33	30	1.86	13.4	1.81	11.9
31	....	....	1.84	12.8	....	....

5 GEORGE V, A. 1915

DAILY GAUGE HEIGHT AND DISCHARGE of Swiftcurrent Creek at Sinclair's Ranch (Lower Station), for 1914.—*Concluded.*

DAY.	July.		August.		September.		October.	
	Gauge Height.	Discharge.	Gauge Height.	Discharge.	Gauge Height.	Discharge.	Gauge Height.	Discharge.
	Feet.	Sec.-ft.	Feet.	Sec.-ft.	Feet.	Sec.-ft.	Feet.	Sec.-ft.
1	1.81	11.90	1.04	0.34	1.42	3.70	1.64	7.6
2	1.76	10.60	1.03	0.28	1.43	3.80	1.68	8.5
3	1.74	10.00	1.03	0.28	1.45	4.10	1.69	8.8
4	1.70	9.00	1.02	0.22	1.43	3.80	2.09	21.0
5	1.69	8.80	1.99	0.09	1.40	3.40	2.92	53.0
6	1.68	8.50	1.98	0.08	1.38	3.20	3.43	73.0
7	1.56	6.00	0.98	0.08	1.37	3.00	3.92	92.0
8	1.45	4.10	0.97	0.07	1.34	2.70	3.98	94.0
9	1.35	2.80	0.95	0.05	1.40	3.40	3.90	91.0
10	1.21	1.48	0.95	0.05	1.45	4.10	3.65	81.0
11	1.17	1.16	0.96	0.06	1.47	4.40	3.52	76.0
12	1.15	1.00	0.95	0.05	1.50	4.90	2.95	54.0
13	1.15	1.00	0.93	0.03	1.64	7.60	2.55	38.0
14	1.14	0.94	0.93	0.03	2.55	38.00	2.42	34.0
15	1.17	1.16	0.94	0.04	2.80	48.00	2.25	27.0
16	1.19	1.32	0.95	0.05	3.20	64.00	2.05	19.9
17	1.19	1.32	0.97	0.07	3.05	58.00	1.98	17.4
18	1.18	1.24	0.99	0.09	2.35	31.00	1.90	14.7
19	1.17	1.16	0.99	0.09	2.21	26.00	1.91	15.0
20	1.15	1.00	0.90	Nil	2.06	20.00	1.91	15.0
21	1.10	0.70	0.90	Nil	1.90	14.70	1.90	14.7
22	1.05	0.40	0.99	0.09	1.82	12.20	1.99	17.8
23	1.08	0.58	1.00	0.10	1.77	10.80	1.96	16.7
24	1.10	0.70	1.45	4.10	1.70	9.00	1.92	15.4
25	1.10	0.70	1.50	4.90	1.67	8.30	1.93	15.7
26	1.11	0.76	1.46	4.30	1.60	6.70	1.98	17.4
27	1.10	0.70	1.44	4.00	1.59	6.50	1.99	17.8
28	1.08	0.58	1.41	3.50	1.52	5.40	1.99	17.8
29	1.06	0.46	1.40	3.40	1.55	5.80	2.02	18.8
30	1.05	0.40	1.41	3.50	1.60	6.70	2.00	18.1
31	1.05	0.40	1.42	3.70	....	....	2.00	18.1

MONTHLY DISCHARGE of Swiftcurrent Creek at Sinclair's Ranch (Lower Station), for 1914.

(Drainage area 366 square miles.)

MONTH.	DISCHARGE IN SECOND-FEET.				RUN-OFF.	
	Maximum.	Minimum.	Mean.	Per square Mile.	Depth in inches on Drainage Area.	Total in Acre-feet.
April	210.0	30.00	102.00	0.280	0.310	6,069
May	37.0	12.80	22.00	0.060	0.070	1,371
June	45.0	8.80	1.86	0.050	0.060	1,107
July	11.9	0.40	2.90	0.008	0.009	180
August	4.9	Nil	1.08	0.003	0.004	66
September	64.0	2.70	14.10	0.038	0.040	839
October	94.0	7.60	33.00	0.091	0.010	2,041
The period	....	....	....	....	0.503	11,673

SWIFTCURRENT CREEK NEAR SWIFT CURRENT (UPPER STATION).

Location.—On the SW. ¼ Sec. 12, Tp. 15, Rge. 14, W. 3rd Mer., above the city of Swift Current's water-supply dam.

Records available.—January 16, 1914, to December 31, 1914.

Gauge.—Vertical staff at old section; zero elevation 91.72 feet since establishment. Vertical staff at weir; zero elevation 89.90 feet since establishment. Crest of weir at elevation 98.58 feet.

Bench-mark.—On top of a pile at upstream face of left abutment, marked D.*I.*; assumed elevation, 100 00 feet. Bench-mark for weir measurements on granite rock on left bank; assumed elevation, 100 00 feet.

Channel.—Pérmanent.

Discharge measurements.—At high stages from bridge; at low stages by wading or by weir.

Winter flow.—Affected by ice.

Observer.—Mrs. Mackintosh.

DISCHARGE MEASUREMENTS of Swiftcurrent Creek near Swift Current (Upper Station), in 1914.

Date.	Engineer.	Width.	Area of Section.	Mean Velocity.	Gauge Height.	Discharge.
		Feet.	*Sq. ft.*	*Ft. per sec.*	*Feet.*	*Sec.-ft.*
Jan. 16	F. R. Steinberger	4.7	3 25	0.46	3.00	1.48
Feb. 6	do				2.36	a
Feb. 25	do	6.5	2.88	0.51	2.90	1.47
Mar. 19	do	64.0	74.80	1.59	4.78	119.00
May 4	W. H. Storey.	66.0	111.00	0.60	2.63	66.00
June 12	do	68.0	111.00	0.39	2.55	45.00
July 7	do	35.5	21.19	0.83	2.35	17.60
Aug. 4	do	17.0	4.60	0.11	1.86	0.52
Sept. 3	do	6.0	2.60	0.82	1.98	2.10
Oct. 5	F. R. Steinberger	40.5	38.20	0.69	2.48	26.00
Nov. 12	do	7.9	8.97	2.97	2.41	24.00
Nov. 16	do	9.7	8.18	1.47	2.31	12.10
Dec. 2	J. E. Caughey	36.0	33.60	0.70	2.54	24.00
Dec. 21	do	30.0	15.50	0.43	9.34	6.60

a Frozen solid.

5 GEORGE V, A. 1915

DAILY GAUGE HEIGHT AND DISCHARGE of Swiftcurrent Creek near Swift Current (Upper Station), for 1914.

DAY.	January.		February.		March.		April.		May.		June.	
	Gauge Height	Dis-charge	Gauge Height.	Dis-charge.	Gauge Height	Dis-charge.	Gauge Height.	Dis-charge	Gauge Height.	Dis-charge.	Gauge Height.	Dis-charge.
	Feet.	*Sec.-ft.*	*Feet.*	*Sec.-ft.*	*Feet.*	*Sec.-ft.*	*Feet.*	*Sec.-ft.*	*Feet.*	*Sec.-ft.*	*Feet.*	*Sec.-ft.*
1			2 65	0 50	3.21	4.0	4.70	200 0	2.56a	48 0	2 31	15.3
2			2 60	0.40	3.31	5.3	4.85	215.0	2.58a	52.0	2.27	11 5
3			2.55	0.30	3.36	6.6	5 00	268.0	2.60a	57.0	2 30	7.9
4			2 50	0 20	3 56	8 0	5 00	270.0	2.63	67.0	2.30	7 9
5			2.45	0 07	3 91	9 2	6 00	240.0	2.63	67.0	2.35	13 0
6			2.36	0.01	4.01	10.5	6.50	370 0	2.62	64.0	2.43	25.0
7			2.31	0.01	4.31	11.7	6.82	360 0	2.64	71.0	2.50	34.0
8			2.21	0.08	4.61	13.0	6.70	360.0	2.63	67.0	2.45	27.0
9			2.16	0.19	4.71	14.4	6.70	390.0	2.61	60 0	2.45	27 0
10			2.11	0.39	4.61	15.7	6.75	325.0	2 59	55 0	2 45	27.0
11			2 01	0.65	4.66	35.0	6.70	320.0	2.61	60.0	2.44	26 0
12			3 76	1 10	5.01	54 0	6.50	285.0	2.63	67.0	2.55	45 0
13			4.01	1 50	5 31	77.0	6.00	310.0	2.63	67.0	2.46	28 0
14			4.01	1 84	5.21	92 0	5.81	310 0	2.59	53.0	2.51	36 0
15			3.31	2.00	5.26	104 0b	5.25	290 0	2.54	43.0	2.54	43 0
16	3 01	1 48b	3 21	2 00	4.75	119.0	4.95	290 0	2 53	41.0	2.50	34 0
17	3 01	1.40	3.11	2.00	4.10	220 0c	4.38	240 0	2.53	41.0	2.50	34 0
18	3.01	1.30	3 01	1.93	4.30	330 0	4.15	255.0	2.52	39.0	2.49	33 0
19	3.00	1.20	3 01	1.74	4.15	328 0	3.95	255 0	2.52	39 0	2.48	31 0
20	2.90	1 07	2.96	1.52	4 64	340.0	3 52	220 0	2.49	33 0	2.47	30 0
21	2 90	0 97	2.91	1.45	4.99	270 0	3.10	165 0	2 49	33.0	2.47	30 0
22	2.71	0.90	2 91	1.40	5 30	260 0	3 00	150 0c	2.49	33.0	2.48	31 0
23	2.71	0 82	3 01	1 40	4 90	185 5	2 70	92 0	2.47	30.0	2.48	31 0
24	2 71	0 77	3.06	1 45	4.70	180 0	2 68	85.0	2.44	26.0	2 48	31.0
25	2 62	0.73	3 01	1.50	4.70	170 0	2 55	42 0	2.42	23.0	2.48	31 0
26	2.62	0 71	3 01	1.60	4 90	160 0	2 45	27 0	2 39	20.0	2 48	31 0
27	2.73	0 70	3 11	1.80	4.50	150.0	2 36	17.6	2 38	19.2	2.48	31 0
28	2 72	0 68	3.16	2.50	4 40	150.0	2.40a	21.0	2.34	16.1	2.47	30.0
29	2 76	0.66			4 40	140 0	2 44a	26.0	2.34	16.1	2.47	30 0
30	2 71	0 62			4.35	130.0	2.48a	31.0	2.33	15.3	2.46	28 0
31	2.66	0 57			4 50	140.0			2.33	15 3		

a Gauge height interpolated.
b Ice conditions Jan. 16 to March 16.
c Discharge estimated March 17 to April 22.

SESSIONAL PAPER No. 25c

DAILY GAUGE HEIGHT AND DISCHARGE of Swiftcurrent Creek near Swift Current (Upper Station), for 1914.

DAY.	July. Gauge Height.	July. Dis- charge.	August. Gauge Height.	August. Dis- charge	September. Gauge Height.	September. Dis- charge	October. Gauge Height.	October. Dis- charge	November. Gauge Height	November. Dis- charge	December. Gauge Height.	December. Dis- charge.
	Feet.	*Sec.-ft.*	*Feet.*	*Sec.-ft.*	*Feet.*	*Sec.-ft.*	*Feet.*	*Sec.-ft.*	*Feet.*	*Sec.-ft.*	*Feet.*	*Sec.-ft.*
1.	2.45	27.0	1 94	1.60	1.97	2.05	2.32	14 5	2.37	18.4	2.69	24.0
2.	2 44	26.0	1 91	1 15	1 99	2 40	2.31	13 8	2.36	17.6	2.63	24.0
3.	2.42	23 0	1 89	0.95	2.02	3.00	2.32	14 5	2.36	17.6	2.60	23.0
4.	2 40	20.7	1.86	0 80	2.01	2.70	2.37	18.4	2 36	17.6	2.58	22.0
5.	2.37	18.4	1 84	0 70	1 99	2.30	2.46	28.0	2.37	18.4	2.55	20.0
6.	2 36	17.6	1.83	.65	1.98	2.20	2.48	31.0	2.38	19.2	2.57	18 8
7.	2.33	15.3	1.81	.55	1.97	2 00	2.49	33 0	2 40	21.0	2.57	17.3
8.	2.31	13.8	1.78	.46	1.96	1.90	2.52	39.0	2.41	22 0	2.58	16.4
9.	2.28	12 0	1.76	0.42	1.96	1.90	2.57	50.0	2 36	17.6	2.58	15 6
10.	2 27	11.5	1.73	0 36	1 97	2.00	2.58	52.0	2.38	19.2	2.59	14.2
11.	2.24	9.9	1.70	.30	1.97	2.00	2.61	61 0	2.41	22.0	2.60	12 2
12.	2.22	8.9	1.67	.27	1.98	2.20	2.65	74.0	2.38	19.2	2.60	9.0
13.	2.20	7.9	1 65	.25	2 03	3 20	2.71	96.0	2.37	18.4	2.60	7.0
14.	2.18	7.3	1 63	0.23	2.53	41.00	2 75	111.0	2.36	17.6	2.60	6.8
15.	2.15	6 4	1.61	0.21	2.60	57.00	2.72	100.0	2.34	16.1	2.61	6.7
16.	2.14	.0	1.59	.19	2.62	64 00	2.71	96 0	2.31	12.1	2.61	6.9
17.	2.14	0	1.57	.17	2.66	78 00	2.66	78.0	2.30	12.7	2.62	8.0
18.	2.13	.7	1.56	.16	2.69	88 00	2.61	60.0	2.28	13 3	2 62	8.5
19.	2.13	.7	1.56	0.16	2 71	96.00	2.57	50.0	2 28	15 5	2.63	8.0
20.	2.12	6.4	1.54	0.14	2.68	85.00	2.52	39 0	2.31	19.5	2.63	7.0
21.	2.12	.4	1.52	.12	2.64	71 00	2.50	34.0	2 35	21.0	9.34d	6 9
22.	2.11	.1	1.51	.11	2.62	64.00	2.47	30 0	2.41	22.0	9.40	7.8
23.	2.08	.3	1.50	10	2.58	52 00	2.46	29 0	2.47	23 0	9 40	7.8
24.	2.07	.1	1.50	0.10	2.53	41.00	2.45	27 0	2.52	25.0	9.39	7 7
25.	2.05	5.6	1.50	0.10	2.48	31.00	2.45	27.0	2.54	27.0	9 39	7.7
26.	2.03	3.2	1.57	0 17	2.44	26 00	2.45	27.0	2.65	28.0	9.35	7.1
27.	2.02	3.0	1.74	0.38	2.41	22 00	2.44	26 0	2.65	28 0	9.35	7.1
28.	2.01	2.7	1 83	0 65	2.38	19 20	2.44	26.0	2.65	27.0	9 30	6.3
29.	2.00	2.5	1 92	1.30	2.35	16 80	2.43	25 0	2.68	26.0	9.30	6.3
30.	1.99	2 3	1 96	1.90	2.34	16.10	3 42	23.0	2 67	25.0	9.35	7.1
31.	1.98	2 2	1.97	2 00	....	....	2 40	21.0	....	....	9.40d	7.7

d to *d* Weir measurements—new rod.

MONTHLY DISCHARGE of Swiftcurrent Creek near Swift Current (Upper Station), for 1914.
(Drainage area 995 square miles.)

MONTH.	DISCHARGE IN SECOND-FEET. Maximum	DISCHARGE IN SECOND-FEET. Minimum.	DISCHARGE IN SECOND-FEET. Mean.	DISCHARGE IN SECOND-FEET. Per square Mile.	RUN-OFF. Depth in inches on Drainage Area.	RUN-OFF. Total in Acre-feet.
January	1.48	0.57	0.91	0.0009	0.0005	29
February	2.50	0.01	1.14	0.0011	0.0011	63
March	340.00	4.00	120.00	0.1210	0.1400	7,378
April	390.00	17.60	214.00	0.2150	0.2400	12,734
May	71.00	15.30	43.00	0.0430	0.0500	2,644
June	45.00	7.90	28.00	0.0280	0.0300	1,666
July	27.00	2.20	9.40	0.0094	0.0010	578
August	2.00	0.10	0.54	0.0005	0.0006	33
September	96.00	1.90	30.00	0.0302	0.0340	1,785
October	111.00	13.80	44.00	0.0442	0.0500	2,705
November	28.00	12.10	20.00	0.0201	0.0200	1,190
December	24.00	6.30	11.40	0.0114	0.0100	701
The year	....	....	....	....	0 5800	31,506

SWIFTCURRENT CREEK NEAR SWIFT CURRENT (LOWER STATION).

Location.—On the NW. ¼ Sec. 18, Tp. 15, Rge. 13, W. 3rd Mer., below the water supply dam of the city of Swift Current.

Records available.—May 5, 1913, to December 31, 1914.

Gauge.—Vertical staff; elevation of zero has been maintained at 87.195 feet since establishment.

No. 25c—27

5 GEORGE V, A. 1915

Bench-mark.—On rock; assumed elevation up to June 11, 1914, 100.00 feet. From June 12, 1914, to December 31, 1914, rock near creek used, with an elevation of 97.24 feet.

Channel.—Permanent.

Discharge measurements.—By wading or from bridge.

Winter flow.—Affected by ice.

Artificial control.—The flow of the creek at this point is affected to some extent by the city water supply dam.

Observer.—Stanley Tite.

DISCHARGE MEASUREMENTS of Swiftcurrent Creek near Swift Current (Lower Station), in 1914.

Date.	Engineer.	Width.	Area of Section.	Mean Velocity.	Gauge Height.	Discharge.
		Feet.	*Sq. feet.*	*Ft. per sec.*	*Feet.*	*Sec.-ft.*
Jan. 17	F. R. Steinberger				0.83	1.92a
Feb. 6	do	5.8	5.2	0.48	1.65	2.50
Feb. 25	do	7.2	2.1	0.66	2.10	1.38
March 16	do	45.0	42.0	2.77	1.92	116.00
May 4	W. H. Storey	55.0	100.0	0.65	1.27	65.00
June 12	do	55.0	96.0	0.46	1.20	44.00
July 7	do	55.0	74.0	0.23	0.84	17.10
Aug. 4	do	11.5	2.7	1.11	0.62	3.00
Sept. 3	do	100.0	2.2	0.62	0.46	1.32
Oct. 5	F. R. Steinberger	29.0	20.6	1.25	1.05	26.00
Nov. 16	do	20.0	10.6	1.07	0.89	11.40
Dec. 2	J. E. Caughey	44.0	50.0	0.71	1.10	35.00
Dec. 21	do	22.0	13.0	0.52	0.59	6.80

a Weir measurement.

DAILY GAUGE HEIGHT AND DISCHARGE of Swiftcurrent Creek near Swift Current (Lower Station), for 1914.

DAY.	January. Gauge Height.	January. Dis- charge.	February. Gauge Height.	February. Dis- charge	March. Gauge Height.	March. Dis- charge	April. Gauge Height.	April. Dis- charge.	May. Gauge Height.	May. Dis- charge.	June Gauge Height.	June Dis- charge.
	Feet.	*Sec.-ft.*	*Feet.*	*Sec.-ft.*	*Feet.*	*Sec.-ft.*	*Feet.*	*Sec.-ft.*	*Feet.*	*Sec.-ft.*	*Feet.*	*Sec.-ft.*
1	1.21	1.05c	0.40a	2.40	3.05	4.0	1.23	55	1 29	71.0	0.93	13.9
2	1.32	1.10	0.50a	2.27	3.04	6.0	1.78	218	1.25	60.0	0.90	15.2
3	1.21	1.12	0.60a	2.24	3.06	7.5	1.94	266	1 25	60 0	0.95	18.4
4	1.20	1.15	1.00a	2.26	3.20	9.0	1.94	266	1.24	58.0	0.95	18.4
5	0.88	1.18	1.42a	2.40	3.19	11 0	2 18	238	1 24	58.0	1.00	22.0
6	0.83	1.20	1.83	2.54	3.16	12.5	2.28	368	1.23	55.0	1.08	29.0
7	0.79	1.25	2.05	2.58	4.05	14.0	2.26	362	1.25	60.0	1.15	40.0
8	0.77	1.30	2.19	2.60	3.70	16.0	2 24	356	1.24	58.0	1.10	32.0
9	0.76	1.35	2.36	2 58	3.80	18.0b	2.34	386	1.22	53.0	1.10	32.0
10	0.79	1.40	2 31	2.50	3.83	20 0	2.14	326	1.20	48.0	1.10	32.0
11	0.81	1.44	2.26	2.42	3.85	30.0	2 12	320	1.22	53.0	1.09	30.0
12	0.85	1.48	2 16	2.30	3.18a	40.0	2.01	287	1.24	58.0	1.20	48.0
13	0.82	1.51	1.96	2.23	2.16a	50.0	2.09	311	1.24	58.0	1.15	40.0
14	0.72	1.60	1.92	2.23	2 14a	100 0	2.08	308	1.20	48.0	1.10	32.0
15	0.72	1.70	1.66	2.25	2.16	144.0cb	2 02	290	1.15	40.0	1.09	30.0
16	0.67	1.82	1.63	2.26	3.02	216.0	2.02	290	1.14	38.0	1.65	179.0
17	0.90	1.90	1 66	2.21	2.11	317.0	1.85	239	1.14	38.0	1.00	22.0
18	0.73	1.94	1.53	2.15	2.11	317.0	1 90	254	1.13	37.0	1.45	119.0
19	0.58a	1.96	1 31	2 00	2.20	344.0	1 90	254	1.13	37.0	0.60	3.3
20	0.58	1.98	0.66	1.70	1 94	266.0	1.79	221	1.10	32.0	0.80	9.8
21	0.51	2.01	0.46a	1.45	1.91	257.0	1.60	164	1.10	32.0	1.00	22.0
22	0.48	2.04	1.90a	1 20	1.61	167.0	1.56	152	1.10	32.0	1.20	48.0
23	0.44a	2.10	2.20a	1.20	1.56	152.0	1.55	149	1.08	30.0	0.65	4.4
24	0.32a	2.18	2.70a	1.30	1.48a	128	1.53	143	1.05	27.0	0.60	3.3
25	0.33a	2.28	3.10a	1.40	1.44	116.0	1.49	131	1.03	25.0	0.55	2.4
26	0.37a	2.42	3.05	1.43	1.29	71.0	1.45	119	1.00	22.0	0.65	4.4
27	0.40a	2.50	3.06	1.55	1.20	48.0	1.40	104	0.99	21.0	0.60	3.3
28	0.35a	2.58	3.07	2.10	1.27	66 0	1.38	98	0.95	18.4	0.55	2.4
29	0.30a	2.63			1.27	66.0	1.36	92	0.95	18.4	0.90	15.2
30	0.40a	2.61			1.27	66.0	1.30	74	0.94	17.2	0.84	11.3
31	0.30a	2.51			1.28	68.0			0.94	17.2		

a Interpolated.

b to b Estimated.

c Ice conditions Jan. 1 to March 15.

SESSIONAL PAPER No. 25c

DAILY GAUGE HEIGHT AND DISCHARGE of Swiftcurrent Creek near Swift Current (Lower Station), for 1914.—*Concluded.*

DAY.	July.		August.		September.		October.		November.		December.	
	Gauge Height.	Dis-charge	Gauge Height.	Dis-charge.	Gauge Height.	Dis-charge.	Gauge Height.	Dis-charge.	Gauge Height.	Dis-charge.	Gauge Height.	Dis-charge.
	Feet.	*Sec.-ft.*	*Feet.*	*Sec.-ft.*	*Feet.*	*Sec.-ft.*	*Feet.*	*Sec.-ft.*	*Feet.*	*Sec.-ft.*	*Feet.*	*Sec.-ft.*
1	0.85	12.3	0.65	4.40	0.31	0.13	0.87	13.4	1.04	26.0	1.05	36.0
2	0.86	12.9	0.60	3.30	0.31	0.13	0.87	13.4	1.03	25.0	1.05	35.0
3	0.86	12.9	0.63	3.90	0.46	1.27	0.85	12.3	1.02	24.0	1.00	22.0
4	0.85	12.3	0.62	3.70	0.43	0.87	0.95a	18.4	1.00	22.0	0.90	15.6
5	0.90	15.2	0.50	2.40	0.45	1.05	1.05	27.0	1.00	22.0	0.88	14.4
6	0.85	12.3	0.38	0.46	0.45	1.05	1.07	29.0	1.00	22.0	0.86	13.3
7	0.80	9.8	0.36	0.32	0.45	1.05	1.06	28.0	1.00	22.0	0.80	12.1
8	0.78	9.0	0.34	0.22	0.45	1.05	1.05	27.0	1.00	22.0	0.80	12.1
9	0.76	8.1	0.31	0.13	0.49	1.49	1.15	40.0	0.90	15.2	0.82	12.7
10	0.73	7.0	0.31	0.13	0.52	1.92	1.15	40.0	0.96	20.0	0.80	12.1
11	0.70	6.0	0.31	0.13	0.55	2.40	1.17	43.0	1.00	22.0	0.75	10.6
12	0.75	7.7	0.31	0.13	0.60	3.30	1.33	83.0	1.00	22.0	0.70	9.1
13	0.73	7.0	0.31	0.13	0.80a	9.80	1.35	89.0	1.00	22.0	0.70	9.0
14	0.66	4.7	0.31	0.13	1.00	22.00	1.30	74.0	0.90	15.2	0.70	9.0
15	0.60	3.3	0.31	0.13	1.15	40.00	1.25	60.0	0.80	12.0b	0.65	8.5
16	0.60	3.3	0.32	0.16	1.10	32.00	1.25	60.0	0.80	12.0	0.66	7.7
17	0.55	2.4	0.32	0.16	1.35	89.00	1.20	48.0	0.85	14.6	0.60	6.8
18	0.60	3.3	0.32	0.16	1.30	74.00	1.15	40.0	0.85	15.7	0.58	6.5
19	0.63	4.4	0.31	0.13	1.26	63.00	1.10	32.0	0.90	16.5	0.60	6.8
20	0.60	3.3	0.31	0.13	1.15	40.00	1.05	27.0	0.87	15.3	0.60	6.8
21	0.65	4.4	0.30	0.10	1.15	40.00	1.03	25.0	0.87	15.3	0.59	6.8
22	0.65	4.4	0.32	0.16	1.10	32.00	1.05	27.0	0.90	15.7	0.59	6.7
23	0.65	4.4	0.34	0.22	1.05	27.00	1.05	27.0	0.90	16.2	0.60	6.7
24	0.65	4.4	0.38	0.46	1.05	27.00	1.05	27.0	0.90	16.9	0.60a	6.8
25	0.63	3.9	0.36	0.32	0.95	18.40	1.05	27.0	1.00	23.0	0.59	7.0
26	0.60	3.3	0.33	0.19	0.95	18.40	1.05	27.0	1.05	29.0	0.60	7.0
27	0.65	4.4	0.32	0.16	0.95	18.40	1.05	27.0	1.05	32.0	0.57	6.4
28	0.61	3.5	0.31	0.13	0.90	15.20	1.05	27.0	1.10	35.0	0.54	5.8
29	0.60	3.3	0.31	0.13	0.90	15.20	1.04	26.0	1.10	36.0	0.50	5.3
30	0.60	3.3	0.31	0.13	0.88	14.00	1.04	26.0	1.10	36.0	0.50	5.3
31	0.65	4.4	0.31	0.13			1.04	26.0			0.50	5.3b

a Interpolated.
b Ice conditions Nov. 15 to Dec. 31.

MONTHLY DISCHARGE of Swiftcurrent Creek near Swift Current (Lower Station), for 1914.

(Drainage area 1,000 square miles.)

MONTH.	DISCHARGE IN SECOND-*FEET*.				RUN-OFF.	
	Maximum.	Minimum.	Mean.	Per square Mile.	Depth in inches on Drainage Area.	Total in Acre-feet.
January	2.6	1.05	1.77	0.0018	0.0020	109
February	2.6	1.20	2.07	0.0020	0.0020	115
March	344.0	4.00	102.00	0.1020	0.1200	6,272
April	386.0	55.00	228.00	0.2280	0.2500	13,567
May	71.0	17.20	41.00	0.0410	0.0500	2,521
June	179.0	2.40	29.00	0.0290	0.0300	1,726
July	15.2	2.40	6.50	0.0065	0.0100	400
August	4.4	0.10	0.73	0.0007	0.0008	45
September	89.0	0.13	20.00	0.0200	0.0200	1,190
October	89.0	12.30	35.00	0.0350	0.0400	2,152
November	36.0	12.00	21.00	0.0210	0.0200	1,250
December	36.0	5.30	10.80	0.0110	0.0100	664
The year					0.5550	30,011

5 GEORGE V. A. 1915

ANTELOPE LAKE DRAINAGE BASIN.

General description.

Antelope Lake is a small body of saline water, six miles long and from one to one-and-one-half miles wide, situated at an elevation of 2,300 feet above sea level. It lies in a deep depression north of the main line of the Canadian Pacific Railway, in Township 15, Range 18, West of the 3rd Meridian, and drains an area of about 350 square miles.

The lake receives its supply from Bridge Creek, which rises in the Cypress Hills. The altitude of the source of this creek is 2,800 feet, and it has an average fall of 15 feet per mile.

The valley traversed by Bridge Creek is narrow and quite shallow, rarely exceeding 100 feet in depth. The land lying along the creek bottom is very flat, and liable to become inundated during periods of flood. The bench land is rolling prairie, cut up by innumerable coulees, which drain the surrounding country into the main valley.

The mean annual rainfall amounts to about 14 inches, most of which occurs during May, June and July. The creek has only a small flow, and is dry along most of its course for several months during the year.

BRIDGE CREEK AT RAYMOND'S RANCH.

Location.—On the SE. ¼ of Sec. 33, Tp. 10, Rge. 22, W. 3rd Mer.
Records available.—April 8, 1911, to October 31, 1914.
Gauge.—Vertical staff; the elevation of the zero of the gauge has been maintained at 89.42 feet since establishment.
Bench-mark.—Permanent iron bench-mark; assumed elevation, 100.00 feet.
Discharge measurements.—Made with meter at flood stages, and with weir at ordinary stages.
Winter flow.—This station is not maintained during the winter.
Observer.—Mrs. C. Raymond.

DISCHARGE MEASUREMENTS of Bridge Creek at Raymond's Ranch, in 1914.

Date.	Engineer.	Width.	Area of Section.	Mean Velocity.	Gauge Height.	Discharge.
		Feet.	*Sq. ft.*	*Ft. per sec.*	*Feet.*	*Sec.-ft.*
Mar. 20	H. O. Brown		1.96		0.90	0.50
Mar. 30	do	3.3	1.96	0.64	1.02	1.26
April 1	do	8.1	4.64	0.98	1.22	4.50
April 11	do	3.2	1.72	0.67	0.84	1.16
April 24	F. R. Steinberger				0.69	0.47a
May 16	do				0.55	0.19a
June 15	do				0.53	0.17a
July 6	do				0.41	0.03a
July 29	do					Nil.
Sept. 8	E. W. W. Hughes				0.48	0.09a
Sept. 28	do				0.50	0.11a
Nov. 4	do				0.55	0.22a

a Weir measurement.

SESSIONAL PAPER No. 25c

DAILY GAUGE HEIGHT AND DISCHARGE of Bridge Creek at Raymond's Ranch, for 1914.

DAY.	March.		April.		May.		June.	
	Gauge Height.	Dis- charge.	Gauge Height.	Dis- charge.	Gauge Height.	Dis- charge.	Gauge Height.	Dis- charge.
	Feet.	*Sec.-ft.*	*Feet.*	*Sec.-ft.*	*Feet.*	*Sec.-ft.*	*Feet.*	*Sec.-ft.*
1	2.80	18.60a	1.26	3.20	0.56	0.20	0.40	0.02
2	3.05	21.00	1.18	2.40a	0.54	0.18	0.38	Nil.
3	3.15	22.00	1.10	3.30	0.58	0.23	0.42	0.04
4	3.20	23.00	1.12	3.50	0.60	0.26	0.45	0.07
5	3.15	22.00	1.04	2.80	0.66	0.39	0.53	0.16
6	2.90	19.60	1.08	3.20	0.68	0.44	0.56	0.20
7	3.18	22.00	1.05	2.90	0.69	0.46	0.50	0.12
8	2.90	19.60	1.00	2.40	0.68	0.44	0.58	0.23
9	3.05	21.00	0.98	2.20	0.60	0.26	0.56	0.20
10	3.00	21.00	0.80	0.86	0.63	0.33	0.56	0.20
11	2.85	19.10	0.85	1.17	0.59	0.25	0.58	0.23
12	2.90	19.60	1.05	2.90	0.58	0.23	0.53	0.16
13	2.55	16.10	1.00	2.40	0.56	0.20	0.58	0.23
14	2.60	16.60	0.95	1.93	0.54	0.18	0.53	0.16
15	2.05	11.10	0.98	2.20	0.50	0.12	0.53	0.16
16	1.50	5.60	0.90	1.48	0.55	0.19	0.50	0.12
17	1.80	8.60	0.88	1.36	0.53	0.16	0.48	0.10
18	1.35	4.10	0.83	1.05	0.55	0.19	0.50	0.12
19	1.05	1.35	0.80	0.86	0.53	0.16	0.56	0.20
20	0.88	0.53	0.78	0.78	0.50	0.12	0.55	0.19
21	0.85	0.45	0.70	0.48	0.52	0.15	0.53	0.16
22	0.85	0.45	0.63	0.33	0.48	0.10	0.50	0.12
23	0.85	0.45	0.60	0.26	0.50	0.12	0.50	0.12
24	0.85	0.45	0.69	0.46	0.46	0.08	0.53	0.16
25	0.80	0.32	0.63	0.33	0.43	0.05	0.48	0.10
26	0.80	0.32	0.60	0.26	0.50	0.12	0.47	0.09
27	0.80	0.32	0.63	0.33	0.46	0.08	0.50	0.12
28	0.80	0.32	0.60	0.26	0.43	0.05	0.53	0.16
29	0.80	0.32	0.58	0.23	0.40	0.02	0.51	0.13
30	1.32	3.80	0.56	0.20	0.38	Nil.	0.50	0.12
31	1.80	8.60	....	....	0.40	0.02	....	....

a to *a* Ice conditions.

5 GEORGE V, A. 1915

DAILY GAUGE HEIGHT AND DISCHARGE of Bridge Creek at Raymond's Ranch, for 1914.
—*Concluded.*

DAY.	July.		August.		September.		October.	
	Gauge Height.	Dis- charge.	Gauge Height.	Dis- charge.	Gauge Height.	Dis- charge.	Gauge Height.	Dis- charge.
	Feet.	*Sec.-ft.*	*Feet.*	*Sec.-ft.*	*Feet.*	*Sec.-ft.*	*Feet.*	*Sec.-ft.*
1	0.48	0.10	Dry.	Nil.	0.53	0.16	0.48	0.10
2	0.46	0.08	"	"	0.53	0.16	0.51	0.13
3	0.45	0.07	"	"	0.52	0.15	0.78	0.78
4	0.43	0.05	"	"	0.54	0.18	0.88	1.36
5	0.39	0.01	"	"	0.55	0.19	0.75	0.67
6	0.41	0.03	"	"	0.52	0.15	0.90	1.48
7	0.44	0.06	"	"	0.50	0.12	1.40	6.30
8	0.42	0.04	"	"	0.50	0.12	1.50	7.30
9	0.40	0.02	0.37	"	0.51	0.13	1.20	4.30
10	0.40	0.02	0.37	"	0.48	0.10	1.03	2.70
11	0.38	Nil.	0.40	0.02	0.49	0.11	0.90	1.48
12	0.37	"	0.38	Nil.	0.55	0.19	0.87	1.29
13	0.36	"	0.38	"	0.88	1.36	0.80	0.86
14	Dry.	"	0.39	0.01	1.10	3.30	0.71	0.62
15	0.37	"	0.37	Nil.	0.73	0.59	0.65	0.37
16	0.38	"	0.36	"	0.70	0.48	0.63	0.33
17	0.40	0.02	0.39	0.01	0.68	0.44	0.60	0.26
18	0.36	Nil.	0.41	0.03	0.70	0.48	0.57	0.22
19	0.36	"	0.42	0.04	0.65	0.37	0.56	0.20
20	0.39	0.01	0.43	0.05	0.68	0.44	0.58	0.23
21	Dry.	Nil.	0.41	0.03	0.65	0.37	0.60	0.26
22	"	"	0.43	0.05	0.63	0.33	0.54	0.18
23	0.36	"	0.46	0.08	0.60	0.26	0.55	0.19
24	0.36	"	0.48	0.10	0.62	0.30	0.60	0.26
25	0.36	"	0.46	0.08	0.60	0.26	0.58	0.23
26	Dry.	"	0.47	0.09	0.58	0.23	0.56	0.20
27	"	"	0.45	0.07	0.53	0.16	0.55	0.19
28	"	"	0.49	0.11	0.50	0.12	0.58	0.23
29	"	"	0.52	0.15	0.48	0.10	0.55	0.19
30	"	"	0.55	0.19	0.47	0.09	0.54	0.18
31	"	"	0.57	0.22	....	....	0.55	0.19

MONTHLY DISCHARGE of Bridge Creek at Raymond's Ranch, for 1914.

(Drainage area 6 square miles.)

MONTH.	DISCHARGE IN SECOND-FEET.				RUN-OFF.	
	Maximum.	Minimum	Mean.	Per square Mile.	Depth in inches on Drainage Area.	Total in Acre-feet.
March	23.00	0.32	10.60	1.760	2.030	651
April	3.50	0.20	1.53	0.256	0.200	91
May	0.46	....	0.19	0.031	0.040	11
June	0.23	....	0.14	0.023	0.030	8
July	0.10	....	0.02	0.003	0.003	1
August	0.22	....	0.04	0.007	0.008	3
September	3.30	0.09	0.38	0.063	0.070	23
October	7.30	0.10	1.07	0.180	0.210	66
The period	....	....	....	....	2,687	854

BRIDGE CREEK NEAR SKULL CREEK.

Location.—On the NW. ¼ Sec. 12, Tp. 11, Rge. 22, W. 3rd Mer., near Skull Creek post office.

Records available.—August 1, 1909, to October 31, 1914.

Gauge.—Vertical staff; the elevation of the zero of the gauge has been maintained at 87.51 feet since establishment.

Bench-mark.—Permanent iron bench-mark; assumed elevation, 100.00 feet.

Discharge measurements.—Made with meter at high stages, and with weir at ordinary stages.

Winter flow.—This station is not maintained during the winter.

Observer.—J. Mann.

DISCHARGE MEASUREMENTS of Bridge Creek near Skull Creek, in 1914.

Date.	Engineer.	Width.	Area of Section.	Mean Velocity.	Gauge Height.	Discharge.
		Feet.	*Sq. ft.*	*Ft. per sec.*	*Feet.*	*Sec.-ft.*
Mar. 20	H. O. Brown				1.45	0.65a
April 1	do	20.2	31.10	0.69	3.18	22.00
April 11	do	8.1	4.20	0.44	1.82	1.84
April 24	F. R. Steinberger				1.52	0.68b
May 16	do				1.07	Nil.
June 15	do					"
July 6	do					"
July 29	do					"
Sept. 8	E. W. W. Hughes					"
Sept. 28	do					"
Nov. 4	do				0.94	0.05a

a Discharge estimated.
b Weir measurement.

DAILY GAUGE HEIGHT AND DISCHARGE of Bridge Creek near Skull Creek, for 1914.

DAY.	March.		April.		May.	
	Gauge Height.	Dis- charge.	Gauge Height.	Dis- charge.	Gauge Height.	Dis- charge.
	Feet.	*Sec.-ft.*	*Feet.*	*Sec.-ft.*	*Feet.*	*Sec.-ft.*
1			3.18	22.00	1.36	0.39
2			2.30	6.30	1.35	0.38
3			2.20	5.10	1.25	0.25
4			2.50	9.40	1.18	0.19
5			2.35b	7.00	1.20	0.20
6			2.20	5.10	1.44	0.53
7			1.94	2.60	1.40	0.45
8			1.78	1.65	1.39	0.44
9			1.70	1.25	1.35	0.38
10			1.52	0.70	1.34b	0.36
11			1.82	1.87	1.34	0.36
12			1.86b	2.10	1.34	0.36
13	3.83	33.00	1.90	2.40	1.29	0.29
14	4.44	44.00	1.92	2.50	1.26	0.26
15	3.98	36.00	2.00	3.10	1.20	0.20
16	3.70	31.00	2.14	4.40	1.07	0.14
17	3.20	22.00	1.80	1.75	1.05b	0.12
18	2.35	7.00	1.75	1.50	1.04	0.12
19	1.74	1.45	1.76b	1.55	1.02	0.11
20	1.45	0.55	1.78	1.65	0.98	0.09
21	1.45	0.55	1.77	1.60	0.94	0.07
22	1.38	0.46	1.80	1.75	0.90	0.05
23	1.34a	0.36	1.62	0.97	0.85	0.02
24		Nil.	1.52	0.70	0.81b	Nil.
25			1.48	0.61	0.78	"
26		"	1.49b	0.63	0.77	"
27		"	1.50	0.65	0.77	"
28		"	1.46	0.57	0.76	"
29		"	1.37	0.40	0.76	"
30	a	"	1.37	0.40	Dry c	"
31	2.69	12.70			"	"

a to a Channel frozen.
b Gauge height interpolated.
c Dry to Oct. 31.

5 GEORGE V, A. 1915

MONTHLY DISCHARGE of Bridge Creek near Skull Creek, for 1914.

(Drainage area 15 square miles.)

MONTH.	DISCHARGE IN SECOND-FEET.				RUN-OFF.	
	Maximum.	Minimum.	Mean.	Per square Mile.	Depth in inches on Drainage Area.	Total in Acre-feet.
March (13-31).........................	44.00	0.00	10.00	0.663	0.47	375
April..............................	22.00	0.40	3.10	0.205	0.23	183
May...............................	0.53	0.00	0.19	0.012	0.01	11
June..............................	....	....	....	....	....	Nil.
July..............................	....	....	....	....	....	"
August............................	....	....	....	....	....	"
September	....	....	....	....	....	"
October...........................	....	....	....	....	....	"
The period....	....	....	....	....	0.71	569

BRIDGE CREEK AT GULL LAKE.

Location.—On highway bridge on the SE. ¼ Sec. 23, Tp. 13, Rge. 19, W. 3rd Mer., near the Canadian Pacific Railway station.
Records available.—March 29, 1911, to December 31, 1914.
Gauge.—Staff; zero of gauge has been maintained at 95.63 feet since establishment.
Bench-mark.—Permanent iron bench-mark; assumed elevation, 100.00 feet.
Channel.—Permanent.
Discharge measurements.—From bridge, or by wading, at station.
Winter flow.—No winter observations have been taken.
Observer.—J. R. Gaskell.

DISCHARGE MEASUREMENTS of Bridge Creek at Gull Lake, in 1914.

Date.	Engineer.	Width.	Area of Section.	Mean Velocity.	Gauge Height.	Discharge.
		Feet.	*Sq. ft.*	*Ft. per sec.*	*Feet.*	*Sec.-ft.*
Mar. 18..........	F. R. Steinberger.	3.9	1.26	0.21	0.75	0.29
Mar. 18...........	do	13.0	5.07	0.66	1.05	3.35
May 5....	W. H. Storey................	....	....	....	Dry.	Nil.
June 13.	do	12.0	6.60	0.22	0.65	1.45
July 8...........	do	....	....	....	Dry.	Nil.
Aug. 4...........	do	....	....	....	"	"
Sept. 4..........	do	....	....	....	"	"

SESSIONAL PAPER No. 25c

DAILY GAUGE HEIGHT AND DISCHARGE of Bridge Creek at Gull Lake, for 1914.

DAY.	March.		April.		May.		June.	
	Gauge Height.	Dis- charge.	Gauge Height.	Dis- charge.	Gauge Height.	Dis- charge.	Gauge Height.	Dis- charge.
	Feet.	*Sec.-ft.*	*Feet.*	*Sec.-ft.*	*Feet.*	*Sec.-ft.*	*Feet.*	*Sec.-ft.*
1	.. ..	....	1.14	....	Dry.	Nil.	Dry.	Nil.
2	.. ..	....	1.24	....	"	"	"	"
3		....	1.02	....	"	"	"	"
4		....	1.01a	....	"	"	"	"
5		....	1.00	5.50c	"	"	"	"
6		....	0.96	4.90	"	"	"	"
7	.....	....	0.95	4.80	"	"	"	"
8		....	0.75	2.40	"	"	"	"
9		....	0.63	1.44	"	"	"	"
10		....	0.56	1.12	"	"	"	"
11	.	....	0.52	0.84	"	"	1.59	21.00
12	.. ..	....	0.47	0.58	"	"	0.70	2.00
13		....	0.42	0.38	"	"	0.44	0.46
14		....	0.36	0.22	"	"	Dry.	Nil.
15		....	0.31	0.12	"	"	"	" d
16		....	0.28	Nil.	"	"	"	"
17		....	0.27	"	"	"	"	"
18	0.66	.....b	0.24	"	"	"	"	"
19	0.85		0.24	"	"	"	"	"
20	0.85		0.33	0.16	"	"	"	"
21	0.78	....	0.34	0.18	"	"	"	"
22	0.80	....	0.30	0.10	"	"	"	"
23	0.80	....	0.30	Nil.	"	"	"	"
24	0.80	....	0.28	"	"	"	"	"
25	0.82a	....	0.28	"	"	"	"	"
26	0.84a	....	0.34	0.18	"	"	"	"
27	0.86a	....	0.32	0.14	"	"	"	"
28	0.88a	....	0.29	Nil.	"	"	"	"
29	0.90a	....	0.26	"	"	"	"	"
30	0.92	....	0.24	"	"	"	"	"
31	0.93	....	....	....	"	"	"	"

a Interpolated.
b to *c* Ice conditions—insufficient data to compute discharge.
d Creek dry from June 14 to end of year.

MONTHLY DISCHARGE of Bridge Creek at Gull Lake, for 1914.

(Drainage area 213 square miles.)

MONTH.	DISCHARGE IN SECOND-FEET.				RUN-OFF.	
	Maximum.	Minimum.	Mean.	Per square Mile.	Depth in inches on Drainage Area.	Total in Acre-feet.
April	5.5	....	0.77	0 0036	0 004	46
May		....			....	Nil.
June	21.0	....	0.78	0 0037	0 004	46
July		....			....	Nil.
August		....			....	"
September		....			....	"
October		....			....	"
The period	....	....	....	....	0 008	92

5 GEORGE V, A. 1915

Miscellaneous Discharge Measurements made in Antelope Lake drainage basin, in 1914.

Date.	Engineer.	Stream.	Location.	Dis-charge.
				Sec.-ft.
April 30....	M. H. French ..	Spring No. 2...........	NE. 27-12-19-3............	0.072
May 11............	do	do 1...........	NW. 32-12-18-3..........	0.124
May 11............	do	do 2...........	NE. 27-12-19-3............	0.065
May 11............	do	do 2...........	NE. 27-12-19-3............	0.071
May 11......,.....	do	do 2...........	NE. 27-12-19-3............	0.074
May 11............	do	do 3....	SW. 27-12-19-3............	0.020
June 15..	W. H. Storey.	do 1...........	NW. 32-12-18-3..........	0.105
June 15............	do	do 2........	NE. 27-12-19-3............	0.065
June 15....	do	do 3...........	SW. 27-12-19-3............	0.004
July 8............	do	do 1...........	NW. 32-12-18-3..........	0.010
July 8............	do	do 2...........	NE. 27-12-19-3............	0.041
July 8............	do	do 2...........	SW. 27-12-19-3............	Nil.
Aug. 5............	do	do 1...........	NW. 32-12-18-3..........	"
Aug. 5............	do	do 2....	NE. 27-12-19-3............	0.018
Aug. 5............	do	do 3...........	SW. 27-12-19-3............	Nil.
Sept. 4............	do	do 1...........	NW. 32-12-18-3..........	0.020
Sept. 4............	do	do 2	NE. 27-12-19-3............	0.064
Sept. 4............	do	do 3....	SW. 27-12-19-3............	Nil.
Nov. 25..........	J. E. Caughey...... ..	do 1...........	NW. 32-12-18-3..........	0.180
Nov. 26............	do	do 2...........	NE. 27-12-19-3............	0.079
Nov. 26....	do	do 3...........	SW. 27-12-19-3............	Nil.
Dec. 19............	do	do 1....	NW. 32-12-18-3..........	0.161
Dec. 19............	do	do 3...........	SW. 27-12-19-3............	Nil.
Dec. 20............	do	do 2...........	NE. 27-12-19-3............	0.094

Note.—All the above are Weir measurements.

LAKE OF THE NARROWS DRAINAGE BASIN.

Description.

Lake of the Narrows is a small lake, three miles long and one and a half miles wide, in Township 3, Range 23, West of the 3rd Meridian. It has a drainage area of about 200 square miles.

The principal stream in the basin is Skull Creek, which rises in the eastern slope of Cypress Hills. It flows through a narrow valley for the greater part of its course, but, as it nears the lake, the valley widens out into large meadows. The surrounding country is rolling prairie.

In very dry years, such as 1910 and 1914, Skull Creek goes dry for a short time. The mean annual precipitation in the drainage basin is about 13 inches.

SKULL CREEK AT DOYLE'S RANCH.

Location.—On the NE. ¼ Sec. 29, Tp. 10, Rge. 22, W. 3rd Mer., near Skull Creek post office.

Records available.—April 8, 1911, to October 31, 1914.

Gauge.—Vertical staff; the elevation of the zero of the gauge was maintained at 87.20 feet during 1911; 86.82 feet during 1912-14.

Bench-mark.—Permanent iron bench-mark; assumed elevation, 100.00 feet.

Discharge measurements.—Made with meter, and with weir at low stages.

Winter flow.—This station is not maintained during the winter.

Artificial control.—A control for the gauge was constructed at this station during August, 1913, and is still in good repair. The flood of April did very little damage to the control itself, but washed the east bank behind the abutment. This was repaired on April 24th.

Observer.—Thos. Doyle.

DISCHARGE MEASUREMENTS of Skull Creek at Doyle's Ranch, for 1914.

Date.	Engineer.	Width.	Area of Section.	Mean Velocity.	Gauge Height.	Discharge.
		Feet.	*Sq. ft.*	*Ft. per sec.*	*Feet.*	*Sec.-ft.*
Mar. 19............	H. O. Brown........	12.0	6.11	1.03	2.10	6.30
Mar. 23............	do	8.6	3.88	0.75	1.96	2.80
Mar. 30............	do	8.5	3.31	0.67	1.82	2.20
April 1............	do	16.2	19.00	2.18	2.59	41.40
April 2............	do	14.4	12.80	1.65	2.34	21.00
April 11.	do	10.5	6.32	1.59	1.99	10.00
April 24............	F. R. Steinberger............	15.3	7.79	0.73	1.84	5.70
May 16............	do	14.3	6.57	0.44	1.84	2.90
June 16............	do	14.9	5.96	0.27	1.75	1.60
July 6............	do	....	....	....	1.60	0.30a
July 29............	do	....	....	....	....	Nil.
Sept. 7............	E. W. W. Hughes... ...	....	....	....	1.64	0.17a
Sept. 29............	do	....	....	....	1.71	0.33a
Nov. 4............	do	....	....	....	1.77	0.83a

a Weir measurement.

DAILY GAUGE HEIGHT AND DISCHARGE of Skull Creek at Doyle's Ranch, for 1914.

DAY.	March.		April.		May.		June.	
	Gauge Height.	Dis-charge.	Gauge Height.	Dis-charge.	Gauge Height.	Dis-charge.	Gauge Height.	Dis-charge.
	Feet.	*Sec.-ft.*	*Feet.*	*Sec.-ft.*	*Feet.*	*Sec.-ft.*	*Feet.*	*Sec.-ft.*
1............	....	....	2.59	41.0	1.93	5.50	1.72a	1.10
2............	....	....	2.34	23.0	1.94	5.80	1.70	0.80
3............	....	....	2.39	26.0	1.94a	5.80	1.70a	0.80
4............	....	....	2.34	23.0	1.94	5.80	1.71a	0.95
5............	....	....	2.74	55.0	1.95	6.10	1.71	0.95
6............	....	....	2.49	32.0	1.96	6.40	1.72	1.10
7............	....	....	2.44	29.0	2.10	10.60	1.73	1.25
8............	....	....	2.39	26.0	2.05	9.00	1.71	0.95
9............	....	....	2.17a	16.1	2.04	8.70	1.70	0.80
10............	....	....	1.96	9.1	2.06	9.30	1.72	1.10
11............	....	....	2.01	10.5	2.00a	7.50	1.72	1.10
12............	....	....	2.29	21.0	1.95	6.10	1.73	1.25
13............	2.30	2.0b	2.24a	18.7	1.94	5.80	1.73	1.25
14............	2.10	3.0	2.19a	16.8	1.90	4.70	1.74a	1.40
15............	2.18a	4.0	2.13	14.7	1.87a	4.00	1.76	1.73
16............	2.24a	5.0	2.08	12.9	1.84	3.30	1.75	1.55
17............	2.30	6.0	1.98	9.6	1.82	2.90	1.70	0.80
18............	2.20a	6.0	1.93	8.2	1.84	3.30	1.71	0.95
19............	2.10	6.3	1.97a	9.4	1.85	3.50	1.72	1.10
20............	2.00	5.0	2.01	10.5	1.91	5.00	1.72	1.10
21............	2.10	4.0	1.98	9.6	1.82	2.90	1.73	1.25
22............	1.96	3.0	1.93	8.2	1.85	3.50	1.72	1.10
23............	1.96	2.8	1.87	6.6	1.82	2.90	1.71a	0.95
24............	1.90	2.0	1.92	8.0	1.82	2.90	1.70	0.80
25............	....	2.0	1.86	3.7	1.80	2.40	1.70	0.80
26............	....	2.0	1.96	6.4	1.78a	2.10	1.70	0.80
27............	....	2.0	1.98	6.9	1.76	1.73	1.68	0.58
28............	....	2.0	1.97	6.7	1.75	1.55	1.65	0.25
29............	1.83	2.0	1.93	5.5	1.74	1.40	1.65	0.25
30............	1.82	2.2b	1.96	6.4	1.74	1.40	1.65	0.25
31............	2.70	51.0	....		1.72a	1.10	....	

a Gauge height interpolated.
b Ice conditions March 13 to 30; discharge estimated.

5 GEORGE V, A. 1915

DAILY GAUGE HEIGHT AND DISCHARGE of Skull Creek at Doyle's Ranch, for 1914.—*Concluded.*

DAY.	July.		August.		September.		October.	
	Gauge Height.	Dis-charge.	Gauge Height.	Dis-charge.	Gauge Height.	Dis-charge.	Gauge Height.	Dis-charge.
	Feet.	Sec.-ft.	Feet.	Sec.-ft.	Feet.	Sec.-ft.	Feet.	Sec.-ft.
1	1.64a	0.20	Dry.	Nil.	1.71a	0.95	1.72	1.10
2	1.64	0.20	"	"	1.70	0.80	1.72	1.10
3	1.64a	0.20	"	"	1.70	0.80	1.72	1.10
4	1.64a	0.20	"	"	1.78	2.10	1.78a	2.10
5	1.64	0.20	"	"	1.77a	1.91	1.85	3.50
6	1.66	0.36	"	"	1.76a	1.73	1.90	4.70
7	1.66a	0.36	"	"	1.65	0.25	2.10	10.60
8	1.66a	0.36	"	"	1.65	0.25	2.35	20.00
9	1.66	0.36	"	"	1.65	0.25	2.40	23.00
10	1.64	0.20	"	"	1.65a	0.25	2.35	20.00
11	1.64	0.20	"	"	1.65	0.25	2.12a	11.30
12	1.64	0.20	"	"	1.65a	0.25	1.90	4.70
13	1.64	0.20	"	"	1.95	6.10	1.90	4.70
14	1.64a	0.20	"	"	2.00	7.50	1.87a	4.00
15	1.64a	0.20	"	"	1.86	3.70	1.85	3.50
16	1.64	0.20	"	"	1.80	2.40	1.80	2.40
17	1.64	0.20	"	"	1.75	1.55	1.80a	2.40
18	1.64	0.20	"	"	1.75	1.55	1.80	2.40
19	1.65	0.25	"	"	1.72	1.10	1.82	2.90
20	Dry.	Nil.	"	"	1.74	1.40	1.80	2.40
21	"	"	"	"	1.72	1.10	1.78	2.10
22	"	"	"	"	1.72	1.10	1.75	1.55
23	"	"	"	"	1.72a	1.10	1.75	1.55
24	"	"	"	"	1.72	1.10	1.75	1.55
25	"	"	1.64	0.20	1.72a	1.10	1.75	1.55
26	"	"	1.65	0.25	1.71a	0.95	1.75	1.55
27	"	"	1.65	0.25	1.70a	0.80	1.75	1.55
28	"	"	1.68	0.58	1.70	0.80	1.75	1.55
29	"	"	1.68	0.58	1.71	0.95	1.75	1.55
30	"	"	1.80	2.40	1.71	0.95	1.75	1.55
31	"	"	1.73	1.25	....	....	1.75	1.55

a Gauge height interpolated.

MONTHLY DISCHARGE of Skull Creek at Doyle's Ranch, for 1914.

(Drainage area 19 square miles.)

MONTH.	DISCHARGE IN SECOND-FEET.				RUN-OFF.	
	Maximum.	Minimum.	Mean.	Per square Mile.	Depth in inches on Drainage Area.	Total in Acre-feet.
March (13-31)	51.00	2.00	5.91	0.311	0.220	223
April	55.00	3.70	16.02	0.843	0.940	952
May	10.60	1.10	4.60	0.243	0.280	283
June	1.73	0.25	0.97	0.051	0.060	58
July	0.36	....	0.14	0.008	0.009	9
August	2.40	....	0.18	0.009	0.010	11
September	7.50	0.25	1.50	0.079	0.090	89
October	23.00	1.10	4.70	0.247	0.280	289
The period	....	....	....	....	1.889	1,914

SESSIONAL PAPER No. 25c

SKULL CREEK NEAR SKULL CREEK.

Location.—On the NW. ¼ Sec. 10, Tp. **11,** Rge. 22, W. 3rd Mer., near Skull Creek post office.
Records available.—July 1, 1908, to October 31, 1914.
Gauge.—Vertical staff; the elevation of the zero of the gauge has been maintained at 88.41 feet since establishment.
Bench-mark.—Permanent iron bench-mark; assumed elevation, 100.00 feet.
Discharge measurements.—Made with meter, and by weir at low stages.
Winter flow.—This station is not maintained during the winter.
Observer.—J. Mann.

DISCHARGE MEASUREMENTS of Skull Creek near Skull Creek, in 1914.

Date.	Engineer.	Width.	Area of Section.	Mean Velocity.	Gauge Height.	Discharge.
		Feet.	*Sq. ft.*	*Ft. per sec.*	*Feet.*	*Sec.-ft.*
Mar. 20	H. O. Brown	9.7	11.20	0.37	2.57	4.10
April 1	do	37.7	63.20	0.80	4.56	51.00
April 11	do	10.4	13.30	0.69	1.73	9.20
April 24.	F. R. Steinberger. . . .	10.0	6.79	0.63	1.06	4.30
May 16.	do	7.5	3.93	0.57	0.74	2.20
June 15.	do				0.70	1.35*a*
July 7.	do					Nil.
July 20.	do					"
Sept. 8.	E. W. W. Hughes. . ·					"
Sept. 28.	do				0.32	0.22*a*
Nov. 4	do	8.1	3.78	0.34	0.62	1.28

a Weir measurement.

DAILY GAUGE HEIGHT AND DISCHARGE of Skull Creek near Skull Creek, for 1914.

DAY.	March.		April.		May.		June.	
	Gauge Height.	Dis-charge.	Gauge Height.	Dis-charge.	Gauge Height.	Dis-charge.	Gauge Height.	Dis-charge.
	Feet.	*Sec.-ft.*	*Feet.*	*Sec.-ft.*	*Feet.*	*Sec.-ft.*	*Feet.*	*Sec.-ft.*
1.			4 56	46 0	0.84	2.50	0.43	0.62
2.			3 57	30.0	0.82	2.40	0.42	0.58
3.			3.32	27.0	0.81	2.40	0.50	0.90
4.			3.72	35 0	0.80	2.30	0.65	1.55
5.			3 57*b*	33 0	0.82	2.40	0.70	1.80
6.			3.42	31.0*a*	0.86	2.70	0.78	2.20
7.			2.96	24 0	0.87	2 70	0.54	1.06
8.			3.46	32 0	0.84	2 50	0.52	0.98
9.			2.12	13.2	0.84	2.50	0.56	1.14
10.			2.06	12 6	0.84*b*	2.50	0.60	1.30
11.			1.72	9.2	0.85	2.60	0.60	1.30
12.			1.71*b*	9.1	0.84	2.50	0.61	1.35
13.	3.86	15.90*a*	1.70	9.0	0.83	2.50	0.62	1.40
14.	4.61	26.00	1.71	9.1	0.82	2.40	0.70	1.80
15.	3.90	16.50	1 63	8.4	0.82	2.40	0.70	1.80
16.	3.12 ·	8.40	1.55	7.6	0.86	2.70	0.67	1.65
17.	3.02	7.60	1.62	8.3	0.78*b*	2.20	0.65	1.55
18.	2.82	5.90	1.27	5.4	0.70	1.80	0.64	1.50
19.	2.13	1.60	1.34*b*	5.9	0.69	1.75	0.60	1.30
20.	2.57	4.10	1.42	6.6	0.67	1.65	0.55	1.10
21.	2.52	5.20	1.43	6.6	0.67	1.65	0.51*b*	0.94
22.	2.34*b*	5.60	1.32	5.8	0.66	1.60	0.48	0.82
23.	2.16	5.00	1.17	4.7	0.65	1.55	0.48	0.82
24.	. . . . . .*c*	. . . .	1.06	3.9	0.62*b*	1.40	0.48	0.82
25.	. . . .	. . . .	1.09	4.1	0.60	1.30	0.48	0.82
26.	. . . .	. . . .	1.17	4.7	0.59	1.26	0.48	0.82
27.	. . . .	. . . .	1.12	4.3	0.59	1.26	0.48	0.82
28.	. . . .	. . . .	1.02	3.6	0.54	1.06	0.49*b*	0.86
29.	. . . .	. . . .	0.86	2.7	0.54	1.06	0.50	0.90
30.	. . . . .*c*	. . . .	0.86	2.7	0.52	0.98	0.48	0.82
31.	3.69	30.00	. . . .	. . . .	0.47*b*	0.80	. . . .	

a to *a* Ice conditions.
b Gauge height interpolated.
c to *c* Channel frozen.

5 GEORGE V. A. 1915

DAILY GAUGE HEIGHT AND DISCHARGE of Skull Creek near Skull Creek, for 1914.—*Concluded.*

DAY.	July.		August.		September.		October.	
	Gauge Height.	Dis- charge.	Gauge Height.	Dis- charge.	Gauge Height.	Dis- charge.	Gauge Height.	Dis- charge.
	Feet.	*Sec.-ft.*	*Feet.*	*Sec.-ft.*	*Feet.*	*Sec.-ft.*	*Feet.*	*Sec.-ft.*
1	0.46a	0.74	Dry.	Nil.	Dry.	Nil.	0.37	0.41
2	0.45	0.70	"	"	"	"	0.37	0.41
3	0.40	0.50	"	"	"	"	0.52	0.98
4	Dry.	Nil.	"	"	"	"	0.72a	1.90
5	"	"	"	"	"	"	0.92	3.00
6	"	"	"	"	"	"	0.90	2.90
7	"	"	"	"	"	"	1.39	6.30
8	"	"	"	"	"	"	2.85	22.00
9	"	"	"	"	"	"	2.50	17.60
10	"	"	"	"	"	"	1.57	7.80
11	"	"	"	"	"	"	1.55a	7.60
12	"	"	"	"	"	"	1.53	7.50
13	"	"	"	"	1.55	7.60	1.50	7.20
14	"	"	"	"	1.12	4.30	1.48	7.00
15	"	"	"	"	0.70	1.80	1.42	6.60
16	"	"	"	"	0.57	1.18	1.10	4.20
17	"	"	"	"	0.49	0.86	0.69	1.75
18	"	"	"	"	0.48	0.82	0.67	1.65
19	"	"	"	"	0.48	0.82	0.65	1.55
20	"	"	"	"	0.46a	0.74	0.64	1.50
21	"	"	"	"	0.45	0.70	0.64	1.50
22	"	"	"	"	0.40	0.50	0.63	1.43
23	"	"	"	"	0.34	0.32	0.60	1.30
24	"	"	"	"	0.34	0.32	0.60	1.30
25	"	"	"	"	0.35	0.35	0.59	1.26
26	"	"	"	"	0.38	0.44	0.58	1.22
27	"	"	"	"	0.36	0.38	0.58	1.22
28	"	"	"	"	0.39	0.47	0.58	1.22
29	"	"	"	"	0.38	0.44	0.59a	1.26
30	"	"	"	"	0.38	0.44	0.60	1.30
31	"	"	"	"	....	....	0.64	1.50

a Gauge height interpolated.

MONTHLY DISCHARGE of Skull Creek near Skull Creek, for 1914.

(Drainage area 32 square miles.)

MONTH.	DISCHARGE IN SECOND-FEET.				RUN-OFF.	
	Maximum.	Minimum	Mean.	Per square Mile.	Depth in inches on Drainage Area	Acre-feet.
March (13-31)	30.00	....	6.90	0.217	0.150	261
April	46.00	2.70	13.50	0.422	0.470	803
May	2.70	0.80	1.98	0.062	0.070	122
June	2.20	0.58	1.18	0.037	0.040	70
July	0.74	....	0.06	0.002	0.002	4
August						Nil.
September	7.60		0.75	0.023	0.030	45
October	22.00	0.41	4.00	0.125	0.140	247
The period					0.902	1,552

CRANE LAKE DRAINAGE BASIN.

General Description.

Crane Lake is one of the largest of the lakes which receive their supply from the drainage of the northern slope of the Cypress Hills. It is situated in Township 13, Range 23, West of the 3rd Meridian, and covers an area of 25 square miles.

The lake has no outlet, is shallow, and the water is saline in character. It is fed by Piapot Creek, which rises in the Cypress Hills, flows northeastward, and is joined by the Bear Creek in Section 7, Township 12, Range 22, West of the 3rd Meridian, before it reaches the lake.

The country to the north of the lake is rolling and of little use for agriculture, being the eastern end of a range of sandhills which extend northwestward some 40 miles. South of the lake the country is rolling prairie, which is bare of tree growth except along the creeks, where there is a small growth of willow and shrub. As it gets closer to the hills the country becomes more broken and the tree growth increases; making the ravines and coulees at the head of the creeks natural reservoirs, which regulate the spring run-off considerably.

There are a number of irrigation schemes, in operation and proposed, in this basin, also one or two industrial schemes along the main line of the Canadian Pacific Railway.

The mean annual precipitation of the northern part of the basin is about 12 inches, but in the hills this is exceeded. During the winter season, from November to April, the streams are frozen over.

EAST BRANCH OF BEAR CREEK AT JOHNSON'S RANCH.

Location.—On the SE. ¼ Sec. 21, Tp. 10, Rge. 23, W. 3rd Mer.
Records available.—August 18th, 1909, to October 31, 1914.
Gauge.—Vertical staff; the elevation of the zero of the gauge was maintained at 92.63 feet during 1909, 1910, 1911, 1913 and 1914, and at 92.26 feet during 1912.
Bench-mark.—Permanent iron bench-mark; assumed elevation, 100.00 feet.
Discharge measurements.—Made with meter, and with weir at low stages.
Winter flow.—This station is not maintained during the winter.
Observer.—T. Johnson.

DISCHARGE MEASUREMENTS of *E*ast Branch of Bear Creek at Johnson's Ranch, in 1914.

Date.	Engineer	Width.	Area of Section.	Mean Velocity.	Gauge Height.	Discharge.
		Feet.	*Sq. ft.*	*Ft. per sec.*	*Feet.*	*Sec.-ft.*
Mar. 18	H. O. Brown	12.2	7.70	0.92	1.45	7.20a
Mar. 23	do	10.6	4.89	0.76	1.39	3.70b
Mar. 30	do	8.8	3.86	0.78	3.51	3.00a
April 2	do	15.1	13.05	2.01	1.71	26.00
April 13	do	14.3	12.90	1.88	1.68	24.00
April 23	F. R. Steinberger	11.0	7.88	0.66	1.26	5.20
May 15	do	10.2	4.41	0.69	1.16	3.00
June 15	do	6.9	2.41	0.69	1.12	1.65
July 4	do				0.85	1.52b
July 28	do					Nil.
Sept. 27	E. W. W. Hughes				0.92	0.72b
Nov. 5	do	10.7	4.00	0.49	1.09	1.96

a Ice conditions.
b Weir measurement.

5 GEORGE V, A. 1915

DAILY GAUGE HEIGHT AND DISCHARGE of *E*ast Branch of Bear Creek at Johnson's Ranch, for 1914.

DAY.	March.		April.		May.		June.	
	Gauge Height.	Dis-charge.	Gauge Height.	Dis-charge.	Gauge Height.	Dis-charge.	Gauge Height.	Dis-charge.
	Feet.	*Sec.-ft.*	*Feet.*	*Sec.-ft.*	*Feet.*	*Sec.-ft.*	*Feet.*	*Sec.-ft.*
1	......	......	1.96	10.0	1.21	4.0	1.18	3.40
2	......	......	2.08	26.0	1.22	4.3	1.17	3.30
3	......	......	2.00	35.0	1.20	3.8	1.15	2.90
4	......	......	1.94	40.0a	1.23	4.5	1.19	3.60
5	......	......	2.08	47.0	1.24	4.8	1.21	4.00
6	......	......	1.94	39.0	1.21	4.0	1.23	4.50
7	......	......	1.78	30.0	1.27	5.6	1.21	4.00
8	......	......	1.76	29.0	1.25	5.0	1.20	3.80
9	......	......	1.74	28.0	1.26	5.3	1.19	3.60
10	......	......	1.77	29.0	1.24	4.8	1.20	3.80
11	......	......	1.76	29.0	1.23	4.5	1.18	3.40
12	......	......	1.86	34.0	1.23	4.5	1.21	4.00
13	......	......	1.53	16.4	1.23	4.5	1.20	3.80
14	......	......	1.51	15.4	1.22	4.3	1.18	3.40
15	......	......	1.52	15.9	1.20	3.8	1.16	3.00
16	......	......	1.48	13.8	1.22	4.3	1.12	2.40
17	......	......	1.37	8.9	1.21	4.0	1.10	2.10
18	1.43	6.4a	1.35	8.1	1.22	4.3	1.08	1.90
19	1.61	13.3	1.33	7.9	1.23	4.5	1.07	1.80
20	1.61	12.8	1.35	8.1	1.24	4.8	1.07	1.80
21	1.52	8.6	1.36	8.5	1.22	4.3	1.08	1.90
22	1.52	7.8	1.28	5.8	1.21	4.0	1.06	1.70
23	1.42	4.4	1.29	6.1	1.22	4.3	1.05	1.60
24	1.39	3.5	1.27	5.6	1.22	4.3	1.02	1.30
25	1.49	3.5	1.24	4.8	1.22	4.3	1.04	1.50
26	1.46	3.0	1.28	5.8	1.22	4.3	1.03	1.40
27	1.44	3.0	1.25	5.0	1.21	4.0	1.05	1.60
28	1.46	3.0	1.26	5.3	1.20	3.8	1.07	1.80
29	1.48	3.0	1.25	5.0	1.20	3.8	1.08	1.90
30	1.85	3.0	1.23	4.5	1.18	3.4	1.06	1.70
31	2.04	3.0	......	......	1.18	3.4	......	......

a Ice conditions March 18 to April 4; discharge estimated.

DAILY GAUGE HEIGHT AND DISCHARGE of East Branch of Bear Creek at Johnson's Ranch,
for 1914.

MONTH.	July.		August.		September.		October.	
	Gauge Height.	Dis-charge.	Gauge Height.	Dis-charge.	Gauge Height.	Dis-charge.	Gauge Height.	Dis-charge.
	Feet.	*Sec.-ft.*	*Feet.*	*Sec.-ft.*	*Feet.*	*Sec.-ft.*	*Feet.*	*Sec.-ft*
1	1.02	1.30	Dry.	Nil.	0.87	0.38	1.00	1.10
2	1.03	1.40	"	"	0.88	0.42	1.03	1.40
3	1.01	1.20	"	"	0.87	0.38	1.08	1.90
4	1.01	1.20	"	"	0.84	0 26	1.18	3.40
5	1.00	1.10	"	"	0.86	0 34	1.15	2.90
6	1.09	2.00	"	"	0.88	0.42	1.18	3.40
7	0.97	0.86	"	"	0.89	0.46	1.20	3.80
8	0.95	0.70	"	"	0.90	0.50	1.37	8.90
9	0.92	0.58	"	"	0.92	0.58	1.84	33.00
10	0.85	0.30	"	"	0.91	0.54	1.50	14.80
11	0.85	0.30	"	"	0.93	0.62	1.22	4.30
12	0.83	0.22	"	"	0.94	0.66	1.21	4.00
13	0.81	0.14	"	"	0.88	0.42	1.16	3.00
14	Dry.	Nil.	"	"	0.85	0.30	1.20	3.80
15	0.75	"	"	"	0.83	0.22	1.19	3.60
16	0.85	0.30	"	"	0.78	0.06	1.21	4.00
17	0.82	0.18	"	"	0.73	Nil.	1.18	3.40
18	0.78	0.06	"	"	0.71	"	1.16	3.00
19	0.75	Nil.	"	"	0.73	"	1.15	2.90
20	Dry.	"	"	"	0.73	"	1.18	3.40
21	"	"	"	"	0.70	"	1.19	3.60
22	"	"	"	"	0.66	"	1.17	3.30
23	"	"	"	"	0.63	"	1.19	3.60
24	"	"	"	"	0.60	"	1.18	3.40
25	"	"	0.92	0.58	0.90	0.50	1.16	3.00
26	"	"	0.90	0.50	1.01	1.20	1.17	3.30
27	"	"	0.85	0.30	1.02	1.30	1.18	3.40
28	"	"	0.85	0.30	1.00	1.10	1.16	3.00
29	"	"	0.81	0.14	0.97	0.86	1.17	3.30
30	"	"	0.83	0.22	0.98	0.94	1.16	3.00
31	"	"	0.89	0.46	....	....	1.18	3.40

MONTHLY DISCHARGE of East Branch of Bear Creek at Johnson's Ranch, for 1914.
(Drainage area 22 square miles.)

MONTH.	DISCHARGE IN SECOND-FEET.				RUN-OFF.	
	Maximum.	Minimum.	Mean.	Per square Mile.	Depth in inches on Drainage Area.	Total in Acre-feet.
March (18-31)	13.30	3.00	5.60	0.254	0.130	155
April	47.00	4.50	17.60	0.800	0.890	1,047
May	5.60	3.40	4.30	0.195	0.220	264
June	4.50	1.30	2.70	0.122	0.140	161
July	2.00	....	0.38	0.017	0.020	23
August	0.58	....	0.08	0.004	0.005	5
September	1.30	....	0.42	0.019	0.020	25
October	33.00	1.10	4.70	0.214	0.250	290
The period	....	....	....	....	1.675	1,970

WEST BRANCH OF BEAR CREEK AT BERTRAM'S RANCH.

Location.—On the SW. ¼ of Sec. 32, Tp. 10, Rge. 23, W. 3rd Mer.

Records available.—September 16, 1909, to October 31, 1914.

Gauge.—Vertical staff; the elevation of the zero of the gauge has been maintained at 92.25 feet since establishment.

Bench-mark.—Permanent iron bench-mark; assumed elevation, 100.00 feet.

Channel.—Slightly shifting.

Discharge measurements.—Made with meter, and with weir at very low stages.

Winter flow.—This station is not maintained during the winter.

Observer.—R. McKenzie and W. L. Taylor.

No. 25c—28

STREAM MEASUREMENTS, 1914

5 GEORGE V, A. 1915

DISCHARGE MEASUREMENTS of West Branch of Bear Creek at Bertram's Ranch, in 1914.

Date.	Engineer.	Width.	Area of Section.	Mean Velocity.	Gauge Height.	Discharge.
		Feet.	*Sq. ft.*	*Ft. per sec.*	*Feet.*	*Sec.-ft.*
Mar. 18	H. O. Brown	13.1	11.40	1.63	1.57	18.60
Mar. 23	do	11.5	7.02	1.05	1.29	7.40
Mar. 30	do	11.8	8.21	1.07	1.41	8.80
April 2	do	15.1	16.10	2.32	1.77	37.00
April 13	do	16.2	16.80	2.16	1.76	36.00
April 23	F. R. Steinberger	12.3	8.86	1.44	1.39	12.80
May 15	do	13.0	6.60	1.19	1.29	7.80
June 15	do	11.5	5.65	0.85	1.16	4.80
July 4	do	...	...	...	0.81	0.13a
July 28	do	...	...	...	0.75	Nil.
Sept. 27	E. W. W. Hughes	8.0	2.40	0.60	1.03	1.43
Nov. 5	do	11.6	4.72	0.95	1.19	4.50

a Weir measurement.

DAILY GAUGE HEIGHT AND DISCHARGE of West Branch of Bear Creek at Bertram's Ranch, for 1914.

DAY.	March.		April.		May.		June.	
	Gauge Height.	Dis- charge.	Gauge Height.	Dis- charge.	Gauge Height.	Dis- charge.	Gauge Height.	Dis- charge.
	Feet.	*Sec.-ft.*	*Feet.*	*Sec.-ft.*	*Feet.*	*Sec.-ft.*	*Feet.*	*Sec.-ft.*
1			1.87	42.0	1.35	10.5	1.13	4.00
2			1.77	37.0a	1.35	10.5	1.13	4.00
3			1.68	30.0	1.35	10.5	1.13	4.00
4			2.16	69.0	1.37	11.4	1.15	4.40
5			1.96	52.0	1.40	12.7	1.14	4.20
6			1.91	48.0	1.35	10.5	1.18	5.10
7			1.51	18.6	1.33	9.8	1.16	4.60
8			1.44	14.7	1.32	9.4	1.15	4.40
9			1.40	12.7	1.44	14.7	1.13	4.00
10			1.33	9.8	1.39	12.3	1.17	4.90
11			1.29	8.4	1.36	10.9	1.15	4.40
12			1.44	14.7	1.33	9.8	1.16	4.60
13			1.70	32.0	1.32	9.4	1.14	4.20
14			1.85	44.0	1.32	9.4	1.15c	4.40
15			1.70	32.0	1.31	9.1	1.16	4.60
16			1.50	18.0	1.31	9.1	1.15	4.40
17			1.45	15.2	1.31	9.1	1.14	4.20
18	1.55	17.6a	1.45	15.2	1.30	8.7	1.13	4.00
19	1.84	39.0	1.44	14.7	1.30	8.7	1.13	4.00
20	1.79	36.0	1.49	17.4	1.32	9.4	1.13	4.00
21	1.69	25.0	1.44	14.7	1.31	9.1	1.13	4.00
22	1.59	22.0	1.41	13.2	1.29	8.4	1.13	4.00
23	1.28	7.4	1.40	12.7	1.25	7.0	1.13	4.00
24	1.19	4.6	1.40	12.7	1.23	6.4	1.13	4.00
25	...b		1.40	12.7	1.21	5.9	1.13	4.00
26			1.40	12.7	1.19	5.4	1.14	4.20
27			1.40	12.7	1.16	4.6	1.13	4.00
28			1.40	12.7	1.14	4.2	1.05	2.60
29	...b		1.40	12.7	1.13	4.0	1.00	1.80
30	1.39	8.0	1.37	11.4	1.13	4.0	0.95	1.20
31	1.77	36.0	...	...	1.13	4.0	...	...

a to *a* Ice conditions.
b to *b* Channel frozen.
c Gauge height interpolated.

DAILY GAUGE HEIGHT AND DISCHARGE of West Branch of Bear Creek at Bertram's Ranch, for 1914.—*Concluded.*

DAY.	July. Gauge Height.	July. Discharge.	August. Gauge Height.	August. Discharge.	September. Gauge Height.	September. Discharge.	October. Gauge Height.	October. Discharge.
	Feet.	*Sec.-ft.*	*Feet.*	*Sec.-ft.*	*Feet.*	*Sec.-ft.*	*Feet.*	*Sec.-ft.*
1	0.90	0.70	Dry.	Nil.	Dry.	Nil.	1.07	2.1
2	0.86	0.46	"	"	"	"	1.07	2.1
3	0.81	0.16	"	"	"	"	1.10	2.6
4	0.81	0.16	"	"	"	"	1.22	5.2
5	0.80	0.10	"	"	"	"	1.27	6.6
6	0.80	1.10	"	"	"	"	1.24	5.7
7	0.79	0.08	"	"	"	"	1.35	9.3
8	0.79	0.08	"	"	"	"	1.79	35.0
9	0.78	0.06	"	"	"	"	1.66	25.0
10	0.77	0.04	"	"	"	"	1.55	18.7
11	0.76	0.02	"	"	"	"	1.42	12.1
12	0.76	0.02	"	"	*a*	....	1.37	10.1
13	0.76	0.02	"	"	....	....	1.34	8.9
14	0.75	Nil.	"	"	....	....	1.32	8.3
15	0.75	"	"	"	....	....	1.29	7.2
16	0.75	"	"	"	....	....	1.28	6.9
17	0.75	"	"	"	....	....	1.26	6.3
18	0.75	"	"	"	....	....	1.24	5.7
19	0.75	"	"	"	....	....	1.23	5.5
20	0.75	"	"	"	....	....	1.23	5.5
21	0.75	"	"	"	....	....	1.23	5.5
22	0.75	"	"	"	....	....	1.23	5.5
23	0.75	"	"	"	....	....	1.22	5.2
24	0.75	"	"	"	....	....	1.22	5.2
25	0.75	"	"	"	....	....	1.21	5.0
26	0.75	"	"	"	....	....	1.24	5.7
27	0.75	"	"	"	1.03	1.42	1.22	5.2
28	0.75	"	"	"	1.05	1.70	1.22	5.2
29	Dry.	"	"	"	1.05	1.70	1.21	5.0
30	"	"	"	"	1.06	1.88	1.21	5.0
31	"	"	"	"	....	....	1.20	4.7

a Stream commenced to flow about this date; no observer obtainable until September 27.

MONTHLY DISCHARGE of West Branch of Bear Creek at Bertram's Ranch, for 1914.

(Drainage area 45 square miles).

MONTH.	DISCHARGE IN SECOND-FEET. Maximum	Minimum	Mean.	Per square Mile.	RUN-OFF. Depth in inches on Drainage Area.	Total in Acre-feet
March (18–31)	39.00	....	14.00	0.311	0.160	389
April	69.00	8.40	22.00	0.499	0.560	1,335
May	14.70	4.00	8.70	0.193	0.220	534
June	5.10	1.20	4.00	0.089	0.100	238
July	0.70	....	0.07	0.001	0.001	4
August						Nil.
September (1–11; 27–30)	1.88	....	1.68	0.037	0.006	13
October	35.00	2.10	7.90	0.176	0.200	488
The period	....	....	....	....	1.247	3,001

5 GEORGE V, A. 1915

BEAR CREEK AT UNSWORTH'S RANCH.

Location.—On the SE. ¼ of Sec. 18, Tp. 11, Rge. 23, W. 3rd Mer.
Records available.—June 22, 1908, to October 1, 1914.
Gauge.—Vertical staff; the elevation of the zero of the gauge has been maintained at 85.95 feet since establishment.
Bench-mark.—A circle of nails in the top of the stringer at the left abutment of the bridge, on the downstream side; assumed elevation, 100.00 feet.
Discharge measurements.—Made with meter from the bridge; by wading, or with a weir, at very low stages.
Winter flow.—This station is not maintained during winter.
Artificial control.—Messrs. Needham Bros. have a dam below this station, but the backwater does not affect the station.
Observer.—S. Unsworth.

DISCHARGE MEASUREMENTS of Bear Creek at Unsworth's Ranch, in 1914.

Date.	Engineer.	Width.	Area of Section.	Mean Velocity.	Gauge Height.	Discharge.
		Feet.	*Sq. feet.*	*Ft. per sec.*	*Feet.*	*Sec.-ft.*
March 17........	H. O. Brown......	12.5	33.80	1.15	4.29	39.00a
March 23........	do	15.5	16.20	0.71	2.27	11.40a
March 30........	do	6.8	14.40	1.04	2.15	15.00a
March 31	do	8.5	8.30	1.64	2.58	13.70a
April 1..........	do	8.4	12.70	2.04	4.33	26.00a
April 2..........	do	12.5	41.60	1.16	4.00	48.00
April 10........	do	11.3	29.80	0.93	2.76	28.00
April 13...... ..	do	15.5	70.60	1.15	5.05	81.00
April 13..........	do	20.0	73.70	1.30	5.70	96.00
April 23........	F. R. Steinberger..	9.2	19.20	0.70	2.13	13.40
May 12..........	M. H. French.... ..	8.5	11.10	0.93	2.88	10.30
May 15..........	F. R. Steinberger.... ..	10.0	17.00	0.51	1.74	8.70
June 10..	do	4.8	2.59	1.66	1.03	4.30
July 4..........	do	....	....	....	0.80	0.88b
July 28..........	do	....	....	....	0.56	Nil.
Sept. 27..........	E. W. W. Hughes .	....	....	....	1.35	0.44b
Nov. 5..........	do	12.5	8.10	0.62	1.75	5.00

a Ice conditions.
b Weir measurement.

SESSIONAL PAPER No. 25c

DAILY GAUGE HEIGHT AND DISCHARGE of Bear Creek at Unsworth's Ranch, for 1914.

DAY.	March.		April.		May.		June.	
	Gauge Height.	Dis-charge.	Gauge Height.	Dis-charge.	Gauge Height.	Dis-charge.	Gauge Height.	Dis-charge.
	Feet.	*Sec.-ft.*	*Feet.*	*Sec.-ft.*	*Feet.*	*Sec.-ft.*	*Feet.*	*Sec.-ft.*
1			3.78	16.0	1.98	11.4	1.38	5.4
2			3.95	47.0	1.98	11.4	1.33	5.0
3			3.53	40.0a	1.98	11.4	1.33	5.0
4			4.03	52.0	1.98	11.4	1.28	4.7
5			5.83	101.0	1.98	11.4	1.23	4.3
6			5.68	96.0	2.03	12.1	1.53	6.6
7			3.83	47.0	2.08	12.7	1.43	5.8
8			3.53	40.0	2.33	16.5	1.38	5.4
9			3.23	33.0	2.23	14.9	1.33	5.0
10			3.13	31.0	2.18	14.1	1.15	3.8
11			2.63	21.0	2.13	13.4	1.15b	4.3
12	2.88	13.2a	4.58	66.0	2.06	12.5	1.15	4.2
13	4.18	36.0	5.36	87.0	2.03	12.1	1.20	5.4
14	6.83	105.0	3.90	48.0	1.98	11.4	1.25	5.6
15	7.23	117.0	3.56	40.0	1.93	10.8	1.30	6.0
16	8.63	159.0	3.38	36.0	1.88	10.2	1.25	5.5
17	4.29	39.0	3.03	29.0	1.83	9.6	1.15	4.6
18	3.93	35.0	2.53	19.7	1.78	9.0	1.10	4.2
19	3.53	28.0	2.45	18.4	1.76	8.8	1.05	3.8
20	3.33	26.0	2.38	17.3	1.73	8.5	1.05	3.6
21	3.13	22.0	2.28	15.7	1.73	8.5	1.00	3.2
22	2.63	16.2	2.18	14.1	1.71	8.3	1.00	3.0
23	2.27	11.4	2.13	13.4	1.68	8.0	0.95	2.6
24	2.18	11.0	2.08	12.7	1.63	7.5	0.95	2.4
25	2.13	11.0	2.08	12.7	1.63	7.5	0.95	2.3
26	2.13	11.6	2.08	12.7	1.58	7.0	1.00	2.7
27	2.18	12.8	2.03	12.1	1.58	7.0	1.00	2.6
28	2.18	13.8	2.03	12.1	1.53	6.6	1.05	2.8
29	2.23	15.2	1.98	11.4	1.48	6.2	1.10	2.9
30	2.15	15.0	1.98	11.4	1.43	5.8	1.05b	2.3
31	3.30	25.0			1.38	5.4		

a to *a* Ice conditions.
b to *b* Shifting conditions.

DAILY GAUGE HEIGHT AND DISCHARGE of Bear Creek at Unsworth's Ranch, for 1914.
—*Concluded.*

DAY.	July.		August.		September.		October.	
	Gauge Height.	Dis- charge.	Gauge Height.	Dis- charge.	Gauge Height.	Dis- charge.	Gauge Height.	Dis- charge.
	Feet.	*Sec.-ft.*	*Feet.*	*Sec.-ft.*	*Feet.*	*Sec.-ft.*	*Feet.*	*Sec.-ft.*
1	1.00a	2.00	0.30	Nil.	0.30	Nil.	1.50	1.10
2	0.90	1.60	0.30	"	0.30	"	1.50	1.20
3	0.80	1.20	0.30	"	0.30	"	1.50	1.20
4	0.70	0.80	0.30	"	0.30	"	1.75	2.20
5	0.65	0.60	0.30	"	0.30	"	1.95	3.80
6	0.60	0.30	0.30	"	0.30	"	2.05	4.40
7	0.60	0.20	0.30	"	0.30	"	4.25	38.00
8	0.60	0.10	0.30	"	0.30	"	3.75	28.00
9	0.60	Nil.	0.30	"	0.30	"	3.10	17.60
10	0.60	"	0.30	"	0.30	"	2.65	11.40
11	0.60	"	0.30	"	0.30	"	2.35	8.00
12	0.60	"	0.30	"	0.30	"	2.15	6.80
13	0.60	"	0.30	"	0.60	"	2.05	6.00
14	0.70	"	0.30	"	1.20	0.60	2.00	5.50
15	0.70	"	0.30	"	1.80	2.60	1.90	5.00
16	0.70	"	0.30	"	1.80	2.60	1.90	5.20
17	0.70	"	0.30	"	1.70	2.00	1.85	4.50
18	0.70	"	0.30	"	1.60	1.60	1.85	4.60
19	0.70	"	0.30	"	1.60	1.60	1.85	4.70
20	0.65	"	0.30	"	1.55	1.20	1.85	4.80
21	0.65	"	0.30	"	1.55	1.20	1.80	4.50
22	0.65	"	0.30	"	1.55	1.20	1.80	4.50
23	0.65	"	0.30	"	1.50	1.00	1.80	4.50
24	0.65	"	0.30	"	1.50	1.00	1.80	4.50
25	0.65	"	0.30	"	1.45	0.64	1.80	4.50
26	0.65	"	0.30	"	1.40	0.60	1.80	4.60
27	0.65	"	0.30	"	1.45	0.65	1.80	4.60
28	0.65	"	0.30	"	1.50	1 00	1.80	4.60
29	0.30	"	0.30	"	1.50	1.10	1.80	4.60
30	0.30	"	0.30	"	1.50	1.10	1.80	4.60
31	0.30	"	0.30	"	....	....	1.80a	4.60

a Shifting conditions July 1 to October 31.

MONTHLY DISCHARGE of Bear Creek at Unsworth's Ranch, for 1914.

(Drainage area 100 square miles).

Month.	DISCHARGE IN SECOND-FEET.				RUN-OFF.	
	Maximum.	Minimum.	Mean.	Per square Mile.	Depth in inches on Drainage Area.	Total in Acre-feet.
March (12–31)	159.0	11.00	36.20	0.362	0.270	1,434
April	101.0	11.40	34.00	0.338	0.380	2,010
May	16.5	5.40	10.00	0.100	0.120	615
June	6.6	2.30	4.20	0.042	0.050	248
July	2.0	....	0.22	0.002	0.002	14
August	....	....	....	....	....	Nil.
September	2.6	....	0.72	0.007	0.008	43
October	38.0	1.10	6.90	0.069	0.080	425
The period	....	....	....	....	0.910	4,789

MONTHLY DISCHARGE of Bear Creek near Unsworth's Ranch, for 1913.

(Drainage area 100 square miles.)

MONTH.	DISCHARGE IN SECOND-FEET.				RUN-OFF.	
	Maximum.	Minimum.	Mean.	Per square Mile.	Depth in inches on Drainage Area.	Total in Acre-feet.
April....................................	314.00	15.50	126.00	1.260	1.400	7,468
May.....................................	22.00	7.40	13.70	0.137	0.158	842
June....................................	9.10	2.70	5.40	0.054	0.062	322
July....................................	12.40	0.54	4.00	0.040	0.046	244
August..................................	1.63	0.10	0.99	0.010	0.011	61
September...............................	1.60	0.10	0.52	0.005	0.006	30
October.................................	4.40	1.85	3.40	0.034	0.039	210
The period..............................	....	....	....	....	1.722	9,177

NOTE.—This table is inserted in this report to correct a table which was published on page 343 of the report for 1913, the total run-off in acre-feet for April and the period being incorrect as then published.

SESSIONAL PAPER No. 25c

BRANIFF DITCH FROM BEAR CREEK.

Location.—On the SE. ¼ Sec. 30, Tp. 11, Rge. 23, W. 3rd Mer.
Records available.—One discharge measurement in 1914.
Gauge.—Vertical staff, at headgate; elevation of zero, 95.91 feet.
Bench-mark.—Stump on right bank; assumed elevation, 100.00 feet.
Discharge measurements.—Made by wading.
Observer.—No observations in 1914.

DISCHARGE MEASUREMENTS of Braniff Ditch from Piapot Creek, in 1914.

Date.	Engineer.	Width.	Area of Section.	Mean Velocity.	Gauge Height.	Discharge.
		Feet.	*Sq. feet.*	*Ft. per sec.*	*Feet.*	*Sec.-ft.*
June 12.............	F. R. Steinberger............	4.0	6.10	0.81	1.42	4.9

PIAPOT CREEK AT CUMBERLAND'S RANCH.

Location.—On the *NE.* ¼ Sec. 18, Tp. 11. Rge. 24, W. 3rd Mer.
Records available.—May 13, 1909, to October 31, 1914; from July 4, 1908, to May 12, 1909, records on this creek were obtained at a station three-quarters of a mile upstream from the present gauge.
Gauge.—Vertical staff; the zero of the gauge was maintained at 89.75 feet during 1909-11, and at 88.75 feet during 1912-14.
Bench-mark.—Permanent iron bench-mark; assumed elevation, 100.00 feet.
Discharge measurements.—Made with weir at low stages, and with meter at ordinary stages.
Winter flow.—This station is not maintained during the winter.
Artificial control.—A log buried in the bed of the stream, about 40 feet below the gauge, forms a control at this station.
Diversions.—Messrs. Fearon and Moorhead, D. Beveridge, Geo. Tranter and *A.* Cumberland divert water for irrigation purposes above this station.
Observer.—A. Cumberland.

DISCHARGE MEASUREMENTS of Piapot Creek at Cumberland's Ranch, in 1914.

Date.	Engineer.	Width.	Area of Section.	Mean Velocity.	Gauge Height.	Discharge.
		Feet.	*Sq. feet.*	*Ft. per sec.*	*Feet.*	*Sec.-ft.*
March 12............	M. H. French..............	7.5	2.25	2.00	4.28	4.50a
March 17............	H. O. Brown..............	12.8	6.11	1.56	3.56	9.50a
March 31............	do	8.9	12.00	0.62	3.55	7.50a
April 3............	do	7.9	10.70	0.81	3.44	8.70a
April 9............	do	10.5	8.53	0.79	1.54	6.80
April 13............	do	12.7	16.00	1.17	2.03	18.80
May 15........ ..	F. R. Steinberger............				1.16	1.66b
June 10............	do				1.04	0.15b
July 4............	do				0.97	0.12b
July 27............	do					Nil.
Sept. 26............	E. W. W. Hughes..............				1.00	0.33b

a Ice conditions.
b Weir measurement.

STREAM MEASUREMENTS, 1914

5 GEORGE V, A. 1915

DAILY GAUGE HEIGHT AND DISCHARGE of Piapot Creek at Cumberland's Ranch, for 1914.

DAY.	March.		April.		May.		June.	
	Gauge Height.	Dis- charge.	Gauge Height.	Dis- charge.	Gauge Height.	Dis- charge.	Gauge Height.	Dis- charge.
	Feet.	*Sec.-ft.*	*Feet.*	*Sec.-ft.*	*Feet.*	*Sec.-ft.*	*Feet.*	*Sec.-ft.*
1	......	......	3.70	11.6	1.31	3.30	0.87	Nil.
2	......	......	3.46	8.0	1.26	2.70	0.87	*a*
3	......	......	3.36*a*	7.2	1.26	2.70	1.02	0.49
4	......	......	3.21	6.0	1.19	1.95	0.98	0.21
5	......	......	3.10	7.5	1.23	2.40	1.05	0.70
6	......	......	2.10	6.6	1.23	2.40	1.03	0.56
7	......	......	1.51	6.2	1.19	1.95	1.05	0.70
8	......	......	1.40	4.6	1.16	1.65	0.93	Nil.
9	......	......	1.66	9.0	1.14	1.46	0.89	*a*
10	......	......	1.44	5.2	1.14	1.46	1.04	0.63
11	......	......	1.49	5.9	1.14	1.46	1.07*b*	0.86
12	4.28*a*	4.5	1.51	6.3	1.13	1.37	1.10	1.10
13	4.48	12.0	1.43	5.0	1.11	1.19	1.15	1.55
14	4.28	12.6	1.69	9.6	1.12	1.28	1.22	2.30
15	4.12	13.8	1.74	10.7	1.16	1.65	1.12	1.28
16	4.53	29.0	1.63	8.4	1.15	1.55	1.10	1.10
17	3.94	18.4	1.53	6.6	1.17*b*	1.75	1.05	0.70
18	4.18	25.0	1.49	5.9	1.18	1.85	1.03	0.56
19	3.58	9.6	1.48	5.8	1.17	1.75	0.99	0.28
20	3.58	9.5	1.56	7.1	1.16	1.65	0.97	0.14
21	3.58	9.4	1.46	5.5	1.15	1.55	0.93	Nil.
22	3.58	9.3	1.53	6.6	1.14	1.46	1.05	0.70
23	3.71	12.1	1.39	4.4	1.15	1.55	0.99	0.28
24	3.57	8.9	1.39	4.4	1.14	1.46	0.88	Nil.
25	3.57	8.8	1.37	4.1	1.13	1.37	0.90	Nil.
26	3.57	8.7	1.46	5.5	1.10	1.10	0.98	0.21
27	3.57	8.6	1.36	4.0	1.05	0.70	0.92	Nil.
28	3.67	10.2	1.34	3.7	1.05	0.70	0.90	*a*
29	3.72	11.2	1.32	3.5	0.98	0.21	0.98	0.21
30	4.07	19.7	1.30	3.2	0.98	0.21	1.07	0.86
31	3.73	11.0	......	......	0.87	Nil.	......	......

a to *b* Ice conditions—discharges estimated.

SESSIONAL PAPER No. 25c

DAILY GAUGE HEIGHT AND DISCHARGE of Piapot Creek at Cumberland's Ranch, for 1914.

DAY.	July.		August.		September.		October.	
	Gauge Height.	Dis- charge.	Gauge Height.	Dis- charge.	Gauge Height.	Dis- charge.	Gauge Height.	Dis- charge.
	Feet.	*Sec.-ft.*	*Feet.*	*Sec.-ft.*	*Feet.*	*Sec.-ft.*	*Feet.*	*Sec.-ft.*
1	1.04	0.63	Dry.	Nil.	0.96	0.07	0.90	Nil.
2	0.95	Nil.	"	"	0.95	Nil.	1.00c	0.35
3	0.89	"	"	"	0.90	"	1.10c	1.10
4	1.00	0.35	"	"	0.85	"	1.15c	1.55
5	0.99	0.28	"	"	0.76	"	1.20c	2.00
6	1.05	0.70	"	"	0.78c	"	1.30c	3.20
7	0.97	0.14	"	"	0.80	"	1.45	5.30
8	0.90	Nil.	"	"	0.90c	"	1.55	7.00
9	0.87	"	"	"	0.99	0.28	1.70	9.80
10	0.84	"	"	"	0.85	Nil.	1.59	7.60
11	0.80	"	"	"	0.81	"	1.56	7.10
12	0.74	"	"	"	1.20	2.00	1.44	5.20
13	0.74	"	"	"	1.59	7.60	1.36	4.00
14	0.97	0.14	"	"	1.25	2.60	1.33	3.60
15	0.83	Nil.	"	"	1.15	1.55	1.30	3.20
16	0.70	"	"	"	1.11	1.19	1.27	2.80
17	0.70	"	"	"	1.06	0.78	1.25	2.60
18	0.70	"	"	"	1.05	0.70	1.20	2.00
19	Dry.	"	"	"	1.04	0.63	1.18	1.85
20	"	"	"	"	1.04	0.63	1.14	1.46
21	"	"	"	"	1.03	0.56	1.14	1.46
22	"	"	"	"	1.04	0.63	1.15	1.55
23	"	"	"	"	1.02	0.49	1.15	1.55
24	"	"	0.95	Nil.	1.03	0.56	1.14	1.46
25	"	"	1.05	0.70	1.01	0.42	1.14	1.46
26	"	"	1.00	0.35	0.99	0.28	1.15	1.55
27	"	"	0.94	Nil.	1.03	0.56	1.14	1.46
28	"	"	0.75	"	1.02	0.49	1.14	1.46
29	"	"	0.74	"	0.90	Nil.	1.14	1.46
30	"	"	0.86c	"	0.90	"	1.14	1.46
31	"	"	1.00	0.35	....	....	1.14	1.46

c Gauge height interpolated.

MONTHLY DISCHARGE of Piapot Creek at Cumberland's Ranch, for 1914.

(Drainage area 55 square miles.)

MONTH.	DISCHARGE IN SECOND-FEET.				RUN-OFF.	
	Maximum.	Minimum	Mean.	Per square Mile.	Depth in inches on Drainage Area.	Total in Acre-feet.
March (12-31) .	29.00	4.50	12.60	0.229	0.170	500
April	11.60	3.20	6.30	0.114	0.130	373
May	3.30	....	1.54	0.028	0.030	95
June	2.30	....	0.51	0.009	0.010	31
July	0.70	....	0.07	0.001	0.001	4
August	0.70	....	0.04	0.001	0.001	3
September	7.60	....	0.73	0.013	0.010	44
October	9.80	....	2.80	0.014	0.060	175
The period	....	....	....	....	0.412	1,225

5 GEORGE V, A. 1915

MISCELLANEOUS DISCHARGE MEASUREMENTS made in Crane Lake drainage basin, in 1914.

Date.	Engineer.	Stream.	Location.	Width.	Area of Section.	Mean Velocity.	Discharge.
				Feet.	*Sq. ft.*	*Ft. per sec.*	*Sec.-ft.*
Mar. 31....	H. O. Brown........	Bear Creek... ...	30-11-23-3........	8.5	8.34	1.64	13.70
Mar. 31....	do	do	do	8.3	9.31	1.88	17.50
April 1....	do	do	do	8.4	12.70	2.04	26.00
April 12....	do	do	do	21.3	41.20	2.50	103.00
July 28....	F. R. Steinberger....	Spring Creek......	S.E. 8-11-23-3....	....	....	....	0.14

HAY LAKE DRAINAGE BASIN.

General Description.

Hay Lake is in Township 11, Range 25, West of the 3rd Meridian, and is fed by Hay Creek, which rises in the Cypress Hills. It is a comparatively small body of saline water of an approximate area of three square miles. Like all lakes in this locality it has no outlet.

The basin supplies water for a number of irrigation schemes, and also to the town of Maple Creek for domestic and industrial purposes, the water being piped some nine miles by means of a gravity system.

The annual precipitation averages about 12 inches; during 1913 and 1914 it was slightly less than this amount.

HAY CREEK AT HAY CREEK SCHOOL.

Location.—On the SW. ¼ Sec. 29, Tp. 10, Rge. 25, W. 3rd Mer.

Records available.—March 24, 1911, to October 31, 1914.

Gauge.—Vertical staff; the elevation of the zero of the gauge has been maintained at 94.79 feet since establishment.

Bench-mark.—Permanent iron bench-mark; assumed elevation, 100.00 feet.

Channel.—Slightly shifting.

Discharge measurements.—Made with weir at ordinary stages, and with a meter in high water periods.

Winter flow.—This station is not maintained during the winter.

Diversions.—The town of Maple Creek takes its water from springs at the head of this creek.

Observer.—Miss K. Jones.

DISCHARGE MEASUREMENTS of Hay Creek at Hay Creek School, in 1914.

Date.	Engineer.	Width.	Area of Section.	Mean Velocity.	Gauge Height.	Discharge.
		Feet.	*Sq. ft.*	*Ft. per sec.*	*Feet.*	*Sec.-ft.*
May 13	F. R. Steinberger...........	....	....	....	1.15	0.19a
June 4..........	do	....	....	....	....	Nil.
July 25..........	do	....	....	....	....	a
Aug. 15..........	do	....	....	....	....	a
Sept. 3..........	E. W. W. Hughes...........	....	....	....	....	a
Sept. 23..........	do	....	....	....	....	a
Nov. 9..........	do	....	....	....	1.09	0.02a

a Weir measurement.

SESSIONAL PAPER No. 25c

DAILY GAUGE HEIGHT AND DISCHARGE of Hay Creek at Hay Creek School, for 1914.

DAY.	March.		April.		May.		June.	
	Gauge Height.	Dis- charge.	Gauge Height.	Dis- charge.	Gauge Height.	Dis- charge.	Gauge Height.	Dis- charge.
	Feet.	*Sec.-ft.*	*Feet.*	*Sec.-ft.*	*Feet.*	*Sec.-ft.*	*Feet.*	*Sec.-ft.*
1	....	....	1.75	8.00	1.44	2.40	1.21	0.45
2	....	....	1.59	4.80	1.45	2.50	1.20	0.40
3	....	....	1.61	5.20	1.45	2.50	1.19	0.35
4	....	....	1.65	6.00	1.46	2.60	1.16	0.20
5	....	....	1.65	6.00	1.48	3.00	1.13	0.11
6	....	....	1.65	6.00	1.49	3.10	1.10	0.05
7	....	....	1.66	6.20	1.50	3.20	1.08	0.03
8	....	....	1.63	5.60	1.51	3.40	1.06	0.01
9	....	....	1.59	4.80	1.52	3.60	1.06	0.01
10	....	....	1.55	4.00	1.51	3.40	1.06	0.01
11	....	....	1.51	3.40	1.53	3.70	1.06	0.01
12	....	....	1.47	2.80	1.50	3.20	1.07	0.02
13	....	....	1.45	2.50	1.30	0.95	1.08	0.03
14	....	....	1.41	2.00	1.30	0.95	1.08	0.03
15	....	....	1.38	1.70	1.30	0.95	1.08	0.03
16	....	....	1.36	1.50	1.30	0.95	1.08	0.03
17	....	....	1.34	1.31	1.30	0.95	1.08	0.03
18	....	....	1.27	0.77	1.31	1.04	1.09	0.04
19	....	....	1.33	1.22	1.30	0.95	1.08	0.03
20	1.67	6.4	1.31	1.04	1.30	0.95	1.09	0.04
21	1.66	6.2	1.29	0.89	1.29	0.89	1.09	0.04
22	1.51	3.4	1.23	0.55	1.29	0.89	1.09	0.04
23	1.50	3.2	1.26	0.71	1.28	0.83	1.09	0.04
24	1.49	3.1	1.43	2.30	1.28	0.83	1.09	0.04
25	1.49	3.1	1.42	2.10	1.26	0.71	1.08	0.03
26	1.49	3.1	1.44	2.40	1.24	0.60	1.08	0.03
27	1.47	2.8	1.45	2.50	1.23	0.55	1.09	0.04
28	1.46	2.6	1.45	2.50	1.22	0.50	1.09	0.04
29	1.45	2.5	1.46	2.60	1.22	0.50	1.09	0.04
30	1.46	2.6	1.45	2.50	1.21	0.45	1.08	0.03
31	1.49	3.1	....	....	1.21	0.45	....	....

5 GEORGE V, A. 1915

DAILY GAUGE HEIGHT AND DISCHARGE of Hay Creek at Hay Creek School, for 1914.
—*Concluded.*

DAY.	July.		August.		September.		October.	
	Gauge Height.	Discharge.	Gauge Height.	Discharge.	Gauge Height.	Discharge.	Gauge Height.	Discharge.
	Feet.	Sec.-ft.	Feet.	Sec.-ft.	Feet.	Sec.-ft.	Feet.	Sec.-ft.
1	1.08	0.03	Dry.	Nil.	Dry.	Nil.	Dry.	Nil.
2	1.07	0.02	"	"	"	"	"	"
3	1.07	0.02	"	"	"	"	"	"
4	1.06	0.01	"	"	"	"	"	"
5	1.06	0.01	"	"	"	"	"	"
6	1.06	0.01	"	"	"	"	"	"
7	1.05	Nil.	"	"	"	"	"	"
8	1.05	"	"	"	"	"	2.00	13.2
9	1.04	"	"	"	"	"	2.01	13.4
10	1.03	"	"	"	"	"	2.02	13.6
11	1.02	"	"	"	"	"	2.03	13.8
12	1.02	"	"	"	"	"	2.03	13.8
13	1.02	"	"	"	"	"	1.02	Nil.
14	1.02	"	"	"	"	"	1.00	"
15	1.02	"	"	"	"	"	Dry.	"
16	1.01	"	"	"	"	"	"	"
17	1.01	"	"	"	"	"	"	"
18	1.01	"	"	"	"	"	"	"
19	1.01	"	"	"	"	"	"	"
20	1.00	"	"	"	"	"	"	"
21	0.99	"	"	"	"	"	"	"
22	0.98	"	"	"	"	"	"	"
23	Dry.	"	"	"	"	"	"	"
24	"	"	"	"	"	"	"	"
25	"	"	"	"	"	"	"	"
26	"	"	"	"	"	"	"	"
27	"	"	"	"	"	"	"	"
28	"	"	"	"	"	"	"	"
29	"	"	"	"	"	"	"	"
30	"	"	"	"	"	"	"	"
31	"	"	"	"	"	"	"	"

MONTHLY DISCHARGE of Hay Creek at Hay Creek School, for 1914.

(Drainage area 22 square miles.)

MONTH.	DISCHARGE IN SECOND-FEET.				RUN-OFF.	
	Maximum.	Minimum.	Mean.	Per square Mile.	Depth in inches on Drainage Area.	Total in Acre-feet.
March (20-31)	6.40	2.50	3.200	0.1480	0.0070	77
April	8.00	0.55	3.100	0.1420	0.1600	186
May	3.70	0.45	1.660	0.0750	0.0900	102
June	0.45	0.01	0.080	0.0030	0.0030	4
July	0.03		0.003	0.0001	0.0001	Nil.
August						"
September						
October	13.80		2.200	0.0990	0.1100	134
The period					0.3701	499

'SESSIONAL PAPER No. 25c

HAY CREEK AT FAUQUIER'S RANCH.

Location.—On the *NE.* ¼ Sec. 30, Tp. 10, Rge. 25, W. 3rd Mer.

Records available.—April 25, 1909, to October 31, 1914.

Gauge.—Vertical staff; the elevation of the zero of the gauge has been maintained at 91.39 feet since establishment.

Bench-mark.—Permanent iron bench-mark; assumed elevation, 100.00 feet.

Channel.—Slightly shifting.

Discharge measurements.—Made with meter by wading, and with a weir at low stages.

Winter flow.—This station is not maintained during winter.

Reservoirs.—The town of Maple Creek takes water from the springs at the head of this creek, and Mr. H. Fauquier diverts water for irrigation purposes above the gauge.

Observer.—Miss M. Fauquier.

DISCHARGE MEASUREMENTS of Hay Creek at Fauquier's Ranch, in 1914.

Date.	Engineer.	Width.	Area of Section.	Mean Velocity.	Gauge Height.	Discharge.
		Feet.	*Sq. ft.*	*Ft. per sec.*	*Feet.*	*Sec.-ft.*
Mar. 14	M. H. French	11.3	11.1	0.93	1.29	10.30
April 3	H. O. Brown	5.5	2.7	1.27	0.91	3.40
April 8	do	5.1	1.9	0.77	0.79	1.49
May 13	F. R. Steinberger					Nil.
July 2	do					"
July 25	do					"
Aug. 14	do					"
Sept. 3	E. W. W. Hughes					"
Sept. 23	do					"
Nov. 9	do					"

DAILY GAUGE HEIGHT AND DISCHARGE of Hay Creek at Fauquier's Ranch, for 1914.

DAY.	March.		April.		May.		June.	
	Gauge Height.	Dis-charge.	Gauge Height.	Dis-charge.	Gauge Height.	Dis-charge.	Gauge Height.	Dis-charge.
	Feet.	*Sec.-ft.*	*Feet.*	*Sec.-ft.*	*Feet.*	*Sec.-ft.*	*Feet.*	*Sec.-ft.*
1			1.51	14.70	0.53	0.03	Dry.	Nil.
2			1.03	5.50	0.21	Nil.	"	"
3			0.77	1.24	Dry.	"	"	"
4			0.89	3.00	"	"	"	"
5			1.27	9.90	"	"	"	"
6			1.01	5.20	"	"	"	"
7			0.93	3.70	"	"	"	"
8			0.56	0.06	"	"	"	"
9			0.71	0.68	"	"	"	"
10			0.89	3.00	"	"	"	"
11			0.61	0.13	"	"	"	"
12	1.16	7.90	1.03	5.50	"	"	"	"
13	1.33	11.10	1.26	9.70	"	"	"	"
14	1.37	11.90	1.16	7.90	"	"	"	"
15	1.03	5.50	1.21	8.80	"	"	"	"
16	0.81	1.76	1.14	7.50	"	"	"	"
17	0.97	4.50	0.93	3.70	"	"	"	"
18	0.81	1.76	0.87	2.70	"	"	"	"
19	*a*		0.82	1.92	"	"	"	"
20			0.81	1.76	"	"	"	"
21			0.75	1.00	"	"	"	"
22			0.67	0.39	"	"	"	"
23			0.66	0.32	"	"	"	"
24			0.67	0.39	"	"	"	"
25			0.63	0.19	"	"	"	"
26			0.68	0.46	"	"	"	"
27			0.65	0.25	"	"	"	"
28			0.60	0.10	"	"	"	"
29	*a*		0.61	0.13	"	"	"	"
30	0.75	1.00	0.59	0.09	"	"	"	"
31	1.21	8.80			"	"	"	"

a to *a* Channel frozen.

5 GEORGE V, A. 1915

DAILY GAUGE HEIGHT AND DISCHARGE of Hay Creek at Fauquier's Ranch, for 1914.
—*Concluded.*

DAY.	July.		August.		September.		October.	
	Gauge Height.	Dis-charge.	Gauge Height.	Dis-charge.	Gauge Height.	Dis-charge.	Gauge Height.	Dis-charge.
	Feet.	Sec.-ft.	Feet.	Sec.-ft.	Feet.	Sec.-ft.	Feet.	Sec.-ft.
1	Dry.	Nil.	Dry.	Nil.	Dry.	Nil.	Dry.	Nil.
2	"	"	"	"	"	"	"	"
3	"	"	"	"	"	"	"	"
4	"	"	"	"	"	"	"	"
5	"	"	"	"	"	"	"	"
6	"	"	"	"	"	"	"	"
7	"	"	"	"	"	"	1.71	18.7
8	"	"	"	"	"	"	1.73	19.3
9	"	"	"	"	"	"	1.04	5.7
10	"	"	"	"	"	"		
11	"	"	"	"	"	"	1.40	12.5
12	"	"	"	"	"	"	0.50	Nil.
13	"	"	"	"	"	"	Dry.	"
14	"	"	"	"	"	"	"	"
15	"	"	"	"	"	"	"	"
16	"	"	"	"	"	"	"	"
17	"	"	"	"	"	"	"	"
18	"	"	"	"	"	"	"	"
19	"	"	"	"	"	"	"	"
20	"	"	"	"	"	"	"	"
21	"	"	"	"	"	"	"	"
22	"	"	"	"	"	"	"	"
23	"	"	"	"	"	"	"	"
24	"	"	"	"	"	"	"	"
25	"	"	"	"	"	"	"	"
26	"	"	"	"	"	"	"	"
27	"	"	"	"	"	"	"	"
28	"	"	"	"	"	"	"	"
29	"	"	"	"	"	"	"	"
30	"	"	"	"	"	"	"	"
31	"	"	"	"	"	"	"	"

MONTHLY DISCHARGE of Hay Creek at Fauquier's Ranch, for 1914.

(Drainage area 24 square miles.)

MONTH.	DISCHARGE IN SECOND-FEET.				RUN-OFF.	
	Maximum	Minimum	Mean.	Per square Mile.	Depth in inches on Drainage Area.	Total in Acre-feet.
March (12-31)	11.90	....	2.70	0.113	0.08	108
April	14.70	0.06	3.30	0.139	0.16	198
May	0.03	....	....	....	....	Nil.
June	....	....	....	....	....	"
July	....	....	....	....	....	"
August	....	....	....	....	....	"
September	....	....	....	....	....	
October	19.3	....	1.81	0.075	0.09	111
The period	....	....	....	....	0.33	417

MISCELLANEOUS DISCHARGE MEASUREMENTS made in Hay Lake drainage basin, in 1914.

Date.	Engineer.	Stream.	Location.	Dis-charge.
				Sec. ft.
Jan. 19	F. R. Steinberger	Saunder's Springs	S.E. 20-10-25-3	0.15
Feb. 7	do	do	do	0.56
Feb. 20	do	do	do	0.35
Mar. 17	do	do	do	0.52
April 17	H. O. Brown	do	do	0.78
May 13	F. R. Steinberger	do	do	1.01
June 6	do	do	do	1.06
July 2	do	do	do	0.82
July 23	do	do	do	0.60
Aug. 15	do	do	do	0.43
Sept. 3	E. W. W. Hughes	do	do	0.38
Sept. 23	do	do	do	0.40
Nov. 9	do	do	do	0.55
Dec. 3	J. E. Caughey	do	do	0.72
Dec. 18	do	do	do	0.56
Jan. 19	F. R. Steinberger	Upper Spring	S.E. 10-10-25-3	0.16
Feb. 7	do	do	do	0.16
Feb. 26	do	do	do	0.20
Mar. 17	do	do	do	0.21
April 8	H. O. Brown	do	do	0.20
May 13	F. R. Steinberger	do	do	0.37
June 6	do	do	do	0.17
July 2	do	do	do	0.17
July 23	do	do	do	0.16
Aug. 15	do	do	do	0.18
Sept. 3	E. W. W. Hughes	do	do	0.20
Sept. 23	do	do	do	0.19
Nov. 9	do	do	do	0.17
Dec. 3	J. E. Caughey	do	do	0.16
Dec. 18	do	do	do	0.15
April 8	H. O. Brown	Hay Creek	S.E. 10-10-25-3	0.45
April 8	do	do	N.W. 9-10-25-3	0.60

BIG STICK LAKE DRAINAGE BASIN.

General Description.

Big Stick is one of the largest lakes in the northern Cypress Hills district. It is situated about Township 15, Range 25, West of the 3rd Meridian, and covers an area of 35 square miles. The lake is alkaline in character and has no outlet.

The only source of supply of the lake is Maple Creek, which with its tributary, Gap Creek, rises in the Cypress Hills 30 miles south. On the south and east the lake is bounded by the sandhills. The drainage area is 820 square miles.

The topography of the drainage basin is for the most part gently rolling, and the creek slope is small except near the source. The basin is bare of trees except in the hills. The channel is flat, wide, and in most places sandy.

There are several small irrigation ditches in the basin.

ADAMS' NORTH DITCH NEAR MAPLE CREEK.

Location.—On the *NE.* ¼ Sec. 10, Tp. 9, Rge. 27, W. 3rd Mer., at Geo. A. Adams' ranch.

Records available.—May 22 to October 31, 1914.

Gauge.—Vertical staff, located near the left bank and 50 feet below the headgate; elevation of zero, 97.14 feet.

Bench-mark.—Top of wooden stake about eight feet from gauge on the left bank; assumed elevation, 100.00 feet.

Control.—A permanent 24-inch sharp-crested weir, with complete end contractions, acts as a control. The crest of the weir is maintained at an elevation of 99.09 feet.

Channel.—Composed of a black, sandy loam.

Discharge measurements.—Computed from the measured head over the weir.

Observer.—Geo. A. Adams.

Remarks.—This ditch was used for three days during 1914, May 24-26, with an estimated total discharge of one acre-foot.

5 GEORGE V, A. 1915

ADAMS' SOUTH DITCH NEAR MAPLE CREEK.

Location.—On the NE. ¼ Sec. 10, Tp. 9, Rge. 27, W. 3rd Mer., at Geo. *A. Adams'* ranch.
Records available.—May 22 to October 31, 1914.
Gauge.—Vertical staff, located near the left bank about 100 feet below the headgate; elevation of zero, 97 64 feet.
Bench-mark.—The top of a wooden stake across the ditch from the gauge rod; assumed elevation, 100.00 feet.
Control.—A permanent 24-inch sharp-crested weir, with complete end contractions, is used as a control; the elevation of the crest is maintained at 99.32 feet.
Channel.—Composed of sandy loam.
Discharge measurements.—Computed from the measured head over the weir.
Observer.—Geo. *A.* Adams.
Remarks.—The ditch was used for eight days, June 7-14, during 1914, with a total estimated discharge of four acre-feet.

GAP CREEK AT SMALL'S RANCH.

Location.—On the SE. ¼ Sec. 4, Tp. 10, Rge. 27, W. 3rd Mer., at Wm. Small's ranch.
Records available.—April 24, 1909, to October 31, 1914.
Gauge.—Vertical staff; the zero of the gauge was maintained at 66.53 feet during 1909-10· 66.62 feet during 1911; 66 63 feet during 1912-14.
Bench-mark.—Permanent iron bench-mark; assumed elevation, 100.00 feet.
Channel.—Composed of loose stones and gravel, and liable to shift during flood stages.
Discharge measurements.—Made from cable car during high stages; by wading or with a weir during low stages.
Winter flow.—Station discontinued during winter season.
Observer.—Wm. Small.

DISCHARGE MEASUREMENTS of Gap Creek at Small's Ranch, in 1914.

Date.	Engineer.	Width.	Area of Section.	Mean Velocity.	Gauge Height.	Discharge.
		Feet.	*Sq. ft.*	*Ft. per sec.*	*Feet.*	*Sec.-ft.*
Mar. 14	H. D. St. A. Smith	55.0	72.0	2.02	3.74	146.00
Mar. 17	H. R. Caracallen.	33.0	33.9	0.63	2.46	21.00
April 16	H. O. Brown	40.0	58.2	1.68	3.00	98.00
May 6	H. W. Rowley	17.0	9.8	0.81	2.25	8.00
June 8	do				1.84	Nil.
June 23	do				1.43	"
July 17	do				Dry.	"
July 24	do				"	"
Sept. 3	do					
Sept. 16	do				2.00	0.78
Oct. 9	do	43.0	66.0	3.11	3.30	205.00
Nov. 6	do				1.90	Nil.

SESSIONAL PAPER No 25c

DAILY GAUGE HEIGHT AND DISCHARGE of Gap Creek at Small's Ranch, for 1914.

DAY.	March.		April.		May.		June.	
	Gauge Height.	Dis-charge.	Gauge Height.	Dis-charge.	Gauge Height.	Dis-charge.	Gauge Height.	Dis-charge.
	Feet.	*Sec.-ft*	*Feet.*	*Sec.-ft.*	*Feet.*	*Sec.-ft.*	*Feet.*	*Sec.-ft.*
1	... ...	... .	2.87	71.0	2.10	2.70	1.84	Nil.
2	... ...	... ...	2.84	65.0	2.10	2.70	1.84	"
3	... ...	... . .	2.72	47.0	2.10	2.70	1.84	"
4	... ...	... ...	2.71	46.0	2.10	2.70	1.84	"
5	... ...	....	3.22	168.0	2.16	4.40	1.86	0.02
6	3.11	127.0	2.96	88.0	2.26	8.40	1.85	Nil.
7	3.06	113.0	2.72	47.0	2.26	8.40	1.84	"
8	3.03	105.0	2.47	21.0	2.36	13.60	1.84	"
9	2.96	88.0	2.49	23.0	2.38	14.80	1.84	"
10	2.66	39.0	2.43	18.0	2.40	16.00	1.84	"
11	2.61	34.0	2.42	17.0	2.36	13.60	1.86	0.02
12	2.71	46.0	2.94	84.0	2.24	7.50	1.90	0.10
13	3.34	227.0	3.08	118.0	2.17	4.80	1.96	0.40
14	3.52	344.0	2.99	96.0	2.09	2.50	1.92	0.18
15	3.14	137.0	2.94	84.0	2.06	1.82	1.90	0.10
16	2.78	56.0	2.92	80.0	2.03	1.28	1.86	0.02
17	2.48	22.0	2.75	52.0	2.02	1.12	1.86	0.02
18	2.40	16.0	2.50	24.0	2.00	0.80	1.82	Nil.
19	2.46	20.0	2.42	17.0	1.98	0.60	1.80	"
20	2.34	12.4	2.47	21.0	1.98	0.60	1.60	"
21	2.21	6.2	2.40	16.0	1.98	0.60	1.80	"
22	2.19	5.5	2.31	10.8	1.97	0.50	1.78	"
23	2.11	3.0	2.28	9.3	1.97	0.50	1.78	"
24	2.17	4.8	2.29	9.7	1.97	0.50	1.78	"
25	2.30	10.2	2.26	8.4	1.96	0.40	1.87	0.04
26	2.29	9.7	2.26	8.4	1.94	0.26	1.86	0.02
27	2.26	8.4	2.21	6.2	1.93	0.22	1.84	Nil.
28	2.19	5.5	2.16	4.4	1.91	0.14	1.82	"
29	2.11	3.0	2.13	3.5	1.89	0.08	1.84	"
30	2.50	24.0	2.12	3.2	1.88	0.06	1.84	"
31	2.50	24.0	....	....	1.86	0.02	....	....

5 GEORGE V. A. 1915

DAILY GAUGE HEIGHT AND DISCHARGE of Gap Creek at Small's Ranch, for 1914.
—*Concluded.*

DAY.	July.		August.		September.		October.	
	Gauge Height.	Dis-charge.	Gauge Height.	Dis-charge.	Gauge Height.	Dis-charge.	Gauge Height.	Dsi-charge.
	Feet.	*Sec.-ft.*	*Feet.*	*Sec.-ft.*	*Feet.*	*Sec.-ft.*	*Feet.*	*Sec.-ft.*
1	1.82	Nil.	1.69	Nil.	1.65	Nil.	1.78	Nil.
2	1.79	"	1.68	"	1.65	"	1.78	"
3	1.79	"	1.68	"	1.65	"	1.78	"
4	1.79	"	1.67	"	1.65	"	2.40	16.00
5	1.79	"	1.68	"	1.65	"	2.20	5.80
6	1.78	"	1.68	"	1.64	"	2.46	20.00
7	1.78	"	1.67	"	1.64	"	2.46	20.00
8	1.78	"	1.69	"	1.64	"	3.45	290.00
9	1.78	"	1.69	"	1.64	"	3.28	196.00
10	1.77	"	1.70	"	1.64	"	2.69	43.00
11	1.76	"	1.70	"	1.63	"	2.50	24.00
12	1.74	"	1.69	"	1.63	Nil.	2.33	11.90
13	1.72	"	1.69	"	2.46	20.00	2.22	6.60
14	1.70	"	1.68	"	2.50	24.00	2.20	5.80
15	1.69	"	1.65	"	2.16	4.40	2.18	5.00
16	1.67	"	1.65	"	2.00	0.80	2.15	4.10
17	1.65	"	1.65	"	1.93	0.22	2.10	2.70
18	1.64	"	1.68	"	1.89	0.08	2.05	1.60
19	1.64	"	1.68	"	1.84	Nil.	2.02	1.12
20	1.64	"	1.68	"	1.83	"	2.02	1.12
21	1.64	"	1.68	"	1.83	"	2.03	1.28
22	1.64	"	1.67	"	1.83	"	2.01	0.96
23	1.63	"	1.67	"	1.83	"	1.99	0.70
24	1.73	"	1.68	"	1.83	"	1.97	0.50
25	1.73	"	1.69	"	1.83	"	1.95	0.30
26	1.73	"	1.68	"	1.83	"	1.94	0.26
27	1.72	"	1.66	"	1.80	"	1.94	0.26
28	1.69	"	1.66	"	1.79	"	1.94	0.26
29	1.69	"	1.66	"	1.79	"	1.94	0.26
30	1.69	"	1.66	"	1.78	"	1.95	0.30
31	1.69	"	1.66	"	....	....	1.95	0.30

MONTHLY DISCHARGE of Gap Creek at Small's Ranch, for 1914.

(Drainage area 108 square miles.)

MONTH.	DISCHARGE IN SECOND-FEET.				RUN-OFF.	
	Maximum.	Minimum.	Mean.	Per square Mile.	Depth in inches on Drainage Area.	Total in Acre-feet.
March (6-31)	344.00	3.00	57.00	0.5310	0.5200	2,956
April	168.00	3.20	42.00	0.3910	0.4400	2,514
May	16.00	0.02	3.70	0.0342	0.0390	227
June	0.40	0.00	0.03	0.0003	0.0003	2
July	....	....	....	....	....	Nil.
August	....	....	....	....	....	"
September	24.00	0.00	1.65	0.0153	0.0200	98
October	290.00	0.00	21.00	0.1970	0.2300	1,309
The period	....	....	....	....	1 2500	7.106

MCSHANE CREEK AT SMALL'S RANCH.

Location.—On the SW. ¼ Sec. 3, Tp. 10, Rge. 27, W. 3rd Mer., at the highway bridge near Wm. Small's house.

Records available.—April 24, 1909, to October 31, 1914.

Gauge.—Vertical staff; zero of gauge was maintained at 86.41 feet during 1909-10; 85.71 feet during 1911-12; 85.21 feet during 1913; 85.74 feet during 1914.

Bench-mark.—Permanent iron bench-mark; assumed elevation, 100.00 feet.

Channel.—Composed of sand and gravel, and shifts during flood stages.

Discharge measurements.—Made by wading, or from the highway bridge during flood stages.

Winter flow.—Station discontinued during winter season.

Observer.—Wm. Small.

DISCHARGE MEASUREMENTS of McShane Creek at Small's Ranch, in 1914.

Date.	Engineer.	Width.	Area of Section.	Mean Velocity.	Gauge Height.	Discharge.
		Feet.	*Sq. ft.*	*Ft. per sec.*	*Feet.*	*Sec.-ft.*
Mar. 14	H. D. St. A. Smith	10.0	5.40	1.79	1.25	9.70
Mar. 17	H. R. Carscallen	12.6	6.87	0.54	1.06	3.70
April 16	H. O. Brown	12.2	6.56	1.54	1.19	10.12
May 6	H. W. Rowley	7.0	2.98	0.70	0.98	1.69
May 29	do				Dry.	Nil.
June 8	do				"	"
June 23	do				"	"
July 17	do				"	"
July 24	do				"	"
Sept. 3	do				"	"
Sept. 16	do				"	"
Oct. 9	do	21.5	30.7	0.65	1.16	20.00
Nov. 6	do				Dry.	Nil.

DAILY GAUGE HEIGHT AND DISCHARGE of McShane Creek at Small's Ranch, for 1914.

DAY.	March.		April.		May.		June.	
	Gauge Height.	Dis-charge.	Gauge Height.	Dis-charge.	Gauge Height.	Dis-charge.	Gauge Height.	Dis-charge.
	Feet.	*Sec.-ft.*	*Feet.*	*Sec.-ft.*	*Feet.*	*Sec.-ft.*	*Feet.*	*Sec.-ft.*
1			1.19	10.10	Dry.	Nil.	Dry.	Nil.
2			1.11	5.80	"	"	"	"
3			0.96	1.42	"	"	"	"
4	1.07	2.20	1.10	5.30	"	"	"	"
5	1.06	2.00	1.20	10.70	0.89	0.63	"	"
6	1.06	2.00	1.16	8.40	0.96	1.42	"	"
7	1.05	1.80	0.95	1.25	0.92	0.92	"	"
8	1.07	2.20	0.88	0.56	0.99	1.93	"	"
9	1.15	4.60	0.91	0.81	1.00	2.10	"	"
10	1.15	4.60	0.90	0.70	0.89	0.63	"	"
11	1.15	4.60	0.91	0.81	0.83	0.25	"	"
12	1.20	6.80	1.13	6.80	0.66	Nil.	"	"
13	1.30	12.70	1.18	9.50	Dry.	"	"	"
14	1.31	13.40	1.18	9.50	"	"	"	"
15	1.26	11.90	1.18	9.50	"	"	"	"
16	1.08	3.90	1.18	9.50	"	"	"	"
17	0.95	1.25	1.10	5.30	"	"	"	"
18	0.98	1.76	1.06	3.80	"	"	"	"
19	0.83	0.25	1.00	2.10	"	"	"	"
20	0.63	Nil.	1.06	3.80	"	"	"	"
21	0.60	"	0.99	1.93	"	"	"	"
22	0.35	"	0.92	0.92	"	"	"	"
23	...a	"	0.99	1.93	"	"	"	"
24	0.75	"	0.95	1.25	"	"	"	"
25	...a	"	0.90	0.70	"	"	"	"
26	...a	"	0.86	0.42	"	"	"	"
27	...a	"	0.81	0.15	"	"	"	"
28	...a	"	0.74	Nil.	"	"	"	"
29	...a	"	0.77	0.04	"	"	"	"
30	1.38	22.00	0.64	Nil.	"	"		
31	1.30	16.70			"	"		

5 GEORGE V. A. 1915

DAILY GAUGE HEIGHT AND DISCHARGE of McShane Creek at Small's Ranch, for 1914.
—Concluded.

DAY.	July.		August.		September.		October.	
	Gauge Height.	Dis- charge.	Gauge Height.	Dis- charge.	Gauge Height.	Dis- charge.	Gauge Height.	Dis- charge.
	Feet.	*Sec.-ft.*	*Feet.*	*Sec.-ft.*	*Feet.*	*Sec.-ft.*	*Feet.*	*Sec.-ft.*
1	Dry.	Nil.	Dry.	Nil.	Dry.	Nil.	Dry.	Nil.
2	"	"	"	"	"	"	"	"
3	"	"	"	"	"	"	"	"
4	"	"	"	"	"	"	1.17	21.00
5	"	"	"	"	"	"	0.97	7.90
6	"	"	"	"	"	"	0.97	7.90
7	"	"	"	"	"	"	1.14	18.70
8	"	"	"	"	"	"	1.92	71.00
9	"	"	"	"	"	"	1.27	27.00
10	"	"	"	"	"	"	0.77	1.20
11	"	"	"	"	"	"	0.62	Nil.
12	"	"	"	"	"	"	0.52	"
13	"	"	"	"	1.23	31.0	0.51	"
14	"	"	"	"	0.86	3.1	0.43	"
15	"	"	"	"	Dry.	Nil.	0.61	"
16	"	"	"	"	"	"	0.52	"
17	"	"	"	"	"	"	0.43	"
18	"	"	"	"	"	"	Dry.	"
19	"	"	"	"	"	"	"	"
20	"	"	"	"	"	"	"	"
21	"	"	"	"	"	"	"	"
22	"	"	"	"	"	"	"	"
23	"	"	"	"	"	"	"	"
24	"	"	"	"	"	"	"	"
25	"	"	"	"	"	"	"	"
26	"	"	"	"	"	"	"	"
27	"	"	"	"	"	"	"	"
28	"	"	"	"	"	"	"	"
29	"	"	"	"	"	"	"	"
30	"	"	"	"	"	"	"	"
31	"	"	"	"	"	"	"	"

MONTHLY DISCHARGE of McShane Creek at Small's Ranch, for 1914.

(Drainage area 28 square miles.)

MONTH.	DISCHARGE IN SECOND-*FEET*.				RUN-OFF.	
	Maximum.	Minimum.	Mean.	Per square Mile.	Depth in inches on Drainage Area.	Total in Acre-feet.
March (4-31)	22.00	0.00	4.10	0.1460	0.15	228
April	10.70	0.00	3.77	0.1350	0.15	224
May	2.10	0.00	0.25	0.0090	0.01	16
June	....	....	....	....	....	Nil.
July	....	....	....	....	....	"
August	....	....	....	....	....	"
September	31.00	0.00	1.14	0.0407	0.04	68
October	71.00	0.00	5.00	0.1800	0.21	307
The period	....	....	....	....	0.56	843

MAPLE CREEK AT MAPLE CREEK (UPPER STATION).

Location.—On the *NE.* ¼ Sec. 16, Tp. 11, Rge. 26, W. 3rd Mer., at the first highway bridge north of the town of Maple Creek.
Records available.—May 13, 1908, to October 31, 1914.
Gauge.—Vertical staff; zero of gauge was maintained at 2,492.64 ft. during 1908-09-10-11-14, and at 2,492.71 feet during the years of 1912 and 1913.

Bench-marks.—Permanent iron bench-mark. *Elevation,* 2,499 875 feet above sea level, which is referred to the Geodetic Survey bench-mark No. 145c, on the northeast corner of the post office at Maple Creek, Sask., the elevation of which is 2,510.39 feet above mean sea level.
Channel.—Composed of sand, and may shift during flood stages.
Discharge measurements.—Made from the bridge, by wading, or with a weir.
Winter flow.—Station discontinued during winter season.
Observer.—Miss Kate Williams.

DISCHARGE MEASUREMENTS of Maple Creek at Maple Creek (Upper Station), in 1914.

Date.	Engineer.	Width.	Area of Section.	Mean Velocity.	Gauge Height.	Discharge.
		Feet.	*Sq. ft.*	*Ft. per sec.*	*Feet.*	*Sec.-ft.*
Mar. 13............	M. H. French.....	8.0	4.90	0.56	1.47	2.70
April 7............	H. O. Brown........... ..	33.0	57.50	0.87	2.76	49.00
April 15............	do	31.7	49.00	1.00	2.83	49.00
April 18............	do	27.5	25.50	0.74	2.05	18.90
May 7............	H. W. Rowley.............	18.0	8.80	0.55	1.45	4.80
May 12............	do	11.0	7.10	0.83	1.51	5.90
May 30...... ...	do				0.56	Nil.
June 10	do				0.87	"
June 26............	do				Dry.	"
July 18............	do				"	"
Aug. 14............	do				"	"
Sept. 4............	do				"	"
Sept. 17............	do				"	"
Oct. 12............	do	19.00	23.30	0.67	2.00	14.90
Nov. 7............	do				0.77	Nil.

DAILY GAUGE HEIGHT AND DISCHARGE of Maple Creek at Maple Creek (Upper Station), for 1914.

DAY.	March.		April.		May.		June.	
	Gauge Height.	Dis-charge.	Gauge Height.	Dis-charge.	Gauge Height.	Dis-charge.	Gauge Height.	Dis-charge.
	Feet.	*Sec.-ft.*	*Feet.*	*Sec.-ft.*	*Feet.*	*Sec.-ft.*	*Feet.*	*Sec.-ft.*
1............			2.45	32.0	1.34	3.40	0.84	0.23
2............			2.55	36.0	1.33	3.30	0.84	0.23
3............			2.43	31.0	1.31	3.10	0.84	0.23
4............			2.27	25.0	1.32	3.20	0.80	0.15
5............			2.60	39.0	1.34	3.40	0.80	0.15
6............			1.95	14.7	1.60	7.00	0.73	0.03
7............			2.80	49.0	1.44	4.60	0.69a	Nil.
8............			2.15	20.0	1.44	4.60	0.65	"
9............			1.80	11.0	1.48	5.10	0.62	"
10............			1.77a	10.4	1.68	8.60	0.65	"
11............			1.75	10.0	1.53	5.90	0.72	0.02
12............			1.72	9.4	1.48	5.10	0.72	0.02
13............	1.45	4.70	2.70	44.0	1.40	4.00	0.74	0.04
14............	2.76	47.00	2.79	48.0	1.35	3.50	0.74	0.04
15............	3.45	92 00	2.70	44.0	1.28	2.80	0.70	Nil.
16............	3.10	67.00	2.58	38.0	1.28	2.80	0.62	"
17............	2.40	30.00	2.36	28.0	1.24	2.40	0.62	"
18............	1.80	11.00	2.14	20.0	1.21	2.10	0.62	"
19............	1.65a	8.00	2.03	16.9	1.18	1.84	0.60	"
20............	1.50	5.40	1.85	12.2	1.13	1.46	0.58	"
21............	1.69	8.80	1.90	13.5	1.10	1.25	0.58	"
22............	1.61	7.20	1.79	10.8	1.08	1.13	0.58	"
23............	1.45	4.70	1.64	7.8	1.02	0.80	0.58	"
24............	1.23	2.30	1.67	8.4	0.96a	0.58	0.58	"
25............	1.17	1.76	1.68	8.6	0.90	0.40	0.58	"
26............	1.19	1.92	1.59	6.8	0.88	0.34	0.58	"
27............	1.21	2.10	1.56	6.4	0.73	0.03	0.58	"
28............	1.23	2.30	1.44	4.6	0.82	0.19	0.58	"
29............	1.25	2.50	1.37	3.7	0.82a	0.19	0.58	"
30............	1.45	4.70	1.34	3.4	0.82	0.19	Dry.	"
31............	1.40	4.00			0.84	0.23		

a Gauge height interpolated.

5 GEORGE V, A. 1915

DAILY GAUGE HEIGHT AND DISCHARGE of Maple Creek at Maple Creek (Upper Station) for 1914.—*Concluded.*

DAY.	July.		August.		September.		October.	
	Gauge Height.	Dis-charge.	Gauge Height.	Dis-charge.	Gauge Height.	Dis-charge.	Gauge Height.	Dis-charge.
	Feet.	Sec.-ft.	Feet.	Sec.-ft.	Feet.	Sec.-ft.	Feet.	Sec.-ft.
1	0.66	Nil.	Dry.	Nil.	Dry.	Nil.	Dry.	Nil.
2	0.66	"	"	"	"	"	"	"
3	0.64	"	"	"	"	"	"	"
4	0.64	"	"	"	"	"	"	"
5	0.62	"	"	"	"	"	"	"
6	0.62	"	"	"	"	"	"	"
7	0.62	"	"	"	"	"	"	"
8	Dry.	"	"	"	"	"	2.16	21.00
9	"	"	"	"	"	"	3.26	78.00
10	"	"	"	"	"	"	3.16	71.00
11	"	"	"	"	"	"	2.60a	39.00
12	"	"	"	"	"	"	1.98	15.50
13	"	"	"	"	"	"	1.90a	13.50
14	"	"	"	"	"	"	1.80	11.00
15	"	"	"	"	"	"	1.50	5.40
16	"	"	"	"	"	"	1.30	3.00
17	"	"	"	"	"	"	1.15	1.60
18	"	"	"	"	"	"	1.00	0.70
19	"	"	"	"	"	"	0.90a	0.40
20	"	"	"	"	"	"	0.83	0.21
21	"	"	"	"	"	"	0.80a	0.15
22	"	"	"	"	"	"	0.78	0.11
23	"	"	"	"	"	"	0.76a	0.07
24	"	"	"	"	"	"	0.74	0.04
25	"	"	"	"	"	"	0.71a	0.01
26	"	"	"	"	"	"	0.68	Nil.
27	"	"	"	"	"	"	0.66a	"
28	"	"	"	"	"	"	0.64	"
29	"	"	"	"	"	"	0.61a	"
30	"	"	"	"	"	"	0.58	"
31	"	"	"	"	....	....	0.55	"

a Gauge height interpolated.

MONTHLY DISCHARGE of Maple Creek at Maple Creek (Upper Station), for 1914.

(Drainage area 81 square miles.)

MONTH.	DISCHARGE IN SECOND-FEET.				RUN-OFF.	
	Maximum.	Minimum.	Mean.	Per square Mile.	Depth in inches on Drainage Area.	Total in Acre-feet.
March (13-31)	92.00	1.76	16.20	0.2000	0.1400	610
April	40.90	3.40	20.00	0.2520	0.2800	1,214
May	8.60	0.03	2.70	0.0330	0.0400	165
June	0.23	0.00	0.04	0.0005	0.0006	2
July	....	....	....	....	....	Nil.
August						"
September						"
October	78.00	0.00	8.40	0.1040	0.1200	517
The period	....	....	....	....	0 5800	2,508

MAPLE CREEK NEAR MAPLE CREEK (LOWER STATION).

Location.—On the SE. ¼ Sec. 28, Tp. 11, Rge. 26, W. 3rd Mer.

Records available.—May 4, 1910, to October 31, 1914.

Gauge.—Vertical staff; zero of the gauge was maintained at 81.64 feet during 1910-11; 81.60 feet during 1912-14.

Bench-mark.—Permanent iron bench-mark; assumed elevation, 100.00 feet.

Channel.—Composed of sand, and liable to shift during flood stage.

Discharge measurements.—Made from the bridge, or by wading, or with a weir.

Winter flow.—Station discontinued during the winter season.

Observer.—Miss Kate Williams.

SESSIONAL PAPER No. 25c

DISCHARGE MEASUREMENTS of Maple Creek near Maple Creek (Lower Station), in 1914.

Date.	Engineer.	Width.	Area of Section.	Mean Velocity.	Gauge Height.	Discharge.
		Feet.	*Sq. ft.*	*Ft. per sec.*	*Feet.*	*Sec.-ft.*
April 15............	H. O. Brown	25.90	28.90	1.23	4.25	35.00
April 18.	do	25.50	20.50	1.15	3.77	24.00
May 7.............	H. W. Rowley....	12.00	5.70	0.78	2.98	4.40
May 12	do	12.00	9.05	0.67	3.05	6.10
May 30.	do	....	....	....	2.52	...........*a*
June 10	do	......*b*	....	....	2.58	0.18
June 26	do	....*b*	....	....	2.55	2.30
July 18....	do	......*b*	....	....	2.81	0.32
July 25..........	do	......*b*	....	....	2.76	0.09
Aug. 14	do	......*b*	....	....	2.67	0.07
Sept. 4	do	......*b*	....	....	2.54	0.04
Sept. 17	do	......*b*	....	....	2.55	0.34
Oct. 10..........	do	36.00	29.80	1.17	5.66	93.40
Oct. 12..........	do	14.50	17.40	0.92	3.76	15.90
Nov. 7	do	......*b*	....	....	2.38	0.40

a Slight flow, too small to measure.
b Weir measurement.

DAILY GAUGE HEIGHT AND DISCHARGE of Maple Creek near Maple Creek (Lower Station), for 1914.

DAY.	March.		April.		May.		June.	
	Gauge Height.	Dis- charge.	Gauge Height.	Dis- charge.	Gauge Height.	Dis- charge.	Gauge Height.	Dis- charge.
	Feet.	*Sec.-ft.*	*Feet.*	*Sec.-ft.*	*Feet.*	*Sec.-ft.*	*Feet.*	*Sec.-ft.*
1....................................	....	....	3.87	23.0	2.98	4.70	2.32	0.20*c*
2....................................	....	....	3.90	24.0	2.95	4.30	2.30	0.20
3....................................	....	....	3.87	23.0	2.83	2.90	2.30	0.20
4....................................	....	....	3.85	23.0	2.88*a*	3.50	2.54	0.18
5....................................	... .	....	4.02	28.0	2.93	4.10	2.54	0.18
6....................................	....	....	4.65	50.0	3.15	7.30	2.54	0.18
7....................................	....	....	4.42	41.0	2.98	4.70	2.54	0.18
8....................................	....	... ...	3.82	22.0	3.00	5.00	2.55	0.18
9....................................	....	.. ..	3.35	11.0	3.15	7.30	2.56	0.18
10....................................	....	. .	3.34*a*	10.8	3.09	6.30	2.61	0.18
11....................................	....	....	3.33	10.6	3.02	5.30	2.62	0.18
12....................................	....	....	3.31	10.2	2.90	3.70	2.61	0.18
13....................................	6.38	129.0	4.48	43.0	2.86	3.30	2.61	0.18
14....................................	6.70	145.0	4.78	55.0	2.70	1.70	2.61	0.18
15....................................	6.70	145.0	4.48	43.0	2.70	1.70	2.62	0.18
16....................................	6.34	127.0	4.11	30.0	2.68*a*	1.57	2.62	0.19
17....................................	4.19	33.0	4.05	29.0	2.65	1.37	2.60	0.20
18....................................	3.50	14.2	3.81	22.0	2.71	1.79	2.60	0.20
19....................................	3.60*a*	16.5	3.67	18.2	2.68	1.57	2.60*a*	0.20
20....................................	3.70	18.9	3.53	14.9	2.62	1.18	2.60	0.20
21....................................	3.67	18.2	3.53	14.9	2.54	0.81	2.56	0.21
22....................................	3.02	5.3	3.39	11.8	2.50	0.65	2.56	0.22
23....................................	3.02	5.3	3.20	8.0	2.40	0.40	2.56	0.23
24....................................	2.98	4.7	3.18	7.7	2.47*a*	0.58	2.50	0.23
25....................................	2.97	4.6	3.19	7.9	2.54	0.81	2.50	0.23
26....................................	2.98*a*	4.7	3.15	7.3	2.58	0.97	2.50	0.23
27....................................	2.99*a*	4.9	3.12	6.8	2.58	0.97	2.40	0.22
28....................................	3.00*a*	5.0	3.07	6.0	2.56	0.89	2.40	0.22
29....................................	3.01	5.2	2.99	4.9	2.46	0.55	2.38	0.20
30....................................	3.54	15.1	2.98	4.7	2.36	0.32	2.30	0.20
31....................................	3.87	23.2	....	....	2.32	0.24	....	....

a Gauge height interpolated.
c Shifting conditions June 1 to Sept. 15.

5 GEORGE V, A. 1915

DAILY GAUGE HEIGHT AND DISCHARGE of Maple Creek near Maple Creek (Lower Station), for 1914.—*Concluded.*

DAY.	July.		August.		September.		October.	
	Gauge Height.	Dis- charge.	Gauge Height.	Dis- charge.	Gauge Height.	Dis- charge.	Gauge Height.	Dis- charge.
	Feet.	*Sec.-ft.*	*Feet.*	*Sec.-ft.*	*Feet.*	*Sec.-ft.*	*Feet.*	*Sec.-ft.*
1	2.30a	0.20	2.22	0.11	2.40	0.40	2.52	0.73
2	2.30	0.20	2.30	0.20	2.20	0.05	2.52	0.73
3	2.30	0.20	2.30	0.20	2.20	0.05	2.99b	4.90
4	2.30	0.20	2.40	0.40	2.40	0.40	3.46b	13.30
5	2.40	0.20	2.45	0.52	2.40	0.40	3.93b	25.00
6	2.40	0.20	2.50	0.65	2.41	0.42	4.40b	40.00
7	2.40	0.20	2.55b	0.85	2.42	0.45	4.87b	59.00
8	2.50	0.21	2.60	1.05	2.44	0.50	5.34b	79.00
9	2.50	0.21	2.60	1.05	2.40	0.40	5.82	101.00
10	2.60	0.22	2.70	1.70	2.53	0.78	5.70	95.00
11	2.70	0.23	2.70	1.70	2.53	0.78	4.10	30.00
12	2.80	0.24	2.77	2.30	2.60b	1.05	3.80	22.00
13	2.90	0.26	2.77	2.30	2.65b	1.37	3.00	5 00
14	2.90	0.28	2.67	1.46	2.72b	1.88	2.90b	3.70
15	2.90	0.30	2.70	1.70	2.78	2.40c	2.80	2.60
16	2.90	0.33	2.70	1.70	2.76	2.20	2.80b	2.60
17	2.90	0.35	2.68b	1.57	2.61	1.12	2.80	2.60
18	2.81	0.32	2.66	1.44	2.60	1.05	2.80b	2.60
19	2.81	0.32	2.66b	1.44	2.57	0.93	2.80	2.60
20	2.80	0.31	2.66	1.44	2.57	0.93	2.70b	1.70
21	2.79	0.30	2.70	1.70	2.55	0.85	2.60	1.05
22	2.78	0.23	2.70	1.70	2.54b	0.81	2.60b	1.05
23	2.78	0.20	2.70	1.70	2.53	0.77	2.60	1.05
24	2.77	0.15	2.64	1.31	2.53b	0.77	2.59b	1.01
25	2.76	0.10	2.68	1.57	2.53	0.77	2.58	0.97
26	2.76	0.10	2.68	1.57	2.52	0.73	2.58b	0.97
27	2.74	0.09	2.65	1.37	2.53	0.77	2.58	0.97
28	2.60	0.08	2.65	1.37	2.53	0.77	2.58	0.97
29	2.50	0.08	2.60	1.05	2.52b	0.73	2.58	0.97
30	2.40	0.09	2.55	0.85	2.50	0.65	2.58b	0.97
31	2.40	0.10	2.50	0.65	....	....	2.59	1.01

a Gauge heights unreliable Aug. 1 to 31; correction applied.
b Gauge height interpolated.
c Shifting conditions June 1 to Sept. 15.

MONTHLY DISCHARGE of Maple Creek near Maple Creek (Lower Station), for 1914.

(Drainage area 86 square miles.)

MONTH.	DISCHARGE IN SECOND-FEET.				RUN-OFF.	
	Maximum.	Minimum	Mean.	Per square Mile.	Depth in inches on Drainage Area.	Total in Acre-feet.
March (13-31)	145.00	4.60	38.10	0.4430	0.310	1,437
April	55.00	4.70	20.40	0.2370	0.260	1,214
May	7.30	0.24	2.60	0.0302	0.035	160
June	0.23	0.18	0.20	0.0023	0.003	12
July	0.35	0.08	0.21	0.0024	0.003	13
August	2.30	0.11	1.25	0.0145	0.017	77
September	2.40	0.05	0.84	0.0098	0.010	50
October	101.00	0.73	16.30	0.1900	0.220	1,002
The period	....	....	....	....	0.860	3,965

GAP CREEK NEAR MAPLE CREEK.

Location.—On the road allowance east of the NE. ¼ Sec. 31, Tp. 11, Rge. 26, W. 3rd Mer., at the highway traffic bridge.

Records available.—May 4, 1910, to October 31, 1914.

Gauge.—Vertical staff; the zero of the gauge was maintained at 81.44 feet during 1910-11; 81.61 feet during 1912-14.

Beñch-mark.—Permanent iron bench-mark; assumed elevation, 100.00 feet.
Channel.—Composed of sand, and shifting.
Discharge measurements.—Made from bridge, by wading, or with a weir.
Winter flow.—Station discontinued during winter season.
Observer.—Miss Kate Williams.

DISCHARGE MEASUREMENTS of Gap Creek near Maple Creek, in 1914.

Date.	Engineer.	Width.	Area of Section.	Mean Velocity.	Gauge Height.	Discharge.
		Feet.	*Sq. ft.*	*Ft. per sec.*	*Feet.*	*Sec.-ft.*
Mar. 14.	M. H. French.....	47.0	104.0	1.76	3.69	183.00
April 7..	H. O. Brown.......	47.6	88.8	1.36	2.97	121.00
April 15	do	24.0	58.1	1.59	3.07	93.00
April 18..	do	35.8	34.3	1.37	2.30	47.00
May 7............	H. W. Rowley..............	10.0	6.4	1.36	1.47	8.70
May 12	do	11.0	9.2	1.82	1.72	16.70
May 30............	do	........*a*			0.97	0.05
June 10.... .. .	do	....	....	....	Dry.	Nil.
June 26.........	do	....	....	....	"	"
July 18.........	do	....	....	....	"	"
July 25.........	do	....	....	....	"	"
Aug. 14........ .	do	....	....	....	"	*a*
Sept. 4.........	do	....	....	....	"	"
Sept. 17	do	....*a*	....	....	1.32	2.20
Oct. 12..........	do	22.0	21.1	1.30	2.08	28.00
Oct. 14...........,..	do	11.0	8.4	1.41	1.64	11.80
Nov. 7..,.........	do	....	....	....	0.99	Nil.

a Weir measurement.

DAILY GAUGE HEIGHT AND DISCHARGE of Gap Creek near Maple Creek, for 1914.

DAY.	March.		April.		May.		June.	
	Gauge Height.	Dis- charge.	Gauge Height.	Dis- charge.	Gauge Height.	Dis- charge.	Gauge Height.	Dis- charge.
	Feet.	*Sec.-ft.*	*Feet.*	*Sec.-ft.*	*Feet.*	*Sec.-ft.*	*Feet.*	*Sec.-ft.*
1............	....	.. ..	3.32	139.0	1.30	5.10	0.95	Nil.
2............	....	.. ..	2.72	79.0	1.31	5.30	0.95	"
3............	....	.. ..	2.81	87.0	1.31	5.30	0.95	"
4............	....	....	2.35	50.0	1.30*a*	5.10	0.98	0.20
5............	....	....	3.40	149.0	1.30	5.10	0.98	0.20
6............	....	....	3.26	133.0	1.32	5.50	0.98	0.20
7............	....	....	2.85	90.0	1.41	7.30	0.94	Nil.
8............	....	....	2.42	55.0	1.49	9.30	0.90	"
9............	....	....	1.99	30.0	1.47	8.80	0.91	"
10............	....	....	1.94*a*	27.0	1.50	9.60	0.95	"
11............	....	....	1.89	24.0	1.56	11.30	0.95	"
12............	....	....	1.82	21.0	1.61	12.80	0.91	"
13............	2.17	40.0	2.86	91.0	1.39	6.90	0.91	"
14............	3.77	193.0	2.97	102.0	1.35	6.10	0.91	"
15............	3.75	191.0	2.91	96.0	1.33	5.70	0.91	"
16............	4.43	273.0	3.15	120.0	1.32	5.50	0.91	"
17............	2.55	65.0	2.75	82.0	1.17	2.90	0.91	"
18............	2.35	50.0	2.26	45.0	1.15	2.60	0.91	"
19............	2.20	41.0	2.08	37.0	1.12	2.10	0.91	"
20............	2.02	31.0	1.87	24.0	1.09	1.66	0.91	"
21............	2.04	32.0	1.93	26.0	1.05	1.10	0.91	"
22............	1.92	26.0	1.78	19.3	1.03	0.82	0.91	"
23............	1.72	16.8	1.61	12.8	0.97	0.10	0.91	"
24............	1.59	12.2	1.60	12.5	1.95*a*	Nil.	0.91	"
25............	1.50*a*	9.6	1.57	11.6	0.93	"	Dry.	"
26............	1.45*a*	8.3	1.53	10.4	0.99	0.30	"	"
27............	1.40*a*	7.1	1.49	9.3	0.98*a*	0.20	"	"
28............	1.40*a*	7.1	1.45	8.3	0.97	0.10	"	"
29............	1.50*a*	9.6	1.41	7.3	0.97	0.10	"	"
30............	1.95	28.0	1.35	6.1	0.97	0.10	"	"
31............	2.01	31.0	....	....	0.95	0.00	....	....

a Gauge height interpolated.

5 GEORGE V, A. 1915

DAILY GAUGE HEIGHT AND DISCHARGE of Gap Creek near Maple Creek, for 1914.
—*Concluded.*

DAY.	July.		August.		September.		October.	
	Gauge Height.	Dis-charge.	Gauge Height.	Dis-charge.	Gauge Height.	Dis-charge.	Gauge Height.	Dis-charge.
	Feet.	*Sec.-ft.*	*Feet.*	*Sec.-ft.*	*Feet.*	*Sec.-ft.*	*Feet.*	*Sec.-ft.*
1	0.91	Nil.	Dry.	Nil.	Dry.	Nil.	Dry.	Nil.
2	0.91	"	"	"	"	"	"	"
3	0.91	"	"	"	"	"	"	"
4	0.91	"	"	"	"	"	"	"
5	0.91	"	"	"	"	"	"	"
6	0.91	"	"	"	"	"	"	"
7	Dry.	"	"	"	"	"	"	"
8	"	"	"	"	"	"	"	"
9	"	"	"	"	"	"	"	"
10	"	"	"	"	"	"	2.00	27.0
11	"	"	"	"	"	"	2.04a	29.0
12	"	"	"	"	"	"	2.08	31.0
13	"	"	"	"	"	"	1.87a	21.0
14	"	"	"	"	"	"	1.66	12.7
15	"	"	"	"	2.00	27.0	1.48a	7.2
16	"	"	"	"	1.50	7.7	1.30	3.3
17	"	"	"	"	1.32	3.5	Dry.	Nil.
18	"	"	"	"	Dry.	Nil.	"	"
19	"	"	"	"	"	"	"	"
20	"	"	"	"	"	"	"	"
21	"	"	"	"	"	"	"	"
22	"	"	"	"	"	"	"	"
23	"	"	"	"	"	"	"	"
24	"	"	"	"	"	"	"	"
25	"	"	"	"	"	"	"	"
26	"	"	"	"	"	"	"	"
27	"	"	"	"	"	"	"	"
28	"	"	"	"	"	"	"	"
29	"	"	"	"	"	"	"	"
30	"	"	"	"	"	"	"	"
31	"	"	"	"	....	....	"	"

a Gauge height interpolated.

MONTHLY DISCHARGE of Gap Creek near Maple Creek, for 1914.

(Drainage area 274 square miles.)

MONTH.	DISCHARGE IN SECOND-FEET.				RUN-OFF.	
	Maximum.	Minimum	Mean.	Per square Mile.	Depth in inches on Drainage Area.	Total in Acre-feet.
March (13-31)	373.00	7.10	56.00	0.2060	0.140	2,126
April	149.00	6.10	53.00	0.1950	0.220	3,178
May	12.80	0.00	4.10	0.0149	0.020	252
June	0.20	0.00	0.02	Nil.	0.000	Nil.
July	....	....	....	....	....	"
August	....	....	....	....	....	..
September	27.00	0.00	1.27	0.0046	0.005	76
October	31.00	0.00	4.20	0.0154	0.020	260
The period	....	....	....	....	0 400	5,892

MISCELLANEOUS DISCHARGE MEASUREMENTS made in Bigstake Lake drainage basin, in 1914.

Date.	Engineer.	Stream.	Location.	Width.	Area of Section.	Mean Velocity.	Discharge.
				Feet.	*Sq. ft.*	*Ft. per sec.*	*Sec.-ft.*
Apr. 6....	H. O. Brown......	Maple Creek......	8-10-26-3.........	18.3	14.5	1.75	25.00
Apr. 6....	do	A Coulee.........	5-10-26-3.........				0.14
July 24....	H. W. Rowley....	Branch Gap Creek.	NE. 20-8-27-3.....				0.18
Sept. 8 ...	do	do	NE. 2-9-28-3......				0.69
Sept. 16...	do	do	SE. 33-8-28-3.....				0.39
Oct. 9....	do	do	13-9-28-3.........	25.2	61.5	1.66	102.00

MANY ISLAND LAKE DRAINAGE BASIN.

General Description.

Many Island Lake, about 25 square miles in area, is situated on the boundary line between the provinces of Alberta and Saskatchewan, about 10 miles north of the town of Walsh. It is the farthest west of the several lakes which receive the drainage of the north slope of the Cypress Hills. The water is shallow and alkaline. Its only source of water supply is Mackay Creek with its tributaries, Stony and Boxelder Creeks.

The topography of the basin is very rough, and the creek slopes are heavy. The basin is bare of trees except in the hills near the sources of the streams. The creek channels are deep, and the beds are mostly gravel.

As is the case in all prairie basins, the highest discharge occurs in April. All the streams of this drainage basin stop running in June or July and generally remain so for the remainder of the season.

In the lower part of the drainage basin near the lake, irrigation has been developed to some extent on hay meadows. In the upper part there are few irrigation schemes.

EAST BRANCH OF MACKAY CREEK AT GRANT'S RANCH.

Location.—On the NW. ¼ Sec. 36, Tp. 10, Rge. 1, W. 4th Mer., at Arthur Grant's ranch.
Records available.—From October 13, 1911, to October 31, 1914.
Gauge.—Vertical staff; the zero of the gauge was maintained at 75.65 feet during 1911; 75.85 feet during 1912-14.
Bench-mark.—Permanent iron bench-mark; assumed elevation, 100.00 feet.
Channel.—Practically permanent..
Discharge measurements.—Made by wading or with a weir.
Winter flow.—Station discontinued during winter season.
Observer.—Mrs. I. B. Grant.

DISCHARGE MEASUREMENTS of East Branch of Mackay Creek at Grant's Ranch, in 1914·

Date.	Engineer.	Width.	Area of Section.	Mean Velocity.	Gauge Height.	Discharge.
		Feet.	*Sq. ft.*	*Ft. per sec.*	*Feet.*	*Sec.-ft.*
Mar. 20...........	R. J. Srigley...............	10.00	4.70	0.46	0.71	2.17
Mar. 30...........	do	13.00	6.40	0.88	0.83	5.61
May 13...........	H. W. Rowley.............	12.00	7.45	0.64	0.86	4.80
June 11...........	do				0.33	Nil.
June 27...........	do				Dry.	"
July 28...........	do				"	"
Aug. 15...........	do				"	"
Sept. 18...........	do				"	"
Oct. 15...........	do	8.00*a*	2.80	0.83	0.73	2.32

a Measurement made 500 feet above gauge.

STREAM MEASUREMENTS, 1914

5 GEORGE V. A. 1915

DAILY GAUGE HEIGHT AND DISCHARGE of East Branch of Mackay Creek at Grant's Ranch, for 1914.

DAY.	March.		April.		May.		June.	
	Gauge Height.	Dis-charge.	Gauge Height.	Dis-charge.	Gauge Height.	Dis-charge.	Gauge Height.	Dis-charge.
	Feet.	Sec.-ft.	Feet.	Sec.-ft.	Feet.	Sec.-ft.	Feet.	Sec.-ft.
1	.	......	1.66	36.00	0.72	2.30	0.34	0.03
2	.	.. . .	1.39	24.00	0.72	2.30	0.36	0.04
3	. ..	......	1.38	24.00	0.68	1.78	0.38	0.06
4	.. . .	....	1.36	22.00	0.68	1.78	0.36	0.04
5	.....	....	2.61	79.00	0.84	4.30	0.38	0.06
6	....	......	1.59	33.00	0.82	4.00	0.38	0.06
7	....	....	1.45	27.00	0.86	4.70	0.38	0.06
8	....	....	1.23	16.90	0.98	7.90	0.37	0.05
9	....	....	1.23	16.90	1.17	14.40	0.37	0.05
10	.. . .	....	0.98	7.90	1.11	12.10	0.36	0.04
11	.. .	....	0.98	7.90	0.91	6.00	0.36	0.04
12			1.41	25.00	0.88	5.20	0.38	0.05
13	1.61	34.00	1.72	39.00	0.86	4.70	0.38	0.05
14	2.36	68.00	1.66	36.00	0.82	4.00	0.38	0.05
15	2.26	60.00	1.65	36.00	0.79	3.40	0.84	4.30
16	1.11	12.10	1.66	36.00	0.74	2.60	0.80	3.60
17	1.18	14.80	1.36	22.00	0.68	1.78	0.71	2.10
18	1.19	15.20	1.28	19.00	0.65	1.45	0.61	1.09
19	1.00a	8.50	1.12	12.50	0.64	1.36	0.54	0.60
20	0.81	3.70	1.16	14.00	0.62	1.18	0.38	0.06
21	0.66	1.56	1.06	10.40	0.59	0.93	0.37	0.05
22	0.61	1.09	0.94	6.60	0.59a	0.93	0.34	0.04
23	0.61	1.09	0.91	6.00	0.59	0.93	0.34	0.04
24	0.71	2.10	0.91	6.00	0.58	0.86	0.34	0.04
25	0.71	2.10	0.90	5.70	0.55	0.65	0.36	0.04
26	0.71	2.10	0.88	5.20	0.50	0.38	0.40	0.08
27	0.71	2.10	0.82	4.00	0.46	0.22	0.37	0.05
28	0.71	2.10	0.78	3.20	0.40	0.08	0.37	0.05
29	0.71	2.10	0.74	2.60	0.38	0.06	0.37	0.05
30	0.83	4.10	0.75	2.70	0.36	0.04	0.36	0.04
31	1.47	28.60	......	....	0.36	0.04	..:....	....

a Gauge height interpolated.

SESSIONAL PAPER No. 25c

DAILY GAUGE HEIGHT AND DISCHARGE of *E*ast Branch of Mackay Creek at Grant's Ranch, for 1914.

	July.		August.		September.		October.	
DAY.	Gauge Height.	Dis- charge.	Gauge Height.	Dis- charge.	Gauge Height.	Dis- charge.	Gauge Height.	Dis- charge.
	Feet.	*Sec.-ft.*	*Feet.*	*Sec.-ft.*	*Feet.*	*Sec.-ft.*	*Feet.*	*Sec.-ft.*
1	0.36	0.04	Dry.	Nil.	Dry.	Nil.	Dry.	Nil.
2	0.35	0.03	"	"	"	"	"	"
3	0.35	0.03	"	"	"	"	"	"
4	0.34	0.02	"	"	"	"	"	"
5	0.34	0.02	"	"	"	"	"	"
6	0.34	0.02	"	"	"	"	0.69	1.89
7	0.34	0.02	"	"	"	"	1.37	23.00
8	0.33	0.02	" .	"	"	"	2.80	87.00
9	0.30a	Nil.	"	"	"	"	1.72	39.00
10	0.27a	"	"	"	"	"	1.29	19.40
11	0.23	"	"	"	"	"	1.02	9.10
12	0.22	"	"	"	"	"	0.84	4.30
13	0.19	"	"	"	"	"	0.70	2.00
14	Dry.	"	"	"	"	"	0.72	2.30
15	"	"	"	"	"	"	0.71	.2.10
16	"	"	"	"	"	"	0.64	1.36
17	"	"	"	"	"	"	0.59	0.93
18	"	"	"	"	"	"	0.64	1.36
19	"	"	"	"	"	"	0.64	1.36
20	"	"	"	"	"	"	0.60	1.00
21	"	"	"	"	"	"	0.59	0.93
22	"	"	"	"	"	"	0.60	1.00
23	"	"	"	"	"	"	0.55	0.65
24	"	"	"	"	"	"	0.50	0.38
25	"	"	"	"	"	"	0.49	0.34
26	"	"	"	"	"	"	0.49	0.34
27	"	"	"	"	"	"	0.44	0.16
28	"	"	"	"	"	"	0.39	0.07
29	"	"	"	"	"	"	0.39	0.07
30	"	"	"	"	"	"	0.37	0.05
31	"	"	"	"	....	....	0.35	0.03

a Gauge height interpolated.

MONTHLY DISCHARGE of East Branch of Mackay Creek at Grant's Ranch, for 1914.

(Drainage area 75 square miles.)

	DISCHARGE IN SECOND-FEET.				RUN-OFF.	
MONTH.	Maximum.	Minimum.	Mean.	Per square Mile.	Depth in inches on Drainage Area.	Total in Acre-feet.
March (13-31)	68.00	1.09	14.00	0.18700	0.130	526
April	79.00	2.70	19.60	0.26100	0.290	1,163
May	14.40	0.04	3.00	0.03970	0.050	183
June	4.30	0.03	0.43	0.00573	0.006	26
July	0.04	0.00	0.01	0.00009	Nil.	Nil.
August	....	....	....	....		"
September	....	....	....	....		"
October	87.00	0.00	6.40	0.08600	0.100	397
The period	....	....	....	....	0.58	2,295

5 GEORGE V, A. 1915

WEST BRANCH OF MACKAY CREEK AT SCHNELL'S RANCH.

Location.—On the NE. ¼ Sec. 27, Tp. 10, Rge. 1, W. 4th Mer., at Chris. Schnell's ranch.
Records available.—From September 20, 1912, to October 31, 1914.
Gauge.—Vertical staff; the zero of the gauge has been maintained at 91.66 feet, remaining unchanged since the station was established.
Bench-mark.—Permanent iron bench-mark; assumed elevation, 100.00 feet.
Channel.—Composed of loose stones and gravel; liable to shift during flood stages.
Discharge measurements.—Made by wading or with a weir.
Winter flow.—Station discontinued during the winter season.
Observer.—Chris. Schnell.

DISCHARGE MEASUREMENTS of West Branch of Mackay Creek at Schnell's Ranch, in 1914.

Date.	Engineer.	Width.	Area of Section.	Mean Velocity.	Gauge Height.	Discharge.
		Feet.	*Sq. ft.*	*Ft. per sec.*	*Feet.*	*Sec.-ft.*
May 13............	H. W. Rowley................	........a	....	....	1.14	0.14
June 11............	do	....	....	....	0.85	Nil.
June 29............	do	....	....	....	Dry.	"
July 28............	do	....	....	....	"	"
Aug. 15............	do	....	....	....	"	"
Sept. 18............	do	....	....	....	"	"
Oct. 16............	do	........a	....	....	1.37	1.98

a Weir measurement.

DAILY GAUGE HEIGHT AND DISCHARGE of West Branch of Mackay Creek at Schnell's Ranch, for 1914.

DAY.	March.		April.		May.		June.	
	Gauge Height.	Dis-charge.	Gauge Height.	Dis-charge.	Gauge Height.	Dis-charge.	Gauge Height.	Dis-charge.
	Feet.	*Sec.-ft.*	*Feet.*	*Sec.-ft.*	*Feet.*	*Sec.-ft.*	*Feet.*	*Sec.-ft.*
1	0.00	Nil.	2.22	21.00	1.06	0.02	0.95	Nil.
2	1.63	7.70	1.73	10.00	1.06	0.02	0.92	"
3	1.58	6.50	1.38	2.20	1.06	0.02	0.96	"
4	1.57	6.30	1.59	6.70	1.06	0.02	0.89	"
5	1.44	3.30	1.78	11.10	1.07	0.03	0.96	"
6	1.43	3.10	1.70	9.30	1.07	0.03	1.03	"
7	1.30	1.04	1.51	4.90	1.06	0.02	0.96	"
8	1.20	0.34	1.38	2.20	1.07	0.03	0.88	"
9	1.31	1.17	1.36	1.86	1.06	0.02	0.82	"
10	1.23	0.52	1.27	0.80	1.05	0.01	0.93	"
11	1.15	0.16	1.25	0.64	1.07	0.03	0.92	"
12	1.19	0.30	1.20	0.34	1.07	0.03	0.90	"
13	1.21	0.40	1.19	0.30	1.09	0.05	0.87	"
14	1.26	0.72	1.40	2.50	1.14	0.14	0.92	"
15	1.33	1.40	1.48	4.20	1.13	0.12	0.80	"
16	1.35	1.70	1.41	2.70	1.11	0.08	0.70	"
17	1.31	1.17	1.35	1.70	1.09	0.05	0.55	"
18	1.26	0.72	1.36	1.86	1.09	0.05	0.50	"
19	1.17	0.23	1.31	1.17	1.07	0.03	0.29	"
20	1.02	Nil.	1.24	0.58	1.06	0.02	0.23	"
21	1.04	"	1.18	0.27	1.06	0.02	0.21	"
22	1.00	"	1.16	0.20	1.06	0.02	0.19	"
23	0.98	"	1.14	0.14	1.05	0.01	0.18	"
24	0.97	"	1.13	0.12	1.08	0.04	0.17	"
25	0.96	"	1.09	0.05	1.08	0.04	0.16	"
26	0.96	"	1.09	0.05	1.06	0.02	0.44	"
27	1.04	"	1.08	0.04	1.04	Nil.	0.38	"
28	1.03	"	1.08	0.04	1.03	"	Dry.	"
29	0.98	"	1.07	0.03	1.02	"	"	"
30	1.00	"	1.07	0.03	1.00	"	"	"
31	2.47	27.00	....	....	0.99	"	....	....

DAILY GAUGE HEIGHT AND DISCHARGE of West Branch of Mackay Creek at Schnell's Ranch, for 1914.—*Concluded.*

DAY.	July.		August.		September.		October.	
	Gauge Height.	Dis-charge.	Gauge Height.	Dis-charge.	Gauge Height.	Dis-charge.	Gauge Height.	Dis-charge.
	Feet.	*Sec.-ft.*	*Feet.*	*Sec.-ft.*	*Feet.*	*Sec.-ft.*	*Feet.*	*Sec.-ft.*
1	Dry.	Nil.	Dry.	Nil.	Dry.	Nil.	Dry.	Nil.
2	"	"	"	"	"	"	"	"
3	"	"	"	"	"	"	"	"
4	"	"	"	"	"	"	"	"
5	"	"	"	"	"	"	"	"
6	"	"	"	"	"	"	"	"
7	"	"	"	"	"	"	"	"
8	"	"	"	"	"	"	2.78	34.00
9	"	"	"	"	"	"	2.30	23.00
10	"	"	"	"	"	"	2.12	19.00
11	"	"	"	"	"	"	1.70	9.30
12	"	"	"	"	"	"	1.45	3.60
13	"	"	"	"	"	"	1.30	1.04
14	"	"	"	"	"	"	1.15	0.16
15	"	"	"	"	"	"	1.50	4.70
16	"	"	"	"	"	"	1.36	1.86
17	"	"	"	"	"	"	1.22	0.46
18	"	"	"	"	"	"	1.09	0.05
19	"	"	"	"	"	"	1.06	0.02
20	"	"	"	"	"	"	1.03	Nil.
21	"	"	"	"	"	"	1.00	"
22	"	"	"	"	"	"	0.97	"
23	"	"	"	"	"	"	0.92	"
24	"	"	"	"	"	"	0.87	"
25	"	"	"	"	"	"	0.86	"
26	"	"	"	"	"	"	0.85	"
27	"	"	"	"	"	"	0.84	"
28	"	"	"	"	"	"	0.81	"
29	"	"	"	"	"	"	0.79	"
30	"	"	"	"	"	"	0.89	"
31	"	"	"	"	....	....	0.86	"

MONTHLY DISCHARGE of West Branch of Mackay Creek at Schnell's Ranch, for 1914.

(Drainage area 88 square miles.)

MONTH.	DISCHARGE IN SECOND-FEET.				RUN-OFF.	
	Maximum.	Minimum	Mean.	Per square Mile.	Depth in inches on Drainage Area.	Total in Acre-feet.
March	27.00	0.00	2.06	0.0234	0.030	127
April	21.00	0.03	2.90	0.0330	0.040	173
May	0.14	0.00	0.31	0.0036	0.004	19
June	....	....	....	....	....	Nil.
July	....	....	....	....	....	"
August	....	....	....	....	....	"
September	....	....	....	....	....	"
October	34.00	0.00	3.14	0.0357	0.040	193
The period	....	....	....	....	0.110	512

5 GEORGE V, A. 1915

MACKAY CREEK AT WALSH.

Location.—On NW. ¼ Sec. 26, Tp. 11, Rge. 1, W. 4th Mer., at traffic bridge.
Records available.—July 29, 1909, to October 31, 1914.
Gauge.—Vertical staff; elevation, 2,432 65 feet above mean sea level, maintained since establishment.
Bench-mark.—Permanent iron bench-mark; elevation, 2,443.73 feet above mean sea level (Geodetic Survey of Canada).
Channel.—Composed of clay.
Discharge measurements.—Made from bridge, by wading, or with a weir.
Winter flow.—Station not maintained during winter.
Observer.—Edward Sept.

DISCHARGE MEASUREMENTS of Mackay Creek at Walsh, in 1914.

Date.	Engineer.	Width.	Area of Section.	Mean Velocity.	Gauge Height.	Discharge.
		Feet.	*Sq. ft.*	*Ft. per sec.*	*Feet.*	*Sec.-ft.*
Mar. 19............	R. J. Srigley	15.0	14.8	0.96	1.28	14.10
Mar. 30............	do	....	....	....	0.63	0.40
April 1............	do	42.0	81.4	1.13	2.72	92.00
May 15............	H. S. Kerby................	9.1	14.3	0.31	0.75	4.50
June 11............	do	....	....	....	Dry.	Nil.
July 28............	do	....	....	....	"	"
Sept. 18............	do	....	....	....	"	"
Oct. 15............	H. W. Rowley..............	....	....	....	0.43	0.69

DAILY GAUGE HEIGHT AND DISCHARGE of Mackay Creek at Walsh, for 1914.

DAY.	March.		April.		May.		June.	
	Gauge Height.	Dis- charge.	Gauge Height.	Dis- charge.	Gauge Height.	Dis- charge.	Gauge Height.	Dis- charge.
	Feet.	*Sec.ft.*	*Feet.*	*Sec.ft.*	*Feet.*	*Sec.ft.*	*Feet.*	*Sec.-ft.*
1............	....	....	2.71	91.00	0.60	2.20	Dry.	Nil.
2............	....	....	2.14	47.00	0.58	2.00	"	"
3............	....	....	1.78	31.00	0.56	1.80	"	"
4............	....	....	1.35	16.00	0.55	1.70	"	"
5............	....	....	1.86	34.00	0.54	1.62	"	"
6............	....	....	2.50	72.00	0.80	4.90	"	"
7............	....	....	1.78	31.00	0.78	4.60	"	"
8............	....	....	1.36	16.30	0.84	5.50	"	"
9............	....	....	1.06	9.40	1.02	8.60	"	"
10............	....	....	1.02	8.60	1.29	14.60	"	"
11............	0.44	0.94	0.99	8.00	1.15	11.30	"	"
12............	0.36	0.46	1.05	9.20	0.98	7.80	"	"
13............	0.39	0.64	1.48	19.80	0.88	6.10	"	"
14............	2.02	41.00	1.67	27.00	0.78	4.60	"	"
15............	2.14	47.00	1.90	36.00	0.72	3.80	"	"
16............	1.52	21.00	1.60	24.00	0.64	2.70	"	"
17............	0.94	7.10	1.70	28.00	0.60	2.20	"	"
18............	0.94	7.10	1.44	18.60	0.56	1.80	"	"
19............	1.12	10.60	1.25	13.60	0.52	1.46	"	"
20............	0.77	4.50	1.19	12.20	0.44	0.94	"	"
21............	0.46	1.06	1.26	13.80	0.39	0.64	"	"
22............	0.46	1.06	1.06	9.40	0.38	0.58	"	"
23............	0.32	0.28	0.94	7.10	0.35	0.40	"	"
24............	0.29	0.18	0 92	6.80	0.40	0.70	"	"
25............	0.52	0.14a	0.92	6.80	0.30	0.20	"	"
26............	0 52	0.10a	0.86	5.80	0.17	0.02	"	"
27............	0 04	0.05a	0.80	4.90	0.08	0.00	"	"
28............	0 00	0 01a	0.72	3.80	0.02	0.00	"	"
29............	0 04	0.05a	0.66	2.90	Dry.	Nil.	"	"
30............	0 34	0 40a	0.63	2.60	"	"	"	"
31............	2.22	52.00	....	....	"	"	....	....

a Stream frozen; discharge estimated.

SESSIONAL PAPER No. 25c

DAILY GAUGE HEIGHT AND DISCHARGE of Mackay Creek at Walsh, for 1914.—*Concluded.*

DAY.	July.		August.		September.		October.	
	Gauge Height.	Dis-charge.	Gauge Height.	Dis-charge.	Gauge Height.	Dis-charge.	Gauge Height	Dis-charge.
	Feet.	*Sec.-ft*	*Feet.*	*Sec.-ft.*	*Feet.*	*Sec.-ft.*	*Feet.*	*Sec.-ft.*
1	Dry.	Nil.	Dry.	Nil.	Dry.	Nil.	Dry.	Nil.
2	"	"	"	"	"	"	"	"
3	"	"	"	"	"	"	"	"
4	"	"	"	"	"	"	0.89	6.20
5	"	"	"	"	"	"	0.86	5.80
6	"	"	"	"	"	"	0.67	3.10
7	"	"	"	"	"	"	0.86	5.80
8	"	"	"	"	"	"	2.74	94.00
9	"	"	"	"	"	"	3.06	126.00
10	"	"	"	"	"	"	2.28	56.00
11	"	"	"	"	"	"	1.50	20.00
12	"	"	"	"	"	"	1.06	9.40
13	"	"	"	"	0.94	7.10	0.79	4.80
14	"	"	"	"	0.64	2.70	0.55	1.70
15	"	"	"	"	0.16	0.01	0.44	0.94
16	"	"	"	"	0.06	0.00	0.50	1.30
17	"	"	"	"	0.01	0.00	0.48	1.18
18	"	"	"	"	Dry.	Nil.	0.30	0.20
19	"	"	"	"	"	"	0.22	0.07
20	"	"	"	"	"	"	0.15	0.00
21	"	"	"	"	"	"	0.11	0.00
22	"	"	"	"	"	"	0.08	0.00
23	"	"	"	"	"	"	0.06	0.00
24	"	"	"	"	"	"	0.02	0.00
25	"	"	"	"	"	"	Dry.	Nil.
26	"	"	"	"	"	"	"	"
27	"	"	"	"	"	"	"	"
28	"	"	"	"	"	"	"	"
29	"	"	"	"	"	"	"	"
30	"	"	"	"	"	"	"	"
31	"	"	"	"			"	"

MONTHLY DISCHARGE of Mackay Creek at Walsh, for 1914.

(Drainage area 200 square miles.)

MONTH.	DISCHARGE IN SECOND-*FEET.*				RUN-OFF.	
	Maximum.	Minimum.	Mean.	Per square Mile.	Depth in inches on Drainage Area.	Total in Acre-feet.
March (11-31)	52.00	0.01	9.32	0.047	0.036	387
April	91.00	2.60	20.60	0.103	0.115	1,226
May	14.60	0.00	2.99	0.015	0.017	184
June	....	....	....	....	....	Nil.
July	....	....	....	....	....	"
August	....	....	....	....	....	"
September	7.10	0.00	0.33	0.016	0.018	196
October	126.00	0.00	10.80	0.054	0.062	664
The period	....	....	....	....	0.248	2,657

No. 25c—30

BOXELDER CREEK AT YOUNG'S RANCH.

Location.—On the NE. ¼ Sec. 2, Tp. 12, Rge. 30, W. 3rd Mer., two miles east of W
Records available.—March 11, 1911, to October 31, 1914. Discharge measurmen
1909.
Gauge.—Vertical staff; elevation of zero maintained at 88.83 feet since estahsh
Bench-mark.—Permanent iron bench-mark; assumed elevation, 100 00 feet.
Channel.—Clay.
Discharge measurements.—Made by wading; during flood stages, from raiway
downstream.
Winter flow.—Station not maintained during the winter.
Observer.—John Young.

DISCHARGE MEASUREMENTS of Boxelder Creek at Young's Ranch, in 191

Date.	Engineer.	Width.	Area of Section.	Mean Velocity.	Gauge Height.	D
		Feet.	*Sq. ft.*	*Ft. per sec.*	*Feet.*	*S*
Mar. 30	R. J. Srigley				Dry.	
April 1	do	14.5	22 90	0.78	2.54	1
May 15	H. S. Kerby					
June 11	do				Dry.	
July 28	H. W. Rowley				"	
Sept. 18	do				"	

a Water standing in pools.

DAILY GAUGE HEIGHT AND DISCHARGE of Boxelder Creek at Young's Ranch, fc 19

DAY.	March.		April.		May.		
	Gauge Height.	Dis-charge.	Gauge Height.	Dis-charge.	Gauge Height.	Dis-charge.	Gaug Heigh.
	Feet.	*Sec.-ft.*	*Feet.*	*Sec.-ft.*	*Feet.*	*Sec.-ft.*	*Fee*
1			2.54	17.90		Nil.	Dr
2			2.25	11.80		"	"
3	2.40	14.80	1.95	7.10		"	"
4	2.70	22.00	1.82	5.60		"	"
5	2.35	13.80	1.88	6.20		"	"
6	2.05	8.50	2.92	27.00		"	"
7	2.05	8 50	2.40	14.80		"	"
8	1.45	2.30	1.72	4.60		"	"
9	1.35	1.72	1.42	2.10		"	"
10	1.20	1.05	1.40	2.00		"	"
11	1.15	0.88	1.30	1.45	1.70	4.30	"
12	1.30	1.45	1.25	1.25	1.75	4.80	"
13	1.42	2.10	1.55	3.00	1 42	2.10	"
14	2.40	14.80	2.15	10.10	1.00	0.45	"
15	2.75	23.00	2.05	8.50	0.60	0.02a	"
16	2.78	24.00	2.20	10.90	0.40	Nil.b	"
17	1.68	4.20	1.95	7.10	Dry.	"	"
18	1.35	1.72	1.75	4.80	"	"	"
19	0.95	0.38	1.60	3.40	"	"	"
20	0.65	0 04	1.45	2.30	"	"	"
21	0.60	0.02	1.28	1.37	"	"	"
22	0.50	0.00	1.20	1 05	"	"	"
23	0.15	0.00	1.15	0.88	"	"	"
24	0.00	0.00	0.90	0.30	"	"	"
25		Nil.a	0 50	0.00	"	"	"
26		"	0.15	0.00	"	"	"
27		"		Nil.a	"	"	"
28		"		"	"	"	"
29		"		"	"	"	"
30	Dry.	"		"	"	"	"
31		"			"	"	

a Water standing in pools.
b Creek dry from May 16th to October 7th.

DAILY GAUGE HEIGHT AND DISCHARGE of Boxelder Creek at Young's Ranch, for 1914.
—*Concluded.*

DAY.	July.		August.		September.		October.	
	Gauge Height.	Dis- charge.	Gauge Height.	Dis- charge.	Gauge Height.	Dis- charge.	Gauge Height.	Dis- charge.
	Feet.	*Sec.-ft.*	*Feet.*	*Sec.-ft.*	*Feet.*	*Sec.-ft.*	*Feet.*	*Sec.-ft.*
1....	Dry.	Nil.	Dry.	Nil.	Dry.	Nil.	Dry.	Nil.
2....	"	"	"	"	"	"	"	"
3....	"	"	"	"	"	"	"	"
4....	"	"	"	"	"	"	"	"
5....	"	"	"	"	"	"	"	"
6....	"	"	"	"	"	"	"	"
7....	"	"	"	"	"	"	"	"
8....	"	"	"	"	"	"	1.70	4.30
9....	"	"	"	"	"	"	3.20	35.00
10....	"	"	"	"	"	"	3.55	47.00
11....	"	"	"	"	"	"	2.22	11.30
12....	"	"	"	"	"	"	1.55	3.00
13....	"	"	"	"	"	"	1.52	2.80
14....	"	"	"	"	"	"	1.35	1.72
15....	"	"	"	"	"	"	0.96	0.39
16....	"	"	"	"	"	"	0.65	0.04
17....	"	"	"	"	"	"	0.20	0.00
18....	"	"	"	"	"	"	....	Nil. *a*
19....	"	"	"	"	"	"	....	"
20....	"	"	"	"	"	"	....	"
21....	"	"	"	"	"	"	....	"
22....	"	"	"	"	"	"	....	"
23....	"	"	"	"	"	"	....	"
24....	"	"	"	"	"	"	....	"
25....	"	"	"	"	"	"	....	"
26....	"	"	"	"	"	"	....	"
27....	"	"	"	"	"	"	"	"
28....	"	"	"	"	"	"	....	"
29....	"	"	"	"	"	"	....	"
30....	"	"	"	"	"	"	....	"
31....	"	"	"	"	....	....	....	"

a Water standing in pools.

MONTHLY DISCHARGE of Boxelder Creek at Young's Ranch, for 1914.

(Drainage area 104 square miles.)

MONTH.	DISCHARGE IN SECOND-FEET.				RUN-OFF.	
	Maximum.	Minimum.	Mean.	Per square Mile.	Depth in inches on Drainage Area.	Total in Acre-feet.
March 3-31)........................	24.00	Nil.	5.01	0.048	0.052	288
April	27.00	"	5.19	0.050	0.056	309
May	4.80	"	0.38	0.004	0.005	23
June	....	....	....	....	....	Nil.
July	....	....	....	....	....	"
Aug	....	....	....	....	....	"
September........................						
October........................	47.00	Nil.	3.41	0.033	0.038	210
The period........................	....	....	....	0.151	830

5 GEORGE V, A. 1915

BOXELDER CREEK AT YOUNG'S RANCH.

Location.—On the NE. ¼ Sec. 2, Tp. 12, Rge. 30, W. 3rd Mer., two miles east of Walsh.
Records available.—March 11, 1911, to October 31, 1914. Discharge measurements from 1909.
Gauge.—Vertical staff; elevation of zero maintained at 88 83 feet since establishment.
Bench-mark.—Permanent iron bench-mark; assumed elevation, 100.00 feet.
Channel.—Clay.
Discharge measurements.—Made by wading; during flood stages, from railway bridge downstream.
Winter flow.—Station not maintained during the winter.
Observer.—John Young.

DISCHARGE MEASUREMENTS of Boxelder Creek at Young's Ranch, in 1914.

Date.	Engineer.	Width.	Area of Section.	Mean Velocity.	Gauge Height.	Discharge.
		Feet.	*Sq. ft.*	*Ft. per sec.*	*Feet.*	*Sec.-ft.*
Mar. 30	R. J. Srigley				Dry.	Nil.
April 1	do	14.5	22 90	0˙78	2.54	17.80
May 15	H. S. Kerby					Nil. *a*
June 11	do				Dry.	" *a*
July 28	H. W. Rowley				"	" *a*
Sept. 18	do				"	" *a*

a Water standing in pools.

DAILY GAUGE HEIGHT AND DISCHARGE of Boxelder Creek at Young's Ranch, for 1914.

DAY.	March.		April.		May.		June.	
	Gauge Height.	Dis- charge.	Gauge Height.	Dis- charge.	Gauge Height.	Dis- charge.	Gauge Height.	Dis- charge.
	Feet.	*Sec.-ft.*	*Feet.*	*Sec.-ft.*	*Feet.*	*Sec.-ft.*	*Feet.*	*Sec.-ft.*
1			2.54	17.90		Nil.	Dry.	Nil.
2			2.25	11.80		"	"	"
3	2.40	14.80	1.95	7.10		"	"	"
4	2.70	22.00	1.82	5.60		"	"	"
5	2.35	13.80	1.88	6.20		"	"	"
6	2.05	8.50	2.92	27.00		"	"	"
7	2.05	8.50	2.40	14.80		"	"	"
8	1.45	2.30	1.72	4.60		"	"	"
9	1.35	1.72	1.42	2.10		"	"	"
10	1.20	1.05	1.40	2.00		"	"	"
11	1.15	0.88	1.30	1.45	1.70	4.30	"	"
12	1.30	1.45	1.25	1.25	1.75	4.80	"	"
13	1.42	2.10	1.55	3.00	1.42	2.10	"	"
14	2.40	14.80	2.15	10.10	1.00	0.45	"	"
15	2.75	23.00	2.03	8.50	0.60	0.02*a*	"	"
16	2.78	24.00	2.20	10.90	0.40	Nil.*b*	"	"
17	1.68	4.20	1.95	7.10	Dry.	"	"	"
18	1.35	1.72	1.75	4.80	"	"	"	"
19	0.95	0.38	1.60	3.40	"	"	"	"
20	0.65	0.04	1.45	2.30	"	"	"	"
21	0.60	0.02	1.28	1.37	"	"	"	"
22	0.50	0.00	1.20	1.05	"	"	"	"
23	0.15	0.00	1.15	0.88	"	"	"	"
24	0.00	0.00	0.90	0.30	"	"	"	"
25		Nil.*a*	0.50	0.00	"	"	"	"
26		"	0.15	0.00	"	"	"	"
27		"		Nil.*a*	"	"	"	"
28		"		"	"	"	"	"
29		"		"	"	"	"	"
30	Dry.	"		"	"	"	"	"
31	"	"			"	"		

a Water standing in pools.
b Creek dry from May 16th to October 7th.

DAILY GAUGE HEIGHT AND DISCHARGE of Boxelder Creek at Young's Ranch, for 1914.
—*Concluded.*

DAY.	July.		August.		September.		October.	
	Gauge Height.	Dis-charge.	Gauge Height.	Dis-charge.	Gauge Height.	Dis-charge.	Gauge Height.	Dis-charge.
	Feet.	*Sec.-ft.*	*Feet.*	*Sec.-ft.*	*Feet.*	*Sec.-ft.*	*Feet.*	*Sec.-ft.*
1	Dry.	Nil.	Dry.	Nil.	Dry.	Nil.	Dry.	Nil.
2	"	"	"	"	"	"	"	"
3	"	"	"	"	"	"	"	"
4	"	"	"	"	"	"	"	"
5	"	"	"	"	"	"	"	"
6	"	"	"	"	"	"	"	"
7	"	"	"	"	"	"	"	"
8	"	"	"	"	"	"	1.70	4.30
9	"	"	"	"	"	"	3.20	35.00
10	"	"	"	"	"	"	3.55	47.00
11	"	"	"	"	"	"	2.22	11.30
12	"	"	"	"	"	"	1.55	3.00
13	"	"	"	"	"	"	1.52	2.80
14	"	"	"	"	"	"	1.35	1.72
15	"	"	"	"	"	"	0.96	0.39
16	"	"	"	"	"	"	0.65	0.04
17	"	"	"	"	"	"	0.20	0.00
18	"	"	"	"	"	"	....	Nil. *a*
19	"	"	"	"	"	"	....	"
20	"	"	"	"	"	"	....	"
21	"	"	"	"	"	"	....	"
22	"	"	"	"	"	"	....	"
23	"	"	"	"	"	"	....	"
24	"	"	"	"	"	"	....	"
25	"	"	"	"	"	"	....	"
26	"	"	"	"	"	"	....	"
27	"	"	"	"	"	"	"	"
28	"	"	"	"	"	"	....	"
29	"	"	"	"	"	"	....	"
30	"	"	"	"	"	"	....	"
31	"	"	"	"	....	....	....	"

a Water standing in pools.

MONTHLY DISCHARGE of Boxelder Creek at Young's Ranch, for 1914.

(Drainage area 104 square miles.)

MONTH.	DISCHARGE IN SECOND-FEET.				RUN-OFF.	
	Maximum.	Minimum	Mean.	Per square Mile.	Depth in inches on Drainage Area.	Total in Acre-feet.
March (3-31)	24.00	Nil.	5.01	0.048	0.052	288
April	27.00	"	5.19	0.050	0.056	309
May	4.80	"	0.38	0.004	0.005	23
June	....	....	....	....	....	Nil.
July	....	....	....	....	....	"
August	....	....	....	....	....	"
September	....	....	....	....	....	
October	47.00	Nil.	3.41	0.033	0.038	210
The period	....	....	....	....	0.151	830

5 GEORGE V, A. 1915

ROSS CREEK DRAINAGE BASIN.

General Description.

Ross Creek rises in Elkwater Lake, a small body of water covering an area of approximately two square miles, situated in Township 8, Range 3, West of the 4th Meridian. The creek flows in a northerly direction as far as Irvine, and then turns sharply to the westward and closely parallels the main line of the Canadian Pacific Railway to Medicine Hat. Here it is joined by Sevenpersons River, and the combined flow empties into the South Saskatchewan in Section 32, Township 12, Range 5, West of the 4th Meridian. The tributaries of Ross Creek are Bullshead Creek, which joins it in Section 21, Township 12, Range 5, West of the 4th Meridian, and Gros Ventre Creek, which joins it in Section 14, Township 11, Range 3, West of the 4th Meridian.

The topography of this basin is exceedingly rough and rolling, and almost totally devoid of tree growth. The one exception is a small area of the Forest Reserve just south of Elkwater Lake, which has a good stand of pine and spruce.

The Canadian Pacific Railway takes the water supply for its tank at Irvine from Ross Creek.

ROSS CREEK AT KOENIG'S RANCH.

Location.—On the SE. ¼ Sec. 36, Tp. 9, Rge. 3, W. 4th Mer., at G. Koenig's ranch, one mile below the former station on Ross Creek at James Robinson's ranch.

Records available.—At the original station at Robinson's ranch, NW. ¼ Sec. 24, Tp. 9, Rge. 3, W. 4th Mer., from October 11, 1911, to May 6, 1914; at the new station, established May 15, 1914, at Koenig's ranch, SE. ¼ Sec. 36, Tp. 9, Rge. 3, W. 4th Mer., from May 15 to October 31, 1914.

Gauge.—Vertical staff at both stations. Station at Robinson's ranch: The zero of the gauge was maintained at 93.34 feet during 1911; at 93.00 feet during 1912; and at 93.12 feet during 1913 and to May 6, 1914. Station at Koenig's ranch: The zero of the gauge was maintained at 94.94 feet during 1914.

Bench-marks.—Permanent iron bench-marks at both locations of stations. At Koenig's ranch the bench-mark is located on the left bank 150 feet NE. of the NE. corner of G. Koenig's orse barn, and 495 feet north of section line between Secs. 25 and 36; assumed elevation, 100.00 feet.

Channel.—Practically permanent.

Winter flow.—Station discontinued during winter season.

Observer.—Mr. G. Koenig.

DISCHARGE MEASUREMENTS of Ross Creek at Koenig's Ranch, in 1914.

Date.	Engineer.	Width.	Area of Section.	Mean Velocity.	Gauge Height.	Discharge.
		Feet.	*Sq. ft.*	*Ft. per sec.*	*Feet.*	*Sec.-ft.*
Mar. 23b	R. J. Srigley				3.85	3.00a
May 15	H. W. Rowley	10.5	3.78	0.64	1.16	3.68
June 12	do	10.0	4.80	0.40	1.05	1.92
June 29	do	5.5c	1.15	0.84	0.98	0.96
June 29b	do	6.5	2.12	0.56	1.38	1.19
July 29	do					Nil.
July 29b	do					0.31
Aug. 15	do	d				Nil.
Aug. 15b	do	d			1.27	0.24
Sept. 19	do	d			0.83	0.30
Sept. 19b	do	d			1.28	0.40
Oct. 16	do	12.0	7.90	0.91	1.29	6.99
Oct. 17b	do	12.0	6.00	1.16	1.59	6.90

a Discharge estimated; ice conditions.
b Measurement and gauge height taken at station at Robinson's ranch.
c Measurement made below gauge.
d Weir measurement.

SESSIONAL PAPER No. 25c

DAILY GAUGE HEIGHT AND DISCHARGE of Ross Creek at *K*oenig's Ranch, for 1914.

DAY.	March.		April.		May.		June.	
	Gauge Height.	Dis- charge.	Gauge Height.	Dis- charge.	Gauge Height	Dis- charge.	Gauge Height.	Dis- charge.
	Feet.	*Sec.-ft.*	*Feet.*	*Sec.-ft.*	*Feet.*	*Sec.-ft.*	*Feet.*	*Sec.-ft.*
1			4.38a	9.00	0.97	0.00	0.88	0.46
2			4.33a	10.00	1.13	0.02	1.04	1.60
3			2.83a	12.00	1.22	0.11	1.14	3.20
4			2.78a	10.00	1.26	0.25	1.18	4.10
5			1.55	4.90	1.28	0.35	1.20	4.60
6			2.40	56.00	1.32	0.61	1.24	5.60
7			1.89	25.00	.....b	....	1.20	4.60
8			1.44	2.10	.....b	....	1.17	3.90
9			1.17	0.01	.....b	....	1.11	2.70
10			1.10	0.00	.....b	....	1.06	1.86
11			1.50	3.40	.....b	....	1.05	1.70
12			1.71·	14.10	.....b	....	1.04	1.60
13			1.62	8.70	.....b	...	1.10	2.50
14			1.57	5.90	.....b	....	1.14	3.20
15			1.56	5.40	1.15	3.40	1.14	3.20
16			1.61	8.10	1.14	3.20	1.12	2.90
17			1.71	14.10	1.12	2.90	1.02	1.40
18			1.66	11.10	1.10	2.50	0.97	0.98
19			1.69	12.90	1.08	2.20	0.90	0.54
20			1.66	11.10	1.08	2.20	0.83	0.29
21			1.64	9.90	1.08	2.20	0.84	0.32
22			1.64	9.90	1.09	2.30	0.87	0.42
23			1.63	9.30	1.08	2.20	0.80	0.22
24			1.60	7.50	1.06	1.86	0.78	0.19
25			1.58	6.50	1.02	1.40	1.03	1.50
26			1.56	5.40	1.00	1.20	1.01	1.30
27			1.56	5.40	0.98	1.06	0.98	1.06
28			1.55	4.90	0.95	0.84	0.96	0.91
29	4.24a	7.00	1.54	4.60	0.92	0.66	0.98	1.06
30	4.40a	8.00	1.54	4.60	0.90	0.54	0.93	0.72
31	4.34a	8.00	....	....	0.88	0.46	....	....

a Ice conditions; discharge estimated.
b No gauge height records.
c March 29 to May 6, records are for the station at Robinson's ranch; May 15 to October 31, records are for the station at Koenig's ranch.

5 GEORGE V, A. 1915

DAILY GAUGE HEIGHT AND DISCHARGE of Ross Creek at Koenig's Ranch, for 1914.—*Concluded.*

DAY.	July.		August.		September.		October.	
	Gauge Height.	Dis- charge.	Gauge Height.	Dis- charge.	Gauge Height.	Dis- charge.	Gauge Height.	Dis- charge.
	Feet.	*Sec.-ft.*	*Feet.*	*Sec.-ft.*	*Feet.*	*Sec.-ft.*	*Feet.*	*Sec.-ft.*
1	0.88	0.46	Dry.	Nil.	0.80	0.22	0.84	0.32
2	0.78	0.19	"	"	0.84	0.32	0.85	0.34
3	0.70	0.08	"	"	0.80	0.22	0.92	0.66
4	0.55	0.01	"	"	0.78	0.19	0.96	0.91
5	0.46	0.00	"	"	0.79	0.20	1.02	1.40
6	0.78	0.19	"	"	0.80	0.22	1.10	2.50
7	0.71	0.09	"	"	0.79	0.20	1.16	3.60
8	0.62	0.03	"	"	0.82	0.27	1.32	7.90
9	0.46	Nil.	"	"	0.82	0.27	1.38	9.50
10	Dry.	"	"	"	0.82	0.27	1.43	10.90
11	"	"	"	"	0.82	0.27	1.34	8.40
12	"	"	"	"	0.88	0.46	1.23	5.40
13	"	"	"	"	1.36	9.00	1.32	7.90
14	"	"	0.60	0.02	1.30	7.30	1.38	9.50
15	"	"	Dry.	Nil.	1.30	7.30	1.32	7.90
16	"	"	"	"	0.88	0.46	1.27	6.50
17	"	"	"	"	0.86	0.38	1.24	5.60
18	"	"	"	"	0.84	0.32	1.20	4.60
19	"	"	0.72	0.10	0.83	0.29	1.21	4.90
20	"	"	0.73	0.12	0.85	0.34	1.19	4.40
21	"	"	0.70	0.08	0.86	0.38	0.15	3.40
22	"	"	0.75	0.14	0.84	0.32	1.14	3.20
23	"	"	0.98	1.06	0.84	0.32	1.11	2.70
24	"	"	0.99	1.13	0.84	0.32	1.10	2.50
25	"	"	1.00	1.20	0.84	0.32	1.06	1.86
26	"	"	0.87	0.42	0.85	0.34	1.04	1.60
27	"	"	0.94	0.78	0.84	0.32	1.06	1.86
28	"	"	0.91	0.60	0.84	0.32	1.05	1.70
29	"	"	0.91	0.60	0.85	0.34	1.05	1.70
30	"	"	0.88	0.46	0.84	0.32	1.05	1.70
31	"	"	0.80	0.22	....	....	1.01	1.30

MONTHLY DISCHARGE of Ross Creek at Koenig's Ranch, for 1914.

(Drainage area 43 square miles.)

MONTH.	DISCHARGE IN SECOND-FEET.				RUN-OFF.	
	Maximum.	Minimum.	Mean.	Per square Mile.	Depth in inches on Drainage Area.	Total in Acre-feet.
March (29-31)	8.00	7.00	7.70	0.1780	0.0200	46
April	56.00	0.00	9.70	0.2260	0.2500	579
May (1-6a) (15-31)	3.40	0.00	1.41	0.0328	0.0300	64
June	5.60	0.19	1.95	0.0450	0.0500	116
July	0.46	0.00	0.03	0.0008	0.0009	2
August	1.20	0.00	0.22	0.0050	0.0060	14
September	9.00	0.19	1.06	0.0200	0.0300	63
October	10.90	0.32	4.10	0.1000	0.1100	251
The period	....	....	....	....	0 5000	1,135

a Records, March 29 to May 6, are for the original station at Robinson's ranch; May 15 to October 31, are for the new station at Koenig's ranch.

SESSIONAL PAPER No. 25c

GROS VENTRE CREEK AT TOTHILL'S RANCH.

Location.—On the SE. ¼ Sec. 27, Tp. 9, Rge. 4, W. 4th Mer., at Alf. Tothill's ranch.
Records available.—October 10, 1911, to October 31, 1914.
Gauge.—Vertical staff; the zero of the gauge has been maintained at 82.89 feet since the station was established.
Bench-mark.—Permanent iron bench-mark; assumed elevation, 100.00 feet.
Channel.—Practically permanent.
Observer.—Mrs. Kate Tothill.

DISCHARGE MEASUREMENTS of Gros Ventre Creek at Tothill's Ranch, in 1914.

Date.	Engineer.	Width.	Area of Section.	Mean Velocity.	Gauge Height.	Discharge.
		Feet.	*Sq. ft.*	*Ft. per sec.*	*Feet.*	*Sec.-ft.*
May 15.............	H. W. Rowley...............	......a	....	....	0.60	0.44
June 12.............	do	......a	....	....	0.50	0.11
June 30.............	do	....	....	....	....	Nil.
July 29.............	do	....	....	....	....	"
Aug. 15.............	do	....	....	....	....	"
Sept. 19.............	do	....	....	....	....	"
Oct. 17.............	do	......a	....	....	0.60	0.70

a Weir measurement.

DAILY GAUGE HEIGHT AND DISCHARGE of Gros Ventre Creek at Tothill's Ranch, for 1914.

DAY.	March.		April.		May.		June.	
	Gauge Height.	Dis-charge.	Gauge Height.	Dis-charge.	Gauge Height.	Dis-charge.	Gauge Height.	Dis-charge.
	Feet.	*Sec.-ft.*	*Feet.*	*Sec.-ft.*	*Feet.*	*Sec.-ft.*	*Feet.*	*Sec.-ft.*
1.............	....	....	1.93	76.00	0.61	0.58	......a	Nil.
2.............	....	....	1.33	26.00	0.60	0.50	......a	"
3.............	....	....	1.24	20.00	0.58	0.40	......a	"
4.............	....	....	1.36	28.00	0.68	1.20	0.47	0.07
5.............	....	....	1.62	49.00	0.70	1.40	0.54	0.22
6.............	....	....	1.30	24.00	0.68	1.20	0.59	0.45
7.............	....	....	1.11	13.50	0.78	2.60	0.62	0.66
8.............	....	....	0.93	6.20	0.94	6.50	0.60	0.50
9.............	....	....	0.88	4.70	0.99	8.20	0.56	0.30
10.............	....	....	0.84	3.70	0.94	6.50	0.52	0.16
11.............	....	....	0.78	2.60	0.80	2.90	0.50	0.10
12.............	....	....	0.88	4.70	0.73	1.80	0.50	0.10
13.............	1.82	66.00	0.96	7.10	0.70	1.40	0.47	0.07
14.............	1.68	54.00	0.97	7.50	0.65	0.90	0.49	0.09
15.............	1.34	27.00	0.91	5.50	0.62	0.66	0.46	0.06
16.............	1.36	28.00	0.94	6.50	0.58	0.40	0.44	0.05
17.............	1.32	25.00	0.84	3.70	0.56	0.30	0.41	0.02
18.............	1.29	23.00	0.78	2.60	0.54	0.22	0.38	0.01
19.............	1.46	36.00	0.76	2.20	0.53	0.19	......a	Nil.
20.............	1.40	31.00	0.78	2.60	0.52	0.16	......a	"
21.............	1.42	32.00	0.78	2.60	0.52	0.16	......a	"
22.............	1.52	40.00	0.72	1.66	0.52	0.16	......a	"
23.............	1.44	34.00	0.71	1.53	0.51	0.13	......a	"
24.............	1.18	16.70	0.74	1.92	0.52	0.16	......a	"
25.............	1.04	10.10	0.74	1.92	0.50	0.10	......a	"
26.............	1.09	12.20	0.71	1.53	0.44	0.05	......a	"
27.............	0.83	3.50	0.67	1.10	0.40	0.02	......a	"
28.............	0.87	4.40	0.66	1.00	0.38	0.01	......a	"
29.............	1.12	13.70	0.66	1.00	......a	Nil.	......a	"
30.............	2.73	145.00	0.62	0.66	......a	"	......a	"
31.............	2.39	116.00	....	....	......a	"	....	....

a Water standing in pools.

5 GEORGE V, A. 1915

DAILY GAUGE HEIGHT AND DISCHARGE at Gros Ventre Creek at Tothill's Ranch, for 1914.
—*Concluded.*

DAY.	July.		August.		September.		October.	
	Gauge Height.	Dis-charge.	Gauge Height.	Dis-charge.	Gauge Height.	Dis-charge.	Gauge Height.	Dis-charge.
	Feet.	*Sec.-ft.*	*Feet.*	*Sec.-ft.*	*Feet.*	*Sec.-ft.*	*Feet.*	*Sec.-ft.*
1	.....a	Nil.	Dry.	Nil.	Dry.	Nil.	.... a	Nil.
2	.....a	"	"	"	"	"	.....a	"
3	.....a	"	"	"	"	"	.....a	"
4	.....a	"	"	"	"	"	.... a	
5	.....a		"	"	"	"	0.88	4.70
6	.....a	"	"	"	"	"	0.68	1.20
7	Dry.	"	"	"	"	"	0.70	1.40
8	"	"	"	"	"	"	0.98	7.80
9	"	"	"	"	"	"	1.07	11.40
10	"	. "	"	"	"	"	1.16	15.60
11	"	"	"	"	"	"	0.96	7.10
12	"	"	"	"	"	"	0.80	2.90
13	"	"	"	"	"	"	0.74	1.92
14	"	"	"	"	0.72	1.66	0.73	1.80
15	"	"	"	"	0.50	0.10	0.66	1.00
16	"	"	"	"	0.42	0.03	0.62	0.66
17	"	"	"	"	0.34	0.00	0.60	0.50
18	"	"	"	"	0.32	0.00	0.60	0.50
19	"	"	"	"	.....a	Nil.	0.58	0.40
20	"	"	"	"	.....a	"	0.54	0.22
21	"	"	"	"	.....a	"	0.54	0.22
22	"	"	"	"	.....a	"	0.53	0.19
23	"	"	"	"	.....a	"	0.52	0.16
24	"	"	"	"	.....a	"	0.52	0.16
25	"	"	"	"	.....a	"	0.52	0.16
26	"	"	"	"	.....a	"	0.51	0.13
27	"	"	"	"	.....a	"	0.52	0.16
28	"	"	"	"	.....a	"	0.52	0.16
29	"	"	"	"	.....a	"	0.51	0.13
30	"	"	"	"	.....a	"	0.51	0.13
31	"	"	"	"	....	....	0.51	0.13

a Water standing in pools.

MONTHLY DISCHARGE of Gros Ventre Creek at Tothill's Ranch, for 1914.

(Drainage area 39 square miles.)

MONTH.	DISCHARGE IN SECOND-FEET.				RUN-OFF.	
	Maximum.	Minimum.	Mean.	Per square Mile.	Depth in inches on Drainage Area.	Total in Acre-feet.
March (13-31)	145.00	3.50	38.00	0.9700	0.690	1,421
April	76.00	0.66	10.40	0.2660	0.300	618
May	8.20	0.00	1.25	0.0320	0.040	77
June	0.66	0.00	0.10	0.0024	0.003	6
July						Nil.
August						"
September	1.66	Nil.	0.06	0.0015	0.002	4
October	15.60	"	1.96	0.0500	0.060	120
The period	....	....	....	....	1.100	2,246

ROSS CREEK AT IRVINE.

Location.—On NW. ¼ Sec. 31, Tp. 11, Rge. 2, W. 4th Mer., at traffic bridge in town of *Irvine*, and about 400 yards below the Canadian Pacific Railway Company's dam.

Records available.—July 28, 1909, to October 31, 1914.

Gauge.—Staff; the elevation of the zero of the gauge (2,477.79 feet) has been unchanged since establishment.

Bench-mark.—Permanent iron bench-mark; elevation, 2,500.43 feet above mean sea level (Geodetic Survey).
Channel.—Shifting.
Discharge measurements.—From traffic bridge, by wading, or with weir.
Winter flow.—Observations discontinued during winter.
Artificial control.—Canadian Pacific Railway Company have a dam about 400 yards above station.
Diversions.—Canadian Pacific Railway Company pump water from creek for their water tank at *Irvine.*
Observer.—H. J. Price.

DISCHARGE MEASUREMENTS of Ross Creek at *Irvine,* in 1914.

Date.	Engineer.	Width.	Area of Section.	Mean Velocity.	Gauge Height.	Discharge.
		Feet.	*Sq. ft.*	*Ft. per sec.*	*Feet.*	*Sec.-ft.*
Mar. 18............	R. J. Srigley	9.5	9.28	1.24	1.52	11.50
Mar. 21............	do	9.5	4.67	0.79	1.14	3.70
Mar. 27............	do	5.0	1.00	0.25	0.79	0.25
Mar. 31............	do	43.0	178.00	1.72	6.83	306.00
April 2............	H. S. Kerby........	25.0	49.90	1.82	3.43	90.40
May 15......'.....	do	6.7	5.61	1.02	1.18	5.76
June 11	do	....	....	....	0.85	0.63a
June 30	do	....	....	....	0.70	Nil.
July 31...........	do	....	....	....	0.70	"
Oct. 12...........	do	10.4	14.1	1.21	1.56	17.00

a Weir measurement.

DAILY GAUGE HEIGHT AND DISCHARGE of Ross Creek at *Irvine,* for 1914.

DAY.	March.		April.		May.		June.	
	Gauge Height.	Dis-charge.	Gauge Height.	Dis-charge.	Gauge Height.	Dis-charge.	Gauge Height.	Dis-charge.
	Feet.	*Sec.-ft.*	*Feet.*	*Sec.-ft.*	*Feet.*	*Sec.-ft.*	*Feet.*	*Sec.-ft.*
1............	3.00	69.0	7 20	331.0	1.07	3.40	0.70	Nil.
2............	2.80	60.0	3 50	95.0	1.04	2.80	0.69	"
3............	2.64	52.0	2.73	56.0	1.02	2.40	0.68	"
4............	2.40	42.0	2 72	56 0	1.00	2.00	0.66	"
5............	2.28	37.0	2 70	55 0	1.00	2.00	0.64	"
6............	2.00	27.0	2.70	55.0	1.07	3.40	0.58	"
7............	1.94	25.0	2.68	54.0	2.00	27.00	0.56	"
8............	1.90	24.0	2.65	52.0	2.50	46.00	0.65	"
9............	1.76	20.0	2.60	50.0	2.20	34.00	0.69	"
10............	1.69	17.7	2.55	48.0	1.90	24.00	0.75	0.15
11............	1.64	16.2	2.50	46.0	1.62	15.60	0.85	0.60
12............	1.58	14.5	2.45	44.0	1.54	13.50	0.84	0.54
13............	1.50	12.5	2.42	43.0	1.50	12.50	0.83	0.48
14............	1.50	12.5	2.38	41.0	1.46	11.50	0.82	0.42
15............	1.50	12.5	2.30	38.0	1.19	5.80	0.81	0.36
16............	1.67	17.1	2.25	36.0	1.09	3.80	0.80	0.30
17............	1.67	17.1	2.13	31.0	1.07	3.40	0.79	0.27
18............	1.66	16.8	2.00	27.0	1.04	2.80	0.78	0.24
19............	1.25	7.0	1.80	21.0	0.98	1.78	0.77	0.21
20............	1.28	7.6	1.64	16.2	0.93	1.23	0.75	0.15
21............	1.27	7.4	1.45	11.2	0.89	0.84	0.74	0.12
22............	1.27	7.4	1.37	9.4	0.84	0.54	0.73	0.09
23............	1.27	7.4	1.30	8.0	0.81	0.36	0.70	Nil.
24............	1.40	10.0	1.30	8.0	0.79	0.27	0.70	"
25............	1.52	13.0	1.32	8.4	0.79	0.27	0.70	"
26............	1.79	21.0	1.29	7.8	0.76	0.18	0.70	"
27............	1.42	10.5	1.24	6.8	0.76	0.18	0.70	"
28............	1.44	11.0	1.21	6.2	0.72	0.06	0.70	"
29............	1.46	11.5	1.18	5.6	0.71	0.03	0.70	"
30............	2.52	47.0	1.12	4.4	0.71	0.03	0.70	"
31............	5.40	213.0	....	....	0.71	0.03	....	....

STREAM MEASUREMENTS, 1914

5 GEORGE V. A. 1915

DAILY GAUGE HEIGHT AND DISCHARGE of Ross Creek at Irvine, for 1914.—*Concluded.*

DAY.	July.		August.		September.		October.	
	Gauge Height.	Dis-charge.	Gauge Height.	Dis-charge.	Gauge Height.	Dis-charge.	Gauge Height.	Dis-charge.
	Feet.	*Sec.-ft.*	*Feet.*	*Sec.-ft.*	*Feet.*	*Sec.-ft.*	*Feet.*	*Sec.-ft.*
1	0.70	Nil.	0.70	Nil.	0.70	Nil.	0.70	Nil.
2	0.70	"	0.70	"	0.70	"	0.70	"
3	0.70	"	0.70	"	0.70	"	0.70	"
4	0.70	"	0.70	"	0.70	"	2.10	30.00
5	0.70	"	0.70	"	0.70	"	2.20	34.00
6	0.70	"	0.70	"	0.70	"	2.25	36.00
7	0.70	"	0.70	"	0.70	"	2.25	36.00
8	0.70	"	0.70	"	0.70	"	2.08	29.00
9	0.70	"	0.70	"	0.70	"	2.00	27.00
10	0.70	"	0.70	"	0.70	"	1.80	21.00
11	0.70	"	0.70	"	0.70	"	1.56	14.00
12	0.70	"	0.70	"	0.70	"	1.45	11.20
13	0.70	"	0.70	"	0.70	"	1.40	10.00
14	0.70	"	0.70	"	0.70	"	1.30	8.00
15	0.70	"	0.70	"	0.70	"	1.20	6.00
16	0.70	"	0.70	"	0.70	"	1.10	4.00
17	0.70	"	0.70	"	0.70	"	1.00	2.00
18	0.70	"	0.70	"	0.70	"	0.98	1.78
19	0.70	"	0.70	"	0.70	"	0.96	1.56
20	0.70	"	0.70	"	0.70	"	0.90	0.90
21	0.70	"	0.70	"	0.70	"	0.90	0.90
22	0.70	"	0.70	"	0.70	"	0.86	0.66
23	0.70	"	0.70	"	0.70	"	0.85	0.60
24	0.70	"	0.70	"	0.70	"	0.83	0.48
25	0.70	"	0.70	"	0.70	"	0.82	0.42
26	0.70	"	0.70	"	0.70	"	0.80	0.30
27	0.70	"	0.70	"	0.70	"	0.75	0.15
28	0.70	"	0.70	"	0.70	"	0.78	0.24
29	0.70	"	0.70	"	0.70	"	0.74	0.12
30	0.70	"	0.70	"	0.70	"	0.70	Nil.
31	0.70	"	0.70	"	....	....	0.70	"

MONTHLY DISCHARGE of Ross Creek at Irvine, for 1914.

(Drainage area 248 square miles.)

MONTH.	DISCHARGE IN SECOND-FEET.				RUN-OFF.	
	Maximum.	Minimum	Mean.	Per square Mile.	Depth in inches on Drainage Area.	Total in Acre-feet.
March	213.0	7.00	28.00	0.1130	0.1300	1,722
April	331.0	4.40	42.00	0.1690	0.1890	2,499
May	46.0	0.03	7.20	0.0290	0.0330	442
June	0.6	....	0.13	0.0005	0.0006	8
July	....	....	....	....	....	Nil.
August	....	....	....	....	....	"
September	....	....	....	....	....	"
October	36.0	....	9.90	0.0400	0.0460	609
The period	....	....	....	....	0.3986	5,280

SESSIONAL PAPER No. 25c

BULLSHEAD CREEK AT CLARK'S RANCH.

Location.—On the NW. ¼ Sec. 15, Tp. 9, Rge. 5, W. 4th Mer., at Clark's ranch.
Records available.—October 9, 1911, to October 31, 1914.
Gauge.—Vertical staff; the zero of the gauge has been maintained at 88.45 feet since the station was established.
Bench-mark.—Permanent iron bench-mark; assumed elevation, 100.00 feet.
Channel.—Practically permanent.
Winter flow.—Station discontinued during winter season.
Diversions.—Water is diverted by Clark Brothers above this station for irrigation purposes.
Observer.—W. E. Clark.

DISCHARGE MEASUREMENTS of Bullshead Creek at Clark's Ranch, in 1914.

Date.	Engineer.	Width.	Area of Section.	Mean Velocity.	Gauge Height.	Discharge.
		Feet.	*Sq. ft.*	*Ft. per sec.*	*Feet.*	*Sec.-ft.*
Mar. 17............	R. J. Srigley...	30.0	28.5	0.66	1.95	18.70
April 7............	do	26.0	22.5	0.65	1.73	14.80
May 16............	H. W. Rowley	........a			1.13	0.78
June 12............	do	........a			1.08	0.26
July 3............	do	........a			0.92	Nil.
July 29	do				0.56	"
Aug. 21	do				0.54	"
Sept. 23............	do	........a			0.95	0.02
Oct. 17............	do	........a			1.22	1.74

a Weir measurement.

DAILY GAUGE HEIGHT AND DISCHARGE of Bullshead Creek at Clark's Ranch, for 1914.

DAY.	March.		April.		May.		June.	
	Gauge Height.	Dis- charge.	Gauge Height.	Dis- charge.	Gauge Height.	Dis- charge.	Gauge Height.	Dis- charge.
	Feet.	*Sec.-ft.*	*Feet.*	*Sec.-ft.*	*Feet.*	*Sec.-ft.*	*Feet.*	*Sec.-ft.*
1............	....	....	1.90a	20.00	1.18	1.18	0.92	Nil.
2............	....	....	1.90a	20.00	1.17	1.07	1.12	0.61
3............	....	....	2.00a	25.00	1.15	0.85	1.17	1.07
4............	....	....	2.30a	34.00	1.15	0.85	1.13	0.69
5............	....	....	1.65a	11.70	1.17	1.07	1.13	0.69
6............	.. ..	... ...	1.50a	7.40	1.22	1.68	1.13	0.69
7............	....	....	1.86	19.70	1.27	2.50	1.13	0.69
8............	....	....	1.72	14.40	1.33	3.60	1.10	0.45
9............	....	....	1.68	13.00	1.40	5.10	1.03	0.14
10............	....	....	1.49	7.30	1.44	6.10	0.96	0.01
11............	....	....	1.68	13.00	1.33	3.60	0.96	0.01
12............	....	....	1.84	18.90	1.22	1.68	1.04	0.17
13............	....	....	1.92	22.00	1.18	1.18	1.06	0.25
14............	....	....	1.87	20.00	1.14	0.77	1.03	0.14
15............	....	....	1.80	17.40	1.13	0.69	1.03	0.14
16............	....	....	1.68	13.00	1.13	0.69	1.01	0.08
17............	2.00	21.00	1.57	9.60	1.13	0.69	1.00	0.05
18............	1.85	15.20	1.49	7.30	1.12	0.61	0.96	0.01
19............	1.76	12.30	1.46	6.60	1.10	0.45	0.95	Nil.
20............	1.65	9.20	1.41	5.30	1.08	0.35	0.98	0.03
21............	1.55	6.80	1.34	3.80	1.08	0.35	0.98	0.03
22............	1.50	5.60	1.34	3.80	1.08	0.35	0.98	0.03
23............	1.64	9.40	1.33	3.60	1.06	0.25	0.98	0.03
24............	1.68	10.80	1.31	3.20	1.03	0.14	0.97	0.02
25............	1.70	11.70	1.30	3.00	1.01	0.08	1.02	0.11
26............	1.70	11.80	1.27	2.50	0.98	0.03	1.03	0.14
27............	1.70	12.00	1.24	1.96	0.96	0.01	1.02	0.11
28............	1.68	11.60	1.23	1.88	0.93	Nil.	0.99	0.04
29............	2.00a	23.00	1.22	1.68	0.93	"	0.95	Nil.
30............	2.40	42.00	1.19	1.29	0.91	"	0.94	"
31............	2.10a	29.00..	....	....	0.90	"	....	....

a Rod out; gauge heights interpolated.

5 GEORGE V. A. 1915

DAILY GAUGE HEIGHT AND DISCHARGE of Bullshead Creek at Clark's Ranch, for 1914.
—Concluded.

DAY.	July.		August.		September.		October.	
	Gauge Height.	Dis-charge.	Gauge Height.	Dis-charge.	Gauge Height.	Dis-charge.	Gauge Height.	Dis-charge.
	Feet.	*Sec.-ft.*	*Feet.*	*Sec.-ft.*	*Feet.*	*Sec.-ft.*	*Feet.*	*Sec.-ft.*
1	Dry.	Nil.	Dry.	Nil.	Dry.	Nil.	0.95	Nil.
2	"	"	"	"	"	....	0.95	"
3	0.93	"	"	"	"	....	1.07	0.30
4	Dry.	"	"	"	"	....	1.14	0.77
5	"	"	"	"	"	....	1.19	1.29
6	"	"	"	"	"	....	1.19	1.29
7	"	"	"	"	"	....	1.41	5.30
8	"	"	"	"	"	....	1.87	20.00
9	"	"	"	"	"	....	1.89	21.00
10	"	"	"	"	"	....	1.99	25.00
11	"	"	"	"	"	....	1.45	6.30
12	"	"	"	"	"	....	1.41	5.30
13	"	"	"	"	1.14	0.77	1.38	4.70
14	"	"	"	"	1.28	2.60	1.35	4.00
15	"	"	"	"	1.30	3.00	1.27	2.50
16	"	"	"	"	1.18	1.18	1.24	1.96
17	"	"	"	"	1.12	0.61	1.24	1.96
18	"	"	"	"	1.04	0.17	1.24	1.96
19	"	"	"	"	1.03	0.14	1.24	1.96
20	"	"	"	"	1.00	0.05	1.24	1.96
21	"	"	0.54	"	0.98	0.03	1.24	1.96
22	"	"	Dry.	"	0 98	0.03	1.22	1.68
23	"	"	"	"	0.96	0.01	1.19	1.29
24	"	"	"	"	0.95	Nil.	1.19	1.29
25	"	"	"	"	0.95	"	1.17	1.07
26	"	"	"	"	0.95	"	1.12	0.61
27	"	"	"	"	0.95	"	1.12	0.61
28	"	"	"	"	0.95	"	1.12	0.61
29	"	"	"	"	0.95	"	1.11	0.53
30	"	"	"	"	0.95	"	1.09	0.40
31	"	"	"	"	....	....	1.09	0.40

MONTHLY DISCHARGE of Bullshead Creek at Clark's Ranch, for 1914.

(Drainage area 56 square miles.)

MONTH.	DISCHARGE IN SECOND-FEET.				RUN-OFF.	
	Maximum.	Mimimun.	Mean.	Per square Mile.	Depth in inches on Drainage Area.	Total in Acre-feet.
March (17-31)	42.00	5.60	15.40	0.275	0.150	457
April	34.00	1.29	11.10	0.198	0.220	660
May	6.10	0.00	1.16	0.021	0.020	71
June	1.07	0.00	0.21	0.004	0.004	13
July	....	....	....	....	....	Nil.
August	....	....	....	....	....	"
September	3.00	0.00	0.29	0.005	0.006	17
October	25.00	0.00	3.80	0.068	0.080	234
The period	....	....	....	....	0.480	1,452

STARK AND BURTON DITCH FROM BULLSHEAD CREEK.

Location.—On the SE. ¼ Sec. 17, Tp. 11, Rge. 5, W. 4th Mer., at Stark and Burton's ranch near Medicine Hat.

Records available.—As sufficient discharge measurements have not been made to complete the discharge of this ditch, only estimates are available for the years of 1912-14.

Gauge.—Vertical staff; the zero of the gauge has been maintained at 97.87 feet since establishment.

Bench-mark.—The head of a nail in a five-inch post, six feet upstream from the gauge; assumed elevation, 100 00 feet.

Channel.—Composed of sand and gravel.

Discharge measurements.—Made with a meter by wading.

Observer.—R. E. Stark.

Remarks.—During September, 1914, Mr. Stark increased the width of this ditch, which has changed the cross-section at the station. The ditch was used for about 24 days in April (April 7-30), but as no discharge measurements were made there are not sufficient data to estimate the daily discharge.

BULLSHEAD CREEK NEAR DUNMORE.

Location.—On SW. ¼ Sec. 16, Tp. 12, Rge. 5, W. 4th Mer., at the traffic bridge about four miles east of Medicine Hat and about one mile above the junction of Ross and Bullshead Creeks.

Records available.—July 26, 1909, to October 31, 1914.

Gauge.—Staff; elevation of zero of gauge 2,295.65 feet during 1909-11; 2,295.01 feet during 1912; 2,295.06 feet during 1913-14.

Bench-mark.—Permanent iron bench-mark; elevation, 2,305 53 feet above mean sea level (Geodetic Survey).

Channel.—Shifting.

Discharge measurements.—From bridge, by wading, or with weir.

Gauge heights.—Owing to it being impossible to obtain an observer, no records were obtained during 1914.

Winter flow.—Observations discontinued during winter.

DISCHARGE MEASUREMENTS of Bullshead Creek near Dunmore, in 1914.

Date.	Engineer.	Width.	Area of Section.	Mean Velocity.	Gauge Height.	Discharge.
		Feet.	*Sq. ft.*	*Ft. per sec.*	*Feet.*	*Sec.-ft.*
Mar. 16	R. J. Srigley	20.0	20.4	1.42	1.95	28.00
Mar. 26	do	16.0	9.5	1.40	1.35	12.90
April 3	do	35.0	34.6	1.50	2.19	52.00
May 14	H. S. Kerby					0.02*a*
June 10	do					Nil.
June 30	do					"
July 31	do					"
Oct. 12	do	17.0	13.3	1.17	1.76	15.60

a Weir measurement.

MISCELLANEOUS DISCHARGE MEASUREMENTS made in Ross Creek drainage basin, in 1914.

Date.	Engineer.	Stream.	Location.	Width.	Area of Section.	Mean Velocity.	Discharge.
				Feet.	*Sq. ft.*	*Ft. per sec.*	*Sec.-ft.*
July 6	H. W. Rowley	Elkwater Creek	½ mile above Elkwater Lake				0.39

5 GEORGE V, A. 1915

SEVENPERSONS R*I*VER DRAINAGE BASIN.

General Description.

Sevenpersons River lies between the South Saskatchewan River and the Cypress Hills, and empties into the South Saskatchewan River at Medicine Hat. The drainage area consists mostly of open, level prairie, which has a small rainfall and a run-off confined chiefly to the spring freshet.

The creek has a considerable flow during the month of April, but the discharge decreases to nil about June.

There are no irrigation works of importance on this stream, and the records are valuable chiefly for statistical purposes.

SEVENPERSONS RIVER AT MEDICINE HAT.

Location.—On N*E*. ¼ Sec. 30,Tp. 12, Rge. 5, W. 4th Mer., at the bridge on the road between Medicine Hat and Dunmore and about one and one-half miles east of the Canadian Pacific Railway station at Medicine Hat.

Records available.—April 27, 1910, to October 31, 1914.

Gauge.—Staff; elevation of zero of gauge 86.68 feet, unchanged since establishment.

Bench-mark.—Permanent iron bench-mark; assumed elevation, 100.00 feet.

Channel.—Shifting.

Discharge measurements.—From bridge, by wading, or with weir.

Winter flow.—Observations discontinued during the winter.

Observer.—J. W. Pickering.

DISCHARGE MEASUREMENTS of Sevenpersons River at Medicine Hat, in 1914.

Date.	Engineer.	Width.	Area of Section.	Mean Velocity.	Gauge Height.	Discharge.
		Feet.	*Sq. ft.*	*Ft. per sec.*	*Feet.*	*Sec.-ft.*
Mar. 16............	R. J. Srigley......	5.0	1.60	0.98	2.94	1.56
Mar. 25............	do	5.0	1.70	0.93	2.94	1.58
April 3............	do	15.5	14.90	2.26	2.91	33.80
April 8............	do	44.0	58.80	2.17	3.26	128.00
May 14............	H. S. Kerby...... ....*a*	........*a*	....	....	1.72	0.40
June 10............	do	....	....	....	Dry.	Nil.
June 30............	do	....	....	....	"	"
July 31............	do	....	....	....	"	"
Oct. 12............	do	....	....	....	"	"

a Weir measurement.

MONTHLY DISCHARGE of Sevenpersons River at Medicine Hat, for 1912-13.

(Drainage area 797 square miles.)

MONTH.	DISCHARGE IN SECOND-FEET.				RUN-OFF.	
	Maximum.	Minimum.	Mean.	Per square Mile.	Depth in inches on Drainage Area.	Total in Acre-feet.
1912.						
July (21-31)...........................	10.8	Nil.	2.07	0.003	0.001	45
August................................	7.9	"	1.41	0.002	0.002	86
September............................	4.5	"	1.37	0.002	0.002	82
October...............................	2.0	0.42	1.13	0.001	0.001	69
November (1-15)......................	1.0	1.00	1.00	0.001	0.001	30
The period............................	....	....	....	....	0.007	312
1913.						
April (3-30)...........................	400.00	7.90	155.20	0.194	0.20	8,619
May..................................	11.20	0.05	5.11	0.006	0.01	314
June..................................	2.60	0.00	0.32	0.000	0.00	19
July (1-12)...........................	0.38	0.00	0.09	0.000	0.00	2
August a.............................	....	....	....	....	....	....
September a..........................	....	....	....	....	....	....
October (5-31)........................	0.10	0.07	0.08	0.000	0.00	4
The period............................	....	....	....	....	0.21	8,958

a No observations in these months.

NOTE.—These tables are inserted in this report to correct tables which were published in the reports for 1912 and 1913. The drainage area used for those years was in error.

DAILY GAUGE HEIGHT AND DISCHARGE of Sevenpersons River at Medicine Hat, for 1914.

| | March. | | April. | | May. | |
DAY.	Gauge Height.	Dis- charge.	Gauge Height.	Dis- charge.	Gauge Height.	Dis- charge.
	Feet.	*Sec.-ft.*	*Feet.*	*Sec.-ft.*	*Feet.*	*Sec.-ft.*
1			2 65	13.5	1.79	2.30
2			2.87	29.0	1.77	1.85
3			2.90	34.0	1.75	1.42
4			3.21	77.0	1.75	1.42
5			3.29	102 0	1.76	1.64
6			3.10	86.0	1.75	1.42
7			3.10	94.0	1.75	1.42
8			3.17	110.0	1.73	1.03
9			3.11	102.0	1.73	1.03
10			2.99	83.0	1.73a	1.03
11			2.69	50.0	1.72a	0.78
12			2.39	27.0	1.72a	0.78
13			2.34	24.0	1.71a	0.56
14			2.29	21.0	1.71a	0.56
15			2.24	19.0	1.70a	0.35
16	3.00	3.5	2.27	20.0	1.70a	0.35
17	2.99	3.2	2.27	20.0	1.69	0.32
18	2.98	3.0	2.31	23.0	1.67	0.24
19	2.97	2.8	2.29	21.0	1.63	0.10
20	2.97	2.8	2.23	18.0	1.49	Nil.b
21	2.94	2.2	2.18	16.1	1.49	"
22	2.94a	2.2	2.07	10.9	1.49	"
23	2.94a	2.2	2.00	8.5	1.49	"
24	2.93a	2.0	1.97	7.4	1.48	"
25	2.93a	2.0	1.91	5.3	1.45	"
26	2.82a	2.7	1.87	4.2	1.44	"
27	2.77a	4.5	1.85	3.7	1.42	"
28	2.62a	3.5	1.84	3.5	1.40	"
29	2.47	1.5	1.83	3.2	1.40	"
30	2.52	4.5	1.81	2.7	1.40	"
31	2.59	9.0			1.40	"

a Gauge height interpolated.
b River dry from May 20.

MONTHLY DISCHARGE of Sevenpersons River at Medicine Hat, for 1914.

(Drainage area 797 square miles.)

| | DISCHARGE IN SECOND-FEET. | | | | RUN-OFF. | |
MONTH.	Maximum.	Minimum.	Mean.	Per square Mile.	Depth in inches on Drainage Area.	Total in Acre-feet.
March (16-31)	9.0	1.5	3.20	0.004	0.002	101
April	110.0	2.7	35.00	0.044	0.049	2,082
May	2.3	Nil.	0.63	0.002	0.002	37
June						Nil.
July						"
August						"
September						"
October						"
The period					0.053	2,220

5 GEORGE V, A. 1915

LAKE JOHNSTON DRAINAGE BASIN.

General Description.

Lake Johnston lies about 20 miles southwest of the city of Moosejaw. *It* is about 25 miles long and 15 wide, and covers an area of nearly five townships. *Almost all the* drainage into the lake comes from the south and west through Wood River. The main tributaries of Wood River are Wiwa Creek, Notukeu Creek, Pinto Creek and Wood Creek. These drain a large area, but, owing to the limited rainfall and the small slope of the drainage basin, the run-off is comparatively small.

Lake Johnston has no surface outlet, and there has been no surface flow from Lake Chaplin to Lake Johnston for several years, but it is noted that the elevations of the two lakes are the same. There is often considerable flow in Wood River in the spring, and there is always some discharge at all seasons; nevertheless, the lake has during recent years receded.

The lower part of Wood River has a very small fall, and is more of the nature of a long slough than that of a running stream. The channel is from twenty to fifty feet wide, and is from two to five feet deep. The bottom is composed of soft clay, and is covered with weeds and grass. There is so little fall that it would be impossible to take out water by gravity, and a dam would flood a large area of good agricultural land. There is, therefore, little possibility of irrigation development in this basin.

This drainage basin includes a large area of very good agricultural land. This is pretty well taken up by settlers and is being farmed with good results. There is one irrigation scheme on Pearce Creek.

NOTUKEU CREEK NEAR VANGUARD.

Location.—On NW. ¼ Sec. 10, Tp. 11, Rge. 10, W. 3rd Mer., at the traffic bridge south of the town.

Records available.—August 6, 1914, to December 31, 1914.

Gauge.—Staff; zero elevation of gauge was maintained at 77.94 feet during 1914.

Bench-mark.—Top of large bolt on plate, top of left pier downstream side; assumed elevation, 100 00 feet.

Channel.—Permanent.

Discharge measurements.—From traffic bridge during high water, or by wading.

Winter flow.—Affected by ice.

Observer.—Miss Ripley.

DISCHARGE MEASUREMENTS of Notukeu Creek near Vanguard, in 1914.

Date.	Engineer.	Width.	Area of Section.	Mean Velocity.	Gauge Height.	Discharge.
		Feet.	*Sq. ft.*	*Ft. per sec.*	*Feet.*	*Sec.-ft.*
Aug.　6	W. H. Storey					.... a
Sept.　5	do	26	10.0	0.19	1.27	1.87
Dec.　1	J. E. Caughey	26	16.0	0.29	1.53	4.62
Dec.　22	do	21	3.4	0.12	1.38	0.42

a Water in pools; no flow.

LAKE JOHNSTON DRAINAGE BASIN   475

SESSIONAL PAPER No. 25c

DAILY GAUGE HEIGHT AND DISCHARGE of Notukeu Creek near Vanguard, for 1914.

DAY.	August. Gauge Height.	August. Dis-charge.	September. Gauge Height.	September. Dis-charge.	October. Gauge Height.	October. Dis-charge.	November. Gauge Height.	November. Dis-charge.	December. Gauge Height.	December. Dis-charge.
	Feet.	Sec.-ft.	Feet.	Sec.-ft.	Feet.	Sec.-ft.	Feet.	Sec.-ft.	Feet.	Sec.-ft.
1	....	....	1.41	3.20	1.26	1.82	1.44	3.5	1.52	4.60a
2	....	....	1.40	3.10	1.27	1.89	1.40	3.1	1.52	4.50
3	....	....	1.37	2.80	1.33	2.40	1.40	3.1	1.52	4.30
4	....	....	1.31	2.20	1.36	2.70	1.38	2.9	1.52	4.10
5	....	....	1.27	1.89	1.40	3.10	1.38	2.9	1.52	3.80
6	Dry.	Nil.	1.26	1.82	1.43	3.40	1.38	2.9	1.52	3.40
7	"	"	1.26	1.82	1.48	4.00	1.40	3.1	1.50	3.10
8	"	"	1.26	1.82	1.53	4.60	1.40	3.1	1.50	2.70
9	"	"	1.23	1.61	1.59	5.30	1.41	3.2	1.50	2.40
10	"	"	1.20	1.40	1.62	5.70	1.42	3.3	1.52	2.00
11	"	"	1.19	1.35	1.62	5.70	1.42	3.3	1.52	1.70
12	"	"	1.20	1.40	1.60	5.40	1.42	3.3	1.52	1.35
13	"	"	1.16	1.20	1.55	4.80	1.42	3.3	1.52	1.00
14	"	"	1.28	1.96	1.54	4.70	1.43	3.4	1.53	0.80
15	"	"	1.38	2.90	1.57	5.00	1.41	3.2	1.53	0.70
16	"	"	1.44	3.50	1.61	5.50	1.41	3.2	1.53	0.62
17	"	"	1.40	3.10	1.63	5.80	1.41	3.2	1.53	0.57
18	"	"	1.38	2.90	1.61	5.50	1.39	3.0	1.53	0.54
19	"	"	1.34	2.50	1.58	5.20	1.39	3.0	1.55	0.48
20	"	"	1.31	2.20	1.55	4.80	1.37	2.8	1.55	0.45
21	"	"	1.31	2.20	1.53	4.60	1.37	2.8	1.53	0.44
22	1.19	1.35	1.29	2.00	1.51	4.30	1.36	2.7	1.38	0.42
23	1.53	4.60	1.27	1.89	1.51	4.30	1.35	2.6	1.38	0.37
24	1.84	8.50	1.27	1.89	1.50	4.20	1.35	2.6	1.38	0.33
25	2.01	10.70	1.28	1.96	1.49	4.10	1.34	2.5	1.37	0.28
26	1.93	9.70	1.28	1.96	1.48	4.00	1.33	2.4	1.37	0.24
27	1.80	8.00	1.28	1.96	1.47	3.90	1.36	2.7	1.37	0.20
28	1.65	6.00	1.27	1.89	1.47	3.90	1.38	2.9	1.35	0.15
29	1.55	4.80	1.26	1.82	1.47	3.90	1.39	3.0	1.35	0.10
30	1.48	4.00	1.25	1.75	1.46	3.80	1.42	3.3	1.36	0.05
31	1.41	3.20	....	....	1.46	3.80	....	....	1.36	0.01a

a Ice conditions Dec. 1 to 31.

MONTHLY DISCHARGE of Notukeu Creek near Vanguard, for 1914.

(Drainage area 1,406 square miles.)

MONTH.	DISCHARGE IN SECOND-FEET. Maximum.	DISCHARGE IN SECOND-FEET. Minimum	DISCHARGE IN SECOND-FEET. Mean.	DISCHARGE IN SECOND-FEET. Per square Mile.	RUN-OFF. Depth in inches on Drainage Area.	RUN-OFF. Total in Acre-feet.
August	10.7	Nil.	2.30	0.0016	0.002	119
September	3.5	1.20	2.10	0.0014	0.002	125
October	5.8	1.82	4.30	0.0030	0.003	264
November	3.5	2.40	3.00	0.0021	0.002	178
December	4.6	0.01	1.48	0.0010	0.001	91
The period	....	....	....	....	0.010	777

• 5 GEORGE V, A. 1915

QU'APPELLE RIVER DRAINAGE BASIN.

General Description.

Qu'Appelle River rises in Township 23, Range 4, West of the 3rd Meridian, and flows eastward into the Assiniboine River in Township 28, Range 17, West of the Principal Meridian. These waters eventually find their way into Hudson's Bay through the Red River, Lake Winnipeg and Nelson River.

The chief tributaries of Qu'Appelle River are Moosejaw Creek, Last Mountain Lake, Waskana Creek and Loon Creek. Last Mountain is the largest lake in the basin, being some sixty miles long and from one to three miles wide.

The valley of the main stream is from 200 to 300 feet deep, with a flat from one to three miles wide along the river. This flat is covered in many places with brush, and the side hills are in many places well wooded. The bench lands above the river are mostly level prairie, much of which is now under cultivation.

The mean annual rainfall at Moosejaw is 14 inches; at Regina, 15 inches; and at Indian Head, 19 inches. The streams are frozen during the winter months, and there is usually an abundant snowfall.

There are several irrigation and many industrial water rights in this basin.

QU'APPELLE RIVER AT LUMSDEN.

Location.—On NW. ¼ Sec. 33, Tp. 19, Rge. 21, W. 2nd Mer., at farm near Lumsden, Sask.
Records available.—May 12, 1911, to December 31, 1914.
Gauge.—Vertical staff; zero of gauge maintained at 85.33 feet during 1911-13; and at 85.16 feet during 1914.
Bench-mark.—Permanent iron bench-mark; assumed elevation, 100.00 feet.
Channel.—Permanent.
Discharge measurements.—From bridge or by wading.
Winter flow.—Affected by ice.
Observer.—J. G. Miller.

DISCHARGE MEASUREMENTS of Qu'Appelle River at Lumsden, in 1914.

Date.	Engineer.	Width.	Area of Section.	Mean Velocity.	Gauge Height.	Discharge.
		Feet.	*Sq. ft.*	*Ft. per sec.*	*Feet.*	*Sec.-ft.*
Jan. 14..........	F. R. Steinberger.	13.5	7.16	0.075	2.56	0.54
Feb. 3..........	do	13.0	8.90	0.000	2.60	0.00
Feb. 21..........	do	10.9	5.10	0.000	2.54	0.00
Mar. 12..........	do	10.5	7.90	0.180	2.55	1.43
April 7..........	do	27.0	77.00	1.000	5.81	77.10
May 18..........	W. H. Storey...	27.0	116.00	0.220	3.11	25.60
July 4..........	do	27.0	114.00	0.180	3.02	20.60
July 16....... .	do	27.0	123.00	.......·...	3.29	..........a
Aug. 11...	do	24.0	20.70	0.210	2.34	4.34
Oct. 8......... .	F. R. Steinberger...... .	24.0	24.60	0.350	2.50	8.56
Nov. 19..........	do	18.0	10.20	0.281	2.16	2.90
Dec. 9..	do	15.5	9.80	0.390	2.31	3.82

a Measurement could not be made, due to low velocity.

SESSIONAL PAPER No. 25c

DAILY GAUGE HEIGHT AND DISCHARGE of Qu'Appelle River at Lumsden, for 1914.

DAY.	January.		February.		March.		April.		May.		June.	
	Gauge Height.	Dis-charge.	Gauge Height.	Dis-charge.	Gauge Height.	Dis-charge	Gauge Height.	Dis-charge.	Gauge Height.	Dis-charge.	Gauge Height.	Dis-charge .
	Feet.	Sec.-ft.	Feet.	Sec.-ft.	Feet.	Sec.-ft.	Feet.	Sec.-ft.	Feet.	Sec -ft.	Feet.	Sec.-ft.
1	2.83	2.70c	2 86	0.06	2.54	0 09	4.38	7 5	3 33	34.0	3 00	22.0
2	2.83	2.67	2.79	0.01	2.56	0.14	5.40	10 4	3 26	31.0	3.00	22.0
3	2.78	2.61	2 74	Nil.	2.56	0.22	5.06	13 0	3.18	28.0	3.02	22 0
4	2.77	2.53	2 74	"	2.62	0.30	5.88	15.7	3 33	34.0	2.82	15.6
5	2.77	2.44	2.74	"	2.62	0.40	6.22	26.0a	3 93	65 0	2.97	20.0
6	2.78	2.33	2.72	"	2.61	0 50	6.04	38.0	3 90	63 0	3.06	24.0
7	2.86	2.23	2.70	"	2.61	0.64	5.93	56.0	3 89	62.0	3 20	29.0
8	2.83	2.08	2.70	"	2.55	0.77	5.64	69.0	3 60	47 0	3.32	34 0
9	2.83	1.87	2.65	"	2.36	0.94	5.52	84 0	3.49	42.0	3.41	38 0
10	2.84	1.65	2.65	"	2.58	1 09	5 89	98 0	3.40	37 0	3 25	31.0
11	2.86	1.44	2.68	"	2.54	1 28	7 88	112 0	3.36	35 0	3 10	25 0
12	2.87	1.45	2.67	"	2 59	1.43	7 69	116 0	3.32	34 0	3.01	22.0
13	2.85	1.50	2.69	"	2.84	1 75	7.72	132 0	3.31	33.0	3 00	22 0
14	2.84	1.30	2.71	"	2 95	2.10	7 85	150 0	3 06	24.0	3.04	23.0
15	2.86	1.00	2.69	"	4 22	2 50	6 77	160.0	2.83	15.9	3 05	23.0
16	2.88	0.75	2.66	"	4 64	2.90	6.24	175 0ac	2 84	16.2	3 06	24 0
17	2.82	0.54	2.69	"	4 35	3 00	5 97	187.0	3 21	29 0	3.02	22.0
18	2.77	0.48	2.67	"	4.86	2.95	5 75	174.0	3.11	25.0	3 06	24 0
19	2.81	0.40	2.65	"	4 61	2 90	5 21	142.0	3 19	29 0	3 08	24 0
20	2.85	0.32	2.63	"	4 28	2 82	5.01	130.0	3.22	30 0	3 08	24 0
21	2.83	0.27	2.65	"	4 12	2.77	4.86	121 0	3 15	27.0	2.90	18.0
22	2.77	0.23	2.63	"	3 75	2 70	4.67	109 0	3 14	27.0	2.98	21.0
23	2.77	0.22	2.63	"	3 64	2 60	4 24	83 0	3 11	25.0	3.10	25 0
24	2.82	0.24	2.58	"	3 54	2 50	3.95	66 0	3 06	24.0	3.12	26.0
25	2.85	0.27	2.54	"	3 34	2.42	3 90	63 0	3 12	26.0	2.88	17.4
26	2.81	0.32	2.53	"	3.05	2 32	3.81	58 0	3 29	33 0	2 86	16.8
27	2.82	0.40	2.53	"	2 96	2.22	3.73	54 0	3 12	26.0	2 94	19 4
28	2.82	0.45	2.53	0.02	2 91	2.16	3.65	50 0	3 26	31 0	3.08	24 0
29	2.79	0.41	....	....	2 84	2.24	3 53	44 0	3 30	33.0	3.10	25 0
30	2.80	0.27	....	....	3 08	2.40	3.43	38.0	3 39	37.0	3.03	23 0
31	2.86	0.15	....	....	3 78	4 30	....	....	3.15	27 0	....	....

a to a Estimated.
c Ice conditions Jan. 1 to April 16.

5 GEORGE V, A. 1915

DAILY GAUGE HEIGHT AND DISCHARGE of Qu'Appelle River at Lumsden, for 1914.
—Concluded.

DAY.	July.		August.		September.		October.		November.		December.	
	Gauge Height.	Dis-charge	Gauge Height.	Dis-charge	Gauge Height	Dis-charge	Gauge Height.	Dis-charge.	Gauge Height.	Dis-charge.	Gauge Height.	Dis-charge.
	Feet.	*Sec.-ft.*	*Feet.*	*Sec.-ft.*	*Feet.*	*Sec.-ft.*	*Feet.*	*Sec.-ft.*	*Feet.*	*Sec.-ft.*	*Feet.*	*Sec.-ft.*
1.........	2 98	22.0	2.70	12.5	2.61	10.2	2.32	4 8	2.31	4.6	2.45	4.40
2.........	3 00	22.0	2.70	12.5	2.51	8.2	2.36	5.4	2.33	5.0	2.41	4 00
3.........	3.02	22.0	2.70	12.5	2.49	7.8	2.35	5.2	2.35	5.2	2.36	4.30
4.........	3.02	22 0	2 66	11.5	2.36	5.4	2.39	5.8	2 36	5.4	2.34	4.10
5.........	3.01	22.0	2.60	10.0	2.29	4.4	2.44	0.8	2.36	5.4	2.32	4.00
6.........	3.20	29.0	2 68	12.0	2.34	5.1	2 48	7.6	2.31	4.6	2.32	4.00
7.........	2.88	17 4	2 62	10.5	2.33	5 0	2.44	6.8	2.30	4.5	2.33	4.10
8.........	2.92	18 7	2 61	10 2	2 30	4 5	2.50	8.0	2 32	4.8	2.33	4.00
9.........	2.98	21 0	2 59	9.8	2.48	7.6	2.58	9.6	2 34	5.1	2.33	3.80
10.........	2.99	21 0	2 51	8 2	2.95	19.6	2 66	11.5	2.31	4.6	2.30	3.90
11.........	3.09	25.0	2.39	5.8	2.36	5.4	2.53	8.6	2.33	5.0	2.29	3.00
12.........	3.04	23.0	2.48	7.6	2.32	4.8	2.45	7.0	2.31	4.6	2.27	2.00
13.........	2.95	19.8	2.42	6.4	2.80	4.5	2.42	6.4	2.30	4.5	2.27	2.30
14.........	2.98	21.0	2.34	5.1	2.26	3.9	2.40	6.0	2.30	4.5	2.27	2.20
15.........	3.14	27.0	2.17	2.6	2.19	2.8	2.38	5.7	2.29	3.3a	2.25	1.66
16.........	3.36	35.0	2.42	6.4	2.47	7.4	2.35	5.2	2.26	3.1	2.25	1.30
17........	3.14	27.0	2.45	7.0	2.25	3.8	2.35	5.2	2.20	3.2	2.20	1.65
18.........	2.90	18.0	2.44	6.8	2.25	3.8	2.35	5.2	2.18	3.3	2.18	2.60
19.........	2.76	14.0	2.38	5.7	2.24	3.6	2.35	5.2	2.16	2.9	2.18	2.20
20.........	2.92	18.7	2.47	7.4	2.27	4.0	2.32	4.8	2.14	3.5	2.15	1.78
21.........	2.99	21.0	2.42	6.4	2.32	4.8	2 30	4.5	2.14	4.3	2.15	1.76
22.........	2.90	18.0	2.42	6.4	2.31	4.6	2.32	4.8	2.13	4.3	2.14	1.48
23.........	2.86	16.8	2.37	5.6	2.28	4.2	2.38	5.7	2.15	4.0	2.14	0.77
24.........	2.85	16.5	2.38	5.7	2.28	4.2	2.31	4.6	2.16	4.3	2.12	0.91
25.........	2.81	15.3	2.32	4.8	2.26	3.9	2.32	4.8	2.18	4.4	2.10	1.02
26.........	2.78	14.5	2.26	3.9	2.25	3.8	2.34	5.1	2.20	4.6	2.05	1.08
27.........	2.76	14.0	2.32	4.8	2.26	3.9	2.32	4.8	2.23	4.8	1.95	0.95
28.........	2.74	13.5	2.34	5.1	2.25	3.8	2.30	4.5	2.27	4.3	2.02	0.95
29.........	2.71	12.8	2.39	5.8	2.25	3.8	2.33	5.0	2.35	4.6	1.94	0.99
30.........	2.70	12.5	2.42	6.4	2.27	4.0	2.35	5.2	2.37	4.6	1.95	1.04
31.........	2.70	12.5	2.54	8.8	......	......	2.32	4.8	......	......	1.95	1.05a

a Ice conditions Nov. 15 to Dec. 31.

MONTHLY DISCHARGE of Qu'Appelle River at Lumsden, for 1914.

(Drainage area 6,160 square miles.)

MONTH.	DISCHARGE IN SECOND-*FEET.*				RUN-OFF.	
	Maximum.	Minimum.	Mean.	Per square Mile.	Depth in inches on Drainage Area.	Total in Acre-feet.
January................................	2.70	0.15	1.140	0 000200	0.0002	70
February..............................	0.06	0.02	0.007	0.000001	0.0000	0
March.................................	4.30	0.09	1.850	.000300	0 0003	114
April..................................	187.00	7.50	86.000	.014000	0.0160	5,117
May...................................	65.00	15.90	33.000	005400	0.0060	2,029
June...................................	38.00	15.60	24.000	003900	0 0040	1,428
July...................................	35.00	12.50	19.800	.003200	0 0040	1,218
August................................	12.50	2.60	7.500	.001200	0 0010	461
September.............................	19.60	2.80	5.400	.000900	0 0010	321
October...............................	11.50	4.50	6.000	.001000	0.0010	369
November.............................	5.40	2.90	4.400	0.000700	0 0008	262
December..............................	4.40	0.77	2 400	0.000400	0.0005	148
The year..............................	....	....	....	....	0.0348	11,537

MOOSEJAW CREEK DRAINAGE BASIN.

General Description.

Moosejaw Creek rises in the Yellowgrass Marsh, which lies in Townships 9 and 10, Range 17, West of the 2nd Meridian, and flows in a north and westerly direction until it reaches the city of Moosejaw, where it is joined by Thunder Creek. From Moosejaw it follows an easterly and northerly course, finally emptying into the Qu'Appelle River near Buffalo Pound Lake. From the headwaters to the city of Moosejaw the drainage area is estimated at about 1,830 square miles. This area is almost entirely devoid of tree growth, except in the vicinity of Moosejaw, where the valley is lined with brush.

Throughout its entire length the creek flows in a very crooked but well-defined channel. The upper portion of the valley is small, being merely a depression, but it gradually increases in size until at Drinkwater it is about 30 feet deep and at Moosejaw about 80 feet deep. The fall in the creek is very small, and particularly so between Drinkwater and Moosejaw, where the total fall is only 67.5 feet, or an average of 2 3 feet per mile of valley.

The Canadian Pacific Railway Company has dams at Milestone, Rouleau, Drinkwater, two at Moosejaw and one at Pasqua. There is also a municipality dam in Section 19, Township 15, Range 24, West of the 2nd Meridian, which supplies water to the neighbourhood during periods when there is no flow in the creek. In 1913 the Canadian Pacific Railway Company constructed a new dam to replace their present dam in Moosejaw.

MOOSEJAW CREEK NEAR LANG.

Location.—At traffic bridge on road allowance east of the *NE.* ¼ Sec. 24, Tp. 11, Rge. 19, W. 2nd Mer., four miles west of the village of Lang.

Records available.—From June 21, 1911, to October 31, 1914.

Gauge.—Vertical staff; zero of gauge was maintained at 94.80 feet during 1911; 95.07 feet during 1912-13; 95 04 feet during 1914.

Bench-mark.—Permanent iron bench-mark; assumed elevation, 100.00 feet.

Channel.—Permanent.

Discharge measurements.—From bridge or by wading.

Winter flow.—No winter observations have been taken.

Observer.—Miss *I*rene *I*rvine.

DISCHARGE MEASUREMENTS of Moosejaw Creek near Lang, in 1914.

Date.	Engineer.	Width.	Area of Section.	Mean Velocity.	Gauge Height.	Discharge.
		Feet.	*Sq. ft.*	*Ft. per sec.*	*Feet.*	*Sec.-ft.*
Mar. 20	F. R. Steinberger	14	10.8	0.260	2.41	2.820
May 10	W. H. Storey	20	10.0	0.343	1.55	3.430
June 16	do	15	3.9	0.210	0.89	0.802
July 10	do				Dry.	Nil.
July 27	do				"	"
Aug. 28	do				"	"

5 GEORGE V, A. 1915

DAILY GAUGE HEIGHT AND DISCHARGE of Moosejaw Creek near Lang, for 1914.

DAY.	March.		April.		May.		June.		July.	
	Gauge Height.	Dis-charge.	Gauge Height.	Dis-charge.	Gauge Height.	Dis-charge.	Gauge Height.	Dis-charge.	Gauge Height.	Dis-charge.
	Feet.	*Sec.-ft.*	*Feet.*	*Sec.-ft.*	*Feet.*	*Sec.-ft.*	*Feet.*	*Sec.-ft.*	*Feet.*	*Sec.-ft.*
1.	......	......	3.25	51.0	1.74	5.80	0.95	0.92	0.49	0.53
2.	......	......	3.40	56.0	1.72	5.40	0.88	0.83	0.44	0.51
3.	......	......	3.19	50.0	1.66	4.60	1.06	1.13	0.38	0.48
4.	......	......	3.14	47.0	1.71	5.30	1.07	1.15	0.29	0.44
5.	......	......	3.41	56.0	1.72	5.40	1.09	1.20	0.24	0.42
6.	......	......	3.34	54.0	1.72	5.40	1.06	1.13	0.19	0.40
7.	......	......	3.29	52.0	1.60	3.90	1.05	1.11	0.14	0.38
8.	......	......	3.22	50.0	1.58	3.70	1.04	1.09	0.09	0.36
9.	......	......	3.03	44.0	1.56	3.50	0.99	0.98	.....b	......
10.	......	......	2.93	41.0	1.61	4.00	0.96	0.94	......	......
11.	......	......	2.78	36.0	1.59	3.80	0.94	0.91	......	......
12.	......	......	2.92	41.0	1.56	3.50	0.92	0.88	......	......
13.	......	......	2.72	35.0	1.54	3.40	0.89	0.84	......	......
14.	......	......	2.92	41.0	1.51	3.10	0.88	0.83	......	......
15.	1.50	......	2.66	33.0	1.51	3.10	0.87	0.82	......	......
16.	2.87	......	2.66	33.0	1.50	3.00	0.84	0.79	......	......
17.	2.95	......	2.56	29.0	1.50	3.00	0.81	0.76	......	......
18.	2.85	......	2.41	25.0	1.50	3.00	0.77	0.73	......	......
19.	2.82	......	2.30	22.0	1.50	3.00	0.74	0.70	......	......
20.	2.53	......	2.40	25.0	1.47	2.80	0.71	0.68	......	......
21.	2.38	......	2.19	18.1	1.44	2.60	0.69	0.66	......	......
22.	2.26	......	2.15	16.9	1.41	2.50	0.64	0.63	......	......
23.	2.25	......	2.09	15.0	1.36	2.20	0.59	0.59	......	......
24.	2.25	......	2.00	12.2	1.31	1.95	0.55	0.57	......	......
25.	2.22	......	1.94	10.3	1.27	1.80	0.51	0.55	......	......
26.	2.22	......	1.88	8.6	1.22	1.59	0.49	0.53	......	......
27.	2.21	......	1.85	7.9	1.15	1.37	0.51	0.55	......	......
28.	2.21	......	1.83	7.5	1.10	1.22	0.54	0.56	......	......
29.	2.21	......	1.80	6.8	1.05	1.11	0.59	0.59	......	......
30.	2.96a	......	1.77	6.3	1.01	1.02	0.54	0.56	......	......
31.	3.05	......	......	......	0.99	0.98	......	......	......	......

a Creek clear of ice March 31 to April 24, estimated.
b Creek dry after July 8.

MONTHLY DISCHARGE of Moosejaw Creek near Lang, for 1914.

(Drainage area 189 square miles.)

MONTH.	DISCHARGE IN SECOND-FEET.				RUN-OFF.	
	Maximum.	Minimum.	Mean.	Per square Mile.	Depth in inches on Drainage Area.	Total in Acre-feet.
April	56.00	6.30	31.00	0.1640	0.1830	1,845
May	5.80	0.98	3.10	0.0164	0.0189	191
June	1.20	0.53	0.80	0.0042	0.0047	48
July	0.53	0.36	0.44	0.0023	0.0007	7
The period	....	....	....	....	0 2073	2,091

SESSIONAL PAPER No. 25c

MOOSEJAW CREEK AT MCCARTHY'S FARM.

Location.—On the NW. ¼ Sec. 16, Tp. 16, Rge. 26, W. 2nd Mer., about three miles south of Moosejaw.

Records available.—April 7, 1910, to December 31, 1914.

Gauge.—Vertical staff; elevation of zero was maintained at 83.03 feet during 1910-11; 82.99 feet during 1912-13; 81.99 feet during 1914.

Bench-mark.—Permanent iron bench-mark; assumed elevation, 100.00 feet.

Channel.—Permanent.

Discharge measurements.—From bridge or by wading.

Winter flow.—Affected by ice.

Observer.—V. J. McCarthy.

DISCHARGE MEASUREMENTS of Moosejaw Creek at McCarthy's Farm, in 1914.

Date.	Engineer.	Width.	Area of Section.	Mean. Velocity.	Gauge Height.	Discharge.
		Feet.	*Sq ft.*	*Ft. per sec.*	*Feet.*	*Sec.-ft.*
Jan. 15	F. R. Steinberger				1.20	Nil.
Feb. 5	do				1.02	"
Feb. 23	do				0.95	"
Mar. 13	do				1.66	"
April 4	do	36.9	49.80	0.57	2.64	28.00
May 8	W. H. Storey	23.0	6.00	0.80	1.67	4.80
June 10	do	20.0	4.70	1.15	1.65	5.40
July 6	do	15.0	3.40	0.25	1.45	0.85
Aug. 1	do				Dry.	Nil.
Aug. 27	do				"	"
Oct. 7	F. R. Steinberger				"	"
Nov. 18	do				"	"
Dec. 5	do	10.5	3.23	0.31	1.34	1.00
Dec. 28	do				1.10	Nil.

DAILY GAUGE HEIGHT AND DISCHARGE of Moosejaw Creek at McCarthy's Farm, for 1914.

DAY.	January.		February.		March.		April.		May.		June.	
	Gauge Height.	Dis-charge	Gauge Height.	Dis-charge.	Gauge Height.	Dis-charge	Gauge Height.	Dis-charge.	Gauge Height.	Dis-charge.	Gauge Height.	Dis-charge.
	Feet.	*Sec.-ft.*	*Feet.*	*Sec.-ft.*	*Feet.*	*Sec -ft.*	*Feet.*	*Sec.-ft.*	*Feet.*	*Sec.-ft.*	*Feet.*	*Sec -ft.*
1	1.10	Nil.*a*	1.00	Nil.	1.10	Nil.	2.90	19 0	1.89	13.60	1 51	1 52
2	1.02	"	1.00	"	1.40	"	2.78	25 0	1 87	12 80	1 50	1 30
3	1.10	"	1.01	"	1.49	"	2.90	28 0	1 84	11.60	1.51	1.52
4	1.05	"	1.00	"	1.65	"	2.86	30 0	1.83	11 20	1.63	4 40
5	1.33	"	1.00	"	1.65	"	2.62	41 0	1.79	9.60	1.61	3.80
6	1.32	"	0.98	"	1.62	"	2.58	54.0	1.75	8.20	1.63	4.40
7	1.25	"	0.97	"	1.64	"	2.71	67.0	1.75	8.20	1.74	7.90
8	1.30	"	0.95	"	1.68	"	2.88	81.0	1.71	6.90	1.78	9.30
9	1.31	"	0.92	"	1.55	"	3.54	145.0	1.71	6.90	1.73	7.60
10	1.29	"	0.93	"	1.40	"	4.02	198.0*b*	1.73	7.60	1.66	5.30
11	1.28	"	0.90	"	1.70	"	3.87	182 0	1.78	9.30	1.63	4.40
12	1.22	"	0.89	"	1.75	"	3.57	149.0	1.73	7.60	1.60	3.30
13	1.25	"	0.80	"	1.65	"	3.41	138.0	1.71	6.90	1.59	3.30
14	1.20	"	0.75	"	1.75	"	3.30	121.0	1.67	5.60	1.56	2.60
15	1.20	"	0.74	"	1.85	"	3.21	112.0	1.63	4.40	1.55	2.40
16	1.23	"	1.01	"	1.85	"	3.07	98.0	1.62	4.10	1.55	2.40
17	1.23	"	0.90	"	1.75	"	2.91	84.0	1.61	3.80	1.53	2.00
18	1.23	"	0.85	"	1.62	"	2.71	67.0	1.61	3.80	1.52	1.74
19	1.22	"	0.85	"	1.65	"	2.53	52.0	1.63	4.40	1.52	1.74
20	1.21	"	0.85	"	1.65	"	2.41	44.0	1.61	3.80	1.54	2.20
21	1.20	"	0.83	"	1.92	"	2.37	41.0	1.59	3.30	1.57	2.84
22	1.20	"	0.70	"	1.90	"	2.23	33.0	1.57	2.84	1.56	2.60
23	1.20	"	0.67	"	1.85	"	2.23	33.0	1.57	2.84	1.51	1.52
24	1.20	"	0.85	"	1.70	"	2.19	30.0	1.55	2.40	1.50	1.30
25	1.25	"	0.95	"	1.66	"	2.11	26.0	1.53	2.00	1.50	1.30
26	1.10	"	0.95	"	1.66	"	2.02	20.0	1.51	1.52	1.54	2.20
27	1.05	"	1.40	"	1.67	"	1.89	13.6	1.51	1.52	1.57	2.84
28	1.08	"	1.10	"	1.68	"*a*	1.81	10.4	1.52	1.64	1.51	1.52
29	1.10	"			3.20	8*b*	1.91	14.5	1.53	2.00	1.65	5.00
30	1.08	"			3.00	11	1.92	15.0	1.55	2.40	1.60	3.50
31	1.05	"			2.85	15			1.53	2.00		

a Ice conditions Jan. 1 to March 28; no discharge
b March 29 to April 10, ice break-up; discharge estimated.

5 GEORGE V, A. 1915

DAILY GAUGE HEIGHT AND DISCHARGE of Moosejaw Creek near McCarthy's Farm, for 1914.
—*Concluded.*

DAY.	July.		August.		September.		October.		November.		December.	
	Gauge Height.	Dis-charge	Gauge Height.	Dis-charge	Gauge Height.	Dis-charge.	Gauge Height.	Dis-charge.	Gauge Height.	Dis-charge.	Gauge Height.	Dis-charge.
	Feet.	*Sec.-ft.*	*Feet.*	*Sec.-ft*	*Feet.*	*Sec.-ft*	*Feet.*	*Sec.-ft.*	*Feet.*	*Scc.-ft.*	*Feet.*	*Sec.-ft.*
1.............	1.54	1.39	1 11	0 01	Dry.	Nil.	Dry.	Nil.	Dry.	Nil.	1.39	0.45
2.............	1.51	1.32	1 14	0 04	"	"	"	"	"	"	1.38	0.35
3.............	1 48	1.10	1 13	0 03	"	"	"	"	"	"	1.35	0.11
4.............	1 46	0 90	1 10	Nil.	"	"	"	"	"	"	1.32	0.00
5.............	1.46	0 90	Dry.	" a	"	"	"	"	"	"	1.43	1.00
6.............	1.44	0.70	"	"	"	"	"	"	"	"	1.42	0.85
7.............	1.44	0.70	"	"	"	"	"	"	"	"	1.42	0.85
8.............	1.44	0.70	"	"	"	"	"	"	"	"	1.42	0.85
9.............	1.42	0.50	"	"	"	"	"	"	"	"	1.42	0.85
10.......	1.42	0.50	"	"	"	"	"	"	"	"	1.40	0.57
11.	1.42	0.50	"	"	"	"	"	"	"	"	1.39	0.45
12.. . ..	1.42	0.50	"	"	"	"	"	"	"	"	1.39	0.45
13.........	1.41	0.40	"	"	"	"	"	"	"	"	1.38	0.35
14.........	1.41	0.40	"	"	"	"	"	"	"	"	1.38	0.35
15........ .	1.40	0.30	"	"	"	"	"	"	1.33	"	1.39	0.45
16.........	1.38	0.28	"	"	"	"	"	"	1.33	"	1.39	0.45
17........	1.36	0.26	"	"	"	"	"	"	1.32	"	1.40	0.57
18.	1.35	0.25	"	"	"	"	"	"	1.30	"	1.40	0.57
19.........	1.34	0.24	"	"	"	"	"	"	1.31	"	1.38	0.35
20.........	1.32	0.22	"	"	"	"	"	"	1.30	"	1.37	0.25
21.........	1.31	0.21	"	"	"	"	"	"	1.30	"	1.35	0 11
22.... . .	1.30	0.20	"	"	"	"	"	"	1.30	"	1.34	0 06
23.........	1.28	0.18	"	"	"	"	"	"	1.30	" a	1 34	0 06
24.........	1.25	0.15	"	"	"	"	"	"	2.00	19.0b	1 33	0.03
25.........	1.24	0.14	"	"	"	"	"	"	1.99	18.5	1 31	Nil.
26..... ..	1.24	0.14	"	"	"	"	"	"	1.88	13.2	1.29	"
27.... .	1.20	0.10	"	"	"	"	"	"	1.72	7.2	1.29	"
28.........	1.18	0.08	"	"	"	"	"	"	1.69	6.2	1.29	"
29.........	1.14	0.04	"	"	"	"	"	"	1.69	6.2	1.28	"
30.........	1.12	0.02	"	"	"	"	"	"	1.58	3.1b	1.28	"
31.........	1.12	0.02	"	"	"	"	"	"	......	......	1.27	"

a Water in pools only from Aug. 5 to Nov. 23.
b Ice went out on Nov. 24, and commenced to re-form Nov. 30. Winter conditions from Dec. 1.

MONTHLY DISCHARGE of Moosejaw Creek at McCarthy's Farm, for 1914.

(Drainage area 1,719 square miles.)

MONTH.	DISCHARGE IN SECOND FEET.				RUN-OFF.	
	Maximum.	Minimum	Mean.	Per square Mile.	Depth in inches on Drainage Area.	Total in Acre-feet.
January	....	....	....	....	....	Nil.
February	....	....	....	....	....	"
March..............	111.00	0.00	9.100	0.0050	0.0056	559
April...	198.00	10.40	73.000	0.0420	0.0468	4,344
May..	13.60	1.52	5.600	0.0032	0.0037	344
June............	9.30	1.30	3.400	0.0020	0.0022	202
July..............	1.39	0.04	0.430	0.0003	0.0003	26
August	0.04	0.00	0.003	0.0000	0.0000	Nil.
September	....	....	....	....	....	"
October...............	....	....	....	....	....	"
November.........	19.00	0.00	2.400	0.0010	0.0012	146
December.....	1.00	0.00	0.340	0.0002	C.0002	21
The year..............................	....	....	....	....	0 0600	5,642

SOURIS RIVER DRAINAGE BASIN.

General Description.

The source of the Souris River is in marshes near Yellow Grass, Saskatchewan. From here it flows in a southeasterly direction almost parallel to the Soo line of the Canadian Pacific Railway to Estevan. It then flows east to Oxbow. then it turns south and crosses the international boundary in Range 34, West of the Principal Meridian. After making a loop into North Dakota, it recrosses the international boundary in Range 27, West of the Principal Meridian, and flows in a northeasterly direction to Souris, Manitoba, where it turns east, and finally joins the Assiniboine River in Township 8, Range 15, West of the 1st Meridian.

The chief tributaries of Souris River are: Long Creek, which joins it near Estevan, Moose Mountain Creek near Oxbow, North and South Antler Creeks near Sourisford, and Pipestone Creek near Souris.

This stream drains a large tract of typical western plains. The rainfall will probably average very little over fifteen inches, and is usually sufficiently divided over the year to prevent excessive run-off or floods. At times when there is an unusual amount of rainfall, and in the early spring, the water drains into the streams very rapidly and causes a flood of short duration.

There are towns, villages, and farms all along the course of this stream and its tributaries which depend on it for a domestic and industrial water supply. The Canadian Pacific Railway is a large consumer. The town of Estevan is establishing a waterworks system, and there is a proposed system at Weyburn to divert water from Souris River. In North Dakota it has been proposed to divert water for irrigation purposes.

LONG CREEK NEAR ESTEVAN.

Location.—At bridge on SE. ¼ Sec. 10, Tp. 2, Rge. 8, W. 2nd Mer., 2½ miles south of the town of Estevan.

Records available.—June 22, 1911, to December 31, 1914.

Gauge.—Staff; zero of gauge maintained at 83 87 feet during 1911-12; at 83.90 feet during 1913; at 83.87 feet from January 1, 1914, to October 28, 1914; at elevation of weir crest from October 29, 1914, to December 31, 1914.

Bench-mark.—Permanent iron bench-mark; assumed elevation, 100.00 feet.

Channel.—Permanent.

Discharge measurements.—From bridge, by wading below bridge, or by weir.

Winter flow.—Winter observations were taken in 1913-14 by a two-foot rectangular weir.

Observer.—Geo. Pawson.

DISCHARGE MEASUREMENTS of Long Creek near Estevan, in 1914.

Date.	Engineer.	Width.	Area of Section.	Mean Velocity.	Gauge Height.	Discharge.
		Feet.	*Sq. ft.*	*Ft. per sec.*	*Feet.*	*Sec.-ft.*
Mar. 24............	F. R. Steinberger	39.5	98.60	0.580	5.35	57.10
May 12............	W. H. Storey...............	36.0	86.40	0.480	2.21	41.60
June 17............	do	36.0	77.20	0.484	1.99	37.20
July 11............	do	34.0	69.20	0.267	1.54	18.40
July 28......	do	6.6	2.42	0.880	0.79	2.16
Aug. 29............	do	6.0	2.30	1.170	1.13	2.70
Oct. 28...........a	F. R. Steinberger..........a	....	....	....	0.27	0.91
Dec. 8...........a	do ....a	....	....	....	0.31	1.12
Dec. 30...........a	do ....a	....	....	....	0.30	1.06

a Weir measurement.

Daily Gauge Height and Discharge of Long Creek near Estevan, for 1914.

Day.	July.		August.		September.		October.		November.		December.	
	Gauge Height.	Dis-charge.	Gauge Height.	Dis-charge.	Gauge Height.	Dis-charge.	Gauge Height.	Dis-charge.	Gauge Height.	Dis-charge.	Gauge Height.	Dis-charge.
	Feet.	Sec.-ft.	Feet.	Sec.-ft.	Feet.	Sec.-ft.	Feet.	Sec.-ft.	Feet.	Sec.-ft.	Feet.	Sec.-ft.
1	1.86		1.78									
2	1.84		1.78									
3	1.82		1.78									
4	1.58		1.74									
5	1.54		1.72									
6	1.48		1.71									
7	1.44											
8	1.39											
9	1.52											
10	1.44											
11	1.49											
12	1.44											
13	1.54											
14	1.44											
15	1.36											
16	1.30											
17	1.24											
18	1.19											
19	1.11											
20	1.06											
21	1.02											
22	0.99											
23	0.98											
24	0.94											
25	0.98											
26	0.98											
27	0.98											
28	0.87											
29	0.78											
30	0.78											
31	0.78											

Note.—Weir measurements after Oct. 28; gauge reading gives the head or 5-inch weir. Interpolated.

Monthly Discharge of Long Creek near Estevan, for 1914

Drainage area 1,830 square miles.

5 GEORGE V, A. 1915

DAILY GAUGE HEIGHT AND DISCHARGE of Long Creek near Estevan, for 1914.

DAY.	March. Gauge Height.	March. Discharge.	April. Gauge Height.	April. Discharge.	May. Gauge Height.	May. Discharge.	June. Gauge Height.	June. Discharge.
	Feet.	Sec.-ft.	Feet.	Sec.-ft.	Feet.	Sec.-ft.	Feet.	Sec.-ft.
1	....	....	4.71	.....	2.14	41.0	1.37	13.4
2			4.56	.....	2.07	38.0	1.37	13.4
3			4.82	.....	2.01	35.0	1.24	10.0
4			6.02	.....	2.12	40.0	1.98	34.0
5			6.89	.....	2.13	40.0	7.13	244.0
6			6.34	.....	2.38	50.0	7.53	260.0
7			5.69	.....	2.55	57.0	6.18	202.0
8			5.44	.....	2.91	71.0	5.18	162.0
9			5.42	.....	2.70	63.0	4.88	150.0
10			6.44	.....	2.41	51.0	4.08	118.0
11			6.32	.....	2.29	47.0	3.64	101.0
12			5.46	.....	2.19	43.0	3.48	94.0
13			4.89	.....	2.14	41.0	3.33	88.0
14	2.04	.....b	4.55	.....	2.01	35.0	2.74	65.0
15	2.63		3.95	.....b	1.91	31.0	2.34	40.0
16	6.04	....a	3.65	101	1.80	27.0	2.23	44.0
17			3.51	95	1.73	25.0	2.04	37.0
18			3.03	76	1.71	24.0	1.94	33.0
19			3.02	76	1.64	22.0	1.77	26.0
20			3.03	76	1.64	22.0	1.69	23.0
21	....a		2.79	67	1.60	20.0	1.64	22.0
22			2.63	60	1.57	19.4	1.53	18.2
23	5.94		2.43	52	1.53	18.2	1.54	18.5
24	5.24		2.35	49	1.52	17.8	1.54	18.5
25	5.19		2.31	47	1.53	18.2	1.54	18.5
26	3.74		2.23	44	1.48	16.6	1.66	22.0
27	2.86		2.15	41	1.47	16.3	1.76	26.0
28	3.56		2.13	40	1.43	15.1	1.77	26.0
29	6.19		2.23	44	1.38	13.7	1.79	27.0
30	5.72		2.30	47	1.38	13.7	1.74	25.0
31	4.99		....	....	1.27	10.8	....	....

a to a Water over gauge.
b Ice conditions to April 16, and not sufficient data to compute the discharge.

SESSIONAL PAPER No. 25c

DAILY GAUGE HEIGHT AND DISCHARGE of Long Creek near *Estevan*, for 1914.

DAY.	July. Gauge Height.	July. Dis-charge	August. Gauge Height.	August. Dis-charge	September. Gauge Height.	September. Dis-charge	October. Gauge Height.	October. Dis-charge	November. Gauge Height.	November. Dis-charge	December. Gauge Height.	December. Dis-charge
	Feet.	*Sec.-ft.*	*Feet.*	*Sec.-ft.*	*Feet.*	*Sec.-ft*	*Feet.*	*Sec.-ft.*	*Feet.*	*Sec.-ft.*	*Feet.*	*Sec.-ft.*
1	1.66	22 00	0 76	1.86	1.33	.0	1 68	2 80	0.30c	1.06	0.33	1.22
2	1.64	22.00	0.76	1.86	1.38	.5	1.68	2.50	0.26	0.86	0.32	1.17
3	1.62	21.00	0 76	1.86	1.43	.0	1.73	2.90	0.26	0.86	0.32	1.17
4	1 58	20 00	0 74	1 64	1 43	.8	1.78	3.40	0.26	0.86	0.31	1.12
5	1.54	18 50	0.73	1.53	1 43	6.6	1 78	3.20	0.25	0.81	0.30	1.06
6	1.48	16 60	0.71	1.31	1.48	6.3	1.78	3.00	0 25	0.81	0.30	1 06
7	1 44	15.40	0 69	1 12	1.48	5.8	1.78	2.80	0.25	0.81	0.32	1 17
8	1.39	13 90	0 68	1.04	1.58	7 4	1.78	2.60	0.23	0 72	0.32	1 17
9	1.34	12.60	0.68	1.04	1 53	6.2	1 83	3 00	0 25	0 81	0.33	1.22
10	1.44	15.40	0 67	0 96	1 53	6 0	1.88	3 50	0 30	1 06	0.31	1.12
11	1.49	16.90	0 66	0.88	1.53	5 7	1 88	3.30	0.29	1.00	0.29	1.00
12	1.64	22 00	0.64	0 72	1.53	5.3	1.88	3.00	0.29	1.00	0.27	0.91
13	1.54	18 50	0 63	0.64	1 53	4.8	1.88	2.70	0.31	1 12	0.27	0 91
14	1.44	15.40	0.63	0.64	1 53	4 6	1.85	2.20	0.35	1 33	0 24	0.76
15	1.36	13 10	0 63	0.64	1 53	4.4	1.88	2 40	0 32	1.17	0.26	0 86
16	1 30	11.50	0 62	0 56	1.53	4 2	1.93	2.70	0.30	1 06	0.26	0.86
17	1.24	10 00	0.62	0.56	1.48	3.3	1.93	2.50	0.29	1 00	0 24	0 76
18	1.19	8.80	0.61	0 48	1.43	2 3	1.93	2.40	0 29	1 00	0 23	0 72
19	1 14	7 80	0.61	0.48	1 48	2 7	1.93	2 20	0 25	0 81	0 23	0.72
20	1.08	6.00	0.65	0 80	1.53	3 3	1 88	1.60	0.26	0.86	0.22	0 67
21	1.02	5 50	0.61	0 48	1.58	3.9	1 88	1.40	0 30	1 06	0.22	0 67
22	0.99	5.00	0 67	0.96	1 58	3.6	1 88	1 20	0.33	1.22	0.21	0.63
23	0.96	4.50	0.71	1 31	1.58	5 4	1.88	0 80	0.34	1 27	0 20	0.58
24	0.94	4.20	0.74	1.64	1 58	3.2	2 08	2.70	0.31	1.12	0 21	0.63
25	0.88	3.30	0.83	2.70	1 68	4 4	1 93	1 00	0.30	1 06	0 21	0.63
26	0.86	3.10	0 83	2 70	1 68	4 1	1 93	0 92	0 34	1.27	0 21	0.63
27	0.84	2 80	0 83	2.70	1 68	3 9	1 93	0.75	0.35	1.33	0 26	0.86
28	0.81	2 40	1.03	3 50	1.73	4 2	1 98	0 91	0 35	1.33	0 29	1 00
29	0.79	2 20	1.13	2.70	1.73	4 0	0 27	0 91	0 35	1.33	0 29	1.00
30	0.78	2 10	1 18	3.20	1.73	3.7	0 33	1 22	0.34	1.27	0 29	1.00
31	0.76	1 86	1.28	4.50	......	...	0 33	1.22	......	......	0 30	1.06

NOTE.—Weir measurements after Oct. 29; gauge reading gives the head on 2-foot Weir.
c Interpolated.

MONTHLY DISCHARGE of Long Creek near *Estevan*, for 1914.

(Drainage area 1,380 square miles.)

MONTH.	DISCHARGE IN SECOND-FEET. Maximum.	Minimum	Mean.	Per square Mile.	RUN-OFF. Depth in inches on Drainage Area.	Total in Acre-feet.
April	101.00	40.00	61.00	0.0442	0.0250	1,815
May	71.00	10.80	32.00	0.0232	0.0300	1,968
June	260.00	10.00	66.00	0.4800	0.0500	3,927
July	22.00	1.86	11.10	0.0080	0.0090	682
August	4.50	0.48	1.52	0.0011	0.0010	93
September	7.40	2.30	4.70	0.0034	0.0040	280
October	3.50	0.75	2.20	0.0016	0.0020	135
November	1.33	0.72	1.04	0.0008	0.0009	62
December	1.22	0.58	0.91	0.0007	0.0008	56
The period	......	......	......	......	0 1227	9,018

5 GEORGE V, A. 1915

SOURIS RIVER NEAR ESTEVAN.

Location.—On *NE.* ¼ Sec. 11, Tp. 2, Rge. 8, W. 2nd Mer., near the pumping plant of the Canadian Pacific Railway.

Records available.—June 23, 1911, to December 31, 1914.

Gauge.—Staff; elevation of zero was maintained at 82.45 feet during 1911-12; and at 82.55 feet during 1913-14.

Bench-mark.—Permanent iron bench-mark; assumed elevation, 100 00 feet.

Channel.—Permanent.

Discharge measurements.—From bridge about one mile upstream, or by wading at gauge.

Winter flow.—Affected by ice.

Observer.—W. Bevan.

DISCHARGE MEASUREMENTS of Souris River near *Estevan*, in 1914.

Date.	Engineer.	Width.	Area of Section.	Mean Velocity.	Gauge Height.	Discharge.
		Feet.	*Sq. ft.*	*Ft. per sec.*	*Feet.*	*Sec.-ft.*
Jan. 2............	F. R. Steinberger.	2.6	0.52	0.15	0.87	0.08
Jan. 21........	do	2.5	0.87	0.47	1.12	0.41
Feb. 10...........	do	3.4	0.98	0.58	0.96	0.57
Feb. 28...........	do	3.3	0.84	0.58	0.95	0.49
Mar. 23...........	do	71.0	133.00	1.37	11.23	182.00
May 12...........	W. H. Storey..............	45.0	312.00	0.20	2.72	61.00
June 17...........	do	50.0	296.00	0.20	2.25	58.00
July 11........	do	14.5	9.80	1.98	1.40	19.40
July 28...........	do	9.0	3.50	0.81	0.81	2.80
Aug. 29...........	do	8.0	2.60	1.03	0.70	2.70
Oct. 27...........	F. R. Steinberger	....	....	....	0.21a	0.63
Dec. 9...........	do	....	....	....	0.28a	0.96
Dec. 30...........	do	....	....	....	0.27a	0.91 -

a Weir rod.

DAILY GAUGE HEIGHT AND DISCHARGE of Souris River near *Estevan*, for 1914.

DAY.	January.		February.		March.		April.		May.		June.	
	Gauge Height.	Dis- charge.	Gauge Height.	Dis- charge	Gauge Height.	Dis- charge.	Gauge Height.	Dis- charge	Gauge Height.	Dis- charge.	Gauge Height.	Dis- charge.
	Feet.	*Sec.-ft.*	*Feet.*	*Sec.-ft.*	*Feet.*	*Sec.-ft.*	*Feet.*	*Sec.-ft.*	*Feet.*	*Sec.-ft.*	*Feet.*	*Sec.-ft.*
1...........	0.74	0.10a	1.03	0.34	0.95	0.49	5.50	170	3.60	132	1.86	34
2...........	0.73	0.10	1.03	0.35	0.99	0.50	7.00	190	3.60	132	1.86	34
3...........	0.85	0.08	1.07	0.37	0.99	0.50	8.50	210	3.20	103	2.24	50
4...........	0.89	0.07	1.07	0.42	1.01	0.50	10.00	230	2.90	83	3.70	140
5...........	0.89	0.10	1.05	0.45	1.41	0.50	11.00	250	2.95	86	6.00	343
6...........	0.91	0.12	1.03	0.47	1.56	1.50	10.50	270	2.90	83	8.55	572
7...........	0.95	0.14	1.01	0.52	1.61	2.00	10.00	290	2.85	80	9.00	613
8...........	0.95	0 18	1.01	0.55	1 66	3.00	9.00	310	2.60	66	9.00	613
9...........	0.95	0.18	0 99	0.56	2.11	5.00	10.00	400	2.40	56	8.50	568
10...........	0.95	0.20	0.96	0.57	2.16	8.00	10.00	420	2.50	61	6.00	343
11...........	0.95	0.22	0.96	0.57	2.61	10.00	9.50	440	2.55	63	5.24	275
12...........	1.01	0.26	0.96	0.57	2.91	20.00	9.50	480	2.72	72	3.65	136
13...........	1.01	0.28	0.98	0.57	3.11	30.00	8.00	500	2.67	70	3.65	136
14...........	1.01	0.32	0.98	0.56	4 67	40.00	7.70	450a	2.65	68	3.20	103
15...........	1.01	0.36	0.98	0.56	5.51	50.00	6.00	343	2.65	68	3.00	89
16...........	1.01	0 38	0.96	0 55	6.11	60.00	5 50	298	2.65	68	3.00	89
17...........	1.00	0.41	0.98	0.54	7.00	80.00	4 20	181	2.60	66	2.25	50
18...........	1.00	0 42	0.98	0 53	9.00	100.00	4 20	181	2.42	57	2.20	48
19...........	1.00	0.42	0.99	0.52	11.00	150.00	4 20	181	2.40	56	2.10	44
20.	1 00	0 42	0.99	0.51	11.50	160.00	4.00	164	2.38	55	2.00	40
21...........	0.99	0.42	0.99	0.50	11.00	160 00	3.40	117	2.38	55	2.00	40
22...........	0.99	0.42	0 99	0.49	11.50	170.00	3 20	10?	2.30	52	1.96	38
23...........	1.00	0.42	0.98	0.48	11.00	180.00	2 80	77	2.25	50	1.96	38
24...........	1.00	0.42	0.97	0.47	11.00	200.00	2 80	77	2.23	49	1.90	36
25...........	1.01	0.40	0 97	0.47	10 00	200.00	2.90	83	2.23	49	1.90	36
26...........	1.01	0.35	0.96	0.47	9.50	200.00	2.90	83	2.10	44	1.87	35
27...........	1.01	0.37	0.97	0.48	7.50	180.00	3 00	89	2.10	40	1.87	35
28...........	1 03	0.40	0.95	0.49	7.00	170 00	3.25	107	1.96	38	1.70	29
29...........	1 03	0.43	......	....	7.00	170.00	3.00	89	1.96	38	1.70	29
30...........	1 02	0.42	......	....	6 50	150.00	3.00	89	1.90	36	1.6S	2S
31...........	1.02	0.36	......	....	6.00	150.00	......	....	1.90	36	......	....

a Ice conditions Jan. 1 to April 14.

SESSIONAL PAPER No. 25c

DAILY GAUGE HEIGHT AND DISCHARGE of Souris River near Estevan, for 1914.—*Concluded.*

DAY.	July.		August.		September.		October.		November.		December.	
	Gauge Height.	Dis-charge.	Gauge Height.	Dis-charge.	Gauge Height.	Dis-charge.	Gauge Height.	Dis-charge.	Gauge Height.	Dis-charge.	Gauge Height	Dis-charge.
	Feet.	*Sec.-ft.*	*Feet.*	*Sec.-ft.*	*Feet.*	*Sec.-ft.*	*Feet.*	*Sec.-ft.*	*Feet.*	*Sec.-ft.*	*Feet.*	*Sec.-ft.*
1	1.86	34.0	0.78	3.60	.65	1.50	0 64	1.40	0.21	0.63	0.30	1.05
2	1.70	29.0	0.76	3.20	65	1.50	0 64	1.40	0.21	0.63	0.30	1.05
3	1.67	28.0	0.76	3.20	.65	1.50	0.65	1.50	0.21	0.63	0.30	1.05
4	1.66	28.0	0.75	3.00	0 64	1.40	0.65	1 50	0.20	0.59	0.31	1.10
5	1.66	28.0	0.75	3.00	0.60	1.00	0.66	1.60	0.19	0.53	0.30	1.05
6	1.64	27.0	0.72	2.40	.60	1.00	.66	1 60	0.19	0.53	0.29	1.00
7	1.62	27.0	0.70	2.00	.57	0.85	.66	1.60	0.19	0.53	0.30	1.05
8	1.58	25.0	0.70	2.00	.57	3 85	68	1.80	0.20	0.59	0.28	0.96
9	1.58	25.0	0.70	2.00	0.54	0.70	0.68	1.80	0.20	0.59	0.28	0.96
10	1.50	23.0	0.70	2.00	0.54	0.70	0.69	1.90	0.20	0.59	0.28	0.96
11	1.50	23.0	0.68	1.80	.52	.60	.70	2.00	0.21	0.63	0.28	0.96
12	1.48	22.0	0.68	1.80	.52	.60	.70	2.00	0.21	0.63	0.28	0.96
13	1.20	14.0	0.68	1.80	.50	.50	.70	2.00	0.21	0.63	0.28	0.96
14	1.14	12.2	0.67	1.70	0.50	0.50	0 68	1.80	0.21	0.63	0.28	0.96
15	1.10	11.0	0.67	1.70	0.50	0.50	0 68	1.80	0.21	0.63	0.28	0.96
16	1.05	9.5	0.67	1.70	0.50	.50	.65	1.50d	0.21	0.63	0.28	0.96
17	1.00	8.0	0.65	1.50	0.49	.48	.72	1.43	0.21	0.63	0.28	0.96
18	0.97	7.4	0.65	1.50	0.49	.48	.74	1.36	0.21	0.63	0.28	0.96
19	0.97	7.4	0.60	1.00	0 48	0.46	0.70	1.29	0.22	0.67	0.28	0.96
20	0.94	6.8	0.58	0.90	0.50	0.50	0.72	1.22	0.25	0.81	0.28	0.96
21	0.94	6.8	0.58	0.90	0.50	.50	.76	1.15	0.25	0.81	0.28	0.96
22	0.90	6.0	0.56	0.80	0.54	.70	.76	1.08	0.27	0.90	0.28	0.96
23	0.86	5.2	0.56	0.80	0.58	.90	.76	1.01	0.27	0.90	0.28	0.96
24	0.85	5.0	0.86	5.20	0.58	0.90	0 76	0.94	0.30	1.05	0.28	0.96
25	0.80	4.0	0.86	5.20	0.58	0.90	0.78	0.87	0.30	1.05	0.28	0.96
26	0.80	4.0	0.86	5.20	.59	0.95	0.78	0 80d	0.30	1.05	0.28	0.96
27	0.80	4.0	0.70	2.00	.59	0.95	0.78a	0.71	0.31	1.10	0.28	0.96
28	0.78	3.6	0.70	2.00	.60	1.00	0.21b	0.63	0.32	1.15	0.27	0.90
29	0.78	3.6	0.69	1.90	0.60	1.00	0 21	0.63	0.33	1.20	0.27	0.90
30	0.80	4.0	0.69	1.90	0.61	1.10	0.20	0.59	0.33	1.20	0.27	0.90
31	0.82	4.4	0.67	1.70	....	....	0.20	0.59	....	....	0.27c	0.90

a 0.78 on summer gauge rod—0.21 on weir rod.
b to c Weir measurements.
d to d Ice conditions.

MONTHLY DISCHARGE of Souris River near Estevan, for 1914.

(Drainage area 4,550 square miles.)

MONTH.	DISCHARGE IN SECOND-FEET.				RUN-OFF.	
	Maximum.	Minimum.	Mean.	Per square Mile.	Depth in inches on Drainage Area.	Total in Acre-feet.
January	0.43	0.07	0.30	0.00007	0.00008	18
February	0.57	0.34	0.50	0.00011	0.00011	28
March	200.00	0.49	86.00	0.01900	0.02000	5,288
April	500.00	77.00	229.00	0.05000	0.06000	13,626
May	132.00	36.00	65.00	.01400	0.02000	3,997
June	613.00	28.00	155.00	03400	0.04000	9,223
July	34.00	3.60	14.40	00320	0.00400	885
August	5.20	0.80	2 20	00050	0 00060	135
September	1.50	0.46	0.83	00018	0 00020	49
October	2.00	0.59	1.35	00030	0 00030	83
November	1.20	0.53	0.76	0.00017	0 00020	45
December	1.10	0.90	1.00	0.00022	0.00030	61
The year	....	....	....	....	0.14579	33,438

5 GEORGE V, A. 1915

MOOSE MOUNTAIN CREEK NEAR OXBOW.

Location.—On *NE*. ¼ Sec. 15, Tp. 3, Rge. 2, W. 2nd Mer., one mile south and one-half mile west of the Canadian Pacific Railway station at Oxbow.

Records available.—From September 4, 1913, to October 31, 1914.

Gauge.—Vertical staff; elevation of zero was 91.94 feet during 1913-14.

Bench-mark.—On stump of tree 50 feet upstream from gauge, painted white; assumed elevation 100.00 feet.

Channel.—Permanent.

Discharge measurements.—From bridge one-quarter mile upstream, or by wading.

Winter flow.—No winter observations have been taken.

Observer.—W. E. Chrismas.

DISCHARGE MEASUREMENTS of Moose Mountain Creek near Oxbow, in 1914.

Date	Engineer.	Width.	Area of Section.	Mean Velocity.	Gauge Height.	Discharge.
		Feet.	*Sq. ft.*	*Ft. per sec.*	*Feet.*	*Sec.-ft.*
May 13	W. H. Storey....	37	63.0	1.82	2.86	116.0
June 20	do	28	26.0	1.71	2.02	45.0
July 14	do	26	19.0	1.76	1.65	33.0
July 30	G. H. Whyte and W. H. Storey	13	4.9	0.87	0.91	4.2
Sept. 1	W. H. Storey....	13	4.9	0.75	0.97	4.2

DAILY GAUGE HEIGHT AND DISCHARGE of Moose Mountain Creek near Oxbow, for 1914.

DAY	March.		April.		May.		June.	
	Gauge Height.	Dis- charge.	Gauge Height.	Dis- charge.	Gauge Height.	Dis- charge.	Gauge Height.	Dis- charge.
	Feet.	*Sec.-ft.*	*Feet.*	*Sec.-ft.*	*Feet.*	*Sec.-ft.*	*Feet.*	*Sec.-ft.*
1			4.92	140*b*	2.97	126	1.93	43
2			6.07	150	3.00	129	1.91	42
3			6.70	160	3.01	130	1.81	35
4			5.30	180	3.05	134	2.10	55
5	3 43	......*a*	5.05	190	3.03	132	2.18	61
6	4.22	...:....	4.55	200	3.23	150	2.38	77
7	4.17	....	4.48	210	3.21	148	2.87	147
8	3.90	....	4.54	230	3.26	152	3.43	168
9	3.24	....	5.10	300	3.33	159	3.52	176
10	3.24	....	6.20	340	3.20	147	3.33	159
11	3.31	....	6.10	350	3.11	139	3.02	131
12	2.55	....	5.56	350*h*	3.06	134	2.83	114
13	3.86	....	5.84	385*c*	2.85	116	2.50	87
14	5.13	....	5.58	361	2.78	109	2.54	90
15	6.60	....	5.16	323	2.72	105	2.35	75
16	5.74	....	4.79	290	2.67	101	2.22	65
17	6.63	....	4.59	272	2.63	97	2.12	57
18	6.69	....	4.32	248	2.64	98	2.06	52
19	5.86	....	4.16	233	2.55	91	2.07	53
20	5.10	....	4.08	226	2.68	101	2.02	49
21	4.75	....	3.91	211	2.62	97	1.99	47
22	5.37	....	3.66	188	2.53	89	1.95	44
23	5.30	....	3.59	182	2.48	85	1.90	41
24	4.68	....	3.49	173	2.41	80	1.87	39
25	4.88	....	3.35	161	2.38	77	1.90	41
26	4.60	....	3.18	145	2.34	74	1.88	39
27	4.81	....	3.12	140	2.27	69	1.88	39
28	4.56	....	3.00	129	2.13	58	1.79	34
29	4.44	....	2.99	128	2.17	61	1.95	44
30	4.37	....	2.93	123	2.13	58	1.78	33
31	4.79	......*a*			2.05	52		

a March 5 to 31—not estimated; insufficient data.
b April 1 to 12—discharge estimated.
c April 13—creek clear of ice.

SESSIONAL PAPER No. 25c

DAILY GAUGE HEIGHT AND DISCHARGE of Moose Mountain Creek near Oxbow, for 1914.
—*Concluded.*

DAY.	July.		August.		September.		October.	
	Gauge Height.	Dis- charge.	Gauge Height.	Dis- charge.	Gauge Height.	Dis- charge.	Gauge Height.	Dis- charge.
	Feet.	*Sec.-ft.*	*Feet.*	*Sec.-ft.*	*Feet.*	*Sec.-ft.*	*Feet.*	*Sec.-ft.*
1	1.74	31.0	0.83	3.10	0.96	4.7	0.76	2.50
2	1.68	27.0	0.85	3.40	0.94	4.4	0.74	2.30
3	1.62	25.0	0.86	3.50	0.93	4.3	0.74	2.30
4	1.60	24.0	0.78	2.60	0.94	4.4	0.74	2.30
5	1.57	22.0	0.74	2.30	1.02	5.6	0.74	2.30
6	1.59	23.0	0.70	2.00	1.00	5.2	0.74	2.30
7	1.60	24.0	0.69	1.94	1.01	5.4	0.74	2.30
8	1.57	22.0	0.67	1.82	1.00	5.2	0.74	2.30
9	1.58	22.0	0.64	1.64	0.98	4.9	0.64	1.64
10	1.62	25.0	0.63	1.58	0.96	4.7	0.64	1.64
11	1.65	26.0	0.61	1.46	0.94	4.4	0.49	0.86
12	1.95	44.0	0.59	1.35	0.94	4.4	0.48	0.82
13	1.83	36.0	0.57	1.25	0.94	4.4	0.48	0.82
14	1.68	28.0	0.56	1.20	0.93	4.3	0.48	0.82
15	1.65	26.0	0.48	0.82	0.92	4.2	0.48	0.82
16	1.53	21.0	0.47	0.78	0.90a	3.9	0.47	0.78
17	1.47	18.0	0.50	0.90	0.89	3.8	0.47	0.78
18	1.45	17.2	0.52	1.00	0.87	3.6	0.47	0.78
19	1.40	15.2	0.51	0.95	0.86	3.5	0.47	0.78
20	1.35	13.6	0.51	0.95	0.84	3.2	0.47	0.78
21	1.35	13.6	0.51	0.95	0.86	3.5	0.45	0.70
22	1.34	13.3	0.55	1.15	0.84	3.2	0.46	0.74
23	1.31	12.3	1.08	6.60	0.83	3.1	0.46	0.74
24	1.29	11.7	0.79	2.70	0.82	3.0	0.46	0.74
25	1.25	10.6	0.96	4.70	0.82	3.0	0.46	0.74
26	1.22	9.8	1.03	5.70	0.79	2.7	0.46	0.74
27	1.20	9.2	1.00	5.20	0.78	2.6	0.46	0.74
28	1.08	6.6	0.99	5.10	0.77	2.6	0.45	0.70
29	1.06	6.3	1.04	5.90	0.78	2.6	0.46a	0.74
30	0.91	4.1	1.02	5.60	0.76	2.5	0.45	0.70
31	0.86	3.5	0.98	4.90	....	....	0.74	2.32

a Interpolated.

MONTHLY DISCHARGE of Moose Mountain Creek near Oxbow, for 1914.

(Drainage area 2,953 square miles.)

MONTH.	DISCHARGE IN SECOND-FEET.				RUN-OFF.	
	Maximum.	Minimum.	Mean.	Per square Mile.	Depth in inches on Drainage Area.	Total in Acre-feet.
April	385.0	123.00	224.0	0.0760	0.0848	13,329
May	159.0	52.00	106.0	0.0360	0.0415	6,518
June	176.0	33.00	71.0	0.0240	0.0268	4,225
July	44.0	3.50	19.0	0.0060	0.0069	1,168
August	6.6	0.78	2.7	0.0010	0.0012	166
September	5.6	2.50	3.9	0.0013	0.0014	232
October	2.5	0.74	1.3	0.0004	0.0005	80
The period	....	....	....	....	0.1631	25,718

5 GEORGE V, A. 1915

SOURIS RIVER NEAR GLEN EWEN.

Location.—On *NE.* ¼ Sec. 36, Tp. 2, Rge. 1, W. 2nd Mer., two miles south and one mile east of Canadian Pacific Railway station at Glen Ewen.

Records available.—June 26, 1911, to October 31, 1914.

Gauge.—Staff; zero of gauge was maintained at 79.32 feet during 1911, and at 78.98 feet during 1912-14.

Bench-mark.—Permanent iron bench-mark; assumed elevation, 100.00 feet.

Channel.—Permanent.

Discharge measurements.—From bridge, which is about one mile above the gauge, or by wading at or near the gauge.

Winter flow.—No winter observations have been taken.

Observer.—D. F. Preston.

DISCHARGE MEASUREMENTS of Souris River near Glen Ewen, in 1914.

Date.	Engineer.	Width.	Area of Section.	Mean Velocity.	Gauge Height.	Discharge.
		Feet.	*Sq. ft.*	*Ft. per sec.*	*Feet.*	*Sec.-ft.*
Mar. 26	F. R. Steinberger		180	1.26	9.65	227.00a
May 14	W. H. Storey	56	204	1.06	4.02	216.00
June 17	do	55	160	0.85	3.22	136.00
July 13	do	50	62	1.11	2.69	69.00
July 29	G. H. Whyte and W. H. Storey	45	42	0.48	2.04	20.20
Aug. 31	W. H. Storey	33	24	0.32	1.70	7.70
Oct. 29	F. R. Steinberger	46	13	0.21	2.00	2.80

a Float measurement.

DAILY GAUGE HEIGHT AND DISCHARGE of Souris River near Glen Ewen, for 1914.

DAY.	March.		April.		May.		June.	
	Gauge Height.	Dis- charge.	Gauge Height.	Dis- charge.	Gauge Height.	Dis- charge.	Gauge Height.	Dis- charge.
	Feet.	*Sec.-ft.*	*Feet.*	*Sec.-ft.*	*Feet.*	*Sec.-ft.*	*Feet.*	*Sec.-ft.*
1			7.30		3.91	203	2.79	80
2			7.95		3.85	197	2.75	76
3			10.00		3.85	197	2.75	76
4			9.15		3.80	191	2.79	80
5			9.10		3.98	211	2.91	92
6			9.00		4.30	246	2.98	100
7			9.08		4.35	251	3.50	157
8			9.85		4.28	244	5.20	345
9			10.12		4.60	279	6.45	483
10			10.87		4.70	290	6.60	499
11			11.25		4.61	280	5.60	389
12			12.20		4.45	262	5.34	360
13			10.35		4.23	238	4.75	295
14			10.75		4.00	213	4.24	239
15	7.10	a	10.49	a	3.88	200	3.93	205
16	9.65		8.57	716	3.78	188	3.81	192
17	9.53		7.80	631	3.73	182	3.59	167
18	10.30		6.95	538	3.68	177	3.30	135
19	10.15		6.46	484	3.61	169	3.24	128
20	10.07		6.20	455	3.58	166	3.19	123
21	8.45		5.69	399	3.50	157	3.06	109
22	8.65		5.30	356	3.43	149	3.03	105
23	9.75		4.88	310	3.37	143	2.90	91
24	10.05		4.69	289	3.30	135	2.81	82
25	10.00		4.53	271	3.25	129	2.80	81
26	10.30		4.30	246	3.05	107	2.81	82
27	9.80		4.19	234	3.09	112	2.80	81
28	9.95		4.13	227	2.98	100	2.78	79
29	9.02		4.05	218	2.90	91	2.77	78
30	7.95		4.10	224	2.90	91	2.79	80
31	7.15				2.82	83		

a March 15 to April 15, ice conditions; insufficient data to estimate discharge.

SESSIONAL PAPER No. 25c

DAILY GAUGE HEIGHT AND DISCHARGE of Souris River near Glen Ewen, for 1914.—*Concluded.*

DAY.	July.		August.		September.		October.	
	Gauge Height.	Dis- charge.	Gauge Height.	Dis- charge.	Gauge Height.	Dis- charge.	Gauge Height.	Dis- charge.
	Feet.	*Sec.-ft.*	*Feet.*	*Sec.-ft.*	*Feet.*	*Sec.-ft.*	*Feet.*	*Sec.-ft.*
1	2.79	80.0	1.85	12.5	1.72	7.7	1.88	13.7
2	2.74	75.0	1.85	12.5	1.71	7.4	1.88	13.7
3	2.70	71.0	1.85	12.5	1.71	7.4	1.88	13.7
4	2.64	65.0	1.84	12.1	1.70	7.0	1.88	13.7
5	2.62	63.0	1.85	12.5	1.68	6.6	1.89	14.1
6	2.63	64.0	1.83	11.7	1.71	7.4	1.88	13.7
7	2.59	60.0	1.81	10.9	1.75	8.7	1.85	12.5
8	2.59	60.0	1.80	10.5	1.80	10.5	1.85	12.5
9	2.58	59.0	1.78	9.8	1.80	10.5	1.84	12.1
10	2.56	57.0	1.77	9.4	1.79	10.1	1.84	12.1
11	2.59	60.0	1.75	8.7	1.80	10.5	1.85	12.5
12	2.61	62.0	1.74	8.4	1.79	10.1	1.90	14.5
13	2.69	70.0	1.71	7.4	1.76	9.1	1.90	14.5
14	2.62	63.0	1.69	6.8	1.77	9.4	1.91	14.9
15	2.59	60.0	1.67	6.4	1.78	9.8	1.86	12.9
16	2.54	56.0	1.66	6.2	1.81	10.9	1.87	13.3
17	2.49	51.0	1.67	6.4	1.76	9.1	1.87	13.3
18	2.44	47.0	1.68	6.6	1.77	9.4	1.86	12.9
19	2.41	45.0	1.68	6.6	1.80	10.5	1.90	14.5
20	2.34	40.0	1.67	6.4	1.82	11.3	1.91	14.9
21	2.29	36.0	1.67	6.4	1.85	12.5	1.92	15.4
22	2.19	29.0	1.78	9.8	1.90	14.5	1.93	15.8
23	2.19	29.0	1.85	12.5	1.88	13.7	1.92	15.4
24	2.19	29.0	1.86	12.9	1.88	13.7	1.95	16.7
25	2.18	29.0	1.81	10.9	1.88	13.7	1.96	17.2
26	2.14	26.0	1.78	9.8	1.89	14.1	1.98	18.1
27	2.11	25.0	1.74	8.4	1.90	14.5	1.98	18.1
28	2.17	28.0	1.71	7.4	1.90	14.5	1.99	18.5
29	1.96	17.2	1.78	9.8	1.90	14.5	1.99	18.5
30	1.86	12.9	1.78	9.8	1.90	14.5	2.14	26.0
31	1.85	12.5	1.72	7.7	....	....	2.10	24.0

MONTHLY DISCHARGE of Souris River near Glen Ewen, for 1914.

(Drainage area 7,500 square miles.)

MONTH.	DISCHARGE IN SECOND-FEET.				RUN-OFF.	
	Maximum.	Minimum	Mean.	Per square Mile.	Depth in inches on Drainage Area.	Total in Acre-feet.
April	716.0	218.0	373.0	0.0500	0.028	11,097
May	290.0	83.0	183.0	0.0244	0.028	11,252
June	499.0	76.0	170.0	0.0230	0.026	10,116
July	80.0	12.5	48.0	0.0064	0.007	2,951
August	12.9	6.2	9.4	0.0012	0.001	578
September	14.5	6.6	10.8	0.0014	0.002	643
October	26.0	12.1	15.3	0.0020	0.002	940
The period	....	....	....	....	0.094	37,577

STREAM MEASUREMENTS, 1914

5 GEORGE V, A. 1915

SOURIS RIVER NEAR MELITA.

Location.—On SW. ¼ Sec. 6, Tp. 4, Rge. 26, W. Pr. Mer., on traffic bridge in park, close to town of Melita, Man.

Records available.—July 20, 1911, to October 31, 1914.

Gauge.—Staff; zero of gauge was maintained at 84.02 feet during 1911; 84.13 feet during 1912; 84.45 feet during 1913-14.

Bench-mark.—Permanent iron bench-mark; assumed elevation, 100.00 feet.

Channel.—Permanent.

Discharge measurements.—From bridge or by wading.

Winter flow.—No winter observations have been taken.

Observer.—Walter Kay.

DISCHARGE MEASUREMENTS of Souris River near Melita, in 1914.

Date.	Engineer.	Width.	Area of Section.	Mean Velocity.	Gauge Height.	Discharge.
		Feet.	*Sq. ft.*	*Ft. per sec.*	*Feet.*	*Sec.-ft.*
May 15.	W. H. Storey.	98	431.0	1.180	4.99	509
June 20	do	86	220.0	0.696	2.58	153
July 14.	do	86	222.0	0.690	2.56	154
July 30.	do	87	225.0	0.660	2.52	148
Sept. 1.	do	80	145.0	0.500	1.70	72
Oct. 30.	F. R. Steinberger.	58	66.2	0.340	1.05	23

DAILY GAUGE HEIGHT AND DISCHARGE of Souris River near Melita, for 1914.

DAY.	June.		July.		August.		September.		October.	
	Gauge Height.	Dis-charge.	Gauge Height.	Dis-charge.	Gauge Height.	Dis-charge.	Gauge Height.	Dis-charge.	Gauge Height.	Dis-charge.
	Feet.	*Sec.-ft.*	*Feet.*	*Sec.-ft.*	*Feet.*	*Sec.-ft.*	*Feet.*	*Sec.-ft.*	*Feet.*	*Sec.-ft.*
1.			2.70	169	2.40	137	1.70	72	1.02	21.0
2.			2.68	167	2.35	132	1.68	70	1.00	20.0
3.			2.64	162	2.34	131	1.67	69	0.99	19.5
4.			2.60	158	2.34	131	1.65	68	0.98	19.0
5.			2.60	158	2.32	129	1.62	65	0.98	19.0
6.			2.67	166	2.30	127	1.58	61	0.97	18.5
7.			2.58	156	2.29	126	1.55	59	0.97	18.5
8.			2.59	157	2.27	124	1.50	55	0.96	18.0
9.			2.58	156	2.24	121	1.40	48	0.95	17.5
10.			2.57	155	2.22	119	1.38	47	1.00	20.0
11.			2.57	155	2.21	118	1.36	45	1.16	31.0
12.			2.56	154	2.20	117	1.35	44	1.16	31.0
13.			2.55	152	2.19	116	1.35	44	1.15	30.0
14.			2.56	154	2.16	113	1.37	46	1.08	26.0
15.			2.55	152	2.12	110	1.36	45	1.00	20.0
16.			2.54	151	2.10	108	1.33	43	0.96	18.0
17.			2.53	150	2.09	107	1.30	41	0.94	17.0
18.			2.52	149	2.06	104	1.28	40	0.92	16.0
19.			2.52	149	2.03	102	1.25	37	0.93	16.5
20.	2.58 *a*	156	2.45	142	2.00	99	1.22	35	0.90	15.0
21.	2.50*b*	147	2.48	145	1.99	98	1.15	31	0.92	16.0
22.	2.45	142	2.47	144	1.98	97	1.08	26	0.91	15.5
23	2.49	146	2.46	143	2.00	99	1.08	26	0.92	16.0
24.	2.47	144	2.45	142	2.10	108	1.07	25	0.93	16.5
25.	2.55	152	2.44	141	2.08	106	1.05	23	0.90	15.0
26	2.52	149	2.42	139	2.10	108	1.02	21	0.92	16.0
27.	2.50	147	2.40	137	2.06	104	1.01	21	0.94	17.0
28.	2.59	157	2.38	135	2.00	99	1.00	20	0.93	16.5
29.	2.75	175	2.50	147	1.95	94	1.02	21	0.95	17.5
30.	2.74	174	2.49	146	1.90	90	1.03	22	1.05	24.0
31			2.42	139	1.80	81			1.09	26.0

a No observations previous to June 20; no observer obtainable.
b Interpolated.

MONTHLY DISCHARGE of Souris River near Melita, for 1914.

(Drainage area 10,673 square miles)

MONTH.	DISCHARGE IN SECOND-FEET.				RUN-OFF.	
	Maximum.	Minimum	Mean.	Per square Mile.	Depth in inches on Drainage Area.	Total in Acre-feet.
June	175	142	153.0	0.0140	0.0057	3,338
July	169	135	151.0	0.0141	0.0163	9,285
August	137	81	111.0	0.0104	0.0120	6,825
September	72	20	42.0	0.0040	0.0045	2,499
October	31	15	19.6	0.0019	0.0022	1,205
The period					0.0407	23,152

MISCELLANEOUS DISCHARGE MEASUREMENTS made in Souris River drainage basin, in 1914.

Date.	Engineer.	Stream.	Location.	Width.	Area of Section.	Mean Velocity.	Discharge.
				Feet.	Sq. ft.	Ft. per sec.	Sec.-ft
Jan. 1	F. R. Steinberger	Souris River	At Weyburn	10.3	3.45		a
Feb. 9	do	do	do			b	Nil.
Mar. 21	do	do	do				1.00
May 11	W. H. Storey	do	do	47.0	121.00		Nil.
June 17	do	do	do			b	"
July 11	do	do	do			b	"
July 27	do	do	do			b	"
Aug. 29	do	do	do			b	"
Oct. 26	F. R. Steinberger	do	do			b	"
Dec. 30	do	do	do			b	"

a Small discharge.
b Water standing in pools.

5 GEORGE V, A. 1915

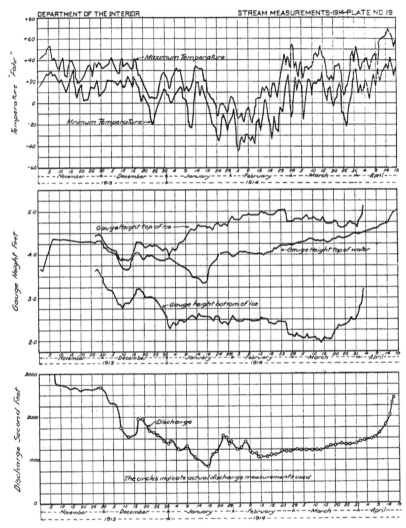

OBSERVATIONS OF GAUGE HEIGHTS ON NORTH SASKATCHEWAN RIVER AT PRINCE ALBERT
SASKATCHEWAN WITH CORRESPONDING MAXIMUM AND MINIMUM TEMPERATURES AND THE
ESTIMATED DAILY DISCHARGES FOR THE WINTER 1913-1914.

SESSIONAL PAPER No. 25c

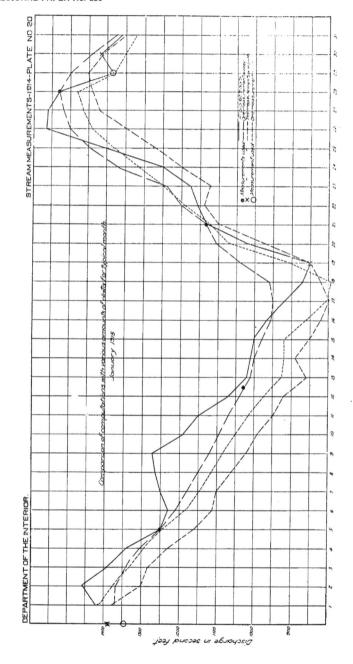

5 GEORGE V, A. 1915

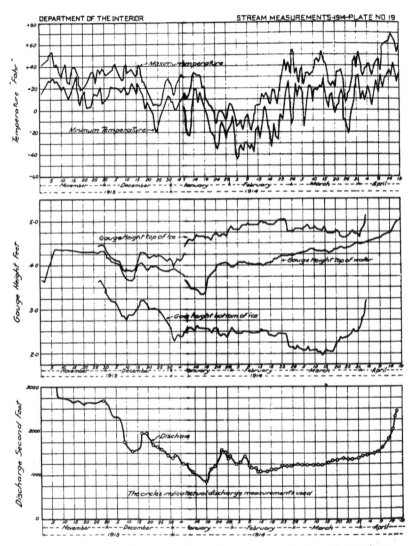

OBSERVATIONS OF GAUGE HEIGHTS ON NORTH SASKATCHEWAN RIVER AT PRINCE ALBE
SASKATCHEWAN WITH CORRESPONDIN MAXIMUM AND MINIMUM TEMPERATURES AND
ESTIMATED DAILY DISCHARGES FOR TH WINTER 1913-1914.

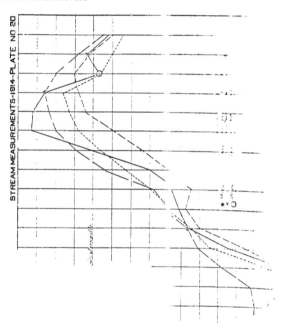

E. INTERIOR.

5 GEORGE V, A. 1915

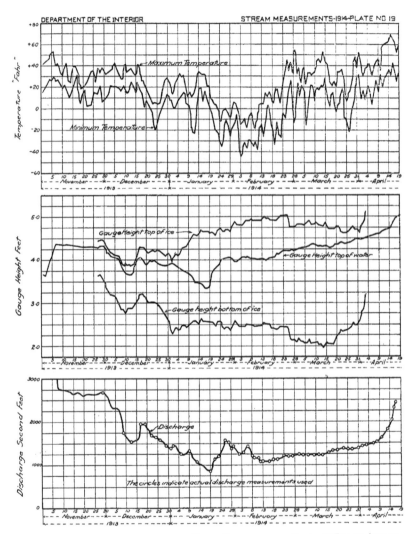

OBSERVATIONS OF GAUGE HEIGHTS ON NORTH SASKATCHEWAN RIVER AT PRINCE ALBERT SASKATCHEWAN WITH CORRESPONDING MAXIMUM AND MINIMUM TEMPERATURES AND THE ESTIMATED DAILY DISCHARGES FOR THE WINTER 1913-1914.

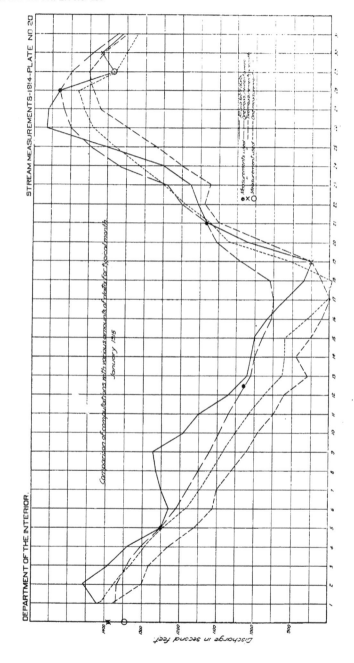

APPENDIX.

BRIEF REPORT AS TO NUMBER OF DISCHARGE MEASUREMENTS REQUIRED TO
OBTAIN RECORDS OF THE DAILY DISCHARGE OF THE NORTH SAS-
KATCHEWAN RIVER AT PRINCE ALBERT, SASK., DURING THE
WINTER PERIOD.

By G. H. WHYTE.

The following is a brief discussion of the methods of computing stream flow under ice conditions from gauge heights, temperatures and a few discharge measurements as applied to the North Saskatchewan River at Prince Albert, Saskatchewan, during the winter of 1913-14.

At the urgent request of the Water Power Branch of the department and the city of Prince Albert, it was decided early in December, 1913, to place a resident hydrometric engineer at Prince Albert for the purpose of making discharge measurements of the North Saskatchewan River at that point every second or third day throughout the winter season. Mr. W. H. Storey was chosen for this work, and on December 8th and 9th made the first discharge measurement, which was followed by further measurements every two or three days until the stream was clear of ice in April. Including a gauging made by Mr. O. H. Hoover, on November 29th, a total of 55 discharge measurements were made during the period of ice cover, divided by months as follows: November, 1; December, 10; January, 11; February, 13; March, 13; and April, 7. The stream froze over on November 6th, and began to break up on April 16th, being clear of all ice on April 23rd.

The North Saskatchewan River at Prince Albert was on an average 600 feet wide and 3½ feet deep, with a mean velocity of some seven-tenths feet per second, with an ice cover of from 1 foot to 2¾ feet during the winter. Discharge measurements were made with current meters of the Gurley Price Pattern No. 623, by suspending with rods through holes in the ice, and taking velocities at from 4 to 9 points in the vertical for periods from 40 to 70 seconds or more at each point. Two newly rated meters were used in this work, and one instrument was checked against the other throughout the year to eliminate all chance of error. Both instruments were re-rated in the spring and found to calibrate the same as at the beginning of the work. Every precaution was also taken while making the gaugings to ensure accuracy.

The gauging section was some 600 yards below the bridge at which open-water records are obtained. Most of the holes were about 20 feet apart, but some near the edge of the stream, where the water was shallow, were 5 to 10 feet apart. The average number of holes was about 35.

The velocities obtained in each vertical were plotted and a velocity curve drawn, and the mean velocity from this curve taken as the mean in the vertical. This work was done by Mr. Storey on days between gaugings, and the notes forwarded to the office, where they were carefully examined and checked. The areas were obtained in the usual manner, and included only the area of the cross-section under the ice.

Gauge heights were taken three times a day by Mr. Storey with the regular chain gauge at the bridge. This included top of ice, thickness of ice and water surface. The gauge was checked with a level once a week and kept at the proper datum. The thickness of ice was measured with our regular ice scale, and was taken at various points near the gauge so that a true thickness was obtained.

Temperatures were obtained from the Dominion Government meterological stations at Edmonton, Battleford, and Prince Albert.

The records as published in this report and used in the comparisons were computed by Messrs. W. H. Storey and O. H. Hoover from all available data, and are assumed to be very nearly accurate. The method used was that fully described by Mr. W. G. Hoyt of the United States Geological Survey in Water Supply Paper No. 337, page 51, published by that Survey, and is known as the eye method. It was found that this method gave the best results under the conditions found at this station, and it may be briefly described as plotting graphs of the records of maximum and minimum temperatures, and the records of gauge heights of water surface and top and bottom of the ice. The discharges obtained by actual discharge measurements are plotted, and the discharge graph is completed by estimating the daily discharge for the periods between measurements by referring to the temperature and gauge height graphs. The engineer making this estimate should have a good idea as to the conditions of flow of the stream at the station during the winter period. Where the stream flow is regular and there are sufficient measurements, fairly accurate results may be obtained. Plate 19 shows the records as completed by this method and used in these results.

5 GEORGE V, A. 1915

It was desired to determine to what degree of accuracy estimates by this method could be made by using actual measurements obtained at various periods of time. The full temperature and gauge height records were given to each engineer assigned to this work, but only a certain number of the discharge measurements. Mr. P. H. Daniells was given one measurement a week, I took two measurements a month (the first made and the one made nearest the middle of the month), and Mr. J. M. Paul was given one measurement a month.

Plate 20 shows the results obtained for the month of January, and is typical of the period estimates. The following tables give a comparison of the monthly means and period mean from the four estimates. It will be noted that only the months of December, January, February and March were used, as it was not considered advisable to use the periods when ice was forming or breaking up, as they are liable to errors in estimates under any method.

The results show that for a single day there are likely to be quite large errors, but for a month or winter the error in the mean is not of any size. At stations on the North Saskatchewan River or streams of a similar type, which are a considerable distance from the source of supply, it is seen that discharge measurements made once every two or three weeks will supply sufficient data, with daily temperature and gauge height records, to make estimates close enough for almost any use. However, nearer the source of supply of a stream it is often desired that more frequent discharge measurements be made, as such streams are not as likely to maintain a uniform flow.

COMPARISON OF DAILY AND MONTHLY MEAN DISCHARGE of the North Saskatchewan River at Prince Albert, Sask., obtained with various amounts of data.

METHOD.	Mean discharge in second-feet.	Difference from Method I in sec.-ft. and per cent.	Greatest difference from Method I for single day in sec.-ft. and per cent.
December 1913.			
I. All data available............	1,819.00		
II. One measurement a week...............	1,753.00	− 66 or − 3.68%	−370 or −18%
III. Two measurements a month...........	1,953.00	+134 or + 7.37%	+383 or +22%
IV. One measurement a month...............	1,436.00	−383 or −21.06%	−800 or −35%
January 1914.			
I. All available data.......................	1,221.00		
II. One measurement a week.................	1,218.00	− 3 or −0.25%	+190 or +22%
III. Two measurements a month...............	1,117.00	−104 or −8.52%	−252 or −20%
IV. One measurement a month...........	1,166.00	− 55 or −4.5%	−187 or −15%
February 1914.			
I. All available data...........	1,191.00		
II. One measurement a week.................	1,188.00	− 3 or −0.25%	−130 or −10%
III. Two measurements a month...............	1,155.00	−36 or −3.02%	−273 or −19%
IV. One measurement a month...............	1,256.00	+65 or +5.46%	+140 or +12%
March 1911.			
I. All available data.....	1.295.00		
II. One measurement a week.................	1,302.00	+ 7 or +0.54%	+ 30 or +2%
III. Two measurements a week...............	1,297.00	+ 2 or +0.15%	− 83 or −6%
IV. One measurement a month...............	1,279.00	−16 or −1.24%	−116 or −9%
Period, December to March.			
I. All available data.......................	1,381.50		
II. One measurement a week.................	1,365.25	−16.25 or −1.17%	
III. Two measurements a month...............	1,380.50	− 1.00 or −0 072%	
IV. One measurement a month...............	1,284.25	−97.25 or −7.04%	

INDEX

5 GEORGE V, A. 1915

SESSIONAL PAPER No. 25c

5 GEORGE V, A. 1915

5 GEORGE V, A. 1915

508   *NDEX*